BLACK'S
MEDICAL DICTIONARY

BY

WILLIAM A. R. THOMSON, M.D.

TWENTY-EIGHTH EDITION

WITH 426 ILLUSTRATIONS IN THE TEXT
AND EIGHTEEN PLATES (FOUR IN COLOUR)

LONDON
ADAM & CHARLES BLACK
1968

PUBLISHED BY A. AND C. BLACK LTD
4, 5 AND 6 SOHO SQUARE LONDON W.I

© 1965, 1967, 1968 A. AND C. BLACK LTD

FIRST EDITION (BY J. D. COMRIE, M.D.) 1906
SECOND EDITION 1906
THIRD EDITION 1907
FOURTH EDITION 1910
FIFTH EDITION 1914, REPRINTED 1916
SIXTH EDITION 1918, REPRINTED 1920
SEVENTH EDITION 1922, REPRINTED 1924
EIGHTH EDITION (ENTIRELY RESET) 1926
REPRINTED 1928 (TWICE)
NINTH EDITION 1930
TENTH EDITION 1931
ELEVENTH EDITION 1933
TWELFTH EDITION 1934
THIRTEENTH EDITION 1936
FOURTEENTH EDITION (COMPLETING 100,000) 1937
FIFTEENTH EDITION 1939
SIXTEENTH EDITION 1941
SEVENTEENTH EDITION 1942
REPRINTED 1943

REVISED BY H. A. CLEGG, F.R.C.P. :
EIGHTEENTH EDITION 1944
REPRINTED 1945
REPRINTED, WITH SLIGHT CHANGES, 1946
REPRINTED 1947

REVISED BY W. A. R. THOMSON, M.D. :
NINETEENTH EDITION 1948
TWENTIETH EDITION (ENTIRELY RESET) 1951
TWENTY-FIRST EDITION 1953
TWENTY-SECOND EDITION 1955
TWENTY-THIRD EDITION 1958
TWENTY-FOURTH EDITION 1961
TWENTY-FIFTH EDITION 1963
TWENTY-SIXTH EDITION 1965
TWENTY-SEVENTH EDITION 1967
TWENTY-EIGHTH EDITION 1968

SBN 7136 0997 4

MADE IN GREAT BRITAIN

PREFACE TO
THE TWENTY-EIGHTH EDITION

IN spite of the fact that it is not yet two years since the last edition of this Dictionary appeared, this new edition contains over forty new entries. In addition, alterations have been made to many other sections in order to bring them up to date, and several new illustrations have been included. This, of course, is merely a sign of the times as exemplified in the rapidly changing face of medicine.

Yet behind this façade the essentials of good medical practice remain relatively unchanged. The human body has not changed; neither have the symptoms and signs of disease. New drugs may come and go ; new methods of investigation may be introduced, and the laboratory may appear to play an ever-increasing role in the diagnosis and treatment of disease. But the fundamentals underlying the maintenance of a healthy mind in a healthy body remain inviolate, and it is these that have always been stressed in this Dictionary since its inception in 1906.

Among the many subjects covered by the new sections are chromosomes, dermatoglyphics, perinatal mortality, pleoptics, pigeon breeder's lung, and polymer fume fever, whilst among the sections rewritten are those on abortion, amphetamines, infant feeding, and mongolism. In order to avoid the currently popular middle-age spread, deletions have been made to compensate for the added new material. As a result there has been no increase in the number of pages.

As in previous editions the aim has been to preserve a balance between the old and the new by retaining what is good in the old and only adding such advances as appear to be standing the test of time. The balance becomes increasingly like a razor edge, but the continuing popularity of the Dictionary suggests that the right balance is still being preserved.

W. A. R. T.

LONDON, 1968

SPECIAL SUGGESTIONS

Black's Medical Dictionary

I. **ACCIDENTS.**—In cases of injury, treat first any bleeding that may be present (see **Hæmorrhage**). Next dress the wound (see **Wounds and Bandages**). If a broken bone, dislocation, or sprain be present, for the treatment see under **Fractures**; **Dislocations**; or **Joints, Diseases of**. In cases of internal injury, see **Abdomen, Injuries of**, and **Chest, Injuries of**. For methods of conveyance, see **Injured, Removal of**. For accidents with electricity, see **Electrical Injuries**.

II. **BURNS AND SCALDS.**—In cases of burning, extinguish the flames by laying the person down and covering with some woollen article, *e.g.*, a blanket. For the treatment, see **Burns and Scalds**.

III. **DROWNING.**—For treatment after immersion in water, see **Drowning, Recovery from**.

IV. **GASSING.**—For treatment, see under **Coal-gas**, **Drowning**, and **Oxygen**.

V. **POISONING.**—For the general treatment of poisoning, see the article on **Poisons**, and also special articles under the headings of **Food Poisoning**, of **Fungus Poisoning**, and of the names of various dangerous substances.

VI. **FITS AND CONVULSIONS.**—In cases of fits and other convulsive seizures, for treatment see the article on **Convulsions** in Children; also that on **Epilepsy** and that on **Hysteria**. For a list of the various conditions that may produce spasm, see **Spasm**.

VII. **UNCONSCIOUSNESS.**—In cases of unconsciousness from some unknown cause, see under the heading **Unconsciousness**. Apart from faints, the most important causes are alcoholism, apoplexy, and diabetic coma. Appropriate treatment will be found under the headings—**Fainting**; **Alcoholism, Acute**; **Apoplexy**; **Diabetes mellitus**; **Brain, Diseases and Injuries of**; and **Uræmia**.

VIII. **DEATH.**—In cases of supposed death, see the article on **Death, Signs of**.

IX. **PERSONAL HEALTH.**—With regard to the preservation of personal health, the article **Health** may be consulted.

X. **SANITATION.**—When information is desired on matters affecting public health, the general article on **Sanitation** may be first consulted. In it numerous references to other subjects are given.

XI. **SYMPTOMS OF DISEASE.**—The symptoms most likely to attract attention are mentioned, and the diseases which most commonly produce them are indicated, under the following headings: **Diarrhœa; Vomiting; Expectoration; Breathlessness; Urine; Stools; Inflammation; Fever; Headache; Backache; Colic; Dropsy; Paralysis; Tremor; Abdomen, Diseases of; Chest, Diseases of; Nervous Diseases.** Under these headings references are given to other places where the individual diseases are fully treated.

XII. **NURSING.**—Directions regarding attendance on the sick are given in the article on **Nursing**, from which references are also made to various special subjects and descriptions of applications such as **Bandages, Bed-changing, Feeding, Fomentations, Poultices, Blisters,** etc.

XIII. **MANAGEMENT OF CHILDREN.**—Information regarding the avoidance or remedying of defects incidental to early life will be found under **Infant Feeding; Infection; Incubation** (of infectious diseases); **Children, Peculiarities of; School Children; Mental Defectiveness; Deafness; Ear, Diseases of; Nose, Diseases of** (section Adenoids); **Vision, Disorders of; Squinting; Palate, Malformations of; Spine and Spinal Cord Diseases.** Some of the more important diseases of children are described under **Bronchitis; Croup; Glands, Diseases of; Joints, Diseases of; Rickets;** and under the names of the various infectious diseases.

XIV. **ACTION OF DRUGS.**—The mode of action of various drugs and applications is given under such headings as — **Anodynes; Anæsthetics; Antiseptics; Demulcents; Disinfection; Hypnotics; Purgatives; Tonics;** etc.; the amounts commonly administered are given under **Dosage;** and the more important drugs are described at greater length under their own names.

XV. **ANATOMY AND PHYSIOLOGY.**—The anatomy and physiology of the body are dealt with under the headings of the various organs, and of such general functions as **Circulation; Perspiration; Respiration; Temperature; Touch; Pain; Sleep; Vision.**

NOTE.—Each of the more important diseases is fully considered under the heading of its own name; those of less frequent occurrence are included in groups under the heading of the organ affected. For example, **Bronchitis, Tuberculosis, Pneumonia** are all dealt with under these heads, while the less important abscess, tumours, wounds, etc., of the lungs are dismissed in a few words under **Lungs, Diseases of.**

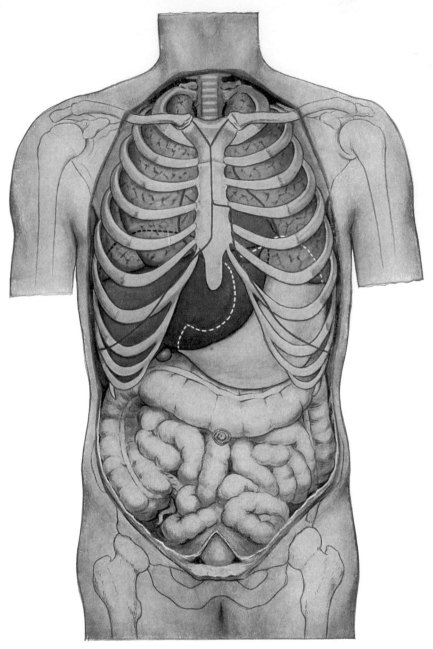

GENERAL VIEW OF THE ABDOMINAL AND THORACIC VISCERA
The lines of pleural reflection are shown in blue.

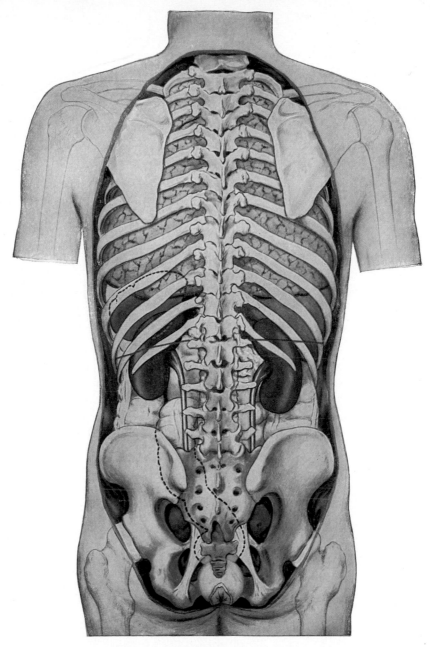

THE ABDOMINAL AND THORACIC VISCERA, FROM BEHIND

The lower limit of the pleural sac is indicated by the blue line. Note the relation of the pleura to the spleen and to the twelfth rib.

A

ABDOMEN is the lower part of the trunk. Above, and separated from it by the diaphragm or midriff, lies the thorax or chest, and below lies the pelvis, or basin, generally described as a separate cavity though directly continuous with that of the abdomen. Behind lie the spinal column and lower ribs which come within a few inches of the iliac or haunch bones ; at the sides the protection afforded to the contained organs by the iliac bones and downsloping ribs is still more effective ; but in front the whole extent is protected only by soft tissues. The latter consist of the skin, a varying amount of fat, three layers of broad, flat muscle, another layer of fat, and finally the smooth, thin peritoneum which lines the whole cavity. The absence of rigidity allows of the necessary distension when food is taken into the stomach, and of the various important movements of the organs associated with digestion. The shape of the abdomen varies ; in children it may protrude considerably, though if this be too marked it may indicate disease, e.g. the presence of fluid ; in healthy young adults it should be either very slightly prominent or slightly indrawn, and should show the outline of the muscular layer, especially of the pair of muscles running vertically (recti), which are divided into four or five sections by transverse lines ; while with advance of age it is quite natural that a considerable amount of fat should be deposited both on and inside the abdomen.

Contents.—The principal contents of the abdominal cavity are the digestive organs, *i.e.* stomach, intestines, and the associated glands the liver and pancreas (Plate III). The position of the stomach is above and to the left when the individual is recumbent, but may be much lower in the erect position. The liver lies above and to the right, lying to a large extent under cover of the ribs, and occupying the hollow of the diaphragm, by which alone both it and the stomach are separated from the lungs and heart. Against the back wall on either side lie the kidneys, protected also to a great extent by the last two ribs ; and from the kidneys run the ureters or urinary ducts down along the back wall to the

bladder in the pelvis. The pancreas lies across the spine between the kidneys, and upon the upper end of each kidney lies a suprarenal gland. High up on the left and partly behind the stomach lies the spleen. The great blood-vessels and nerves, the absorbent vessels and the glands connected with them, lie on the back wall, and the remainder of the space is taken up by the intestines or bowels (*see* INTESTINE), the large intestine lying in the flanks on either side in front of the kidneys and crossing below the stomach from right to left, while the small intestine hangs from the back wall in coils which fill up all spaces between the other organs. Hanging down from the stomach in front of the bowels is the omentum, or apron, containing a considerable amount of fat, and helping to protect the bowels from cold and injury. In the condition of pregnancy the womb, as it increases in size, rises up from the pelvis into the abdomen, lifting the coils of the small intestine above it.

The *pelvis* is that portion of the abdomen which lies within the bony pelvis (*see* BONES), and contains the rectum or end part of the intestine, the bladder, and, in the male the prostate, in the female the womb, ovaries, and Fallopian tubes.

ABDOMEN, DISEASES OF.—(*See under* STOMACH, DISEASES OF ; INTESTINE, DISEASES OF ; DIARRHŒA ; LIVER, DISEASES OF ; PANCREAS, DISEASES OF ; KIDNEY, DISEASES OF ; BLADDER, DISEASES OF ; HERNIA ; PERITONITIS ; APPENDICITIS ; TUMOURS.)

Symptoms.—The symptoms of various diseases will be found under the above headings, and only some general symptoms of abdominal disease, or symptoms, the meaning of which is not plain, but which nevertheless point to trouble in definite organs, will be mentioned here.

PAIN.—This is a most important symptom, because the internal organs being devoid of ordinary sensation, pain in them generally means a considerable interference with structure or function. The *site* of the pain may indicate the organ affected. Thus pain under the ribs on the left, or in the pit of

1

the stomach, generally points to the stomach as being at fault. When it is felt on the right high up, and shoots through to the right shoulder, it indicates trouble connected with the liver or gall-bladder. Pain situated on the right, and low down in the iliac region, may arise from a diseased appendix. On the left, and low down, or at the exit of the bowel, it means some rectal trouble. Finally, pain situated vaguely all over the front of the abdomen, especially round the navel, points to inflammation of the peritoneal lining of the abdomen, or to irregularity in movement of the small intestine.

The *character* of the pain is also important. A dull, aching pain is not generally serious, though it may indicate chronic peritonitis or obstruction. (*See* PERITONITIS *and* INTESTINE, DISEASES OF.) A twisting, griping pain is generally, *e.g.* in babies, due to spasmodic movements of the small intestine, often produced by errors in diet, and called colic. A straining pain with frequent calls to stool indicates irritation low down in the large bowel. The pains of stomach trouble are of varied nature. (*See* DYSPEPSIA.) Sudden, colicky, agonizing pain is very often due to the passage of a gall-stone, if situated high up on the right, shooting through towards the back, or to the passage of a renal calculus, if shooting from the back down into the groin. Pain of a dull character slightly to the right of the pit of the stomach, especially when it is relieved by taking food, suggests some trouble in the duodenum.

TENDERNESS on pressure is generally a sign of inflammation either of an organ situated beneath the tender spot or of the peritoneum. (*See* APPENDICITIS, PERITONITIS.)

VOMITING is an important symptom. (*See* VOMITING.) When due to irritation of the stomach, it usually ceases as the contents of this organ are brought up. If it persists, it may be due to some obstruction in the bowels, or may be of nervous origin, *e.g.* in sea-sickness, or cerebral tumour, and have no direct connection with the abdomen.

DIARRHŒA is a very important symptom, and may be of serious import. (*See* DIARRHŒA.)

SWELLING of the abdomen may be so

2

marked as to call the patient's attention to it. This may be due merely to excessive deposit of fat, especially in elderly people—for example, in women at the menopause. (*See* CORPULENCE, DIET.) Enlargement, of course, occurs in pregnancy. The abdomen in habitual constipation may become more distended, partly by the undischarged remnant of the food and partly by gases arising from its decomposition, or this condition may be due to chronic obstruction of the bowels. (*See* CONSTIPATION *and* INTESTINE, DISEASES OF.) Finally, a collection of fluid may produce the swelling (*see* DROPSY; LIVER, DISEASES OF; HEART, DISEASES OF; PERITONITIS), or it may be due to enlargement of a single organ.

INDRAWING of the abdomen occurs in wasting diseases, and also to a marked extent in meningitis. (*See* MENINGITIS.)

DISTENSION OF THE VEINS on the surface of the abdomen indicates some interference with the circulation in the portal vein or in the inferior vena cava.

VISIBLE MOVEMENTS are sometimes seen, due to the bowels or stomach being distended and contracting forcibly in the attempt to drive their contents onwards. They indicate (unless they are visible merely on account of extreme thinness of the abdominal wall) some obstruction in the bowel or stomach. (*See* PERISTALSIS.)

The differentiation of abdominal diseases is often one of the most difficult problems with which even an expert has to deal, and frequently it is only after a period of observation, lasting in difficult cases perhaps some weeks, that a diagnosis of approximate accuracy can be arrived at. This is partly due to the difficulty or impossibility of feeling the surface and dimensions of the contained organs, *e.g.* the kidneys, especially in stout persons ; partly to the vagueness of symptoms set up in organs which are very little sensitive to even extreme changes in their structure ; and partly to the readiness with which the organs change their relative positions, and to the great changes in shape and position often brought about by previous disease.

Treatment.—Details of treatment are given under the headings of the various diseases. On the whole, people are rather too much given to regarding abdominal symptoms as trivial and amenable to home treatment. In many a case incurable dyspepsia would have been got rid of in its early stages if its symptoms had not been neglected, and not infrequently patients with acute obstruction of the bowels die because a dose of castor oil was taken when a doctor should have been consulted. In this connection one may say that whenever the three symptoms of (a) abdominal pain, (b) vomiting or retching, and (c) stoppage of the bowels for a day or two, or stoppage followed by a little diarrhœa, have occurred together, the case demands the attention of a skilled medical adviser. If severe abdominal pain be directly traceable to some dietetic indiscretion, the offending material should be got rid off speedily by an emetic, if it is still in the stomach (see EMETICS) ; or by a purgative if the symptoms are referable to the bowels (see PURGATIVES). If the pain be griping in character, e.g. in babies, relief is often given by pressure ; thus nurses often lay their charges stomach downwards across the arm, or adults get some relief by lying face downwards on a pillow. (See COLIC, LEAD-POISONING.) The application of heat, in the form of a hot-water bottle, may also give relief. When the pain is of an agonizing nature, stronger remedies are necessary. (See COLIC.)

ABDOMEN, INJURIES OF.—When one considers the exposed nature of the abdomen to the front and the thinness of the wall covering the viscera, it is surprising how seldom blows and crushes damage the contained organs. This is explained by the fact that the firm muscles, which are perhaps half an inch (12 mm.) in thickness, offer the same type of protection as would be given by a slab of india-rubber of like thickness tightly stretched, while the fat still further dissipates the effect of violence. When a kick or blow causes rupture of an organ, the violence has generally been unexpected, and the muscles have been surprised in a lax condition. It is true that instantaneous death may follow a comparatively trivial blow on the epigastrium or pit of the stomach, and this is due to shock (see SHOCK) caused by injury to a nerve-plexus situated in the back of the abdomen in

that region. Rupture of the liver, kidney, or spleen may occur, with hæmorrhage into the surrounding tissues, from severe crushes between railway-carriage buffers, from falls from a height, motorcar accidents, etc. ; but these are not necessarily fatal unless some large blood-vessel be torn. Rupture of the bowel occasionally follows a blow or wound and is almost necessarily fatal in a few days, unless the abdomen be opened by a surgeon and the torn bowel stitched within a few hours of the accident.

Persons run over by carts or cars are liable to have the bladder ruptured. This occurs especially in the case of children, and it happens only when the bladder is full, or nearly so, of urine. In such a case the inability to pass water soon after the accident, provided that it was not passed for some hours previously, or the passage of blood, indicates the necessity of a speedy operation to stitch the torn bladder.

Straining to lift a weight beyond the strength, or excessive straining at stool, may force a loop of the intestine through the muscular part of the abdominal wall, so producing a hernia or rupture (see HERNIA).

ABDOMEN, REGIONS OF. — For convenience of reference the abdomen is divided into regions by artificial lines. Two are vertical, passing through the middle of Poupart's (inguinal) ligament, a band which crosses the groin obliquely and divides thigh from abdomen ; and two are horizontal : the subcostal plane which passes through the lowest part of the costal margin, and the intertubercular plane which passes through the most outwardly projecting points of the iliac or haunch bones. These divide off nine regions named as follows : Epigastrium or pit of the stomach (E), two Hypochondriac regions (H), Umbilical or Navel region (U), two Lumbar or Loin regions (L), Hypogastric region (Hy), and two Iliac regions or Groins (I) (see Plate IV). The inguinal region on each side is the lower part of the hypogastric. This contains the inguinal canal which pierces the abdominal wall obliquely.

ABDUCENT NERVE (abducens) is the sixth nerve rising from the brain and controls the external rectus muscle of the eye, which turns the eye out-

3

wards. It is particularly liable to be paralysed in diseases of the nervous system, thus leading to an inward squint.

ABLATION means the removal of any part of the body by a surgical operation.

ABORTIFACIENT is a drug which causes artificial abortion.

ABORTION (from *aborior*, I perish), or MISCARRIAGE, means the separation and expulsion of the contents of the pregnant uterus before the 28th week of pregnancy. The frequency of abortion is not known, but it is estimated that 10 to 15 per cent. of pregnancies end in abortion. The common time for abortion to occur is from the 8th to 13th week of pregnancy.

Causes.—The cause of the abortion may be found in the mother or in the germ cells, or in some completely extraneous factor.

So far as the mother is concerned, the most common cause is an abnormality of the hormonal balance which controls the course of pregnancy (*q.v.*). The main defect is a lack of progesterone (*q.v.*). This hormone is secreted by the corpus luteum (*q.v.*) in the early weeks of pregnancy and subsequently by the placenta (*q.v.*). The function of progesterone is to ensure the safe embedding of the fertilized ovum in the mother's uterus, and then to ensure that the uterus does not start contracting until the time for labour is due. It is thus obvious why a defective supply of progesterone can result in abortion.

Other maternal causes of abortion include disturbances of other endocrine glands, or hormones, such as hypothyroidism, or myxœdema (*q.v.*), and diabetes mellitus (*q.v.*) ; high blood pressure ; Bright's disease (*q.v.*) ; any acute illness ; congenital abnormalities of the uterus, and any severe emotional disturbance.

Two oft-quoted classical causes of abortion are syphilis and drugs. Syphilis is certainly a dangerous disease for a pregnant mother to have, but it is more likely to cause the death of the fœtus after the 28th week of pregnancy ; and technically this is not an

abortion. Several drugs have achieved a popular reputation as abortifacients, or inducers of abortion, but the reputation is usually fallacious. As many a misled woman has found, it is incredibly difficult to induce an abortion by means of drugs in a healthy pregnancy. This even applies to pills containing lead, though there is no doubt that lead can induce an abortion.

Any defect in the germ cells, whether ovum or spermatozoon, may lead to abortion if it is severe enough to cause gross malformation of the embryo.

Finally, reference must be made to criminally induced abortion. This may be attempted in a variety of ways, particularly the introduction of fluids or instruments into the uterus. It is a dangerous practice, as shown by a Ministry of Health investigation into 294 fatal abortions. At least 199 of these were criminal abortions, 105 (53 per cent.) of whom died from sepsis.

Treatment.—The treatment depends largely upon whether the abortion is threatened or inevitable. In the case of the former, often a few days rest in bed is all that is necessary, following which the mother takes particular care at the next two period times. If an abortion is inevitable, the treatment is that of a miniature labour. More complicated, and requiring skilled supervision, is the treatment of what is known as an incomplete abortion (that is, when part of the fœtus and/or placenta have been retained in the uterus), and—most dangerous of all—the treatment of a septic abortion.

The Abortion Act.—The whole outlook on abortion has been changed by the Abortion Act which came into force on April 27, 1968. Under the terms of this Act, a pregnancy can be terminated, in other words, an abortion can be induced, by a ' registered medical practitioner if two registered medical practitioners are of the opinion, formed in good faith, (*a*) that the continuance of the pregnancy would involve risk to the life of the pregnant woman or of injury to the physical or mental health of the pregnant woman or any existing children of her family greater than if the pregnancy were terminated ; or (*b*) that there is a substantial risk that if the child were born it would suffer from such physical or mental abnormalities as to be seriously handi-capped '.

ABRASION means the rubbing off of the surface of the skin or of a mucous membrane due to some mechanical injury. Such injuries, though slight in themselves, are very apt to allow entrance of dirt containing organisms and so to lead to an abscess or some severer form of inflammation.

Treatment.—The most effective form of treatment consists in the thorough and immediate cleansing of the wound with soap and water. An antiseptic such as 1 per cent. cetrimide can then be applied, and a sterile dry dressing.

ABSCESS (*abscessus*) is a localized collection of pus. A minute abscess is known as a pustule (*see* PUSTULE), a diffused production of pus is known as cellulitis or erysipelas (*see* ERYSIPELAS). An abscess may be acute or chronic.

ABSCESS, ACUTE.—An acute abscess is one which develops rapidly within the course of a few days or hours. It is characterized by a definite set of symptoms.

Causes.—The direct cause is various bacteria. In a few cases the presence of foreign bodies, such as bullets or splinters, or contact with poisonous plants, such as poison ivy, may produce abscesses, but these foreign bodies, may remain for life buried in the tissues without causing any trouble provided they are not contaminated with bacteria or other micro-organisms.

The micro-organisms most frequently found are *staphylococci*, and next to these *streptococci*, though the latter cause more virulent abscesses, or in general the more serious condition of erysipelas or cellulitis. Other abscess-forming organisms are *Pseudomonas pyocyanea*, which produces blue or green-ish pus ; and *Escherichia coli*, which lives always in the bowels, probably aiding digestion, and under certain conditions wanders into the surround-ing tissues and produces abscesses.

The mere presence of micro-organisms is not sufficient to produce suppura-tion (*see* IMMUNITY *and* INFECTION) ; indeed streptococci, which upon oc-casion produce most disastrous effects, can often be found on the skin and

in the skin glands of perfectly healthy individuals. Given the proper micro-organisms in the tissues, whether they will produce abscesses or not depends upon two factors : (1) the virulence of the organism at the time, and (2) the resisting power of the indi-vidual. In the case of bad health, in diabetes, in fever, in Bright's disease, the tissues are much less resistant, and cold, injury, or previous disease of a part renders that particular part less able to cope with bacterial invasion. On the other hand, good food, vigorous exercise, and healthy open-air life help to render the individual more or less immune from the ill-effects of these bacteria. They are communicated, principally in a virulent form, from one wound to another ; but they live also in the air, in dust, and in water. They enter the body generally by a wound, but may also come through the mucous membrane of the intestine when this is rendered less resistant by conditions such as appendicitis ; they may also pass through the mucous membranes of the nose, mouth, respiratory and urinary passages, and cause local abscesses, or even through the skin by way of its minute lubricating glands.

When bacteria have gained access, for example, to a wound, they rapidly multiply, and, by the formation of poisonous substances, irritate the sur-rounding tissues, and so produce local dilatation of the blood-vessels, slowing of the blood-stream, and exudation of blood corpuscles and fluid. The leuco-cytes, or white corpuscles of the blood, collect around the invaded area, appar-ently under some attracting influence of the bacteria (chemotaxis), and destroy the latter either by actually devouring and digesting them (*see* PHAGOCYTOSIS), or by forming some substances which cause their death. These white cor-puscles undergo a granular fatty de-generation, and in turn die, and form the white constituent of the pus (pus corpuscles). Meanwhile, the area where these changes have been taking place has been cut off from communication with the rest of the body by plugging of the blood and lymphatic vessels around it. The tissues of the affected area die and are digested by the action of the white corpuscles, and the cavity so produced is distended by fluid and

5

by the white corpuscles which flock to it in increasing numbers till all bacteria have disappeared. The abscess is shut off from healthy tissue by what is known as the abscess wall. The bacteria may find their way along a vessel to some little distance, where the same process takes place, and these secondary abscess cavities may coalesce with the original one.

Symptoms.—The classic symptoms of inflammation are *rubor, calor, tumor,* and *dolor, i.e.* redness, warmth, swelling, and pain ; and, besides these, when the abscess is well developed a considerable amount of fever, perhaps with delirium, sets in, and the temperature rises to 100° to 104° F. (38° to 40° C.). When the cavity containing fluid has been formed, a sign, known as fluctuation, can be made out. Later, as the abscess is dis-

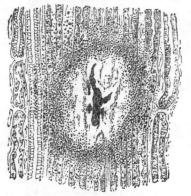

Fig. 1.—Small abscess in the kidney. In the centre is a mass of bacteria ; round it is an area of dead tissue ; at the margin of this the surrounding tissues are infiltrated with leucocytes. Magnified by 162. (Thoma's *Pathology.*)

tended almost to bursting, the skin becomes reddish blue, glazed, and thin ; and this is known as ' pointing ' of the abscess ; or if the abscess is very deep-seated the skin over it becomes swollen, and pits on pressure. The lymphatic glands in the neighbourhood may be swollen and tender. Immediately the abscess is opened, or bursts, the pain disappears, the temperature falls rapidly to normal, the elasticity of the tissues around the cavity diminishes its bulk, and the healing of the small space left proceeds rapidly. If, however, the ab-

scess discharge into an internal cavity, such as the bowel or bladder, it may heal very slowly, and the reabsorption of its poisonous products may cause general ill-health for long. When an abscess is deep-seated an important sign for diagnosis is provided by examination of the blood. (*See* LEUCOCYTOSIS.)

Treatment.—As soon as there is evidence that pus has formed, we know that Nature's attempt to destroy the bacteria has been successful, and, as the further formation of pus is designed simply to burst a passage to the exterior, we can relieve pain, stop unnecessary destruction of tissue, and shorten the process by opening the abscess. This is done as soon as there is evidence from fluctuation, redness, or pitting of the skin that pus has formed. Previous to this it may be advisable to give a course of injections of penicillin, and these may prevent the formation of an abscess. Nature's efforts may be aided by the application of heat. This has the effect of diminishing the pain ; of aiding resolution, if abscess formation is not going to take place ; and of hastening the formation of an abscess cavity, and softening the overlying tissues if the latter process has already begun.

When the abscess is opened three things are attended to :

(1) That important structures such as arteries in the neighbourhood are not damaged.

(2) That the opening is as far away as possible from a new source of infection like the mouth or anus.

(3) That the opening is large and so situated that the cavity can drain itself completely ; otherwise, if the abscess cavity be large or irregular, a further collection of pus takes place, and the wound will not heal but forms a sinus (*see* SINUS) ; for this reason it may be necessary to make two or more ' counter-openings '.

After the abscess is opened a simple wet dressing, of moist lint covered by gutta-percha tissue, and this again covered by absorbent wool (to absorb the remaining discharge) and a bandage, should be applied and changed daily. If the cavity be large it may be necessary to ' pack ' the opening with a strip of gauze or lint, or to insert a drainage tube, so as to ensure healing from the bottom of the cavity. The injection of penicillin into the abscess cavity may be of value in some cases.

Special varieties of acute abscess : ABSCESS IN ABDOMEN.—When this occurs in the iliac region it is generally a result of appendicitis (*see* APPENDICITIS) ; when in the lumbar region it may be the result of this disease ' pointing ' backwards, or may be the result of inflammation in the loose tissue around the kidney (perinephric abscess). In the upper part of the abdomen it is known as a subphrenic abscess, and may be the consequence of ulceration from the stomach or bowels, or of abscess in the liver. All these conditions are very grave.

ABSCESS IN BONE (*see* BONE, DISEASES OF).

ABSCESS OF BREAST (*see* BREAST, DISEASES OF).

CEREBRAL AND CEREBELLAR ABSCESS. —These are apt to come on suddenly in cases in which the middle ear is diseased, generally after long-standing discharge from the ear. The stoppage of the discharge in such a case is a warning of danger. (*See* EAR, DISEASES OF.)

ABSCESS IN THE FINGER (*see* WHITLOW).

ILIAC ABSCESS (*see* APPENDICITIS).

ABSCESS OF THE JAW (*see* GUMBOIL).

ABSCESS OF THE LUNG may follow pneumonia or the drawing of some foreign body, such as food, down the windpipe. Being deep-seated, its presence may be hard to diagnose. It may burst either into a bronchus, when pus will be spat up, or into the pleural cavity.

ABSCESS IN THE PLEURAL CAVITY is known as empyema. (*See* EMPYEMA.)

ABSCESS, CHRONIC.—A chronic abscess is one which takes weeks or months for its development. In the vast majority of cases it is tuberculous.

Causes.—Some acute abscesses, instead of bursting, may settle down, become surrounded by dense fibrous tissue, and so form chronic abscesses, but these are rare. Abscesses may form in the liver as a complication of amœbic dysentery. (*See* DYSENTERY.) The tubercle bacillus, or *Mycobacterium tuberculosis*, as it is now known, however, is generally the cause. How

it obtains entrance is still in dispute ; in the case of abscesses of the neck it is probably through the throat or tonsil, and in the case of abscesses elsewhere, through the circulation from the lung or intestinal canal, owing to polluted air or food. A common source of infection is milk which has not been boiled or pasteurized. Abscesses arise most commonly from tuberculous deposits in glands or bones, especially in the vertebræ or bones of the spine, the epiphyses or large ends of long bones near a joint, and the ribs. They may start also in the synovial membranes, *i.e.* membranes lining a joint (*see* JOINT DISEASES), in the loose tissue beneath the skin, quite apart from disease of any other structure, and, not uncommonly, in the testicle.

Symptoms.—There is far less in the way of symptoms than in acute abscess. Sometimes the swelling is noticed by accident ; it is not hot, red, or in general painful, as is an acute abscess. The skin becomes red only a short time before the abscess bursts. If the temperature be taken every four hours it will generally be found that there is a slight rise either in the forenoon or late afternoon. If the abscess be untreated it generally enlarges till it bursts, then a ragged wound is left, infection with other organisms takes place, and the resulting sinus with ' mixed infection ' becomes extremely difficult to heal. If such a sinus be large, as in a psoas abscess, it may persist for years, and the patient becomes exhausted by the resulting hectic fever ; or waxy disease (*see* WAXY DISEASE) attacks the liver and kidneys, and causes wasting and death.

Characters of the pus.—The fluid is thin and watery (not thick and white as in an acute abscess) and contains little curdy masses. It is not really ' pus ', as pus corpuscles are almost entirely absent, and only fragments of the dead tissues are found under the microscope.

Treatment.—For the purpose of discussing treatment it will be assumed that the abscess is tuberculous.

The introduction of the anti-tuberculous drugs, streptomycin (*q.v.*), para-aminosalicylic acid (*q.v.*), and isoniazid (*q.v.*), has revolutionized the outlook in tuberculous abscesses and has removed

7

many of the hazards which attached to them at one time. The general rules for improving the health of the individual and resting the affected part still apply, but the administration of these drugs shortens the period of treatment and convalescence very considerably. Further details will be found under GLANDS and JOINT DISEASES.

Special varieties of chronic abscess :
ABSCESS OF THE LIVER.—This occurs in persons who have been the subject of amœbic dysentery (see DYSENTERY), frequently after returning in apparently fair health to a temperate region where dysentery does not occur. The liver becomes enlarged and tender, and there is a degree of ill-health and slight jaundice. When threatening, it is treated by emetine, rest, and light diet ; and when it has formed should be at once operated on, lest it burst into lung or peritoneal cavity.

ISCHIO-RECTAL ABSCESS.—This forms at the side of the rectum. Whether it bursts or is opened it is very difficult to keep clean, on account of its position, and so forms a sinus ; or if it open into the bowel, a fistula. (See FISTULA.) It may occur late in a case of pulmonary tuberculosis, but may also occur as the first manifestation of tuberculosis.

RETROPHARYNGEAL ABSCESS.—This is due generally to disease of the spinal column in the neck. It is opened from the side of the neck ; otherwise it bursts into the mouth, and the discharges from it being constantly swallowed, lead to rapid falling-off in health, and to death.

ILIO-PSOAS ABSCESS.—This is a common form of large chronic abscess. It arises generally from tuberculous disease of the spinal column in the lumbar region, and though this may cure itself, the abscess bursts into the sheath of the psoas muscle and passes along the muscle through the iliac region into the thigh, on the inner side of which it generally ' points '. Its early symptoms resemble those of hip-joint desease. (See JOINT DISEASES.) The opening and scraping of such an abscess often require large incisions in the thigh, groin, and lumbar region, and if, unfortunately, the wound become the seat of mixed infection the resulting sinus may last months or years.

8

ACTINOMYCOTIC ABSCESS.—This is another form of chronic abscess, which occurs about the jaw or mouth. (See ACTINOMYCOSIS.)

ABSINTHISM.—Absinthe is a liquor prepared by steeping several herbs, especially anise and wormwood, in alcohol for several days. It is greenish in colour. It was first introduced into France by soldiers stationed in Algiers between 1830 and 1850, for whom it had been prescribed as a febrifuge, and its employment spread thence into other countries. Its use becomes a habit like that of alcohol, but its effects are more demoralizing. Its habitual use brings on tremors and paralysis, in the arms especially, with delusional insanity.

ABSTRACT.—This is a dry powdered extract produced by extracting the active principles from a crude drug with strong alcohol, mixing with sugar of milk, and drying. Abstracts are standardized so as to be twice the strength of the crude drug.

ACACIA GUM, or GUM ARABIC, is a gummy exudation from various species of the acacia tree, which, dissolved in water to form mucilage, is largely used in coughs and sore throat and in states of irritation of the stomach and bowels. The dose of mucilage of acacia is one to four teaspoonfuls. Gum acacia, 6 per cent. in normal salt solution, is sometimes injected into the veins after severe haemorrhage to make up for loss of blood.

ACANTHOSIS NIGRICANS is a rare disease in which pigmented warty growths appear on the skin in different parts of the body and in the mouth.

ACAPNIA (ά, neg. ; καπνός, smoke) means a condition of diminished carbon dioxide in the blood.

ACARUS (ἀκαρί, a mite).—The group of animal parasites which includes *Sarcoptes scabiei*, the cause of the skin disease known as Itch, or Scabies. This parasite used to be known as *Acarus scabiei*. (See ITCH.)

ACCOMMODATION is the faculty possessed by the eye of altering its refractive power so that rays of light, whether from a near or distant point, are brought accurately to a focus on the retina. (See EYE.) It is effected by means of the elasticity of the crystalline lens. If the eye be directed towards a distant object the rays of light entering it should be focused exactly on the retina ; if now the eye be turned towards an object a few inches off, the elastic, circular ligament, in the centre of which the lens is suspended, is drawn together by the circular ciliary muscle, allowing the lens to become more globular (Fig. 2), as it constantly tends to do. The lens becomes, therefore, of higher power, and the diverging rays from the near object are still brought to a focus on the retina. The amount of power possessed by the eye of thus suiting itself for objects far off and near at hand is known as range of accommodation. At the age of forty-five the lens has lost much of its elasticity, though this change has been gradually proceeding throughout life ; and by

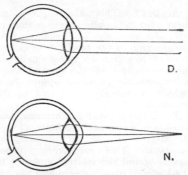

D.

N.

FIG. 2.—Diagram illustrating resting position of eye for distant vision (D), and increased convexity of lens for vision of a near object (N).

the age of sixty, even though it be quite clear, it is incapable of this accommodative change in shape ; consequently a natural change with advancing years is that persons become unable to read, sew, or do other fine work near at hand without glasses, though for distant vision no such assistance is necessary. This natural change is known as ' presbyopia ' (q.v.).

In addition to this, there are three errors in the refractive power of the eye which may be either present at birth or come on early in life and persist through

life, and in which these movements of the lens are not always sufficient to focus the rays of light accurately on the retina. These are astigmatism (see ASTIGMATISM), hypermetropia (see HYPERMETROPIA) or long sight, in which the eyeball is too short, and myopia (see MYOPIA) or short sight, in which the eyeball is too long. (See also SPECTACLES.)

ACCOUCHEUR is a physician who specializes in the practice of midwifery.

A.C.E. MIXTURE is an anæsthetic mixture containing one part of alcohol, two of chloroform, and three of ether.

ACETABULUM (acetabulum, a cup) is the cup-shaped socket on the pelvis in which rests the head of the femur or thigh-bone, the two forming the hip joint. (See HIP JOINT.)

ACETARSOL, also known as STO-VARSOL, is an organic arsenical preparation used in the treatment of infections of the vagina due to Trichomonas vaginalis.

ACETAZOLAMIDE, also known as DIAMOX, is a drug which acts by inhibiting the enzyme carbonic anhydrase. This enzyme is of great importance in the production of acid and alkaline secretions in the body and in the metabolism of the central nervous system. Acetazolamide has proved of value as a diuretic, as an anticonvulsant in the treatment of epilepsy, and in the treatment of glaucoma.

ACETIC ACID (acetum, vinegar), also called pyroligneous acid, is prepared in large quantities by the distillation of wood and subsequent separation from tar. In the pure form it is solid, being then known as glacial acetic acid. It is the active principle of vinegar, which is prepared from wine by the action of a particular ferment discovered by Pasteur. This grows on the surface of the vine, taking from the air oxygen which it gives up to the alcohol of the wine, so producing acetic acid. Weak acetic acid has all the actions of vinegar, and is less expensive. Strong acetic acid is a caustic and irritant poison.

Uses.—In strong solution acetic acid is used to destroy warts or raise blisters. In cases of great and weakening sweating the weak acid is of value, because, sponged over the skin, it checks perspiration and produces a sense of grateful coolness ; for this purpose a few tablespoonfuls of vinegar may be added to a quart of water. Used similarly it is good for headache.

ACETOHEXAMIDE is one of the new oral hypoglycæmic drugs being used in the treatment of diabetes mellitus. It is thought to act by increasing the output of insulin.

ACETONE is a chemical substance found in the urine in wasting conditions like cancer, in diabetes, in prolonged vomiting, and in acute fevers—especially in children. With it occur in the urine β-hydroxy-butyric and aceto-acetic acids, particularly in severe cases of diabetes. A large quantity of these acids and of acetone in the urine in diabetes indicates approaching coma. Acetone is sometimes used externally as an antiseptic. (*See also* ACIDOSIS.)

ACETYLCHOLINE is a substance constantly found in small quantities in the muscles and necessary for the transmission of nervous influences for their contraction. It appears to be responsible for the transmission of nervous impulses at the synapses and terminals of the parasympathetic nervous system. Various preparations of choline are used as stimulants of this system, causing vasodilatation, slowing of the heart, increased activity of the gastro-intestinal tract. Acetylcholine is rapidly destroyed by cholinesterase, an enzyme present in the blood.

ACETYLSALICYLIC ACID (*see* ASPIRIN).

ACHALASIA (*ά*, neg. ; *χάλασις*, slackening) is another term for spasm, but indicates not so much an active spasm of muscle as a failure to relax.

ACHALASIA OF THE CARDIA is a condition in which there is a failure to relax of the muscle fibres round the opening of the œsophagus into the stomach.

10

ACHLORHYDRIA means an absence of hydrochloric acid from the stomach juice ; it occurs in about 4 per cent. of healthy people and in several conditions, including pernicious anæmia, carcinoma of the stomach, and gastritis.

ACHONDROPLASIA (*ά*, neg. ; *χόνδρος*, cartilage ; *πλάσσω*, I form) is the name of a form of dwarfing in which the arms and legs are abnormally short and the head large.

ACHORION (*άχωρ*, dandruff) is the name of the micro-organism causing favus or honeycomb ringworm. (*See* RINGWORM.)

ACHYLIA GASTRICA (*ά*, neg. ; *χυλός*, juice) means the complete absence of ferments and of hydrochloric acid from the gastric juice, so that in this condition the food is passed from the stomach in a state of incomplete digestion.

ACIDITY.—This is a vague term, more used in popular language than in scientific medicine, and meaning that the reaction of the blood, or of one or more of the secretions, is less alkaline or more strongly acid than normal, while a considerable number of symptoms is rightly or wrongly attributed to the condition.

The blood in health is alkaline, and an elaborate chemical mechanism keeps the degree of alkalinity remarkably constant. This mechanism hinges largely round the relative amounts in the blood of carbonic acid and sodium bicarbonate, $H_2CO_3/NaHCO_3$. By this and other mechanisms the acids formed in metabolism are neutralized and got rid of through the kidneys and the lungs. These acids are the fixed acids, such as lactic, sulphuric, phosphoric, and carbonic acid which is produced in large amounts daily as a result of tissue activity. The blood in disease never becomes actually acid, except in the last stages. But the blood may become *less alkaline*, and the patient in this state is said to have acidæmia—although the blood is not acid.

ACIDOSIS is a condition in which there is either (i) a production in the body of two abnormal acids—β-oxy-butyric and aceto-acetic acids, or (ii) a diminution in the alkali reserve of the blood.

Causes.—The condition is usually due to faulty metabolism of fat which results in the production of β-oxy-butyric and aceto-acetic acids. It occurs in diabetes mellitus when this is either untreated or inadequately treated, starvation, persistent vomiting, and delayed anæsthetic vomiting. It also occurs in the terminal stages of Bright's disease when it is due to failure of the kidneys. A milder form of it may occur in severe fevers, particularly in children. (*See also* ACETONE.)

Symptoms.—General lassitude, vomiting, thirst, restlessness, and the presence of acetone in the urine form the earliest manifestations of the condition. In diabetes a state of coma may ensue and the disease end fatally.

Treatment.—The underlying condition must always be treated, *e.g.*, if the acidosis is due to diabetes mellitus insulin must be given. For the acidosis, alkalis should be given, *e.g.* bicarbonate of soda, either by mouth, or by injection if there is persistent vomiting or if the patient is unconscious. Glucose should also be given, and adequate fluids.

ACIDS.—These are substances which combine with alkalis to form salts. Most are oxygen compounds, have a sour taste, and turn blue litmus red. They are divided into (*a*) mineral or inorganic, and (*b*) vegetable or organic. In strong solution the mineral acids act upon stomach and bowels as irritant poisons, but small quantities in weak solution aid digestion, diminish the alkalinity of the blood, are excreted in the urine, the acidity of which they increase, act as mild astringents and refrigerants, and check excessive sweating. The action of the organic acids varies, but the best known, viz. acetic, citric, lactic, tartaric, while in strong solution acting like mineral acids, in weaker solution after absorption into the blood become decomposed into carbonates, and have precisely the opposite actions, *i.e.* those of alkalis.

Varieties commonly used.—(*a*) *Inorganic* : boracic or boric, chromic,

hydrochloric, hydrobromic, nitric, nitro-hydrochloric, phosphoric, sulphuric, sulphurous. (*b*) *Organic* : acetic, carbolic, carbonic, chrysophanic, citric, gallic, hydrocyanic or prussic, lactic, salicylic, tannic or tannin, tartaric.

Uses.—The strong mineral acids, especially chromic and nitric, with pure acetic and carbolic from among the organic acids, are used as caustics to remove outgrowths such as corns, warts, piles, and also to destroy diseased tissue in poisoned wounds and spreading sores. In using them, care must be taken not to let the action extend too far and destroy healthy tissue ; they are usually applied on a glass rod, and an alkali, oil, or glycerin should be at hand to apply in case a drop falls on the healthy surface.

Weak acids are given in dyspepsia (*see* DYSPEPSIA), usually after meals, to stimulate digestion in the stomach. For this action hydrochloric acid (the acid naturally present in the gastric juice), or nitrohydrochloric acid, is chiefly used.

The astringent action is utilized in excessive sweating. (*See also* ACETIC ACID.) When the urine is very alkaline there is a tendency to the formation of phosphate calculi, and catarrh of the bladder is often present ; these are relieved by acids among various other substances.

In fevers and in cases in which an increase in the output of urine is desirable, the vegetable acids or their acid salts are given, *e.g.* citrate, tartrate, or acetate of potash, because they lessen dryness of the mouth and thirst, cause a feeling of refreshment, stimulate the kidneys and sweat glands, and lower the temperature. In general acidity (*see* ACIDITY) the vegetable acids are used as indirect alkalis.

For the use of special acids see under ACETIC ACID, CARBOLIC ACID, SALICYLIC ACID, etc.

ACIDS, POISONING BY.—Although most acids have an extremely sour and burning taste, which warns a person drinking one of his error before very much is swallowed, several are so much used in commercial processes, and so easily obtained, that accidental and intentional poisoning by acids is not uncommon.

Symptoms. — The symptoms produced are destruction of the skin and mucous membrane about the mouth, great pain in the mouth, throat, and stomach, and sometimes fainting or collapse. There is also later a risk of scarring and contraction of the throat. These are especially the symptoms of poisoning by strong mineral acids, or by citric, or tartaric in large quantities, while several, such as prussic and carbolic, have symptoms peculiar to themselves and not due to irritation.

Treatment.—Give large quantities of water by mouth, and if possible add alkalis to it—such as bicarbonate of soda, baking soda, plaster from the ceiling, whitewash from the walls, or finely powdered egg shells. These neutralize the acid taken and form harmless salts, and also soothe the irritated mucous membrane. On no account must emetics be given. The patient must be treated for shock. Soothing or demulcent substances, such as milk in oil, or barley water, must also be given.

ACINUS (*acinus*, a grape) is the name applied to each of the minute sacs of which secreting glands are composed, and which usually cluster round the branches of the gland-duct like grapes on their stem.

ACNE is a chronic skin disease affecting the sebaceous glands of the forehead, nose, chin, chest, back of the shoulders, and outer side of the thighs, or one or more of these regions.

Causes.—The condition occurs in individuals with seborrhœa (*q.v.*). Although a micro-organism known as the acne bacillus is found in the comedones, which are the characteristic lesion, this is not the entire cause. There is an individual predisposition to the disease and it is dependent upon the development of the sebaceous glands which takes place at puberty. It occurs in both sexes and usually between the ages of fourteen and twenty. The condition is often associated with dyspepsia, constipation, and lack of fresh air and exercise. In women it tends to become worse during menstruation.

Symptoms.—The eruption itself consists of little black spots (blackheads or comedones) which indicate the mouth of small sebaceous ducts choked with dust or dirt, from which a long, wormy-looking, fatty mass can be squeezed ; hard pimples generally showing one of these blackheads on the top ; little pustules surrounded by a slight degree of inflammation, which gradually grow, burst, and then heal ; and hard lumps, sometimes half an inch (12 mm.) across, which last for weeks or months, slowly suppurate, and leave a permanent hardness or scar.

Treatment.—The general health must be looked to, and dyspepsia, constipation, and similar errors treated. Excess of fats and sweets should be avoided, particularly nuts and chocolates. If there is any tendency to overweight, this should be dealt with by a reducing diet. Sometimes anæmia needs treatment by iron. If the subject of the disease leads a sedentary or inactive life, active exercise should be taken, and the hygiene of the whole skin should be attended to. The most important point in treatment is the daily washing of the affected areas with soap and *hot* water, followed by brisk rubbing with a soft towel. The exact type of soap is unimportant, but the addition of borax or sodium bicarbonate to the water is helpful. After washing and drying, a lotion containing sulphur is applied to the affected areas. The contents of the sebaceous glands, wherever a blackhead shows, may be regularly squeezed out, by gentle pressure with a fine tube or 'comedo-extractor', after washing. In severe cases, more drastic treatment may be required, such as ultra-violet light or X-rays, but such treatment, of course, can only be used under medical supervision.

ACNE ROSACEA is a condition in which chronic congestion of the face, especially of the nose, leading to enlargement of the minute blood-vessels, lumpiness, and a red or dusky-copper colour, is associated with dyspepsia.

Causes.—It generally occurs in the subjects of dyspepsia, and often occurs in women at the time of the menopause. Severer forms, due to abuse of alcohol, are popularly known as ' grog-blossoms '.

Symptoms.—In the milder forms there is simple redness, burning, and tingling of the nose, the redness lasting at first only for a few hours every day, but later tending to become permanent, and also to appear upon the cheeks. In the severer form the nose becomes very red and the skin thick and lumpy, while the openings of the sebaceous glands are seen as quite wide pits.

Treatment.—The mild form is lessened by attending to the dyspepsia which is its cause ; avoiding exposure to cold winds ; and by painting with Goulard's water, or calamine lotion. In the more severe forms the dilated veins may be destroyed by electrolysis. When there is much overgrowth of the skin, it may be necessary to remove some of the overgrown tissue.

ACONITE (also known as ' Wolf's-bane ', or ' Blue rocket ' or ' Monk's hood ') is an extremely poisonous plant found in different species all over the world, and largely grown for its appearance in gardens. All parts of the plant are poisonous. The root has been mistaken for horse-radish, although the resemblance, to those who know horse-radish by sight, is not very great. The root of the horse-radish is long, whitish outside, when scraped remains white, and has the well-known pungent odour. Aconite root is short and stumpy, brown, and when scraped the white cut surface speedily turns pinkish ; if it be chewed, the tongue in a few minutes tingles, then becomes numb and swollen, and a burning sensation is felt in the mouth. The action of aconitine, its active principle, is produced by smaller doses than in the case of any other drug ; accordingly aconite is a favourite homœopathic remedy.

Uses.—Aconite is seldom used at the present day, although in the form of a liniment it is sometimes used externally to relieve pain, sprains, and rheumatism. Tincture of aconite, which is still kept in some households, should never be used without the sanction of a doctor.

ACONITE POISONING.—This may occur, as stated above, by mistaking the root for horse-radish, by children eating parts of the plant, or by the administration of too large a dose.

Symptoms.—There are characteristic symptoms in the mouth (*see* ACONITE) after chewing parts of the plant. If a large amount of the poison has been taken into the stomach, vomiting and purging follow after some time. Numbness is felt all over the body. The pulse becomes weak, the breathing laboured, and the face livid. Convulsions may come on, but consciousness is retained.

Treatment.—Give plenty of warm water to drink. The poison must be got rid of at once by an emetic, one of the handiest being a tablespoonful of mustard in a cupful of cold water ; or, best of all, one or two tablespoonfuls of sal volatile in water, this being also a stimulant. Stimulants, such as picrotoxin or atropine, may be given by injection, or brandy may be given by the mouth, with black coffee or strong tea after the vomiting has stopped. Artificial respiration may be necessary.

ACRIDINE is a colourless crystalline compound occurring in coal-tar. Its formula is $C_{13}H_9N$. From this are derived the valuable acridine dyes or flavines, used as antiseptics.

ACRIFLAVINE is an aniline derivative, the hydrochloride of diaminomethylacridine chloride. It is an orange-red crystalline powder, readily soluble in water, which gives a rich yellow colour to substances brought into contact with it, and in a solution of 1 in 1000 of water, possesses strong antiseptic powers.

ACROCYANOSIS is a condition, occurring especially in young women, in which there is persistent blueness of hands, feet, nose, and ears.

ACRODYNIA (*see* ERYTHRŒDEMA).

ACROMEGALY (ἄκρον, an extremity; μέγας, large) is a chronic disease characterized by increased massiveness of the bones, most noticeable in the jaws, hands, and feet. The bones of the chest and elsewhere are also lengthened and thickened so that the whole person becomes more massive. It was first described in 1866, and is not uncommon. It is associated with tumours or other disorders causing increase in size of the front part of the pituitary gland inside the skull on the base of the brain. The condition is due to an excessive secretion by this gland of a substance, known as the growth hormone, which has the effect of stimulating the growth of bones, so that if it begins in early life great stature results ; if later, a thickening of the bones, most noticeable in the hands and feet. Treatment has little or no effect, but the disease advances very slowly, and frequently it stops its progress after the bones are slightly enlarged. A disorder of vision, involving limitation of the field of vision at its outer sides, is apt to be caused by interference with the optic tracts through the increase in size of the gland in advanced stages of the disease.

Treatment.—Surgical removal of the front portion of the pituitary gland is sometimes practised in advanced cases when the vision is seriously affected. In other cases treatment consists of irradiation of the gland with X-rays.

ACROMION (ἀκρώμιον) is the part of the scapula or shoulder blade forming the tip of the shoulder and giving its squareness to the latter. It projects forward from the scapula, and, with the clavicle or collar-bone in front, forms a protecting arch of bone over the shoulder joint.

ACROPARÆSTHESIA is a disorder occurring predominantly in middle-aged women in which there are numbness and tingling of the fingers.

A.C.T.H. is the commonly used abbreviation for corticotrophin, the adrenocorticotrophic hormone of the pituitary gland. It is so called because it stimulates the functions of the cortex of the suprarenal glands. This results, among other things, in an increased output of cortisone. Although it was first isolated from the pituitary gland in 1933, it was not until the discovery, in 1949, of the dramatic effect of cortisone and A.C.T.H. in rheumatoid arthritis that it came into general use. No means of synthesis has yet been discovered, and the only available source are the pituitary glands of animals. It is only active when given by intravenous or intramuscular injection. As its action is predominantly the same as that of cortisone, the action of the two is discussed together in the section on cortisone (q.v.).

ACTINOMYCIN D is an antibiotic isolated from *Streptomyces chrysomalis* which has an inhibitory action on neoplastic cells.

14

ACTINOMYCOSIS (ἀκτίς, a ray ; μύκης, a fungus) is an acute or chronic suppurative disease affecting cattle, in which it is known as ' Woody Tongue ', and sometimes found in man.

Causes.—The direct cause is the ray-fungus or actinomyces known as *Actinomyces israeli*, which occurs as a commensal (q.v.) in the mouth. In certain circumstances still rather obscure, but one of which is undoubtedly trauma, such as a fractured jaw or extraction of a tooth, the *A. israeli* becomes active. It then causes hard swellings, abscesses, and ulcers, in the pus of which the fungus is found in little yellow balls of a size which can just be made out by the naked eye. These little balls are found to consist of masses of thread-like material matted together, and of club-shaped bodies radiating from a common centre, hence the name of ray-fungus. It used to be thought that the human infection arose from the chewing of straw or grain, or was caught from cattle, but this is now known not to be the case. In over 50 per cent. of cases the disease occurs in or about the mouth ; in 20 per cent. it occurs in the abdomen, and in 15 per cent. in the thorax.

Symptoms.—These are general bad health, the presence of hard fibrous masses about the mouth or tongue, or in other organs, and the development sooner or later in these masses of abscesses which after bursting form sinuses or ulcers that will not heal.

Treatment.—The outlook has been changed completely since the introduction of the antibiotics. The best results are usually obtained with large doses of penicillin, but in some cases chlortetracycline is more effective. Surgical treatment may be required, as in the draining of abscesses.

ACTIVE PRINCIPLES.—These are the portions of a drug which produce its effect, being administered for convenience, or of necessity, with the water, oils, vegetable fibre, etc., which make the bulk of the drug. They are of various chemical nature, but, in general, alkaloids. (*See* ALKALOIDS.)

ACUPUNCTURE (*acus*, a needle ; *punctum*, a prick) is a method of treatment by puncture of a part with needles two to three inches long. It is little used, but in obstinate sciatica is sometimes successful. The needles are pushed into the sciatic nerve and left in for twenty to thirty minutes. Their insertion causes very little pain.

ACUTE DISEASE.—A disease is said to be acute in contradistinction to chronic when it comes on rapidly and produces death rapidly, or goes on to speedy recovery, e.g. acute bronchitis ; or the word is used, though less often, in the sense of severe or sharply painful, e.g. acute sciatica, acute neuralgia.

ADDISONIAN ANÆMIA is another term for pernicious anæmia. (*See* ANÆMIA.)

ADDISON'S DISEASE.—This disease, described by Addison of Guy's Hospital, London, in 1855, is not uncommon. It consists of a state of anæmia, extreme weakness, low blood-pressure, dyspepsia, wasting, pigmentation of the skin and mucous membranes, and subnormal temperature. It is due to disease of the suprarenal glands (*q.v.*), resulting in destruction of the cortical section of the gland.

Causes.—Men, and especially young adults, suffer oftener than women in the proportion of two to one. The condition found after death is generally tuberculosis or atrophy of the suprarenal glands, causing their destruction to a greater or less extent. More rarely it is caused by other diseases, such as atrophy or cancer of, or hæmorrhage into, the glands. The disease destroys the secreting tissue of the glands, especially the cortex, and so checks the formation of the very powerful secretion which these glands have been shown to produce in health, and which is necessary for the proper functions of the body, as for example for the maintenance of the blood-pressure and the contractile power of the muscles.

Symptoms.—In the words of Addison, the main symptoms are : ' Anæmia, general languor or debility, remarkable feebleness of the heart's action, irritability of the stomach, and a peculiar change of colour in the skin '. The colour ranges from yellow to dark brown, or even black, and though at first marked on the exposed surface

(*i.e.* face and hands), and on regions where pigment occurs naturally (groins, armpits, etc.), it gradually increases in area and in depth of tint. The next most prominent symptom is weakness on the least exertion, with giddiness, noises in the ears, or even faintings when efforts are made. Nausea, vomiting, occasional diarrhœa are also symptoms, and there is palpitation of the heart and feebleness of the pulse. The sufferer in general gets gradually worse, though there may be periods of betterment lasting some months. Untreated the disease rarely lasts longer than three or four years, and it may prove fatal within some months. Sometimes recovery may occur.

Several other diseases cause a limited pigmentation, especially of the face, so that this symptom must not always be taken as a sign of Addison's disease. Such conditions are cirrhosis of the liver, abdominal cancer, menstrual irregularity, exophthalmic goitre ; while pregnancy brings on the so-called ' masques des femmes enceintes ', which fades after delivery.

Treatment.—The outlook in this disease has improved so considerably as a result of substitution therapy that it is now possible for many patients with this disease to lead more or less normal lives. Treatment consists of the regular administration of deoxycortone acetate (*q.v.*) and of cortisone (*q.v.*). In all cases the administration of common salt is essential, as there is a depletion of this salt in the disease.

ADENITIS (ἀδήν, a gland) means inflammation of a gland. (*See* LYMPHATICS.)

ADENO- (ἀδήν, a gland) is a prefix denoting relation to a gland or glands.

ADENOIDS (ἀδήν, a gland ; εἶδος, form). (*See* NOSE, DISEASES OF.)

ADENOMA (ἀδήν, a gland ; oma, a termination adopted to signify tumour) means a benign tumour composed of glandular tissue. It may arise in any part of the body in which glandular tissue occurs, *e.g.* the thyroid gland. It must be differentiated from an adenocarcinoma, which is a malignant tumour

15

composed of glandular tissue. (*See* TUMOURS.)

ADENOVIRUSES are a group of viruses which cause infections of the upper respiratory tract resembling the common cold, and often referred to as febrile catarrh.

ADHESION.—This means the uniting together of structures which should normally be separate and freely movable. It is the result of acute or chronic inflammation. The medium by which the attachment takes place may at first be fibrin (as a result of acute inflammation), but later is, in every case, fibrous tissue either in masses or in bands.

Causes.—The most important adhesions are those taking place in serous and joint cavities. When one of these structures becomes inflamed there is a great exudation of fluid into the cavity. From this fluid a solid material separates and becomes deposited upon the smooth surface of the cavity. This solid 'fibrin' should, in the course of recovery, be reabsorbed ; but, if the inflammation be very severe, or if there be repeated attacks of it, this absorption does not completely take place, the two layers of fibrin on the opposing surfaces of the cavity stick together, and the united mass is 'organized' into the less absorbable fibrous tissue (*see* FIBROUS TISSUE). As a result there is restricted movement in the parts concerned ; thus in the case of a joint there is ankylosis (*see* JOINT DISEASES) ; if the inflammation has been pleurisy the lung becomes adherent to the chest wall ; if peritonitis, bands are formed between stomach, bowels, and other abdominal organs.

Symptoms.—It is generally difficult to tell, except from the history of an inflammatory attack and from the presence of disordered function of internal organs, that adhesions are present (*see* PLEURISY, PERITONITIS). Sometimes adhesions between loops of bowels may be very serious and cause obstruction, if an old-standing and rigid fibrous band becomes twisted round a loop of bowel (*see* INTESTINE, DISEASES OF).

Treatment.—While the adhesions are still *fibrinous* one expects complete ab-

16

sorption if the inflammation be speedily subdued. If the adhesions are *fibrous*, and show their presence by interference with the function of the organs concerned, one can seldom expect their complete absorption. Some drugs, *e.g.* potassium iodide, act as absorbents when given internally, and counter-irritation (*see* BLISTERS) may be applied locally over the site of the adhesion. Sometimes, *e.g.* when obstruction of the bowels is due to an adhesion, an immediate operation is necessary, and the adhesion is then divided. Adhesions causing limitation of movement in joints can often be broken down by means of manipulation.

ADHESIVE PLASTERS.—These are made by spreading upon cotton cloth, linen, or leather some sticky substance containing drugs of various sorts. The sticky material, which may consist either of resin, beeswax, pitch, or lead-soap (diachylon), or generally of two of these mixed, becomes more adhesive by the action of gentle heat. Rubber plasters which are highly adhesive are also obtainable, usually in a long strip on a spool. 'Court plaster' is a thin silk tissue.

Uses.—Plasters are generally useful on account of their power of gripping a part and exerting steady pressure on it. In cases where a part is weak, such as the muscles of the back after a slight injury, a large plaster, 12 by 8 inches (30 × 20 cm.), gives great support, and may be worn for a fortnight or so, till the plaster gets loose. Such large plasters are spread on leather or strong linen and have numerous holes for evaporation of moisture (porous plaster). Plasters are sometimes used to obtain the absorbent effect of steady pressure combined with warmth and moisture in the treatment of chronic callous ulcers (*see* ULCERS). In this case the plaster is put on in strips, each of which overlaps the last, and has no holes ; it must be changed every few days if it cover an unclean ulcer. Belladonna plaster is used for soothing pain. To support a sprained joint, *e.g.* the ankle, a plaster is often applied in overlapping strips passing round the leg and instep. Cantharides plaster and mustard plaster are used as counter-irritants on account of their blistering action. Capsicum plaster is used as a milder form of counter-irritant. Plasters of felt are employed to protect corns, bunions, and small sores from abrasion ; and ' corn plasters ', containing salicylic acid in various strengths, are used to soften and remove corns. (*See* BLISTERS.)

Mode of application.—Most plasters with a rubber basis stick by simply laying the plaster with the adhesive side next the skin, but some must be warmed. If the plaster be wide, or the surface to be covered be rounded, it is necessary to cut deep notches into the plaster before heating (*see* Fig. 3), and the edges so formed are

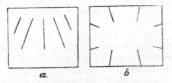

a   *b*

FIG. 3.—Diagram showing the method of slitting an adhesive plaster : *a*, to support the breast ; *b*, for the back.

allowed to overlap or separate. In applying a plaster for support to the back, the person must bend backwards as far as possible ; then when he tends to stoop forwards the plaster is a real

support. On the other hand, in applying it for support to the breast, the breast must be lifted as high as possible, and the skin which the plaster is to cover stretched, slits having been cut in the plaster beforehand. Plaster strips used to support the ankle or leg should be applied like a bandage (*q.v.*).

ADIE'S SYNDROME is the term given to the condition described by the late W. J. Adie in 1931 in which absence of tendon reflexes is associated with pupils which do not react to light in a person who has not had syphilis.

ADIPOCERE (*adeps*, fat ; *cera*, wax). (*See* PUTREFACTION.)

ADIPOSE TISSUE or FAT (*adeps*, fat) is a loose variety of fibrous tissue, in the meshes of which lie cells, each of which is distended by several small drops, or one large drop of fat (Fig. 4). This tissue replaces the fibrous tissue when the amount of food taken is in excess of the bodily requirements. (*See* DIET, CORPULENCE.)

ADIPOSIS DOLOROSA, also known as Dercum's disease, is a condition in which painful masses of fat develop

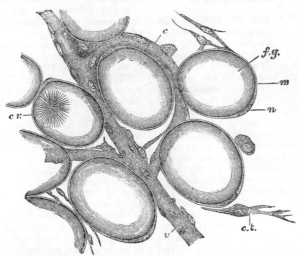

FIG. 4.—Adipose tissue. Highly magnified. *m*, membrane of fat-cell consisting of cytoplasm and nucleus (*n*) and enclosing fat-globule (*f.g.*) ; *cr.*, crystals of fatty acid ; *c*, a capillary joining a venule (*v*) ; *c.t.*, a connective-tissue cell. (From Quain, *Elements of Anatomy*. Longmans, Green & Co. Ltd.)

under the skin. It is commoner in women than in men and is thought to be caused by some disturbance of the pituitary gland.

ADRENAL GLANDS, also known as SUPRARENAL or EPINEPHRIC GLANDS. (*See* SUPRARENAL GLANDS.)

ADRENALINE is an extract derived from the suprarenal glands of animals. (*See* SUPRARENAL GLANDS.)

It was first prepared by Takamine in 1901. Similar extracts are made under such names as epinephrine ; and the substance is now prepared synthetically. When injected it produces the same effect as stimulation of the sympathetic nervous system (*q.v.*). Among its important effects are raising of the blood-pressure, increasing the amount of glucose in the blood, and constricting the smaller blood-vessels. It is applied directly to wounds on gauze or lint to check hæmorrhage. Injected along with some local anæsthetic it permits of painless, bloodless operations being performed on the eye, nose, etc. It is injected hypodermically to relieve asthma, and to stimulate the heart in collapsed conditions. It is also injected as an antidote in the condition of hypoglycæmia, when too large a dose of insulin has been given.

ADULTERATION OF FOOD.—The incidence of adulteration of food has decreased considerably during the last eighty years. Thus, in 1875 about 20 per cent. of foods examined by public analysts were found to be adulterated, whilst in 1938 the figure was only 5·8 per cent. (*i.e.* 8433 samples out of 149,073 analysed). The procedure for the inspection of food is laid down in the Food and Drugs Act, 1955, which empowers local authorities to appoint public analysts. A ' sampling officer ' is an authorized officer of the local authority, and he may purchase any sample of food (or drug) and submit it for analysis to the local public analyst. In making such a purchase for analysis the following procedure must be followed, otherwise it will not be possible to obtain a conviction of the seller. After the purchase has been completed the purchaser must immediately inform the vendor that he

proposes to have the sample analysed. The article must then be divided into three portions and each portion must be separately packed and sealed. One portion is then handed to the vendor, one is sent to the public analyst, and the third is retained by the purchaser.

Examples of adulteration.—MILK.—Milk which contains less than 3 per cent. of fat or 8·5 per cent. of milk solids other than fat is presumed to be adulterated. The addition of the following to milk is prohibited by law : colouring matter, water, dried or condensed milk or any fluid constituted therefrom, skimmed or separated milk, preservatives of any kind, any thickening substance (except cane or beet sugar to cream). The most common forms of adulteration of milk are the addition of water or the removal of fat. The most satisfactory method of deciding whether or not adulteration with water has taken place is the freezing point method. Milk which freezes above $-0·53°$ C. can be considered to be adulterated. Even more important is the problem of milk-borne disease. (*See* MILK.)

BUTTER.—No preservative may be added to butter and not more than 16 per cent. of moisture is permitted by the legal standard. The two most common forms of adulteration of butter are the addition of other fats, *e.g.* cotton-seed oil, and excessive amounts of water.

MARGARINE must not contain more than 16 per cent. of moisture or 10 per cent. of butter fat. It must be reinforced with 760-940 international units of vitamin A and 80-100 international units of vitamin D per ounce.

BREAD is usually fairly pure. All flour intended for human consumption must contain not less than 1·6 mg. of iron, 0·24 mg. of vitamin B_1, and 1·60 mg. of nicotinic acid or nicotinamide per 100 grammes, and, except in the case of flour containing the whole of the products derived from the milling of wheat, 235 to 390 mg. of creta præparata per 100 grammes. If wheat flour should be adulterated with flour of other grains, *e.g.* barley, maize, rye, these can be easily recognized under the microscope.

BAKING POWDERS consist of an acid

18

salt, such as cream of tartar in acid calcium phosphate, and bicarbonate of soda and starch. If carelessly prepared, the acid salt may contain an excess of arsenic. They may also contain alum.

EGG SUBSTITUTE POWDERS, to give them their correct designation, are virtually baking powders coloured yellow with turmeric or a coal-tar dye. Lead chromate has occasionally been found in them.

CUSTARD POWDERS usually consist of coloured and flavoured maize starch, but they have been known to contain sago, rice, or potato.

COCOA.—There is no standard for cocoa in Great Britain. As sold it usually contains cornflour (or some similar material) and sugar. This is done because pure cocoa is rather indigestible on account of its high fat content.

COFFEE, unless bought as beans, is liable to contain chicory. Chicory can be recognized by the fact that in water it sinks and colours the water brown, whereas coffee floats in the water and scarcely stains it. They can also be differentiated under the microscope.

TEA.—Because of the careful examination to which it is submitted by Customs officers, tea is seldom adulterated now as it used to be in the old days with exhausted leaves, leaves from other sources or from green tea 'faced' with indigo or Prussian blue. Cheap tea may still contain a high proportion of tea dust. Unadulterated tea should contain 1·5 to 5 per cent. of theine, the alkaloid to which it owes its stimulating action.

SUGAR is usually pure. Sometimes flour may be mixed with it, but this can easily be detected by the presence of a sediment when the sugar dissolves. Cane sugar (the ordinary white sugar) may be coloured by caramelization or vegetable dyes and sold as Demerara sugar.

CHOCOLATES AND SWEETS.—Chocolate should contain not less than 10 per cent. of ground cocoa nib or 5 per cent. of essence of cocoa, to which are added cocoa fat, starch, sugar, and milk. Inferior chocolate (usually imported) contains only 2 to 3 per cent. of ground cocoa nib ; when exposed to a strong light it appears to have a greyish or bluish-grey bloom. Ultra-violet light and X-rays can be used to reveal chemical impurities. Inferior boiled sweets may be contaminated with minute traces of arsenic due to the use of impure glucose instead of sugar.

HONEY may be adulterated with cane sugar or glucose.

JAMS AND MARMALADE are seldom adulterated at the present day. The unofficial standards for jams adopted by the manufacturers are that ' full fruit standard ' contains 30 to 45 per cent. of fruit, whilst ' lower fruit standard ' contains 20 per cent. of fruit.

MEAT cannot readily be adulterated except by the sale of unsound or diseased meat. Horseflesh can be distinguished by the fact that it is dark and coarse, has a sickly odour and a soapy feel, and the fat is yellow. As horseflesh contains more glycogen (q.v.) than oxflesh, the addition of a few drops of a solution of iodine potassium iodide to a decoction of the flesh will produce a violet coloration.

ARROWROOT may be adulterated with potato starch, rice, or wheat flour.

CINNAMON and other similar spices are adulterated with flour and may contain sand.

GROUND GINGER may contain pepper.

PEPPER often contains 1·5 to 3 per cent. of sand and grit. This is an example of unavoidable adulteration.

PICKLES, SAUCES, AND CHUTNEY often consist principally of vinegar thickened with curry powder, pea-flour, and caramel.

MUSTARD is sold mixed with cornflour to keep the mustard grains separate ; otherwise it would go solid.

VINEGAR is sometimes adulterated with cheap acetic acid. It should contain 4 to 8 per cent. of glacial acetic acid. Reduction of the acid to below 4 per cent. by the addition of water should be regarded as adulteration. It may also be adulterated with sulphuric acid. Although some authorities contend that the presence of any sulphuric acid constitutes adulteration, the more generally held view is that there should not be more than 0·1 per cent. of sulphuric acid.

ALCOHOLIC BEVERAGES.—Whisky may be diluted with water legally ; it must not be more than 35 degrees under proof. Some low-grade whiskies may contain potato spirit. *Brandy* is made from fermented grape juice but inferior brands are made from potato spirit, coloured with burnt sugar and flavoured with various agents, or a little real brandy. *Beer* may contain arsenic if chemically prepared glucose is used in its manufacture. It may also contain an excessive amount of common salt or excessive preservative : the amount of preservative is limited by Regulations to 70 parts of sulphur dioxide per million. *Wines* should be made from the fermented juice of the grape. Calcium sulphate is sometimes added to wine to increase its dryness and improve its keeping properties ; this is known as ' plastering '. If excess is added, this may lead to the formation of sufficient potassium sulphate to produce a purgative effect. To avoid this, not more than 2 grammes of calcium sulphate is permitted per litre in France. There is relatively little tampering with foreign wines in Britain, but fraudulent imitations are sometimes sold under the title of ' British wines ', *e.g.* water coloured with cochineal, flavoured with essences and thickened with sugar. *Cider*, because of its acidity, may become contaminated with lead.

Preservatives in food.—Preservatives, such as boric acid, borax, formaldehyde, benzoic acid, and sulphur dioxide, used to be added often to foodstuffs. Their indiscriminate use led to much trouble and their use is now forbidden by Regulations, with the exception of sulphur dioxide and benzoic acid in specified amounts in specified foods, and sodium or potassium nitrite in ham, bacon, and cooked pickled meat. In the case of cooked pickled meat not more than 200 parts per million may be added. Under these Regulations the term ' preservative ' does not include salt, saltpetre, sugar, glycerin, alcohol, vinegar, acetic acid, and spices. Up to 70 parts of sulphur dioxide or 120 parts of benzoic acid may be added to sweetened mineral waters, but cordials and fruit juices can contain only up to 350 parts of sulphur dioxide or 600 parts of benzoic acid per million parts. Alcoholic wines are not allowed to contain more than 450 parts of sulphur dioxide per million ; for beer the upper limit is 70 parts per million, whilst for cider it is 200 parts per million. Sulphur dioxide is also used in jams and marmalade, the limit being 40 parts per million. Pickles, sauces, and chutney may not contain more than 250 parts of benzoic acid per million. Sausages may have sulphur dioxide added as a preservative (450 parts per million).

AËDES EGYPTI (or STEGOMYIA FASCIATA) is the scientific name of the mosquito which conveys to man (by biting) the viruses of yellow fever and of dengue or ' breakbone fever '. (*See* Fig. 426, page 1011.)

ÆGOPHONY (αἴξ, a goat ; φωνή, voice) is the bleating or punchinello tone given to the voice as heard by auscultation, when there is a small amount of fluid in the pleural cavity.

ÆROPHAGY means air-swallowing, and is the name applied to a habit which some persons, especially when suffering from dyspepsia, contract of swallowing mouthfuls of air. This at first gives relief to the discomfort and pain of indigestion, but later prolongs and aggravates it. The resulting breathlessness can be relieved to some extent by taking peppermint water or chloroform water in doses of a tablespoonful, but the chief necessity is to overcome the habit of swallowing air.

ÆROSOL is a suspension of very fine liquid (or rarely solid) particles in a gas such as air or oxygen. The size of ærosol particles ranges from 30 microns (a micron$= \frac{1}{1000}$ millimetre) down to a fraction of a micron. The fine mist of an ærosol can be produced by either a hand spray or by a special machine known as a nebulizer. There are three main uses for ærosols in medicine. (i) To destroy pests such as malaria- or yellow-fever-carrying mosquitoes, and lice which transmit typhus. D.D.T. is a usual constituent of such ærosols. (ii) To sterilize premises such as hospital wards, schoolrooms, and cinemas, to prevent the spread of airborne droplet infections. The usual constituents of such ærosols are sodium hypochlorite, hexylresorcinol, or propylene glycol. (iii) To combat diseases of the lungs such as asthma and chronic bronchitis, by producing an ærosol which is inhaled by the patient. Such ærosols may contain one of the drugs used for the relief of an asthmatic attack such as adrenaline or isoprenaline. The inhalation of ærosols containing ardenaline and iso-prenaline is proving most useful in the treatment of bronchial asthma.

ÆSTHESIOMETER is an instrument for measuring the sensation of touch in a person.

ÆTIOLOGY (*airía*, cause ; *λόγος,* discourse) is the part of medical science dealing with the causes of disease.

AFFUSION is a method of treatment by pouring water upon the body. (*See* BATHS ; COLD, EFFECTS OF ; DOUCHES.)

AFIBRINOGENÆMIA is a condition in which the blood is incoagulable as a result of absence of fibrin (*q.v.*). It is characterized by hæmorrhage. There are two forms : (*a*) a congenital form, and (*b*) an acquired form. The latter may be associated with advanced liver disease, or may occur as a complication of labour. Treatment consists of the intravenous injection of fibrinogen and blood transfusion.

AFTERBIRTH, or PLACENTA, is the name given to the thick, spongy disc-like cake of tissue which connects the embryo with the inner surface of the womb, the embryo otherwise lying free in the amniotic fluid. (*See* AMNION.) The placenta is mainly a new structure growing with the embryo, but, when it separates, a portion of the inner surface of the womb, called the maternal placenta, comes away with it. It is mainly composed of loops of veins belonging to the embryo, lying in blood-sinuses, in which circulates maternal blood. So that, though no mixing of the blood of embryo and mother takes place, there is ample opportunity for the exchange of fluids, gases, and the nutriment brought by the mother's blood. The width of the full-sized placenta is about eight inches (20 cm.), its thickness one inch (2·5 cm.). One surface is rough and studded with villi, which constis of the loops of fœtal veins ; the other is smooth, and has implanted in its centre the umbilical

cord, or navel string, which is about as thick as a finger and 20 inches (50 cm.) long, contains two arteries and a vein, enters the fœtus at the navel, and forms the sole connection between the bodies of mother and fœtus. The name ' afterbirth ' is given to the structure because it is expelled from the womb in the third stage of labour (*see* LABOUR).

AFTERPAINS are pains similar to but feebler than those of labour, occurring in the two or three days following childbirth.
Causes are generally the presence of a blood-clot or retained piece of placenta which the womb is attempting to expel.

AGAMMAGLOBULINÆMIA is a condition found in children, in which there is no gamma-globulin (*q.v.*) in the blood. These children are particularly susceptible to infections as they are unable to form antibodies to the infecting micro-organism.

AGAR is a gelatinous substance prepared from Ceylon moss and other East Indian seaweed. It is used in preparing culture-media for use in bacteriological laboratories. It is sometimes given for relieving constipation.

AGE, NATURAL CHANGES IN.— The tissues, as age advances, become more rigid and less elastic. The bones become more brittle. The ligaments are stiffer, so that contortions of the body and limbs, as in gymnastic feats, become impossible. Fat is deposited beneath the skin in middle life and absorbed again in old age, leaving the skin wrinkled. Deposition of fat also occurs in internal organs, *e.g.* the heart, weakening their activity. The skin becomes thin, is less well lubricated, and its vessels do not react properly to heat and cold, so that cold is more acutely felt. The chief change is in the blood-vessels, the walls of which become first thicker, then more brittle, so that hæmorrhage (*e.g.* into the brain, with apoplexy) more readily occurs. This change is hastened by alcoholic excesses and some diseases, and the extent to which it has occurred is the measure of the interference with the employments of active life, so that it has been said, ' A man is as old as his arteries '. This thickening of the arteries in the brain and consequent narrowing of their calibre, causing a poorer blood-supply to the brain, is one of the chief reasons of mental feebleness in old age. The menopause occurs in women between forty-five and fifty (*see* MENSTRUATION), and men sometimes about the age of sixty have some months' illness and feebleness, after which strength again returns. Loss of elasticity in the lens of the eye brings about the need of spectacles for reading from forty upwards. Another eye-change occurs after fifty in the appearance of a whitish ring (arcus senilis) round the cornea, near its edge. After sixty the teeth, if still good, may begin to fall out, and the hair whitens. (*See also* CLIMACTERIC.)

AGENE is nitrogen trichloride and has been used for many years as a flour improver and bleacher. As a result of experiments that showed that agene produced hysteria in dogs and some other animals, the British and U.S. governments have prohibited the use of agene as a flour improver, substituting chlorine dioxide as an alternative improver.

AGENESIA, or AGENESIS, means incomplete development or the failure of any part or organ of the body to develop normally.

AGGLUTINATION (*agglutino*, I cause to adhere) is the adherence together of small bodies in a fluid. Thus, blood corpuscles agglutinate into heaps (rouleaux) when added to the serum of a person belonging to an incompatible blood-group. Bacteria agglutinate into clumps and die when exposed to the presence of antibodies in the blood. This is important in regard to diagnosis of certain diseases due to bacteria. In typhoid fever, for example, the blood of an animal is immunized against typhoid bacilli by repeated injections of these. The blood-serum of the animal, known now as anti-typhoid serum, is issued to laboratories for use when bacilli are found in the excretions of a patient who is possibly suffering from typhoid fever. The bacilli are exposed to the action of a drop of the serum ; if the serum shows the power of agglutinating

these bacteria, this forms evidence that the bacteria in question are typhoid bacilli. The reaction may also be carried out in the contrary manner ; that is to say, the serum from the blood of a patient, who may be suffering from typhoid fever, but in regard to whom the diagnosis is still a matter of doubt, is added to a drop of fluid containing bacteria known to be typhoid bacilli ; if these are agglutinated into clumps by the patient's serum, the patient is then known to be suffering from typhoid fever ; if they do not agglutinate, his symptoms are due to some other condition. This reaction for typhoid fever is known as Widal's reaction. Comparable agglutination reactions, using an appropriate serum, are used in the diagnosis of a number of diseases, including glandular fever (when it is known as the Paul-Bunnell reaction) typhus fever (when it is known as the Weil-Felix reaction), undulant fever, and Weil's disease.

AGNOSIA is the term given to the condition in which, in certain diseases of the brain, the patient loses the ability to recognize the character of objects through the senses—touch, taste, sight, hearing.

AGONY (ἀγών, struggle) is excessive pain associated with struggling.

AGORAPHOBIA (ἀγορά, market place ; φόβος, fear) means a sense of fear experienced in crossing large open spaces, such as public squares, and is a symptom of psychological disorder.

AGRANULOCYTOSIS is a condition in which the white corpuscles in the blood of the polynuclear or granular variety become greatly lessened in numbers or disappear altogether. This change is found accompanying long-standing suppurative conditions, especially about the throat and mouth, and is a very serious one. It is also caused in some cases by taking such drugs as amidopyrine, thiourea, sulphonamides, and chloramphenicol.

AGRAPHIA (ἀ, neg. ; γράφω, I write) is the loss of power to express the ideas by writing. (*See* APHASIA.)

AGUE (*see* MALARIA). The term is also sometimes applied to neuralgia (brow ague) and to a state of tremor of the muscles found in various diseases (such as brass founders' ague).

AGUE CAKE is the old term applied to the enlarged spleen found in malaria.

AIR is of very uniform composition both in towns and country as regards its general constituents. These are :

Oxygen	. .	20·94 per cent.
Nitrogen	. .	78·09 ,,
Argon .	. .	0·94 ,,
Carbonic Acid	.	0·03 ,,

Besides these there are always ozone, minerals, and organic matters in small and variable amounts, and more or less water vapour according to the weather. In the air of towns, sulphurous acid and sulphuretted hydrogen are important impurities derived from combustion. After air has been respired once, the oxygen falls by about 4 per cent. and the carbonic acid rises to about 4 per cent., while organic matters and water vapour are greatly increased and the air rises in temperature. The cause of the discomfort felt in badly ventilated rooms and crowded halls is associated with the increase in the temperature and moisture of the air, but a high percentage of carbonic acid may be present without causing any noticeable discomfort or appreciable quickening of the respiration. Microbes are found especially in dusty air, and during coughing, sneezing, and loud talking they are expelled from the air passages on droplets of moisture. When epidemic diseases such as influenza are rife, infection is apt to be conveyed through the air by these means, especially in badly ventilated and over-warmed rooms. When the amount of carbonic acid present in the air exceeds 0·1 per cent. there is usually a distinct sense of ' stuffiness ', which forms the best guide as to the necessity for increased ventilation. The continued breathing day after day of ' stuffy ' atmosphere is apt to produce headache, drowsiness, depression, inability to concentrate on work, dryness of the throat, and a tendency to ' catch cold ' easily, thus resulting in a gradual deterioration of health. Inadequate ventilation has much to do with the onset of pulmonary tuberculosis as well as with infection by other diseases such as influenza and the common cold. (*See* TUBERCULOSIS *and* VENTILATION.)

Uses (*see* CLIMATE, INHALATIONS, RESPIRATION, VENTILATION).

AIR-BEDS consist of stout rubber perforated in numerous places by rubber tubes which open on the upper and lower surfaces and add strength to the bed. The bed is blown up from one end by means of an automobile or bicycle pump to the desired hardness. Such a bed is both easier for the nurse to manage and more comfortable to the patient than a water-bed.

Uses.—In general an air-bed is placed under a bedridden person or one suffering from some devitalizing disease of the nervous system, in order to prevent the formation of bed sores, by distributing pressure all over the patient's back. Apart from the tendency to bed sores, a patient who is long confined to bed, who is fevered, or who is much emaciated, derives a sense of great coolness and comfort from an air-bed.

AIR PASSAGES.—These are the nose, pharynx or throat (the large cavity behind the nose and mouth), larynx, trachea or windpipe, and bronchi or bronchial tubes. The air, on entering the nose (Fig. 5), passes through a high narrow passage on each side, the outer wall of which projects along three lines (the turbinate processes), so as almost to touch the dividing septum between the nostrils, thus making on each side three passages or meatuses, in which the air is warmed, moistened, and relieved of particles of dust. Mouth-breathing is, accordingly, a bad habit because the air is not prepared for entrance to the lungs. In the pharynx the food and air passages meet and cross. The larynx lies in front of the lower part of the pharynx and is the organ where the voice is produced (*see* VOICE) by aid of the vocal cords. The opening between the cords is called the ' glottis ', and shortly after passing this the air reaches the trachea or windpipe, a tube four to five inches long (10 to 12·5 cm.), and ¾ inch (2 cm.) wide (Plate VI).

This leads into the chest and divides above the heart into two bronchi, one of which goes to each lung, in which it splits into finer and finer tubes (*see* LUNGS). The larynx is enclosed in two strong cartilages, the thyroid

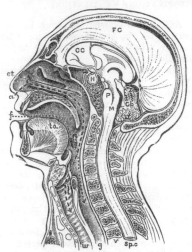

FIG. 5.—Vertical section through the middle of the head and neck, showing the upper air passages. The passages for air, *a*, are indicated by a heavy dotted line, those for the food, *f*, by a fainter line ; *et*, Eustachian tube ; *l*, larynx ; *w*, windpipe ; *t*, tonsil ; *to*, tongue ; *g*, gullet. For other letters, *see* Fig. 71. (After Braune.)

(of which the most projecting part, the Adam's apple, is a prominent point on the front of the neck) and the cricoid (which can be felt as a hard ring about an inch below). Beneath this, the trachea, which is stiffened by rings of cartilage, so that it is never closed in any position of the body, can be traced down till it disappears behind the breast-bone.

AIR-SICKNESS. — The manifestations of this condition are very similar to those of SEA-SICKNESS (*q.v.*). The most satisfactory remedy is hyoscine hydrobromide, 1/60 to 1/120 grain (1 to 0·5 mg.)

ALASTRIM, or VARIOLA MINOR, is a form of smallpox which differs from ordinary smallpox in being milder and having a low mortality.

ALBINISM (*albus*, white) is a state of poverty (or absence) of pigment in the superficial tissues of the body, producing a pale pink colour of the skin, whiteness of the hair, and redness of the iris and interior of the eye. A person showing these peculiarities is called an ' albino '. It may also occur only in patches.

Causes.—It is generally congenital, existing from birth, though the parents of an albino are not necessarily subjects of albinism. It is most marked amongst the dark races, such as the Negroes of West Africa, and is said to be due, in some cases, to poor food and unhealthy surroundings of the mother.

Symptoms.—An albino may show nothing remarkable beyond white hair, delicate skin, and pink eyes, but many are physically and mentally feeble. Usually the absence of pigment to screen the eye from bright light gives rise to trouble, and the person has a tendency to inflammation of the eyes. (*See* EYE, DISEASES OF.)

Treatment.—There is no remedy. The eyes should be protected in bright light by wearing smoked glasses.

ALBUMINS (*albus*, white) are proteins. They enter into the composition of all the tissues of the body. Their characters are that they are soluble in pure water ; can be dried into a light, flaky, non-crystalline powder ; are coagulated by heat, and precipitated by various agents like nitric acid, tannin, alcohol, or perchloride of mercury.

Varieties.—Albumins are generally divided according to their source of origin, as muscle - albumin, milk-albumin, blood- or serum-albumin, egg-albumin, vegetable-albumin, etc. These differ both in chemical reactions and also physiologically, for though serum-albumin occurs in the blood, some albumins, *e.g.* egg-albumin, injected direct into the blood are highly poisonous.

Uses.—When taken into the stomach they are all converted into a soluble form by the process of digestion, and are then absorbed into the blood, whence they go to build up the tissues gradually worn out in the activity of the body. (*See* ALBUMINURIA, BRIGHT'S DISEASE.)

ALBUMINURIA means a condition in which albumin is present in the urine. It is of immense importance, both because it is itself a drain upon the health, and because it is often a symptom of serious heart or kidney disease.

Causes.—(1) *Kidney disease* is the most important cause of albuminuria, and in some cases the discovery of albuminuria may be the first evidence of such disease. This is why an examination of the urine for the presence of albumin constitutes an essential part of every medical examination. Almost any form of kidney disease will cause albuminuria, but the most frequent form to do this is Bright's disease. In the subacute (or nephrotic) stage of Bright's disease the most marked albuminuria of all may be found. Albuminuria is also found in infections of the kidney (pyelitis) as well as in infections of the bladder (cystitis) and of the urethra (urethritis). The development of albuminuria in pregnancy is always an indication for the individual receiving careful medical treatment, as it may be the first sign of one of the most dangerous complications of pregnancy: toxæmia of pregnancy, Bright's disease, or eclampsia (*q.v.*).

(2) *Heart failure* is always accompanied by albuminuria, particularly when the right side of the heart is failing. In severe cases of failure, accompanied by dropsy, the albuminuria may be marked. It is due to congestion of the kidneys.

(3) *Fever* is practically always accompanied by albuminuria, even though there is not actual kidney disease. The albuminuria disappears soon after the temperature becomes normal.

(4) *Drugs and poisons.*—These include arsenic, lead, mercury, gold, copaiba, salicylic acid, and quinine.

(5) *Anæmia.*—A trace of albumin may be found in the urine in severe cases of anæmia.

(6) *Functional or orthostatic albuminuria.*—Almost any normal person may have a transitory albuminuria after severe muscular exertion or after a cold bath, and it may occasionally appear after eating a large amount of protein, *e.g.* raw eggs. The form commonly known as *orthostatic* or postural albuminuria is much more common and is of importance because, if the true cause is not recognized, it may be taken

as a sign of kidney disease. In the 1914–18 War it was found in 4 per cent. of healthy British soldiers, and in an American investigation it was found in 5 per cent. of healthy University freshmen. The cause is still doubtful, but it is probably due to temporary congestion of the kidneys caused by adoption of the upright position in individuals with some slight disturbance of the circulation of the blood in the kidneys. At one time it was thought that individuals with this type of albuminuria were more prone to develop Bright's disease later in life than individuals in whom it was not present, but this has now been definitely disproved. The features of this type of albuminuria are that it occurs in young people, usually between the ages of 8 and 18 years, and that it is not present while the patient is at rest. Thus, the specimen of urine obtained the first thing in the morning, before the individual gets up, contains no albumin, whilst a specimen obtained later in the day, after the individual has been up and about, will contain albumin.

Albuminuria and Life Assurance.— Most companies will not issue a life policy to anyone with permanent albuminuria lest this be due to Bright's disease. Even cases in which no serious disease manifests itself have, if the albuminuria persists, a shorter expectation of life than other people, and so require a higher premium. In cases of doubt, tests to measure the function of the kidney may be carried out. If the tests show normal function, then the albuminuria takes on a much less serious aspect.

Treatment.—The treatment is that of the underlying disease. (*See* BRIGHT'S DISEASE, etc.) In the case of functional albuminuria due to excessive exercise, cold baths, or excessive ingestion of protein, treatment consists of removal of the cause. Individuals who have orthostatic or postural albuminuria are usually adolescents or young adults who are not in good training, and the treatment consists of getting them into good condition. Unless bathing is found to produce albuminuria, they should be encouraged to have a cold plunge every morning, followed by rapid friction with a towel. ' Early to bed, early to rise ' is sound advice for these individuals, in addition to regular exercise in the open air.

ALBUMIN WATER is used for administration as a light form of nourishment to patients with weak digestion or suffering from diarrhœa or some condition in which only very small amounts of food can be borne. To prepare albumin water a raw egg is broken in two on the edge of a cup. The white is allowed to escape by passing the yolk from one half of the shell to the other. The white is then whisked for 10 minutes to a stiff froth, ½ pint of cold water is added, and it is allowed to stand for an hour to dissolve. Lemon juice may be added to flavour, and a cupful may be given at one time.

ALBUMOSE is the term applied to the products of digestion of protein foods, differing from albumin in not being coagulable by heat. Albumose is further converted by digestion into peptone.

ALCOHOL (Arabic word), more correctly ETHYL ALCOHOL, is a liquid obtained by the action of yeast on solutions of sugar, especially of grape sugar or glucose. Carbonic acid gas is also formed in the process and escapes. After fermentation of the sugary fluid has taken place, the alcohol is separated from the water by distillation and from the last traces of water by the action of lime, which absorbs the latter. Absolute (or water-free) alcohol is very expensive owing to the difficulty of complete separation. It is a powerful irritant, and even in moderate quantities a poison. Rectified spirit, or spirit of wine, contains 90 per cent. of alcohol by volume, and is used to make essences, tinctures, and weaker spirits of 80, 70, 60, 50, 45, 25 and 20 per cent. strength. The alcohol dilutum of the U.S. Pharmacopœia contains 64·5 per cent. of alcohol by volume. Proof spirit contains 57 per cent. (by volume) of alcohol. It is called ' proof ' spirit, because an old test of its strength was to drench gunpowder with it, set fire to it, and if the gunpowder was ignited the alcohol stood the proof. If stronger, a spirit is over-proof—if weaker, under-

26

proof. Alcohol freezes at a very low temperature, and so is used for thermometers for the Arctic regions. It dissolves many things which water does not dissolve, such as fats, oils, and resins. Mixed with wood-spirit, it forms methylated spirit, on which no duty is payable but which is, of course, unfit for drinking. It coagulates the tissues, and so has a hardening effect upon skin, wounds, etc. Like several substances closely related to it chemically, such as chloroform and ether, alcohol causes, when taken internally, first of all a gentle stimulation of the bodily and mental functions, in larger doses excitement, then loss of feeling,

	Total Consumption in Gallons	
	1897	1953
Beer . .	1,208,916,000	911,520,000
Wine . .	15,810,000	10,340,000
Spirits .	47,927,000	10,200,000

	Consumption in Gallons per Head of Population	
	1897	1953
Beer . .	30·2	17·9
Wine . .	0·4	0·2
Spirits .	1·2	0·2

TABLE 1.—Consumption of Alcoholic Liquors in Great Britain.

and, finally, paralysis with unconsciousness ; but the interval between these is wider with alcohol, and far larger quantities of the drug are necessary than in the case of the others. Alcohol taken into the body is almost all used up. The amount of alcohol used in Great Britain has decreased greatly in recent years. This is shown by a comparison of the amounts of beer, wine, and spirits consumed in 1897 and 1953 in the United Kingdom.

Varieties of alcoholic liquors.—Spirits and wines sold under various names differ very much in the amount of alcohol contained in different samples under the same name, but the following table gives a general idea of the percentages of alcohol by volume present in the various forms of beverage. Many of the stronger forms are sold commonly in a more diluted state than that indicated in the table. Some of the weaker wines, on the other hand, are 'fortified' by the addition of spirit to confer on them more stimulating properties.

Rum, Whisky ⎫ Brandy, Gin ⎭	. . .	40 per cent.
Liqueurs .	. .	about 50 ,,
Port, Sherry ⎫ Madeira ⎭	. .	about 20 ,,
Champagne	. . .	10 per cent.
Burgundy .	. .	about 14 ,,
Claret ⎫ Moselle, Hock ⎭	. .	about 10 ,,
Strong ale .	. .	about 8 ,,
Cider ⎫ Porter, Beer ⎭	. .	2 to 5 ,,
Ginger beer	. .	1 to 3 ,,

TABLE 2.—Alcoholic Content of Alcoholic Liquors.

Various wines, manufactured or home-made, are produced by fermenting mixtures of fruit and sugar, e.g. cowslip wine, ginger wine, orange bitters, raisin wine, raspberry wine, red currant wine. In a report issued by the Ministry of Health on an analysis of these British wines, it appears that the percentage of alcohol is usually about 10 or 12, rising in some of the stronger forms to over 20 per cent.

SPIRITS, including *rum* from molasses, *brandy* from wine, *whisky* from malted grain, and *gin* from grain and juniper berries, are prepared by fermentation followed by distillation. They contain in their raw state more or less 'fusel oil', an oily substance consisting of amyl and butyl alcohols which have a more harmful effect upon the nervous system than ethyl alcohol. These, however, are slowly converted to ethers, which give to long-kept spirit its prized flavour and aroma, and are harmless. Spirits are by law prohibited from being delivered for consumption in Britain until they have been warehoused for at least three years.

LIQUEURS are spirits in which have been steeped various spices, leaves, and fruits, and which have, in addition to the properties of alcohol, those of the various ingredients.

PORT, SHERRY, MADEIRA, and other Portuguese and Hungarian wines, are known as 'fortified wines', because spirit is added to them for preservation. They are therefore stronger, and containing much unchanged grape-juice have more 'body' and bouquet than those in which the alcohol is simply derived from the grape-juice, which is completely used up in fermentation. They improve by keeping, as the tannin and other harsh-tasting substances separate out gradually as a 'crust'.

CHAMPAGNE and other effervescent wines are white wines to which much sugar has been added after bottling, so that fermentation goes on and carbonic acid gas is produced, which becomes, on long keeping, intimately blended with the wine, and adds greatly to its effect. Hence champagne is far more stimulating and its effects more rapid than in the case of other wines much stronger in alcohol.

CLARET, BURGUNDY, MOSELLE, HOCK, and other wines from the northern vineyards, are thin and acidulous from cream of tartar, and so form refreshing drinks with no special virtue beyond the stimulating effect of the alcohol they contain. They are, however, less harmful in gout, etc., than the wines with much 'body', and there is not the same necessity for keeping them many years before using.

BEER, in addition to being weakly alcoholic, contains an infusion of hops which gives it bitterness.

Effects of alcohol.—Alcohol, when taken as a food, is very quickly and completely absorbed. About one-fifth of any dose taken is absorbed from the stomach, and almost the whole of the remainder is absorbed in the upper part of the small intestine within two or three hours of having been taken. Very little is excreted by the breath, urine, and other channels. This never amounts to more than one-tenth of the quantity swallowed and may be as little as one-hundredth. The remainder is completely used up within twenty-four hours, being oxidized mainly to produce heat. Atwater and Benedict have shown that the body can derive one-fifth of the total energy it requires from alcohol, and in this way alcohol spares carbohydrates and fats taken in the food. There is a tendency, therefore, for both of these to be deposited in the tissues as superfluous fat when alcohol is habitually added to the diet without a decrease of the other food.

With regard to the mental effect of alcohol, this is dependent partly upon its effect on the circulation and partly on its anæsthetic action on the nervous system, dulling small pains and the sense of worry and anxiety. Owing to a similar dulling action upon the higher intellectual faculties, self-criticism and self-control are also to a considerable extent lessened. If a larger dose be taken, the functions of sense perception and skilled movement are to a certain extent dulled and deteriorated, with the result that there is a certain clumsiness of behaviour. The person now begins to make ill-adjusted movements, shows some slurring of speech, and becomes less quick and less capable in performing acts which require decision and promptitude, e.g. avoiding a collision when driving a motor-car. In a further stage the intellectual processes of judgment, self-criticism, and self-control are largely suspended and the functions of sense perception and skilled movement become very greatly impaired, until ultimately a heavy sleep supervenes which lasts until the alcohol absorbed by the nervous system has been oxidized and consumed. The effects of alcohol on the performance of muscular acts are of great importance in relation to the individual's capacity for work and for action of a responsible nature. A dose of alcohol not exceeding 40 millilitres, or about as much as would be taken in 2¾ oz. of whisky at proof or in 1¾ pints of beer in an adult accustomed to moderate use of alcohol, exerts very little effect on the performance by him of muscular acts not demanding great precision, although even smaller doses than these may to a certain extent diminish the speed and nicety with which very delicate actions can be carried out. There does not seem to be any proof that alcohol in any dose improves the efficiency with which either skilled or unskilled work can be carried out during the few hours while the alcohol acts.

With regard to the action on digestion, moderate doses of alcohol increase the secretions of the stomach and thus may aid digestion in persons in whom these secretions are defective. At the same time wines appear to slow the process of digestion, although this has the effect of rendering absorption of the food slower and thus making it of greater nutritive value. Different wines have very varying effect on different persons in this respect, probably on account of the substances other than alcohol which they contain. When alcoholic beverages are taken habitually over long periods, and especially in the more concentrated form of spirits, they exert a pronounced effect of irritation upon the mucous membrane of the stomach and thus lead to chronic indigestion.

With regard to the action of alcohol on respiration and circulation of the blood, moderate doses have practically no effect upon the breathing, although very large doses have a paralysing effect, and when death occurs from alcohol it is brought about by stoppage of the respiration. As to its stimulating action on the circulation, this is in part brought about by its effect in the blood when swallowed, and in part to the lessening of mental strain brought about through its narcotic and sedative action. It is also due in part to its action in dilating the small blood-vessels, and thus reducing the blood-pressure and possibly relieving strain on the heart.

The popular reputation of alcohol as a means of 'warding off cold' is due largely to its power of dilating the superficial blood-vessels and of dulling the sensory nerves of the skin, so that the skin actually becomes warm, while external impressions are not felt. If at the same time as the alcohol is administered, warmth is applied to the surface of the body by hot blankets, hot bottles, etc., the skin becomes more capable of absorbing the external heat and thus the alcohol acts as a restorative.

The official statistics issued by the Registrar-General indicate a heavy mortality among persons occupied in the liquor trade, who are known to consume more than the average amount of alcohol. The experience of insurance companies has made them adverse to admitting on ordinary terms persons who are habitual users of alcoholic beverages in large amount.

Alcohol and Driving.—During recent years increasing attention has been devoted to the effect of alcohol upon the ability to drive a motor-car. It is now recognized that even quite small amounts of alcohol may be sufficient to impair those standards of watchfulness and efficiency which are vitally important if accidents are to be reduced to a minimum in these days of ever-increasing congestion on the roads and ever-increasing speed of cars.

Careful attention is therefore being given to means of detecting whether or not a car-driver has had sufficient alcohol to interfere with his capacity as a driver. Particular attention has been devoted to means of estimating the amount of alcohol that has been consumed and correlating this with the ability to drive. It is now generally accepted that the amount of alcohol in the blood is a reliable guide, and that this can be estimated directly, or indirectly, by estimating the amount of alcohol in the urine or in the expired breath of the individual. The last of these is the most unreliable.

In October 1967, the Road Safety Act came into force, making it an offence for a motorist to drive, attempt to drive, or be in charge of a vehicle if his (or her) blood alcohol level is over 80 mg. per 100 millilitres or his (or her) urine alcohol is over 107 mg. per 100 millilitres.

These figures must not be taken to mean that it is safe to drive a car if one's blood or urine alcohol is below these levels. Equally dangerous is it to attempt to correlate one's consumption of alcohol with one's blood or urine alcohol levels. The only safe rule is not to drive after drinking.

Uses of Alcohol.—*Externally* it is used in the cheap form of methylated spirit to cleanse the skin of oily, fatty, or resinous substances, which water will not remove. Also to harden the skin of the feet before a long walk, or that of the back in persons confined to bed for long periods, and so prevent bed sores.

A whisky pack or brandy pack is an old-fashioned remedy to stimulate infants reduced to a state of collapse by diarrhœa or bronchitis.

Internally there are few, if any, absolute indications for the use of alcohol, and during the last fifty years the use of alcohol as a medicine has declined rapidly.

Alcohol may be of value in stimulating the appetite during convalescence. It is also a useful sedative sometimes in old people, particularly in an individual who is used to taking alcohol regularly in moderation. Its value as a stimulant of the heart is doubtful. There is a certain amount of justification for the use of undiluted whisky or brandy in the treatment of fainting, provided this is not due to some serious condition such as hæmorrhage. It should never be given to a patient who is suffering from shock. Champagne and brandy-and-soda have a traditional reputation for the relief of vomiting, including sea-sickness.

The popular habit of taking spirits ' to keep the cold out ' is a delusion. Alcohol gives a sense of warmth to the skin by bringing the blood there ; but, as the blood is rapidly cooled in cold air, the risk of frost-bite and even death by freezing is increased, so that experienced hunters and mountaineers will on no account touch spirits on biting days or at high altitudes.

In health, there is no necessity for alcohol, and, as so many persons contract the alcohol habit, it would be well for every one to consider the question carefully before embarking on its habitual use. Even far short of drunkenness its constant use in large quantities certainly shortens life. (*See* ALCOHOLISM, CHRONIC.)

ALCOHOLISM, ACUTE.—This is the condition produced by taking excessive quantities of alcohol over a short period. The effects vary greatly according to the hereditary and nervous constitution of the person concerned, his or her age and social surroundings, and to a great extent with the kind of liquor taken, whether it is taken with food, and whether it has been taken for a long time previously.

Varieties.—There are many curious effects produced and phases of character brought to light by the disturbance of mental balance, but the three important forms are ordinary drunkenness, alcoholic mania, and ' delirium tremens '.

Symptoms. — ORDINARY DRUNKENNESS is too common to need much description. First the person is brightened, his spirits rise, his conversation is witty, the skin becomes flushed, and there is a general sense of well-being. As he becomes really drunk a phase of depression-excitement comes on : one person becomes angry, resents fancied affronts, and tries to pick quarrels, another becomes melancholy and lugubrious, a third grows maudlin, and weepingly recounts the secrets of his family to perfect strangers, while a fourth type assumes a regal manner and gives away his money and valuables or makes promises which he cannot possibly fulfil ; and all lose the controlling power of reason. A third stage is that in which all feeling of shame is lost, and there is dullness of sense and loss of power, the drunk man or woman reeling or falling and rising with difficulty. The fourth stage is popularly known as ' dead drunk ' ; the person lies in a state of insensibility, with stertorous breathing and dilated pupils.

ALCOHOLIC MANIA is the form which often affects neurotic young men or women with a family taint of insanity. A state of excitement and fury, leading sometimes to attempts at murder or suicide, comes on after, it may be, only a few glasses of spirits or wine, and lasts some hours or days, without any tendency to dullness or sleep. Some persons who are liable to epileptic attacks have a fit when alcohol is taken even in moderate amount.

DELIRIUM TREMENS is the most serious form, and is popularly known as ' blue-devils ', because of the hallucinations accompanying the state. It follows on a long course of drinking which has ended in a bout, or may be brought on by an injury or business worries in a heavy drinker ; but it does not follow a single ' spree '. Tremors all over the body, but especially in the hands and tongue, are the first sign of its onset, then complete loss of appetite, sickness, rise of temperature, weak pulse, and constant purposeless movements. Finally hallucinations come on; spiders, flies, mice, rats are described on the clothes or floor, or disgusting objects like snakes, toads, and demons ; or the bystanders are taken for policemen, hangmen, etc., and the furniture distorts itself into weird shapes. Lastly, delirium of a terrified or raging type comes on, in which there is more or less danger of suicide or homicide. Pneumonia of a serious type is apt to ensue, and if these two be combined the case is usually fatal. When a case of

delirium tremens follows upon a very prolonged course of chronic alcoholism the mental state sometimes passes into one of permanent mental feebleness, due to organic changes in the brain.

Treatment.—Ordinary drunkenness is best treated by letting the person sleep it off, or, if great quantities of alcohol have been rapidly taken, the stomach should be washed out with the stomach-tube. In the second or excited stage, and in alcoholic mania, if the person be uncontrollable, he is to be treated as in *delirium tremens*. In the latter, admission to hospital is necessary, with careful nursing and constant supervision. Paraldehyde is the best sedative in the acute phase, and promising results are being reported from the use of tranquillizers. If any infection, such as pneumonia is present, full doses of antibiotics are given. A high-calorie, high-vitamin diet should be given, with particular emphasis on a high intake of vitamin B_1 (aneurine).

ALCOHOLISM, CHRONIC.—This is the condition of mind and body produced by taking too much alcohol over long periods. It is estimated that 33,000,000 of the population of Britain drink alcoholic beverages and that over 400,000 of them are alcoholics. The annual cost to industry in Britain of absenteeism, accident proneness and inefficiency due to excessive drinking is estimated to be over £40,000,000, and over a third of our prison population is in prison for crimes connected with alcohol.

Chronic alcoholism is a disease, but it is necessary to differentiate between the chronic alcoholic and the excessive drinker. The latter is able to stop drinking if he is given sufficient good reason for doing so, whereas the chronic alcoholic cannot voluntarily abstain for more than a short while. As one expert has put it : ' The regular heavy drinker lives to drink, but the alcoholic *must* drink to live '.

Whatever the reason for drinking, the long-continued consumption of alcohol can result in many medical disorders. The most frequent of these is *gastritis* (*q.v.*). Indeed, the most common cause of acute and chronic gastritis is over-indulgence in alcohol, Cirrhosis of the liver (*see* LIVER.

DISEASES OF) is a frequent complication. Injurious effects on the heart from habitual spirit drinking are not uncommon, and there is an increased tendency for alcoholics to suffer from diseases of the arteries (*q.v.*). Peripheral neuritis (*q.v.*) is also common. In the early stages this manifests itself by pains in the feet and hands, and tenderness in the calves of the legs, followed later by wrist-drop and foot-drop. In severe cases the cranial nerves may be involved and this may be accompanied by blindness. The fiery visage (*see* ACNE ROSACEA) is a well-known sign of the chronic alcoholic. Finally, there may be severe mental disturbance, such as Korsakow's syndrome (*q.v.*) and delirium tremens (*see* ALCOHOLISM, ACUTE).

There are four types of chronic alcoholics : (i) The alcoholic with a good previous personality ; about 80 per cent. of these make a successful recovery : i.e., remain totally abstinent. (ii) The alcoholic whose basic personality is neurotic. About 30 per cent. recover, but they are prone to relapse before they finally become abstinent. (iii) The alcoholic whose basic personality is psychotic. The outlook in this group depends entirely upon the psychosis. In a sense they are not true alcoholics, and treatment is aimed primarily at the psychosis. (iv) The alcoholic whose basic personality is psychopathic. The outlook for this group is extremely bad. The woman psychopath is particularly addicted to alcohol, and she often attempts suicide —and often succeeds.

The prognosis is good if the patient has a happy home and a good job to return to. Those who are separated or divorced, or the bachelor living on his own, find it more difficult to maintain sobriety. The patient who seeks help has the best chance to recover. Undergoing treatment simply to pacify or please the marital partner, or to avoid being cut out of a will, is a poor prognostic sign. Patients of poor, or limited, intelligence, are unlikely to respond to treatment. Excessive drinking in early adult life is usually found in the neurotic. Violent abnormal behaviour of young people under the influence of alcohol suggests an underlying psychosis, such as schizophrenia, or epilepsy. Alcoholism developing at the menopause suggests a depressive state; if it develops in later life it suggests a senile depressive state and has a poor prognosis. A feature of the chronic alcoholic is that he has few hobbies, few outside interests, and little interest in other people. His entire life is centred round drinking.

Treatment.—To be successful this must practically always be carried out in the first instance in hospital or special clinic. Very few, if any, can be treated at home, and even outpatient treatment is seldom successful without a preliminary period of inpatient treatment.

The essential feature of treatment is the immediate withdrawal of all alcohol over a period not exceeding forty-eight hours. To overcome, or prevent, the inevitable disturbances this causes, the patient is given tranquillizers and intensive vitamin therapy. The disruption of the drinking pattern is then completed either by the so-called vomiting technique, using apomorphine, or by the use of antabuse, or disulfiram to give it its approved name. This is a drug which so upsets the patient when he takes alcohol in addition that he develops an aversion to alcohol.

Once the drinking pattern has been disrupted, the patient then undergoes a course of psychotherapy. Hypnosis is proving particularly useful in this respect. In addition, group therapy is valuable, especially once the patient has recovered and has returned to his normal surroundings. This is the basis of Alcoholics Anonymous, an informal organization of men and women ' for whom alcohol has become a major problem, and who, admitting it, have decided to do something about it '. The address is BM/AAL, London, W.C.1.

Finally, it must be stressed that there can be no compromise with the alcoholic if he is to be considered cured. Total abstinence is essential for life in every case. There are no exceptions to this rule.

ALCURONIUM is a recently introduced relaxant drug which is being used by anæsthetists in relatively short operations of around twenty minutes' duration.

ALDOSTERONE is a hormone secreted by the adrenal cortex. It plays an important part in maintaining the electrolyte balance of the body by promoting the reabsorption of sodium and the secretion of potassium by the renal tubules. It is thus of primary importance in controlling the volume of the body fluids.

ALEXIA (ά, neg.; λέξις, word) is another name for 'word-blindness'. (*See* APHASIA.)

ALGESIMETER (ἄλγησις, sense of pain; μέτρον, measure) is the name of an instrument used in measuring the sensitiveness of areas of the skin.

ALGID (*algidus*, cold) stage of cholera and ague, is that in which extreme coldness of the body occurs. (*See* CHOLERA, MALARIA.)

ALIENATION (*alienatio*) means insanity or mental derangement.

ALIENIST means an expert in the treatment of insanity.

ALIMENTARY CANAL is the passage along which the food passes, in which it is digested (*see* DIGESTION), and from which it is absorbed by lymphatics and blood-vessels into the circulation. The canal consists of the mouth, pharynx or throat, œsophagus or gullet, stomach, small intestine, and large intestine, in this order (Fig. 6). For details see articles under these heads. The total length of the alimentary canal is about 30 feet (9 metres) in man.

ALKALÆMIA means an increase in the alkalinity of the blood, or, more accurately, a decrease in the concentration of hydrogen ions in the blood. It occurs, for example, in patients who have had large doses of alkalis for the treatment of gastric ulcer. Another term for this condition is alkalosis.

ALKALI (Arabic word) is a substance which neutralizes an acid to form a salt, and turns litmus and other vegetable dyes blue. Alkalis are generally oxides or carbonates of metals.
Varieties.—Ammonia, lithia, potash, and soda are the principal ; the carbonates of these act as weaker alkalis, and their bicarbonates still weaker. Lime,

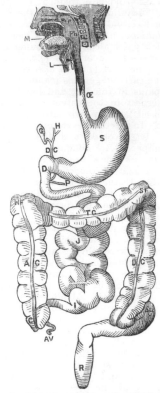

FIG. 6.—Alimentary canal. *M*, Mouth ; *Ph*, pharynx ; *L*, larynx ; *Œ*, œsophagus ; *S*, stomach ; *D, J, I*, small intestine ; *AV, AC, HF, TC, SF, DC, Sg, R*, parts of large intestine. (For further details, *see* INTESTINE.) (*Ency. Brit.*)

magnesia, baryta, and strontium are called alkaline earths, and act as alkalis. Further, substances which in the body are converted into alkalis, such as acetates, citrates, and tartrates, are called ' indirect ' alkalis. In the body protein substances also act as alkalis, absorbing acids and thus preventing the development of general acidosis.

Uses.—In poisoning by acids, one at once administers dilute alkaline solutions (*see* ACIDS, POISONING BY). Caustic, *i.e.* undiluted, alkalis are used to destroy warts. Bee-stings and insect-bites cause irritation because of an acid injected by the insect, and consequently are relieved by weak alkaline applications. Very weak solutions of sodium

PLATE III

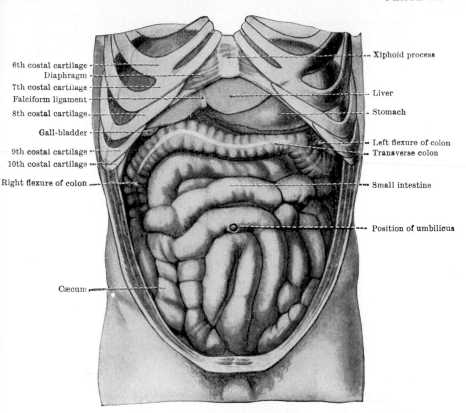

6th costal cartilage
Diaphragm
7th costal cartilage
Falciform ligament
8th costal cartilage
Gall-bladder
9th costal cartilage
10th costal cartilage
Right flexure of colon
Cæcum

Xiphoid process
Liver
Stomach
Left flexure of colon
Transverse colon
Small intestine
Position of umbilicus

Contents of the abdomen in position, the front wall of the abdomen and the omentum removed. (From Cunningham's *Anatomy*. Oxford University Press.) *See* ABDOMEN.

Section of blood clot, showing network of strings of fibrin. Magnified 400 times. (From Schafer's *Histology*. Longmans, Green & Co., Ltd.) *See* BLOOD, COAGULATION and FIBRIN.

PLATE IV

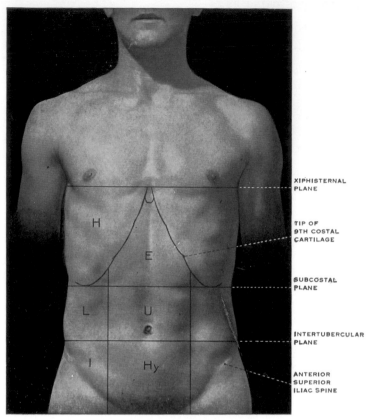

XIPHISTERNAL
PLANE

TIP OF
9TH COSTAL
CARTILAGE

SUBCOSTAL
PLANE

INTERTUBERCULAR
PLANE

ANTERIOR
SUPERIOR
ILIAC SPINE

Diagram of regions of abdomen. (For meaning of letters, *see* text, page 3.) (From Appleton, etc., *Surface and Radiological Anatomy*. W. Heffer & Sons, Ltd.) *See* ABDOMEN, REGIONS OF.

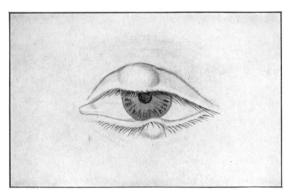

Meibomian cysts.

Trachoma.

(From Parsons and Duke-Elder, *Diseases of the Eye.*
J. & A. Churchill, Ltd.) *See* EYE DISEASES.

or potassium bicarbonate are given internally for bronchitis, when the phlegm is thick. In heartburn, bicarbonate of soda (20 grains [1·2 G.], or as much as can be heaped on a sixpence or dime-piece) is taken after a meal, to soothe irritation and spasm of the stomach. The largest use of alkalis is in the treatment of duodenal ulcer and other forms of dyspepsia associated with hyperchlorhydria (q.v.). The most commonly used alkalis for this purpose are magnesium trisilicate, magnesium carbonate, and aluminium hydroxide.

ALKALIS, POISONING BY. — Persons may drink soap-lye, ammonia, caustic soda, caustic potash, washing soda, pearl ash, spirit of hartshorn, by mistake, and, when this has been done, plenty of water should be given to drink, to which should be added, if available, weak acids such as vinegar, lime juice, or lemon juice. Oily substances, such as olive oil, may thereafter be administered. On no account must any attempt be made to make the patient vomit.

ALKALOIDS are substances found commonly in various plants. They are natural nitrogenous organic bases and combine with acids to form crystalline salts. Among alkaloids, morphine was discovered in 1805, strychnine in 1818, quinine and caffeine in 1820, nicotine in 1829, atropine in 1833. Only a few alkaloids occur in the animal kingdom, the outstanding example being adrenaline (or epinephrine), which is formed in the medulla of the suprarenal, or adrenal, gland. Alkaloids are often used for medicinal purposes. They are slightly soluble in water but readily dissolved by alcohol, which is therefore used in their extraction from the plants containing them. Most alkaloids have a bitter taste and have a strong action on the body. The name of an alkaloid ends in ' ine ' (in Latin ina).

NEUTRAL PRINCIPLES are crystalline substances with actions similar to those of alkaloids but having a neutral reaction. The name of a neutral principle ends in ' in ', e.g. digitalin, aloin.

Most alkaloids are obtained pure from their plants by a complicated process involving extraction with alcohol, the formation of a salt by addition of

an acid, and solution of this in water which is subsequently driven off by evaporation. The following are the most important active principles, with the plants from which they come :

Aconite, from Monk's-hood.
Atropine, from Belladonna (juice of Deadly Nightshade).
Cocaine, from Coca leaves.
Hyoscine, from Henbane.
Morphine ⎫
Codeine ⎬ from Opium (juice of Poppy).
Thebaine ⎭
Nicotine, from Tobacco.
Physostigmine, from Calabar bean.
Pilocarpine, from Jaborandi leaves.
Quinine ⎱ from Cinchona or Peruvian
Quinidine ⎰ bark.
Strychnine, from Nux Vomica seeds.

ALKALOSIS (see ALKALÆMIA).

ALKAPTONURIA (see OCHRONOSIS).

ALKYLATING AGENTS are so named because they alkylate or react with certain biochemical entities, particularly those concerned with the synthesis of nucleic acid. Alkylation is the substitution of an organic grouping in place of another grouping in a molecule.

The importance of the alkylating agents in medicine is that by interfering with the growth of cells they have proved of value in the treatment of various forms of malignant disease. Unfortunately they interfere with the growth of normal cells as well as malignant cells, and this restricts their use to a considerable extent.

Nevertheless several of them, including mustine (q.v.) and thiotepa (q.v.) have proved of considerable value in the chemotherapy of malignant disease.

ALLANTIASIS (ἀλλᾶς, sausage) is a name for sausage-poisoning. (*See* FOOD POISONING.)

ALLANTOIN is a crystallizable substance obtained from allantoic fluid, fœtal urine, etc., and also prepared by the oxidation of uric acid. It is used in the treatment of ulcers to stimulate the formation of the surface epithelial layer of the skin.

ALLANTOIS (ἀλλᾶς, sausage ; εἶδος, form) is a vascular structure which, very early in the life of the embryo, grows out from its hind-gut. The end becomes attached to the wall of the womb. It spreads out at the end, becomes stalked, and develops later into the placenta and umbilical cord (*see* AFTERBIRTH), which forms the only connection between the mother and embryo.

ALLERGEN is the term applied to any substance, usually a protein, which, taken into the body, makes the body hypersensitive or ' allergic ' to it. Thus in hay-fever the allergen is pollen.

ALLERGY (ἄλλος, different ; ἔργον, reaction) means special sensitiveness of an individual to certain foods, pollens or other products of plants, animal emanations, insect bites, etc., so that in such an individual conditions like asthma, dyspepsia, nettle-rash, hay fever, eczema, and headache are produced. The term anaphylaxis is given to a similar serious reaction following the injection of serum. (*See* ANAPHYLAXIS.) The substances that produce allergy are generally of protein nature and include such ordinary foods as eggs, milk, flour, and potatoes ; also strawberries, tomatoes, cauliflower, walnuts, pork, shell-fish, salmon, coffee, etc. ; it may also be caused by inhalation of dust from feathers (in pillows), of the hair of horses, dogs or cats, of face powder containing orris root, and of pollen, especially from grasses and certain flowers.

Symptoms.—The reaction in sensitive persons usually appears within a few minutes, but may be delayed for hours. One of the most common effects is nettle-rash or dropsical swellings in various parts ; hay fever is another common result ; sometimes there is swelling in a joint. Another type of reaction consists in spasmodic contractions of unstriped muscle so that the person affected may become urgently ill with asthma, or may develop spasms in the stomach with painful dyspepsia and vomiting, or in the intestine with symptoms resembling obstruction or severe diarrhœa, or may be troubled by irritability of the bladder. In other cases, neuralgia, headache or attacks of giddiness may come on.

Treatment.—It is important to find out the food or other substance to which the individual is sensitive. Sometimes this has been discovered by long per-

sonal experience. Skin testing may also be carried out by inoculating into a series of scratches extracts of various foods, etc., likely to cause allergy, and the substance responsible produces a weal surrounded by redness within a few minutes. When the substance is discovered, it should in future be carefully avoided, or, if it is an ordinary food, the sensitiveness can sometimes be abolished by taking this food constantly in small quantities, very gradually increased. Severe symptoms, as in asthma, may be relieved by an injection of adrenaline, 5 to 10 minims (0·3 to 0·6 ml.). There is now available a range of antihistamine drugs (*q.v.*) which are of value in treating cases in which the cause of the condition cannot be avoided or is not known.

ALLOCHEIRIA (ἄλλος, another ; χείρ, the hand) is the name for a disorder of sensation in which sensations are referred to the wrong part of the body.

ALLOPATHY (ἄλλος, another ; πάθη, condition) is a term applied sometimes by homœopathists to the methods used by regular practitioners of medicine and surgery. The term literally means curing by inducing a different kind of action in the body, and is an erroneous designation.

ALLOPURINOL is a drug which is proving of value in the treatment of gout. It acts by suppressing the formation of uric acid.

ALOES is the dried juice of a plant which grows in the West Indies (*Aloe vera*) and East Africa (*Aloe Perryi*). It acts as a purgative, and, taken in the evening, it acts next morning. The dose is 2 to 5 grains (125 to 300 mg.) of aloes, or 4 to 8 grains (250 to 500 mg.) of aloes pill. Since it tends to cause griping, it is usually combined with other drugs. (*See* CONSTIPATION.)

ALOIN is an extract from aloes much used in pills ; the dose is from $\frac{1}{4}$ to 1 grain (15 to 60 mg.).

ALOPECIA (ἀλώπηξ, a fox), is another name for baldness. (*See* BALDNESS.)

ALOPECIA AREATA is the term given to the disorder in which the hair comes out in patches, resulting in shiny, smooth, bald areas. (*See* BALDNESS.)

ALPENSTICH (German word) is a term applied to pneumonia which is apt to affect persons exposed to the cold of high regions.

ALUM is the sulphate of aluminium and potassium. Ammonia alum is the sulphate of aluminium and ammonium. Alum is an astringent, and may be used in powder to rub into wounds, *e.g.* of the head, when bleeding will not stop of itself. As an emetic, a teaspoonful of powdered alum may be given in water. A valuable use is in an eye-wash for inflamed, painful, and bloodshot eyes, the strength being about 4 grains (250 mg.) to the ounce (30 ml.) of water. It is also used sometimes in double that strength to form an astringent douche.

ALUMINIUM is a light whitish metal which is very malleable and ductile and is much used for the manufacture of surgical instruments and as a base for artificial dentures. It is quickly destroyed by exposure to salt, iodine, and some other substances commonly used as antiseptics. Aluminium acetate is used in solution as an astringent and antiseptic. Aluminium hydroxide is used internally as an antacid and absorbent in dyspepsia in doses of 3 to 15 grains (200 mg. to 1 G.).

ALVEOLAR ABSCESS (*see* GUM-BOIL).

ALVEOLUS (*alveoli*) is a term applied to the sockets of the teeth in the jaw-bone. The term is also applied to the minute divisions of glands and to the air sacs of the lungs.

AMANTADINE is a drug which is being used in the treatment of certain virus infections, such as influenza, but hitherto with only moderate success.

AMAUROSIS (ἀμαύρωσις) is the term applied to blindness in which there is no obvious lesion of the eye, the blindness being caused by disease of the optic nerve, retina, or brain, or being due to hysteria.

AMBIVALENCE is the term applied to the psychological state in which a person concurrently hates and loves the same object or person.

AMBLYOPIA (ἀμβλυωπία) means defective vision for which no recognizable cause exists in any part of the eye. It may be due to such causes as defective development, hysteria, excessive use of tobacco or alcohol, etc. The most important form is that associated with squinting (or strabismus), or gross difference in refraction (*q.v.*) between the two eyes. It has been estimated that in Britain 5.7 per cent. of young adults have amblyopia due to this cause.

AMBULANCE (*ambulo*, I move about) is a vehicle for conveying sick or injured individuals. Under the National Health Service a comprehensive ambulance service is available for the whole country. There is no charge for this except in the case of patients who are being taken to a nursing home or the pay wards of a hospital. The responsibility for arranging for the ambulance rests with the doctor in charge of the patient. In the case of an emergency, *e.g.* an accident or sudden illness in the street, an emergency ambulance service is available and the quickest way of obtaining an ambulance is through the police. The ambulance service is provided by local health authorities, which not only provide their own ambulances but are allowed to provide them through the agency of other bodies, such as the British Red Cross Society.

There is also a Hospital Car Service run by persons who use their own cars to take patients to and from hospital. They are paid an approved mileage allowance by the appropriate local health authority.

Ambulance classes.—Courses of instruction in first aid comprise six to twelve sessions, each of about two hours' duration. Syllabuses of instruction are published by various organizations, the principal ones being the British Red Cross Society, the St. John Ambulance Association, and the St. Andrew's Ambulance Association. For full details reference should be made to the secretary of one of these associations.

(For subjects connected with first-aid, *see under* INJURED, REMOVAL OF; BANDAGES, BURNS, CONVULSIONS, DROWNING, FAINTING, FRACTURES, HÆMORRHAGE, NURSING, POISONING, WOUNDS.)

AMBULATORY FEVER (*ambulo*, l move about) is one in which the attack is at first so mild that the person keeps on going about as usual. It occurs especially in typhoid fever, and then the sick person forms a source of infection.

AMENORRHŒA (*à*, neg. ; μήν, a month ; ῥέω, I flow) is the absence of the menstrual flow during the time of life at which it should occur. (*See* MENSTRUATION.)

AMENT is an idiot or mentally deficient person—one having no mind.

AMENTIA is the state of being an ament : mental deficiency from failure of the mind to develop normally.

AMETHOCAINE is a powerful local anæsthetic which is used when a prolonged effect is required. It is also used as a spinal anæsthetic.

AMETROPIA (*à*, neg. ; μέτρον, proportion ; ὄψις, sight) means an error in the refractive power of the eye so that images are not properly focused on the retina. It may occur as long-sightedness (hypermetropia), short-sightedness (myopia), or astigmatism, or as a combination of either of the first two with astigmatism. It is corrected by appropriate lenses.

AMIDOPYRINE, or PYRAMIDON, is an analgesic and antipyretic remedy, which is seldom used now because of the risk of its causing agranulocytosis (*q.v.*).

AMINACRINE HYDROCHLORIDE is a derivative of acridine and is used as a local antiseptic.

AMINO-ACID is the name given to substances which are derived from the ultimate products of digestion of protein foods and from which the protein materials of the body are again built up. They are organic acids in which one or more hydrogen atoms have been replaced by the chemical group NH_2.

AMINOCAPROIC ACID is one of a group of drugs which have recently been introduced for the control of bleeding. These drugs act by inhibiting what is known as the fibrinolytic enzyme. This is a complex system which helps to maintain the coagulation mechanism of the blood in such a state that clotting of the blood only occurs when it is necessary. Thus, if fibrinolysis is prevented then the blood will clot more easily and bleeding will stop.

AMINOMETRADINE is a synthetic, non-mercurial diuretic which is effective when taken by mouth.

AMINOPHYLLINE is the name given to a combination of theophylline and ethylene diamine. It has a fourfold use : (*a*) as a diuretic ; (*b*) in the treatment of angina pectoris by virtue of its action in improving the blood supply to the heart muscle ; (*c*) in the treatment of bronchial asthma ; (*d*) in the treatment of Cheyne-Stokes respiration.

AMINOPTERIN is an antimetabolite (*q.v.*) which is proving of value in the treatment of acute leukæmia (*q.v.*).

AMITRIPTYLINE is one of the antidepressant drugs. It has also been used in the treatment of severe hiccup.

AMMONIA is a pungent gas formed by heating a mixture of sal-ammoniac and quicklime. Dissolved in water it forms the well-known spirits of hartshorn, or liquor ammoniæ. It is given off slowly from carbonate of ammonia, which is used as a smelling salts. Carbonate of ammonia is the chief ingredient in aromatic spirits of ammonia or sal volatile. In chloride of ammonia or sal-ammoniac it is fixed. (For ammonia poisoning, *see* ALKALIS, POISONING BY.)

Uses.—Externally, strong ammonia produces blistering. For bee-stings, weak ammonia is applied locally to relieve the pain. (*See* ALKALI.) Internally it is a powerful stimulant, and, therefore, a teaspoonful of sal volatile in water is given, or smelling salts are applied to the nose, when fainting

AMMONIAC

AMPHETAMINES

threatens. The chloride and the carbonate of ammonia are used as expectorants (*q.v.*), whilst the former is also a diuretic (*q.v.*).

AMMONIAC is a resinous gum obtained from *Dorema ammoniacum*, and possessed of a slightly irritant action. It is now little used.

AMNESIA (*ἀμνησία*, forgetfulness) means loss of memory. (*See* APHASIA.)

AMNION (*ἀμνίον*) is the tough fibrous membrane which lines the cavity of the womb during pregnancy, and contains from one to two pints (0·5 to 1 litre) of fluid in which the embryo floats. It is formed from the ovum along with the embryo, and in labour the part of it at the mouth of the womb forms the 'bag of waters'. (*See* LABOUR.) When a child is 'born with a caul', the caul is a piece of amnion.

AMNIOSCOPY is the method whereby the volume and the colour of the fluid in the amniotic sac (*see* AMNION) can be assessed without interfering with the course of pregnancy. It is of value in determining whether the fœtus is distressed and therefore whether or not labour should be induced.

AMNIOPLASTIN is the name given to the membrane prepared from the AMNION (*q.v.*) and used in surgery to prevent, for example, the brain adhering to the skull after operations on it. The amnioplastin is placed between the skull and the brain. It is also wrapped round nerves which have been operated on, to prevent their being bound down by scar tissue.

AMODIAQUINE is a member of the 4-aminoquinoline series of substances, and is widely used in the prevention, and treatment, of malaria.

AMŒBA is the name applied to a minute protozoan animal consisting of a single cell, in which is a nucleus surrounded by protoplasm that changes its shape as the animal progresses or absorbs nourishment. Several varieties of this organism are found under different conditions within the human body, these forms being known as

entamœbæ. One variety, *Entamœba coli* (Fig. 7), is found in the large intestine of man without any associated disease;

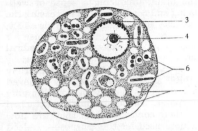

FIG. 7.—*Entamœba coli*, unencysted. 1, ectoplasm; 2, endoplasm; 3, nucleus; 4, karyosome; 5, vacuoles; 6, ingested bacteria. (From Blacklock and Southwell, *A Guide to Human Parasitology*. H. K. Lewis & Co. Ltd.)

another, *Amœba dentalis*, is found in the sockets of the teeth associated with pyorrhœa; another, *Entamœba histolytica* (Fig. 8), is the causative organism of amœbic dysentery (*see* DYSENTERY). Other forms are found in the genital organs.

AMŒBIASIS (*see* DYSENTERY).

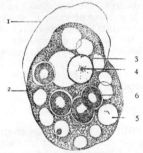

FIG. 8.—*Entamœba histolytica*, unencysted. 1, ectoplasm; 2, endoplasm; 3, nucleus; 4, karyosome; 5, vacuoles; 6, ingested red blood cells. (From Blacklock and Southwell, *A Guide to Human Parasitology*. H. K. Lewis & Co. Ltd.)

AMPHETAMINES are a group of drugs closely related to adrenaline and act by stimulating the sympathetic nervous system. There are now more than fifty preparations of amphetamine substances.

On being inhaled, they constrict the blood-vessels in the nose and so ease the congestion or 'stuffiness' of nasal catarrh. Their indiscriminate use for this purpose is harmful and they should only be used under medical supervision. When taken by mouth they have a profound stimulating effect on the brain, producing a sense of well-being and confidence and increasing the capacity for mental work. This effect, however, is temporary, and its use for this purpose, except under medical supervision, is fraught with danger.

By virtue of the fact that they inhibit appetite, they rapidly achieved a widespread reputation for slimming purposes. In view of the risks attached to their continued use, they are now seldom used for this purpose. Indeed there is growing evidence that the dangers of the amphetamines including the risk of becoming addicted to them, far outweigh their advantages.

AMPHORIC is an adjective denoting the kind of breathing heard over a cavity in the lung. Amphoric breathing is common in advanced cases of pulmonary tuberculosis, and the sound is like that made by blowing over the mouth of a narrow-necked vase.

AMPHOTERICIN B is an antibiotic, derived from *Streptomyces nodosus*, which is proving of value in the treatment of certain of the diseases classified under the heading of mycosis (*q.v.*). It is, however, a very toxic substance and is therefore only used in those infections in which the outlook is otherwise hopeless.

AMPICILLIN (*see* PENICILLIN).

AMPOULE is a small glass container having one end drawn out into a point capable of being sealed so as to preserve its contents sterile. It is used for containing solutions for hypodermic injection.

AMPUTATION (*amputo*, I prune) means the severing of any limb or part completely from the body. In the case of organs other than limbs the word ' excision ' is generally used. An amputation through a joint without sawing of bone is called a ' disarticulation '.

Objects of Amputation.—In the great majority of cases a limb is amputated because it has been damaged beyond the hope of recovery. It is not always easy to say at once that a limb should,

38

or should not, be removed after an injury, but the three chief points are, as to whether (1) extensive portions of muscle, skin, and bone are so crushed and torn as to make their death and separation inevitable ; (2) the great nerves and blood-vessels are divided so as to destroy the vitality of the limb ; and (3) the laceration is so extensive, or involves joint cavities so as to render cleaning of the wound impossible and endanger the patient from blood-poisoning due to septic absorption. (*See* BLOOD-POISONING.) Often after gunshot wounds, crushes in machinery, or railway accidents, where a decision cannot be made at once, the injured limb is cleaned (vessels tied, sinews stitched, etc.), and then is put in a weak antiseptic bath for some days to see if healing will take place. This is done, especially in the case of the hand, where every fragment of tissue is valuable because of the delicate movements the limb executes, and where fortunately circulation by anastomosis is good. (*See* ANASTOMOSIS.) But in the lower limbs, the chief point is to have a small scar and a sound stump, so that the weight of the body can be borne, and therefore a few inches of length are, if necessary, sacrificed and amputation oftener performed.

Not infrequently, when bones or joints are diseased, especially with persistent discharges, or when gangrene has taken place, amputation of part of a limb is necessary. Another object of amputation is to remove malignant tumours entirely, such as those in the foot. Still another case for amputation is where a limb is paralysed completely, and a more useful artificial substitute can be fashioned. Owing to improvements in surgery which have taken place in recent years, many injured limbs can now be saved which previously would have required to be amputated.

Methods of amputation.—When a limb is to be amputated, it is elevated to empty it of blood as far as possible, then a tight or elastic band called a tourniquet is applied, to prevent bleeding ; and, the limb being cut off by one of the following methods, the cut ends of the blood-vessels are ligatured, the tourniquet removed, the muscles and sinews stitched over the bone, and finally the edges of the skin stitched together. Thus there may be almost no blood lost. The *circular method* is one in which skin, muscles or flesh, and bone are cut or sawn at successively higher levels, so that the skin meets afterwards over the other tissues. It is an old method, and, being rapid, was used before the days of chloroform. In the *elliptical method* the tissues are divided in the form of an oblique circle, so that one side of the cut is much lower down the limb than the other. This has the advantage of bringing the resulting scar over to one side of the limb, and thus providing a better covering for the end of the sawn bone. The *flap method* is one in which a large flap of skin and fibrous tissue is carefully dissected up from the underlying muscles, and, after the limb is removed, laid across the cut surface and stitched at its sides and end. Only one flap may be made, or more often two, which meet end to end and side to side. Sometimes the flap consists of muscle as well as of skin, and occasionally a slice of bone with its covering membrane is included in the flap so as to produce a broad surface of bone when the flap is turned into its final position, and thus to form a better support in the case of lower-limb amputations. The flap method is that most frequently used, partly because with it the scar does not fall opposite the end of the bone, and also because a limb seldom being injured at the same level all round, the formation of a flap enables a larger part to be saved. The ' *racquet* ' *method* consists of a circular cut running round the limb and a long cut, like the handle of a racquet, up its side ; the two edges are drawn apart, the bone divided high up, and then the sides of the racquet stitched together.

The wound is generally healed completely in three weeks and an artificial limb can be fitted at the end of three to six months. (*see* ARTIFICIAL LIMBS). The avoidance of suppuration in an amputation following an injury is of great importance. Sometimes a ' conical stump ' forms, owing to the bone continuing to grow, and thus tending to stretch the other parts over its end. In such a case an operation must be performed later to remove part of the bone.

AMYL NITRITE is a volatile, oily liquid prepared by the action of nitric and nitrous acids upon amylic alcohol. It resembles other nitrites in its power of relieving spasms and dilating blood-vessels, and it acts with great rapidity when inhaled, producing its effects in a few seconds. (*See* NITROGLYCERIN.)

AMYLOBARBITONE, or AMYTAL, is one of the barbiturate group of drugs. Its approximate duration of action is 6 to 8 hours. The dose is 100 to 200 mg.

AMYLOCAINE, or STOVAINE, is an alkaloidal substance resembling cocaine but prepared artificially. It has an anæsthetic action similar to that of cocaine, but has the great advantage over the latter that it is much less toxic and is therefore not so liable to cause headaches, sickness, and fainting. It is used to produce anæsthesia for operations either by injection beneath the skin or by injection into the spinal canal.

AMYLOID (*see* WAXY DISEASE).

AMYLOID BODIES (ἄμυλον, starch ; εἶδος, form) is the collective name for starch, dextrin, glycogen or animal starch, and similar substances.

AMYLOSE is the name applied to any carbohydrate of the starch group.

AMYLUM (ἄμυλον) is another name for starch.

AMYOTROPHIC LATERAL SCLER-OSIS is a disease of the nervous sytem in which, as a result of degeneration of nerve cells in the spine and brain, there is progressive wasting of the muscles of the body, with spastic paralysis.

AMYOTROPHY means atrophy or loss of substance of a muscle.

ANÆMIA. No simple classification of anæmia can be wholly accurate, but the most useful method is to divide anæmias into : (*a*) microcytic hypochromic anæmia, (*b*) megaloblastic hyperchromic anæmia, (*c*) aplastic anæmia, (*d*) hæmolytic anæmia.

MICROCYTIC HYPOCHROMIC ANÆMIA.

—This corresponds to a large extent with what used to be known as ' secondary anæmia '. It takes its name from the characteristic changes in the blood, which will be discussed shortly.

Causes.—(1) *Loss of blood.* (a) As a result of trauma. This is perhaps the simplest example of all, when, as a result of an accident involving a large artery, there is severe hæmorrhage.

(b) Menstruation. The regular monthly loss of blood which women sustain as a result of menstruation always puts a strain on the blood-forming organs. If this loss is excessive, then over a period of time it may lead to quite severe anæmia.

(c) Child - birth. A considerable amount of blood is always lost at childbirth, and if this is severe, or if the woman was anæmic during pregnancy, a severe degree of anæmia may develop.

(d) Bleeding from the gastro-intestinal tract. The best example here is anæmia due to ' bleeding piles '. Such bleeding, even though slight, if maintained over a long period of time, is a common cause of anæmia in both men and women. The hæmorrhage may be more acute and occur from a duodenal or gastric ulcer, when it is known as hæmatemesis.

(e) Certain blood diseases, such as purpura and hæmophilia (q.v.), which are characterized by bleeding.

(2) *Defective blood formation.*—(a) This is the main cause of anæmia in infections. The organism responsible for the infection has a deleterious effect upon the blood-forming organs, just as it does upon other parts of the body.

(b) Toxins. In conditions such as chronic Bright's disease and uræmia there is a severe anæmia due to the effect of the disease upon blood-formation.

(c) Drugs. Certain drugs, such as lead, depress blood-formation.

(3) *Inadequate intake of iron.*—The daily requirement of iron for an adult is 12 mg., and 15-20 mg. during pregnancy. This is well covered by an ordinary diet, so that by itself it is not a common cause. But if there is a steady loss of blood, as a result of heavy menstrual loss or ' bleeding piles ', the intake of iron in the diet may not be sufficient to maintain adequate formation of hæmoglobin.

40

(4) *Inadequate absorption of iron.*—This may occur in diseases of the stomach or bowels, e.g. ulcerative colitis.

In many cases the anæmia is found to be due to a combination of two or more of these causes. A severe form of this anæmia in women, known as CHLOROSIS, used to be common, but it is seldom seen nowadays.

Symptoms. — These depend upon whether the anæmia is sudden in onset, as in severe hæmorrhage, or gradual. In all cases, however, the striking sign is pallor, the depth of which depends upon the severity of the anæmia. The colour of the skin may be misleading, except in cases due to severe hæmorrhage, as the skin of many people is normally pale. The best guide is the colour of the internal lining of the eyelid. When the onset of the anæmia is sudden the patient complains of weakness and giddiness, and he loses consciousness if he tries to stand or sit up. The breathing is rapid and distressed, the pulse is rapid, and the blood pressure is low. The tongue is often sore (glossitis), and the nails of the fingers may be brittle and concave instead of convex (koilonychia). In some cases, particularly in women, the Plummer-Vinson syndrome is present. This consists of difficulty in swallowing and may be accompanied by huskiness ; in these cases glossitis is also present. There may be slight enlargement of the spleen, and there is usually some diminution in gastric acidity.

Changes in the blood.—The characteristic change is a diminution in both the hæmoglobin and the red cell content of the blood. There is a relatively greater fall in the hæmoglobin than in the red cell count, so that the colour index is less than unity. The colour index is the percentage of hæmoglobin stated in terms of the amount contained in each red cell. In health it is 1·0 (or unity). If the blood is examined under a microscope the red cells are seen to be paler and smaller than normal. These small red cells are known as microcytes.

Treatment consists primarily of giving sufficient iron by mouth to restore, and then maintain, a normal blood picture. The main iron preparation now used is Ferrous Sulphate, 3 to 6 grains (200 to 400 mg.), thrice daily. When the blood picture has become

PLATE V

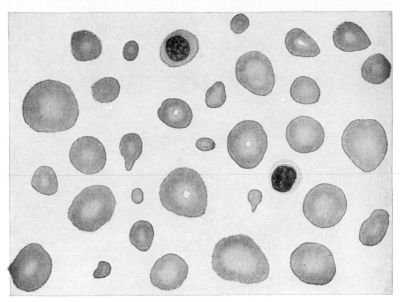

Blood film in Pernicious Anæmia

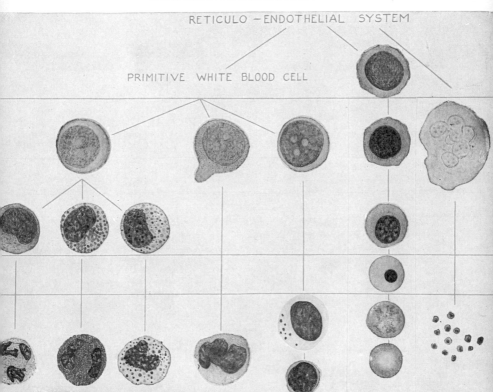

RETICULO — ENDOTHELIAL SYSTEM

PRIMITIVE WHITE BLOOD CELL

Origin of Blood Cells

From Whitby and Britton's *Disorders of the Blood* (Churchill).

normal, the dosage is gradually re-duced. A preparation of iron is now available which can be given intra-venously, but this is only used in cases which do not respond to iron given by mouth, or in cases in which it is essential to obtain a quick response.

If, of course, there is hæmorrhage, this must be arrested, and if the loss of blood has been severe it may be neces-sary to give a blood transfusion. Care must be taken to ensure that the patient is having an adequate diet, and a period of rest in hospital, fol-owed by a holiday, is often beneficial. If there is any underlying toxic or infective condition, this, of course, must be adequately treated.

MEGALOBLASTIC HYPER-CHROMIC ANÆMIA. — There are various forms of anæmia of this type, such as those due to nutritional defects and those associated with ex-cessive destruction of red cells in the body, but the most important is that known as PERNICIOUS ANÆMIA.

PERNICIOUS ANÆMIA, or ADDI-SONIAN ANÆMIA, is found in all civilized countries. Up until about forty years ago its cause was unknown and it was an invariably fatal disease. In 1926, two Americans, G. R. Minot and W. P. Murphy, published an article showing that pernicious anæmia re-sponded to treatment with liver. This discovery is one of the greatest in the history of medicine and ranks in im-portance with that of insulin in the treatment of diabetes mellitus. This form of treatment is based upon the now well-proved fact that pernicious anæmia is due to lack of what is known as the *intrinsic factor*. For the forma-tion of normal red blood corpuscles a substance known as the hæmatinic principle, or *anti-anæmic factor*, is necessary (Fig. 9). This factor is formed as a result of two other factors—the *extrinsic factor* and the *intrinsic factor*. The former is present in any well-balanced diet, being present in beef, marmite, etc. The *intrinsic factor* is pro-duced normally by the mucosa lining the distal part of the stomach. It is the inability of the patient to produce the intrinsic factor that leads to the onset of pernicious anæmia. The *hæmatinic principle*, normally produced in the stomach by the interaction of the

2 a

extrinsic and the intrinsic factor, is stored in the liver ready for use when supplies are required for the formation of red blood corpuscles in the bone marrow.

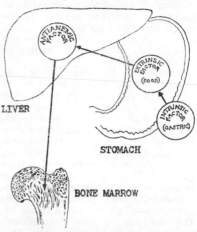

FIG. 9.—Diagram illustrating factors responsible for normal red blood corpuscles. (From Best and Taylor, *The Physiological Basis of Medical Practice.* Baillière, Tindall & Cox.)

Symptoms.—Pernicious anæmia is a disease of middle age, being rare under the age of 40 years. It affects both men and women. The onset is usually insidious, so that the anæmia is usually well developed before medical advice is sought. In addition to the general symptoms and signs already described in the section on microcytic anæmia, the important features of pernicious anæmia are as follows. The patient, who is often prematurely grey-haired, has a characteristic lemon-yellow com-plexion. The tongue is often sore and appears thinner, smoother, and redder than usual—a condition which makes it very like that of a dog. There is often soreness and excoriation of the corners of the mouth—a condition known as cheilosis. There may be slight enlargement of the spleen. There is a complete absence of free hydrochloric acid in the stomach, even after the injection of histamine; this is one of the most important points in the diagnosis of pernicious anæmia. One of the most serious complica-tions of pernicious anæmia is a disease with the cumbersome title of SUBACUTE COMBINED DEGENERATION OF THE CORD. This, as the name indicates, is a degenerative condition of the spinal cord, and the importance of recognizing its onset is that it can be cured by adequate treatment of the anæmia. Its early manifestations are a sensation of tingling or 'pins and needles' in the legs, accompanied by stiffness. Later, if untreated, the stiffness becomes progressively worse, finally leading to paralysis.

Changes in the blood.—The important finding in the blood is an anæmia in which there is a relatively greater diminution in the number of red cells than in the hæmoglobin content of each cell, so that the colour index is 1·0 or more. The red cells are larger than normal, *i.e.* megalocytes, and they appear to be redder than normal. They also vary in shape (*poikilocytosis*) and in size (*anisocytosis*). Occasionally a few primitive red cells (normoblasts) may be found (Plate V). The total white cell count is diminished, *i.e.* there is leucopenia. The final diagnosis depends upon an examination of the bone marrow, which is found to contain many very primitive red cells, *i.e.* megaloblasts.

Treatment consists of the administration of vitamin B_{12}, or cyanocobalamin as it is now known. Its precise mode of action is not known, but it is probably the extrinsic factor. It is given by injection. Preparations are available which can be given by mouth, but the general consensus of expert opinion is that these are not satisfactory for efficient control of the disease. The dosage usually depends mainly upon the severity of the anæmia, but there is also considerable personal variation in different patients, so that treatment must be supervised by a physician and checked by repeated examinations of the blood. It must always be remembered that a patient with pernicious anæmia requires to take cyanocobalamin for the rest of his life.

An alternative to cyanocobalamin is now available : namely, hydroxocobalamin. This has the advantage over cyanocobalamin that it is better retained in the body and therefore less frequent injections are necessary.

APLASTIC ANÆMIA is a disease in which the red blood corpuscles are very greatly reduced and in which no attempt

appears to be made in the bone marrow towards their regeneration. The cause in many cases is not known, but in rather less than half the cases the condition is due to some toxic substance, such as benzol or certain drugs, or ionizing radiations. The patient becomes very pale, with a tendency to hæmorrhages under the skin and mucous membranes, and the temperature may at times be raised. The red blood corpuscles diminish steadily in numbers. Treatment consists primarily of regular blood transfusions. Although the disease is often fatal, the outlook has improved in recent years. About 25 per cent. of patients recover when adequately treated, and others survive for several years.

HÆMOLYTIC ANÆMIA results from the excessive destruction or hæmolysis (*q.v.*) of the red blood cells. This hæmolysis may be due to undue fragility of the red blood cells, when the condition is known as congenital hæmolytic anæmia, or acholuric jaundice. Another important form is hæmolytic disease of the newborn (*q.v.*). In other cases it is due to transfusion with incompatible blood (*see* TRANSFUSION OF BLOOD).

ANÆROBE (ἀ, neg. ; ἀήρ, air ; βιόω, I live) is the term applied to bacteria having the power to live without air. Such organisms are found growing freely, deep in the soil, as, for example, the tetanus bacillus.

ANÆSTHESIA (ἀναισθησία) means loss of the power of feeling. The word is applied either to loss over a limited area of skin produced by certain nervous diseases, by freezing, by cocaine, etc., or to a total loss of feeling and consciousness, in the state produced by chloroform, ether. and similar drugs. When only loss of the sense of pain is meant, without loss of the sense of touch, the correct term is analgesia.

ANÆSTHETICS are drugs and other measures which produce insensibility to external impressions.

Historical.—Although it is mainly owing to the researches of distinguished chemists and physicians of last century that the employment of anæsthesia has come to occupy a foremost place among remedies, there is abundant evidence to show that it is a practice of great antiquity. Besides the mention by Homer of the anæsthetic effects of nepenthe, and the reference by Herodotus to the practice of the Scythians of inhaling the vapours of a certain kind of hemp to produce intoxication, the employment of anæsthetics in surgery by the use of mandrake is particularly noted by Dioscorides and Pliny. It also appears, from an old Chinese manuscript, that a physician named Hoa-tho, who lived in the third century, gave his patients a preparation of hemp, whereby they were rendered insensible during the performance of surgical operations. Mandrake was extensively used as an anæsthetic by Hugo de Lucca, who practised in the thirteenth century. The soporific effects of mandrake are remarked by Shakespeare, who also makes frequent mention of anæsthetizing draughts, the composition of which is not specified.

In 1800 Sir Humphry Davy, experimenting on nitrous oxide gas, discovered its anæsthetic properties, and described the effects it had on himself when inhaled with the view of relieving local pain. He suggested its employment in surgery, but his suggestion remained unheeded for nearly half a century.

The inhalation of sulphuric ether for the relief of asthma and other lung affections had been employed by Dr. Pearson, of Birmingham, as early as 1785 ; in 1818 Faraday showed that the inhalation of the vapour of sulphuric ether produced anæsthetic effects similar to those of nitrous oxide gas ; and this property of ether was confirmed by the American physicians, Godman (1822), Jackson (1833), Wood and Bache (1834).

These observations, however, appear to have been regarded as mere scientific curiosities till December 1844, when Dr. Horace Wells, a dentist of Hartford, Connecticut, underwent in his own person the operation of tooth extraction while rendered insensible by nitrous oxide gas. On September 30, 1846, Dr. Morton, a dentist of Boston, employed the vapour of sulphuric ether to procure general anæsthesia in a case of tooth extraction, and thereafter administered it with complete success in cases requiring surgical operation. This great achievement marked a new era in surgery. Operations were performed in America in numerous instances under ether inhalation, the result being only to establish more firmly its value as a successful anæsthetic. The news of the discovery reached England on December 17, 1846. On December 19, Mr. Robinson, a dentist in London, and on the 21st, Mr. Liston, the eminent surgeon, operated on patients anæsthetized by ether ; and the practice soon became general both in Great Britain and on the Continent.

Sir James Y. Simpson, of Edinburgh, was the first to apply anæsthesia by ether in midwifery practice. This he did on January 19, 1847, and he subsequently employed ether inhalation in numerous cases of both easy and difficult parturition, an account of which he published, containing much important information.

These observations excited great interest in the medical world, and led to the extensive employment of ether inhalation till November 15, 1847, when Simpson announced his discovery of the anæsthetic properties of chloroform (the trial of which had been suggested to him by Mr. Waldie, a chemist of Liverpool). He proposed it as a substitute for sulphuric ether, which for a time it almost completely displaced for anæsthetic purposes in Britain. In America, however, ether remained the favourite drug for this object. In 1858 Dr. Snow, of St. Thomas's Hospital, London, published a work, *On Chloroform and other Anæsthetics*, which was the first attempt to place the whole subject on a scientific basis. The number of fatalities which took place during the administration of various anæsthetics had by this time begun to attract attention, and mechanical inhalers designed to prevent the administration of too concentrated a vapour were invented by Clover in 1862 and Junker in 1867, modifications of which are still in use (Fig. 10). Experiments with various other drugs were made by other men, and during the period 1860–70 a movement, starting in the United States, took place in favour of nitrous oxide, or 'laughing-gas', for dental work, and this anæsthetic, firmly installed towards the end of the decade for tooth extractions and other short operations, has never gone out of use, being reckoned one of the safest anæsthetics we possess. In 1876, Clover introduced an apparatus whereby

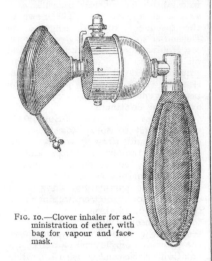

Fig. 10.—Clover inhaler for administration of ether, with bag for vapour and face-mask.

nitrous oxide and ether could be inhaled in succession, and as the initial stages of ether administration are difficult and unpleasant, and are obviated by beginning with the gas, this instrument and method proved of great usefulness.

Choice of Anæsthetic.—At the present day there is a large range of anæsthetics to choose from. Many of these require complicated apparatus for their administration, whilst others are potentially dangerous unless used by an experienced anæsthetist. The choice of anæsthetic in any one particular case often requires considerable judgement, and, except with a highly skilled anæsthetist, the sound working rule is that the doctor should use the anæsthetic of which he has had most experience. In the case of the general practitioner called upon in an emergency to administer an anæsthetic for a surgical operation, this usually means ether or chloroform.

The following is a useful classification of the present range of anæsthetics.

VOLATILE ANÆSTHETICS.—These include ether, chloroform, nitrous oxide, ethyl chloride, vinyl ether, trichlorethylene, cyclopropane, and

halothane. The last four should only be used by anæsthetists experienced in their use. Mixtures of chloroform and ether are sometimes used. Nitrous oxide has two great advantages: the patient recovers quickly from the anæsthetic, and there is relatively little nausea and vomiting. Its use for major surgical operations requires considerable skill and special apparatus, and for this purpose, therefore, it can only be used by an experienced anæsthetist. Actually, it is tending to be replaced by cyclopropane. Nitrous oxide is an excellent anæsthetic for minor surgical operations, for dentistry, and in midwifery, but in the first of these it is tending to be replaced by the basal narcotics. It is often used in endotracheal anæsthesia, *i.e.* when the anæsthetic is introduced directly into the lungs by means of a tube passed into the trachea. Endotracheal anæsthesia is employed in operations in the head or neck where a mask or any other anæsthetic apparatus would get in the way of the surgeon. Ethyl chloride is seldom used to maintain anæsthesia; it is more commonly used to induce anæsthesia, especially in children.

BASAL NARCOTICS.—These are used to induce, without any distress to the patient, a degree of unconsciousness which permits of operations being carried out under nitrous oxide or small amounts of ether or chloroform. It is seldom safe to use these basal narcotics to produce a degree of anæsthesia which is sufficient to permit of operations being performed without the addition of some other anæsthetic. Their great advantage is that the induction of anæsthesia is much more pleasant for the patient than by inhalation of an anæsthetic, and that their use often reduces the amount of volatile anæsthetic necessary for the operation. They are given either per rectum or intravenously. Amongst those given per rectum are paraldehyde and bromethol, whilst hexobarbitone sodium and thiopentone sodium are the two most frequently given intravenously.

STEROID ANÆSTHETICS.—Some years ago it was discovered that a state of anæsthesia could be induced by large doses of steroid hormones. A derivative of **one** of these hormones has now been prepared in which the anæsthetic action can be obtained without the hormone action. This preparation, known as hydroxydione, promises to be a useful adjunct to anæsthesia. It is given intravenously and appears to have certain advantages over other anæsthetics.

LOCAL ANÆSTHETICS are given by injection to induce loss of sensation in the area to be operated upon, without any general loss of consciousness. For major operations they are more commonly used on the Continent than in this country, but they have tended to be used more frequently in Great Britain of recent years, particularly in operations on the stomach. Cocaine was the first local anæsthetic to be used, but on account of its toxic properties it has been almost entirely replaced by synthetic preparations. These include procaine hydrochloride, lignocaine, and cinchocaine hydrochloride.

SPINAL ANÆSTHETICS are used when it is considered inadvisable to induce general anæsthesia and local anæsthesia is contra-indicated. Their two main advantages are that they can be used in patients with diseases of the lung in whom a general anæsthetic may lead to complications, and that they produce excellent relaxation of the muscles. The same anæsthetics are used for inducing local anæsthesia, with the exception of cocaine, which is never used as a spinal anæsthetic. The two most frequently used are cinchocaine hydrochloride and amylocaine hydrochloride. The solution is injected into the spinal canal by the same technique as in use for lumbar puncture (*q.v.*).

Stages of anæsthesia.—Whatever be the anæsthetic employed, the effects are much the same, though some symptoms are more prominent with one anæsthetic, others with another, and in the case of nitrous oxide the initial stages are hurried over and the patient plunged almost at once into deep unconsciousness.

STAGE I.—There is great rapidity of thought, but disturbance of judgement and power of control. Giddiness, tingling, and other peculiar or pleasant sensations are felt. The patient may be emotional, or may sing, shout, or struggle, and then passes off into a dreamy state, with partial loss of sensation. The heart's action becomes stronger and the pupils dilate.

STAGE II.—There is complete loss of consciousness. The speech becomes unintelligible, changing to a mere muttering. There may be muscular spasms of various sorts, also coughing, retching, and possibly vomiting. The pupils become small.

STAGE III.—There is absolute unconsciousness and complete muscular relaxation, and in this stage surgical operations are performed. The heart's action is weakened, most reflex movements abolished, and the pupil dilates again but is still capable of contracting when the eyelid is raised so that light enters the eye.

STAGE IV.—This is the stage of danger, the breathing becomes shallow, the face pallid or livid, the heart weak and irregular, and the pupils widely dilated. If the anæsthetic be not at once removed, breathing and pulse then stop and the person dies.

Uses of anæsthetics. — The most evident use of anæsthetics is to relieve the pain of surgical operations and of convulsive diseases. Their use has made possible much more prolonged and delicate operations than could be performed upon the conscious and suffering body. An anæsthetic is also an aid in diagnosis, particularly of abdominal conditions, producing muscular relaxation and allowing the free handling of painful regions. Anæsthetics are also used in medical practice to quiet violent spasmodic states, as in the uræmia of Bright's disease, in a succession of epileptic fits, in lock-jaw, and in strychnine poisoning. (For the use of local anæsthetics, *see* ANALGESICS.)

ANALEPTIC (ἀναληπτικός) means a restorative medicine, or one which acts as a stimulant of the central nervous system, for example caffeine.

ANALGESIA (ἀ, neg. ; ἄλγος, pain) means loss of the power to feel pain without loss of consciousness, *e.g.* in some nervous diseases or due to some drugs. (*See also* AUDIOANALGESIA).

ANALGESICS are drugs or other measures which cause temporary loss of the sense of pain without unconsciousness and without necessarily loss of the sense of touch. Some act generally on the brain or the nerves to dull pain which is already present (*see* ANODYNES) ; others act locally, such as cocaine, benzamine, amylocaine, and the process of freezing, which are used to prevent pain which would otherwise necessarily be caused by operations. In a position between that of a general anæsthetic and a local analgesic stand drugs such as morphine and scopolamine which are used for the production of a torpid, semi-insensible state like that sometimes used in child-birth (*see* TWILIGHT SLEEP).

Uses.—Local insensibility to pain may be produced in a considerable variety of ways, but most of these fall into one of four classes : (1) infiltration of the region to be operated upon by a solution of the analgesic drug ; (2) injection of the solution into or near the nerve trunks which convey the sensations of the part ; (3) painting, spraying, or rubbing the surface, especially of mucous membrane, with the drug ; and (4) the application of intense cold.

The first drug to be used for local anæsthesia or analgesia in operations was cocaine, which has certain disadvantages in that it is destroyed by boiling and that it readily causes symptoms of poisoning, so that it cannot be safely used in doses over $\frac{1}{2}$ grain (30 mg.) Procaine, also known as ethocaine, planocaine and novocain, which is an artificially prepared substance, has largely displaced cocaine because it is many times less poisonous and so can be used in larger doses. Amethocaine is largely used for spinal analgesia. Benzamine, also known as eucaine, is a synthetic compound, devoid of irritating properties, which is used for application to the eye, especially combined with adrenaline, which, by its constricting effect on the blood-vessels, diminishes congestion and bleeding in operations. One of the most widely used local anæsthetics at the present moment is lignocaine, which is also known by the proprietary name of xylocaine. Quinine and urea hydrochloride has been employed as an analgesic in cases where a prolonged effect is desired, as its results last for several days.

When *infiltration analgesia* is em-

ployed, a weak solution of procaine is generally used to which a small amount of adrenaline is added. A long hypodermic needle is used to inject this solution in large quantity (several ounces) into and especially around the part upon which the operation is to be performed. By this means tumours can be removed, the abdomen opened, and similar serious operations, which do not involve great shock to the patient and in which general unconsciousness is not desirable, can be performed.

When general loss of sensation in a region is to be brought about by injecting a nerve trunk or its neighbourhood, stronger solutions (*e.g.* procaine 2 per cent.) are used in similar quantities. The large nerves of a limb are sometimes treated in this way for the prevention of the shock caused by a severe operation, even when a general anæsthetic is also employed. This method is much used for painless tooth extraction. The two methods of infiltration and regional analgesia are often combined, for example, to perform amputations below the knee or elbow or in removal of a goitre.

Another way of applying the injection method is by *spinal analgesia*, in which sensation is abolished temporarily in the lower limbs by injection of the drug into the spinal canal.

The *surface application* of analgesics is in general only useful in cases in which operations are to be performed upon mucous membranes, such as those of the nose or throat, where cocaine and eucaine can readily be applied by painting or spraying.

A transitory analgesia is produced by *freezing* the skin. This is usually effected by spraying a small area with ethyl chloride, which very quickly evaporates, with the production of intense cold.

ANALYSIS (ἀνάλυσις) means a separation into component parts by determination of the chemical constituents of a substance. The process of analysis is carried out by various means, *e.g.* chromatographic analysis by means of the adsorption column ; colorimetric analysis by means of various colour tests ; densimetric analysis by estimation of the specific gravity ;

gasometric analysis by estimating the different gases given off in some process ; polariscopic analysis by means of the polariscope ; volumetric analysis by measuring volumes of liquids. Analysis is also sometimes used as an abbreviation for psycho-analysis.

ANAMNESIS (ἀνάμνησις) is the term applied to the statement of the past history of some particular case of disease.

ANAPHYLAXIS (φύλαξις, guarding) is a condition of excessive sensitiveness exhibited by certain persons or animals to the injection of foreign material into their tissues. A common example is the pain, swelling, eruption, feverishness, and general prostration which occasionally follow the injection of serum containing the diphtheria or tetanus antitoxin. An example of a slighter form of anaphylaxis is afforded by persons who suffer from nettle-rash, asthma, and similar symptoms when they take some food of which their system is intolerant, or by other persons who present similar symptoms when exposed to the emanations of certain animals, *e.g.* horses, cats, or fowls (*see* ALLERGY).

ANAPLASIA means the state in which a body cell loses its distinctive characters and takes on a more primitive form ; it occurs, for example, in cancer, when cells proliferate rapidly.

ANASARCA (ἀνά, up ; σάρξ, the flesh) is a condition of general dropsy.

ANASTOMOSIS (ἀναστόμωσις, an outlet) is a term describing the means by which circulation is carried on when large vessels are narrowed or closed, as by pressure. In the limbs, especially around joints, and in internal organs, small arteries open freely into their neighbours to form a network from which the smallest vessels carry off the blood. By this means pressure from one side, or even the ligature of the main artery to a limb, is prevented from stopping the flow of blood to any part, because so soon as one artery is closed, the other arteries of the limb dilate, through relaxation of their muscle fibres, and the supply of blood passes on as before, but by new

channels. Anastomosis is also a term describing the joining together (by operation) of any two parts of the alimentary tract, so that an artificial communication is formed between them.

ANATOMY (ἀνατομή) is the science which deals with the structure of the bodies of men and animals. Brief descriptions of the anatomy of each important organ are given under the headings of the various organs. It is studied by dissection of bodies specially bequeathed for the purpose or of the bodies of those who die in hospitals and similar institutions, unclaimed by relatives.

ANATOXIN, or FORMOL TOXOID, is a preparation of diphtheria toxin which has been made non-toxic by heat or by formalin. Injected into a person, it makes him immune to diphtheria.

ANDROGEN is the general term for any one of a group of hormones which govern the development of the sexual organs and the secondary sexual characteristics of the male.

ANENCEPHALY is the term given to the condition in which a child is born with a defect of the skull and absence of the brain.

ANEURINE is the *British Pharmacopœia* name for vitamin B_1 (*see* VITAMIN).

ANEURYSM, or ANEURISM (ἀνεύρυσμα), means a dilatation upon an artery, due to yielding of the vessel-wall and gradual stretching by the pressure of the blood.

Varieties.—There are several ways of classifying aneurysms. With reference to structure, they have been separated into *true aneurysms*, in which the vessel-wall is merely thinned and stretched but still intact, and *false aneurysms*, in which the wall has been thinned away with the increase of the hollow, till all the coats of the artery (*see* ARTERIES) have given way, and the blood is enclosed only by the greatly thickened fibrous tissues surrounding the artery. With reference to shape, they are called *fusiform* when the

47

artery is dilated all round for some distance (Fig. 11), this form being common on the thoracic aorta ; *sacculated* when a spot on one side has been pushed out gradually to form a sort of pouch, which is the usual form when medium-sized arteries are affected ; *dissecting* when the inner coat has given way

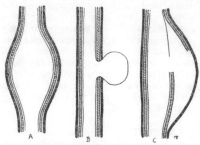

Fig. 11.— Diagram showing A, a fusiform aneurysm; B, a saccular aneurysm; C, a dissecting aneurysm. (From Handfield-Jones and Porritt, *The Essentials of Modern Surgery.* E. & S. Livingstone, Ltd.)

somewhat suddenly and blood has passed between the coats and torn its way some distance along the vessel ; *miliary* when the aneurysm is very small and looks like a millet seed on the side of the vessel, which is a form often found on the vessels in the brain. An *arterio-venous aneurysm* is one where there is a communication between an artery and a vein. Further, they are called after the regions in which they occur—*abdominal, thoracic, gluteal, popliteal, axillary,* etc.

Causes.—The two main factors responsible for the formation of an aneurysm are (1) strain ; (2) weakening of the wall of the artery. This latter is the more important. No amount of strain, whether due to a raised blood-pressure or to muscular effort, will lead to aneurysm formation unless there is some local weakening of the wall of the artery. The most important cause of weakening of the arterial wall is syphilis, and practically all aneurysms in the thoracic aorta (the most common site for aneurysms) are due to this factor. Next in order of importance comes atheroma (*q.v.*) and this is responsible for about 50 per cent. of aneurysms in the abdominal aorta. Aneurysms may also be due to loss of the support provided by the surrounding tissues, *e.g.* in the lungs,

48

where an aneurysm may form in one of the branches of the pulmonary artery as a result of destruction of the surrounding tissue by tuberculosis. Occasionally they may be due to congenital defects in the arterial wall : the most common site for such aneurysms is the Circle of Willis (*q.v.*) at the base of the brain. More rarely they may arise as a result of repeated small traumata and strain in exposed arteries, such as the popliteal artery, which have not much support from the surrounding tissues ; popliteal aneurysms were more common in the old coaching days among those who spent most of their working lives on horseback. Small aneurysms may also arise in cases of severe sepsis, as a result of infection of the arterial wall. Aneurysms are more common in men than in women, and particularly among those who indulge in hard physical labour, such as labourers and stevedores.

Symptoms.—These vary greatly with the size and position of the aneurysm, but there are some which are characteristic of all forms. The *type of person* who suffers is usually a man in his forties or fifties, who has had an arduous or irregular life and has often indulged in high living. There may be other signs of arterial disease, such as cirrhotic Bright's disease (*see* BRIGHT'S DISEASE), or a previous apoplexy. If the aneurysm be in a limb, a round *swelling* is noticed, perhaps as large as a walnut or Mandarin orange, which expands and diminishes with each heart-beat. The swelling is generally painless, and the skin over it is unchanged (unlike an abscess). Aneurysms rarely occur farther from the trunk than elbow or knee. If the aneurysm be internal it is situated upon a great vessel, and is often very large in size before it causes any definite symptoms, which are mainly due to interference with surrounding organs. *Pain* is felt only when the swelling presses upon nerves, upon the air passages, causing great breathlessness, or upon bone, wearing it gradually away. In the latter case pain may be agonizing, although in early cases it is not infrequently taken for mere rheumatic pain. *Breathlessness* or *difficulty in swallowing* may occur where there is a large thoracic aneurysm, from pressure on the windpipe or gullet, also *cough* of a barking, irritating nature, and changes in the voice, from irritation or paralysis of the left recurrent laryngeal nerve. In thoracic and abdominal aneurysm there may be a *bulging* in the upper part of chest or abdomen, as the case may be, which can be felt to throb when one hand is placed on it in front and the other on the back; in a later stage pulsation can also be seen. The *aneurysmal tippet* is the name given to a network of dilated veins which appears upon the chest and shoulders, owing to obstruction of the circulation through the great veins, by a thoracic aneurysm. *Swelling of the skin* or œdema is found with all aneurysms sooner or later from the same cause. Many other signs, such as inequality of the pupils, difference in the pulse on the two sides of the body, and murmurs heard over the swelling, are present in different aneurysms, but can be appreciated only by the trained observer.

Aneurysm is a serious disease : it is apt to cause great interference with other organs ; it may at any time burst and cause sudden death from bleeding into the loose tissues or cavities of the body ; it is a sign that the arteries are extensively diseased, and the person unfit for active work. The duration of life is generally only a few years, although it may be prolonged for twenty if the aneurysm fills up with clot, which forms a natural method of cure.

Treatment. — (*a*)   MEDICAL. — Although the aneurysm tends constantly to increase, another tendency is for the blood in contact with the unhealthy wall to clot. If this be encouraged, the aneurysm may become a solid mass, which practically may be looked on as a cure, because there is no more tendency to grow or to burst. To this end the circulation must be quieted by rest in bed, freedom from worry, and a bland diet. Potassium iodide is often of value, particularly if the aneurysm is syphilitic in origin, and in cases due to this cause penicillin is given.

(*b*) SURGICAL. — Tremendous advances have been achieved in recent years in the surgical treatment of aneurysms. In many cases, as in aneurysms of arteries in the limbs, all that is required is to ligature the artery above and below the aneurysm, the circulation to the limb being maintained by anastomosis (*q.v.*) of the other arteries in the limb. In the case of other major arteries, such as the aorta, the aneurysm is replaced by a graft so that the circulation through the artery can be maintained. This graft may consist of a piece of an artery removed from a cadaver, or of synthetic material such as orlon.

ANGINA (ἄγχω, I strangle) means literally choking, and is a term applied to swellings of the throat or other cause of difficulty in breathing, as *tonsillar angina* or quinsy, *laryngeal angina* or laryngitis, *membranous angina* or croup, *anginal scarlatina* or scarlet fever with abscesses round the throat.

ANGINA PECTORIS is a term applied to a violent paroxysm of painful sensations in the chest, arising for the most part in connection with disease of the coronary arteries.

Causes. — Angina pectoris is generally held to be due to an inadequate blood-supply to the myocardium, *i.e.* the heart muscle. The myocardium receives its blood-supply through the coronary arteries. Thus angina pectoris may be due to spasm of the coronary arteries or to narrowing of the lumen of these arteries as a result of arteriosclerosis (*q.v.*) or atheroma (*q.v.*). It is probably seldom due to spasm alone. In the majority of cases it is due either to spasm plus arteriosclerosis (or atheroma) or to arteriosclerosis (or atheroma). Occasionally the defective blood-supply may be the result of disease of the first part of the aorta or of the aortic valve. Because of its association with coronary artery disease, angina pectoris is predominantly a disease of middle age and is much more common in men than in women.

Symptoms. — The characteristic feature of angina pectoris is the occurrence of pain behind the chest-bone, arising as a result of exertion and relieved by rest. This pain often spreads into the left arm. The amount of exertion necessary to induce the pain varies considerably, and to a certain extent gives some idea of the severity of the condition. Thus, it may only occur on hurrying, whilst in other cases the blood-supply to the myocardium may be so defective that the least exertion, *e.g.* turning over in bed, may be sufficient to induce a severe paroxysm of pain. Aggravating factors are exposure to cold, or exertion immediately following a meal. The paroxysm of pain seldom lasts for more than a few minutes, provided the affected individual remains at complete rest. In most instances the pain is so severe that the affected individual is unable to continue any exertion. Occasionally it is accompanied by a feeling of impending dissolution, often referred to as *angor animi*.

Treatment.—The aim of treatment is to prevent the occurrence of pain by persuading the patient to restrict his activities. Thus, he should always rest for at least half an hour after a meal. He should always be warmly clad when he goes out of doors in cold weather. In more severe cases his bedroom should be on the ground floor and should be warmed in the winter. He should always allow himself plenty of time so that he never needs to hurry. If he is overweight he should restrict his diet so as to bring his weight down. Even with all these precautions, attacks of pain may still occur, and for the relief of these tabella trinitrini, grain $\frac{1}{100}$ (0·6 mg.), is the most satisfactory. A tablet should be placed in the mouth, as soon as pain is felt, and allowed to melt in the mouth. It should not be swallowed intact, as this delays the onset of relief. Most patients with angina pectoris carry a small supply of these tablets about with them wherever they go, so that they are always available for immediate use. An alternative form of treatment is amyl nitrite, which is supplied in the form of small glass ' perles '. One of these, held in a handkerchief, is broken between the fingers and the contents then inhaled. Whilst usually as effective as trinitrin tablets, amyl nitrite is more liable to produce unpleasant side-effects such as headache and giddiness. Both these preparations bring relief in angina pectoris by virtue of the fact that they cause vasodilatation of the coronary arteries and thereby improve the blood-supply to the myocardium.

ANGIOGRAPHY means rendering the blood-vessels visible on an X-ray

film by injecting into them a radio-opaque substance. In the case of arteries this is known as *arteriography* ; the corresponding term for veins being *venography* or *phlebography*. This procedure demonstrates whether there is any narrowing of the lumen of the vessel.

ANGIOMA (ἀγγεῖον, a blood-vessel) is a tumour composed of blood-vessels. (*See* TUMOUR *and* NÆVUS.)

ANGIONEUROTIC ŒDEMA is a condition of localized dropsy, similar in many ways to nettle-rash. The precise cause is not known. (*See* NETTLE-RASH.)

ANGITIS, or ANGIITIS (ἀγγεῖον, a vessel), means inflammation of a vessel such as a blood-vessel, lymph-vessel, or bile-duct.

ÅNGSTRÖM UNIT, A.U. (called after Swedish physicist), is a measurement of length and equals $\frac{1}{10000}$ micron, or one hundred-millionth of a centimetre. It is represented by the symbol λ and is used to give the length of electromagnetic waves, light waves lying within the range of 4000 to 8000 A.U.

ANHIDROSIS is the condition in which there is an abnormal diminution in the secretion of sweat.

ANHYDRÆMIA is the term used to describe an abnormal loss of water from the blood.

ANILINE is a substance derived from indigo by distillation, from coal - tar by extraction, or manufactured from benzene. It is a colourless liquid, with peculiar aromatic smell and burning taste. From it many vivid and beautiful dyes are made and extensively used, such as fuchsine or rosaniline, eosine, magenta, Congo red, methyl blue, Hofmann's violet. Aniline itself is a narcotic poison, though most of the colours are harmless in moderate amount. In some persons the dyes, when brought into constant touch with the skin, as in coloured stockings, scarves, etc. (especially red and black goods), cause excessive irritation and eruptions, such as eczema, boils, weals, which are very difficult to get rid of.

Probably these are due, not to the aniline, but to the presence of arsenic, which is used in the process of manufacture, and in cheap dyes is not completely removed.

ANISE is the dried fruit of *Pimpinella anisum* or of *Illicium anisatum,* a Chinese plant, from which is obtained a volatile oil used in the form of anise water and spirit of anise for a flavouring agent in some mixtures, and especially as a remedy for colic in children. (*See* OILS.)

ANISINDIONE, or MIRADON, is one of the newer anticoagulants which is active when taken by mouth. Its maximum effect occurs in about 36 hours, and its action passes off within 48 hours of cessation of treatment.

ANKLE is the joint between the leg bones (tibia and fibula) above, and the astragalus (the Roman dice-bone or talus) below. It is a very strong joint with powerful ligaments binding the bones together at either side, many sinews running over it, and bony projections from the leg bones, which form large bosses on either side, called the outer and inner malleoli, extending about half an inch below the actual joint. Two common injuries near the ankle are a sprain, on the inner side, consisting of tearing of the internal ligament ; and fracture of the fibula (Pott's fracture) on the outer side. (*See also* JOINT DISEASES.)

ANKYLOSIS (ἀγκύλος, crooked) is a term meaning the condition of a joint in which the movements are restricteɒ by fibrous bands, or by malformation, or by actual union of the bones. (*See* JOINT DISEASES.)

ANKYLOSTOMA (ἀγκύλος, crooked ; στόμα, mouth) is a parasitic worm. (*See* PARASITES.)

ANODYNES (ἀ, neg. ; ὀδύνη, pain) are curative measures which soothe pain. They act by removing the cause of pain, by soothing the irritated nerves of the painful part, or by paralysing the part of the brain by which the painful impression is received. Substances which destroy the power of feeling altogether are called anæsthetics (*q.v.*), those which destroy only the power of feeling pain are analgesics (*q.v.*).

Varieties.—Alkaline applications are anodynes to gouty joints, bee-stings, etc. Prolonged application of either cold or heat is an anodyne in inflammation. Chloroform, cocaine, eucaine, camphor and menthol, are local anodynes, while internally butyl chloral, Indian hemp, gelsemium, hyoscyamus, and various synthetic products like phenacetin, aspirin, and phenazone, soothe pain in distant parts.

Uses.—Opium is the oldest and most powerful anodyne, but can only be used in cases of excessive pain, because of its tendency to habit-formation. Bromides and chloral dull pain, but with it the mental faculties, so that they also interfere with the performance of everyday duties. Aspirin, phenacetin, and paracetamol seem to have the power of dulling only that part of the brain which perceives the pain, and so are most suitable in slighter pains which do not incapacitate though they interfere with ordinary duties. Butyl chloral and gelsemium (derived from the jasmine plant) have a reputed soothing action in facial neuralgia. (For further details, *see* NEURALGIA, HEADACHE, INFLAMMATION, etc.)

ANOPHELES is the generic name of a widely distributed group of mosquitoes, certain species of which transmit to man the infecting agent of malaria. *Anopheles maculipennis* and *A. bifurcatus* are both found in England and can both transmit the malaria parasite. (*See* Fig. 235, page 481.)

ANOREXIA (ἀ, neg. ; ὄρεξις, appetite) means loss of appetite. (*See* APPETITE.)

ANOREXIA NERVOSA. (*See* APPETITE.)

ANOREXIANT DRUGS are drugs which reduce appetite by an action on the brain. They are all synthetic sympathomimetic amines—*i.e.* produce effects simulating those produced by stimulation of the sympathetic nerves. Typical examples are amphetamine (*q.v.*), chlorphentermine (*q.v.*), and phenmetrazine (*q.v.*). In no circumstances should they ever be used except under strict medical supervision.

ANOSMIA (ἀ, neg.; ὀσμή, smell) means loss of sense of smell. (*See* NOSE, DISEASES OF.)

ANOXÆMIA means reduction of the oxygen content of the blood below normal limits.

ANOXIA is the term applied to that state in which the body tissues have an inadequate supply of oxygen. This may be because the blood in the lungs does not receive enough oxygen, or because there is not enough blood to receive the oxygen, or because the blood stagnates in the body.

ANTABUSE (*see* DISULFIRAM).

ANTACIDS are medicines which correct acidity, either general or stomachic. (*See* ACIDITY, ALKALI, DYSPEPSIA.)

ANTE- (*ante*) is a prefix meaning before or forwards.

ANTEFLEXION (*ante*, before; *flexio*, a bend) means the abnormal forward curvature of an organ in which the upper part is sharply bent forward. The term is especially applied to forward displacement of the uterus.

ANTENATAL (*ante*, before; *natus*, born) is a term applied to conditions occurring before birth. It is used with reference both to mother and child. (For Antenatal Clinics, *see* MATERNITY AND CHILD WELFARE.)

ANTEVERSION (*ante*, before; *verto*, I turn) is the term applied to the forward tilting of an organ, especially of the uterus.

ANTHELMINTICS (ἀντί, against; ἕλμινς, a worm) are substances which cause the death or expulsion of parasitic worms. (*See* PARASITES.)

ANTHIOMALINE is lithium antimony thiomalate, in a 6 per cent. solution. A drug which has been used in the treatment of lymphogranuloma inguinale, schistosomiasis, and filariasis.

ANTHRACOSIS (ἄνθραξ, coal) is the change which takes place in the lungs and bronchial glands of miners, and others, who inhale coal dust constantly.

The affected tissues change in colour from greyish pink to jet black, owing to loading with minute carbon particles. This fine form of dust appears to be almost devoid of any harmful effect.

ANTHRAX (ἄνθραξ, coal) is a very serious disease occurring in sheep and cattle, and in those who tend them or handle the skins and fleeces, even long after removal of the latter from the animals. It has also broken out occasionally in epidemics among woolsorters or cattle-tenders. In 1966, 10 cases were notified in England and Wales. It is sometimes referred to as malignant pustule, woolsorters' disease, splenic fever of animals, or murrain.

Causes.—The cause is a bacillus (*B. anthracis*) which grows in long chains (Plate VIII) and produces spores of great vitality. These spores retain their life for years, in dried skins and fleeces; they are not destroyed by boiling, freezing, 5 per cent. carbolic lotion, or, like many bacilli, by the gastric juice. The disease is communicated from a diseased animal to a crack in the skin, *e.g.* of a shepherd or butcher, or from contact with contaminated skins or fleeces. Nowadays skins are handled wet, but if they are allowed to dry so, that dust laden with spoes is inhaled by the workers, an internal form of the disease results. Instances have occurred of the disease being conveyed on shaving brushes made from bristles of diseased animals.

Symptoms.—(*a*) EXTERNAL FORM. —This is the 'malignant pustule'. After inoculation of some small wound, a few hours or days elapse, and then a red, inflamed swelling appears, which grows larger till it covers half the face or the breadth of the arm, as the case may be. Upon its summit appears a bleb of pus, which bursts and leaves a black scab, perhaps half an inch wide. There is at the same time great prostration and fever. The inflammation may last ten days or so, when it slowly subsides and the patient recovers, if surviving the fever and prostration.

(*b*) INTERNAL FORM.—This takes the form of pneumonia with hæmorrhages, when the spores have been drawn into the lungs, or of ulcers of the stomach and intestines, with gangrene of the spleen, when they have been swallowed. It is usually fatal in two or three days.

Treatment.—Prevention is most important by disinfecting all hides, wool and hair coming from areas of the world, such as the Middle and Far East, where the disease is commonly found. All hides should be handled wet, so that spores cannot be present in dust ; for the internal form is four times as fatal as the external. The hands of workmen must be carefully washed before eating, and working clothes changed. By these means the number of deaths from anthrax, in the English woollen manufacturing districts has been reduced to a tenth of the number that occurred fifty years ago, before the disease was understood. An efficient vaccine is now available. Treatment consists of the administration of large doses of penicillin or of one of the tetracyclines. There is also an anti-serum which can be given in addition to penicillin. If there is a pustule, this is kept clean, but must not be cauterized or incised.

ANTI- (ἀντί, against) is a prefix meaning against.

ANTIBIOTIC is the term used to describe any anti-bacterial agent derived from micro-organisms, such as penicillin, streptomycin, chloramphenicol, and chlortetracycline.

ANTIBODIES are substances in the blood which destroy or neutralize various toxins or ' bodies ' (*e.g.* bacteria), known generally as antigens. The antibodies are formed, usually, as a result of the introduction into the body of the antigens to which they are antagonistic, as in all infectious diseases.

ANTICOAGULANTS are drugs which prevent coagulation of the blood. The main ones now in use are heparin (*q.v.*), anisindione (*q.v.*), cyclocoumarol dicoumarol (*q.v.*), ethyl biscoumacetate (*q.v.*), phenindione (*q.v.*), and warfarin (*q.v.*).

ANTIDEPRESSANTS are drugs which relieve depression by a direct antagonizing action on the depression. They include drugs such as imipramine and phenelzine.

ANTIDOTES (ἀντί, against ; δίδωμι, I give) are remedies which neutralize the effects of poisons either (*a*) by changing the poisons into harmless substances through chemical action, or (*b*) by setting up an action in the body opposite to that caused by the poison.

Uses.—(*a*) The first class, in which the poisons are acted on by the antidote in the stomach, includes most of the poisons except the very deadly vegetable alkaloids. Thus acids have alkalis as antidote and vice versa ; arsenious acid has dialysed iron or magnesia ; corrosive sublimate has white of egg, milk, or flour ; oxalic acid has chalk or magnesia ; sugar of lead has Epsom salts ; tartar emetic has tannin. (*b*) Among the very deadly poisons (*see* ALKALOIDS) the antidote to one is generally a powerful poison itself, and the actions do not neutralize one another precisely in every respect. Calabar bean has for its antidote atropine ; prussic acid also has atropine ; muscarine (the poison of toadstools) also has atropine ; opium and morphine too have atropine ; strychnine has chloral or chloroform ; chloral has strychnine ; chloroform has amyl nitrite ; curare or Indian arrow-poison has strychnine ; cocaine has morphine; and digitalis has aconite and nitrites.

ANTIGEN is the term applied to a substance which causes the formation of antibodies, that is bodies which act in opposition to poisons formed in the body or introduced from outside.

ANTIHISTAMINE DRUGS are drugs which antagonize the action of histamine (*q.v.*) and are therefore of value in the treatment of certain allergic conditions such as hay fever, nettle-rash, and certain forms of eczema.

A selection of those available in Great Britain is given in Table 3, where they are classified according to their sedative effect. This classification has been used because the degree of sedation produced by the drug, through its action on the central nervous system, is often the deciding factor in selecting the preparation to be used in a given case. It should be noted that those in Group III are also liable to cause a dry mouth and

53

blurring of the vision, just as hyoscine does.

APPROVED NAME	PROPRIETARY NAME
Group I. Least Sedative	
Antazoline	Anstitin
	Ben-hist
	Histostab
Buclizine	Vibazine
Chlorcyclizine	Diparalene
Chlorpheniramine	Piriton
Halopyramine	Synopen
Phenindamine	Theophorin
Triprolidine	Actidil
Group II. Moderate Sedative	
Bromazine	Ambodryl
Dimenhydrinate	Dramamine
Mepyramine	Anthisan
Promethazine chlorophyllinate	Avomine
Tripelenamine	Pyribenzamine
Group III. Highly Sedative	
Diphenhydramine	Benadryl
Promethazine	Phenergan

TABLE 3.—Classification of Antihistamine Drugs (*The Practitioner*).

ANTIKAMNIA is a remedy of antipyretic properties containing sodium bicarbonate, caffeine, and acetanilide.

ANTIKETOGENIC is the term applied to foods and remedies which prevent or decrease the formation of ketones, *i.e.* bodies related to acetone.

ANTIMETABOLITES are a group of drugs which have been introduced for the treatment of certain forms of malignant disease. Chemically, they closely resemble substances (or metabolites) which are essential for the life and growth of cells. When introduced into the body they are 'mistaken', so to speak, by the cell for the corresponding metabolite, thereby preventing the cell from making use of the metabolite, or substance, which is essential for its growth. By this means the life of the cell is affected and it ultimately dies.

ANTIMONY is the name applied to a metal and also to its sulphide, a black powder found in nature. The tartrate of potassium and antimony is com-

monly known as 'tartar emetic' in reference to its chief property. The preparations of antimony are all irritants; hence in large doses they are poisons, producing vomiting, purging, and also paralysis of the heart and nervous system. In moderate amounts they stimulate secretions from the bronchial tubes, intestine, and skin, and thus ease cough, move the bowels, and cause free perspiration.

Uses.—Once a popular constituent, in the form of antimonial wine and James's powder (antimonial powder), of preparations for the treatment of fever and bronchitis, antimony is only used now in the treatment of certain tropical diseases such as kala-azar and schistosomiasis. For this purpose either the trivalent or pentavalent salts are used. These include antimony and sodium tartrate, antimony and potassium tartrate, stibophen, and neostam.

ANTIPERIODICS are drugs which tend to prevent the repetition of attacks of diseases occurring at stated periods. The term is used generally with reference to malaria.

ANTIPERISTALSIS is a term meaning a movement in the bowels and stomach by which the food and other contents are passed upwards, instead of in the proper direction. (*See* PERISTALSIS.)

ANTIPHLOGISTICS (ἀντί, against; φλέγω, I burn) is an old term meaning remedies used against inflammation, fever, and similar conditions.

ANTIPYRETICS (ἀντί, against; πυρετός, a fever) are measures used to reduce temperature in fever.

Varieties.—Cold-sponging, wet-pack, baths, alcohol, diaphoretic drugs, phenazone, phenacetin, quinine, salicylate of soda, and aspirin.

Uses (*see under above headings*).

ANTIPYRIN is another name for PHENAZONE (*q.v.*).

ANTISEPTICS (ἀντί, against, and σηπτός, putrid, from σήπω, I make rotten) are substances which have the property of preventing or arresting putrefaction in dead animal or vegetable matter. The access of air, together with a moderate amount of warmth and of moisture, is necessary for the occurrence of the putrefactive changes, which consist essentially in the breaking up of the complex organic material, and the formation of new and simpler combinations among its constituent elements. During the process, various gases and vapours are evolved, and the lower forms of animal and vegetable life are observed to grow and multiply in the putrefying substance. The exciting causes of putrefaction formed, fer centuries, a subject of scientific discussion, but the changes which take place are now known, as the result of Pasteur and Tyndall's labours, to depend upon the growth and activity of micro-organisms (*see* BACTERIOLOGY). The changes which take place in a wound when organisms gain entrance to it and flourish upon its discharges were first demonstrated by Semmelweiss in 1847 and are collectively known as sepsis or septic processes (*see* ABSCESS).

Varieties.—By exclusion of the air, or even by covering from germ-laden dust, dead matter that does not already contain bacteria may be kept intact for an indefinite time, as shown in the method of preserving meat by hermetically sealing the jars, after destruction of all germs by heat. Again, the preservative influence of a low temperature is well known ; and extreme cold is a powerful antiseptic, as proved in the case of the frozen mammoths of northern Asia. Furthermore, the abstraction of moisture will prevent corruption in dead material. In warm and dry climates, animal food may be preserved by exposure to the sun. In the ancient practice of embalming the dead, which is the earliest illustration of the systematic use of antiseptics, the moister portions of the body were removed before the preservative agents were added. The action of direct sunlight is highly destructive to bacteria, having more effect upon some kinds than upon others.

Reliance is chiefly placed, for practical purposes, on heat and chemical substances which destroy bacteria. Many substances which are strong antiseptics are of little practical use, either because they produce changes in the fluids with which they come in contact of such a nature as to hinder their further action, or because they are too irritating or too destructive when they come in contact with tissues of the body. Further, some antiseptics act strongly upon certain organisms and less effectively upon others, so that the value of an antiseptic varies in different circumstances.

HEAT is one of the most effective antiseptics and may be applied at a temperature of 100° to 150° C. Dry articles to be disinfected may be brought into contact with steam under pressure, or more simple articles to be preserved from decomposition or sterilized may be boiled for a short period. This method is, however, obviously inapplicable to the living body and to many fragile articles.

BORIC ACID is a weak antiseptic which is used because of its nonpoisonous and unirritating qualities. It may be used up to the full strength at which it dissolves in cold water, *i.e.* 1 part in 25 of water.

CARBOLIC ACID, originally introduced by Lord Lister, is a powerful antiseptic. 1 part in 100 of water will in the course of some hours kill most bacteria. Up to a strength of 1 part in 20 of water it may be brought in contact with tissues for a short time, but even this strength is dangerous for prolonged application.

MERCURIC SALTS are among the most powerful antiseptics. Perchloride of mercury may be used for washing the hands in a strength of 1 in 1000 of water. For lotions to be applied to the eyes, nose, and mouth, or for vaginal douching, it may be used in a strength of 1 in 10,000. Even in the strength of 1 part in 100,000 of water it kills almost all bacteria in a few minutes. The biniodide and cyanide of mercury are also used, either in lotions of similar strength or by saturating lint, gauze, or wool for application to wounds. The disadvantage of mercuric salts is that though very powerful they are highly irritating, and secondly, that they are precipitated and rendered useless by the albumens of discharges with which they come in contact.

CRESOL, TRICRESOL, or CRESYLIC ACID is a mixture of substances obtained from coal-tar, which is both stronger and less poisonous than carbolic acid. Various preparations sold under proprietary names, such as CREOLIN, CYLLIN, JEYES' FLUID, ACROSYL, and IZAL, are of similar nature and widely used. They are all dark oily liquids which form a white milky emulsion in water. LYSOL and some others contain fluid soap which aids their cleansing and penetrating action. For surgical purposes the usual strength is 1 part in 100 or 200 of water. For general disinfection these substances may be used weaker. TAR WATER is a popular antiseptic often used because of the cresols and similar substances that it contains.

HYDROGEN PEROXIDE has the double merit of being a strong antiseptic and at the same time non-irritating. It may be freely applied to mucous membranes in the full pharmacopoeial strength, although, even when considerably diluted with water, it is still a powerful germicide. It is essential that it should be fresh, as it rapidly deteriorates by losing oxygen.

IODINE is a strong antiseptic and is specially used in the form of weak solution of iodine ($2\frac{1}{2}$ per cent. strength).

IODOFORM has the power of checking septic changes when discharges come in contact with it, probably by its power of giving off iodine. It is sometimes used to impregnate gauze for filling abscesses and other cavities.

CHLORINE GAS is a powerful antiseptic often used to disinfect a room, while CHLORINATED LIME, which gives off chlorine gas, is much used to disinfect drains. Chlorine has the disadvantage of being very irritating and of bleaching and destroying many substances, e.g. cloth, leather, etc., with which it comes in contact.

SULPHUR DIOXIDE GAS, obtained from burning sulphur, is highly antiseptic and is used in the same way.

FORMALDEHYDE is one of the most powerful antiseptics, and dissolved in water is used as a spray for disinfection of walls and furniture. It is also used in throat lozenges. It is excessively irritating, and therefore cannot be used as an antiseptic for application to the tissues.

POTASSIUM PERMANGANATE is one of the most commonly used antiseptics in strength of 1 part in 1000 of water or weaker as a gargle, douche, and as a wash for the hands, etc.

ACRIFLAVINE, PROFLAVINE, BRIL-
56

LIANT GREEN, and other aniline dyes have a powerful action as antiseptics, and have also a gentle stimulating action on the tissues. They can be used in strength of 1 part in 1000 of normal saline, and they can be mixed with various other antiseptics without detriment.

HYPOCHLOROUS ACID, under such names as EUSOL, DAKIN'S SOLUTION, is much used and very effective for septic wounds.

ALCOHOL is a powerful antiseptic, and, like ETHER, is used for removing septic matter and grease from the skin.

NITRATE OF SILVER is a powerful antiseptic much used for lotions, eye drops, etc., in the strength of 1 part in 500 or 1000 of water. Other silver salts which are less irritating to the tissues are used in a similar way.

SALTS OF COPPER, SALTS OF IRON, SALTS OF LEAD, CHLORIDE OF ZINC, and compounds of most of the heavy metals act as strong antiseptics, but most of them, on account of their irritating or poisonous action, are not readily applicable for this purpose.

BALSAM OF TOLU, BALSAM OF PERU, and other aromatic substances are antiseptics for application to surface wounds, but are too expensive for general use.

CETRIMIDE, a mixture of alkyl ammonium bromides, is most effective for cleaning and disinfecting wounds and as a first-aid dressing in burns. It is also suitable for disinfecting utensils.

CHLORHEXIDINE is a recently introduced antiseptic which has proved particularly valuable in obstetric practice, as a skin disinfectant, and in the treatment of burns.

CHLOROXYLENOL is a powerful antiseptic, though its range of action is somewhat limited. It is non-irritating and is widely used in obstetric practice.

Uses.—Antiseptics act in various ways. Some of them kill bacteria by drying them, e.g. common salt and syrup used as preservatives extract water from bacteria and thus kill them; other antiseptics kill bacteria by oxidation, e.g. hydrogen peroxide, potassium permanganate; others coagulate the fluids in and around bacteria, e.g. perchloride of mercury; and still others act as bacterial poisons, e.g. cresol. The practice of using antiseptics has been in vogue for thousands of years. Thus cedar oil, tar, and resins were in use among the Egyptians. Pitch, copper salts, vinegar, etc., were used for wounds by the Romans, while the fumes of sulphur for purification and salt as a preservative of food have been employed from the earliest times. Many of the stronger and more irritating antiseptics are now used as disinfectants (*see* DISINFECTION). Lord Lister was the first, in 1865, to place the subject upon a scientific basis. The method of applying antiseptics in surgery is somewhat as follows : The surgeon's hands, and those of every one who is to handle the patient or any instrument or dressing, are purified by washing most thoroughly with soap and water, special care being taken to clean the crevices about the nails. Then some use ethereal soap, and the majority complete the procedure by steeping the hands in solution of perchloride of mercury. The skin of the patient is cleansed by shaving and then washing in a similar manner, the cleansing being generally, if possible performed on the day prior to the operation, after which the skin is covered by a dressing and often painted with iodine solution before the operation. Instruments are sterilized by boiling or by steeping in alcohol or cresol lotion, and all dressings are sterilized by steam or dry heat. By these means it is ensured that no substance which contains germs comes in contact with the operation wound. (*See also* ASEPSIS.)

ANTISPASMODICS (ἀντί, against ; σπάσμα, a spasm), or SPASMOLYTICS, are remedies which diminish spasm. The majority act upon muscular tissue to relax it, or make its contractions regular ; others dull the nervous system when its irritability is the cause of the spasm. Antispasmodics which relieve the spasm of colic are called carminatives.

Varieties.—Essential vegetable oils, such as oil of lavender, of peppermint, of cloves, and also valerian and camphor, diminish the sensitiveness of the nerve endings and so check irritable spasm of the heart and bowels. Alcohol, ether, chloroform, and amyl nitrite have a powerful paralysing action on nerve endings and on muscle. Belladonna, and hyoscyamus are often used for the relief of gall-stone or renal colic, or, in small quantity, with purgatives which cause griping, so as to diminish this unpleasant effect. Amyl nitrite quickly relieves the spasm of angina pectoris. Conium, lobelia, stramonium, and tobacco, in burning, give off sedative substances, and are used in various ' asthma cures '. Barbiturates are general sedatives to the brain and nerves, and are used in epilepsy and convulsions generally. In addition, a large number of synthetic preparations with antispasmodic actions have been introduced during recent years.

ANTITOXINS, ANTITOXIC SERUM (ἀντί, against ; τοξικόν, arrow poison). (*See* SERUM THERAPY.)

ANTIVENINE is a substance produced by the injection of snake venom into animals in small but increasing doses. In course of time the animal becomes immune to the particular venom injected, and the antivenine prepared from its serum is highly effective in neutralizing venom injected by the bite of a snake of the same species. To be of any use, it must be administered within one hour of the snake bite.

ANTROSTOMY is the term applied to the operation in which an opening is made through the nose into the maxillary antrum. (*See* ANTRUM.)

ANTRUM (ἄντρον, a cave) means a natural hollow in a bone. The *maxillary antrum* (antrum of Highmore) is situated in the upper jaw-bone between the eye and mouth and to the side of the nose, its dimensions being about one inch (25 mm.) each way (see NOSE, DISEASES OF). It communicates by a small opening with the nose. The *mastoid antrum* is situated in the mastoid process, the mass of bone felt behind the ear, and is much smaller. The latter may become the seat of an abscess in cases of suppuration of the middle ear (*see* EAR, DISEASES OF).

ANURIA is a condition in which no urine is voided. (*See* BRIGHT'S DISEASE, URINE.)

ANUS is the opening at the lower end of the bowel. It is kept closed by two muscles, the external and internal sphincters. The latter is a muscular ring which extends about an inch (25 mm.) up the bowel, is nearly $\frac{1}{4}$ inch (6 mm.) thick, and is kept constantly contracted by the action of a nerve centre in the spinal cord. Constipation is sometimes due to its failure to relax ; while in disease of the spinal cord the muscle may be paralysed, and inability to retain the motions results.

ANUS, DISEASES OF (*see* RECTUM, DISEASES OF).

AORTA (ἀορτή) is the large vessel which opens out of the left ventricle of the heart and carries blood to all the body (Fig. 12). It is about $1\frac{1}{2}$ feet (45 cm.) long and 1 inch (2·5 cm.) wide. Like other arteries it possesses three coats, of which the middle one is much the thickest. This consists partly of

FIG. 12.—Aorta with its branches, showing its position in front of the spinal column. *A*, Ascending part of arch ; *DA*, descending thoracic aorta ; *AA*, abdominal aorta ; *M*, middle sacral artery ; *SS*, subclavian arteries ; *C*, carotid arteries ; *I*, common iliac, dividing into *EI*, external, and *II*, internal iliac arteries ; *c*, coronary artery ; *d*, obliterated ductus arteriosus uniting the aorta to the pulmonary artery ; *b*, bronchial artery ; *oe*, œsophageal artery ; *ai*, series of aortic intercostal arteries ; *l*, series of lumbar arteries ; *p*, phrenic arteries to diaphragm ; *ax*, opposite cœliac axis ; *r*, renal arteries, with suprarenal arteries above ; *s*, spermatic arteries ; *sm*, opposite superior mesenteric artery lying between the renal arteries ; *im*, inferior mesenteric artery. (Turner's *Anatomy*.)

muscle fibre, but is mainly composed of an elastic substance, called elastin. The aorta passes first to the right, and lies nearest the surface behind the end of the second right rib-cartilage ; then it curves backwards and to the left, passes down behind the left lung close to the backbone, and through an opening in the diaphragm into the abdomen, where

it divides, at the level of the navel, into the two iliac arteries, which carry blood to the lower limbs. Its branches, in order, are : two coronary arteries to the heart wall ; the innominate, left common carotid, and left subclavian arteries to the head, neck, and upper limbs ; several small branches to the œsophagus, bronchi, and other organs of the chest ; nine intercostal arteries which run round the body between the ribs ; five lumbar arteries to the muscles of the loins ; cœliac axis to the stomach, liver, and pancreas ; two mesenteric arteries to the bowels ; and suprarenal, renal, and spermatic arteries to the suprarenal body, kidney, and testicle on each side. From the termination of the aorta rises a small branch, the middle sacral artery, which runs down into the pelvis, and may, in a sense, be regarded as the continuation of the aorta. In the female the ovarian arteries replace the spermatic.

The chief diseases of the aorta are atheroma and aneurysm. (*See* ARTERIES, DISEASES OF, ANEURYSM, *and* COARCTATION OF THE AORTA.)

AORTITIS means a degenerative condition of the lining of the aorta. It is usually produced by syphilis.

AORTOGRAPHY is the technique of rendering the aorta visible in an X-ray film by injecting a radio-opaque substance into it. (*See also* ANGIOGRAPHY).

APERIENTS (*aperio*, I open) are medicines which produce a natural movement of the bowels. (*See* CONSTIPATION *and* PURGATIVES.)

APEX is the pointed portion of any organ which has a conical shape. The apex of each lung reaches about one and a half or two inches (3·5 to 5·0 cm.) above the collar-bone into the neck. (*See* TUBERCULOSIS.) The apex of the heart should be found beneath the fifth rib immediately inside the nipple. It is displaced in some diseases. (*See* HEART DISEASE.)

APHAKIA is a term which means absence of the lens of the eye.

APHASIA (ἀ, neg.; φημί, I speak) means a loss of the power of speech, due to injury to the centres which govern this act in the brain (Fig. 13). The higher of these centres, which have to do with forming the ideas of speech, putting words together in sentences, and governing the movements of mouth, tongue, and larynx, lie on the surface of the cerebral hemispheres, especially of the left; while the lower centres, which directly bring the muscles of the voice organs into action, under superintendence of the higher ones, are in the medulla or hind brain.

Causes.—The cause is destruction of a portion of the brain, including one of these higher centres, owing to rupture of a blood-vessel, and hæmorrhage into the brain tissue; or owing to blocking of a blood-vessel by an embolus (*see* EMBOLISM), or by clotting of the blood on the diseased wall of a vessel (*see* THROMBOSIS), any one of which cuts off the supply of blood to the part concerned. The causes are thus the same as in apoplexy, and aphasia may be one of the symptoms of an apoplectic seizure, especially when the right side

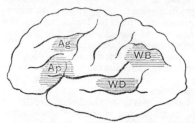

FIG. 13.—Diagram showing the areas of the brain affected in various forms of aphasia. *Ap*, with motor aphasia; *Ag*, with loss of power to write correctly; *WB*, with word blindness; *WD*, with word deafness.

of the body is paralysed, or may occur by itself, according to the extent of brain involved. Other diseases, such as tumours, may also be the cause, the important factor being interference with the functions of certain definite areas of the brain.

Varieties.—It was first pointed out by Broca that the inferior frontal convolution on the left side of the brain in right-handed persons, and vice versa, is, after death, found to be diseased in those who have, in life, suffered from inability to speak, although the intelligence and powers of silent reading and of writing may have remained. Such a

condition is known as *motor aphasia*. But the state is generally more complicated. In addition to Broca's convolution, which governs the movements of the tongue, mouth, and larynx that frame words to express ideas, there is a centre in the middle frontal convolution of the left side, which regulates the power of writing intelligibly, and disease of this region produces loss of power to write rationally, even though the hand remain quite able to hold a pen, this condition being known as *agraphia*. These two forms involve loss of power of *production* of speech and writing, but there are corresponding losses of power of *perception* known as *word blindness* and *word deafness*, the two conditions being grouped together as *sensory aphasia*. In the former of these the afflicted person is unable to read correctly, though his vision is perfect, and he may be able to spell and even to write, though not to read what he writes. This condition is due to disease in the angular convolution. In word deafness the disability consists in failure to understand what is said, and, though the sufferer hears perfectly, the sounds are to him like those of a foreign tongue which he does not understand; in this case the disease lies in the superior temporal convolution. There are still more complicated forms in which the disease affects, not the surface of the brain, but the strands of nerve fibres, which run from one centre to another and reduce the working of the whole arrangement to a system.

Symptoms.—The disorder generally follows an attack of apoplexy and exists along with some paralysis on the right side of the body. When the right side of the brain, on the other hand, is injured, the result is paralysis on the left side of the body, accompanied usually by more or less *amnesia* or forgetfulness. *Aphasia* may come on suddenly and last only a few hours or days, being due then to a passing congestion of the brain, or to a block in the circulation, which is later swept away. Generally it is permanent, and, naturally, a person with aphasia has always some mental impairment. Sometimes he is absolutely without the power of speech, though often a few interjections, like ' Oh dear ', ' Yes ', or ' No ', or meaningless sounds, or even oaths, can be pronounced. When the condition is one of *sensory aphasia* (*see* above) names of persons, of places, even of the commonest household articles, are forgotten, a cat is called 'a brush', a bell 'a pen', and so forth, or the person gives meaningless answers to questions, so that conversation becomes very slow or quite impossible.

Treatment. — This is just as in apoplexy, of which the condition often forms a part (*see* APOPLEXY). The condition is seldom much improved if it has lasted more than a week without betterment. But in some cases, after the hæmorrhage or other cause is long past, brilliant results are achieved by teaching the afflicted person to read and speak just as one would teach a child, a new part of the brain apparently being educated.

APHEMIA (*ἀ*, neg. ; *φημί*, I speak) means loss of the power of speech due to disease in the brain.

APHONIA (*ἀ*, neg. ; *φωνή*, the voice) means loss of voice. It is caused by some disorder in the throat or in the nerves proceeding to the throat muscles, or by hysteria. (*See* VOICE.)

APHTHÆ (*see* THRUSH).

APICOLYSIS is the term describing the operation for bringing about the collapse or compression of the apex of the lung—for example, in pulmonary tuberculosis—thus 'knocking out' the diseased area.

APNŒA (*ἀ*, neg. ; *πνέω*, I breathe) means stoppage of breathing, such as occurs when the blood is artificially supplied with too much oxygen ; for example, by taking several deep breaths in quick succession. (*See* ASPHYXIA.)

APO- (*ἀπό*, from) is a prefix implying separation or derivation from.

APOMORPHINE is a crystalline alkaloid closely related to morphine and having a powerful emetic action. Apomorphine hydrochloride is given hypodermically in doses of $\frac{1}{32}$ to $\frac{1}{8}$ grain (2 to 7·5 mg.) in cases of poisoning in which the patient is unable to swallow or a very rapid emetic action is desired. It is also used in the treatment of alcoholism.

APONEUROSIS is the term applied to the white fibrous membrane which serves as an investment for the muscles and which covers the skull beneath the scalp.

APOPLEXY (*ἀποπληξία*) is a term introduced by Hippocrates, meaning a stroke of sudden insensibility or of bodily disablement connected with some diseased condition of the brain.

Causes.—In persons who are the subject of heart disease, a clot may form in the cavities or on a valve of the heart, and being carried away by the blood-stream may lodge in a vessel of the brain so as to form a plug which prevents blood from reaching the part supplied by the vessel in question. The occurrence of this *embolism* is absolutely sudden and produces all the symptoms of apoplexy. When it occurs, the prospect of improvement is better than when the apoplectic symptoms are due to haemorrhage. In elderly people whose blood-vessels are extensively diseased and whose circulation is feeble, a type of apoplexy, of more gradual onset, may appear in consequence of the blood clotting in the interior of the vessels, this process being known as *thrombosis*.

The most important occasion of apoplexy is *hæmorrhage* into the brain by the rupture of blood-vessels. The blood-vessels of the brain, like those in other parts of the body, are liable to undergo degenerative changes after middle life (Fig. 14). These changes affect the minute arteries as well as the larger vessels, rendering their

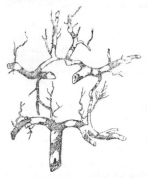

FIG. 14.—Arteries from the base of the brain, showing advanced atheromatous disease. The white areas are patches of atheroma.

texture fragile, and at the same time impairing their function in carrying on the healthy nutrition of the brain. Hence, in the immediate vicinity of the diseased blood-vessels the substance of the brain itself undergoes degeneration and becomes softened. The small vessels having thus lost the natural support of the surrounding tissues, and being here and there distended into aneurysms by disease, are liable to give way, and blood escapes into the brain. The hæmorrhage may be slight in amount and in parts of the brain where its presence gives rise to little disturbance; but where a large blood-vessel has ruptured, and more especially where the blood has been extravasated in or around the important structures at the base of the brain, the result is a stroke or apoplexy, as described below, and death not infrequently follows within a short period. In favourable cases, where a certain measure of recovery takes place, the effused blood undergoes gradual absorption, or becomes enveloped in a sort of capsule formed by the surrounding brain substance, and ceases to cause further disturbance. But even in such cases some degree of paralysis remains. Moreover, the nutrition of the brain is so impaired as to render probable a recurrence of the hæmorrhage, and thus the danger to life, as is well known, increases with each successive attack.

From what has been stated above, it will be observed that apoplexy is usually a disease of advanced life. Nevertheless it may occur at any period of life, and cases of true apoplexy in very young children have, for example, sometimes followed whooping-cough. It is more common in men than in women. What has from early times been described as the apoplectic habit of body, consisting of a stout build, a short neck, and florid complexion, is now generally discredited, it being admitted that apoplexy occurs about as frequently in thin and spare persons who present no such peculiarity of conformation. A hereditary tendency is acknowledged as one of the predisposing causes of apoplexy, and the most important factor is progressive disease of the kidneys with changes in the heart and blood-vessels and raised blood-pressure. With respect to the exciting causes of a stroke of apoplexy, it may be stated generally that whatever tends directly or indirectly to increase the tension within the cerebral blood-vessels may bring on an attack. Hence, such causes as immoderate eating or drinking, severe exertion of body or mind, violent emotions, much stooping, overheated rooms, over-exposure of the head to the sun, and sudden shocks to the body, may precipitate the attack in a susceptible individual. Many cases in elderly people occur while some violent exertion is being made, such as hurrying to catch a train or during straining at stool.

Symptoms.—Apoplectic attacks vary both as regards their intensity, the particular symptoms shown, and the after-effects, but well-marked cases present the following symptoms. The person attacked becomes, more or less suddenly, deprived of consciousness and all power of voluntary motion. He lies as if in a deep sleep, with a flushed face, a slow pulse, stertorous breathing, accompanied with puffing of the cheeks during expiration, and with the pupils of the eyes insensible to light and contracted or unequal. This state in many respects resembles the coma of narcotic poisoning, and is unfortunately too often mistaken by unskilled persons for alcoholic intoxication. The symptoms and history of the case, however, are usually sufficient to enable a medical man to form a correct diagnosis.

The presence of complete paralysis down one or other side is a point which in general differentiates apoplexy from narcotic poisoning and alcoholic intoxication, the paralysis being demonstrable even during unconsciousness by lifting the limbs and noting the characteristic suddenness and helplessness with which those on the affected side fall when not supported. The fact that in either of the last-named conditions the person can generally be partially roused, while in apoplexy unconsciousness is complete, is also valuable. Assistance is also gained by observing the state of the pupils, which in narcotic poisoning are usually much contracted, while in alcoholic intoxication they are widely dilated.

In this condition of insensibility death may occur within a few hours, or there may be a gradual return to consciousness, in which case it is usually found that the result of the attack remains in the form of paralysis of one side of the body (hemiplegia), while occasionally there may also be noticed some impairment of the mental powers, pointing to damage done to the brain. (*See* PARALYSIS *and* APHASIA.)

An attack of apoplexy may occur without unconsciousness, a sudden paralysis of one side of the body being the only manifestation. Occasionally, when the hæmorrhage takes place gently, the symptoms are gradually developed over a period of several hours (*ingravescent apoplexy*). Sometimes premonitory symptoms occur. Persistent headache of a dull throbbing character, a sense of fullness in the head, vomiting, giddiness, noises in the ears, slight confusion of mind, and numbness of a limb or of one side of the body are among the more important premonitory symptoms ; and these may exist for a variable length of time before the attack comes on. Such symptoms, especially in a person known to be gouty or the subject of high blood pressure with or without kidney disease, at or beyond middle life, indicate danger of an apoplectic seizure.

The effects of a stroke or apoplexy, as regards the paralysis which remains after the immediate attack is over, are described under *Hemiplegia* in the article on PARALYSIS. The dangerous period of an apoplectic attack is during the first two or three days and especially during the first twenty-four hours, when the hæmorrhage in the brain may be increased or even started again, after it has ceased, by injudicious disturbance of the patient, such as may be caused by his removal to a distance. A certain amount of danger remains for a period of three weeks or thereabout while the process of absorption and organization of the blood clot is taking place. During this period also such improvement in the patient's condition of paralysis, as will take place reaches almost its full extent.

Treatment.—A knowledge of these facts is of the utmost importance in the treatment of apoplexy, as obviously much can be done in the way of warding off a stroke when it appears to threaten, and of preventing a recurrence in cases

where there have been previous attacks. With respect to the treatment of apoplexy, it must be admitted that little can be done during the state of unconsciousness, apart from skilled nursing. The great importance of absolute quiet, with the body in the recumbent position and the head supported on a low pillow, cannot be too strongly emphasized. Care must be taken that the patient receive nothing of a stimulant nature, which would tend to raise the general blood-pressure and increase the hæmorrhage in the brain. If the blood-pressure is very high, the administration of hypotensive drugs may be of value. (*See* ESSENTIAL HYPERTENSION.)

The patient must be carefully watched, and symptoms treated as they arise. When consciousness returns care and quietness are necessary to prevent recurrence of the hæmorrhage. The diet must be light for some time after the attack, and the period of convalescence should be prolonged. In the after-treatment of the resulting paralysis much may be done to prevent stiffness and to preserve the power of the muscles in the weakened limbs by physiotherapy, including exercises, massage and electrical treatment, and continuing reassurance.

APOSTEMA (ἀπόστημα) is an old term for abscess.

APOTHECARIES' WEIGHT (*see* WEIGHTS AND MEASURES).

APPENDICECTOMY, or appendectomy, is the operation for the removal of the appendix vermiformis.

APPENDICITIS is the name of an inflammatory disease starting in the appendix vermiformis. (*See* INTESTINE.)

Varieties.—The disease is classified in many ways with regard to its treatment and its anatomical characters. First of all, one must separate the *acute* from the *chronic* or *relapsing form.* In the latter the person affected is troubled by repeated slight attacks of pain in the right iliac region, perhaps never bad enough to keep him from moderate work, but sufficient to be a burden ; or there is a sense of constant indefinable weakness and discomfort in this situation. In some cases the slightly inflamed appendix undergoes at times spasmodic, painful contractions, the so-called *appendicular colic*. This may be associated with the presence of concretions in the interior of the appendix or with adhesions between it and neighbouring parts. In other cases the inflammatory process is so mild that no symptoms directly referable to the appendix ever occur, but the patient suffers from constipation, indigestion, or general abdominal dis-

dicitis are operated upon as soon as possible.

Causes.—The disease is said by many authorities to have increased much in the last forty years, and, if this be so, it must be owing to some widespread change of social habits or of diet. But the apparent increase is, if not entirely, at all events very largely, due to avoidance of such vague names as ' perityphlitis ', ' inflammation of the bowels ', ' gastric seizure ', etc. *Constipation*, and the retention in the cæcum of undigested food, together with overeating,

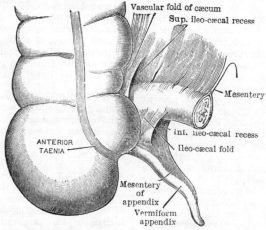

Fig. 15.—Part of the bowel situated in the right iliac region showing the relations of the appendix to the ileum (the last part of the small intestine) and the cæcum (the first part of the large intestine). The anterior tænia is one of the three bands of longitudinal muscle fibres which run along the entire length of the large intestine. (From Cunningham, *Textbook of Anatomy*. Oxford University Press.)

comfort produced in a reflex manner by the disturbance of the appendix. The *acute form* is that which is usually known as an ' attack of appendicitis '. Unless adequately and properly treated, this form may proceed to two very serious forms. *Gangrenous appendicitis* is one in which the inflammation is so intense that the appendix sloughs away, and the bowels communicate, through the opening, with the peritoneal cavity. The other form is *suppurative appendicitis*, in which the inflammation is not quite so severe but the appendix becomes the centre of an abscess. Both of these latter forms are extremely dangerous to life and are often very sudden in their development. It is for this reason that the vast majority of cases of acute appen-

may have a close connection with the onset of an attack. The great modern increase in the habit of meat-eating has also been credited as the main factor responsible for the constipation and inflammation. It is predominantly a disease of western civilization.

When congestion and inflammation of the appendix or neighbouring organs have been started the condition is continued and augmented by the presence of various *bacteria*. The severity of an attack depends largely upon the nature of the bacteria present. The widespread popular idea that grape-seeds, apple-pips, date-stones, and similar small objects have a special faculty for finding out the appendix, lodging there, and setting up appendicitis, is fallacious. Though such objects are found there occasionally, these cases are exceptional, and the small masses of hardened fæces or minute concretions of lime, which are very common, are a result of, rather than the cause of, the appendicitis. Although the disease is specially one of *youth*, 80 per cent. of all cases occurring under the age of thirty, it may occur at any age.

Symptoms.—An attack of appendicitis comes on as a rule suddenly, without the early feelings of languor and malaise common to most acute diseases. The principal symptoms are four in number : (*a*) sudden pain in the abdomen, often vague in situation at first, but usually settling in the right iliac region. It is generally very severe, and the patient has to lie constantly on his back with the right leg drawn up. (*b*) Disturbance of the digestive functions, consisting in loss of appetite, nausea, often vomiting, and constipation, which has usually been present for a day or two. (*c*) Tenderness to touch in the right iliac region, which in very many cases has its point of greatest intensity defined with curious exactitude at a point called Munro's or M'Burney's point, situated about half-way between the spine of the iliac bone and the navel. (*d*) Fever of a moderate amount, generally about 102° F. (39° C.). The first three of these occur with varying intensity in other diseases of the abdomen, in which, however, fever is uncommon. Distinct resistance and hardness of the muscles in the right lower quarter of the abdomen can be made out on pressure, and swelling is usually visible in the right iliac region after two or three days. In *gangrenous appendicitis* the symptoms are extreme, the fever high, and death may come on with startling rapidity, if an operation be not performed. In *suppurative appendicitis* an abscess forms with marked swelling, though rarely before the end of the first week, and this also calls for operation.

In some cases an attack is very slight, the bowels around become matted together, an abscess collects in the cavity so formed, and only when it comes near the surface is the condition diagnosed.

Treatment. — In no circumstances should a purgative be given. A patient with acute appendicitis seen within

thirty-six hours of the onset should be operated on forthwith, the mortality in the hands of good surgeons being very low. If the case is seen after forty-eight hours of the onset and improvement has set in, some surgeons recommend postponement of the operation until the inflammation has completely subsided ; others hold that operation should be done at once. If operation is refused or impossible, the patient should be kept quiet in bed, be given only water by mouth, and perhaps have an injection of morphine. If the case is one of gangrenous appendicitis immediate operation is the only possible course ; for the great danger of the disease consists in the production of a general peritonitis through the escape of bacteria and putrescent material in large amount from the interior of the appendix (*see* PERITONITIS).

APPENDICOSTOMY is the term describing the operation whereby an artificial opening is made into the appendix vermiformis, through which the bowel may be irrigated in certain diseases of the colon.

APPENDIX is a term applied to appendages of several hollow organs. The epiploic appendices are a number of tags of fat hanging from the outer surface of the large intestine. The appendices of the larynx are two pouches, one on either side between the false and true vocal cords. The term appendix is most commonly applied to the appendix vermiformis of the large intestine (Fig. 15). It is a tubular prolongation of the large intestine with an average length of 9 or 10 cm. and a width of 6 mm. It lies in the right lower corner of the abdomen and has peritoneal, muscular, and mucous coats similar to those of the rest of the intestine.

APPETITE is the craving for the food necessary to maintain the body and to supply it with sufficient energy to carry on its functions. The ultimate cause of appetite is a question of supply and demand in the muscles and various organs, but the proximate cause is doubtful. Unlike hunger, it is probably an acquired, rather than an inborn, sensation. Thus, a new-born infant

PLATE VI

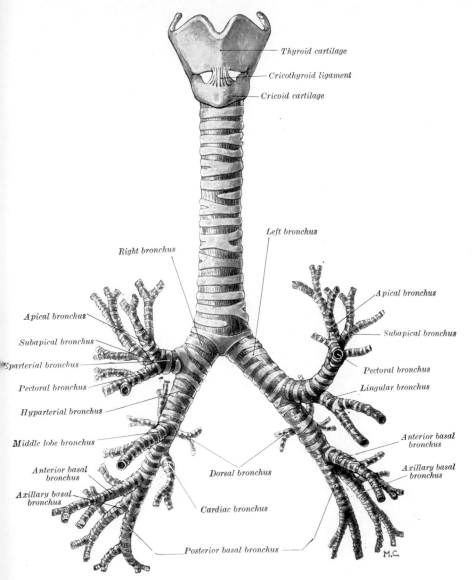

Thyroid cartilage

Cricothyroid ligament

Cricoid cartilage

Left bronchus

Right bronchus

Apical bronchus

Apical bronchus

Subapical bronchus

Subapical bronchus

Eparterial bronchus

Pectoral bronchus

Pectoral bronchus

Lingular bronchus

Hyparterial bronchus

Middle lobe bronchus

Anterior basal bronchus

Anterior basal bronchus

Axillary basal bronchus

Dorsal bronchus

Axillary basal bronchus

Cardiac bronchus

Posterior basal bronchus

M.C.

The lower air passages. (From Gray's *Anatomy*. Longmans, Green & Co., Ltd.) *See* AIR PASSAGES and LUNGS.

PLATE VII

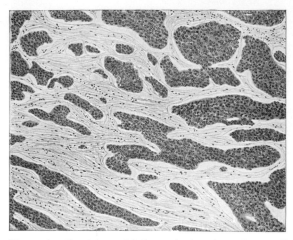

Microscopic section of cancer of the breast, showing columns of cancer cells surrounded by fibrous tissue. *See* CANCER and TUMOUR.

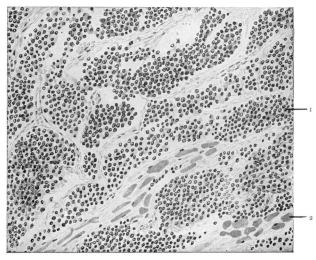

Small round-celled sarcoma of muscle. (1) Sarcoma cells, (2) muscle fibres. (Both from Kettle's *Pathology of Tumours*. H. K. Lewis & Co. Ltd.) *See* CANCER, MUSCLE and TUMOUR.

experiences hunger, but probably not appetite. Whatever other factors may be concerned, the tone of the stomach is of importance. This is supported by the fact that in conditions associated with poor appetite the tone of the stomach is poor, whilst in conditions such as duodenal ulcer which are characterized by a good, or even excessive appetite, the stomach is often hypertonic. Important factors in stimulating appetite are anticipation and the sight and smell of well cooked food. Just as, conversely, the sight or smell of badly cooked food may remove all desire for food. Undoubtedly a good appetite is necessary to good digestion, and a perfectly healthy taste and appetite ought to be both a guide to the suitability of foods and a gauge of the amount required. Like every other bodily function, appetite may be out of order. It may be depraved, and may indicate quite unsuitable articles of diet, from toasted cheese in dyspeptics, who know by experience that such an article disorders their stomach functions, to cinders, hair, pebbles, etc., in the condition known as *pica*, which occurs sometimes during pregnancy, in hysteria, and frequently in mental disorders. The two chief disorders are, however, excessive increase of appetite and diminution or loss of appetite.

Excessive appetite may be simply a bad habit, due to habitual over-indulgence in good food, and resulting in gout, obesity, etc., according to the other habits and constitution of the person. It is often a sign of acid dyspepsia (*see* DYSPEPSIA), diabetes, or thyrotoxicosis.

Diminished appetite is a sign common to almost all diseases causing general weakness, because the activity of the stomach and the secretion of gastric juice fail early when vital power is low. It is the most common sign of dyspepsia due to gastritis (*see* DYSPEPSIA) and of cancer of the stomach. In some cases it is a manifestation of stress or strain such as domestic worry or difficulties at work. Indeed, appetite seems to be particularly susceptible to emotional disturbances.

There is one peculiar condition known as *anorexia nervosa*, in which the sufferer, usually a young woman, sleeps little, eats almost nothing,

but is constantly exerting energy upon some favourite pursuit; this condition is very liable to end in a total nervous breakdown. Diminished appetite in feverish states is a salutary thing, as the digestive functions are reduced in power, and people in these circumstances should restrict themselves to a light diet, consisting mainly of milk and fruit juices, and should rest quietly at the same time.

APPROVED NAMES is the term used for names devised or selected by the *British Pharmacopœia* Commission for new drugs. The intention is that if any of the drugs to which these Approved Names are applied should eventually be included in the *British Pharmacopœia* the Approved Name should be its official title. The issue of an Approved Name, however, does not imply that the substance will necessarily be included in the *British Pharmacopœia* or that the Commission is prepared to recommend the use of the substance.

APRAXIA (ἀπραξία) means loss of power to carry out regulated movements.

APYREXIA (ἀ, neg.; πυρέσσω, I am fevered) means absence of fever.

ARACHIS OIL, also known as peanut oil, is the oil expressed from the seeds of *Arachis hypogœa*. It is sometimes used to replace olive oil when the latter is in short supply. It is commonly used as the vehicle for the intramuscular injection of drugs, *e.g.* penicillin.

ARACHNOID MEMBRANE (ἀράχνη, a spider; εἶδος, form) is one of the membranes covering the brain and spinal cord (*see* BRAIN). Arachnoiditis is the name applied to inflammation of this membrane.

ARCUS SENILIS is the white line which appears round the cornea of the eye with advancing years. (*See* AGE, NATURAL CHANGES IN.)

AREOLA literally means a small space, and is the term applied to the red or dusky ring round the nipple, or round an inflamed part. Increase in the duskiness of the areola on the breast is an important early sign of pregnancy.

ARGENTUM is the Latin word for silver.

ARGYLL ROBERTSON PUPIL is a condition (described originally by Dr. Argyll Robertson) in which the pupils contract when the eyes converge on a near object, but fail to contract when a bright light falls on the eye. It is found in several diseases, especially in locomotor ataxia and general paralysis.

ARGYRIA (ἄργυρος, silver) means the effect produced by taking silver salts over a long period, and consists of a deep duskiness of the skin, especially of the exposed parts.

ARGYROL (*see* SILVER).

ARM is the part of the upper limb between the shoulder and elbow, but is generally taken to include also the forearm and shoulder regions. The upper limb is attached to the body by the strong pectoral muscles in front and by several powerful muscles springing from the spine and ribs behind. The great mobility of the shoulder is largely due to the fact that the only contact with the bones of the trunk takes place between the collar-bone and the upper end of the sternum or breast - bone, the shoulder - blade sliding freely between the muscles of the back as the arm is raised and lowered. The bones of the arm (Fig. 76) are the clavicle or collar-bone and the scapula or shoulder-blade lying at the upper part of the chest, the humerus, a single bone in the upper arm, and the radius and ulna lying side by side in the forearm. Eight small bones compose the wrist and connect the hand with the lower end of the radius. The shoulder-joint is of the ball - and - socket variety, the head of the humerus resting against the glenoid cavity of the shoulder-blade. The elbow is a hinged joint formed at the lower end of the humerus above, while the ulna forms the chief part of the joint below, the radius resting lightly against the humerus.

When the hand is rotated so as to lie palm up and back up, the radius in the first case lies alongside the ulna and in the latter crosses over it. The chief muscle which bends the elbow is the biceps in front of the upper arm, while the triceps lying behind straightens the limb (Fig. 287, 298). A group of muscles attached at the inner side of the elbow act to bend the wrist and fingers ; another group of muscles attached to the outer side of the elbow have the general action of straightening and bending backwards the wrist and fingers. One large artery (brachial artery) runs down the inner side of the upper arm, corresponding to the seam of the coat sleeve in position (Fig. 16). At the elbow this divides into two branches, the radial and ulnar arteries. The radial artery can be felt pulsating near the wrist and is generally known as the pulse. The ulnar artery lies to the inner side of the forearm, deeply imbedded in muscles. A large group of nerves lies at the inner side of the armpit, and these nerves run downwards to supply the muscles and skin of the arm. The ulnar nerve can readily be felt behind the inner side of the elbow, where it is exposed to bruising and is popularly known as the ' funny bone '. The large radial nerve runs down the back of the upper arm and the outer side of the forearm. At the back of the upper arm it is frequently damaged, leading then to the condition known as drop-wrist, in which the hand hangs helpless and cannot be raised. The collar-bone, by reason of its exposed position, is very liable to fracture from falls on the shoulder, and the radius is frequently broken by falls on the palm of the hand. The shoulder-joint, on account of its great mobility, is prone to be dislocated in twists of the upper arm, but the elbow-joint is seldom injured. A small bursa or cavity lies between the skin and the end of the ulna at the point of the elbow, and this is frequently inflamed as the result of injury, and in the same way as the bursa in front of the knee is affected in the condition known as housemaid's knee (*see* BURSITIS).

ARMENIAN BOLE is a pale reddish earth used in tooth powders and sometimes administered internally for irritable conditions of the stomach.

ARMPIT, or AXILLA, is the pyramidal hollow between the upper arm and chest, bounded in front by the pectoral or breast muscles, behind by the shoulder-blade and its muscles, and running up to a point beneath the collar-bone. It contains the axillary vessels and nerves which run to the arm, also much fatty tissue and lymphatic glands. The latter are important, because in poisoned wounds of the arm they may become inflamed, resulting in abscess ; and still more, because in cancer of the breast they become infected with cancer, and have to be removed with the breast. Wounds in the armpit are dangerous on the outer, front, and back walls, because large blood vessels run there.

ARNICA is a medicine derived from *Arnica montana*, a plant of the Western United States and Europe. The tincture of arnica is used as a domestic remedy. Externally the tincture is used as a lotion for application to sprains and bruises, which it relieves by virtue of its weakly irritant action. It is seldom used internally, though sometimes it is given to stimulate digestion.

AROMATICS form a group of chemical substances containing carbon and a relatively small amount of hydrogen, some also containing oxygen. The group includes most of the essential oils of plants, *e.g.* anise, cloves, turpentine, camphor, thymol (hence the name, as these all have an aroma), and also benzene (derived from coal-tar) and its derivatives, such as phenol or carbolic acid, aniline, etc. These substances are almost all strongly antiseptic.

ARRHYTHMIA (ἀρρυθμία, want of rhythm) means any variation from the normal regular rhythm of the heart-beat. The condition is produced by some affection interfering with the mechanism which controls the beating of the heart, and includes the following disorders : sinus arrhythmia, atrial (or auricular) fibrillation, atrial flutter, heart block, extrasystole, pulsus alter-

nans, and paroxysmal tachycardia. (*See* HEART DISEASES.)

ARROW POISON (*see* BITES, etc.).

ARROWROOT is a West Indian plant (*Maranta arundinacea*). As sold, it is a white powder, consisting of almost pure starch, derived from the root of the plant. It is much used as an invalid food, because the particular form of the starch renders it easy of digestion, but it must, of course, be combined with other forms of nourishment. (*See* FARINACEOUS FOODS.)

ARSENIC is a metal, but is better known by its oxide, white arsenic, by two arsenites of copper, Scheele's green and emerald green, and by two sulphides of arsenic, orpiment or king's yellow, and realgar. It is extensively used in dyeworks, in the manufacture of chemicals, in making enamel, in hardening shot and type, in fly-papers, sheep-dips, yellow and green paints, and is further given to horses to improve their coat. It is also used in medicine. Applied pure, it is a strong germicide and caustic, and in large doses is a powerful irritant to stomach and intestines. When taken over long periods, larger and larger doses can be tolerated, till at last a quantity many times the poisonous dose has no apparent ill-effect. In some parts of the world, as among the mountaineers of Styria, its use has become a habit, and in these people it produces a sense of well-being and greater capacity for sustaining fatigue.

From the medical point of view its important action is that it interferes with the life processes of micro-organisms by inhibiting metabolic processes essential to their survival. It also produces dilatation of the capillaries.

Uses.—In medicine, arsenic is used in two forms : inorganic and organic.

Inorganic arsenical compounds. — Once used on a large scale for a variety of conditions, including anæmia, asthma, indigestion and skin diseases, and as a ' tonic ', the inorganic compounds are practically only used now in the treatment of certain skin diseases. For this purpose the preparation commonly used is Fowler's solution (*q.v.*) which contains arsenic trioxide.

Organic arsenical compounds.—These first came to the fore in 1909, when Ehrlich discovered that an organic arsenical compound, Salvarsan, was effective in the treatment of syphilis. For practically forty years, Salvarsan (or arsphenamine (*q.v.*), to give it its official name), and a less toxic derivative (neoarsphenamine) were the standard drugs for the treatment of syphilis.

Today, they have been completely replaced by penicillin, and practically their only use, in the form of neoarsphenamine, is in the treatment of certain forms of relapsing fever (*q.v.*). Another organic arsenical preparation which is sometimes used in the treatment of relapsing fever is oxophenarsine (*q.v.*).

Other organic arsenical compounds include tryparsamide (*q.v.*) used in the treatment of sleeping sickness (*q.v.*), acetarsol (*q.v.*) used in the treatment of trichomonal infections of the vagina, and carbarsone (*q.v.*) in the treatment of chronic amœbic dysentery.

ARSENIC POISONING may be acute or chronic.

Acute.—The symptoms are violent purging, vomiting, and great prostration. The treatment is to administer freshly prepared dialysed iron or peroxide of iron, or magnesia, and then give an emetic, followed by soothing drinks like milk, gruel, etc.

Chronic poisoning occurs among dyers and paperhangers, or from contamination of food by, or other contact with, green or yellow paint, or wall-paper containing arsenic. The symptoms are irritability of the eyes and throat, with cough, tendency to sickness, diarrhœa, prostration, and skin eruptions, and often headache, tremors, paralyses, and other nervous signs (*see* NEURITIS). The treatment is first of all discovery and removal of the source of poisoning, after which one must wait till the arsenic has been gradually expelled from the system by help of fresh air, good food, and tonics. Persons who have been subjects of arsenic poisoning may be left in a very debilitated condition with weak digestion and symptoms of neuritis lasting several years.

In both acute and chronic arsenical poisoning, in addition to the measures

outlined, a course of dimercaprol (*q.v.*), is now given. This is the most efficient known antidote to arsenic.

ARTERIES (ἀήρ, air ; τηρέω, I keep) are vessels which convey blood away from the heart to the tissues of the body, limbs, and internal organs. In the case of most arteries, the blood has been purified by passing through the lungs, and is consequently bright red in colour, but in the pulmonary arteries which convey it to the lungs it is

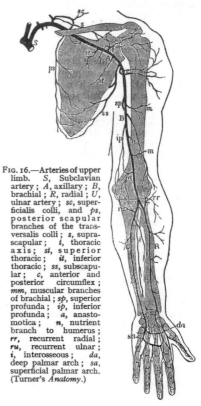

FIG. 16.—Arteries of upper limb. *S*, Subclavian artery ; *A*, axillary ; *B*, brachial ; *R*, radial ; *U*, ulnar artery ; *sc*, superficialis colli, and *ps*, posterior scapular branches of the transversalis colli ; *s*, suprascapular ; *t*, thoracic axis ; *st*, superior thoracic ; *it*, inferior thoracic ; *ss*, subscapular ; *c*, anterior and posterior circumflex ; *mm*, muscular branches of brachial ; *sp*, superior profunda ; *ip*, inferior profunda ; *a*, anastomotica ; *n*, nutrient branch to humerus ; *rr*, recurrent radial ; *ru*, recurrent ulnar ; *i*, interosseous ; *da*, deep palmar arch ; *sa*, superficial palmar arch. (Turner's *Anatomy*.)

impure, dark, and like the blood in veins, therefore called venous blood. The arterial system begins at the left ventricle of the heart with the aorta (*see* AORTA), which gives off branches that subdivide into smaller and smaller vessels, the final divisions, called arterioles, being microscopic, and ending in a network of ' capillaries ', which perforate the tissues like the

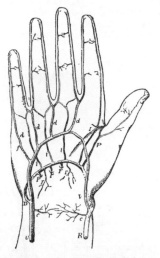

FIG. 18.—Arteries of hand. *R*, Radial artery ; *U*, ulnar artery ; *V*, superficial volar ; *P*, a large artery of the thumb ; *I*, radial artery of forefinger ; *D*, deep branch of ulnar artery ; *cc*, anterior carpal branches ; *dddd*, digital branches from superficial palmar arch ; *iii*, interosseous branches from the deep arch ; *ppp*, perforating branches ; *rr*, recurrent branches. (Turner's *Anatomy*.)

FIG. 19.—Arteries of the sole of the foot. 1 Posterior tibial artery, dividing into 2, internal, and 3, external plantar arteries ; 4 4 4, posterior perforating branches ; 5 5 5 5, digital branches ; 6, dorsal artery of the foot appearing in the sole between the first and second toes. The letters refer to the corresponding plantar nerves and their branches. (Turner's *Anatomy*.)

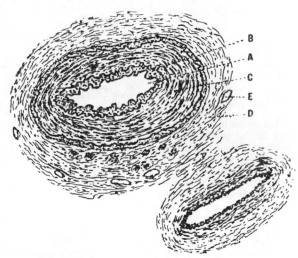

FIG. 20.—Diagram to show the structure of an artery. *A*, lumen of artery lined with endothelial cells ; *B*, elastic membrane ; *C*, muscular coat, or media ; *D*, adventitia ; *E*, capillary supplying adventitia with blood. (From Hill, *Manual of Human Physiology*. Edward Arnold & Co.)

pores of a sponge, and bathe them in blood that is collected and brought back to the heart by veins. (*See* CIRCULATION.)

The chief arteries after the *aorta* and its branches (*see* AORTA) are : (1) the *common carotid*, running up each side of the neck and dividing into *internal carotid* to the brain, and *external carotid* to the neck and face ; (2) the *subclavian* (Fig. 16) to each arm, continued by the *axillary* in the armpit, and the *brachial* along the inner side of the arm, dividing at the elbow into *radial* and *ulnar*, which unite across the palm of the hand in arches that give branches to the fingers (Fig. 18) ; (3) the two *common iliacs* (Fig. 21) in which the aorta ends, each of which divides into the *internal iliac* to the organs in the pelvis, and the *external iliac* to the lower limb, continued by the *femoral* in the thigh, and the *popliteal* behind the knee, dividing into *anterior* and *posterior tibial* arteries to the front and back of the leg. The latter passes behind the

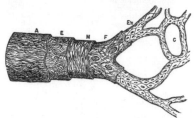

FIG. 17.—Diagram to show the structure of an artery. *A*, Tunica adventitia ; *E*, elastic layers, and *M*, muscular fibres of the tunica media ; *F*, elastic layer, and *En*, endothelial cells of the tunica intima. The last are continuous with the cells forming *C*, the capillaries. (Turner's *Anatomy*.)

inner ankle to the sole of the foot, where it forms arches similar to those in the hand, and supplies the foot and toes by *plantar branches* (Fig. 19).

Structure.—The arteries are highly elastic, dilating at each heart-beat as blood is driven into them, and forcing it on by their resiliency (*see* PULSE). Every artery has *three coats* (Figs. 17, 20): (*a*) the outer or adventitia, consisting of ordinary strong fibrous tissue ; (*b*) the middle or media, consisting of muscular fibre supported by elastic fibres, which in some of the larger arteries form distinct membranes ; and (*c*) the inner or intima, consisting of a layer of

70

yellow elastic tissue on whose inner surface rests a layer of smooth plate-like endothelial cells, over which flows the blood. In the larger arteries the muscle of the middle coat is largely replaced

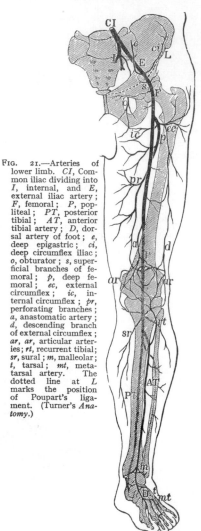

FIG. 21.—Arteries of lower limb. *CI*, Common iliac dividing into *I*, internal, and *E*, external iliac artery ; *F*, femoral ; *P*, popliteal ; *PT*, posterior tibial ; *AT*, anterior tibial artery ; *D*, dorsal artery of foot ; *e*, deep epigastric ; *ci*, deep circumflex iliac ; *o*, obturator ; *s*, superficial branches of femoral ; *p*, deep femoral ; *ec*, external circumflex ; *ic*, internal circumflex ; *pr*, perforating branches ; *a*, anastomatic artery ; *d*, descending branch of external circumflex ; *ar*, *ar*, articular arteries ; *rt*, recurrent tibial ; *sr*, sural ; *m*, malleolar ; *t*, tarsal ; *mt*, metatarsal artery. The dotted line at *L* marks the position of Poupart's ligament. (Turner's *Anatomy*.)

by elastic fibres, which render the artery still more expansile and elastic. When an artery is cut across, the muscular coat instantly shrinks, drawing the cut end within a fibrous sheath that surrounds the artery, and bunching it up, so that a very small hole is left to be closed by blood-clot (*see* HÆMORRHAGE).

ARTERIES, DISEASES OF.—

Arteriosclerosis, which is a condition of thickening and rigidity involving predominantly the middle coat of medium-sized arteries, occurs as a natural change in old age. In some individuals, however, the change occurs earlier. Hence the old adage that a man is as old as his arteries. The cause is still obscure, but certain facts are well established, even though they may only be predisposing factors. There is a hereditary tendency, and this is most marked in cases in which it develops at a relatively early age. There is a definite association with high blood-pressure in many cases, but arteriosclerosis can occur without a high blood-pressure. It is much more common in patients with diabetes mellitus than in individuals without this disease. It is also a common finding in gout. The traditional association with alcoholism and lead poisoning is not so certain. The distribution of arteriosclerosis throughout the arterial tree varies considerably. It may give rise to no symptoms, and only does so if it involves certain arteries. Thus, if it involves the arteries to the brain, the individual is liable to have a stroke; if it involves the coronary arteries which nourish the muscle of the heart, it may result in angina pectoris or a coronary thrombosis; if the arteries of the kidney are involved, a form of Bright's disease may develop; whilst if the arteries to the legs and feet are involved, gangrene may occur.

Atherosclerosis is a condition characterized by the presence in the inner coat, or intima, of arteries of the degenerative condition known as atheroma. This manifests itself by nodes, or plaques, of yellowish material containing a high proportion of cholesterol (*q.v.*) and other lipids (*q.v.*). As these plaques enlarge, and the intima increases in thickness, the lumen of the artery becomes smaller and smaller. In due course the lumen of the artery may be so narrowed that it becomes blocked. If this occurs in the coronary arteries, which supply the heart muscle, the result is the all too common coronary thrombosis. If it occurs in the arteries in the brain it causes a stroke. The cause of atherosclerosis is not known, but one factor is undoubtedly the consumption of excessive saturated fats.

Following on atheroma, plates of lime may form in the arteries, or these vessels may, in extreme states, be changed into brittle calcareous tubes, very liable to tearing from slight injuries. When this condition occurs in older people, it is confined to the middle coat and is accompanied by marked calcification; it is known as *Mönckeberg's sclerosis*.

Syphilis and other inflammatory diseases may bring about an *obliterative inflammation*, in which the internal coat becomes greatly thickened (*endarteritis*) and in which the artery is more or less completely blocked. This leads to very serious effects, particularly in the case of arteries supplying the heart and brain. (*See also* THROMBOANGIITIS OBLITERANS, ANEURYSM.)

ARTERIOGRAPHY (*see* ANGIOGRAPHY).

ARTERIO-VENOUS ANEURYSM is an abnormal communication between an artery and a vein. It is usually the result of an injury, such as a stab or a gunshot wound, which involves both a neighbouring artery and vein.

ARTERITIS means inflammation of an artery.

ARTHRITIS (ἄρθρον, a joint) means inflammation of a joint or joints. The chief forms are osteoarthritis, rheumatoid, gouty, gonorrhœal, tuberculous, and traumatic. (*See* JOINTS, DISEASES OF.)

ARTHROPATHY is a term applied to any form of joint disease.

ARTICULAR means anything connected with a joint, *e.g.* articular rheumatism.

ARTICULATION is a term employed in two senses in medicine, either meaning the enunciation of words and sentences or meaning a joint.

ARTIFICIAL INSEMINATION is the introduction of semen into the vagina by artificial means. It has long been used in animal breeding, and of recent years has been used to an increasing extent in human beings in an attempt to allow a married woman to become pregnant who cannot do so by the normal method. There are two forms of artificial insemination : A.I.H. and A.I.D. In A.I.H. (artificial insemination by the husband) the semen is obtained from the husband. In A.I.D. (artificial insemination by a donor) the semen is obtained from a man other than the woman's husband. The former is used when the husband can produce healthy semen but is unable to impregnate his wife ; the latter (A.I.D.) when the husband is sterile.

ARTIFICIAL LIMBS AND OTHER PARTS.—It is often necessary, for æsthetic or practical reasons, to replace a portion of the body, lost by injury or disease, with more or less efficient copies of the natural part. From the most ancient times this has been the case : Herodotus speaks of a man who had a wooden foot ; the Romans carried the manufacture of limbs to a high degree of efficiency, as witnessed by a leg, neatly formed of thin bronze plates, found in a tomb at Capua ; the Etruscans fashioned gold teeth five centuries before our era ; Goetz von Berlichingen, to supply his lost right hand, had one made of iron ; and Ambroise Paré, who wrote on surgery in the sixteenth century, has a chapter upon artificial limbs.

Arms.—Owing to the very delicate movements which the upper limb has to carry out, it is never amputated if there is any possibility of its being of any use. When amputation is decided upon, as little as possible of the arm is removed. Great strides have been made in the provision of artificial arms and hands, and it is now found that 50 per cent. efficiency can be obtained when the amputation has been above the elbow, and 75 per cent. efficiency when it is below the elbow. Appliances are now available which allow an individual who has lost an arm to engage in carpentry, many branches of engineering, and the electrical trades.

Such an individual can also write, shoot, play golf and cricket, and even fly-fish.

Legs.—An artificial substitute can come much nearer to the usefulness of the original in the lower than in the upper limb. As a result of experience gained in the two World Wars artificial lower limbs are now so efficient that the individual often suffers little disability. This applies particularly to amputations below the knee, but even in the case of amputations high in the thigh many individuals can often resume their old occupations. In addition, they can often ride a bicycle or a horse, or drive a motor car, whilst in the field of recreation, tennis and golf are quite normal pastimes. One of the great secrets of success in the fitting of artificial limbs is to restore the patient's morale and to stimulate his sense of independence.

Eyes.—Artificial eyes are worn both for appearance and to protect the socket from dust, though, of course, vision is impossible. They are made of glass or plastic, and are thin shells of a boat-shape, representing the front half of the eye which has been removed. The stump which is left has still the eye-muscles in it, and so the artificial eye still has the power of moving with the other, though to a less extent, and it is often difficult for this reason to tell at a short distance that a person has a false eye. A glass eye has to be replaced by a new one every year. Plastic eyes have the advantage of being more comfortable to wear, and more durable and of being unbreakable.

Teeth.—Where a single tooth is false it is often fitted by a gold peg to the fang of the lost natural one. Where a number are fitted, a plate, either adhering accurately to the gum by suction, or attached to neighbouring teeth by ' crown and bridge work ', is employed to carry them. It has been found that in the case of elaborate artificial attachments to roots of teeth suppurative processes of a harmful nature are apt to take place, leading to rheumatism and similar conditions. Less dental work is, therefore, done at the present day in the form of ' crowning ' teeth and attaching artificial teeth by pegs than was formerly carried out.

Nose.—Through disease the nose may be eaten away, leaving the nostrils projecting forward in an unsightly manner. Often a triangular flap of skin is raised from the forehead, turned downwards over the gap, allowed to grow there, and then the small bridge which has maintained its nutrition is cut through, and the edges of the wound in the forehead are simply drawn together. Recently a method has been introduced for improving the shape of noses with sunken bridge by injecting under the skin melted, hard paraffin, that solidifies as it cools, or a new bridge is fashioned from a piece of cartilage of a rib inserted under the skin.

ARTIFICIAL RESPIRATION (*see* DROWNING, RECOVERY FROM).

ARYTENOID (ἀρυταινοειδής, shaped like a ladle) is the name applied to two cartilages in the larynx.

ASAFŒTIDA is a gum resin of unpleasant odour, obtained from the root of *Ferula fœtida*. It used to be given as an expectorant to increase the secretion of mucus in the air-passages or as an anti-spasmodic in colic with flatulence.

ASBESTOSIS is a disease of the lungs caused by the inhalation of asbestos particles. Victims of asbestosis are particularly liable to develop cancer of the lungs.

ASCARIS is the name of a roundworm, sometimes nearly a foot (30 cm.) in length, which is parasitic in the human intestine and that of the horse, and very much resembles a large earthworm. (*See* PARASITES.)

ASCITES (ἀσκός, a wine-skin) means dropsical swelling of the abdomen. (*See* DROPSY.)

ASCORBIC ACID is a crystalline substance extracted from various vegetables, or synthetically prepared, and has the same action as vitamin C. (*See* VITAMIN.)

ASEPSIS (ἀ, neg.; σήπω, I make putrid) is a term, used in distinction from ' antisepsis ', to mean that principle in surgery by which, instead of strong germicides like corrosive sublimate or carbolic acid being applied to wounds, all the dressings, sponges, and instruments used are simply purified by steaming, boiling, or dry heat. Thin sterilized india-rubber gloves are worn by surgeons and prevent risk of infection from the hands. Aseptic surgery has the advantage that the germ-destroying activity of the tissues and their healing power after wounds are not lessened by antiseptics which decrease the vitality of the tissues ; and therefore healing is surer and more rapid after an aseptic operation. (*See* also ANTISEPTICS.)

ASEPTOL is the name applied to a reddish oily disinfectant, phenolsulphonic acid, which is used in the strength of 1 to 10 per cent. in water.

ASPERGILLUS is the name applied to a group of fungi including the common moulds. Several of these are capable of infecting the lungs and producing a disease resembling pulmonary tuberculosis.

ASPHYXIA (ἀ, neg.; σφύξις, pulse) means literally absence of pulse, but is the name given to the whole series of symptoms which follow stoppage of breathing and of the heart's action.

Causes.—For practical consideration by far the most important cause is *drowning*. Human beings are not adapted to extract the oxygen dissolved in water—first, because the amount is only one-third of that required to supply the needs of the processes of diffusion which take place in the lungs ; and, secondly, because the air or fluid taken in through the mouth must return the same way, there being no second opening and rapid constant stream like that by which in fishes a great quantity of water passes over the gills in a short time. *Blockage of the air passages* occurs in some diseases, such as croup, diphtheria, swelling of the throat due to wounds or inflammation, asthma (to a partial extent), tumours in the chest (causing slow asphyxia), and the external conditions of suffocation and strangling. *Poisonous gases* also cause asphyxia.

Carbonic acid gas in excessive amount in the air, due to the breathing of a number of individuals in a small space, as in the Black Hole of Calcutta, or to the fumes given off in fermentation vats, has often caused death. Carbon monoxide gas is still more deadly, and in the form of ' water gas ', or when it is given off, for example, by a stove or charcoal brazier in a badly ventilated room, has killed many persons during sleep. (*See* COAL - GAS POISONING.) Several gases, such as sulphurous acid (from burning sulphur), ammonia, and chlorine (from bleaching-powder), cause involuntary closure of the entrance to the larynx, and thus prevent breathing. Other gases, such as nitrous oxide (or laughing-gas), chloroform, and ether, in poisonous quantity, cause stoppage of breathing by paralysing the respiration centre in the brain.

Symptoms.—In the vast majority of cases death from asphyxia is due to insufficiency of oxygen supplied to the blood. The first signs—apart from instinctive efforts to escape from the cause, such as the struggles of a drowning man—are rapid pulse and gasping for breath. Next comes great increase in the pressure of the blood, causing throbbing in the head, with lividity or blueness of the skin, due to failure of aëration of the blood, followed by still greater struggles for breath and by general convulsions. In this stage, the veins and right side of the heart become overfilled with blood, owing to stoppage of the circulation, which follows contraction of the minute arteries all over the body from the irritation of the impure blood in them. Accordingly, the heart becomes over-distended and gradually weaker, a paralytic stage sets in, and all struggling and breathing slowly cease. When, on the other hand, asphyxia is due to charcoal fumes, coal-gas, and other narcotic influences, there is no convulsive stage, and death ensues gently and may occur in the course of sleep. After death, the right side of the heart, the large veins, and the pulmonary artery are found distended by blood, and this blood is fluid instead of in clots, as it is after a gradual death. These are the chief signs of death by asphyxia, but each cause produces distinguishing signs of its own.

74

Treatment.—So long as the heart continues to beat, recovery may be looked for under prompt treatment. The one essential of treatment is to get the impure blood aërated by artificial respiration. Besides this, the feeble circulation can be helped by various methods. (*See under* DROWNING, RECOVERY FROM.) When the heart is very feeble or even stopped, the face extremely blue, and the veins of the neck and arms swollen, the person's life may possibly be saved by opening a vein in the arm or neck, and so allowing some blood to escape and the heart to contract again.

ASPHXYIA NEONATORUM is imperfect breathing in the new-born infant. It has been estimated that it plays a part in about half the deaths which occur during the first month of life. The main causes are serious illness of the mother during the latter months of pregnancy, anæsthetics or analgesics given to the mother during labour, prolonged labour, obstruction to the circulation in the umbilical cord, obstruction of the infant's air passages, intracranial hæmorrhage, and congenital heart disease.

ASPIDIUM is the name of the genus of ferns called shield-ferns. The root of *Aspidium filix-mas* (male fern) is used as a remedy for tapeworms. It is administered in the form of a fluid extract in doses of 45 to 90 minims (3 to 6 ml.).

ASPIRATION (*aspiro*, I breathe) means the withdrawal of fluid or gases from the natural cavities of the body or from cavities produced by disease. It may be performed either for curative purposes, or, very often, a small amount is drawn off for diagnosis of the nature or origin of the fluid.

Uses.—*Dropsy* used to be one of the most common conditions requiring its application, but since the introduction of efficient diuretics (*q.v.*) it is much less frequently required. When in the abdomen, dropsy which persists in spite of the administration of diuretics (*q.v.*) can be relieved by means of a metal tube or cannula about the size of a small quill, which is provided with a sharp point or trocar capable of being drawn out. After careful cleansing of the skin, and having ensured that the bladder is empty, the trocar and cannula are plunged boldly into the lower part of the abdomen. There is practically no pain, and only a local anæsthetic is necessary. After the cannula, with the trocar inserted in it, has been pushed through the skin the trocar is withdrawn, leaving the tube in place. To this tube is attached an india-rubber tube leading to a bottle, which is air-tight, and in which a vacuum can be produced by a hand air-pump. The fluid is drawn out into the bottle, and 1, 2 or more litres may be withdrawn at one time. When the dropsy is in the legs, Southey's tubes are still occasionally used. Here the cannula is very fine, and has about a yard of fine india-rubber tubing attached, which draws the water slowly off (in the course of several hours) by siphon action. *Pleurisy with effusion* is another condition requiring aspiration, and a litre or more of fluid may be drawn off by an aspirator or a large syringe and needle. *Chronic abscesses* and *tuberculous joints* may call for its use, the operation being done with a small syringe and hollow needle. *Pericarditis* with effusion is another condition in which aspiration is sometimes performed. The spinal canal is aspirated by the operation of lumbar puncture. (*See* LUMBAR PUNCTURE.) In children the ventricles of the brain are sometimes similarly relieved from excess of fluid by piercing the fontanelle (soft spot) on the infant's head. (*See* HYDROCEPHALUS.)

ASPIRIN, or ACETYLSALICYLIC ACID, is a white crystalline powder which is used like sodium salicylate as a remedy for rheumatism, chorea, neuralgia, etc., also to reduce fever in infectious diseases. It has some action in relieving pain and producing sleep and is therefore frequently used for headache and slighter degrees of insomnia. The dose is 5 to 15 grains (300 mg. to 1 G.).

ASPIRIN POISONING may not be common in relation to the vast amounts that are consumed every year, but nevertheless it is a worrying problem.

In ordinary doses it may induce bleeding from the stomach. This is usually quite mild, but it can be severe. In small doses it can produce a severe allergic reaction in individuals who are sensitive to it. This takes the form of asthma and angioneurotic oedema.

When an overdose is taken there is marked over-breathing, sweating and vomiting. Later the individual becomes restless and irritable, and there may be convulsions before consciousness is finally lost.

Treatment.—The stomach should be washed out, preferably with an alkaline solution, and a litre of 5 per cent. sodium bicarbonate should be left in the stomach. If there has been much loss of fluid by sweating and vomiting, fluids may need to be given intravenously. In severe cases oxygen may need to be administered.

ASSIMILATION (*see* DIGESTION).

ASTASIA-ABASIA is the term applied to the condition in which a person is unable, because of loss of willpower through hysteria, to stand or to walk.

ASTEREOGNOSIS means the loss of the capacity to recognize the nature of an object by feeling it, and indicates a lesion (*e.g.* tumour) of the brain.

ASTHENIA (ἀ, neg. ; σθένος, strength) means want of strength in the system. (*See* DEBILITY.)

ASTHENOPIA (ἀ, neg. ; σθένος strength ; ὤψ, the eye) means a sense of weakness in the eyes, coming on when they are used. As a rule it is due to long-sightedness, slight inflammation, or weakness of the muscles that move the eyes. (*See* VISION.)

ASTHMA (ἄσθμα, a gasping: ἀσθμαίνω, I gasp for breath) is a disorder of respiration characterized by severe paroxysms of difficult breathing, usually followed by a period of complete relief, with recurrence of the attacks at more or less frequent intervals. The term is often incorrectly employed in reference to states of embarrassed respiration, which are plainly due to permanent organic disease within the chest, and which have none of the distinctive characters of true asthma.

Cause.—Asthma is an anaphylactic reaction which manifests itself by spasmodic contraction of the smaller bronchial tubes (see ANAPHYLAXIS). It is this narrowing of the bronchial tubes, often accentuated by swelling of the lining epithelium, that is responsible for the great difficulty in breathing which is the characteristic feature of the condition. There is a large number of substances to which the asthmatic subject may be hypersensitive, contact with which is responsible for an attack. These include pollens ; the emanations of certain animals such as cats, dogs, horses, etc. ; certain articles of diet ; bacteria. The discovery of the substance to which the individual is susceptible may sometimes be difficult. Thus, it may be noted that attacks of asthma occur when the patient goes to bed, and it may be found that these occur because he is susceptible to horse hair, with which the pillow is filled. In other instances the difficulty may be due to the fact that the individual is hypersensitive to more than one substance. In many cases the specific susceptibility of the individual may be enhanced by some non-specific conditions, such as emotional disturbance, worry, indigestion or an infection such as a sore throat or a ' cold in the head '. There is another group of asthmatic subjects in whom the asthma is due to sensitization to bacteria responsible for some chronic or repeated infection. For instance, an individual who is subject to repeated attacks of tonsillitis, sinusitis, or nasal catarrh may become sensitized to the causative organism, so that whenever he becomes infected with this organism he is liable to develop attacks of asthma. The reason why asthma does not develop in all such individuals subject to repeated infections, is that such attacks only occur in the individual who has the tendency to develop hypersensitivity. This tendency is usually hereditary, and it will often be found that the asthmatic subject suffers from other allergic conditions such as hay fever and urticaria (or nettle-rash). Asthma is more common in males than in females, and the first attack usually occurs in childhood.

76

There is a form of asthma which may not develop until later in life. This occurs in individuals who suffer from chronic bronchitis. A certain proportion of these people ultimately become sensitized to the organisms responsible for their chronic bronchitis, and this sensitization may not develop until middle age.

Two other conditions to which the term asthma is applied must be carefully differentiated from the condition that has just been described. These are *cardiac asthma* and *renal asthma*. The former consists of sudden attacks of shortness of breath while the patient is resting ; it is a grave sign, as it is due to severe heart failure. Renal asthma, which is probably similar in causation to cardiac asthma, occurs in the terminal stages of chronic Bright's disease, and, again, is a sign of extremely grave significance.

Symptoms.—The onset of an attack of asthma is usually sudden, although there may exist certain premonitory symptoms which warn the sufferer of its approach, such as a feeling of discomfort, drowsiness, irritability, and depression of spirits. The period when the asthmatic paroxysm comes on is generally during the night, or rather in the early hours of morning. The patient then awakes in a state of great anxiety and alarm, with a sense of weight and tightness across the chest, which he feels himself unable to expand with freedom. Respiration is performed with great difficulty, and is accompanied by wheezing noises. His distress rapidly increases, and he can no longer retain the recumbent position, but gets up, and sits or stands with his shoulders raised, his head thrown back, and his whole body heaving with his desperate efforts to breathe. His countenance is pale or livid, and wet with perspiration, while his extremities are cold ; his pulse is rapid, and may be irregular or intermitting. All his clothing must be loose about him ; he cannot bear to be touched, and the very presence of others around him seems to aggravate his distress. His one desire is to breathe fresh air ; and he will place himself by an open window and sit for hours in the middle of the night, unmindful of the exposure. The paroxysm, after continuing for a variable length of time, often extending over many hours, begins to abate, the breathing becomes easier, and the subsidence of the attack is often marked by the occurrence of coughing with expectoration.

After the cessation of the attack the patient appears to be, and feels, comparatively well. In cases of long standing, however, the subject of asthma comes to bear permanent evidence of its effects. He is easily put out of breath on exertion and he requires to lie with his head elevated, circumstances to be ascribed to organic changes in the chest, which oft-recurring attacks of asthma are liable to induce (*see* EMPHYSEMA). The asthmatic paroxysms, although occasionally periodic, do not generally observe any regularity in their return. They may recur each successive night for several days, or there may be no return for many weeks or months, this being to a large extent dependent on a renewal of the exciting cause.

Treatment. — The treatment of asthma consists in the employment of remedies to allay the paroxysms, and in the adoption of measures likely to prevent their recurrence. During the attack the patient should be placed in as favourable circumstances for breathing as practicable. He usually selects the position easiest for himself. Abundance of air should be admitted to the apartment, and he should be interfered with as little as possible. The household remedial agents employed with the view of relieving the paroxysms are very numerous, and only a few of the more important of them can be mentioned. Much value is attached by some to the smoking of stramonium and even tobacco smoking appears in some instances to give relief. The fumes of nitre-paper (blotting-paper prepared by being dipped in a saturated solution of nitre and dried) burnt in the apartment may succeed in mitigating the paroxysm. (*See* NITRE.) Glass capsules containing amyl nitrite, which are crushed and held beneath the nostrils, sometimes give considerable relief in bad cases ; so too does the tincture of lobelia. Coffee is a popular and useful remedy, but, to do good, the infusion must be very strong, and taken upon an empty stomach. Dry cupping of the back, and placing of the hands in very hot water contained in basins placed at the side of the bed, are other household remedies.

In the majority of cases, however, certain drugs are required which should only be taken under medical supervision. These include adrenaline (by injection), ephedrine, aminophylline, and isoprenaline. In severe cases, corticotrophin, or one of the cortisone group of drugs, is often of value.

To prevent the recurrence of the paroxysms special care must be taken by the sufferer to avoid those influences, whether connected with locality or mode of life, which his experience may have proved to have been the occasion of former attacks. Particularly must care be taken to avoid exposure to those influences apt to bring on bronchitis. Breathing exercises are often of value in reducing the frequency of attacks. In the group of cases found to be due to a particular animal emanation or article of diet, care should be taken to avoid this cause. The sensitiveness of the individual can sometimes be diminished by a course of treatment by vaccine prepared from the bacteria present in his expectoration.

ASTIGMATISM (*ἀ*, neg. ; *στίγμα*, a point) is an error of refraction in the eye due to the cornea (the clear membrane in front of the eye) being unequally curved in different directions, so that rays of light in different meridians cannot be brought to a focus together on the retina. The curvature, instead of being globular, is egg-shaped, longer in one axis than the other. The condition causes objects to seem distorted and out of place, a ball for instance looking like an egg, a circle like an ellipse. The condition is remedied by suitable spectacles of which one surface forms part of a cylinder. (*See* SPECTACLES.)

ASTRAGALUS is the name applied to the somewhat square-shaped bone which forms the lower part of the ankle-joint and unites the leg bones to the foot.

ASTRINGENTS (*astringo*, I bind) are substances which cause contraction of mucous surfaces, blood - vessels, or tissues, or which stop secretions and check discharges.

Varieties. — Dilute acids ; soluble salts of the heavy metals, such as perchloride of mercury, acetate of lead (sugar of lead), nitrate of silver (lunar caustic), sulphate of copper (bluestone), perchloride of iron, sulphate of zinc ; also alum, lime-water, some vegetable products, like tannic and gallic acids and witch hazel, and adrenaline.

Uses.—Locally, perchloride of mercury, nitrate of silver, and sulphate of copper are applied in very weak solutions to ulcers to harden the healing tissues. Perchloride of iron, tannic and gallic acids, and witch hazel are used to control bleeding from the throat, from wounds, etc., or to diminish congestion. Adrenaline is particularly valuable in controlling bleeding in the mouth or throat provided the bleeding is not occurring from a large artery. Alum and sulphate of zinc are used as astringent eyewashes. In diarrhoea, sulphate of copper, tannic acid, and lime-water are among the chief remedies. For piles, acetate of lead is a useful astringent.

ASYNERGIA means the absence of harmonious and co-ordinated movements between muscles having opposite actions—*e.g.* the flexors and extensors of a joint—and is a sign of disease of the nervous system.

ASYSTOLE (ἀ, neg. ; συστολή, a contraction) means arrest of the action of the heart.

ATARACTIC (*ataraktos*, without disturbance) is the term used to describe drugs which induce peace of mind. For all practical purposes it is synonymous with tranquillizer (*q.v.*). It has never been widely adopted in Britain.

ATAVISM (*atavus*, a grandfather) means the principle of inheritance of disease or bodily characters from grandparents or remoter ancestors, the parents not having been affected by these.

ATAXIA (ἀ, neg.; τάξις, order) means loss of power of governing movements,

78

though the power necessary to make the movements is still present. Thus an ataxic person may have a good grip in each hand but be unable to do any fine movements with the fingers, or, if the ataxia be in the legs, he throws these about a great deal in walking, though he can lift the legs and take steps quite well. This is due to a sensory defect. (*See* FRIEDRICH'S ATAXIA *and* LOCOMOTOR ATAXIA.)

ATELECTASIS (ἀτελής, imperfect ; ἔκτασις, expansion) means collapse of a part of the lung, or failure of the lung to expand at birth.

ATHEROMA (ἀθήρη, porridge) is a degenerative change in the inner and middle coats of arteries. (*See* ARTERIES, DISEASES OF.)

ATHEROSCLEROSIS is a form of arteriosclerosis (*q.v.*), in which there is fatty degeneration of the middle coat of the arterial wall.

ATHETOSIS (ἄθετος, without fixed position) is the name for slow, involuntary, writhing, and repeated movements of the hands and feet, caused by disease of the brain.

ATLAS is the name applied to the first cervical vertebra.

ATONY (ἀ, neg.; τόνος, strength) means want of tone or vigour in muscles and other organs. (*See* TONICS.)

ATOPHAN is a yellowish powder which is used in the treatment of gout and rheumatic conditions.

ATRESIA (ἀ, neg. ; τίτρημι, I pierce) means the absence of a natural opening or closure of it by a membrane. Thus atresia may be found in new - born infants preventing the bowels from moving, and, in young girls after puberty, absence of the menstrual flow may be due to such a malformation.

ATRIUM is the name now given to the two upper cavities of the heart. These used to be known as the auricles of the heart. The term is also applied to the part of the ear immediately internal to the drum of the ear.

ATROPHY (ἀ, neg.; τρέφω, I nourish) is a term in medicine used to describe a state of wasting due to some interference with the function of healthy nutrition. It is essential for the maintenance of health that a due relation exist between the processes of waste and repair, so that the one may not be in excess of the other. When the appropriation of nutriment exceeds the waste, hypertrophy or increase in bulk of the tissues takes place. (*See* HYPERTROPHY.) When, on the other hand, the supply of nutritive matter is suspended or diminished, or when the power of assimilation is impaired, atrophy or wasting is the result. Thus the whole body becomes atrophied in many diseases ; and in old age every part of the frame, with the exception of the heart, undergoes atrophic change. Atrophy may, however, affect single organs or parts of the body, irrespective of the general state of nutrition, and this may be brought about in a variety of ways. One of the most frequently observed of such instances is atrophy from disuse, or cessation of function. Thus, when a limb is deprived of the natural power of motion, either by paralysis or by painful joint disease, atrophy of all its tissues sooner or later takes place. This form of atrophy is likewise well exemplified in the case of those organs and structures of the body which subserve important ends during fœtal life, but which, ceasing to be necessary after birth, undergo a sort of natural atrophy, such as the thymus gland, and certain vessels specially concerned in the fœtal circulation. The uterus after parturition undergoes atrophy, and the ovaries, after the child-bearing period, become shrunken. Atrophy of a part may also be caused by interruption to its normal blood supply, as in the case of the ligature or obstruction of an artery. Again, long-standing disease, by affecting the nutrition of an organ and by inducing the deposit of morbid products, may result in atrophy, as frequently happens in affections of the liver and kidneys. Parts that are subjected to continuous pressure are liable to become atrophied, as is sometimes seen in internal organs which have been compressed by tumours or other morbid growths, and as was well illustrated in the case of the feet of Chinese ladies, which were prevented from growing by persistent compression exercised from birth. Atrophy may manifest itself simply by loss of substance ; but, on the other hand, it is often found to co-exist with degenerative changes and the formation of fibrous or fatty growth, so that the part may not be reduced in bulk, although atrophied as regards its proper structure. Thus, in the case of the heart, when affected with fatty degeneration, there is atrophy of the proper muscular texture, but this, being largely replaced by fatty material, the organ may undergo no diminution in volume, but may, on the contrary, be increased in size. Atrophy is usually a gradual and slow process, but sometimes it proceeds rapidly. In the disease known by the name of *acute yellow atrophy of the liver*, that organ undergoes such rapidly destructive change as results in its shrinking to half, or one-third, of its normal size in the course of a few days.

The term *progressive muscular atrophy* (*wasting* or *creeping palsy*) is applied to an affection of the muscular system, which is characterized by the atrophy and subsequent paralysis of certain muscles, or groups of muscles, and is associated with morbid changes in the anterior part of the grey matter in the spinal cord. This disease begins insidiously, and is often first observed to affect the muscles of one hand, generally the right. Gradually other muscles in the arms and legs become affected in a similar manner, their atrophy being attended with a corresponding diminution in power. (*See* PROGRESSIVE MUSCULAR ATROPHY *under* PARALYSIS.)

The term *idiopathic muscular atrophy* (also known as *muscular dystrophy*) is applied to a somewhat similar condition affecting young people in whom a progressive degeneration of the muscles occurs. In this condition no change is found in the nervous system after death, the cause apparently acting directly upon the muscles. (*See* MUSCLES, DISEASES OF.)

ATROPINE (Ἄτροπος, fate) is the active principle of belladonna, the juice of the deadly nightshade. It is said to be used as a cosmetic to give the eyes a full, lustrous appearance, but, in addition to this effect, it temporarily impairs vision by paralysing accommodative power. (*See* ACCOMMODATION.) It has the effect of checking the activity of almost all the glands of the body, including the sweat glands of the skin and the salivary glands in the mouth. It relieves spasm by paralysing nerves in the muscle of the intestine, bile-ducts, bladder, stomach, etc. It has the power, in moderate doses, of markedly increasing the rate of the heart-beats, though by very large doses the heart, along with all other muscles, is paralysed and stopped.

Uses.—Externally, liniment of belladonna is used in neuralgia, and other painful conditions. Plaster of belladonna is used in muscular rheumatism. To the breasts, a plaster of belladonna is applied to stop the milk formation in threatened abscess. It is doubtful, however, whether the belladonna in either the liniment or the plaster is of any real value. In eye troubles, atropine drops are used to dilate the pupil for more thorough examination of the interior of the eye, or to draw the iris away from wounds and ulcers on the centre of the eye ; they also soothe the pain due to light falling on an inflamed eye, and are further used to paralyse the ciliary muscle and so prevent accommodative changes in the eye while the eye is being examined with the ophthalmoscope (*q.v.*). Belladonna is employed in cough-mixtures for bronchitis and whooping-cough to dry up the mucus and check spasmodic coughing. In renal colic, gall-stone colic, and other agonizing spasmodic conditions, atropine is given along with morphine by hypodermic injection. It is also used to decrease the amount of gastric secretion in peptic ulcer. It has been used as an antidote in opium poisoning and to muscarine, the poisonous principle of some toadstools.

ATROPINE or **BELLADONNA POISONING.**—This may occur from children eating the berries or leaves of the deadly nightshade (*see* BERRIES, POISONOUS). The warning symptoms are : (1) great dryness of the mouth and throat, (2) wide dilatation of the pupils, (3) increased rate of the heart's action. There is sickness later, and the poisoned person has an excited

delirium with, at the same time, bodily languor and weakness. If the dose has been very large, paralysis, unconsciousness, and gradual stoppage of heart and breathing ensue.

Treatment.—An emetic should be given as soon as possible ; such as a tablespoonful of mustard in cold water. After vomiting has ceased, large draughts of water and stimulant, such as alcohol and sal volatile, are administered, and if breathing becomes feeble, artificial respiration must be performed. The patient should be made to pass water frequently, as the poison is excreted by the kidneys, and may otherwise be reabsorbed.

AUDIOANALGESIA is a method of relieving the pains of childbirth. It is produced by the patient listening through headphones to a combination of white sound and high-fidelity music. The intensity of the sound is controlled by the woman herself according to the intensity of her pain. Experience suggests that the method is successful in women who are well adapted, like music and have some understanding of labour and delivery.

AUDIOMETRY is the testing of hearing.

AUDITORY NERVE, or NERVE OF HEARING, is the eighth of the cranial nerves. It begins on the floor of the fourth ventricle in the medulla or hind brain, though it has numerous connections with other parts of the brain. It runs outwards, enters the temporal bone of the skull, and is distributed to various parts of the internal ear. It really consists of two branches ; one of these is concerned with hearing, while the other is distributed to the vestibule and semicircular canals of the internal ear, and is concerned with the sense of balancing. Disturbance of the former causes deafness and of the latter giddiness.

AURA (*aura*, a breeze) is a peculiar feeling which persons, subject to epileptic seizures, have just before the onset of an attack. It may be a sensation of a cold breeze, a peculiar smell, a vision of some animal or person, an undefinable sense of disgust, or the like, but it is very important for persons who experience it, because it gives warning that a fit is coming and may enable a place of safety or seclusion to be reached.

AURAL DISEASES (*see* EAR, DISEASES OF).

AUREOMYCIN (*see* CHLORTETRACYCLINE).

AURICLE is a term applied both to the pinna or flap of the ear and also to the ear-shaped tip of the atrium of the heart.

AURISCOPE is an instrument for examining the ear. The source of illumination may be incorporated in the instrument, as in the electric auriscope

Fig. 22.—Electric auriscope. The battery is situated in the handle. (From Pye, *Surgical Handicraft.* John Wright & Sons, Ltd.)

(Fig. 22), or it may be an independent light which is reflected into the ear by means of a forehead mirror.

AURISTILLÆ are ear-drops.

AURUM is the Latin name for gold.

AUSCULTATION (*ausculto*, I listen) is a term in medicine applied to the method employed by physicians for determining, by the sense of hearing, the condition of certain internal organs. The ancient physicians appear to have practised a kind of auscultation, by which they were able to detect the presence of air or fluids in the cavities of the chest and abdomen. In 1761

Auenbrugger of Vienna introduced the art of *percussion* in reference more especially to diseases of the chest. This consisted in tapping with the fingers the surface of the body, so as to elicit sounds by which the comparative resonance of the subjacent parts or organs might be estimated.

In 1819 the distinguished French physician, Laennec, introduced the method of auscultation by means of the stethoscope (στῆθος, the chest, and σκοπέω, I examine), with which his name stands permanently associated. For some time previously, physicians, more especially in the hospitals of Paris, had been in the habit of applying the ear over the region of the heart for the purpose of listening to the sounds of that organ, and it was in the employment of this method that Laennec conceived the idea that these sounds might be better conveyed through the medium of some solid body interposed between his ear and the patient's chest. He accordingly, by way of experiment, rolled up a quire of paper into the form of a cylinder and applied it in the manner just mentioned, when he found, as he states, that he was able to perceive the action of the heart more distinctly than he had ever been able to do by the immediate application of his ear. He thence inferred that not merely the heart's sounds. but also those of other organs of the chest might be brought within reach of the ear by some such instrument, and he therefore had constructed the wooden cylinder, or stethoscope, which bears his name. This instrument was subsequently modified by Piorry to the form of a thin narrow cylinder of about 7 inches (18 cm.) long, with an expansion at one end for applying to the chest, and a more or less flattened surface at the other for the ear of the listener.

The binaural stethoscope (Fig. 23), consisting of a small expanded chestpiece and two flexible tubes with ivory or vulcanite ends that fit tightly into the ears of the observer, is the type now generally used. This form is, in some ways, more convenient to use, though the sounds are no more clearly heard than with Piorry's instrument, and, in some cases, are less distinct, as the conduction of sound by the flexible tubes is entirely aerial. Various modifications of the binaural stethoscope have been introduced, such as the phonendoscope, in which the place of the chest-piece is taken by a small drum. An electrical stethoscope has

FIG. 23.—Binaural stethoscope.

been devised, through which, by the help of microphone, telephone, and electric valves, the beating of the heart, murmurs, etc., may be heard at a distance from the patient with any desired intensity.

The numerous conditions affecting the lungs can be recognized and discriminated from each other by means of auscultation and the stethoscope. The same holds good in the case of the heart, whose varied and often complex forms of disease can, by auscultation, be identified with striking accuracy. But in addition to these, its main uses, auscultation is found to render great assistance in the investigation of many obscure internal affections, such as aneurysms and certain diseases of the œsophagus and stomach. To the accoucheur the stethoscope yields valuable aid in the detection of some forms of uterine tumours, and especially in the diagnosis of pregnancy—the auscultatory evidence afforded by the sounds of the fœtal heart being one of the most reliable of the many signs of pregnancy and giving valuable information concerning the viability of the fœtus.

AUTACOID (αὐτός, self ; ἄκος, remedy) is a term applied to an organic substance formed by the cells of one organ and passed into the circulation to produce effects like those of drugs upon other organs at a distance. Some autacoids have a stimulating property and are then known as hormones ; others have a controlling or inhibitory influence and are then known as chalones or colyones. An example of the former group is insulin and of the latter group the substance in the placenta which prevents secretion of milk.

82

AUTO- (αὐτός, self) is a prefix meaning self.

AUTISM is a form of mental disturbance in children, in which there is a severance from reality, with relative or absolute preponderance of the inner life. The child grows up in an inner world of his own, cut off from human relationships and contact.

AUTOCLAVE.—This is one of the most effective ways of ensuring that material, e.g. surgical dressings, is completely sterilized and that even the most resistant bacteria with which it may be contaminated, are destroyed. Its use is based upon the fact that water boils when its vapour pressure is equal to the pressure of the surrounding atmosphere. This means that if the pressure inside a closed vessel be increased, the temperature at which water inside the vessel boils, will rise above 100° C. By adjusting the pressure, almost any temperature for the boiling of the water will be obtained. This is now one of the most widely used methods of sterilization in hospitals and laboratories.

AUTOGENOUS (αὐτογενής, self-produced) means self-generated and is the term applied to products which arise within the body. It is applied especially to bacterial vaccines manufactured from the organisms found in discharges from the body and used for the treatment of the person from whom the bacteria were derived.

AUTO-IMMUNITY is the process whereby an individual develops antibodies to his own tissues. Normally an individual does not develop antibodies to his own tissues, but only to invaders of the body such as micro-organisms. The precise reason why some individuals develop this unfortunate propensity is still obscure but it is proving a fruitful line of investigation into the cause of some diseases of hitherto unknown origin.

AUTO-INTOXICATION (αὐτός, self ; τοξικόν, poison) means literally self-poisoning, and is any condition of poisoning brought about by substances formed in or by the body.

AUTOLYSIS means the disintegration and softening of dead cells brought about by enzymes in the cells themselves.

AUTOMATISM means the performance of acts without conscious will, as, for example, after an attack of epilepsy or concussion of the brain. In such conditions the person may perform acts of which he is neither conscious at the time nor has any memory afterwards. The condition is of considerable importance from a legal point of view, because acts done in this state, and for which the person committing them is not responsible, may be of a criminal nature.

AUTONOMIC NERVOUS SYSTEM (αὐτόνομος, independent) is the term applied to that part of the nervous system which regulates the functions of some of the internal organs independently of the will power. It consists of two main divisions—the SYMPATHETIC and the PARASYMPATHETIC SYSTEMS (*q.v.*).

AUTOPSY (αὐτοψία, a seeing with one's own eyes) means the examination of the internal organs of a dead body. It is carried out in such a way as to produce almost no disfigurement. The brain is examined by an opening across the scalp, afterwards hidden by the hair, and the contents of chest and abdomen are inspected through an opening down the middle line in front. If necessary minute pieces of organs are removed for microscopic examinations. It is a social duty of the deceased person's relatives to permit or request a *post-mortem* examination in cases where the disease was a matter of uncertainty. Nothing causes so much doubt in diagnosis, and therefore in treatment, as the inability of a medical man to confirm his opinions, owing to sentiment on the part of a deceased person's relatives.

AUTO-SUGGESTION is the term applied to a peculiar mental state, which sometimes occurs after accidents, in which the will and judgement are partially perverted, so that slight or temporary injuries are greatly exaggerated in the imagination, and the person believes himself to be affected by some serious disability. Examples of this are found in paralysed and insensitive limbs following some minor bruise, for example in a railway accident, and the blindness, deafness, or inability to speak, which sometimes followed concussion in soldiers, especially when the injury was received in the dark. This state is also called ' traumatic suggestion '. The condition frequently approaches very near to, or is mingled with, the condition of malingering, in which the person consciously suggests to himself or produces some disability from an ulterior motive, as, for example, in some of the prolonged cases of disability following a trifling injury for which a person is in receipt of compensation. The term is also applied to the reverse process, by which, either as a result of suggestion by another person, or suggestion applied by the will power of the person affected, a cure of such a condition is accomplished.

AVITAMINOSIS is the term applied to the condition of a human being or an animal deprived of one or more vitamins.

AVOMINE is the trade name for promethazine - 8 - chlorotheophyllinate, which is widely, and successfully, used as a remedy for travel sickness.

AXILLA is the anatomical name for the armpit. (*See* ARMPIT.)

AZOCHLORAMIDE is a chlorine antiseptic.

AZOOSPERMIA is the condition characterized by lack of spermatozoa in the semen.

AZOTÆMIA means the presence of urea and other nitrogenous bodies in greater concentration than normal in the blood. The condition is generally associated with advanced types of kidney disease.

AZOTE (ἀ, neg. ; ζωτικός, capable of maintaining life) is another name for nitrogen.

AZOTIZED bodies are bodies containing nitrogen or azote. The principal are the proteins, substances which form most the bodily of tissues, of which albumin is the chief. (*See* PROTEINS, ALBUMINS, NITROGENOUS FOODS.)

B

BABINSKI REFLEX is the name applied to an abnormal response of the plantar reflex. When a sharp body is drawn along the sole of the foot, instead of the toes bending down towards the sole as usual, the great toe is turned upwards and the other toes tend to spread apart. This response may be obtained in normal infants, but after the age of about two years its presence indicates some severe disturbance in the upper part of the central nervous system.

BACILLÆMIA is the term given to the condition in which bacilli are present in the blood but do not multiply therein. (More usually called BACTERIÆMIA.)

BACILLI (*bacillus*, a little rod) are micro-organisms which are rod-like in form. (*See under* BACTERIOLOGY.)

BACILLURIA means the presence of bacilli in the urine, the result, usually, of infection of the kidney or the bladder.

BACITRACIN is a polypeptide antibiotic derived from *Bacillus licheniformis*. It is active against the same range of bacteria as penicillin.

BACK.—The back consists mainly of the spinal column and hinder parts of the ribs and the wide-spreading iliac or haunch bones with the sacrum below. The bones are covered by thick and powerful muscles, which above support and move the head and which below pass round the flanks and downwards into the lower limbs. The skin covering the back is very insensitive and is not greatly subject to painful conditions. The powerful muscles, of which the chief is the erector spinæ, are much subject to minor injuries, the result of twists and strains, and also to rheumatic affections (*see* LUMBAGO). Diseases and injuries of the spinal column and spinal cord are of a very serious nature (*see* SPINAL COLUMN *and* SPINAL CORD). A theory has been advanced by unqualified medical practitioners that many painful disorders and diseases are due to pressure upon nerves issuing between the vertebræ of the spine resulting from displacements of these bones. This idea is, however, without foundation.

BACKACHE is a symptom of many diseases. In addition to being the result of local causes, pain referred to the back is often due to disease or disorder in deep-seated organs.

Causes.—(*a*) LOCAL.—*Lumbago*, or a rheumatic condition in the muscles or nerves of the loins, which may be of a chronic aching nature, or may come on suddenly, feeling like a blow, is the commonest cause. A similar condition is often set up by unwonted exercise of these muscles in golfing, rowing, and the like. *Weakness* in growing boys or girls may cause a feeling of extreme weariness every day, and may be associated with lateral curvature of the spine, if not attended to. *Spinal disease* sometimes causes backache, and is associated with rigidity of the back, and often with great tenderness to the touch, with or without any deformity. Stiffness with pain sometimes follows some long-continued fever which has led to weakness in the back, especially found after typhoid fever ; a state of permanent stiffness is sometimes found in old people in whom the spine has become the seat of chronic rheumatic changes leading to the formation of bony outgrowths between the different vertebræ.

(*b*) INDIRECT. — *Kidney disease* is sometimes a cause of pain in the loins. All sorts of *pelvic trouble* in women, such as menstrual disorders, prolapse of the womb, and ovarian inflammation and tumours, are constantly accompanied by a dull, dragging-down pain in the back. *Gall-stones* sometimes cause an acute pain high up near the right shoulder. *Stomach ulcers* may cause a pain above the level of the last rib and close to the left side of the spine. Backache may also be one of the first symptoms of *smallpox*, and of several other febrile diseases.

Treatment.—This is of course the treatment of the disease causing the

84

pain. When the pain is due to a local cause, such as lumbago, the loins must be kept warm by extra clothing or a flannel belt. Belladonna plaster (*see* ADHESIVE PLASTERS) relieves it, also massage, ironing with a flat-iron through a piece of cloth, and, in acute cases, application of mustard leaf, hot fomentations, or a hot-water bottle or thermophore. Weakness in young persons is rectified by calisthenics and other forms of exercise, with regular daily periods of rest, and the careful avoidance of stooping or a twisted position at lessons. Perhaps the best exercise of all for strengthening the muscles of the back is the use of a skipping-rope.

BACTERIA (βακτήριον, a rod) is a term which at first meant micro-organisms in the form of short rods, but the word is now vaguely used to cover a great variety of low microscopic forms of plant life. It is equivalent to terms such as 'germs', 'microbes', 'micro-organisms'.

BACTERICIDE strictly means anything which kills bacteria, but is usually applied to drugs and antiseptics which do this. Hence BACTERICIDAL.

BACTERIOLOGY is the branch of biological science concerned with the study of the lowest forms of plant life, particularly of those which cause disease in men and animals, and putrefaction. (For details on INFECTION, IMMUNITY, ANTISEPTICS, VACCINATION, SERUM THERAPY, and OPSONINS, *see* these headings.) Although bacteria had been noticed about 1687 by Leeuwenhoek and others after the introduction of the microscope, they were not definitely associated with disease until the nineteenth century. Goodsir in 1842 described *sarcinæ* in the stomach, and Davaine in 1865 noticed the large organisms of anthrax, but Pasteur was the first, about 1865, to make a complete study of the manner in which micro-organisms multiply and produce disease. He was followed by Koch, who in 1876 worked out the complete life-history and spore formation of the bacillus of anthrax. In 1877 Koch published his methods of staining films of bacteria ; in 1878 his great memoir on the cause of infectious diseases, describing those kinds of bacteria which produce suppuration in wounds; and in 1881 his method of obtaining pure cultures of different organisms. Koch's methods founded the science of bacteriology, and with little change they are still in use.

Classification of micro-organisms.—If we include the viruses under the heading of 'bacteria', the micro-organisms of the vegetable kingdom which cause disease may be grouped as follows : (1) *Moulds*, of which penicillium, the green cheese-mould, and mucor, a white mould, are examples. These grow on leather, bread, and in fact anything of a nutritious nature which happens to be damp, their spores floating everywhere in the air. One mould is sometimes a cause of pneumonia, another causes disease in salmon, and others produce the various forms of ringworm. (2) *Yeasts*, of which one is of great importance as being the producer of alcohol. (3) *Bacteria* proper (Plate VIII). The latter are again divided, mainly owing to their shape, into *cocci*, which are round ; *bacilli*, long, slender rods ; *spirilla*, curved or wavy. They have secondary names according to some physical property, such as the power of producing colour, as *Staphylococcus aureus*, which appears under the microscope in grape-like clusters, produces pus in the body, and grows in golden-yellow masses when artificially cultivated. *Streptococci* are cocci arranged in chains ; *diplococci* occur in pairs. (4) *Rickettsiæ*, named after the bacteriologist Ricketts, are disease-causing micro-organisms, coccal or rod-shaped, and intermediate in size between bacteria and viruses. Rickettsiæ are the infecting agents in typhus and typhus-like fevers, and also of trench fever. *Rickettsia prowazeki*, the infecting agent of typhus, is conveyed to man by infected lice. Other Rickettsial infections—such as Rocky Mountain fever—are conveyed by ticks or fleas. (5) *Viruses* are living agents which cause disease and are so minute that they pass through porcelain filters impassable by ordinary bacteria and cannot be seen with ordinary microscopic methods (ultramicroscopic).

They appear to be living crystals of protein, and cause such diseases as poliomyelitis, measles, mumps, chicken-pox, the common cold, and influenza.

Properties of bacteria.—MOTION.—It is doubtful if cocci have this power, but most of the bacilli and spirilla move rapidly and freely, either by quick contortions similar to those of a fish-tail, or by beating the fluid in which they lie by flagella, long whip-like lashes, with which many, such as the bacillus of typhoid fever and the spirillum of cholera, are provided. This power of movement is of immense importance in the spread of disease. The movements become more active if the temperature is raised and bacteria are attracted to certain substances and repelled by others, this property being known as *positive* and *negative chemiotaxis*.

SIZE.—It is difficult at first to grasp the extreme smallness of these bodies. Many thousands of them may lie upon the smallest visible speck of dust. The round forms or cocci are not more than $\frac{1}{25000}$ inch in breadth. The bacillus of anthrax, much the largest disease-producing bacillus, is less than $\frac{1}{3000}$ inch in length, and most of the bacilli are only $\frac{1}{50000}$ inch, or a little more, in breadth.

REPRODUCTION.—The moulds have special filaments which produce hundreds of spores, and the yeasts give off little buds from their surface which produce new chains of yeast, but most of the simpler bacteria multiply by growing in size and then splitting into two. As a result of this, long chains are formed in which the individuals lie end to end, or masses, in which they lie side by side. A bacterium may grow and split in about half an hour, with the result that, given favourable circumstances of warmth, food, etc., a single bacillus could, in the course of twenty-four hours, produce nearly 300,000,000,000,000 individuals. Fortunately such favourable circumstances are seldom completely attained in nature. Another important method of reproduction possessed by some bacilli, such as that of anthrax, is by spores. Each bacillus produces only one spore, which, however, is much more tenacious of life than the bacillus and often capable of surviving after being boiled, or after drying for months or years.

Each spore again produces a bacillus when it lights in a suitable germinating ground. This explains many obscure cases of infection.

Effects of growth.—Diseases are due, in many cases, to the growth of the bacteria and their irritation or destruction of the tissues in which they lie, as, for example, in tuberculosis, leprosy, abscess ; in other cases to the production by them of poisonous substances called ' toxins ', which circulate in the blood, and cause fever, delirium, paralysis, and other general effects. In this manner the serious results of diphtheria, tetanus, and many other acute infectious diseases are produced. Many bacilli produce acids by their growth, such as that which turns milk sour, and may be of great commercial value, as the bacillus which produces vinegar. Alcohol, as is well known, is the product of the activity of yeast. Many bacteria also produce brilliant pigments of red, yellow, blue, green, or purple colour, such as the *Bacillus prodigiosus*, which turns milk red, and the *Bacillus pyocyaneus*, which produces blue pus in abscesses. Many bacteria produce gases from the substances in which they develop such as sulphuretted hydrogen, carbon dioxide, marsh gas, etc. Others liquefy solid substances, such as gelatin, and in this manner the common bacillus of the intestine, which inhabits the alimentary canal from a few days after birth till the end of life, probably plays a useful and necessary part in digestion, although it also, from time to time, when other factors aid it, produces untoward results in appendicitis, peritonitis, and other diseases in the neighbourhood of the bowels. Many of the actions of bacteria depend upon ferments which are produced by them and exercise a complicated action. These ferments are sometimes set free in the fluid surrounding the bacteria, and sometimes retained for a time within the bacteria themselves. Most bacteria produce substances which finally stop their growth and activity ; thus vinegar, alcohol, and the evil-smelling substances resulting from the activity of the intestinal bacillus check the excessive growth of, and finally kill their respective bacteria, and a similar result explains the crisis in, and recovery from many diseases like pneumonia and relapsing fever

Conditions of growth.—FOOD.—Some bacteria live by taking carbonic acid and nitrogen from the air and producing complex organic substances in their growth, so that these bacteria are of great importance in some of the operations of farming. Most, however, break down the complex plant and animal bodies into simpler substances. All require some moisture for their growth. Some bacteria are readily killed by drying, thus the spirillum of cholera is killed by two or three hours of drying, but the ordinary bacteria of suppuration may be dried for at least several days, and anthrax spores still survive after drying for several years. A few bacteria live best, or only, in living bodies, being then called parasitic, or, if they produce disease, pathogenic. Others live only in dead matter, and are called saprophytic. The substances on which they grow best are gelatinous or starchy matters containing a little soluble animal substance, like peptone, and a trace of salts, or in fluids like broth, containing much animal or vegetable matter.

WARMTH.—The bacteria of putrefaction flourish best at the ordinary temperature found inside a house—*i.e.* about 20° C. ; the disease-producing bacteria at the temperature of the body —*i.e.* 37° C. Freezing, though it stops growth for the time, does not kill most bacteria, which afterwards take on new activity ; but a process of thawing and freezing repeated several times in succession kills all organisms. Boiling, on the other hand, is more deadly to them, and, if continued for a few minutes, kills most bacteria, though not their spores. The latter are killed by superheated steam at 120° C. Dry heat can be survived at much higher temperatures. The surest method of destruction is Koch's plan of sterilizing dishes, instruments, etc. These are exposed for twenty minutes to steam rising from boiling water, in a special apparatus, or, equally efficiently, in an ordinary pot with a lid. This kills all bacteria. Next day they are similarly treated, when any spores which have been present have developed into bacteria, and these are likewise killed. A third application of steam, on the day again following, renders certain the freedom from spores and bacteria.

LIGHT.—Bacteria develop best in the dark, though some produce their special effects only when exposed to light. Direct sunlight stops their growth, and exposure for several hours to the full light of the sun kills most bacteria, notably those of plague and tuberculosis. The effect of sunlight is increased by dryness, and it has been found, for example, that even anthrax spores, which possess greater vitality than almost any other bacteria, are killed when dried and exposed to sunlight for one and a half hours, although, if moisture is present, a much longer exposure to sunlight is necessary. The effect is still further increased by heat, so that bacteria live for a very short time only in hot, dry, and sunshiny localities. Electric light has a similar, although weaker action, the violet rays being most powerful in killing bacteria, but the X-rays have very little effect in checking bacterial growth.

AIR.—Most bacteria grow with or without fresh air. A certain amount of fresh air is necessary to rapid putrefaction, but a very free supply, and certainly the presence of pure oxygen, tends to destroy bacteria. Bacteria, such as those of tetanus (lock-jaw) and of gas gangrene, can develop only deep in the earth or in deep wounds where oxygen is absent, and these are known as ' anaerobic bacteria '.

Relation to disease.—The first bacterium stated to be connected with disease was the anthrax bacillus. Since the introduction of modern bacteriological methods about 1880, a great number of bacteria responsible for disease have been demonstrated. The proof that a bacterium is the direct cause of any disease depends upon the fulfilment of three conditions laid down by Koch : (1) that the bacterium be always found in the body or its discharges when a certain disease is present ; (2) that the bacterium can be isolated and cultivated under laboratory conditions and thus freed from other possible causes of the disease ; and (3) that on the inoculation of a healthy man or animal with a culture of the bacterium, which is now free from any possible contamination, symptoms of the original disease appear in the animal inoculated. Thus complete proof has been obtained in the case of a large number of diseases, while in the case of other diseases for some technical reason, such as that the organism cannot be grown in the laboratory or because no animal can be found to suffer typically from the disease, an absolute proof of the connection between the disease and the organism is so far wanting.

Among the diseases which have been definitely shown to be due to particular organisms are the following (Fig. 24) :

ACUTE INFLAMMATION AND SUPPURATION.—Localized inflammation may be due to a great variety of organisms, of which the various *staphylococci* and *streptococci* are the chief. Staphylococci are the most common agents in producing pustules on the skin, boils, and catarrhs of mucous surfaces. Streptococci commonly produce more deep-seated, serious, and spreading diseases, such as erysipelas. They also occur in broncho-pneumonia and ulcerative endocarditis. The streptococcus is a common cause of tonsillitis, is responsible for puerperal fever, often starts infection of wounds (especially those sustained in war), and indeed may attack any part of the body, resulting in such conditions as peritonitis, meningitis, empyema. Suppuration may also be produced by several bacteria mentioned below as associated with particular diseases.

PNEUMONIA of the acute lobar type is usually due to the pneumococcus or *Diplococcus pneumoniæ*. This organism is of several different types, types I and II being much the most common, while type III is found in about 12 per cent. of cases of pneumonia. A few cases of pneumonia are due to the *streptococcus*, the *bacillus of influenza* (or *Hæmophilus influenzæ*, as it is now known), and the *pneumobacillus*. There is also a form of pneumonia, known as primary atypical pneumonia, which is due to a virus.

CEREBRO-SPINAL FEVER.—This disease is due to the *Meningococcus*, which occurs in four types. It appears to gain entrance to the body through the nasal passages, where it is frequently found even in people who do not suffer from the disease.

88

RHEUMATIC FEVER, especially that variety associated with severe disorders of the heart valves, is commonly associated with a hæmolytic streptococcus.

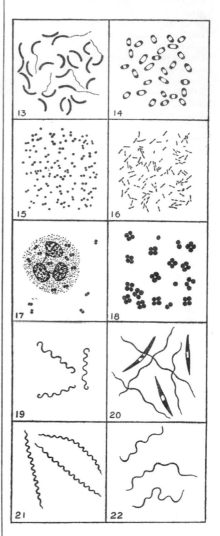

FIG. 24.—Various bacteria of disease. (13) Cholera vibrio, showing flagella. (14) Plague bacillus. (15) *Brucella melitensis*. (16) Influenza bacillus. (17) Diplococcus of cerebro-spinal meningitis. (18) *Micrococcus tetragenus*. (19) Spirochæte of epidemic jaundice. (20) Spirochæte and fusiform bacillus of Vincent's angina (septic sore throat). (21) Spirochæte of syphilis. (22) *Spirochæte refringens*. (Drawn by R. Muir.)

PLATE VIII

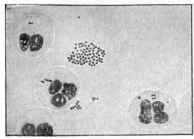

Staphylococci
In Pus from Abscess of Neck.
(Carbol-thionin.)

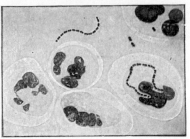

Streptococci
In Pus from a case of Cellulitis.
(Carbol-thionin.)

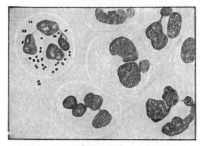

Gonococci
From a Urethral Discharge.
(Carbol-thionin.)

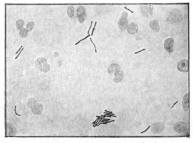

Mycobacteria Tuberculosis
In Sputum.
(Carbol Fuchsin and Methylene Blue.)

Corynebacteria Diphtheriae
Culture on Blood Serum.
(Löffler's Methylene Blue.)

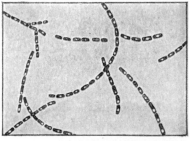

Anthrax Bacilli
Culture on Gelatin.
(Carbol-thionin.)

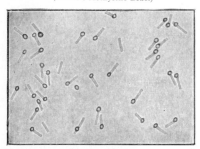

Tetanus Bacilli
Anærobic Culture on Agar.
(Carbol Fuchsin and Methylene Blue.)

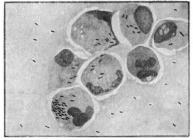

Influenza Bacilli
In Pus from Knee Joint.
(Carbol Fuchsin.)

From Panton and Marrack's *Clinical Pathology* (Churchill).

SCARLATINA and some allied infections are due to a hæmolytic streptococcus.

GONORRHŒA is due to a diplococcus—the gonococcus—which is found to a large extent inside the cells of the discharge.

SYPHILIS is caused by a minute spiral-shaped organism, or spirochæte, known as *Treponema pallidum*. Other diseases due to different varieties of spirochætes are RELAPSING FEVER, YAWS, SPIROCHÆTAL JAUNDICE, and RAT-BITE FEVER.

TUBERCULOSIS is due to one or other of two bacilli, or mycobacteria, known as the 'human tubercle bacillus' and the 'bovine tubercle bacillus'. Tuberculosis in the lung is almost always caused by the human type, while abdominal tuberculosis, as well as tuberculosis of bones and joints, found in children, is due in a good many cases to the bovine type derived from milk, and tuberculosis of the glands in young children is due to the latter type. Other types of tubercle bacilli cause similar diseases in birds and fish, while closely allied bacilli are found subsisting in grass.

LEPROSY is caused by a bacillus presenting certain close resemblances to the bacillus of tuberculosis.

GLANDERS, or FARCY, is caused by *Bacillus mallei*.

ACTINOMYCOSIS, or WOODY TONGUE is caused by *Actinomyces bovis*, which is one of a genus of micro-organisms known as actinomyces. The MADURA FOOT OF INDIA is caused by an organism belonging to a closely associated genus.

ANTHRAX, or WOOLSORTERS' DISEASE, is due to a relatively large organism, the *Bacillus anthracis*, which produces spores that may retain their vitality when dried for several years.

TYPHOID FEVER and the group of diseases related to it, such as para-typhoid fever A and B, bacillary dysentery, and forms of food poisoning, are due to *Salmonella typhosa*, *Salmonella paratyphi*, and *Shigella sonnei*, and a number of other organisms which resemble one another considerably in their mode of growth, cultural characters, and, broadly speaking, in the effects which they produce on the intestine and the body generally.

DIPHTHERIA is due to the *Bacillus diphtheriæ* (or *Corynebacterium diph-*

theriæ, as it is now known), which is often found in the throat of healthy persons, but which in susceptible persons produces a very severe type of surface inflammation with general toxic effects throughout the body.

TETANUS, or LOCK-JAW, is produced by the *Bacillus tetani* (or *Clostridium tetani*, as it is now known), which is an anaerobic bacillus growing especially deep in the soil or in dung-heaps. It produces spores which, like those of anthrax, are extremely tenacious of life.

GAS GANGRENE is a disease produced by various anaerobic bacilli, especially the *Bacillus welchii* (or *Clostridium welchii*), which grow deep in highly cultivated soil, and, like the tetanus bacillus, cause infection when such soil is disturbed.

CHOLERA is due to the cholera vibrio, an organism of S-shaped appearance which is very readily destroyed by drying or by weak antiseptics.

PLAGUE is caused by a rod-shaped bacillus, *Pasteurella pestis*, which is transmitted to man through rodents and fleas.

INFLUENZA is due to a virus. Three specific viruses have, so far, been isolated, and others that may take part in the infection are under investigation. At one time it was thought that influenza was due to the *Hæmophilus influenzæ* (Pfeiffer's bacillus), but it is now known that this is only one of the secondarily infecting organisms that are often found in influenza.

WHOOPING-COUGH is due to a minute oval bacterium, the *Hæmophilus pertussis*, or *Bordetella pertussis* as it is now known.

MALTA FEVER is due to a minute coccus, the *Brucella melitensis*.

MALARIA is due to an organism known as the *Plasmodium*. Three different but closely related types cause the three varieties of malaria. The plasmodia belong to a group of micro-organisms known as protozoa. Other diseases which are due to protozoa are : AMŒBIC DYSENTERY, due to the *Entamœba histolytica* ; SLEEPING SICK-NESS, due to the *Trypanosoma gambiense* ; KALA-AZAR, due to the *Leishmania donovani*, and other closely allied diseases.

89

Study of bacteria.—It is impossible to go more than very briefly into the highly technical methods employed in a bacteriological laboratory. The material to be examined must be collected in such a way as to prevent contamination by organisms from outside sources, *e.g.* the skin or the air. For example, in collecting matter from the throat to find if the diphtheria bacillus is present, a glass tube plugged with cotton-wool and containing a cotton-wool swab at the end of a piece of wire is used. The throat is rubbed with the swab, which is then carefully returned, reinserted in the tube, and sent to the laboratory. When the urine is to be examined for the presence of bacteria, it is carefully drawn off under aseptic precautions by means of a catheter into a sterile bottle closed with a sterilized stopper and similarly sent to the laboratory. Similar precautions are taken in the case of material from other sources. The bacteriological methods used fall into four groups.

(1) EXAMINATION BY THE MICRO-SCOPE.—If bacteria are placed in a little fluid upon a glass slide and examined with the aid of a microscope, they appear when magnified some hundreds of times as clear, transparent, often quickly moving particles or lines. For careful observation they must be killed by heat or by some powerful chemical substance, and thereafter stained with appropriate reagents. These are usually aniline dyes of different colours ; and the bacteria of different diseases, apart from their size, shape, and general appearance, can often be recognized from the way in which they become stained or fail to stain with certain dyes. Methylene blue is a simple dye generally used for all bacteria. The tubercle bacillus is distinguished by the peculiar tenacity with which it retains the red fuchsin stain when treated by sulphuric acid and spirit, while from other bacteria this dye can be readily extracted by these reagents. The majority of bacteria are stained a deep purple colour by Gram's stain (successive application of gentian-violet, iodine, and alcohol), but some are readily recognized by being negative to this stain, *e.g.* the gonococcus, meningococcus, and the typhoid bacillus. Neisser's stain is

much used for the recognition of the diphtheria bacillus ; it consists of two stains (methylene blue and Bismarck brown) which stain this bacillus in a characteristic variegated manner. Many other bacteria have similar special staining properties by which they can be recognized without further trouble.

(2) CULTIVATION.—In general, however, it is not possible to identify an organism with certainty, simply by its appearance, even if suitably stained, and the changes which its growth in large masses produces upon various nutrient substances contained in glass culture tubes must also be observed. In doing this the first necessity is to prepare a nutrient medium and place it in flat covered plates or in glass tubes of which the open end is plugged with a piece of cotton-wool so as to exclude organisms that might enter from the air, while freely admitting the air itself. These tubes and their contents must be carefully sterilized in the manner already indicated ; they are then inoculated, by means of a previously sterilized platinum needle or a glass rod, with material. containing the organism which it is desired to study ; and are finally placed inside an incubator maintained day and night at the temperature of the body. After being incubated for several days the bacteria have multiplied so as to form colonies easily visible to the naked eye, and from these, small fragments are removed by the platinum needle, stained, and microscopically examined.

Among the nutrient substances on which bacteria are grown in the laboratory, the chief are broth, gelatin, agar, potato, and milk. The turbidity produced in broth after some days' growth, the power to liquefy gelatin, the colours produced on the surface of agar or of cut potato, and the curdling of milk form distinctive characters of different bacteria. Again, various sugars may be added to these substances and the bacteria are thus divided into classes according to their power of fermenting the sugar as they grow. The formation of acid by other bacteria is tested by adding to the tubes litmus or some other reagent which changes its colour when acidified, and the development of gas-bubbles is also an important distinguishing mark.

Some bacteria (known as anaerobic bacteria) fail to grow unless the oxygen be extracted from the tubes in which they are placed or an atmosphere of hydrogen gas be provided by means of a special apparatus.

Since many different types of bacteria are as a rule mingled together in the discharge from a diseased part of the body, it becomes necessary to separate these and to obtain for study cultures of each, free from contamination by the others. For this separation, the organisms are either grown upon a medium to which have been added substances that destroy some kinds of bacteria while sparing others ; or they are diluted by mixture with a large quantity of sterile fluid, and, drops of this being stroked over the surface of some nutrient material lying on a broad covered glass plate (Petri dish), the individual bacteria produce within a few days widely separated colonies that can be seen by the naked eye and removed for further examination.

(3) AGGLUTINATION OR PRECIPITATION is a method much used for the identification of certain bacteria. The manner in which it is carried out is described in the article AGGLUTINATION. It is usually performed by making a uniform emulsion with water of the bacteria to be identified, and then adding a drop of this emulsion to a drop of immune serum on a microscopic slide. Various stock sera are kept in the laboratory, and one of these is chosen corresponding to the disease to which the bacterium is supposed to belong. If the bacteria on microscopic examination are seen to clump together under the action of the serum, this identifies the bacteria as belonging to the disease from which the serum has been prepared. If the bacteria do not clump, the same process is carried out with another serum until the appropriate serum is found. The same process may be carried out without microscopic examination by placing the bacterial emulsion in small test tubes and adding drops of the sera to these. Precipitation of the bacteria to the bottom of the tube can be seen to take place in a tube containing the corresponding bacteria and serum. This

method is much used in identifying the meningococcus, typhoid bacillus, diphtheria bacillus, dysentery bacillus, and others.

(4) INOCULATION OF ANIMALS.—For the purpose of making certain which of the many kinds of bacteria derived from a case of disease is its actual cause, or in some instances when the bacteria are so few in number or so difficult to cultivate that they cannot be found, it becomes necessary to inoculate animals like mice, guinea-pigs, or rabbits with material containing the bacteria, in order, if possible, to reproduce the disease. This inoculation is effected through pricking the skin or puncturing the abdomen by means of a needle and syringe charged with the material in question. Subsequently the animal is killed and its organs examined for signs of the disease.

BACTERIOPHAGE was the name given by d'Herelle to an agent which affects growing bacteria so as to break up and destroy them. It is now known to be a virus.

BACTERIOSTATIC.—Bringing bacteria to a standstill by preventing their nourishment and growth.

BAGASSOSIS is an industrial lung disease occurring in those who work with ' Bagasse ', which is the name given to the broken sugar cane after sugar has been extracted from it. Bagasse, which contains 6 per cent. silica, is used in board-making. The inhalation of dust causes an acute lung affection, and subsequently in some cases a chronic lung disease.

B.A.L. is the abbreviation for BRITISH ANTI-LEWISITE. (*See* DIMERCAPROL.)

BALANITIS means inflammation of the parts covered by the prepuce.

BALBUTIES is a medical term for stammering or stuttering.

BALDNESS is generally partial and slowly progressive, and is so universal that it may be looked on as a natural change in age. It may also occur rapidly in patches, or even every hair on the body may be lost, in the disease called alopecia areata.

Causes.—Certain *serious diseases* are associated with partial loss of hair as one of their symptoms ; but these diseases are of so much greater importance that the thinness of hair is not taken account of, and as a rule remedies itself as these diseases wear off. Such diseases are acute fevers, myxœdema, syphilis, influenza, anæmia, and great anxiety or nervous shock. Gradual premature baldness is, to a considerable extent, hereditary, and it is preceded for some years by seborrhœic eczema, a condition of dandruff on the scalp set up by bacterial decomposition of the natural oil of the hair. Every day, in the healthy scalp, a certain number of hairs reach the end of their existence, and are combed out, being replaced in time by others growing up from below. Each hair-follicle in this way produces many hairs in the course of a person's life, but, if the change is too rapid, the hairs become gradually finer, then downy, and lastly the hair-producing power of the follicle wears out. This rapid change is due to the eczematous condition of the scalp. Many skin diseases, like lupus, erysipelas, ringworm, which leave a hardened condition of the scalp behind them, cause baldness, and such cases are made worse by the various stimulating hair washes sold for baldness.

Treatment.—The earlier the condition is attacked, the more promising the outlook, for there is little hope of obtaining more than a downy growth, by any treatment, from a shiny, bald scalp. A hard hat should be worn as little as possible, and in summer, in the country, or by the seaside, no cap should be worn. No hard brush or sharp comb should be used, as their irritation induces dandruff. The head should be frequently washed, say once a week, with extract of quillayia and hot water, or super-fatted soap, or a whipped-up egg. The hair should be always thoroughly dried after washing, and, if it remains hard and brittle, a little hair-oil composed of lanolin (1 part) and sesame oil (16 parts) may be applied. If baldness is definitely appearing, the hair, in boys, may be

cut short and bay rum or spirit used daily to wash the scalp. This treatment makes the hair hard and bristly, and removes all dandruff. In people who prefer to wear the hair longer, the head may be daily washed, till the hair ceases coming out, with Hebra's soap, consisting of green soap (2 parts), rectified spirit (1 part), filtered and perfumed. After washing, the soap must be thoroughly rinsed out and the hair dried, and oiled as above. A pomade consisting of tannin 60 minims (4 ml.), lanolin 360 minims (24 ml.), sesame oil 120 minims (8 ml.), is also good for checking the loss of hair. Perchloride of mercury is one of the best substances for removing dandruff, either in a wash containing 5 ounces (142 ml.) of water, 1 ounce (28·5 ml.) of eau-de-Cologne, and 1 grain (60 mg.) of perchloride of mercury, or in a pomade like that given above, to which 2 or 3 grains (120 or 180 mg.) of the perchloride of mercury may be added. The many vaunted hair restorers contain either a little Goulard's water or, more generally, tincture of cantharides or Spanish fly. The latter is very stimulating in advanced cases, 60 minims (4 ml.) of vinegar of cantharides being used in 1 ounce (28·5 ml.) of spirit to dab on the scalp, coupled with the washing mentioned above. It is of great importance to attend to the general health, for baldness advances more rapidly in those of poor health than in the robust. The hair should further be frequently cut (every three weeks), and singeing may do good.

ALOPECIA AREATA, or patchy baldness, is common on the scalp, but may affect the hair all over the body. It occurs principally in adolescents and young adults. Many authorities regard it as an infective condition, but it is not infectious. Others, again, believe that it is due to disturbance of the sympathetic nervous system. In some cases it appears to be associated with general debility or with disease of the teeth, throat, or eye. These should be examined and, if necessary, treated. It is doubtful whether treatment makes any difference. The hair regrows spontaneously in more than 99 per cent. of cases, sometimes lighter in colour, or even white. Ultra-violet light is beneficial in some cases.

BALNEOLOGY (βαλανεῖον, bath ; λόγος, discourse) is the department of medical science which deals with the giving of baths. (*See* BATHS.)

BALSAMS (βάλσαμον) are substances which contain resins and benzoic acid. Balsam of Peru, balsam of Tolu, and Friar's balsam or compound tincture of benzoin are the chief. They are given internally for colds, and aid expectoration, while locally they are used to cover abrasions and stimulate ulcers. Friar's balsam, one teaspoonful, inhaled from a jug of boiling water, is of value in the alleviation of the common cold. Balsam of Peru is given internally in doses of 5 to 15 drops with beaten-up egg ; balsam of Tolu is similarly administered in doses of 5 to 15 grains (300 mg. to 1 G.), or is given as the more familiar syrup of Tolu in doses of one teaspoonful.

BANDAGES are pieces of flannel, calico, muslin, etc., used to support injured parts or retain dressings on wounds. The two usual forms are the triangular and the roller bandage.

Triangular bandages are used in ambulance work, on the battlefield, and

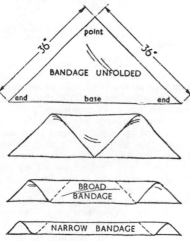

FIG. 25.—Triangular bandage unfolded and folded.

whenever an easily applied temporary bandage is wanted. They are made by

taking a piece of calico 1 yard (1 metre square and cutting it across cornerwise to form two triangles (Fig. 25). The cut side of each is called the ' base ', and the right-angled corner opposite, the ' point '. The bandage, either singly or two together, can be used for almost any part of the body, but is merely a covering intended to retain a dressing, and does not exert much pressure. A triangular bandage may be applied in one of three forms : (*a*) *open* as a

FIG. 26.—Bandage for shoulder. Two triangles : one folded into sling for wrist ; the second open with point on neck and ends tied round arm.

triangle, sometimes with a hem turned over at the base, according to the size of the part to be covered ; (*b*) *folded broad*, with the point turned in twice towards the centre of the base ; and (*c*) *folded narrow*, like a cravat, the point being turned in three times. These bandages are of great use for first aid and for military work, as they take up little room, can be readily applied, and can be taken off easily without disturbing the injured part. Their mode of application is readily seen from the diagrams.

The flat hand may be covered in by a bandage similar to that for the foot, the wrist being placed on the centre of the base and the fingers towards the point, which is turned back over them ; the ends are folded in and tied off round the wrist.

Bandages similar to those shown for

FIG. 27.—Bandage for arm. Triangle folded broad is carried three times round and tied.

FIG. 28.—Bandage for open hand. Triangle is folded narrow; centre placed on palm of hand, ends carried round to back, crossed, carried round wrist twice, and tied.

FIG. 29.—Bandage for elbow. Triangle folded broad is laid with centre on elbow; ends are crossed in front, carried round forearm, crossed again in front, carried round upper arm, and tied.

the arm and elbow may be applied to the leg and knee of a person who is not going about; but in walking, triangular bandages applied to these parts are apt to slip down.

It is well that the knots of all triangular bandages should be reef-knots, which are much more easily undone than the other form; and it is essential that they should always be tied on the outer side of a limb, or in such a position that they can be easily removed without disturbing the injured part.

94

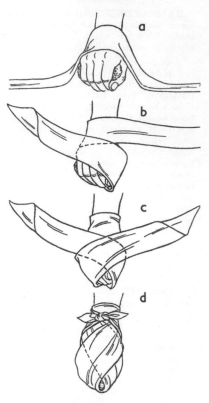

FIG. 30.—Bandage for closed fist, in which a roll of cotton-wool, lint, etc., is grasped. Four stages.

The applications of the triangular bandage in the treatment of fractures are described under FRACTURES, and for their adjustment as slings (q.v.).

Roller Bandages are strips 10, 15, or 20 feet (3, 4·5, 6 metres) long, and varying in width from 2 to 4 inches (5 to 10 cm.), according as a limb or the body is to be covered. They are generally sterilized before use, or impregnated with some antiseptic (see ANTISEPTICS), and may be of flannel, which can be washed and used repeatedly, of calico, or of cheesecloth. The chief methods of applying roller bandages are: Simple spiral, in which the bandage circles up the limb, each turn overlapping half of that preceding. This is used for a cylindrical part of the body like the upper arm.

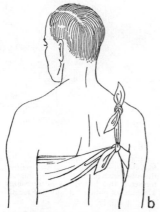

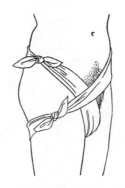

FIG. 32.—Bandage for groin. Two triangles, folded narrow and tied end to end.

FIG. 31.—Bandage to cover the chest. One triangle: the point is laid over one shoulder, the ends carried round the sides and tied over the same shoulder-blade; the longer of the two ends is carried up and tied to the point; *a*, front; *b*, back. To cover the back the same bandage is used with knots in front.

Spiral with reverses, in which the bandage is turned sharply over on itself at each circle so as to lie smooth when the circles tend to separate widely. It is used for conical parts like the forearm or calf (Fig. 41). *Figure of 8,* in which the bandage loops alternately round two parts of the body. It is used to cover a projection or hollow such as the shoulder or armpit, by looping round trunk and arm alternately. *Spica,* which is used for a joint, the turns covering one another completely in the

FIG. 33.—Bandage for hip. Two triangles: one folded narrow and tied round waist; the other with point on the side and ends tied round thigh; *a*, first stage; *b*, finished.

95

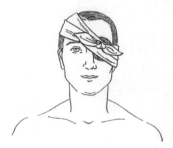

FIG. 35.—Bandage for eye. Triangle folded narrow ; centre is placed over the eye, and carried round head, crossed, carried forwards, and tied.

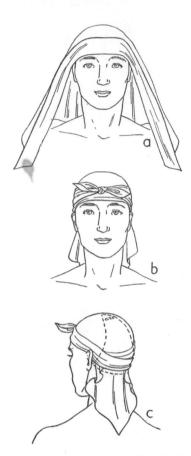

FIG. 34.—Bandage for head. (*a*) Triangle with a hem turned up on base is placed with centre of base on forehead and point on back of neck ; (*b*) ends are carried behind head, crossed on neck, carried forward, and tied on forehead. (*c*) Point is finally pinned up. Three stages.

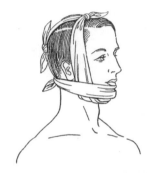

FIG. 36.—Bandage for lower jaw. Two triangles folded narrow ; place one with centre below, the other with centre in front of the chin. The former is tied above, the latter behind head. The ends of both are finally tied together.

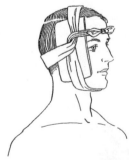

FIG. 37.—Bandage for side of head. Triangle folded narrow ; centre is placed over one ear, one end carried over top of head, the other beneath chin ; the two turn round one another above ear, and are then carried round forehead and back of head and tied over centre of forehead.

bend of the joint, and separating partly over the prominence like the arrangement in a coat-of-mail (Figs. 42, 53, 54). It is simply a modified figure of 8. *Trefoil* is a bandage applied to the head, and is the same in principle as the figure of 8, though it has three loops instead of two (Figs. 49 50).

In applying a roller bandage the first circle must be firmly fixed by covering it completely with the next to prevent slipping ; or a still better method of

44 and 45, and covering this with the subsequent turns of the bandage. The

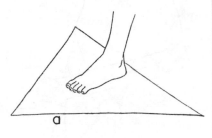

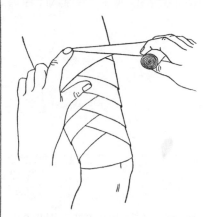

FIG. 40.—Spiral with reverses for thigh.

FIG. 38.—Bandage for foot. Foot is placed on triangle with heel near the centre of base; ends are folded over three times to lie along side of heel; point is turned up over front of ankle, ends tied round ankle, and point is finally pinned down over the knot. *a*, First stage; *b*, second stage; *c*, finished.

bandage must pass upwards or the limb will become blue owing to the

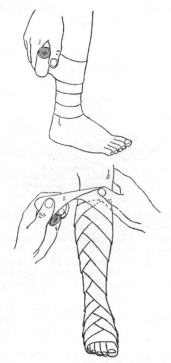

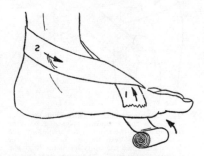

FIG. 39.—Method of 'fixing' bandage firmly for application to foot.

fixing consists in taking a figure of 8 turn round the limb, as shown in Figs.

4

FIG. 41.— Spiral with reverses for leg.

blood in the superficial veins being pressed backwards towards the extremity of the limb. It should cross

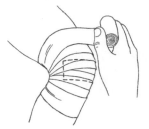

FIG. 42.—Roller bandages for the lower limb. The first is a bandage for the lower part of the leg (simple spiral); the second for the whole leg (spiral with reverses); and the third for the knee (spica). The dotted outline in above figure shows the beginning of bandage.

the front of the limb from within outwards in order to give more room for making reverses towards the outer side. Where skin surfaces come into contact, one should be separated from the other by cotton wool, as otherwise moisture accumulates and the surfaces readily become abraded. This should be done,

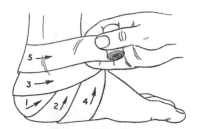

FIG. 43.—Bandage covering heel. First turn covers heel, second and third bind down its loose edges; fourth and fifth bind down the loose edges of second and third.

for example, between the fingers, behind the ear, in the armpit, etc. In order to make the bandage lie smoothly it is important in applying it that the head of the bandage should always, except in reversing, remain in contact with the part that is being bandaged, round which it is simply rolled.

The *width* of roller bandages varies: for the finger 1 inch (2·5 cm.); for the head 2 inches (5 cm.); for the arm 2½ inches (6 cm.); for the leg 3 inches (7·5 cm.); for the abdomen or chest 4 or 5 inches (10 or 12·5 cm.).

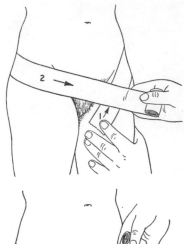

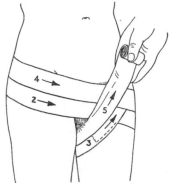

FIG. 44.—Ascending spica for groin.

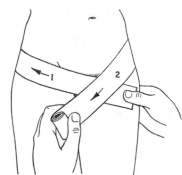

FIG. 45.—Commencement of descending spica for groin. In the ascending spica the bandage runs up across the front of the thigh and each turn is higher than the one before. In the descending spica the turns across the thigh run down and each turn is at a lower level than its predecessor. The body turns pass round the pelvis, not round the waist. When both groins are to be bandaged, a turn of ascending spica on one alternates with a turn of descending spica on the other; after each pair of turns a complete circular turn is made round the pelvis.

Bandages of special shape are used for certain parts of the body. The

stitching the middle of a 4-foot (1·2-metre) strip of roller bandage to the

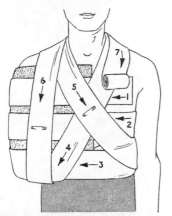

FIG. 46.—Bandage to fix a dressing on the chest, and cover in the arm. In actual practice a wider bandage would be used, and the turns would overlap. For clearness they are here shown separated.

four-tailed bandage is made for the jaw or the crown of the head by tearing a 4-foot (1·2-metre) -strip of roller bandage up the middle from both ends, leaving 4 inches (10 cm.) untorn in the

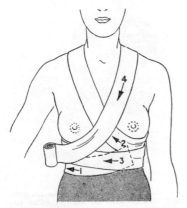

FIG. 47.—Bandage to support the breasts. A wide bandage is used. After each pair of turns beneath the breasts a circle to fix is taken round the waist.

centre ; it is applied in the same manner as the two triangular bandages shown in Fig. 36. The *T-shaped bandage* (Fig. 59 *a*) for the fork is made by

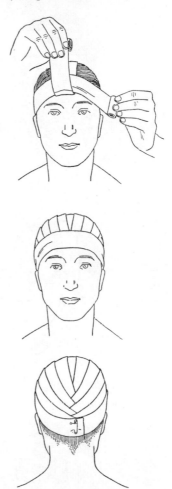

FIG. 48.—Capelline Bandage for head. Two bandages are stitched end to end. The bandage is rolled off one to the other till one roller is half as large again as the other. The larger part circles round the head close above the eyebrows and ears, and low down on the back of the head, binding down at each turn a strip of the other, which passes alternately backward and forward on either side.

end of a similar strip which is torn up the middle for the greater part of its length; the untorn strip forms a waist belt, the divided part passes down through the fork and its ends are pinned to the part that forms the waist belt. The *many-tailed* bandage (Fig. 59 *b*) for the

several 4-foot (1·2-metre) strips, each of which overlaps one-half of that

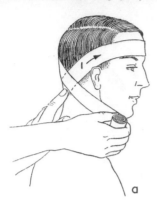

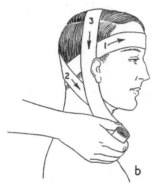

FIG. 49.—Bandage for head (trefoil). This consists essentially of three turns repeated in order. *a* shows commencement on the nape of the neck and first turn ; *b* shows second and third turns, the bandage next passing below chin and round to nape of neck ; *c* shows the gradual covering in of head ; and *d* a further stage. To fix all, a final turn in the position of the first should be made low down on the nape of the neck behind and close above the eyebrows in front.

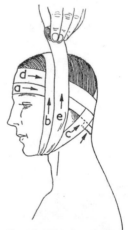

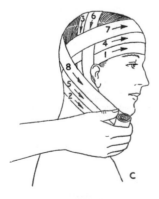

FIG. 50.—Same bandage (trefoil) from the other side. Shows that the vertical turns pass behind the ear on one side, in front of it on the other. When bandage is used to cover in one ear, the first turn should pass round the other side of the head, as shown. This bandage cannot be used to cover in the part of the head shown bare in Fig. 49 *d*, for which the capelline bandage or a four-tailed bandage may be used.

abdomen is made by stitching a strip of roller bandage down the middle of

below ; shorter strips are used for fractured or painful limbs.

Plaster bandages.—When a very rigid support is required, calico roller

bubbles cease to rise from them, and then, being applied wet, set quite

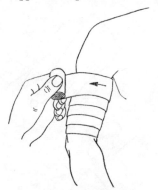

FIG. 51.—Simple spiral for arm.

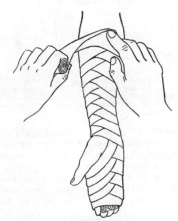

FIG. 52.—Spiral with reverses for hand and forearm.

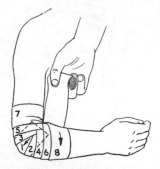

FIG. 53.—Spica for elbow.

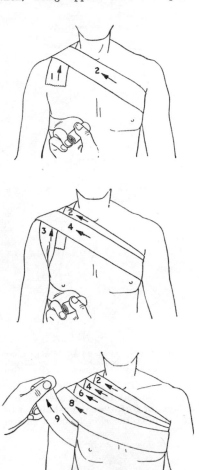

FIG. 54.—Spica for shoulder or armpit.

hard and can be worn for months; or they are painted with waterglass,

bandages are rubbed with plaster of Paris in powder, dipped in water till

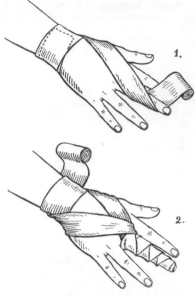

FIG. 57.—Bandage for finger. It starts round wrist for the purpose of fixing, passes in an open spiral down to the point of the finger (1), then upwards again as a spiral with reverse at each turn (2), and ends round wrist.

FIG. 55.—Bandage for closed fist, in which a pad of wool should be placed. There are alternate loops round wrist and round knuckles. Four stages.

which also sets hard. A piece of lint or layer of cotton-wool must always be placed next the skin before a plaster

bandage is applied. Great care is necessary that plaster bandages are put on smoothly, so as not to press upon any one place and so possibly produce an ulcer, and also that they are applied without stretching, so that they may not be too tight. The part to be

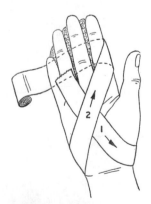

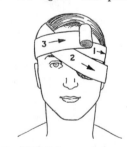

FIG. 58.—Bandage for eye ; turns pass alternately round forehead and down over eye.

bandaged must be supported so that the bandage can pass freely round without moving it ; and it must remain motionless for twenty to thirty minutes after the bandage is applied, so that the latter may harden.

FIG. 56.—Method of ' fixing ' bandage before commencing spiral with reverses for hand.

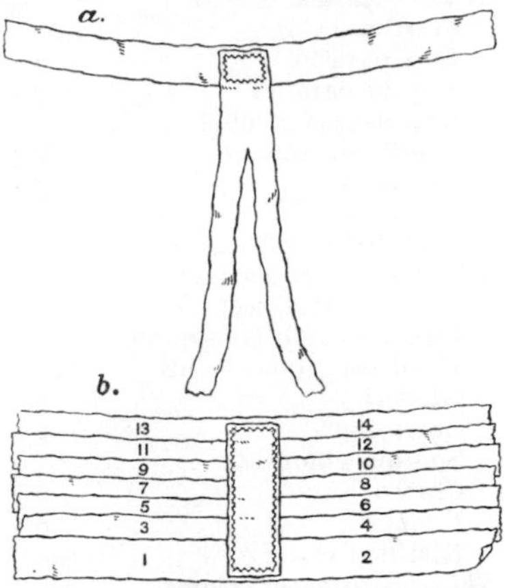

FIG. 59.—Two special bandages. *a*, T-bandage ; *b*, many-tailed bandage ; the central strip is placed behind the part to be bandaged, and the numbers indicate the order in which the 'tails' of the bandage are applied.

The various forms of elastic bandages are treated under VEINS, DISEASES OF.

BANTI'S DISEASE (*see* SPLENIC ANÆMIA).

BARAGNOSIS means the inability on the part of a patient to recognize that an object placed in the hand has weight, a condition due to disease of the brain.

BARANY'S TEST is a test for gauging the efficiency of the balancing mechanism (the vestibular apparatus) by applying hot or cold air or water to the external ear.

BARBER'S ITCH (*see* SYCOSIS).

BARBITONE, or DIETHYL-MALONYL-UREA, also known as VERONAL, is one of the barbiturate group of drugs. It has a prolonged action, lasting for 10 to 20 hours. The dose is 0·3 to 0·6 G. (5 to 10 grains). Caution must be exercised in taking barbitone or any of its derivatives, because of the danger of over-dosage, and of habit-formation.

BARBITURATES.—The barbiturate drugs, which are all derivatives of bar-bituric acid (malonyl-urea), form one of the most extensive series of sedative, hypnotic, and anæsthetic drugs at present in use. The more important ones, with their duration of action and dosage, are listed in Table 4.

BARIUM SULPHATE is a heavy white powder used in X-ray diagnosis

	Approved or *British Pharmacopœia* Name	Proprietary Name	Dose	Approximate Duration of Action in Hours
Long acting	Phenobarbitone	Gardenal; Luminal	30 to 120 mg.	12 to 24
	Phenobarbitone sodium	Gardenal sodium; Luminal sodium	60 to 200 mg. intramuscularly	12 to 24
	Barbitone	Veronal	250 to 500 mg.	10 to 20
	Barbitone sodium	Medinal; Veronal sodium	250 to 500 mg.	8 to 16
Intermediate acting	Allobarbitone	Dial	100 to 200 mg.	8 to 10
	Butobarbitone	Soneryl	100 to 200 mg.	8 to 10
	Amylobarbitone	Amytal	100 to 200 mg.	6 to 8
	Pentobarbitone	Nembutal	100 to 200 mg.	6 to 8
Short acting	Cyclobarbitone	Phanodorm	100 to 200 mg.	4 to 6
	Quinalbarbitone	Seconal	100 to 200 mg.	4 to 6
	Hexobarbitone	Cyclonal; Evipan	250 to 500 mg.	3 to 4

TABLE 4.—Dosage and Duration of Action of the Barbiturates (*The Practitioner*).

The mass of barium forms an opaque shadow and shows the outline of the cavity in which it lies. Thus the physician can see the size and position of the stomach in an X-ray photograph, or can trace a meal in its passage through the bowels.

BARLEY-WATER is a beverage made by allowing 2 ounces (57 g.) of pearly barley to simmer for two hours with a quart (1 litre) of water, then adding sugar and lemon to flavour, and straining.

BARLOW'S DISEASE is another term for infantile scurvy. It is so-called after Sir Thomas Barlow (1845–1945), the distinguished English pædiatrician, whose classical paper published in 1883 gave the first clear-cut description of infantile scurvy. Previously it had been confused with rickets.

BARRIER CREAMS are substances applied to the skin before work to prevent damage to the skin by irritants handled at work. They are also used in medicine : e.g., for the prevention of bedsores and napkin rashes.

There are three main types of barrier creams :—

A **dust barrier** to protect the skin against sensitizing dusts and against substances which, if absorbed, will produce systemic poisoning.

A **water-repellent barrier** for those whose hands are constantly exposed to water, alkalis, and water-soluble oils.

An **oil-repellent or water-miscible barrier**, which is a protective against oils, greases and solvents, and which facilitates their removal without the use of abrasives or oil solvents.

The following formulæ, prepared by the barrier substances subcommittee of the *British Pharmacopœia Codex* revision committee are now in wide use :

Dust barrier :

Casein (Rennet finely powdered)	3
Sodium alginate	2
Glycerin	6
Stearic acid	10
Triethanolamine	1·55
Chlorocresol	0·2
Phenol	0·5
Distilled water	to 100

Water-repellent barrier :

Hard paraffin	25
Soft paraffin	11·75
Liquid paraffin	3·5
Cetostearyl alcohol	5
Triethanolamine	0·7
Stearic acid	1·8
Chlorocresol	0·2
Distilled water	to 100

Water-repellent barrier :

Kaolin (sterilized)	20
Fuller's earth (200 mesh)	3
Hard soap (powdered)	12
Glycerin	6
Stearic acid	2
Sodium chloride	1
Chlorocresol	0·2
Phenol	0·5
Distilled water	to 100

Skin-conditioning cream :

Monostearin, self-emulsifying	10
Glycerin	6
Triethanolamine ricinoleate	1
Wool alcohols	6
Chlorocresol	0·2
Oleyl alcohol	3
Distilled water	to 100

The skin-conditioning cream is used after work if the hands are dry and degreased.

Silicones (*q.v.*), which are water repellent, are being used increasingly as barrier creams.

The hands should be clean and dry before applying a barrier cream. The cream should be applied sparingly to the whole of the hands, and not just rubbed into the palms. It is essential to coat the backs of the hands, paying special attention to the sides of the fingers and the webs between. The cream should be well rubbed into the nail folds and under the free edges of the nails. To get the full value from silicone creams, they should be applied twice daily for ten days before exposing the hands to irritants ; after this a once-daily application should be sufficient.

A point which is being increasingly emphasized by the experts is that the use of barrier creams must not be allowed to lead to any slackening in the attention paid to other more important protective measures, such as standards of cleanliness in workshops and the wearing of protective clothing.

BASAL METABOLISM (*see* META-BOLISM).

BASEDOW'S DISEASE is another name for exophthalmic goitre or Graves's disease.

BASILIC VEIN (βασιλικός, royal) is the prominent vein which runs from near the bend of the elbow upwards along the inner side of the upper arm. It is generally the vein opened in venesection for blood-letting.

BASILICON OINTMENT (βασιλικός, royal) is an old name for an ointment of resin, lard, wax, and almond oil.

BASOPHILIA is a term applied to the bluish appearance under the microscope of immature red blood corpuscles when stained by certain dyes. This appearance, with the blue areas collected in points, is seen in lead poisoning, and the condition is called punctate basophilia. The term basophilia may also mean an increase in the numbers of basophil cells in the blood.

BAT EARS is the term commonly applied to prominent ears. The condition may be familial, but this is by no means the rule. Strapping the ears firmly back has no effect and is merely a waste of time and an embarrassment to the child. In cases in which the condition is proving a definite embarrassment to the child, it can be rectified by plastic surgery.

BATHER'S ITCH, also called SWIMMER'S ITCH, WATER ITCH, and SCHISTOSOME DERMATITIS, is the term given to a blotchy rash on the skin occurring in those bathing in water which is infested with the larvæ of certain trematode worms known as *Schistosomes* (*see* PARASITES). The worm is parasitic in snails. The skin rash is caused by penetration of the skin by the free-swimming larval cercaria. Bather's itch is common in many parts of the world, including U.S.A., Canada, Central and South America, Australasia, Malaysia and Japan. It has also been found in Wales, France, and Germany.

BATHS.—The main action of water on the skin is as a vehicle for heat, and

baths act largely either by extracting heat from, or adding it to, the body. The sweat glands of the skin excrete some 30 ounces (850 ml.) of water daily, containing about one-twentieth part of the nitrogenous waste of the body, and their excretory activity may be greatly increased by baths of high temperature. Baths also exert a mechanical effect by virtue of the fact that water is slightly denser than the human body and therefore causes the body to float on its surface. They also exert an important psychological effect, the heat of a warm bath and the buoyancy of the water allowing a paralysed patient to perform movements of which he thought he was no longer capable.

A. WATER BATHS.—(1) COLD.— This is a bath about 60° F. or 16° C. (cold tap temperature). It should be taken while the body is warm, and its daily use is a healthy habit and helps to prevent colds. The average person should go straight from bed to a plunge bath of the above temperature; or, if preferred, a warm bath of about 100° F. or 38° C. may be first taken, and then a cold douche or sponge from the cold-water-tap. The cold bath should last from a few seconds to two minutes, and the warm bath preceding it up to ten minutes. The bather should rub himself vigorously in both baths, and must at once rub himself dry with a coarse towel and quickly dress. During drying the skin becomes rosy, and a delightful warm glow comes on and lasts several hours. Persons whose blood-vessels do not react properly to changes of temperature are apt to suffer one or other of two things after a bath. The 'reaction' is due to a quick contraction, followed by a moderate dilatation of the blood-vessels in the skin, and in persons with poor 'tone' of the arteries, either an excessive dilatation follows a hot bath, which the cold bath cannot overcome, and the blood being unduly cooled in the full vessels of the skin, a 'chill' results; or the vessels contract too firmly after the cold bath, so that cold hands and feet result. The latter can be got over by taking the cold bath in two stages, first a tepid bath on getting out of bed, and then a sponge or douche from the cold tap. Even the weakest person may get part of the benefits of a cold bath without

4 a

any ill effect, by taking a tepid bath at 90° F. or 32° C., and cooling it down by running in tap water in the course of five minutes to 75° F. or 24° C., rubbing the body and legs vigorously all the while, or having them rubbed by an attendant, and afterwards drying rapidly. Very cold baths must be avoided by those with a tendency to apoplexy.

(2) TEPID.—A tepid bath is one slightly below the body temperature, viz. about 90° F. or 32° C. It is the convenient temperature for large baths. Prolonged tepid baths have a soothing effect. The patient is placed in a bath at 95° F. or 35° C., cooled down slowly to about 92° F. or 33·3° C. ; at first he remains in it for half an hour and on subsequent days gradually longer, up to eight hours daily.

(3) WARM.—A warm bath is one ranging from about the body temperature, 99° F. or 37° C., to about 110° F. or 43° C. Water at 115° F. (46° C.) can just be borne by the hand, but not by the whole body. A warm bath quickens the pulse, and lowers the blood-pressure. It also causes free perspiration. A warm bath of about 104° F. (40° C.) for ten or fifteen minutes, followed by a cold douche, in the robust, is one of the best means of preventing the stiffness which follows prolonged muscular effort, or of warding off a cold. But very warm baths are dangerous to those suffering from disease of the heart.

B. VAPOUR BATHS.—(1) AROMATIC.—The patient sits in a special box, his head protruding through a hole in the lid, while steam from water containing fir-balsam, lavender, etc., circulates round him. Beyond acting as a hot bath this form is of no therapeutic value.

(2) RUSSIAN BATHS have much the same effect as warm-water baths. The bath is generally taken in a room which is filled with vapour, but as good an effect may be obtained from a cabinet, or a tent of blankets, in which the patient sits on a chair some inches over boiling water. In a vapour bath 120° F. (49° C.) can be borne readily, and the person should remain in the vapour until he breaks into a copious perspiration, usually about fifteen or twenty minutes. Subsequently a cold douche or bath should be taken, according to the state of his ' reaction '. In Russia it is a common practice immediately

after the vapour bath to pour a stream of ice-cold water all over the surface of the body.

C. DRY BATHS. — (1) HOT-AIR BATHS may be taken as the TURKISH or ROMAN bath, in a specially constructed building heated by pipes in the walls, with tepid room, hot room, washing room, and cooling room, through which the bather goes in succession. A hot bath may also be taken in an electric-light cabinet, where the person sits exposed to brilliant light and heat till he sweats copiously, when he takes a cold-water bath.

Such a bath may also be given in bed, the patient lying under a curved wire shield. In hospitals the under-surface of the shield is provided with numerous electric-light bulbs which speedily raise the temperature of the enclosed air to a high degree (Fig. 60).

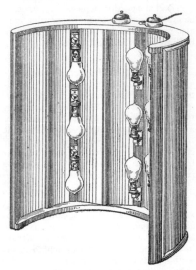

FIG. 60.—Radiant heat bath with electric-light bulbs under curved asbestos shield to cover patient.

The duration of a Roman bath is about two hours, and it leaves a feeling of great freshness. In either of these baths one may lose 6 pounds (2·7 kg.) at one time by sweating. They are useful for reducing weight, and for rheumatism, while the hot-air bath, given in bed for fifteen minutes at a time, promotes the action of the skin in Bright's disease. The electric-light bath can be given in bed, the lights being underneath a curved shield, 5 feet (152 cm.) long, which covers the patient, and there are also smaller shields for single limbs. A dry temperature of 200° F. (93° C.) can be borne without discomfort for a quarter of an hour, and has excellent results in chronic rheumatism, rheumatoid arthritis, and sciatica. When a sick person is being treated by such a high temperature bath, it is necessary that his pulse should be frequently examined, in case the heart's action should become enfeebled.

(2) SAND BATHS are used for rheumatic conditions, the sand being made very hot to purify it, and heaped on the patient when moderately cool.

D. MEDICINAL BATHS. — (1) ALKALINE BATHS are used to soften the skin in certain skin diseases like general eczema. Six ounces (170 G.) of washing soda are added to 30 gallons (135 litres) of tepid water.

(2) BRAN BATHS are used to soothe general irritation of the skin. Four pounds (1·8 kg.) of bran are boiled and the liquor added to a tepid bath, in which the patient soaks for half an hour.

(3) PEAT and MUD BATHS are used generally for rheumatism at various spas. The patient is covered with a layer of warmed mud, such as fango, lies in it for perhaps twenty minutes, and is then washed clean by a cold douche. Such baths can be taken at a much higher temperature than water baths (102° to 112° F. (39° to 44° C.)).

(4) MUSTARD BATHS are used for the feet to check colds, and for the whole body as a good general stimulant. For this, a handful of mustard is made into a paste with cold water and stirred into the warm bath.

(5) PINE-NEEDLE BATHS are pleasant and stimulating. They are prepared by adding to a tepid bath the water in which several pounds of fresh pine needles have been boiled.

(6) SEA-WATER BATHS are best taken in the sea. Brine baths are found at various spas. Failing that, about 9 pounds (4 kg.) of common salt are added to 30 gallons (135 litres) of water. The effect is very stimulating. Such baths are used in cases of chronic rheumatism. They are also of value in the treatment of the so-called decubitus ulcers which are liable to occur in patients with spinal cord injuries. The recommended strength for this purpose is 5 per cent. crude rock salt and 2·5 per cent. magnesium sulphate.

(7) CARBONIC ACID BATHS are used for their stimulating effect upon the skin and upon the body generally. They may be administered by the aid of water which is naturally effervescent, as at Royat, St. Moritz, Spa, Marienbad, where they are specially in vogue for the treatment of heart disorders ; or the carbonic acid may be allowed to escape from cylinders in the bathwater ; or weak formic acid is mixed with the water in which small cotton bags of washing soda are placed. Such effervescent baths, especially when taken warm, have a marked action in increasing the circulation in the skin and diminishing general arterial blood-pressure.

(8) FOAM BATHS contain some soapy substance such as an extract of quillaia bark which on stirring produces a copious froth. They usually contain also some substance which adds to the frothy effect by development of carbonic acid gas, and they then have the effects mentioned above under carbonic acid baths.

(9) SULPHUR BATHS are used for the presence in the water of sulphuretted hydrogen, which not only stimulates the skin but is to some extent absorbed. The bath may be prepared artificially by adding from ¼ to ½ pound (112 to 224 G.) of sulphuret of potassium or of yellow sulphur to 30 gallons (135 litres) of hot water. Sulphur baths are specially used in the treatment of skin diseases and in rheumatism.

E. ELECTRIC BATHS may be given in earthenware, stone, or wooden baths. The bath is filled with tepid water, in which the patient lies. An electrode hangs in the water at either end, not touching the patient, and a moderate current is passed through the water. This bath is useful in cases of debility and neurasthenia. (*See* ELECTRICITY IN MEDICINE.)

B.C.G. VACCINE.—B.C.G. (*Bacille Calmette-Guérin*) vaccine, which was introduced in France in 1908, is the only vaccine that has produced significant immunity against the tubercle bacillus and at the same time has proved safe enough for use in human subjects. The original work of Calmette and Guérin has now been amply confirmed by investigators in many parts of the world. There are two main indications for the use of B.C.G. vaccine : (a) for the protection of new-born infants or children exposed to special risks of infection ; (b) for the immunization of adolescents or young adults, such as nurses, who are known to have developed no natural immunity to tuberculosis and who are exposed to particularly heavy infections.

BEARBERRY, or *Arctostaphylos uva-ursi*, is an old remedy used in chronic inflammation of the bladder, in doses of $\frac{1}{2}$ ounce (14 ml.) or more of the infusion.

BEAT ELBOW, BEAT HAND, and BEAT KNEE are terms applied by miners to an inflamed condition with swelling of the elbow, hand, or knee. The condition is particularly common in miners, but occurs in other trades also from constant pressure and the ingraining of particles of dirt, caused by the constant use of a tool or pressure in resting on the joints at work. The condition sometimes proceeds to suppuration, but usually subsides under soothing and antiseptic applications.

BED.—The bed used in cases of sickness should consist of an iron *frame* of at least 6 feet (183 cm.) in length and 3 feet 3 inches to 3 feet 6 inches (99 to 107 cm.) in width, and should be provided with a stiff *wire mattress*. A piece of canvas or felt, fixed to the mattress, should form a *mattress cover* to prevent rusting of the wire. Upon this is a mattress of wool, or, preferably, of hair. The mattress should have a loose cover of cotton, which can be washed from time to time as required. Over the mattress is placed a sheet which is tucked in firmly beneath the mattress all round to form the *under sheet*. The bed is completed by the *upper sheet* and *blankets*, varying in number according to the season of the year, and by a light *bedcover*. Two thin *pillows*, each covered by a linen or cotton pillow-slip, should be supplied, but it is important both in health and

in disease that the support for the head should not be too high, and the pillows should simply be sufficient to fill up the distance between the head and shoulder when the patient lies on the side.

The bed should stand with its head towards the wall and the foot towards the centre of the room or ward, and there should be a free passage up either side for access by the attendants. In some diseases and injuries the bed requires special modification. In all cases confined to bed for longer than a few days a *draw sheet* is required. The draw sheet is formed as follows : An ordinary sheet is folded lengthwise so that the folded sheet is sufficiently wide to extend from the patient's shoulders to behind the knees. Between the folds of this is placed a mackintosh sheet one yard (0.9 metre) square, or it is often more convenient to place the mackintosh sheet beneath the draw sheet, directly upon the under sheet. This folded sheet is pushed at one end under the mattress, carried across the bed, and the superfluous length is folded up and pushed out of the way under the mattress at the other side. From time to time the sheet is pulled through beneath the patient towards the shorter end, thus bringing a fresh piece of sheet beneath the back. In *rheumatic fever*, *Bright's disease*, and other conditions in which the patient perspires profusely, the patient lies directly upon and is covered by a blanket, as the woollen material absorbs the perspiration better than sheets. In cases of *fracture* of a lower limb it is necessary to make the bed more rigid, and for this purpose boards are placed across the wire mattress. In cases of *bronchitis* it is frequently necessary to erect a tent over the bed, to cut off draughts or to retain a moist atmosphere produced by a steam kettle. This can be effected by a light screen placed round the bed and covered with a blanket.

In cases of paralysis, prolonged fever, and other *devitalizing conditions*, the patient may require to be placed upon a mattress which supports his body evenly instead of allowing pressure to come upon its most projecting parts. For this purpose a *water-bed* (*q.v.*) may be employed, or, better, an *air-bed* (*q.v.*). The water-bed is filled with warm water after it is placed upon the mattress, and care is taken to expel all bubbles of air by stroking it with the hand towards the inlet through which the water is poured. The pneumatic or air bed is much more easily managed, and is pumped up by an ordinary bicycle pump from time to time without the necessity of removing the patient. The under sheet is laid directly on top of the water-bed, or air-bed.

A *bed rest* must sometimes be provided for patients unable to breathe comfortably in a recumbent position, or in order to change the position from time to time of a patient permanently confined to bed. For this purpose, four or five pillows may be placed behind the patient's back, or, preferably, a rest, consisting of a horizontal part hinged to a cane-backed rest resembling the back of a chair and supported on a strut, is used and furnished with a couple of pillows. In order to give a still further change of position, a *bed table* may be used. This is supported on four legs some 3 feet 6 inches (107 cm.) high and is of sufficient width (about 4 feet (120 cm.)) to enable each pair of legs to stand on either side of the bed. Upon this the patient can lean forward.

BED BUG, or *Cimex lectularius*, is a wingless, blood-sucking insect, parasitic on man. The bed bug remains hidden during the day in cracks in walls and floors, and in beds. Eggs hatch out into larvæ in 6 to 10 days, which become adult within about 6 weeks. Various agents have been used to disinfect premises, such as sulphur dioxide, ethylene oxide mixed with carbon dioxide, hydrogen cyanide and heavy naphtha. D.D.T. is most effective for this purpose.

BED CHANGING.—Two methods are adopted for changing the bedclothes without removing the sick person from the bed. One of these, called medical changing, is generally applicable when the upper part of the body or head is affected. The other, known as surgical changing, is generally used when the lower part of the body is affected or when the lower limbs are the site of fracture or similar disability.

MEDICAL CHANGING.—The pillows

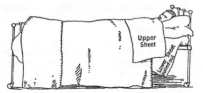

FIG. 61.—Sheet changing, first stage.

are first removed ; the patient is then turned upon one side (right) near the right edge of the bed (Fig. 62). The

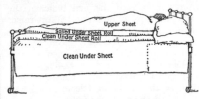

FIG. 62.—Patient turned on right side and sheets rolled against his back.

soiled sheet with the draw sheet is then rolled up lengthwise from the right edge of the bed until the roll lies against the patient's back. The fresh sheet is made into a roll lengthwise ; one edge is tucked in under the right edge of the mattress and the sheet is unrolled across the bed towards the left until the roll lies alongside the roll of soiled

FIG. 63.—Patient turned on left side, and sheet rolls pulled through beneath him to be spread out.

sheet. The patient is next turned on the back and then on the left side near the left-hand side of the bed (Fig. 63). He now lies upon the unrolled portion of the fresh sheet. The soiled sheet, which now lies behind his back, is pulled off the bed and the roll of fresh sheet is unrolled and its edge tucked beneath the left-hand edge of the mattress. During this procedure the patient remains covered by the upper sheet and blankets. A fresh draw sheet is introduced by similar procedure. The pillows, having been placed in fresh pillow-slips, are again set under the patient's head.

SURGICAL CHANGING.—In some cases the under sheet is more conveniently changed from the top or bottom of the bed. To do this the edges of the soiled sheet are pulled out all round from under the edges of the mattress. The sheet is then pulled down under the patient's hips, and, finally, from under the legs. The fresh sheet is now rolled up from top and bottom to the middle, and the double roll is pushed through from the side of the bed beneath the patient's hips while an attendant raises these slightly from the bed. By gently easing up the patient's shoulders the upper half of the sheet is unrolled and tucked in at the top of the mattress, and by similarly elevating his legs slightly the lower half is unrolled and tucked in at the foot of the bed.

CHANGING DRAW SHEET.—When it is necessary to insert a fresh draw sheet, the draw sheet is folded up as in the method for changing the under sheet and is introduced either by rolling the patient over or slightly elevating his hips. When the draw sheet requires to be replaced frequently, it is more convenient to place the square of mackintosh on the under sheet and to insert the draw sheet above it separately.

CHANGING NIGHTDRESS.—When it is necessary to change the nightdress of a person confined to bed, the fresh nightdress should be warmed; one arm is then slipped out of the soiled nightdress and inserted into the corresponding sleeve of the fresh nightdress. The soiled nightdress is then slipped over the patient's head and removed, and the fresh one is slipped on and arranged. This should be carried out without removing the upper sheet and blankets. In the case of patients too ill to be much disturbed, the nightdress may conveniently be slit down the back.

BED SORES are areas of inflamed skin, tending to ulcerate, which appear upon the body or limbs of those long confined to bed, and especially of those much weakened by disease.

Causes. — Sores seldom occur in vigorous persons confined to bed by a fractured limb or other minor cause. They appear in those who have not

much fat between bones and skin, in the aged, in those suffering from prostrating weakness, like that of typhoid fever, and especially in those whose nervous system is at fault and the nutrition of whose skin is consequently impaired, for example in persons with fractured spine, or with degeneration of the spinal cord, or in general paralytics. The direct cause may be wrinkles left in the bed-clothes, discharges allowed to soil the invalid's back, and want of daily observation of the places where sores are likely to form.

Symptoms.—Very often the invalid feels no pain, sometimes he complains only of a hard place or wrinkle in the bed - clothes. The sites where sores commonly form are where the bones show plainly through the skin in the lower part of the back, on the heels, on the haunch, on one ankle, on the elbows, or on the shoulder blades. At first, for one or two days, there is redness of the skin over a prominence, which quickly turns blue and dusky. Then a black slough forms, and comes away, leaving a raw surface, which widens if not carefully treated.

Treatment. — The best treatment is preventive, by keeping the patient's back scrupulously clean and dry, by washing it daily with soap and water, sponging it with spirit in order to dry and harden the skin, and, finally, dusting it with a powder of zinc oxide or boric acid (or instead of using spirit and dusting powder, the skin may be preserved by rubbing in daily a little zinc oxide ointment) ; by examining night and morning for any sign of redness ; and especially by changing the invalid's position, so as to relieve the various prominences from constant pressure. Recently it has been reported that better results are obtained from the twice-daily smearing of the skin with barrier creams containing silicone.

If redness appear over a prominent part, this must be wrapped in dry cotton-wool and the patient at once put on an air ring or air bed. Superficial sores are treated with 1 per cent. gentian violet or zinc and castor-oil cream. Deeper sores can be treated with cetrimide. When a black, hard slough is forming, and the surface is breaking, infection is almost invariably present and the type of dressing must be changed. Amongst those that have been recommended are : cod-liver oil ; picric acid solutions ; tannic acid solutions ; eusol ; one of the flavine group of antiseptics, *e.g.* proflavine, flavazole. Irradiation of the affected area with ultra-violet light has also been used, in addition to one of these dressings. Whatever dressing is used, sloughs are removed as they become loosened. When the area has become clean again, a return is made to dry dressings.

BEEF-TEA (*see* NITROGENOUS FOODS) forms a valuable stimulant for invalids, although, when it has been boiled for a prolonged period, the protein matters are coagulated and left in the meat.

To prepare beef-tea take 1 pound (454 G.) of lean beef, cut into shreds, and place it in a jar with 1 pint (570 ml.) of cold water. Allow to stand for about half an hour, then tightly cover the jar and place it in a saucepan of water. Heat gradually, but for the first hour do not allow the temperature to exceed 167° F. (75° C.). From time to time stir the mixture and squeeze the lumps of meat against the side of the jar. At the end of an hour bring the mixture to the boil and then remove it at once from the stove. The beef-tea is then poured off, not strained. The residue is then squeezed firmly with a wooden spoon in a coarse strainer and the juice so obtained added to the tea, which is then set aside to cool. The fat which settles on the top is removed with a warm spoon. Beef-tea is usually administered in quantities of one teacupful at a time, *i.e.* 5 or 6 ounces (140 to 170 ml.).

BEE STINGS (*see* BITES).

BELLADONNA (*see* ATROPINE).

BELL'S PARALYSIS is paralysis of the muscles of the face on one or both sides, causing inability to close the eye, to smile, to show the teeth, and the like, on the affected side. The paralysis is due to damage of the seventh or facial nerve. When due to inflammation, it is often temporary, and complete recovery may ensue, but when due to a wound in front of the ear, to fracture of the base of the skull, or to a stroke of apoplexy, it is apt to be permanent, although apoplectic paralysis of the face is more favourable for recovery than that due to injury. (*See* PARALYSIS.)

BELTS AND BINDERS are commonly worn, not only as articles of dress, but as supports and curative agents.

Uses.—Flannel or linen binders are worn by infants for warmth, as a support to the body, and because, for some time after birth, the region of the navel remains thin and weak ; such a binder should extend from the middle of the chest well on to the hips. Women, after labour, wear a binder because it gives a feeling of support ; it should be of similar extent to the infant's, and it is very important that it should be as tight as possible below, and very loose in its upper half. In the case of both infants and mothers after labour, however, the practice of using binders is being gradually discarded unless there is some special indication for them.

Narrower flannel binders give great comfort in cases of lumbago when worn next the skin. Persons of all ages, with weak and easily tired backs, get great support from wearing a broad belt round the waist. When, however, the upper part of the body is subject to great muscular efforts, as in athletes and navvies, it is a great mistake to encircle the waist tightly with a narrow belt, which ought to run round in the hollow on either side between the summit of the haunch-bone and the hip-joint, and so give full play to the abdominal muscles and those of the loins. Elderly persons who have a large, flabby abdomen often suffer from a form of dyspepsia due to want of support of the abdominal organs, which is relieved speedily by wearing a broad, shaped belt round the lower part of the abdomen, or corsets with such a belt attached. This abdominal belt should be tight in its lower part, and loose above the navel, to allow free movement of the stomach in digestion.

BEMEGRIDE is a drug which antagonizes the hypnotic and respiratory depressant action of the barbiturates, and has proved of value in the treatment of barbiturate poisoning.

BENDS (*see* CAISSON DISEASE).

BENEDICT'S TEST for glycosuria (*see* URINE).

BENNETT'S FRACTURE, so-called after an Irish surgeon, Edward Hallaran Bennett (1837–1907), is a longitudinal fracture of the first metacarpal bone, which also involves the carpo-metacarpal joint.

BENZAMINE HYDROCHLORIDE is a substance closely resembling cocaine both in chemical composition and in action upon the body. It has two advantages over cocaine : it can be boiled, and so sterilized for injection, without being destroyed, and it has four-tenths the toxicity of cocaine. It has, however, a greater irritant, and a slightly less anæsthetic, effect.

BENZATHINE PENICILLIN (*see* PENICILLIN).

BENZEDRINE is a proprietary name for amphetamine sulphate (*see* AMPHETAMINE).

BENZENE HEXACHLORIDE is an insecticide which acts more rapidly than D.D.T. but not for such a long time. When first sprayed it is 10 times as toxic to insects as D.D.T., but its action wears off in 3 to 4 months, whereas that of D.D.T. will persist for up to a year.

BENZINE, or BENZOL, is a colourless volatile liquid used as a remedy for tapeworm, and in leukæmia.

BENZOCAINE is a white powder with soothing properties used as a sedative for inflamed and painful surfaces.

BENZOIC ACID is an antiseptic. It, or benzoate of sodium, is given internally in doses of 5 to 15 grains (300 mg. to 1 G.) in cases of suppuration along the urinary tract, especially in

inflammation of the bladder with decomposition of the urine. Other acids are neutralized in the blood, but benzoic acid is excreted as hippuric acid and acidifies the urine. (For benzoin, *see* BALSAM.) It is also used as a preservative in certain foodstuffs and beverages, *e.g.* fruit cordials, pickles.

BENZTHIADIAZINES are a group of recently introduced diuretics which are effective when taken by mouth. They act by virtue of inhibiting the re-absorption of sodium and chloride in the renal tubules. Chlorothiazide was the first member of this group to be introduced.

BENZYL BENZOATE is widely used as a lotion in the treatment of scabies.

BENZYLPENICILLIN (*see* PENICILLIN).

BERGER RHYTHM is the term applied to normal rhythmical changes of electric potential in the brain. The electrical ' waves ' can be recorded graphically. A person with epilepsy has abnormal waves.

BERIBERI, called by the Japanese KARKÉ, is a disease found in Japan, Malaya, China, Manila, Fiji Islands, India, West Africa, Western Australia, and round the Gulf of Mexico, and consists in inflammation of the nerves all over the body. (*See* NEURITIS.)

Causes.—It is found among those living in certain parts of the tropics, whose diet consists mainly of highly milled rice. It also occurs in Newfoundland and Labrador, where the inhabitants' main item of diet is white wheaten flour. In both groups of population the removal of the husk of rice and of the wheat berry leaves the diet very deficient in vitamin B_I. It is the lack of this vitamin that causes the trouble.

Symptoms. — The affected person becomes, first of all, for some days feverish and weak ; then, though feeling better in general health, he gradually develops symptoms of paralysis, especially of hands and feet, dropsy, palpitation of the heart, and loss of sensation in large areas of skin, especially about the legs. These pass off, in general, in the course of some weeks, and the sufferer gradually recovers health, or occasionally they get worse, and he dies from cardiac failure.

Treatment.—The treatment required is large doses of vitamin B_1 (aneurine), plenty of nourishing food, and complete rest.

BERKEFELD FILTER is a candle-shaped filter made of diatomaceous earth. It restrains ordinary bacteria but lets through viruses.

BERRIES, POISONOUS.—As most berries in Britain are either red or blackish in colour when ripe, their colour is one of the simplest ways of distinguishing them.

Black poisonous berries.—One of the most poisonous of these is the *deadly nightshade* (*Atropa belladonna*) (Fig. 64). Three berries are sufficient to kill a

FIG. 64.—Atropa belladonna.

child. Ripening from July onwards, they are dull black in colour, often as large as a small marble, and surrounded by a persistent withered calyx. The plant usually grows in semi-shaded

sites and is up to three feet in height. Even more poisonous, but fortunately less common, is the *baneberry* (*Actæa spicata*) which grows in woods on limestone in Yorkshire, Lancashire, and Westmorland. The berries are nearly a quarter of an inch in diameter and grow on stems one or two feet long. More common is *Herb Paris* (*Paris quadrifolia*), which grows in semi-shaded sites, and has stems up to two feet high. The berries are up to a quarter of an inch in diameter and contain 16 to 20 dark-coloured seeds. The *buckthorn* (*Rhamnus cathartica*) and the *alder buckthorn* (*Rhamnus frangula*) (Fig. 65) are shrubs up to 20 feet in height which grow in woody thickets

FIG. 65.—Rhamnus frangula.

on peaty soil. The berries grow in clusters and are about the size of black-currants. Each berry contains four seeds. Only on unpruned *privets* (*Ligustrum vulgare* (Fig. 66) and *Ligustrum ovaliform*) are berries found in quantity. About the size of a pea, the berry has two chambers inside, usually with one or two seeds in each. These berries have caused fatal poisoning in children. The *cherry laurel* (*Prunus laurocerasus*), commonly grown in gardens and parks, produces in late summer small berries very like small black cherries except that the fruit stalk is short and rigid and the berries, up to about twelve in number, are borne along a common stalk four inches long. The *spurge laurel* (*Daphne laureola*), which grows

sparingly in woodlands in England, produces egg-shaped blue-black berries on

Fig. 66.—Ligustrum vulgare.

stems which grow to about four feet in
height. The *ivy* (*Hedera helix*) (Fig. 67)
produces berries about the size of a pea
which ripen in early spring.

Fig. 67.—Hedera helix.

Red poisonous berries.—These are
even more dangerous because their
colour is so much more attractive to
children. The *woody nightshade* or
bittersweet (*Solanum dulcamara*) (Fig.
68), which is common in South and Central England, is a straggling plant
which bears clusters of six to eight
bright-red translucent berries. These

114

are very like redcurrants except that
there is no tuft of old flower parts at

Fig. 68.—Solanum dulcamara.

the upper end of the fruit and they contain numerous seeds, compared with
the six or eight in the redcurrant. The
white bryony (*Bryonia dioica*) is another
scrambling plant of the wayside and
wasteland. It is most commonly found
in Southern England and is almost entirely absent in the North. The berry
is dull scarlet in colour, about a centimetre in diameter and contains three to
six large flat, yellow-and-black mottled
berries. The *black bryony* (*Tamus communis*) (Fig. 69) is another straggling

Fig. 69.—Tamus communis.

plant. The berries are bright crimson
in colour and grow in small bunches.

Superficially they are like redcurrants. The *cuckoo-pint* or *lords and ladies* (*Arum maculatum*) (Fig. 70), which

Fig. 70.—Arum maculatum.

grows in damp woodlands, sometimes in hedgerows, especially on basic soils, produces bright-red berries which ripen from August onwards. The berries, about the size of a pea, grow in clusters of eight to twenty at the upper end of a sturdy, naked, green stem about six to nine inches long, and bear three small marks at the apex and usually contain three brownish, rough-coated seeds. The *dwarf baytree* (*Daphne mezereum*) (Fig. 71), which is usually cul-

Fig. 71.—Daphne mezereum.

tivated in gardens because of its heavily scented, pink or purplish flowers from

January onwards, bears small clusters of red berries from August onwards. They may be mistaken for redcurrants but can be distinguished by the lack of a tuft of withered flower parts at the upper end of the fruit. The berry of the *yew* (*Taxus baccata*) (Fig. 72), which grows naturally in Southern Britain,

Fig. 72.—Taxus baccata.

and is planted widely elsewhere for ornament, ripens from August onwards. The pale, half-inch-long seed is half submerged in a soft, red, juicy cup. This fleshy cup, which has a sickly sweet taste, is not particularly poisonous, but the seed is highly poisonous.

[The nine illustrations in this section are reproduced by courtesy of L. Reeve & Co. Ltd., from *Illustrations of the British Flora*, fifth edition, by W. H. Fitch and W. G. Smith.]

BERYLLIOSIS is a disease of the lungs caused by the inhalation of particles of beryllium oxide.

BETHANIDINE is a hypotensive drug which acts by blocking the sympathetic nervous system.

BEZOAR is a concretion found in the stomach and intestines of animals, especially goats, which was formerly used as a remedy against poisoning. It is also occasionally found in man.

BICARBONATE OF SODA, or BAKING SODA. (*See* ALKALI.)

BIDET is a fixed sitz-bath raised on legs which is used for administering douches and enemas.

BILE is a thick, bitter, golden-brown or greenish-yellow fluid, secreted by the liver, and stored in the gall-bladder. It consists of water, mucus, brown and green pigments (bilirubin and biliverdin), salts of two complex acids (glycocholic and taurocholic acids), and some mineral salts, and it is discharged through the bile-ducts into the intestine, a few inches below the opening from the stomach. This discharge is constant, but is much increased shortly after food is taken, and again, some hours later, when the food is digested. Bile is partly an excretion of waste material thrown out by the liver, partly a secretion endowed with some functions in digestion, especially that of fats, and it further aids the absorption of nourishment from the food passing down the bowels, and prevents excessive decomposition by destroying various organisms, especially micrococci. About a pint to a quart is daily secreted in man, but the greater part of this is reabsorbed with the food, passes into the blood, and ultimately circulates back to the liver, to be again excreted, and so on.

Jaundice is a condition in which the flow of bile becomes obstructed, so that the bile is not poured into the intestine, but circulates in the blood. As a consequence, the bile pigments are deposited in the tissues, and the skin becomes yellow or olive-green, while, at the same time, the stools become grey or white and the urine dark. (*See* JAUNDICE.)

Bilious headache, or biliousness, is rather a vague term, applied either to migraine (*see* HEADACHE) or to the headache and vomiting which occur in acute catarrh of the stomach set up by errors in diet. (*See* DYSPEPSIA.)

Vomiting of bile occurs in the two last-named conditions, and also is a sign of obstruction of the bowels, but bile may be brought up in any case of persistent vomiting or retching.

BILHARZIA (*see* PARASITES).

BILIRUBIN is the chief pigment in human bile. It is derived from hæmoglobin (*q.v.*) which is the red pigment of the red blood corpuscles. The main site of manufacture of bilirubin is the

116

bone marrow, but it is also made in the liver, the spleen, and the lymph glands. When bile is passed into the intestine from the gall-bladder, part of the bilirubin is converted into stercobilin and excreted in the fæces. The remainder is reabsorbed into the bloodstream, and of this portion the bulk goes back to the liver to be re-excreted into the bile, whilst a small proportion is excreted in the urine as urobilinogen.

BILIVERDIN is the chief pigment of bile in carnivora. It is an oxidative derivative of bilirubin, and there is a small amount in human bile.

BINOVULAR TWINS is the term applied to twins who result from the fertilization of two separate ova.

BIOCHEMISTRY means the chemistry of living organisms and of vital processes.

BIOPSY means the removal and examination of tissue from the living body for diagnostic purposes. For example, a piece of a tumour may be cut out and examined to determine whether it is cancerous.

BIOTIN is one of the dozen or so vitamins included in the vitamin B complex. It is found in liver, eggs, and meat, and it is also synthesized by bacteria in the gut. Absorption from the gut is prevented by avidin, a constituent of egg-white. The daily requirement is small: a fraction of a milligramme daily. Gross deficiency results in disturbances of the skin, a smooth tongue and lassitude.

BIPP is a colloquial term used to designate an antiseptic and soothing paste applied to wounds and consisting of bismuth subnitrate, iodoform, and paraffin. It was much used in the war of 1914–18.

BIRD FANCIER'S LUNG (*see* PIGEON BREEDER'S LUNG.)

BIRTH (*see* LABOUR).—The average length of a child at birth is about 21 inches (53 cm.), and its weight 7 pounds

(3·2 kg.). A *stillborn* child is 'any child which has issued forth from its mother after the twenty-eighth week of pregnancy and which did not at any time after being completely expelled from its mother breathe or show any other sign of life'. *Premature birth* is one which takes place before the natural time (*see* PREGNANCY), but in which the child is capable of surviving. A birth which takes place so prematurely that the child must necessarily die is known as an abortion or *miscarriage* (*see* MISCARRIAGE).

BIRTH-MARKS are of various kinds. The most common are port-wine marks (*see* NÆVUS). Pigment spots are found, very often raised above the surface and more or less hairy, being then called moles (*see* MOLES).

BISACODYL, also known as DULCO-LAX, has the chemical formula : [2 - (4 : 4^1 - diaetoxydiphenylmethyl) pyridine]. It is a laxative which acts by stimulation of the nerve endings in the colon by direct contact with the mucous lining.

BISMUTH is a metal, of which the carbonate, subnitrate, salicylate, and oxychloride are used in medicine.

Uses.—In irritative and painful conditions of the stomach or of the bowels, *e.g.* when diarrhœa or vomiting is present, they have a marked sedative action. The salicylate of bismuth especially is used to check diarrhœa, the usual medicinal dose of it or of the subnitrate being about 20 grains (1·2 G.). Given internally, bismuth salts turn the stools black.

Externally, as dusting powder, they are used, both as a cosmetic and in eczema and other moist conditions of the skin, being commonly mixed, in equal proportions, with starch powder or oxide of zinc, or both.

BITES, STINGS, AND POISONED WOUNDS.—Bites of animals are in general to be treated as punctured or lacerated wounds (*see* WOUNDS), but as animals' teeth are, in general, foul, suppuration is very apt to arise if the bite be deep. The bite of some reptiles, scorpions, spiders, etc., causes definite symptoms of poisoning, while,

after the bites of several animals, especially the wolf and the dog, there is often a risk of hydrophobia. Wounds which are *septic*, *i.e.* poisoned by bacteria, are dealt with in the section on WOUNDS.

Dog bites in Britain are treated by washing (not scrubbing) the bite with soap and water, and then applying hydrogen peroxide or cetrimide. The bite is then covered with a dressing. Penicillin is also given as a rule, and measures taken to prevent tetanus. Overseas, more active treatment is required in view of the risk of rabies (*q.v.*).

Snake bites are not necessarily poisonous, for not only are many snakes harmless, but persons can, like the snake-charmers of India, render themselves immune by the injection under the skin of gradually increasing doses of the poison. It is estimated that the annual death rate from snake bites, throughout the world, is 25,000 to 35,000, of which 20,000 to 25,000 occur in India. In Europe there are probably only 2 or 3 fatal cases every year. The last two fatal cases reported in England and Wales occurred in 1941, and in the previous fifty years only five deaths due to snake bite had been reported.

The principal poisonous snakes belong to the viper and cobra families, and all inject their poison through a pair of grooved or hollow teeth connected with poison glands. These include in Asia the cobra, the king cobra, the krait, the deboia, and the phoorsa ; in America the rattlesnake, the copperhead, and the moccasin ; in South America the fer-de-lance and the coral snake ; in Africa cobras, vipers, and the puff-adder ; and in Australia the death-adder, tiger snake, copperhead, brown snake, and black snake. The sea snakes of the Pacific and Indian Oceans are almost all poisonous. The only poisonous snake in Britain is the adder (*Vipera berus*). It is chiefly found in Scotland, Dartmoor and the New Forest.

The symptoms of snake-poisoning are swelling and paralysis of the bitten part, with general depression, palpitation, difficulty of breathing, faintness, and later paralysis and convulsions, followed, in bad cases, by death. These symptoms appear within fifteen minutes to an hour after the bite. After the bite of a deboia or of one of the rattlesnakes very severe suppuration may occur in the neighbourhood of the bite in people who recover.

Treatment of an adder bite in Britain consists of immobilizing the limb by splinting, washing the wound with water, and giving an analgesic to relieve the pain. Antivenine should not be given. Outside Britain, where the consequences can be much more serious, treatment consists of applying a tourniquet between the bite and the body, to prevent the poison being absorbed into the body. This should be released for a few seconds every fifteen minutes, in order to prevent gangrene. The bite should then be sucked vigorously for five-minute periods at frequent intervals. A serum known as *antivenine* is now available as an antidote against many snake bites, and this should be injected intravenously in liberal amounts as soon as possible. It should also be injected under the skin around the bitten area. The individual should also be treated as for shock, *i.e.* resting quietly, kept warm, and given a blood transfusion and oxygen if necessary. As stimulants, sal volatile, strong tea, or coffee may be given, *not* alcohol.

Poisonous fishes exist in most tropical waters, especially around the islands of the Pacific and Indian Oceans, and their venom may be conveyed to man either by poisonous stings or by their bite. The action of the poison is mostly a depressing one upon the heart, and in the case of some of the tropical fishes convulsions and even death may be produced.

Toads and salamanders secrete a milky fluid from the skin of the back which is irritating locally, and which, in small animals and weakly children, is said to kill if introduced by a wound.

Centipedes, scorpions, and tarantulas (large tropical spiders) kill their prey by poison, and can inflict a very painful, though probably seldom fatal, bite on human beings. The treatment is to apply a ligature as for snake bite at once, and to suck the wound or wash it well with a strong solution of permanganate of potassium. Some other substances have also a reputation as antidotes, such as ammonia, spirit of camphor, tobacco juice, turpentine, and camphor and chloral rubbed up together. An antitoxic serum has been prepared for use against scorpion bite in Egypt. If an abscess forms it is treated like an abscess from any other cause.

Harvest-bugs, fleas, lice, and mosquitoes often cause great irritation of the skin by their bite. Harvest-bugs may bury themselves in the skin and have to be picked out with a needle. Dimethyl phthallate applied to the skin or clothing is an effective repellent. Lice may be got rid of, if in the hair, by the application of a 2 per cent. emulsion of D.D.T. They may be got rid of from the clothes by baking these in an oven or fumigating with burning sulphur for several hours, or by the use of D.D.T. (*See further under* INSECTS IN RELATION TO DISEASE.) Bites by mosquitoes or bugs are soothed by bathing with salt water, by painting with sal volatile or cool calamine lotion, or by applying an antihistamine cream or ointment. They may be prevented by smearing the skin with dimethyl phthallate (*q.v.*), or, if this is not available, camphor water, lime juice, or one of the oils of pennyroyal, lavender, cloves, or cinnamon.

Ants, bees, wasps, and hornets cause great irritation by the stings with which the females and workers are provided. Those of ants are allayed by eau-de-Cologne, vinegar, or lemon juice. Bees sometimes leave a part of their sting as well as poison in the skin, and this should be looked for first of all and pressed out. The sting of a wasp in the throat, the insect having been taken into the mouth in biting a fruit, has caused death owing to rapid swelling, which blocks the air passage. For bee stings the treatment is the dabbing on of ammonia, bicarbonate of soda, or washing blue. For wasp and hornet stings the treatment is the application of vinegar or lemon juice.

Jellyfish and hairy-caterpillars, the former by threads which they discharge and the latter by brittle, poisoned hairs, cause an itchy red rash after contact. It is relieved by vinegar or olive oil.

Nettle stings are relieved by bruised dock leaves or raw onion juice.

Arrow poison is sometimes dreaded when children have been playing with arrows from the East Indies. Unless, however, the arrow has been actually driven into the flesh, the amount of poison absorbed would probably be insufficient to do any harm. The wound should be washed out with permanganate of potassium solution. The poison on these arrows is sometimes one causing convulsions, in which the general treatment is that for strychnine poisoning, or more generally it is of the nature of curare, causing paralysis, in which case, if the breathing should begin to fail, the proper treatment would be artificial respiration (*see under* DROWNING).

BITTERS.—The two most bitter substances are probably strychnine and quinine, which have other still more powerful properties. But when one speaks of ' bitters ' one means substances of milder properties, which are used to stimulate the functions of the stomach and so give an appetite and aid digestion. Calumba, chiretta, gentian, and quassia are the chief pure bitters ; others contain tannin and are also astringent.

BLACK DEATH is an old name for plague. (*See* PLAGUE.)

BLACK-DRAUGHT is a powerful purgative preparation, known also as compound senna mixture, and containing Epsom salts, senna, and liquorice. The dose is two to three tablespoonfuls.

BLACK DROP is another name for laudanum or tincture of opium. (*See* OPIUM.)

BLACKHEADS (*see* ACNE).

BLACK MOTIONS are passed when there is great constipation, and when bismuth or iron is being taken ; but the most important cause is blood changed by the digestive processes, and proceeding generally from ulceration somewhere in the stomach or bowels.

BLACK VOMIT is due to the presence of blood in the stomach. There may be dark masses, as in yellow fever, or a small amount of black sediment like coffee-grounds, as in ulcer of the stomach.

BLACKWATER FEVER is an acute illness characterized by hæmoglobinuria (' black water '), jaundice, fever, vomiting, anæmia, and severe hæmolysis. It is associated with malignant tertian malaria, and occurs in Central Africa, India, and the Far East.

Although the precise cause is still obscure, it is known that the disease may be precipitated in malarial subjects by the taking of quinine or by exposure to cold, by fatigue, and by trauma. Predisposing factors include exposure by non-immune individuals to virulent strains of the malarial parasite and irregular and inadequate treatment of such infections. The mortality rate usually varies between 10 and 20 per cent., but may be as high as 40 per cent.

Symptoms.—These are fever, rigor, nausea, bilious vomiting, epigastric discomfort, jaundice, and the passage of pinkish, red, or port-wine coloured urine—hæmoglobinuria. The spleen and liver are enlarged and tender. After a few hours the temperature falls, there is profuse sweating, and the skin becomes jaundiced. Mild cases may recover in a day or two. Severe cases have a succession of attacks.

Treatment.—Consists in (1) absolute rest in bed; (2) administration of plenty of alkaline fluids ; (3) glucose given intravenously (and sodium bicarbonate if necessary) ; (4) blood transfusion, and subsequent remedies for anæmia. Recent evidence suggests that corticosteroids are of value. Careful nursing is most important.

BLADDERS are sacs formed of muscular and fibrous tissue and lined by a mucous membrane, which is united loosely to the muscular coat, so as to allow freely of increase and decrease in the contained cavity. Bladders are designed to contain some secretion or excretion, and communicate with the exterior by a narrow opening through which their contents can be discharged. In man there are two, the *gall-bladder* and the *urinary bladder*.

GALL-BLADDER.—This is situated under the liver in the upper part of the abdomen, and its function is to store the bile, which it discharges into the intestine by the bile duct. For further details, see LIVER.

URINARY BLADDER. — This is situated in the pelvis, in front of the last part of the bowel. The bladder, in the full state, rises up into the abdomen and holds about a pint (570 ml.) of urine. Two fine tubes, called the ureters, lead into the bladder, one from each kidney ; and the urethra, a tube as wide as a lead pencil when distended, leads from it to the exterior, a distance of $1\text{-}1\frac{1}{2}$ inches (25 to 37·5 cm.) in the female and 8 inches (200 cm.) in the male.

Structure.—The wall of the bladder is similar in structure to that of the bowels, and consists of four coats. The inner surface is lined by a soft mucous membrane covered by epithelial cells of irregular shape. This is attached to the muscular coat by a loose, fibrous, sub-mucous coat, in which run numerous blood-vessels. In the muscular coat the muscle fibres are arranged in several layers, and run in various directions, thereby adding greatly to the strength of the wall. On its upper and back part, the bladder possesses a covering of serous membrane, formed by part of the general peritoneal lining of the abdominal cavity, but this outermost coat does not extend down to the base of the bladder, where the latter lies in close contact with the other pelvic organs. The bladder is suspended in position by numerous ligaments, four of which are fibrous bands, while the remaining five are formed by thickened portions of the peritoneum. The base of the bladder is directed downwards and backwards, and in this part are the three openings of the ureters and urethra. The exit from the bladder is kept closed by a muscular ring, which is relaxed every time water is passed.

BLADDER, DISEASES OF.—For diseases of the gall-bladder see GALL-BLADDER. (See also URINE.) The urinary bladder is subject to several diseases, but, partly through its general freedom from disease, partly owing to its inaccessibility, as it lies deep in the pelvis behind the pubic bones, partly owing to general ignorance as to its site

and functions, symptoms set up in it are very often attributed to the bowels and other organs. Diseased conditions in it are diagnosed in part by the symptoms they set up, in part by chemical and microscopical examination of the urine, and in the more obscure conditions by means of the cystoscope. The *cystoscope* consists of a narrow metal tube fitted up as a telescope, and bearing at its end a small electric lamp by which the cavity is lighted up. The instrument is introduced through the urethra, and shows any tumour or ulcer which may exist, and also whether blood in the urine comes from the bladder wall or runs out of the ureters from the kidneys. *Sounding* is another process, consisting in the introduction of a curved solid metal rod, when the presence of a stone is suspected, against which the sound can be felt or heard to strike. *Catheters* are tubes about the thickness of quills, which are made of metal, vulcanite, india-rubber, etc., and are used to draw off the water when it is not possible to expel this voluntarily, or, when the bladder is to be washed out for some diseased condition. (See CATHETERS.) The following are some of the chief diseased conditions :

CYSTITIS, or INFLAMMATION OF THE BLADDER. — **Causes.** — Bacteria live readily in the urine but they do not multiply in the healthy bladder. When some cause is present to weaken the bladder wall, or, when bacteria are introduced in large numbers, for example on a dirty catheter, they multiply inside this organ and set up inflammation.

There may be direct infection from neighbouring organs, as the urethra in gonorrhœa. Any cause that prevents the free voiding of the urine, such as stricture or narrowing of the urethra, or enlargement of the prostate gland at the outlet of the bladder, which is a common occurrence in elderly men, may produce a chronic form of cystitis. In women it is commonly associated with prolapse of the womb. A stone, if present, is apt by its irritation to do the same. One of the most frequent organisms found in the urine in cases of cystitis is the common colon bacillus (or *Escherichia coli*, as it is now known). Tuberculous cystitis may be found, due to the *Mycobacterium tuberculosis* which produces a chronic ulcer on the bladder wall. Another very chronic form is caused by bilharzia, a small parasitic worm which may settle in the minute blood-vessels of the bladder wall. This form is very common in Egypt and South Africa, and is sometimes found in those who have resided in those countries.

Symptoms.—Pain in the region of the bladder or in the small of the back, frequency of making water, and a condition of bad smell, turbidity, and whitish sediment in the urine, are the chief facts noticed by the sufferer. There may, in acute cases, be high temperature and shivering fits. In the chronic form the very frequent desire to pass small quantities of urine is the most marked symptom.

Treatment.—Rest in bed, hot hip baths, and hot applications, like poultices or fomentations to the lower part of the abdomen, along with simple diet and large quantities of fluid, such as barley water, to drink, may be all that is necessary. Large doses of potassium citrate are also helpful, usually combined in a mixture with tincture of hyoscyamus. In the majority of cases, however, it is necessary to give drugs that will destroy the causative organism. In practice this means one of the sulphonamides or antibiotics. The choice is dependent upon which organism is responsible for the infection, and this is determined by submitting a specimen of urine to bacteriological investigation.

STONE, or CALCULUS, in the bladder may be of any size up to that of a hen's or goose's egg, but those which set up symptoms severe enough to necessitate operation are seldom smaller than a cherry or a pigeon's egg. There are three varieties of stone : (*a*) URATIC, associated with acidity (*see* ACIDITY) or with the gouty constitution ; (*b*) OXALIC, composed of oxalate of lime, and often associated with a nervous dyspeptic type of temperament; (*c*) PHOSPHATIC, which occur in long-standing cases of inflammation of the bladder, accompanied by constant decomposition of the urine. This is the most common type of stone found in the bladder.

Symptoms.—The symptoms of in-

flammation of the bladder, together with discomfort on movement, and sudden pain immediately after the passing of water, are those generally found.

Treatment.—Although control of the diet may reduce the tendency to the formation of stones in the bladder, the only method of treatment once they have formed is surgical removal. In spite of many vaunted claims, there is no drug known which can remove, or dissolve, stones in the bladder. In 1739 a secret remedy sold by Mrs. Joanna Stephens was considered so effectual in stones that the secret was bought by the British Government for £5000. It was found to consist of calcined egg shells, soap, and aromatic bitters— that is, its essentials were lime, phosphates, and alkalies. Surgical removal of the stone (or stones) is carried out by either *litholapaxy* or *lithotomy*. Litholapaxy consists of passing into the bladder through the urethra an instrument known as a lithotrite which crushes the stone, after which the small pieces are removed through the urethra. The advantage of this method is that no incision is required and the patient is only laid up for one or two days. If the stone is larger than 2 inches (5 cm.) in diameter, however, or if there are too many stones present, lithotomy has to be performed : *i.e.* the bladder is opened through an incision in the lower abdominal wall and the stone (or stones) are removed in this way.

TUMOURS in the bladder are often the cause of large quantities of bright blood being passed with the urine. For their removal the bladder is opened through the lower part of the abdomen.

RUPTURE of the bladder may occur in old men who have long suffered from difficulty in passing water and cystitis, or in healthy persons owing to a blow or crush. (*See* ABDOMEN, INJURIES OF.)

BLAUD'S PILL is a pill containing carbonate of iron, used in the treatment of anæmia.

BLEEDER is a term applied to persons in whom it is difficult to stop bleeding when some small wound has been sustained. (*See* HÆMOPHILIA.)

BLEEDING (*see* HÆMORRHAGE *and* BLOOD-LETTING).

BLENORRHŒA (βλέννα, mucus; ρέω, I flow) means an excessive discharge of mucus or slimy material from a surface, such as that of the eye, nose, bowel, etc. The word catarrh is used with the same meaning, but also includes the idea of inflammation as the cause of such discharge.

BLEPHARITIS means inflammation of the eyelids. (*See* EYE DISEASES AND INJURIES.)

BLEPHAROSPASM means spasm of the eyelids.

BLINDNESS.—In the National Assistance Act, 1948, a 'blind person' is defined as one 'so blind as to be unable to perform any work for which eyesight is essential'. In the case of children, the term 'blind' includes not only the totally blind, but also those who cannot be taught by visual methods which make use of large print, blackboard writing, or lenses for magnifying ordinary print. At December 31, 1960, the number of registered blind, according to these definitions, in England and Wales was 97,469. These included 10 infants aged under one year, 312 children aged one to four years, 1950 aged five to fifteen, and 55,400 adults aged 70 and over. Of those registered as blind during 1960, 3·0 per cent. were totally blind (*i.e.* had no perception of light), 9·2 per cent. had perception of light, and 58·9 per cent. could perceive hand movements. The most common cause of blindness was senile macular degeneration, a degenerative process involving the most sensitive part of the retina, which was responsible for 28·9 per cent. of cases, whilst cataract accounted for 20·9 per cent., and glaucoma accounted for 12·7 per cent. Diabetes mellitus was the cause in 7·5 per cent. Congenital syphilis accounted for 0·4 per cent. (*See also* VISION.)

BLIND SPOT (*see* EYE).

BLISTERS AND COUNTER - IRRITANTS.—These are employed in cases of both acute and chronic inflammation, on the principle that irritation of the skin causes congestion of the parts immediately below the skin, while it relieves congestion of deep - seated organs through an action upon the nerves that regulate the size of the minute blood-vessels.

Varieties.—Substances so employed are spoken of generally as counter-irritants, and divided into *rubefacients*, or substances which merely redden the skin and cause it to peel off ; and *vesicants*, or blistering applications, when, in addition, they produce a collection of fluid under the horny layer of the skin ; but there is no sharp division between them, most rubefacients producing blisters if left on long enough. The chief *rubefacients* are : mustard, turpentine, cajuput oil, capsicum, tincture of iodine, and liniments of ammonia, chloroform, etc., and of *vesicants* we have cantharides or Spanish fly, pure acetic acid, ammonia, and chloroform.

The CAUTERY is also used for this purpose. (*See* CAUTERY.)

Uses.—MILDER COUNTER-IRRITANTS are used in cases of bronchitis, congestion of the stomach with vomiting, vague rheumatic pain, sprains, and when a prolonged application is desired, so that some swelling or thickening due to chronic inflammation may be absorbed, or some continued pain lessened.

BLISTERS are used (1) to subdue severer forms of pain and inflammation, for example, in pleurisy, pericarditis, and sciatica, in which case they are applied a little distance away from the seat of pain ; and (2) to promote absorption of thickenings and effusions in joints, etc., in which case the blister is applied to the skin immediately over the affected part.

How to apply a blister or counter-irritant.—*Mustard* is made into a paste and spread on muslin or brown paper, and so applied directly to the skin for twenty to thirty minutes, until a warm glow is felt. Mustard leaves can also be purchased and similarly used after moistening. If a more powerful action be desired, mustard may be dusted thickly over the surface of a linseed-meal poultice, and this applied for a similar length of time. After-redness is less if muslin has been placed between the mustard and the skin.

One must be careful not to apply mustard too long in weak persons and children, or a slough may result. For a milder effect the paste may be made with equal quantities of mustard and flour. The skin should be sponged with warm water, dried, and anointed with a little vaseline after the mustard is removed.

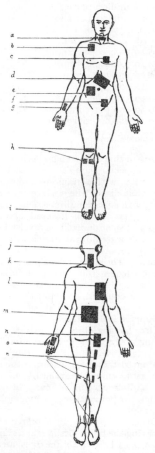

time, upon flannel cloths, which are then wrung out of hot water, and used for pain in the abdomen or back. (*See* POULTICES *and* FOMENTATIONS.)

Tincture of iodine is usually painted on the skin once or twice a day till the cuticle comes off in flakes, but just short of blistering. It is used over joints,

Cantharides blisters are produced by painting on Liquor Epispasticus (blistering fluid), or by applying cantharides plaster, the black surface of which is oiled and then placed against the dried skin ; the plaster is then secured with strips of adhesive plaster or with a bandage or handkerchief. Sometimes cantharides is applied in an ointment containing the powdered insects. Care must be taken not to apply a blister over a bony prominence in a person who is weakly or confined to bed, or healing may be very slow. Fig. 73 shows the sites in which blisters are oftenest ordered. The application is left in position for some hours (if large), or over night (if small), and, when it is removed, olive oil should be applied to remove any particles of cantharides still in the skin, and prevent another blister rising. The bleb should be pricked at once, but on no account should the raised skin be cut away till the skin beneath is hard—that is, after two or three days. The blistered area should be dressed for a day or two with some simple ointment spread on lint.

In persons who are the subject of Bright's disease, and in the case of paralysed limbs, cantharides blisters are unsuitable applications.

Acetic acid, ammonia, and *chloroform* are used by soaking a piece of lint of the required size in one of these fluids, applying it, and covering with a watch-glass till the blister rises.

BLOOD is a fluid which circulates through the arteries, capillaries, and veins, exchanging fluid and gases with the bodily tissues. The latter receive the products absorbed from the food and oxygen taken up by the blood in its passage through the lungs, while the blood removes from the tissues carbonic acid gas to discharge it in the lungs, and various waste products, of which it rids itself in its passage through the kidneys.

Composition.—The blood consists, in

FIG. 73.—Diagram illustrating various positions where blisters, etc., are commonly applied. The larger areas correspond in size to weaker irritants, such as mustard leaves ; the smaller indicate the size of blisters. *a*, For laryngitis ; *b*, for pleurisy ; *c*, for pericarditis ; *d*, for vomiting ; *e*, for appendicitis ; *f*, for ovaritis ; *g*, *h*, *i*, *o*, for rheumatism or gout ; *j*, for headache ; *k*, for epilepsy ; *l*, for pleurisy ; *m*, for lumbago ; *n*, for sciatica.

Turpentine and *cajuput oil* are generally sprinkled, about a teaspoonful at a addition to the fluid, of corpuscles, minute bodies $\frac{1}{3000}$ of an inch (8 microns), or less, in size. These are of three kinds : red corpuscles, white corpuscles, and blood platelets. In the *fluid* are dissolved the various salts and proteins which nourish the tissues (*see* LYMPH), and also the waste

The range of the normal blood count is shown in table 5.

Examination of blood.—The corpuscles of the blood may be counted. For this purpose a minute drop is drawn up into a special graduated tube provided with a bulb in which the blood is mixed with a suitable diluting fluid.

Red corpuscles : Men	4·5 to 6·5 million per c.mm.
Women	4·0 to 5·5 million per c.mm.
Hæmoglobin : Men	13·5 to 18 G. per 100 ml.
Women	11·5 to 16 G. per 100 ml.
White corpuscles	4,000 to 10,000 per c.mm.
Neutrophils	2,500 to 7,000 per c.mm.
Eosinophils	50 to 400 per c.mm.
Basophils	20 to 200 per c.mm.
Lymphocytes	1,500 to 3,000 per c.mm.
Monocytes	200 to 800 per c.mm.
Platelets	150,000 to 500,000 per c.mm.

TABLE 5.—Range of Normal Blood Count.

products, such as uric acid, destined for removal from the body. The *red corpuscles* act as the carriers of oxygen ; each is a disc, hollowed out on either surface, and contains a substance called hæmoglobin, which acts as a medium of interchange between the oxygen of the air in the lungs, and the tissues requiring it. There are about 5,000,000 red corpuscles in every cubic millimetre of blood, the blood of women containing slightly fewer than that of men. The *white corpuscles* are of several different kinds, and wander through the walls of the small blood-vessels, upon occasion, into the tissues ; here they have many functions to perform, of which the chief are the repair of wounds, the absorption of foreign bodies, and the destruction of bacteria ; their dead bodies form, when in large numbers, the matter or pus of abscesses. Their number is less than 1 to 500 of the red corpuscles. The chief varieties of white corpuscles are those with a single large nucleus (large mononuclear), those with a nucleus consisting of several variously shaped parts (polymorphonuclear), and small corpuscles resembling those formed in the lymphatic glands (lymphocytes). Also they are classed according to whether the granules they contain stain with a blue alkaline dye (basophil) or with a red acid dye (eosinophil). The *blood platelets* are extremely minute, and play some important part in clotting.

A drop of this diluted blood is blown out upon a special glass slide on which have been ruled with a diamond a number of lines that divide the surface into areas of a 400th square millimetre in size. A cover glass is then lowered upon the drop and so supported on a raised glass rim that a definite distance (0·1 millimetre) separates it from the ruled surface. The slide is then placed under a microscope, the average number of corpuscles that have settled on each square is counted, and thus the number in one four-thousandth of a cubic millimetre is ascertained.

The hæmoglobin is estimated by taking a drop in a fine measured tube, diluting it with distilled water in a graduated tube till it assumes the same tint as a known standard, and then, by reading off the amount of water added, the percentage of hæmoglobin is obtained.

Dried films are also prepared by smearing the blood on slides and staining these, usually with aniline dyes, methylene blue, and eosin dissolved in methyl alcohol ; in these dried films the corpuscles can be examined by a high magnifying power and a differential count can be made of the various forms (*see* Plate V).

Formation of blood.—The life of a corpuscle is probably about three or four weeks ; at all events the blood-forming organs can restore the blood after extreme hæmorrhage to its normal

124

state in this time. To renew the wear, as well as to make good losses by wounds, a constant manufacture is going on in the marrow of the smaller bones, in some glands, and also probably in the spleen.

Amount of blood.—In health this is around 85 millilitres per kilogram (2·2 pounds) of body weight, or 9 per cent. ($\frac{1}{11}$th) of the weight of the body.

Clotting of blood occurs when blood is shed, and is due to the formation of threads of fibrin, which, as it shrinks, squeezes out from its interstices a clear, faintly straw-coloured fluid —serum. (For details of clotting, *see* COAGULATION.)

Functions of blood. — The red corpuscles act as oxygen carriers; the white corpuscles have mainly a defensive action against the onset of infection. The fluid of the blood carries in solution various waste-products such as carbonic acid gas to be exhaled by the lungs, urea and salts to be removed by the kidneys ; also it distributes foodstuffs, such as sugar and proteins absorbed from the intestine and elaborated by various glands ; and it forms a general medium of communication between organs that are chemically interdependent ; for example, carrying to the stomach the materials for the gastric juice, to the muscles ferments formed in the pancreas, etc., and absorbing secretions needed for the general purposes of the body, like those of the thyroid gland and suprarenal glands.

BLOOD, DISEASES OF (*see* ANÆMIA and LEUKÆMIA).

BLOOD GROUPS.—People are divided, in respect of a certain reaction of the blood, into four main groups. This depends upon the capacity of the serum of one person's blood to agglutinate the red blood corpuscles of another's in certain circumstances. The reaction depends on antigens, known as agglutinogens, in the red corpuscles and antibodies, known as agglutinins, in the serum. There are two of each, the agglutinogens being known as A and B. Anyone's blood corpuscles may have (1) no agglutinogens, (2) agglutinogen A, (3) agglutinogen B, (4) agglutinogens A and B : these are the four groups (*see* Table 6).

The practical importance is that, in blood transfusion, the person giving and the person receiving the blood should belong to the same blood group, or a dangerous reaction will take place from the agglutination that occurs when blood of a different group is present.

Rhesus factor.—In addition to these A and B agglutinogens (or antigens) there is another one known as the

Group	Agglutinogens in the Corpuscles.	Agglutinins in the Plasma.	Frequency in Great Britain.
AB	A and B	None	2 per cent.
A	A	Anti-B	46 per cent.
B	B	Anti-A	8 per cent.
O	Neither A nor B	Anti-A and Anti-B	44 per cent.

TABLE 6.—The Four Main Blood Groups (Bayliss).

Rhesus (or Rh) factor, so named because there is a similar antigen in the red blood corpuscles of the Rhesus monkey. About 84 per cent. of the population have this Rh factor in their blood and are therefore known as ' Rhpositive '. The remaining 16 per cent. who do not possess the factor are known as ' Rh-negative '.

The practical importance of the Rh factor is that, unlike the A and B agglutinogens, there are no naturally occurring Rh antibodies, but such antibodies may develop in an Rh-negative person if the Rh antigen is introduced into his or her circulation. This can occur (*a*) if an Rh-negative person is given a transfusion of Rh-positive blood, (*b*) if an Rh-negative mother married to an Rh-positive husband becomes pregnant and the foetus is Rhpositive. If this happens, the mother's Rh antibodies can pass into the foetal circulation, where they react with the baby's Rh antigen and cause hæmolytic disease of the foetus and newborn. This means that the child may be stillborn or become jaundiced shortly after birth (*see* HÆMOLYTIC DISEASE OF THE NEWBORN).

As about one in six expectant mothers is Rh-negative, this explains why a blood-group examination is now considered an essential part of the antenatal examination of a pregnant woman. It also explains why Rh-positive blood should never be transfused to an Rh-negative girl or woman.

BLOODLESSNESS (see ANÆMIA).

BLOOD-LETTING was a practice much in vogue for various ailments a century ago. Indeed, many people had themselves bled regularly for the purpose of avoiding the bad health consequent on over-eating and over-drinking. It came, in time, to be so much abused—many sick people undoubtedly having died, not of the original disease, but of the excessive bleeding practised for its cure—that it fell into almost complete disuse. Certain conditions are, however, benefited by withdrawing blood either from the affected part or from the general circulation. The chief methods of blood-letting are three in number.

Vein puncture is employed when it is desired to obtain a small quantity of blood for analysis or the performance of various tests. For this purpose a hollow hypodermic needle is pushed into a vein, one of those at the bend of the elbow usually being chosen, while pressure by a band or by the fingers is exerted on the veins in the upper arm. If it is desired to obtain the serum of the blood, the blood is run off into a test tube and allowed to clot. If the blood is required for analysis, clotting may be prevented by adding to the tube, before the blood is drawn off, a few crystals of potassium oxalate or potassium citrate.

Venesection consists in the opening of a vein, usually, owing to its superficial position, one of the veins just above the bend of the elbow. After the desired amount has flowed out, a pad and tight bandage are used to stop the bleeding. This method is of use in certain cases of acute heart failure, when life may depend upon quickly and temporarily relieving the strain on the heart. It is also used in the treatment of polycythæmia (q.v.).

Cupping was at one time used either as dry-cupping to draw blood to the surface, or as wet-cupping to withdraw blood from a congested area. (See CUPPING.)

Leeches were formerly used to draw

126

blood. After they are removed, bleeding is generally free, and may be encouraged, if desired, by warm poultices. They are seldom used at the present day.

BLOOD-POISONING is, in general, a very serious condition, and is known as 'septicæmia' or 'pyæmia', according as the sufferer is simply poisoned by substances circulating in the blood, or as he develops, in addition, abscesses at different points over his body, owing to bacteria deposited from the blood. There is a slighter form called 'sapræmia', in which the person becomes fevered and ill owing to the absorption of foul or putrid substances from the bowels or from wounds, but is not dangerously affected, and there is a chronic form called 'hectic fever', in which constant absorption of poisonous material takes place from cavities in the lungs, from diseased bones, etc. (see TUBERCULOSIS).

Causes.—Wounds or inflamed areas, especially in bones, joints, and veins, may be invaded by specially virulent bacteria, or, owing to great constitutional weakness of the person, for example, in alcoholics or diabetics, the bacteria may find a specially congenial soil for their growth. Women after delivery are specially liable to infection —the condition known as puerperal fever—but this is much less common nowadays as a result of more efficient methods of prevention.

Symptoms. — In septicæmia very high temperature, followed speedily by death, may be the only sign. In pyæmia there are, in addition, shivering (rigor), profuse sweating, pains in the joints and muscles, and the signs of abscesses at different points, which may last over days or weeks,

Treatment.—The introduction of antiseptic surgery by Lord Lister immensely reduced the frequency of blood-poisoning, but the position has been improved out of all recognition by the introduction of the sulphonamides and antibiotics. Which of these should be used in a given case depends upon the causative organism, but in the majority of cases penicillin given intramuscularly is the treatment of choice. Active surgical treatment by amputation, opening of abscesses, antiseptic douches, etc., according to circumstances, is also necessary.

BLOOD-PRESSURE is the name given to the pressure that must be applied to an artery, say in the arm, in order to stop the pulse in the vessel beyond the point of pressure. It is generally assumed to be equivalent to the pressure to which the blood is subjected by the force of the heart and the elasticity of the vessels, but it is also dependent on the thickness and hardness of the vessel wall, and on the volume of blood thrown out of the heart at each beat.

The blood-pressure is greatest at each heart-beat (systolic pressure) and falls somewhat between the beats (diastolic pressure). The systolic pressure in children is equal to that of a mercury column about 100 mm. high, in young adults about 120, and it tends to increase with advancing age as the arteries get thicker and harder, but this is by no means always the case.

The blood-pressure is raised temporarily by exposure to cold, and permanently by kidney disease, by some disorders of the ductless glands, and in the condition known as essential hypertension (q.v.). A blood-pressure of 180 is not uncommon in cases of chronic kidney disease, and it may, in advanced cases, be as high as 250 or occasionally even 300 mm. Mental worry combined with lack of sufficient exercise has also an important effect in producing raised blood-pressure. The pressure is below the normal as the result of warmth, e.g. after a hot bath, as well as in exhaustion, weakening diseases, fevers, and generally in heart failure.

The blood-pressure may be estimated roughly by the pressure with which it is necessary to apply the finger at the wrist in order to obliterate the pulse. It is more exactly measured by means of an instrument known as the *sphygmomanometer*. This consists of a flat rubber bag which is strapped round the arm, and the interior of which communicates by two tubes with either a pressure gauge or a mercury manometer, and with a hand pump. The bag is pumped up so as to constrict the arm, and the systolic pressure is taken as that at which the pulse dis-

appears from the vessel farther down the arm.

An abnormally high blood-pressure is often accompanied by disease of the arteries, so that persons with greatly raised pressure are specially liable to apoplexy. In cases associated with advanced disease of the kidneys, the heightened blood-pressure is to some extent a salutary matter, because the circulation of the blood through the diminished vessels of the kidneys is thereby increased. In such a case the general health of the patient is better while the pressure remains moderately high, and if it be reduced too much by drugs and other means the general health deteriorates.

BLOOD-SPITTING or HÆMOPTYSIS. —(For the means of distinguishing this from vomiting of blood, *see* EXPECTORATION, for its treatment, *see* HÆMORRHAGE.)

BLOOD TRANSFUSION (*see* TRANSFUSION OF BLOOD).

'BLOWING' OF CANS means the presence of gas in cans of food, the gas resulting from putrefaction or fermentation of the food, or from the action of fruit on the metal of the container, producing hydrogen. The ends of the can or tin bulge and give a tympanitic note on percussion. The food in such cans should not be eaten.

BLUE DISEASE is a popular term for cyanosis. (*See* CYANOSIS.)

BLUE PILL, or MERCURY PILL, is a purgative. It contains mercury, confection of roses, and liquorice. It is also said to stimulate the activity of the liver. The dose is from 4 to 8 grains (250 to 500 mg.).

BOILS, or FURUNCLES, are small areas of inflammation starting in the roots of hairs, and due to the growth of a micro-organism (generally that known as a staphylococcus). When a large number of boils form close together at one time the mass is called a 'carbuncle'.

Causes.—The essential cause is bacterial, as stated, but many circumstances predispose to the growth of bacteria around the sheath of the hair, within which they are constantly found, though harmless. Diabetics and the subjects of Bright's disease are specially troubled with boils, so that any one liable to recurrence of boils should submit himself to medical examination in case he may be suffering from one of these diseases. Persons who eat too much food, or who are recovering from an exhausting illness, are also liable to them. Friction, which irritates the hair roots, is a very important cause, and therefore boils are commonest on the back of the neck, on the forearm, and on the leg, while those who row or ride have them about the buttocks.

Symptoms.—A red swelling forms round a hair, and causes a good deal of irritation and scratching. It gets larger for some days, being, as a rule, not very painful, unless subject to chafing. When, however, the boil begins on the head, in the ear, or in the nose, where the tissues will not stretch readily, the pain may be very great. Even after two or three days the swelling may slowly subside, and the inflammation gradually pass off, the boil being said to 'abort'. In most cases, about the sixth or seventh day the top of the boil breaks, and some thin fluid, and perhaps matter, oozes out. The yellowish 'core', consisting of a small mass of dead tissue, is now seen occupying the interior of the boil, and this comes away about a couple of days later, after which the boil speedily heals. If the boil be not treated, however, the first is apt to be followed by a crop of others in the neighbourhood, owing to the discharge from the first boil infecting other hairs. There is a special danger in boils of the upper lip and nose ; for these may lead to inflammation within the head. Generally a boil, though its presence causes great annoyance, does not lead to fever or other general symptoms. But in boils of the ear, or about the face, there may be high temperature and great prostration, which are serious signs. Carbuncles are exhausting, and, in old people, very dangerous.

Treatment.—At first the boil should be kept as still as possible, and to this end a piece of antiseptic sticking-plaster with a small hole cut in the centre, through which any discharge can pass, may be applied over the boil and kept in position for several days, when the

boil very often aborts. Another method to prevent boils coming to a head is to paint the boil and a small area of skin round it night and morning for several days with strong tincture of iodine (10 per cent.). If, however, the boil is painful, or if it is proceeding to suppuration, hot fomentations should be applied, or magnesium sulphate paste. Magnesium sulphate paste is very effective, but must be freshly made. Carbuncles, painful boils and boils about the lip and nose may become very dangerous and should on no account be squeezed or fingered. As penicillin is so effective against staphylococcal infection, it has proved of value in the treatment of severe boils and carbuncles. General treatment in the form of good food, and avoidance of alcohol is also necessary. The taking of yeast is said to be of value. New boils are more effectively prevented from forming by rubbing powdered boric acid gently into the skin around the old boil twice a day after washing and drying. In recurrent cases a course of injections of a specially made vaccine or of toxoid may be of value.

BONE forms the framework upon which the rest of the body is built up. The bones are generally called the skeleton, though this term also includes the cartilages which join the ribs to the breast-bone, protect the larynx, etc.

Structure of bone.—Bone is composed partly of fibrous tissue, partly of bone earth (phosphate and carbonate of lime), intimately mixed together. As the bones of a child are composed to the extent of about two-thirds of fibrous tissue, whilst those of the aged contain two-thirds of bone earth, one readily understands the toughness of the former and the brittleness of the latter. One speaks of *dense bone*, of which the shafts of the limb bones are composed, the bone being a hard tube surrounded by a membrane, the periosteum, and enclosing a fatty substance, the marrow ; and of *cancellous bone*, which forms the short bones and the ends of long bones, in which a fine lace-work of bone fills up the whole interior, enclosing marrow in its meshes. The marrow of the smaller bones is of great importance. It is red in colour, and in it red blood corpuscles are formed. Even the densest bone is tunnelled by fine canals (Haversian canals)

FIG. 74.—Transverse section of dried bone. The open spaces are Haversian canals surrounded by lamellæ; the lacunæ and canaliculi are shown blank. Magnified by about 200. (Turner's *Anatomy*.)

in which run small blood-vessels, nerves and lymphatics, for the maintenance and repair of the bone (Fig. 74). Round these Haversian canals the bone is arranged in circular plates called lamellæ, the lamellæ being separated from one another by clefts, known as lacunæ, in which single bone-cells are contained. Even the lamellæ are pierced by fine tubes known as canaliculi lodging processes of these cells. Each lamella is composed of very fine interlacing fibres.

Growth of bones.—Bones grow in thickness from the fibrous tissue and lime salts laid down by cells in their substance (Figs. 75, 77); while the long bones grow in length from a plate of cartilage (epiphyseal cartilage) which runs across the bone about half an inch

or more from its ends, and which on one surface is also constantly forming bone till the bone ceases to lengthen about the age of sixteen or eighteen. The existence of this cartilage is important to bear in mind, because in children an injury to it may lead to diminished growth of the limb.

Repair of bone is effected by cells of microscopic size : some called osteoblasts, elaborating the materials brought by the blood, and laying down strands of fibrous tissue, between which bone earth is later deposited ; while other cells, known as osteoclasts, dissolve and break up dead or damaged bone. When a fracture has occurred, and the broken ends have been brought into contact, these are surrounded by a mass of blood at first ; this is partly absorbed and partly organized by these cells, first into fibrous tissue and later into bone. The mass surrounding the fractured ends is called the callus, and for some months it forms a distinct thickening, which is gradually smoothed away, leaving the bone as before the fracture. If the ends have not been brought accurately in contact a permanent thickening results.

Varieties of bones.—Apart from the structural varieties, bones fall into four classes : (*a*) long bones like those of the limbs ; (*b*) short bones composed of cancellous tissue like those of wrist and ankle ; (*c*) flat bones like those of the skull ; (*d*) irregular bones like those of the face or the vertebræ.

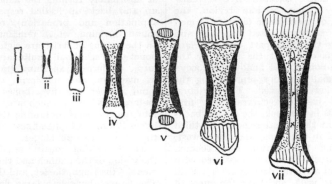

FIG. 75.—Diagram to show growth of a long bone. Cartilage, white. Subperiosteal bone, black. Other sites of bone formation, dotted and vertical lines. (i) Shows the original cartilage model and successive drawings show the development of the bone until in (vii) the only cartilage left is that at the ends of the bone. In (vii) X indicates the bone marrow cavity. (From Schafer, *Essentials of Histology* (after Mathias Duval). (Longmans, Green & Co., Ltd.)

The **skeleton** consists of over 200 bones (Fig. 76). It is divided into an AXIAL part, consisting of the skull, the vertebral column, the ribs with their cartilages,

FIG. 77.—Surface of a growing bone. *SP*, Superficial fibrous layer of periosteum; *DP*, deep cellular layer forming bone; *V*, blood-vessel entering the bone; *HH*, Haversian canals. Magnified by about 200. (Turner's *Anatomy*.)

and the breast-bone, and an APPENDICULAR portion consisting of the four limbs. The hyoid bone in the neck, together with the cartilages protecting the larynx and windpipe, may be described as the VISCERAL skeleton.

AXIAL SKELETON.—The *skull* consists of the cranium, which has eight bones, viz. occipital, two parietal, two temporal, one frontal, ethmoid, and sphenoid ; and of the face, which has fourteen bones, viz. maxillæ or two upper jaw-bones and one lower jaw-bone, two malar or cheek bones, two nasal, two lacrimal, two turbinal, two palate bones, and one vomer bone. (For further details, *see* SKULL.) The *vertebral column* consists of seven vertebræ in the cervical or neck region, twelve dorsal vertebræ, five vertebræ in the lumbar or loin region, the sacrum or sacral bone (a mass formed of five vertebræ fused together and forming the back part of the *pelvis*, which is closed at the sides by the haunch-bones), and finally the coccyx (four small vertebræ representing the tail of lower animals). The vertebral column has four curves : the first forwards in the neck, the second backwards in the dorsal region, the third forward in the loins, and the lowest, involving the sacrum and coccyx, backwards. These are associated with the erect attitude, develop after a child learns to walk, and have the effect of diminishing jars and shocks before these reach internal organs, much as carriage springs protect the contents of a vehicle from injury. This is still further aided

by discs of cartilage placed between each pair of vertebræ. Each vertebra has a solid part, the ' body ' in front, and behind this a ring of bone, the series of rings one above another forming a bony canal, up which runs the spinal cord to pass through an opening in the cranium at the upper end of the canal and there join the brain. (For further details, *see* SPINAL COLUMN.) The *ribs*, twelve in number, on each side, are attached behind to the twelve dorsal vertebræ, while in front they end a few inches away from the breast-bone, but are continued forwards by cartilages. Of these the upper seven reach the breast-bone, these ribs being called ' true ribs ', the next three are joined each to the cartilage above it, while the last two have their ends free and are called ' floating ribs '. The *breast-bone* is shaped something like a short sword, about 6 inches (15 cm.) long, and rather over an inch wide.

APPENDICULAR SKELETON. — The *upper limb* consists of the shoulder region and three segments—the upper arm, the forearm, and the wrist with the hand, separated from each other by joints. In the shoulder lie the clavicle or collar-bone (which is immediately beneath the skin, and forms a prominent object on the front of the neck), and the scapula or shoulder-blade behind the chest. In the upper arm is a single bone, the humerus. In the forearm are two bones, the radius and ulna ; the radius, in the movements of alternately turning the hand palm up and back up (called respectively supination and pronation), rotating round the ulna, which remains fixed. In the carpus or wrist are eight small bones—the scaphoid, semilunar, cuneiform, pisiform, trapezium, trapezoid, os magnum, and unciform. In the hand proper are five bones called metacarpals, upon which are set the four fingers, each containing the three bones known as phalanges, and the thumb with two phalanges.

The *lower limb* consists similarly of the region of the haunch and three segments—the thigh, the leg, and the foot. The haunch-bone is a large flat bone made up of three—the ilium, the ischium, and the pubes, fused together, and forms the side of the pelvis or basin which encloses some of the abdominal

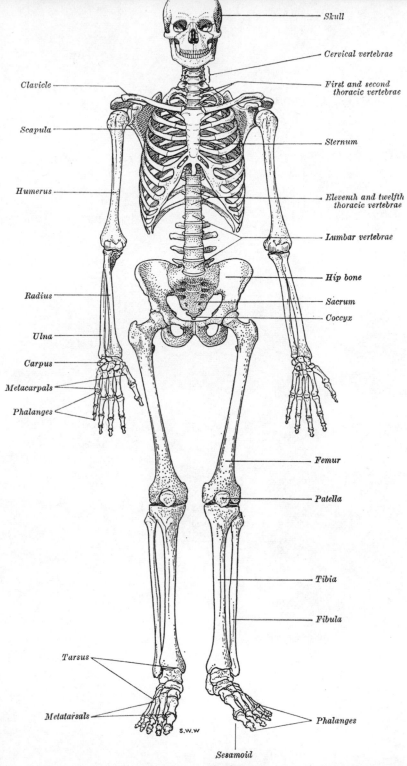

Skull

Cervical vertebrae

First and second
thoracic vertebrae

Clavicle

Scapula

Sternum

Humerus

Eleventh and twelfth
thoracic vertebrae

Lumbar vertebrae

Hip bone

Radius

Sacrum

Coccyx

Ulna

Carpus

Metacarpals

Phalanges

Femur

Patella

Tibia

Fibula

Tarsus

Metatarsals

Phalanges

S.W.W

Sesamoid

FIG. 76 —Human skeleton. (From Gray's *Anatomy*. Longmans, Green & Co., Ltd.) 131

organs. The thigh contains the femur, and the leg contains two bones—the tibia and fibula. In the tarsus are seven bones : the astragalus (which enters into the ankle-joint), calcaneum or heel-bone, scaphoid, external, middle and internal cuneiforms, and the cuboid. These bones are so shaped as to form a distinct arch in the foot both from before back and from side to side. Finally, as in the hand, there are five metatarsals and fourteen phalanges, of which the great toe has two, the other toes three each.

Besides these named bones there are others sometimes found in sinews called 'sesamoid' bones, while the numbers of the regular bones may be increased by extra ribs or diminished by the fusion together of two or more bones.

BONE, DISEASES OF.—Owing to the facts that most bones are deeply buried in the muscles, and that they contain in their earthy matter so much indifferent material, diseases in the bones are both apt to escape notice for a long time, and are actually much slower in their progress than similar diseases in other organs.

ACUTE INFLAMMATION is the disease which produces the most rapid effects. It is divided into acute *periostitis*, or inflammation of the surface of the bone and its enveloping membrane; acute *osteitis*, or inflammation of the bony substance itself ; and acute *osteomyelitis*, or inflammation in the bone and its central cavity. Of these three conditions, osteomyelitis is by far the most important.

Causes.—Osteomyelitis is usually due to infection with the *Staphylococcus aureus*. There is usually a history of a fall or a knock involving the affected limb. The disease is predominantly one of childhood.

Symptoms.—In the slighter forms there is pain and tenderness to touch over some bone, which on examination is found swollen, but there are no general symptoms. In more serious cases severe pain comes on suddenly in a limb, one day perhaps after a slight accident. There is much fever, the temperature rising to 104° or 105° F. (40° or 40·5° C.), and often shivering, and at night delirium. After two or three days the limb becomes swollen, hot, and ten-

der to touch, and still later the skin becomes inflamed and red. If the condition be not treated, general blood-poisoning may result, or abscesses may form in other parts, and death may follow.

Treatment.—As the *Staphylococcus aureus* is one of the organisms most sensitive to penicillin, the introduction of penicillin has revolutionized the treatment. Instead of being a condition practically always demanding operation and often causing prolonged invalidism, it can now be controlled by penicillin within a short space of time. The earlier treatment with penicillin is instituted, the better the results. Unless penicillin is given at an early stage, it may still be necessary to operate to remove any part of the bone that has been completely destroyed as a result of the infection. Such a dead portion of bone is known as a sequestrum (*q.v.*).

CHRONIC INFLAMMATION includes several quite distinct conditions, viz. abscess, necrosis, and exostosis, these conditions usually being due to injury, syphilis, or tuberculosis.

ABSCESS occurs generally in boys about the age of fourteen or fifteen, and the bone usually affected is one of those in the lower limb. The cause is either some local injury or local tuberculous disease.

Symptoms.—There is a painful swelling on the bone usually at the outer or inner side of the knee, and the temperature of the limb may be raised. The pain is generally worse at night and may prevent sleep. This may persist for months or years.

Treatment.—The treatment is surgical, by having the abscess opened, and the administration of the appropriate antibiotic.

NECROSIS means death of a bone. As stated above, it generally follows acute bone inflammation. It also follows severe fractures, occurs from contact with phosphorus (*see* TRADE DISEASES), in syphilis, and occasionally at the end of some severe infectious disease like scarlatina or typhoid fever.

Symptoms.—Usually in the course of suppuration a passage is burst to the exterior, and remains as a constantly discharging ' sinus '. At the bottom of this lies the dead bone or ' sequestrum ', and an operation must be performed for its removal. Usually about three to six months elapse after the original injury before it is loose and ready for removal. If it be not removed the sinus continues to discharge and waxy disease of various internal organs may develop.

EXOSTOSIS is an outgrowth upon a bone, which may be produced by long-continued irritation, *e.g.* the bony growths on the inner side of the knee of those who ride much ; or may be a symptom of syphilis ; or may be of the nature of a tumour. (*See below.*)

SYPHILITIC DISEASE of bone in the secondary stage of this disease takes the form of 'nodes' or swellings due to localized inflammation of the periosteal membrane, and in the tertiary stage there are often areas of great hardening with necrosis of pieces of bone.

TUBERCULOUS DISEASE in bone as a rule occurs in young people, but it also is found now and then in a person well up in years (senile tuberculosis). It may occur (*a*) in the bones of the hand or foot, in which case several may be affected ; (*b*) in the ends of the long bones, when it is very apt to lead to disease of the neighbouring joint; (*c*) in the vertebræ, where it often results in curvature of the spine, or produces a chronic abscess. (*See* ABSCESS, CHRONIC.) 'Caries' is the name given to a crumbling condition of the bone produced by this or any other disease.

Symptoms.—Generally the health is not first-rate and there may be a history of tuberculosis in other organs. There are generally pain, tenderness, and swelling of the affected part. The whole limb, when a toe or finger is affected, may feel hot. Later the skin may get red and thin and a chronic abscess form and burst, leaving a sinus. Or the condition may heal, leaving the bone only a little thickened. The progress is in any case slow, lasting many weeks or months.

Treatment.—The administration of anti-tuberculous drugs is all-important. Rest to the part affected, general exercise of the body in the fresh air, and good food are necessary. When the skin threatens to break, this should be anticipated by an operation, in which the diseased bone, etc., is all scraped away, or even amputation may be advisable in very bad

cases. (*See further under* JOINTS, DISEASES OF.)

TUMOURS.—CHONDROMA, a small tumour of cartilage and bone, grows sometimes under the nail of a finger or toe, and causes a good deal of pain and annoyance. It is easily removed, generally by splitting the nail, and does not return. CANCER rarely if ever begins in a bone, though secondary cancers commonly develop inside bones ; for example cancer of the breast may be followed by secondary cancer in the bone of the arm or elsewhere. SARCOMA is a tumour sometimes found, especially in the larger bones, causing the bone to break readily, or dilating it to a great size ; amputation is necessary for its removal.

RICKETS is a disease of childhood in which the bones do not harden as they ought to do. (*See* RICKETS.)

ACROMEGALY is a disease in which the bones enlarge in size. (*See* ACROMEGALY.)

OSTEITIS is a general term applied to inflammatory conditions of bone. It includes *osteitis deformans* (*q.v.*), in which the long bones become curved and the skull thickened ; also *osteitis fibrosa cystica generalisata* (*q.v.*), in which bones become weakened as a result of the presence of cysts.

OSTEOMALACIA is a disease characterized by a gradual loss of lime salts in the bones, so that these become soft and lose their proper form. It is due to lack of vitamin D and of calcium in the diet. (*See* OSTEOMALACIA.)

OSTEOPOROSIS is a condition characterized by rarefaction and brittleness of bone due to lack of calcium. (*See* OSTEOPOROSIS.)

BORAX, or BIBORATE OF SODA, acts in much the same ways as boric acid, but has not its acid reaction.

Uses.—Its chief use is in the form of a lotion (about 1 part to 30 of water) in all forms of itching and chapping of the skin. In 'thrush' and other forms of irritation about the mouth in children the honey of borax, smeared on several times a day, is very soothing. To clean the mouth as well as soothe it, borax in honey wiped over the gums and tongue is very efficient. As in the case of boric acid, it should not be used in infants and young children.

BORBORYGMUS (βορβορύζω, I rumble) means flatulence in the bowels.

BORIC ACID, or BORACIC ACID, is found in volcanic districts, or is prepared from borax. It is a mild antiseptic.

Uses.—It is used for dressing wounds, either dusted on as powder or in a lotion (1 part in 30). This lotion, mixed with an equal quantity of warm water, makes an extremely good eyewash for painful and inflamed eyes. Lint is sold ready soaked in boric lotion, dried, and generally dyed pink ; it requires only to be dipped in water and applied. Offensive perspiration of the feet is checked by dipping the stockings in boric lotion and drying them before wearing. Because of the risk of toxic effects it should not be used in infants and young children. Boric ointment is used for dressing ulcers or for lubricating instruments.

BORNHOLM DISEASE, also known as devil's grip, and epidemic myalgia, is an acute infective disease due to Coxsackie viruses (q.v.), and characterized by the abrupt onset of pain around the lower margin of the ribs, headache, and fever. It occurs in epidemics, usually during warm weather, and it is more common in young people than the old. The illness usually lasts seven to ten days. It is practically never fatal. The disease is named after the island of Bornholm in the Baltic, where several epidemics have been described.

BOROGLYCERIDE is a clear unctuous antiseptic, made by dissolving boric acid crystals in glycerin while hot.

BOTHRIOCEPHALUS (βοθρίον, a pit; κεφαλή, the head) is the old name for a parasitic worm now known as *Diphyllobochrium latum*. (*See* PARASITES.)

BOTULISM (*botulus*, sausage) is a term applied to a rare type of food-poisoning caused by the toxin arising from the presence in improperly preserved foods of the *Clostridium botulinum*. The first symptoms come on a few hours after the food has been taken and consist of vomiting, abdominal pain, and difficulty of vision. Later, nervous symptoms consisting of double vision, drooping of the eyelids, weakness of the facial muscles, dilatation of the pupils, and difficulty in swallowing and breathing appear. The prognosis is extremely grave, the mortality rate being higher than 50 per cent. Fortunately, the condition is rare in Britain. Since the outbreak at Loch Maree in 1922, when eight fishermen died of the disease after eating sandwiches containing duck paste, only seven cases have occurred in Great Britain.

Treatment.—An antitoxic serum is available, and this should be given, along with full doses of antibiotics. Because of the nervous signs, such as difficulty in swallowing, skilled nursing is essential.

BOUGIES are solid instruments for introduction into natural passages in the body either in order to apply medicaments which they contain or with which they are coated, or, more usually, in order to dilate a narrow part or ' stricture ' of the passage. Thus we have urethral bougies, œsophageal bougies, rectal bougies, etc., made usually of flexible rubber or, in the case of the urethra, of steel.

BOUILLON is a broth or soup prepared from flesh. It is much used in various food preparations and also as a medium for cultivating organisms in bacteriological laboratories.

BOULIMIA, or BULIMIA (βουλιμία), means exaggerated appetite. (*See* APPETITE.)

BOWELS (*see* INTESTINE).

BOXING INJURIES rank eighth in frequency among sports injuries. In the 1957–1958 season there were 137 injuries among the 4,350 contests held under the auspices of the London Amateur Boxing Association. These included 42 cuts in or about the face, five sprains of the fingers, three fractured metacarpals, two fractured noses, 60 knock-outs, and nine cases of amnesia without loss of consciousness.

There has been no death in amateur boxing in Great Britain during the last seven years. In the United States of

America, in 1962, two boxers died after professional fights and two after amateur bouts, compared with 32 killed in football and six in baseball.

The commonest boxing injury is simple nose-bleeding. This can easily be stopped by sitting the boxer upright, pinching the nose, and applying a cold sponge. If it persists after the bout, the nose is plugged with adrenaline gauze or adrenaline-soaked cotton-wool. In the case of abrasions on the face and head, bleeding is stopped by firm pressure. The wound is then bathed with warm saline, and this is followed by application of 1 per cent. cetrimide, and then a light dusting with sulphathiazole powder.

Many boxing injuries can be prevented by the wearing of bandages over the metacarpals, the use of gum shields and laceless gloves weighing 8 ounces (225 grammes), and by having a 'Sorbo' rubber covering under the canvas of the ring.

BRACHIAL means 'belonging to the upper arm'. There are, for example, a brachial artery, and a brachial plexus of nerves through which run all the nerves to the arm. The brachial plexus lies along the outer side of the armpit, and is liable to be damaged in dislocation at the shoulder.

BRACHYCEPHALIC means shortheaded and is a term applied to skulls the breadth of which is at least four-fifths of the length. BRACHYCEPHALY is a characteristic of the Alpine race.

BRACHYDACTYLY is a term applied to the conditions in which the fingers or toes are abnormally short.

BRADYCARDIA (βραδύς, slow; καρδία, the heart) means slowness of the beating of the heart with corresponding slowness of the pulse (below 60 per minute). (*See* HEART DISEASES.)

BRADYKINESIA is a term used to describe the condition in which the movements of the body and limbs are abnormally slow.

BRAIDISM, after James Braid, who introduced it into medicine, is another name for hypnotism. (*See* HYPNOTISM.)

136

BRAIN.—The brain and spinal cord together form the central nervous system, the twelve nerves passing on each side from the brain, and the thirty-one from the cord being called the peripheral nervous system, while the complex chains of nerves and ganglia lying within the chest and abdomen, and acting to a large extent independently of the other two systems, though closely connected with them, make up the autonomic system, and govern the activity of the viscera.

Divisions.—The brain in its simplest form in lowly vertebrate animals is a

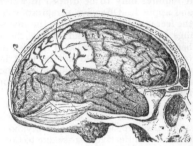

FIG. 78.—Side view of the brain in position within the skull. *F*, Frontal; *P*, parietal; *O*, occipital regions; *R*, fissure of Rolando; *S*, fissure of Sylvius; *PO*, parieto-occipital fissure. (Turner's *Anatomy*.)

thickened part at the front end of the spinal cord, developed in order to govern the organs of special sense, viz. smell, sight, hearing, and taste, lodged near at hand. Higher in the scale, in fishes for example, there are marked bulgings of nervous matter forming the fore-brain, the mid-brain, and the hind-brain, and that part connected with the nerves of the eyes appears to be the highest governing part. In man, however, the part in front of this is specially developed, and not only forms the great bulk of the entire brain, but governs the activities of the rest. This part is called the cerebrum. The brain may be divided into five parts :

(1) CEREBRUM, or *fore-brain* or *prosencephalon*. This forms the great bulk of the brain in amount and consists of two 'cerebral hemispheres' which occupy the entire vault of the cranium and are separated from one another by a deep cleft, the 'median longitudinal fissure'. At the bottom of this cleft the two hemispheres are united by a

thick band of transverse nerve fibres : the corpus callosum. Other fissures or sulci make deep impressions, dividing the cerebrum into lobes. Of these the chief are the fissure of Sylvius and the fissure of Rolando. The lobes of the cerebrum are the frontal lobe in the forehead region, the parietal lobe on the side and upper part of the brain, the occipital lobe to the back, the temporal lobe lying just above the region

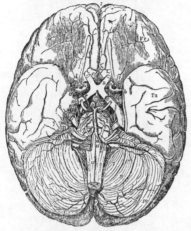

FIG. 79.—The base of the brain viewed from below, with its nerves and arteries. *Fr*, Frontal ; *Ts*, temporo-sphenoidal ; *Oc*, occipital lobes of cerebrum ; *g*, pons ; *m*, medulla ; 7, 8, 9, 10, cerebellum. (Turner's *Anatomy*.)

of the ear, the central lobe or island of Reil lying at the bottom of the Sylvian fissure, and the falciform lobe on the surface towards the longitudinal fissure.

Numbers of shallower infoldings of the surface called furrows or sulci separate raised areas called convolutions or gyri. The outer ⅛ inch (3 mm.) or thereabouts of the cerebral hemispheres consists of grey matter largely made up of ganglion cells, while in the deeper part the white matter consists of medullated nerve fibres connecting different parts of the surface and passing down to the lower parts of the brain. Amongst the white matter lie several rounded masses of grey matter, the ' lenticular ' and ' caudate ' nuclei. In the centre of each cerebral hemisphere is an irregular cavity, the lateral ventricle, each of which communicates with that on the other side and behind with the 3rd

5 *a*

ventricle through a small opening, the foramen of Monro.

(2) BASAL GANGLIA, or *twixt-brain* or *thalamencephalon*, consists of two large masses of grey matter imbedded in the base of the cerebral hemispheres in man, but forming the chief part of the brain in many of the animals. Between these masses lies the 3rd ventricle, from which the infundibulum, a funnel - shaped process, projects downwards into the pituitary body, and above lies the pineal gland. This region includes the important *hypothalamus*.

(3) MID-BRAIN, or *mesencephalon*, is a stalk about ¾ inch (20 mm.) long connecting the cerebrum with the hind-

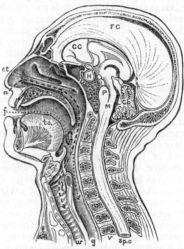

FIG. 80.—Vertical section through the middle of the head and neck. *Cb*, Cerebellum ; *CC*, corpus callosum ; *FC*, falx cerebri, the process of dura mater lying between the two cerebral hemispheres ; *H*, pituitary body ; *M*, medulla oblongata ; *P*, pons Varolii ; *Sp.c*, spinal cord ; *v*, vertebral column. For other letters, see AIR PASSAGES. (After Braune.)

brain. Down its centre lies a tube, the aqueduct of Sylvius, connecting the 3rd and 4th ventricles. Above this aqueduct lie the corpora quadrigemina, and beneath it are the ' crura cerebri ', strong bands of white matter in which important nerve fibres pass downwards from the cerebrum.

(4) CEREBELLUM and PONS VAROLII form the *hind-brain* or *epencephalon*. The pons Varolii is a mass of nerve fibres, some of which run crosswise and others are the continuation of the crura cerebri downwards. The cerebellum

lies towards the back, being placed underneath the occipital lobes of the cerebrum.

(5) MEDULLA or BULB, also known as the *after-brain* or *metencephalon*, is the lowest part of the brain, in structure resembling the spinal cord, with white matter on the surface and grey matter in its interior. This is continuous through the large opening in the skull, foramen magnum, with the spinal cord. Between the medulla, pons, and cerebellum lies the 4th ventricle of the brain.

Structure.—The brain is made up of grey and white matter. In the cerebrum and cerebellum the grey matter is arranged mainly in a layer on the surface, though both have certain grey masses imbedded in the white matter. In the other parts the grey matter is found in definite masses called 'nuclei', from which the nerves spring. The grey matter consists mainly of cells in which all the activities of the brain commence. These cells vary considerably in size and shape in different parts of the brain, though all give off a number of processes, some of which form nerve fibres. The cells on the surface of the cerebral hemispheres, for example, are very numerous, being set in layers five or six deep (Fig. 81). In shape these cells are pyramidal, giving off processes from the apex, from the centre of the base, and from various projections elsewhere on the cell. The grey matter is everywhere penetrated by a rich supply of blood-vessels, and the nerve cells and blood-vessels are supported in a fine network of fibres, known as neuroglia. The white matter consists of nerve fibres, each of which is attached, at one end, to a cell in the grey matter, while, at the other end, it splits up into a tree-like structure round another cell in another part of the grey matter in the brain or spinal cord. The fibres have insulating sheaths of a fatty material, which, in the mass, gives the white matter its colour, and they convey messages from one part of the brain to the other (association fibres), or, grouped into bundles, leave the brain as nerves, or pass down into the spinal cord, where they end near, and exert a control upon, cells from which in turn spring the nerves to the body. Both grey and white matter are

138

bound together by a felt-work called neuroglia. The general arrangement of fibres can be best understood by describing the course of a motor nerve fibre. Arising in a cell on the surface in front of the fissure of Rolando, such a fibre passes inwards towards the centre of the cerebral hemisphere, the collected

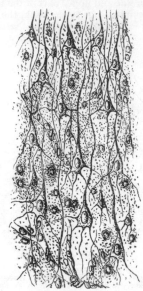

FIG. 81.—Vertical section through the cerebral cortex of the frontal region, showing the pyramidal cells and their processes. (Turner's *Anatomy.*)

mass of fibres as they lie between the lenticular nucleus and optic thalamus being known as the internal capsule. Hence the fibre passes down through the crus cerebri, giving off various small connecting fibres as it passes downwards. After passing through the pons it reaches the medulla, and at this point crosses to the opposite side (decussation of the pyramids). Entering the spinal cord, it passes downwards to end finally in a series of branches (arborization) which meet and touch (synapsis) similar branches from one or more of the cells in the grey matter of the cord (*see* SPINAL CORD).

Size.—The weight of the average male brain is 49½ ounces (1·4 kg.), of the female brain 44½ ounces (1·25 kg.), but brains have been found as heavy as 60 ounces (1·7 kg.). Although the weight of the brain is not in absolute proportion to intellectual power, on the whole the higher races have the heavier brains.

Functions.—The cerebrum is associated with the intellectual faculties in man, and also exerts a guiding influence over the rest of the nervous system. It is not, however, necessary to actual life. If the cerebrum of a frog be destroyed it still breathes and its heart beats, it can hop if pinched, and swim if put in water, but when left alone it sits still till it perishes. If the same happen to a pigeon it can fly when thrown in the air, and can alight, but it does not fly away when threatened, nor will it take food, having lost even the instinct to preserve life. If, on the other hand, the cerebellum of a pigeon be destroyed, the bird cannot maintain its balance, the cerebellum being concerned in the regulation of muscular movements and in preserving the equilibrium.

Plato recognized three mental faculties, which he placed respectively in the liver, heart, and brain, these organs being supposed to secrete the ' animal spirits' appropriate to each faculty; and this view was accepted by the medical writers of antiquity. In the Middle Ages the Arabian physicians, however, following Galen's opinion, placed the different mental faculties in the several ventricles of the brain, this theory being adopted by Duns Scotus, Thomas of Aquino, and referred to by Burton in his *Anatomy of Melancholy*.

Descartes (1596–1650) had the fanciful idea that the pineal body was the seat of the mind, though this structure is now supposed to be the vestige of a third eye. After his time it was fancied that the whole brain must act together in every process, from the fact that, in cases of severe injury to the head, much substance has been lost from some parts of the brain without impairment of any one definite function or memory.

But it has recently been proved that definite areas of surface are associated with definite functions. The earliest systematic attempt to localize the functions of the brain to certain areas was made by Gall and Spurzheim, who founded the system of phrenology in the first quarter of the nineteenth century. Although this system was proved to be wrong both as regards the functions of the brain and the philo-sophic analysis of mental processes, still the criticism it called forth gave a great impetus to the attempt to localize the functions of the brain in definite spots. Between 1820 and 1840 it became established that, in persons who have lost the power of speech during life, the brain shows some disease in the left frontal lobe after death, and in 1861 Broca made the first definite discovery in cerebral localization, by proving that the faculty of speech is governed by a centre in the left inferior frontal convolution, named after him

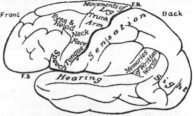

FIG. 82.—Diagram showing areas upon the left surface of the cerebrum associated with definite functions. *FR*, Fissure of Rolando; *FS*, fissure of Sylvius. (Partly after Osler.)

Broca's convolution. His discovery was followed later by the important observation of Hughlings Jackson that certain forms of epilepsy, associated with movements beginning in a definite limb, are caused by disease affecting the part of the brain that borders on the fissure of Rolando, and this discovery has been confirmed and extended by many experimenters and physicians. Fritsch, Hitzig, Ferrier, Sherrington, Grünbaum and others have shown that definite areas near the fissure of Rolando are associated with the movement of definite parts. (*See* Fig. 82.) Further, the occipital lobes are associated with the sense of sight, the temporal lobe with hearing, and the inner surface of the same lobe with taste and smell. The purely intellectual faculties probably are associated with the frontal lobes, which seem to govern nothing else. The functions of the cerebellum have been much disputed, but at least this is sure, that it has to do with the powers of balancing and of regulating movements. The medulla and pons have very important functions, governing many of the processes most essential to life, *e.g.* those of respiration, rate of the heart, swallowing, vomiting, etc., and giving off all the nerves which arise from the brain, except the first four.

Membranes.—The brain is separated from the skull by three membranes—the dura mater, a thick fibrous membrane; the arachnoid mater, a more delicate structure; and the pia mater, adhering to the surface of the brain, and containing the blood-vessels which nourish it. Between each pair is a space containing fluid on which the brain floats as on a water-bed. The fluid beneath the arachnoid membrane mixes with that inside the ventricles through a small opening in the 4th ventricle, called the foramen of Magendie.

These fluid arrangements have a great influence in preserving the brain from injury.

Nerves.—The nerves which come off the brain are twelve in number :

I. Olfactory, to the nose (smell).
II. Optic, to the eye (sight).
III. Oculomotor ⎫
IV. Trochlear ⎬ to eye-muscles.
VI. Abducent ⎭
V. Trigeminal, to skin of face.
VII. Facial, to muscles of face.
VIII. Auditory, to ear (hearing and balancing).
IX. Glossopharyngeal, to tongue (taste).
X. Vagus, to heart, larynx, lungs, and stomach.
XI. Spinal Accessory, to muscles in neck.
XII. Hypoglossal, to muscles of tongue.

Blood-vessels.—Four vessels carry blood to the brain, two internal carotid arteries in front, and two vertebral arteries behind. These communicate to form a circle (circle of Willis) inside the skull, so that if one be blocked the others, by dilating, supply its place. The chief branch of the internal carotid artery on each side is the middle cerebral, and this gives off a small but very important branch which pierces the base of the brain and supplies the region of the basal ganglia with blood. The chief importance of this vessel lies in the fact that the blood in it is under specially high pressure, owing to its close connection with the carotid artery, so that hæmorrhage from it is very liable to occur and thus give rise to apoplexy. Two veins, the veins of Galen, bring the blood away from the interior of the brain, but most of the

140

small veins come to the surface and open into large 'venous sinuses', which run in grooves in the skull, and finally pour their blood into the internal jugular vein that accompanies the carotid artery on each side of the neck.

BRAIN, DISEASES AND INJURIES OF.—The signs of brain disease are in general very indirect, being manifested by some defect in sensation or in the power of action, or by some peculiarity of conduct. The symptoms are more fully discussed under NERVOUS DIS-EASES. (*See also* APHASIA, APOPLEXY, ENCEPHALITIS, EPILEPSY, HEADACHE, HYDROCEPHALUS, MENINGITIS, MENTAL ILLNESS, PARALYSIS.) The following are some of the conditions more exclusively connected with the brain.

ABSCESS is a very serious condition. It results from wounds of the scalp which suppurate and in which the matter does not get free exit, or from suppurating ear disease, in which the discharge from the ear has been stopped. The symptoms are rather vague, but sooner or later there are great headache and vomiting, with rise of temperature, and often some interference with vision. When the abscess lies in the temporal lobe the temperature is often below normal. The treatment should be prevention, by keeping every scalp wound clean, and by having every case of discharging ear disease under medical supervision (*see* EAR, DISEASES OF). When it is recognized that an abscess has occurred in the brain, it is customary to tre-phine the skull and evacuate the abscess, after which recovery often takes place.

ANÆMIA OF THE BRAIN is the cause of fainting when suddenly brought on by weakness of the heart's action. Anæmia of a more chronic type is a cause of sleeplessness in elderly persons, accompanied by weakness of mental power and drowsiness during working hours. It causes also headache, giddi-ness, and ringing in the ears.

COMPRESSION OF THE BRAIN may be caused by the growth of a tumour in the brain, a collection of blood between the brain and skull from injury of the membranes, or suppuration in the same locality from a neglected scalp wound or fracture of the skull.

Unconsciousness coming on some hours after a blow on the side of the head is generally due to a fracture tearing one of the arteries in the membranes and producing a large clot between the skull and brain. The symptoms are vague, but, in addition to unconsciousness, there are generally difficulty of breathing, feeble pulse, and paralysis down one side of the body. The treatment is trephining of the skull (see TREPHINING).

CONCUSSION is a bruising of part of the brain as the result of a blow on the head (generally at the back) or a severe shake of the body. Cases vary in severity from mere giddiness and headache for an hour or two, to complete loss of consciousness lasting for weeks, and include those curious instances of lost memory for facts or even for personal identity which have been much used by novelists. The person lies unconscious and can be roused with difficulty. If he answers questions at all he does so irrelevantly, and shows great irritability of temper, going off to sleep again at once. He lies turned away from the light, with his knees drawn up on the body. Consciousness and convalescence come on very gradually, and for months there may be loss of memory, bad temper, and great susceptibility to the effects of alcohol. Recovery is generally good, but a tendency to epilepsy may remain. The treatment is complete rest in a darkened room, fluid food, cold to the head ; the urine often requires to be drawn off by catheter, and purgatives may be necessary.

BRAIN FEVER is a popular name for several conditions. One is a state of prostration following some severe mental strain, which is not very serious and passes off in the course of a few weeks of rest. Another condition known under this name is encephalitis lethargica, also known popularly as ' sleepy sickness ', in which inflammatory changes accompanied by œdema and hæmorrhages take place in parts of the brain, causing a serious and often fatal disorder. (See ENCEPHALITIS LETHARGICA.) Another condition often called by this name is inflammation of the membranes of the brain, or meningitis, which occurs most commonly in children or in persons suffering from tuberculosis, and which may be a very fatal disease (see MENINGITIS).

HÆMORRHAGE into the brain causes apoplexy. (See APOPLEXY.)

LACERATION of the brain may occur in fracture of the skull. When the injury affects the upper part of the cerebrum, it is not of so great importance as the fact of whether the wound is kept clean and free from suppuration, although near the fissure of Rolando damage to the brain may result in paralysis of a limb. When it occurs at the base of the skull serious injury of the brain is apt to result, very often ending in death (see FRACTURES).

SOFTENING of the brain is a term used in a strictly scientific sense and in a popular sense. In the former case an actual area of brain tissue softens owing to its blood supply being cut off by plugging of its blood-vessels, or in consequence of some long - standing inflammatory process. The symptoms are then those of apoplexy, though not so sudden as if the cause were hæmorrhage. In the popular sense, when persons who have been the subjects of gout, alcoholism, or syphilis, especially elderly persons, become gradually dull in intellect, drowsy, absent-minded, emotional, and finally demented, because of their diseased blood-vessels diminishing the blood supply to, and causing deterioration of, the brain, these symptoms are also attributed to ' softening of the brain '.

TUMOURS of the brain produce very insidious and very complex symptoms, depending on the region they affect. Among the general symptoms are headache, giddiness, vomiting independent of food, and tenderness of the head on pressure. Blindness and mental symptoms come on later, owing to rise of pressure inside the skull. Sometimes these tumours are tuberculous or syphilitic in origin, when the general treatment for these diseases may be of some help In other cases. little good can be done, except palliation of the pain and other symptoms —sometimes by trephining to relieve the pressure. Occasionally a tumour produces definite ' localizing ' symptoms indicating its position in the brain. In such cases an operation may occasionally be performed for the complete and successful removal of the tumour.

BRAN is the meal derived from the outer covering of a cereal grain. It contains little or no carbohydrate, and is mainly used to provide roughage in certain cases of constipation.

BRANDY (*see* ALCOHOL).

BREAD is usually prepared from wheat flour which contains about 15 per cent. of water, 8 to 12 per cent. of gluten (vegetable albumin), and about 70 per cent. of starch, together with small quantities of sugar and dextrin. The whitest flour is very deficient in salts and vitamin B₁, because the husk and the germ of the wheat grain have been separated from it in the process of milling. The separated outer part of the grain, known as ' offal ' or ' bran ', contains about 15 per cent. of nitrogenous substance, 3 per cent. of fat, and 5 per cent. of salts. In the separation of the bran, therefore, much nutritious material is lost, but at the same time the bread is rendered more digestible. When the entire grain is ground up, the resulting flour is known as ' whole meal '. In ' fine meal ' or ' entire white flour ' a portion of the bran only is removed. In ' standard flour ' 20 per cent. of the flour is removed as bran and the flour consists of 80 per cent. of the grain. It has a distinctly brownish colour in consequence of the small amount of bran remaining in it. ' Patent grade flour ' is almost pure white and is that most used by bakers for bread-making as it contains practically no bran, absorbs a large amount of water, and makes a large white loaf. In ' aerated bread ' carbonic acid gas is forced through the dough under pressure instead of the flour being fermented by the addition of yeast. A similar result is produced by baking powders.

Other grains used for bread-making are barley, which is slightly deficient in albuminous material but richer in mineral matter than wheat ; rye, which produces a dark-coloured, sour bread equal in nutrition to that of wheat but somewhat liable to produce diarrhœa in those unaccustomed to it ; oats, which produces a granular type of

bread, with laxative properties, that is much richer than wheat in fat and mineral matters ; and maize, which is richer in fat but poorer in mineral matter than wheat, and of which the albuminous material seems to be defective in nutritive qualities.

With regard to nutritive value, white wheaten bread of 70-72 per cent. extraction contains on an average 7·9 per cent. of protein, 0·7 per cent. of fat, and 53·7 per cent. of carbohydrate, giving a total calorie value per 100 grams of 260 calories. When bread is toasted so that water is driven off, the calorie value is raised to over 300 calories per 100 grammes. Oatmeal (dry) has an average value of about 390 calories per 100 grammes.

In the war of 1939–45 the extraction of the wheatberry was increased from 72 per cent. to 85 per cent. During the post-war years the rate of extraction varied between 80 and 90 per cent., and in 1949 it was 85 per cent. National flour at this time was reinforced with calcium (*creta preparata*) at the rate of 14 oz. per 280 lb. In 1953, arrangements were made whereby two flours became available : a National flour of 80 per cent. extraction, and a ' white ' flour of 70 per cent. extraction to which were added calcium carbonate, aneurine (vitamin B₁), nicotinic acid, and iron. In 1956, new regulations were introduced which, for all practical purposes, abolished ' National flour ' as such, and decreed that all flour intended for human consumption should contain not less than 1·65 mg. of iron, 0·24 mg. of vitamin B₁, and 1·6 mg. of nicotinic acid or nicotinamide per 100 grammes, and, except in the case of flour containing the whole of the products derived from the milling of wheat, 235-390 mg. of chalk per 100 grammes.

BREAK-BONE FEVER is another name for dengue (*q.v.*).

BREASTS, or MAMMARY GLANDS, are found in the most highly developed class of animals, called the Mammalia, for the purpose of suckling the young. As a rule they are confined to the female sex, though the male has rudimentary nipples, and, even in man, individuals occur in the male sex who have well-developed glands and have been known to produce milk. These glands are developed in the skin of the chest, and, in the full-grown female, extend from the second to the sixth or seventh rib, being at the centre about 2 inches (5 cm.) thick. There is usually one on each side, but small supplementary breasts are occasionally found in the armpit or low down on the abdomen. In the centre is a dark patch, called the ' areola ', which surrounds the nipple. This areola darkens during pregnancy. This, together with enlargement of the whole breast and dilatation of its veins, forms an important and early sign of this condition. In structure each breast consists of from twelve to twenty compartments, each of which contains a system of branching tubes lined by cells that form the fatty and fluid materials composing the milk. In each section the tubes open on the surface of the nipple by a single small tube, or duct, of which therefore there are twelve to twenty in all. Between these gland tubes lie muscle fibres (which give the breasts their firmness), fibrous tissue, and fat (which is specially plentiful in elderly women).

BREASTS, DISEASES OF.—These glands go through great changes during the course of life, becoming considerably enlarged about the age of puberty, afterwards congested at each monthly period, then undergoing great development during pregnancy, so as to be double the usual size during the time of suckling, and finally, with advancing years, undergoing gradual absorption, though, in stout persons, their actual size increases from deposit of fat.

ACUTE INFLAMMATION AND ABSCESS. — **Causes.** — This is most common during the period of suckling a child, and particularly during the first two months. The infection usually reaches the breast from the nipple, as a result of cracks of the nipple and lack of cleanliness. Another common cause is an indrawn nipple. Passing congestion, producing swelling and tenderness, sometimes appears in boys or girls at the time of puberty, but rarely goes on to abscess.

Symptoms.—Discomfort in some part of the breast, with increased hardness and fullness, usually towards the lower edge, is first noticed, and, if treatment

be then begun, the majority of cases do not go on to abscess. If the condition remains untreated, definite pain next comes on, especially when the infant sucks, along with redness, swelling, and heat, the general signs of abscess. Finally, the skin over one spot, usually about a couple of inches from the nipple, turns purple, and here the abscess bursts.

Treatment.—It is essential that every care should be taken to prevent infection of the breast, by scrupulous attention to cleansing of the breast during the later stages of pregnancy and during suckling. This is best done by careful washing with soap and water ; scrubbing with a brush is usually unnecessary. If the nipples are retracted during pregnancy, they should be drawn out every day. During suckling, the nipples should be carefully cleaned with sterile (*i.e.* boiled) water each time the baby is put to the breast.

If, in spite of these precautions, the breast becomes hard, tender, or congested, a kaolin poultice should be applied, and every care taken to ensure that the breast is emptied completely at every feed, preferably by the baby. Occasionally it may be necessary to use a breast pump to empty the breast. If the condition does not respond to this treatment, penicillin is used. If an abscess forms, it is opened and drained. In severe cases in which it is necessary to wean the baby, the secretion of milk is stopped by taking one of the œstrogenic hormones, *e.g.* stilbœstrol (*q.v.*).

CHRONIC INFLAMMATION, or MASTITIS, may take the form of a chronic abscess, but, more commonly, it consists of simple swelling and pain in one part of the breast, often erroneously believed by the affected person to be cancer.

Symptoms.—This condition is not due to infection, but to some disturbance of the normal control of the breast exerted by the ovaries and the pituitary gland. It occurs with increasing frequency after the age of 30 years, and is more liable to occur in women who have borne children. Pain is the principal symptom. This is worse just before the monthly period or during the early days of the period. It may be confined to one part of the breast or may involve the whole breast. Both breasts may be involved. One or more swellings may be seen or felt in the breast.

Treatment.—The condition is made much worse by the patient allowing her mind to dwell on it and by constant handling of the swelling, so that when the breast is completely covered up and supported by a well-fitting brassière, complete recovery may speedily take place. The first essential, however, is that medical advice is sought, to decide whether or not the pain and swelling are due to cancer of the breast.

NEURALGIA may be very painful during pregnancy, in pelvic disorders, or in general troubles like anæmia and rheumatism. It is treated like neuralgia elsewhere.

CRACKED NIPPLES are sometimes very troublesome. For their treatment see under Acute Inflammation above. When there is a chronic eczematous condition, a nipple-shield should be applied and fixed with plaster or tapes.

TUMOURS.—In consequence of the fact that the breast is one of the organs most frequently attacked by cancer, many women render themselves unnecessarily unhappy over some swelling in the breast, taking for cancer what is often simply chronic inflammation, or a cyst or adenoma, the two latter being common non-malignant growths. In every case, immediately a woman discovers a small nodule in her breast she should consult a surgeon. If the swelling be not cancer—and usually it is not—her mind will be relieved, and the treatment, whether by operation or not, will not in general necessitate the removal of the breast. If cancer be present, then the earlier an operation be done the more chance there is of a complete cure. In such cases it is now the practice to remove the entire breast, part of the muscle under it, and the glands and fat of the armpit, because the cancer is apt to have long rootlets or secondary growths in neighbouring glands.

BREATH, DISORDERS OF.—The composition of the breath and the changes that air undergoes when it is breathed are described under AIR; the manner in which breathing is

effected is described under RESPIRATION. (*See also* BREATHLESSNESS, CHEST DISEASES, *and* LUNG DISEASES.)

BAD BREATH, or HALITOSIS, is sometimes extremely unpleasant to those around the subject of the trouble, although the smell may be extremely foul without the person himself being conscious of it.

Causes.—Frequent causes are bad teeth, infections of the gums (*e.g.* Vincent's angina), chronic tonsillitis, and indigestion. Besides these, an excessively fœtid condition is caused by bronchiectasis (*see* LUNGS, DISEASES OF), by ulceration about the bones of the nose, and by a disease of the nose, known as ozœna, in which crusts constantly form there (*see* NOSE, DISEASES OF).

Treatment.—Careful attention to the hygiene of the mouth is the first essential (*see* TEETH), or the dental treatment of any defective teeth or infection of the gums. Tonsillectomy may be required if the tonsils are chronically inflamed. In one form of tonsillitis, small cheesy pellets of secretion collect in the hollows of the tonsils and putrefy; the tendency to this is lessened by using daily some solvent or antiseptic gargle (*see* GARGLES). Indigestion with furred tongue is also credited with being a frequent cause of bad breath (*see* DYSPEPSIA). The smell may be temporarily relieved by placing a small drop of some essential oil, such as cloves, occasionally on the tongue, or by various scented sweets, or by means of a mouth wash containing one teaspoonful of concentrated peppermint water B.P., and one teaspoonful of salt in 8 ounces (200 millilitres) of water.

BREATH-HOLDING. — Breath-holding attacks are not uncommon in infants and toddlers. They are characterized by the child suddenly stopping breathing in the midst of a bout of crying evoked by pain, some emotional upset, or loss of temper. The breath may be held so long that the child goes blue in the face. The attack is never fatal and the condition disappears spontaneously after the age of 3 to 5 years, but once a child has acquired the habit it may recur quite often.

The attacks require no treatment as recovery is spontaneous and rapid. In no circumstances should the parents dramatize the situation by slapping, pinching, or drenching the child with water.

BREATHLESSNESS may be due to any condition which renders the blood impure or deficient in oxygen, and which therefore produces excessive involuntary efforts to gain more air.

Causes.—Many diseased *conditions of the lungs* diminish the area available for breathing, *e.g.* pneumonia, tuberculosis, emphysema, bronchitis, collections of fluid in the pleural cavities, and pressure by a tumour or aneurysm.

Pleurisy causes short, rapid breathing to avoid the pain of deep inspiration.

Narrowing of the air passages may produce sudden and alarming attacks of difficult breathing, especially among children ; *e.g.* in laryngismus, croup, asthma, and diphtheria (*see these headings*).

Almost all *affections of the heart* cause breathlessness when the person undergoes any special exertion.

Anæmia is a frequent cause.

Obesity is often associated with shortness of breath.

Among the *general diseases* which may interfere with breathing, the uræmia of Bright's disease and the coma which may occur in diabetes mellitus must be noted.

Treatment.—In young girls who become breathless on very slight exertion the treatment is generally that for bloodlessness. (*See* ANÆMIA.) For the treatment of breathlessness in stout people, see CORPULENCE. In all conditions of breathlessness due to disease of a lung, the patient finds most ease in breathing when he lies upon the affected side. In most inflammatory conditions of the air passages much relief is gained from steam inhalations. The subjects of heart disease, if able to go about, should not unduly exert themselves, and are benefited by one of the forms of treatment mentioned under HEART DISEASES. Patients confined to bed by a cardiac affection are frequently unable to lie down, and must be provided with a comfortable bed-rest. Their difficulty of breathing is often due to bronchitis (*see* BRONCHITIS), or to collection of fluid in the chest (*see* DROPSY), which requires special and energetic treatment. For breathlessness with lividity, oxygen inhalation is often usefully employed.

BRETYLIUM TOSYLATE is one of the newer drugs introduced for the treatment for hypertension. It acts by inhibiting sympathetic nerve action.

BRIGHT'S DISEASE is a term applied to a class of diseases of the kidneys which have as their most common symptom the presence of albumin in the urine, and frequently also the presence of dropsy. These associated symptoms, in connection with kidney disease, were first described in 1827 by Dr. Richard Bright. Since that time the subject has been investigated by many able physicians, and it is now well established that the above-named symptoms may be dependent on various causes. (*See* ALBUMINURIA.) Further, one or both of these symptoms may be absent in cases of Bright's disease which are readily recognizable as such from other symptoms.

There is still considerable confusion in the classification of this group of diseases but, speaking generally, it may be said that the terms nephritis or glomerulonephritis are synonymous with Bright's disease, and that these are subdivided into :

Acute Bright's Disease or Acute Glomerulonephritis.

Subacute Bright's Disease or Subacute Glomerulonephritis.

Chronic Bright's Disease or Chronic Glomerulonephritis.

ACUTE BRIGHT'S DISEASE (ACUTE GLOMERULONEPHRITIS).

Cause.—This is a disease predominantly of childhood. It is practically always associated with an infection of the throat, tonsils, sinuses, or some other part of the upper respiratory tract by the hæmolytic streptococcus. As this is the causative organism of scarlet fever and of erysipelas, acute glomerulonephritis may also occur in association with these two diseases. The first signs of kidney involvement usually occur 7-21 days after the original infection with the hæmolytic streptococcus. In view of this fact, taken in conjunction with the fact that no infecting organism is ever found in the urine or in the kidneys, it is now assumed that glomerulonephritis is an allergic reaction on the part of the kidneys to the hæmolytic streptococcus. Predisposing factors are exposure to cold or general poor health, but it will often be found that the condition occurs in a previously healthy child without any warning apart from the fact that he has had a 'sore throat' for some days. In this form of the disease the kidneys are red, swollen, and congested. There is a diffuse congestion of the blood-vessels throughout the kidneys, and this results in degeneration and swelling of the lining cells of the glomeruli. Later the renal tubules are involved. These damaged lining cells of the glomeruli and the tubules are passed in the urine, and, glued together in the inflammatory process with red blood corpuscles, they unite to form casts of the renal tubules through which they have passed.

There is another form of acute glomerulonephritis in which there is a less diffuse involvement of the kidneys —what is sometimes termed acute focal glomerulonephritis. This occurs in conditions such as subacute bacterial endocarditis (q.v.), in which small clots (or emboli) are discharged from the damaged heart valve, and some of these emboli lodge in the kidneys.

Symptoms.—The symptoms to which the condition gives rise are usually of a severe character, although frequently cases of acute Bright's disease, occurring, for example, in the course of scarlet fever, are so mild as to escape notice at the time, and only cause trouble when the condition becomes chronic in later life. Vomiting very frequently ushers in the attack, pain in the back of a moderate degree is also a common symptom, and there is often for the first day or two a slight febrile disturbance. Dropsy, varying in degree from slight puffiness under the eyes to an accumulation of fluid distending the body cavities and causing serious embarrassment to respiration, is a very common accompaniment. The digestion is almost invariably disordered, the appetite is poor, and the

146

patient is troubled with headache. There is also a rise in the blood-pressure. The urine is reduced in quantity, is of dark, smoky, or blood-stained colour, and, when it is tested, is found to contain a large amount of albumin, while under the microscope blood corpuscles with hyaline and epithelial casts, as above mentioned, are found in abundance.

This state of acute inflammation, if very severe, may lead to stoppage of the excretion of the urine to such an extent that waste products accumulate in the blood and paralyse vital activity. Death is then generally preceded by severe headache followed by unconsciousness and frequently by convulsions, a condition known as 'acute uræmia'. Even in extreme cases, however, energetic treatment may save the patient's life. Death may also result from heart failure. More frequently the acute disease partially subsides and gradually results in the establishment of subacute or chronic Bright's disease. In other cases an arrest of the inflammatory action occurs, the urine increases in amount, the blood and later the albumin and other abnormal constituents disappear from the urine, the dropsy subsides, the strength returns, and the disease entirely disappears.

Treatment.—The greatest care must be taken of a person showing for the first time the symptoms of acute Bright's disease, because, although the condition is seldom fatal in a first attack, if it be allowed to pass on to the chronic form the person must in future live the life of a semi-invalid, or, at all events, is very greatly limited in the extent of his activities. The patient must remain in the equable temperature of bed, carefully protected from all chance of chill, and is usually placed directly between blankets and clothed in woollen garments. It is essential to maintain the free action of the skin, and to this end, in addition to confinement in bed, hot-water bottles, hot-air baths, or hot wet packs which produce free perspiration are administered, particularly if the onset of uræmia threatens. (See BATHS.) Free movement of the bowels is also important, and this can best be achieved by an enema every other morning. During the acute phase of the disease the diet should be light and there should be some restriction of the fluid intake. Unless the daily output of urine is very low, however, it is seldom advisable to restrict the fluid intake to much less than two pints daily. At first the diet should consist principally of milk and glucose drinks flavoured with fruit juices. As the condition improves, the diet should be gradually supplemented by the addition of milk puddings, jelly, bread and butter, and steamed fish. Although restriction of protein is not now considered as essential as it used to be, meat should not be given during the first few weeks.

Local means of relieving congestion of the kidneys, such as warm fomentations upon, or cupping of, the loins may be adopted. Hot sponging, followed by friction with warm, dry towels, will encourage the skin to act. If acute uræmia threatens, a hot-air bath may be of great help.

When dropsy is a troublesome feature, the abolition of salt from the diet and the substitution of salt-free bread and of potatoes, fresh butter, fruit, and green vegetables for the milk is recommended by some authorities. During the period of convalescence from this disease special care must be exercised in the avoidance of animal food in large quantity, of alcoholic stimulants, and of chills to the surface of the body. It is essential that the patient should be kept in bed until the urine has become normal again. A change for a time to a dry, warm climate is often beneficial.

SUBACUTE BRIGHT'S DISEASE (Subacute Glomerulonephritis) may occur as a direct sequel of the acute stage of the disease, the patient passing direct from the acute to the subacute phase. In other cases the transition is more gradual: the patient never recovers completely from the acute phase, and over a period of months, or even years, gradually passes into the subacute stage. In yet another small group of cases subacute glomerulonephritis appears to develop without any preceding acute glomerulonephritis. The probable explanation of these cases is that the acute stage has been so mild as to be overlooked, but the pathological process has been present all the time, gradually producing exten-

sive enough changes in the kidney to result in all the typical signs and symptoms of subacute glomerulonephritis. The brunt of the process in this stage falls on the renal tubules, which are the site of marked degenerative changes, resulting in swelling and desquamation of the lining cells. The kidneys are large and white. The urine contains large amounts of albumin, many fatty and hyaline casts, but practically no blood This stage of Bright's disease is sometimes referred to as the nephrotic stage, ' nephrosis ' being a term introduced by Muller in 1905 to designate a degenerative lesion confined to the kidney tubules.

Symptoms. — The characteristic features are dropsy, which may be generalized and include ascites (fluid in the abdomen) and effusions in the pleural cavity ; pallor, which is partly due to anæmia and partly due to the subcutaneous œdema ; normal or low blood-pressure ; diminution in the daily output of urine, and marked albuminuria. Indeed, there are few other conditions in which such gross albuminuria is found. Unlike the acute stage, there is little or no blood in the urine, and the nitrogenous contents of the blood are only slightly raised in amount, if at all. The protein content of the blood is much decreased owing to the steady loss of protein in the urine, and this hypoproteinæmia, as it is called, is one of the principal causes of the dropsy. Patients in this stage of Bright's disease are very susceptible to infections, especially of the lungs and the intestines, and such an infection may be responsible for a fatal termination.

Treatment.—The essentials of treatment are rest in bed, relief of the œdema (or dropsy) and alleviation of the anæmia. As the œdema is primarily due to a deficient concentration of protein in the blood, treatment should consist of a high protein diet, *i.e.* one containing 100-120 grammes of protein daily. The less salt the diet contains the better, but a ' salt-free ' diet is most unpalatable. If the dropsy does not respond to such a diet, then diuretics should be administered : urea, the organic mercurial diuretics (mersalyl), or theophylline ethylenediamine (aminophylline). Full doses of iron are given to relieve the anæmia. In certain cases the administration of cortisone, or one of its analogues, is of value.

CHRONIC BRIGHT'S DISEASE (CHRONIC GLOMERULONEPHRITIS) is the final stage of the disease. It may follow directly upon the subacute stage, or may arise as a result of repeated recurrence of the acute stage. In other cases there may be a long period intervening between the subacute and the chronic stage, whilst in others again there may be no history of previous kidney disease. Here the probable explanation is that the original stages of the disease have been so slight as to be overlooked. The kidneys in this stage are small, contracted, and usually white in appearance because of the diminution in the number of active blood-vessels. This characteristic appearance is due to gradual replacement of the active kidney tissue by fibrous, or scar, tissue. It should be pointed out that a similar condition, both pathologically and clinically, may arise as a result of long-continued degenerative changes in the kidneys produced by arterial disease. This is the condition now commonly referred to as *nephrosclerosis*.

Symptoms.—These vary considerably, depending upon the stage the changes in the kidney have reached. In the early stages they may be similar to those of the subacute stage, but gradually the blood-pressure tends to rise, the albuminuria decreases in amount, the dropsy diminishes (until heart failure sets in), and the nitrogenous contents of the blood (*e.g.* urea) increase. Because of the inability of the kidneys to concentrate the urine, the specific gravity of the urine falls to 1005 (or less) and there is not the normal variation between the concentration of the urine voided during the night and that voided during the day. Very often in the later stages the patient complains of symptoms not apparently directly connected with the kidney, *e.g.* headache, shortness of breath, failing vision, loss of appetite, indigestion, or even apoplexy. Many of these symptoms are due to the associated arteriosclerosis or high blood-pressure. The dimness of vision is due to retinitis, which arises as a result of arteriosclerosis of the retinal artery. The apoplexy is a result of arterio-

sclerosis of the arteries supplying the brain. This may lead to blockage of the arteries (cerebral thrombosis) or rupture of the arteries (cerebral hæmorrhage). If the patient does not die of some intercurrent infection, heart failure, or a stroke, the final stage is uræmia (*q.v.*).

Treatment.—As the condition is incurable, the treatment is palliative, *i.e.* it is directed to relieving as much as possible the strain on the kidneys and the heart. Thus the patient should lead as quiet and as sheltered a life as possible, preferably in a warm, dry climate. He should avoid exposure to cold and damp, and in the winter should always be warmly clad. A certain amount of quiet exercise should be encouraged, except when there are exacerbations of the condition; these are indications for a period of rest in bed. The diet should not contain too much protein, but it is a mistake to impose too rigid restrictions. The appetite is often poor and requires stimulating rather than the reverse. Condiments, spices, strong tea and coffee should be avoided. Alcohol in moderation, especially in the form of spirits and light wines, does no harm. If signs of heart failure develop, then digitalis should be given. Dropsy may be so marked as to require treatment, and here theophylline ethylenediamine (aminophylline) is the safest diuretic. If this fails, then mersalyl may be given, but in view of its action in the kidneys its use must be carefully controlled. Sedatives are often required, and of these the barbiturates are usually the most effective: *e.g.* phenobarbitone. In some cases chloralamide or chloral hydrate and one of the bromides in combination may be more effective. Iron should be given if there is any anæmia, but the anæmia in chronic glomerulonephritis is very resistant to treatment. If constipation is troublesome, the best treatment is an enema every other day; in other cases regular doses of liquid paraffin or of one of the saline purgatives may be preferred, but excessive purgation must always be avoided.

BROMIDES are salts of bromine. The bromides of potassium, sodium, strontium, and ammonium are used in medicine. They act chiefly by depressing activity, and dull sensibility of the brain.

Uses.—Introduced to clinical medicine just over a hundred years ago, the bromides were for long the standard treatment of epilepsy. For this purpose they have now been largely replaced by the barbiturates, or more recent anti-convulsant drugs, but they are still of value in occasional cases of epilepsy which do not respond satisfactorily to the newer drugs. Their other main use to-day is as an occasional sedative in mild cases of insomnia : either alone in a dosage of 10 to 20 grains (0·6 to 1·2 G.), or in combination with chloral hydrate.

They have the disadvantage of tending to produce an eruption, especially about the face. They must not be taken recklessly, or their use may become a habit. As a result of taking bromides for a long time some people may show symptoms of a disturbed balance of mind, which pass off when the drug is omitted.

BROMIDROSIS (βρῶμος, stench ; ἱδρώς, sweat) means the excretion of evil-smelling perspiration. (*See* PERSPIRATION, DISORDERS OF.)

BROMISM is the name given to a group of symptoms consisting of acne on the face, mental dullness, sleepiness, weakness, unsteady gait, and bad breath, which shows that too much bromide is being taken.

BROMPTON MIXTURE is a prescription containing, morphine, cocaine and whisky (or rum) which for long has had a high reputation as a most effective pain-reliever, particularly in the terminal stages of painful diseases such as cancer.

BRONCHIAL TUBES (*see* AIR PASSAGES, LUNGS).

BRONCHIECTASIS (βρόγχος, windpipe ; ἔκτασις, lengthening). (*See* LUNGS, DISEASES OF.)

BRONCHIOLECTASIS is the term applied to the morbid dilatation of the bronchioles as a result of disease of their walls.

BRONCHIOLES is the term applied to the finest divisions of the bronchial tubes.

BRONCHIOLITIS is a name sometimes applied to bronchitis affecting the finest bronchial tubes, also known as capillary bronchitis.

BRONCHITIS (βρόγχος, windpipe) means inflammation of the mucous membrane of the bronchial tubes. Well known as one of the most common diseases of the climate of Great Britain, bronchitis exists in either an *acute* or a *chronic* form.

(*a*) ACUTE BRONCHITIS, like other inflammatory affections of the chest, often develops following exposure to cold, particularly if accompanied with damp, or sudden change from a heated to a cool atmosphere. It may also arise as the result of inhaling irritating dust or vapours. The exciting cause is infection of the bronchial tree with one or more of the catarrh-producing organisms, and great numbers of these bacteria are commonly found in the expectoration.

Symptoms. — The symptoms vary according to the severity of the attack, and more especially according to the extent to which the inflammatory action spreads in the bronchial tubes. The disease usually manifests itself at first in the form of catarrh, or common cold ; but the accompanying feverishness and general constitutional disturbance proclaim the attack to be something more severe, and symptoms denoting the onset of bronchitis soon present themselves. A short, painful, dry cough, accompanied with rapid and wheezing respiration, a feeling of rawness and pain in the throat and behind the breast-bone, and of oppression or tightness throughout the chest, mark the early stages of the disease.

After a few days, expectoration begins to come with the cough, at first scanty and viscid or frothy, but soon becoming copious and of purulent character. In general, after free expectoration has been established the more urgent and distressing symptoms abate; and, while the cough may persist for a length of time, often extending to three or four weeks, in the majority of instances convalescence advances, and the patient is ultimately restored to health, although not infrequently a tendency is left to a recurrence of the disease on exposure to its exciting causes.

When the ear or the stethoscope is applied to the chest of a person suffering from such an attack as that now described, there are heard in the earlier stages snoring or cooing sounds, mixed up with others of wheezing or fine whistling quality, accompanying respiration. These are named dry sounds or rhonchi, and they are occasionally so abundant and distinct as to convey their vibrations to the hand applied to the chest, as well as to be audible to a bystander at some distance. As the disease progresses these sounds become to a large extent replaced by others of crackling or bubbling character, which are termed moist sounds or crepitations. Both these kinds of abnormal sounds are readily explained by a reference to the pathological condition of the parts. One of the first effects of inflammation upon the bronchial mucous membrane is to cause some degree of swelling, which, together with the presence of a tough secretion closely adhering to it, tends to narrow the tubes. The respired air as it passes through the narrowed tubes gives rise to the dry or sonorous breath sounds, the coarser being generated in the large, and the finer or wheezing sounds in the small divisions of the bronchi. Before long, however, the discharge from the bronchial mucous membrane becomes more abundant and less glutinous, and accumulates in the tubes till dislodged by coughing. The respired air, as it passes through this fluid, causes the moist *râles*, or crepitations, above described. In most instances both moist and dry sounds are heard abundantly in the same case, since different portions of the bronchial tubes are affected at different times in the course of the disease.

Such are briefly the main characteristics presented by an ordinary attack of acute bronchitis running a favourable course.

The case is, however, very different when the inflammation spreads into, or when it primarily affects, the minute ramifications of the bronchial tubes which are in immediate relation to the air-cells of the lungs, giving rise to that form of the disease known as *capillary bronchitis*. When this takes place all the symptoms already detailed become greatly intensified, and the outlook becomes much more serious in consequence of the interruption to the entrance of air into the lungs, and thus to the due aeration of the blood. Indeed the condition may become indistinguishable from broncho-pneumonia. The feverishness and restlessness increase, the cough becomes incessant, the respiration extremely rapid and laboured, the nostrils dilating with each effort, and evidence of impending suffocation appears. The surface of the body is pale or dusky, the lips are livid, while breathing becomes increasingly difficult and is attended with suffocative paroxysms which render the recumbent posture impossible. Unless speedy relief is obtained by coughing and expectoration, the patient's strength gives way, somnolence and delirium set in, and death ensues. All this may be brought about in a few days, and such cases, particularly among the very young or the aged, sometimes prove fatal within forty-eight hours.

In addition to the auscultatory signs present in ordinary bronchitis, there generally exist in this form of the disease abundant fine crepitations at the bases of both lungs; and the appearance of these organs after death shows the minute bronchi and many of the air-cells to be filled with matter similar to that which had been expectorated, and which has thus acted as a mechanical hindrance to the entrance of the air and caused death by asphyxia.

Acute bronchitis is pre-eminently dangerous at the extremes of life, and mortality statistics show it to be one of the most fatal of the diseases of those periods. This is to be explained not only by the well-recognized fact that all acute diseases tell with great severity on the feeble frames alike of infants and aged people, but more particularly by the tendency which bronchitis undoubtedly has, in them, to assume the capillary form, and, when it does so, to prove quickly fatal. The importance, therefore, of early attention to the slightest evidence of bronchitis among the very young or the aged can scarcely be overrated.

Bronchitis is also apt to be very severe when it occurs in persons who are addicted to intemperance. Again, in those who suffer from any disease affecting directly or indirectly the respiratory functions, such as tuberculosis or heart disease, the supervention of an attack of acute bronchitis is an alarming complication, increasing, as it necessarily does, the embarrassment of breathing. The same remark is applicable to those numerous instances of its occurrence in children who are, or have been, suffering from such diseases as have always associated with them a certain degree of bronchial irritation, such as measles and whooping-cough.

One other source of danger of a special character in bronchitis remains to be mentioned, viz. collapse of the lung. Occasionally a branch of a bronchial tube becomes plugged up with secretion, so that the area of the lung to which this branch brings air ceases to be inflated on inspiration. The small quantity of air imprisoned in the portion of lung gradually escapes, but no fresh air enters, and the part collapses and becomes of solid consistence. Increased difficulty of breathing is the result, and when a large portion of lung is affected by the plugging up of a large bronchus, a fatal result may rapidly follow, the danger being specially great in the case of children. Fortunately, the obstruction may sometimes be removed by vigorous coughing, and relief is then obtained.

Treatment.—In those mild cases which are more of the nature of a simple catarrh little else will be found necessary than confinement in a warm room, or in bed, for a few days, and the use of light diet, together with warm diluent drinks, warm milk being specially beneficial. Additional measures are, however, called for when the disease is more markedly developed. Either penicillin or one of the sulphonamides should be given. In the early stages of the disease, when the cough is harsh and unproductive, linctuses give considerable relief. Sedatives are also usually required at night, *e.g.* chloralamide or phenobarbitone. Opium or morphine must never be given to a patient with bronchitis, because of its depressant effect upon the respiratory centre. In the later stages

of the disease, as the cough becomes looser, expectorants (*q.v.*) are of value. From the outset of the attack the employment of warm applications to the chest, in the form of fomentations or poultices, affords great relief. In children, rubbing the chest with some stimulating liniment such as camphorated oil has a similar effect.

In the earlier stages few remedial measures are of greater value than the frequent inhalation of steam. This is accomplished readily enough in the case of adults by the use of an inhaler or simply by breathing over an open-mouthed vessel containing boiling water. In children, in whom this plan cannot be carried out in the same manner, there is in general no difficulty in surrounding them with an atmosphere of steam by erecting over the bed or cot a tent, formed by a screen and blanket, under which can be led the orifice of a tin kettle heated by a

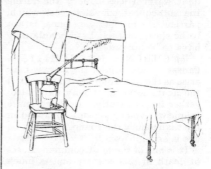

Fig. 83.—Bronchitis tent and steam kettle.

spirit lamp or electric heater, and provided with a spout 2 or 3 feet (60 or 90 cm.) long. Various drugs of soothing or expectorant qualities, such as tincture of benzoin and menthol, can also be added to the water in the kettle, or poured upon a sponge which is placed in the end of the spout, and so inhaled in the steam.

The relief to the cough and breathing, and the aid to expectoration afforded by this simple plan are often surprising, and the cases are rare where it cannot be borne.

Should the cough persist for a length of time, and the disease threaten to become chronic, counter-irritant applications to the chest in front and behind, in the form of stimulating liniments or painting with tincture of iodine, will be rendered necessary.

When the bronchitis is of the capillary form, the great object is to overcome the infection as quickly as possible by means of full doses of the sulphonamides, penicillin, or one of the other antibiotics, to maintain the patient's strength, and to endeavour to secure the expulsion of the morbid secretion from the fine bronchi. In addition to the remedies already mentioned, stimulants are called for frequently; and should the cough be ineffectual in relieving the bronchial tubes, the administration of an emetic dose of sulphate of zinc, or especially of ipecacuanha wine, often clears out the expectoration when the patient vomits, and so gives great relief.

During the whole course of any attack of bronchitis attention must be paid to the due nourishment of the patient by light, warm articles of diet; and during the subsequent convalescence, which, particularly in elderly persons, is apt to be slow, tonics and stimulants may have to be prescribed.

(b) CHRONIC BRONCHITIS.—
Causes.—This form of the disease may arise as the result of repeated attacks of the acute form, or it may exist altogether independently. It occurs more frequently among persons advanced in life than among the young, although no age is exempt from it.

It is one of the most common causes of death in this country and is much more common than in any other country. Hence its international reputation as the 'English disease'. Whilst there is probably a constitutional predisposition to the disease, there are in addition six important contributory factors:—

(1) Exposure to irritant dust, smoke or fumes either as an occupational hazard or as part of the atmospheric pollution prevalent in industrial areas.

(2) Excessive cigarette smoking.

(3) Bad housing.

(4) A cold, damp, foggy climate.

(5) Obesity.

(6) Recurring respiratory infections.

The usual history of this form of bronchitis is that of a cough recurring during the colder seasons of the year, and in its earlier stages, departing

152

entirely in summer, so that it is frequently called 'winter cough'. In many persons subject to it, however, attacks are apt to be excited at any time by very slight causes, such as changes in the weather; and in advanced cases of the disease the cough is seldom altogether absent.

Chronic bronchitis may arise secondarily to some other ailment. This is especially the case in Bright's disease of the kidneys, and in heart disease, in both of which maladies it often proves a serious complication.

Symptoms.—The symptoms and auscultatory signs of chronic bronchitis are on the whole similar to those pertaining to the acute form, except that the febrile disturbance and pain are much less marked. The cough is usually more troublesome in the morning than during the day. There is usually free and copious expectoration of a thin frothy fluid, and occasionally this is so abundant as to constitute what is termed *bronchorrhœa*.

Chronic bronchitis leads to alterations of structure in the affected bronchial tubes, their mucous membrane becoming thickened or even ulcerated, while occasionally permanent dilatation of the bronchi takes place, often accompanied with profuse fœtid expectoration. In long-standing cases of chronic bronchitis, the nutrition of the lungs becomes impaired, and dilatation of the air-sacs (*emphysema*) and other complications result, giving rise to more or less constant breathlessness and leading to deformity of the chest (*barrel-shaped chest*). Chronic bronchitis is liable, in some instances, particularly when accompanied with loss of flesh and strength, to be mistaken for tuberculosis; but, whilst this is a possibility which must always be borne in mind, the physician who carefully regards the history of the case and observes the physical signs and symptoms, will in general be able to distinguish the one disease from the other. In this, too, the examination of the sputum for the presence of the tubercle bacillus is of great importance, the discovery of this organism at once indicating the tuberculous nature of the malady.

Chronic bronchitis does not often prove directly fatal, nor is it necessarily inconsistent with long life. Its chief danger lies in the tendency to intercurrent acute attacks, particularly in the aged ; and in this manner it frequently causes death.

Treatment.—The treatment to be adopted in chronic bronchitis depends upon the severity of the case, the age of the patient, and the presence or absence of complications. Attention to the general health is a matter of prime importance in all cases of the disease, more particularly among persons whose work entails exposure. As severe bronchitis is seldom found in one who has never smoked, smoking—certainly of cigarettes—should be given up. If the victim is overweight, he should take steps to get his weight down. The use of a respirator, from which pine oil and other aromatic substances can be inhaled, is occasionally helpful. In those aggravated forms of chronic bronchitis in which the slightest exposure to cold air brings on fresh attacks, it may become necessary, where circumstances permit, to enjoin confinement to a warm room, or removal to a more genial climate during the winter months.

When expectoration is difficult, such remedies as squill combined with carbonate of ammonia may prove useful. When, on the other hand, expectoration is excessive, astringents are called for. The inhalation of vapour containing friar's balsam or menthol is often followed by marked benefit in this way. Where breathlessness accompanies the disease, relief is often obtained from the use of iodide of potassium, or of ethereal preparations. Counter-irritation of the chest with mustard, turpentine, or croton liniment is generally attended by good results.

The value of antibiotics in chronic bronchitis is still undecided. Some recommend their routine use every winter, whilst others contend that this is unnecessary and not without its drawbacks. In many cases infection plays a relatively unimportant part, and for such patients antibiotics are obviously of little value, and treatment must consist of the general measures outlined above. In the presence of infection, as exemplified by a purulent sputum and/or the finding of antibiotic - sensitive organisms in the sputum, antibiotics may be of great value.

In the aged, and in weak persons, stimulants are an indispensable part of the treatment. Acute attacks of the disease, which are so apt to arise in the chronic form, must be dealt with on the principles already indicated in treating of acute bronchitis.

BRONCHOPHONY (βρόγχος, windpipe ; φωνή, voice) means the resonance of the voice as heard by auscultation over the site of the large bronchial tubes, and, in diseased conditions, conveyed beyond these by cavities or solidification of parts of the lung.

BRONCHO-PNEUMONIA (see PNEUMONIA).

BRONCHOSCOPE (βρόγχος, windpipe ; σκοπέω, I examine) is an instrument constructed on the principle of the telescope, which on introduction into the mouth is passed down through the larynx and windpipe and enables the observer to see the interior of the larger bronchial tubes.

BRONCHUS (βρόγχος, windpipe), or bronchial tube, is the name applied to tubes into which the windpipe divides, one going to either lung. The name is also applied to the divisions of these tubes distributed throughout the lungs, the smallest being called bronchioles.

BRONZED SKIN is one of the symptoms of Addison's disease. (See ADDISON'S DISEASE.)

BROW AGUE is a term used to denote both frontal neuralgia or tic douloureux (see NEURALGIA) and migraine or megrim (see MIGRAINE).

BRUCELLA ABORTUS is a bacterium closely related to *Brucella melitensis*, the causative organism of Malta or undulant fever. *Br. abortus* causes infectious abortion in cattle, and is excreted in cow's milk, whence it finds its way into the human intestinal tract, giving rise to the most troublesome disease, undulant fever. Attempts are being made by vaccination to control *abortus* fever in cattle, and by pasteurization of milk to prevent human infection.

BRUCELLA MELITENSIS is the name of a bacterium (Fig. 24) present in the milk of the goats of Malta and causing Malta or undulant fever among those drinking the milk. Undulant fever is common along the shores of the Mediterranean.

BRUCELLOSIS, also known as UN-DULANT FEVER, MALTA FEVER, MEDI-TERRANEAN FEVER, ROCK FEVER, NEAPOLITAN FEVER, and LEVANT FEVER, is a long-continued fever which occurs on the shores and islands of the Mediterranean principally, but is found also in many other countries.

Causes.—In Malta and the Mediterranean littoral the causative organism is the *Brucella melitensis* (Fig. 24) which is conveyed in goat's milk. In Great Britain, the U.S.A., and South Africa, the causative organism is the *Brucella abortus*, which is conveyed in cow's milk. This is the organism which is responsible for contagious abortion in cattle. The incubation period is about 14 days. The number of cases confirmed in England and Wales in recent years is : 136 in 1963, 124 in 1964, 123 in 1965, 169 in 1966, and 242 (provisional) in 1967.

Symptoms.—For the first week or so the person has headache, sickness, loss of appetite, constipation, and a feeling of tenderness over the liver and spleen, which are both enlarged. There is generally cough also, and the person perspires freely. Later, fever comes on and may resemble either that of typhoid or that of malaria in type, and it may be very difficult to distinguish a case of brucellosis, especially from typhoid. It tends to last a long time, its average duration being about three months, during which time the fever continues, the sweating is very profuse, the person gets extremely thin and weak, and rheumatic affections in the joints may appear. The convalescence is equally tedious, but death very seldom occurs, only about one case in fifty being fatal.

Treatment.—The disease has practically been abolished from Malta by ceasing to use goat's milk. Treatment is directed towards relieving the sleeplessness, pain in the joints, and other symptoms. The strength must also be supported by careful dieting, and, during convalescence, removal to a cool climate quickens recovery. The condition responds well to one of the tetracycline antibiotics, and also to chloramphenicol. In chronic cases a combination of streptomycin and one of the tetracyclines is often more effective.

It can be prevented by boiling or pasteurizing all milk used for human consumption.

BRUISES, or CONTUSIONS, are more or less extensive injuries of the deeper parts of the skin and underlying tissues, accompanied generally by outpouring of blood from damaged vessels, but unattended by corresponding open wounds.

Varieties.—An extensive bruise may be accompanied by a wound, in which case the injury is known as a ' contused wound '. (*See* WOUNDS.)

The simplest type of bruise is one in which only the deeper layers of the skin are damaged, causing a slight bluish discoloration due to the tearing of minute vessels and the escape of blood into the cellular spaces of the skin. As the result of a severe blow, the muscles may be bruised and torn without any wound in the skin, and the resulting effusion of blood may cause a large swelling which sometimes, though not usually, results in the formation of an abscess. When a bone is bruised, as by a kick on the shin or by a fall upon the knee or elbow, changes similar to those which follow an actual fracture are produced and a permanent thickening of the bone may result. Bruises of this type are of great importance, because an effusion of blood into the cavity of a joint leads to stiffness lasting some weeks, which may, if absorption of the blood be not complete, remain in some degree permanent owing to the formation of adhesions (*see* ADHESIONS *and* JOINTS, DISEASES OF). Further, it is held by many authorities that some slight injury of this nature is sometimes the starting-point of the tuberculous disease which attacks the bones of children. Severe bruises of internal organs, as from a crush or run-over accident, sometimes occur even when the skin has escaped injury and shows no mark (*see* ABDO-MEN, INJURIES OF). Bruising of the brain or spinal cord occasionally occurs in consequence of a severe shaking, as in a railway accident, and is known as ' concussion ' (*see* BRAIN, DISEASES OF).

Appearance of a bruise.—The extent of a bruise and the depth of its tint depend upon the amount of blood which has escaped from the vessels, and this again varies according to the violence of the blow and peculiarities of the person injured. In some diseases, like hæmophilia and scurvy, extensive bruises are produced by little or no violence. Sometimes a bruise is so sharply limited that it gives a distinct impression of the instrument with which it has been inflicted, whilst in other cases the blood runs downwards and produces a black mark at some distance from the injured part, as seen, for example, in the blackness beneath the eye which may follow an injury of the forehead or temple.

The colour of a bruise is at first black or bluish, later becoming brown, and finally changing to yellow, which fades away as alterations take place in, and absorption occurs of, the blood pigment. The time occupied in disappearance of a bruise depends largely upon the amount of blood effused, but in moderate bruises ten days or a fortnight must elapse before the injury ceases to be noticeable.

Treatment of slight bruises consists chiefly in preventing the effusion of blood after an injury, by means of cold compresses firmly fixed in position by suitable bandages. Ice may also be applied with good results. If it be not convenient to apply cold, various astringent substances may be used in the form of evaporating lotions kept in contact with the part for eight or ten hours ; thus a cloth may be wrung out in Goulard's water and applied to the bruise, or the skin may be painted with hazeline or tincture of arnica. In painful bruises one of the best applications is lead and opium lotion. (*See* GOULARD'S WATER.) The injured part, if a limb, should be elevated in a sling or on a couch.

Mere surface bruises and abrasions are benefited by application of hazeline, or if the skin be much ruffled or ingrained with dirt it is well to apply for a few days a piece of boracic lint in the form of a water-dressing. (*See* POULTICES.)

BRUIT and MURMUR are words used to describe abnormal sounds heard in connection with the heart, arteries, and veins on auscultation.

BUBO (βουβών, the groin) means a swelling of a lymphatic gland in the groin in venereal disease or in plague. (*See* PLAGUE.)

BUCHU is a remedy derived from the leaves of *Barosma betulina* and similar plants. It contains volatile oil and mucilage and is administered especially in inflammatory conditions of the bladder. The infusion of buchu is given in doses of 1 to 2 ounces (28·5 to 57 ml.)

BUERGER'S DISEASE (*see* THROMBOANGIITIS OBLITERANS).

BULIMIA (*see* BOULIMIA).

BULLA is another word for blister.

BUNDLE OF HIS.—This is a bundle of special muscle fibres which pass from the atria to the ventricles of the heart and which form the pathway for the impulse which makes the ventricles contract, the impulse originating in the part of the atria known as the sino-atrial node.

BUNIONS (*see* CORNS AND BUNIONS).

BURKITT'S LYMPHOMA is the most commonly found tumour in children in Africa, and is so called after the surgeon who first described it. Because of its geographical distribution it is thought to be due to a virus which is transmitted by mosquitoes, but no virus has yet been definitely isolated from the tumour. (*See* LYMPHOMA.)

BURNING FEET is a syndrome (*q.v.*) characterized by a burning sensation in the soles of the feet. It is rare in temperate climes but widespread in India and the Far East. The precise cause is not known, but it is undoubtedly associated with malnutrition, and lack of one or more components of the vitamin B complex is the likeliest cause.

BURNS and SCALDS.—Burns are injuries caused by dry heat, scalds by moist heat, but the two are similar in symptoms and treatment. Severe burns are also caused by contact with electric wires, and by the action of acids and other chemicals. The burn caused by chemicals differs from a burn by fire only in the fact that it is more favourable than the latter, because the chemical destroys the bacteria on the part, so that less suppuration follows.

Severe and extensive burns are most frequently produced by the clothes, for example, of a child, catching fire. This applies especially to cotton garments, which blaze up quickly. It should be remembered that such a flame can immediately be extinguished by making the individual lie on the floor so that the flames are uppermost, and wrapping him in a rug, mat, or blanket. As prevention is always better than cure, particular care should always be exercised with electric fires and kettles or pots of boiling water in houses where there are young children or old people. Equally important is it that children's night-clothes and frocks be made of non-inflammable material. Pyjamas are also much safer than nightdresses. Severe scalds are usually produced by escape of steam in boiler explosions.

Degrees of burns.—The French surgeon Dupuytren divided burns into six degrees, according to their depth.

1ST DEGREE.—There is simply redness. Such burns may be painful for a day or two. Similar effects are produced by prolonged exposure to sunlight and to X-rays.

2ND DEGREE.—There is great redness, and the surface is raised up in blebs. There is much pain, but healing occurs without a scar.

3RD DEGREE.—The scarf-skin or epidermis is all peeled off, and the true skin below is in part destroyed, so as to expose the endings of the sensory nerves. This is a very painful form of burn, and a scar follows on healing.

4TH DEGREE.—The entire skin of an area is destroyed, with its nerves, so that there is much less pain than in the last form. A scar forms, later contracts, and may produce great deformity.

5TH DEGREE.—The muscles also are burned, and still greater deformity follows.

6TH DEGREE.—A whole limb is charred. It separates as in gangrene.

Symptoms.—For the first two days

the chief symptoms are pain, varying with the degree of the burn, and in severe cases shock (*see* SHOCK). It is said that even superficial burns of as much as one-third of the skin-surface are always fatal. After forty-eight hours, in cases of the 3rd and higher degrees, inflammation of the part and fever are very apt to come on, and, in extensive burns over the head, chest, or abdomen, there is great risk of inflammation in the membranes covering the internal organs beneath the burn. Such conditions as bronchitis, pneumonia, and pleurisy are apt to develop when the burns are over the chest, and meningitis in the case of burns about the head and neck. Albuminuria is very frequently found owing to congestion of the kidneys. In burns about the face and mouth œdema of the larynx is a dangerous complication accompanied by the risk of suffocation. Later, when the burnt parts slough away there is much suppuration until the gap finally heals. All through this stage there is, in extensive burns, a liability to death from ulceration of the bowels or from general blood-poisoning. Healing is slow, and if the burn is deep, there is often terrible deformity.

The danger of burns depends chiefly upon their surface extent and to a less degree upon the depth of the burn. Burns over the chest, abdomen, or head are much more dangerous than larger burns on the limbs. The age is also a matter of importance, because children and old people are more liable to succumb to shock in the early stage of the burn than are adults of full health and strength. At a later stage the presence or absence of septic changes is the most important factor in regard to recovery.

Treatment.—Slight burns are soothed by protecting them from the air with a dressing (*e.g.* gauze, wool, and bandage). For severer burns it is important that any dressings applied should be of such a nature as (*a*) to relieve pain, (*b*) prevent septic changes, and (*c*) aid the healing of the resulting ulcer. If pain is very severe, it may be necessary to inject some soothing remedy such as morphine. The treatment of shock, if it is present, must at this stage be undertaken on the general principles applicable to this condition (*see* COLLAPSE). The clothing must in the first place be carefully removed, the whole of the burned area being gently but thoroughly washed with a solution of cetrimide (1 per cent.) or of chlorhexidine, or, if neither of these is available, some other mild, warm, antiseptic lotion. By this means the charred clothing is separated. The burn may thereafter be treated on the following lines :

In the case of an uninfected burn the best dressing is a single layer of non-greasy, open-mesh tulle gras, covered with thick gauze swabs and cotton-wool. It is essential to ensure that this dressing is firmly fixed, and the best way of doing this is by means of Elastoplast. Opinion varies as to whether it is necessary to use an antibiotic in the case of an apparently uninfected burn. If it should be decided that this is necessary, the safest method is to use a powder consisting of 1000 units of penicillin to a gramme of lactose. In the case of a relatively superficial and uninfected burn, current practice is to leave this original dressing on for 12 to 14 days, by which time it will be healed or virtually so. Indications for earlier removal of the dressing are unexplained pain or temperature, suggesting infection; inadequacy of the dressing resulting in exposure of the burn ; and seepage of serum through the dressing.

In the case of a burn seen at an early stage, which is thought to be infected, an alternative to penicillin in powder form is a cream containing a combination of antibiotics, *e.g.* penicillin and chlorhexidine, or chlorhexidine, neomycin, and polymyxin. In the case of a neglected infected burn more active treatment is required. The slough should be removed as it forms and firm compresses of eusol in a saturated solution of sodium sulphate applied. When all sloughs have been removed, an antibiotic is applied to the burn.

Children sometimes scald the mouth and gullet by drinking from the spout of a kettle, and for this, teaspoonful doses of a mixture of cod-liver oil and lime-water, from time to time, give relief.

The rapidly fatal result which sometimes follows upon extensive superficial burns is explained in some cases by general shock to the nervous system. This makes it of great importance to maintain quietness and to relieve pain as much as possible at the very beginning of the treatment. Another explanation which has been advanced to explain death in cases where there does not seem to be a great amount of shock, is that some poisonous substance is produced in the burnt tissues which is absorbed, and produces a general toxic effect. For this reason, some surgeons make it a practice in the case of very extensive burns in children to transfuse the patient with fresh blood obtained from another person at an early stage of the treatment.

BURSÆ are natural hollows in the fibrous tissues, lined by smooth cells and containing a little fluid. They are situated at points where there is much pressure or friction, and their purpose is to allow free movement without stretching or straining the tissues—for example, on the knee-cap or the point of the elbow, and, generally speaking, where one muscle rubs against another or against a bone. They develop also beneath corns and bunions, or where a bone comes to press in an unwonted manner on the skin.

BURSITIS means inflammation within a bursa. Acute bursitis is of the nature of an abscess, being produced by injury of a bursa, especially on the

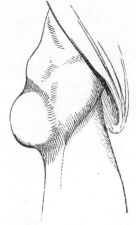

FIG. 84.—Housemaid's knee. (Miller's *Surgery*.)

knee or elbow, when the prominent part of the joint becomes swollen, hot, painful, and red. It is treated as an abscess (*see* ABSCESS).

Chronic bursitis is due to too much movement of, or pressure on, a bursa. For example, the condition of housemaid's knee (Fig. 89) is a chronic inflammation of the patellar bursa in front of the knee, due to too much kneeling. This condition may consist of either a collection of fluid in the bursa, or, less frequently, in thickening of its walls, producing in either case an elastic swelling over the joint, with pain. In the former case, resting the limb, with counter-irritation (*see* BLISTERS) over the swelling, or injection of some irritant substance into its interior, forms the treatment; in the latter case, removal by operation.

Chronic bursitis about the sinews round the wrist and ankle is generally called a ' ganglion '. (*See* GANGLION.)

BUSULPHAN, or myleran, is a preparation allied to the nitrogen mustard group of compounds (*q.v.*), with an action on dividing cells similar to that of irradiation. It is proving of value in the treatment of chronic myeloid leukæmia.

BUTTER (*see* DIET).

BUTYL CHLORAL HYDRATE is similar to chloral hydrate but has a special action upon the fifth cranial nerve, and is used for facial neuralgia.

BYSSINOSIS is a pneumoconiosis (*q.v.*), or chronic inflammatory thickening of the lung tissue, due to the inhalation of dust in textile factories. It is found chiefly among cotton and flax workers and, to a lesser extent, among workers in soft hemp. It is rare or absent in workers in jute and the hard fibres of hemp and sisal.

C

CABBAGE is a vegetable much used in Great Britain. It contains about 5 per cent. of carbohydrates, the remainder being largely indigestible vegetable fibre and water. It is a good source of vitamin C (*see* DIET.).

CACAO is the name given to the seeds of *Theobroma cacao*, which yield cocoa, chocolate, and cocoa butter.

CACHET means an oval capsule, generally made of rice paper, for enclosing a dose of unpleasant medicine. Cachets are softened by moistening with water prior to swallowing.

CACHEXIA (κακός, bad; ἕξις, condition) is the feeble state produced by serious disease, such as cancer.

CACODYLE is the name given to certain organic compounds of arsenic which have been used both internally and by hypodermic administration for various chronic diseases.

CACOLET is the name given to a chair suspended from a pack-saddle for transporting wounded.

CADAVERIC RIGIDITY is the stiffness which comes on after death. (*See* DEATH, SIGNS OF.)

CÆCUM is the dilated commencement of the large intestine lying in the right lower corner of the abdomen. Into it the small intestine and the appendix vermiformis open, and it is continued upwards through the right flank as the ascending colon.

CÆSAREAN SECTION means the delivery of a child by opening the abdomen and womb from in front. It is supposed to get its name from the traditional, but unproven, story that Julius Cæsar was so delivered. It is performed when delivery by the natural passage is undesirable because of the risk to mother and child : for example, because of bony deformity of the pelvis; also when the mother has died just before labour, so as to save the child.

CAFFEINE is a white crystalline substance obtained from coffee, of which it is the active principle. Its main uses are as a cerebral stimulant, a cardiac stimulant, and as a diuretic. It is also of value in some cases of asthma. It is a constituent of many tablets for the relief of headache, usually combined with aspirin and phenacetin. Granular effervescent citrate of caffeine forms a useful, non-intoxicating stimulant in headache due to tiredness.

CAISSON DISEASE affects workers in compressed air. Its chief symptoms are pains in the joints and limbs (bends), pain in the stomach, headache and dizziness, and paralysis. Sudden death may occur. The condition is caused by the accumulation of bubbles of nitrogen in different parts of the body.

CAJUPUT OIL is a green oil with camphor-like smell, much used for rubbing over diseased and painful joints. Spirit of cajuput in teaspoonful doses is useful for severe colic.

CALABAR BEAN is another name for physostigmine (*q.v.*).

CALAMINE, or CARBONATE OF ZINC, is a mild astringent used to soothe and protect the rough and weeping skin in eczema, as calamine lotion or ointment.

CALCANEUM is the name of the heel-bone or os calcis.

CALCICOSIS is the term applied to disease of the lung caused by the inhalation of marble dust by marble-cutters.

CALCIFEROL, or VITAMIN D$_2$, is a crystalline substance extracted from irradiated ergosterol, and has the same action as vitamin D. (*See* VITAMIN.)

CALCIFICATION is the process of deposit of lime salts. This occurs in old scars, as, for example, in the scars left by healed tuberculosis.

CALCIUM is the metal present in chalk and other forms of lime. The chief preparations used in medicine are calcium carbonate (precipitated), calcium chloride, calcium hydroxide (slaked lime), liquor of calcium hydroxide (lime-water), calcium lactate, and calcium phosphate (*see* LIME). Although still commonly used in the treatment of chilblains, there is little evidence that calcium is of any real value in this condition. Calcium gluconate is freely soluble in water and is used in conditions in which calcium should be given by injection.

Calcium is a most important element in diet, and the chief sources of it are milk, cheese, and green vegetables. Calcium is especially needed by the growing child and the pregnant and nursing mother.

CALCULI (*calculus*, a pebble) is the general name given to concretions in the bladder, kidneys, gall-bladder, etc.

CALLIPER SPLINT is one that is applied to the broken leg in such a way that in walking the weight of the body is taken by the hip bone and not by the foot.

CALLOSITIES (*callosus*, thick-skinned) are thickenings of the outer skin or cuticle. (*See* CORNS.)

CALLOUS ULCER (*see* ULCER).

CALLUS is the new tissue formed round the ends of a broken bone. (*See* FRACTURES.)

CALOMEL, or SUBCHLORIDE OF MERCURY, is not to be confounded with corrosive sublimate or perchloride of mercury, a far more active drug and deadly poison. (*See* MERCURY.)

CALORIE is the name applied to a unit of energy. Two units are called by this name—the small calorie, gramme calorie, or standard calorie is the amount of heat required to raise one gramme of water one degree centigrade in temperature ; the large calorie or kilocalorie, which is used in the study of dietetics and physiological processes, is the amount of heat required to raise one kilogram of water one degree centigrade in temperature. The number of calories required to carry on the processes necessary for life and body warmth, such as the beating of the heart, the movements of the chest in breathing, and the chemical activities of the secreting glands, is, for an adult person of ordinary weight, somewhere in the neighbourhood of 1600 calories.

For ordinary sedentary occupations an individual requires about 2500 calories, for light muscular work slightly over 3000 calories, and for hard continuous labour about 4000 calories daily.

CALUMBA ROOT is one of the pure bitters (*see* BITTERS).

CALVARIA, or CALVARIUM, is another name for the skull cap or vault of the head.

CALX is another name for lime or chalk. It is also the anatomical term for the heel.

CALYX (*calix*) means a cup-shaped cavity, the term being especially applied to the recesses of the pelvis of the kidney.

CAMPHINE is another name for oil of turpentine.

CAMPHOR is a solid, crystalline, oily substance distilled from the wood of a species of laurel grown in Japan and Formosa. It is sold in the form of cubes, or in powder known as flowers of camphor.

Uses.—Externally, it is frequently placed among bed-clothes to keep off fleas, lice, and other insect pests, but for this purpose it has now been largely replaced by the much more efficient D.D.T. (*q.v.*). In gout, and various painful skin conditions, it is rubbed up with chloral, menthol, thymol, or salol to form an oily liquid which can be smeared over the surface with great relief. Liniment of camphor and camphorated oil (1 ounce (28·5 G.) camphor in 8 ounces (228 ml.) olive oil) are likewise useful in painful conditions or as mild counter-irritants to produce a warm glow when rubbed into the chest in bronchitis and similar conditions.

Internally, spirit of camphor in 5 to 30 drop doses and camphor water in tablespoonful doses are used to relieve spasms like hiccup and colic, and to ward off colds in the head.

Dissolved in oil camphor is sometimes used by hypodermic injection in the treatment of serious conditions in which heart failure threatens to take place, but this practice has largely died out in Britain.

CANALICULUS means a small channel, and is applied to (*a*) the minute passage leading from the lacrimal pore on each eyelid to the lacrimal sac on the side of the nose ; (*b*) to any one of the minute canals in bone.

CANCELLOUS is a term applied to loose bony tissues as found in the ends of the long bones.

CANCER (*cancer*, a crab), **CAR-CINOMA** (καρκίνωμα) **and SARCOMA** (σάρκωμα) are general names for forms of tumour to which the term ' malignant ' is applied. They are differentiated from benign tumours by four principal criteria : (1) They are not encapsulated, or surrounded by a capsule, and invade and destroy the tissues in which they arise. (2) They have an unlimited power of disorderly reproduction, quite unlike the orderly way in which the healthy cells of an organ are reproduced. (3) Their cells usually show some loss of differentiation of their structure and tend to become more like primitive cells. (4) They are capable of producing metastases, or secondary growths, at a distance from the parent, or primary, tumour. Cancer or carcinoma is composed mainly of epithelial cells, or cells similar to those of skin or of the mucous membrane lining the stomach and bowels, or of secreting glands ; but these cells are imperfect in form and arrangement, although they generally retain their characters sufficiently to allow of the organ from which they have come being recognized when a section of the cancer is examined under the microscope (Plate VII). A sarcoma is a tumour developing in the connective tissue of bones, muscles, sinews, etc., and in structure resembling imperfect connective tissue (Plate VII). Sarcoma is less common than cancer in the proportion of about one case of the former to twenty of the latter.

Cancers are classified mainly according to the structure they present on microscopic examination. A cancer growing on skin surface is generally known as an EPITHELIOMA. A cancer arising in the stomach or intestine and presenting an appearance resembling imperfectly formed gland tubules is known as ADENOCARCINOMA. A cancer composed almost entirely of cells

without supporting tissue is known as a SOFT CANCER ; and one in which the cells are much compressed and obliterated by development of fibrous tissue is known as a HARD or SCIRRHUS CANCER. These occur particularly in the breast. Various degenerations also occur in cancers, such as glue-like degeneration, COLLOID CANCER, cystic degeneration, calcareous degeneration, etc. Sarcoma is classified into ROUND-CELLED SARCOMA, SPINDLE-CELLED SARCOMA, etc., according to the microscopic appearances.

Causes.—The cause of malignant growths is still undiscovered. Many theories have been advanced, and, considering the fact that cancer is gradually becoming more frequent, it has become of great importance to establish the nature of the cause as a first step towards prevention and treatment. Much has been done in the last few years by various cancer research laboratories to increase our knowledge as to the distribution of cancer in the animal kingdom and among different races, and also to study the mode of spread and conditions of growth in this disease. It has been found that cancers occur in animals as well as among human beings, and that no race is exempt from the disease. It appears, however, that the disease occurs more commonly in civilized communities than among more primitive races. It has been found by experiments on animals that cancer can be transferred directly from one animal to another by inoculating a healthy animal with a small piece of cancerous tissue, and it has further been found that, when transferred in this way through a long succession of animals, the type of cancer produced remains always the same. An important step was taken by the Japanese workers who found that cancer could be produced in experimental animals by painting the skin with tar. British workers then isolated the actual chemical substance in tar which produces the cancer, and it was found that this substance is chemically similar to substances present in the healthy body. Does some chemical twist take place and make these normal substances carcinogenic or cancer-producing? Another important factor to be investigated is infection. Many micro-organisms

6

have been incriminated, but the only one that has stood the test of serious investigation is a virus. For example, there is a type of cancer in fowls which is caused by a virus. Another factor in the causation of cancer is the influence of the hormones of the ductless glands. It appears, for example, that the female sex hormone has an effect on the development of breast cancer. Still another factor is heredity. All this, and other work, suggests that cancer is not one disease with one cause, but an abnormal reaction of the tissues to a variety of exciting agents. Some scientists have supposed that no external cause is necessary, but that in early or embryonic life parts of the developing body come to rest, only to start sudden and irregular growth at a later period of life. The structure of some cancers, in which a cancerous growth develops in one part of the body resembling an embryonic structure or some other organ at a distance, lends support to this view. It would appear as if the cause of cancer growth were a complicated one, in which several factors, including degeneration or scar formation in the tissues and at the same time some external cause of the nature of an organism, were at work.

Several facts, though not to be regarded as direct causes, are important considerations in the origin of the disease.

INJURY.—Smoking a clay pipe has been observed to bring on cancer of the lip, constant alcoholic indulgence to favour cancer of the throat and stomach, while a scar, e.g. of an old ulcer, may be the starting-point. Chimney-sweeps, paraffin workers, and workers in some other special employments have a great liability to cancer of the skin, apparently from long-continued irritation. It has also been found by experiments on animals that the prolonged application of tar to an area of skin may result ultimately in development of cancer. There does not seem any reason to suppose that cancer follows mechanical damage caused by a blow or wound, although there is ground for the belief that sarcoma occasionally follows some severe injury, such as fracture of a bone.

LOCALITY.—There are undoubtedly

wide variations in the incidence of cancer in different parts of the country, apart from the fact that death rates for a given age are higher in urban than in rural areas. The explanation of these geographical differences is still not known.

HEREDITY. — Although, strictly speaking, there is no evidence that, in man, cancer is inherited, there is a growing volume of evidence that there may be a familial tendency to develop cancer. Thus, it has been shown that women with carcinoma of the breast or of the uterus have a larger proportion of female relatives with such cancers than would be expected in women in general.

AGE.—Cancer is rare before adolescence, the commonest age being between fifty and sixty years. Although cancer is tending to increase in prevalence, there appears from the returns of the Registrar-General for England to be no tendency for the number of persons affected below the age of forty-five years to rise, and cancer is now more a disease of old age than formerly. Sarcoma is commoner in younger persons.

SEX.—In 1964, in England and Wales, the deaths from malignant disease in men were 56,247, compared with 48,451 in women. These figures correspond to a crude death-rate per million living of 2,441 males and 1,989 females. There is a marked difference in the site of cancer in the two sexes. Thus, in males the most commonly involved site is the gastro-intestinal tract, followed by the lungs and the prostate. In women, on the other hand, the breasts and uterus account for one-third of all cancers. The lungs and the tongue are much less commonly involved among women than among men.

Symptoms.—These vary according to the organs with which the growth interferes, thus cancer of the stomach tends to cause dyspepsia and, it may be, severe pain ; cancer in the bowels is apt to lead to gradually increasing obstruction, which may produce either diarrhœa or constipation ; cancer affecting the jaw is apt to set up neuralgia ; when the growth originates in the womb, flooding is one of the principal early symptoms ; when pressure is exercised upon a vein, dropsy results, and so forth. When the growth takes place on the surface there is a hard swelling, which in time is liable to break down and ulcerate. In any case, the growth tends to spread by the lymphatic vessels, and the glands in the neighbourhood soon become affected by secondary growths if the original one be not speedily removed. This applies especially to cancer, and is one reason why cancer is so liable to return after apparently complete removal. Sarcoma tends less to spread along the lymphatic vessels, but occasionally minute fragments are carried away to distant organs in the circulating blood. When a cancer begins to ulcerate by invading the skin or an internal mucous membrane, a state of very bad health and weakness, called cachexia, results. The duration of symptoms of cancer is extremely variable. When the stomach is affected, these seldom last much longer than six months. When the breast is affected, the duration may be very much longer, especially if the main part of the growth has been removed, and life is then frequently prolonged for several years. The same applies to cancer of the rectum, when an artificial opening is made so that the growth is not irritated by the passage over it of intestinal contents.

Mortality.—The following table, compiled from the annual returns of the Registrar-General for England, shows the steady increase in the number of reported deaths from cancer at five-yearly intervals in the eighty years following 1880 in England and Wales :

Year	Deaths	Death-rate per Million Living
1881	13,542	520
1886	16,243	590
1891	20,117	692
1896	23,521	764
1901	27,487	842
1906	31,668	913
1911	35,902	1103*
1916	40,630	1161*
1921	46,022	1215*
1926	53,220	1362*
1931	59,346	1484*
1936	66,354	1625
1940	70,371	...
1945	75,712	...
1950	85,270	...
1955	91,340	...
1960	98,788	...
1965	106,338	...

* From 1911 onwards these rates are standardized for age, so as to take into account the rapidly increasing number of elderly persons in the population.

TABLE 7.—Cancer Mortality Rates.

It is evident, from table 7 that the number of deaths recorded from cancer has in eighty years increased more than eight times, though the population is just over one and a half times as large (increase from 26,046,000 in 1881 to 47,762,800 in 1965).

The organs in which cancer has chiefly increased are the stomach, intestine, breast, and lungs.

Cancer now stands second in importance as a cause of death, having in 1966 caused 108,158 deaths as compared with 114,766 due to arteriosclerotic heart disease, including coronary disease, while tuberculosis accounted for 2354, bronchitis and pneumonia, for 67,904 and vascular lesions of the nervous system, including cerebral hæmorrhage, for 78,824.

The increase in cancer is partly explained by the fact that diagnosis is now more precise and many deaths are registered as due to cancer which formerly would have been attributed to ' old age ', ' obstruction of the bowels ', etc. ; and partly by the fact that more people now reach the ages at which cancer prevails.

Treatment.—It should be strongly urged that any person finding a hard swelling under the skin should consult a surgeon. In the event of the swelling not being cancer, mental relief will be gained ; and if it be cancer, there is at an early stage the chance of the only completely successful remedy at present known, that is thorough removal. The improvement of modern surgical technique and early diagnosis lead now to the possibility of operations which greatly prolong the life of persons affected by cancer, and in some cases permit of permanent recovery. In the case of certain internal cancers, e.g. of the stomach, attempts at complete removal have not, taking all cases together, attained a great measure of success, but much can be done in the way of operations designed for relief of symptoms, which thus prolong life. Much greater success has attended modern operations for complete removal of cancer of the breast and the womb.

Many cures have from time to time been vaunted, such as arsenic paste, turpentine, injections of trypsin, adrenaline, lead salts, etc., but these have all proved useless on trial. In many cases much benefit accrues from combined treatment by surgery, X-rays, and radium. (*See* RADIUM, *also* RADIOTHERAPY *under* X-RAYS.) Radioactive isotopes are also proving of value in many cases (*see* ISOTOPES).

The most recent development in the treatment of cancer, and also the most promising, is chemotherapy. Several chemical substances have been discovered to have an effect on malignant tumours. These include nitrogen mustard and a group of substances known as pterins. Some of these have been tried in the treatment of cancer in man, and, although none of them ' cure ' cancer, the results obtained with them suggest that it may not be very long before a substance will be found which will destroy malignant cells and yet have no harmful effect upon healthy cells.

At a late stage the administration of morphine and other sedatives, as well as the application of various antiseptic and soothing dressings, relieve the pain and discomfort of the patient.

CANCRUM ORIS (*cancrum*, a sore ; *oris*, of the mouth), also called WATER-CANKER or NOMA, is a gangrenous ulcer about the mouth which affects weakly children, especially after some severe disease, such as measles. It is due to the growth of bacteria in the tissues.

CANINE TEETH, or EYE-TEETH (*see* TEETH).

CANKER is a name applied to small ulcers which form about the mouth and lips as the result of some local irritation, *e.g.* a jagged tooth, or in a condition of dyspepsia and deteriorated general health. (*See* MOUTH DISEASES.)

CANNABIS INDICA, or INDIAN HEMP, also known in India as GUNJAH, and in other parts of the East as BHANG and HASHISH, consists of the flowering tops of *Cannabis sativa*.

Action.—It is, in small doses, a stimulant and intoxicant, and in larger doses a narcotic. In the stage of intoxication persons under its influence become much more excited than do the devotees of alcohol, and one name of the drug, hashish, is associated with the name of the sect of ' Assassins ', whose crimes were perpetrated in the

fury induced by the drug. Others, according to their temperament, show an access of politeness, and ' salaam ' to bystanders till exhausted, while still others become extravagantly merry, losing the sense of personality and assuming extraordinary attitudes. Finally sleep comes on, attended by dreams of a sensuous character. Its use as a drug of addiction, always widespread in the East, is spreading to the Western hemisphere, where it is giving rise to some concern.

Uses.—At one time used in combination with other anodyne and soporific drugs to relieve spasm and dull pain, it is seldom used now in view of its unreliability of action and its tendency to produce drug addiction.

CANNED FOOD.—The canning of food has increased tremendously of recent years, and indeed it is difficult to imagine the modern civilized world without canned food. Originally popularized in the United States of America, it had to overcome considerable prejudice in Great Britain. Such prejudice still persists to a certain extent, but, irrespective of the merits of the controversy of fresh versus preserved food, it must be recognized that the advantages of canned food far outweigh the disadvantages. Modern methods of canning are so efficient that not only is the purity of the food preserved but its nutritional value is retained. There is, of course, some loss of vitamin content but this has been much reduced of recent years. Indeed there is probably less loss of vitamins in canning than in the average domestic cooking. The further great advantage of canning is that it makes available to many people foodstuffs which otherwise they would either never be able to obtain or could only obtain at certain seasons of the year.

Methods of canning vary according to the foodstuff, but the two essentials of all canning processes are (1) heat treatment of the food and (2) expulsion of all air, after which the can is hermetically sealed. Cans are made of tinplate, which is steel coated with tin. In order to prevent any interaction with highly acid foods and to preserve the colour of the food, the tinplate is usually lacquered. Many canned foods will keep for long periods : *e.g.* canned fish, meat preparations, and soups will keep for five years, whilst canned vegetables will keep for two years.

Dangers of canned food.—The main danger is food poisoning. In 1956, in England and Wales, thirty-two of the 268 outbreaks of food poisoning, for which information was available, were due to canned food : canned meat on nineteen occasions, canned fish on six occasions, canned vegetables on six occasions, and canned fruit on one occasion. The organism most commonly responsible was the staphylococcus. In other cases decomposition of canned fish or meat may occur due to faulty cans, whilst the acid in fruits or vegetables may lead to erosion of faulty tinplate or soldering, with contamination of the foodstuff with tin or lead.

Examination of canned food.—Most cases of ' poisoning ' with canned food could be avoided if cans were examined before use. Canned food is carefully inspected either in the canning factory if made in this country or at the port of entry if imported. About 1·5 per cent. of canned meat is rejected in this country. It is a sound rule never to buy a canned food which does not bear a manufacturer's name. Another sound rule is that good cans usually contain good food. Any can which is leaking should be immediately discarded, and much rusting should be regarded with suspicion. ' Blowing ' or bulging of the ends of the can is the most important sign of faulty carriers, but this must be differentiated from the bulging of one side of a can due to an indentation in the opposite side. Tapping of a sound can should produce a dull note ; if the note is drum-like, this suggests gas-formation in the can due to decomposition. Shaking should produce no sound in a can of meat, but this test, of course, is of no value in the case of canned fruit, which contains syrup. If on opening the can an unpleasant or a stale odour is noted, or if, in the case of meat, there is a loss of firmness of the contents or a fading of the colour, the contents should be discarded.

CANNULA, or CANULA, is a tube for insertion into the body, designed to fit tightly round a trocar, a sharp pointed instrument which is withdrawn from the cannula after insertion, so that fluid may run out through the latter.

CANTHARIDES, or SPANISH FLY, is a powder made of the body and wings of a dried beetle, *Cantharis vesicatoria*, which inhabits Spain, Italy, Sicily, and Southern Russia.

Action.—It is an irritant, first, to the part with which it is brought in contact, whether the skin surface or the stomach, and, secondly, to the genital and urinary organs by which it is discharged from the body.

Uses.—Its only use is for blistering (*see* BLISTERS), and it may be applied as a plaster, in a paste, or painted on in ethereal solution called liquor epispasticus.

CANTHUS (κανθός) is the name applied to the angle at either end of the aperture between the eyelids.

CAPILLARIES are the minute vessels which join the ends of the arteries to the commencement of the veins. Their walls consist of a single layer of fine, flat transparent cells, bound together at the edges (Fig. 85), and the vessels form a

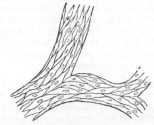

FIG. 85.—The endothelial cell wall of capillaries from the retina. Magnified by 300. (Turner's *Anatomy.*)

mesh-work all through the tissues of the body, bathing the latter in blood with only the thin capillary wall interposed, through which gases and fluids readily pass. These vessels are less than $\frac{1}{1000}$ inch (0·025 mm.) in width. (*See* BLOOD *and* CIRCULATION.)

CAPREOMYCIN is an antibiotic derived from *Streptomyces capreolus*, which is proving of value in the treatment of tuberculosis.

CAPSICUM, or CAYENNE PEPPER consists of small orange-coloured pods containing whitish seeds. It is irritating when applied either internally or to the skin.

Uses. — Externally the powdered pepper is used in an ointment, or in the form of ' Chilli paste ', to rub over sprains and bruises, the discoloration of which it helps to remove. Internally, tincture of capsicum is given for some forms of dyspepsia, and is said to be useful (in 15-drop doses before meals) to allay the craving for alcohol.

CAPSULE (*capsula*, a little box) is a term used in several senses in medicine. The term is applied to a soluble case, usually of gelatine, for enclosing small doses of unpleasant medicine. The term is also applied to the fibrous or membranous envelope of various organs, as of the spleen, liver, or kidney. It is also applied to the ligamentous bag surrounding various joints and attached by its edge to the bones on either side.

CAPUT MEDUSÆ is the term describing the abnormally dilated veins that form round the umbilicus in cirrhosis of the liver.

CAPUT SUCCEDANEUM is the temporary swelling which is sometimes found on the head of the new-born infant. It is due to œdema in and around the scalp, caused by pressure on the head as the child is born. It is of no significance and quickly disappears spontaneously.

CARAWAY FRUIT, generally called caraway seed, is used to prepare caraway water and caraway oil. A tablespoonful of the former or 2 drops of the latter on sugar is useful for checking colic, griping pains in children, and flatulence.

CARBACHOL, or CARBAMYLCHOLINE CHLORIDE, also known under the proprietary name of ' doryl ', is a drug which stimulates the parasympathetic nervous system. It is given, for example, for paralysis of the gut and for retention of urine due to atony.

CARBAMAZEPINE is a drug which is proving of value in the treatment of trigeminal neuralgia (*see* NEURALGIA.) It is also of value in the treatment of certain cases of epilepsy. Because of its occasional action in causing aplastic anæmia and jaundice it must only be used under careful medical supervision.

CARBENOXOLONE is a derivative of liquorice, which is proving of value in the treatment of gastric ulcer.

CARBIMAZOLE is at present one of the most widely used drugs in the treatment of hyperthyroidism. It acts by interfering with the synthesis of thyroid hormone in the thyroid gland.

CARBOHYDRATE is the term applied to an organic substance in which the hydrogen and oxygen are usually in the proportion to form water. Carbohydrates are all, chemically considered, derivations from simple forms of sugar and are classified as monosaccharides (*e.g.* glucose), disaccharides (*e.g.* cane sugar), polysaccharides (*e.g.* starch). Many of the cheaper and most important foods are included in this group, which comprises sugars, starches, celluloses, and gums. When one of these foods is digested, it is converted into a simple kind of sugar and absorbed in this form. In the disease known as diabetes, the most marked feature consists of an inability on the part of the tissues to assimilate and utilize the carbohydrate material. Each gramme of carbohydrate is capable of furnishing slightly over 4 calories of energy. (*See* DIET.)

CARBOLIC ACID, or PHENOL, is a coal-tar preparation, first introduced into medicine by Lord Lister some time prior to 1867

Action.—Carbolic acid first paralyses and then destroys all forms of life, having a specially destructive action upon lowly organisms like bacteria. It has a softening action upon tissues, pus, etc., and it also vaporizes readily, so that it has much greater penetrating power than alcohol, perchloride of mercury, and other powerful antiseptics, which have a hardening action that retards their germicidal power. It dulls pain greatly, when applied to an inflamed part, by benumbing the nerves around.

It must never be forgotten that pure carbolic acid, or even a weak lotion too long applied, may painlessly kill the skin and cause it to slough. This effect is lessened by smearing the damaged part with glycerin or with oil.

Internally it has similar actions, and even in moderate doses it is a poison, being first of all an irritant and on absorption a narcotic.

Carbolic acid is used as a standard antiseptic for comparison of the power of other substances to kill germs.

Uses.—Because of the risk of producing gangrene or ulceration, carbolic acid must never be used in a compress or dressing on the skin. In the pure form it is sometimes used as a cauterizing agent to sterilize septic areas. In the pure form it is also used in minute amounts in the treatment of ulcers of the cornea. In very weak solution it is used as a throat gargle. As a $2\frac{1}{2}$ per cent. solution in glycerin it is useful in treatment of infections of the ear. A further use is in the treatment of hæmorrhoids and varicose veins. As a 1 per cent. lotion it is of value in the treatment of itching conditions of the skin. As a disinfectant 1 in 20 of water (or 5 per cent.) is the convenient strength, and is used to put in the bottom of the sputum-dish of consumptives, to steep the sheets soiled by typhoid-fever cases, to swab the floors and walls of sickrooms. Lysol is now more commonly used for this purpose.

CARBOLIC ACID POISONING, due to accident or suicide, became fairly common with the use of the acid for disinfection and dressing wounds. No bottle containing carbolic lotion should ever be kept near other medicine bottles, as a few teaspoonfuls may cause death. Carbolic acid poisoning may also come on slowly through gradual absorption from dressings by a wound. The urine generally is black for a day or two before the case gets serious.

Symptoms.—If the acid has been swallowed there is a sense of burning about the mouth and throat, followed by numbness, and the skin and mucous membrane of the mouth show white where the acid has touched them. Unconsciousness and stupor soon come on, and death follows usually in a few hours.

Treatment.—Olive oil, or any fatty substance like milk or cream, should be administered at once, and the stomach washed out or emptied by an emetic in several tumblerfuls of tepid water.

Large doses are also given internally of Epsom salts or sulphate of magnesium, which combines with the carbolic acid and renders it harmless.

CARBON (*carbo*, coal) (*see* CHARCOAL).

CARBON DIOXIDE SNOW is formed when CO_2, stored under pressure in a cylinder, is allowed to escape through a small nozzle. This sudden expansion lowers its temperature to about $-70°$ C. and the CO_2 is obtained as a white powder or 'snow', which is then compressed into a cake or tube for application to the skin. It is a most effective method of freezing a localized area, and is most commonly used in the treatment of warts (*q.v.*).

CARBONIC ACID, or CARBON DI-OXIDE, is the gas formed by the tissues and exhaled by the lungs (*see* AIR *and* VENTILATION). It effervesces from aerated waters and sparkling wines, and is used in baths for stimulation to the skin (*see* BATHS). Carbon dioxide in cylinders, combined with oxygen, is used to control breathing in anæsthesia and in cases of carbon monoxide poisoning (*see* COAL-GAS).

CARBON MONOXIDE, or CARBONIC OXIDE (*see* COAL-GAS).

CARBON TETRACHLORIDE is a colourless liquid with strong odour, used against hook-worms and other parasites in doses of 30 to 60 minims (2 to 4 ml.)

CARBOXYHÆMOGLOBINÆMIA is the term applied to the state of the blood in carbon monoxide poisoning, in which this gas combines with the hæmoglobin, displacing oxygen from it.

CARBROMAL is a white powder with soporific action, given in doses of 5 to 15 grains (300 mg. to 1 G.).

CARBUNCLE (*carbunculus*, a small coal), like a boil, is an infection of a hair follicle and sebaceous gland or of a sweat gland, but unlike a boil it does not remain localized but spreads more deeply. The infecting organism is usually a staphylococcus. (*See* BOILS.)

CARBUTAMIDE is sulphonyl-n-butyl urea, a sulphonamide derivative. It was the first to be introduced of a new series of drugs known as 'oral hypoglycæmic agents': *i.e.* drugs which, when taken by mouth, lower the level of the blood sugar in diabetes mellitus. Their mode of action is not known, but it has been suggested that they may either stimulate the production of insulin by the pancreas, or potentiate in some way the action of insulin. With the exception of phenethyldiguanide (*q.v.*), they lower the blood sugar only if the patient's pancreas is capable of producing some insulin.

Because of its toxicity, carbutamide is now being given up in favour of the other oral hypoglycæmic agents. (*See* DIABETES MELLITUS, CHLORPROPAMIDE, PHENETHYLDIGUANIDE, and TOLBUTAMIDE.)

CARCINOMA (καρκίνωμα, a gnawing sore) is another name for cancer.

CARDAMOM, TINCTURE OF, is a bright red fluid, prepared from the seeds of *Elettaria repens*, useful to relieve spasm and flatulence, and much used to colour medicines.

CARDIA (καρδία, the heart) is a term applied to the upper opening of the stomach which lies immediately behind the heart.

CARDIAC DISEASE (*see* HEART).

CARDIAC MASSAGE is the procedure used to restart the action of the heart if it is suddenly arrested. For long the only recognized method of doing this was by opening the chest wall and massaging the heart directly by hand. This is perfectly feasible if the heart stops beating during an operation. Elsewhere, however, it is seldom a practicable proposition.

Recently it has been shown that in many cases the arrested heart can be made to start beating again by rhythmic compression of the chest wall.

This is done by placing the patient on a hard surface—a table or the floor —and then placing the heel of the hand over the lower part of the sternum and compressing the chest wall forcibly at the rate of 60 to 80 times a minute. At the same time artificial respiration must be started by the mouth-to-mouth method. (*See* DROWNING, RECOVERY FROM.)

CARDIAC PACEMAKER.—The rate and rhythm of the heart are controlled by a small collection of specialized nervous tissue known as the sinuatrial node, situated at the base of the heart (*see* HEART). This is the natural pacemaker of the heart—or cardiac pacemaker. When the impulse sent out by this pacemaker cannot reach all parts of the heart (a condition known as heart-block), the heart either stops or contracts in an irregular manner (*see* HEART DISEASES).

In these cases the natural pacemaker can be replaced by an artificial pacemaker which, for all practical purposes, is a battery which stimulates the heart and allows it to beat at normal speeds. The majority of cardiac pacemaker units are of the constant voltage type, powered by 3 or 4 mercury batteries which are potted in an epoxy resin and coated with silicone rubber (Fig. 85A). They are normally adjusted to deliver 65 to 75 impulses a minute. The pacemaker is either fixed to the outside of the chest or implanted in the armpit, and connected to an electrode catheter which is passed through the main vein in the neck into the heart.

CARDIOLOGY is the term applied to that branch of medical science devoted to the study of the diseases of the heart.

CARDIOSPASM means the spasmodic contraction of the muscle surrounding the opening of the œsophagus into the stomach : also termed ACHALASIA OF THE CARDIA.

CARIES (*caries*, decay) is a progress of gradual decay in bones, analogous to ulceration in the soft tissues. (*See* BONE, DISEASES OF, *and* TEETH.)

CARLSBAD SALT is the salt derived from Carlsbad water, with aperient properties. An artificial Carlsbad salt can be prepared by taking sodium sulphate 22 parts, potassium sulphate 1 part, sodium chloride 9 parts, sodium bicarbonate 18 parts, and mixing. If 53 grains (3·5 G.) of the salt be added to 1 pint (500 ml.) of water, a fluid closely resembling the natural Carlsbad water is obtained.

CARMINATIVES (*carmen*, a charm) are remedies which relieve griping and expel flatulence. (*See* ANTISPASMODICS.)

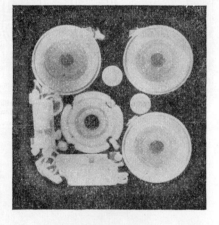

FIG. 85A (*above*).—A Cardiac Pacemaker beside a half-crown piece. (*right*) An X-ray of the Pacemaker showing three mercury batteries occupying three corners and electronic components occupying the fourth corner (*lower left*).   (*The Practitioner*)

CARNEOUS MOLE is an ovum which has died in the early months of pregnnacy. It usually requires no treatment and evacuates itself.

CAROTENE is a colouring matter of carrots, other plants, butter, and yolk of egg, and is the precursor of vitamin A, which is formed from carotene in the liver. (*See* VITAMIN.)

CARPUS is the Latin term for the wrist, composed of eight small bones firmly joined together with ligaments, but capable of a certain amount of sliding movement over one another.

CARRAGEEN, or IRISH MOSS, is derived from a kind of sea-weed, *Chondrus crispus*. It is pleasantly soothing and in the form of a jelly is sometimes added to an invalid diet. Half an ounce of the moss is added to $1\frac{1}{2}$ pints (850 ml.) of water and boiled down to 1 pint (500 ml.). Its main dietetic value is on account of the iron, calcium, and iodine which it contains.

CARRIERS OF DISEASE (*see* INFECTION).

CARTILAGE is a hard but pliant substance forming parts of the skeleton, *e.g.* the cartilages of the ribs, of the larynx, and of the ears. Microscopically, cartilage is found to consist of cells arranged in twos or in rows, and embedded in a ground-glass-like material devoid of blood-vessels and nerves (Figs. 86, 87). The end of every long bone has a smooth layer of cartilage on it where it forms a joint with other bones (articular cartilage), and in young persons up to about the age of sixteen there is a plate of cartilage (epiphyseal cartilage) running right across the bone about half an inch from each end. The latter, by constantly thickening and changing into bone, causes the increase in length

of the bone. (*See* BONES.) In some situations there is found a combination of cartilage and fibrous tissue, as in the discs between the vertebræ of the spine. This fibro-cartilage combines the pliability of fibrous tissue with the elasticity of cartilage. The bones of fishes are mostly formed of cartilage. Cartilage when boiled for a long time yields a substance like gelatine. (For cartilages of the knee, *see* KNEE.)

CARUNCLE is the name applied to any small fleshy eminence, whether normal or abnormal.

CASCARA SAGRADA is the bark derived from *Rhamnus purshiana*, or *Rhamnus frangula*, from which a liquid and a solid extract of powerful purga-

FIG. 86.—Diagram to show division of cartilage cells. (From Hewer, *Textbook of Histology*. William Heinemann, Ltd.)

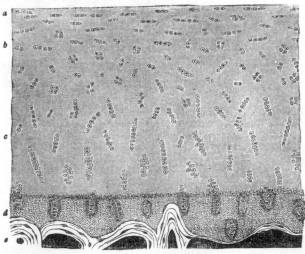

FIG. 87.—Vertical section of articular cartilage covering end of tibia. Magnified 30 times. *a, b, c,* Groups o cartilage cells embedded in matrix ; *d,* layer of calcified cartilage; *e,* bone. (From Schafer, *Essentials of Histology.* Longmans, Green & Co. Ltd.)

tive action are prepared. The full dose for one administration is a teaspoonful of the fluid extract or about 4 grains (250 mg.) of the solid. But it is best taken in small doses of 5 or 10 drops of the fluid extract after each meal, or night and morning ; gradually this may be decreased and finally left off, the bowels continuing regular in action. The elixir of cascara is a pleasanter preparation, of which the dose is ½ to 1 teaspoonful.

CASCARILLA is an aromatic bitter tonic derived from the bark of *Croton eluteria* (*see* BITTERS). The dry bark has been used as a substitute for tobacco during attempts to break off the habit of smoking.

CASEATION (*caseus*, cheese) is a process which takes place in the tissues in tuberculosis and some other chronic diseases. The central part of a diseased area, instead of changing into pus and so forming an abscess, changes to a firm cheese-like mass which may next be absorbed or may be converted into calcareous deposit and fibrous tissue, and so healing results with the formation of a scar.

CASEIN is that part of milk which forms cheese or curds. It is produced by the union of a substance, ' caseinogen ', dissolved in the milk, with lime salts also dissolved in the milk, the union being produced by the action of rennin, a ferment from the stomach of the calf. The same change occurs in the human stomach as the first step in the digestion of milk, and therefore when milk is vomited curdled it merely shows that digestion has begun.

CASSIA is a dried pulp obtained from the pods of *Cassia fistula*, which is used as a mild aperient.

CASTOREUM is a strong-smelling, brownish substance obtained from the beaver, *Castor fiber*. It is an antispasmodic.

CASTOR OIL is a thick colourless oil pressed from the seeds of *Ricinus communis*, the castor-oil plant. Owing to its general action over the whole intestine it is perhaps the best purgative for a single administration, though, in consequence of the fact that its action is often followed by slight constipation, it is unsuitable for frequently repeated use.

The dose for an adult is from one teaspoonful to two tablespoonfuls. To a child one year old a teaspoonful may be given. The cup in which it is given should be scalded out with hot water, of which a little remains in the bottom ; the oil is next poured in, and upon it a little brandy or whisky. The oil may be then swallowed without leaving much taste behind. Lemon juice also helps to remove the taste.

CASTRATION (*castratio*) is the term applied to an operation for removal of the testicles or ovaries.

CASTS of hollow organs are found in various diseases. Membranous casts of the air passages are found in diphtheria and in one form of bronchitis, and are sometimes coughed up entire. Casts of the interior of the bowels are passed in cases of mucous colitis associated with constipation, and casts of the microscopic tubules in the kidneys passed in the urine form one of the surest signs of Bright's disease.

CATALEPSY (from κατάληψις, a seizure) is a term applied to a nervous affection characterized by the sudden suspension of sensation and volition, accompanied by a peculiar rigidity of the whole or of certain muscles of the body. The subjects of catalepsy are in most instances females of highly nervous or hysterical temperament. The exciting cause of an attack is usually **mental** emotion operating either suddenly, as in the case of a fright, or more gradually in the way of prolonged depression. Sometimes the typical features of the disease are exhibited in a state of complete insensibility, together with a statue-like appearance of the body, which will retain any attitude it may be made to assume during the continuance of the attack. In this condition the whole organic and vital functions appear to be reduced to the lowest possible limit consistent with life, and to such a degree as to simulate actual death. The attack may be of short duration, passing off within a few minutes. It may, however, last for many hours, and in rare instances persist for several days ; and it is conceivable that in such cases the appearances presented might be mistaken for real death, as is alleged to have happened occasionally. Catalepsy is sometimes associated with epilepsy and with grave forms of mental disease. From what has been stated it follows that the successful treatment of such a disease as catalepsy must depend upon the due recognition of both its corporeal and mental relations. (*See* ECSTASY, HYSTERIA, SLEEP.)

CATAMENIA (καταμήνια) is another term for menstruation.

CATAPHORESIS (καταφορέω, I carry down) is the term applied to a method of treatment by introduction of medicine through the unbroken skin by means of an electric current. (*See* IONIZATION.)

CATAPLASM (κατάπλασμα) is another name for poultice.

CATAPLEXY is the term applied to a condition in which the patient has a sudden attack of weakness and falls to the ground, where he remains immobile, speechless, but fully conscious. (*See also* NARCOLEPSY.)

CATARACT (*cataracta*, a waterfall or portcullis) is an opacity of the crystalline lens of the eye, more or less completely obscuring vision.

Causes and Varieties.—The most common form is *senile cataract*, which begins about the age of fifty in eyes which may have been perfectly healthy. In every eye, the lens from childhood onward slowly hardens and loses its power of focusing for near objects, and in the cataractous eye there is a special hardening and rapid shrinking at the centre of the lens, which leads to splitting up and gradual disintegration of the lens, with consequent loss of transparency. Senile cataract, then, has nothing to do with loss of general health, or with disease of the rest of the eye. *Cataract in children* may be found at birth, and there may or may not be other disease of the eye, so that the result of operation is not so promising. *Diabetic cataract* appears sometimes in persons suffering from diabetes. *Black cataract* is one in which the lens is black in colour, due to deposition of pigment. *Partial cataracts* of various forms occur, obscuring vision in one direction but not requiring operation. *Posterior cortical cataract* is one at the back of

the lens, and is a rare form which is important because it follows disease in the back of the eye, and, though there is impairment of vision, this is not due to the cataract nor cured by its removal. It comes on in fairly young persons.

Cataract from injury (*traumatic cataract*) is caused by almost any wound of the lens, and sometimes by severe blows on the eye. *Heat* (*infra-red*) *cataract* occurs in glass-workers who have long been engaged in glass manufacture, and in certain iron-workers. *Irradiation cataract* is caused by X-rays, radium, or nuclear energy. *Electric cataract* may develop rapidly after the passage through the body of a powerful electric current.

Symptoms.—The first thing noticed is the appearance of motes in the vision, not floating, like those seen by almost every healthy eye against a white background, but stationary.

Bright objects are seen multiplied, especially bright lights at a distance in the dark. A moderate degree of short-sightedness may come on, which is relieved for a time by spectacles. Gradually increasing blindness is the most apparent symptom, and in the early stages the person may be less blind in the dusk than in bright light, because, the centre only of the lens being affected, a clear part round the edge admits the rays of light when the pupil, *i.e.* the opening in the iris, dilates, as it does in dull light.

Finally, when the cataract is well advanced, it becomes visible to bystanders as a ground-glass-like mass filling up the pupil.

Treatment.—No medicines or eye-washes or ointments are of any use against cataract. Atropine drops, which dilate the pupil, are much resorted to by quacks, because their use is followed for a time by better vision, for the reason given above. The cataract is unaffected by such applications, and can be removed only by operation. This is performed when the cataract reaches the stage of interfering with vision to an extent that prevents the reading of newsprint. There is a great variety of operations, but the chief are *extracapsular extraction* of the lens by opening the anterior capsule and expressing the lens through the pupil and hooking it out ; *intracapsular extraction* by grasping the anterior capsule with toothless forceps and gently tearing away the capsule so that the entire cataract enclosed in its intact membranes comes away. The operation is usually done under a local anæsthetic and is very safe and successful even in very old persons, though demanding great skill. Patients are usually allowed out of bed on the second or third post-operative day, and the stay in hospital is usually less than a fortnight.

The latest advance in the treatment of cataract is the insertion of acrylic lenses within the eye after extraction of the cataract. This gives the patient much better sight than did the old operation.

Sometimes after an operation for cataract disappointment is experienced because the sight is not restored. In such cases the retina also is diseased, and though the removal of the cataract admits light to the eye, the defective retina is unable to perceive objects clearly. To avoid this disappointment the eyes should be carefully examined by an expert before the cataract becomes sufficiently dense to obscure the back of the eye.

CATARRH (κατά, down ; ῥέω, I flow) is a term employed to describe a state of irritation of the mucous membranes, particularly those of the air passages, associated with a copious secretion of mucus. This complaint, so prevalent in damp and cold weather, usually begins as a nasal catarrh or coryza, with a feeling of weight about the forehead and some difficulty in breathing through the nose, increased on lying down. Fits of sneezing, accompanied with a profuse watery discharge from the nostrils and eyes, soon follow, while the sense of smell and to some extent that of taste become considerably impaired. There is usually present some amount of sore throat and of bronchial irritation, causing hoarseness and cough. Sometimes the vocal apparatus becomes so much inflamed (laryngeal catarrh) that temporary loss of voice results. There is always more or less feverishness and discomfort, and frequently an extreme sensitiveness to cold. After two or three days the symptoms begin to abate, the discharge from the nostrils and

chest becoming thicker and of purulent character, and producing when dislodged considerable relief to the breathing. On the other hand, the catarrh may assume a more severe aspect and pass into some form of pulmonary inflammation. (*See* BRONCHITIS *and* CHILLS AND COLDS.)

The term catarrh is also applied to describe a state of irritation, accompanied by abnormal secretion of mucus, in the stomach (*see* DYSPEPSIA), in the bowels (*see* DIARRHŒA *and* INTESTINE, DISEASES OF), in the bladder (*see* Cystitis *under* BLADDER DISEASES), and in other mucous surfaces.

CATATONIA (κατά, according to τόνος, bracing) is a term applied to a symptom of mental disease in which the patient remains rigidly in the same position, behaving very much like a statue. Catatonia minor is a term applied to the group of symptoms occurring in the mental disease dementia præcox, in which the patient shows peculiar mannerisms, continuing to repeat the same words or actions.

CATECHU is a reddish extract from the leaves of the *Uncaria gambier*, containing much tannin and acting as a powerful astringent. Compound catechu powder, containing catechu, kino, rhatany, cinnamon and nutmeg, and tincture of catechu are given in diarrhœa, and catechu lozenges are useful in relaxed sore throat.

CATGUT is used in surgery for tying cut arteries and stitching wounds. It is made from the fibrous coat of the intestines of animals, especially of the sheep, requires very careful purification, and in the tissues is gradually absorbed—in about five to ten days—as it is itself an animal substance. ' Hardened ' catgut is catgut which has been treated with a suitable hardening agent to prolong the time taken for it to be absorbed ; catgut hardened by treatment with chromium compounds is known as ' chromicized ' catgut.

CATHARTICS (καθαρτικόν) (*see* PURGATIVES) are substances which produce an evacuation of the bowels.

CATHETERS (καθετήρ) are tubes used for passing along the urethra, the narrow passage from the bladder to the exterior, in order to draw off urine, when for some reason the natural void-ance is impossible. The tube is about 14 inches (35 cm.) long, open at one end (the outer end) and closed at the other (the point), near which is an oval opening in the side (the eye). Catheters are, in England, graduated according to an arbitrary scale, numbers 6 to 10 being those in most common use.

FIG. 88.—Metal catheter.

Varieties.—*Rigid* catheters are generally made of silver, silverized metal, or glass ; the greater part is straight, but there is a sweeping curve towards the point. These require for use a considerable knowledge of anatomy, and since great damage may be done by unskilful manipulation they are suited only for a surgeon's use. A rigid catheter may often be passed where a softer one fails, especially where there is a stricture, or narrowing of the urethra. *Flexible* catheters are made of linen or silk web covered with an elastic material, or of hard black rubber. They soften in hot water, but are spoiled by boiling. This form (gum - elastic catheter) is that generally used by those elderly persons in whom the prostate gland blocks the outlet from the bladder. *Enamel* catheters are made of fabric thickly coated with composition and may be boiled for sterilization. These have to a great extent displaced the flexible catheters formerly used. *Soft* catheters are made of red india-rubber. They are used in cases where there is no obstruction to the passage, but where the urine, owing to weakness or paralysis of the bladder, for example, in cases of fractured spine, cannot be passed. They can be easily sterilized as they do not spoil by boiling. *Self-retaining* catheters are made of soft rubber with an enlargement near the inner end which expands when the stilet, on which the catheter has been introduced, is removed.

The *Eustachian catheter* is a smaller instrument, of similar shape, but open at both ends. It is used to pass along the floor of the nose into the Eustachian tube, in order to inflate the middle ear with air, or to introduce into it some volatile medicaments.

Use.—Sterilization is most important, because inflammation of the bladder is very apt to be caused by bacteria introduced on a soiled catheter. Rigid and soft catheters should be boiled each time before use, and then handled as little as possible, and only by perfectly clean hands. Just before introduction the urethral opening is washed and the point of the catheter dipped in an antiseptic lubricant, such as boracic ointment or antiseptic jelly. The flexible catheter is passed straight on without force, the soft catheter introduced by a slight screwing movement. After use the catheter is dipped at once into hot water and then wiped clean of grease, and a stream of antiseptic lotion is passed through it by means of a syringe. To keep a gum-elastic catheter clean and ready for use it should be suspended in, or laid full length in, a glass vessel containing perchloride of mercury lotion (1 in 4000), which is washed off the catheter immediately before use with hot sterile water. But perchloride of mercury lotion must not touch a metal catheter, which it corrodes. A catheter must be at once discarded when it gets rough or begins to break, otherwise a fragment may remain in the bladder and provide a nucleus round which a stone can form.

CAT-SCRATCH FEVER is a disease, probably due to a virus, which is characterized by enlargement of the glands. In spite of the name, there is a history of a cat scratch in only about half the cases ; in others the infection is acquired through a puncture of the skin by a splinter or thorn. The glandular swelling is usually slight and of short duration, but in some cases may go on to abscess formation which requires aspiration. The infection is not controlled by penicillin.

CAUL (*see* AMNION).

CAUSTICS and CAUTERIES (καίω, I burn) are bodies used to burn diseased tissues, the former by chemical action, the latter by their high temperature.

Varieties.—The chief chemical caustics in use are acetic, lactic, chromic, carbolic, and nitric acids, caustic soda and caustic potash, arsenic in paste, and nitrate of silver or lunar caustic. Of cauteries there are Corrigan's button cautery, the red-hot iron, the electro-cautery, consisting of a platinum point heated by an electric current, the galvano-cautery, in which a wire is heated with a galvanic current, and Paquelin's cautery, which has a hollow metal point kept hot by benzine constantly blown into it, and diathermy (*see* DIATHERMY).

Uses.—Caustics are used to destroy warts, small tumours, etc. The cautery is used, mildly heated, as a counter-irritant instead of a blister in sciatica, neuralgia, rheumatic pains, etc. (*see* BLISTERS). The galvanocautery is used to reduce inflamed tissues about the nose and throat. The Paquelin's cautery or red-hot iron was at one time much in vogue for removal of small growths, conversion of foul ulcers and poisoned wounds into healthy burns, and operations upon very vascular organs like hæmorrhoids.

CAVERNOUS BREATHING indicates a peculiar quality of the respiratory sounds heard on auscultation over a cavity in the lung.

CELLS (*cella*, a cell in a honeycomb) are the microscopic particles which build up the tissues, of which they are the smallest structural divisions. The term was originally applied in botany to the hollow particles of which plants are built up, and was extended to include the corresponding structures in animal bodies, though these are seldom hollow.

Every cell consists essentially of a cell-body of soft albuminous material called protoplasm, in which lies a kernel or nucleus which seems to direct all the activities of the cell. Within the nucleus may be seen a minute body, the nucleolus ; and there may or may not be a cell-envelope around all (Fig. 89).

Cells vary much in size, ranging in the human body from $\frac{1}{10000}$ inch (0·0025 mm.) to about $\frac{1}{1000}$ inch (0·025 mm.). But the egg of a hen is still a simple cell, though enormously distended by food material.

All animals and plants consist at first of a single cell (the egg-cell, or *ovum*), which begins to develop when fertilized by the sperm-cell derived from the opposite sex. Development begins by a division into two new cells, then into four, and so on till a large mass is formed. These cells then arrange them-

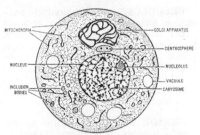

FIG. 89—The Cell. (From Best and Taylor's The Living Body. Holt Rinehart and Wilson Inc.).

selves into layers, and form various tubes, rods, and masses which represent in the embryo the organs of the fully developed animal. (*See* FŒTUS.)

When the individual organs have been laid down on a scaffolding of cells, these gradually change in shape and in chemical composition. The cells in the nervous system send out long processes to form the nerves, those in the muscles become long and striped in appearance, and those which form fat become filled with fat droplets which distend the cells. Further, they begin to produce, between one another, the substances which give the various tissues their special character. Thus, in the future bones, some cells deposit lime salts, and others form cartilage ; while, in tendons, they produce long white fibres of a gelatinous substance. In some organs the cells change little : thus the liver consists of columns of large cells packed together, while many cells, like the white blood corpuscles, retain their primitive characters almost entire.

Thus cells are the active agents in forming the body, and they have a similar function in repairing its wear and tear. Tumours, and especially malignant tumours, have a highly cellular structure, the cells being of an embryonic type, or, at best, forming poor imitations of the tissues in which they grow.

CELLULAR TISSUE is an old name for the loose fibrous tissue which forms, so to speak, packing between the skin and muscles and round the different organs.

CELLULITIS means an inflammation taking place in cellular tissue. (*See* ABSCESS *and* ERYSIPELAS.)

CELLULOSE is a carbohydrate substance forming the skeleton of most plant structures. It is colourless, transparent, insoluble in water, and is practically unaffected by digestion. In vegetable foods it therefore adds to the bulk, but it is of no value as a food-stuff. It is found in practically a pure state in cotton-wool.

CENSOR is a term applied to the mental influence which prevents certain subconscious thoughts and wishes from coming into consciousness unless they are disguised so as to be unrecognizable.

CENTRE is a term applied to a collection of nerve cells which give off nerve fibres and control some particular function, *e.g.* the speech centre and the vision centre in the brain.

CEPHALORIDINE is the semi-synthetic derivative of the nucleus of an antibiotic known as cephalosporin C, originally derived from a sewage out-fall in Sardinia. This nucleus, 7-aminocephalosporanic acid, is closely related to the penicillin nucleus (*see* PENICILLIN). It has a wide antibacterial range and is active against penicillin-resistant micro-organisms. It is therefore often the antibiotic of first choice in treating fulminating infections in which the causative organism has not been identified. It has to be given by injection.

CERATE (*cera*, wax) is a medicinal preparation, intended for external application, made with a basis consisting of wax in whole or in part which can be spread on the skin without melting, *e.g.* camphor cerate, cantharides cerate.

CERCOMONAS is the term applied to a genus of minute protozoan animals found in the intestine and other cavities of man and animals. One form is said to be responsible for occasional cases of diarrhœa.

CEREAL (*cerealis*) is the term applied to any plant of the nature of grass bearing an edible seed. The important cereals are wheat, oats, barley, maize, rice, and millet. Along with these are usually included tapioca (derived from the cassava plant), sago (derived from the pith of the sago palm), and arrow-

root (derived from the root of a West Indian plant), all of which consist almost entirely of starch. Semolina, farola, and macaroni are preparations of wheat.

Cereals consist predominantly of carbohydrate, their general composition being :

Water . .	10 to 12 per cent.
Protein . .	10 to 12 ,,
Carbohydrate .	65 to 75 ,,
Fat . . .	0·5 to 8 ,,
Mineral matter .	2 ,,

TABLE 8.—Composition of Cereals.

They are therefore an excellent source of energy, and indeed can be regarded as the mainstay of civilization. On the other hand, their deficiency in protein and fat means that to provide a balanced diet, they must be supplemented by other foods rich in protein and fat, such as meat, milk, and eggs. The percentage composition of the more important cereals is as follows :

	Water	Protein	Fat	Carbohydrate	Cellulose	Ash
Wheat .	12·0	11·0	1·7	71·2	2·2	1·9
Oatmeal	7·2	14·2	7·3	65·9	3·5	1·9
Barley .	12·3	10·1	1·9	69·5	3·8	2·4
Rye	11·0	10·2	2·3	72·3	2·1	2·1
Maize .	12·5	9·7	5·4	68·9	2·0	1·5
Rice (polished)	12·4	6·9	0·4	79·4	0·4	0·5
Millet .	12·3	10·4	3·9	68·3	2·9	2·2
Buckwheat	13·0	10·2	2·2	61·3	11·1	2·2

TABLE 9.—Composition of certain Cereals.

Wheat is mainly used in the form of bread (*q.v.*). The reason why other cereals, with the exception of rye, are not used for bread-making is that they do not contain gluten, a protein which becomes viscid and adhesive when mixed with water. In the process of producing white flour much of the vitamin B complex, the iron and the calcium, is lost, so that, from the nutritional point of view, ' whole-meal ' bread should be eaten. *Rye* is the other great bread-making cereal of the world. Compared with wheat-flour, rye-flour is deficient in protein. Preparations such as Ryvita are made from crushed whole rye. *Oats* are used in the form of oatmeal for human consumption. Although oats and oatmeal are amongst the richest of cereals from the point of view of analysis, in practice when taken as porridge they are not particularly nutritious. This is because of the large amount of water in porridge, *e.g.* a 7-oz. helping of porridge will contain only 3–4 oz. of oatmeal (*i.e.* 90 calories). It is the milk (and sugar) taken as a rule with porridge which enhances its food value. *Maize*, a staple article of diet in America, compares favourably with other cereals as a source of energy. In Great Britain it is used mainly in the form of *cornflour* and custard powder, in the preparation of which practically all the protein and the fat in the maize is removed. *Barley* is now used more for malting and for fodder than for human consumption. The ' barley water ' so popular in the sick-room is merely a pleasant drink and is of practically no value as a food ; it contains over 99 per cent. of water. *Rice*, the staple article of diet in the East, is the poorest of all cereals in fat and protein. On the other hand, because of the small amount of cellulose it contains, it is almost completely absorbed during the course of digestion. This renders it a useful food in certain diseases of the alimentary tract.

CEREBELLUM AND CEREBRUM (*see* BRAIN).

CEREBRO-SPINAL FEVER is another name for cerebro-spinal meningitis. (*See under* MENINGITIS.)

CEREBRO-SPINAL FLUID is the fluid within the ventricles of the brain and bathing its surface and that of the spinal cord. It is normally under a pressure of 60 to 150 mm. of water and contains 0 to 5 lymphocytes per c.mm. In each 100 millilitres of cerebro-spinal fluid there are normally between 10 to 20 mg. of protein (mostly albumin), 50 to 80 mg. of glucose, and 725 to 750 mg. of chlorides.

CERECLOTH means linen or cotton cloth impregnated with wax and made antiseptic for use in dressing wounds.

CEREVISIA, Latin name for yeast.

CERUMEN, Latin name for the wax-like secretion found in the external ear.

CERVICAL (*cervicalis*) means anything pertaining to the neck, or to the neck of the womb.

CERVICITIS means inflammation of the cervix uteri or neck of the womb.

CERVIX UTERI is the neck of the womb or uterus and is placed partly above and partly within the vagina.

CETRARIA, or ICELAND MOSS, is a substance used in the form of decoctions, jellies, or lozenges in irritable states of the mouth and throat.

CETRIMIDE (also known as CETAVLON) is the official name for a mixture of alkyl ammonium bromides. It is a potent antiseptic, and as a 1 per cent. solution is used for cleaning and disinfecting wounds, and in the first-aid treatment of burns. As it is also a detergent, it is particularly useful for cleaning the skin, and also for cleansing and disinfecting greasy and infected bowls and baths.

CHAFING OF THE SKIN occurs in infants at the natural folds, *e.g.* groins, armpits, elbows, where two moist surfaces constantly rub one another ; in stout elderly people at similar positions ; and generally where the clothes cause friction or pressure, as in the armpits or on the feet of those who walk great distances.

To prevent chafing the folds, the skin should be kept specially clean by washing with warm water and superfatted soap, carefully dried, and then dusted with fuller's earth or any dusting-powder, such as a mixture of starch, zinc oxide, and subnitrate of bismuth in equal parts.

CHAGA'S DISEASE, or American trypanosomiasis, a disease widespread in Central and South America, and caused by the *Trypanosoma cruzi*. The disease is transmitted by the biting bugs, *Panstrongylus megistus* and *Triatoma infestans*.

CHALAZION (χαλάζιον) is a small swelling of the eyelid, formed by the distension of a gland with secretion.

CHALICOSIS (χάλιξ, gravel) is a term applied to a disorder of the lungs found amongst stone-cutters, and due to the inhalation of fine particles of stone.

CHALK (*see* CRETA *and* LIME).

CHALK-STONES (*see* GOUT).

CHALONE ($\chi\alpha\lambda\acute{\alpha}\omega$, I loosen), or *coly-one*, is an organic substance formed by the cells of one organ, which after being absorbed into the circulation produces an effect upon the cells of some other organ at a distance to inhibit or prevent them from forming their proper secretion. (*See also* AUTACOID.)

CHALYBEATE tonics or waters ($\chi\acute{\alpha}\lambda\nu\psi$, steel) are those containing salts of iron. (*See* IRON.)

CHAMOMILE TEA is a 'bitter' made by infusing half an ounce of dried chamomile flowers in half a pint of boiling water for fifteen minutes and then straining. It is used cold in wineglassful doses.

CHANCRE means the primary lesion of syphilis.

CHANCROID means a soft or non-syphilitic venereal sore.

CHANGE OF LIFE (*see* CLIMACTERIC *and* MENSTRUATION).

CHAPPED HANDS occur in cold weather, when the activity of the sweat and sebaceous glands is reduced and there is therefore less natural protection of the skin. If the hands are then degreased by prolonged immersion in soapy water, and afterwards exposed to cold air, the skin becomes inelastic and cracks.

Prevention.—A mop should be used for washing up, and household rubber gloves worn when using strong bleaching solutions, ammonia, or degreasing compounds for cleaning ovens. A barrier cream (*q.v.*), such as petroleum jelly or lanolin, may be used, but most housewives find these too greasy. A more effective, and less greasy barrier cream is the *British Pharmacopœia* Oily Cream. Adequate drying of the hands is essential, and the hands should be protected from cold weather so far as possible.

Treatment.—Once chapping has occurred, a cream, such as the Oily Cream just mentioned or another *British Pharmacopœia* preparation, Aqueous Cream, should be applied every night at bedtime. After it has been applied, the hands should be covered with thin cotton gloves. The painful cracks which are so liable to form at the finger-

178

tips are best treated with a paint consisting of equal parts of tincture of benzoin and collodion.

CHAPPED LIPS (*see* LIPS).

CHAPPED NIPPLES (*see* BREASTS).

CHARCOAL, or CARBON, is obtainable in two forms, bone-charcoal and wood-charcoal. They are made by burning bones or wood without access of air, the bone-charcoal being afterwards purified from bone-earth by washing with hydrochloric acid. Bone-charcoal, which has much finer pores than wood-charcoal, has the same properties, and these in addition, that it destroys vegetable dyes and so is a bleacher, and that it destroys alkaloidal poisons and so may be given as an antidote to morphine, strychnine, etc. (half an ounce (14 G.) of charcoal neutralizing about 1 grain (60 mg.) of poison). The mode of action of charcoal is that it is porous, and so absorbs discharges, etc., with which it comes in contact, and that, in its dry state, it has the power of condensing in its pores large quantities of oxygen, which combines with organic substances, like evil-smelling gases, to form simpler, innocuous substances.

Uses.—Dry charcoal forms a good application in poultices to foul ulcers, the charcoal being sprinkled dry on the surface of a linseed poultice. Internally it is given in 20- to 60-grain (1·2 to 4 G.) doses by cachets, or in charcoal biscuits, to relieve dyspepsia associated with flatulence, and must be taken dry.

CHARCOT - LEYDEN CRYSTALS are sharp crystals found in the sputum of those suffering from asthma, and of those affected by some blood diseases.

CHARCOT'S DISEASE is the name applied to a swelling and disorganization of the joints which comes on late in locomotor ataxia (*q.v.*).

CHARPIE is linen waste, formerly used to absorb discharges, but now replaced by absorbent cotton-wool.

CHAULMOOGRA OIL is a volatile oil obtained from the seeds of an Asiatic shrub, *Gynocardia odorata*, and used in cases of leprosy.

CHEILOSIS is the term applied to an eczematous condition of the lips, especially at the angles of the mouth, and believed to be due to deficiency in the diet of one of the vitamins in the vitamin B complex—riboflavin. ANGULAR STOMATITIS and PERLÈCHE are other terms used to describe the condition, which may be associated with a red, sore tongue ; fine desquamation at the junction of nose and lip, just inside the nose, and in the ears ; eczema of the scrotum and perineum.

CHEIROPOMPHOLYX is the term applied to a disease of the skin in which little blisters filled with clear fluid suddenly appear on the hands and sometimes on the feet.

CHELOID (χηλή, a claw) is a special type of tumour formation starting in scars, especially in those of burns. It consists of an overgrowth of scar tissue, and gets its name from its claw-like offshoots, which pucker up the surrounding skin. It is found especially over parts where the skin is stretched, like the front of the chest, and is sometimes painful, sometimes painless. Often these growths disappear spontaneously after a period of activity. Massage, application of radium, or electrolysis sometimes aids their disappearance.

CHELSEA PENSIONER (see CONFECTIONS).

CHEMOSIS (χήμη, a hole) means swelling of the conjunctival membrane that covers the white of the eye, leaving the cornea depressed. (*See* EYE.)

CHEMOTAXIS (χημεία, chemistry ; τάξις, arrangement) means the property possessed by certain cells of attracting or repelling other cells.

CHEMOTHERAPY means the treatment of disease by chemical substances. In the modern sense it dates from the discovery by Paul Ehrlich, in 1910, of the action of Salvarsan (' 606 ') in destroying the spirochæte of syphilis. This organic arsenical preparation revolutionized the treatment of syphilis. The next great advance in chemotherapy was the introduction of the sulphonamides in 1935. Just as Salvarsan had revolutionized the treatment of syphilis so did the sulphonamides revolutionize the treatment of infections with the streptococcus, pneumococcus, gono-

coccus and similar organisms. They remained supreme in the treatment of such infections as septicæmia, pneumonia, and certain forms of meningitis, until the introduction of penicillin during the 1939–45 War. Subsequently a series of new antibiotics (*q.v.*) have been discovered, including streptomycin, chloramphenicol, and the tetracyclines.

Chemotherapy has also played an important rôle in tropical medicine : *e.g.* mepacrine and proguanil for the treatment of malaria ; the amidines in the treatment of sleeping sickness in man, and the sulphones in the treatment of leprosy.

CHENOPODIUM OIL, distilled from American wormseed, is used in the treatment of round-worms and hook-worms in doses of 3 to 15 minims (0·2 to 1 ml.).

CHEST, or THORAX, is the upper part of the trunk. It is enclosed by the breast-bone and rib-cartilages in front, by the twelve ribs at each side, and by the hinder parts of these along with the spinal column behind. Above, it is

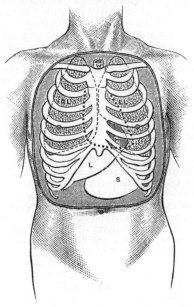

FIG. 90.—Chest with the skin and muscles removed from the front, showing the position of heart and lungs. *H,* Heart ; *LL,* left lung ; *RL,* right lung ; *W,* windpipe ; *L,* liver ; *S,* stomach.

continued by an opening a few inches wide, through which pass the windpipe, gullet, and large blood-vessels, into the root of the neck ; while, below, its cavity is separated from that of the abdomen by a thin dome-shaped plate of muscle, the diaphragm or midriff. Between each pair of ribs lie two thin muscular layers, the intercostal muscles, which fill up the spaces between the ribs, and move the chest wall in respiration. Its outlines are further covered and moulded behind by four layers of muscles, sometimes several inches thick, and by the shoulder-blade with its muscles, and in front by the two pectoral muscles which pass from the ribs to the upper arm. Further, there is a more or less plentiful layer of fat beneath the skin, and in this fat lie the breasts, extending in the female from the second rib down to the seventh.

Contents.—The chest contains the lungs, one on each side, with the end of the windpipe, which divides into right and left bronchial tubes, to the two lungs ; the heart in the middle and projecting on the left almost to the nipple, with the great vessels which carry blood from and to it ; the gullet, which passes down on the left side of the spinal column to enter the abdomen through an opening in the diaphragm ; the thoracic duct of the absorbent system, which runs up to enter a vein in the neck ; and various important nerves which control the contained organs. Each lung is enclosed in a smooth, double membrane, the pleura (*see* LUNGS), and the heart in a similar membrane, the pericardium.

CHEST, DEFORMITIES OF.—The healthy chest is gently rounded all over, its contour being still more rounded in women by the breasts, and in transverse outline it should present an oval shape slightly flattened behind and having a proportion of about 10 to 7·5 between its side - to - side and front - to - back measurements. The angle at the lower end of the breast-bone formed between the edges of the rib cartilages of the two sides should be about four-fifths of a right angle. An interval of about two inches should exist between the twelfth rib and the haunch-bone. The circumference varies from 33 inches (84 cm.) for a man of 5 feet (152 cm.) in

height to about 40 inches (102 cm.) for a man of 6 feet (183 cm.).

Long chest is one in which the shoulders slope downwards, the ribs incline downwards as they come forwards more than they should do, the lower ribs touch or almost touch the haunch-bones, and the circumference is small. Further, the neck is long, the throat prominent, and the shoulder-blades stand out behind, the chest for this reason being also called the winged or ‘ alar ’ chest. Traditionally, this form is said to predispose to tuberculosis and other lung diseases, probably because the lungs are never properly expanded, but this long chest can be much improved and the circumference rapidly increased by proper exercises.

Flat chest is often a consequence of lung diseases, and flatness is sometimes found along with too great length. In this form, the ribs and their cartilages grow too straight in front, so that the chest loses in fullness. This form is partly curable in youth by exercises.

Barrel chest is one in which the ribs are too horizontal, the shoulders raised, and the chest short. It is the opposite in every respect of the ‘ long chest ’.

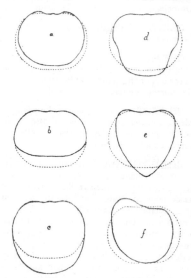

FIG. 91.—Outline of various forms of chest in transverse section, the dotted line in each case showing the normal shape. *a*, Long chest ; *b*, flat chest ; *c*, barrel-shaped ; *d*, rickety chest ; *e*, pigeon breast ; *f*, bulged chest in curvature of the spine.

The curves of the chest resemble those of a barrel and the ribs the hoops. This form is due to too great expansion of the lungs, especially in the disease called emphysema. The chest being blown out almost to its full capacity at expiration, inspiration is made very laborious.

Rickety chest is due to rickets in early life, and usually the head and other bones are also affected. (*See* RICKETS.) There is a hollow down each side owing to the yielding of the soft growing ribs in early life under the pressure of the atmosphere. There is, however, a protrusion of the front of the chest, so that the lungs are not pressed on, nor specially liable to disease. Frequently the chest shows, down each side, a row of nodules placed at the junction of the ribs with their cartilages, and known as the 'rickety rosary'. Sometimes the lower part of the chest is much bulged out from moulding over the liver and other abdominal organs.

Pigeon breast is one in which the cross-section of the chest becomes triangular, the breast-bone forming a sort of keel in front, like that in the pigeon's breast. It is due to the ribs becoming straightened so as to push the breast-bone straight forwards, and is caused by some obstacle to the entrance of air in early life, such as enlarged tonsils and adenoids in the throat.

Bulging of the chest may be due to curvature of the spine, which makes a projection behind, and consequently, the chest being shortened, causes the breast-bone to bend on itself and project in front. When the spine twists to one side, that side becomes flattened, the other side bulging and the contained organs being pushed into it.

Hollowing of the chest is found in many conditions. In tuberculosis, when the lung becomes chronically solidified in its upper part, and later probably develops a cavity, it shrinks, and the chest wall to some extent falls in beneath the collar-bone. In pleurisy of long standing the lung is apt to collapse, *i.e.* undergo a shrinking process and lose its air spaces, so that the whole chest wall of that side sinks inwards under atmosphere pressure.

CHEST DEVELOPMENT is of great practical importance in view of the fact that persons with 'long' and 'flat' chests undoubtedly suffer more often from serious lung disease than those who have good chest capacity. The art of full breathing also confers a feeling of exhilaration upon those who practise it, and adds ease to the carriage of the body. Many persons, debarred from entering one of the public services through having too small a chest circumference, owe this largely to a faulty manner of carrying the chest, the ribs being allowed to droop and the shoulders to slope downwards and forwards, although one or two inches might be added to the girth in a few days or weeks by proper exercises. (*See* CHEST, DEFORMITIES OF.) The muscles which come into action in taking a breath fall into two classes : (1) the muscles of ordinary inspiration, including the diaphragm, and the intercostal muscles, which suspend one rib from that next above it ; and (2) the muscles of forced inspiration, including most of the muscles of the neck, the shoulder, and the abdomen, which come into play in taking an extra deep breath.

The lungs rise a distance of half an inch to one and a half inches above the collar-bone into the root of the neck, and this portion is little expanded except in forced breathing. It is just here that tuberculosis is liable to make its first appearance, and though cause and effect are not quite clear in this matter, it is beyond doubt that the deficient expansion, and consequently sluggish circulation, play an important part.

Although violent exercise like football has an indirect influence in expanding the chest by necessitating deep breathing, other forms of athletics add mainly to the size and strength of the muscles on the chest without increasing its capacity. Probably the only exercise which attains the latter thoroughly is forced breathing.

Every one, whether of athletic build or not, may practise this by the following three movements, recommended by Checkley (Fig. 92). These should be carried out night and morning, with the upper part of the body bare, or covered only by a loose or elastic undervest :

(*a*) The person standing erect holds the hands in front of him, backs upwards, on a level with his hips. As he begins to breathe he raises them till, at the end of an inspiration, they are straight above his head. As he breathes out he lets them slowly fall to their

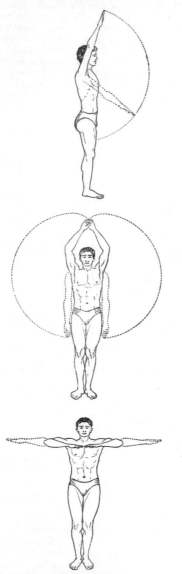

Fig. 92.—Movements for expansion of the chest. (After Checkley.)

former position. This he repeats with each breath, making the breaths as deep as possible.

182

(b) Standing with the hands by the sides, palms forwards, he raises them away from the sides as he breathes in, to the same position as in the first movement, and lets them descend slowly outwards as he breathes out.

(c) Standing with elbows bent, the thumbs pressed against the upper part of the chest, and the finger-tips of opposite hands touching, he carries the arms outwards and as far backwards as possible, keeping them always on a level with the shoulders, as he draws a deep breath, and brings them forwards again as he breathes out.

In performing these movements a light pair of dumb-bells (not exceeding 2 pounds each) may, if desired, be used, and the movements will then be a better exercise for the arm muscles.

It is of the utmost importance that the movements should be slow : not quicker than six to the minute, and preferably about three per minute, and each movement should be a conscious effort, not made automatically. If each movement be performed twenty times, a fair amount of exercise will be obtained in about a quarter of an hour.

Further, the person should cultivate the habit of breathing deeply at all times, and of standing, sitting, or walking with the shoulders well braced back, so as to take the weight of the shoulder blade and upper limb off the expansile part of the chest.

CHEST DISEASES (*see* LUNGS, DISEASES OF ; HEART DISEASES, ANEURYSM, ANGINA PECTORIS, PLEURISY, PNEUMONIA, BRONCHITIS, TUBERCULOSIS).

Chest diseases are of special importance, because the lungs and heart are perhaps the most important organs in the body, and are especially difficult to treat, as these are the only organs which cannot rest for a few minutes without death becoming imminent. Further, they are so closely placed and so intimately associated by the circulation of the blood, that when one suffers from disease, either acute or chronic, the other is rarely unaffected.

Symptoms.—Owing to the rigid nature of the chest wall, changes in the enclosed organs rarely become visible to the eye. *Pain* is a very important symptom. Very severe pain may, it is true, be caused by muscular rheumatism in the chest wall (the condition called pleurodynia) or by neuralgia, but when of a stabbing character and felt at the end of every breath it suggests pleurisy as a cause. Pain about the heart may be caused by indigestion, but if severe, and especially if brought on by exertion, seldom is found without some slight or serious heart disease. An agonizing spasm of the heart, often coupled with a feeling of impending death, is known as angina pectoris (*see* ANGINA PECTORIS). Severe persistent pain of a boring character is suggestive of an aneurysm (*see* ANEURYSM). *Expectoration* of blood may occur both in heart and in lung disease, and various other characters are noteworthy in the sputum (*see* EXPECTORATION). *Breathlessness* is an important sign of lung and heart diseases (*see* BREATHLESSNESS). *Other organs* are prone to be affected by disease of either heart or lungs ; thus in tuberculosis the digestive system sometimes gives the first sign of ill-health, and in heart disease congestion of the liver, or swelling of the feet, may be for long the main trouble. *Cough* is one of the best-known symptoms of lung mischief, either of tuberculosis or of bronchitis, but it may be due to irritation of other parts of the respiratory system, or even of the stomach.

Treatment.—Rest is the most important factor in the treatment of all chest conditions, because, when the body is quiet, the circulation of the blood becomes slower, the rate of pulse and respiration slackens, and so the heart and lungs have a partial rest. Pain is soothed by the application of fomentations, poultices, ice-bags, or counter-irritants to the chest. Fresh air is specially necessary in lung disease (*see* TUBERCULOSIS). Infections are controlled by the sulphonamides or antibiotics. Various drugs called expectorants are given to act upon the lungs, or similar drugs are inhaled (*see* EXPECTORANTS *and* INHALATIONS). Oxygen is much used both in affections of the heart and of the lungs. In the case of the heart, there are several drugs by which the action of this organ can be slowed, or quickened, or made more regular, for example, digitalis, strophanthus, atropine.

CHEST INJURIES.—Injuries due to moderate violence are not usually serious, resulting generally in muscular bruises or in fractured rib (*see* FRACTURES). If the ribs do not penetrate the lung, union and recovery are rapid, but, if the lung be injured, various complications, such as emphysema, effusion of blood and entrance of air into the pleural cavity, abscess in the lung, traumatic pneumonia, etc., may ensue. Penetrating wounds of the lungs, as by a bullet or stab, are apt to lead to similar complications, but do not necessarily produce serious effects unless a large vessel be severed. Simple fractures of ribs may be serious in old people, and bronchitis often follows their occurrence. Wounds of the heart are generally at once fatal from hæmorrhage, but this organ has been so seriously injured as even to require stitching, and yet recovery has ensued.

CHEYNE-STOKES' BREATHING is a type of breathing seen in some serious nervous affections, such as brain

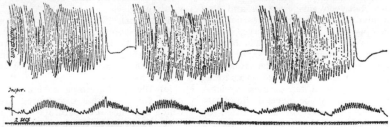

FIG. 93.—Tracing of Cheyne-Stokes' Breathing. Note two periods in tracing when breathing stops completely. (From Best and Taylor, *The Physiological Basis of Medical Practice.* The Williams & Wilkins Co.)

tumours and apoplexy, and also in the case of persons with advanced disease of the heart or kidneys. When well marked it is a sign that death is impending, though milder degrees of it do not carry such a serious implication in elderly patients. The breathing gets very faint for a short time, then gradually deepens till full expirations are taken for a few seconds, and then gradually dies away to another quiet period, again increasing in depth after a few seconds and so on in cycles (Fig. 93).

CHICKENPOX, or VARICELLA, is an acute contagious disease of children, characterized by feverishness and an eruption on the skin.

Causes.—The disease occurs in epidemics affecting especially children under the age of ten years. It has no connection with smallpox, to which it bears a superficial resemblance. It is due to a virus, and the condition is an extremely infectious one from child to child.

Symptoms.—There is an incubation period of eleven to twenty-one days after infection, and then the child becomes feverish or has a slight shivering, or may feel more severely ill with vomiting and pains in the back and legs. Almost at the same time, and at all events within twenty-four hours, an eruption consisting of red pimples which quickly change into vesicles filled with clear fluid appears on the back and chest, sometimes about the forehead, and less frequently on the limbs. These vesicles during the second day may show a change of their contents to turbid, purulent fluid and within a day or two they burst, or, at all events, shrivel up and become covered with brownish crusts. An important point of difference between this eruption and that of smallpox is that these vesicles keep on appearing for several days, so that vesicles are seen at all stages of development, whilst in those of smallpox all parts of the rash are at the same stage at one time. In a slight case there may be only eight or ten of these vesicles, or there may be several hundreds. The small crusts have all dried up and fallen off in little more than a week and recovery is almost always complete.

184

Treatment.—The child must be isolated from other children for fourteen days from the appearance of the rash or until all the vesicles are dry, but there is no need to wait until the scabs have separated. A patient need not be confined to bed unless the temperature is raised, but he should be kept in one room. If the rash appear on the face, care must be taken to prevent scratching or pock marks may remain. A lotion of calamine or of carbolic acid, or a simple dusting powder, relieves the itchiness. No other treatment beyond isolation is required. If children have been exposed to the risk of infection, it is usual to keep them under observation for twenty days.

CHICORY (*see* ADULTERATION OF FOOD).

CHIGGER is another name for the harvest mite (*see* PARASITES).

CHILBLAIN, or ERYTHEMA PERNIO, is an inflamed condition of the skin of hands or feet, or even of the ears, occurring in persons of defective circulation and in those of poor health.

Causes.—Chilblains are found especially in childhood and adolescence. Under-feeding, poor clothing, and a defective circulation favour their appearance. Persons who suffer from them habitually have cold and numb hands and feet, and are subject to chills and colds in the head. In these persons, tight boots often are sufficient to bring on chilblains of the feet, and warming the hands at the fire when they are cold produces chilblains on the fingers, the skin becoming engorged with blood in consequence of the irritation or warmth, and later losing its vitality.

Symptoms.—There are three stages in the development of a chilblain :

(1) The skin, usually of the little toe, the outer side of the foot, or the inner side of the hand, becomes purple and very itchy.

(2) Blebs, containing a thin yellow fluid, form on this discoloured area, which becomes very painful.

(3) These blebs break and leave behind an ulcerated surface very difficult to heal.

True chilblains should not be confounded with a cracked or 'chapped' condition of the hands, feet, lips, or ears brought on by cold wind, or washing with hot water during cold weather in persons of robust constitution but delicate skin.

Treatment. — Preventive treatment is the best. Good food and warm clothing improve the general condition upon which chilblains depend. Regular exercise, and a cold or modified cold bath every day (*see* BATHS) improve the circulation. The person liable to chilblains should wear wide boots and thick woollen socks in winter, and, before going into the open air, should always pull on a pair of woollen gloves. Garters and constrictions round the wrist or ankle, which interfere with the circulation, should be abolished, and india-rubber shoes should not be worn. If the hands and feet are cold they should be rubbed for warmth, not held before the fire. In the first stage the chilblain may be rubbed with hazeline snow or cream, or painted with tincture of iodine. Carefully controlled irradiation with ultra-violet light from a carbon-arc lamp is often beneficial. Voyagers to the Arctic regions rub the part with a mixture of whisky and soap. In the second and third stages some simple ointment, like boracic, and a dressing of wool are best, or the part may be painted with compound tincture of benzoin.

CHILD-CROWING is another name for laryngismus. (*See* LARYNGISMUS.)

CHILDREN, FEEDING OF (*see* INFANT FEEDING).

CHILDREN, PECULIARITIES OF.— The fact that children cannot put into words, or cannot correctly estimate the nature of troubles and pains from which they suffer, coupled with the great importance of remedying as early in life as possible any physical or mental defect, or any bad habit, makes the observation of their peculiarities of great importance.

Activity.—For some weeks after an infant is born the only signs of intelligence, apart from the performance of the merely animal functions, consist in *constant movements* of the lips, head, and limbs. The fingers are constantly opened and shut, the legs drawn up and down, and the lips pouted, while the child is awake ; and the vigour of these movements gives a good idea of the vitality of the child. At about the third or fourth month the child should begin to develop the power of attention, as shown by his staring fixedly at any bright or moving object presented to him and ceasing other movements while his attention is so engaged. During the sixth month teething begins. A delay in teething is one of the signs of rickets (*see* TEETH). About the end of the first year of life the child should be gaining the power to stand and walk (*see* GAIT.)

Crying in early childhood is a manifestation of either pain, or hunger, or discomfort. The most common pain is that known as 'gripes' and associated with indigestion, in which the cry is of a wailing character, with a note of ill-temper (*see* COLIC). In head pain the cry is of a sharp, piercing nature. In older children frowning is a common symptom of headache, especially when it is due to eye-strain (*see* VISION, DISORDERS OF).

Temperature is not much of a guide to disease in children, because the temperature-regulating mechanism is easily thrown out of gear.

Fullness under the eyes may be a symptom of Bright's disease.

An open mouth in breathing, especially when deafness and shortness of breath accompany it, is usually due to enlargement of the tonsils and adenoids in the throat. A child so affected is generally found to snore when asleep. (*See* NOSE, DISEASES OF.)

Accompanying these symptoms in older children we find broadening of the bridge of the nose, narrow nostrils, and often narrowing of the roof of the mouth with projecting front teeth.

The expression of the face is often of great importance. Brain disease causes contractions of the facial muscles producing the appearance of emotions quite foreign to childhood, and causing the deep lines which, in middle-aged persons, are supposed to denote character. The head, too, is often drawn back in such a case, and the back arched. Deep hollowing of the eyes during an attack of summer diarrhœa and vomiting is a grave sign, indicating great exhaustion. The size of the cranium is large in children compared with that of the face. At birth the proportion is about eight to one, though the face rapidly grows in size. On the top of the head is the ' fontanelle ' or soft spot, which is at birth about a square inch in size, and gradually closes as the bones grow till, at the end of the second year, it should have disappeared. Premature closure, with narrowing of the forehead, is often, though not necessarily, associated with menta deficiency. Late closure, with the development of a lofty, ' intellectual '- looking forehead, is one of the signs of rickets.

Bad postures in children, such as standing on one leg, stooping at the shoulders, and leaning the left elbow on the table at lessons, should be discouraged as tending to produce deformities. The latter habit may produce considerable curvature of the spine and defective development of one side of the chest.

Nervousness may show itself by twitching movements of hands and feet, and a shy, nervous child is apt to be unintentionally clumsy. Twitchings and grimaces very often show the beginning of St. Vitus's dance, and children are apt to be punished for these quite involuntary peculiarities, such punishment only aggravating the condition. Grinning on every occasion, however, shows a want of control over the muscles of expression, and indicates a low-class brain and necessity for careful upbringing. Convulsions in young children are due to many causes (*see* CONVULSIONS), and when some nervous disease is the cause they form a serious symptom. Although much more common in children, they are not by any means as grave as fits of similar severity in adults. The involuntary or unconscious passing of urine (or enuresis), showing itself generally by wetting of the bed, is usually a bad habit in a nervous child and capable of correction by careful psychological treatment, but is occasionally due to physical conditions needing correction.

Bad habits in children include such

186

actions as persistent sucking of the thumb or tongue, biting the nails, rolling or nodding the head in a rhythmic manner, knocking the head violently on the pillow, rhythmic swaying of the body, eating of dirt. These habits all consist in a morbid exaggeration of some normal action which has an extraordinary fascination for the children who practise it. They should be corrected at an early stage, firmly yet tactfully and without any fuss, by checking the child and making him carry out some other activity on each occasion when the habit is noticed. Advice should be sought at a child-guidance clinic or from the family doctor if the habit persists.

Left-handedness is often taken for a sign of stupidity, and children are punished when they do not use the right. This is a great mistake, because the condition is due to the fact that the side of the brain governing the left hand has developed in advance of the other. The child may, however, be taught to do certain things with the right, and so attain a condition of ambidexterity.

The teaching of children should not be forced before the age of seven, and up to this age should be directed rather to teaching habits of study, orderliness, and regularity. The teaching of good habits should begin at birth. This may be done, for example, in the matter of feeding. The periods at which the child is to be fed having been determined upon, these should be rigidly adhered to, despite the child's crying. It is astonishing how soon the child accepts this discipline and ceases to cry for food at irregular times. Present-day teaching in the kindergartens and primary schools is directed towards instructing children how to observe and study rather than towards cramming them with facts. After the age of seven is reached, the child's brain is quite capable of enduring some fatigue, and regular lessons should be begun, or the child will learn idle, loafing habits.

Sleep should be longer the younger the child, and nervous children should have a specially good allowance. The following table gives approximately the minimum periods of sleep at different ages :

	Hours a Day
During first year . . .	20
During second year .	14-16
From second to fourth year .	12-14
From fourth to sixth year .	10-12
From sixth to twelfth year .	10
From twelfth to sixteenth year	9

TABLE 10.—Minimum Requirements of Sleep at Different Ages.

CHILLS and COLDS form a subject of some importance because, although in general trivial ailments, they are often the prelude to serious diseases.

Causes. — The so - called ' common cold ' may follow some chill to the surface, such as exposure to a draught of cold air, breathing in a foggy atmosphere, wetting of the feet on a cold day, sudden immersion in water, etc., some persons being specially liable after one of these to develop a catarrh of the respiratory passages and feverish state. These, however, are only predisposing factors, and the primary cause is a virus. Often a ' cold in the head ' runs through all the members of a family or school or a group of persons employed together, and such an ' infectious cold ' is due to the causative virus passed from one person to another by sneezing or coughing.

Varieties and symptoms.—A cold in the head with catarrh of the nose is known to every one ; the catarrh sometimes extending up into the frontal sinuses and causing a severe browache, or involving the maxillary sinuses (*see* ANTRUM) and causing faceache, or even spreading up the Eustachian tubes and causing inflammation of the middle ear with painful earache. Generally, these secondary affections disappear as the cold gets well, but suppuration may result in these various cavities, most commonly in the middle ear, though seldom in the frontal sinus. When the throat is the part affected, inflammation of the tonsils may result. (*See* TONSILLITIS.) In persons who use the voice much, or in those who indulge overmuch in alcohol, the larynx is a weak point, and laryngitis, with huskiness or even temporary loss of voice, is the common result of a chill. The cold may affect the respiratory passages farther down and bronchitis then results, or if the surfaces of the air spaces in the lungs be inflamed, pneumonia is the condition produced. When the air passages from the larynx downwards contain mucus, coughing results, this being a series of involuntary explosive expirations designed to force the irritating substance up into the mouth, from which it is spat out. Some persons have a liability, as the result of a chill, to catarrh not of the respiratory, but of the alimentary system, as shown by ensuing dyspepsia or diarrhœa. It should be remembered that a so-called 'cold' is the commencement of several infectious and serious diseases, such as measles, whooping-cough, influenza, and tuberculosis. Medical advice should therefore be sought whenever this apparently trivial malady lasts more than a few weeks. Finally a chilly sensation is a frequent accompaniment of some nervous shock either of a severe nature or even of some minor type.

Treatment.—There is very little one can do in the treatment of a cold. Most people have their pet remedies, and most of these are harmless. On ' catching a cold ', with a temperature above normal, the best thing to do is to go to bed and stay there at least 24 hours, if not two days. In this way the course of the cold will be cut short, and at the same time the sufferer will not be exposing other people to his infection. The best way to prevent colds is to isolate the infected by keeping them in bed. Vaccines seem to be ineffectual in the prevention of colds.

CHINCOUGH (Dutch, *kind*, a child ; *kuch*, cough) is another name for whooping-cough. (*See* WHOOPING-COUGH.)

CHIRAGRA (χειράγρα) is an ancient term applied to gout affecting the hand.

CHIRETTA, or CHIRATA, is a favourite bitter, resembling gentian. (*See* BITTERS.)

CHIROPODIST (χείρ, hand ; πούς, foot) is the name applied to one who treats corns, bunions, and other minor affections of the hands and feet.

CHIROPRACTOR (χείρ, the hand ; πράσσω, I practise) is a term applied to a person who practises chiropractic, which is a system of adjustment by

187

hand of supposed minor displacements of the spinal column in order to relieve pressure upon the nerves issuing at the intervertebral foramina. The essential fallacy of this system lies in the fact that the foramina for the exit of the spinal nerves are so large that pressure upon these nerves is only possible in gross displacements caused by very severe injury or disease.

CHIRURGEON ($\chi\epsilon\iota\rho\text{ου}\rho\gamma\acute{o}\varsigma$) is an obsolete method of spelling surgeon.

CHITTENDEN'S DIET is the name applied to a diet containing about half the amount of protein which the ordinary diet of healthy persons includes.

CHLOASMA ($\chi\lambda\acute{o}\alpha$, a green plant) is a condition in which brown blotches appear, especially on the face. It occurs chiefly in pregnant women, in whom the spots fade after delivery, and also in those who suffer from various abdominal complaints.

CHLORALAMIDE is a crystalline powder with faintly bitter taste which is generally regarded as a safe hypnotic, It is given in doses of 15 to 45 grains (1 to 3 G.).

CHLORAL HYDRATE is a substance prepared by prolonged action upon alcohol with chlorine gas. It is a clear, crystalline substance, with sweetish taste, which dissolves rapidly in water. When taken internally in moderate doses it produces sound, dreamless, refreshing sleep, like natural sleep. It is, however, dangerous in large doses, and persons taking it frequently are liable to contract a habit for it. In safe doses it does not lessen pain appreciably, as opium does, and so will not cure sleeplessness due to this cause. In dangerous doses it paralyses and slows the heart, slows respiration, and reduces body temperature.
Uses.—Chloral is chiefly used to produce sleep in those suffering from worry, overwork, or delirium tremens. It is given in doses of 5 to 20 grains (300 mg. to 1·2 G.), or in the form of syrup of chloral, a teaspoonful, but for the reasons mentioned above, should only be taken under medical observation. It is also used in small doses for relief from convulsions, astham, seasickness, etc. *Externally* chloral is an
188

antiseptic, and a lotion of strength 8 grains (500 mg.) of chloral to each ounce (28·5 ml.) of water is used for cleansing unhealthy ulcers, and some forms of eczema. Chloral and camphor, rubbed together in equal parts, form a clear fluid, so do chloral and menthol, and either of these is useful for painting on to the skin in cases of neuralgia or of gouty pain.

CHLORAL POISONING is by no means infrequent, because, the sleep-producing effect of the drug passing off after repeated administrations, the sleepless person is apt to increase the dose too far.
Symptoms. — Occasionally, though seldom, there is gastric pain and sickness after a large dose. Usually the result is a speedy and deep sleep, passing gradually into coma, the pulse growing feebler, and the respirations embarrassed till death peacefully ensues.
Treatment.—The patient must be persistently irritated and roused as in opium poisoning. The stomach should be at once emptied by stomach-tube or emetic. The extremities of the body must be kept warm, and stimulants given. Leptazol and ephedrine are said to be useful. Artificial respiration may be needed.

CHLORALUM, or CHLORIDE OF ALUMINIUM, is used as a disinfectant for drains and excreta, in strength of 1 pound (450 G.) to a gallon (4·5 litres) of water.

CHLORAMBUCIL is a derivative of nitrogen mustard (*q.v.*), which is proving of value in the treatment of chronic lymphatic leukæmia (*q.v.*) and Hodgkin's disease (*q.v.*). It is given by mouth.

CHLORAMINE is a white powder with powerful antiseptic action, which is non-irritant and non-poisonous.

CHLORAMPHENICOL, or CHLOROMYCETIN, is an antibiotic derived from a soil organism, *Streptomyces venezuelæ*. It is also prepared synthetically. It is active against a wide range of organisms, but its most striking feature is its activity against certain rickettsiæ (*q.v.*). It has proved effective in the treatment of typhus, scrub typhus, Rocky Mountain spotted fever, typhoid and paratyphoid fevers. Its activity against certain organisms not susceptible to the sulphonamides and penicillin is proving of great value. Particularly is this true of its use in the treatment of meningitis due to *H. influenzæ*. It is given by mouth.

It is an antibiotic, however, that must be administered with discrimination because in certain individuals it may cause aplastic anæmia (*q.v.*), particularly if given for too long a period or in repeated courses.

CHLORDANE is an insecticide which has been used successfully against flies and mosquitoes resistant to D.D.T., and for the control of ticks and mites. It requires special handing as it is toxic to man when applied to the skin.

CHLORDIAZEPOXIDE, the proprietary name of which is librium, is a widely used anti-anxiety drug.

CHLORETONE, or CHLORBUTOL, is a white powder with an odour like camphor. Applied to the surface of the skin or mucous membrane it has a soothing and antiseptic effect, and internally it acts as a hypnotic.

CHLORHEXIDINE, also known as HIBITANE, is a bisdiguanide which has a powerful bacteriostatic action against many bacteria, including *Staphylococcus aureus*. It is proving particularly useful as a skin disinfectant.

CHLORIDE OF ZINC is the main constituent of Burnett's disinfectant.

CHLORINATED LIME, generally known as CHLORIDE OF LIME, is a white powder made by passing chlorine gas over slaked lime. Chlorine is a greenish gas, heavier than air, with a pungent, choking smell, and highly poisonous to all forms of bacterial life. By virtue of its power to give off chlorine, chlorinated lime is a powerful bleaching agent and disinfectant, especially when mixed with an acid.

To disinfect rooms, chlorinated lime may be mixed with an equal bulk of water acidulated with sulphuric acid, and exposed on flat dishes for some hours.

To disinfect water-closets and drains, 1 pound (450 G.) of the chlorinated lime may be mixed with a gallon (4·5 litres) of water and poured down the drain.

CHLORINE WATER, is a solution of chlorine gas in water. It is used as a gargle in suppurating sore throat, as an inhalation when the expectoration is very offensive, and for an antiseptic application to foul-smelling ulcers.

Preparation.—Ten grains (600 mg.) of chlorate of potash and thirty drops of strong hydrochloric acid are mixed in the bottom of a pint (500 ml.) bottle. Chlorine gas is produced, and replaces the air in the bottle. When this yellow gas begins to issue from the bottle the latter is corked, allowed to stand for two minutes to cool, and then the bottle filled little by little with water, being corked and well shaken after each addition, so that the gas may be absorbed by the water.

CHLORMERODRIN is a mercurial diuretic which is active when given by mouth. (*See* DIURETICS.)

CHLORODYNE is a proprietary soothing remedy said to contain chloroform, hydrocyanic acid, morphine, capsicum, and Indian hemp. It is similar to the pharmacopœial preparation of compound tincture of chloroform and morphia, which is used in doses of 5 to 15 minims (0·3 to 1 ml.).

CHLOROFORM is a colourless, volatile liquid, half as heavy again as water, and, unlike ether, non-inflammable. It was discovered by Liebig in 1831, and is manufactured by distilling alcohol with a mixture of slaked lime and chloride of lime, being a compound of carbon, hydrogen, and chlorine. It does not dissolve to a large amount in water, but mixes readily with alcohol or ether. It dissolves sulphur, phosphorus, fats, resins, and most substances which contain a large proportion of carbon; it is therefore very useful as a cleansing agent. It was introduced into medicine in 1847 by Sir J. Y. Simpson, who was then in search of a substance which could produce unconsciousness for operative purposes more conveniently than ether, introduced a short time previously by Morton in America. (See ANÆSTHETICS.)

Uses.—Chloroform is used as a solvent of fats, resins, etc., in many chemical processes.

Externally it may be used to produce blisters (*see* BLISTERS), and the liniment of chloroform is a useful application for rheumatic and similar pains, having both a soothing and a mildly counter-irritant action.

Internally its chief use is by inhalation to produce insensibility to pain during surgical operations, in painful and convulsive diseases such as gall-stone colic, and during child-birth. By the mouth, small doses have also the effect of relieving pain and producing sleep, so that it is useful for soothing headache and relieving vomiting, especially in seasickness. For this purpose 1 to 5 drops may be taken on a lump of sugar, but care is needful, for in large doses, chloroform is a violent irritant and narcotic poison. Spirit of chloroform is a frequent component of cough and digestive mixtures, for its stimulating and soothing effects upon the interior of the stomach and bronchial tubes.

CHLOROMA, or GREEN CANCER, is the name of a disease in which greenish growths appear under the skin, and in which a change takes place in the blood resembling that in leukæmia.

CHLOROMYCETIN is another name for CHLORAMPHENICOL (*q.v.*).

CHLOROPHYLL (χλωρός, green ; φύλλον, leaf) is the name of the green colouring matter of plants. It is being found of value as a deodorant dressing to remove, or diminish, the unpleasant odour of heavily infected sores and wounds.

CHLOROQUINE, which is a 4-aminoquinoline, was introduced during the 1939–45 War, for the treatment of malaria. It has also been found of value in the treatment of amœbic abscess in the liver, of the skin condition known as chronic discoid lupus erythematosus, and of rheumatoid arthritis.

CHLOROSIS (χλωρός, greenish-yellow) is a form of anæmia which receives its name from the yellow or faintly

190

greenish-grey complexion of those suffering from it. Very common before the 1914–18 War, it is scarcely ever seen now. (See ANÆMIA.)

CHLOROTHIAZIDE is a potent benzthiadiazine (*q.v.*) diuretic which is active when taken by mouth. It has also a blood-pressure lowering effect when used in conjunction with other hypotensive drugs.

CHLOROXYLENOL is an antiseptic which is used for treating cuts, abrasions, and wounds. It is also widely used in obstetric practice. It is only slightly soluble in water (1 in 3000).

CHLORPHENTERMINE is a synthetic amphetamine derivative which is proving of value in the management of obesity.

CHLORPROMAZINE, or LARGACTIL, is chemically related to the antihistamine drug, promethazine. It is one of the so-called ' tranquillizers (*q.v.*), and is being used extensively in psychiatry on account of its action in calming psychotic activity without producing undue general depression or clouding of consciousness.

CHLORPROPAMIDE is one of the new oral hypoglycæmic agents. Like carbutamide (*q.v.*) it is a sulphonamide derivative, but it is less toxic. As it has a prolonged action, it need only be given once a day. It is said to be more effective than tolbutamide (*q.v.*). (*See also* DIABETES MELLITUS.)

CHLORTETRACYCLINE, also known as aureomycin, is an antibiotic derived from a soil organism, *Streptomyces aureofaciens*. (*See* TETRACYCLINES.)

CHOCOLATE is a solid substance made by grinding cocoa nibs to powder and mixing with a large amount of sugar and some flavouring substance, such as vanilla. It consists, roughly, half of sugar, starch, and protein, and half of a fat known as cocoa-butter, with small quantities of water and salts, and about 1 per cent. of theobromine, an alkaloid of stimulating properties similar to those of tea and coffee.

Chocolate has been used in England since the time of Charles II, when it was very popular. It forms a compact and easily carried food, suitable for sustaining hard labour and for protecting against cold. The energy value of chocolate is about 600 calories per 100 grammes.

CHOKE-DAMP (*see* DAMP).

CHOKING is the process which results from an obstruction to breathing situated in the larynx (*see* AIR PASSAGES). It may occur as the result of disease causing swelling round the glottis (the entrance to the larynx), or of some nervous disorders that interfere with the regulation of the muscles which open and shut the larynx, but generally it is due to the irritation of a piece of food or other substance introduced by the mouth, which provokes coughing but only partly interferes with breathing. In the act of swallowing, all food passes over the top of the larynx, and, as a preliminary to swallowing, the glottis is automatically closed by approximation of the sides of the larynx at their upper edge, over which the bolus of food is shot into the gullet (Fig. 94). When, as the result of some nervous disease, such as a form of para-

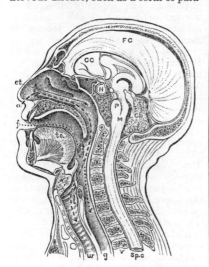

FIG. 94.--Vertical section through the middle of the head and neck, showing the upper air passages. The passages for air *a*, are indicated by a heavy dotted line, those for the food *f*, by a fainter line; *et*, Eustachian tube; *l*, larynx; *w*, windpipe; *t*, tonsil; *to*, tongue; *g*, gullet. (For other letters, *see* BRAIN.) (After Braune.)

lysis of the mouth and throat muscles, or simply of an attempt to speak or laugh during eating, this preliminary closure is not complete, a piece of food is apt to lodge in, or some fluid to trickle down into, the larynx. The mucous membrane lining the upper part of the latter being specially sensitive, coughing results in order to expel the cause of irritation. At the same time, if the foreign body be of any size, lividity of the face appears, due to partial suffocation (*see* ASPHYXIA).

Treatment.—If coughing be vigorous the choking person should be let alone, a glass of water being put within his reach, because a gulp of cold water often dislodges the particle, and, at all events, stimulates more vigorous coughing. The choking person should take slow, deep inspirations, which do not force the particle farther in (as sudden catchings of the breath between the coughs do), and which produce more powerful coughs. If the coughing be weak, one or two strong blows with the palm of the hand over either shoulder blade, timed to coincide with coughs aid the effect of the coughing. In the case of a child the patient may be held up by the legs, when the substance causing the obstruction is more readily dislodged. Finally, if the coughing be getting weak, lividity of the face and finger-nails coming on, and especially if unconsciousness has supervened, death is imminent within a few minutes unless the obstruction be removed.

For this purpose the bystander should pass his right forefinger along the side of the patient's tongue, forcing the teeth apart first, if necessary, with a knife handle, and keeping them apart by the fingers of the other hand with a napkin rolled round them. The forefinger should be passed as far down the throat as possible, its point then turned towards the middle line and hooked forwards towards the root of the tongue. After a few attempts the foreign body will very likely be dislodged and pulled up into the mouth.

Sometimes, however, the foreign body may be too small to catch; for example, death has been recorded in consequence of a fragment of cabbage leaf which lay over the opening of the larynx like a valve, completely preventing the entrance of air, and, the opening being only a slit about a quarter of an inch (6 mm.) from side to side and less than an inch (25 mm.) from before backwards, such an accident may readily happen. In this case, if the sufferer be livid and unconscious, and if no medical man be obtained within five minutes, someone at hand may undertake to open the larynx below the obstruction, and admit air to the lungs, but, on account of its dangers, this is suitable only in extremest cases. For this purpose a sharp-pointed knife, such as a penknife, should be taken, the prominent Adam's apple in front of the neck felt for, and the knife pushed boldly into the throat at a point half an inch (12 mm.) below the prominence (in a full-grown person). The knife must be pushed in exactly in the middle line, straight backwards to the depth of half an inch (12 mm.), and the cut extended half an inch (12 mm.) downwards. After this, artificial respiration (see DROWNING) may be necessary, and, if there be any bleeding from the wound in the neck, a bystander should press gently with his finger on the edge from which it comes, at the same time pressing the edges of the wound apart so as to allow the air to enter. By this procedure, lives have been saved when the obstruction could not be dislodged through the mouth.

CHOLÆMIA (χολή, bile; αἷμα, blood) is a vague term applied to conditions in which the bile is not excreted from the body to its usual extent, but circulates in the blood. (*See* JAUNDICE.)

CHOLAGOGUES (χολή, bile; ἄγω, I move) are substances which increase the flow of bile. The great majority of these act only by increasing the activity of the digestive organs, and so producing a flow of bile already stored up in the gall-bladder, but a few actually stimulate the liver to secrete more bile, and so have the effect of clearing the system of various injurious substances circulating in the blood.

Varieties and Uses.—Among the former class are blue pill, calomel, aloes, ipecacuanha, rhubarb, and Epsom salts. The only true cholagogues are bile and bile salts.

CHOLANGITIS (χολή, bile; ἀγγεῖον, vessel) is the term applied to inflammation of the bile ducts.

CHOLECYSTECTOMY means the removal of the gall-bladder by operation.

CHOLECYSTITIS (χολή, bile; κύστις, a bladder) means inflammation of the gall-bladder (*q.v.*).

CHOLECYSTOGRAPHY is the term applied to the process whereby the gall-bladder is rendered radio-opaque and therefore visible on an X-ray film. (*See* PHENIODOL.)

CHOLELITHIASIS (χολή, bile; λίθος, a stone) means the presence of gall-stones in the bile-ducts and/or in the gall-bladder. (*See* GALL-STONES.)

CHOLERA (from χολή, bile; and ῥέω, I flow) is one of the most severe and fatal of all diseases. Cholera belongs originally to Asia, more particularly to India and East Pakistan, where epidemics are known to have occurred at various times for several centuries. It was not, however, till 1817 that the attention of European physicians was specially directed to the disease by the outbreak of a violent epidemic of cholera at Jessore in Bengal. This was followed by its rapid spread over a large portion of British India, where it caused immense destruction of life among both natives and Europeans. By 1823 it had extended into Asia Minor and Russia in Asia, and it continued to advance steadily though slowly westwards, and spread onwards to England, appearing in Sunderland in October 1831, and in London in January 1832. The disease subsequently spread through North and Central America, reaching even to the military posts on the upper Mississippi. In 1835 it was general throughout North Africa, after which this epidemic disappeared.

About the year 1841 another great epidemic of cholera appeared in India and China, and soon began to extend in the direction traversed by the former, but involving a still wider area. This epidemic appears to have been even more deadly than the former, especially as regards Great Britain and France.

A third great outbreak of cholera

took place in the East in 1850, entering Europe in 1853. It was specially severe throughout both North and South America.

A fourth epidemic visited Europe again in 1865–66, but was on the whole less extensive and destructive than its predecessors. In 1884, and again in 1892 and 1893, there were outbreaks in the middle of Europe, the last one being specially severe in Hamburg and some other cities, but, apart from occasional cases brought by ship, there has been no epidemic in Britain or in the United States for many years.

Causes.—The cause of the disease is the *Vibrio choleræ* or ' comma-bacillus ' discovered by Koch (Fig. 24). This organism is constantly found in the discharges from the bowels of those suffering from the disease. The most important mode of transmission is by means of contaminated water, but the infection is also conveyed by flies, which contaminate food with infected fæces. The crowding which occurs under conditions of war and famine also favours epidemics.

Symptoms.—The incubation period is a few hours to five days. The disease varies in severity from mild cases which do not feel ill enough to take to bed, to cases which are fatal within twenty-four hours. Over 90 per cent. of cases, however, are of the so-called *Cholera gravis* type, in which three stages are recognized.

The *first stage*, which lasts for three to twelve hours, is of sudden onset with painless diarrhœa and vomiting. The stools rapidly become frequent and copious, resembling rice-water and containing flakes of fibrin. This is soon followed by agonizing cramps, first in the limbs and then in the abdomen. The patient complains bitterly of thirst and becomes restless and exhausted, with cold bluish skin, sunken eyeballs, and husky voice. The pulse is weak and the temperature taken in the rectum is 101° to 104° F. (38.3° to 40° C.).

The *second stage* is termed the stage of collapse or algid stage. The symptoms now advance with rapidity. The signs of collapse increase. The surface of the body becomes colder and assumes a dusky blue or purple hue, the skin is dry and wrinkled, indicating the intense

draining away, in the evacuations, of the fluids of the body. The features are pinched and the eyes more deeply sunken, the pulse at the wrist is imperceptible, and the voice is reduced to a hoarse whisper (the ' vox cholerica '). There may be complete suppression of the urine.

In this condition, death often takes place in less than one day, but, in epidemics, cases are sometimes observed in which the collapse is so sudden and complete as to prove fatal in one or two hours without any great amount of previous purging or vomiting. In most instances the mental faculties are comparatively unaffected, although in the later stages there is generally more or less apathy.

Reaction may, however, take place, and this constitutes the *third stage*. It consists in the arrest of the alarming symptoms of the second stage, and the gradual but evident improvement in the patient's condition. The pulse returns, the surface assumes a natural hue, and the bodily heat is restored. Before long, the vomiting ceases, and, though diarrhœa may continue for a time, it is not of a severe character and soon subsides, as do also the cramps. The urine may remain suppressed for some time, and on returning is often found to be albuminous.

Even in this stage, however, the danger is not past, for relapses sometimes occur which speedily prove fatal; while, again, the reaction may be of imperfect character, and there may succeed an exhausting fever (the so-called *typhoid stage* of cholera), which may greatly retard recovery, and under which the patient may sink at a period even as late as two or three weeks from the commencement of the illness.

The bodies of persons dying of cholera are found to remain long warm, and the temperature may even rise after death. Muscular contractions have been observed to take place after death, so that the position of the limbs may become altered.

Treatment. — PREVENTIVE TREATMENT. — When cholera threatens to invade any place, however favourably circumstanced as to its hygienic condition, increased vigilance will be requisite on the part of those entrusted with the care of the public health.

7

Cholera may be introduced into a community by one or more individuals who have themselves only suffered from the first or milder stage of the disease (cholera diarrhœa), since the discharges from the bowels abound in the infective organisms, and, where sanitary arrangements are deficient, may readily contaminate the water of a locality.

Where suspicion attaches to the water, it should be boiled or chlorinated before being used ; milk should also be boiled. Water and food should be protected against pollution with flies, and houses should be fly-proofed. Instructions should be issued by the authorities warning all persons against the use of unwholesome food, unripe fruit, and excesses of every kind, and recommending early application for medical advice where there is any tendency to diarrhœa. The discharges from cholera patients should be treated, as soon as passed, with strong disinfectants (*see* DISINFECTION), and special care should be taken that they are not disposed of in places where they can contaminate drinking-water. In 1893 Haffkine introduced a vaccine for preventive inoculation against cholera, and this seems to afford a certain amount of protection over a period of some months.

CURATIVE TREATMENT.—Strict rest in bed is essential and for the first few days only water and rice or barley water is given by mouth—in the form of frequent drinks not exceeding 2 ounces (60 ml.). The basic treatment is the rapid replacement of water and electrolytes lost in the frequent watery stools, by means of intravenous hypertonic or isotonic saline. The hypertonic saline consists of 120 grains (8 G.) of sodium chloride and 4 grains (250 mg.) of calcium chloride in a pint (500 ml.) of water. A blood-pressure below 70 mm. of mercury, especially if there is associated cyanosis, restlessness, cramps, and cold extremities, is an indication for immediate transfusion with isotonic saline solution.

Chemotherapy is useful only in reducing the period during which the vibrio remains in the stool. For this purpose, chloramphenicol, chlortetracycline, or one of the insoluble sulphonamides (*e.g.* sulphaguanidine) should be used.

194

CHOLERINE is the name given to cases which occur during an epidemic of cholera with very slight symptoms of the latter, and which are either mild cases of cholera or are due to fright.

CHOLESTEROL, or CHOLESTERIN (χολή, bile ; στερεός, solid), is a substance derivable from many tissues of the body, from fat, blood, tumours, and several secretions such as the bile. It can be obtained pure by extraction with alcohol or ether, and is then found to be chemically a complex alcohol, which crystallizes in colourless rhombic plates. Gall-stones consist mainly of masses of cholesterol mixed with more or less bile pigment, and are produced either by its sedimentation from the bile or by degeneration in the mucous membrane of the bile ducts. Of recent years there has been increasing evidence of a correlation between a high level of cholesterol in the blood and the incidence of coronary artery disease.

CHOLINE, one of the many constituents of the vitamin B complex, is of importance because lack of it in the experimental animal produces a fatty liver. It is found in egg-yolk, liver, and meat, and the probable daily human requirement is 250 mg. It has been used recently in the treatment of cirrhosis of the liver, but there is no evidence that it is of any value in this condition.

CHONDROMA (χόνδρος, cartilage) is a tumour composed in part of cartilage. (*See* TUMOURS.)

CHORDOTOMY is the term applied to the operation of cutting the nerves in the spinal cord which convey the sensation of pain to the brain. This operation is done for the relief of severe and intractable pain.

CHOREA (χόρεια, a dance). The medical name for St. Vitus's dance. (*See* ST. VITUS'S DANCE.)

CHORIOCARCINOMA is a form of cancer affecting the chorion (*q.v.*).

CHORION (χόριον) is the name applied to the more external of the two fœtal membranes.

CHOROID, or Chorioid (χόριον, a membrane ; εἶδος, form), is the middle of the three coats of the eye, and consists chiefly of blood - vessels, which effect the nourishment of this organ. (*See* Eye.)

CHOROIDITIS, or Chorioditis, means inflammation of the choroid coat of the eye, and is sometimes associated with inflammation of the iris. (*See* Eye, Diseases of ; Iritis ; *and* Vision.) It may be syphilitic or tuberculous in origin, or it may be due to infection with some other microorganism. It may also be allergic in origin. In its early stages it may produce no symptoms. When well advanced, it produces inflammation in the retina and then causes interference with sight in various ways, such as dark spots in the field of vision, loss of vision for particular colours, etc. Its effects vary greatly, according to the position of the inflamed patches, for wide stretches of inflammation may occur situated towards the front of the eye without causing much interference with vision, whilst a very small patch, occurring on or near the macula or spot of clearest vision in the centre of the back of the eye (*see* Eye), may cause great visual defect. The condition is easily made out by examination with the ophthalmoscope, even in early stages ; but, though treatment retards, or completely stops the progress of the disease, little improvement in vision is to be expected.

CHRISTMAS DISEASE is a hereditary disorder of blood coagulation which can only be distinguished from hæmophilia (*q.v.*) by laboratory tests. It is so called after the surname of the first case reported in this country. About one out of every ten patients clinically diagnosed as hæmophilia have in fact Christmas disease. One of the differences between the two diseases is that patients with Christmas disease can be treated with stored blood, whereas those with hæmophilia only respond to fresh blood.

CHROMAFFIN is a term applied to certain cells and organs in the body, such as part of the adrenal glands, which have a peculiar affinity for chrome salts. These cells and tissues generally are supposed to secrete substances which have an important action in maintaining the tone and elasticity of the blood-vessels and muscles.

CHROMIC ACID is used in several industries, particularly in chromium plating. Unless precautions are taken it may lead to dermatitis of the hands, arms, chest and face. It may also cause deep ulcers, especially of the nasal septum and knuckles.

Uses.—The chief medicinal use of chromic acid is as a caustic for the treatment of warts and indolent ulcers. It is also sometimes used in a 2 or 3 per cent. solution for the treatment of sweating feet.

CHROMOSOMES are the rod-shaped bodies to be found in the nucleus of every cell in the body. They contain the genes, or hereditary elements, which establish the characteristics of an individual. They occur in pairs, and human beings possess forty-six, made up of twenty-three pairs (Plate X). The number of chromosomes is specific for each species of animal. (*See* Heredity *and* Sex Chromosomes.)

CHRYSAROBIN, or Goa powder, is a substance got from Brazil, being a concretion which forms on the stems of the *Araroba* plant, powdered and purified. It is used in various skin diseases, especially psoriasis, either in the form of an ointment or plaster, or made into a paste with vinegar. Whilst efficacious, it has the drawback that it stains the clothes a deep violet colour. These stains, however, may be removed with benzol or weak chlorinated lime in water.

CHYLE (χυλός) is the name given to the partly digested food as it passes down the small intestine, and also to that part of it which is absorbed by the lymphatic vessels of the intestine. The absorbed portion consists of fats in very fine emulsion, like milk, so that these vessels receive the name of lacteals (L. *lac*, milk). This absorbed chyle mixes with the lymph and is discharged into the thoracic duct, a vessel as large as a quill, which passes up through the chest to open into the jugular vein on the left side of the neck, where the chyle mixes with the blood.

CHYME (χυμός, juice) is the name given to the partly digested food as it issues from the stomach into the intestine. It is very acid and grey in colour, containing salts and sugars in solution, and the animal food softened into a semi-liquid mass. It is next converted into chyle.

CICATRIX (*cicatrix*) is another word for scar.

CIDER is an alcoholic beverage made from apples. (*See* ALCOHOL.)

CILIA (*cilium*, eyelash) is a term applied to minute, lash-like processes which are seen with the aid of the microscope upon the cells covering certain mucous membranes, *e.g.* the trachea (or windpipe), and which maintain movement in the fluid passing over these membranes. They are also found upon certain bacteria which have the power of rapid movement.

CIMEX LECTULARIUS (*see* BED BUG *and* PARASITES).

CINCHONA is the general name for several trees in the bark of which quinine is found. This bark is also known as Jesuit's bark, having been brought first to notice by Spanish priests in South America and brought to Europe first by the Countess of Cinchon, wife of the Viceroy of Peru, in 1640. The red cinchona bark is that which contains most quinine, and from which it is usually prepared. (*See* QUININE.) Various extracts and tinctures are made direct from cinchona bark, and used in place of quinine.

CINCHOPHEN, also known as atophan, is described chemically as phenyl-quinoline-carboxylic acid. It is used in gout by virtue of its power to promote the excretion of uric acid. One of its risks is that it is toxic to the liver.

CINNAMON is the bark of *Cinnamomum Zeylandicum*, a species of laurel grown in Ceylon. It has a stimulating action upon the stomach, and assists digestion, hence its use as a condiment. It is also an antispasmodic.

Uses.—In flatulent dyspepsia and in sea-sickness, cinnamon powder (10 grains (600 mg.)) is very useful. For the same purposes, or for relieving griping, four drops of oil of cinnamon may be
196

taken on sugar, or one tablespoonful of cinnamon water (distilled) may be similarly used.

CIRCLE OF WILLIS, or CIRCULUS ARTERIOSUS, is a circle of arteries at the base of the brain, which is formed by the junction of the basilar, posterior cerebral, internal carotid, and anterior cerebral arteries. Congenital defects may occur in these arteries and lead to the formation of aneurysms (*q.v.*).

CIRCULATION OF THE BLOOD.— This principle, demonstrated for the first time by William Harvey in 1628, was the result of many years of careful reasoning and experimentation. The proof of the facts of circulation was certainly one of the most important discoveries in medical science. Before Harvey's discovery the generally accepted view was that the arteries contained a mixture of air and 'vital spirits', with only an accidental admixture of blood, and that the heart

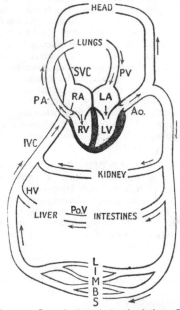

FIG. 95.—General plan of the circulation. PA, pulmonary artery. PV, pulmonary vein. LA, left atrium. LV, left ventricle. Ao, aorta, PoV, portal vein. HV, hepatic vein. IVC, inferior vena cava. SVC, superior vena cava. RA, right atrium. RV, right ventricle. (From Bell, Davidson, and Scarborough, *Textbook of Physiology and Biochemistry*. E. & S. Livingstone Ltd.)

by its motions alternately sucked in more air through the pores of the skin and those of the lungs, and through the same channels expelled ' fuliginous vapours '. The ' vital spirits ' were assumed to be manufactured by the heart and to be the origin of all activity, whilst the ' fuliginous vapours ' were a form of smoke resulting from the bodily motions. The blood in the veins was supposed to be derived from the

passes in a constant stream to all the members of the body, and does not return by the same route. (3) The blood in the veins flows incessantly to the heart, and does not ebb and flow, as is shown by the valves in veins and in the heart, and by the fact that veins when pressed on do not fill from above. Having proved these points, he assumed there must be ' pores in the flesh ' through which the blood ' percolated '

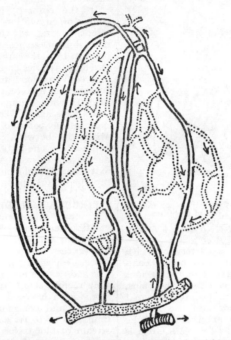

FIG. 96.—Drawing to show capillary network between a small artery (arteriole) and a small vein (venule) magnified 35 times. (From Hewer, *Textbook of Histology*. William Heinemann, Ltd.)

liver, which absorbed the ' juices of the food ', and to ebb and flow in and out of the various organs for their nourishment. Harvey proved, first of all, mainly by the examination of living animals, that the arteries contain only blood. Secondly, he showed by three main propositions that this blood must go round from arteries to veins in a continuous circuit. (1) The quantity of blood passing from the veins into the heart in the course of a whole day is so great that it is quite impossible it could all be manufactured from the food. (2) The blood in the arteries

from the ends of the arteries to the commencements of the veins. The last link in the evidence was supplied some thirty years later by Malpighi, an Italian scientist, who with the help of the microscope showed these ' pores ' to be the minute vessels now called ' capillaries '.

The course of the circulation is as follows (Fig. 95): The veins pour their blood, coming from the head, trunk, limbs, and abdominal organs, into the right atrium of the heart. This contracts and drives the blood into the right ventricle, which then forces the

197

blood into the lungs by way of the pulmonary artery. Here it is contained in thin-walled capillaries, over which the air plays freely, and through which gases pass readily out and in. The blood gives off CO_2 and takes up oxygen (*see* RESPIRATION), and passes on by the pulmonary veins to the left atrium of the heart. The left atrium expels it into the left ventricle, which forces it on

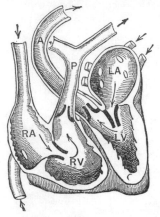

FIG. 97.—Diagram of the heart opened from in front to show the action of the valves. *RA*, Right atrium; *RV*, right ventricle; *P*, pulmonary artery; *LA*, left atrium; *LV*, left ventricle; *A*, aorta.

into the aorta, or great artery, by which it is distributed all over the body. Passing through capillaries in the various tissues (Fig. 96) it enters the veins, which ultimately unite into two great veins, the superior and the inferior vena cava, these emptying into the right atrium. This complete circle is accomplished by any particular drop of blood in about half a minute.

In one part of the body there is a further complication. The veins coming from the bowels, charged with food material and other products, split up, and their blood undergoes a second capillary circulation through the liver. Here it is relieved of some food material and purified, and then passes into the inferior vena cava, and so to the right auricle. This is known as the ' portal circulation '.

The circle is maintained always in one direction by four valves, situated one at the outlet from each cavity of the heart (Fig. 97). (*See* HEART.)

The blood in the arteries going to

the body generally is bright red, that in the veins dull red in colour, owing to the former being charged with oxygen, the latter with carbonic acid (*see* RESPIRATION). For the same reason the blood in the pulmonary artery is dark, that in the pulmonary veins bright. There is no direct communication between the right and left sides of the heart, the blood passing from the right ventricle to the left atrium through the lungs.

In the embryo, before birth, the course of circulation is somewhat different, owing to the fact that no nourishment comes from the bowels nor air into the lungs. Accordingly, two large arteries pass out of the navel, and convey blood to be changed by contact with maternal blood (*see* AFTER-BIRTH), while a large vein brings this blood back again. There are also communications between the right and left atria, and between pulmonary artery and aorta. The latter is known as the ductus arteriosus. At birth all these extra vessels and connections close and rapidly shrivel up.

CIRCULATION, DISORDERS OF.—
The steady maintenance of the circulation depends upon two factors : (1) the power and regularity of the heart ; and (2) the condition of the walls of the vessels, especially of the small arteries. The arteries are not rigid tubes, nor are they merely elastic tubes of a definite size, for each vessel has the power of dilating and contracting within wide limits, so as to let a larger or smaller stream of blood pass through. These motions are controlled by constricting and dilating nerves governed by the nervous system, and upon the action of these, more than upon the heart, depends the state of circulation in various parts. For example, when cold strikes the skin the constrictor nerves are stimulated, the vessels contract, and the blood is driven from the skin, which becomes pallid. On the other hand, ' blushing ' is due to loss of control by these nerves over the vessels, or, when the redness is extreme, to stimulation of the dilating nerves by some emotion powerfully affecting the nervous system. Similar changes occur, under other conditions, in all the organs.

Causes and Symptoms.—*Inflammation* in its early stages is associated with great redness and swelling, due to excessive inflow of blood to the inflamed part through widely dilated arteries. *Congestion* is a condition sometimes due to inflammation, sometimes to an obstruction to the veins which should carry off the blood, or very often to the feebleness of the heart, which cannot drive the blood upwards from dependent parts like the feet, or like the back portions of the lungs in bed-ridden persons. In old persons with diseased vessels, in which blood-clots are liable to form, congestion of the brain readily takes place from such obstructions. In weak persons, or those exhausted by illness, lying constantly on the back, congestion of the lungs is very apt to come on. Congestion of the lungs with bronchitis, and congestion of the liver and stomach with various disorders of digestion, are common results of valvular disease of the heart (*see* HEART DISEASES). *Dropsy* and *varicose veins* are similar disorders often due to obstruction to veins. Dropsy is also a usual result of heart disease and of kidney disease (*see* DROPSY *and* VEINS, DISEASES OF). *Bloodlessness* of parts is a disorder in the opposite direction, due to spasm and extreme narrowing of arteries (*see* RAYNAUD'S DISEASE). A local blanching often precedes *chilblains*, which occur in persons of sluggish circulation. *Cold feet and hands*, especially at night, form a milder variety of the same condition. *Insomnia* in elderly persons is sometimes due to disordered circulation in the brain, because the vessels are extremely narrowed by disease.

Treatment.—Where any failure of the heart is present, the case is treated by various cardiac drugs, by rest, and by graduated exercises. Some cases of disordered circulation depending on the vessels are benefited by cold baths (*see* BATHS) and daily vigorous exercises, while good diet, warm clothing, and tonics are of importance for their cure. (*See also* CHILBLAIN.)

CIRCUMCISION (*circum*, around ; *caedo*, I cut) means the cutting round and removal of the foreskin. It is performed as a religious rite among many tribes, notably by the Jews, and is advisable when the foreskin is so narrow at the opening, or so adherent, as to render its drawing back, for washing impossible. If done in infancy, it is a trivial operation.

CIRRHOSIS, or FIBROSIS (κιρρός, yellow), is a diseased condition of various internal organs, in which the proper tissue is replaced by fibrous tissue similar to scar tissue. The name 'Cirrhosis' was originally given by Laennec to the disease as occurring in the liver, because of its yellow colour, but it is now applied to a similar condition in the lung, kidney, stomach, etc.

Causes.—The cause of cirrhosis of the liver is still obscure. Experimentally it has been shown that the condition can be produced by a deficiency of certain of the amino-acids found in protein, but this only explains a small proportion of the cases found in man. It is probable that in most cases three factors are involved in varying degrees : a nutritional deficiency, a toxic factor, and an infective factor. The classical rôle of alcohol in its causation is probably an indirect one, accentuating a nutritional deficiency through its deleterious action on the digestive tract. Cirrhosis of the kidney is associated with disease of the blood-vessels, and with gout (*see* BRIGHT'S DISEASE).

Symptoms.—In one form of cirrhosis the liver is much contracted (atrophic or coarse cirrhosis), its blood-vessels are pressed upon, and dropsy results. In another form there is great enlargement of the organ (hypertrophic or biliary cirrhosis) and jaundice appears. Cirrhosis of the kidney is the most serious form of Bright's disease.

Treatment.—Nothing can be done to repair a cirrhosed organ, but the cause, if known, must be removed and further advance of the process thus prevented. In the case of the liver a high-protein, high-carbohydrate diet is given, supplemented by liver extract and vitamin B. In cirrhosis of the kidney, a farinaceous diet, warm clothing, and careful hygiene of the skin and bowels are the essentials.

CIRSOID ANEURYSM is the term applied to the condition in which a group of arteries become abnormally dilated and tortuous.

CITRIC ACID is the acid which gives their sharp taste to lemons, limes, unripe oranges, currants, and raspberries. It is practically identical in action and appearance with tartaric acid, which is obtained from grapes and other fruits, although the two differ in chemical composition. They are similar also to malic acid, found in apples, pears, and the berries of the mountain ash.

Uses.—These vegetable acids and their salts (citrates and tartrates) are changed, on absorption into the blood, into alkaline substances, and act, therefore, to correct acidity (*see* ACIDITY). The acids themselves have the power of allaying thirst by stimulating the flow of saliva, and also of creating a feeling of coolness. For both these reasons they are much used for cooling drinks in fever. When, in addition, the stomach is irritable, they are best taken in the form of effervescing drinks, which soothe this organ.

For feverish conditions a few slices of lemon may be put in a tumbler of drinking water, or ' Imperial Drink ' made as follows : To one pint (500 ml.) of cold water add a teaspoonful of cream of tartar, a squeeze of lemon, and two lumps of sugar.

For an effervescing draught 20 grains (1·2 G.) of citric acid or the juice of one fresh lemon may be mixed with a large wineglassful of water ; 30 grains (2 G.) of bicarbonate of potash or 24 grains (1·6 G.) of bicarbonate of soda (*i.e.* about as much baking soda as will lie heaped up on a shilling-piece) are dissolved in another wineglassful of water ; a third wineglassful of water is sweetened with sugar ; the contents of the three wine glasses are mixed just before drinking.

CITRINE OINTMENT, or NITRATE OF MERCURY OINTMENT, is used for stimulating sluggish ulcers, and also, diluted with olive oil, in cases of eczema.

CLAUSTROPHOBIA means the fear of being in a confined space, or the fear experienced while in it.

CLAVICLE (*clavicula*, a twig) is another name for the collar-bone (*q.v.*.)

CLAVUS (*clavus*, a nail) is a form of neuralgia about the head, often found in hysterical persons and others, compared by them to the pain of driving in a nail (*see* NEURALGIA). The term is also applied to a corn, or thickening of the horny epithelium upon the foot (*see* CORNS).

CLAW-HAND is a condition of bending and wasting of the hand and fingers, especially of the ring and little fingers. The condition is generally due to paralysis of the ulnar nerve. A somewhat similar condition is produced by contraction of the fibrous tissues in the palm of the hand, partly due to rheumatic changes and partly to injury caused by the constant pressure of a tool against the palm of the hand (*see* DUPUYTREN'S CONTRACTION).

CLEANLINESS (*see* ASEPSIS, ANTISEPTICS, BATHS, DISINFECTION).

CLEFT PALATE is the term applied to a fissure of the roof of the mouth sometimes present at birth and very often combined with hare-lip. (*See* PALATE MALFORMATIONS.)

CLERGYMAN'S SORE THROAT is the name given to a complication of throat ailments, which gradually comes on in those who do much public speaking, and who possess weak vocal organs. Persons who suffer from it, as a rule, produce the voice badly, using the throat as a resonating chamber instead of gaining the full volume of the voice by keeping the lungs expanded. Speaking, accordingly, is performed with great effort, the more so as the muscles of the larynx and throat become soon tired. The mucous membrane of the throat and even of the nose becomes congested, and catarrh follows on very slight provocation, chronic laryngitis, and pharyngitis being set up. Still greater vocal efforts of an incorrect kind being made to overcome the consequent huskiness and feebleness, the condition gets inevitably worse and worse, till public speaking may become an utter impossibility.

Treatment.—The first essential is to obtain correct voice-production, by expansion of the chest (*see* CHEST, DEVELOPMENT OF), and by a course of lessons on elocution from a good teacher (*see* VOICE AND SPEECH). The affected person must also get out of the bad habit of straining the throat in speaking. Secondly, the mucous membrane of the throat must be got back to its original state by such measures as gargles of potassium chlorate, or of common salt and baking soda (one teaspoonful of each in a tumblerful of cold water), or of aromatic substances, painting the throat with tincture of iodine or glycerin of tannin, and similar procedures. When the chronic inflammatory condition has proceeded further, and has set up considerable laryngitis and pharyngitis, the case should be under the care of a throat specialist, for local astringent applications to the larynx, throat, and nose are necessary, or even the reduction of swollen mucous membrane by the cautery. In advanced stages, complete rest of the voice may be essential, and a change to some climate where the air is warm, moderately moist, and quite free from dust, may be advisable. Such a climate is found along the south coast of England, on the Mediterranean shores, or in Florida.

CLIMACTERIC (κλιμακτήρ, the step of a ladder) was a word originally applied to the end of certain epochs or stages in the life of an individual, at which some great change was supposed to take place. Thus the Greeks supposed the whole body was renewed every seven years, and looked upon certain of these periods as of special importance. There is some justification for such a view, since fourteen is the age about which puberty, *i.e.* the commencement of sexual activity, appears ; about twenty-one full sexual maturity is usually attained, which renders this the most approved age for marriage, and the age at which legal majority is fixed in most countries ; at or after forty-two takes place in women the ' grand climacteric ', when menstruation and the power of bearing children cease ; whilst about sixty-three there sometimes appears in men a transitory enfeeblement to which the name of ' climacteric ' has also been given, and a Hebrew writer has fixed the utmost span of robust life at ' threescore years and ten '.

7 *a*

CLIMATE IN RELATION TO DISEASE. Climate is of great medical importance, both because various diseases are found in one part of the world and not in others, so that it becomes necessary to know the reasons for this difference, and because removal of a diseased person to new conditions of air, warmth, moisture, etc., is often a most valuable means of cure.

The broad division of climates is into hot, temperate, and cold climates.

(*a*) **Hot climates** are generally considered as extending to about 35° from the equator, and possessing an average temperature throughout the year of about 84° F. (29° C.). In the Southern Hemisphere, Monte Video, Cape Town, and Sydney lie just at the edge of this band, while north of the equator the limit divides the northern from the southern states of North America, skirts the south of Algeria, the north of India, and excludes Japan from the hot region. Generally speaking, there are, in this region, a wet and a dry season, but near the equator, two wet and two dry seasons. It is a generally held but mistaken idea that the equator is the place of greatest heat on the earth's surface. At the tropics, some 1500 miles north and south of the equator, it is both much hotter and much drier than at the line itself. This corresponds north of the equator with Central Mexico, the centre of the Red Sea, Central India, and Hong Kong ; while south of the line it passes through Rio de Janeiro, Damaraland, and Central Australia. These places are the hottest on the earth's surface, but far less unhealthy than the damp and steamy climate of the Amazon Valley, the Gold Coast, the Congo Valley, and Borneo, which lie on or near the line. The general character of the natives of these hot climates is lethargic and indolent ; the skin and digestive organs are particularly active and specially liable to disease ; dysentery, yellow fever, malaria, degenerations of the liver and diseases due to parasites being specially common, whilst, on the other hand, lung diseases are comparatively rare.

(*b*) **Temperate climates** are those from about 35° to 55° of latitude, and have a mean temperature of about 38° F. (3·3° C.) in winter and 68° F. (31° C.) in summer. Including, as these regions do, the Northern American States and south of Canada, Central and Southern Europe, and, in the East, Japan, they comprise the peoples who have been most distinguished for physical and mental attainment.

(c) **Cold climates** are those from 55° latitude to the poles. The cold is much modified, however, in some localities by ocean currents, so that Scotland, at the same latitude as Labrador, enjoys a temperate though moist climate, the surrounding seas and air being warmed by the Gulf Stream. The people of these northern latitudes are hardy and vigorous, and, though chest and kidney disorders are more common than in the temperate climes, they suffer from fewer diseases.

But, in estimating the effect of climate, far more than mere distance from the equator has to be considered. The degree of moisture in the air and presence of the sea near at hand, the rarefaction of the air in consequence of elevation, the difference between night and day temperatures, and the presence or absence of dust and bacteria are all of vital importance. For these reasons climates are classed into four sub-varieties : (1) seaboard and ocean climates ; (2) inland low climates ; (3) mountain climates ; (4) dry climates.

(1) SEABOARD AND OCEAN CLIMATES.—The important features of these climates are the large amount of moisture in the air, the density of the latter compared with that of mountain air, and the presence of more or less salt. The air of the high seas is also free from dust and bacteria, a point of great importance in lung diseases. The cases for which seaside air is most suitable are those convalescent from acute diseases, those worn out by business or social worries, and, above all, those of a scrofulous tendency (*i.e.* troubled with enlarged glands, etc.). Holidays at the seaside, especially if the holidays be perforce short, as a rule benefit the jaded dweller in towns more than any other form of ' change of air ', although, for the youthful and vigorous, mountain air is often better.

Perhaps the mildest climate in existence is that of the Mediterranean shores from Spain to Greece on the north, and in Algeria on the south. The proper time to seek this part is from October

to May, so as to avoid the colder northern winter.

Ocean voyages are specially valuable for patients who are convalescent from pulmonary tuberculosis, or for persons who are simply delicate and are thereby more susceptible to lung disease. Various other chronic lung diseases benefit immensely from a long voyage, and so do those persons broken down by overwork. One of the best voyages for English people is that to Australia or New Zealand, which takes over one month, and on which the patient experiences a variety of climates with corresponding stimulation to the system. By leaving England in the late autumn and returning in the late spring, the patient escapes the winter altogether, and has two or three months at the Antipodes, which should be spent in the mountains of Australia or New Zealand. In going to Australia, one should choose a cabin on the port side, and, in returning, one to starboard, for, by this means, the cool breeze is secured both ways. From the United States perhaps the usual voyage is to the West Indies and thence across to Europe, and back. Another good variety of climate is got by the voyage in which call is made at Lisbon, Teneriffe, Rio de Janeiro, Monte Video, and often a North American port.

(2) INLAND LOW CLIMATES include most of the health resorts to which people go in order to drink mineral waters. The general character of inland climates is the great variation between the summer and winter temperature, but, as most of these places are resorted to only in the open part of the year, the climate goes often by the vague name of ' relaxing ', in contradistinction to the ' bracing ' climate of mountains. In such a climate, the moistness and density of the air, the warmth, and the absence of stimulating sea breezes combine to reduce the pressure at which life is carried on, to diminish the appetite, and to give the organs which discharge waste products from the body a better chance to carry out their functions. This is aided by the various waters peculiar to these spas. The diseases for which this type of climate is most suitable are rheumatism, gout, skin diseases, and other chronic constitutional troubles. Ex-

amples of this climate are given by Harrogate, Bath, and the watering-places of the Rhine basin. Diseases of the heart and other parts of the circulatory system are treated at some of the less depressing of these resorts, such as Nauheim, Schwalbach, etc., where tonic treatment and graduated exercises aid the restful action of the climate.

(3) MOUNTAIN CLIMATES have, as their chief character, the rarity of the air, by reason of which the breathing and heart-beats are increased in rate, and a feeling of buoyancy and increased strength given to the whole system. Further, the air is drier and less laden with dust and bacteria, and there is greater difference between the day and night and between the sun and shade temperatures than at lower levels. Accordingly the mountains are suitable for persons who, though over-worked and broken-down, are young and of good physique; for those who are young but delicate, disposed to lung disease, and who have outgrown their strength; for those also who suffer from chronic lung diseases with a certain amount of fever, and for whom sea-voyages are unsuitable. But for the weak and aged, for those with heart diseases, and for those with kidney diseases, mountain climates are unsuitable.

(4) DRY CLIMATES OR DESERT CLIMATES combine warmth and dryness. In addition, the air is relatively clear of bacteria, though apt to be dusty, and the nights are cold. Such climates are found in Egypt, Australia, some of the Western States of the U.S.A., and, in a milder degree, on the Pampas of South America and the tablelands of Cape Province in South Africa. These are suited especially for kidney diseases and chronic rheumatism, in both of which a maximum of perspiration is desirable, and *par excellence* for tuberculous cases.

CLINICAL (κλίνη, a bed) means literally ' belonging to a bed ', but the word is used to denote anything associated with the practical study or observation of sick persons, as clinical medicine, clinical thermometers.

CLINICS (*see* MATERNITY AND CHILD WELFARE).

CLONIC (κλόνος, a tumult) is a word applied to short spasmodic movements

CLOT is the term applied to any semi-solid mass of blood, lymph, or other body fluid. Clotting in the blood is due to the formation of strings of fibrin produced by the action of a ferment (Plate III). Milk clots in a similar manner in the stomach when exposed to the action of the ferment rennin. Clotting occurs naturally when blood is shed and comes in contact with tissues outside the blood-vessels. It occurs also at times in diseased vessels (*thrombosis*), producing serious effects upon the organs supplied by these vessels. Clots also form sometimes in the heart when the circulation is feeble and the blood passes slowly through this organ, especially when some form of blood poisoning is present. (*See* COAGULATION, EMBOLISM, THROMBOSIS.)

CLOTHING has certain medical aspects in its relation to the preservation of health.

Five chief substances are used in manufacturing clothes, viz.: *sheep's wool*, from which worsted, flannel, and alpaca are made; *silk*, from which also velvet, satin, and crêpe are produced; *flax*, from which linen and the finer cambric and lawn originate; *cotton*, giving us, by various forms of weaving, calico, jean, flannelette, fustian, and muslin; and so-called man-made fibres, such as nylon.

However these are manufactured, each of the five has certain properties which render it more or less suitable for clothing purposes in different circumstances.

(a) **Warmth.**—Those materials which conduct heat badly, retain the animal heat of the body, and so preserve its warmth best. The worst conductor is wool, and with it, furs and down; next come silk and cotton; while linen, conducting heat away most readily, is coolest. Wool, in fact, makes twice as warm a covering as linen of equal thickness. Colour, however, has a most important influence on the coolness of clothing, quite apart from material, and if the body be exposed to the sun's rays clad in black or dark blue, more than twice the amount of heat is absorbed that would be absorbed if the clothing were of the same material but white in colour. Thus white clothes are twice as cool as black or blue material in the heat of summer. Red stands about half-way between, while yellow is almost as cool as white. The texture has also much to do with warmth, quite apart from the actual weight of material employed. Thus material so made as to contain many spaces in the meshes of its threads, such as cotton-wool, knitted clothes, and 'cellular' underclothing, is much warmer than the same weight of closely woven calico, or flannel. The reason is that the intervening air is a still worse conductor of heat than the material. For the same reason, a single garment is not so warm as two garments each of half its thickness, which have a layer of air between them. Another cause of the warmth of woollen underclothing lies in the scratching action of its rough hairs upon the skin. Persons with sensitive skin, who cannot bear this, may avoid it, and still wear wool, by having next the skin one of the network garments now much used for summer wear.

(b) **Absorptive power** is of immense importance, and varies greatly in the different materials. During perspiration, the garments absorb the moisture from the skin surface, and give it off into the surrounding air. Wool absorbs moisture twice as rapidly as cotton, and almost twice as rapidly as silk or linen. Accordingly, if a person be exerting himself vigorously in the sun, or in a hot room, he experiences a much more cooling effect at first if wearing linen or cotton next the skin, because these conduct away the heat more rapidly than wool; but, as he begins to perspire, woollen clothes, which carry off the perspiration better, render him both cooler and less clammy. If, in a state of free perspiration, he now goes out into the cold air, provided he be wearing cotton underclothing, this and the skin are reduced speedily to a dangerous condition of damp cold; whereas, if he be clothed in woollen material, the gradual cooling goes on much as before, and a dangerous reduction of heat is prevented by the poor conducting power of the wool. Waterproofs have absolutely no absorptive power, and prevent not only rain from passing in-

204

wards, but perspiration from getting out. Accordingly, exertion in a waterproof produces much heat and soaking perspiration, but as the thin waterproof allows the heat to pass off quickly, it is a very undesirable costume for more than merely temporary use.

(c) **Non-inflammability** of clothing is a point of great importance. Linen, cotton, flannelette, and viscose rayon are all flammable. Silk burns more slowly, and even wool may smoulder away without catching flame. Treating a fabric with a solution of borax and boric acid will prevent its bursting into flame, although it will char as long as it is in contact with the source of heat. Unfortunately the proofing salts are removed when the fabric is washed. Progress in fire-proofing, however, is being made and more satisfactory methods are now available for cellulosic fabrics. The newer man-made fabrics are the least inflammable of all. Polyvinyl chloride, for instance, is virtually non-inflammable, and nylon, though it can be made to burn in certain circumstances, is difficult to ignite.

General considerations.—From what has been stated, it will appear that, for outdoor clothes, sheep's wool is warmest in winter. For *summer wear* light-coloured clothes are coolest, and for much exercise with periods of rest, such as at cricket, tennis, etc., the clothes should be of white wool. For *underclothing*, one should wear wool next the skin both summer and winter, persons with irritable skin choosing fine merino wool or placing a network garment beneath the woollen one. Alternatively, some form of 'cellular' underwear should be worn. Loose-fitting underwear is both more comfortable and warmer than tight-fitting. For *nightwear*, linen, cotton, or silk is better than flannel, because the warmth is maintained by the bed-clothes and the sleeper does not, or should not, perspire.

Corsets are of doubtful value. For young and healthy women they are quite unnecessary. The feeling of limpness, felt when they are discarded, is simply begotten of their constant use. For elderly women who possess much fatty tissue, corsets, combined especially with an abdominal belt, give relief from many minor troubles and improve the figure. An abdominal binder or cholera belt of woollen material is useful for persons subject to intestinal disorders. An abdominal belt is also helpful in the case of displacements of various organs, such as the kidney and stomach. *Boots often form a badly made article of clothing (see* CORNS AND BUNIONS). Children, especially when growing rapidly, may show a tendency to 'weak ankles' or 'flat-foot'. They should wear shoes or sandals, because boots prevent the natural action of the ligaments and muscles at the ankle; the shoes should also have low heels.

CLOVES are the unexpanded flower-buds of a species of myrtle, *Caryophyllus aromaticus,* from the Indian Archipelago. Oil of cloves is an antiseptic, checks griping, and masks bad breath. It may be taken in doses of 2 or 3 drops on a lump of sugar, or one tablespoonful of infusion of cloves may be similarly used. Cotton-wool dipped in clove oil and put in a hollow tooth relieves toothache temporarily.

CLOXACILLIN (*See* PENICILLIN.)

CLUB-FOOT, or TALIPES (*talus*, the ankle; *pes*, the foot), is a deformity in which the foot is permanently twisted at the ankle-joint, so that the sole no longer rests on the ground in standing.

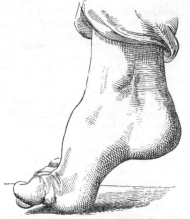

FIG. 98.—Talipes equinus. (Miller's *Surgery*.)

Varieties.—The foot can be twisted in four directions. The heel may be pulled

up so that the person walks on his toes (*talipes equinus*) (Fig. 98), or the toes may be bent up so that he walks on his heel only (*talipes calcaneus*), or the sole may look inwards so that he walks on the outer edge of the foot (*talipes varus*), or outwards so that he walks on the inside of the foot (*talipes valgus*). These are usually combined, the heel being drawn up and the sole turned inwards

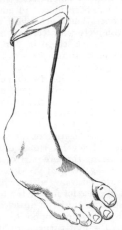

FIG. 99.—Talipes equino-varus. (Miller's *Surgery*.)

(*equino-varus*) (Fig. 99), or the heel resting on the ground and the sole looking outwards (*calcaneo-valgus*). A more important division is into those cases in which the deformity exists at birth, which are generally at first fairly easily rectified; and into those cases which are acquired later in life as the result of some disease, which do not yield to such simple treatment.

Causes.—The cases found at birth are due to some arrest of development, or some faulty position of the fœtus in the womb. The popular idea, that a fright received by the mother may cause the deformity, is improbable. Those which are acquired later may be caused by some spasm in the muscles of one side of the leg, or especially by paralysis of the muscles on the side of the leg away from the deformity (infantile paralysis), or by rigidity due to the scar following a burn or inflammation.

Treatment.—For the cases acquired after birth, an elaborate treatment, including one or several operations, or the wearing of some special appliance to support the ankle in the correct position, is usually necessary. When the deformity is due to paralysis, the application of massage and electricity to the affected muscles is often requisite. When it is caused by scars or muscular spasms, the muscles or their tendons must be divided before replacement in the correct position is possible. In all cases it must be remembered that, after the foot has been placed in good position by operation or otherwise, the cure is not complete till after several years of care, because there is, for long, a great tendency to relapse.

The cases found deformed at birth have some distortion in shape of the bones about the ankle, but, as these bones are very soft in the young child, the condition is often quite remediable by attention on the part of the mother or nurse. The position of the foot must be corrected several times daily, the nurse grasping the fore part of the foot and pressing it gently, slowly, and firmly into position, after which she holds it in place for five or ten minutes. In addition to this, the muscles of the leg, especially those opposite the side to which the foot turns, should be repeatedly massaged every day. Generally it is also necessary to apply a splint which holds the foot in the correct position, so that, as growth goes on, the bones are moulded to the proper shape in a few months.

If the condition be not attended to at once after birth, and also in bad cases, an operation may become necessary, consisting, during the first few months of life, in the division of tendons, and if deferred till later, in the removal of parts of the deformed bones, so that the foot may be brought to its natural position.

CLYSTER (κλυστήρ) is another name for enema.

COAGULATION of the blood is the process whereby bleeding (or hæmorrhage) is normally arrested in the body. The process is summarized in the accompanying diagram :

PROTHROMBIN + CALCIUM + THROMBOPLASTIN
↓
THROMBIN + FIBRINOGEN
↓
FIBRIN

Prothrombin and calcium are normally present in the blood. Thromboplastin is an enzyme which is normally found in the blood platelets and in tissue cells. When bleeding occurs from a blood-vessel there is always some damage to tissue cells and to the blood platelets. As a result of this damage, thromboplastin is released and comes in contact with the prothrombin and calcium in the blood. In the presence of thromboplastin and calcium prothrombin is converted into thrombin, which in turn interacts with fibrinogen, a protein always present in the blood, to form fibrin. Fibrin consists of needle-shaped crystals, which, with the assistance of the blood platelets, form a fine network (Plate III) in which the blood corpuscles become enmeshed. This meshwork, or clot as it is known, gradually retracts until it forms a tight mass which prevents any further bleeding. It will thus be seen that clotting, or coagulation, does not occur in the healthy blood-vessel because there is no thromboplastin present. There is now evidence suggesting that there is an anti-thrombin substance present in the blood in small amounts, and that this substance antagonizes any small amounts of thrombin that may be formed as a result of small amounts of thromboplastin being released.

COAGULUM is the Latin term for a clot.

COAL-GAS is a mixture of several gases, but owes its dangerous properties to carbonic oxide or carbon monoxide gas, which is present to the extent of 5 or 10 per cent. Water-gas, which is sometimes mixed with coal-gas, contains a still larger proportion of this dangerous substance. It has two dangers, that of explosion and that of poisoning. Explosion takes place when gas has escaped into a closed space to such extent as to make a mixture of 1 part of gas to 10 parts of air, and when a light is brought into the mixture. But a mixture of 1 part of gas to 100 of air is a dangerous poison to inhale. The burning of one cubic foot of wood is enough, in the absence of a ventilating draft, to poison a mine gallery one-quarter mile long. When a person enters such an atmosphere death may be almost instantaneous ; but if only small traces of the gas are present the poisoning comes on very insidiously. Carbon monoxide has a special action upon the ganglia at the base of the brain, and large quantities cause destructive changes in this part of the nervous system.

Carbon monoxide is dangerous because it has practically 300 times the affinity of oxygen for hæmoglobin. This means that it converts the hæmoglobin of the blood into carboxyhæmoglobin and thereby deprives the tissues of the body of oxygen. Its danger is increased by the fact that it has no smell and therefore the individual exposed to it is unaware of the fact—often until it is too late because he loses consciousness before he can move from the affected area. An individual suffering from carbon monoxide poisoning has a cherry-red appearance due to the large amount of carboxyhæmoglobin in his blood.

Treatment of gas poisoning consists of artificial respiration and fresh air (*see* DROWNING). The inhalation of oxygen or air containing a small quantity of carbon dioxide (4 to 6 per cent.) has been found especially valuable in mine-rescue work for freeing the blood quickly from carbon monoxide gas.

COAL-MINER'S LUNG (*see* ANTHRACOSIS).

COARCTATION OF THE AORTA (*co*, together ; *ar(c)tare*, to make tight) is a narrowing of the aorta in the vicinity of the insertion of the ductus arteriosus. It is a congenital abnormality. Recently, satisfactory results have been obtained from surgical treatment.

COBALAMINS.—The cobalamins are a group of substances which have an enzyme action (*q.v.*) and are essential for normal growth and nutrition. (*See also* CYANOCOBALIN and HYDROXOCOBALAMIN.)

COBALT 60 is a radioactive isotope which is being used as a substitute for radium and high-voltage X-rays in the treatment of malignant disease. (*See* RADIOTHERAPY.)

COCAINE.—Coca leaves are obtained from two South American plants, *Erythroxylon coca* and *Erythroxylon bolivianum*, and contain an alkaloid, COCAINE,

which has most marked effects as a stimulant, and, locally applied, as an anæsthetic by paralysing nerves of sensation. The dried leaves have been used from time immemorial by the South American Indians, who chew them mixed with a little lime. Their effect is to dull the mucous surfaces of mouth and stomach, with which the saliva, produced by chewing them, comes into contact, thus blunting, for long, all feeling of hunger. The cocaine, being absorbed, produces on the central nervous system a stimulating effect, so that all sense of fatigue and breathlessness vanishes for the time. It was by the use of coca that the Indian post-runners of South America were able to achieve their extraordinary feats of endurance, using half an ounce or thereabout of the leaves daily. The continued use of the drug, however, results in emaciation, loss of memory, sleeplessness, and general breakdown.

Uses.—Before the serious effects that result from its habitual use were realized the drug was sometimes used by hunters, travellers, and others to relieve exhaustion and breathlessness in climbing mountains, to steady the nerves, and to dull hunger. The chief use in medicine is by local application to dull pain. Internally, it relieves the pain of cancer and other diseases of the stomach. Cocaine ointment is useful to relieve pain in cases where the skin surface is broken : for example, in eczema, shingles, piles, and itchiness. Discs of cocaine (in gelatin), or a 4 per cent. watery solution, is used to soothe pain in the eye caused by foreign bodies and the like, or to enable operations to be performed, painlessly, on this organ. Artificial chemical compounds closely allied to cocaine are injected hypodermically in order to render painless small operations, such as amputation of the fingers, and by injection into the spinal canal to enable major operations to be done on the lower limbs without pain (*see* PROCAINE HYDROCHLORIDE).

COCCUS (*κόκκος*, a berry) is the name applied to a rounded form of bacterium. (*See* BACTERIOLOGY.)

COCCYDYNIA, or COCCYGODYNIA, means the sensation of severe pain in the coccyx.

207

COCCYX (κόκκυξ, a cuckoo) is the lower end of the spinal column, resembling a bird's beak and consisting of four nodules of bone, which represent vertebræ, and correspond to the tail in lower animals. They are deeply buried in the muscles in man, but in occasional cases they project backwards, and are surrounded by a fold of skin, so as to form an actual tail.

COCHINEAL, or CARMINE, is a bright red powder derived from a dried American insect, *Coccus cacti*. It is used to colour various medicinal preparations.

COCILLANA is the bark of *Guarrea swartzii*, a South American plant with properties similar to those of ipecacuanha. It is used as a remedy in coughs and also as an aperient.

COCOA, or CACAO, is a West Indian plant, *Theobroma cacao*, first brought to Europe by Columbus. It bears a fruit containing pulp in which are embedded seeds, each as large as a bean. The seeds are fermented for some days, then roasted to loosen their husk, after which the two halves of each are pressed out as 'cocoa-nibs'. The nibs consist, half of a fat called cocoa-butter, and half of albuminous material, starch, tannin, gum, and water in varying proportions. There is an alkaloid named theobromine, very similar to the caffeine of tea and coffee, present to the amount of 1 per cent., which gives to cocoa and chocolate their stimulating properties. Of tannin, there is about half the amount that is present in tea leaves. The 'soluble-cocoa', sold for domestic use, has much of the fat removed, and consists about one-half of sugar and starchy material, one-quarter of fat, one-fifth of albuminous material, and of moisture, salts, etc., in small amounts. The cocoas of different makers are all very similar. As a food, cocoa is much overrated, although it contains a fair amount of fat, and, when made with milk and sugar, forms a valuable food. As it contains little tannin, it is sometimes tolerated by a weak stomach better than tea. (For uses, *see* CHOCOLATE.)

CODEINE is one of the active principles of opium (*q.v.*). In the form of codeine phosphate it is widely prescribed for the relief of a useless, ir-

ritative cough, and also along with aspirin and phenacetin for the relief of headaches and rheumatic pains.

COD-LIVER OIL is made by purification of the oil pressed from the fresh liver of the cod (*Gadus callarias*). Its principal value in medicine arises out of its high content of vitamin D, the vitamin used in the prevention and treatment of rickets. The official cod-liver oil of the *British Pharmacopœia* contains not less than 85 international units per gramme. Cod-liver oil is also a rich source of vitamin A, the official cod-liver oil of the *British Pharmacopœia* containing not less than 600 units of vitamin A activity per gramme. The protective dose of vitamin D for infants and children is not less than 700 units daily. This is best given in the form of cod-liver oil itself. It is sometimes objected that the taste is so unpleasant that an infant or child will not take it. Experience has shown, however, that if the oil is given from the second week of life there is seldom any real difficulty in persuading the infant to take it. Should it be preferred, however, to give it in a more palatable form, it may be given as cod-liver oil emulsion or cod-liver oil and malt. The amount of cod-liver oil in some of these preparations, however, varies considerably, and if they are used, care must be taken to ensure that the child is receiving sufficient of the oil. This applies particularly to cod-liver oil and malt preparations, most of which contain only 15 per cent. of the oil.

There are some who contend that cod-liver oil and malt is a useful remedy in the treatment of chronic bronchitis.

COELIAC DISEASE is a wasting disease of childhood in which there is inability to absorb fat from the intestines ; there is therefore an excess of fat in the stools. (*See also* GLUTEN *and* MALABSORPTION SYNDROME.)

COELIOSCOPY is the term applied to a method of viewing the interior of the abdomen in patients in whom a tumour or some other condition requiring operation may be present but cannot with certainty be diagnosed. The examination is carried out by making a minute opening under local anæsthesia, inserting an instrument bearing an electric lamp and telescopic lenses like that for examining the bladder (cystoscope) and blowing into the abdominal cavity. Certain of the abdominal organs can then be directly inspected in turn.

COFFEE and TEA.—Tea was introduced into Europe in 1610, but for long was so expensive that its use did not become general till during the course of the last century. Coffee, introduced rather later, has become the general beverage among the Latin and Teuton races, while tea has become the favourite with the whole British stock.

Coffee is a bean, obtained from the seed of a plant, *Coffee arabica*, originally hailing from Arabia, and now cultivated in tropical climes all round the world. Tea is the leaf of a plant, *Camellia thea*, brought first from China and now cultivated in Japan, India, Ceylon, and Uganda. It contains caffeine or theine, and tannic acid (or tannin), in addition to vegetable fibre, albuminous matters, and volatile oils. It is these volatile oils which give ' China ' and ' Indian ' tea their characteristic aroma and flavour. The same alkaloid gives their stimulating properties to *maté*, or Paraguay tea, derived from the leaves of *Ilex paraguayensis*, and to kola, derived from the seeds of *Cola acuminata*, a West African plant. As to caffeine, which has the action of stimulating the intellectual powers, and increasing the force of the heart's action and the functions of the kidneys, see CAFFEINE ; tea-leaves contain from 2 to 4 per cent. while coffee-berries have about half that amount. As to tannic acid, tea-leaves have about 10 per cent., and coffee-berries half this amount. But as regards the liquids, since coffee is made about twice as strong as tea in general, a strong teacupful of either will contain nearly two grains (125 mg.) of caffeine and over three grains of tannic acid. Coffee is, however, often extensively adulterated with chicory (see ADULTERATION OF FOOD), which has no virtue beyond imparting a dark colour to the mixture and changing its flavour somewhat.

COLCHICUM, the bulb of *Colchicum autumnale*, or meadow-saffron, has long been used as a remedy for gout in all the forms of this disease. How it acts is not quite certain.

Uses.—Its main use is in gout, for which colchicine, the active principle of colchicum, in doses of 0·5 mg. every one or two hours until the pain is relieved, followed by 0·5 mg. thrice daily for about a week, is the form generally employed. Demecolcine, a derivative of colchicine, is sometimes of value in the treatment of chronic myelogenous leukæmia.

COLD, INJURIES FROM (*see* CHILBLAIN, FROST-BITE, *also* CHILLS AND COLDS).

COLD, USES OF.—The application of cold to the surface of the body is capable of influencing the progress of disease in deep-seated parts to a considerable extent by acting on the blood at the surface, or through the nerves which end in the skin. Cold is applied for five chief purposes :

(*a*) **To subdue pain.**—In headache, a wet cloth to the forehead, or sponging with an evaporating mixture of vinegar and water, or eau-de-Cologne and water, is a well-known remedy. Sprains, if treated by holding the injured joint at once under running water, are much relieved. Later on, however, cold applications do harm, rather than good, by preventing the absorption of the effused blood. Pleurisy is often speedily rendered painless by the application of an ice-bag to the side. Small operations may be done painlessly after freezing the skin of the part by spraying ethyl chloride over it.

(*b*) **To lessen inflammation.**—Ice-bags are used in many inflammatory conditions to prevent the formation of an abscess. In meningitis, or inflammation of the membranes of the brain, a coil of tubing, through which iced water runs, laid on the head, often gives some relief.

(*c*) **To reduce high temperature.**—In any fever, sponging the arms and legs, one by one, with tepid water, is harmless and often very soothing. When the temperature runs very high, *e.g.* to 105° or 107° F. (40·5 to 41·8° C.) death is often averted by wrapping the patient in a wet sheet and rubbing it with ice, or by putting him in a cold bath. (*See also under* TYPHOID FEVER *and* WET PACK.)

(*d*) **To stop hæmorrhage.**—In cases of increasing hæmorrhage under the skin, for example, a bruised and blackening eye or a sprain, the amount of bleeding, and consequent discoloration, is lessened by applying compresses containing ice or some cooling lotion.

(*e*) **As a general stimulant.**—Some diseases are systematically treated in certain countries by cold bathing : for example, typhoid fever. Others are benefited by an alternation of hot and cold bathing : for example, chronic rheumatism. In general debility, one of the best curative agents is the daily cold bath (*see* BATHS.)

(*See also* HYPOTHERMIA and CRYOSURGERY.)

COLDS (*see* CHILLS AND COLDS).

COLECTOMY is the operation for removing the colon.

COLIC (from κόλον, the large intestine).—By this term is generally understood an attack of pain in the abdomen, usually seated in the neighbourhood of the navel, of spasmodic character, and attended for the most part with constipation.

SIMPLE COLIC commonly arises from the presence in the alimentary canal of some indigestible matter, which excites spasmodic contraction of the muscular coats of the intestines. The pain of colic is relieved by pressure over the abdomen, and there is no attendant fever—points which are of importance in distinguishing it from inflammation.

Attacks of this form of colic may occur in connection with a variety of causes other than that above mentioned, *e.g.* from accumulations of fæculent matter in the intestines in the case of those who suffer from habitual constipation ; also as an accompaniment of nervous and hysterical ailments and not infrequently as the result of exposure to cold and damp, particularly where the feet become chilled, as in walking through snow. Similar attacks of colic are apt to occur in infants, especially those who are fed artificially ; and in such cases it will generally be found that a temporary change of diet

will be necessary. The duration of an attack of simple colic is seldom long, and in general no ill consequences follow from it. It is, however, not free from risk, especially that of sudden obstruction of the bowel from twisting, or invagination of one part within another (intussusception) during the spasmodic seizure, giving rise to a very grave condition. Colic is also a serious symptom when due to obstruction of the bowel by a tumour or similar condition. (*See* INTESTINE, DISEASES OF ; INTUSSUSCEPTION.)

LEAD COLIC is of greater importance and interest from a medical point of view (*Syn*, painters' colic, *colica Pictonum*, Devonshire colic, dry belly-ache), since it has been clearly ascertained to be due to the absorption of lead into the system. This disease had been observed and described long before its cause was discovered. Its occurrence in an epidemic form among the inhabitants of Poitou was recorded by Francis Citois, in 1617, and the disease was thereafter termed *colica Pictonum*. It was supposed to be due to the acidity of the native wines, but it was afterwards found to depend on lead contained in them. About the middle of the eighteenth century this disease, which had long been known to prevail in Devonshire, was carefully investigated by Sir George Baker, who traced it to the contamination of the native beverage, cider, with lead, either accidentally from the lead-work of the vats and other apparatus for preparing the liquor, or from its being sweetened with litharge. (*See* LEAD-POISONING.)

BILIARY COLIC and RENAL COLIC are the terms applied to that violent pain which is produced, in the one case where a biliary calculus or gall-stone passes down from the gall-bladder into the intestine, and in the other where a renal calculus descends from the kidney along the ureter into the bladder. (*See* GALLSTONES *and* KIDNEY, DISEASES OF.)

Treatment.—The treatment of colic consists in means to relieve the spasmodic pain, and in the removal, where possible, of the cause upon which it depends. When the attack appears to depend on accumulations of irritating matter in the alimentary canal, a brisk purgative, such as castor oil, will in addition, be called for. It must be borne in mind that abdominal pain may indicate the onset of acute appendicitis or be a sign of, say, perforation of a peptic ulcer : in such cases purgatives must on no account be given.

Pressure upon the abdomen may relieve the pain partially if not completely. It may be effected, in the case of a child, by laying him face downwards across the nurse's arm, and in the case of older people by laying a hot-water bottle upon the abdomen, or by lying face downward upon a folded-up pillow. The various substances known as carminatives or antispasmodics (*see* ANTISPASMODICS) also aid in giving relief. (For the treatment of lead colic, *see* LEAD-POISONING.)

COLIMYCIN is an antibiotic isolated from the soil organism, *Bacillus colistinus*. It is active against many Gram-negative organisms, and is proving of value in the treatment of gastro-intestinal and genito-urinary infections.

COLITIS (κόλον, the large intestine) means inflammation of the colon or first part of the large intestine. *Mucous colitis*, once a fashionable disease, is now recognized not to be a form of colitis and has been named *muco-membranous colic*, or *spastic colon*. It is caused by painful spasms of the colon and occurs in nervous types of individuals. Treatment consists of dealing with the underlying nervous condition, the avoidance of all aperients, and a full diet without an excess of roughage. *Acute catarrhal colitis* occurs as part of an acute gastro-enteritis, usually due to food poisoning. The treatment is as for acute diarrhœa (*q.v.*). *Chronic catarrhal colitis* is usually due to the abuse of aperients and purgatives.

ULCERATIVE COLITIS is the most important form of colitis. It is an acute condition, the cause of which is not known. Although apparently precipitated at times by exposure to cold or damp or by dietetic indiscretions, these are not the primary cause. It is predominantly a disease of young adults. Once an individual has had the disease, he is very liable to relapses.

Symptoms.—The onset may be sudden or insidious. In the acute form there is severe diarrhœa and the patient may pass up to twenty stools a day. The stools, which may be small in quantity, are fluid and contain blood, pus, and mucus. There is always fever, which runs an irregular course. In other cases the patient first notices some irregularity of the movement of the bowels, with the passage of blood. This becomes gradually more marked. There is seldom actual pain except immediately prior to the passage of a stool, but there is always a varying amount of abdominal discomfort. The constant diarrhœa leads to emaciation and weakness, and there is always a well-marked anæmia. The acute forms may be rapidly fatal, but as a rule the acute phase passes into a chronic stage. The chronic form is liable to run a prolonged course, and the majority of cases are subject to relapses for many years.

Treatment.—Rest in bed is essential during the acute stage and as long as there is fever. The diarrhœa is controlled by mixtures containing bismuth salts and opium, and by starch and opium enemas. The diet should be bland and nourishing and should contain a minimum of roughage, *i.e.* a low-residue diet (*see* DIETS). The anæmia which is always present is treated by means of iron preparations. In some cases it may be necessary to use surgical measures to control the condition ; this usually consists of the operation known as ileostomy (*q.v.*). In some cases excellent results are obtained from the use of cortisone or its analogues. Once a patient has recovered and is back to work again, it is essential for him to remain on a low-residue diet, and to be particularly careful in avoiding unnecessary exposure to cold and damp ; otherwise the condition is liable to recur.

COLLAGEN is the protein material of which the white fibres of the connective tissue of the body are composed. On boiling it is converted into gelatin (*see* FIBROUS TISSUE).

COLLAGEN DISEASES is a term which has come into general use since the introduction to medicine of cortisone and A.C.T.H. It includes a group of diseases, including acute rheumatism and rheumatoid arthritis, which are characterized by changes in the collagen of the tissues. The precise cause of these changes is not known, but they are probably a sensitization reaction to an unknown toxin, and they respond to cortisone and A.C.T.H.

COLLAPSE is a condition of extreme weakness of all the bodily powers, and especially of the nervous system. It forms the termination of many severe diseases, such as cholera, typhoid fever, irritant poisoning, etc. It is closely allied to the condition of surgical shock, but, whilst in collapse from the conditions mentioned the chief feature is feebleness of the heart's action, in shock there are numerous other prominent symptoms. (*See* SHOCK.)

Symptoms.—The face is pale and drawn, the forehead sometimes covered with cold sweat, the eyes sunken and glassy. The voice is weak, the breathing shallow, and the pulse rapid and feeble or imperceptible. The temperature is usually reduced to 96° or 97° F. (35·6 or 36·1° C.). Generally the patient lies on his back, paying no attention to what is proceeding around him.

Treatment.—The patient should be allowed to lie quietly on his back in a darkened room, well covered, and surrounded by hot bottles to maintain the body heat. Stimulants are also necessary.

COLLAPSE THERAPY is the term applied to the method of treating diseases of the lung by bringing about collapse of the diseased part through removing the supporting ribs (thoracoplasty), or introducing air into the pleural cavity (artificial pneumothorax).

COLLAR-BONE, or CLAVICLE, is the bone which runs from the upper end of the breast-bone towards the tip of the shoulder across the root of the neck. It serves to support the upper limb, to keep it out from the side, and to give breadth to the shoulders. The bone is shaped like an '*f*' with two curves, which give it increased strength. It is, however, very liable to be broken by falls on the hand or on the shoulder, and is the most frequently fractured bone in the body (*see* FRACTURES).

COLLARGOL is a form of colloidal silver which mixes readily with water and any albuminous fluids, and has an antiseptic action. It is used especially

for application to the eyes in inflammatory conditions.

COLLATERAL CIRCULATION (*see* ANASTOMOSIS).

COLLES'S FRACTURE is a fracture of the lower end of the radius close to the wrist, caused usually by a fall forwards on the palm of the hand, in which the lower fragment is displaced backwards. (Plate X, C.)

COLLODION (κόλλα, glue) is a thick, colourless, syrupy liquid, made by dissolving gun-cotton in a mixture of ether and alcohol or with acetone. When painted on the skin the solvent evaporates, leaving a tough film behind. *Flexible collodion*, made by adding some castor oil and colophony, is more elastic, and does not crack through the movements of the skin. *Blistering collodion* contains cantharides, and, being painted on, raises a blister, to which at the same time it affords protection. *Medicated collodion* has various substances, such as salicylic acid, benzoin, etc., added to it, in order that these may remain in contact with the skin for a prolonged period.

Uses.—Collodion is mainly used as a covering for wounds, after these have been purified. The objection to its use is that, if a wound, or the surface round it, be not absolutely clean, the discharges from the wound are retained by the collodion, and may carry infection deeply into the tissues. Medicated collodion is used in many skin diseases.

Mode of application.—The wound having been cleaned thoroughly, dried, and all bleeding stopped, collodion is painted over it with a camel's-hair brush. Before this has time to dry, a very thin film of cotton-wool is laid on it and painted down with more collodion. Then another film of cotton-wool, followed by collodion, and so on till five or six layers of each have been applied, the successful application depending on the films of wool being as thin as possible, and upon each layer being applied before that beneath it has had time to dry completely.

COLLOID (κόλλα, glue ; εἶδος, form) is the name given to a type of cancer of internal organs, in which a glue-like substance collects in the interior of the tumour. The term is also applied to substances existing in a colloidal solution, and to the viscid iodine-containing material in the spaces of the thyroid gland.

COLLOIDAL SOLUTIONS are solutions in which a substance very finely divided into particles is suspended in another substance, as, for example, metals like silver and iron suspended in the form of minute particles in water or glycerin. The two constituents of the colloidal solution are called phases—the particles being known as the internal phase, and the medium in which they are suspended, the continuous or external phase. The term suspensoid is applied to colloids in which the particles consist of pure solid, and the term emulsoid is applied to those in which the particles absorb some of the liquid in which they are suspended.

COLLYRIUM (κολλύριον) means an eye-lotion.

COLOBOMA (κολόβωμα, a missing part) is the term applied to a congenital defect or fissure in the lens, iris, or retina of the eye.

COLOCYNTH, or BITTER APPLE, is the fruit of a species of cucumber, *Citrullus colocynthis*, growing on the Mediterranean shores. The dried white pulp is a powerful purgative. It is administered usually as colocynth and hyoscyamus pill, taken in doses of 4 to 8 grains (250 to 500 mg.).

COLON (κόλον) is the first part of the large intestine. (*See* INTESTINE.)

COLOPHONY is another name for resin. Resin plaster is now called colophony plaster.

COLOSTRUM (*colustrum*) is the first fluid secreted by the mammary glands for two or three days after childbirth. It contains less casein and more albumin than ordinary milk.

COLOUR BLINDNESS (*see* VISION).

COLOUR INDEX is one of the criteria used in assessing the degree and type of anæmia. It signifies the per-

centage of hæmoglobin in terms of the amount contained in each red blood corpuscle. (*See* ANÆMIA.)

COLPITIS is a term applied to inflammation of the vagina. (*See* WHITES.)

COLPORRHAPHY (κόλπος, the vagina ; ῥαφή, stitch) is a term applied to an operation designed to strengthen the pelvic floor in cases of prolapse of the uterus.

COLPOSCOPY is the method of examining the vagina and cervix by means of the binocular instrument known as the colposcope. It is proving of particular value in the early detection of cancer of the cervix.

COLT'S-FOOT is the name given to the leaves of *Tussilago farfara* or *Tussilago petasites*, the butter burr, a composite plant used in the form of a decoction for the treatment of coughs.

COMA (κῶμα, deep sleep) is a state of profound unconsciousness, in which not only can the sufferer not be roused, but there are not even reflex movements when the skin is pinched, the eyeball touched, etc. The breathing is generally stertorous, but deep, and the heart's action is strong. The cause of coma is usually apoplexy, but it may also be due to high fever, diabetes mellitus, Bright's disease, alcohol, epilepsy, cerebral tumour, meningitis, injury to the head, overdose of insulin, carbon monoxide poisoning, poisoning from opium and other narcotic drugs. If the condition does not begin to pass off in twenty-four hours, death is generally near at hand. (*See* UNCONSCIOUSNESS.)

COMEDONES (*see* ACNE).

COMMENSAL (*com*, together ; *mensa*, table) is the term applied to micro-organisms which live in or on the body (*e.g.* in the gut or respiratory tract, or on the skin) without doing any harm to the individual.

COMMISSURE (*committo*, I join) means a joining, and is a term applied to strands of nerve fibres which join one side of the brain to the other, to the band joining one optic nerve to the other, to the junctions of the lips at the corners of the mouth, etc.

COMMOTIO CEREBRI is another term for concussion of the brain.

COMPENSATION is a term applied to the counterbalancing of some defect of structure or function by some other special bodily development. The body possesses a remarkable power of adapting itself to even serious defects, so that disability due to these passes off after a time. The term is most frequently applied to the ability possessed by the heart to increase in size, and therefore in power, when the need for greater pumping action arises in consequence of a defective valve or some other abnormality in the circulation. A heart in this condition is, however, more liable to be prejudicially affected by strains and diseased processes, and the term ' failure of compensation ' is applied to the symptoms that result when this power becomes temporarily insufficient.

COMPLEMENT is a normal constituent of blood serum which plays an important part in the antibody-antigen reaction which is the basis of many immunity processes. (*See* IMMUNITY.)

COMPLEX is the term applied to a combination of various actions or symptoms. The term is particularly applied to a set of symptoms occurring together in mental disease with such regularity as to receive a special name.

COMPLEXION (*see* ACNE, SKIN DISEASES, SUNBURN).

COMPOSITOR'S DISEASE is a form of lead poisoning which occasionally attacks those who handle type. (*See* LEAD-POISONING.)

COMPRESS is the name given to a pad of linen or flannel wrung out of water and bound to the body. It is generally wrung out of cold water, and may be covered with a piece of waterproof. It is used to subdue pain or inflammation (*see* COLD). A hot compress is generally called a 'fomentation' (*see* FOMENTATIONS).

COMPRESSED AIR ILLNESS (*see* CAISSON DISEASE).

CONCEPTION signifies the complex set of changes which occur in the ovum and in the body of the mother at the beginning of pregnancy. The precise moment of conception is that at which the male element, or spermatozoon, and the female element, or ovum, fuse together. (*See* FŒTUS.)

CONCRETIONS (*con*, together; *cresco*, I grow) are masses of various sizes and substances which form in many of the tissues and smaller cavities of the body, in certain circumstances.

Varieties and causes.—There is a special liability to the deposit of lime-salts in damaged or degenerating tissues. The reason for this is probably much the same as that for the similar deposit from hard water inside kettles and boilers. The tissues in question being inactive do not produce sufficient carbonic acid gas to keep dissolved the lime salts in the fluids circulating past and through them. Accordingly, healed-up areas in the lungs, which have been the seat of tuberculosis, the remains of dead parasites and other foreign bodies, degenerated blood-vessels, tumours, and scars generally, are apt to have lime deposited in and around them till masses of considerable size are formed. The tartar on the teeth, some stones in the bladder, and the calculi sometimes found in the ducts of salivary glands in the cheek or beneath the tongue, are examples of a similar deposit of lime and phosphates, due to the action of bacteria.

Hair-balls, which are common in the stomachs of lower animals that lick themselves, occur sometimes in mentally deranged patients who have a habit of chewing their hair, and may reach the size of walnuts or larger. (*See also* BEZOAR.)

Various glands produce secretions, which, by a gradual process of sedimentation build up solid masses in the ducts of these glands. Examples of this are found in the gall-stones, formed of cholesterin separated from the bile, in the uratic stones found in the kidney or bladder of persons suffering from acidity, in the plugs of hardened wax which often give trouble in the ear, and in the cheese-like masses which accumulate in the tonsils and give rise to fœtor of the breath.

Gout is a disease in which the pain is due to sharp uratic crystals which are deposited on the surfaces of joints, the same crystals being deposited in other tissues also, at a later stage of the disease, so that large solid masses called ' chalk-stones ' are ultimately formed. (*See* GOUT.)

CONCUSSION OF THE BRAIN (*see* BRAIN).

CONDIMENTS (*see* DIET).

CONDURANGO is the bark of *Gonolobus condurango*, a South American plant which is used as a bitter tonic, the tincture being given in doses of 60 to 120 minims (4 to 8 ml.).

CONDYLE (κόνδυλος, a knuckle) is the name given to a rounded prominence at the end of a bone : for example, the prominences at the outer and inner sides of the elbow upon the humerus, and the prominences at the outer and inner sides of the knee on the thighbone.

CONDYLOMA (κονδύλωμα, a knob) means a localized, rounded swelling of mucous membrane often found about the opening of the bowel, especially in cases of syphilis, and disappearing slowly as this disease is treated, or requiring removal by caustics or by cutting.

CONDY'S FLUID is a powerful disinfectant containing permanganate of sodium in water. (For its action and uses, *see* PERMANGANATE OF POTASSIUM.) Green Condy's fluid contains manganate of sodium, which has a similar action.

CONFECTIONS, also known as conserves and electuaries, form a method of prescribing certain bulky drugs mixed into a paste with sugar or honey. The best-known confections are those of senna and sulphur, both of which are aperient in action. Compound confection of guaiacum, better known as ' Chelsea Pensioner ', is an old remedy for constipation and rheumatic pains in elderly people, having received its name from the success of its use among the men of that hospital. It contains guaiacum resin, rhubarb, potassium acid tartrate, nutmeg, sublimed sulphur, and honey. The dose of all these confections is about a teaspoonful or more.

CONFLUENT SMALLPOX (*confluo*, I run together) is a very severe form of this malady, in which the individual pustules of the eruption run together. (*See* SMALLPOX.)

CONGENITAL (*con*, together ; *genitus*, begotten) deformities, diseases, etc., are those which are either present at birth, or which, being transmitted direct from the parents, show themselves some time after birth.

CONGESTION (*congero*, I accumulate) means the accumulation of blood in a part due to over-filling of its bloodvessels. The condition may be due to some weakness of the circulation (*see* CIRCULATION, DISORDERS OF), but as a rule is one of the early signs of inflammation (*see* ABSCESS, INFLAMMATION).

CONGESTION TREATMENT is a method sometimes used to stimulate the process of repair in both acute and chronic states of inflammation. It depends upon the principle that when the blood-vessels of an inflamed part are artificially dilated the number, and consequently the activity, of phagocytes (*see* PHAGOCYTOSIS) are increased. The congestion is brought about either by obstructing the return of blood (*e.g.* in a limb) by means of an elastic bandage, or by diminishing the atmospheric pressure in the case of flat or outlying parts (*e.g.* the back or the finger) by means of a suction cup or cylinder from which a rubber tube leads to a suction pump.

CONIUM (*see* HEMLOCK).

CONJUGATE DEVIATION is the term for describing the persistent and involuntary turning of both eyes in any one direction, and is a sign of a lesion in the brain.

CONJUNCTIVA (*conjungo*, I join together) is the membrane which covers the front of the eye. Beginning at the edge of the lower lid, it clothes the inner surface of that lid, and, at the line where the latter joins the cheek, forms a shallow pocket and passes on to the eyeball. Covering the front of the ball it then passes forward to the upper lid, forming a much deeper pocket between this lid and the ball, and so down to the margin of the upper lid, where it meets the skin. The membrane is transparent, especially over the centre of the eye, where a specialized portion, the cornea, admits light to the interior. The ' white ' of the eye is formed by the sclerotic or outer coat of the eyeball shining through the conjunctiva. The membrane is richly supplied with nerves of sensation, and is extremely sensitive, so that the slightest touch produces a reflex closure of the lids.

CONJUNCTIVITIS means inflammation of the conjunctiva. (*See* EYE, DISEASES OF.)

CONOVID (*see* NORETHYNODREL).

CONSOLIDATION is a term applied to solidification of an organ, especially of a lung. The consolidation may be of a permanent nature due to formation of fibrous tissue, or may be temporary, as in acute pneumonia.

CONSTIPATION, or COSTIVENESS (*con*, together ; *stipo*, I cram), means a condition in which the bowels are opened too seldom or incompletely, the motions as a consequence being dry and hard. It should, however, be borne in mind that, though most persons have in health one daily movement of the bowels, some perform this act twice, while in others a motion once in two or more days is perfectly natural. Constipation is a chronic condition, and must be carefully distinguished from acute obstruction of the bowels, a much more serious condition (*see* INTESTINE, DISEASES OF). The stool of a healthy person, with good appetite, should be light brown in colour, about 5 ounces (140 grammes) in weight, and about 5 inches (12 cm.) long, should cohere in one or two pieces but should be sufficiently light to float in water. Great variations, however, take place in colour (*see* STOOLS), in amount, and in consistence, according to the nature and quantity of the food and drink taken.

Causes.—The uncommon causes of constipation are mechanical—that is, obstruction by stricture of the bowel, by tumour, by adhesive bands. The

common causes are (1) habit, (2) ' a greedy colon ', which absorbs water too quickly, (3) a spastic colon, the muscle of which remains in a state of spasm, (4) lack of tone of the colon muscle, sometimes because of too little vitamin B_1 in the diet, (5) a diet which has not enough ' roughage ' in it to stimulate the intestine to activity. Of these, habit is probably most important. Constant neglect to respond to the sensation in the rectum which indicates that it is full and needs emptying leads to retention of fæces, which become dry and hard. The condition is aggravated by the use of purgatives.

Symptoms and effects.—The stools are, as is well known, dark, hard, and passed with difficulty, and in small amount. In severe, persistent cases there may be swelling of the abdomen, from the retention of large masses of the remnants from digestion. Colic is not uncommon. Piles, which are a cause of increasing constipation, are often brought on by inattention to the bowels to begin with. When the condition has become habitual, the whole digestion may be thrown out of gear, with foul tongue, bad breath, and loss of appetite. Headache and lassitude may also be present.

Treatment.—Assuming that there is no organic cause, such as tumour or other source of mechanical obstruction, the most important matter is the regulation of the daily habits. The person concerned should take a certain amount of exercise daily. Above all things, a habit of opening the bowels, at the same time every day, should be cultivated; a definite hour should be fixed, preferably after a meal, and best after breakfast, and, no matter whether there be a sensation that the bowels will move or not, the attempt should unfailingly be made. The diet is of importance. On the whole, in cases of constipation this errs in being too concentrated and too unirritating, although the same trouble exists among country-people who use a coarse vegetable dietary. As a rule, however, the diet should be changed to include oatmeal porridge, brown bread, green vegetables, and fruit, especially fruit like prunes or brambles, which have a large indigestible residue, while a considerable amount of fluid should be taken. The juice of an orange or grapefruit, or a glass of water, first thing in the morning may help.

The use of aperients and purgatives has usually exaggerated the condition, and as a general rule should be given up.

CONSTITUTION, or DIATHESIS (διάθεσις, a disposition), means the general condition of the body, especially with reference to its liability to certain diseases. A sound constitution is one in which the structure and functions of the various parts and organs are so evenly maintained that there is no apparent liability to any disease. The term 'constitutional' is sometimes vaguely applied to diseases which present knowledge does not permit of our attributing to any definite organ or system. A constitution such as the gouty constitution may be inherited, or it may develop as the result of improper food, habits, and environment ; or, on the other hand, a heredity towards some disease may be gradually eliminated by a careful and regular life.

CONSUMPTION (*see* TUBERCULOSIS).

CONTACT LENSES are lenses shaped to fit the eyeball. They fit in direct contact with the eye, behind the eyelids, and move with the eye. Their advantages, compared with spectacles, are twofold : optical and cosmetic. In certain disturbances of vision they provide better results than do ordinary spectacles. They are invisible, except on close examination, and are therefore preferred by some people, *e.g.* actors and actresses. Other advantages they possess are that they cannot be knocked off, and can, therefore, be worn for even strenuous sports, such as football, and that they do not steam in a warm, moist atmosphere. On the other hand, some people find them troublesome to wear for more than a few hours at a time. They require careful fitting, and should, therefore, only be worn on the recommendation of an experienced ophthalmologist.

CONTAGION (*contagio*, pollution by touching) means the principle of spread of disease by direct contact with the body of an affected person, while by infection is meant the spread through the air or by other distant means.

CONTINUED FEVERS are typhus, typhoid, and relapsing fevers, so called because of their continuing over a more or less definite space of time.

CONTRACEPTION is the prevention by artificial means of fertilization of the ovum ensuing from sexual intercourse. Five main groups of contraceptives are in general use : (1) The occlusive (or Dutch) cap, which covers the entrance to the womb and thereby prevents entrance of spermatozoa to the womb. (2) The sheath (or condom), which prevents spermatozoa entering the vagina. (3) Chemical pessaries or solutions, which, when placed in the vagina, destroy the spermatozoa. (4) The oral contraceptives : these are steroid hormones which are taken in the form of a pill. (*See also* NORETHYNODREL.) (5) The intra-uterine contraceptive devices which prevent implantation of the fertilized ovum in the uterus. The method of *coitus interruptus* is universally condemned by the medical profession as being harmful to both husband and wife.

CONTRACTURE means the permanent shortening of a muscle or of fibrous tissue. Contraction is the name given to the temporary shortening of a muscle.

CONTRE-COUP means an injury in which a bone, generally the skull, is fractured, not at the spot where the violence is applied, but at the exactly opposite point.

CONTUSION (*see* BRUISES).

CONVALESCENCE means the condition through which a person passes after having suffered from some acute disease, and before complete health and strength are regained. Many diseases have special dangers during convalescence, for example, after typhoid fever the effects of over-eating may be disastrous ; after measles, pneumonia, and other diseases of the respiratory tract, there is a greater risk than usual of the onset of tuberculosis in susceptible individuals ; and, while convalescence from scarlatina is proceeding, there is a special risk of kidney inflammation. These are guarded against by working the body at low pressure for a time, exposing it to no strain, partaking of a moderate diet, and taking an ample allowance of rest and sleep, till all the functions have regained their usual activity and vigour. For further details see under each disease.

CONVOLUTIONS (*convolvo*, I roll up) (*see* BRAIN).

CONVULSIONS (*convello*, I tear) are rapidly alternating contractions and relaxations of the muscles, causing irregular movements of the limbs or body generally, and usually accompanied by unconsciousness. They form really only a symptom of some other trouble, often, in children, of a trifling nature, but, on account of the alarm they cause and their occasional seriousness, they are treated often as a disease by themselves.

Causes.—The most common cause of convulsions in adults is epilepsy (*q.v.*). As the vast majority of convulsive seizures occur in children, however, only these will be dealt with here. The relative frequency of convulsions in infants and young children is probably due to an instability of the immature nervous system. An American investigation showed that in a group of 8823 otherwise normal children, some 6 per cent. had had one or more convulsions. Some children are more liable to develop convulsions than others, and this is probably due to a neurotic inheritance. In young infants convulsions may be due to *birth injuries*, usually the result of a difficult labour. The convulsions in these cases are due to damage of the brain, either by bleeding from torn blood-vessels or concussion of the brain. In older infants convulsions may be due to the irritability of the brain often associated with *rickets*. This is the condition known as tetany, and before the introduction of the routine administration of vitamin D to infants and children, it was one of the most common causes of convulsions in older infants and young children.

A sudden *rise of temperature*, such as may occur in any infection, may induce convulsions in an infant and young child. This is most likely in pneumonia, and it would appear as if in the child a convulsion was the equivalent of the chill or rigor which occurs in adults. *Irritation* elsewhere in the body may cause convulsions in the

predisposed child. This is most likely to occur with irritation in the bowels, *e.g.* the eating of unripe or indigestible food, colic, worms, or even constipation. Infection of the kidneys or bladder may also be responsible, as may be earache, particularly if of sudden onset. The rôle of teething as a cause of convulsions has been exaggerated, but there is no doubt that, if painful, the teething process may occasionally produce convulsions.

Diseases of the brain, such as meningitis, encephalitis, and tumours, or any disturbance of the brain due to bleeding, blockage of a blood-vessel, or irritation of the brain by a fracture of the skull, may also be responsible for convulsions.

Asphyxia, such as may occur in a young child during a paroxysm of whooping-cough, may also bring on convulsions. Breath-holding, a not uncommon condition in infants and young children, may also persist long enough to bring on convulsions. These breath-holding attacks follow a severe bout of crying, at the end of which the infant holds its breath. As a rule, the worst that happens is that the infant holds his breath until he is blue in the face, and then starts breathing again. Occasionally, however, the breath-holding persists until there is a convulsion. An occasional breath-holding attack need not be taken too seriously, but if it is repeated, medical advice should be sought.

Finally, it must never be forgotten that *epilepsy* can occur in infants and young children.

Treatment.—Convulsions are rarely dangerous to life unless they occur as part of a dangerous condition which is already threatening the child's life. The time-honoured custom is to put the child in a hot bath, but this is seldom necessary. On the other hand, tepid sponging may help if there is fever. If there is any possibility of the child biting his tongue, a spoon or a spatula should be put between the teeth. There is seldom any need to restrain the movements unless they are severe enough to throw the child off the bed or couch. If the convulsions persist, it may be necessary to give inhalations of chloroform. As a rule a sedative, such as chloral hydrate or an injection of one of the barbiturates, controls the convulsions. Once these are under control, the cause of the convulsions must be sought and the necessary treatment given.

COOLEY'S ANÆMIA, or THALASSÆMIA, is a condition in which there is an inherited defect in the production of normal hæmoglobin, resulting in a severe degree of anæmia.

CO-ORDINATION means the governing power exercised by the brain as a whole, or by certain centres in the nervous system, to make various muscles contract in harmony, and so produce definite actions, instead of meaningless movements. It is bound up intimately with the complex sense of localization, which enables a person with his eyes shut to tell, by sensations received from the bones, joints, and muscles, the position of the various parts of his body. The power is impaired in various diseases, such as in locomotor ataxia. It is tested by making the patient shut his eyes, moving his hand in various directions, and then telling him to bring the point of the forefinger steadily to the tip of the nose, or by other simple movements.

COPAIBA, or COPAIVA, is a mixture of oil and resin in a thick yellow fluid, obtained by cutting into the bark of *Copaifera langsdorfii*, a South American tree. It is excreted by the mucous membranes, especially of the urinary and respiratory organs, which it stimulates. **Uses.**—It is used in various chronic inflammations of the urinary organs, and as an expectorant in chronic bronchitis.

COPPER is used in medicine in the two salts, sulphate of copper and nitrate of copper. The former is, in small doses, a powerful astringent, and in larger doses an irritant. Both are caustics when applied externally. **Uses.**—Externally, either is used to rub on unhealthy ulcers and growths, with the view of stimulating the granulation tissue to more rapid healing. In very small amounts copper is necessary for the formation of red blood corpuscles. It is, therefore, sometimes necessary to give copper as well as iron to cases of anæmia, especially in children.

COPPER POISONING is rare. Copper itself is harmless, but sulphate of copper (blue vitriol) and acetate of copper (verdigris) are now and then taken as poisons, while their use in very small quantities to colour peas and other green vegetables put up in bottles is said to lead to occasional unpleasant symptoms.
Treatment.—If one of the salts above named has been taken by mistake, the treatment is that for any irritant poison, viz. milk or white of egg as an antidote, followed by washing out the stomach.

COPROLALIA is the condition in which insane people give utterance to filthy and obscene words.

CORDOTOMY, or CHORDOTOMY, is the surgical operation of cutting the antero-lateral tracts of the spinal cord to relieve otherwise intractable pain. It is also sometimes known as TRACTOTOMY.

CORNEA (*cornu*, horn) is the clear membrane in front of the eye through which light passes to its interior. (*See* EYE.)

CORNEAL GRAFTING is the method of treating certain conditions of the cornea by replacing the damaged cornea with a cornea which has been taken from a human body. An Act of Parliament passed in 1952 authorized the removal of the eyes from a body for the purpose of corneal grafting, unless the deceased person previous to his death, or a surviving relative, had expressed an objection. If the eye, or cornea, is removed within ten hours of death it can be kept in a corneal bank for as long as twenty days before being used. A corneal graft can be used to restore vision in many diseases of the cornea, including interstitial keratitis (*q.v.*), scarring of the cornea, or damage to the cornea due to agents such as lime and ammonia.
The Ministry of Health has drawn up a list of suitable eye-banks to which people can apply to bequeath their eyes, and an official form is now available for the bequest of eyes.

CORNS and BUNIONS.—A corn is a localized thickening of the cuticle or epidermis, of a conical shape, the point of the cone being directed inwards and being known as the 'eye' of the corn. A general thickening over a wider area is called a 'callosity'. 'Bunion' is a condition found over the joint at the base of the great toe, in which not only is there thickening of the skin, but the head of the metatarsal bone, in consequence of bending outwards of the toe by pointed or too short boots, becomes unduly prominent beneath the thickened skin (Fig. 100). 'Hammer-toe' is a condition of the second toe, caused by short boots, in which the toe becomes bent at its two joints in such a way as to resemble a hammer, while corns form over the bends.

Causes.—The cause of bunions is the wearing of ill-fitting boots. Corns are due similarly to the pressure of tight or badly fitting boots, or, when on the under surface of the foot, to unevenness in the sole. The skin grows more rapidly in consequence of the irritation, and becomes changed by the pressure into a species of horn. Where the corns are between the toes, they become moist and sodden, and are called soft corns.

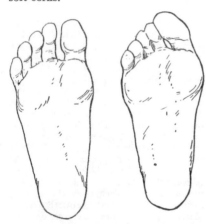

Fig. 100.—Two foot-soles, showing on left natural appearance, on right distortion of toes produced by badly fitting boot, with tendency to bunion.

Treatment.—The first requisite is to wear sufficiently large and properly shaped boots. The inner side of the sole should be straight, not cut away to a point, and the width of the sole at the level of the little toe should be as great

as that of the bare foot when the weight of the body is thrown on it. Relief from the pain of a corn may be obtained by wearing a ring of felt (corn plaster) round the corn, so as to free it from pressure and distribute the pressure of the boot over the surrounding skin. To remove the corn, the foot should be soaked in hot soapy water, and the corn then cut or scraped away with a knife or pair of scissors. After drying, the site of the corn should be covered with a small piece of soap plaster, or painted inside the felt ring with salicylic acid collodion. This consists of salicylic acid (8 parts), extract of cannabis indica (1 part), and flexile collodion (60 parts). This preparation softens and breaks up the corn, which may be picked away gradually or rubbed down with pumice-stone. After the corn is removed, the skin of the foot should be hardened by daily bathing for some time in salt water or in spirit. A tendency to bunions, flat foot, and corns can sometimes be checked by wearing boots of which the sole is slightly thicker along the inner side than on the outer side.

Soft corns and the deformities of bunion and hammer-toe should be treated by wearing socks made like gloves with a compartment for each toe, or in slighter cases by inserting a piece of boracic lint each morning in the spaces between the toes. In bad cases of bunion the opening of the boot should run forwards to between the first and second toes, where the lace, or a peg known as a 'toe-post', is fixed to the sole in order to keep the great toe in its proper place; or a rubber pad may be worn between the toes. In old-standing cases of bunion and hammer-toe, an operation in which the protruding toe joint is excised may be necessary for cure.

CORONARY (*coronarius*, crown-like) is a term applied to several structures in the body encircling an organ in the manner of a crown. The coronary arteries are the arteries of supply to the heart which arise from the aorta, just beyond the aortic valve, and through which the blood is delivered with great pressure to the muscle of the heart. Disease of the coronary arteries is a very serious condition producing various abnormal forms of heart action and the disease angina pectoris. (*See also* THROMBOSIS.)

CORONARY THROMBOSIS.—When the coronary arteries are diseased in arteriosclerosis they may become so narrow that the blood, slowing down in its flow, clots or thromboses. This cuts off the supply of blood to part of the heart, and the result may be fatal. This condition—coronary thrombosis— has become much more common during the last two or three decades. (*See also* THROMBOSIS.)

CORPORA QUADRIGEMINA form part of the mid-brain. (*See* BRAIN.)

CORPULENCE, or OBESITY, is a condition of the body characterized by over-accumulation of fat under the skin and around certain of the internal organs. The extent to which obesity may proceed is illustrated by numerous well-authenticated examples, of which only a few can be here mentioned. Thus Bright, a grocer of Maldon, in Essex, who died in 1750, in his twenty-ninth year, weighed 616 lb. In the *Philosophical Transactions* for 1813 a case is recorded of a girl four years of age who weighed 256 lb. But the most celebrated case is that of Daniel Lambert of Leicester, who died in 1809 in his fortieth year. He is said to have been the heaviest man who ever lived, his weight being 739 lb. (52 st. 11 lb.). Lambert had publicly exhibited himself for some years prior to his death, which occurred suddenly at Stamford. At the inn where he died two suits of his clothes were preserved, from which some idea of his enormous dimensions may be obtained when it is stated that his waistcoat could easily enclose seven persons of ordinary size. Lambert ate moderately, drank only water, and slept less than most persons. He is said to have had an excellent tenor voice.

For some persons, and particularly among some races, a degree of corpulence is natural, and though the following table represents the average weight for men of twenty-five years of age and over, of varying height, it must be accepted as true for health only with a wide margin. A person's weight may be one-fifth over the figures given

and yet within the limit of health, while, on the other hand, if the weight is not more than one-fifth below the average weight this is not indicative of bad health. The average woman should weigh rather less for her height than the average male, as a comparison of Tables 11 and 12 makes clear.

The average weight of the clothing is $\frac{1}{24}$ of the male body, and the above

Height		Small Frame	Medium Frame	Large Frame
Feet	Inches	lb.	lb.	lb.
5	2	116–125	124–133	131–142
5	3	119–128	127–136	133–144
5	4	122–132	130–140	137–149
5	5	126–136	134–144	141–153
5	6	129–139	137–147	145–157
5	7	133–143	141–151	149–162
5	8	136–147	145–156	153–166
5	9	140–151	149–160	157–170
5	10	144–155	153–164	161–175
5	11	148–159	157–168	165–180
6	0	152–164	161–173	169–185
6	1	157–169	166–178	174–190
6	2	163–175	171–184	179–196
6	3	168–180	176–189	184–202

TABLE 11.—Ideal Weights for Men of Ages 25 and Over. Height, with shoes on. Weight, dressed. (Metropolitan Life Insurance Company, 1943.)

weights include clothing. An addition of about three pounds for every four years of age over thirty must be made to the above figures, as the weight tends to increase naturally until old age sets in. (*See* WEIGHT AND HEIGHT.)

Causes.—Various causes are assigned for the production of corpulence. Thus, in some instances it may be due to disturbances of some of the endocrine glands, such as the thyroid, pituitary and sex glands. In some families there appears to be a hereditary predisposition to an obese habit of

Height		Small Frame	Medium Frame	Large Frame
Feet	Inches	lb.	lb.	lb.
4	11	104–111	110–118	117–127
5	0	105–113	112–120	119–129
5	1	107–115	114–122	121–131
5	2	110–118	117–125	124–135
5	3	113–121	120–128	127–138
5	4	116–125	124–132	131–142
5	5	119–128	127–135	133–145
5	6	123–132	130–140	138–150
5	7	126–136	134–144	142–154
5	8	129–139	137–147	145–158
5	9	133–143	141–151	149–162
5	10	136–147	145–155	152–166
5	11	139–150	148–158	155–169

TABLE 12.—Ideal Weights for Women of Ages 25 and Over. Height, with shoes on. Weight, dressed. (Metropolitan Life Insurance Company, 1942.)

body, upon which precautions in living seem to have little effect. But, beyond this, it is unquestionable that certain habits favour the occurrence of corpulence.

A luxurious, inactive, or sedentary life is a well-recognized predisposing cause. The more immediate exciting causes are over-feeding and the large use of fluids of any kind, but especially alcoholic liquors. Fat persons are not always great eaters, although many of them are ; while again, leanness and inordinate appetite are not infrequently associated. Still, it may be stated generally that indulgence in food beyond what is requisite to repair daily waste goes towards the increase of fat. This is more especially the case when the non-nitrogenous (the fatty, sugary, and starchy) elements of the food are in excess. It is generally held that the fat of the body is mainly, if not entirely, formed from these foods, while nitrogenous (albuminous) foods increase oxidation and lead to tissue waste. Alcoholic liquors, when taken to a considerable extent, also tend to the formation of fat, partly because many of them, *e.g.* beer, contain much sugar, and partly no doubt because a portion of the body heat is derived from the alcohol and a corresponding amount of the starchy and sugary food spared and converted into fat.

Women are prone to become more corpulent than men, and appear to take on this condition more readily after having borne a child, and after the cessation of menstruation.

In young persons excessive corpulence is sometimes associated with defective action of some of the endocrine glands, especially the pituitary and thyroid glands. In slighter cases of such defect the gland usually gains its full development as life advances, and the corpulence passes off when adult age is reached.

Defective muscular exertion has been mentioned as a cause of corpulence, but it is sometimes observed that stout men, when they begin to take active exercise, become fatter still, the reason being that the appetite is sharpened and still more food is taken.

Symptoms.—Health cannot be long maintained under excessive obesity, for the increase in bulk of the body, rendering exercise more difficult, leads to relaxation and defective nutrition of muscle, while the accumulations of fat in the chest and abdomen occasion serious embarrassment to the functions of the various organs in these cavities. In general, the mental activity of the highly corpulent becomes impaired, although there have always been notable exceptions to this rule.

The corpulent are at least as liable as the spare to be attacked by acute diseases, and they succumb much more readily to them than do the latter. Diabetes, gall-stones, gout, arterial disease, high blood pressure, and varicose veins are all more common in the obese individual. Various skin conditions, such as eczema, and particularly a chafed and painful condition of the skin at folds where two surfaces meet (*see* CHAFING) are also troublesome. It is therefore not surprising that the corpulent have a poor expectation of life. Life insurance statistics show that an increase of 25 pounds above standard weight reduces the life expectancy of a man of 45 by 25 per cent. This means that he is likely to die at 60, whereas he might have expected to live until 80 if he had not been obese.

Treatment.—For the prevention of corpulence and the reduction of superfluous fat, many expedients have been resorted to, and numerous remedies recommended. These have embraced such regimens as bleeding, purging, starving, the use of different kinds of baths, and of drugs innumerable, most of which means have been found to fail in accomplishing the desired object.

The drinking of vinegar was long popularly supposed to be a remedy for obesity. It is related of the Marquis of Cortona, a noted general of the Duke of Alba, that by drinking vinegar he so reduced his body from a condition of enormous obesity that he could fold his skin around him like a garment. Such a result was only a proof of the injury done to his health, and probably to his digestive organs, by the excessive use of vinegar.

When the obesity is due to myxœdema (*q.v.*), excellent results are obtained from the administration of thyroid gland, but this form of treatment should not be used for the treatment of obesity except under careful medical supervision.

Of far greater importance than any drugs is the question of the regulation of habits as to diet, exercise, and sleep. In 1863 a pamphlet appeared, entitled a *Letter on Corpulence, Addressed to the Public by William Banting*, in which was narrated the remarkable experience of the writer in accomplishing the reduction of his own weight in a short time, by the adoption of a particular kind of diet. Mr. Banting described the condition of obesity in which he was in August 1862, and which, although certainly less than those examples above mentioned, appears to have been sufficient to prove a source of much discomfort and even of actual suffering. After trying almost every known remedy without effect, he placed himself upon an entirely new form of diet, which consisted chiefly in the removal as far as possible, of all sugary, starchy, and fat food, the reduction of liquids, and the substitution of meat or fish and fruit in moderate quantity at each meal, together with the daily use of an antacid draught. Under this regimen his weight was reduced 35 lb. in the course of a few weeks, while his health underwent a marked improvement. Mr. Banting's experience induced many to follow his example, and in numerous instances the effects were all that could be desired. Such a rapid loss of weight is, however, apt to be attended with serious impairment of health, and, generally speaking, it is not advisable to aim at losing weight at a greater rate than about three or four pounds in each week.

Various Continental bathing-places have elaborate courses of treatment, in which rigid rules are laid down. Since a person submits himself more easily to, and obeys more implicitly, the rules in these places than he would do at home, such a ' cure ' is attended with special benefit.

Unless the individual is grossly overweight it is inadvisable to reduce weight too rapidly. Provided the diet is carefully adhered to, it is seldom necessary to give a diet containing less than 1000 to 1200 calories. Fats and carbohydrates must be reduced as much as possible. This means that sugar, sweets, jams, tinned fruit, pota-

toes and fried food must be banned. It is advisable to exclude all alcoholic liquors, but if the individual is so used to these that complete abstinence would be a real hardship, then a little dry wine may be allowed. Beer, sweet wines, spirits, and aerated waters must not be taken. Items which can be partaken of freely, include green vegetables (salad dressings must be made with vinegar or lemon juice, *not* olive oil), coffee (without milk), tea, and clear soups. Saccharine, of course, can be used freely for sweetening purposes.

The following is a sample diet which contains approximately 1100 calories :

Early Morning.—Glass of water.

Breakfast.—Orange or ½ grapefruit ; 1 thin slice of wholemeal bread ; 1 egg or 1 oz. of lean ham (cold) ; tea or black coffee.

Mid-morning.—One cup of tea.

Lunch.—Lean meat, liver, kidney, chicken, white fish or tripe (small helping) ; potatoes (small helping) and green vegetables ; stewed apple or pear with junket.

Tea.—1 thin slice of brown or wholemeal bread ; tomato, cress, or lettuce ; tea.

Dinner.—Clear soup ; small helping of white fish ; small helping of lean meat, chicken, or rabbit ; green vegetable ; fruit.

The amount of milk allowed daily is ½ to 1 pint, whilst not more than 1 ounce of butter (or margarine) must be taken every day,

Exercise should be abundant, and clothing should be light when an attempt is made to reduce corpulence, but care must be taken that the food is not at the same time increased to satisfy the sharpened appetite, or the effect of exercise is defeated. Sleep is a matter of importance. The person should go to bed early, and should limit the duration of rest to seven or at most eight hours, while the habit of sleeping during the day should be broken off.

In no circumstances should so-called ' slimming drugs ', such as amphetamine, be taken except under medical supervision.

COR PULMONALE is another name for pulmonary heart disease, which is characterized by hypertrophy and failure of the right ventricle of the heart as a result of disease of the lungs or disorder of the pulmonary circulation.

CORPUSCLE (*corpusculum*) means a small body. (*See* BLOOD.)

CORPUS LUTEUM is the mass of cells formed in the ruptured Graafian follicle in the ovary from which the ovum is discharged about fifteen days before the onset of the next menstrual period. When the ovum escapes the follicle fills up with blood. This is soon replaced by cells which contain a yellow fatty material. The follicle and its luteal cells constitute the corpus luteum. In the human the corpus luteum begins to disappear after ten days, unless the discharged ovum is fertilized and pregnancy ensues. In pregnancy the corpus luteum persists and grows and secretes the hormone progesterone (*q.v.*).

CORRIGAN PULSE is the name applied to the throbbing pulse found with incompetence of the aortic valve. It is so called after Sir Dominic John Corrigan (1802-80), the famous Dublin physician, who first described it.

CORROSIVES are poisonous substances which corrode or eat away the mucous surfaces of mouth, gullet, and stomach with which they come in contact. Examples are strong mineral acids like sulphuric, nitric, and hydrochloric acids, caustic alkalies, and some salts like chlorides of mercury and zinc. (*See* POISONS.)

CORROSIVE SUBLIMATE, or PERCHLORIDE OF MERCURY, is a powerful antiseptic and an irritant poison. It is not to be confounded with subchloride of mercury, or calomel. (*See* ANTISEPTICS, DISINFECTION, MERCURY.)

CORTICOSTEROIDS is the generic term for the group of hormones with a cortisone-like action.

CORTICOTROPHIN is the 'approved name' for A.C.T.H. (*q.v.*).

CORTISOL is another name for hydrocortisone (*q.v.*).

CORTISONE, originally known as Compound E, was isolated from beef adrenal glands in 1936 by workers at the Mayo Clinic. Its chemical name is 11-dehydro-17-hydroxycorticosterone. Mainly because of difficulties in obtaining adequate amounts, little interest was taken in it until, in 1949, Hench and Kendall and their colleagues demonstrated its dramatic, if transitory, effect in rheumatoid arthritis. The precise mode of action of cortisone is still not known, but it would appear to have a direct action on the tissues. Among other things, it prevents (or delays) the proliferative changes in the tissues which are the normal response to infection and in allergic conditions.

Among the conditions which have been shown to benefit from cortisone are rheumatoid arthritis, rheumatic fever, gout, certain eye conditions, and Addison's disease.

Cortisone has two disadvantages which will always tend to restrict its use. One is that in chronic conditions such as rheumatoid arthritis the effect of cortisone is merely temporary, and tends to stop when administration is stopped. The other is that cortisone has certain toxic effects, and therefore it must only be used under medical supervision.

For all practical purposes, A.C.T.H. (*q.v.*) and cortisone have the same action. (*See also* DEXAMETHASONE, HYDROCORTISONE, PREDNISOLONE, PREDNISONE, *and* TRIAMCINOLONE.

CORYZA (κόρυζα, a running at the nose) is the technical name of a 'cold in the head'.

COSTAL (*costa*, a rib) means anything pertaining to the ribs.

COSTALGIA means pain in the ribs.

COSTIVENESS (*see* CONSTIPATION).

COTTON-WOOL is a downy material made from the hairs on cotton plant seeds (*Gossypium barbadense*). Ordinary cotton-wool is non-absorbent, owing to its containing a considerable quantity of cotton-seed oil. The absorbent form is produced by removing this oil with alkalies. The non-absorbent wool is of great use for purposes of protection to injured parts by reason of its combined warmth and cheapness. It is highly inflammable. The absorbent wool is medicated with various substances, such as perchloride of mercury (sublimated wool), salicylic acid, etc., for use in dressings.

Cotton-seed oil can be used for purposes similar to those of olive oil, and taken in doses of ½ to 1 fluid ounce (14 to 28 ml.).

COUNTER-IRRITANTS (*see* BLISTERS AND COUNTER-IRRITANTS)

COW-POX is a disease affecting the udders of cows, on which it produces vesicles. It is communicable to man, and there has for centuries been a tradition that persons who have caught this cow-pox from cows do not suffer afterwards from smallpox. This formed the basis for Jenner's experiments on vaccination. (*See* VACCINATION.)

COXALGIA (*coxa*, the hip ; ἄλγος, pain) means pain in the hip-joint.

COXA VARA (*coxa*, the hip ; *varus*, bent outwards) is a condition in which the neck of the thigh-bone is bent so that the lower limbs are turned very much outwards and lameness results.

COXSACKIE VIRUSES are a group of viruses so-called because they were first isolated from two patients with a disease resembling paralytic poliomyelitis, in the village of Coxsackie in New York State. At least twenty-five distinct types have now been identified. They constitute one of the three groups of viruses included in the family of enteroviruses (*q.v.*). They are divided into two groups—A and B. Despite the large number of types of group A virus (19) in existence, evidence of their rôle in causing human disease is limited. Some, however, cause aseptic meningitis, and others cause a condition known as herpangina (*q.v.*). All 6 types of group B virus have been associated with outbreaks of aseptic meningitis, and they are also the cause of Bornholm disease (*q.v.*).

CRAB-LOUSE is another name for PHTHIRIUS INGUINALIS, a louse that infests the pubic region. (*See* INSECTS.)

CRACKED-POT SOUND is a peculiar resonance heard sometimes on percussion of the chest over a cavity in the lung, resembling the jarring sound heard on striking a cracked pot or bell.

CRADLE is the name applied to the cage which is placed over the legs of a patient in bed, in order to take the weight of the bed-clothes off the legs.

CRADLE CAP, or CRUSTA LACTEA as it is technically known, is the form of seborrhœa of the scalp which is not uncommon in nursing infants. It usually responds to an ointment containing equal parts of salicylic acid ointment of the *British National Formulary*, sulphur ointment B.P., and white soft paraffin B.P.

CRAMP is a painful spasmodic contraction of muscles, most frequently occurring in the limbs, but also apt to affect certain internal organs. This disorder belongs to the class of diseases known as local spasms, of which other varieties exist in such affections as spasmodic asthma, tetany, and colic. The cause of these painful seizures resides in the nervous system, and operates either directly from the great nerve centres, or, as is generally the case, indirectly by reflex action, as, for example, when attacks are brought on by some derangement of the digestive organs.

TEMPORARY CRAMP.—In its most common form, that of cramp in the limbs, this disorder comes on suddenly, often during sleep, the patient being aroused by an agonizing feeling of pain in the calf of the leg or back of the thigh. During the paroxysm the muscular fibres affected can often be felt gathered up into a hard knot. The attack in general lasts but a few seconds and then suddenly departs, the spasmodic contraction of the muscles ceasing entirely ; or, on the other hand, relief may come more gradually during a period of minutes or even hours. A liability to cramp is often associated with a rheumatic or gouty tendency, but occasional attacks are common enough apart from this, and are often induced by some special posture which a limb has assumed during sleep. Exposure of the limbs to cold will also bring on cramp. It is likewise of frequent occurrence in the process of parturition.

Treatment.—This painful disorder can be greatly relieved and often entirely removed by firmly grasping or briskly rubbing the affected part with the hand, or by anything which makes an impression on the nerves, such as the application of some cold substance

8

to the part, or occasionally by warmth. Even a sudden and vigorous movement of the limb, in such a direction as to stretch the affected muscle, will often succeed in terminating the attack.

CRAMP OF SWIMMERS includes usually spasm of the arteries as well as of the muscles, due to cold and exertion, so that death is apt to occur from stoppage of the heart. If treatment can be applied, friction of the limbs, warmth, and hot drinks are essential.

CRAMP OF THE STOMACH, or GASTRALGIA, usually is a symptom in connection with some form of gastric disorder (*see* STOMACH, DISEASES OF). For cramp affecting the muscular wall of the bowels, see COLIC.

HABIT SPASMS, or FUNCTIONAL SPASMS, are liable to occur in individuals of almost any handicraft, and are often extremely troublesome.

Writer's Cramp, or *Scrivener's Palsy,* is a spasm which affects certain muscles when engaged in the performance of acts the result of education and long usage, and which does not occur when the same muscles are employed in acts of a different kind. This disorder owes its name to the relative frequency with which it develops in persons who write much, although it is by no means confined to them.

The symptoms are in the first instance a gradually increasing difficulty experienced in conducting the movements required for executing the work in hand. At an early stage of the disease the difficulty may be to a large extent overcome by persevering efforts, but ultimately, when the attempt is persisted in, the muscles of the fingers, and occasionally also those of the forearm, are seized with spasm or cramp, so that the act of writing is rendered impossible. Sometimes the fingers, instead of being cramped, move in a disorderly manner and the pen cannot be grasped, while in other rare instances a kind of paralysis affects the muscles of the fingers, and they are powerless to make the movements necessary for holding the pen. It is to be noted that it is only in the act of writing that these phenomena present themselves, and that, for all other movements, the fingers and arms possess their natural power. Similar symptoms are observed and similar remarks apply

226

in the case of musicians, typists, telegraphists, artists, compositors, seamstresses, tailors, and many mechanics.

Spasmodic Wry-neck is one of the most frequent forms which the disease takes. This comes on in shoemakers, tailors, and persons generally whose employment necessitates their following, with the head, movements which the hands are making. The result is that the muscles of the neck assume the unpleasant habit of drawing the head to one side whenever the slightest attempt is made to turn and look at anything. Indeed, although actually a rare disease, no muscle or group of muscles which is specially called into action in any particular occupation is exempt from liability to this functional spasm, which is therefore ascribed to over-use of the parts concerned.

Treatment.—In the treatment of habit spasms, the only effectual remedy is absolute cessation for a time (it may be a month or longer) from the work with which the attack is associated. It is sometimes recommended that the opposite hand or limb be used, so as to afford the affected part entire rest, but this may be followed by the extension of the disorder to that locality also. Special forms of penholder and other mechanical contrivances have been suggested so as to enable the occupation to be carried on, but they do not afford any relief to the disease, for the cure of which entire rest is important. There is often a strong psychological element in such cases, and psychotherapy is indicated. Where the spasmodically acting muscles are not of great importance to the bodily economy, their action can be controlled by division of their nerves of supply. For example, spasmodic wry-neck can be checked by division of the spinal accessory nerve on one side of the neck. Such a procedure is out of the question in the case of the hand.

HEAT CRAMPS are painful contractions of muscles occurring in men (*e.g.* stokers) working in high temperatures. The cramps are due to excessive loss of salt in the sweat, and can be cured by giving salt water to drink.

CRANIAL NERVES (*see* BRAIN) are those arising from the brain.

CRANIUM (κρανίον) means the part of the skull enclosing the brain as distinguished from the face.

CRASIS (κρᾶσις, blend) is the term applied to the individual temperament or constitution. (*See* CONSTITUTION.)

CREAM is the oily or fatty part of milk from which butter is prepared. Average cream when purchased contains about 18 per cent. of fat. A food known as ' 20 per cent. cream ' consists of the upper 4 oz. skimmed off a quart of milk which has stood for twenty-four hours. Heavy cream or whipped cream may contain about 48 per cent. of fat. (*See* MILK.)
Various medicinal preparations are known also as cream, *e.g.* cold cream, which is a simple ointment containing rose-water, beeswax, borax, and almond oil scented with oil of rose.

CREAM OF TARTAR is another name for bitartrate of potassium.
Imperial Drink consists of a teaspoonful of cream of tartar, a squeeze of lemon, two lumps of sugar, and a pint of cold water.

CREATINE (κρέας, flesh) is a nitrogenous substance, methyl-guanidine-acetic-acid. In the adult human body there are about 120 grammes of it, and 98 per cent. of this is present in the muscles. Much of the creatine in muscle is combined with phosphoric acid as phosphocreatine, which plays an important part in the chemistry of muscular contraction.

CREATININE is the anhydride of creatine and is derived from it. It is purely a waste product.

CREMATION (*see* DEAD, DISPOSAL OF THE)

CREOLIN is a coal-tar product, useful for removing smells, if a few teaspoonfuls be added to a pint of water and the mixture be sprinkled on floors, etc. It has a powerful antiseptic action.

CREOSOTE, or CREASOTE, is a clear, yellow liquid, of aromatic smell and burning taste, prepared by distillation from pine-wood or from beech-wood, the product of the latter being of better quality. It mixes readily with alcohol, ether, chloroform, glycerin, and oils.

It is a powerful antiseptic and disinfectant. It has also a soothing action upon parts with which it is brought into contact. It is unchanged after absorption into the blood, and, being excreted by the lungs and exhaled on the breath, it exercises an effect upon these organs.

Uses.—Creosote is an ingredient of some disinfectant fluids ; it is also used in the form of a vapour, containing creosote 80 drops, light carbonate of magnesia 30 grains (2 G.), water 1 ounce (28·5 ml.), of which a teaspoonful is added to a pint (500 ml.) of hot water and inhaled in cases of suppurating throat, fœtid breath, etc. In cases of sea-sickness, it is sometimes given in doses of 2 to 10 drops o check the vomiting.

CREPITATIONS (*crepito*, I rattle) is the name applied to certain sounds which occur along with the breath sounds, as heard by auscultation, in various diseases of the lungs. They are signs of the presence of moist exudations in the lungs or in the bronchial tubes, are classified as fine, medium, and coarse crepitations, and resemble the sound made by bursting bubbles of various sizes.

CREPITUS (*crepitus*) means a grating sound. It is found in cases of fractured bones when the ends rub together ; also in cases of severe chronic arthritis by the rubbing together of the dried internal surfaces of the joints.

CRESOL, or METHYL PHENOL, is an oily liquid obtained from the tar distilled out of coal, beechwood, or pine. It is a powerful antiseptic and disinfectant.
Uses.—It is used combined with soap to form a clear saponaceous fluid which can be mixed with water in any proportions. For the disinfection of linen, bed-pans, drains, or surgical instruments a convenient strength is 2 per cent. (one tablespoonful to 1¼ pints (600 ml.) of water) ; for washing the hands 1 per cent. (one tablespoonful to 2½ pints (1·25 litres)) and for a douche ½ per cent. (one tablespoonful to 5 pints (2·5 litres are)) commonly used.

CRETA is a Latin name for chalk.

227

CRETINISM (Swiss *crétin*, a Christian) is a disease which is due to defective thyroid function in fœtal life or early in infancy. It can usually be recognized within a few weeks of birth. Not only is the mind feeble, but the whole body remains undeveloped, and there are deformities of the bones, changes in the thyroid gland, and a swollen condition of the skin. The defect in the thyroid gland is responsible for most of the other bodily and mental peculiarities. If untreated, the affected child rarely reaches middle age. The condition is met with particularly in Switzerland, Northern Italy, and Tyrol, but cases crop up now and then in England, America, etc.

Treatment consists in giving extract of thyroid regularly and in attending to the general health : it is important for the disease to be diagnosed at an early stage if treatment is to have effect.

CRISIS (κρίσις, a decision) is a word used with several distinct meanings.

1. The usual meaning is that of a rapid loss of fever and return to comparative health in certain acute diseases. For example, pneumonia, if allowed to run its natural course, ends by a ' crisis ', usually on the eighth day, the temperature falling in twenty-four hours to normal, the pulse and breathing becoming slow and regular, and the patient passing from a partly delirious state into natural sleep. The opposite mode of ending to crisis is by ' lysis ', for example, in typhoid fever, where the patient slowly improves during a period of a week or more, without any sudden change.

2. A popular use of the word 'crisis', and still more frequently of ' critical ', is to signify a dangerous state of illness in which it is uncertain whether the sufferer will recover or not.

3. The word ' crisis ' is also used to signify a paroxysm of pain in the larynx, stomach, or bowels occurring during the course of locomotor ataxia.

CROHN'S DISEASE (*see* ILEITIS).

CROTON OIL is a powerful purgative, seldom used now, producing copious watery evacuations, and, in large quantities, acting as an irritant poison.

Externally, croton liniment is used as a counter-irritant.

CROUP is a household term for a group of diseases characterized by swelling and partial blockage of the entrance to the larynx, occurring in children and characterized by crowing inspiration. There are various causes including diphtheritic laryngitis (*see* DIPHTHERIA), acute laryngitis, laryngismus stridulus (*q.v.*), and laryngo-tracheo-bronchitis (*q.v.*), and the condition known as spasmodic croup or laryngismus stridulosa. It is an account of this last condition which will be given here.

The important thing to remember about any form of croup is that it is always potentially dangerous—particularly in the case of an infant—because of the narrowness of the entrance to the larynx and therefore the comparative ease with which it may be blocked, thereby leading to suffocation of the infant.

Symptoms. — The attack usually comes on at night, when the child is in bed, and follows a chill caught during the day, or an ordinary cold that has lasted perhaps for some days. The breathing is hoarse and croaking (hence the name of the disease), the voice thin, the cough paroxysmal and metallic in tone, and the air passes in with a harsh, loud noise. The child is frightened and excited at first, but later gets feeble and livid. Still later, pallor, sweating, and great struggling for breath come on, and may last half an hour or several hours. After this the symptoms begin to abate, gradually pass away, and the child falls asleep, but there is always a danger that the larynx may become completely blocked, in which case death ensues in a few minutes. A fatal termination is rare if the child receives proper treatment, and the alarming symptoms usually abate on the day following the attack, to return, it may be, on the succeeding night. A child who has once had croup is liable to have future attacks, and so should be specially guarded against cold and damp till he has outgrown the tendency.

Treatment.—The child should be put into a hot bath to which a tablespoonful of mustard has been added, and a tent should be made with a blanket over the bath, so that he may inhale the steam. When he is put back into bed the tent should be put over the bed and the nozzle of a steam kettle brought within it. To the water in the kettle may be added a teaspoonful of compound tincture of benzoin, of vapour of creosote (*see* CREOSOTE), or of other soothing substance. At the commencement, an attack is often checked by the administration of a teaspoonful of ipecacuanha wine every ten minutes till vomiting takes place. Sometimes, when the spasm of the laryngeal muscles seems very great, inhalation of chloroform is resorted to.

CRYOSURGERY is the use of cold in surgery. Its main scope is in the fields of brain and eye surgery. For this purpose liquid nitrogen is usually used, with which temperatures as low as − 140° C. can be obtained.

CRUCIATE LIGAMENTS (*crux*, a cross) are two strong ligaments in the interior of the knee-joint, which cross one another like the limbs of the letter X. They are so attached as to become taut when the lower limb is straightened, and they prevent over-extension or bending forwards at the knee.

CRURAL (*crus*, the leg) means something connected with the leg.

CRUSH SYNDROME is the term given to a condition in which kidney failure occurs in patients who have been the victims of severe crushing accidents. The fundamental injury is damage to muscle. The limb swells. The blood volume falls. Blood urea rises ; there is also a rise in the potassium content of the blood. The patient may survive ; or he dies with renal failure. Post - mortem examination shows degeneration of the tubules of the kidney, and the presence in them of pigment casts.

CRUTCH-PALSY (*see* DROP-WRIST).

CRYMOTHERAPY is the term applied to the treatment of disease by refrigeration. The two main forms in which it is now used are HYPOTHERMIA (*q.v.*) and REFRIGERATION ANÆSTHESIA. Perhaps the best example of the latter is when a gangrenous leg in chronic diabetes or arteriosclerosis is kept by means of ice bags at a temperature of 5° C. for from 1 to 5 hours. This form of anæsthesia much reduces the risks of shock and infection.

CRYOSCOPY (κρύος, frost ; σκοπέω, I examine) means the method of finding the concentration of blood, urine, etc., by observing their freezing-point.

CUBEBS is the fruit of *Piper cubeba*, used similarly to copaiba (*q.v.*).

CULDOSCOPY is the term applied to the method of examining the pelvic organs in women by means of an instrument comparable to a cystoscope (*q.v.*) inserted into the pelvic cavity through the vagina. The instrument used for this purpose is known as a culdoscope.

CUPPING is used in cases of deep-seated congestion to draw blood to the surface. It causes sudden dilatation of the superficial blood-vessels, and so probably contracts those of underlying organs. But whatever the explanation, it gives relief in difficulty of breathing due to asthma, bronchitis, and heart disease, and relieves congestion of the kidneys in acute Bright's disease. Cupping is of two kinds, *dry-cupping* and *wet-cupping*. To dry-cup, one takes a cupping-glass (or an ordinary thick glass tumbler), puts a few drops of methylated spirit upon a fragment of blotting-paper into it, ignites this, and, while it is still burning, claps the mouth of the glass tightly on the back of the patient. A vacuum is produced, and the skin swells up into the glass as blood rushes into its small blood-vessels. This is repeated four, six, or eight times in different places. Wet-cupping is rarely used these days. The skin is first dry-cupped, the swollen skin is next scarified with a lancet or a special instrument for the purpose, and then the cupping-glass is again applied, and blood drawn off into it. The vacuum for dry- or wet-cupping may also be produced by a suction bulb.

CUPRALUM is a disinfectant, composed of copper sulphate, alum, bichromate of potassium, and terebene.

CUPRUM is the Latin word for copper.

CURARE, known also as CURARA, WOORARI, WOURALI, URARI, and TICUNAS, is a dark-coloured extract from some trees of the *Strychnos* family. It is used by the South American Indians

229

as an arrow poison, and is extremely potent, its action depending upon a crystalline alkaloid—d-tubocurarine chloride. This alkaloid paralyses the nerve endings in muscle. For many years it was considered to be much too dangerous for use in man, but recent research has shown that the pure alkaloid can be used with safety, and it is now being used on an increasing scale. Its main use is in anæsthesia. where the muscular relaxation it produces is of invaluable assistance to the surgeon. With the aid of tubocurarine adequate muscular relaxation can be obtained with a lesser degree of anæsthesia than would be required were the drug not being used. It is a drug, however, that should only be used by a skilled anæsthetist. Its action is antagonized by prostigmine. It has also been used in the treatment of spastic conditions.

CURDLED MILK (see CASEIN).

CURETTE, or CURET, is a spoon-shaped instrument used in surgery for scooping out the contents of any cavity of the body, e.g. the uterine cavity.

CUSHING'S SYNDROME is the term applied to the changes that take place in the body as the result of a tumour of the pituitary gland. The changes are : obesity, hairiness, curvature of the spine, impotence, and the appearance of red lines in the skin. Cushing was a famous American brain surgeon who died in 1939.

CUSPARIA, or ANGOSTURA, is the dried bark of Galipea cusparia, a tree of tropical America. An infusion is used as a bitter, in doses of one, two, or more tablespoonfuls.

CUTANEOUS (cutis, the skin) means belonging to the skin. (See SKIN DISEASES.)

CUTICLE (see SKIN).

CUTS (see WOUNDS).

CUT-THROAT is an injury which may be due to suicide or murder, an expert being able to tell at a glance the one from the other. Death, when it occurs at once, is usually due to bleeding from the large vessels of the neck, and later may be caused by inflamma-

230

tion of the air passages. Another danger is that air will enter the large veins in such amount as to bring the circulation of the blood to a standstill. In a case of cut-throat, if any vessel be seen to bleed, the hæmorrhage should be checked by pressure with the finger till surgical assistance can be obtained.

CYANIDES are salts of hydrocyanic or prussic acid. They are highly poisonous, and are also powerful antiseptics. (See PRUSSIC ACID, WOUNDS.) Double cyanide of mercury and zinc is specially powerful as an antiseptic used to impregnate gauze and cotton - wool for dressing wounds.

CYANOCOBALAMIN is the name given by the British Pharmacopœia Commission to vitamin B_{12}. It is a red cobalt-containing substance, and it owes its name to the fact that it contains cyanide and cobalt. Vitamin B_{12} was first isolated in 1948 and was found to be an effective substitute for liver in the treatment of pernicious anæmia (see ANÆMIA). Its precise mode of action in pernicious anæmia is not known, but either it or hydroxocobalamin (q.v.) is now the standard treatment for this condition. (See COBALAMINS.)

CYANOSIS (κυάνεος, blue) is a condition of blueness seen particularly about the face and extremities, accompanying states in which the blood is not properly oxygenated in the lungs. It appears earliest through the nails, on the tips of the ears, and over the cheeks. It may be due to blockage of the air passages, or to disease in the lungs, or to a feeble circulation, as in heart disease.

CYBERNETICS is the science of communication and control in the animal and in the machine—a science which has come very much to the fore since the introduction of the modern computers.

CYCLOPHOSPHAMIDE is a nitrogen mustard derivative (q.v.) which is proving of value in the treatment of various forms of malignant disease, including Hodgkin's disease.

CYCLOPLEGIA denotes paralysis of the ciliary muscle of the eye, which results in the loss of power of accommodation in the eye. (*See* ACCOM-MODATION.)

CYCLOPROPANE ($CH_2 . CH_2 . CH_2$) is an anæsthetic gas which has come into increasing use during recent years.

CYCLOSERINE is an antibiotic, derived from an actinomycete, which is of value in the treatment of certain infections of the genito-urinary tract, and of limited value in the treatment of tuberculosis.

CYCLOTHYMIA is the state characterized by extreme swings of mood from elation to depression, and vice-versa.

CYESIS is another term for pregnancy.

CYNANCHE (κυνάγκη) is an old name for severe sore throat with choking. (*See* QUINSY.)

CYRTOMETER (κυρτός, curved ; μέτρον, a measure) is an instrument for measuring the shape of the chest.

CYSTITIS (κύστις, a bladder) means inflammation of the bladder. (*See* BLADDER, DISEASES OF.)

CYSTOSCOPE (κύστις, the bladder ; σκοπέω, I view) is an instrument for viewing the interior of the bladder. It consists of a narrow tube carrying a small electric lamp at its end, a small mirror set obliquely opposite an opening near the end of the tube, and a telescope which is passed down the tube and by which the reflection of the brightly illuminated bladder wall in the

FIG. 101.—Cystoscope, showing (above) the telescope which is passed down the interior in order to see the interior of the bladder ; also two catheters which can be passed up the ureters to the kidneys.

mirror is examined. It is of great value in the diagnosis of conditions like ulcers and small tumours of the bladder.

Fine catheters can be passed along the cystoscope, and by the aid of vision can be inserted into each ureter and pushed up to the kidney, so that the urine from each kidney may be obtained and examined separately in order to diagnose which of these organs is diseased.

CYSTS (κύστις, a bladder) are hollow tumours, containing fluid or soft material. They are almost always simple in nature and seldom return after removal, though in the case of certain types there are apt to be several of various sizes.

Varieties.—(*a*) RETENTION CYSTS.— In these some cavity which ought naturally to contain a little fluid becomes, in consequence of irritation or other cause, distended to a great extent, or the natural outlet from the cavity becomes blocked. Wens are caused by the blockage of the outlet from sebaceous glands in the skin, so that an accumulation of fatty matter takes place. Ranula is a clear swelling under the tongue, due to a collection of saliva in consequence of an obstruction to a salivary duct. Cysts in the breasts are, in many cases, the result of blockage in milk ducts, due to inflammation. Cysts also form in the kidney as a result of obstruction to the free outflow of the urine.

(*b*) DEVELOPMENTAL CYSTS. — Of these the most important are the huge cysts that originate in the ovaries. The cause is doubtful, but the cyst commences probably at a very early period of life, gradually enlarges, and buds off smaller cysts from its wall. The contents are usually a clear gelatinous fluid. Very often both ovaries are affected, and the cysts may slowly reach a great size, often, however, taking a lifetime to do so.

A similar condition sometimes occurs in the kidney, and the tumour may have reached a great size in an infant even before birth (congenital cystic kidney).

Dermoid cysts are small cavities, which also originate probably early in life, but do not reach any great size till fairly late in life. They appear about parts of the body where clefts occur in the embryo and close up before birth, such as the corner of the eyes, the side of the neck, the middle line of the body. They contain hair, fatty matter, fragments of bone, scraps of skin, even numerous teeth.

(c) HYDATID CYSTS are produced in many organs, particularly in the liver, by a parasite which is the larval stage of a tapeworm found in dogs. They occur in people who keep dogs and allow them to contaminate their food. (*See* PARASITES.)

CYTO- (κύτος, a cell) is a prefix meaning something connected with a cell or cells.

CYTODIAGNOSIS means diagnosis of disease by examining the cells found in blood effusions from cavities, etc.

CYTOMETER is an instrument for counting and measuring cells.

D

DA COSTA'S SYNDROME is another name for the EFFORT SYNDROME (*q.v.*).

DACRYOCYSTITIS (δάκρυον, a tear ; κύστις, a bladder) means inflammation of the tear-sac at the side of the nose, near the inner angle of the eye.

DACTYLITIS (δάκτυλος, a finger) means inflammation of a finger or toe.

D.A.H. is an abbreviation for DISORDERED ACTION OF THE HEART. (*See* EFFORT SYNDROME.)

DAMP is the name applied generally by miners to noxious gases in a mine. ' Fire damp ' is an explosive mixture of gases, chiefly marsh gas. ' After damp ' or ' white damp ' is the term applied to carbon monoxide. ' Choke damp ' and ' stink damp ' are terms applied to an evil-smelling mixture of gases following the use of explosives containing sulphuretted hydrogen and other irritating compounds. ' Black damp ' is the name applied to the stagnant air of old workings and wells from which the oxygen has disappeared, and which consists of nitrogen and carbon dioxide. (*See* AIR, VENTILATION, COAL-GAS, ASPHYXIA.)

DANDELION (*see* TARAXACUM).

DANDRUFF (*see* BALDNESS).

DANDY-FEVER is another name for dengue (*q.v.*).

DANGEROUS DRUGS. This term is applied to certain drugs which are scheduled under the Dangerous Drugs Act, and which must be dispensed only under certain stringent regulations. These include morphine, cocaine, ecgonine, diamorphine (commonly known as heroin), extracts and tinctures of Indian hemp and opium, as well as any preparation containing one part in 500 or more of morphine or one part in 1000 or more of cocaine, ecgonine, or diamorphine. Certain preparations of opium are exempted, such as opium plaster, liniment of opium, Dover's powder and ointment of galls and opium, and hospitals are also exempted from the provisions of the regulations in regard to these drugs. Prescriptions containing any of these drugs must be written, dated, and signed by a practitioner, and must give the name and address of the person for whom the prescription is intended, as well as the total amount of the drug to be supplied.

All other poisonous substances are scheduled in twelve classes, the important ones from the medical point of view being those included in the first and fourth schedules. The substances included in the First Schedule are those containing the more deadly poisons, which may not be sold by chemists except to persons known to the seller, and regarding which the name and address of the purchaser must be entered in a book. The Fourth Schedule includes less potent poisons, such as amidopyrine, barbituric acid and its derivatives, dinitrophenol, sulphonal, and tridione. A prescription for any substance in Schedule Four must contain the prescriber's name, the name and address of the seller, and the date on which the prescription was dispensed. It must not be dispensed more than once unless the prescriber directs that it be dispensed a stated number of times or at stated intervals.

DAPSONE is the *British Pharmacopœia* name for 4 : 4'–diaminodiphenylsulphone, which is proving one of the most effective drugs in the treatment of leprosy.

DARTOS is the thin muscle just under the skin of the scrotum which enables the scrotum to alter its shape.

DAY BLINDNESS is a condition in which the patient sees better in a dim light or by night than in daylight. It is only found in conditions in which the light is very glaring, as in the desert and on snow, and is relieved by resting the retina, for example by wearing coloured glasses for a time.

D.D.T. is the generally used abbreviation for the compound 1, 1 bis (4 chlorophenyl) 2, 2, 2-trichloroethane, which has now been given the official name of dicophane. It was first synthesized in 1874, but it was not until 1940 that, as a result of research work in Switzerland, its remarkable toxic action on insects was discovered. This work was taken up and rapidly expanded in Great Britain and America, and one of its first practical applications was in controlling the spread of typhus. This disease is transmitted by the louse, one of the insects for which D.D.T. is most toxic. Its toxic action against the mosquito has also been amply proved, and it is thus rapidly becoming one of the most effective measures in controlling malaria. D.D.T. is toxic to a large range of insects in addition to the louse and the mosquito; these include house-flies, bed-bugs, clothes-moths, fleas, cockroaches, and ants. It is also active against many agricultural and horticultural pests, including weevils, flour beetles, pine sawfly, and most varieties of scale insect.

D.D.T. has thus a wide use in medicine, public health, veterinary medicine, horticulture, and agriculture, both in temperate and tropical zones. Like all potent preparations, however, its indiscriminate use is not without danger. Thus, it is toxic to bees and a number of parasites of fruit pests, and may therefore do as much harm as good if used indiscriminately as a horticultural spray. Again, if used to kill fleas in animals such as cats, which lick themselves, care must be taken in using it, as it may be toxic when swallowed. It is quite safe when applied to the skin, either in man or animals, in a watery solution, but if applied in an oily solution it may be rapidly absorbed and produce toxic effects. When used for domestic purposes or on animals, it is usually applied as a 5 per cent. dust. Full details concerning its use may be obtained from the many leaflets and booklets issued by the manufacturers, by government departments, and by agricultural and horticultural institutes.

Finally, there is the most worrying factor of all : the increasing number of species of insects which are becoming resistant to D.D.T. Fortunately, to date newer insecticides have been introduced which are toxic to D.D.T.-resistant insects, but there is a certain amount of anxiety as to whether this supply of new insecticides can be maintained.

DEAD, DISPOSAL OF THE. — Practically, only three methods have

been used from the earliest times : (a) burial ; (b) embalming ; (c) cremation.

(a) **Burial** is perhaps the earliest and most primitive method, and, because of its practice among the Jews, and the popularly accepted idea as to the resurrection of the body, has become intimately bound up with the Christian religion. It was customary to bury the bodies of the dead in consecrated ground around the churches till the earlier half of the nineteenth century, when the utterly insanitary state of churchyards led to legislation for their better control, and now that cemeteries are supposed to be situated outside towns and in proper sites, the interment of the dead should seldom be a menace to the health of the living. If a light coffin and porous soil surround the body its decay should be rapid and harmless, and in a year or two only the bones should remain (see PUTREFACTION). Burials in Britain take place usually upon production of a certificate from a registrar of deaths, to whom notice of the death, accompanied by a medical certificate, must be given without delay by the nearest relatives.

(b) **Embalming** was practised by several races of antiquity, notably by the Egyptians, with the view of preserving from decay the bodies of dead friends. It is still used to a certain extent. The process consists in removing the internal organs by small openings and filling the body cavities with various aromatics of antiseptic power, the skin being swathed in bandages or otherwise protected from the action of the air. Bodies are also preserved by injecting the blood-vessels with strong antiseptics like perchloride of mercury. In certain circumstances bodies become naturally changed to a non-putrefying substance known as adipocere.

(c) **Cremation** was practised among the Greeks and the early Aryan races generally, and furnishes a much speedier reduction of the body to its simple components than does burial, and one devoid of any harmful tendencies to the living. Not the least of its advantages is the amount of space that is saved and can thereby be devoted to more useful and practical purposes. It is being used to an increasing extent.

In order to prevent any abuse, special certificates are required, and the necessary forms for these are obtained from the cremating authority. The law does not distinguish in England or America between cremation and burial, but special formalities are insisted upon by the crematorium authorities. The ceremony is conducted similarly to a burial ceremony, the coffin is lowered from the mortuary chapel, through an opening, on to a trolley which bears it direct to the furnace. The process of incineration takes between one and two hours. About five to seven pounds of ash result from the combustion of the body, and there is no admixture with that from the fuel.

DEAD FINGERS (*see* RAYNAUD'S DISEASE).

DEADLY NIGHTSHADE is the popular name of *Atropa belladonna*, from which atropine is procured. Its poisonous black berries are sometimes eaten by children. (*See* ATROPINE, *and* BERRIES, POISONOUS.)

DEAFNESS is divided into three classes, according to the section of the ear at fault.

EXTERNAL EAR is the passage, about 1½ inches in length, leading inward from the surface to the drum. When the deafness has its cause in this part, it is due simply to obstruction of the passage by a tumour, by a foreign body, such as a pea, or a polypus, or, most commonly of all, by a plug of hardened wax.

MIDDLE EAR is the tympanic cavity separated by the tympanic membrane from the outer ear, and communicating with the mastoid antrum, a hollow in the skull, behind, and with the Eustachian tube, which leads to the throat, beneath. These communications are important, because the connection with the throat explains the deafness that accompanies cold in the head and other forms of inflammation which spread from the nose and throat up into the middle ear; while the connection with the antrum shows why suppuration in the antrum causes great destruction of the delicate mechanism in the middle ear. Acute inflammation in the throat, for example in scarlatina and measles, or chronic conditions like adenoids in children, are very liable to produce middle-ear disease, perforation of the drum, and deafness. Tearing of the drum in consequence of a box on the ear, or of an explosion, as a rule heals and leaves no deafness; but a perforation following inflammation in the antrum or middle ear is accompanied by suppuration, discharge from the ear, and other changes, and generally attended by impairment of hearing. It is a peculi-

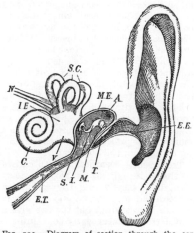

FIG. 102.—Diagram of section through the ear. *EE*, external, *ME*, middle, *IE*, internal ear; *T*, tympanic membrane; *M*, malleus; *I*, incus; *S*, stapes; *A*, opening to mastoid antrum; *ET*, Eustachian tube; *C*, cochlea; *SC*, semicircular canals; *V*, utricle; *N*, auditory nerve. (Schmeil's *Zoology*.)

arity of deafness in middle-ear disease that the hearing is often better during a loud noise; for example, a conversation is more clearly heard while church bells are ringing, or in the noise of a railway train.

INTERNAL EAR AND BRAIN constitute the receptive and perceptive apparatus for sound, the outer and middle ear forming parts of the conducting and collecting apparatus. Certain fevers like typhus and typhoid, tumours of the brain, meningitis, Ménière's disease, mumps, and fractures of the base of the skull may all bring on a greater or less degree of deafness by interference with the perceptive apparatus. Some drugs produce a temporary deafness, notably quinine and salicin.

Boiler-maker's disease is a condition

of deafness due apparently to a gradual wearing out of the nervous mechanism by the constant noise of hammering, and comes on in a few years, especially in boiler-makers, but also in sawyers, threshing-mill tenders, and persons similarly subject to constant noise. The term, boiler-maker's disease, is now a misnomer as there are so many working conditions under which noise is a major hazard to hearing. The amount of deafness due to excessive noise at work is turning out to be much higher than was suspected, and at long last steps are being taken to reduce to a minimum the amount of unnecessary noise in industry. Where the amount of noise cannot be reduced to a safe level, then workmen must be supplied with effective ear-protection. No ear-protector, however, is an effective substitute for a safe level of sound.

The hereditary form of deafness known as otosclerosis (q.v.) comes on in several members of some families shortly after puberty, owing to hardening changes in the inner ear.

Treatment.—Deafness due to causes in the external ear is readily dealt with, and, considering the frequency of hardened wax, it is a good and safe procedure to syringe out the ear with a tumblerful of warm water containing a teaspoonful of baking soda (bicarbonate). The stream of water is directed along the upper wall of the passage and flows out below. In cases where deafness accompanies nasal catarrh, adenoids, enlarged tonsils, etc., these conditions must be remedied by nasal douches, gargles, operation, etc. (see NOSE, DISEASES OF). In a case of perforation of the drum, accompanied by a chronic discharge, particular care must be taken to keep the ear clean, because there is otherwise a danger not only of increased deafness but of retained matter infecting some neighbouring part, and causing dangerous abscess in the brain, meningitis, or suppuration in the mastoid antrum (see EAR, DISEASES OF). Boiler-maker's deafness generally improves if the occupation be changed, otherwise it grows steadily worse. Deaf-mutism is a condition where deafness has been complete from early life, usually from birth, and the child has never learned to speak, though the voice-producing

236

organs are perfect. Such children can with patience, be taught to carry on a fluent conversation by means of 'lip-reading', or by the finger language and signs (see DUMBNESS).

Various aids to hearing have been devised. Speaking-tubes and trumpets give some help and have the great advantage of simplicity and low cost. On the other hand, amplification is limited and they are cumbersome to carry about. There are now several satisfactory midget valve amplifier hearing aids available. These instruments are highly successful in the case of many deaf persons, though not of great use in others. Each instrument requires to be carefully tuned for the deaf person using it. Before deciding to use a hearing aid the advice of an ear specialist should be obtained. The National Institute for the Deaf, 105 Gower Street, London, W.C.1, provides a list of clinics where such a specialist can be consulted. It also gives reliable advice concerning the purchase and use of hearing aids.

DEAMINATION is the term applied to the process of removal of the amino group, NH_2, from amino-acids not required for building up body protein. This is carried out mainly in the liver by means of an enzyme, deaminase. The fatty acid residue is either ' burnt up ' to yield energy, or is converted into glucose.

DEATH, CAUSES OF. — Although the final cause of death is usually failure

	1948	1952	1954	1956	1966
Tuberculosis .	4·6	2·1	1·6	1·0	0·4
Cancer .	17·4	17·6	18·0	17·8	19·2
Circulatory disease .	33·7	36·8	37·1	37·2	37·0
Respiratory disease .	9·9	10·5	10·0	11·5	13·6
Digestive disease .	3·7	3·3	3·2	3·0	2·7
Genito-urinary disease .	3·0	2·6	2·5	2·2	1·6
Accidents, poisonings, and violence .	3·9	3·8	4·2	4·2	3·0

TABLE 13.—Percentage Contribution of Nine Principal Causes of Death to all Causes, in England and Wales in 1948–66.

of the vital centres which govern the beating of the heart and the act of breathing, the practical question is the disease or injury which leads to this failure. A general idea of the extent to which different causes operate in terminating life can be obtained from table 13.

DEATH SIGNS OF.—There are some minor signs, such as relaxation of the facial muscles, which produces the staring eye and gaping mouth of the *Hippocratic countenance*, as well as a loss of the curves of the back, which becomes flat by contact with the bed or table ; *discoloration of the skin*, which becomes of a wax-yellow hue, and loses its pink transparency at the finger-webs ; *absence of blistering and redness* if the skin be burned (Christison's sign) ; and *failure of a ligature* tied round the finger to produce, after its removal, the usual change of a white ring, which, after a few seconds, becomes redder than the surrounding skin in a living person.

Most important for the immediate recognition of death are *stoppage of the heart* for five minutes, as listened for by placing the ear on the chest at the inner side of the left nipple, and *cessation of breathing*, as noted by observing that a mirror held before the mouth shows no haze, that a feather placed on the upper lip does not flutter, or that the reflection on the ceiling from a cup of water placed on the chest of the dead person shows no movement. An important sign is that if a cut be made in the skin or a vessel be opened no bleeding takes place after death.

Four points are important in determining the time that has elapsed since death. *Hypostasis*, or congestion, begins to appear as livid spots on the back, often mistaken for bruises, four hours or more after death. It is due to the blood running into the vessels in the lowest parts. *Loss of heat* begins at once after death, and the body has become as cold as the surrounding air after 15 or 20 hours, though this is delayed by hot weather, death from asphyxia, and some other causes. *Rigidity* begins at 4 to 10 hours after death in the muscles of the neck, spreads to the other muscles, and is complete a few hours later, remaining for 2 to 4 days, and passing gradually off. It comes on more quickly after death from wasting diseases, and often

suddenly after injuries to the brain, so that a suicide may be found firmly grasping the revolver with which he has shot himself. If a joint be forcibly bent, rigidity does not return, while in the rigidity of catalepsy such a joint becomes as stiff as before. *Putrefaction* is a certain sign, and begins in 2 or 3 days, as a greenish tint over the abdomen (*see* PUTREFACTION).

DEBILITY (*debilitas*) means a state of weakness in which the body or one of its systems becomes unable to bear strains put upon it, or even, in severe cases, to discharge the ordinary functions of life. The condition may be hereditary, or may be an early stage of some disease, such as tuberculosis, or come on as a developmental change.

Treatment.—The cause must, so far as possible, be removed. The essential is rest, combined with regulated exercises, and good food. The person must be specially guarded, for the time being, from strains of all sorts and exposure to infectious diseases.

DEBRISOQUINE is one of the many new hypotensive agents which is proving of value in the treatment of high blood pressure.

DECAPSULATION is the term applied to an operation performed upon the kidney in some cases of Bright's disease. The capsule is stripped off, so that the kidney may expand.

DECHOLIN is a proprietary term for dehydrocholic acid, obtained from bile acid. Administration of dehydrocholic acid is said to raise the pressure in the bile passages and thus to be of possible value in expelling gall-stones from them.

DECIBEL is the unit of hearing. One decibel is the least intensity of sound at which a given note can be heard. The usual abbreviation for decibel is db.

DECIDUA (*decido*, I fall off) is the name of the soft coat which lines the interior of the womb during pregnancy and which is cast off at birth.

DECOCTION (*decoquo*, I boil down) is the name for a preparation made by boiling various plants in water and straining the fluid. Examples are decoction of broom-tops, of cinchona, and of sarsaparilla. The dose of all is from one to several tablespoonfuls.

DECOMPENSATION means a failing condition of the heart after compensation has been established in a case of valvular disease.

DECUBITUS (*decumbo*, I lie down) is the name applied to the peculiar positions taken up in bed by patients suffering from various conditions. For example, patients with pleurisy or pneumonia prefer to lie upon the affected side ; patients suffering from peritonitis, on the back ; much exhausted persons, far down in the bed. The bed sores (*q.v.*) which such patients are liable to develop are known as decubitus ulcers (*see* BATHS).

DECUSSATION (*decussatio*) is a term applied to any point in the nervous system at which nerve fibres cross from one side to the other, *e.g.* the decussation of the pyramidal tracts in the medulla, where the motor fibres from one side of the brain cross to the other side of the spinal cord.

DEFÆCATION (*defæco*, I cleanse) means the act of opening the bowels. (*See* CONSTIPATION, DIARRHŒA.)

DEFICIENCY DISEASE is the term applied to any disease resulting from the absence from the diet of any substance essential to good health, *e.g.* one of the vitamins.

DEFORMITIES may be present at birth, or they may be the result of injuries, of disease, or simply produced by bad habits, like the curved spine occasionally found in children. (*See* BURNS ; CHEST, DEFORMITIES OF ; CLUB-FOOT ; FINGERS ; FLAT-FOOT ; KNOCK-KNEE ; LEPROSY ; PALATE, DEFECTS OF : PARALYSIS ; RICKETS ; SCAR ; SKULL ; SPINE, DISEASES OF : JOINTS, DISEASES OF.)

DEGENERATION (*degenero*, I degenerate) means a change in structure or in chemical composition of a tissue or organ by which its vitality is lowered or its function interfered with. Degeneration is of various kinds, the chief being fatty, fibroid (*see* CIRRHOSIS),

238

calcareous (*see* CONCRETIONS), waxy (*see* WAXY DISEASE), colloid, and mucoid.

Causes of degeneration are, in many cases, very obscure. In some cases heredity plays a part, particular organs, for example the kidneys, tending to show fibroid changes in successive generations. Fatty, fibroid, and calcareous degenerations are part of the natural change in old age. Defective nutrition may bring them on prematurely, so may excessive and long-continued strain upon an organ like the heart. Various poisons, like alcohol, play a special part in producing the changes, and so do the poisons produced by various diseases, particularly syphilis and tuberculosis.

DEGLUTITION (*deglutio*, I swallow) means the act of swallowing. (*See* CHOKING.)

DELHI BOIL is a form of chronic sore occurring in Eastern countries, caused by a protozoan parasite, *Leishmania tropica*.

DELIRIUM (*deliro*, I rave) is a state of perverted consciousness in which an irregular discharge of nervous energy goes on, causing incoherent talk, delusions, and ill-regulated muscular action.

Varieties.—There are three types :

Low DELIRIUM is associated with exhaustion, and consists mainly of muttering or rambling talk, in which past events are jumbled together. Surrounding persons and objects are not heeded, or their identity is totally mistaken. The fingers are sometimes busily employed in picking at the bed-clothes, or there is a constant twitching of the muscles in the arms, legs, and face, which is a sign of great weakness.

TREMBLING DELIRIUM (delirium tremens) is the form most commonly due to alcoholism (*see* ALCOHOLISM, ACUTE). In this form the mind is more active and delusions more extraordinary. Trembling is a specially marked feature, particularly in the early stages.

RAVING DELIRIUM sometimes appears in acute fevers, often is due to alcoholism, and is characterized by violent activity of the muscular system, acting in response to such wild delusions that it may result in suicide or homicide.

Treatment is, as a rule, the treatment of the fever, etc., which causes the delirium. (*See also* ALCOHOLISM, ACUTE.) As the delirium in fevers is due partly to high temperature but mainly to nervous exhaustion, good feeding, careful nursing, and stimulants are specially necessary. When delirium banishes sleep and aggravates exhaustion, sleeping draughts are often necessary, such as paraldehyde or one of the barbiturates, and in severe cases even morphine and/or hyoscine.

DELIVERY means the final expulsion of the child in the act of birth. (*See* LABOUR.)

DELTA WAVES is the term given to abnormal electrical 'waves' observed in the electro - encephalogram (*see* ELECTRO-ENCEPHALOGRAPHY). The frequency of the normal ' alpha ' waves is ten per second. That of the delta waves is seven or less per second. They occur in the region of tumours of the brain, and in the brains of epileptics.

DELTOID (the letter Δ; εἶδος, form) muscle is the powerful triangular muscle attached above to the collarbone and shoulder-blade, and below, by its point, to the humerus, nearly half-way down the outer side of the upper arm. Its action is to raise the arm from the side, and it covers and gives roundness to the shoulder.

DELUSIONS (*deludo*, I mock) are errors in judgment, regarding simple facts, which interfere with the ordinary conduct of life. Thus a man may have the delusion that he has no stomach and refuse to take food. No amount of argument or demonstration will convince the subject of a delusion as to the error of his belief. The existence of a delusion, of such a nature as to influence conduct seriously, in the mind of a mentally disordered person, is one of the most important signs in certifying the case as one of insanity.

DEMENTIA (*dementia*, folly) is a form of insanity consisting of mental feebleness rather than derangement. It may come on acutely after some illness like influenza, but, as a rule, is chronic, and often succeeds other forms of insanity like melancholia and mania. Dementia is one of the changes almost natural in old age, and, whatever be the cause, it is one of the least hopeful forms of insanity. (*See* MENTAL ILLNESS.)

DEMENTIA PRÆCOX—now more often referred to as schizophrenia (split mind) —is a form of insanity appearing in young persons, especially between twenty and thirty, in which introversion is marked and the personality is ' split '. There is disorder in thinking and behaviour. Thinking becomes incoherent ; morbid ideas and delusions and hallucinations are common. Behaviour may be peculiar, bizarre, excited, impulsive. There is increasing withdrawal from the outside world to an exclusive preoccupation with the self. Finally there is gradual deterioration until the patient lives little more than a vegetative existence. Until recent years, treatment was of little avail, but the method of administering shocks to the brain either by electricity or by injections of insulin or of leptazol has brought about improvement in a number of cases.

DEMENTIA PARALYTICA is another name for general paralysis of the insane. (*See* GENERAL PARALYSIS.)

DEMETHYL CHLORTETRACYCLINE, or LEDERMYCIN, is a tetracydine (*q.v.*) preparation which is effective in relatively low dosage and is said to be more stable than other tetracycline preparations.

DEMULCENTS (*demulceo*, I stroke down) are substances which exert a soothing or protective influence upon the surface of the alimentary canal.

Varieties.—Mucilaginous substances like gum, isinglass, Iceland moss ; oils like olive, linseed, and almond oils ; starchy substances like arrowroot ; also glycerin, borax, and mild alkalies, and fine powders like subnitrate of bismuth.

Uses.—They are used in cases of inflammation, particularly of the throat and stomach, in gargles or draughts, to protect these parts from the irritation of their own secretions ; and after injury, such as that due to swallowing a corrosive poison, in order to soothe the pain and encourage healing in the injured part.

DENGUE (Spanish word), also called BREAK - BONE FEVER, DANDY - FEVER, and THREE-DAY FEVER, is a disease of tropical and subtropical regions caused by a virus transmitted to man by the mosquito *Aëdes egypti*. It is a sudden and short infectious fever, characterized mainly by swelling and pains in the joints, and by eruptions.

Symptoms.—It usually begins suddenly with pain in a joint and fever. Next appears redness of the face, spreading later over the body, very much like the rash of scarlatina. There are also sore throat and running of the eyes, and the muscles and joints generally become very painful. These symptoms endure for about three days, and then gradually pass off, leaving the person very weak. After two or three days a relapse generally takes place, very similar to the first attack, except that the rash more resembles that of measles. There may be a third or even a fourth relapse, and recovery from the weakness and pains in the joints is often slow, often lasting over months. Death hardly ever occurs.

Treatment.—Salicylate of soda, or phenacetin, relieves the pains and reduces the temperature. If the fever be marked, liquor ammoniæ acetatis (Mindererus spirit), in tablespoonful doses, with spirit of nitrous ether in teaspoonful doses, may be given three or four times in the day, and cold sponging of the limbs and body is very beneficial.

DENTINE is the dense white material of which the greater part of the teeth is composed, and which constitutes ivory. The dentine is pierced by numberless fine tubules which communicate with the sensitive pulp in the central hollow of the tooth, hence its sensitiveness when the enamel, which covers the dentine with a thin transparent shell, is eaten away or broken. The dentine is specially liable to decay, so that when the enamel is defective in one spot, a large cavity is apt to form beneath it. (*See* TEETH.)

DENTITION (*see* TEETH).

DEODORANTS (*de*, from ; *odoro*, I make a perfume) are substances which remove or lessen objectionable odours. Some, which have a powerful odour, simply cover other smells, but the most effective act by giving off oxygen, so as to convert the objectionable substances into simple and harmless ones.

Varieties.—Volatile oils of plants, such as eucalyptus and turpentine,

chlorine water and chlorinated lime, peroxide of hydrogen, charcoal, dry earth, sawdust, and permanganate of potassium, are among the most powerful.

Uses.—The main use is to purify sewage, bilge-water, and water-closets. Many powerful deodorants act, at the same time, as disinfectants. They are also used in sick-rooms to cover the smell of discharges, and the like. For the manner of use see under the individual deodorants.

DEOXYCORTONE ACETATE is a synthetic chemical compound having the same action as ' cortin ', the extract of the cortex of the suprarenal gland. It is used successfully in the treatment of Addison's disease.

DEPILATION (*de*, from ; *pilo*, I make bald) is the process of destroying hair ; substances and processes used for this purpose being known as depilatories. The purpose may be effected in three ways : (1) by removing the hairs at the level of the skin surface ; (2) by pulling the hairs out (epilation) ; (3) by destroying the roots and so preventing the growth of new hairs.

Shaving is the most effective way of removing superfluous hairs. Rubbing morning and night with a smooth pumice-stone is said to be helpful. The alkaline sulphides used as depilatories tend to erode the skin as well as the hairs. Electrolysis and diathermy have a limited use. In some cases of excessive hairiness in women the cortices of the suprarenal glands may be hypertrophied. Surgical correction of this is sometimes followed by a dropping out of the excessive hairs.

DEPRESSOR is the name given to a nerve by whose stimulation motion, secretion, or some other function is restrained or prevented, *e.g.* the depressor nerve of the heart slows the beating of this organ.

DEQUALINIUM CHLORIDE is an antibacterial and antifungal compound which is of value in the treatment of infections of the mouth, gums, and throat, and in certain skin conditions.

DERBYSHIRE NECK is a name for goitre, which is fairly common in Derbyshire. (*See* GOITRE.)

240

DERMABRASION, or 'surgical planing', is a method of removing the superfical layers of the skin which is sometimes useful in the removal of tattoos and superficial blemishes of the skin.

DERMATITIS (δέρμα, skin) means any inflammation of the skin, although the name is usually restricted to those affections in which the cuticle comes off in large flakes, leaving a red surface behind. (*See* SKIN DISEASES.)

DERMATOGLYPHICS is the study of the patterns made by the ridges and crevices of the hands and the soles of the feet. It has become an important study in medicine because of the help it provides in the diagnosis of certain diseases, such as mongolism. It is also proving of value in certain other congenital diseases. Thus, a recent study showed abnormal palmar findings in 64 per cent. of patients with congenital heart disease (*q.v.*) compared with only 17 per cent. of patients with acquired heart disease.

DERMOGRAPHIA (δέρμα, skin; γράφω, I write) also known as DERMO-GRAPHISM and URTICARIA FACTITIA, is a condition in which tracings made on the skin leave a distinct swollen, reddish mark. It occurs in allergic individuals, in whom the stimulus of scratching the skin produces an excessive amount of histamine (*see* ALLERGY).

DERMOID CYST (*see* CYSTS).

DESFERRIOXAMINE is a preparation which is proving of value in the treatment of iron poisoning.

DESQUAMATION (*de*, away; *squama*, a scale) means the scaling off of the superficial layer of the cuticle, particularly after scarlatina.

DETERGENTS (*detergo*, I cleanse) are substances which clean the skin surface. This means that, strictly speaking, any soap, or soap-like substance used in washing, is a detergent. At the present day, however, the term is largely used for the synthetic detergents which are now used on such a large scale. These are prepared by the cracking and oxidation of high petroleum waxes with sulphuric acid. The commoner ones in commercial preparations are aryl alkyl sulphate or sulphonate and secondary alkyl sulphate.

DETOXICATION (*de*, away from; *toxicum*, poison) means reduction or removal of the toxic properties of poisons or remedies. (*See* VACCINES.)

DEVONSHIRE COLIC is caused by drinking cider which has been stored in contact with lead, so that colic comes on as a result of lead poisoning. (*See* COLIC, LEAD-POISONING.)

DEXAMETHASONE is a corticosteroid derivative, which has the formula 16α-methyl-9α-fluoro-prednisolone. As an anti-inflammatory agent it is approximately 30 times as effective as cortisone and eight times as effective as prednisolone. On the other hand, it has practically none of the salt-retaining properties of cortisone.

DEXTRAN is the name given to a group of polysaccharides which was first discovered in sugar-beet preparations which had become infected with certain bacteria. Of recent years, a homogeneous preparation of it, with a consistent molecular weight and free from protein, has been introduced as a substitute for plasma for transfusion purposes.

DEXTRIN (*dexter*, right) is a soluble carbohydrate substance into which starch is converted by diastatic ferment or by heat. It is thus contained in toast, the crust of bread, biscuits, and breakfast foods. It is a white or yellowish powder which, dissolved in water, forms mucilage. Animal dextrin, also known as glycogen, is a carbohydrate stored in the liver after meals, often to considerable amount.

DEXTROMORAMIDE is a potent analgesic, or pain-reliever, which is active whether taken by mouth or given by injection.

DEXTROSE is another name for purified grape sugar or glucose.

DIA- (διά, through) is a prefix meaning through or thoroughly.

DIABETES (διαβήτης, from διαβαίνω, I pass through) **INSIPIDUS** is a disease characterized by excessive thirst and the passing of large volumes of urine which has a low specific gravity and

241

contains no abnormal constituents. It is due to lack or diminution of the anti-diuretic hormone normally produced by the posterior lobe of the pituitary gland (*q.v.*). This faulty secretion may result from a lesion involving the posterior lobe of the pituitary gland or a lesion in the base of the brain adjacent to this gland. The condition may be hereditary or due to some pathological process, such as inflammation, a tumour, or syphilis, involving the base of the brain. Treatment consists of the administration of posterior pituitary extracts, either by injection or by nasal insufflation. This condition, which is relatively rare, must be carefully differentiated from the other form of diabetes—DIABETES MELLITUS—which is an entirely different disease.

DIABETES MELLITUS (*mellitus*, honeyed) is a constitutional disorder in which the power of the muscles and other tissues to utilize sugar for purposes of nutrition is greatly diminished or lost, as a result of lack of insulin, the internal secretion of the pancreas. In consequence of this, weakness and various other symptoms appear, while the sugar accumulates in the blood and is excreted in the urine and lost to the system.

Causes.—In 1889 Mering and Minkowski found that diabetes very frequently followed removal of the pancreas from animals. Subsequent work gradually established that, in all cases of diabetes, there is a defect in the chemistry of the body, whereby the muscles cannot absorb the sugar derived from the food, so that a gradual wastage takes place in the muscular tissue all over the body. This defect was attributed by Sharpey-Schafer, so long ago as 1909, to the failure of the pancreas to produce a hormone for which he proposed the name of ' insulin '. Depite the general acceptance of this theory, insulin was not isolated until the year 1921, when it was successfully obtained for the first time by Banting and Best taking advantage of the degeneration in the pancreas of an animal which follows ligature of the duct of the gland. Insulin, which is produced by the cells in the pancreas known as the Islets of Langerhans, is

242

obtained from the pancreas of cattle by a special process of extraction.

It is important to remember that glycosuria (*i.e.* sugar in the urine) can occur in conditions other than diabetes mellitus. Thus, it is a common finding in thyrotoxicosis (*q.v.*) and in certain disorders of the pituitary gland. Emotional disturbance may also cause temporary glycosuria in certain individuals. Glycosuria, which is not due to diabetes, may also occur during pregnancy.

Diabetes is more prevalent during middle age in corpulent people than in persons of average physique. In adults the disease usually appears insidiously and has in most cases been present for some time before an examination of the urine reveals the condition by chance. On the other hand, in children the onset may be sudden. Exposure to wet and cold, privation, depressing mental conditions or mental overwork are predisposing causes to the onset of diabetes mellitus in susceptible individuals, but, of all predisposing causes, infection is the most important. Obesity is another important predisposing factor. There appears to be a distinct tendency for diabetes to run in families. It is most common among adults and occurs more frequently in men than in women. Certain races are particularly prone to this disease, such as the Jewish race and Hindus, but this increased liability is probably in large part due to habits of life and diet.

Symptoms.—The symptoms of diabetes are usually gradual in onset, and the disease is often discovered by chance before the patient complains of any definite symptoms. The first symptoms which attract attention are usually failure of strength and loss of weight, along with great thirst and passage of an increased amount of urine. Dryness of the skin and mouth and constipation also form frequent complaints. The urine, from the normal quantity of between 2 and 3 pints in 24 hours, may be increased to 10, or even 20 pints. It is usually clear, pale in colour, and is of high specific gravity (1030 to 1050). When diabetic urine is boiled with cupric salt, which has a bluish or green colour, the latter is reduced to a cuprous salt having a brown or yellow colour, and a process depending upon this chemical reaction forms the usual method of recognizing and estimating the amount of sugar present in the urine. The sugar can also be tested by measuring the amount of carbonic acid gas set free on fermentation by yeast, and by the extent to which a specimen of the urine rotates the plane of polarized light. The quantity of sugar passed in 24 hours may vary from a few ounces to several pounds, and it is of course markedly increased after sugary or starchy food has been taken. The amount of sugar circulating in the blood rises from about 0·1 per cent., which is normal, to 0·2, 0·3, or more per cent., and it remains high for several hours after a meal instead of being rapidly absorbed.

A troublesome symptom is the intense thirst, which the patient is constantly seeking to allay, and the quantity of liquid consumed is proportional to the amount of urine passed. There is sometimes a voracious appetite. The mouth is always parched and in severe cases a faint sweetish odour can be recognized at times on the breath, owing to the escape of acetone and diacetic acid from the blood into the air in the lungs. The patient gradually becomes more and more emaciated and suffers from increasing muscular weakness ; dyspepsia and constipation are commonly present. Owing to the poor vitality of the tissues, various skin eruptions appear, boils and carbuncles being especially common, and, in fact, sometimes giving the first sign of the presence of disease. The sugar deposited from the urine is liable to cause itching about the groins, and eczema of various parts of the body is set up by the presence of sugar in the sweat. The skin, as the disease advances, becomes dry and harsh, with a papery consistency. There is a special tendency to gangrene of the skin of the feet, beginning with the toes, and this forms a very serious complication of diabetes.

Diabetes, as a rule, advances comparatively slowly except in the case of young people, in whom its progress is apt to be rapid. Indeed, in a general way, it is more serious the younger the subject of the disease. Various complications arise in its course, among which may be mentioned dimness of vision due to cataract, weakness and pains in the limbs due to neuritis, inflammatory chest affections, of which pulmonary tuberculosis is the most important and may be the cause of death. Occasionally death occurs from exhaustion or from the condition known as diabetic coma, in which acetone and similar bodies known as ketones, accumulate in the system, and in which the breathing becomes slower and slower, the person gradually more deeply unconscious, and death ensuing in a few hours or days.

Cases may continue for many years without material change for the worse, especially in elderly subjects. The most unfavourable cases are those in which serious chest or other complications have arisen, and cases in which the disease has already become of severe and established character before it is recognized.

Treatment.—The aim of treatment is to restore carbohydrate metabolism to as near normal as possible, and the two main guides as to how successfully this is being attained are the blood-sugar concentration and the amount of sugar and ketone bodies (*e.g.* acetone) in the urine. The patient's general health is also of importance here, but it will usually be found that there is a direct correlation between the first two and the patient's sense of well-being. The one important exception to this occurs in the case of middle-aged and elderly diabetics, many of whom feel better with a rather high blood-sugar level than they do when the blood-sugar level is brought down to within normal limits. In other words, the diabetic must not become too introspective about the amount of sugar he finds on testing his urine, nor must the doctor attach all his interest to the concentration of sugar in the blood of his diabetic patients. Generally speaking, once a diabetic patient has been stabilized in his treatment, there is no need for him to test his own urine provided he is feeling well and is attending his doctor or his diabetic clinic at regular intervals. Conversely, it is equally important that the moment he begins to feel unwell, *e.g.* develops dyspepsia, a cough, or ' a cold ', he should report at once to his doctor.

The treatment of uncomplicated diabetes mellitus can be divided into two sections : (1) diet ; (2) insulin. These can, again, be divided into two stages : (a) stabilization ; (b) maintenance.

DIET.—Of recent years the tendency has been to give the diabetic patient as liberal a diet as possible, except in the case of the obese patient in whom it is essential to obtain a reduction of weight. It has also been recognized that, as diabetes mellitus practically always persists for the rest of the patient's life, dietetic restrictions should be reduced to a minimum so that he should be able to lead as normal a life as possible. The simplest and most satisfactory way of attaining this is to control the amount of carbohydrate in the diet and not to worry (except in special cases) with the relative proportions of fat and protein in the diet. If the ordinary diabetic patient is taking an ordinary mixed diet in which the carbohydrate content is controlled, then there is seldom any need to worry about the fat and protein. If bread is used as the standard, and it is remembered that 1 oz. of bread contains 15 grammes of carbohydrate, there is little difficulty in working out the daily diet from the following data, once it has been decided how much carbohydrate is to be taken each day and how this amount is to be divided between the four main meals of the day.

Butter	Green vegetables
Cheese	Asparagus
Eggs	Celery
Bacon	Marrow
Meat	Mushrooms
Fish	Leeks
Clear soup	Tomatoes
Tea	Cranberry
Coffee	Grapefruit
	Green gooseberries
	Loganberry
	Melon
	Red currants
	Rhubarb

TABLE 14.—Articles of Food that can be taken freely.

The following amounts of some of the commoner articles of diet are equivalent in carbohydrate content to 1 oz. of bread :—

Cereals

Flour	3 dessert-spoons
Porridge	3 ,,

244

Rice	1 dessert-spoon
Semolina	1 ,,
Tapioca	1 ,,

Fruit

$\frac{1}{2}$ lb. of : apples, figs, pears, pineapple.
1 lb. of : apricots, blackberries, black currants, cherries, damsons, greengages, peaches, plums, raspberries, strawberries.
1 oz. of : prunes.
2 oz. of : dates.
2 oranges.
2 bananas.

Vegetables

$\frac{1}{2}$ lb. of : beetroot, broad beans, carrots, onions, peas.
3 oz. of : potatoes.

Miscellaneous

$\frac{1}{2}$ pint of milk.
1 dessert-spoon of jam or marmalade.

TABLE 15.—Carbohydrate Equivalents.

When diabetes mellitus is first diagnosed, it is usual to initiate treatment by diet alone unless the condition is very severe, when the immediate use of insulin may be called for. The usual initial diet is one containing 100 grammes of carbohydrate (i.e. 6-7 oz. of bread or its equivalent) daily. If the diabetes improves on this diet, then it is gradually increased by 50-gramme stages every two or three weeks, so long as the blood-sugar level remains satisfactory. In milder cases such dietetic control may be all that is necessary, but if it is impossible to control the diabetes in this way, then insulin is necessary.

INSULIN.—Seven forms of insulin are now available : soluble insulin ; protamine zinc insulin ; globin insulin ; isophane insulin ; insulin zinc suspension ; insulin zinc suspension (amorphous) ; insulin zinc suspension (crystalline). All these have to be given by injection. The essential difference between these seven forms is their duration of action. Thus, the action of soluble insulin begins in 20 to 30 minutes and reaches its maximum in 4 to 5 hours. With protamine zinc insulin the blood sugar begins to fall in 5 to 11 hours, and the maximum effect is obtained in 15 to 20 hours. With globin insulin the effect begins in 1 to 2 hours, and reaches a maximum in 8 to 16 hours. Isophane insulin begins to act in 2 hours and its action persists for

24 hours. Insulin zinc suspension has a fairly rapid onset of action which persists for 24 hours. Insulin zinc suspension (amorphous) has also a fairly rapid onset of action, but this lasts for only 12 to 16 hours. Insulin zinc suspension (crystalline) has a somewhat delayed onset of action which persists for 24 hours.

In stabilizing a new case of diabetes which requires insulin, it is advisable to use soluble insulin. A usual initial dose is 10 to 20 units night and morning. This involves an alteration in the distribution of the daily allowance of carbohydrate, the greater part having to be equally divided between the two meals corresponding to the injections of insulin, *i.e.* breakfast and supper. The amount of insulin is gradually increased every four or five days until a satisfactory blood-sugar level is attained. The subsequent course of treatment depends upon the individual response of each patient. The aim in an active patient, who is not over weight, is to allow him to take a diet containing 200 to 300 grammes of carbohydrate daily. In the case of children, 300 grammes of carbohydrate daily should be considered the minimum if full health and adequate growth are to be maintained. In the case of the obese patient, a diet of 1100 calories, containing 60 grammes of carbohydrate daily, is the optimum one to obtain a reduction in weight without undue discomfort to the patient.

Once the patient is stabilized on a given diet and soluble insulin, a decision is then taken as to whether the maintenance insulin is to be soluble insulin or one of the other six. The theoretical advantage of the delayed-action insulins is that they maintain a steadier blood-sugar level throughout the 24 hours ; their practical advantage is that they involve only one injection every day instead of two. The final decision in each case as to which form of insulin to use is one to be decided by the medical attendant in charge of the case.

Oral hypoglycæmic agents.—Certain sulphonamide and diguanide derivatives have recently been introduced which, when taken by mouth, lower the level of the blood sugar. The available evidence indicates that, as a substitute for insulin, they are only of value in a certain proportion of mild cases of diabetes mellitus. The great majority of severe, and, the majority of moderately severe, diabetics fail to respond to these oral agents. The use of these agents should therefore be restricted to those mild, or relatively mild, diabetics in whom : (i) Diet alone fails to bring the blood sugar within or near normal limits. (ii) The dietary restriction required to control the diabetes causes progressive loss of weight or severe hunger. (iii) The withdrawal of insulin is not followed by relapse into significant acidosis. The dose of insulin that can be replaced by these oral agents seldom exceeds 30 units. (*See* CARBUTAMIDE, CHLORPROPAMIDE, PHENETHYLDIGUANIDE, *and* TOLBUTAMIDE.)

Dangers. — The danger which is always present in cases of diabetes is the occurrence of *acidosis*, which, in severe cases, proceeds to *diabetic coma*. An indication of the presence of this condition is given when a large amount of acetone along with sugar is found in the urine. This is a dangerous condition unless it is immediately treated with full doses of insulin.

This type of coma must be carefully differentiated from *hypoglycæmic coma*, which is due to an overdose of insulin resulting in an extreme fall in the blood-sugar concentration. Milder forms of hypoglycæmia are relatively common, manifesting themselves by a sinking feeling, a sensation of hunger, a feeling of sickness, giddiness, or breaking out in a sweat. The treatment consists of the administration of sugar in some form—by mouth if the patient is conscious, by intravenous injection if the patient is unconscious. Every diabetic subject who is subject to hypoglycæmia should carry sugar about with him, in the form of a lump of sugar or barley sugar, so that he can easily avert an attack should he feel it coming on.

Another serious danger incurred by the subject of diabetes is the occurrence of *gangrene* in the skin, especially about the toes. In order to avoid this, special care must be taken to keep the feet in a healthy condition by frequent washing, treatment of corns and abrasions, and avoidance of tight shoes. Other forms of infection, such as boils, must also be treated with special care on ordinary principles. In consequence of the generally poor vitality of the tissues, diabetic patients often form bad subjects for *surgical operations*, but since the introduction of insulin the outlook has improved considerably, and, with careful pre-operative care, there is seldom much need for worry, The frequency with which *chest complications* supervene in diabetes has been mentioned, and special precautions must be taken to avoid catarrhs.

DIACHYLON (*see* LEAD).

DIAGNOSIS (διάγνωσις) is the art of distinguishing one disease from another, and is essential to scientific and successful treatment. The name is also given to the opinion arrived at as to the nature of a disease. It is in diagnosis more than in treatment that the highest medical skill is required, and, for a diagnosis, the past and hereditary history of a case, the symptoms complained of, and the signs of disease found upon examination are all weighed. Many methods of laboratory examination are also used at the present day in aiding diagnosis.

DIAMIDINO-STILBENE is an aromatic diamidine which has been successfully used in the treatment of trypanosomiasis and kala-azar. (*See* CHEMOTHERAPY.)

DIAMINODIPHENYLSULPHONE is a sulphone derivative which is proving of value in the treatment of leprosy.

DIAMORPHINE and DIACETYL-MORPHINE are other names for heroin (*q.v.*).

DIAPEDESIS (*see* INFLAMMATION).

DIAPHORESIS (διά, through; φορέω, I carry) is another name for perspiration. (*See* PERSPIRATION.)

DIAPHORETICS (from διαφορέω, I carry through) are remedies which promote perspiration. By imperceptible perspiration, the body loses over a pint (500 ml.) of moisture daily. Under exertion or in a heated atmosphere, this natural function of the skin is increased, sweating more or less profuse follows, and, evaporation gingo

246

on rapidly over the whole surface, little or no rise in the temperature of the body takes place. In many forms of disease, such as fevers and inflammatory affections, the action of the skin is arrested, and the surface of the body feels harsh and dry, while the temperature is greatly elevated. The occurrence of perspiration frequently marks a crisis in such diseases, and is in general regarded as a favourable event. In some chronic diseases, such as diabetes mellitus and some cases of Bright's disease, the absence of perspiration is a marked feature (*see* PERSPIRATION).

Varieties and uses.—Many means can be used to induce perspiration, among the best known being baths, either in the form of hot-vapour or hot-water baths, or the exposure of the body to a dry and hot atmosphere or to beams of electric light in a special apparatus (*see* BATHS). Such measures, particularly if followed by the drinking of hot liquids and the wrapping of the body in warm clothing, seldom fail to excite copious perspiration. Numerous medicinal substances have a similar effect, such as the well-known diaphoretics—Mindererus spirit (acetate of ammonia), guaiacum, nitrous ether, and jaborandi. Opium acts as a diaphoretic, especially when in combination with ipecacuanha, as in Dover's powder, and alcohol, as well as phenacetin, aspirin, and similar drugs, also produces perspiration (*see under these headings*). When employed at the commencement of a catarrh or common cold, diaphoretics sometimes check it. In Bright's disease, diaphoretics are not used as widely as they were at one time, although hot packs are still sometimes used in acute cases. In certain circumstances, diaphoretics, particularly in the form of baths, may be unsafe, especially where there is any affection of the heart or lungs attended with embarrassed respiration.

DIAPHRAGM (διάφραγμα) is the muscular partition which separates the cavity of the abdomen from that of the chest. It is only a small fraction of an inch in thickness, and is of a dome shape, extending up on the right side to the space beneath the fourth rib, on the left to that beneath the fifth. In contact with its lower surface are, on the right side, the liver, right kidney, and suprarenal body, and to the left the stomach, pancreas, left kidney, suprarenal body, and spleen ; while upon its upper surface lies the heart, with a lung on either side. The diaphragm is attached by its edge to the lower margin of the chest all round, and consists of muscular fibres meeting round a trefoil-shaped piece of fibrous tissue in the centre. It completely shuts off the above-named cavities from one another, being pierced only by openings for the gullet, the aorta, and the inferior vena cava, with a few minute openings for nerves and small vessels. The diaphragm is of great importance in respiration, playing the chief part in filling the lungs. During deep respiration its movements are responsible for 60 per cent. of the total amount of air breathed.

DIAPHYSECTOMY is the term applied to the operation whereby a part of the shaft of a long bone (*e.g.* humerus, femur) is excised.

DIARRHŒA (διαρρέω, I flow away), or looseness of the bowels, is, except in its mildest forms, a most serious condition. It is really a symptom of some disease situated in the bowels, but deserves special mention because of its serious import.

Varieties and causes. — Diarrhœa forms the chief symptom of several *serious diseases*, but it would be a great mistake to imagine that, by checking the diarrhœa, the disease is of necessity successfully treated. For example, the severity of an attack of cholera or dysentery is gauged mainly by the extent to which diarrhœa is present; in typhoid fever, persons fed upon ordinary diet have much diarrhœa, so that this is a usual feature in early stages of this diserse ; in tuberculous ulceration of the intestine diarrhœa occurs which speedily brings down the sufferer. In some diseases of the liver, kidneys, lungs, or heart, diarrhœa ensues as a result of congestion of the bowels, or through the bowels taking up in part the eliminating functions of the damaged organs. In such cases the diarrhœa may actually be a salutary thing. These special forms are considered under the headings of the respective diseases which produce them. Recur-

ring attacks of diarrhœa occur in some cases of habitual constipation, owing to irritation caused by the presence of hard fæcal masses.

Catarrhal diarrhœa is the ordinary form, and in it the intestinal mucous membrane is in much the same condition of congestion and swelling as the nasal mucous membrane during a ' cold in the head ', and secretes, in great amount, clear, viscid mucus of a similar nature. This catarrhal diarrhœa may be produced in a slight degree by indigestible food, by nervous excitement, or as the result of a chill. In a severer form, it may be due to infection by micro-organisms of the food-poisoning group (*see* SALMONELLA GROUP), or to drugs such as mercury and arsenic. Atmospheric conditions may also play a part, some persons developing an attack of diarrhœa upon a change of weather, just as others develop a catarrhal condition in the air-passages.

Diarrhœa in infants is such a serious condition that it requires separate consideration. One of its features is that it is usually accompanied by vomiting. Some ten per cent. of the cases in this country are due to the dysentery organisms (*q.v.*) and will not be considered here. The remainder constitute the group of cases now usually referred to as infantile gastroenteritis. The condition is rare after the age of fifteen months, and the majority of cases occur between the ages of two and four months. The younger the infant, the higher the mortality rate. This is the type of diarrhœa which used to be known as ' summer diarrhœa ' because of its high incidence in the late summer, but during recent years this seasonal incidence has tended to disappear. The precise cause is still obscure, but certain strains of the organism known as *Escherichia coli* (*E. coli*) are responsible for some cases, whilst in others a virus may be the cause. One important predisposing factor is artificial feeding. The condition is rare in breast-fed babies, and when it does occur in these it is usually less severe. The environment of the infant is also important : the condition occurs most commonly in industrial areas and in institutions. A third factor is infection elsewhere in the body, particularly in the ear or the mastoid.

Choleraic diarrhœa, or 'cholera nostras', is an extremely severe type of diarrhœa, resulting very often in death. Its symptoms are hardly distinguishable from those of true cholera. (*See* CHOLERA.)

Lienteric diarrhœa is a chronic form, in which a movement of the bowels occurs shortly after every meal. The condition may become so aggravated that food passes rapidly and undigested through the body, and the sufferer becomes very thin.

Pancreatic diarrhœa is a form occasionally met in children of imperfect development, in consequence of failure by the pancreas to secrete its proper digestive fluid.

Ulcerative colitis is a serious condition characterized by the passage of frequent stools containing blood. (*See* COLITIS.)

Diarrhœa may also be a symptom of ulceration or gangrene of the bowels, and is then associated with the passage of *blood and mucus*, or even of shreds of membrane produced by the destruction of the inner surface of the bowels.

Treatment.—The treatment of diarrhœa which is an incident of special diseases like cholera, typhoid fever, dysentery, etc., is considered under these heads.

ACUTE DIARRHŒA, it must be remembered, is often merely a symptom either of one of the above diseases or of some local disease like intussusception, so that if the symptom be treated as if it were the real disease, the consequence may be disastrous to the sick person. Assuming that we are dealing simply with cases of uncomplicated *catarrhal diarrhœa*, we may consider the treatment of an adult and child separately. In the case of both, rest in bed is essential until the diarrhœa has subsided.

In adults, if the attack has followed the eating of some indigestible substance, a dose of castor oil (two tablespoonfuls) may be given, together with, or followed in an hour or two by, 15 drops of laudanum. To control the diarrhœa the two most effective drugs are kaolin and opium. Kaolin may be given in doses of one tablespoonful thrice daily ; alternatively, in doses of 30 grains (2 G.) it may be combined in a mixture with 10 minims (0·6 ml.) of chlorodyne. If the diarrhœa lasts more

248

than a couple of days, an enema consisting of starch cream (4 ounces (115 G.)) with laudanum (20 drops) is useful, given every six hours. If there is much discomfort with distension of the abdomen, a turpentine stupe (*q.v.*) may be of value. During the first twenty-four hours of an acute attack, no food should be given, but the individual must be given ample water. In less acute cases barley water may be given. This, as in the case of water, should be given in small amounts at frequent intervals. Later, arrowroot made with water is given. After the severer symptoms of diarrhœa have passed off, the affected person must exercise great caution for several days in respect to diet. A gradual return should be made to ordinary food, consisting at first of eggs, milk, and milk puddings, followed later by fish, and only after the lapse of several days by meat and vegetables.

In infants treatment is highly specialized, and much depends upon efficient nursing. Drugs play little part in the treatment, which is largely dietetic. Opium and its derivatives are badly tolerated by these infants and should not be used. The evidence concerning the value of the sulphonamide drugs and antibiotics is contradictory, but recent reports suggest that when the infant is not responding to dietetic treatment and the temperature is raised, one of the sulphonamides or one of the antibiotics should be given. Severe cases should receive such therapy from the outset. If there is any evidence of infection elsewhere in the body, *e.g.* the ear, this must be treated at once. When there is no evidence of dehydration, *i.e.* the infant has not lost much fluid in the stools or the vomit, the infant should be starved for twelve to twenty-four hours, but during this period should be given plenty ¼-strength saline and 5 per cent. glucose, either together or alternating with each other, by mouth. When feeding is reinstituted, this should consist of half-strength, half-cream National Dried Milk, alternating with the glucose-saline mixture, in frequent small feeds. After 24 hours, if progress is maintained the infant is given half-strength, half-cream milk. The strength of the milk is gradually increased until, usually within a matter of five to seven days, the infant is able to take all feeds of full-strength National Dried Milk.

When dehydration is present, the outlook is much more serious, and adequate fluid must be given either subcutaneously or intravenously. The fluid is usually glucose in saline, but some prefer to use Hartman's solution (isotonic sodium lactate) instead of the saline. During the first twelve or twenty-four hours of intravenous administration, nothing is given by mouth. By the end of this time vomiting has usually stopped, and then feeding by mouth can be started very gradually.

CHRONIC DIARRHŒA requires, above all things, full investigation to try and determine the cause, complete rest in bed and a simple diet, such as peptonized milk, or white of egg in water, or tea and toast. Washing out of the lower bowel through a soft rubber tube, and the injection of various soothing and astringent fluids, may be of benefit. Kaolin in doses of 1 teaspoonful or more in water after meals has sometimes a beneficial effect.

DIASTASE is the name of a ferment found in germinating seeds, and is contained in large quantity in malt, which has the property of converting starch into sugar. It can be extracted as a white soluble powder. *Takadiastase* is a diastatic ferment produced by the action of a fungus, *Aspergillus oryzae*, upon wheat bran. It is used as a medicine in cases where starch is improperly digested through deficiency of saliva or owing to gastric acidity.

DIASTASIS (διάστασις, separation) is a term applied to separation of the end of a growing bone from the shaft. The condition resembles a fracture, but is more serious because of the damage done to the growing cartilage through which the separation takes place, so that the future growth of the bone is considerably diminished.

DIASTOLE (διαστολή) means the relaxation of a hollow organ. The term is applied in particular to the heart, to indicate the resting period between the beats (systoles), while blood is flowing into the organ.

DIATHERMY (διά, through ; θέρμη, heat) is a process by which electric currents can be passed into the deeper parts of the body so as to produce

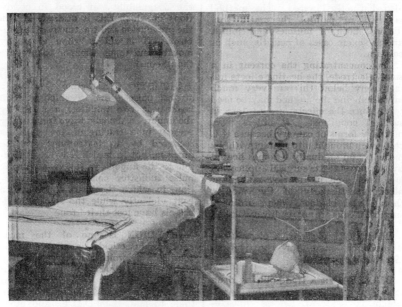

FIG. 103.—A microwave diathermy machine. (*The Practitioner.*)

internal warmth and relieve pain ; or, by using powerful currents, to destroy tumours and diseased parts bloodlessly. The form of electricity used consists of high-frequency oscillations, the frequency of oscillation ranging from 10 million to 25,000 million oscillations per second.

The so-called ultra-short-wave diathermy (or short-wave diathermy, as it is usually referred to) has replaced the original long-wave diathermy, as it is produced consistently at a stable wave-length (11 metres) and is easier to apply. In recent years microwave diathermy (Fig. 103) has been developed, which has a still higher oscillating current (25,000 million cycles per second, compared with 500 million for short-wave diathermy. It has two practical advantages : there is no danger of producing deep-seated burns, and it can be given to a fully dressed patient.

When the current passes, a distinct sensation of increasing warmth is experienced and the temperature of the body gradually rises ; the heart's action becomes quicker ; there is sweating and increased excretion of waste products. The general blood-pressure is also distinctly lowered. The method is used in painful rheumatic conditions, both of muscles and joints, and in severe cases of neuritis, such as sciatica.

By concentrating the current in a small electrode, the heating effects immediately below this are very much increased, and the method may be used to produce the effects of a cautery in surgical conditions. It differs from ordinary forms of cautery because it is cold when brought into contact with the patient, and gradually becomes heated by the current. Its surgical application has been used in treating malignant ulcers, particularly of the mouth, throat, and bladder, where ordinary surgical means are not readily available.

DIATHESIS ($\delta\iota\acute{a}\theta\epsilon\sigma\iota\varsigma$, a disposition) is another name for constitution. (*See* CONSTITUTION.)

DIAZEPAM is a tranquillizing drug related to chlordiazepoxide (*q.v.*), which is said to possess muscle-relaxant properties and therefore to be of value in the treatment of muscular rheumatism.

DICEPHALUS is the term applied to a fœtal ' monster ' having two heads.

DICHLORAL PHENAZONE is a non-barbiturate sedative, consisting of a complex of chloral hydrate (*q.v.*) and phenazone (*q.v.*).

DICHLOROPHEN, 2 : 2'-dehydroxy-5 : 5' - dichlorodiphenylmethane, is a drug for the treatment of tapeworm infestations. The dose is 70 mg. per kg. body weight, given as a single dose or in three divided doses eight-hourly.

DICK TEST is a test devised for discovering those children who are specially susceptible to contract scarlet fever. (*See* SCARLET FEVER.)

DICOPHANE is the official name for D.D.T. (*q.v.*).

DICOUMAROL is a substance isolated from spoiled sweet clover which causes a hæmorrhagic disease in cattle. Dicoumarol has been synthesized and is used in clinical medicine to reduce the coagulability of blood in conditions in which this is desired—*e.g.* in the prevention and treatment of thrombosis. It is active when given by mouth, and much cheaper to prepare than heparin.

DICROTIC ($\delta\iota\varsigma$, double ; $\kappa\rho\acute{o}\tau\circ\varsigma$, a stroke) pulse is one in which at each heart-beat two impulses are felt by the finger. A dicrotic wave is naturally present in a tracing of any pulse as recorded by an instrument for the purpose, but in health it is imperceptible to the finger. In fevers, a dicrotic pulse indicates considerable prostration, in which the heart continues to beat violently while the small blood-vessels have lost their ' tone '.

DIELDRIN is one of the most effective insecticides available as it combines a prolonged action with a highly lethal action on insects. In addition, it is toxic to a wide range of insects. On the other hand, it is more toxic to man than D.D.T., and must therefore be handled with care.

DIENŒSTROL is a synthetic œstrogen closely related to stilbœstrol (*q.v.*). It is not as potent as stilbœstrol, but as it would appear to be less toxic, it may, for this reason, have certain advantages over stilbœstrol.

DIET (δίαιτα, way of life) is a subject of the greatest importance. Information as to the change in diet necessary in special diseases will be found in the section on these diseases, and what will be said here refers to general principles of feeding. Details regarding the diet of young children are given under INFANT FEEDING.

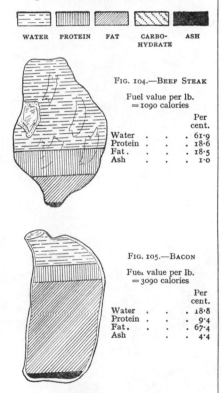

| WATER | PROTEIN | FAT | CARBO-HYDRATE | ASH |

FIG. 104.—BEEF STEAK

Fuel value per lb. = 1090 calories

		Per cent.
Water	. .	61·9
Protein	.	18·6
Fat	. .	18·5
Ash	. .	1·0

FIG. 105.—BACON

Fuel value per lb. = 3090 calories

		Per cent.
Water	. .	18·8
Protein	. .	9·4
Fat	. .	67·4
Ash	.	4·4

Dietetic principles.—The body is, in many respects, comparable to an engine. Like a piece of machinery it requires fuel to supply the muscles, etc., with energizing power for the various bodily activities, and it likewise needs building materials to repair loss from wear and tear. For the latter purpose, food containing nitrogen is necessary, the protein of which the muscles and other tissues are composed being replaceable only by fresh nitrogen-containing protein. For the necessary supply of energy, on the other hand, protein would suffice ; but, as its use for this purpose would throw

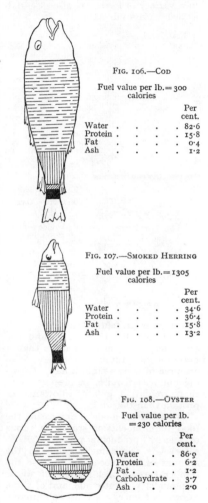

FIG. 106.—COD

Fuel value per lb. = 300 calories

		Per cent.
Water	. . .	82·6
Protein	. . .	15·8
Fat	. . .	0·4
Ash	. . .	1·2

FIG. 107.—SMOKED HERRING

Fuel value per lb. = 1305 calories

		Per cent.
Water	. . .	34·6
Protein	. . .	36·4
Fat	. . .	15·8
Ash	. . .	13·2

FIG. 108.—OYSTER

Fuel value per lb. = 230 calories

		Per cent.
Water	.	86·9
Protein	.	6·2
Fat	.	1·2
Carbohydrate	.	3·7
Ash	. .	2·0

upon the kidneys and other excretory organs the necessity of getting rid of a large residue, fats and carbohydrates (including starch and sugars), which contain only carbon, hydrogen, and oxygen, are more convenient for the purpose. In addition to these three varieties of food, water must be taken in sufficient quantity to make up for the loss by the urine, sweat, etc., and also various salts, of which, however, there is always a surplus in the food. Certain substances known as vitamins, which are present in small quantities in a variety of foods, are also essential, as are certain minerals.

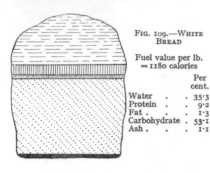

FIG. 109.—WHITE BREAD

Fuel value per lb. = 1180 calories

		Per cent.
Water	.	35·3
Protein	.	9·2
Fat	.	1·3
Carbohydrate	.	53·1
Ash	.	1·1

FIG. 110.—OATS (DRY)

Fuel value per lb. = 1670 calories

		Per cent.
Water	.	11·0
Protein	.	11·8
Fat	.	5.0
Carbohydrate	.	69·2
Ash	.	3·0

The daily protein requirement of the average man lies between 70 and 100 grammes a day, or a bit more than 1 gramme of protein for every kilogramme of body weight a day. Growing children require, in proportion to their weight, a greater allowance of protein than the adult.

The scientific mode of expressing the food requirements is stated in terms of energy - producing power. 'Kilocalory' is the name applied to the amount of heat necessary to raise the temperature of a kilogram of water (2 pounds) 1° Centigrade, and of these calories of energy 4·1 are obtainable by burning a gramme of protein or of carbohydrate, and 9·3 by combustion of the same amount of fat. In estimating the energy expended by an individual in climbing a mountain, doing his daily work, etc., one expresses it as so many 'calories', while the

252

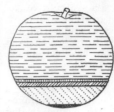

FIG. 111.—APPLE

Fuel value per lb. = 285 calories

		Per cent.
Water	.	84·6
Protein	.	0·4
Fat	.	0·5
Carbohydrate	.	14·2
Ash	.	0·3

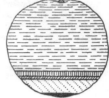

FIG. 112.—ORANGE

Fuel value per lb. = 233 calories

		Per cent.
Water	.	87·7
Protein	.	0·8
Fat	.	0·2
Carbohydrate	.	10·6
Ash	.	0·7

FIG. 113.—BANANA

Fuel value per lb. = 445 calories

		Per cent.
Water	.	75·3
Protein	.	1·3
Fat	.	0·6
Carbohydrate	.	22·0
Ash	.	0·8

FIG. 114.—GRAPES

Fuel value per lb. = 435 calories

		Per cent.
Water	.	77·4
Protein	.	1·3
Fat	.	1·6
Carbohydrate	.	19·2
Ash	.	0·5

FIG. 115.—RAISINS

Fuel value per lb. = 1560 calories

		Per cent.
Water	.	14·6
Protein	.	2·6
Fat	.	3·3
Carbohydrate	.	76·1
Ash	.	3·4

amount of food which is burned up in the body by the process may be similarly stated.

Quantity of food.—The total daily amount of food necessary for a fair-sized man, doing average hard work, should provide over 3000 calories of energy, and since about 4 ounces of the daily food must, as above stated, be protein, to supply wear and tear, this leaves 2500 calories to be supplied by carbohydrate and fat together. The proportion of these to one another depends upon minor considerations ; for example, the Esquimaux make it up in fat, because, in the northern regions, sugar and cereals are unobtainable. The natives of India, and the poorer classes of the world in general, use cereal food because of its great cheapness as compared with fat, and persons of feeble digestive power consume large quantities of soft fats, because—fat being, bulk for bulk, more than double the caloric value of carbohydrate — the digestion of a sufficiency of food is rendered easier by the use of the former in excess. For a diet giving about 3000 calories a day these may be suitably provided thus : carbohydrate, 400 grammes ; fat, 110 grammes ; protein, 90 grammes, —providing respectively 1640, 1120, and 360 calories.

Atwater made investigations upon this subject ; the proportions in the diet of various classes are selected from his researches as follows :—

	Pro-tein Grms.	Fat Grms.	Carbo-hydrate Grms.	Energy Calories.
Trappist monk with little exercise	68	11	469	2304
Japanese students	97	16	438	2343
German soldiers	114	39	480	2798
English blacksmith	176	71	667	4117
College football team	181	292	557	5742
Average of 53 Americans	103	138	436	3494

TABLE 16.—Diets of various Races and Social Classes.

To contrast these figures with the ideal. The Trappist monk and the Japanese students led a life that was free both from wear and from hard bodily work, and so they needed little

protein and little energizing food. The German soldier came nearest the ideal, but had a slightly diminished diet on account of his passive barrack life.

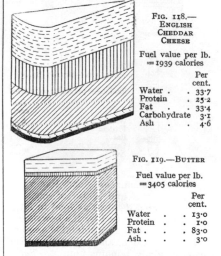

FIG. 116.—FRESH MILK

Fuel value per lb. (roughly ¼ pint) = 315 calories

		Per cent.
Water	. .	87·0
Protein	.	3·3
Fat	.	4·0
Carbohydrate	.	5·0
Ash	. .	0·7

FIG. 117.—EGG

Fuel value per lb. = 695 calories (80 calories each)

		Per cent.
Water	. .	73·7
Protein	. .	14·8
Fat	. .	10·5
Ash	. .	1·0

The English blacksmith and college football team had an increase all round to maintain their exertions, although the latter probably ate far too much fat. The average American took too much fat, as richer classes tend to do, substituting fat for the cheaper, less palatable, and more bulky carbohydrate.

FIG. 118.— ENGLISH CHEDDAR CHEESE

Fuel value per lb. = 1939 calories

		Per cent.
Water	.	33·7
Protein	.	25·2
Fat	.	33·4
Carbohydrate		3·1
Ash	.	4·6

FIG. 119.—BUTTER

Fuel value per lb. = 3405 calories

		Per cent.
Water	.	13·0
Protein	.	1·0
Fat	.	83·0
Ash	.	3·0

Quality of food.—After the energizing power of a substance has been ascer-

253

tained, there remain several other factors which determine its suitability as a food. *Digestibility* is one of the most important, for, while petroleum, sawdust, and the like have a high energy - producing power, they are absolutely useless as foods. *Absorbability* is also of importance, for few substances are completely absorbed

food and partly upon its preparation. Food should not be capable of too rapid digestion, or it cannot be fully utilized by the tissues ; hence a food like oatmeal is more sustaining, in persons of good digestive power, than meat essences ; and hence also the value of cooking certain foods with fat, which, when it penetrates the other food, retards digestion. As a rule, the more satisfying a food is, the less digestible it proves ; and this is one of the chief reasons that different

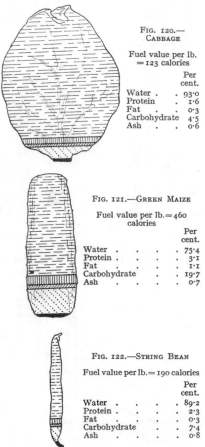

Fig. 120.—
Cabbage

Fuel value per lb.
= 123 calories

		Per cent.
Water	.	93·0
Protein	.	1·6
Fat	.	0·3
Carbohydrate		4·5
Ash	.	0·6

Fig. 121.—Green Maize

Fuel value per lb. = 460 calories

			Per cent.
Water	.	.	75·4
Protein	.	.	3·1
Fat	.	.	1·1
Carbohydrate		.	19·7
Ash	.	.	0·7

Fig. 122.—String Bean

Fuel value per lb. = 190 calories

			Per cent.
Water	.	.	89·2
Protein	.	.	2·3
Fat	.	.	0·3
Carbohydrate		.	7·4
Ash	.	.	0·8

Fig. 123.—Potato

Fuel value per lb.
= 375 calories

			Per cent.
Water	.	.	78·3
Protein	.	.	2·2
Fat	.	.	0·1
Carbohydrate		.	18·4
Ash	.	.	1·0

Fig. 124.—Chestnut

Fuel value per lb.
= 1820 calories

			Per cent.
Water	.	.	5·9
Protein	.	.	10·7
Fat	.	.	7·0
Carbohydrate		.	74·2
Ash	.	.	2·2

Fig. 125.—Walnut

Fuel value per lb.
= 3180 calories

			Per cent.
Water	.	.	2·5
Protein	.	.	16·6
Fat	.	.	63·4
Carbohydrate		.	16·1
Ash	.	.	1·4

into the system, and some, like vegetable proteins and white of egg, are even rejected if taken as food in large amounts, and passed by the bowels unchanged. Thus a considerable amount of all food eaten, and especially of the coarser kinds, remains unused. *Satisfying power* is of great importance, and depends partly upon the bulk of the

foods and different methods of cooking suit persons of diverse physique and digestive powers. *Preparation* by grinding, cooking, etc., is also important. The effect of cooking is partly to develop flavours in the food, and so make it more palatable and digestible ; partly to kill organisms and animal parasites which may be present in it ; and, mainly, in the case of meats, to soften the connective tissues which bind the meat proper, and, in the case of vegetables, to burst or tear the fibres and capsules of cellulose which surround the starchy and sugary material. *Cheapness* is of immense importance to the working classes. Animal protein, as beef, forms the dearest food, and bread is by far the cheapest, well deserving the name of ' the staff of life '. Among the cheapest and most efficient forms of protein food are skimmed milk, cheese, and fish. Fat has double the energy - producing power of carbo-hydrates, but butter is more than four times as expensive as its equivalent in bread. Hence fatty foods are called ' rich foods '. Nevertheless margarine falls into the list of cheap foods and is quite as nutritious as butter, and, since September 1939, all margarine has had the vitamins A and D added up to the level of some butter. *Freshness* is important, since preserved foods tend to lose their vitamins, and the daily diet should include vegetables, fruit, milk, butter, cheese.

The *source* of food is not indifferent. It might be thought that a person well fed on peas would have the same powers as one fed on their equivalent in beef, but those races and individuals who feed upon a largely animal diet are characterized by the power of doing work more rapidly, by greater spirit, and by greater power of resisting disease. Although, as a general principle, this is undeniably true, and although it forms the main argument against the suitability of vegetarianism for those doing severe work involving any mental or highly skilled effort, it may be carried to a very fanciful extreme, as in the case of Kean, the actor, who would choose his dinner according to the part he was to play, taking pork for a tyrant, beef for a murderer, and mutton for a lover. Probably, in such a case, ease of digestion had more to do with the effect of the food than its source.

The great objection to *vegetarianism*, apart from that stated above, lies in the enormous bulk of vegetable food necessary, mainly in consequence of the relatively large amount of water it contains. Thus, if one were to subsist on nothing but lentil porridge, about 5 pounds of it would be necessary daily ; or if one lived solely on green vegetables and succulent fruits, the impossible weight of about 30 lb. every day would be necessary to a fairly hard-working healthy man. Those vegetarians who add milk, eggs, and cheese to their food reach at once a healthy and rational diet, and one which, in those liable to gout and rheumatism—and for most people—is more salutary than a full ordinary diet.

External conditions produce great differences in the need for food. In cold climates, or in those persons unusually exposed to the weather, a special addition of fats or carbo-hydrates must be made to the diet in order to maintain the body heat. For the same reason a tall, spare man requires a much greater supply of these foods than a short, fat man of the same weight. Such a difference in con-figuration may mean the necessity for adding one quarter or more of the amount of food.

Age and sex are important considerations. A woman requires about four-fifths of the diet of a man about the same size and build, the reduction affecting chiefly the starchy and sugary elements of her food. Children require much more protein—*i.e.* building material—in proportion to their size than adults ; whilst old people, on the other hand, if they wish to keep healthy, must be very sparing eaters, particularly of animal foods.

Thus, according to the National Research Council of America, if a moderately active male, weighing 70 kg., has 3000 calories daily, including 70 grammes of protein, the corresponding figures are :

A woman (weight 56 kg.), 2500 cal., 60 grammes of protein

Children aged 10 to 12 years, 2500 cal., 70 grammes of protein

Adolescent aged 13 to 15 years, 3200 cal., 85 grammes of protein

Adolescent aged 16 to 20 years, 5800 cal., 100 grammes of protein

Articles of diet.—Further details, regarding the various articles in common use as foods, are given under BREAD, TINNED FOODS, CEREAL, MILK, NITROGENOUS FOODS, INFANT FEED-ING. Some of the substances more frequently added to foods are mentioned under ADULTERATION OF FOODS. The articles which may most suitably be taken in various diseased conditions are mentioned under the headings of the various diseases.

Diet for athletes and manual workers. —For long it has been traditional for athletes in training to eat large amounts of meat. There is, however, no evidence to suggest that this is necessary. Carbohydrate, and not protein, is the best source of energy. Although there is still considerable difference between theory and practice, the views of dietitians and athletes are now converging, and it is now generally accepted that a simple and sufficient diet is what is required. The same holds true for manual workers. In the case of an athlete, it is probably advisable for him to go on a lighter diet for a day or two before the contest for which he is training, making certain that this contains ample carbohydrate. There is probably also much to be said in favour of taking glucose shortly before the event. There is also some evidence that the requirements of certain components of the vitamin B complex increase with exercise, so that care should be taken to ensure that there is ample vitamin B in the diet. Ample fluids should also be taken, but there is no evidence that alcohol is of any advantage.

The total daily calories should be about 4500, and the following list (modified from one published by Mottram) gives some indication of the foods to be taken :

Foods for calories.—Dripping, suet, butter, margarine, bacon, cheese, bread, flour, sugar, jam, syrup, dried fruits, potatoes, cereals.

Foods for first-class proteins.—Milk, eggs, meat, fish.

Foods for vitamins.—Vitamin A : Dairy foods, liver, tomatoes, green and yellow vegetables. Vitamin B : yeast, liver, kidney, whole-meal bread, bacon, ham, wheat germ. Vitamin C : Citrus fruits, swedes, potatoes, green vegetables, liver. Vitamin D : Fat fish, summer milk, and butter.

Invalid diet.—One of the greatest advances of recent years has been the recognition of the importance of diet in the treatment of disease. Whilst this is best exemplified in the case of

diabetes mellitus, there are many other conditions in which special diets are ordered. Thus, in chronic cholecystitis a low-fat diet is necessary, whilst in jaundice a diet rich in first-class protein and carbohydrate is prescribed. Low-calorie diets are the most effective for obesity, whilst a low-sodium diet is an essential part of the treatment of dropsy.

In febrile conditions the diet depends upon the expected duration of the fever. Thus, in a long-continued fever, such as typhoid fever, the essentials are that the diet should have a high calorie value (3000 calories), a large proportion of carbohydrate (380 grammes), adequate protein (70-80 grammes), and be given in easily digestible form in small amounts every two hours.

On the other hand, in fevers of short duration, e.g. pneumonia, the amount of nourishment taken is not of such importance. If the individual is receiving ample fluid, including at least two pints of milk daily, there is little to worry about for several days. Again, small feeds should be given every two hours. To increase the nutritional value of the diet, and yet still impose no strain upon the digestive organs, glucose may be added to the water the patient drinks, and this can be flavoured with fruit juice, the addition of which ensures an adequate intake of vitamin C. If the patient desires more food, this may be given in the form of eggs (lightly boiled or poached), milk puddings (e.g. junket, arrowroot), or jellies.

During convalescence it is necessary to give as nourishing a diet as possible. On the other hand, the digestion is sometimes not satisfactory, and the appetite is fickle. The following is a typical convalescent diet which provides approximately 2500 calories :

Early morning.—Sweetened orange juice.
Breakfast.—Fruit, breakfast cereal with milk, egg, toast with butter and marmalade (or honey), weak tea (or coffee) with milk and sugar.
Mid-morning.—Glass of milk, biscuit (or sandwich) and marmite.
Lunch.—Steamed white fish, or chicken, or rabbit, or sweetbreads, or tripe; potatoes (mashed with milk), vegetable purée, milk pudding or custard with stewed fruit.

Tea.—Sandwiches—cress or marmite, bis-
    cuits or sponge-cake, weak tea with
    milk and sugar.
Dinner (or Supper).—As for lunch. An
    egg-dish may be preferred to fish or
    meat, *e.g.* an omelette.
Bed-time.—Glass of hot milk, or Horlicks,
    or Ovaltine, biscuit if desired.

**DIETHYLCARBAMAZINE CIT-
RATE** is a derivative of piperazine,
which is proving of value in the treatment of filariasis.

DIETL'S CRISES (*see* KIDNEY DIS-
EASES *under* MOVABLE KIDNEY).

**DIGESTION, ABSORPTION, and
ASSIMILATION** are the three processes by which food is incorporated in
the living body. In digestion, the food
is softened and converted into a form
which is soluble in the watery fluids of
the body, or, in the case of fat, into
very minute globules. In absorption,
the substances formed are taken up
from the bowels and carried throughout
the body by the blood. In assimilation, these substances, deposited from
the blood, are united with the various
tissues for their growth and repair. For
the maintenance of health each of these
must proceed in a regular manner.

SALIVARY DIGESTION begins
as soon as the food enters the mouth.
Saliva runs from the minute orifices
of the salivary gland ducts, and contains a ferment named ptyalin, which
actively changes the starch of bread,
potatoes, and the like, into sugar.
The object of chewing is not only to
bruise the food, and make it more permeable for the gastric juice, but also
to mix the starchy parts thoroughly
with saliva. This process goes on, after
swallowing, for the first twenty minutes
or half-hour that the food remains in
the stomach, after which the action of
the saliva is checked by the acid of the
gastric juice.

GASTRIC DIGESTION begins a
little time after the food enters the
stomach, the gastric juice exuding
rapidly from the openings of the minute
glands with which the interior surface
of this organ is covered. The gastric
juice begins to be secreted even before
the food enters the stomach, at the sight
and smell of food (psychic secretion).
This juice contains two ferments,
named pepsin and rennin, the former

9

having the power of breaking down
the proteins of food into smaller molecules containing fewer amino-acids,
the latter being concerned with the
digestion of milk. There are also

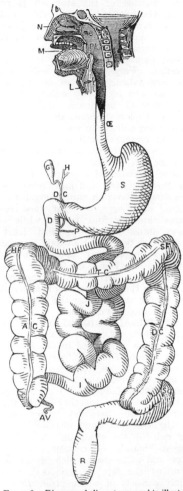

FIG. 126.—Diagram of alimentary canal to illustrate
the organs concerned in digestion. *M*, Mouth;
Ph, pharynx ; *Œ*, œsophagus ; *S*, stomach;
D, J, I, small intestine ; into the duodenum
D open *P*, the pancreatic duct, and *DC*, the
common bile duct ; *G*, gall-bladder ; *H*,
hepatic duct ; *C, AC, TC, DC*, large intestine ;
R, rectum ; *AV*, appendix. (*Ency. Brit.*)

present free hydrochloric acid, which
aids the action of the pepsin and prevents putrefaction of the food, and
acid salts, such as phosphate of soda,
which have a similar action. The

slow, churning movements which take place in the walls of the stomach have the effect of thoroughly mixing the food and gastric juice, and, to a slight extent, of breaking up the former. The main function of the stomach is to render the ingested food soluble, and mix it thoroughly with the gastric juice until it assumes a gruel-like consistency. This material, known as *chyme*, is then passed through the pylorus into the intestine. Very soon after soft food has been taken, waves of movement may be seen on X-ray examination, the orifice at the lower end of the stomach (pylorus) opens, and the food is squeezed quickly in small quantities into the bowel; but if any hard food comes in contact with the stomach wall near the exit the orifice at once closes. Gastric digestion of a simple meal of tea, bread, butter, and jam should be complete in about an hour, a meal containing milk, eggs, or light meat requires three or four hours, while a heavy dinner with soup, meat, fruit, and wine or beer is not entirely treated by the stomach till six or seven hours have elapsed. Hence the English plan of taking the heavy meal of the day (dinner) in the early evening is a sound one, giving time during the night for the later stages of digestion.

INTESTINAL DIGESTION. — The softened food, or chyme, which leaves the stomach is exposed in the bowels to the action of four factors—(a) bile, (b) pancreatic juice, (c) intestinal juice, (d) bacteria. Bile is collected from the liver and gall-bladder into the common bile-duct, which, together with the duct from the pancreas, opens into the duodenum a short distance from the exit of the stomach. The bile consists mainly of certain complex salts and pigments, which assist in digesting the fats of the food, and partly consists of waste products removed from the blood. The pancreatic juice contains four powerful ferments, which have the following effects: lipase breaks down fats into glycerin and fatty acids; chymotrypsin curdles milk; amylase completes the digestion of starch; and trypsin carries on the breaking down of proteins begun in the stomach. Intestinal juice contains ferments (enzymes) which (1) complete the breakdown of proteins into the con-

stituent amino-acids; (2) act upon the disaccharides maltose, sucrose, and lactose, converting them into the monosaccharide glucose; (3) split fats into fatty acids and glycerin. Bacteria are normal inhabitants of both small and large intestine. In the former they have a fermentative, in the latter a putrefactive, action. In the former they act upon carbohydrate to

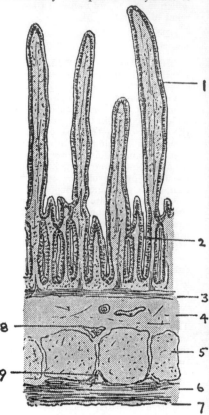

FIG. 127.—Section of small intestine (jejunum), showing four of the villi with which the inner surface is covered. Magnified 110 times. 1, villus; 2, crypt of Lieberkühn; 3, muscularis mucosæ; 4, submucosa; 5, circular muscular coat; 6, longitudinal muscular coat; 7, serous coat; 8, 9, nerve plexuses. (From Hewer, *Textbook of Histology*. William Heinemann, Ltd.)

produce acetic, butyric, and lactic acids. In the latter, bacteria decompose protein into such products as histamine, phenol, cresol, indole, skatole, etc. These are no longer, however, believed to be responsible for the ill-effects of constipation. The intestinal bacteria also play an important and valuable rôle in the manufacture of certain components of the vitamin B complex.

ABSORPTION. — The only substance absorbed from the stomach to any extent is alcohol. Water is quickly passed from the stomach into the intestine, and considerable quantities are there absorbed in a few minutes. But it is only after subjection to digestion in the intestine for several hours that the bulk of the food is taken up into the system. The semi-solid chyme which leaves the stomach is converted into a yellowish fluid of creamy consistence called ' chyle ' by the action of bile and pancreatic fluid. From this the fats, in the form of a fine emulsion, are taken up by lymph vessels called ' lacteals ', and ultimately reach the blood, while sugars, salts, and amino-acids formed from proteins pass directly into the small blood-vessels of the intestine. The process is facilitated by the extreme unevenness of the intestinal wall, which is folded into many ridges and pockets, while, in microscopic structure, the surface is covered by fine finger-like processes named ' villi ' (Fig. 127), which are bathed in the fluids passing down the intestine. Further, absorption is probably assisted by the ' leucocytes ', or white cells of the blood, which are increased in numbers after a meal, and which have the power of wandering out of the blood-stream and taking up particles into their substance. Food materials are absorbed almost exclusively by the small intestine. The large intestine, or colon, absorbs water and salts. The food is passed down the intestine by the contractions of its muscular coat, and, finally, the indigestible residue, together with various waste substances excreted from the liver and intestinal walls, is cast out of the body in the stools.

ASSIMILATION takes place more slowly, the blood circulating through every organ, and each taking from it what is necessary for its own growth and repair. Thus the cells in the bones extract lime salts, muscles extract sugar and protein, and so forth. When the supply of food is much in excess of the immediate bodily requirements it is stored up for future use, fat being deposited in various sites, sugar being converted into glycogen in the liver. The greater bulk of nutriment is assimilated by the muscles for heat production and work, the sugar and amino-acids being built up into a substance which forms the permanent part of the muscle. The substance so formed undergoes chemical changes, and is broken down to form carbonic acid, lactic acid, and other waste products as the muscle does work. Various hormones, such as insulin, which is an internal secretion of the pancreas, circulate in the blood and are concerned in these processes. For all these processes to function satisfactorily an adequate daily intake of water is necessary ; about three pints are drunk or taken with the food and absorbed daily, a similar amount being discharged from the body in the urine, perspiration, and other excretions.

DIGITALIS is the leaf of the wild foxglove, *Digitalis purpurea*, gathered when the flowers are at a certain stage, dried, and powdered. The leaf contains several active principles, which can be extracted in various ways. Its action is to strengthen involuntary muscular contraction, particularly that of the muscle fibres in the heart and blood-vessels. It is one of the most valuable remedies we have in cases of disease of the heart, associated with rapid or irregular beating of this organ, and with dropsy. Upon the heart it has the double action of increasing the strength of each beat and of lengthening each intervening pause (diastole), so that the muscle of the damaged organ obtains longer periods for rest and repair. It also lessens the ' conductivity ' of the heart muscle, so that feeble and ineffective beats tend to disappear, when the action is irregular. By thus acting on the heart, it causes the production of more urine by the kidneys and a consequent decrease of existing dropsy in cases in which the dropsy is due to heart failure.

Uses.—Digitalis may be given as a powder, as tincture, as infusion, and also in the form of sugar-coated ' granules ' which contain the active principle of the drug. The most common form of administration is the powder given in the form of a tablet. It is the great stand-by in the treatment of heart failure accompanied by, or likely to be accompanied by, dropsy. Its action is particularly useful when the heart failure is due to atrial fibrillation, the condition in which the heart rate is wholly irregular. In such cases the digitalis slows the heart rate by abolishing many of the weak heart-beats which, although of no value in helping to maintain an efficient circulation, yet put an additional and useless strain on the heart muscle.

DIGITALIS POISONING may occur from taking medicinal doses over too long a period, or from taking a single overdose. In the two cases the symptoms are similar. The heart, which is made slower and more regular by taking small doses, becomes again quicker and more irregular as the result of excessive administration. At the same time breathing gets more difficult, and there may be convulsions or unconsciousness. The amount of urine passed gets less and less, thus causing retention in the system of the drug, which is naturally got rid of by the kidneys.

Treatment. — The drug must be stopped. If a single overdose has been swallowed, the stomach should be washed out with weak potassium permanganate solution and stimulants administered.

DIGOXIN is a crystalline glycoside obtained from *Digitalis lanata*. It is used for the same purpose as digitalis, and has the advantage that it can be given by intravenous injection as well as by mouth.

DI-IODOHYDROXYQUINOLINE is a drug used in the treatment of chronic amœbic dysentery, usually as a supplement to treatment with emetine.

DILAUDID is a derivative of morphine (dihydromorphinone hydrochloride). It has the same action as morphine but is given in a smaller dose. It is said to be less apt to start a drug habit in the patient.

DILUENTS (*diluo*, I wash) are watery fluids of an unirritating nature,

which are given to increase the amount of perspiration or of urine, and carry solids with them from the system. Examples are water, milk, barley-water, and solutions of alkaline salts.

DIMENHYDRINATE is the British Pharmacopœia Commission approved name for dramamine (*q.v.*).

DIMERCAPROL is the official name for B.A.L. (British Anti-Lewisite), the antidote to lewisite poisoning which was discovered during the 1939–45 War. It was subsequently found to be an excellent antidote to poisoning with certain heavy metals, including arsenic, mercury, and gold, and it is now widely used for this purpose.

DIMETHYLPHTHALATE is an organic compound which was found, during the 1939–45 War, to be a most effective repellent for mosquitoes. It is equally effective against flies and midges. Under the proprietary names of MYLOL and SKEETOFAX, it is available as a cream and as a liquid. This is smeared on the face, arms, hands, legs, or other exposed parts of the body. Care must be taken not to allow it to get into the eyes or to come into contact with plastic spectacle-frames. It does not kill flies, but merely prevents them from alighting on the skin.

DIODONE is a complex organic preparation, containing 49·8 per cent. iodine. It is used primarily for contrast radiography of the kidney passages, but can also be used for contrast radiography of the biliary tract, arteries, veins, and joints.

DIOPTER is a term used in the measurement of the refractive or focusing power of lenses ; one diopter is the power of a lens with a focal distance of one metre and is the unit of refractive power. As a stronger lens has a greater refractive power, this means that the focal distance will be shorter. The strength in diopters therefore is the reciprocal of the focal length expressed in metres.

DIPHENHYDRAMINE (*see* BENADRYL).

DIPHTHERIA (διφθέρα, a skin or membrane) is the term applied to an acute infectious disease, which is accompanied by a membranous exudation on a mucous surface, generally on the tonsils and back of the throat or pharynx.

Causes.—The infection is essentially a local one in the throat due to the development there of the *Corynebacterium diphtheriæ* (Plate VIII), and the general symptoms are referable to the absorption of toxins (*q.v.*) which damage the heart muscle and the nerves. Among the first signs of the disease appears an inflammation of the throat, where a false membrane develops, composed partly of the dead surface of mucous membrane and partly of products effused from the blood and lymph. In this membrane the causative organisms swarm, along with many other varieties of organism, particularly streptococci.

The disease is generally conveyed by direct contagion, as by kissing an affected person, using his cup or spoon, or receiving a drop of saliva or fragment of membrane upon the lips or face through incautiously approaching him when he is coughing. The organism grows freely in milk, and infection may be conveyed in this way.

Three strains of *Corynebacterium diphtheriæ* are now recognized as causing clinical diphtheria : *gravis, intermedius, mitis*. *Gravis* and *intermedius* strains are almost always virulent ; about 10 per cent. of *mitis* strains are non-virulent.

It is predominantly a disease of the autumn and winter and, although it occurs at all ages, it is commonest in childhood. It is rare under six months of age as the young infant has a transmitted immunity from the mother.

A method known as the ' *Schick test* ' has been devised for detecting the susceptibility of individuals to diphtheria. A minute quantity of toxin filtered off from growing diphtheria bacilli is injected with a very fine needle into the skin of the arm. Individuals possessing naturally a considerable amount of antitoxic power show no reaction, but if the individual has very little resisting power to diphtheria, an area of inflammation is produced on the skin at the site of the injection.

In 1966 there were only 20 cases of diphtheria, with 5 deaths, in England and Wales, compared with over 45,000 cases and 2400 deaths in 1940, the year in which a national immunization campaign was launched by the Ministry of Health. The substance injected is diphtheria toxoid, which is diphtheria toxin so treated that it is harmless but will produce antibodies to the diphtheria bacillus and thereby give the injected individual an immunity to the disease.

Very few children are immunized solely against diphtheria at the present day They are more usually given a combined vaccine against diphtheria, tetanus and whooping-cough. (*See* VACCINES.)

Symptoms.—The severity of diphtheritic inflammation in general, and the fact that it is accompanied by serious constitutional symptoms, suffice usually to distinguish this disease from croup, which, although resembling diphtheria, differs from it in being a merely local inflammation of the larynx. There are several other diseases of the throat, such as acute suppurative quinsy, which are even more liable to be mistaken for diphtheria. The diagnosis is often difficult, even for a skilled physician.

In doubtful cases, the deciding point is the taking of a throat swab. A swab of cotton-wool mounted on a wire is rubbed against the throat, and then sent to a skilled bacteriologist for examination. A culture of the organisms from the swab is made upon dried serum, for 16 to 24 hours at body temperature, and if the organisms found in the resulting culture be pronounced to be diphtheria bacilli, the case can be safely diagnosed as one in which this disease is present.

Cases of diphtheria differ as to their intensity from the mildest forms, which resemble an ordinary catarrhal sore throat, to those of the most severe character (such as the gangrenous form), in which the disease is hopelessly intractable from the first.

Following an incubation period of two to four days (extremes one to six days) after infection, symptoms set in like those commonly accompanying a cold, viz. chilliness and depression. Sometimes very severe disturbances usher in an attack, such as vomiting and diarrhœa. A slight feeling of easiness in the throat is experienced along with some stiffness of the back of the neck. When looked at, the throat appears reddened and somewhat swollen, particularly in the neighbourhood of the tonsils, the soft palate, and upper part of pharynx, while along with this there is tenderness and swelling of the glands at the angles of the jaw. The affection of the throat spreads rapidly, and soon the characteristic exudation appears on the inflamed surface in the form of greyish-white specks or patches, increasing in extent and thickness until a yellowish-looking false membrane is formed. This deposit is firmly adherent to the mucous membrane beneath, or is incorporated with it, and, if forcibly removed, it leaves a raw, bleeding, ulcerated surface, upon which it is reproduced in a short period. The appearance of the exudation has been compared to wet parchment or washed leather, and it is dense in texture. It may cover the whole of the back of the throat, the cavity of the mouth, and the posterior nares, and may spread downwards into the air passages and into the alimentary canal, while any wound on the surface of the body is liable to become covered with it. As it loosens, it becomes decomposed, giving a most offensive and characteristic odour to the breath. There are pain and difficulty in swallowing, but, unless the disease has affected the larynx, no affection of the breathing. The voice acquires a snuffling character. When the disease invades the posterior nares, an acrid, fetid discharge, and sometimes also copious bleeding, take place from the nostrils. Along with these local phenomena there is evidence of constitutional disturbance of the most severe character. There may be no great fever, and the temperature seldom rises above 102° or 103° F. (39° to 39·5° C.), but there are marked depression and loss of strength. The pulse becomes small and rapid, the countenance pale, the swelling of the glands in the neck increases, which, along with the presence of albumin in the urine, testifies to a condition of blood-poisoning. Unless favourable symptoms emerge, death takes place within three or four days or sooner, either from the rapid extension of the false membrane into the air passages,

giving rise to asphyxia, or from a condition of general collapse, which is sometimes remarkably sudden owing to sudden failure of the heart, for which the diphtheria toxin has a special predilection. For the same reason death occasionally takes place suddenly during convalescence, from acute dilatation of the weakened heart, if a considerable effort be made at too early a period. Death may also ensue if the temperature rises excessively.

In cases of recovery, the change for the better is marked by an arrest in the extension of the false membrane, the detachment and expectoration of that already formed, and the healing of the ulcerated mucous membrane beneath. Along with this, there is a general improvement in the symptoms, the power of swallowing returns, and the strength gradually increases, while the glandular enlargement of the neck diminishes, and the albumin disappears from the urine. These favourable symptoms should appear within three or four days, but recovery is generally slow, and it may be many weeks before full convalescence is established. During this period it is particularly necessary in the case of diphtheria to guard against premature over-exertion, and for this reason patients are kept in bed for several weeks even though feeling quite well.

Even when diphtheria ends quite favourably, certain sequels are apt to follow, generally in a period of two or three weeks after all the local evidence of the disease has disappeared. These effects, which are due to neuritis caused by the effect of the diphtheria toxin upon various nerves, may occur after mild as well as after severe attacks, and they are principally in the form of paralysis affecting the soft palate and throat, causing difficulty in swallowing, with regurgitation of fluid through the nose, and giving a peculiar nasal character to the voice. Another form of paralysis is one affecting the muscles of the eye, and producing loss of the power of accommodation and consequent difficulty in reading without glasses, which often lasts for a period of several months; another form may be paralysis of a limb, or of both legs, or even of the respiratory muscles. These symptoms, however, after continuing for a variable length of time, almost always ultimately disappear.

Treatment.—The first essential of treatment is the immediate injection of *antitoxin* (*see* SERUM THERAPY). Every moment of delay increases the danger to the patient. As diphtheria antitoxin contains horse serum, the possibility of an anaphylactic reaction (*see* ANAPHYLAXIS) must be borne in mind. In addition to antitoxin, the patient is given penicillin daily for five days, as this antibiotic has a bactericidal action on *C. diphtheriæ.*

The second essential is *complete rest in bed* for at least three weeks. Adequate nourishment should be freely administered in the form of milk, soup, etc., as long as there exists the power of swallowing, and when this fails, fluids, in the form of Hartmann's solution (*q.v.*), glucose and plasma, should be given by infusion or by nasal catheter. The strict maintenance of the recumbent position is of great importance in preserving the strength of the heart. If the infection spreads to the larynx (laryngeal diphtheria), additional antitoxin is given and the patient is kept in a steam tent. If obstruction to breathing is not relieved by this, it may be necessary to perform the operation of tracheotomy.

Most cases of diphtheritic paralysis recover without special treatment. In cases where the respiratory muscles are paralysed, it may be necessary for a time to resort to artificial respiration till the paralysis passes off, by means of some form of apparatus which rhythmically inflates and deflates the chest.

As the disease is notifiable a case of diphtheria should be notified immediately to the medical officer of health, and arrangements made for urgent admission to a hospital for infectious diseases. Cases are isolated until cultures from three successive nose and throat swabs, taken at intervals of not less than two days, are negative.

If a case of diphtheria occurs in a closed community, such as a school, a daily examination of the throats of all contacts should be made during the incubation period, and throat swabs should be taken. Those with positive throat swabs should be given an intramuscular injection of 8000 units of antitoxin and also penicillin. They must also be isolated until three successive throat swabs free of virulent *C. diphtheriæ* are obtained. The Schick test should also be carried out on all contacts, and those who give a positive reaction should be given a course of toxoid immunization.

DIPLEGIA (δίς, twice; πληγή, a blow) means extensive paralysis on both sides of the body. (*See* PARALYSIS.)

DIPLO- (διπλόος, double) is a prefix meaning twofold.

DIPLOCOCCUS (διπλόος, double; κόκκος, berry) is the term applied to a group of bacterial organisms which have a tendency to occur in pairs, *e.g.* pneumococci.

DIPLOE (διπλόη, a doubling) is the layer of spongy bone which intervenes between the compact outer and inner tables of the skull.

DIPLOPIA (διπλόος, double; ὄπτομαι, I see) means double vision. It is due to some irregularity in action of the muscles which move the eyeball, in consequence of which the eyes are placed so that rays of light from one object do not fall upon corresponding parts of the two retinæ, and two images are produced. It is a symptom of several nervous diseases, and often a temporary attack follows an injury to the eye, intoxication, or some febrile disease like diphtheria.

DIPROSOPUS is the term applied to a fœtus which has two faces instead of one.

DIPSOMANIA (δίψα, thirst; μανία, madness) is a morbid and insatiable craving for alcohol. (*See* ALCOHOLISM, CHRONIC.)

DIPYGUS is the term applied to a fœtus which has a double pelvis.

DISARTICULATION is the amputation of a bone by cutting through the joint of which the bone forms a part.

DISCHARGE is the term applied to abnormal emissions from any part of the body. It usually applies to purulent material, *e.g.* the septic material which comes away from an infected ear, nose, etc.

DISCISSION is the term applied to an operation for destroying a structure by tearing it without removal, *e.g.* the operation of needling the lens of the eye for cataract.

DISINFECTION is the process of rendering harmless any persons, articles, rooms, etc., which are liable to communicate disease. *Disinfectants* are procedures, or substances, used for this purpose by virtue of their capacity for killing the organisms responsible for the disease. The word is sometimes confused with *antiseptics*, which denotes substances used to prevent or check putrefaction, but which do not necessarily kill the causative organism. Thus, although most antiseptics are disinfectant, this is not necesarily the case. *Germicides* are measures directed towards killing bacterial life. *Deodorants* are substances which suppress foul smells, and, although many deodorants are disinfectants, they are so only on much more effective application than is necessary to subdue smell. Thus charcoal exposed in a sick-room clears away smell but does not disinfect the room, and eucalyptus sprinkled on the floor renders the air of a room sweet, but does not destroy all the germs of disease in the room.

FORMS OF DISINFECTANT. — **Light and fresh air** are too apt to be neglected. There can hardly be found a more powerful disinfectant than direct sunlight, for few bacteria can survive exposure to it in the open for an hour. This applies, for example, with special force to the tubercle bacillus.

Heat is of great importance. Exposure to moist heat at 212° F. or 100° C. (*i.e.* boiling in water) kills bacteria in five to ten minutes, whilst for absolute purification Koch's method of boiling on three successive days (*see* BACTERIOLOGY) may be employed. Some articles which would spoil by boiling may be steamed in a closed, though not air-tight, vessel, steam being allowed to pass freely over them for twenty minutes after it has begun to rise ; metal articles, for example, do not rust so quickly in steam as in boiling water, and cotton or linen materials do not become so wet as in water. In the expensive forms of sterilizer the steam used is subjected to

pressure, which renders its action much more effective. Articles which will not stand moisture at all may be subjected to dry heat at a temperature of 250° F. (120° C.) for an hour, for example, in Ransom's apparatus ; but this form of heat has little penetrating power, so that clothes, etc., subjected to it must not be made up into thick bundles.

CRUDE CARBOLIC in a dilution of 1 in 20 is used for disinfecting clothing and bedding. Although it does not harm fabrics or affect colours or metals, it is liable to stain, due to the presence of impurities.

PURE PHENOL is a satisfactory disinfectant in a dilution of 1 in 100. Although not as efficient as crude carbolic, it has the advantage of not staining.

CRESOL, in the form of a 1 per cent. emulsion of saponified cresol, is an excellent disinfectant.

IZAL, CYLLIN, AND LYSOL are other satisfactory coal-tar disinfectants. Izal and cyllin, which have a carbolic coefficient of 20, are used in a dilution of 0·5 per cent., whilst lysol, with a carbolic coefficient of 5 to 10, is used in a 1 per cent. solution.

PERCHLORIDE OF MERCURY in a 1 in 1000 solution is a potent disinfectant, killing organisms in thirty minutes. Its use is restricted by the fact that it corrodes metals, and is not suitable for disinfecting faeces and sputum, as it forms insoluble compounds with albuminous material. Because of its extreme toxicity and the fact that it forms a colourless solution like water, it is coloured blue to prevent accidents. The following formula, recommended by the Ministry of Health, gives a 1 in 960 solution : mercury perchloride 0·5 ounce (14 grammes), hydrochloric acid 1 ounce (28·5 ml.), aniline blue 5 grains (300 mg.), water 3 gallons (13·5 litres).

FORMALDEHYDE may be used either as a gaseous disinfectant or in solution as formalin (40 per cent. solution). The simplest way of producing gaseous formaldehyde is by heating paraform tablets (25 to 30 per 1000 cubic feet of space).

POTASSIUM PERMANGANATE, which is a disinfectant by virtue of being a powerful oxidizing agent, is a useful and safe disinfectant. Its use is restricted by the fact that it is rendered inert by organic matter. Five minutes in a 1 in 1000 solution of permanganate is an effective way of sterilizing drinking and eating utensils. Although it stains textiles, the stain can be removed by oxalic acid or lemon juice. The well-known Condy's fluid contains potassium permanganate.

SODIUM HYPOCHLORITE is unstable in solution and corrodes metal, but in 1 in 3000 solution it is a useful disinfectant for floors and latrines.

LIME, one of the cheapest of disinfectants, kills organisms in a few hours in a 1 per cent. solution.

CHLORINATED LIME (bleaching powder) is less stable than lime. It has the further disadvantage of being destructive to fabrics. In a 0·5 to 1 per cent. solution it kills most organisms in one to five minutes.

HYDROGEN CYANIDE, which, because of its intense toxicity, must only be used by experienced personnel, is used for destroying bed bugs and for fumigating ships.

SULPHUR DIOXIDE is also used for fumigating ships.

METHODS OF DISINFECTION.—
The person.—The hands must always be carefully disinfected after being in contact with an individual suffering from an infectious disease, or before dressing a wound. The best method is to wash the hands thoroughly in plenty of warm water, using clean soap and a sterilized nail-brush. There is no particular merit in antiseptic soap, e.g. carbolic soap. The hands should then be carefully rinsed in one of the following : pink potassium permanganate solution; perchloride of mercury solution (1 in 2000) ; biniodide of mercury solution (1 in 1000 solution in water, or 1 in 500 parts of 90 per cent. alcohol). For a mouth disinfectant either a pink potassium permanganate solution may be used or hydrogen peroxide.

Dressings and instruments. — The former are now sterilized by high-pressure steam sterilization. Surgical instruments, including syringes and needles, are sterilized by boiling in water for ten to twenty minutes.

Rooms.—Provided reasonable precautions are taken during the illness, disinfection of the sick-room is not now considered necessary in the case of

ordinary infectious diseases such as measles and diphtheria. Thorough washing with soap and water and plenty of fresh air are all that are required. At the beginning all unnecessary ornaments and hangings should be removed and the room should be kept well ventilated. During the illness dusting and sweeping must be reduced to a minimum and carried out only with damp dusters and mops. Recent work has shown that certain organisms remain alive in dust and in fluff from blankets for considerable periods. To overcome spread of infection by this means blankets and floors are now being treated by oil in hospitals. If it is considered necessary to disinfect a room after an infectious illness, the first preliminary is to burn articles of little value and to send bedding and mattresses for steam disinfection. The only satisfactory way of disinfecting a room is by a spray, and for this purpose the best is formalin : 8 ounces to the gallon of water (230 ml. to 4·5 litres), and 1 gallon (4·5 litres) for every 400 square feet (111 square metres) of surface. A room sprayed in this way in the morning can be occupied again the same evening, provided all windows and doors are kept open during the spraying.

Clothes and bedding.—Bed linen, blankets, and similar articles should be soaked in cresol or a 5 per cent. solution of carbolic acid for twelve hours before being washed. Other articles, such as boots and leather materials, which cannot be soaked in disinfectant or destroyed, should be left in the room during disinfection and afterwards exposed to the open air for an entire day. Where a central disinfecting station exists, arrangements should be made with the local health authorities to have the disinfecting done there.

Sputum, stools, and other discharges.
—Sputum and discharges from the nose should be collected in gauze and burnt. If there is sufficient sputum to justify a sputum flask, this should contain a 5 per cent. solution of carbolic acid. The bed-pan should also contain 5 per cent. solution of carbolic acid, or cresol. After use, more disinfectant should be added, well mixed with the contents and allowed to stand for two hours before being emptied down the water-closet.

DISINFESTATION means the destruction of insect pests, especially lice, whether on the person or in dwelling-places.

DISLOCATIONS (*dis*, apart ; *loco*, I place) are injuries to joints of such a nature that the ends of the opposed bones are forced more or less out of connection with one another. Besides displacement of the bones, there is more or less bruising of the tissues around them, and tearing of the ligaments which bind the bones together.

Varieties.—Dislocations, like fractures, are divided into simple and compound, the bone in the latter case being forced through the skin. This seldom occurs, since the round head of the bone has not the same power to wound as the sharp end of a broken bone. Dislocations are also divided according as they are (1) congenital, *i.e.* present at birth in consequence of some malformation, or (2) acquired at a later period in consequence of injury, the great majority falling into the latter class.

An important distinction is drawn between recent and old-standing dislocations. In old-standing dislocations. the accident has occurred perhaps some weeks previously, and has either been unrecognized on account of surrounding swelling, or, at all events, untreated, so that not only has the dislocated bone formed adhesions in its new position, but the smooth, cartilage - covered surfaces have lost, to a great extent, their power of moving evenly over one another if again properly brought in contact. The treatment of such old-standing dislocations is always a difficult problem, and the decision as to which form of treatment should be adopted depends upon various factors, including the age of the person, the presence or absence of pain. the usefulness of the limb in its new position, etc.

Causes.—The causes of dislocation are similar to those of fracture, the fact as to whether a bone or a joint gives way depending upon the manner in which force is applied, and still more upon the relative strength of bones and joints. Thus in very young and very old persons dislocations are extremely rare, because the bones are relatively easily broken, and thereby

the joints are saved from damage. Congenital dislocations are mainly due to some defect in development of the bones.

Signs and symptoms.—The injured limb is useless, but, as a rule, there is little pain, unless the dislocated bone presses upon some nerve trunk. When the limb is compared with that of the opposite side, the joint is found to be unduly prominent in one place, and shows an abnormal hollow in another. Further, there is loss of movement at the joint in question, but no grating (crepitus) as in a case of fracture. Each joint shows further special symptoms dependent upon its conformation.

Treatment.—So far as temporary treatment is concerned, nothing is necessary but a splint, bandage, sling, or the like, to keep the injured part moderately quiet, because there is not the same danger of damage to nerves, vessels, etc., by the rounded head of the bone as by the sharp fragments of a fracture. The greatest care is necessary in reduction, *i.e.* putting the dislocated bone back in place, for great damage may be done by an unskilled person in the way of breaking the bone, tearing nerves and vessels, or even leaving the bone dislocated in a new direction. After reduction to the natural position, the limb must be fixed for a time so as to prevent a recurrence, which will take place if it be used at once. The length of time depends upon the severity of the injury ; as a rule, after about ten days, gentle movements are made to prevent the joint becoming stiff, and the bandages, etc., left off after about three weeks. But care in using the limb is necessary for long.

SHOULDER.—This may be reduced in one of two methods. (*a*) By *manipulation*, in which the bone is gently worked back into place by a method too complicated for description here. (*b*) By *extension*. The injured person lies on his back upon a couch or upon the floor. The operator then, sitting down by the injured side opposite the patient's hip and facing towards his shoulder, grasps the limb with one hand by the wrist, with the other above the elbow, while at the same time he places his foot, from which the shoe has been removed, in the armpit, on the edge of the shoulder-blade, to steady it, and give him something against which to pull. He then pulls on the injured arm gently, steadily, and strongly, first in a direction parallel with the injured person's body, and, if this be unsuccessful, at right angles to it, pressing all the while with his foot against the edge of the shoulder-blade. The injured person must at the same time relax all his shoulder muscles. The bone goes into place generally with a snap, and the appearance of the joint is then like that of its fellow.

ELBOW.—This joint may be dislocated backwards by a fall on the hand, or forwards by a fall on the point of the elbow (Plate X, B). In both cases it is reduced by bending steadily across the knee of the operator, who at the same time pulls on the forearm.

WRIST.—This joint is seldom dislocated, and the dislocation is readily replaced by pressure, and is then kept in position by a well-padded splint on the palm and front of forearm. A fracture of the lower end of the radius (Colles's fracture) (Plate X, C) is sometimes mistaken for a dislocated wrist.

FINGERS AND TOES may be dislocated and are difficult to reduce, because the tight ligaments close round the displaced bone, and because of the difficulty in grasping the finger to pull on it. This may be overcome by winding strips of sticking-plaster round the finger, or by a device of interlacing tapes known as the ' Indian puzzle '. Dislocation of the thumb at its base is particularly hard to reduce, and may even require an operation to enlarge the opening through which the bone has passed.

HIP.—This joint, being extremely strong, is seldom dislocated, and, when dislocated, is very difficult to reduce. The head of the thigh bone usually passes backwards and upwards, so that the limb appears much shortened and the toes turned inward. Reduction is effected by a special form of manipulation, or, failing this, by extension. For the latter, the injured person lying on his back, the limb is pulled straight downwards, one assistant steadying the pelvis by pressing one of his hands upon each iliac spine, and another pulling the whole thigh outwards by means of a towel passed round it as high up as possible. A very steady, powerful pull is necessary if reduction is to be effected.

CONGENITAL DISLOCATION OF THE HIP is the commonest form of congenital dislocation. The earlier it is detected, the better the results of treatment.

KNEE.—This joint is very seldom dislocated, and such an injury to it is specially severe, being accompanied by the tearing of strong ligaments.

ANKLE.—This joint is hardly ever dislocated, most severe injuries near it being fractures of the leg bones.

SPINE.—Dislocation of the spine is only produced by great violence, such as that of a horse rolling over a man, and is usually combined with fracture. Very often pressure on, or tearing of, the spinal cord takes place, which may produce paralysis of the lower limbs, or even death from shock.

JAW.—This joint is sometimes dislocated forwards when the mouth is very widely opened, as in yawning or singing. It can usually be replaced by a person pressing downwards with his thumbs upon the farthest back teeth and at the same time pressing up the chin. He should take care that his thumbs do not get bitten.

DISORIENTATION is a term applied to a symptom in mental disease or delirium in which the patient is confused as to sense of time or place.

DISPLACEMENT is a term used in psychological medicine to describe the mental process of attaching to one object painful emotions associated with another object.

DISSEMINATED SCLEROSIS (*dissemino*, I scatter about, σκληρός, hard), also called MULTIPLE and INSULAR SCLEROSIS, is a disease of the brain and spinal cord, which, though slow in its onset, in time produces marked symptoms, such as paralysis and tremors, and ultimately renders persons suffering from it confirmed invalids. It consists of hardened patches, from the size of a pin-head to that of a pea or larger, scattered here and there irregularly through the brain and cord, each patch being made up of a mass of the connective tissue (neuroglia), which should be present only in sufficient amount to bind the nerve-cells and fibres together. In the earliest stage, the insulating sheaths of the nerve-fibres in the hardened patches break up, are absorbed, and leave the nerve-fibres bare, the connective tissue being later formed between these.

Cause.—Although this is one of the most common diseases of the central nervous system in Europe, the cause is still not known. The disease comes on in young people (onset being rare after the age of forty), apparently without previous illness ; and although it occurs sometimes in persons with a heredity of nervous disorder, this is not always so. The actual changes in the nervous system appear to be due to the action of some substance which dissolves or breaks up the fatty matter of the nerve-sheaths.

Symptoms.—These depend greatly upon the part of the brain and cord affected by the sclerotic patches. Temporary paralysis of a limb, or of an eye muscle, causing double vision, and tremors upon exertion, first in the affected parts, and later in all parts of the body, are early symptoms. Stiffness of the lower limbs causing the toes to catch on small irregularities in the ground and trip the person in walking, is frequently an annoying symptom and one of the first to be noticed. Great activity is shown in the reflex movements obtained by striking the tendons and by stroking the soles of the feet. The latter reflex shows a characteristic sign (Babinski sign) in which the great toe bends upwards and the other toes spread apart as the sole is stroked, instead of the toes collectively bending downwards as in the normal person. Tremor of the eye movements (nystagmus) is usually found. Trembling handwriting, interference with the functions of the bladder, giddiness, and a peculiar 'staccato' or 'scanning' speech are common symptoms at a later stage. Numbness and tingling in the extremities occur commonly, particularly in the early stages of the disease. As the disease progresses, the paralyses, which were before transitory, now become confirmed, often with great rigidity in the limbs. Many cases progress very slowly and show little or no tendency to shortening of the duration of life.

Treatment is unsatisfactory, because the most that can be done is, by means of careful dieting, plenty of sleep, and especially by leading a life as free from strain as possible, to check the progress of the disease. It is important to keep the nerves and muscles functioning, and therefore the patient should remain at his work as long as he is capable of doing it, and in any case should regularly exercise the lower limbs by walking and the upper limbs by carrying out movements requiring co-ordination, such as knitting or embroidery. In some cases protein shock by injections of peptone or anti-typhoid vaccine in doses sufficient to produce a moderate rise of temperature may help (*see* PROTEIN SHOCK). Arsenic, usually as Fowler's solution, is sometimes of temporary value. Injections of liver extract and vitamin B_1 have also been recommended. Corticosteroids seem to be as effective a means as any of slowing up the progress of the disease, but they can only be used under skilled medical supervision.

DISTEMPER is the name applied to several infectious diseases of animals, especially a contagious catarrhal disease affecting young dogs, caused by a virus.

DISTICHIASIS is the term applied to the condition in which there are two complete rows of eyelashes in one eyelid (or in both).

DISTOMA (δίς, twice; στόμα, mouth) is a general term including various forms of trematodes or fluke-worms parasitic in the intestine, lung, and other organs.

DISULFIRAM, or ANTABUSE, the full chemical name of which is tetraethylthiuram disulphide is used in the treatment of alcoholism. It is relatively non-toxic by itself, but when taken in conjunction with alcohol it produces most unpleasant effects : *e.g.* flushing of the face, palpitations, a sense of oppression and distress, and ultimately sickness and vomiting. The rationale of treatment, therefore, is to give the alcoholic subject a course of disulfiram and then demonstrate, by letting him take some alcoholic liquor, how unpleasant are the effects. If the patient is co-operative, the results of treatment are often very satisfactory It is a form of treatment, however, that is not without risk, and it must therefore be given under skilled medical supervision.

DIURETICS (διά, through ; οὐρέω, I pass water) are substances which produce diuresis, that is, a copious excretion of urine by the kidneys.

Varieties.—There is a host of substances which can produce diuresis, although only a small proportion of these are now used. Water, for instance, is an excellent diuretic, and if the diminished output of urine is due to inadequate intake of fluid or excessive loss of fluid through other channels, *e.g.* sweating, diarrhœa, water is often the best diuretic to rectify matters. Salts of potassium, calcium chloride, and ammonium chloride produce diuresis by temporarily altering the chemistry of the blood. Urea acts as a diuretic by stimulating the glomeruli of the kidneys. Vasodilators (*q.v.*) act as diuretics by increasing the blood supply to the kidneys. Among the vasodilators used for this purpose are caffeine, theophylline, aminophylline, and theobromine. Spirit of nitrous ether, a popular constituent of fever mixtures, falls into this group, but is a much weaker diuretic than the others mentioned. Gin used to be a commonly used diuretic ; here there was a twofold action—the alcohol acted as a vasodilator and the oil of juniper acted as a mild irritant of the kidney, thereby acting as a stimulant to the excretion of urine. Needless to say, gin is never used now for this purpose. The digitalis group of drugs act as diuretics in cases of dropsy due to heart failure ; they have no direct action on the kidneys, but by improving the action of the heart they increase the circulation through the kidneys and thereby increase the output of urine.

For many years the most widely used diuretics were the organic mercurial diuretics, *e.g.* mersalyl (*q.v.*), which act by diminishing the activity of the renal tubules. These, however, had certain disadvantages, including the fact that they had to be given by injection. They are now being largely replaced by a new group of diuretics, which are benzthiadiazine (*q.v.*) derivatives, and which are effective when taken by mouth. (*See* CHLOROTHIAZIDE, *and* HYDROFLUMETHIAZIDE.) Like the organic mercurial diuretics, they act on the renal tubules. The most recent addition to the list of diuretics is spironolactone (*q.v.*).

Uses.—The removal of dropsical fluid is the main function of diuretics. If the dropsy is due to heart failure the best diuretics to use are the digitalis group of drugs. These are often supplemented by the organic mercurial diuretics, or the new benzthiadiazine derivatives. In the case of dropsy due to disease of the kidneys, the choice of diuretic depends upon the condition of the kidneys. In febrile conditions, when so much fluid is being lost in the excessive sweating caused by the fever, it is often advisable to give diuretics to maintain the excretion of urine, and for this purpose a combination of the milder diuretics, such as potassium nitrate and spirit of nitrous ether, may be used.

DIVERTICULUM (*diverto*, I turn aside) means a pouch or pocket leading off a main cavity or tube. The term is especially applied to protrusions from the intestine, which may be either present at the time of birth as a developmental peculiarity, or which in some cases develop in numbers upon the large intestine during the course of life, leading to constipation and general symptoms arising from absorption of poisonous products. The process of formation of these pockets is known as diverticulosis, and inflammation of them as diverticulitis.

DIZZINESS (*see* VERTIGO).

DOLICHOCEPHALIC means long-headed and is a term applied to skulls the breadth of which is less than four-fifths of the length.

DOSAGE.—The quantity of medicine given in one dose must vary considerably in different circumstances. Many drugs produce one effect when given in small amount, and quite another effect when administered in larger quantity ; thus antimony potassium tartrate in fractional doses of a grain causes merely profuse perspiration, whilst one or two grains act as an emetic.

Drug.	Dose in Imperial Measure.	Dose in Metric Measure.
Acetarsol	1 to 4 grains	0·06 to 0·25 G.
Acetazolamide	..	250 to 1000 mg.
Acetomenaphthone . . .	..	5 to 20 mg.
Adrenaline (by injection) . . .	..	0·2 to 0·5 mg.
Adrenaline acid tartrate (by injection) .	..	0·4 to 1 mg.
Allobarbitone	..	100 to 200 mg.
Almond oil	½ to 1 fluid ounce	15 to 30 ml.
Aloes, powdered	2 to 5 grains	0·12 to 0·3 G.
Aloin	¼ to 1 grain	15 to 60 mg.
Aluminium hydroxide gel . . .	60 to 120 minims	4 to 8 ml.
Aluminium hydroxide tablets, B.P. .	1 to 2 tablets	..
Aminophylline (Theophylline with Ethyl- enediamine) (by injection) . .	..	0·25 to 0·5 G.
Amiphenazole hydrochloride . .	..	15 to 60 mg.
Ammonia, aromatic solution of . .	15 to 60 minims	1 to 4 ml.
Ammonium bicarbonate . . .	5 to 10 grains	0·3 to 0·6 G.
Ammonium chloride	5 to 30 grains	0·3 to 2 G.
Amodiaquine (base)	..	400 mg.
(weekly prophylactic dose)		
Amphetamine sulphate . . .	..	5 to 10 mg.
Amyl nitrite (by inhalation) . .	2 to 5 minims	0·12 to 0·3 ml.
Amylobarbitone	..	100 to 200 mg.
Aneurine hydrochloride (vitamin B₁) .	..	2 to 5 mg.
(daily prophylactic dose)		
Aneurine hydrochloride . . .	..	25 to 100 mg.
(daily therapeutic dose)		
Aniseed oil	1 to 3 minims	0·06 to 0·2 ml.
Antazoline hydrochloride . . .	..	50 to 100 mg.
Antimony potassium tartrate (as emetic)	½ to 1 grain	30 to 60 mg.
Apomorphine hydrochloride (as emetic) .	1/32 to ⅛ grain	2 to 8 mg.
Arsenical solution (Fowler's solution) .	2 to 8 minims	0·12 to 0·5 ml.
Ascorbic acid (vitamin C) . . .	..	25 to 75 mg.
(daily prophylactic dose)		
Ascorbic acid (daily therapeutic dose) .	..	200 to 500 mg.
Aspirin	5 to 15 grains	0·3 to 1 G.
Atropine methonitrate . . .	..	0·2 to 0·6 mg.
Atropine sulphate	1/240 to 1/60 grain	0·25 to 1 mg.
Barbitone	..	0·3 to 0·6 G.
Belladonna, dry extract of . .	¼ to 1 grain	15 to 60 mg.
Belladonna, tincture of . . .	10 to 30 minims	0·6 to 2 ml.
Bemegride (by injection) . . .	..	40 to 80 mg.
Benactyzine hydrochloride . .	..	1 to 2 mg.
Benzhexol hydrochloride . . .	..	2 to 20 mg. (daily)
Benzoin, compound tincture of . .	30 to 60 minims	2 to 4 ml.
Bismuth carbonate	10 to 30 grains	0·6 to 2 G.
Blackcurrant, syrup of	..	4 to 8 ml.
Butobarbitone	..	100 to 200 mg.
Caffeine	5 to 10 grains	0·3 to 0·6 G.
Cajuput oil	1 to 3 minims	0·06 to 0·2 ml.
Calciferol (daily prophylactic dose) .	..	0·01 to 0·025 mg
Calciferol (daily therapeutic dose) .	..	0·125 to 1·25 mg.
Calcium carbonate	15 to 60 grains	1 to 4 G.
Calcium chloride	10 to 30 grains	0·6 to 2 G.
Calcium gluconate	15 to 60 grains	1 to 4 G.
Calcium gluconate, injection of . .	150 to 300 minims	10 to 20 ml.

mg.=milligramme; G.=gramme; ml.=millilitre

DOSAGE

Drug.	Dose in Imperial Measure.	Dose in Metric Measure.
Calcium lactate	15 to 60 grains	1 to 4 G.
Calomel	$\frac{1}{2}$ to 3 grains	0·03 to 0·2 G.
Camphor water	$\frac{1}{2}$ to 1 fluid ounce	15 to 30 ml.
Capsicum, tincture of	5 to 15 minims	0·3 to 1 ml.
Caraway, oil of	1 to 3 minims	0·06 to 0·2 ml.
Carbachol (subcutaneous injection)	..	0·25 to 0·5 mg.
Carbarsone	2 to 4 grains	0·12 to 0·25 G.
Carbon tetrachloride	30 to 60 minims	2 to 4 ml.
Carbromal	5 to 15 grains	300 to 1000 mg.
Cardamom, compound tincture of	30 to 60 minims	2 to 4 ml.
Cascara sagrada, elixir of	30 to 60 minims	2 to 4 ml.
Cascara sagrada, liquid extract of	30 to 60 minims	2 to 4 ml.
Castor oil	60 to 240 minims	4 to 16 ml.
Catechu, tincture of	30 to 60 minims	2 to 4 ml.
Chalk, aromatic powder of	10 to 60 grains	0·6 to 4 G.
Chalk, aromatic powder of, with opium	10 to 60 grains	0·6 to 4 G.
Charcoal	60 to 120 grains	4 to 8 G.
Chiniofon sodium	..	0·1 to 0·5 G.
Chloral hydrate	5 to 30 grains	0·3 to 2 G.
Chlorbutol (Chloretone)	5 to 20 grains	0·3 to 1·2 G.
Chlorcyclizine hydrochloride	..	50 to 150 mg.
Chloroform, spirit of	5 to 30 minims	0·3 to 2 ml.
Chloroform water	$\frac{1}{2}$ to 1 fluid ounce	15 to 30 ml.
Chloroquine (base) (weekly prophylactic dose)	..	300 mg.
Chlorothiazide	..	0·5 to 2 G.
Chlorpromazine	..	25 to 50 mg.
Choline theophyllinate	..	100 to 400 mg.
Cinnamon, oil of	1 to 3 minims	0·06 to 0·2 ml.
Citric acid	5 to 30 grains	0·3 to 2 G.
Clove, oil of	1 to 3 minims	0·06 to 0·2 ml.
Cocaine hydrochloride	$\frac{1}{8}$ to $\frac{1}{4}$ grain	8 to 16 mg.
Cochineal, tincture of	5 to 15 minims	0·3 to 1 ml.
Cocillana, liquid extract of	5 to 15 minims	0·3 to 1 ml.
Codeine phosphate	$\frac{1}{6}$ to $\frac{1}{2}$ grain	10 to 60 mg.
Cod-liver oil (daily dose)	60 to 240 minims	4 to 16 ml.
Colchicine	..	0·5 mg.
Colchicum, tincture of	8 to 15 minims	0·5 to 1 ml.
Colocynth, compound extract of	2 to 8 grains	0·12 to 0·5 G.
Crystal violet (medicinal gentian violet)	$\frac{1}{6}$ to $\frac{1}{2}$ grain	10 to 30 mg.
Cyclobarbitone	..	100 to 200 mg.
Cyclizine hydrochloride	..	25 to 50 mg.
Dexamphetamine sulphate	..	5 to 10 mg.
Dextromethorphan hydrobromide	..	15 to 30 mg.
Diamorphine hydrochloride	$\frac{1}{12}$ to $\frac{1}{8}$ grain	5 to 10 mg.
Diamorphine, linctus of	30 to 120 minims	2 to 8 ml.
Dicoumarol (daily dose)	..	50 to 300 mg.
Diethylcarbamazine citrate	..	150 to 500 mg.
Digitalis, prepared	$\frac{1}{2}$ to $1\frac{1}{2}$ grains	30 to 100 mg.
Digitalis, tincture of	5 to 15 minims	0·3 to 1 ml.
Digoxin	..	0·25 to 1 mg.
Di-iodohydroxyquinoline	..	1 to 2 G.
Dimenhydrinate	..	25 to 50 mg.
Diphenhydramine hydrochloride	..	25 to 75 mg.
Dover's powder	5 to 10 grains	0·3 to 0·6 G.
Emetine and bismuth iodide	1 to 3 grains	0·06 to 0·2 G.

Drug.	Dose in Imperial Measure.	Dose in Metric Measure.
Emetine hydrochloride (by injection) .	$\frac{1}{2}$ to 1 grain	30 to 60 mg.
Ephedrine hydrochloride . . .	$\frac{1}{4}$ to 1 grain	16 to 60 mg.
Epsom salts	30 to 240 grains	2 to 16 G.
Ergot, liquid extract of . . .	10 to 20 minims	0·6 to 1·2 ml.
Ergotamine tartrate . . .	..	1 to 2 mg.
Ergotamine tartrate (by subcutaneous injection)	..	0·25 to 0·5 mg.
Erythrol tetranitrate . . .	$\frac{1}{4}$ to 1 grain	15 to 60 mg.
Ether, nitrous, spirit of . .	15 to 60 minims	1 to 4 ml.
Ethinylœstradiol (daily dose) . .	..	0·01 to 0·1 mg.
Ethisterone (daily dose) . .	..	25 to 100 mg.
Eucalyptus oil	1 to 3 minims	0·06 to 0·2 ml.
Fern, male, extract of . .	45 to 90 minims	3 to 6 ml.
Figs, compound syrup of . .	30 to 120 minims	2 to 8 ml.
Folic acid	..	5 to 20 mg. (daily)
Gelsemium, tincture of . .	5 to 15 minims	0·3 to 1 ml.
Gentian, compound infusion of .	$\frac{1}{2}$ to 1 fluid ounce	15 to 30 ml.
Ginger, syrup of	30 to 60 minims	2 to 4 ml.
Glauber's salt	30 to 240 grains	2 to 16 G.
Glutethimide	..	250 to 500 mg.
Glycerophosphates, syrup of .	60 to 120 minims	4 to 8 ml.
Glyceryl trinitrate	$\frac{1}{180}$ to $\frac{1}{60}$ grain	0·5 to 1 mg.
Gregory's powder . . .	10 to 60 grains	0·6 to 4 G.
Guaiacol	5 to 10 minims	0·3 to 0·6 ml.
Halibut-liver oil (daily dose) . .	..	0·06 to 0·5 ml.
Hexamine	10 to 30 grains	0·6 to 2 G.
Hexobarbitone	4 to 8 grains	0·25 to 0·5 G.
Hydrochloric acid, dilute . .	10 to 120 minims	0·6 to 8 ml.
Hydrocyanic acid, diluted . .	2 to 5 minims	0·12 to 0·3 ml.
Hyoscine hydrobromide . .	$\frac{1}{200}$ to $\frac{1}{100}$ grain	0·3 to 0·6 mg.
Hyoscyamus, tincture of . .	30 to 60 minims	2 to 4 ml.
Hypophosphites, syrup of . .	60 to 120 minims	4 to 8 ml.
Hypophosphorous acid, dilute .	5 to 15 minims	0·3 to 1 ml.
Iodine, aqueous solution of (Lugol's solution)	5 to 15 minims	0·3 to 1 ml.
Ipecacuanha and opium, powder of (Dover's powder)	5 to 10 grains	0·3 to 0·6 G.
Ipecacuanha, liquid extract of (as emetic)	10 to 30 minims	0·6 to 2 ml.
Ipecacuanha, prepared (as emetic)	15 to 30 grains	1 to 2 G.
Ipecacuanha, tincture of (as emetic) .	$\frac{1}{4}$ to 1 fluid ounce	15 to 30 ml.
Iron and ammonium citrate . .	15 to 45 grains	1 to 3 G.
Iron (ferric), chloride, solution of .	5 to 15 minims	0·3 to 1 ml.
Iron (ferrous) sulphate . . .	3 to 5 grains	0·2 to 0·3 G.
Isoprenaline	..	5 to 20 mg.
Kaolin light	$\frac{1}{2}$ to 2 ounces	15 to 60 G.
Laudanum	5 to 30 minims	0·3 to 2 ml.
Lemon, syrup of	30 to 120 minims	2 to 8 ml.
Leptazol, injection of	..	0·5 to 1 ml
Lime water	1 to 4 fluid ounces	30 to 120 ml.
Liquorice, compound powder of .	60 to 120 grains	4 to 8 G.
Lobelia	3 to 10 grains	0·2 to 0·6 G.

Drug.	Dose in Imperial Measure.	Dose in Metric Measure.
Magnesium bicarbonate solution (fluid magnesia)	1 to 2 fluid ounces	30 to 60 ml.
Magnesium carbonate, heavy . .	5 to 60 grains	0·3 to 4 G.
Magnesium carbonate, light . . .	5 to 60 grains	0·3 to 4 G.
Magnesium hydroxide, mixture of .	60 to 240 minims	4 to 16 ml.
Magnesium oxide, heavy . . .	5 to 60 grains	0·3 to 4 G.
Magnesium oxide, light . . .	5 to 60 grains	0·3 to 4 G.
Magnesium sulphate	30 to 240 grains	2 to 16 G.
Magnesium trisilicate	5 to 30 grains	0·3 to 2 G.
Malt extract	60 minims to 1 fl. oz.	4 to 30 ml.
Mandelic acid	30 to 60 grains	2 to 4 G.
Meclozine hydrochloride . . .	..	25 to 50 mg. (daily)
Menaphthone (by injection) . . .	..	5 to 10 mg. (daily)
Mepacrine hydrochloride . . .	..	100 mg.
(daily prophylactic dose)		
Meprobamate	..	400 to 800 mg.
Mepyramine maleate	..	300 to 800 mg. (daily)
Mercury pill	4 to 8 grains	0·25 to 0·5 G.
Mercury subchloride	½ to 3 grains	30 to 200 mg.
Mersalyl, injection of	..	0·5 to 2 ml.
Metacholine chloride (by injection) .	..	10 to 25 mg.
Methadone	$\frac{1}{12}$ to $\frac{1}{6}$ grain	5 to 10 mg.
Methoin	..	50 to 100 mg.
Methylamphetamine hydrochloride .	..	2·5 to 10 mg.
Methylamphetamine hydrochloride (by injection)	..	10 to 30 mg.
Methylpentynol	..	250 to 1000 mg.
Methylphenobarbitone (Phemitone) .	1 to 3 grains	0·06 to 0·2 G.
Methylthionin chloride (methylene blue)	1 to 5 grains	60 to 300 mg.
Methylthiouracil	..	0·1 to 0·3 G.
Morphine hydrochloride . . .	⅛ to ⅓ grain	8 to 20 mg.
Morphine hydrochloride, solution of .	5 to 30 minims	0·3 to 2 ml.
Morphine sulphate	⅛ to ⅓ grain	8 to 20 mg.
Myrrh, tincture of	30 to 60 minims	2 to 4 ml.
Nalorphine hydrobromide (by injection)	..	5 to 10 mg.
Nicotinamide (daily prophylactic dose) .	..	15 to 30 mg.
Nicotinamide (daily therapeutic dose) .	..	50 to 250 mg.
Nicotinic acid	..	15 to 30 mg.
(daily prophylactic dose)		
Nicotinic acid	..	50 to 250 mg.
(daily therapeutic dose)		
Nikethamide, injection of . . .	..	1 to 4 ml.
Nitroglycerin tablets	$\frac{1}{180}$ to $\frac{1}{60}$ grain	0·5 to 1 mg.
Nitrous ether, spirit of . . .	15 to 60 minims	1 to 4 ml.
Nutmeg, oil of	1 to 3 minims	0·06 to 0·2 ml.
Nux vomica, tincture of . . .	10 to 30 minims	0·6 to 2 ml.
Octyl nitrite (by inhalation) . .	3 to 6 minims	0·2 to 0·4 ml.
Opium, camphorated tincture of (paregoric)	30 to 120 minims	2 to 8 ml.
Opium, powdered	½ to 3 grains	30 to 200 mg.
Opium, tincture of	5 to 30 minims	0·3 to 2 ml.
Oxymel	30 to 120 minims	2 to 8 ml.
Oxymel of squill	30 to 60 minims	2 to 4 ml.
Oxytocin, injection of . . .	..	1 to 5 units

Drug.	Dose in Imperial Measure.	Dose in Metric Measure.
Pancreatin	8 to 15 grains	0·5 to 1 G.
Papaverine hydrochloride	2½ to 5 grains	0·15 to 0·3 G.
Paraffin, liquid	¼ to 1 fluid ounce	8 to 30 ml.
Paraldehyde	30 to 120 minims	2 to 8 ml.
Paregoric	30 to 60 minims	2 to 4 ml.
Pentrobrabitone	..	100 to 200 mg.
Peppermint oil	1 to 3 minims	0·06 to 0·2 ml.
Peppermint water, concentrated	5 to 15 minims	0·3 to 1 ml.
Pepsin	5 to 15 grains	0·3 to 1 G.
Pethidine hydrochloride	..	25 to 100 mg.
Phenacetin	5 to 10 grains	0·3 to 0·6 G.
Phenazone	5 to 10 grains	0·3 to 0·6 G.
Phenindamine tartrate	..	25 to 50 mg.
Phenobarbitone	..	30 to 120 mg.
Phenolphthalein	1 to 5 grains	0·06 to 0·3 G.
Phenylbutazone	..	200 to 400 mg. (daily)
Phenytoin sodium	¾ to 1½ grains	50 to 100 mg.
Pholcodine	..	5 to 15 mg.
Phosphoric acid, dilute	5 to 60 minims	0·3 to 4 ml.
Phthalylsulphathiazole	..	5 to 10 G. (daily)
Physostigmine salicylate	..	3 to 6 mg.
Picrotoxin (by injection)	..	0·6 to 3 mg.
Pilocarpine nitrate	1/20 to ⅕ grain	3 to 12 mg.
Piperazine adipate	..	1 to 2 G. (daily)
Podophyllum resin	¼ to 1 grain	15 to 60 mg.
Potassium acetate	15 to 30 grains	1 to 2 G.
Potassium acid tartrate	15 to 60 grains	1 to 4 G.
Potassium bicarbonate	15 to 30 grains	1 to 2 G.
Potassium bromide	5 to 20 grains	0·3 to 1·2 G.
Potassium citrate	15 to 30 grains	1 to 2 G.
Potassium iodide	5 to 30 grains	0·3 to 2 G.
Prednisolone	..	10 to 50 mg. (daily)
Prednisone	..	10 to 50 mg. (daily)
Primaquine phosphate	..	10 to 15 mg. (daily)
Primidone	..	0·5 to 1·5 G. (daily)
Procyclidine hydrochloride	..	2·5 to 20 mg. (daily)
Proguanil (paludrine) (daily prophylactic dose)	..	100 mg.
Promethazine hydrochloride	..	25 to 75 mg. (daily)
Propantheline bromide	..	15 to 30 mg.
Propylthiouracil	..	50 to 600 mg. (daily)
Pyrimethamine (weekly prophylactic dose)	..	25 mg.
Quassia, fresh infusion of	½ to 1 fluid ounce	15 to 30 ml.
Quinalbarbitone	..	100 to 200 mg.
Quinidine sulphate	1 to 5 grains	0·06 to 0·3 G.
Quinine hydrochloride	5 to 10 grains	0·3 to 0·6 G.
Quinine sulphate	5 to 10 grains	0·3 to 0·6 G.
Reserpine	..	0·25 to 1 mg. (daily)
Rhubarb, compound powder of	10 to 60 grains	0·6 to 4 G.
Riboflavine (prophylactic daily dose)	..	1 to 4 mg.
Riboflavine (therapeutic daily dose)	..	5 to 10 mg.

DOSAGE

Drug.	Dose in Imperial Measure.	Dose in Metric Measure.
Sal volatile, spirit of	15 to 60 minims	1 to 4 ml.
Santonin	1 to 3 grains	0·06 to 0·2 G.
Senega, tincture of	30 to 60 minims	2 to 4 ml.
Senna, compound mixture of . .	1 to 2 fluid ounces	30 to 60 ml.
Senna confection . . .	60 to 120 grains	4 to 8 G.
Senna leaf	10 to 30 grains	0·6 to 2 G.
Sodium acid phosphate . . .	30 to 60 grains	2 to 4 G.
Sodium aurothiomalate (by injection) .	..	10 to 100 mg. (weekly)
Sodium benzoate	5 to 30 grains	0·3 to 2 G.
Sodium bicarbonate	15 to 60 grains	1 to 4 G.
Sodium bromide	5 to 20 grains	0·3 to 1·2 G.
Sodium citrate	15 to 60 grains	1 to 4 G.
Sodium iodide	5 to 30 grains	0·3 to 2 G.
Sodium nitrite	½ to 2 grains	0·03 to 0·12 G.
Sodium potassium tartrate . . .	120 to 240 grains	8 to 16 G.
Sodium salicylate	10 to 30 grains	0·6 to 2 G.
Sodium stibogluconate (by injection) .	..	0·6 to 2 G. (daily)
Sodium sulphate	30 to 240 grains	2 to 16 G.
Solapsone	..	1 to 3 G. (daily)
Solapsone (by injection) . . .	..	0·5 to 1·5 G. (twice (weekly)
Squill, tincture of . . .	10 to 30 minims	0·6 to 2 ml.
Stibophen (by injection) . . .	..	100 to 300 mg.
Stramonium, tincture of . . .	10 to 30 minims	0·6 to 2 ml.
Strychnine hydrochloride . . .	$\frac{1}{30}$ to $\frac{1}{8}$ grain	2 to 8 mg.
Strychnine hydrochloride, solution of .	3 to 12 minims	0·2 to 0·8 ml.
Succinylsulphathiazole . . .	..	10 to 20 G. (daily)
Sulphonal	5 to 20 grains	0·3 to 1·2 G.
Sulphur, sublimed (flowers of sulphur) .	15 to 60 grains	1 to 4 G.
Suramin (by intravenous injection) .	..	1 to 2 G.
Syrup, compound, of iron phosphate (Parrish)	30 to 120 minims	2 to 8 ml.
Syrup of iron phosphate with quinine and strychnine (Easton) . .	30 to 60 minims	2 to 4 ml.
Tartaric acid	5 to 30 grains	0·3 to 2 G.
Terebene	5 to 15 minims	0·3 to 1 ml.
Theobromine and sodium salicylate .	10 to 20 grains	0·6 to 1·2 G.
Theophylline	1 to 3 grains	0·06 to 0·2 G.
Theophylline and sodium acetate . .	2 to 5 grains	0·12 to 0·3 G.
Thiouracil	..	0·1 to 0·2 G.
Thymol (as anthelmintic) . . .	15 to 30 grains	1 to 2 G.
Thyroid	½ to 2 grains	0·03 to 0·12 G.
Thyroxine sodium	..	0·05 to 0·5 mg. (daily)
Tolazoline	..	25 to 75 mg.
Tolu, syrup of	30 to 120 minims	2 to 8 ml.
Totaquina	5 to 10 grains	0·3 to 0·6 G.
Tryparsamide (by injection) . .	..	1 to 2 G.
Urea	..	5 to 15 G.
Vasopressin, injection of . . .	..	0·25 to 0·75 ml.
Yeast, dried	..	1 to 8 G.
Zinc sulphate (as emetic) . . .	10 to 30 grains	0·6 to 2 G.

Many factors, however, influence the activity with which drugs of very definite effect operate ; and instead of having a fixed dose each drug varies in the amount given, according to circumstances, within certain recognized limits. Among the factors which affect the necessary quantity are age, weight, sex, idiosyncrasy, habitual use, disease, fasting, combination with other drugs, and the form in which the drug is given.

Age is perhaps the most important factor of all, for naturally a young child requires a smaller dose than an adult. Again, some of the most potent remedies, such as opium and strychnine, are borne by children very badly. On the other hand, children require nearly the full adult dose of some remedies like arsenic, calomel, belladonna, ipecacuanha, and most purgatives. Various devices have been introduced for calculating roughly and quickly the dose generally suitable for a child of any given age : *e.g.*—

$$\text{adult dose} \times \frac{\text{age next birthday}}{20}$$

According to *Young's Rule* the fraction of the adult dose is measured by dividing the child's age by the age plus 12.

Weight and Sex are of importance, for, as a rule, women require slightly smaller doses than men, and naturally an individual weighing 100 pounds would require much less than a person of double that size.

Idiosyncrasy occasionally causes drugs administered in the ordinary dose to produce unexpected effects. Thus some people are but little affected by even powerful drugs, whilst in others certain drugs, such as iodide of potassium, calomel, or belladonna, produce excessive symptoms in minute doses. Similar facts are noticed in persons of one family or race.

Habitual use of a drug is perhaps the influence that causes the greatest increase in the dose necessary to produce its effect. The most notable examples are found in the large quantities of opium and arsenic that can be tolerated by addicts to these drugs. The conrary holds with regard to some of the most active alkaloidal principles like strychnine, which, after being taken without an interval over a prolonged

period, are liable to accumulate in the system and suddenly to produce an extreme or even dangerous effect.

Disease modifies considerably the dose of many medicines, for their tendency to produce poisonous effects diminishes in circumstances that urgently require their administration.

Fasting aids the rapidity of absorption of, and also makes the system much more susceptible than otherwise to, the action of most remedies. For this reason, as well as to avoid irritation of the stomach, it is usual to prescribe medicines to be taken after meals, and diluted with water.

Combination of different drugs possessing a similar action is sometimes practised in the writing of prescriptions, and frequently this enables the total dose to be more effective with fewer of the undesirable subsidiary symptoms that would accompany the use of one of the drugs given by itself.

Form of Administration is also highly important, for active principles when separated and given by themselves in solution produce more rapid and intense effects than a corresponding amount of the crude drug. Except when specially indicated, the doses given in the accompanying table are those for administration by the mouth to adults.

DOUCHE (French word) is an application of water to the body, directly, through a pipe.

Action. — Douches fall into two divisions : (*a*) those which act by virtue of some substance which they contain, such as astringent douches, cleansing douches, etc. ; (*b*) those which act by virtue of their temperature, producing the effects which have been described under BATHS, and COLD, USES OF, with the distinction that douches act locally and so produce an action, upon one part only, greater than if the application were made to the whole body at one time.

Uses.—(*a*) MEDICATED AND CLEANSING DOUCHES are applied when it is inconvenient to use a general bath. For example, *warm douches* of boric lotion may be used to irrigate wounds or ulcers, either in order to remove dressings which are adherent, or in order to maintain a steady trickle over the broken surface, and prevent accumula-

DOUCHE

tion of putrefactive material. *Bladder douches* are often used in inflammation of this cavity, containing, for example, boric acid solution (1 in 80), or weak potassium permanganate solution. Such a douche is administered by means of

FIG. 128.—Douche-can, tube, and nozzle.

a douche-can holding one quart or more, connected by india-rubber piping with a three-way or T-shaped tube of glass, which, on its other two ends, has an outflow tube and a tube leading to a catheter introduced into the bladder. The douche-can being suspended at a height of 3 feet or so above the bed on which the patient lies, is filled with fluid, which runs into the bladder as soon as the outflow tube is pinched. When sufficient has entered, it can be at once drawn off by pinching the inflow tube and releasing the outflow. This is repeated several times. *Vaginal douches* of sulphate of zinc (40 grains per pint (4·5 grammes per litre)), Condy's fluid of a pink tinge, sodium bicarbonate (60 grains per pint (7 grammes per litre)), are used in cases of leucorrhœa or 'whites'. A quart or larger douche-can is used at a height of 5 or 6 feet. It leads by an india-rubber tube to a large nozzle, which should be made of glass for ready disinfection. Very often such a douche is used at a temperature of 115° F. (46° C.), or as hot as the hand can bear, in order to obtain also the soothing and constricting action of a hot douche on the blood-vessels of the surrounding parts.

DRASTICS

(*b*) TEMPERATURE DOUCHES may be hot or cold, or in general the two alternated. The action upon the circulation has been explained under the heading of BATHS, with the exception that the douche acts strongly upon a single part. Douching, combined with massage, is a useful procedure for rheumatism, neuralgia, and other pains. The Scotch douche consists of an alternate hot water or steam douche and a cold douche. It is used for similar purposes, and it is important that the hot stream should be given first, and that it should last four or five times as long as the cold stream. Such a douche acts powerfully upon the skin and nerves, and can be continued for a few minutes only.

DOVER'S POWDER, also known as POWDER OF IPECACUANHA AND MORPHINE, is made from 10 per cent. each of powdered opium and ipecacuanha, with 80 per cent. of sulphate of potassium (*see* OPIUM). Still one of the most popular remedies in medicine, it was introduced by Captain Thomas Dover (1660–1742), one of the most romantic figures in the history of medicine. Perhaps his greatest claim to fame is that he was a member of the privateering expedition which rescued Alexander Selkirk from Juan Fernandez, an island off the coast of Chile. It was upon the story of Alexander Selkirk that Daniel Defoe based his immortal *Robinson Crusoe*.

Uses.—It is widely used as a diaphoretic, analgesic, and sedative in the treatment of feverish colds and influenza. It is also an excellent remedy for dry, hacking coughs. The dose is 5 to 10 grains (300 to 600 mg.).

DOWN'S SYNDROME (*see* MONGOLISM.)

DRAINS (*see* WATER-CLOSETS, etc.).

DRAMAMINE is the trade name for beta-dimethylaminoethyl-benzohydryl-ether-8-chlorotheophyllinate, a drug which is widely used, with considerable success, in the treatment of travel sickness. The *British Pharmacopœia* Approved Name for it is dimenhydrinate.

DRASTICS (δράω, I act) are substances which have a violent purgative

277

action, such as croton oil, jalap, scammony. (*See* PURGATIVES.)

DRAUGHT, or DRAFT, is a small mixture intended to be taken at one dose. It consists generally of two or four tablespoonfuls of fluid. The best-known is black draft, whose chief constituents are sulphate of magnesium and tincture of senna.

DRAW SHEET (*see* BED).

DREAMS (*see* SLEEP).

DRENCH is an old term still used in parts of England for a draft of medicine.

DREPANOCYTOSIS is another term for sickle-cell anæmia, which is characterized by the presence in the blood of red blood corpuscles sickle-like in shape. The anæmia is a severe one and afflicts the negro race.

DRESSINGS (*see* WOUNDS).

DROP-FOOT is a condition in which there is difficulty in raising the front part of the foot from the ground, or in which, when the condition is severe, the foot hangs limp.

Causes.—The commonest form is that due to neuritis of the nerve (anterior tibial) supplying the muscles on the front of the leg. It may be caused by alcohol, lead poisoning, or trauma to the leg, or it may follow some infection such as typhoid fever or diphtheria. In drop-foot from these causes, there are apt to be disturbances of sensation on the leg also. Drop-foot may occur in children who have had infantile paralysis, but in this condition there is no sensory disturbance. It is also liable to occur in patients who are confined to bed for any length of time. In order to prevent this occurring the weight of the bed-clothes should be taken off the patient's feet by means of a cradle. If the condition is not so severe as to prevent the patient from going about, he walks by lifting the foot high so as to prevent the toes from catching on objects on the ground.

Treatment.—If the condition is due to neuritis, it tends gradually to become better as the neuritis passes off. (*See* NEURITIS.) While the condition lasts, it is usual for the patient to wear a shoe the front part of which is supported by an elastic band attached to the front of the leg, in order to prevent the weak muscles from being overstretched and the toes from dropping. Massage and electrical treatment are also required to maintain the tone of the affected muscles.

DROPPED BEAT means the missing out of a regular beat of the heart. It can be detected either by listening to the heart or by feeling the pulse. It may be due to HEART BLOCK or to an EXTRASYSTOLE. Dropped beat due to extrasystole is of no great significance.

DROPSY, or HYDROPS (ύδρωψ), means an abnormal accumulation of fluid beneath the skin, or in one or more of the cavities of the body. The term is a general one, the accumulation in special localities having special names, *e.g.* dropsy beneath the skin is known, when limited, as *œdema*, when widespread, as *anasarca*; dropsy in the abdomen as *ascites*, in the chest as *hydrothorax*, and in the head as *hydrocephalus*.

Causes.—Dropsy is not a disease, although this is a popular idea, supported by the fact that at one time many deaths were recorded as due to ' dropsy ' without a further statement of the cause. Dropsy may be due to one of three conditions : (1) weakening of the walls of the capillary vessels, by injury of the part in which dropsy occurs, by ill-health of the body generally, by poverty of the blood circulating through and nourishing the vessels, or by poisonous materials in the blood ; (2) obstruction to the blood - flow through the veins ; (3) a watery condition of the blood, allowing fluid to escape through the capillary walls. Dropsy may also result from obstruction to the flow of lymph in the lymph channels.

Heart disease, which produces increased pressure in the veins, and also an impure condition of the blood, in consequence of the defective pumping action of the heart, and *Bright's disease*, in which the kidneys fail in their functions of excreting poisonous substances and a certain amount of water from the blood, are the main causes of general dropsy. In heart disease the dropsy is more marked after exertion, in kidney disease it is found chiefly after resting. Thus one of the chief characters of dropsy due to Bright's disease is that it appears in the morning, affects loose tissues like the skin beneath the eyes, and passes off as the day advances. Dropsy due to heart disease, on the other hand, tends to appear towards evening, affects dependent parts like the feet, and diminishes during the night. When the two diseases are combined, the state of dropsy may become very grave.

In *Hunger œdema*, due to starvation, the dropsy is generalized, but in the earlier stages is most marked in the feet and legs, especially after exertion. The swelling which sometimes follows serpent-bites, bee-stings, or the eating of poisonous shell-fish, and constitutes an extreme and rapidly ensuing form of *nettle-rash*, is a special variety of dropsy. *White-leg*, which may appear after some acute disease like typhoid fever or pneumonia, or after the birth of a child, due to a thrombosis or plugging up of the main vein in the affected limb, is one of the localized forms of dropsy. A similar condition may be caused by a *tumour* pressing upon a large vein of the arm or leg. Dropsy in the legs may be due to varicose veins. *Cirrhosis*, tumours, and other diseases of the liver may, by interference with the circulation through it, cause dropsy, first of the abdomen and later of the lower limbs.

Treatment. — There is no general treatment which will meet every case. The particular cause has, in each case, to be removed. Dropsy due to heart or kidney disease yields as the disease producing it is alleviated. In cases of localized dropsy, elevation of the dropsical part is of great importance, and the person should adopt the recumbent position. In the case of heart disease, digitalis, which improves the action of the heart, and benzthiadiazine diuretics form the chief means employed. In acute kidney disease the treatment of the dropsy consists in the hot-air baths, aperients, and drugs to act upon the skin which form the routine treatment of Bright's disease. In dropsy due to liver conditions, occasional purges with blue-pill or calomel may help the condition. When the dropsy will not yield to drugs, some of the fluid may have to be drawn off (*see* ASPIRATION) ; when this is done partially, the kidneys are sometimes enabled to cope with the remainder of the fluid.

DROP-WRIST is a condition in which, owing to partial or complete paralysis of the muscles which extend the hand, the latter droops at the wrist.

Causes.—Perhaps the commonest form is that known as crutch-palsy, in which, owing to the constant pressure of a crutch in the armpit, the large nerve (musculo - spiral) that controls the extensor muscles of the forearm becomes damaged, and hence the muscles in question are paralysed. The same effect may be produced when a person sleeps with his head resting on the upper arm, or with the arm over the back of a chair. A blow on the back of the arm may produce a similar condition. Poisoning by alcohol or by lead may also cause the condition, which may also be brought about by a chill.

Treatment.—The forms due to pressure on the nerve or to chill require only rest and application of massage and electricity to the muscles to prevent their wasting for recovery usually takes place gradually but surely. In the cases due to lead, the appropriate treatment for lead poisoning is necessary.

DROWNING, RECOVERY FROM. —In Britain, more than a thousand people are drowned every year, practically a third of whom are under the age of 15. In drowning, death as a rule ensues from asphyxia (*see* ASPHYXIA), although, in falls from a height upon water, or in cases where the body in falling has encountered blows upon the head or abdomen, death may be due to 'shock'. In the latter case, instead of the signs of asphyxia, the skin is pale, the face placid, and the lungs are empty of water because no attempts at breathing have taken place. In slight cases of shock the chances of resuscitation are rather more hopeful than in cases of asphyxia, because little water has been drawn into the lungs, and because there has been no struggling. It must be remembered that recovery from drowning may take place even after submersions for as long as half an hour. Artificial respiration must therefore be persisted in until the signs of death are unmistakable. Speed and immediate treatment on withdrawal from the water are of paramount importance.

The specific gravity of the body being slightly greater than that of water, it sinks at first; then if the person is able to struggle, his efforts bring him to the surface, only to sink again as he becomes exhausted. This may be repeated several times. In these struggles, water mixed with air is drawn into the air-passages, and the two are churned up with mucus into a froth which forms a great obstacle to the entrance of air into the lungs during subsequent attempts at resuscitation. The first step in this process should be taken *on the instant the body is drawn from the water*, without delay for any examination, removal of clothing, or the like, and consists in the attempt to restore breathing by *artificial respiration*. Before beginning the actual movements of artificial respiration a few seconds may be spent in getting rid of as much water as possible from the lungs and air-passages: for example, a child may be held up by its heels, and the water will run out of its mouth; when an adult is lying prone on the ground, as in the illustration, the operator's arms can be linked round the patient's middle, which is then raised, and water will flow out of the mouth. Any seaweeds or other matter in the mouth should be quickly removed by the finger. The same methods of artificial respiration are applicable whatever the cause of asphyxia. Six methods are available. According to the St. John Ambulance Association, the St. Andrew's Ambulance Association and the British Red Cross Society, expired air resuscitation, or mouth-to-mouth (or -nose) method is the method of choice.

1. **Schafer's prone-posture method.** —Immediately on removal from the water, place the patient face downwards on the ground, with a folded coat under the lower part of the chest, and lose no time by removing clothing. Turn the patient's face a little to one side, so that the mouth and nose are not obstructed. Let the operator *kneel astride* of, or to one side of, the patient, facing his head, and let him

place his hands over the lower part of the patient's back, one on each side (on the lowest ribs). Let him throw the weight of his body forward upon his hands, so as to press the air (and water if there is any) out of the patient's

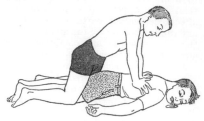

FIG. 129.—Artificial respiration by Schafer's method.

lungs. Then let him immediately raise his body to take the pressure off and allow the patient's chest to expand. Repeat these movements twelve or fifteen times per minute.

This method has the advantages of extreme simplicity and great effectiveness. Further, no time is lost in freeing the air passages of water and mucus, which may drain from the mouth during the whole procedure; there is no trouble caused by the tongue falling backwards into the throat, as in the face-up methods; the patient is not so liable to bruising as in the Marshall Hall method, nor to injury of the ribs or liver, which may be occasioned by the Howard method. The introducer of the method also claimed that while the amount of air taken into the lungs of an average-sized healthy person is about 5850 millilitres per minute, the amount that can be drawn in by this method is about 6760 millilitres, an amount far in excess of that possible by the Silvester or Marshall Hall method. While in the Silvester method force is employed to produce inspiration as well as expiration, in Schafer's method, as in Howard's method, the force is used only to compress the chest, and the chest is allowed to expand by its own elasticity and draw air into the lungs.

2. **Holger-Nielsen's method** is the method now recommended by the British Red Cross Society. The principle is that the chest is compressed against the ground for expiration and raised by the arms for inspiration. The

patient is turned face downwards, with the arms upwards and the elbows flexed, so that his head is turned to the side and rests on his hands. The operator kneels on one knee at the patient's head and facing his feet, with his opposite foot near the patient's elbow. For the inspiratory movement grasp the arms above the elbows and rock backwards, raising the arms until tension is felt. Count 1, 2, 3 while doing this (= 2½ seconds). For expiration drop the arms and put your hands on the patient's back just below the shoulder blades, with the thumbs touching, and count 4 as you do this. Rock forwards with your elbows straight and exert steady pressure on the chest. Count 5, 6, 7 while doing this (= 2½ seconds). Slide your hands off the back and on to the patient's arms as you count 8. This cycle should be repeated 10 to 12 times a minute. If the arm is injured, inspiration is achieved by lifting from the shoulders rather than the upper arms.

3. **Marshall Hall's ready method** is valuable for two reasons: firstly, because it frees one lung thoroughly from its frothy water; and, secondly, because it is a very easy and simple method. A roll about 6 to 8 inches thick is made, for example, out of a rolled-up coat and vest, or a large stone or spar of wood may be used for the purpose. With this under his chest, the patient is placed face downwards, and firm pressure made with both hands upon the back to expel air and water. Then the body, grasped by the shoulders, is turned steadily upon one side, still lying upon the bundle or stone, so that one lung is expanded. Then the body is turned again upon the face so that the air is expelled from the chest, and so forth, each movement being repeated about fifteen times per minute. It is important always to turn the body upon the same side, otherwise water is apt to run from the lung which was previously the lower one, and again choke up the air passages of the one which has been cleared.

4. **Silvester's method** is fairly efficient and quite simple. Its drawbacks are, that in addition to the operator there should be some one to hold the feet of the patient—though this is not absolutely necessary—and that there may

be difficulty in keeping the entrance to the larynx open. To effect the latter,

FIG. 130.—Artificial respiration by rocking method. (From Belilios, *First Aid and Bandaging.* Baillière, Tindall and Cox.)

the tongue must be drawn forward, and if necessary held forwards either by means of a cloth or forceps. The patient after his air passages have been cleared, as in Howard's method, is placed on a flat surface inclined a little

FIG. 131a.

from the feet upwards, with a roll of clothing under his shoulders. The mouth and nose are carefully wiped. Then to produce inspiration the operator, placing himself at the head of the patient, grasps his arms just above the elbows, and draws them upward by the side of the head for two seconds.

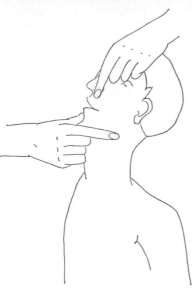

Fig. 131b.

(Note that in Bain's modification of Silvester's method the operator grasps

Fig. 131c.—The mouth-to-mouth method of artificial respiration.
[The Practitioner.]

the pectoral muscles and collar-bone in front of the armpit.) Next, to pro-

duce expiration, he turns down the arms and presses them against the patient's chest for two seconds. This is repeated fifteen times a minute. A caution is necessary that the downward movements must not be made too forcibly ; for serious damage is apt to be done to the internal organs of an unconscious person by violent pressure.

5. **Rocking method,** originally recommended by Dr. F. C. Eve, is carried out by securing the patient face-down on a stretcher. The stretcher is then rocked at the rate of 12 to 15 double rocks per minute (Fig. 130). It is an excellent form of artificial respiration provided the stretcher and suitable appliances for rocking it are available.

6. **Expired-air resuscitation** is a method which has recently come to the fore. It consists of the old Biblical method of breathing direct into the victim's mouth. Careful investigations carried out in the United States, this country, and Australia indicate that it is a more efficient method of artificial respiration than any of the more indirect methods, such as the Holger-Nielsen method.

As in all methods of artificial respiration, speed is the essence of success. Briefly, the technique is as follows :—
(1) Lay the victim on his back and kneel opposite his left ear. (2) Turn his head towards you and extend it to the sniffing position (Fig. 131a). (3) Open his mouth, and sweep a finger round the mouth and throat to remove any obvious debris. (4) Place the thumb of the right hand between the teeth and grip the lower jaw in the centre and hold it forwards so that the lower front teeth protrude (Fig. 131b). (5) Close the victim's nose by pinching the nostrils with the thumb and index fingers of the left hand (Fig. 131b). (6) Take a deep breath and, placing your mouth over the victim's mouth (Fig. 131c), sealing it, blow forcefully in adults, gently in children, and with puffs of the cheeks in infants, so that the chest is seen to rise. (7) Remove your mouth and allow passive expiration. (8) Repeat about 20 times a minute at first ; later slow down to 15.

Three important points to remember are : (i) The victim's head must be extended ; i.e., bent backwards. (ii) The lower jaw must be kept thrust forwards. (iii) You must take a deep breath each time.

After-treatment for drowning.—As soon as the patient makes efforts at breathing, these measures are stopped. But no such effort may be made for twenty minutes, an hour, or even, in some recorded cases, for several hours, and still the person may recover, so that artificial respiration should be persevered with so long as there is the slightest sign of life. Efforts must next be made to restore the feeble circulation, and, in cases where the body has been long in water or much exposed during artificial respiration, to regain the body warmth. To this end the patient should be wrapped in hot blankets, with hot bottles to the sides and feet, and the arms and legs should be rubbed upwards towards the body. So soon as the power of swallowing returns, sips of hot water, and teaspoonfuls of hot brandy and water, or hot coffee, may be administered. Ammonia, nitrite of amyl, or smelling salts may for the same purpose be now and then held to the nose. Finally, if the patient shows a tendency to sleep, this should be encouraged.

DRUG (see DANGEROUS DRUGS and DOSAGE).

DRUG HABITS.—Drugs which have been administered for the relief of pain, for sleeplessness, or as a temporary stimulant, or which have been taken out of curiosity, are sometimes continued for their pleasurable effects or for the temporary sense of increased well-being which they confer, until their use becomes a habit. This habit may be continued either because the addict has not sufficient will-power to resign the pleasure derived from the use of his drug, or, very often, because any attempt to break off the habit leads to severe mental and bodily distress. All such habits lead to a mental and moral deterioration, and, under proper precautions, they may in every case be broken off, although in the case of morphia this may be extremely difficult.

Alcohol habit (see ALCOHOLISM, CHRONIC).

Ether habit.—This is by no means common, but comes into vogue now and then. Several teaspoonfuls are taken with water, and produce quickly a state of excited intoxication, which goes through all the stages of alcoholic intoxication in an hour or thereabout. The treatment is similar to that for alcoholism.

Cocaine habit.—The action of this drug is described under coca. It is generally taken hypodermically by its addicts, or the leaves may be chewed. A hypodermic dose of around 1 grain (60 mg.) may produce after a few minutes a feeling of suffocation, anxiety, and faintness, but this rapidly passes off and is followed by mental exhilaration, rapidity of thought, and a feeling of buoyancy. After a short time, however, this passes off, and as dose after dose is taken, a reaction of deeper and deeper depression ensues upon each. The drug begins to lose its effect, and larger and larger doses have to be taken; while, at the same time, dyspepsia, loss of appetite, restlessness, sleeplessness, forgetfulness, and failure of the power to apply the mind to any task appear. Finally, the person may pass into a state of melancholia or mania. Marked physical deterioration, in the form of emaciation and digestive disorders, is also found. The treatment is similar to that for the morphia habit, but the cocaine habit is the harder to renounce.

Morphia habit, or opium habit, is perhaps the commonest one indulged in. Although the ordinary dose of morphia is about $\frac{1}{4}$ grain (15 mg.), and of laudanum about 30 drops, addicts to the drug become so inured to it that 100 grains (6·5 G.) of the former are sometimes taken daily, and the latter has been drunk as if it were wine. It must be borne in mind, however, that by some Oriental peoples opium is widely used, not in an excessive and pernicious manner, but in the same sense as tobacco is used in Europe and America, The confirmed morphia-eater, who takes excessive doses or uses the drug constantly, speedily degenerates. His face becomes sallow, his appearance prematurely aged, and his muscles wasted. The memory becomes bad, sleep is lost, and conditions resembling neuralgia or ague come on, from which the only relief is given by larger doses. The character changes also, and a person who previously was honest and truthful, becomes in everything utterly untrustworthy. Delusions of various sorts may present themselves, and under their influence criminal acts may be performed. If the drug be suddenly stopped, there is always much suffering. Restlessness and sleeplessness become extreme, neuralgic pains come on, and dyspepsia, diarrhœa, and vomiting appear. Within one day of complete deprivation of the drug a condition of delirium or even serious collapse may ensue.

Treatment.—The longer the habit has lasted, the less hope is there for permanent abandonment of the drug, and persons who have long lost self-control may relinquish one habit only to fall into another, like that of alcohol. It is essential that treatment be carried out in a special institution which caters for the treatment of drug addicts. Nothing but failure awaits those who attempt to treat these unfortunate people at home or in an ordinary nursing home or hospital. The principle of treatment is to replace morphia with some other less habit-forming drug, such as methadone, and so wean him (or her) away from morphia.

Chloral hydrate, Sulphonal, Trional, Bromides, and Paraldehyde have also their devotees, the habit having been contracted through taking the drug for insomnia. Confusion of mind, digestive troubles, and inability to transact business are the symptoms, but these habits are much more easily abandoned than those of cocaine or morphia. The drug should simply be stopped once and for all, the patient resting quietly in bed for some time and being massaged or placed in a wet-pack to induce sleep.

DRUNKENNESS (*see* ALCOHOLISM, ACUTE *and* CHRONIC).

DUBINI'S DISEASE is another name for ELECTRIC CHOREA, a nervous disease acute in onset and characterized by involuntary shock-like movements of the muscles and severe pain.

DUCT is the name applied to a passage leading from a gland into some hollow organ, or on to the surface of the body, by which the secretion of the gland is discharged, *e.g.* pancreatic duct and bile duct opening into the duodenum, and the sweat duct opening on the skin surface.

DUCTLESS GLAND is the term applied to any one of certain glands in the body the secretion of which goes directly into the blood stream and so is carried to different parts of the body. These glands—the pituitary, thyroid, parathyroid, adrenal, and reproductive —are also known as the ENDOCRINE GLANDS. Some glands may be both duct glands and ductless glands. For example, the pancreas manufactures a digestive juice which passes by a duct into the small intestine. It also manufactures, by means of special cells, a substance called insulin which passes straight into the blood and not by way of any duct.

DUCTUS ARTERIOSUS is the blood-vessel in the fœtus through which blood passes from the pulmonary artery to the aorta, thereby by-passing the lungs, which do not function during intra-uterine life (*see* CIRCULATION OF THE BLOOD). The ductus normally ceases to function soon after birth and within a few weeks is converted into a fibrous cord. Occasionally this obliteration does not occur : a condition known as patent ductus arteriosus. This is one of the more common congenital defects of the heart, and one which responds particularly well to surgical treatment. (*See* HEART DISEASES).

DUMBNESS means an inability to pronounce the elementary sounds which make up words.

Varieties. — The important classification of cases of deficient power of speech is into (*a*) those associated with deafness and (*b*) those in which hearing is good. In a case associated with deafness, the person may be dumb merely because he has been born deaf, and, having no knowledge of sound, cannot understand or make intelligible sounds, although provided with good voice mechanism ; or a person who has lost his hearing by some disease in childhood may be unable to speak otherwise than as a child for the same reason. It is estimated that 1 per 1000 deaf children are so deaf that natural speech is impossible. When hearing is good, on the other hand, dumbness is due generally to some mental defect or sometimes to some failure in the organs of voice production.

Causes.—Deafness is the most important cause, because the one most capable of treatment. Of those due to some congenital brain - deficiency, some arise in children of persons who were themselves deaf-mutes. Another class of cases, in which there is also mental deficiency, arises from brain disease, such as that due to syphilis. Those children who are mentally bright and whose hearing is good have occasionally some structural defect, such as tongue-tie or enlarged tonsils and adenoids in the throat, which allow of attempts at speaking but prevent proper formation of words. Dumbness is sometimes a hysterical manifestation. Lisping and lalling speech are slight forms of dumbness due to inefficient control of the voice mechanism, but can generally be cured by careful training (*see* STAMMERING *and* VOICE).

Treatment.—A dumb child is cut off from other people and so cannot develop normally, unless carefully treated ; a careful examination should be made of any child who does not speak by four years of age. Deafness is easily discovered by finding that the child pays no attention to noises made behind its back. Mental ability can be measured by special tests. Physical obstructions, like tongue-tie or large tonsils, should be removed if present.

Deaf-mutes may be trained to read the lips and throat movements of others by sight, and to use their powers of voice through a complicated process, which should begin about the age of six or seven. It is hard for adults to pick this up, and persons who are to be instructed in this method should not learn the finger language first.

The training required for this ' oral ' method is long, and, if the deaf person is to gain a modulated voice and a fair command of language, the constant attention of an expert tutor is necessary all through childhood and youth. In England and Wales a local education authority can compel a parent of any child of two years of age or over to submit the child for medical examination. If this shows that special educational treatment is required, the authority must provide such treatment.

In the case of deaf-mutes, attendance is compulsory between the ages of 5 and 16. Training in lip-reading should be started as soon as possible, and special educational methods should be begun as soon as possible after the age of two years.

DUODENAL ILEUS is the term applied to dilatation of the duodenum due to chronic obstruction of the duodenum, caused by an abnormal position of arteries in the region of the duodenum pressing on it.

DUODENAL ULCER is a condition in which an ulcer similar to an ulcer of the stomach forms in the duodenum usually just beyond the exit from the stomach. The chief symptoms of duodenal ulcer are pain of a spasmodic character commencing from two to three hours after food is taken, and also at night, and relieved by taking more food ; also tenderness below the ribs slightly to the right of the middle line ; and sometimes the passage of dark, tarry material derived from blood, in the stools. There are also general symptoms of failing health and anæmia caused by interference with digestion and by the loss of blood in cases where this is considerable. The treatment of duodenal ulcer is similar to that of gastric ulcer. (*See* STOMACH DISEASES.)

DUODENUM (*duodenum*) is the first part of the intestine immediately beyond the stomach, so named because its length is about twelve finger-breadths. (*See* INTESTINE.)

DUPUYTREN'S CONTRACTURE is a thickening and drawing together of the skin and the underlying tissues in the palm of the hand, which causes gradual and permanent bending of the fingers. The cause of the condition is not known. It is more common among white-collar workers than among manual labourers. The ring and little fingers are most often affected. It is treated in early cases by massage and the occasional wearing of a splint, but the only cure is by means of surgery : by dividing the fibrous bands beneath the skin.

DURA MATER (*durus*, dense ; *mater*, mother) is the outermost and strongest of the three membranes or meninges which envelop the brain and spinal cord. In it run vessels which nourish the inner surface of the skull. (*See* BRAIN.)

DWARF, or DWARFISM, is a term applied to under-development of the body. The causes are either developmental or due to food insufficient in quantity or unsuitable in quality, or to defects in some of the body secretions which can be corrected. The first-named group includes ' pituitary ' dwarfism, the subjects being very small persons with normally proportioned parts, also achondroplastic dwarfs with large globular head and shortened limbs and stumpy fingers. In the class of dwarfism which is partly curable, there are included cretins, whose want of growth in mind and body is attributable to a primary defect of the thyroid gland (*see* CRETINISM). In this class are also included various forms of defective growth associated with defects in the secretions of the digestive organs, especially the pancreas ; this type of defect, often known as pancreatic infantilism, is mainly confined to a retardation of physical development, while the mental changes are little marked. Another form of dwarfism, associated with a deformity of the bones, is produced by rickets in early life, such persons showing high forehead, great bending of the leg bones, and deformity of the chest (*see* RICKETS).

DYNAMOMETER (δύναμις, power ; μέτρον, a measure) is an elliptical ring of steel to which is attached a dial and moving index. It is used to test the strength of the muscles of the forearm, being squeezed in the hand, and registering the pressure in pounds or kilogrammes.

DYS- (δυσ-, badly) is a prefix meaning difficult or painful.

DYSCHEZIA is the term applied to constipation due to retention of fæces in the rectum. This retention is the outcome of irregular habits, which damp down the normal reflex causing defæcation.

DYSCRASIA (the prefix δυσ-, badly ; κρᾶσις, a mixture) means a diseased constitution. (*See* CONSTITUTION.)

DYSDIADOKOKINESIA means loss of the ability to perform rapid alternate movements, such as winding up a watch. It is a sign of a lesion in the cerebellum.

DYSENTERY (from the prefix δυσ-, and ἔντερον, the intestine), also called bloody flux, is an infectious disease with a local lesion in the form of inflammation and ulceration of the lower portion of the bowels. It occurs in two main forms—bacillary dysentery and amœbic dysentery, which will be discussed separately.

BACILLARY DYSENTERY is found in practically every part of the world. **Cause.**—The disease may occur sporadically or in epidemics. The causative organism is the dysentery bacillus, or shigella as it is now known, of which there are several strains, named after their discoverers : Shiga, Flexner, and Sonne. In England and Wales, where there were 21,567 cases, with 20 deaths, in 1966, the Sonne strain (*Shigella sonnei*) is responsible for the vast majority of cases. The infection is spread by flies or by pollution of the water by fæces from infected patients, which contain the bacillus. Epidemics are thus encouraged by overcrowding and insanitary conditions. In the East, uncooked vegetables, especially salads, are a potent source of infection, as are cooks and other food-handlers who are carriers of the disease. The disease tends to assume epidemic dimensions in the hot season. The incubation period is 1 to 7 days. The severity of the disease depends partly upon the strain responsible for the infection. Thus, Shiga infections are usually severe, whilst, except in infants, Flexner and Sonne infections run a more benign course.

The dysentery bacilli affect mainly the large intestine. In mild cases there may be only a catarrh of the intestine with excessive mucoid excretion, whilst in severe cases there may be extensive ulceration involving practically the whole of the large intestine.

Symptoms.—These vary from those

of a mild attack of diarrhœa to those of an acute fulminating infection. The first symptoms usually consist of colicky pain in the abdomen followed by diarrhœa. There may also be nausea, aching pain in the limbs, and shivery feelings. There is always fever. The number of stools varies, but there may be as many as fifty daily in acute cases, The stools consist mainly of mucus and blood. The duration of the diarrhœa varies from a few days to a fortnight, depending upon the severity of the infection. Diagnosis is established by finding dysentery bacilli in the stools. Complications only occur in severe cases, and consist of perforation of the intestine and severe hæmorrhage from the gut. At one time one of the killing diseases of the world, with mortality rates up to 50 per cent. during epidemics, the outlook has been entirely altered by the introduction of the sulphonamides, but it is still a serious condition in young infants, old people, and the malnourished.

Treatment.—PREVENTIVE.—This consists of adequate sanitation, the destruction of flies, careful disposal of all garbage, and careful protection of all food from flies. In addition no carrier of dysentery bacilli should be allowed to handle food.

CURATIVE.—Complete rest in bed is essential, and precautions must be taken to ensure that the stools are disposed of without any risk of their spreading the infection. For the first twenty-four hours only water is given. This is gradually supplemented with milk, milk puddings, and chicken broth, but it is necessary for the diet to be kept light, and to contain as little residue as possible, until the diarrhœa has settled. Purgatives and laxatives are not given. The sheet-anchor of treatment is now the sulphonamides : usually phthalylsulphathiazole or succinylsulphathizole. Alternatively, neomycin may be used. If there is much abdominal pain, morphine may be given during the first day, but usually the application of heat in some form to the abdomen is sufficient.

AMŒBIC DYSENTERY is in some ways a more serious condition than bacillary dysentery, mainly because of the lack of any adequate treatment and the tendency for the condition to involve the liver.

Cause.—The disease is almost entirely confined to tropical and sub-tropical countries. The causative organism is the *Entamœba histolytica* (Fig. 8, page 37). Infection occurs as a result of food, *e.g.* uncooked vegetables, or drinking water which has been contaminated either by a carrier of the disease or by flies. The amœbæ settle in the wall of the large intestine, where they cause first of all inflammatory changes and then ulceration. These ulcers then tend to become infected with other organisms. From the ulcers the amœbæ may spread through the portal vein, where they cause abscesses. An amœbic abscess of the liver is not infrequent. More rarely, the amœbæ may spread elsewhere, *e.g.* to the lungs or brain, and cause abscesses. Occasionally a mass may be formed in the colon, known as an amœboma.

Symptoms.—The incubation period is variable, ranging from three weeks to three months. The onset of the disease is usually gradual, with the passage of several stools daily, which ultimately contain blood. Occasionally there may be an acute sudden onset as described for bacillary dysentery. Even in the cases with gradual onset there is loss of weight, with dyspepsia and anæmia. Complications which may occur include perforation of the intestine, hæmorrhage from the gut, and abscess formation. The condition is very liable to run a chronic course. Any individual who has been in the tropics and who complains of abdominal pain and dyspepsia should have the stools examined for the presence of *Entamœba histolytica*, even though there is no history of dysentery. Involvement of the liver may occur months or years after the occurrence of amœbic dysentery. Such involvement is marked by the occurrence of pain and tenderness over the liver, with fever.

Treatment.—PREVENTIVE.—This consists of the protection of food from flies, the avoidance of contamination of water and uncooked vegetables, and steps to ensure that those handling food are not carriers of the amœba.

CURATIVE.—Emetine, one of the alkaloids of ipecacuanha, is the most effective drug for the treatment of amœbic dysentery. It is usually given in the form of emetine and bismuth iodide given by mouth, or emetine hydrochloride given by injection. A recently introduced drug which is proving of value is diloxanide furoate. Emetine hydrochloride, by intramuscular injection, is given for the treatment of amœbic hepatitis. If an amœbic abscess has formed in the liver, this is aspirated and emetine is given as in the case of amœbic hepatitis. Chloroquine given by mouth is also of value in the treatment of amœbic hepatitis. When amœbic dysentery does not respond to the treatment outlined, this is supplemented by the administration of full doses of oxytetracycline.

DYSIDROSIS, or CHEIROPOMPHOLYX, is a skin eruption in which minute vesicles of clear fluid form in the cuticle.

DYSLEXIA is difficulty in reading or learning to read. It is always accompanied by difficulty in writing and particularly by difficulties in spelling correctly. It is a condition which is attracting increasing attention, particularly the form known as specific dyslexia. This is the name given to difficulties in learning to read and write which affect a minority of children exposed to normal educational processes who do not show backwardness in other school subjects.

Parents of such children would be well advised to get in touch with the Word Blind Centre of the Invalid Children's Aid Association, 93 Guilford Street, London, W.C.1.

DYSMENORRHŒA (δυσ-, with difficulty, μήν, a month; ῥέω, I flow) means painful menstruation. (*See* MENSTRUATION.)

DYSPAREUNIA means painful or difficult coitus.

DYSPEPSIA (δυσ-, with difficulty; πέπτω, I digest) means pain, or any uncomfortable symptom associated with the function of digestion. The term dyspepsia should not be limited to the occurrence of pain while the food remains in the stomach, for (*see* DIGESTION) this period represents only a small part of the digestive

process, and interference with this process, in its wider sense, may produce various symptoms, such as appendicitis, constipation, diarrhœa, upon which information will be found elsewhere. Vagaries of digestion produce symptoms of many sorts, often not at all directly connected with the taking of food. The condition of the teeth is of the utmost importance in regard to dyspepsia, and proper chewing of the food, together with leisurely eating of meals by those accustomed to hurry, frequently suffices to cure indigestion of long standing. Success in treatment of obstinate cases is greatly aided by the administration of test meals, their withdrawal after some time by the stomach tube, and chemical and microscopic examination of the digestive products.

We shall consider here only the broadly marked forms of dyspepsia affecting the stomach, and recognizable by every one as such. *See also* STOMACH, DISEASES OF.

ACUTE DYSPEPSIA sometimes occurs in people who ordinarily digest food with comfort, and, still more frequently, in persons of weak digestive powers. It results from a single serious error in diet, or the irritation of poisonous substances acting upon the interior of the stomach. For the treatment see Acute Gastritis under STOMACH, DISEASES OF.

ACID DYSPEPSIA (ACID GASTRITIS) is one of the commonest forms. It is of several types, but as a rule affects young persons or those in the prime of life, and is due to the presence of an excessive amount of hydrochloric acid, or of acid salts, in the gastric juice. One type affects young persons of sedentary occupation who eat irregularly as to time and amount of food, and who are in the habit of bolting their meals. Another type of sufferer is the nervous, highly strung individual, in whom nervous dyspepsia may take this form.

Symptoms.—As a rule, the dyspeptic is conscious of irregularity in taking his meals, and, having a good appetite, eats at times more food than is good for him. There is no discomfort for perhaps an hour, indeed relief is often gained by eating, and then a sense of heaviness and heat about the pit of

288

the stomach and left side set in and grow gradually worse. There is often a feeling as of strangling in the throat, and a vague sense of constriction in the left side which grows now more and now less intense in conformity with the muscular action of the stomach. Relief is obtained for a few seconds by swallowing saliva, and by gulping mouthfuls of air, but these lead later to distension and greater pain. After perhaps an hour of this discomfort, a burning feeling (heartburn) is experienced about the centre of the chest, and mouthfuls of intensely sour material are brought up into the mouth, leaving a raw feeling in the throat (waterbrash). Now and then vomiting occurs, and this gives temporary relief. The vomit is intensely sour, and may contain streaks of blood in cases where the pain is great, the blood and pain being due to minute ' erosions ' in the mucous membrane of the stomach. If blood comes in any quantity, however, and if sharp pain be experienced immediately upon partaking of solid food, the case is probably one of ulcer. (*See* STOMACH, DISEASES OF.)

Treatment.—Regularity in mealtimes, and in the amount of food taken at each meal, is essential, and regular exercise in the open air, cold baths in the morning, and early rising all play an important part. The food should be chewed deliberately, and small meals, frequently taken, suit this and the following form of dyspepsia better than large meals with long intervals. It is important to avoid condiments, such as vinegar, mustard, pickles, and particularly salt. The food should be of a simple form, which does not stimulate the walls of the stomach to secrete much gastric juice, such as eggs, fish, thick soups, puddings made from tapioca, cornflour, rice, and the like. Above all, milk and cream are well borne, and, in any case where there is bleeding, should form the staple of the diet. Meat, meat essences, and strong (stock) soups should be avoided. The symptoms may be much abated by alkali mixtures or tablets, such as cream of magnesia. Smoking in all forms, if indulged in, should be given up. Constipation should be treated by mild remedies (*see* CONSTIPATION).

10

CHRONIC CATARRH OF THE STOMACH (MUCOUS GASTRITIS) may come on as a late stage of the above. Perhaps its commonest cause is the chronic abuse of alcohol. It is also associated with heart disease, and disorders of the liver, which cause congestion of the stomach, and it is not infrequently produced by gout.

Symptoms.—The appetite is poor, or is capricious, with an inclination for sharp, sour, or salt articles of diet like pickles, pepper, vinegar, salt herrings. The tongue is covered with a thick yellow or brownish fur, especially in the mornings, and, in consequence, the taste of ordinary food is dull and papery. The usual symptoms are discomfort, eructations, and choking sensations after a meal, with occasional vomiting, particularly in the morning. The vomit consists of fragments of half-digested food mixed with strings and lumps of tough mucus, with which the interior of the stomach is coated. Most discomfort is felt after the chief meal of the day, and soup seems specially prone to cause this. Constipation is generally present.

Treatment.—Attention to the diet is here also the most important point. Alcohol and tobacco, which maintain and even cause the condition, must be stopped, and daily exercise should be taken. Salted foods, pickles, and the like may in this case be taken, and are beneficial when a meal contains a considerable amount of meat, because the secretion of gastric juice is feeble and is stimulated by these means. The meat taken should all be scraped down, because the gastric juice has to a large extent lost its power to dissolve fibrous tissue. The following diet is one which is readily digested and non-irritating. The lunch and supper might be interchanged.

7 A.M. *Breakfast.*—Breakfast cup of cocoa made with milk and sugar ; 2 oz. of toast or rusks.

10 A.M. *Lunch.*—3 oz. white fish ; 3 oz. sweetbread or chicken ; 2 oz. bread and 1 oz. butter.

1 P.M. *Dinner.*—Plate of soup made of 1 oz. tapioca-meal, a pat of butter, and an egg ; 3 oz. of chicken-breast, or veal, or fish, or pigeon ; 3 oz. macaroni, or vermicelli, or purée of potatoes,

spinach, or beans ; 3 oz. of milk-pudding or omelette.

4 P.M. *Afternoon tea.*—One teacupful of milk or milk-tea with sugar ; 1 oz. of toast or biscuits.

8 P.M. *Supper.*—A sandwich consisting of 2 oz. bread, 1 oz. butter, and 2 oz. finely scraped meat.

Medicinal treatment is not generally necessary if these rules be attended to, except for the loss of appetite, the pain, and the irregularity of the bowels. Appetite may be gained by taking bitters half an hour before dinner, such as condurango, or calumba with nux vomica. Before breakfast, the patient may take a tumblerful of warm water, to which has been added a small teaspoonful of common salt. This has the effect of dissolving the mucus in the stomach and also of helping the action of the bowels. For the discomfort after meals, ten drops of dilute hydrochloric acid, in water, or added to the bitter, may be taken after meals and repeated every half-hour while digestion is proceeding. For constipation, if present, a glass of an aperient water in the morning may be sufficient, and for diarrhœa, if present, lime-water or chalk mixture.

NERVOUS DYSPEPSIA includes many forms, the cases being due, not to an actual organic deficiency in or injury to the stomach, but to an exaggerated influence of the nervous system in increasing or diminishing the natural movements of the digestive organs, or altering the character of their secretions. There may be no apparent cause for the dyspepsia beyond the fact that the person is of a nervous temperament. These forms of dyspepsia occur also in alcoholics, in brain-workers, and in people subject to constant exhaustion, and are very liable to be associated with mental depression and the moody, critical state known as hypochondriasis. To this class belong the following, among other groups of symptoms : *Acute dilatation* arises readily in some people when food is taken during exhaustion, such as that caused by a long walk or climbing a mountain, or too soon after a severe surgical operation. The stomach distends, and can neither digest nor expel its contents. Ineffectual attempts are made at vomiting, and unless the stomach be relieved of its contents by a smart emetic or by the

290

stomach tube, the result may sometimes be dangerous even to life. *Periodic vomiting* is a similar but slighter condition which comes on now and then in people with irritable stomach, prone at other times to suffer from acid dyspepsia. It is known also as ' acute catarrh ', and as ' bilious attack '. Digestion ceases for the time being, and the stomach contents, often followed by bile from the intestine, are vomited up. It is due usually to an indiscretion in diet, and in women is sometimes associated with irregularity of the menstrual function. *Atonic dyspepsia* is a chronic condition which is practically the reverse of acid dyspepsia. The secretion of juice may fail, or the stomach walls may lose their activity and lapse into a weak, flabby condition of partial dilatation. It occurs especially in people of feeble general health, or is sometimes the result of long-continued abuse of the stomach by over-feeding. *Spasm* is an acute condition of the opposite nature. It comes on from time to time, often associated with acid dyspepsia, and causes severe griping pains very similar to colic. *Flatulence* is a condition which may be due either to fermentation in the intestine or to nervous influences. Persons subject to it are troubled by noisy action of the stomach and bowels, particularly when the limbs are at rest, and are liable to suffer from cold hands and feet, warm and cold flushes, and other signs of bad circulation.

Treatment.—For the conditions associated with vomiting see VOMITING. Atonic dyspepsia requires tonics, nutritious food of little bulk, change of air and scene, and cold baths. Spasm is relieved by hot compresses, mustard leaves to the pit of the stomach, and internally by belladonna, peppermint water, or tincture of valerian. Flatulence requires simple food, an avoidance of certain articles of diet, such as green vegetables, and general tonic treatment (*see* FLATULENCE). It is important to bear in mind that flatulence is often due to a habit of swallowing air, and can be relieved by breaking this habit.

FERMENTATIVE DYSPEPSIA is a condition which is far less common than those already stated. It arises in connection with dilatation of the stomach due to some obstruction at its exit, in consequence of which food is retained, ferments, and distends the organ. In the majority of cases the gastric juice is not deficient. The most common cause is narrowing of the outlet by the scar of a previous and healed ulcer, while other causes are found in various displacements of the organ, pressure by other organs, and even tumours in the stomach wall.

Symptoms.—Great loss of appetite, a feeling of constant fullness and weight increased by food, belching up of foul-smelling gases, repeated vomiting of large quantities of fermenting, frothy, and half-digested food, great thirst, headache, and obstinate constipation are the main symptoms of this form of dyspepsia.

Treatment.—The washing out of the stomach, regularly, for a period of some weeks, either at night or in the morning, is the treatment *par excellence* of this condition. After having been shown a few times how to pass the stomach tube, the patient can do this for himself, and thereby obtain great relief.

The apparatus required for washing out the stomach is : a soft india-rubber stomach tube about 2 feet (60 cm.) long ; a glass tube 3 inches (7 cm.) long to connect it with 4 feet (120 cm.) of rubber tubing ; and a glass or metal funnel to fit into the other end of the long piece of tubing. The method of use is as follows : the stomach tube is dipped in warm water and the end is then passed back into the throat ; swallowing motions are at once made by the patient while the tube is pushed steadily onwards for a distance of 18 or 20 inches (45 or 50 cm.), by which time its end will have reached the stomach. If an inclination to retch be present, it is obviated by drawing deep breaths. Fluid is then poured into the funnel, and this being raised, the fluid runs down into the patient's stomach. Before the tube is quite empty the funnel is depressed into a pail or other receptacle standing on the floor, and the fluid, and other contents of the stomach, run off by siphon action. This is repeated till several quarts of fluid have been run into and out of the stomach,

thoroughly cleansing its walls. The fluid used is generally warm water tinted pink with permanganate of potassium.

Further, a special diet is necessary. The dyspeptic should avoid fats and starchy foods, take all his nourishment in as dry a form as possible, eat only three meals daily, with no food between them, and limit the fluid he drinks to a quart or less each day. Lying upon the right side for half an hour some 2 or 3 hours after a meal enables the stomach to empty itself and so brings relief. The wearing of a supporting belt also helps to counteract the dilatation. (*See* BELTS AND BINDERS.) When the condition of dilatation is great and does not yield to simple treatment, the operation of gastro-enterostomy—by which an opening is made out of the lowest part of the stomach into a neighbouring loop of the small intestine—is sometimes helpful in cases of dilatation caused by narrowing of the scar following an ulcer.

DYSPHAGIA is the medical term for difficulty in swallowing.

DYSPITUITARISM means disordered function of the pituitary body. (*See* PITUITARY BODY.)

DYSPNŒA (δύσπνοια) means difficulty in breathing. Orthopnœa means breathing possible only when sitting up.

DYSTOCIA means slow or painful birth of a child.

DYSTROPHY (δυσ-, badly ; τρέφω, I nourish) means defective or faulty nutrition, and is a term generally applied to some developmental change in the muscles occurring independently of the nervous system. The best-known forms are those known as *progressive muscular dystrophy*, in which the groups of muscles, especially those of the calves and buttocks, undergo a fatty degeneration associated with increase in size but weakness in power ; and *adiposo-genital dystrophy* associated with defect of the pituitary gland.

DYSURIA means difficulty or pain in urination.

E

EAR.—The ear is concerned with two functions. The more evident is that of the sense of hearing, the other is the sense of equilibration and of

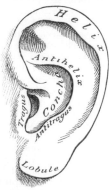

motion. The organ is divided into three parts : (*a*) the external ear, consisting of the auricle on the surface of the head, and the tube which leads inwards to the drum ; (*b*) the middle ear, or drum, separated from the former by the tympanic membrane, and from the internal ear by two other membranes, but communicating with the throat by the Eustachian tube; and (*c*) the internal ear, comprising the complicated labyrinth from which runs the auditory nerve into the brain (Fig. 133).

External ear.—The auricle or pinna, shaped in man something like a crumpled-up funnel, is not essential to the sense of hearing, although in animals it appears to play an important part. It consists of a framework of elastic cartilage covered by skin, the lobule at the lower end being a small mass of fat. The various parts of the auricle are named as in Fig. 132. From the bottom of the concha the external auditory meatus runs inwards for 1 or 1½ inches (25 or 37 mm.), to end blindly at the drum. This passage is short in young children, in whom the drum is almost at the surface, and it lengthens as the skull bones develop. The outer half of the passage is surrounded by cartilage, lined by skin, on which are placed fine hairs pointing

outwards, and glands secreting a small amount of wax. In the inner half, the skin is smooth and lies directly upon the temporal bone, in the substance of which the whole hearing apparatus is enclosed. The two parts meet at a slight angle, so as to give the whole passage a curve, which can be straightened by pulling the auricle upwards and backwards, when the drum can often be clearly seen by a good light.

Middle ear.—The tympanic membrane, forming the drum, is stretched completely across the end of the passage, being placed rather obliquely, so that it makes an angle of about 60° with the floor. It is about one-third of an inch across, as thick as a piece of gold-beater's skin, and white or pale pink in colour, so that it is partly transparent, and some of the contents of the middle ear shine through it. From this description it can be readily understood how easily it is torn, and

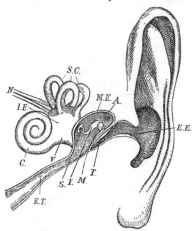

how dangerous are blows on the side of the head, and rough manipulations to remove wax. The cavity of the middle ear is about one-third of an inch (8 mm.) wide and one-sixth of an inch (4 mm.)

in depth from the tympanic membrane to the inner wall of bone. Although important structures, like the facial nerve, which runs down behind it, lie close around, its only important contents are three small bones, the malleus (hammer), incus (anvil), and stapes (stirrup), collectively known as the auditory ossicles, with two minute muscles which regulate their movements, and the chorda tympani nerve which runs across the cavity. The auditory ossicles are of great importance. The malleus has a long spicule of bone, the handle, embedded in the substance of the drum, while its head is in contact with the incus. The incus, suspended by one process of bone, has another affixed to the stapes, and the latter fits, by what would in a real stirrup be the footpiece, into one (fenestra ovalis) of the two openings which lead through the inner wall of the middle ear into the internal ear. Accordingly these three bones form a chain across the middle ear, connecting the drum with the internal ear. Their function is to convert the air-waves, which strike upon the drum, into mechanical movements which can affect the fluid in the inner ear, because air-waves produce little effect upon fluid directly.

The middle ear has two connections which are of great importance as regards disease ; in front, it communicates by a passage $1\frac{1}{2}$ inches (37 mm.) long, the Eustachian tube, with the upper part of the throat, which lies behind the nose ; behind and above, it opens into a cavity known as the mastoid antrum. The Eustachian tube admits air from the throat, and so keeps the pressure on both sides of the drum fairly equal. Serious deafness is produced by its closure, and it also, unfortunately, forms a channel by which acute inflammation in measles, scarlatina, etc., spreads to the ear. The antrum occupies the interior of the projecting mass of bone, the mastoid process, which is felt on the surface of the head behind the ear, and this cavity, along with the middle ear, is separated from the interior of the skull only by a thin plate of bone about the thickness of a calling card.

Internal ear. — This consists of a complex system of hollows in the substance of the temporal bone enclosing a membranous duplicate. Between the membrane and the bone is a fluid known as perilymph, while the membrane is distended by another collection of fluid known as endolymph. This membranous labyrinth, as it is called, consists of two parts (Fig. 134). The hinder part, comprising a sac, the

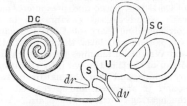

FIG. 134.—Diagram of the membranous labyrinth. *DC*, Ductus cochlearis ; *dr*, ductus reuniens ; *S*, sacculus ; *U*, utriculus ; *dv*, ductus vestibuli ; *SC*, semicircular canals. (Turner's *Anatomy*.)

utricle, and three short semicircular canals opening at each end into it, is the part probably concerned with the balancing sense ; the forward part consists of another small bag, the saccule, and of a still more important part, the cochlea, and is the part concerned in hearing. In the cochlea three tubes, known as the scala tympani, scala media, and scala vestibuli, placed side by side (the middle one being part of the membranous labyrinth), take two and a half spiral turns round a central stem, after the manner of a snail's shell. In the central one (scala media) is placed the apparatus (organ of Corti) on which the sound-waves are finally received and by which the sounds are communicated to the auditory nerve, which ends in filaments to this organ of Corti. The essential parts in the organ of Corti are a double row of rods and several rows of cells furnished with fine hairs of varying length. This organ runs the whole length of the scala media. Different musical notes are perhaps appreciated by different rods and hair cells.

The act of hearing.—When sound-waves in the air reach the ear, the drum is alternately pressed in and pulled out, in consequence of which a to-and-fro movement is communicated to the chain of ossicles. The foot of the stapes communicates these movements to the perilymph in the scala tympani, by which in turn the fluid of the scala media is set in motion. Finally these motions reach the delicate filaments placed in the organ of Corti, and so affect the nerve of hearing, which conveys impressions to the centre in the brain. There are two theories of hearing. The first is that of Helmholtz, who compared the organ of Corti to a piano and presumed that each sound caused a vibration of a corresponding part of Corti's organ. The second and later theory of Keith and Wrightson assumes that the entire organ of Corti is thrown into vibration by sounds, and that the nature of the sound is analysed and perceived by the hearing-centre in the brain. The vibrations in the fluid of the internal ear are prevented from doing damage by the fact that the scala vestibuli, which communicates with the scala tympani at the apex of the cochlea, is separated at its other end from the middle ear only by a membrane in the fenestra rotunda, and this bulges out as the stapes is driven in, and vice versa.

EAR, DISEASES OF. — Troubles connected with the ear should, when possible, be treated early, both on account of this organ's importance, and because, owing to its delicacy and inaccessibility, little can be done for unpleasant symptoms like deafness and ringing due to advanced disease. Mention has been made of the importance of the connection between throat and middle ear by way of the Eustachian tube, both as regards the maintenance of good hearing and as regards the spread of inflammation. There are several simple procedures connected with the management of the ear which demand explanation.

Examination of the external ear is carried out by placing the person's head in a good light near a window, inclining the head away from the window a little, pulling the auricle upwards and backwards, and if a conical speculum be at hand, introducing this with a gentle screwing movement. The drum and deeper part of the external ear may then be viewed. If available, an electric auriscope (*q.v.*) is a much more satis-

factory means of carrying out the examination.

Syringing is done with a large-sized glass or metal syringe provided with a short blunt point (not longer than 1 inch (25 mm.), so that no damage to the drum can result). The auricle is pulled gently up and back, while a steady

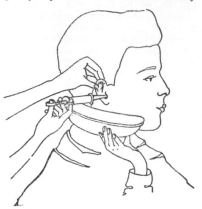

FIG. 135.—Method of syringing ear.

stream from the syringe is directed along the upper wall, and flows out along the lower one (Fig. 135). In syringing the ear of a child the point of the syringe should not be inserted within the shallow passage at all.

Inflation of the middle ear is performed for cases in which the Eustachian tube is partly blocked and the drum indrawn. A catheter is passed along the floor of the nose into the opening of the Eustachian tube in the throat, and forcible inflation made through this by means of an india-rubber bag (Politzer's bag). Or the bag is used to blow up one nostril, the other being closed, while the Eustachian tube is kept open by one of the following devices. The person swallows a mouthful of water, or pronounces some guttural, such as ' Huck ', so as to raise the soft palate and close the opening between the nose and throat ; and at this moment the bag is suddenly squeezed. The middle ear may also be inflated by forcibly expelling air from the chest while the mouth and nose are closed. The fact of whether air enters the middle ear becomes plain to the person himself by a click followed by a slight ringing in the ear, and often by improved hearing, and to the surgeon by means of an india-rubber tube, a couple of feet long, connecting his ear with the patient's ear, through which he hears the click of the distended drum.

Tuning-fork test is used to test the internal ear. When a vibrating fork is placed on the centre of the forehead it is heard equally in both ears, the sound being conducted through the bones of the head. If one ear be closed, it is heard better in that ear. Accordingly, if one ear be deaf, and the sound of the fork placed on the forehead is heard better in that ear, the deafness is due to middle ear disease. While if the ear be deaf to the fork when placed on the forehead, as well as when held near the ear, the internal ear or nerve mechanism is at fault.

General symptoms. — The following are some of the chief symptoms of ear disease :

DEAFNESS (*see* DEAFNESS).

EARACHE is in general due to acute inflammation in the middle ear, but may also be due to chronic inflammation, or to boils, eczema, wax, or neuralgia affecting the outer ear. Pain in this region may also be caused by carious teeth. The treatment varies, of course, with the cause, but the pain may generally be relieved to some extent by applying hot flannel or a hot-water bag to the side of the head. Ear drops consisting of carbolic acid, 10 grains (600 mg.), in glycerin, 120 minims (8 ml.), have a soothing and antiseptic effect when one or two drops are instilled into the ear. A few drops of laudanum have a similar effect when dropped from a warm teaspoon. Warm salt solution (a teaspoonful to every tumblerful of water) may also be gently run into the ear for two hours with soothing effect. A small blister applied to the skin behind the ear often gives relief in prolonged cases. The ear should not be syringed, which is very painful in a case of inflammation, nor should oil be dropped in, as is often done. When inflammation is very acute, it is sometimes necessary for the surgeon to puncture the drum in its lower part.

RINGING in the ear, or 'tinnitus', is sometimes a very annoying symptom. It may take various forms, but is in general accompanied by catarrh of some part of the ear. Pulsating or throbbing in the ear is sometimes due to bloodlessness, or to large doses of quinine or salicylate of soda, and passes off as the bloodlessness is treated or the drugs producing it discontinued. Blowing, hissing, and whistling noises, like those made by an escape of steam or by a boiling kettle, are the most common and most annoying forms. Usually they are associated with middle-ear catarrh, but they are very often due to gout or rheumatism or associated with high blood-pressure, and diminish as the general disease is treated. Accompanied by deafness, ringing is not infrequently due to wax. Musical tinnitus sometimes occurs, in which the sound of bells, or of short passages of music, is repeated constantly. It is due to similar causes. A high crescendo musical note, followed by giddiness, is one of the symptoms of Ménière's disease.

DISCHARGE from the ear may arise in the external ear as the result of eczema, boils, or the irritation caused by a plug of wax or foreign body, but, in the absence of these, comes in the great majority of cases from a chronic suppuration in the middle ear through a perforation in the drum. The suppuration may begin in an acute inflammation of the middle ear arising in the course of a ' cold in the head ', or may result from scarlet fever or measles, or may be due to disease of the bone in or around the ear, or may simply have a slow onset, without apparent cause, in weakly persons, especially in children. The discharge may be thick and yellowish in cases which are fairly acute, or thin and watery in cases which are improving, or brownish and evil-smelling in cases which have been neglected or in which the bone is diseased. There are two common fallacies regarding this condition. One is that a discharge from the ear is a trifling thing, and that, on the whole, it is undesirable to take means to cure it. In reality the presence of suppuration is accompanied usually by increasing deafness, and is attended always by the risk of an abscess in the mastoid antrum, or even within the skull. The other fallacy is that a perforation in the drum necessarily entails great deafness. As a matter of fact, unless the perforation be so large as to interfere with the tension of the drum, it causes little interference with hearing, the real cause of deafness in suppurative middle-ear disease being adhesions which bind down the ossicles and prevent their movements. Treatment depends upon whether the cause of the discharge is in the outer or the middle ear.

If it is in the *outer ear*, the ear is carefully cleaned out with an orange stick with a small narrow tuft of cotton-wool firmly rolled on it. The ear is then lightly packed with half-inch gauze soaked in Argyrol (10 per cent. in saline), or one part of dilute mercury nitrate ointment in 19 parts of olive oil, or 8 per cent. aluminium acetate. This swab is left in the ear for twenty-four hours, and during this time it is moistened several times with whichever solution is being used. At the end of twenty-four hours, it is removed, and replaced by a fresh piece of gauze. An alternative method of treatment is to paint the inside of the outer ear with 2·5 per cent. gentian violet in spirit.

If the infection is in the *middle ear*, treatment consists of the administration of an antibiotic, usually penicillin, in the early stages. The antibiotic is given by injection or by mouth. If the discharge persists, the local treatment consists of that used in the treatment of infection of the outer ear, but the solution must either be a simple drying preparation such as boric and spirit, or 1 per cent. hydrogen peroxide in glycerin saturated with urea.

If these methods fail, it may be necessary for a surgeon, in bad cases, to remove the ossicles and remains of the drum, and so to convert the middle ear into a simple cavity, which can be easily kept clean. Removal of the malleus and incus does not necessarily produce great deafness ; indeed the hearing may be improved after this operation.

WAX in the ear is the commonest cause of deafness, sometimes even of several years' standing. It is to be removed by syringing (Fig. 135) with warm water containing two teaspoonfuls of baking soda to a tumblerful of water. If the wax be very hard it should be softened by making the person lie down on his side for half an hour with the affected ear upwards, into which is poured some of this solution, or a few drops of olive oil. At the end of half an hour the syringing is repeated.

FOREIGN BODIES, such as peas, gravel, or slate pencils are often pushed by children into the ear, and are extremely difficult to remove. An attempt should first of all be made by syringing as for wax. In the case of peas, however, it is better to syringe with warm oil, because water causes the dried pea to swell and block the passage still more. If syringing be ineffectual, no attempt should be made by unskilful persons with hair-pins, bent wires, or the like, to remove the object, which is apt by such means to be pushed through the drum.

BOILS in the skin lining the outer ear give rise to intense pain. This pain is much relieved by running gently into the ear a quantity of warm carbolic lotion (1 in 40), or by packing the ear lightly with a piece of gauze dipped in a 10 per cent. solution of ichthyol in water or glycerin, or in 8 per cent. aluminium acetate. Relief is also gained when the boil is incised.

ECZEMA, consisting of a cracked condition of the skin in the ear, with watery discharge and intense irritation, is common, as an acute affection in infants, and as a chronic one in gouty and rheumatic adults. In children, syringing with Goulard's water and application of vaseline, with care not to bring soap in contact with the ear for a time, affords relief. In adults, weak nitrate of mercury ointment, or tar ointment mixed with vaseline, applied with a brush several times daily, does good.

TUMOURS in the ear are mostly either outgrowths from the surrounding bone or soft polypi. The former may block the passage and interfere with hearing, but have often a narrow neck, so that they can be easily removed. Polypi usually develop as a result of the irritation set up by a chronic discharge, and shrivel up as the discharge is cured, though a large one may have to be removed in order to get to the drum.

ACUTE INFLAMMATION (otitis) is already referred to under Earache.

CHRONIC INFLAMMATION is referred to above, under Discharge from the Ear. There is a form of inflammation (catarrh) in which no true suppuration takes place, and, if the drum is not perforated, there is no discharge outwards. This condition, which leads to adhesions about the ossicles and thickening of the drum, interferes greatly with hearing, and causes a slowly advancing and most intractable form of deafness. It often runs in families, and is frequently preceded by adenoid growths in the postnasal space during childhood.

MASTOID DISEASE is a serious complication of inflammation in the ear. The mastoid antrum and its connection with the middle ear have been mentioned under EAR. As a rule, inflammation in this cavity arises by direct spread of a long-standing suppuration from the middle ear, sometimes in consequence of neglect to keep the ear clean and prevent discharge from accumulating, although in influenza and some other conditions the mastoid antrum has been known to become primarily affected. The signs of this condition are rather vague, but include swelling and tenderness of the skin behind the ear, redness and swelling inside the ear, pain in the side of the head, feverishness, and discharge of foul-smelling, brownish material from the ear. If the condition be left to itself it may, after a period of inflammation, resolve itself without the formation of an abscess, but the dangers are great. More usually an abscess forms, and the pus, if unrelieved, bursts, according to the nature of the surrounding bone, upwards or backwards into the skull at the base of the brain, or outwards through the skin, or downwards among the muscles of the neck. Accordingly, in early cases, the surgeon cuts through the skin behind the ear to relieve congestion, but once an abscess has formed, he chisels down through the bone of the mastoid process till he can clear out the pus, and completes his operation by making a free communication between the antrum and the ear, so that pus cannot collect again when the outside wound heals.

EBURNATION (*ebur*, ivory) is a process of hardening and polishing which takes place at the ends of bones, giving

10 *a*

them an ivory-like appearance. It is caused by the wearing away, in consequence of osteo-arthritis, of the smooth plates of cartilage which in health cover the ends of the bones.

ECBOLICS (ἐκβάλλω, I throw out) are drugs which cause contraction of the womb, such as ergot.

ECCHYMOSIS (ἐκ, out of ; χυμός, juice) means the discoloured patch resulting from escape of blood into the tissues just under the skin, often from bruising.

ECCYESIS is the term applied to the condition in which the egg is impregnated, and the resulting fœtus develops, outside the uterus, the normal place for these events.

ECGONINE is another name for cocaine.

ECHINOCOCCUS (ἐχῖνος, hedgehog ; κόκκος, berry) is the immature form of a small tapeworm, *Taenia echinococcus*, found in dogs, wolves, and jackals from which human beings become infected, so that they harbour the immature parasite in the form known as hydatid cyst. (*See* PARASITES.)

ECHOLALIA is a term applied to the meaningless repetition, by a person suffering from mental degeneration, of words and phrases addressed to him.

ECHO VIRUSES, of which there are at least 28 known types, are a recently discovered group of virus. Their full name is Enteric Cytopathogenic Human Orphan (hence the abbreviation, ECHO, from the first letter of each word). They owe their cumbersome full name to the fact that they were originally found in the stools of children without disease. Their precise significance is not yet known, but they have been responsible for one or two outbreaks of meningitis, and have also been isolated in outbreaks of mild respiratory illness, particularly in children.

ECLAMPSIA (ἐκλάμπω, I explode) is a general name for convulsive seizures of sudden onset. (*See* CONVULSIONS,

297

EPILEPSY, URÆMIA.) The name is now applied only to convulsions arising in connection with pregnancy, which are of a very dangerous type. This condition is said to occur in one out of every 500 cases of pregnancy. It occurs especially in the later months and at the time of delivery, but a certain proportion of cases are manifest only after delivery has taken place. The cause of the condition is not definitely known, but it appears to be of the nature of a poisoning process from products derived either from the after-birth or from defective chemical changes in the blood. In practically all cases the kidneys are profoundly affected, and in this way the condition is much aggravated.

Symptoms.—There are several warning symptoms, such as dizziness, headache, vomiting, and secretion of urine which is found to contain albumin. These symptoms may be present for some days or weeks before the seizure takes place. The seizure consists of rigidity of the body, with unconsciousness, followed by twitching in the face and limbs lasting for one or two minutes and then passing into a state of deep unconsciousness with stertorous breathing. In mild cases there are a few fits at long intervals and the patient recovers consciousness between them, but in severer cases the fits succeed one another so rapidly that there is no appreciable interval. In cases which progress to a fatal termination, the pulse and temperature rise, and cerebral hæmorrhage or pneumonia may supervene, or the breathing may gradually cease. About one-quarter of the cases end in this way.

Treatment.—The treatment of the seizures is that generally applicable to convulsions of any kind, morphine and chloral being especially used as sedatives. Magnesium sulphate given intramuscularly sometimes helps to control the fits. In severe cases oxygen should be given, and, if heart failure threatens, digoxin should be given intravenously. Some authorities recommend that the birth of the child should be hastened, but at the present day the tendency is to leave this part of the treatment to nature.

ECSTASY (ἔκτασις, from ἐξίστημι, I put out of its place, I alter) is a term applied to a morbid mental condition in which the mind is entirely absorbed in the contemplation of one dominant idea or object, and loses for the time its normal self-control. This condition usually presents itself as a kind of temporary religious insanity, and has frequently appeared as an epidemic.

ECTHYMA (ἔκθυμα, a pustule) is the term applied to a pustular eruption accompanied by surrounding inflammation. The pustules burst and discharge, leaving pigmented scars. It is most frequently found on the legs and buttocks.

ECTO- (ἐκτός, without) is a prefix meaning on the outside.

ECTOPIC (ἐκ, out of ; τόπος, place) means out of the usual place. For example, in congenital displacement of the heart outside the thoracic cavity it is said to be ectopic, while an ' ectopic gestation ' means a pregnancy outside of the womb.

ECTROMELIA means the absence of a limb or limbs from congenital causes.

ECTROPION (ἐκ, out of ; τρέπω, I turn) is a condition of the eyelid, usually the lower, in which the skin is contracted so as to turn the inside of the lid outwards. It is caused usually by scars due to burns and the like, and is remedied by operation.

ECZEMA (ἐκζέω, I bubble up) is a superficial disease of the skin of inflammatory nature, characterized by a scaly and fissured condition of the cuticle and a sticky watery discharge, and associated with itching or even pain. The condition is very important, because it is said to embrace about one-half of all the cases of skin disease. It is often called by the more general term of ' dermatitis ' or inflammation of the skin. (*See* SKIN, DISEASES OF.)

EFFERENT (*efferens*, carrying out) is the term applied to vessels which convey away blood or a secretion from a part, or of nerves which carry nerve impulses outwards from the nerve-centres.

EFFERVESCING DRAUGHTS (*see* CITRIC ACID).

EFFLEURAGE is a form of massage by gentle stroking movements.

EFFORT SYNDROME, or D.A.H. (Disordered Action of the Heart), also known as Da Costa's syndrome, is a condition in which symptoms occur, such as palpitations and shortness of breath, which are attributed by the patient to disorder of the heart. There is no evidence, however, of heart disease, and psychological factors are thought to be of importance.

EFFUSION (*effundo*, I pour out) means a pouring out of fluid from the vessels in which it is naturally enclosed into the substance of the organs, or into cavities of the body, as a result of inflammation or of injury : for example, pleurisy with effusion, effusions into joints, and effusion of blood.

EGG is a term applied to any animal ovum. The hen's egg forms an easily digestible article of food, and weighs on an average 2 ounces (57 grammes). One egg consists of 6 grammes of protein and 6 grammes of fat, providing energy equivalent to 80 calories. The yolk of the egg is of special value as a food. The best test for a stale egg is to dissolve 2 ounces (57 grammes) of salt in a pint (500 ml.) of water ; fresh eggs placed in the solution sink ; stale eggs float.

ELBOW is the joint formed between the humerus above and the radius and ulna below. The humerus has at its lower end a rounded surface, against which the head of the radius moves, and a deep groove to which a saddle-shaped surface at the upper end of the ulna fits. The head of the radius rests upon a projection of the ulna and is bound to it by a stout annular ligament, within which it can rotate. Two important movements take place at this joint, a flail-like backward and forward movement of the radius

and ulna moving together upon the humerus, and a rotary movement of the radius on the ulna, by which the lower end of the radius is crossed over the ulna and again brought side by side with it, according as the hand is turned palm downwards and palm upwards. The joint is secured at the sides by strong lateral ligaments, and at the back and front is covered by powerful muscles. The ulnar nerve as it passes down to the forearm has an exposed position behind the inner edge of the humerus at its lower end, and is popularly known as the ' funnybone '. The elbow is seldom dislocated, but a not uncommon accident consists in the chipping off, through a fall on the elbow, of the olecranon process which forms the point behind the joint. *Miner's Elbow* or *Beat Elbow* is the term applied to an inflammatory condition of the bursa over the point of the elbow, caused by resting the weight of the body on the elbow in hewing coal. The condition corresponds to housemaid's knee in the lower limb, and occurs not only in miners but sometimes in school children and other persons who lean upon or bruise the point of the elbow. (*See* BURSITIS.) *Tennis Elbow* is a term applied to a pain over the lower end of the humerus due to mild inflammation in the bone caused by strains and jars in playing tennis and similar games. *Pulled Elbow* is the name applied to a painful condition of the elbow in young children, constituting a slight dislocation of the head of the radius from beneath the ligament which should bind it to the ulna, caused by a jerk of the hand.

ELECTRICAL INJURIES are usually caused by the passage through the body of an electric current of high voltage owing to accidental contact with a live wire or to a discharge of lightning. The general effects produced are included under the term electric shock, but vary greatly in degree. The local effects include spasmodic contraction of muscles, fracture of bones, and in severe cases more or less widespread destruction of tissues which may amount simply to burns of the skin or may include necrosis of masses of muscle and internal organs. Fright due to unexpectedness of the shock and pain due to the sudden cramp of muscles are the commonest symptoms and in most cases pass off in a few minutes or less. In more severe cases, especially when the person has remained in contact with a live wire for some time or has been unable to let go of the electrical contact owing to spasmodic contraction of his muscles, the effects are more pronounced and may be those of concussion of the brain or of compression of the brain (see BRAIN, DISEASES OF). In still severer cases, death may ensue either from paralysis of the respiration or stoppage of the heart's action. In either instance, the condition may be at first one of suspended animation, and death may not ensue if prompt measures are taken for treatment.

With regard to the after-effects of an electric shock, recovery in slighter cases is almost immediate, but in cases in which the discharge of current has been prolonged the process of recovery may be prolonged. The more permanent effects depend upon the extent to which tissues have been destroyed. Fractures and splitting of bones are frequently caused by very powerful currents, but these usually mend rapidly and thoroughly. Dislocation of a joint is sometimes produced by violent muscular spasm. Masses of muscle and areas of skin may be destroyed, and if these injuries are extensive, a long time may be required for the absorption or sloughing away of the dead tissues and for healing. A remarkable fact, however, is that electrical injuries show little tendency to become septic as compared with similar injuries due to other causes, and while loss of a part of the body may take place, healing is in the end usually satisfactory.

With regard to the amount of current necessary to produce serious results, this varies enormously according to circumstances. It has been found by experiment that a current at 100 volts and of $\frac{1}{10}$ ampere invariably kills an animal such as a dog. On the other hand, instances are frequent in human beings of brief contact with a live wire at 250 or more volts which produces merely an unpleasant momentary cramp and a small burn. A current of 500 volts is usually fatal. Contact with high-tension currents (1000 volts

or more) of the alternating type is immediately fatal. The amperage of the current appears to be of more importance than the voltage, and alternating current is more injurious than direct current. Physical factors are important in regard to the effects produced by a given strength of current, and after a shock is received through dry shoes or dry clothing, the effect may be negligible as compared with that of contact made with a bare part of the body, especially when the skin is damp or perspiring, or of contact through wet feet. This is why electrical apparatus should never be allowed in a bathroom unless it is out of all possible contact with individuals using the bathroom. Water is a good conductor of electricity. Therefore if an individual touches an electrical heater or fire with wet hands, he may receive a severe shock. If the contact occurs while the individual is still in his bath the result will probably be fatal. Even touching a faulty switch with dripping hands may prove fatal.

Treatment.—No electrical apparatus or switch should be touched by anyone who is in metallic contact with the ground, such as through a metal pipe, especially, for example, from a bath. The first necessity in regard to a person through whose body a powerful electric current is passing is to break the current. This can sometimes be done by turning off a switch. If the victim is grasping or in contact with a live wire, the contact may be severed with safety only by someone wearing rubber gloves or rubber boots, but as these are not likely to be immediately available, his hands may be protected by a thick wrapping of dry cloth, or the live wire may be hooked or pushed out of the way with a long wooden stick. If the injured person is unconscious, and especially if breathing has stopped, *artificial respiration should be applied and continued even for hours*, as described under DROWNING, RECOVERY FROM. When the patient begins to breathe again, he must be treated for shock, *i.e.* put to bed and given hot-water bottles and hot drinks. Electrical burns are treated on the same lines as ordinary burns. If the patient shows undue excitement and restlessness, sedatives may later be necessary.

The local destructive effects of a powerful current, including burns, fractures, and sloughing of large masses of tissue, are treated later by ordinary surgical means, but strong and irritating antiseptics should be avoided. Bleeding from damaged vessels is liable to occur a few days after a severe injury, and is treated by the ordinary means for arrest of hæmorrhage.

ELECTRICITY IN MEDICINE.—

As electricity has proved to be a form of energy, of great usefulness and extremely convenient in application, it has become widely employed in medicine. Several forms of electricity are of importance also in regard to diagnosis, especially in conditions of the nervous system. In addition, electricity is of great indirect importance in the use of various instruments and forms of apparatus, for example, in lighting small lamps for examination of the eye, throat, etc., in heating cauteries, and in the production of X - rays and ultra - violet rays. It has, however, been credited with powers of healing far beyond those that it is capable of achieving. Electricity is generally spoken of as existing in different forms, but these differ in pressure, in amount, and in duration, rather than in any essential quality. They are named as follows : (a) Static, or Frictional, or Franklinic ; (b) Galvanic or Voltaic ; (c) Faradic or Induced ; (d) Alternating or Sinusoidal ; (e) High Frequency or D'Arsonvalism.

Static electricity has been recognized, by some of its simplest phenomena, from the earliest times. The name electricity is derived from the Greek word ἤλεκτρον, meaning ' amber ', because it is said that Thales of Miletus first discovered this force by noticing that a piece of amber, rubbed with a dry cloth, had the power of attracting other small bodies to itself. Subsequently it was found that other bodies, such as sulphur, wax, and glass, have similar properties, and a treatise, De Magnete, was published on the subject by Gilbert, physician to Queen Elizabeth, in 1600. This form of electricity is often called ' Franklinic ', after Benjamin Franklin, who, in the middle of the eighteenth century, experimented much with it in the

United States. It is also interesting to note that Wesley, the famous preacher, was greatly interested in the subject of electricity, and about the same time published a treatise on its medical applications known as The Desideratum, or Electricity made Plain and Useful, by a Lover of Mankind and Common Sense.

When a glass rod is rubbed with a piece of dry flannel, the two gain certain properties. If the glass rod be brought near a light pith-ball or piece of paper hanging by a dry silk thread, the pith-ball is attracted towards the rod, but if the two be allowed to touch for a moment, the pith-ball is now as energetically repelled when the rod is brought near it. If, however, the piece of flannel be brought near the ball, the latter is attracted to it. To express these facts conveniently it is said that there are two ' kinds ' of electricity, positive and negative, the glass rod becoming positively electrified by the rubbing, the flannel negatively electrified, and further, that like electricities repel one another. Accordingly, when the positively electrified glass rod is brought near the pith-ball, the negative electricity in the latter is supposed to separate from the positive (the ball having till now been uniformly charged with the two) and to collect on that side of the ball nearest to the rod, while the positive electricity is repelled to the point farthest off. When the rod and ball touch, the negative electricity escapes to the rod, leaving the ball positively electrified, so that it is now repelled by the positive electricity of the rod and attracted by the negative electricity of the flannel. Positive electricity is designated shortly by the sign +, and negative by the sign −, while the power possessed by the electricity of passing from pith-ball to glass rod, carrying the ball with it, is known as potential, or pressure, or electro-motive force (E.M.F.). All bodies have these properties, developing, when suddenly separated or broken, this difference of potential, the amount and nature of the force produced depending on the nature of the bodies in question. But while in the case of certain bodies called non-conductors, such as glass, porcelain, sealing - wax, india - rubber, gutta-percha, dry wool, silk, and amber, the electricity remains upon the surface where it is produced, in the case of others, known as conductors, such as metals, salt solutions, and the bodies of animals and plants, it flows away through the body so soon as formed, and therefore does not show its presence. Static electricity is closely related to magnetism, a set of properties possessed only by iron, steel, nickel, cobalt, and an iron-ore called lodestone.

Static electricity may be stored up in large amount by means of the Leyden jar. This consists of two conducting surfaces, such as tinfoil, placed one outside, the other inside, a glass jar, so that they are everywhere separated by a thin plate of glass. The outer one simply rests in contact with the earth, the inner is connected to a metal rod ending in a knob. Electrified bodies, like a rubbed glass rod, may be brought up to the knob time after time till the inner sheet of tinfoil becomes highly charged with positive electricity, which attracts negative electricity from the earth into the outside sheet. If the knob of a charged Leyden-jar be connected with the outside sheet of foil the two electricities combine suddenly, and if this contact be made through the human body, a severe momentary shock is felt.

For practical medical purposes, static electricity is produced by an influence machine consisting of several pairs of circular glass or vulcanite plates, which are driven in opposite directions. Each plate carries at starting a small amount of electricity ; and, as they revolve, the alternate plates generate increasing quantities of + and – electricity, which are drawn off to opposite sides of the machine by fine metal brushes. The electricity can be stored in Leyden jars, or used directly to electrify the body. For the latter purpose, the person sits upon a chair or couch, carefully insulated from the earth by glass legs, india-rubber mats, or other non-conductors, and becomes charged positively or negatively according to the manner in which he is connected with the machine. During the process of charging, a peculiar tingling over the skin is felt and the hair stands upright ;

the breathing becomes more rapid, and during a séance of fifteen to twenty minutes the chemical changes which accompany bodily activity are markedly increased. The electricity is discharged by bringing a metal point or ball gradually towards the charged person, when, in the former case, a spray of air or ' souffle ' passes towards the point as the charge passes off, in the latter case sparks are drawn. Either form of discharge, especially the latter, has a very stimulating effect. Electropathic belts may produce static electricity in small amount, but any benefit derived from them is probably a merely mental one. The atmosphere, both upon high wooded mountains and in the neighbourhood of breaking waves, has, as Lord Kelvin demonstrated, a different electric state from the quiet air of inland plains, so that it is quite possible that some of the advantage derived from summer change to mountain and seaside resorts may be due to stimulation from this cause.

Galvanic electricity is so named after Galvani, professor at Bologna, who published researches upon what he called ' animal electricity ' in 1791. It also received the name ' voltaic ', after Volta, professor at Pavia, who in 1799 published researches showing that this type of electricity is really due to chemical action. He found that dissimilar metals, moistened and brought in contact, became electrified, so that, when parts of these metals not in contact are connected by a conductor, such as copper wire, a constant current passes through the wire. As chemical action proceeds almost continuously, this current is also continuous ; and for this reason, added to the facts that it is of moderate potential or pressure and is easily produced, it is the most convenient for general medical use.

The choice of metals depends upon the fact that one must be very liable to chemical action, the other as little affected as possible by an oxidizing agent. The principal metals may be arranged in a series, thus :

+ Sodium	Iron
Magnesium	Copper
Zinc	Silver
Lead	Gold
Tin	Platinum
	– Carbon

—of which each one is more oxidizable than that following it, and becomes positively electrified when brought into contact with one of those lower down in the series. Zinc and carbon, or zinc and copper, on account of their distance apart in this scale, and their comparative cheapness, are the metals usually selected. A vessel containing two metal plates, for example, zinc and copper, immersed in a fluid which maintains chemical action, for example, sulphuric acid in water, is known as a galvanic cell. A collection of such cells is called a ' battery '. When the plates are joined by a conducting wire an electric current passes along it from the copper (+ pole) to the zinc (– pole). At the same time there is set free, on the surface of the zinc plate, oxygen, which acts upon the zinc, and also produces sulphuric acid ; while hydrogen is set free at the surface of the copper plate and escapes.

It is important to bear in mind also that if the current passing along the wire be passed for some distance through a moist decomposable substance, such as the tissues of the human body, a similar chemical action is produced at the points where the wire enters and leaves the substance, which are called the electrodes. Thus oxygen is set free and acids formed at the electrode connected to the + pole (the anode), while hydrogen is set free and alkalies developed at the other, or – electrode (the cathode). This action, known as electrolysis, is much used in medicine for removing hairs, destroying nævi or birth-marks, and reducing the size of certain tumours, unsuitable for removal by the knife. There is a great difference between the action of the two electrodes, because the substances formed at the anode are caustic and germicidal in action, whilst those produced at the cathode have no such action. Accordingly, the anode (+ pole) is generally applied to the structure which it is desirable to destroy.

Another important property of electric currents, viz. the fact that a powerful current passing through a circuit heats any part which is of feeble conducting power, is utilized to heat cauteries for delicate surgical work, especially about the nose and throat,

and also to light small incandescent lamps for internal examinations. The cautery consists of a piece of platinum (low conducting power), joining the ends of two large copper wires (high conducting power), so that, when the current passes, the former immediately becomes red or white hot, according to the intensity of the current.

Another method in which the galvanic current is employed is in order to carry drugs through the unbroken skin by the process known as iontophoresis (q.v.).

Faradic electricity dates only from 1831, when it was discovered by Faraday that if two coils of wire be placed near one another, and if a galvanic current be suddenly passed

Fig. 136—Urate crystals from a tophus. Magnified 500 times

through one of them and again stopped, a current is induced in the second coil at the moments of closing and of opening the first circuit. This secondary current differs from the continuous galvanic current in two important particulars : (1) it is only momentary in duration ; (2) it has a much higher potential or pressure, and is therefore much more capable of traversing poor conductors like the human body. The currents induced in the secondary coil at opening and closing the primary coil run in opposite directions, and accordingly, if the primary current be very rapidly closed and opened, as, for example, by the vibration of a steel spring, an almost continuous series of alternating currents is obtained in the secondary circuit.

A faradic current sufficient for medical purposes can be obtained from an apparatus consisting of the following : a single galvanic cell connected to a primary coil, with an appliance to make and break the circuit ; a secondary coil, which is connected by wires with two electrodes provided with handles, by which the electrodes can be applied to the surface of the body ; and a core of iron which fits inside the primary coil, and which, becoming magnetized as the current passes through this coil, increases the effect upon the secondary coil. Such an apparatus can be obtained in the small compass of a box 4 or 5 inches each way (Fig. 136).

The faradic current can be administered to the surface of the body generally by immersion of the patient in a warm bath into which two electrodes dip.

For certain purposes, such as X-ray work, secondary coils with an enormous length of wire (even 40 miles) are used, the potential or pressure of the faradic current increasing with the number of turns taken by the wire in the secondary coil. By such coils a spark from 1 to 2 feet in length may be obtained.

The potential of faradic currents is high, in medical coils it may reach 20,000 or 100,000 volts, or about five hundred times as high as that of the powerful current which supplies a town, but the amount of electricity is very small. The difference between faradic and galvanic electricity presents some resemblance to the difference between a shower of swiftly falling raindrops, in which the total amount of water is small, and a large, sluggish river.

Alternating or sinusoidal currents.— An alternating current differs from the faradic current in the fact that the latter consists of a rapid series of sudden impulses or shocks, while with the sinusoidal or alternating current the strength gradually rises from nothing to a maximum, and falls away again to be followed immediately

304

by a current in the reverse direction, which also grows to a maximum and wanes in the same manner. These currents rapidly succeed one another, so that the effect on the body is very much the same as that produced by the faradic current. Most systems of public distribution of electrical energy are carried out by alternating currents of this type, and by means of transformers they can be very readily converted into forms of electricity more suitable for medical use. The sinusoidal current, suitably reduced by apparatus, may be used for the electric bath, or may be used for stimulating nerves or muscles, especially when the current is rhythmically cut off and restored by an instrument known as a rhythmic interrupter. Sinusoidal currents on a small scale can be produced by bringing a magnet rapidly up to and away from a secondary coil, or making the coil move while the magnet remains fixed. Upon this principle are constructed box electric machines driven by hand which were formerly much used for medical purposes. The sinusoidal form of current generally has a very stinging effect on sensory nerves, and in this way is somewhat unpleasant for use.

High-frequency currents.—By apparatus constructed on the principle of the induction coil, but with other complicated arrangements designed to make and break the primary current several hundred thousand times a second, currents, huge in pressure but minute as regards duration, can be produced which have an action similar to that of a discharge of static electricity. The sensation is merely one of slight tingling when sparks are drawn, and there is no stimulation of muscles or nerves. This may possibly be explained by the currents being confined to the surface, and not passing through the substance of the body at all, or more probably by the theory of D'Arsonval, that the nerve endings are incapable of perceiving such extremely short vibrations. These high-frequency currents formed at one time a very popular mode of stimulating treatment.

The apparatus by which these currents are produced consists essentially of Leyden jars, whose outer coats are united through a solenoid or spiral of thick copper wire. The jars are rapidly charged and discharged by some source of high potential electricity ; and, since the discharges from a Leyden jar have the property of taking place in an oscillatory manner, they induce in the solenoid corresponding secondary currents, which are of immensely rapid frequency. A second coil of thick wire, known as a resonator, is in general connected to the solenoid with the purpose of allowing of variations in the potential of the high-frequency discharges.

The currents are applied to the patient in various ways. (a) He may be connected to the two ends of the solenoid by thin wires provided with ordinary flat electrodes, from which the currents are simply passed through his body (direct application). (b) He may lie upon a couch connected with one end of the solenoid, while the cushion of the couch isolates him from a metal plate connected with the other end ; he then becomes rapidly charged and discharged (condensation). (c) He may stand or lie within a wide secondary coil, and have currents induced in his body (auto-conduction). (d) One end of the solenoid may be connected to earth, while to the other end is attached an electrode, which is cautiously approached to any desired part (local application). (e) The method of diathermy or thermo-penetration may be used to produce heat within the body. (See DIATHERMY.)

As already stated, the passage of high-frequency currents through the body produces no stimulation of muscles and no sensation, apart from that of heat caused by the resistance. There is a powerful effect, lasting many minutes, in diminishing the sensitiveness of the skin ; the fullness of the blood-vessels in the skin, the output of body heat and of carbonic acid gas by the lungs are increased, and the quantity of urine passed becomes much greater.

Applications of electricity.—The galvanic and faradic currents are of value as a means of *diagnosis* in many conditions affecting nerves and muscles. In their natural condition nerves react to faradic or to interrupted galvanic currents, muscles to the latter. When excitability by faradization is lost, it shows that the nerves in question are degenerating. The sudden commencement of a weak galvanic current should produce a contraction of muscles to which the cathode is applied, but, if a much stronger current be required, or if a contraction be obtained more readily with the anode, it shows that the muscles in question are also in process of degeneration. This is expressed by the statement that when the anodal closing contraction is stronger than the cathodal closing contraction the reaction of degeneration is present, or, put briefly, $A.C.C. > K.C.C. = R.D.$

PAIN, whether headache, neuralgia, sciatica, a chronic rheumatic condition, or due to several other causes, is almost always relieved temporarily, and sometimes, after a protracted course of treatment, severe pain is entirely removed by one of the following. The static breeze may be tried, applied to the seat of pain for some minutes every day. In painful nerve conditions like neuralgia, greater benefit is often derived from the galvanic current, a strong current of 20-30 milliamperes being used, and the anode (+ electrode) being placed over the course of the affected nerve. In most cases of vague but severe pain the faradic current is the simplest of application, and very effective. A small button electrode or wire-brush is applied to the seat of pain, the other electrode, moistened with common salt solution, to the neck, back, or other convenient part. The séance lasts, perhaps, a quarter of an hour, and is repeated several times daily.

SPASMODIC CONDITIONS of all sorts, such as writer's cramp, are relieved or lessened by the static breeze, and still more by a strong galvanic current arranged so that the anode is close to the nerve or nerves connected with the spasmodically acting muscles. The anode decreases the conducting power of nerves for motor impulses as well as for painful sensations.

PARALYSIS, such as infantile paralysis, or that following a stroke of apoplexy, or injury to a nerve, calls specially for the application of interrupted galvanic currents. The muscles in these and similar cases, where the nervous control usually exerted over them is lost, tend to waste. The application of interrupted galvanic currents of about 10 milliamperes strength, or of these combined with faradization, and assisted in every case by massage, and movements of the neighbouring joints, not only keeps up the nourishment of the paralysed muscles and prevents stiffness and wasting, but actually assists recovery. Treatment should be as far as possible daily, and must extend over very long periods.

DESTRUCTION OF HAIRS is almost painlessly accomplished by electrolysis.

BIRTH-MARKS, consisting of masses of blood-vessels beneath the skin (nævi), are successfully destroyed, with-

effected by a powerful electro-magnet consisting of a soft iron core round which is wound an electric coil, through which a heavy current can be passed.

X-RAYS AND ULTRA-VIOLET RAYS are produced by the aid of electricity, and used in the treatment of many skin and other diseases. (See under LIGHT TREATMENT and X-RAYS.)

ELECTROCARDIOGRAM is the term applied to a record of the variations in electric potential which occur in the heart as it contracts and relaxes. Any muscle in use produces an electric current, but when an individual is at rest the main muscular current in the body is that produced by the heart.

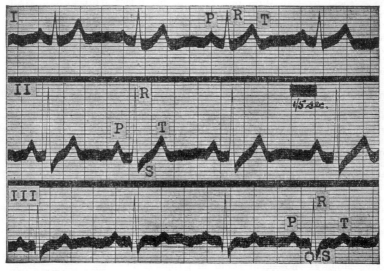

FIG. 137.—Normal electrocardiogram. The wave marked P represents atrial activity. The waves marked Q, R, S, and T represent ventricular activity. (From Evans, *Cardiology*. Butterworth & Co. Ltd.)

out leaving a scar, by electrolysis. The electrodes consist of two needles which are pushed through the skin into the mass, and an anæsthetic is usually given during the process.

STRICTURES of the gullet, bowel, and urethra may, it is claimed, also be painlessly dilated by electrolysis, though the process must be repeated several times at intervals of a fortnight or thereabout, in séances of fifteen minutes.

REMOVAL OF STEEL PARTICLES which have penetrated the eye may often be

This can be recorded by connecting the outside of the body by electrodes with an instrument known as an electrocardiograph. This instrument contains a galvanometer of great delicacy, consisting essentially of a silvered wire which vibrates in a magnetic field in response to these currents. While it is vibrating, an electrographic record is obtained upon a moving photographic plate, and this, being subsequently developed, can be studied by the physician at his convenience. The patient is connected to the electro-cardiograph by leads from either the arms and legs or different points on the chest. The normal electrocardiogram of each heart-beat shows one wave corresponding to the activity of the atria and four waves corresponding to the phases of each ventricular beat (Fig. 137). Various readily recognizable changes are seen in cases in which the heart is acting in an abnormal manner, or in which one or other side of the heart is hypertrophied. This record, therefore, forms a useful aid in many cases of heart disease.

ELECTROCAUTERY (*see* CAUTERY).

ELECTRO-ENCEPHALOGRAPHY.
—It has been found that in the brain there is a regular, rhythmical change of electric potential, due to the rhythmic discharge of energy by nerve cells. These changes can be recorded graphically and the ' brain waves ' examined. These records—electro-encephalograms —are useful in diagnosis. For example, the abnormal electro-encephalogram occurring in epilepsy is characteristic of this disease. The normal waves, known as alpha waves, occur with a frequency of 10 per second. Abnormal waves, with a frequency of 7 or less per second, are known as delta waves and occur in the region of cerebral tumours and in the brains of epileptics.

ELECTRO-OCULOGRAPHY is a method of recording movements of the eyes, which is proving of value in assessing the function of the retina.

ELECTROPHORESIS means the migration of charged particles between electrodes. Of recent years a simple method of electrophoresis, known as paper electrophoresis, has been introduced which is proving of value in examining the proteins in body fluids. This method consists in applying the protein-containing solution as a spot or a streak to a strip of filter paper which has been soaked in buffer solution and across the ends of which a potential difference is then applied for some hours.

ELECTUARY, or CONFECTION, is a soft paste containing drugs mixed with sugar or honey. (*See* CONFECTION.)

ELEPHANTIASIS (synonyms, *Elephantiasis Arabum, Barbados Leg, Boucnemia*) is a term applied to a disease which is characterized by gross overgrowth of the skin and subjacent textures. This condition arises from repeated attacks of inflammation of the skin and subcutaneous tissue, and concurrent obstruction of the lymphatic vessels. A common cause in the tropics is infection with certain parasitic worms (filariæ) which invade the lymphatic vessels. These worms are conveyed to man by mosquitoes. They may attack any portion of the body, but most commonly the leg, which becomes so enlarged and disfigured by the great thickening of its textures as to resemble the leg of an elephant, whence the name of the disease is derived. The thickening is due to excessive increase in the connective tissue, which results from the inflammatory process, and which by pressure on the muscles of the limb causes them to undergo atrophy or degeneration. Hence the limb becomes weak. When affecting the scrotum it frequently produces a tumour of enormous dimensions. The health, however, ultimately suffers, and serious constitutional disturbance is apt to arise. In elephantiasis of the leg much relief is obtained from the use of elastic bandaging, massage, rest, and elevation of the limb. Prevention must be carried out by destruction of mosquitoes. Promising results are now being reported from the use of a drug known as diethylcarbazine (hetrazan).

ELIXIR (*elixo*, I boil) is a diluted tincture made pleasant to the taste by the addition of aromatic substances and sugar. The name was specially applied to several preparations greatly used in the Middle Ages, which had the effect of acting as a tonic to the stomach and relieving constipation, and which were known as the elixir of Paracelsus, elixir of long life, etc. The main constituent of all of these was tincture of aloes. At the present day they are mainly used as a vehicle for potent and nauseous drugs.

EMACIATION (*emacio*, I make lean) means pronounced wasting, and is a common symptom of many diseases, particularly of those which are associated with a prolonged or repeated rise of temperature, such as typhoid fever and tuberculosis. It is also associated with diseases of the alimentary system in which digestion is inefficient, or in which the food is not fully absorbed, for example, in diarrhœa of long-standing, whatever be its cause. It is also a marked feature of malignant disease.

EMBALMING (*see* DEAD, DISPOSAL OF THE).

EMBOLISM (ἔμβολον, a plug) means the plugging of a small blood-vessel by material which has been carried through the larger vessels by the blood stream (Fig. 138). It is due usually to fragments of a clot which has formed in some vessel, or to small portions carried off from the edge of a heart-valve when this organ is diseased ; but the plug may also be a small mass of bacteria, or a fragment of a tumour, or even a

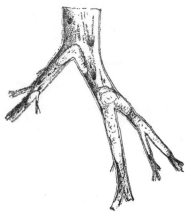

FIG. 138.—Artery from the lung, which has become plugged by emboli, opened lengthwise. (Thoma's *Pathology*.)

mass of air bubbles sucked into the veins during operations on the neck. The result is usually more or less destruction of the organ or part of an organ supplied by the obstructed vessel. This is particularly the case in the brain, where softening of the brain, with aphasia or apoplexy, may be the result. If the plug be a fragment of malignant tumour, a new growth develops at the spot ; and if

it be a mass of bacteria, an abscess forms there. Air-embolism occasionally causes sudden death in the case of wounds in the neck, the air bubbles completely stopping the flow of blood. Fat-embolism is a condition which has been known to cause death, masses of fat, in consequence of such an injury as a fractured bone, finding their way into the circulation and stopping the blood in its passage through the lungs.

EMBROCATIONS (ἐμβρέχω, I soak in) are mixtures, usually of an oily nature, intended for external application in cases of rheumatism, sprains, and other painful conditions. Their action is due partly to the massage employed in rubbing in the embrocations, partly to the counter-irritant action of the drugs which they contain. (*See* LINIMENTS.)

EMBRYO (ἔμβρυον) means the fœtus in the womb prior to the middle of the second month. (*See* FŒTUS.)

EMESIS (ἔμεσις) means vomiting. (*See* VOMITING.)

EMETICS (ἐμετικός, provoking sickness) are drugs or other means which produce vomiting.

Varieties.—Emetics are divided into two important classes : (1) direct emetics, which, being taken by the mouth, irritate the stomach and so cause vomiting, and (2) indirect emetics, which will cause vomiting, even when injected into the blood, by action upon the centre in the brain controlling the act of vomiting. Examples of the first type are sulphate of zinc, mustard in water, alum, sal volatile, sulphate of copper, and even copious draughts of warm salt water. In the second class we have apomorphine, ipecacuanha, and tartar emetic ; to this class also belong such means as tickling the throat, or presenting evil-smelling substances to the nose.

Uses.—Emetics are now relatively seldom used except in certain cases of poisoning to remove the poisonous substance as rapidly as possible from the stomach. Large draughts of warm salt water, or a heaped dessert-spoonful of mustard in a tumblerful of cold water, are simple emetics, but in cases of poisoning, a more rapidly acting and more certain emetic is required. Sulphate of zinc (20 grains (1·2 G.)), repeated if necessary) and sulphate of copper (10 grains (600 mg.)) are rapid and effective. Emetics in smaller doses than will produce vomiting, are often used in cough mixtures, as they render the secretions in the bronchial tubes more fluid and therefore more easily coughed up. Wine of ipecacuanha is most often used for this purpose.

EMETINE is one of the active principles of ipecacuanha. (*See* IPECACUANHA *and* DYSENTERY.)

EMICTORY is a drug which provokes the excretion of urine.

EMMENAGOGUES (ἐμμήνια, the menses ; ἄγω I move) are drugs which restore the flow at the menstrual periods, when this is scanty or absent. Certain substances, which are mainly dangerous irritant poisons, are credited with the power of producing this effect. Other substances act indirectly by removing the state of ill-health to which the failure is due, such as iron in anæmia. (*See* MENSTRUATION.)

EMMETROPIA (ἔμμετρος, regular ; ὄψις, vision) is a term applied to the normal condition of the eye as regards refraction of light rays. In this state when the muscles in the eyeball are completely relaxed the focusing power is accurately adjusted for parallel rays, so that vision is perfect for distant objects.

EMOLLIENTS (*emollio*, I soften) are substances which have a softening and soothing effect upon the skin. They include dusting powders such as French chalk, oils such as olive oil and almond oil, and fats such as the various pharmacopœial preparations of paraffin, suet, and lard. Glycerin is also an excellent emollient.

Uses.—They are used in various inflammatory conditions such as eczema, when the skin becomes hard, cracked, and painful. They may be used either in the form of a dusting powder or an oil, or as an ointment.

EMPHYSEMA (ἐμφύσημα) means an abnormal presence of air in certain parts of the body. In its restricted sense, however, it is generally employed to designate an affection of the lungs, of which there are two forms. In one of these there is over-distension of the air-cells of these organs, and in parts destruction of their walls, giving rise to the formation of large sacs, from the rupture and running together of a number of contiguous air-vesicles. This is much the more common of the two forms and is the one which is usually meant when the term ' emphysema ' is used. In the other form the air is infiltrated into the connective tissue beneath the pleura and between the pulmonary air-cells, constituting what is known as *acute interstitial emphysema*.

Causes.—1. Where a portion of the lung has become wasted, or its vesicular structure permanently obliterated by disease, without corresponding fallingin of the chest wall, the neighbouring air-vesicles, or some of them, undergo dilatation to fill the vacuum.

2. In cases of bronchitis, and especially of bronchial asthma, where numbers of the smaller bronchial tubes become obstructed, the air in the pulmonary vesicles remains imprisoned, the force of expiration being insufficient to expel it ; while, on the other hand, the stronger force of inspiration being adequate to overcome the resistance, the air-cells tend to become more and more distended, and permanent alterations in their structure, including emphysema, are the result.

3. Emphysema also arises from exertion involving expiratory efforts, during which the glottis is constricted, as in paroxysms of coughing, in straining, and in lifting heavy weights. Whooping-cough is well known as the exciting cause of emphysema in many cases.

Symptoms.—In the affected portions of the lungs there are loss of the natural elasticity of the air - cells, the destruction of many of the pulmonary capillary blood - vessels, and diminution of aerating surface for the blood. As a consequence there is a strain on the heart and the venous system generally, leading to dilatation of the right side of the heart, and so to dropsy. The chief symptom in this complaint is shortness of breath, more or less constant but greatly aggravated by exertion, and by attacks of bronchitis, to which persons suffering from emphysema are specially liable. The respiration is of a wheezy character. In severe forms of the disease the patient comes to acquire a peculiar bluish and bloated appearance, and the configuration of the chest is altered, assuming the character known as the *barrel-shaped chest*.

Treatment.—The main element in the treatment of emphysema consists in attention to the general condition of the health, and in the avoidance of all causes likely to aggravate the disease or induce its complications. The same general plan of treatment as that recommended in asthma and bronchitis is applicable in emphysema. During attacks of urgent breathlessness antispasmodic remedies should be given, while dry cupping back and front over the lungs, together with inhalation of oxygen, will often afford marked and speedy relief.

ACUTE INTERSTITIAL EMPHYSEMA, arising from the rupture of air-cells, may occur as a complication of the vesicular form, or separately as the result of some sudden expulsive effort, such as a fit of coughing, or, as has frequently happened, in parturition. Occasionally the air infiltrates the cellular tissue of the mediastinum, and thence comes to distend the integument of the neck and even the whole surface of the body. This air is, however, rapidly absorbed, and the condition soon subsides.

SURGICAL EMPHYSEMA is the term applied when air is present under the skin. It may get there, for example, if the lungs are wounded through the chest wall, or if the wind-pipe is pierced at any point in its path.

EMPIRICAL (ἐμπειρία, experience) treatment is that school of treatment which is founded simply on experience. Because a given remedy has been successful in the treatment of a certain group of symptoms, it is assumed, by those who uphold this principle, that it will be successful in the treatment of other cases presenting similar groups of symptoms, without any inquiry as to the cause of the symptoms or reason underlying the action of the remedy.

It is the contrary of 'rational' or 'scientific' treatment. Sometimes a course of treatment must perforce be empirical for want of knowledge.

EMPLASTRUM is the Latin term for a plaster.

EMPROSTHOTONOS is the term applied to the spasm of the belly muscles that occurs in tetanus, making the body arch forwards.

EMPYEMA (ἐμπύημα, an internal abscess) is a term applied to an accumulation of pus within a cavity, the term being generally reserved for collections of pus within one of the pleural cavities. The condition is virtually an abscess, and therefore gives rise to the general symptoms accompanying that condition ; but, on account of the thick unyielding wall of the chest, it has very little tendency to burst through the surface, and therefore it is of particular importance that the condition should be recognized early, and, as a rule, treated by surgical means.

Causes.—The condition most commonly follows an attack of pneumonia. It may also occur in the advanced stage of pulmonary tuberculosis. Empyema also occurs at times through infection from some serious disease in neighbouring organs, such as cancer of the gullet, or follows upon wounds penetrating the chest wall.

Symptoms.—In empyema following a case of pneumonia, symptoms of the former generally appear as the pneumonia is subsiding, and when an ordinary attack of pneumonia does not come satisfactorily to an end after the lapse of eight to ten days, it is usual for the physician to suspect and search for the signs of empyema. A certain amount of inflammation in the membrane lining the pleural cavity always accompanies pneumonia, and the fluid which is thus produced may show any stage between that of clear yellow serous fluid and thick pus of the consistence of cream. When the fluid is clear or merely turbid, absorption generally takes place naturally in course of time, and the mild type of infection which is present is readily overcome by the ordinary powers of the tissues. When, however, a severe infection, due usually either to a virulent pneumococcus or streptococcus, is present, the fluid is of the thicker purulent variety, and active measures of treatment are required. The temperature of the patient, which should revert to normal at the end of the attack of pneumonia, tends to show a daily rise to 102° or 103° F. (39° to 39.5° C.) ; there is profuse sweating and the patient presents a flushed appearance. The severity of these symptoms is proportional to the degree of virulence in the infection of the pleural membrane, the symptoms generally being less marked the clearer the fluid. On examination of the chest a dull percussion-note, faint or absent breath sounds, and other characteristic signs of the presence of fluid are found. It is usual for the physician to complete the diagnosis by puncturing the chest by means of a fine needle attached to a small aspiration syringe. A sample of the fluid is thus obtained, and its characteristics as regards the bacteria present, etc., are investigated. The collection of fluid may be very small in size and limited by adhesions to a small portion of the chest, especially in those cases due to the pneumococcus, and it may be necessary in such cases to insert the needle at various points before the purulent fluid is definitely located.

Treatment.—In those cases where the fluid is clear or only slightly turbid, the measures commonly employed for pleurisy (see PLEURISY) are very often sufficient to bring about absorption. In cases where the fluid is thick and purulent, and especially those following acute pneumonia, it is usually necessary to perform an operation for the drainage of the cavity, an incision being made through the skin and a portion of rib removed. The fluid is thus evacuated, and the lung can then expand naturally against the chest wall, a drainage tube being left in the wound so that the cavity can be irrigated and any fresh fluid which tends to collect can escape freely until the natural closure of the cavity is completed. Penicillin is also given, both intramuscularly and into the cavity. In the great majority of cases the lung ultimately reverts completely to a normal state

EMULSIONS (*emulgeo*, I milk out) are mixtures containing oily substances in a state of very fine division. The division is effected and the oil kept suspended in the fluid by means of alkalies and sticky ingredients such as albumin, glycerin, or mucilage. Milk is an example of a perfect emulsion of fat globules each surrounded by an envelope of albumin. The various preparations of cod-liver oil are usually emulsified by the aid of glycerin. The oil is not only rendered more devoid of taste, but digestion and absorption are also rendered easier by emulsification.

EMUNCTORY (*emungo*, I cleanse) is a term applied generally to excretory organs, such as the kidneys and bowels.

ENAMEL is a thin, hard, transparent layer which covers the surface of the teeth, at least that part of them which projects above the gums. It is composed almost entirely of the earthy salts found in bone, and is the hardest tissue in the body. It is arranged in the form of long six-sided prisms, each about $\frac{1}{5000}$ inch (5 microns) in thickness, and set on end upon the dentine of the tooth.

ENCEPHALITIS (ἐγκέφαλος, the brain) means inflammation of the brain.

ENCEPHALITIS LETHARGICA, also known as SLEEPY SICKNESS and as EPIDEMIC ENCEPHALITIS, VON ECONOMO'S DISEASE, is a disease that appears from time to time, especially in spring, in the form of epidemics. It is a virus infection, attacking chiefly the basal ganglia, the cerebrum, and the brain stem. These undergo dropsical swelling, hæmorrhages, and ultimately destruction of areas of tissue involving both nerve-cells and fibres. The process may involve other parts of the brain, the spinal cord, and even other organs.

Symptoms.—The illness begins usually with rise of temperature and increasing drowsiness or lethargy, which may gradually proceed to a state of complete unconsciousness. In some cases, however, the patient instead of being drowsy passes at first through a stage of restlessness which may amount to maniacal excitement. As a rule the drowsiness deepens gradually over a period of a week or more, and accompanying it there appear various forms of paralysis, shown by drooping of the eyelids, squint, and weakness of one or both sides of the face. The nerves controlling the muscles of the throat are also sometimes paralysed, causing changes in the voice and difficulty in swallowing. In some cases the disease affects the spinal cord, producing severe pain in one or more of the limbs, and it is frequently followed by partial paralysis. Signs of inflammation are not infrequently found in other organs, and hæmorrhages may be visible beneath the skin and in the muscles, or blood may be vomited up or passed in the stools. The effects last usually for many months, the patient remaining easily tired and somnolent or frequently showing rigidity of muscle, mask-like facies, festinant gait, and rhythmical coarse tremors, resembling the 'clinical picture' of paralysis agitans (q.v.).

Treatment.—There is no specific treatment for the disease. During the acute stage the patient must be kept at rest in bed. After the acute stage is over, physiotherapy in the form of massage, passive movements and exercises should be given to control the muscular rigidity. Prolonged convalescence, i.e. three months, is essential to reduce the risk of relapse.

ENCEPHALOID (ἐγκέφαλος, brain ; εἶδος, form) is the name applied to a form of cancer which, to the naked eye, resembles the tissue of the brain.

ENCEPHALOMYELITIS means inflammation of the substance of both brain and spinal cord.

ENCEPHALOPATHY is the term used to describe certain conditions in which there are signs of cerebral irritation without any localized lesion to account for them. The two best examples are *hypertensive encephalopathy* and *lead encephalopathy*. In the former, which occurs in the later stages of chronic Bright's disease, or uræmia (q.v.), the headache, convulsions, and delirium which constitute the main

symptoms are supposed to be due to a deficient blood-supply to the brain. In the latter the symptoms are probably due to spasm of the arteries in the brain.

ENCHONDROMA (ἐν, in ; χόνδρος, cartilage ; -oma, termination meaning tumour) means a tumour formed of cartilage. (See TUMOURS.)

ENCYSTED (ἐν, in; κύστις, a bladder) means enclosed within a bladder-like wall. The term is applied to parasites, collections of pus, etc., which are shut off from surrounding tissues by a membrane or by adhesions.

ENDARTERITIS (ἔνδον, within ; ἀρτηρία, an artery) means inflammation of the inner coat of an artery. (See ARTERIES, DISEASES OF.)

ENDEMIC (ἐν, in ; δῆμος, the people) is a term applied to diseases which exist in particular localities or amongst certain races. Some diseases which are at times epidemic over wide districts, have a restricted area where they are always endemic, and from which they spread. For example, both cholera and plague are endemic in certain parts of Asia.

ENDO- (ἔνδον, within) is a prefix meaning situated inside.

ENDOCARDITIS (ἔνδον, within ; καρδία, the heart) means inflammation of the smooth membrane lining the heart, especially that over the heart valves. (See HEART, DISEASES OF.)

ENDOCRINE GLANDS (ἔνδον within ; κρίνω, I separate) is a term applied to certain organs whose function is to secrete into the blood or lymph a substance which plays an important part in regard to general chemical changes or to the activities of other organs at a distance. Some organs have a double function, such as the pancreas, which pours digestive secretions by a duct into the intestine, and, at the same time, has an endocrine or internal secretion which is absorbed by the blood. Various diseases arise as the result of defects or excess in the internal secretions of the different glands. The chief endocrine glands are the thyroid gland, adrenal bodies, pituitary body, para-thyroid glands, pancreas, ovaries, and testicles. A certain amount of an-tagonism exists between the different endocrine glands; for example, secre-tion of the adrenal glands checks the action of pancreatic secretion. Other glands have an associated action ; for example, extract of pituitary gland stimulates the production of normal secretion of the thyroid. During healthy bodily activity there appears to be a constant state of balancing between the action of the different endocrine secretions. The structure of these glands is noted elsewhere under the appropriate headings, and only a short account will be given here of the action of their secretion.

THYROID GLAND.—This gland, situ-ated in front of the neck, produces a secretion which has a very important effect in regulating the general nutri-tion of the body. When it is defective, the conditions known as myxœdema and cretinism result ; whilst excess or perversion of the secretion is associated with different types of the condition generally known as exophthalmic goitre. An extract is prepared from the thyroid glands of sheep and other animals, and is used in cases where the secretion is defective. It forms one of the most powerful stimulants of general bodily activity. The active principle of this secretion is thyroxine.

ADRENAL BODIES. — These two glands, also known as SUPRARENAL GLANDS, lie immediately above the kidneys. The central or medullary por-tion of the glands forms the secretions known as adrenaline or epinephrine, and noradrenaline. Adrenaline acts upon structures innervated by sym-pathetic nerves ; its action is ' sympatho-mimetic '. Briefly, the blood-vessels of the skin and of the splanchnic viscera (except the in-testines) are constricted, and at the same time the arteries of the muscles and the coronary arteries are dilated ; systolic blood - pressure rises ; blood-sugar increases ; the metabolic rate rises ; muscle fatigue is diminished. Adrenaline can be synthetically pre-pared in the laboratory. This sub-stance is very widely used in medicine in 1 in 1000 solution, for the purpose of checking bleeding, relieving congestion

of mucous membranes, for the relief of asthma, and in the treatment of ana-phylactic shock. The superficial or cortical part of the glands produce a series of chemical substances, the full range of which is not known. They have as their basis a complicated steroid nucleus. The best known of these are aldosterone, cortisone, hydro-cortisone, and deoxycortone acetate. These substances are essential for the maintenance of life. It is the absence of these substances, due to atrophy or destruction of the suprarenal cortex, that is responsible for the condition known as Addison's disease (q.v.).

PITUITARY GLAND.—This gland is attached to the base of the brain and rests in a hollow on the base of the skull immediately above the hinder part of the throat. The anterior, intermediate, and posterior parts of the gland appear to produce different secretions : that from the intermediate and posterior parts known as ' pitui-trin ' has a powerful action in stimu-lating the contractions of unstriped muscle-fibres found, for example, in the uterus, intestine, and blood-vessels. Pituitary extract (posterior lobe) is therefore greatly employed in obstetric practice for its valuable action in checking bleeding and increasing the contractions of the uterus during delivery. It is also used in the treat-ment of shock on account of its action in contracting blood-vessels and raising the pressure of the blood.

The anterior part secretes hormones which stimulate growth, development of sex, and secretion of milk, and exert a controlling influence on most of the other endocrine glands—thyroid, adrenal, and reproductive glands.

PARATHYROID GLANDS.—These are four minute glands lying at the side of, or behind, the thyroid. They have a certain effect in controlling the ab-sorption of lime salts by the bones and other tissues. When their secretion is defective, tetany occurs.

PANCREAS.—This gland is situated in the upper part of the abdomen and, in addition to the digestive ferments which it produces, a substance known as insulin is absorbed from it into the circulating blood. This has the effect of adapting sugary foods for incorpora-tion in the muscles and other tissues that particularly require such food-stuffs. Its defect is followed by the production of the disease known as diabetes mellitus.

OVARIES AND TESTICLES.—In addition to their main function of producing reproductive cells, these organs secrete substances which have a general effect upon the other bodily tissues.

The ovary secretes at least two hormones, known respectively as œstradiol (follicular hormone) and progesterone (corpus luteum hormone). Œstradiol develops (under the stimulus of the anterior pituitary lobe) each time an ovum in the ovary becomes mature. Œstradiol causes extensive proliferation of the endometrium lining the uterus, a stage ending with shedding of the ovum about 14 days before the onset of menstruation. The corpus

ing' of the ovum—if fertilized. If fertilization does not occur, the corpus luteum degenerates, the hormones cease acting, and menstruation takes place.

The hormone secreted by the testicles is known as testosterone. It is responsible for the growth of the male secondary sex organs.

ENDOMETRITIS (ἔνδον, within; μήτρα, the womb) means inflammation of the mucous membrane lining the womb. (*See* UTERUS, DISEASES OF.)

ENDOMETRIUM is the mucous membrane which lines the interior of the uterus.

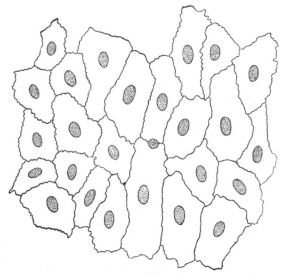

FIG. 139.—Endothelium. (From Schafer, *Essentials of Histology.* Longmans, Green & Co. Ltd.)

FIG. 140.—Endothelial cells of serous membrane in profile. (From Schafer, *Essentials of Histology.* Longmans, Green & Co. Ltd.)

luteum which then forms secretes both progesterone and œstradiol. Progesterone brings about great activity of the glands in the endometrium. The uterus is now ready for the ' nest-

ENDOTHELIUM (ἔνδον, within; θηλή, nipple) is the term applied to the membrane lining various vessels and cavities of the body, such as the pleura, pericardium, peritoneum, lymphatic vessels, blood-vessels, and joints. It consists of a fibrous layer covered with thin flat cells, which render the surface perfectly smooth and secrete the fluid for its lubrication (Figs. 139, 140).

ENEMA (ἔνεμα) means an injection of fluid into the bowel.

Uses. — PURGATIVE ENEMATA are given generally in large bulk, so as to distend the rectum, and they contain also various stimulating substances. For an adult, 1 to 2 pints (450 to 900 ml.) are injected, for a young child about 6 ounces (170 ml.). The process of injection should be slow, and the person should retain the enema as long as he can, in order to obtain the maximum effect. The water should be tepid: about 80° F. (27° C.). The usual constituent is soft green soap (B.P.), 1 ounce (28·5 G.) in 1 pint (450 ml.) of water. Yellow soap is also satisfactory. In some cases an olive oil enema (5 to 8 ounces (140 to 230 ml.) of olive oil) is preferred, or a glycerin enema (not more than 5 ounces (140 ml.) of equal parts of glycerin and water). To expel flatulence, two table-spoonfuls of turpentine may be added to each pint of warm water. The frequent use of enemata is unhealthy, because they gradually distend the bowel, especially if injected warm, and so ultimately increase the constipation.

MINIATURE ENEMATA are coming into increasing use. Their great advantage is that they are of a much smaller volume—only 2 millilitres, and therefore much more comfortable for the patient. They are also prepared much more easily and are supplied ready made up in a plastic container with a soft nozzle. They may be self-administered. As a rule, a movement of the bowels occurs within fifteen minutes. A widely used formula for such a miniature enema is: 5 mg. of bisacodyl; 0·5 millilitre of glycerin; made up to 2 millilitres with sulphonated castor oil B.P.C.

SEDATIVE ENEMATA are used to quiet spasm, and check excessive action of the bowels. When a person is being fed by nutrient enemata, he should receive one sedative enema daily, consisting of a pint of warm water containing two teaspoonfuls of common salt. A

similar enema given in larger quantities is very soothing for many forms of irritation, such as colitis. In very painful conditions of the bowel and of surrounding organs, 4 ounces (115 ml.) of thin starch containing 20 to 60 drops of laudanum and injected tepid gives great relief.

NUTRIENT ENEMATA are given when the stomach is seriously deranged and cannot retain or cannot digest food. A nutrient enema consists of dextrose, 5 per cent. solution in normal saline solution, that is, ½ ounce (14 G. of dextrose and ½ teaspoonful of common salt to ½ pint (220 ml.) of warm water. The enema, which is warmed to 100° F. (38° C.), must be administered very slowly, and preferably run in through a small funnel and catheter tube. It may be given, to the amount of 8 or 10 ounces (230 to 285 ml.), every 4 hours, that is five times in 24 hours.

HEALING ENEMATA are given when ulcers and inflammatory conditions are present in the lower bowel, consisting of such substances as small quantities of starch and laudanum or of nitrate of silver solution (¼ grain to the ounce (15 mg. to 28·5 ml.)). A form of enema known as *irrigation* is often used for healing and cleansing purposes. Several pints of warm, weak salt solution (2 teaspoonfuls of salt to every pint (450 ml.) of water) or boracic acid solution are introduced very slowly, by a douche, into the bowel, and then allowed to run off by lowering the tube, very much in the same way that the stomach is washed out.

FIG. 141.—Enema syringe.

Mode of administration. — The instrument used for nutrient enemata should be an india-rubber tube 3 or 4 feet (90 to 120 cm.) in length, with a funnel at one end, and soft rubber nozzle, with rounded end, at the other. For purgative enemata, the rubber syringe with a ball in the centre may be used, and for small enemata an india-rubber bag which contains the exact amount required. In all cases the old bone or metal nozzle should be replaced by a soft rubber one, because much pain and injury may be inflicted by a rigid one carelessly or forcibly introduced.

The patient lies upon his left side with the hips raised on a thick pillow, and should remain so after the enema has been given. The nozzle is oiled, introduced forwards and upwards with a screwing motion, and should be passed gently up for 3 or 4 inches (75 or 100 mm.). The fluid is now pumped, or, if a tube and funnel be used, allowed to flow gently in by raising the funnel. In the case of nutrient enemata, fully fifteen or twenty minutes should be spent in letting the fluid slowly enter, otherwise the bowels may move and the whole enema be rejected.

ENOPHTHALMOS (ἐν, in ; ὀφθαλμός, eye), is a term applied to abnormal retraction of the eye into its socket, for example, when the sympathetic nerve in the neck is paralysed.

ENTAMŒBA (see AMŒBA).

ENTERALGIA (ἔντερον, the intestine; ἄλγος, pain) is another name for colic.

ENTERIC FEVER, or TYPHOID FEVER (ἔντερον, the intestine), is a continued fever characterized mainly by its insidious onset, by a typical course of the temperature, by marked abdominal symptoms occurring in connection with ulceration of the bowels, by an eruption upon the skin, by its uncertain duration, and by a liability to relapses.

Until the middle of last century typhoid was not distinguished from typhus fever. The distinction between the two diseases appears to have been first accurately made in 1836 by Dr. Gerhard, of Philadelphia, and still more fully demonstrated by Dr. A. P. Stewart, of Glasgow, in 1840. Subsequently all doubt upon the subject was removed by the careful clinical and pathological observations made by Sir William Jenner at the London Fever Hospital (1849–51). At the end

of the nineteenth century it was noticed that cases of fever resembling typhoid but of shorter duration occurred, and these were found to be due to bacilli resembling the typhoid bacillus and are known as paratyphoid fevers. This group of fevers again has a resemblance, both as regards symptoms and as regards the causal bacteria, to cases of food-poisoning, dysentery, and summer diarrhœa.

The number of cases notified in England and Wales in recent years is shown in Table 16A. It is to be noted that 76 of the 112 patients with typhoid fever in 1966 are thought to have contracted the infection abroad, including holidaying in Europe.

Year	Typhoid Fever	Paratyphoid Fever
1957	125	310
1958	147	200
1959	123	379
1960	90	241
1961	97	254
1962	130	126
1963	247	342
1964	124	229
1965	138	832
1966	112	132

TABLE 16A.—Notifications of typhoid fever and paratyphoid fever in England and Wales 1957–1966.

Causes.—A bacillus, discovered first by Eberth in 1880, and known as the *Salmonella typhi*, is the cause of the malady. (*See* BACTERIOLOGY.) The bacilli found to be responsible for cases of paratyphoid fever are known as *Salmonella paratyphi A* and *Salmonella paratyphi B*, the latter being the commoner. Other bacilli which do not altogether correspond to either of these are also responsible for mild attacks of fever, sometimes grouped as paratyphoid C. Where the discharges, sheets, etc., from typhoid patients are carefully disinfected, there is little risk of direct spread from person to person. In many hospitals the typhoid cases are therefore treated in the general wards, with little or no risk to the other patients, provided certain precautions be taken.

All insanitary conditions in respect of drainage of houses and localities furnish the most ready means for the spread of the contagion of typhoid fever. The most certain means of preventing its appearance or checking its spread are the water-carriage system of sewage disposal; prevention of pollution of water-supplies, food, milk, and shell-fish with human excreta; chlorination of drinking water; pasteurization of milk; control of the house-fly; personal cleanliness; detection of carriers of enteric bacilli. The bacillus resides in the stools and urine of typhoid patients. Thus, in badly laid drains, where the contents stagnate, the bacillus may increase indefinitely, and, by the contamination of drinking-water in places where wells or cisterns are exposed to sewage pollution, convey infection to a whole community. Dust may also act as the medium which conveys the bacilli, in cases where the discharges of a typhoid patient or the sewage is allowed to dry, and so get blown into drinking-water or on to food. Milk may readily be contaminated by the bacillus and form the cause of an epidemic, when a case of the fever has occurred in a dairy. The source of an epidemic has also been traced to the eating of oysters taken from oyster-beds near which contaminated sewage is discharged. During an epidemic it can be readily understood that flies may also form a means of contamination between uncovered stools and uncovered food. It may therefore be said that the spread of typhoid fever depends upon food or drink contaminated by a bacillus which is derived more or less directly from the discharges of previous typhoid cases.

The incubation period is usually ten to twelve days, but may be as short as five days or as long as twenty-one days.

The chief symptoms will be better understood by a brief reference to the principal changes that take place in the body during the disease. The bowels are chiefly affected, particularly the lower end of the small intestine, where the 'solitary glands' and 'Peyer's patches' on the inner surface of the bowel (see INTESTINES) pass through changes that bear a distinct relation to the symptoms exhibited by the patient during the course of the disease. (1) During the first eight or ten days of the illness these glands, which in health are comparatively indistinct, become enlarged and prominent as the result of inflammation. (2) During the second week of the

fever these enlarged glands undergo a process of sloughing, being cast off either in fragments or *en masse*. (3) From the second week onwards during the remainder of the fever, and even into the stage of convalescence, the ulcers formed by this process remain open, though slowly healing. The ulcers vary in size according to the gland masses that have sloughed away, and they may be few or many in number. They are frequently, but not always, oblong in shape, with their long axis in that of the bowel, and they have somewhat thin and ragged edges. They may extend through the thickness of the bowel to the peritoneal coat, and they may perforate this, or may erode blood-vessels in their progress. (4) During convalescence the ulcers usually heal, leaving no contraction in the wall of the bowel.

The mesenteric glands associated with the intestine become enlarged, but usually subside without abscess formation as recovery takes place. The spleen becomes soft and enlarged, this enlargement being a useful guide to the physician in cases which are difficult to diagnose. As in other fevers, the muscular tissues soften and waste, and various complications affecting other organs may arise.

Symptoms.—The symptoms at the *onset* of typhoid fever are much less marked than those of most other fevers, and the disease in the majority of instances sets in somewhat insidiously. Indeed, it is no uncommon thing for patients with this fever to go about for a considerable time after it has begun. The most marked of the early symptoms are headache, lassitude, and discomfort, together with sleeplessness and feverishness, particularly at night; this last symptom is that by which the disease is most readily detected in its early stages. Bleeding at the nose is also an early symptom in many cases. The course of *the temperature* is also one of the most important diagnostic evidences (Fig. 142). During the first week it is slightly raised in the morning but in the evening there is a marked ascent, with a fall again towards morning, each morning and evening, however, showing respectively a higher point than that of the previous day, until about the eighth day, when, in an average case, the highest point is attained. This varies according to the severity of the attack ; but it is no unusual thing to register 104° or 105° F. (40° or 40·5° C.) in the evening and 103° or 104° F. (39·5° or 40° C.) in the morning. During the second week the daily range of temperature is comparatively small, a slight morning remission being all that is observed. In the third week the same condition continues more or less ; but frequently a slight tendency to lowering may be discerned, particularly in the morning

100. In severe and protracted cases, where there is evidence of extensive intestinal ulceration, the pulse becomes rapid and weak. The *tongue* has at first a thin whitish fur and is red at the tip and edges. It tends, however, to become dry, brown or glazed-looking, and fissured transversely, while sordes may be present about the lips and teeth. There is much thirst, and, in some cases, vomiting.

From an early period in the disease *abdominal symptoms* show themselves and are frequently of great help in diagnosis. The abdomen is somewhat

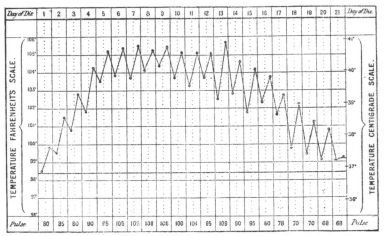

FIG. 142.—Chart showing the ordinary course of temperature and its gradual subsidence in a case of typhoid fever. The higher part of the curve is usually prolonged for a week or so more than is shown.

temperature, and the fever gradually dies down as a rule between the twenty-first and twenty-eight days, although it is liable to recur in the form of a relapse. Although the patient may, during the earlier days of the fever, be able to move about, he feels languid and uneasy ; and usually before the first week is over he has to take to bed, and soon the effects of the attack become more apparent. He is restless, hot, and uncomfortable, particularly as the day advances, and his cheeks show a red flush, especially in the evening or after taking food. The *pulse* in an ordinary case, although more rapid than normal, is not accelerated to an extent corresponding to the height of the temperature, and is, at least in the earlier stages of the fever, rarely above

distended, and pain accompanying some gurgling sounds may be elicited on light pressure about the lower part of the right side close to the groin— the region corresponding to that portion of the intestine in which the morbid changes already referred to are progressing. *Diarrhœa* is a frequent but by no means constant symptom. When present, it may be slight in amount, or, on the other hand, extremely profuse, and it corresponds, as a rule, to the severity of the intestinal ulceration, and to the nature of the diet which the patient has been taking. The discharges are highly characteristic, being of light-yellow colour, resembling ' pea soup ' in appearance. Sometimes, especially in milder cases, constipation is found instead of diarrhœa. Should intestinal hæmorrhage occur, as is not infrequently the case during some stage of the fever, the stools may be dark brown, or composed entirely of blood. Enlargement of the spleen and liver can usually be made out by the physician. The urine is scanty and high-coloured. When the fever is well developed from the second week onwards, the *blood* shows a well-marked feature known as the Widal reaction. (*See* AGGLUTINATION.)

About the beginning, or during the course of the second week of the fever, an *eruption* frequently makes its appearance on the skin. It consists of small isolated spots, oval or round in shape, of a pale pink or rose colour, which are seen chiefly upon the abdomen, chest, and back, and they come out in crops, which continue for four or five days and then fade away. At first they are slightly elevated, and disappear on pressure. In some cases they are very few in number, and their presence is made out with difficulty ; but in others they are numerous and sometimes show themselves upon the limbs as well as upon the body. They do not appear to have any relation to the severity of the attack, and in a large proportion of cases (particularly in children) they are entirely absent. Besides this eruption there are frequently numerous very faint bluish patches or blotches about half an inch in diameter, chiefly upon the body and thighs. When present, the rose-coloured spots continue to come out in crops till nearly the end of the fever, and they may reappear should a relapse subsequently occur.

These various symptoms persist throughout the third week, usually, however, increasing in intensity. The patient becomes prostrate and emaciated ; the tongue is dry and brown, the pulse quickened and feeble, and the abdominal symptoms more marked; while nervous disturbance is exhibited in delirium, in tremors and jerkings of the muscles (*subsultus tendinum*), in drowsiness, and occasionally in ' coma vigil '. (*See* TYPHUS FEVER.) In severe cases the exhaustion reaches an extreme degree, but even in such instances the condition should not be regarded as hopeless. In favourable cases a change for the better may be expected between the twenty-first and twenty-eighth days, although it takes place by a ' lysis ' or gradual subsidence of the symptoms (the morning and evening temperatures descending, the pulse becoming stronger, the diarrhœa passing off, the tongue becoming clean, etc.), not by a ' crisis ' as in typhus fever or pneumonia. Convalescence proceeds slowly, and relapses are apt to occur (due frequently to errors in diet). Such relapses may prolong the fever for two or three months, though this is not common.

Abscesses sometimes arise, especially in connection with inflammation in the periosteum of the bones, found after the patient has been for some time convalescent, and these form a troublesome and prolonged complication. Stiff back, known as ' typhoid spine ', is an occasional sequel to this disease, due either to inflammation in the spine or more commonly to changes in the muscles with development of fibrous tissue, causing the patient for long, it may be for years, to suffer from severe ' rheumatic ' pains. Inflammation of the bile passages, with retention of the bacilli in these and their constant discharge in the stools, is also an occasional sequel ; and, although this may cause no trouble to the patient, it renders him a source of danger to others as a ' carrier ' of the disease (*see* INFECTION).

When death takes place, it is generally due to one of the following causes : (1) Exhaustion in the second or third week or later ; (2) hæmorrhage from the bowels ; (3) perforation of an ulcer and the onset of peritonitis ; (4) excessive rise of temperature ; (5) complications, such as inflammation of the lungs.

Treatment.—The preventive treatment includes all the **municipal and** domestic measures that aim at securing pure supplies of water and milk and well-laid drains. (*See* SANITATION.) Inoculation with anti-typhoid vaccine is a precaution which ought to be adopted by persons about to proceed to a country such as India, where the disease is rife. (*See* VACCINE.)

When an outbreak of typhoid fever occurs in a family, the source of the

319

milk supply especially should be scrutinized. The discharges of a typhoid patient should be mixed so soon as passed with a strong disinfectant (*see* DISINFECTION). Similar care should be taken to sterilize all sheets, towels, etc., soiled by the patient. Special care is necessary on the part of those in attendance upon a typhoid-fever case to cleanse the hands at once after touching the patient, and especially after they have become in any way soiled by contact with his discharges.

Very special care is necessary in typhoid fever with regard to diet. Milk is of great service in typhoid, but it must be administered with due regard to time and to the digestive powers of the patient. The usual quantity given is from 3 to 4 ounces (85 to 112 ml.) regularly administered every two or three hours, that is $1\frac{1}{2}$ to 2 pints (850 to 1100 ml.) daily. In the intervals water or other fever drink may be given from time to time. When given too frequently or in too great quantity, milk may, by its imperfect digestion, prove a source of irritation to the bowels. In such a case its admixture with lime-water, or peptonizing it, may render its digestion less difficult, but sometimes its use must for a time be suspended. Barley water or simple soups, such as chicken-broth, beef-tea, etc., are occasionally useful either as substitutes for, or in addition to, milk. In convalescence, the diet should still be largely milk and soft food, such as custards, light puddings, meat jellies, boiled bread and milk, or one of the numerous proprietary invalids' foods ; but other solid foods, with the exception of fish, should be avoided. In changing the diet it is of importance to note its effect upon the temperature, which may sometimes be considerably disturbed from this cause, even after the apparent subsidence of all fever.

The more prominent symptoms which mark the course of typhoid fever frequently call for special treatment. Thus, when diarrhœa is excessive, it may be restrained by such remedies as Dover's powder or a starch-and-opium enema. In the event of perforation of the bowel, an immediate operation may in some cases

give the patient a chance of life (*see* PERITONITIS), but this chance is very small. With regard to the condition of the mouth and tongue, much comfort is gained if the patient's mouth and teeth be washed occasionally with boric lotion in tepid water, and the lips and tip of the tongue lightly smeared with boroglyceride or some emollient ointment.

The introduction of chloramphenicol (*q.v.*) has revolutionized the outlook in typhoid fever. There is usually a dramatic improvement within 48-60 hours after this antibiotic is administered. Ampicillin (*q.v.*) is also proving of value, but the relative value of these two antibiotics has not been determined. Whichever is used, however, it is still necessary to keep the patient in bed for three weeks, and to keep him on a bland nutritious diet during this period. Otherwise complications may arise. The patient should be considered infective until six consecutive specimens of stools and urine are found to be negative on bacteriological examination.

In the convalescent stage, and even after apparently complete recovery, the utmost care should be observed by the patient as to diet, all hard and indigestible substances being dangerous from their tendency to irritate or reopen unhealed ulcers and bring on a relapse of the fever or cause a sudden perforation. Lastly, the general health demands careful attention for a length of time.

ENTERITIS (ἔντερον, the intestine) means inflammation of the intestines (*See* DIARRHŒA, *and* INTESTINES, DISEASES OF.)

ENTEROBIASIS means infestation with *Enterobius vermicularis*, or Threadworms (*see* PARASITES).

ENTEROCELE (ἔντερον, the intestine ; κήλη, a tumour) means a hernia of the bowel. (*See* HERNIA.)

ENTEROGASTRONE is a hormone derived from the mucosal lining of the small intestine which inhibits the movements and the secretion of the stomach. For this reason it was considered that it might be of value in the treatment of gastric and duodenal ulcers, but so far it has not proved satisfactory for this purpose.

ENTEROGENOUS CYANOSIS.—This is a rare condition characterized by blueness of the lips and face (cyanosis) and the presence in the blood of sulphæmoglobin and methæmoglobin, especially the former. It is usually the result of taking drugs, especially those derived from aniline (*e.g.* phenacetin). Recovery follows discontinuance of the drug.

ENTEROPTOSIS (ἔντερον, the intestine; πτῶσις, a fall) means a condition in which, owing to a lax condition of the mesenteries and ligaments which support the bowels, the latter descend into the lower part of the abdominal cavity. The condition is aggravated by tight lacing and by the lax condition of the abdominal walls which follows repeated child-bearing, and so is commoner in women.

Treatment.—Massage of the abdominal muscles and viscera, and the wearing of a well-shaped abdominal belt (*see* BELTS) give most relief.

ENTEROSTOMY (ἔντερον, intestine; στόμα, mouth) means an operation by which an artificial opening is formed into the intestine.

ENTEROVIRUSES are a family of viruses which include the poliomyelitis, coxsackie and ECHO groups of viruses. Their importance lies in their tendency to invade the central nervous system. They receive their name from the fact that their mode of entry into the body is through the gut.

ENTOZOA (ἐντός, within; ζῷον animal) are animals which are occasionally found within the human body, and derive nourishment from its fluids, or from the digested food. (*See* PARASITES.)

ENTROPION (ἐν, in; τρέπω, I turn) means a condition in which, as a result of disease, the edge of the eyelid is turned inwards towards the ball of the eye.

ENURESIS (ἐν, in; οὐρέω, I make water) means the unconscious or involuntary passage of urine. (*See* NOCTURNAL ENURESIS.)

ENZYME is the name applied to a chemical ferment produced by living cells. Enzymes are present in the digestive fluids and in many of the tissues, and are capable of producing in small amount the transformation on a large scale of various compounds. Examples of enzymes are found in the ptyalin of saliva and diastase of pancreatic juice which split up starch into sugar, the pepsin of the gastric juice and the trypsin of pancreatic juice which break proteins into simpler molecules and eventually into the constituent amino-acids, the thrombin of the blood which causes coagulation, etc.

EOSINOPHIL is any cell in the body with granules in its substance that stain easily with the dye eosin. About 2 per cent. of the white cells of the blood are eosinophils. Eosinophil cells are also present in the pituitary gland.

EOSINOPHILIA means an abnormal increase in the number of eosinophils in the blood. It occurs in Hodgkin's disease, in asthma and hay fever, in some skin diseases, and in parasitic infestation.

EPHEDRINE is an alkaloid derived from the Chinese plant *Ma Huang*, much used for asthma, in doses of $\frac{1}{4}$ to $1\frac{1}{2}$ grains (15 to 100 mg.). It is similar to adrenaline in both chemical constitution and pharmacological action.

EPHELIS means sunburn, or brown discoloration of the skin produced by constant exposure to great heat.

EPHEMERAL FEVER (ἐφήμερος, for one day), or MILK-FEVER, is the name given to a slight feverish attack, which often comes on about the third or fourth day after childbirth, in consequence of constipation, tension of the breasts, or other trifling cause. It lasts only for a day or so, hence its name.

EPI- (ἐπί, upon) is a prefix meaning situated on or outside of.

EPIDEMIC (ἐπί, upon; δῆμος the people) is a term applied to a disease which affects a large number of people in a particular locality at one time. The term is, in a sense, opposed to 'endemic', which means a disease always found in the locality in question.

A disease may, however, be endemic as a rule—for example, malaria in swampy districts, and may become at times epidemic, when an unusually large number of people are affected.

As a rule an epidemic disease is infectious from person to person, but this is not necessarily the case, since many persons in a locality may simply be exposed to the same cause at one time; for example, outbreaks of scurvy or lead-poisoning are epidemic in this sense.

The laws which govern the outbreak of epidemics are by no means fully understood. Infected food supplies, such as drinking water contaminated by the evacuations of persons sick of cholera or typhoid fever, or milk tainted by the organism of scarlatina, have been traced in repeated instances as the cause of outbreaks of these diseases. The migrations of certain of the lower animals, such as rats, are in some cases responsible for the spread of plague, from which these animals die in great numbers. Certain epidemics come with regularity at certain seasons. Thus scarlatina and diphtheria are autumnal complaints, and produce their epidemics in September, October, and November. Whooping-cough, on the other hand, is a spring complaint, and very few cases occur in autumn. Measles produces two epidemics, as a rule, one in midsummer and one in December. Infantile diarrhœa, which is a very fatal complaint, particularly among the children of the poor, appears regularly in June, quickly reaches its height in July, and gradually disappears during August and September. These seasonal variations depend largely, no doubt, upon conditions like the amount of sunshine, the rainfall, and the temperature of the ground, and the aggregation of susceptible individuals.

There is another variation, both as regards the number of persons affected and the number who die in successive epidemics, the severity of successive epidemics, rising and falling over periods of five or ten years. Further, scourges like plague and cholera have swept over whole continents at longer periods, and then died down without apparent cause. The reason for these latter variations is still obscure.

EPIDEMIC ENCEPHALITIS is another term for ENCEPHALITIS LETHARGICA (*q.v.*).

EPIDYDIMIS (ἐπιδιδυμίς) is the name applied to an oblong body attached to the upper part of each testicle, composed of convoluted vessels and ducts. It is liable to be the seat of tuberculous and other inflammation.

EPIGASTRIUM (ἐπί, upon ; γαστήρ, the stomach) is the region lying in the middle of the abdomen over the stomach. (*See* ABDOMEN, REGIONS OF.)

EPIGLOTTIS (ἐπιγλωττίς) is a leaf-like piece of elastic cartilage covered with mucous membrane, which stands upright between the back of the tongue and the glottis, or entrance to the larynx. In the act of swallowing, it prevents fluids and solids from passing off the back of the tongue into the larynx.

EPIGLOTTITIS.—Acute epiglottitis is an acute inflammatory œdema of the epiglottis, due to *Hæmophilus influenzæ*, which causes laryngeal obstruction due to swelling and immobilization of the epiglottis. It is a disease predominantly of children, occurs usually in the winter, and may prove rapidly fatal.

EPIGNATHUS is the term used to describe a mal-development of the fœtus in which the deformed remains of one twin are united to the upper jaw of the other.

EPILATION (*e*, out ; *pilus*, hair) means the removal of hair by the roots. (*See* DEPILATION.)

EPILEPSY (ἐπίληψις), or FALLING SICKNESS, is a term applied to a nervous disorder characterized by a fit of sudden loss of consciousness, attended with convulsions. There may, however, exist manifestations of epilepsy much less marked than this, yet equally characteristic of the disease. On the other hand, it is to be borne in mind that many other attacks of a convulsive nature have the term 'epileptiform' applied to them because they resemble epilepsy.

Epilepsy was well known in ancient times, and was regarded as a special infliction of the gods, hence the names *morbus sacer*, *morbus divus*. It was also termed *morbus Herculeus*, from Hercules being supposed to have been epileptic, and *morbus comitialis*, from the circumstances that when any one at a meeting in the forum was seized with an epileptic fit the assembly was at once broken up. *Morbus caducus*, *morbus lunaticus astralis*, *morbus demoniacus*, *morbus major* were all terms used to designate epilepsy.

There are two well-marked varieties of the epileptic seizure, either of which may exist alone or both may be found to occur in the same individual. To these the terms *le grand mal* and *le petit mal* are generally applied. The former of these, if not the more common, is at least that which attracts most attention, being what is generally known as an epileptic fit. In addition to these two forms there is a type known as *Jacksonian epilepsy*, in which the seizure consists of convulsive movements commencing in a single muscle or group of muscles, consciousness being in general retained. Cases of this type shade off, however, into *grand mal*, and indeed the subjects of Jacksonian epilepsy may, at a later stage, be affected by typical seizures of severe type.

Causes.—In the very rare instances of persons dying in the epileptic fit, the *post-mortem* appearances presented by the brain are in general either entirely negative or of such indefinite character as cerebral congestion ; on the other hand, in chronic cases of epilepsy, such lesions as atrophy and degeneration of brain substance or vascular disease are frequently met with, but are, as is well known, common to many other forms of nervous disease, and are much more probably the consequences rather than the causes of the epileptic attacks. The disease is commonly regarded as one of disordered function of the brain. Those cases, which begin with the Jacksonian type of seizure, appear to be due to some organic disease of the brain, such as

a tumour, inflammation of the membranes of the brain, or the scar of some old injury, but this certainly does not occur in the majority of cases of epilepsy.

Practically all that can be said about the direct cause is that in the healthy brain nerve energy is capable, under control of the will, of being expended in a sudden and explosive but regulated manner, whilst, in the disease known as epilepsy, uncontrolled discharges of energy, devoid of any purposive action, take place from time to time in an unusual manner.

Various predisposing factors must, however, be taken into account. In view of the possible hereditary nature of epilepsy medical men were apt to advise those with a family history of the disease not to marry. But it is now believed that direct transmission of the disease is uncommon, and medical prohibition of marriage and child-bearing is less dogmatically applied.

Age is of importance in reference to the production of epilepsy. The disease may appear at any period of life, but it most frequently first manifests itself before adult life, usually during infancy or at puberty.

Among precipitating factors which are influential in the development of epilepsy in predisposed individuals may be mentioned sudden fright, prolonged mental anxiety, overwork, and alcoholism. Epileptiform fits, which at a later period may develop into typical epileptic seizures, also occur in connection with injuries of the head and organic disease of the brain, as well as with a depraved state of the general health.

Epilepsy is occasionally feigned by malingerers, but an experienced medical practitioner will rarely be deceived ; and when it is stated that although many of the phenomena of an attack, particularly the convulsive movements, can be readily simulated, yet that of the condition of the pupils, which are dilated during the fit, cannot be feigned, and that the impostor seldom bites his tongue or injures himself in falling, choosing some soft object instead of falling headlong like the true epileptic, deception is not likely to succeed even with **non-medical** persons of intelligence. The electro-encephalogram (*see* ELECTRO - ENCE-PHALOGRAPHY) in true epilepsy is characteristic.

Symptoms.—Although in most instances an epileptic attack comes on suddenly, it is in some cases preceded by certain premonitory indications or warnings. These are of very varied character, and may be in the form of some temporary change in the disposition, such as unusual elevation or depression of spirits, or of some alteration in the look. Besides these general symptoms, there are frequently peculiar sensations which immediately precede the onset of the fit, and to such the name of *aura epileptica* is applied. The so-called ' aura ', which occurs in about 50 per cent. of cases, may be of mental character, in the form of an agonizing feeling of momentary duration ; of sensory character, in the form of pain in a limb or in some internal organ, such as the stomach ; or unusual feeling connected with the special senses, such as a strange smell or extraordinary vision ; or, further, of a motor character, in the form of contractions or trembling in some of the muscles. The aura may be so distinct and of such duration as to enable the patient to lie down or seek a place of safety before the attack comes on.

The seizure is usually preceded by a loud scream or cry, which is not to be ascribed, as was at one time supposed, to terror or pain, but is due to the convulsive action of the muscles of the larynx, and the expulsion of air through the narrowed glottis. If the patient is standing he immediately falls, and often sustains serious injury. Unconsciousness is complete, and the muscles generally are in a state of stiffness or tonic contraction, which may be found to affect those on one side of the body in particular. The head is turned towards one or other shoulder, the breathing is for the moment arrested, the countenance first pale then livid, the pupils dilated, and the pulse rapid. This, the first stage of the fit, generally lasts for about half a minute, and is followed by the state of clonic (*i.e.* tumultuous) spasm of the muscles, in which the whole body is thrown into violent agitation. The

eyes roll wildly, the teeth are gnashed together, and the tongue is often severely bitten. The breathing is noisy, and foam (often tinged with blood) issues from the mouth, while even the contents of the bowels and bladder may be ejected. This stage lasts for a period varying from a few seconds to several minutes, when the convulsive movements gradually subside and relaxation of the muscles takes place, together with partial return of consciousness, the patient looking confusedly about him and attempting to speak. This, however, is soon followed by drowsiness and stupor, which may continue for several hours, when he awakes either apparently quite recovered, or fatigued and depressed, and occasionally in a state of excitement which sometimes assumes the form of mania.

Epileptic fits of this sort succeed each other with varying degrees of frequency, and occasionally though not frequently with regular periodicity. In some persons they only occur once in a life-time, or once in the course of many years, while in others they return every week or two, or even are of daily occurrence, and occasionally there are numerous attacks each day. When the fit occurs, it is not uncommon for one seizure to be followed by another within a few hours or days. Occasionally there occurs a constant succession of attacks extending over many hours, and with such rapidity that the patient appears as if he had never come out of the one fit. The term *status epilepticus* is applied to this condition, which is sometimes followed with fatal results. In many epileptics the fits occur during the night as well as during the day, but in some instances they are entirely nocturnal, and in such cases the disease may long exist and yet remain unrecognized either by the patient or by the physician, until observed and described by some other person.

The other manifestation of epilepsy, to which the name *epilepsia mitior* or *le petit mal* is given, differs from that above described in the absence of the convulsive spasms. It consists essentially in the sudden arrest of consciousness, which is of but short duration, and may be accompanied with staggering or some alteration in position or motion, or may simply exhibit itself in a look of absence or confusion, and, should the patient happen to be engaged in conversation, by an abrupt termination of the act. In general, it lasts but a few seconds, and the individual resumes his occupation without perhaps being aware of anything having been the matter. In some instances there is a degree of spasmodic action in certain muscles which may cause the patient to make some unexpected movement, such as turning half round, or walking abruptly aside, or may show itself by some unusual expression of countenance, such as squinting or grinning. There may be some amount of ' aura ' preceding such attacks, and also of faintness following them.

Allusion has already been made to the occasional occurrence of maniacal excitement as one of the results of the epileptic seizure. Such attacks, to which the name of *furor epilepticus* is applied, are generally accompanied with violent acts on the part of the patient, rendering him dangerous, and demanding prompt measures of restraint.

There is another sequel of an epileptic fit, particularly *petit mal*, which may have medico-legal implications. This is what is known as *post-epileptic automatism*. In this state, following an attack, an epileptic may carry out or perform some action, of which he is entirely unaware when he recovers. Thus, he may proceed to undress himself no matter where he may be, or he may pick up the first thing he lays his hands on, or he may attack someone. An interesting feature of this phenomenon is that the action performed by any one epileptic is stereotype : that is, it is always the same odd action he performs. The possible medico-legal implications of this automatism are, of course, obvious.

Treatment. — During the fit, little can be done beyond preventing the patient as far as possible from injuring himself while unconsciousness continues. Tight clothing should be loosened, and a cork or pad inserted between the teeth. When the fit is over, the patient should be allowed to sleep, and have the head and shoulders well raised.

In the intervals between the attacks, the general health of the patient is one of the most important points to be attended to. The strictest hygienic rules should be observed, and all the causes which have been mentioned as favouring the development of the disease should as far as possible be avoided. Of medicinal remedies for epilepsy there are innumerable varieties but only a few deserve mention as possessing any efficacy in controlling or curing the disease. The most commonly used drug is phenobarbitone, either alone or in combination with one of the increasing number of other drugs being introduced for the treatment of epilepsy. The bromides, originally the great stand-by in the treatment of epilepsy, are seldom used for this purpose at the present day. More recent drugs that have proved of value include phenytoin sodium, mesontoin, and primidone. One of the most effective drugs for controlling *petit mal* is troxidone. The secret of success in controlling epilepsy is to remember that every case must be considered individually, and that once a successful means of control has been established, it should not be altered unless there is some special reason for so doing.

The diet should be wholesome and regular and contain ample fruit and vegetables. Alcohol is strictly forbidden.

As few restrictions as possible should be placed on the activities of an epileptic, but there are certain things, such as car-driving and swimming, which must be forbidden because of their obvious danger to the individual.

' Epileptic colonies ' have been established in many places, where persons afflicted in this way can carry out productive work under safe conditions. These colonies are particularly useful for the 20 per cent. or so of epileptics who are mentally retarded.

EPILOIA (*see* TUBEROSE SCLEROSIS).

EPINEPHRINE (*see* ADRENALINE).

EPIPHORA (ἐπί, upon ; φέρω, I carry) means a condition in which tears, instead of passing from the eye down into the nose, run over on the cheek. It is due to blocking of the tear-ducts. (*See* EYE.)

EPIPHYSIS (ἐπίφυσις) means the spongy extremity of a bone, attached to it for the purpose of forming a joint with the similar process of another bone. An epiphysis is covered on its surface by cartilage, is developed from a distinct centre of ossification, and in a young person is connected with the shaft of the bone by a plate of cartilage that disappears in the adult. Separation of an epiphysis is a form of fracture which sometimes occurs in children, and is apt to be more serious than a break through bony tissue because it involves damage to the plate of growing cartilage, so that, although union takes place readily, the subsequent growth of the bone may be interfered with and the full growth of the limb may afterwards fail to be attained.

EPISIOTOMY is the operation of cutting the outlet of the vagina in childbirth so as to facilitate the birth of the child.

EPISPASTICS (ἐπί, upon; σπάω, I draw) are substances which produce blistering of the skin. (*See* BLISTERS.)

EPISTAXIS (ἐπί, upon; στάζω, I drop) means bleeding of the nose. (*See* HÆMORRHAGE.)

EPITHELIOMA (ἐπί, upon; θηλή, the nipple; -*oma*, meaning tumour) is a tumour of malignant nature arising in the epithelium covering the surface of the body. (*See* CANCER.)

EPITHELIUM (ἐπί, upon; θηλή, the nipple) means the cellular layer which forms the cuticle upon the skin, covers the inner surface of the bowels, and forms the lining of ducts and hollow organs, like the bladder. It consists of one or more layers of cells which adhere to one another, and is one of the simplest tissues of the body. It is of several forms : for example, the cuticle is formed of scaly epithelium, the cells being in several layers and more or less flattened (*see* SKIN) ; the bowels are lined by a single layer of columnar epithelium, the cells being long and narrow in shape (Fig. 143) ; the air passages are lined by ciliated epithelium (Fig. 144)— that is to say, each cell is provided with

326

lashes which drive the fluid upon the surface of the passages gradually up-

FIG. 143.—Columnar epithelium. *A*, Side view of a group of cells ; *B*, surface view of the ends of a group of cells ; *C*, a columnar cell from the mucous membrane of the small intestine. (Turner's *Anatomy*.)

wards ; and the inner surface of the bladder consists of cells intermediate in

FIG. 144.—Ciliated epithelial cells. (Turner's *Anatomy*.)

shape between those of the skin and those of the bowel.

EPIZOÖTIC (ἐπί, upon; ζῷον, animal) is a term applied to any disease in animals which diffuses itself widely. The term corresponds to the word epidemic as applied to human beings. In plague, for example, an epizoötic in rats usually precedes the epidemic in human beings.

EPSOM SALTS is the popular name for sulphate of magnesium, which is perhaps the most commonly used saline purgative. For a dose, a heaped teaspoonful or more of the salt should be mixed with as little water as will dissolve it, and taken in the morning before breakfast, or the same quantity may be taken divided into three or four small doses, one of which is taken every quarter of an hour. (*See* PURGATIVES.)

Magnesium sulphate is used for the treatment of inflammatory conditions of the bowels in order to remove by purgation the cause of the irritation. It is sometimes injected through a stomach-tube direct into the duodenum in order to produce a copious flow of bile in disorders of the liver and gall-bladder. External fomentations of 5 to 25 per cent. magnesium sulphate solution are frequently applied in cases of rheumatic joints and other forms of inflammation, whilst a paste of magnesium sulphate in glycerin is a useful form of treatment of boils. It has also been used for injection intramuscularly or into the spinal canal in the treatment of tetanus, eclampsia, and other convulsive disorders.

EPULIS (*ἐπουλίς*, a gumboil) is a term applied to any tumour connected with the jaws.

ERB'S PARALYSIS is a form of paralysis of the arm due to stretching or tearing of the fibres of the brachial nerve plexus. Such damage to the brachial plexus may occur during birth, and it is found that the arm lies by the side of the body with elbow extended, forearm pronated, and the fingers flexed. The infant is unable to raise the arm.

EREPSIN, or EREPTASE, is a ferment secreted by the intestine which breaks up peptides into amino-acids.

ERGOMETRINE is one of the active constituents of ergot (*q.v.*). It has a powerful action in controlling the excessive bleeding from the womb which may occur after childbirth. The official *British Pharmacopœia* preparation is ergometrine maleate.

ERGOSTEROL is a sterol found in yeasts and fungi and in plant and animal fat. Under the action of sunlight or ultra-violet rays it produces vitamin D2. The substance produced in this way is known as calciferol, and is used for the prevention and cure of rickets and osteomalacia. A similar change in the ergosterol of the skin is produced when the body is freely exposed to sunlight. Calciferol is probably not so active as, and differs chemically from, the vitamin D occurring in fish-liver oils.

ERGOT is the spawn of *Claviceps purpurea*, a fungus which grows in the grain of rye. It contains several active principles, including the alkaloids ergometrine, ergotoxine, and ergotamine. The drug causes prolonged contraction of unstriped muscle fibres all over the body, particularly the

muscle fibres of the blood-vessels and of the womb. This action on the womb makes the drug of great value in midwifery, and it has been in use in midwifery since the 16th century.

Uses.—The drug is used mainly to check hæmorrhage, particularly that which is apt to follow upon childbirth. It is also given in small doses for some time after childbirth to reduce the womb to its proper size in cases in which this is not taking place naturally.

ERGOTAMINE is one of the alkaloids in ergot. In the form of ergotamine tartrate it is most effective in the treatment of migraine (*q.v.*). It is usually given by injection, but is sometimes effective when given by mouth. Its continued use is not without risk, occasionally leading to gangrene of the tips of the fingers, so it should only be used under medical supervision. It has also been used for the relief of the itching of the skin which is sometimes such a troublesome feature of uræmia.

ERGOT POISONING occasionally occurs among persons who eat bread made from diseased rye. Several terrible epidemics (*St. Anthony's Fire*) occurred in France and Germany during the Middle Ages. Its symptoms are the occurrence of spasmodic muscular contractions, and the gradual production of gangrene in parts like the fingers, toes, and tips of the ears.

EROSION (*erodo*, I gnaw away) means a process of gradual wearing down of structures in the body. The term is applied to the effect of tumours, when they cause destruction of tissue in their neighbourhood without actually growing into the latter; for example, an aneurysm may 'erode' bones in its neighbourhood. The term is also applied to minute ulcers, for example, 'erosions' of the stomach, caused by extreme acidity of the gastric juice.

ERRHINES (*ἔρρινον*) are drugs which cause running at the nose, *e.g.* iodide of potassium.

ERUCTATION (*eructo*, I belch), or belching, means the sudden escape of gas or of portions of half-digested food from the stomach up into the mouth. The excessive production of gases in the stomach is usually associated with dilatation of that organ. Many nervous persons, however, and also persons who suffer from acid dyspepsia, have a bad habit of gulping down mouthfuls of air when digestion is uncomfortable. This air is, after a little while, belched up again. Eructations of extremely sour fluid prove the existence of acid dyspepsia (see Dys-pepsia). Some persons, especially those in whom dyspepsia occurs from time to time, have at other times the peculiarity of bringing up fragments of food an hour or two after meals.

ERUPTION (*erumpo*, I break out), or Rash, means an outbreak, in a scattered form, upon the surface of the skin, usually raised and red, and, it may be, also covered with scales, or crusts, or vesicles containing fluid. The appearance of an eruption depends, to a certain extent, upon the nature of the disease, or other source of irritation, which causes it ; for example, the eruption of measles is always distinguishable from that of chickenpox. But the same disease may also produce different eruptions in different persons, or in the same person in different states of health, or even on different parts of the body at one time.

Eruptions may be acute or chronic. Most of the acute eruptions belong to the exanthemata, *i.e.* they are bright in colour and burst out suddenly like a flower. These are the eruptions of typhus fever, typhoid fever, scarlatina, measles, German measles, smallpox and chickenpox. In general the severity of these diseases can be measured by the amount of eruption, but in cases where the eruption is ' suppressed ', or, as it is popularly termed, ' goes in ', the disease is apt to be serious.

Some eruptions are very transitory, like nettle-rash, appearing and vanishing again in the course of a few hours. (For chronic eruptions *see* Skin, Diseases of.)

ERYSIPELAS (ἐρυσίπελας, probably derived from ἐρυθρός, red ; and πέλλα, skin)—synonyms, *the Rose, St. Anthony's Fire*—is a disease characterized by diffuse inflammation of the skin, or of the subcutaneous cellular tissue, at-
328

tended with fever. In the Middle Ages this disease was confused with ergot poisoning.

Causes.—It has long been known that the disease is of a highly infectious nature. This contagiousness of erysipelas was often illustrated in the surgical wards of hospitals, where, having once broken out, it was apt to spread with great rapidity, and to produce disastrous results, as well as in lying-in hospitals, where its occurrence gave rise to the spread of a form of puerperal fever of virulent character. Not only is the disease communicated from wounds already the seat of erysipelas, but infection of wounds by various suppurative diseases seems capable of producing it. The infecting organism is the *Streptococcus pyogenes*. Erysipelas is slightly commoner in women than in men, and is commonest between the ages of 50 and 60.

Symptoms.—When the erysipelas is of moderate character, there is simply a redness of the skin, which feels somewhat hard and thickened, and upon which there often appear small vesicles. This redness, though at first circumscribed, tends to spread and affect the neighbouring sound skin, until an entire limb or a large area of the body may become involved in the inflammatory process. There is usually considerable pain, with heat and tingling in the affected part. As the disease advances, the portions of skin first attacked become less inflamed, and exhibit a yellowish appearance, which is followed by slight desquamation of the cuticle. The inflammation in general gradually disappears. Sometimes, however, it breaks out again, and passes over the area originally affected a second time. But besides the skin, the subjacent tissues may become involved in the inflammation and give rise to the formation of pus. This is termed *phlegmonous erysipelas*, and is much more apt to occur when the disease starts in a wound or ulcer. Occasionally the affected parts become gangrenous. Certain complications are apt to arise in erysipelas affecting the surface of the body, particularly inflammation of serous membranes, such as the pericardium, pleura, and peritoneum.

Erysipelas of the face usually begins

with symptoms of general illness, the patient feeling languid, drowsy, and sick, while frequently there is shivering followed by fever, and the temperature may rise to 104° or 105° F. (40° or 40·5° C.). Sore throat is sometimes felt, but, in general, the first indication of the local affection is a red and painful spot at the side of the nose or on one of the cheeks or ears. Occasionally the inflammation begins in the throat, and reaches the face through the nasal fossæ. The redness gradually spreads over the whole surface of the face, and is accompanied with swelling, which, in the lax tissues of the cheeks and eyelids, is so great that the features soon become unrecognizable and the eyes quite closed. The spreading edge of the red area is usually sharply marked and raised. Advancing over the scalp, the disease may invade the neck and pass on to the trunk, but in general the inflammation remains confined to the face and head. While the disease progresses, besides the pain, tenderness, and heat of the affected parts, the constitutional symptoms are very severe. Delirium is a frequent accompaniment. The attack in general lasts for a week or ten days, during which the inflammation subsides in the parts of the skin first attacked, while it spreads onwards in other directions, and after it has passed away there is some slight desquamation of the cuticle.

Although in general the termination is favourable, serious and occasionally fatal results follow from inflammation of the membranes of the brain, and in some rare instances sudden death has occurred from suffocation arising from œdema of the glottis, the inflammation having spread into and extensively involved the throat. Persons who have had one attack of erysipelas appear to enjoy protection from another attack only for a very limited period, probably a few weeks or months. But apart from this, they certainly appear more liable to attacks than those who have never suffered from the disease.

Erysipelas occasionally assumes from the first a violent form, under which the patient sinks rapidly. It is sometimes a complication in certain forms of exhausting disease, such as tuber-

culosis or typhoid fever, and is then to be regarded as of serious import. A very fatal form occasionally attacks new-born infants, particularly in the first four weeks of life (*Erysipelas neonatorum*). In epidemics of puerperal fever, this form of erysipelas has been specially found to prevail.

Treatment.—The patient must be isolated, and great care must be taken to ensure that the infection is not transmitted to others by those in attendance on the patient. The outlook has changed considerably for the better since the introduction of the sulphonamides and of penicillin, and one or other of these should be given in full doses as soon as the condition is recognized. For local application the best preparations are either cold compresses of a saturated solution of magnesium sulphate or a 10 per cent. solution of ichthyol in water. The patient must be kept in bed until the temperature has settled, and as nourishing a diet as possible should be given.

ERYTHEMA (ἐρύθημα) is a general term signifying several conditions in which areas of the skin become congested with blood, and consequently a red eruption appears. The eruption is accompanied by tingling, and often by itching and pain.

Causes.—It may be due to heat, such as exposure to the sun, or the constant exposure, by cooks or iron-workers, of the face, hands, or legs to a blazing fire. Another form, known as 'erythema pernio ', is due to exposure to cold and wet (*see* CHILBLAINS). A third variety, which appears, usually on the front of the legs, in the form of red or livid, tender swellings, often over an inch in breadth, is known as ' erythema nodosum ', and is thought to be a manifestation of rheumatism, or of tuberculosis. In infants suffering from dyspepsia or diarrhœa, a form of erythema, very like the rash of scarlatina, may appear quickly over the whole body. Adults may also, especially in the spring and autumn, owing probably to errors in diet, suffer from a severer form, which begins as red blotches on the hands, and, spreading up the arms to the body, produces lumps and vesicles, or even large blebs full of fluid. This form, on account of the diversity of

11 a

the appearances in different parts, is known as 'erythema multiforme'. It also occurs as a drug-rash from the use of such drugs as belladonna or copaiba.

ERYTHRASMA is a reddish-brown macular eruption of the skin, caused by a fungus known as *Nocardia minutissima*.

ERYTHROBLASTOSIS FŒTALIS (*see* HÆMOLYTIC DISEASE OF THE NEW-BORN).

ERYTHROCYTE (ἐρυθρός, red; κύτος cell) is another name for a red blood corpuscle.

ERYTHRŒDEMA.—Other terms for this condition are ACRODYNIA and PINK DISEASE. This is a disease of infants in which there are the following features : restlessness, weakness, neuritis, and swelling and redness of the face, fingers, and toes. In the vast majority of cases it is a manifestation of mercurial poisoning, often due to the infant having been given teething powders containing a mercurial laxative.

ERYTHROL is a sugar derived from *Rocella tinctoria* and other lichens. It is used in combination with nitric acid to form erythrol tetranitrate, or erythrityl tetranitrate, which produces a prolonged effect in dilating blood-vessels by virtue of the nitrites which are slowly evolved from it. It is used in the treatment of angina pectoris in doses of ¼ to 1 grain (15 to 60 mg.) several times daily.

ERYTHROMELALGIA (ἐρυθρός, red; μέλος, limb; ἄλγος, pain), or RED NEURALGIA, is a condition in which the fingers or toes, or even larger portions of the limbs, become purple, bloated in appearance, and very painful. In persons suffering from this condition, which is not a common one, the attacks come and go, being worse in summer (unlike chilblains), and worse on exertion or when the affected parts are warmed or allowed to hang down. The condition may appear without apparent cause, but is often associated with vascular diseases, such as hypertension and polycythæmia vera. It also occurs in association with certain

diseases of the central nervous system, and in cases of metallic poisoning, e.g. arsenic, mercury, and thallium. Treatment is unsatisfactory. Residence in a moderate climate, the wearing of light-weight stockings or socks, and sandals, and the avoidance of excessive heat help to relieve the discomfort. Aspirin also gives marked relief.

ERYTHROMYCIN is an antibiotic derived from *Streptomyces erythreus*. Its antibacterial range of activity is comparable to that of penicillin, and it is effective when taken by mouth.

ESCHAR (ἐσχάρα, a slough) is a piece of the body killed by heat or caustics.

ESCHAROTICS are the more powerful varieties of caustics, such as mineral acids, which produce death, to some depth, of tissues with which they come in contact. (*See* CAUSTICS.)

ESCHERICHIA is the generic name given to the group of gram-negative, rod-shaped bacteria found as normal inhabitants of the lower bowel : e.g. *Escherichia coli*.

ESMARCH'S BANDAGE is a rubber bandage which is applied to a limb from below upwards in order to drive blood from it.

ESSENCES are strong solutions of active substances, for example, essence of rennet, essence of pancreatin. Some of these are made by solution in water, but the aromatic essences are usually solutions of volatile oils (*e.g.* essence of peppermint, essence of vanilla), in rectified spirit of the strength 1 in 5.

ESSENTIAL HYPERTENSION is the most common form of high blood-pressure. Other causes of a high blood-pressure include kidney disease, especially Bright's disease; certain diseases of the endocrine glands; and a congenital abnormality of the aorta known as coarctation of the aorta.

Cause.—In spite of its being such a common condition, the cause of essential hypertension is still obscure. It has been recognized for a long time that arteriosclerosis and hypertension often occur together, and at one time it was considered that the arteriosclerosis was the primary lesion and that the raised blood-pressure was a compensatory effort on the part of the heart to maintain an adequate circulation of blood through the thickened and narrowed arteries. This view is now considered to be wrong, and the general consensus of opinion is that the raised blood-pressure is the cause of the arteriosclerosis in these cases, although it must be remembered that arteriosclerosis can occur without hypertension. At the present moment it is generally believed that the primary lesion in essential hypertension is spasm of the smaller arteries (or arterioles). What is still undecided is what is responsible for this spasm. We know that such spasm can be produced by adrenaline and that adrenaline is produced by emotional, mental, and physical strain. On the other hand, it has never been possible to demonstrate an excess of adrenaline in the blood of people with hypertension, nor does this theory explain why only some people exposed to strain develop hypertension. Although we still do not know why this spasm of the arterioles is produced in the first instance, there is now evidence that spasm of the arteries to the kidneys results in the production of a substance called *renin* which produces a rise in the blood-pressure. It is therefore possible that the course of events in essential hypertension is as follows :—

spasm of arterioles → renin → hypertension → arteriosclerosis of kidneys.

It must be realized, however, that this is a marked simplification of a most complicated problem, but it is useful as a working basis.

The following are among some of the other factors that we know about essential hypertension. It is much more common among western races than among eastern races. It is more common in males than in females, and it is rare under the age of 40 years. The highest incidence is between the ages of 50 and 60 years. It is also more common among obese individuals than among those who are normal in weight or under-weight. There is no evidence that the consumption of meat has anything to do with essential hypertension.

Symptoms.—Essential hypertension may be present without any symptoms whatsoever, and the condition may be discovered accidentally during a routine medical examination. The basis for a diagnosis of hypertension is usually taken to be a systolic pressure which is persistently greater than 150 mm. of mercury and a diastolic pressure which is persistently greater than 95 mm. of mercury. The emphasis is upon the persistence of the raised pressure, because it is not unusual for the blood-pressure in a normal individual to be raised temporarily by excitement. From the point of view of prognosis, the height of the diastolic pressure is much more important than that of the systolic pressure.

When essential hypertension is accompanied by symptoms, these usually consist of headache, ringing in the ears (tinnitus) and giddiness. When headache is present, it is usually in the back of the head and is worst on wakening in the morning, wearing off during the course of the day, and then becoming worse again towards evening.

When essential hypertension runs its natural course, it usually causes death in the end as a result of heart failure, but a proportion of its victims die of a stroke, whilst some die of failure of the kidneys. To a certain extent it is true to say that the earlier the onset of essential hypertension, the poorer the expectation of life, but many people with this condition live to a ripe old age.

Treatment.—As the cause of essential hypertension is not known, there is no specific treatment. In the majority of cases, treatment consists in the individual leading a quiet life, avoiding undue effort or strain, getting off to bed early at night, and insisting upon resting at the week-ends. Unless there are signs of heart failure there is no need for the individual to take to bed. Sedatives are useful if the individual is worrying unduly, is not sleeping well, or is subject to headaches. If there is overweight, this should be treated dietetically so as to bring the weight down to within normal limits. Of recent years the operation of sympathectomy has been recommended for the treatment of essential hypertension. This operation consists of cutting practically all the sympathetic nerve fibres to the abdominal organs. The rationale of the operation is that it is through these nerve fibres that are carried the impulses which are responsible for producing vasoconstriction, or spasm of the arteries, and thereby hypertension. Whilst there is no doubt that an extensive sympathectomy lowers the blood-pressure in most hypertensive subjects, it is now evident that it is only in a minority of cases that the pressure remains down, but in carefully selected cases the results are sometimes most gratifying.

During recent years, certain drugs have been introduced which are proving of value in the treatment of certain cases. These drugs include bretylium tosylate (q.v.), hydrallazine (q.v.), mecamylamine (q.v.), methonium compounds (see METHONIUM), pempidine (q.v.), rauwolfia (q.v) and veratrum derivatives (see VERATRUM). The decision as to which, if any, of these drugs should be used in any given patient is often a difficult one, and there is no rule of thumb by which this decision can be reached. Each case must be looked upon as an individual problem. Their greatest value is in the treatment of malignant hypertension (q.v.).

ESTER. — An organic compound formed from an alcohol and an acid by the removal of water. A compound formed by the replacement of the hydrogen of an acid by a hydrocarbon radical. Also known as *compound ether, ethereal salt*. Fats, for instance, are esters of fatty acids and glycerol.

ETHACRYNIC ACID is a potent diuretic (q.v.), which is clinically unrelated to any of the other diuretics.

ETHAMBUTOL is a synthetic drug which is proving of value in the treatment of tuberculosis.

ETHER, or ETHYL OXIDE, is a colourless, volatile, highly inflammable liquid formed by the action of sulphuric acid upon alcohol, with the aid of heat. Ether boils below the body temperature, and so, when sprayed over the skin, rapidly evaporates. It dissolves many substances, such as fats, oils, and resins, better than alcohol or water, and is accordingly used in the preparation of many drugs.

332

Uses.—Externally it is used as a cleansing agent before operations. By inhalation it is used as a general anæsthetic. (*See* ANÆSTHETICS.) Internally it is used occasionally for relieving pain such as colic. (For its use as an intoxicant, *see* DRUG HABITS.)

ETHINYLŒSTRADIOL is a highly active œstrogen (q.v.), which is about ten times as active as stilbœstrol (q.v.). It is active when given by mouth.

ETHISTERONE is the name approved by the *British Pharmacopœia* for the orally active analogue of progesterone. Ethisterone is also known as pregneninolone or anhydrohydroxyprogesterone. It is given in certain cases of menorrhagia and habitual abortion, where a deficient secretion of the corpus luteum is suspected. (*See* PROGESTERONE.)

ETHMOID (ἠθμός, a sieve; εἶδος, form) is the name of a bone in the base of the skull which separates the cavity of the nose from the membranes of the brain. It is a spongy bone with numerous cavities or sinuses.

Chronic suppuration in the ethmoidal sinuses causing a nasal discharge is sometimes responsible for inflammation in neighbouring parts such as the eye.

ETHOGLUCID is an alkylating agent (q.v.), which is proving of value in the treatment of cancer.

ETHYL BISCOUMACETATE is the *British Pharmacopœia* name for ethyl 4 : 4' - dihydroxydicoumarin - 3 : 3' - ylacetate, which is also known as TROMEXAN. It is an anticoagulant which is active when taken by mouth. Its action is similar to that of dicoumarol (q.v.), but less prolonged. It is used in the prevention, and treatment, of thrombotic conditions.

ETHYL CHLORIDE is a clear, colourless liquid, produced by treating ethyl alcohol or industrial methylated spirit with hydrogen chloride. It is extremely volatile, and rapidly produces freezing of the surface, when sprayed upon it. Accordingly it is used to produce insensibility to pain for small and short operations. It is put up in graduated glass or metal tubes, with a fine nozzle. The tube is warmed by the hand and the liquid jets out in a fine spray which evaporates at once and so freezes the skin upon which it is sprayed It is also used by inhalation to produce general anæsthesia for very brief operations, such as removal of tonsils and tooth extraction. Unconsciousness is produced in the course of one or two minutes, but consciousness returns after its use with almost equal rapidity. It is also used to induce anæsthesia in patients in whom the anæsthesia is subsequently to be maintained by some other anæsthetic such as nitrous oxide or ether.

ETHYLENE is a colourless inflammable gas used as an anæsthetic, compressed in metal cylinders.

ETIOLOGY, Ætiology (αἰτία, cause; λόγος, discourse), means the group of conditions which form the cause of any disease.

EU- (εὖ, well) is a prefix meaning satisfactory or beneficial.

EUCALYPTUS, or Blue-gum (*Eucalyptus globulus*), is a tree, originally a native of Australia, and now grown all over the world. Its important constituent, oil of eucalyptus, is an oil of pleasant smell and spicy taste, which is obtained by distillation from the leaves of the tree. Similar oils are obtained in varying amount from most species of gum-trees, some of which have peculiar and fragrant odours. Groves of eucalyptus trees exert a marked influence upon the soil and air in their neighbourhood. The trees, which reach a great size, and have wide - spreading roots, remove much moisture from the soil, and have accordingly a powerful action in drying up swampy ground. The oil constantly exhaled from the leaves has the power of oxidizing and destroying large quantities of the foul gases which emanate from swamps, and of checking to some extent the growth of microbes. Accordingly these trees have a beneficial influence upon unhealthy districts in which they are planted.

Uses.—The oil is largely used as a disinfectant and deodorant. Two ounces (57 ml.) of oil of eucalyptus, placed in a porous earthenware vessel so as to impregnate its substance, will keep the air of a water-closet in which the vessel is suspended perfectly free from smell for several months. For a similar purpose, it may be mixed with eight times its weight of sawdust and used to sprinkle on floors.

It is also used as an inhalation or internally in bronchitis and in coryza.

EUGENICS (εὖ, well ; γεννάω, I beget) is a term applied to the study and cultivation of conditions that may improve the physical and moral qualities of future generations.

EUMYDRIN, or atropine methyl nitrate, is an anti-spasmodic which has been used successfully in the treatment of congenital pyloric stenosis. In a certain number of cases it obviates the necessity for operation in this condition.

EUONYMIN is a dry extract made from the bark of the Wahoo-tree (*Euonymus atropurpureus*), a native of the United States. It has a mild purgative action, and to some extent also stimulates the liver.

EUPAD is a mixture of calcium cloride and boric acid, 25 grammes of which, dissolved in 1 litre of water, form ' eusol '.

EUPATORIUM is a drug used in household medicine. It consists of the powdered leaves of the thoroughwort (*Eupatorium perfoliatum*), a native plant of the United States. A hot infusion is given in colds and chills to produce perspiration, and a cold infusion as a bitter.

EUSOL (*see* Hypochlorous Acid).

EUPHORIANTS are drugs which induce a state of euphoria or well-being. A typical example is amphetamine (*q.v.*).

EUSTACHIAN TUBES are the passages, one on each side, leading from the throat to the middle ear. Each is about 1½ inches (38 mm.) long and is large at either end, though at its narrowest part it only admits a fine probe. The tubes open widely in the act of swallowing or yawning. The opening into the throat is situated just behind the lower part of the nose, so that a catheter can be passed through the corresponding nostril into the tube for inflation of the middle ear. (*See also* EAR *and* NOSE.)

EUTHANASIA (εὖ, well ; θάνατος, death) means the procuring of an easy and painless death. It has been advocated in some quarters that a medical man should have the power to put to death painlessly, by means of such drugs as morphine, any person suffering from a painful, distressing, and incurable disease the outcome of which is inevitably fatal, the patient or his relatives consenting. Various legal safeguards have been proposed, but there are obvious moral and religious—not to mention medical— objections to the recognition of such a procedure.

EVACUANT (*evacuans*, making empty) is a name for a purgative medicine.

EXANTHEMATA (ἐξ, out ; ἀνθέω, I blossom) is an old name used to classify the acute infectious diseases distinguished by a characteristic eruption. (*See* ERUPTION.)

EXCIPIENT (*excipio*, I mix with) means any more or less inert substance added to a prescription in order to make the remedy as prescribed more suitable in bulk, consistence, or form for administration.

EXCISION (*excisio*) means literally a cutting out, and is a term applied to the removal of any structure from the body, when such removal necessitates a certain amount of separation from surrounding parts. For example, one speaks of the excision of a tumour, of a gland, of a joint, etc. When an opening is simply made into the body the term ' incision ' is used. When a limb, or part of one, is removed, the term ' amputation ' is employed.

EXCITEMENT (*see* DELIRIUM, HYSTERIA, *and* MENTAL ILLNESS).

EXCITING CAUSE of a disease is the name given to the direct or immediate cause, as opposed to ' predisposing ' causes, which merely render the body more liable to the disease in question. For example, poor expansion of the chest may be a ' pre-

disposing ' cause of tuberculosis, but the ' exciting ' cause is infection with the tubercle bacillus, or *Mycobacterium tuberculosis* as it is now known.

EXCORIATION (*ex*, out of ; *corium*, the skin) means the destruction of small pieces of the surface of skin or mucous membrane. (*See* CHAFING OF THE SKIN.)

EXEIRESIS means the evulsion of a part by operation, especially of the phrenic nerve. Exeiresis of the phrenic nerve is done in order to paralyse one-half of the diaphragm and so give rest to the diseased lung on the side operated on.

EXERCISE is a matter of great importance in the maintenance of health at all ages, but particularly for those who are normally engaged in sedentary occupations. (*See also* CHEST DEVELOPMENT.)

Effects of exercise. — Upon the muscles of the body exercise produces, by their contraction, loss of material and repair by new material, the muscles growing gradually as increased demands are made upon them. Upon the blood-vessels and lymph-vessels the contracting and relaxing muscles exert a pumping action, so that the blood and lymph circulate more rapidly.

It is calculated that the body of a man, 11 stones, *i.e.* 154 pounds, in weight, expends about 3400 foot-tons of energy daily, or sufficient to raise one ton to the top of a high British mountain. Of this, about 260 foot-tons are expended on the work of the internal organs, viz. the beating of the heart, the movements of the chest in breathing, and of the stomach and bowels in digestion. The large amount of 2840 foot-tons is, on an average, necessary to maintain the body heat. The remaining 300 foot-tons represent the natural amount of external work of which the body is capable in health.

Want of exercise.—The failure to perform at least a considerable part of this natural amount of work is followed by many bad results. In the young the muscles and bones do not develop as they should, and although they may increase in length they remain thin and puny. Further, the muscles which support the back become readily tired, producing 'round shoulders', or, since they are, as a rule, more tired on one side than on the other, causing curvature of the spine with elevation and 'throwing forward' of one shoulder. Deficient expansion of the chest is the result of never making special efforts in breathing, and this deformity is one of the chief predisposing causes of diseases of the lungs. Where a single limb or one side of the body is not used in consequence of paralysis, the muscles undergo degeneration and the joints become stiff. In those more advanced in years, faulty chemistry of the body, with bloodlessness, dyspepsia, and constipation, sets in when exercise and fresh air are insufficient. And, in the middle-aged, obesity, accompanied by degeneration of the heart muscle and blood-vessels, with a fat and flabby condition of all the muscles, is the result (*see* CORPULENCE). Further, the person who refrains from exercising his or her body in a rational manner, becomes a prey to all kinds of morbid inclinations.

Over-exercise seldom does any permanent harm except in the rapidly growing adolescent and in the old, provided the individual is healthy. For instance, there is no evidence that a healthy heart can be damaged by exercise. The circulatory system is so adaptable that, if there is any possibility of undue strain being placed upon the heart, certain mechanisms come into play which cause giddiness or fainting, so that the exercise in question is automatically stopped before any real harm is done. On the other hand, should there be any undetected disease of the heart, then undue exercise may produce permanent harm. This is why a careful medical examination is an essential preliminary to any severe form of exercise. This is particularly important, indeed essential, in the case of school children.

The secret of success here, as in most spheres of life, is moderation in all things. The man in his fifties or sixties must realize that he can no longer do many of the things that he did when he was thirty years younger. If he bears this in mind, there is little chance of his damaging himself by exercise. For instance, if he finds that an afternoon's tennis begins to make him

uncomfortably breathless, then he should give up the game for a less exacting one, or alternatively be satisfied with one or two sets instead of several.

In the case of adolescents and young adults, the wise rule is to ensure that the individual, and particularly his heart, is sound, and then to insist upon his undergoing a careful course of training before embarking upon any severe form of exercise such as racing or rugger.

Training involves a certain regimen and practice prior to engaging in special athletic efforts. The objects of training, generally speaking, are :

(1) To accustom certain muscles to perform a spectacular act, as, for example, the thigh and leg muscles to contract sharply and in a particular

FIG. 145.—*Position of attention*, which forms commencement for most exercises. Heels together, feet turned out at an angle of 45°, knees straight, trunk erect, arms hanging naturally from the shoulders, with palms turned towards thighs, neck erect, and eyes looking forwards.

FIG. 146.—*Position of hips firm.* The hands are raised quickly to grasp the waist with fingers in front and thumbs behind. This is the starting position for most arm exercises.

NECK EXERCISES

FIG. 147.—*Head bending backward.* In the position of attention, the head is bent slowly backward as far as possible, and then raised slowly to its former position.

FIG. 148.—*Head turning.* The head is turned slowly but strongly to the left as far as possible, then turned to its former position; then to the right as far as possible, and, finally, the position of attention resumed.

ARM EXERCISES

FIG. 149.—*Arm bending.* Keeping the elbows to the sides, the arms are quickly and sharply bent by carrying the hands up in front of the body and clenching the fists; the arms are then sharply stretched downward to the sides.

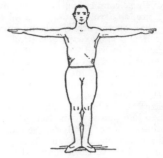

FIG. 150.—*Arms stretching sideways.* The arms are stretched sharply in line with the shoulders, palms downward and fingers fully stretched.

FIG. 151.—*Arms stretching upward.* The arms are stretched sharply upward to their fullest extent, palms inward and fingers fully extended.
The last three exercises strengthen the muscles of the arms and shoulders.

LEG EXERCISES

FIG. 152.—*Rising on tiptoe.* The heels are raised from the ground as high as possible and slowly lowered to the ground again. This develops the calf muscles.

FIG. 153.—*Full knee bending*. Keeping the heels together, these are raised from the ground as high as possible ; the knees are then bent as much as possible, so that the buttocks are lowered to touch the heels ; the original standing position is then slowly resumed. This strengthens the leg and thigh muscles and keeps the ankle, knee, and hip joints supple.

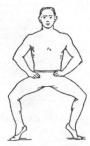

FIG. 154.—*Foot placing sideways with knee bending*. Each foot is carried one foot sideways ; the heels are raised from the ground ; the knees are bent till thigh and leg form a right angle ; the knees are then straightened ; the heels are slowly lowered and the original position of attention resumed. This exercises the adductor muscles of the thigh.

FIG. 155.—*Lunging*. The right foot is kept flat on the ground, and right leg straight ; the left leg is carried three feet to the left and the body sharply inclined over the left foot, the trunk being in line with the right leg. To resume the original position, the left foot is pressed sharply on the ground and then carried back into the position of attention. The lunge may similarly be made to the right by carrying the right foot three feet to the right at starting.

BALANCING EXERCISES

FIG. 156.—*Knee raising*. Standing on the right foot, the left knee is raised till the thigh is at right angles to the body with the leg hanging downward from the knee ; the knee is then straightened and the leg then brought slowly down to its original position. The movement is repeated with the right leg.

FIG. 157.—*Leg raising backward*. Standing on the right foot, the left leg is raised as far as possible backward with the knee straight, and the toe pointed ; the left leg is then slowly lowered to its original position. The movement is repeated with the right leg.

DORSAL EXERCISE

FIG. 158.—*Trunk downward bending*. Assume the position of Fig. 151. Bend the body as far downward as possible from the hips without rounding the back ; slowly resume original position.

337

FIG. 159.—*Trunk turning.* Each foot is carried one foot outward, the hands are placed behind the neck, and, with the feet firm on the ground, the trunk is turned steadily as far as possible to the left; the original position is resumed, and the movement repeated to the right.

FIG. 160.—*Trunk bending sideways.* The arms are stretched upward, each foot is carried one foot outward, and, with the feet firm on the ground, the trunk is then bent steadily as far as possible to the left; the original position is resumed, the trunk is then bent to the right, and the original position again resumed.

FIG. 161.—*Lunging with arms stretched.* Lunge outward as in Fig. 155; at the same time sharply stretch upward the arm corresponding to the forward foot and stretch downward, one hand's-breadth from the thigh, the arm corresponding to the rear foot, the movement of the arms being completed as the forward foot reaches the ground. Resume the position of attention, repeat towards opposite side.

338

FIG. 162.—*Upward jumping.* Assume position of Fig. 153. Suddenly extend the knees and ankles and place the arms straight at the sides, springing from the ground vertically upward; drop to the ground on the toes with the knees practically straight, but allowing the ankles and knees to give, so that the position of Fig. 153 is resumed after landing. Repeat the movement.

ABDOMINAL EXERCISES

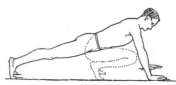

FIG. 163.—*On the hands.* Keeping the heels together, these are raised from the ground and the knees bent; at the same time the palms of the hands are placed on the ground rather more than the width of the shoulders apart, with arms straight. Keeping the arms straight, the feet are shot backward till the body and legs are straight, and fully stretched, the weight supported on the toes and hands.

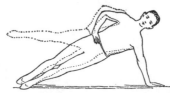

FIG. 164.—*Turning on the hand and leg-raising.* From position of Fig. 163 raise the right hand from the ground and place it on the waist, at the same time turning the body to the right and placing the right foot immediately over the left; keeping left arm straight, raise right leg slowly as high as possible and slowly resume original position. Repeat by turning on the right hand.

PLATE IX

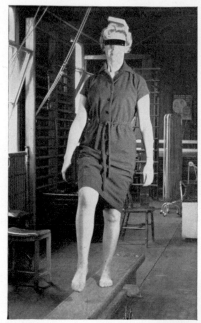

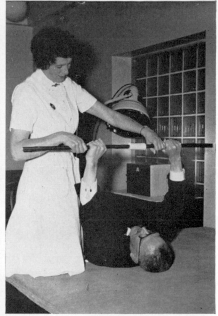

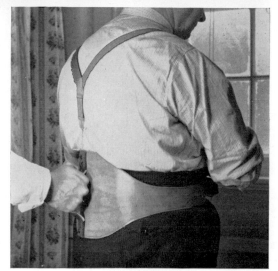

A (*top left*).—A form of balancing
   exercise.
B (*top right*).—Resisted **shoulder**
   exercise.
C (*bottom*).—A Harris belt.

PLATE X

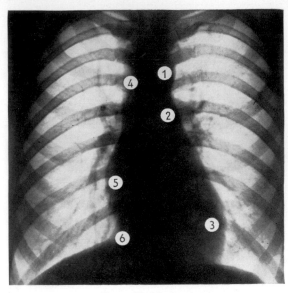

1 Aorta.
2 Pulmonary artery.
3 Left ventricle.
4 Superior vena cava.
5 Right atrium.
6 Inferior vena cava.

X-ray of healthy heart.
(From *Diseases of the Heart and Arteries*
by William Evans. E. & S. Livingstone)

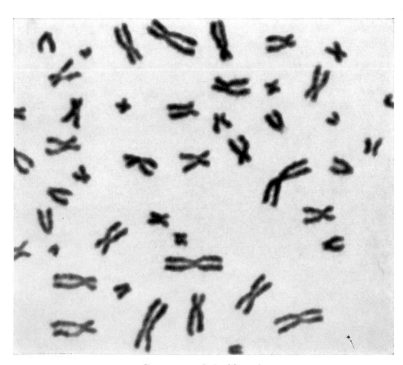

Chromosomes of a healthy male.
(*The Practitioner*)

FIG. 165.—*Trunk backward bending.* Keeping the knees straight, raise the arms above the head and bend the upper part of the trunk slowly backward as far as possible. Slowly resume the original position.

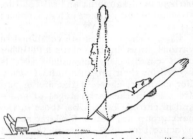

FIG. 166.—*Trunk backward bending with foot support.* Sitting on the ground with feet supported above and arms stretched upwards, bend slowly backward to touch the ground. Slowly resume original position.

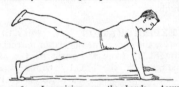

FIG. 167.—*Leg-raising—on the hands.* Assume the position of Fig. 163; keeping the right leg straight, raise it as high as possible with toe pointed. Resume starting position and repeat with left leg.

FIG. 168.—*Leg-raising—on the back.* Assume the position of Fig. 153; place both hands on the ground to the rear and lower the body quickly backward to the ground, shooting the legs to the front. The body is then stretched flat on the back, feet together, and arms to the sides; stretch arms upward, keeping the knees straight, raise the right leg steadily without arching the back, lower the leg, and repeat with left leg. Repeat with both legs at one time.

order for jumping; (2) to strengthen the heart and deepen the breathing for prolonged efforts; and (3) to bring the whole body, and especially the nervous system, to a state of perfect health. For these objects, a course of special practice, combined with various general exercises, lasting usually over three weeks before the event for which the training is intended, is combined with a healthy form of diet. (*See* DIET.) Different trainers have, in addition, special rules of their own, usually founded on experience.

Training exercises.—The chief object of physical training is to produce a state of health and general physical fitness so that the body may be able better to withstand the strain of daily life, and to perform the work required of it without injury. Other objects of physical training are to obtain a good carriage and to prevent the undue accumulation of fat. The effect of physical exercises is important, not only on the muscles but also upon the heart, lungs, and other internal organs, especially when systematic exercises are carried out at the commencement of the day's activity.

The foregoing exercises have been selected from the *Manual of Physical Training* used in the British Army, and include groups of exercises for the different parts of the body. If ten or twelve of these exercises be chosen, and if each movement be carried out ten or twelve times slowly and methodically, this is sufficient to provide fifteen minutes of exercise. If these are carried out during dressing in the morning by business men and others whose duties prevent them from obtaining outdoor exercise by games, sufficient exercise is obtained to maintain a good standard of physical fitness.

Remedial gymnastics.—Equally important is the value of exercises in restoring the physically disabled to health. (*See also* FRENKEL'S EXERCISES.) The accompanying three photographs illustrate those typical forms of remedial exercises.

Plate IX (A) shows one form of balancing exercise, in which a patient with loss of joint sense as a result of multiple sclerosis (*q.v.*) is walking along a bench, balancing a bean bag on her head. Plate IX (B) shows a patient performing resisted shoulder exercises, whilst Plate IX (C) shows a Harris belt which is a useful aid when giving walking exercises.

EXFOLIATION (*ex*, out of ; *folium*, a leaf) means the separation, in layers, of pieces of dead bone or skin.

EXOMPHALOS is the term applied to a hernia formed by the projection of abdominal organs through the umbilicus.

EXOPHTHALMIC GOITRE (ἐξ, out ; ὀφθαλμός, the eye ; *guttur*, throat) is a disease in which there is an enlargement of the thyroid gland, protrusion of the eyes, and other symptoms. (*See* GOITRE.)

EXOPHTHALMOS is abnormal protrusion of the eyeball. The commonest cause is hyperthyroidism (*see* GOITRE). It may also occur as a result of a tumour at the back of the eye pushing the eyeball forwards.

EXOSTOSIS (ἐξ, out of; ὀστέον, a bone) means an outgrowth from a bone ; it may be due to chronic inflammation, constant pressure or tension on the bone, or tumour-formation. (*See* BONE, DISEASES OF.)

EXPECTANT (*expectans*, waiting) is a term applied to a form of treatment in which the cure of the patient is left mainly to nature, while the physician simply watches for any unsatisfactory developments or symptoms, and relieves them if they occur.

EXPECTORANTS (*ex*, out of ; *pectus*, the chest) are drugs which assist the removal of secretions from the air passages.

Varieties.—Most drugs used as expectorants have a very complicated mode of action. (1) Some act chiefly by making the secretion in the bronchial tubes more watery, and therefore less sticky ; (2) others have exactly the opposite action, drying up the secretion where it is very copious ; (3) a third group assists the act of coughing

in feeble persons, and so helps the removal of secretion ; (4) while those in a fourth group soothe the lining membrane of the air passages and quiet ineffectual coughing. Some of the chief drugs, arranged as far as possible in the order of these groups, though several have a double action, are as follows : (1) steam inhalations, draughts of hot milk or water, chloride of ammonium, iodide of potassium, and, generally speaking, all alkalis ; (2) volatile oils like anise, eucalyptus, and turpentine, menthol, balsam of tolu and Friar's balsam, syrup of squills and infusion of senega, inhalation of creosote or tar, and, generally speaking, all acids ; (3) ipecacuanha, carbonate of ammonia and sal volatile, strychnine and tincture of nux vomica ; (4) codeine.

Uses.—These drugs are combined in various ways in bronchitis and other chest conditions, but much skill is needed for their proper administration. For example, those in the first group are used in the early stages of acute and in chronic bronchitis, those in the next group are better for later stages of acute bronchitis, those of the third group are necessary for aged persons with pneumonia and bronchitis, and the members of the fourth group are applicable to a constant hacking cough.

EXPECTORATION (*ex*, out of ; *pectus*, the chest) means either material brought up from the chest by the air passages, or the act by which it is brought up. The term is also used in place of 'sputum' for anything spat out. Expectoration varies considerably in character according to the site in which it is produced, and the disease with which it is associated.

Characters of expectoration.—There may be much cough productive of a very small amount of sputum at the commencement of an acute bronchitis or inflammation of the throat, and it must be remembered that young children and some older persons swallow their expectoration as soon as they have brought it up instead of spitting it out.

The sputum from the throat in catarrh of this region is usually thick and sticky, speckled with black owing to dust and smoke inhaled and deposited on the throat.

Watery, frothy expectoration is brought up in considerable quantities during the greater part of an attack of acute bronchitis, particularly in old people. A similar fluid is spat up when the lungs are œdematous or dropsical, as occurs sometimes in the course of heart or kidney disease. At a later stage of an acute bronchitis the sputum becomes more yellow and thicker in consistence.

When cavities are present in the lungs their contents are often expectorated as thick, yellow, oily-looking material, with few air-bubbles in it; and expectoration from this source, when spat into water, flattens out into a round disc resembling a coin, and hence gets the name of nummular sputum (Lat. *nummulus*, money).

Sputum with a ' rusty ' tinge, and so sticky that it adheres to the dish into which it is expectorated, when the latter is turned upside down, is characteristic of pneumonia.

Bright red blood in large quantities may be brought up from the lungs. This is the condition known as *hæmoptysis* (*q.v.*) and usually indicates the presence of pulmonary tuberculosis, carcinoma of the lung, or certain forms of heart disease. On the other hand, it must be remembered that spitting of blood may be due merely to bleeding in the nose from which the blood has run backward down the throat: or to the rupture of a small vessel on the wall of the throat in cases in which this part of the air passages is inflamed. Bleeding from the stomach has totally different characteristics from those of lung bleeding. That brought up from the lungs is bright red, frothy, and usually comes up with a hawk or with a few suppressed coughs, it may be by mouthfuls. Blood from the stomach is usually dark brown and granular from the action of the gastric juice, and is brought up by a definite act of vomiting. It results generally from some ulcerated or congested state of the stomach.

Expectoration of a ' prune juice ' colour occurring in the course of pneumonia is an ominous sign, and indicates usually that softening of parts of the lungs is setting in.

In some diseases the sputum possesses a very foul smell, particularly in gangrene of the lung and in the condition known as bronchiectasis. (*See* LUNGS, DISEASES OF.)

Microscopic examination of the sputum is of importance chiefly in diagnosing pulmonary tuberculosis by finding tubercle bacilli in it. In cancer of the lung the microscope may disclose malignant cells in the sputum, whilst in pneumonia large numbers of pneumococci are present.

Disposal of expectoration is a matter demanding public attention. The habit of spitting on the ground in public places is one which, in view of the dangerous nature of diseased sputum, should never be tolerated. Where spittoons are provided, these should be washed and disinfected every day.

Most tuberculous patients are supplied with a sputum flask containing a small quantity of some strong antiseptic (*e.g.* carbolic acid solution 1 in 5 or 1 in 20) into which the expectoration is received and by which it is disinfected before it is poured down the drains.

EXTENSION is the term applied to the process of straightening or stretching a limb. In cases of fractured limbs, extension is employed during the application of splints, in order to reduce the displacement caused by the fracture, and prevent movement of the broken ends of bone. It is effected by gently and steadily pulling upon the part of the limb beyond the fracture. Extension of a more permanent type is used in the after-treatment of some fractures, as well as in diseases of the spine, by placing the patient upon an inclined bed and affixing weights to his lower limbs or to his head by means of adhesive plaster or of straps. A similar procedure is often adopted in tuberculous disease of the knee or hip, to prevent the ' starting pains ', which are apt to occur as the affected person is dropping off to sleep.

EXTRA is a Latin prefix meaning outside of or in addition, such as extracapsular, meaning outside the capsule of a joint, and extrasystole, meaning an additional contraction of the heart.

EXTRACTS are preparations, usually of a semi-solid consistence, containing the active parts of various plants extracted in one of several ways. In the case of some extracts the juice of the fresh plant is simply pressed out and purified ; in the case of others the active principles are dissolved out in water, which is then to a great extent driven off by evaporation ; other extracts are similarly made by the help of alcohol, and in some cases ether is the solvent.

EXTRASYSTOLE is a term applied to premature contraction of one or more of the chambers of the heart. A beat of the heart occurs sooner than it should do in the ordinary rhythm and is followed by a longer rest than usual before the next beat. In extrasystole the stimulus to contraction arises in a part of the heart other than the usual. Extrasystoles often give rise to an unpleasant sensation as of the heart stumbling over a beat, but their occurrence is not usually of serious importance.

EXTRAVASATION (*extra*, outside of ; *vas*, a vessel) means an escape of fluid from the vessels or passages which ought to contain it. Extravasation of blood due to tearing of vessel walls is found in apoplexy, and in the commoner condition of the surface known as a bruise. Extravasation of urine takes place when the bladder or the urethra is ruptured by a blow on the abdomen or on the fork, or torn in a fracture of the pelvis.

EXUDATION (*exudo*, I sweat) means the process in which some of the constituents of the blood pass slowly through the walls of the small vessels in the course of inflammation, and also means the accumulation resulting from this process. For example, in pleurisy the solid, rough material deposited on the surface of the lung is an 'exudation'.

EYE.—The eyes are set, one on each side, in a deep four-sided cavity in the

skull, called the ' orbit '. The edges of this are so prominent, especially above and to the inner side, that a flat object resting on them does not touch the eyeball, and therefore the eye is very seldom injured by a blow. The prominence of the eyebrow is largely due to air-spaces known as the ' frontal sinuses ', lying in the substance of the frontal bone, and connected with the interior of the nose. The space behind the eyeball, and between it and the bone, is filled up by loose fat, which supports the ball as on an elastic cushion. The walls of the orbit almost meet in a point behind, leaving only two small gaps, through which pass nerves and vessels. The most prominent point of each eyeball is about $1\frac{1}{4}$ inches (31·5 mm.) from the middle line of the face, so that the two are $2\frac{1}{2}$ inches (63 mm.) apart. The eye is protected by two lids, upper and lower, which cover a varying amount of the globe, leaving usually an almond-shaped opening between their edges, which widens slightly as the eyes are turned up and down. The points where the lids join are known as the outer canthus and inner canthus. The inner canthus is tightly bound to the side of the nose, as may be seen by drawing the lids outwards, when a band stands out beneath the skin, between the nose and inner canthus ; but the outer angle is freely movable up and down. Just within the inner canthus lies a small red swelling, the caruncle, which is merely a soft piece of skin, and often bears a few hairs. Within this, again, is a small fold, the semilunar fold, in the membrane covering the eyeball which in some persons is fairly large, and represents the third eyelid found in birds and some other animals.

Eyelids.—Each of these consists of four layers. On the surface is skin, similar to the skin elsewhere on the body, but specially thin, loose, and pliant. Behind this comes a layer of muscle, the orbicular muscle, the fibres of which run round and round from one lid to the other, and serve to shut the eye. Next comes a stiff, fibrous layer, the tarsal plate, which gives stiffness to the lids, but which does not extend upwards and downwards the whole height of the lids, reaching, in the upper lid, only about one-third of an inch (8 mm.) from the margin, in the lower one about half that distance. In the substance of this plate is embedded a row of straight glands, the Meibomian glands, the openings of which can be seen on the edge of the lid as a row of minute punctures. Small cysts very frequently form as a result of obstruction to these glands, and produce small, round, painless swellings upon the surface of the lid. Farthest back of all is a moist, red layer of mucous membrane, known as the conjunctiva. This rubs over the surface of conjunctiva covering the eyeball, with which that on the lids is in fact continuous, at the upper margin of the upper lid and the lower margin of the lower lid. The conjunctiva, in passing from the lid to the surface of the eyeball, forms a pocket above and below. From the free margin of the lid projects a row of long, curved, elastic hairs, the eyelashes, which very materially protect the eyes from dust, insects, and the like. About one-fifth of the length of each lid away from the inner canthus one sees, on turning the lid a little outward, a small puncture on the margin of the lid. This puncture, the lacrimal puncture, leads off the tears from the surface of the eye.

Front of the eye.—When one separates the lids widely, a large part of the white of the eye comes into view. The white appearance is due to the sclerotic coat, composed of dense, white, fibrous tissue, shining through the translucent conjunctiva. In the centre of the sclerotic is set the clear transparent cornea, through which light passes into the eye. Behind the cornea, again, is the beautifully coloured iris, with a hole in its centre, the pupil, which looks black against the dark interior of the eye. A space is seen to exist between the cornea and iris, particularly if the eye be looked at from a little to one side, this space being filled with a clear transparent fluid. The colour of the iris depends upon the way in which the pigment is arranged in it : blue or grey eyes owe their colour to the presence of pigment at the back of the iris (in the posterior epithelial layer); in brown eyes pigment is present also in the pigmen cells in the middle layer

(the stroma). If one attempts to look in through the pupil, one sees nothing, because, just as in looking into a camera, one obscures the entering light by placing one's head in front of it, and very little of the light which enters from the sides is reflected out again. If, however, one holds a mirror in front of the eye into which one wishes to look, in this way reflecting a bright beam of light into the eye, and if one then looks from behind the mirror through a small hole in its centre, one sees the interior of the eye brightly lighted up. The ophthalmoscope is an instrument constructed on this principle. By its help, one sees the interior as a general red ground. At one point is a round, pale area, the end of the optic nerve, and from the centre of it arteries and veins spread out over the inner surface of the eyeball. The signs of various diseases, not only of diseases of the eye, but also of various constitutional maladies which to some extent affect the structure of this organ, can be minutely studied with the help of the ophthalmoscope, which often therefore is of inestimable value to the physician.

Coats of the eyeball.—The eyeball rests upon a pad of fat in the cavity of the orbit, where it is held in place by the pressure of the eyelids ; by the attachment of the conjunctiva ; by the orbital fascia and an envelope of fibrous tissue known as the Capsule of Tenon ; by six small muscles, which move it in different directions ; and finally by the optic nerve, which enters from behind. The eyeball has three distinct coats (Fig. 169) :

(a) THE SCLEROTIC or fibrous coat is composed of dense white, fibrous tissue, which gives its appearance to the white of the eye. This coat completely encloses the ball, except behind, where the optic nerve pierces it, while in front it is modified so as to form the transparent cornea. It maintains the shape of, and gives its strength to, the ball of the eye, being very hard to cut or tear. The cornea, which has a greater curvature than the rest of the ball, is also formed from fibrous tissue arranged in layers, so as to be quite transparent. In front of and behind these layers is a thin protective membrane, and both surfaces, back and front, are covered by a layer of cells. All these are transparent, and the cornea forms, as it were, a window let into the front of the sclerotic.

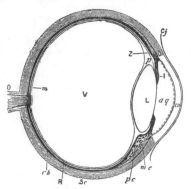

FIG. 169.—Diagrammatic section through the eyeball. *Cj*, Conjunctiva; *co*, cornea; *Sc*, sclerotic coat; *ch*, choroid coat; *pc*, ciliary processes; *mc*, ciliary muscle; *O*, optic nerve; *R*, retina; *I*, iris; *aq*, anterior chamber containing aqueous humour; *L*, lens; *V*, vitreous humour; *Z*, Zonule of Zinn, which supports the lens; *p*, space known as the canal of Petit; *m*, position of the macula, or yellow spot. (Turner's *Anatomy*.)

(*b*) THE UVEA or vascular coat lies within the sclerotic coat, and consists of three parts. The *choroid membrane*, which forms its greatest part, and lines more than two-thirds of the sclerotic, consists mainly of a network of vessels which nourish the sclerotic coat and the interior of the eyeball. It is formed by the endings of a few ciliary vessels which pierce the sclerotic coat on the front and back of the ball. The choroid membrane is prolonged forward into the *ciliary body*, a very complex structure, which forms a thickened ring opposite the line where the sclerotic passes into the cornea. To this line of junction between the sclerotic and cornea the ciliary body is firmly attached by the ciliary muscle, and, from the line of junction as a fixed point the ciliary muscle takes its bearing, and, in contracting, slackens the suspensory ligament of the lens, so as to allow the lens of the eye which is suspended from, or, as it were, 'set' in, the ciliary body, to grow thicker and thinner in the act of accommodation for near and distant vision (*see* ACCOMMODATION). The iris and ciliary body are easily infected,

and injuries to them are more dangerous for the whole eye than injuries to the cornea or to the eyeball farther outwards. The zone over the ciliary body, *i.e.* for a short distance outside of the edge of the cornea, is therefore called the 'dangerous zone' of the eye, and wounds to it frequently necessitate removal of the eye in order to save the sight of the other eye (*see* EYE DISEASES AND INJURIES). The farthest forward part of the choroid coat is known as the *iris*, and, as already stated, it is seen lying behind the cornea and separated from the latter by a slight space. The iris consists partly of fibrous tissue, partly of muscle fibres, interspersed with pigment cells, some of the fibres being arranged in a circular manner, others running from the edge of the pupil to the outer margin of the iris. These fibres, by their contraction, serve to narrow or dilate the pupil, according as the light entering the eye is strong or weak, and according as the eye gazes at a near or distant object. In the sharp angle formed by the meeting of the cornea and iris round their edges the fluids which keep the eyeball naturally tense filter out and in, to and from the neighbouring vessels. In the disease known as glaucoma the angle through which this process takes place is blocked up, and the eyeball becomes very tense, painful, and hard till sight is lost. The iris and ciliary muscle are powerfully acted on by certain drugs. Thus when atropine or belladonna is put in the eye or taken internally the pupil becomes widely dilated, whilst under the influence of moderate doses of opium or morphine, or of eserine locally applied, it contracts. This action is a valuable sign of poisoning by these drugs.

(*c*) THE RETINA or nervous coat is the innermost of the three coats of the eyeball. The optic nerve ends, after piercing the sclerotic and choroid coats, by a sudden spreading out of its fibres in all directions to form this coat, which also contains blood-vessels and nerve and pigment cells. The retina in microscopic section can be seen to consist of no fewer than ten layers (Fig. 170). Of these the outermost is a layer of pigment cells preventing the diffusion of light inside the eye, and the layer next to this is that of the rods and cones upon which light is received, and from which impressions are conveyed by the optic nerve to the brain, where the sensations to which the various forms of light give rise are perceived. The rods are coloured of a purple hue, visual purple, which fades for a time on exposure to bright light. They are excessively minute, being less than $\frac{1}{400}$ inch (0·06 mm.) long and about $\frac{1}{1000}$ inch (25 microns) in

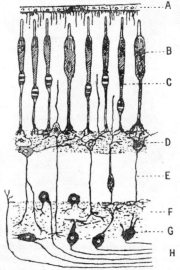

FIG. 170.—Diagrammatic section of the retina showing its various layers. A, pigment cells; B, cones; C, rods; D, F, felt-work of dendrons; E, axon of one of the cells which lie between the rods and cones and G, the ganglion cells; H, axons passing from ganglion cells to optic nerve. (From Hill, *Manual of Human Physiology*. Edward Arnold & Co.)

thickness. The cones are still shorter. The total number of cones in the human retina is about 6,500,000, and there are many more rods—about 115,000,000. It is probably that in order that two points of light may be seen as separate they must be sufficiently far apart for the rays proceeding from them to the eye to affect at least two cones. In the middle of the retina, at the very back of the eye, is a yellow spot, in the centre of which a central pit marks the 'point of clear vision'. Here the retina is very thin, and consists almost entirely of cones. Rods and cones stand closely side by side

over the whole retina, except over the area where the optic nerve enters. As there are none over the ending of the nerve, no light is perceived at this point, which is therefore called the blind spot. The presence of the blind spot in each eye can easily be proved by taking a clean sheet of paper, making an X in the middle of it, and then, while one eye is closed, following with the other eye the point of a pencil which is slowly moved to the right in the case of the left eye and to the left for the right eye. When the pencil is about 3 or 4 inches (75 to 100 mm.) from the X the latter suddenly disappears, reappearing as the pencil is followed farther on.

The contents of the eyeball are simple. The clear fluid separating the cornea from the iris, known as the 'aqueous humour' of the eye, has been already mentioned. Immediately behind the iris and opposite the ciliary body, to which it is attached round its edge by a ligament, known as the zonule of Zinn, lies the lens, a clear elastic body about $\frac{1}{3}$ inch (8mm.) in diameter and convex on both surfaces. If the lens becomes opaque, as it sometimes does in later life, the condition is known as cataract. Behind the lens and filling up the greater part of the interior of the eyeball is a soft, transparent, jelly-like mass known as the vitreous humour. The lens and vitreous humour are both of an albuminoid nature in chemical composition. The vitreous humour usually contains small specks and filaments, which cast shadows upon the retina when the eye looks at a bright cloud or whitened wall. They appear as floating blots or strings, and often cause alarm when noticed for the first time, but are of no importance and occur in almost every eye.

The lacrimal apparatus (Fig. 171) is an attachment to the eye designed to keep its surface clean. In the upper and outer part of the orbit, between the eyeball and the bone, lies the lacrimal gland, which secretes a saltish, clear, watery fluid, which is constantly conveyed, drop by drop, through several fine ducts to the upper part of the sac formed by the conjunctiva, between the upper lid and the eyeball. From here the fluid

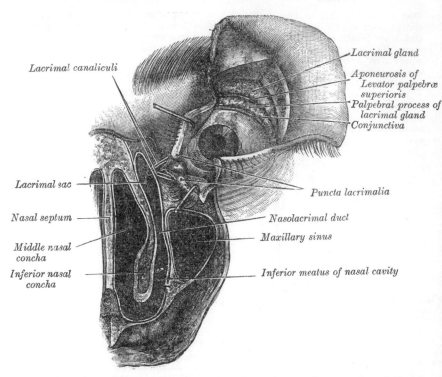

Lacrimal canaliculi

Lacrimal gland

Aponeurosis of
Levator palpebræ
superioris

Palpebral process of
lacrimal gland

Conjunctiva

Lacrimal sac

Nasal septum

Middle nasal
concha

Inferior nasal
concha

Puncta lacrimalia

Nasolacrimal duct

Maxillary sinus

Inferior meatus of nasal cavity

FIG. 171.—Dissection to show lacrimal apparatus. (From Gray's *Anatomy*. Longmans, Green & Co., Ltd.)

spreads out over the front of the eye, and is removed mainly by evaporation and partly through the minute lacrimal punctures which can be seen, one on the margin of each eyelid, about one-fifth of its length from its inner end. When the fluid runs over the margin of the lid it forms tears. From the lacrimal punctures the fluid runs, carrying with it specks of dust, etc., through two small canals into the lacrimal sac and duct, which lie alongside the nose, and thence into the lower part of the nose.

Effect of light.—When rays of light from an object fall upon the eye, they are strongly refracted at the front surface of the cornea ; next, they pass through the aqueous humour and then the lens, by which they should be so much refracted as to be brought to an accurate focus on the retina, producing upon the rods and cones a small inverted image of the object viewed. If a bright light falls upon the eye, the

pupil is narrowed by muscular action of the iris, causing, if the light continues very bright, considerable eye-strain. Therefore, in reading, one should not let a bright light shine full into the eyes, but should set it above one's head, behind one's back, or carefully shade it from the eyes. If the gaze turns to an object close at hand, the eyes look inwards, the pupils narrow, and the lenses become more convex by the automatic action of the muscles outside the eyeball, and of the muscle fibres in the iris and ciliary body. (*See* Accommodation.) As the eyes look at a distant object again, they take up the position of rest, the pupils widening, the ciliary muscle relaxing, and both eyes looking straight forwards. Hence the sensation of restfulness derived from looking in moderate light at a distant scene or even at a landscape picture. The images formed upon the retina are reversed in every way ; thus rays from points towards the right hand fall upon the left side of both retinæ, and vice versa, while rays from the ground affect the upper part, and those from above the lower part of both retinæ. The different colours corresponding to rays of various wave length produce different effects upon the retina, and these, being converted into nerve impulses, are carried along the optic nerves to the hinder part of the brain, where they produce the varied sensations of light and colour, very much in the same way, probably, as the voice is received by a telephone, transmitted along wires in an altered form, and again reproduced in the receiver with all its original tones and modulations.

The sense of distance, solidity, and form implies an act of judgment based upon experience. To an infant the universe is a mass of colour spread before his eyes, but gradually he learns, with the help of other senses, that objects which appear large and distinct are close at hand and may be grasped, those which seem small and indistinct are far off. The impression of solidity is gained by the image of any object upon one retina being slightly different from the image of it upon the other which can, so to speak, see a little way round the side of the object. This principle is utilized in making and viewing stereoscopic photographs. These, being taken from two different points, form, when viewed side by side, different images upon the two retinæ. The two images are combined by the mind into the sensations derived from a single scene which has depth as well as breadth and height. (For further information, *see* VISION.)

EYE DISEASES AND INJURIES.

The delicacy of structure of the eye renders any disorder of this organ highly important. Many of its disorders cannot be cured or can be remedied only to a small extent, such, for example, as loss of transparency in the cornea ; whilst, in the case of others, such as cataract and high errors of refraction, the skill of the specialist may restore the eye from a state of almost complete uselessness to that of good vision. Most of the diseases are intricate in their course and treatment, requiring the highest degree of skill in handling.

In the following account, some of the simpler and commoner diseases are dealt with. The subjects of CATARACT, CHOROIDITIS, GLAUCOMA, IRITIS, VISION, DEFECTS OF, SQUINTING, and SPECTACLES are dealt with under these headings.

STYE consists of an inflammation situated round an eyelash, which occurs especially in young people. It begins as a general swelling of the lid accompanied by pain, and gradually suppurates. Very often as one stye subsides another appears. Styes are most likely to occur in debilitated individuals. Treatment consists of hot compresses. Once the stye has burst, neomycin ointment may be of value.

BLEPHARITIS (βλέφαρα, eyelids), or chronic inflammation of the margin of the lids, occurs in weakly children. It is known by a variety of names, and, if not treated, it may produce, a red, watery condition of the eyelids, with loss of the eyelashes, known as ' blear eyes ', which persists throughout life. It begins with swelling near the edge of the eyelid, usually the upper one, redness and the constant formation of a crust round the roots of the eyelashes. The onset often follows one of the acute diseases of childhood, especially measles. The lower lid becomes infected later.

Treatment consists in removing the crusts from the lids twice a day with warm solution of bicarbonate of soda (a teaspoonful to a tumblerful of water), drying carefully, and at once applying some astringent and antiseptic, of which the favourite is ammoniated mercury ointment or yellow oxide of mercury ointment. Neomycin ointment has proved of value in the treatment of this condition.

CYSTS of the lids often arise in connection with the Meibomian glands

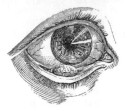

(Plate IV ; Fig. 172). They may last for many years, and give no trouble beyond that of irritation and disfigurement caused by their size, if they be large. They may be removed, when desired, by an opening on the hinder surface of the lid, which is turned outward for the purpose. The contents being scraped out, the cyst does not tend to refill. This small operation is done under local anæsthesia.

PARALYSIS of the lids may occur from many causes, producing a drooping of the upper lid known as ' ptosis ' when the 3rd nerve is affected, or a turning outward of the lower lid, together with inability to close the eye, when the 7th (facial) nerve is injured. (See PARALYSIS.) Paralysis of the muscles that move the eyeballs, causing double vision and an appearance of squinting, is a frequent symptom of chronic nervous diseases, such as multiple sclerosis. It may also be caused by injuries to, and various morbid conditions within, the skull, causing interference with the 3rd, 4th, and 6th cranial nerves, which regulate these muscles.

SPASM of the lid is sometimes a troublesome condition. It may occur either in the form of frequent fluttering of the lid, popularly called 'life' in the eyelid, or there may be a partial closure of the eye, which will not relax. Fluttering of the lid is common and usually has no obvious cause, the person being simply tired or ' run down '.

NYSTAGMUS — involuntary, rapid, rhythmical, usually fine up-and-down or side-to-side flickering movements of the eyeball—is a symptom of many nervous disorders, but, being due to a want of control of the nervous system over the action of the muscles which move the eyeball, is not really an eye disorder. It is observed also in persons who have had bad eyesight from childhood, and in miners.

WATERY EYE, or EPIPHORA (ἐπιφορά), in which the tears overflow on to the face, is a slight but very annoying trouble. It results either from some irritation which causes over-secretion of tears or from some interference with the ducts which should convey the tears away to the lower part of the nose. Sometimes in old people with flabby eyelids, or in cases where

there is a contracting scar on the face, the lower eyelid turns outwards so that the lacrimal puncture is drawn away from the eye and the tears cannot enter it, but collect in the hollow of the lid, and then run over the face. Usually there is a blockage, it may be of the canaliculus by an eyelash or other small object, or, more often, of the duct upon the side of the nose as a result of inflammation. In the latter case a small swelling forms upon the side of the nose, and, if one presses upon this with the finger, tears and mucus ooze back on to the eyeball. If this condition be permitted to continue, not only is there the annoyance of tears constantly trickling down the cheek, but suppuration is very apt to occur in the obstructed duct and to produce a small but unsightly sinus on the side of the nose, which can be closed only with difficulty. The presence of a suppurating tear sac is a source of danger to the eye, because, after any accident to or operation on the eye, virulent organisms are apt to spread from the sac and set up ulceration of the cornea.

Treatment of epiphora.—Where the cause is due to conjunctival irritation, a mild astringent lotion, e.g. tannic acid in the strength of 2 to 5 grains (125 to 300 mg.) to the ounce (28·5 ml.) of water, may be employed. Foreign bodies blocking the lacrimal punctures or canaliculi must be removed. When the lacrimal sac is distended with mucus and pus the canaliculus should be dilated, and a probe passed down the nasal duct into the nose, so as to remove any obstruction and allow free drainage into the nose. Gentle washing out of the sac with a small syringe often helps to restore the parts to a more healthy state. In very bad cases many surgeons advocate removal of the lacrimal sac by operation.

CONJUNCTIVITIS, or inflammation of the conjunctiva, is a very common eye affection. Not in itself a serious condition, it may yet give rise to grave complications, as, for instance, ulceration of the cornea.

A chronic state of redness or congestion of the eye, hardly amounting to conjunctivitis, is common in people whose eyes are much exposed to irritation from dust, smoke, cold winds, etc.

In gouty or plethoric people a similar congested state of the conjunctivæ is often met with. Even the strain upon the eyesight due to errors of refraction may cause the eyes to appear reddened and tender. Cold in the head is often associated with congestion of the conjunctiva, or even with a conjunctivitis more or less severe. In some infectious diseases, and notably in measles, conjunctivitis is a well-recognized symptom. Micro-organisms are the cause of nearly all cases of acute and sub-acute conjunctivitis. This explains why epidemics of conjunctivitis often occur in schools, orphanages, and similar institutions, the infection being readily conveyed on towels, sponges, etc., from one person to another.

Symptoms of conjunctivitis. — The most characteristic sign of conjunctivitis is that the affected eye becomes red or *bloodshot* (Fig. 173). This is due

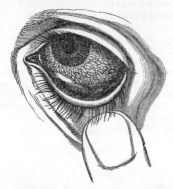

Fig. 173.—Eye showing simple conjunctivitis. Contrast with the more serious condition of iritis shown below. (Miller's *Surgery*.)

to the dilatation of the numerous vessels which ramify over the conjunctival surface. The colour is often described as brick red, and it is specially to be noted that the redness is general, and not most marked round the cornea, as is the case in iritis (Fig. 174). The *swelling* of the conjunctiva in severe cases may be marked, and a thickened fold may form round the edge of the cornea. Hæmorrhages in the conjunctiva from rupture of small blood-vessels are very frequently seen in acute cases, but their presence does not afford any special cause for anxiety. Subjective

symptoms vary greatly in severity. In mild cases there may be merely an

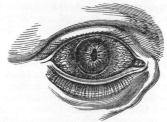

Fig. 174.—Eye showing iritis. (Miller's *Surgery*.)

annoying feeling of roughness or sand in the eyes, while in severe cases there may be very great *pain*. *Photophobia* (dread of light) is a constant symptom. but is not usually so intense as in iritis and keratitis.

The *discharge* from the eyes in the early stages is thin and serous, but

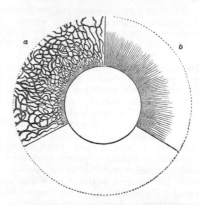

Fig. 175.—Diagram of the white of the eye, illustrating the appearance of the vessels that are congested: *a*, in superficial inflammation (conjunctivitis) ; *b*, in deep-seated inflammation (iritis). (Miller's *Surgery*.)

assumes more or less the character of pus after a few days. The sticky secretions tend to keep the lids gummed together, so that there may be great difficulty in opening the eyes, especially in the morning. Both eyes are usually affected, but very often the disease begins in one eye some days before it attacks the other ; the second eye in such cases becoming infected by accidental contamination with discharges

349

from the inflamed eye. An attack of acute conjunctivitis lasts for one to two weeks.

Varieties of conjunctivitis. — In addition to the type of *simple acute conjunctivitis* above described, there are various more severe forms.

A very severe type of conjunctivitis, *ophthalmia of the new-born* or *ophthalmia neonatorum*, may attack children a few days after birth. It is due to infection with discharges, usually gonorrhœal, from the maternal passages, and may be attended with very severe corneal ulceration, thereby destroying or doing great permanent harm to the eyesight. At one time responsible for practically 50 per cent. of cases of blindness in children, it is now gradually disappearing. In 1966, there were 612 cases in England and Wales. Infection from the genital passages in cases of gonorrhœa may in the adult cause a *gonorrhœal conjunctivitis* of the most severe type.

Trachoma or *granular conjunctivitis* (Egyptian ophthalmia) is a chronic, persistent, and severe form of conjunctivitis very common in the East and in some European countries. It is the greatest single world cause of serious and progressive loss of sight, and it is estimated that there are 400 million victims of the disease. Although one of the oldest known and most widespread of diseases, it was only a few years ago that the cause of it was discovered. It was in 1957 that Chinese workers, in Peking, reported that they had isolated three strains of a virus from the eyes of patients with trachoma. These findings were confirmed by workers in London, and elsewhere. So it is now established that trachoma is a disease due to a known virus. Trachoma is characterized by the appearance of nodules, pale in colour, and often compared to boiled sago grains, situated on the conjunctiva lining the lids (Plate IV). Very often the cornea in its upper half becomes covered with a hazy film containing a network of superficial blood - vessels. In the later stages of the disease there is much scarring and shrinking of the conjunctiva, and the lids are apt to be turned inwards, thereby causing the lashes to rub on the cornea. Loss of transparency of the cornea and

consequent dimness of vision are therefore very frequent results of this disease.

Follicular conjunctivitis is characterized by the presence of numerous small reddish elevations about the size of a pin's head, often arranged in rows on the conjunctiva lining the eyelids. It is often seen in children and young adults, but its effects are not serious, and it must not be confused with trachoma, which it may closely simulate.

Phlyctenular conjunctivitis is a form seen usually in weakly, ill-nourished children. At one time very common, it has now almost disappeared. In this form of the disease little, elevated, yellowish-red, flattened nodules (phlyctenules) are seen on the conjunctiva near the corneal margin. The disease may involve the cornea, producing ulceration and very great irritation and photophobia. It is then known as kerato-conjunctivitis.

Treatment of conjunctivitis. — In *simple cases* all that is needed is to keep the eyes clean by frequent bathing with a mild antiseptic lotion, *e.g.* boracic lotion. The bathing is best done by pledgets of cotton-wool which can be burned after use. A special small flask known as an ' undine ' with a long nozzle may be used to direct a stream of lotion over the eyeball (Fig. 176). A mild antiseptic ointment, *e.g.* boracic

FIG. 176.—Undine for washing eye.

or zinc ointment, should be smeared on the lid margins to prevent gumming of the lids. Bandaging the eye is not good treatment, as it prevents the escape of discharges from the eye, and thus encourages the growth of organisms. Similarly, poultices of bread, porridge, etc., so often employed as a household remedy for inflamed eyes, may do great harm. The eyes may, however, be protected from light and draught by an eye-shade, which at the same time allows access of air.

In *severe cases* of conjunctivitis, and especially in the stage when the secretion is becoming purulent, sulphacetamide or chloramphenicol eye-drops are of the greatest value. Silver salts are also used on account of their astringent and antiseptic actions. Silver nitrate (1-2 per cent.) may be applied gently on a camel-hair brush once or twice. Its application is very painful, and, on this account, an organic salt of silver, *e.g.* protargol, 5 or 10 per cent., or argyrol, 20 per cent., applied twice daily, may be substituted. Thorough and frequent bathing of the eye is of primary importance.

The severe *ophthalmia of infants* can also be treated by these silver salts. These, however, have been almost entirely replaced by penicillin eye-drops, supplemented sometimes in severe cases by sulphonamides given by mouth. In many Maternity Hospitals a few drops of weak nitrate of silver solution ($\frac{1}{2}$ per cent.) are instilled into the eyes of every child at birth. The application should, at all events, be made to the eyes of every infant showing a discharge. This preventive method has greatly diminished the number of these unfortunate cases of destructive inflammation.

Many cases of *subacute conjunctivitis*, accompanied by inflammation of the lid margins, will yield readily to the use of zinc salts. Zinc sulphate lotion (1 to 2 grains (60 to 120 mg.) to the ounce (28·5 ml.) of water) may be instilled thrice daily, and an ointment of zinc oxide rubbed into the lid margins at bedtime.

Trachoma is best treated by the local application to the eye of antibiotics, combined with the administration of sulphonamides by mouth. The usual course of treatment is chlortetracycline, oxytetracycline, or tetracycline, in the form of a 1 per cent. ointment in oily suspensions applied to the eye three times or more daily for two months. In addition, the patient is given a triple sulphonamide mixture by mouth, 40 mg. per kilogram of body weight daily in divided doses, for 20 successive days. This course of sulphonamides is repeated after a ten-day interval.

In *phlyctenular conjunctivitis* the best treatment is the daily application of a 1 per cent. ointment of yellow oxide of mercury. In using the ointment a piece about as large as a small grain of barley should be laid gently within the lower-lid margin, and then the eye, being closed, the lid should be gently massaged so as to rub the ointment over the whole eye. (Similarly, when drops are applied to the eye, the lower lid is pulled down, so as to form a sort of pocket into which the drops are allowed to fall.) Should the cornea be affected, the addition of atropine ($\frac{1}{2}$-1 per cent.) to the ointment will greatly relieve photophobia and promote healing. General treatment is very important in these cases. The diet should be plain and simple, but nourishing, including especially milk, butter, and eggs. Fresh air, sunlight, and the strictest attention to cleanliness are of the greatest importance. Children with this affection tend to suffer from nasal catarrh and overgrowth of the tonsils and adenoid tissue of the nasopharynx. Proper treatment of these affections will do much to improve the general health and expedite the cure of the ocular troubles. (*See* NOSE DISEASES.)

KERATITIS, or INFLAMMATION OF THE CORNEA ($\kappa\acute{\epsilon}\rho\alpha\varsigma$, ' horn '), is due to several causes. It may be caused by an abrasion of the cornea, or it may be caused by a burn from molten metal, acids or alkalis. Such burning accidents are not uncommon in certain industries, such as the heavy metal industries and the chemical industry. If the eye is injured by acids, alkalis, or irritant gases it must be irrigated immediately with a copious gentle stream of water or by blinking under water. This must be continued for up to 20 minutes depending on the severity of the injury. If the eye is still painful after irrigation, a few drops of castor oil may be put into the outer corner of the eye, which is then covered lightly with a sterile pad or bandage. The patient is then sent for immediate further medical attention.

Acute infection of the cornea tends

Fig. 177.—Eye showing corneal opacity before corneal grafting.

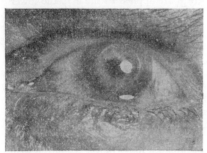

Fig. 178.—Same eye after successful corneal grafting, showing clear cornea.

to lead to corneal ulcer (*q.v.*). Chronic keratitis occurs in association with tuberculosis, syphilis, and leprosy. Perhaps the best known of these is syphilitic interstitial keratitis. It is nearly always a manifestation of inherited syphilis, and comes on between the ages of seven and twenty years. The cornea gets dull and hazy, the sight being a good deal interfered with, and at the same time there are pain and intolerance of light. This disorder lasts usually four to six months, or longer, both eyes being affected, and it is almost always accompanied by iritis, which renders it still more serious. The treatment generally adopted is the use of atropine drops and the wearing of dark glasses. If the condition is syphilitic the appropriate anti-syphilitic treatment must be given. The chief danger of the disorder is that it leaves behind it opaque patches in the cornea, or changes in the choroid membrane, which interfere with vision or even obscure it altogether.

One dramatic advance in treatment has been the grafting of a new cornea (Figs. 177, 178) in place of one that is

so opaque by disease as to hinder vision (*see* CORNEAL GRAFTING).

ULCER of the cornea arises from various causes, several of which have been mentioned. Two chief dangers attend an ulcer here, one being the fact that a white scar, which interferes with vision, especially if the ulcer has been severe, is certain to follow the ulcer ; the other danger being that of perforation of the cornea (which is only about one millimetre in thickness), followed by more or less destruction of the eye.

Treatment of corneal ulcer.—The great essential is to keep the eye clean. Hence bandages, poultices, and such applications are in most cases likely to be harmful. Weak corrosive sublimate lotion (1-6000), or boracic or argyrol lotion, may be used to bathe the eye, and vaseline may be freely smeared on the lid margins. Atropine is used to combat the iritis which always attends severe ulceration of the cornea. If the ulcer is spreading, various methods are adopted to check it, such as application of a cautery to the spreading margin, the division of the ulcer and opening up of the anterior chamber by a fine knife, etc. A corneal ulcer of the severe spreading kind may, if not checked, destroy the cornea in a few days, and with it all hope of useful vision in that eye. Hence the necessity for prompt and efficient treatment. In severe cases penicillin is of value.

XEROPHTHALMIA is the term given to a condition in children characterized by inflammation of the cornea and eyelids, which leads to blindness unless treated in time. It is due to a deficiency of vitamin A in the diet, and is cured, not by local applications, but by giving vitamin A concentrates or food rich in this vitamin—milk, eggs, butter, carrots.

ARCUS SENILIS is the name given to a white ring which forms round the edge of the cornea with advancing years. (*See* AGE, NATURAL CHANGES IN.)

SCLERITIS, or ' HOT-EYE ', is a not uncommon trouble in persons who have a markedly gouty or rheumatic constitution. It consists of an inflammation of the sclerotic coat accompanied by patches of dusky redness over the white of the eye, pain, and watering of the eye. The condition subsides when protective glasses are worn, and the constitutional condition is treated ; but it is very obstinate to cure and liable to recur. In young persons it is often tuberculous.

BLACK-EYE is an effusion of blood under the loose skin over and round the lids, due to a blow. Within the first few hours of a blow on the eye, much may be done to diminish the blackness by a pad of linen wrung out of cold water, or of Goulard's water, and tightly bound on by a handkerchief passing round the head. A time-honoured pad is a raw beef-steak, which is moist and cold. After the first day absorption may be hastened by gentle massage and the bruise may be made less apparent by the application of flesh-coloured grease paint.

WOUNDS OF THE EYE. — The eyebrow, cheek, nose, and even the eyelids are often wounded, but seldom the eye itself, on account of the efficient protection afforded to it by these parts. The danger of a wound to the eye consists, not so much in the wounding of any important structure, which will heal with great rapidity, as in the introduction of organisms which may set up inflammation. The most dangerous position for a wound is in the ciliary region or iris, that is, just outside the margin of the cornea (see EYE), from whence a destructive inflammation not only of the wounded eye but also of the other, causing total blindness, is apt to be set up. (See IRITIS.) Metallic particles which penetrate the eye should always, if possible, be removed, because the fluids of the eye act upon them to form irritating chemical compounds. Most eye hospitals are provided with a powerful electro - magnet, which will draw small particles of iron or steel from the deeper part of the eye into the anterior chamber, where they can be seen by the operator and successfully removed. Cinders or dust may lodge behind one of the lids or may be embedded in the cornea and cause much pain. In this case the eye should not be rubbed, but a handkerchief may be gently pressed against it. The lids should be drawn gently apart, and if the body be seen it should be wiped off the eye with a wet camel-hair brush or clean wet rag. If it cannot be seen, the eyelids should be turned outwards and the inner surface of each lid examined. The lower lid is simply pulled downwards. To examine the upper lid, the person is told to look steadily downwards, a flat pencil, or penholder, or a match is laid horizontally along the centre of the lid, and the lid, being grasped by the eyelashes between the finger and thumb of the person who is looking for the foreign body, is gently and quite painlessly folded upwards over the pencil, etc. (Fig. 179). The irritating body is then

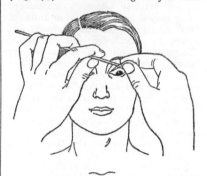

FIG. 179.—Method of turning out the upper eyelid in order to examine its inner surface and the upper part of the ball for cinders, etc.

brushed away, and the lid turned down again. If a piece of lime has got upon the eye it should be sponged with vinegar and water, and if acid has got into the eye it should be copiously bathed with baking-soda in water.

EYE STRAIN (see VISION).

F

FACE is that part of the head extending from the eyebrows to the chin. It is supported by 14 bones, consisting of 2 nasal bones, 2 superior maxillary bones which carry the upper teeth, 2 lacrimal bones, 2 malar bones, 2 palate bones, 2 inferior turbinated bones at the sides of the nose, the vomer, forming a partition between the nostrils, and the inferior maxillary bone carrying the lower teeth. The lower jaw forms a joint of hinge-shape with the temporal bones of the skull, whilst the other bones of the face are firmly fixed together by sutures. The face in man is relatively small, as compared with that in lower animals, on account of the development of the cranium containing the brain. For the same reason, the face has an almost vertical direction instead of being sloped backwards as in animals. This facial angle has formed one means of classifying different races. The angle, which is measured by drawing one line from the centre of the forehead to the projecting part of the upper jaw and another line from the lower margin of the ear to the base of the nasal opening, is in Negroid races an acute angle, in most European races almost a right angle, while in the ancient Greek statues the face has an overhanging character.

The general character of the features depends chiefly upon the presence of air spaces in the frontal bone, situated immediately behind the eyebrows and in the upper jaw-bones. The varying expressions which are connected with the emotions and the general expression denoting character are chiefly due to the action of numerous thin muscles situated around the openings of the eyes, nose, and mouth. (*See* Muscle.) These are controlled by the 7th cranial nerve, which springs from the hinder part of the brain, passes through the skull to the ear, and, emerging immediately below the latter, passes forward on to the face round the edge of the lower jaw. In this position it is very liable to be wounded or to be injured by such conditions as cold, then giving rise to a flat and expressionless appearance of one side

of the face, known as *Bell's Palsy* or *facial paralysis*. The sensory nerve of the face is the 5th nerve, which originates from the neighbouring part of the brain and within the skull divides into three portions called respectively ophthalmic, maxillary, and mandibular divisions. Each of these sends branches on to the face through a notch that can be felt near the inner end of the eyebrow, through an opening immediately beneath the eye, and through another opening near the middle of the chin. On their way to the face these nerves supply the parts about the eye, the teeth, and the muscles which move the lower jaw in chewing. The various parts of this nerve are subject to a particularly painful form of neuralgia, known sometimes as ' tic douloureux ' (*see* Neuralgia).

The face is liable to certain deformities, of which hare-lip and cleft palate are the principal (*see* Palate, Malformations of). The skin of the face, which has an unusually free blood supply, bleeds with great freedom when wounded, but, for the same reason, wounds heal with special rapidity and freedom from suppuration. The contraction of scars after severe injuries, such as burns, sometimes leads to marked deformity of the eyelids, mouth, and nose. The skin condition known as acne (*see* Acne) is very common in young persons about the chin and brow, disappearing as age advances. Boils, carbuncles, and other infectious conditions frequently occur on the face, and, when situated about the upper lip, present a considerable degree of danger from the liability of the infection to spread to the interior of the head. The tuberculous disease known as lupus is more frequent on the face than in any other situation and may lead to unsightly ulceration and scarring. Certain simple tumours, particularly sebaceous cysts and nævi or birth marks, very commonly affect the skin in this region, and cancer, in the form of epithelioma, is not uncommon in the later stages of life about the margins of the lip, nostril, or eyelid. This is also one of the commonest sites of the slow-growing form of cancer known as rodent ulcer.

FACIAL NERVE is the seventh cranial nerve, and supplies the muscles of expression in the face, being purely a motor nerve. It enters the face immediately below the ear after splitting up into several branches (see BELL'S PARALYSIS).

FACIES is a term applied to the expression or appearance of the face, which often gives indications of the presence of disease in other parts of the body. Thus the *abdominal facies* is a pinched, anxious expression associated with severe disease in the abdomen. The *cardiac facies* is a condition present in some valvular defects of the heart, showing bright purplish cheeks and lips, with a sallow hue of the rest of the face. The *typhoid facies* is a vacant, bewildered, and apathetic expression seen in typhoid fever and other debilitating diseases. The *Hippocratic facies* is a cast of countenance originally described by Hippocrates, in which the face is drawn, pinched, and livid, indicating approaching death.

FÆCES (*fæx*, dregs) is another name for the stools. (*See* CONSTIPATION, DIARRHŒA, STOOLS.)

FAINTING, or SYNCOPE, is a temporary loss of consciousness.

Causes.—The manner in which the loss of consciousness is produced appears to be that temporarily there is an inadequate supply of blood to the brain. If the person who threatens to faint lies down, or, still better, if she sits and then bends forward so as to bring the head below the knees, the faint is averted. Fainting may occur as part of the general muscular relaxation which takes place in a hot bath. Powerful emotion, generally of a sorrowful nature, but sometimes even great joy, is a common cause. Extreme pain, such as that due to the crushing of a limb, and shocks to the nervous system, such as a blow on the head or on the abdomen, are apt to cause fainting, or even the more serious condition known as ' shock '. It is very liable to occur on first getting up after a prolonged period of illness with confinement to bed. Another not uncommon cause, particulary in adolescents and young adults, is pro longed standing, *e.g.* on the parade ground. Disgusting smells and sights, breathing of bad air, and general exhaustion are also causes. As a rule, a combination of these causes is necessary, except in hysterical persons, and persons weak from some illness, who are specially liable to faints. Certain drugs, such as tobacco or alcohol, when taken in large amount, produce syncope. Occasionally it may be due to heart disease.

Symptoms are well known. There are certain warning symptoms, such as pallor, feebleness of the pulse, a sinking feeling, and a dullness of sight and hearing. When the faint has occurred, the person lies still, breathing very faintly, with feeble pulse, pallid complexion, and often perspiration standing in drops on the face.

The faint, as a rule, lasts only a few seconds or minutes, but it may last for hours, and hysterical persons may pass from one faint, only to fall into another several times.

Treatment.—The faint may often be prevented by attending to the cause, as stated above. Sitting down and bending forwards so as to bring the head on a level with the knees, or taking rapid gulps of cold water, often is enough to prevent a threatened faint. The person in a faint should be laid flat on the back, and care should be taken that breathing is unimpeded. If care be not taken to leave the fainting person lying flat, death may ensue, but if this be attended to, nothing more is usually necessary. Stimulants may be applied to the skin in the form of cold compresses on the head, slapping of the hands, pinching of the cheeks ; or to the nose in the form of smelling-salts or eau-de-Cologne, or the pungent fumes of burnt feathers. After recovery has taken place from the faint the tendency to its recurrence may be prevented by administration of some stimulant such as sal volatile or brandy.

FALLING SICKNESS is an old name for epilepsy. (*See* EPILEPSY.)

FALLOPIAN TUBES are tubes, one on each side, which are attached at one end to the womb, and have the other unattached but lying close to the ovary. Each is between 4 and 5 inches (10 and 12·5 cm.) long, large at the end next the ovary, but communicating with the womb by an opening which admits only a bristle. These tubes conduct the ova from the ovaries to the interior of the womb.

FALSE MEMBRANE is the name given to the deposit which forms upon the walls of the air passages in cases of diphtheria. It consists partly of fibrin derived from the blood, partly of the destroyed surface of the mucous membrane upon which it rests, and it contains bacteria in enormous numbers. If it be removed, it leaves a raw and bleeding surface upon which new membrane quickly forms.

FANGO is the name of a kind of mud, derived from thermal springs at Battaglio in Italy, which is applied warm to gouty and rheumatic joints.

FARADISM (*see* ELECTRICITY IN MEDICINE).

FARCY is another name for glanders. (*See* GLANDERS.)

FARINACEOUS FOODS (*farina*, meal) are those derived from cereals (*q.v.*).

FARMER'S LUNG is a form of pneumoconiosis (*q.v.*) caused by the inhalation of dust from mouldy hay or straw.

FASCIA is the name applied to sheets or bands of fibrous tissue which enclose and connect the muscles.

FASTIGIUM means the highest temperature reached in a feverish state.

FASTING means the abstention from, or deprivation of, food and drink sufficient to supply the waste resulting from the bodily activity and to maintain the body temperature.

The practice, which some persons carry out, of fasting one day a week or even of changing to a light diet at stated intervals, in the interests of health or of religion, has much to commend it in certain cases, because it gives the digestive organs a periodic rest.

If **food and drink be entirely sus-**

pended, two results quickly follow: the body becomes thinner and lighter as it draws upon its stored-up nourishment, and also the temperature gradually falls. If water be taken, the process of using up the fat and muscles in order to maintain the activity of the heart, lungs, and other vital organs, proceeds to an extreme extent, and the body grows very much emaciated before death. If water be withheld, death results much sooner, and the sufferings are great. If the body be well protected by clothes and blankets, the loss of heat is slower, and life is prolonged beyond the time that it lasts if the fasting person be poorly clad or exposed to severe cold, as in the case of Arctic explorers. It follows, too, that a person fasting and doing no work can survive very much better than one who is compelled at the same time to put forth great exertions, and so use up more of the bodily store of food. Persons are subjected to the worst combination then, when they are not only deprived of food, but have also a poor supply of water, are exposed to severe cold, and must make great muscular efforts.

Under the last - named conditions life could not be prolonged more than two or three days. But in the case of miners imprisoned by a fall of earth or flooding in a mine, and well supplied with water, life and health may be prolonged without any food for over a week. In the case of five miners imprisoned in Redding Pit, Scotland, in September 1923, they were brought up little the worse after being deprived of food for 214 hours.

Dogs may be kept alive with nothing but drinking-water for considerable periods. One case is on record of a dog which was starved for 117 days. At the end of this period it had lost 63 per cent. of its weight but was fairly active. Human beings can also survive long fasts; one of the longest on record, in which the individual survived, being that of Merlotte of Paris, who fasted for fifty days. One of the most historic fasts of modern times is that of Terence McSweeney, the Mayor of Cork, who in 1920 went on hunger strike and died 74 days later.

The professional fasters who profess to subsist entirely without food for a month or six weeks probably have small supplies administered to them in their drinking-water, or by other surreptitious means.

After prolonged fasting the return to food should be gradual, and no heavy meal should be taken for a day or two.

FAT as a food has more energy-producing power weight for weight than any other food. Animal fat is a mixture in varying proportions of stearic, palmitic, and oleic acids combined with glycerin. Butter contains about 80 per cent. of fat, ordinary cream contains 20 per cent. fat, and rich cream 40 per cent., whilst olive oil is practically a pure form of fat. Fat requires, when taken to a large extent in the diet, to be combined with a certain proportion of either carbohydrate or protein in order that it may be completely consumed, otherwise harmful products, known as ketones, are apt to be formed in the blood. Each gramme of fat has an energy-producing equivalent of 9·3 calories.

From the medical point of view, fats are divided into saturated fats, that is, animal fats and dairy produce, and unsaturated fats which include vegetable oils from soya bean, maize and sunflower, and marine oils from fish (*e.g.* cod-liver oil). (*See* ADIPOSE TISSUE, CORPULENCE, LIPID.)

FATIGUE.—Fatigue is brought about in two ways. In the first place muscles become fatigued by the lactic acid accumulating in them as the result of their activity. For the removal of lactic acid in the recovery phase of muscular contraction oxygen is needed. If the supply of oxygen is not plentiful enough, or cannot 'keep pace' with the work the muscle is doing, then lactic acid accumulates and fatigue results. There is also a nervous element in muscular fatigue : it is diminished by stimulation of the sympathetic nervous system.

Industrial workers. — Many factors enter into the maintenance of efficiency and the avoidance of fatigue, mental and physical. Intensity and direction of illumination, ventilation, temperature and humidity of the air, adequate diet, posture at work, rest pauses, monotony, and, above all, hours of work are among some of these factors. There is a level beyond which the human machine can no longer produce work satisfactorily. If this is exceeded it is shown by a reduction in the quantity and quality of the work done. If work is done under conditions of fatigue, damage to health results and accidents may occur. The shortening of unduly long hours of labour under improved hygienic conditions is followed by increased productive efficiency. During night-work productive efficiency is much less than during the day.

Children are especially liable to suffer from over-pressure at work. This applies especially to children of nervous temperament, those who are anæmic or badly fed, those who are rapidly growing, and those who have too little sleep and recreation or have various physical defects in sight, hearing, etc. The time devoted to a lesson in any particular subject should not exceed three-quarters of an hour, and there should be an appropriate variation of subjects, sufficient intervals for rest, recreation, physical exercise and food. Fresh air and quiet in the classroom diminish fatigue. Home work should not be given to children under the age of nine years, and for several years after that age it should not take longer than one hour. The teachers should be carefully on the look-out for imperfections of vision and hearing which cause strain and brain fatigue. (*See* CHILDREN, PECULIARITIES OF, *and* SCHOOL CHILDREN.)

FAT NECROSIS.—In injury to, or inflammation of, the pancreas the fat-splitting enzyme in it may escape into the abdominal cavity, causing death of fat-containing cells.

FATTY DEGENERATION.—As a result of anæmia, interference with blood or nerve supply, or because of the action of various poisons, body cells may undergo abnormal changes accompanied by the appearance in their substance of fat droplets.

FAUCES (*fauces*) is the name given to the somewhat narrowed opening between the mouth and throat. It is bounded above by the soft palate, below by the tongue, and on either side by the tonsil. In front of, and behind, the tonsil are two ridges of mucous membrane, the anterior and posterior pillars of the fauces.

FAVISM is a fulminating hæmolytic anæmia, attacks of which occur within an hour or two of eating broad beans (*Vicia faba*) or inhaling their pollen. It is a hereditary disease which is largely confined to inhabitants of the Mediterranean littoral.

FAVUS (*favus*, a honeycomb) is another name for honeycomb ringworm. (*See* Ringworm.)

FEBRICULA (*febricula*) means a little fever. The term—at one time popular in medical parlance to describe a fever of short duration, the cause of which was obscure—is seldom used now.

FEBRIFUGES (*febris*, a fever ; *fugo*, I drive away), or antipyretics, are remedies employed to reduce the temperature of the body when it has been raised above that found in health (*see* Baths, Cold, Uses of, *and* Fever). In addition to the application of cold, some of the chief febrifuges are aspirin, quinine, and salicylate of soda. (*See also under each of these headings*.)

FEEBLE-MINDEDNESS (*see* Mental Defectiveness).

FEEDING (*see* Cereals, Diet, Digestion, Infant Feeding, *and* Nitrogenous Foods). The manner and times of administering food are matters of considerable importance in illness. In health appetite forms the usual guide to the amount of food and to meal-times. Most persons in health take four meals in the course of the day, one meal being much larger than any of the others and taken either in the middle of the day or in the evening. During the course of a disease or in convalescence, when the digestive powers are weak and a large meal cannot be borne, it is usually found more suitable to feed the patient in

358

small amounts given at frequent intervals. The nature of the food must be such that it is very readily digested and the food is usually fluid. Except in certain special cases, milk is the ideal food for this purpose, supplemented by drinks containing glucose. The quantity of milk given at one time is 6 to 8 ounces (170 to 230 ml.). If milk tends to produuce nasea or vomiting, it may be diluted with equal parts of water and given warm. The total amount of milk given in twenty-four hours should be 2 to 3 pints (1 to 2 litres). Glucose is given in preference to ordinary sugar (*i.e.* sucrose) because it is not so sweet, and therefore it is possible to give larger amounts without making the dish too sweet. In order to produce variety, and at the same time to ensure an adequate amount of vitamin C, the glucose drinks should be flavoured with fresh fruit juice, *e.g.* orange or lemon. Milk puddings and eggs should be added to the diet as soon as possible. Beef tea, although it has no energy value, adds variety to the invalid diet, as do jellies. Small feeds should be given : two-hourly during the day, and during the night if the patient is awake.

It is sometimes convenient to feed the patient by means of a spoon, but, as a rule, the patient's head being raised by the nurse's arm passed beneath the pillow, the spout of a feeding - cup

Fig. 180.—Two forms of feeding-cup. The cup on the left is used for patients who are further advanced in convalescence, and who are partly raised in bed.

is introduced into his mouth and the patient is thus able to drink without spilling the fluid. A form of glass from which the patient can drink more naturally consists of a tumbler with an elongated lip on one side, and this is often preferable. Still another method in which the patient may be fed with thin fluids is through a straw or piece of narrow india-rubber tubing. In this case the straw must be thrown away after use and the rubber tubing carefully boiled before being used again.

Food may be peptonized for administration to invalids. (*See* Peptonized Foods; *see also* Milk, and for preparation of fluid foods for invalids, *see* Albumin Water, Barley Water, Beef-tea, Gruel, Nitrogenous Foods, Rice Water, Toast Water.)

FEHLING'S TEST for glycosuria (*see* Urine).

FEMUR is the bone of the thigh, and is the longest and strongest bone in the body. As the upper end of the femur is set at an angle of about 120 degrees to the rest of the bone, and since the weight of the body is entirely borne by the two femora, fracture of one of these bones close to its upper end is a common accident in old people, whose bones are becoming brittle. The femur fits, at its upper end, into the acetabulum of the pelvis, forming the hipjoint, and, at its lower end, meets the tibia and patella in the knee-joint.

FENESTRATION (φαίνειν, to show). The fenestration operation, whereby a new opening is made into the labyrinth of the ear, is one of the greatest advances in ear surgery of recent years. It has proved most valuable in restoring hearing to patients with otosclerosis (*q.v.*), particularly in young people with this disease.

FENFLURAMINE is one of the more recent anorexiant drugs (*q.v.*), introduced to aid the slimming process by suppressing or reducing appetite. Although less likely to become a drug of addiction than some of the other anorexiant drugs, it is not without its risks and must only be used under skilled medical supervision.

FENNEL is the seed-like fruit of the *Fœniculum vulgare* used as a carminative, *i.e.* to relieve griping, flatulence,

and distension of the stomach. Fennel water used to be a popular remedy for griping.

FERMENTS are substances which produce chemical changes in other bodies while remaining unchanged themselves.

FERN-ROOT, or Filix Mas, is a remedy used for the expulsion of tapeworms. An extract is made from the root of the common male fern (*Aspidium filix mas*). It is taken in the following manner. After the person who harbours the tapeworm has taken a dose of Epsom salts in the morning, he subsists on a fluid diet for 48 hours. Then at 6 A.M. he is given 30 minims (2 ml.) of a fresh extract of filix mas in a capsule, or as an emulsion. This dose is repeated at 6.30 A.M. and 7 A.M. At 8.30 A.M. he is given 2 ounces (60 ml.) of saturated sodium sulphate solution. If the head of the tapeworm has not been passed by 10 A.M., a soap-and-water enema is given. The patient is given an ordinary meal as soon as the head has been passed, or by 10.30 A.M. in any case.

FERRUM is the Latin name for iron.

FESTER is a popular term used to mean any collection or formation of pus. It is applied to both abscesses and ulcers (*see* Abscess, Ulcer, Whitlow).

FESTINATION is the term applied to the involuntary quickening of gait seen in some nervous diseases, especially in Paralysis agitans and Parkinsonism (*q.v.*)

FEVER (*ferveo*, I burn). This term, which may be defined as a condition of the body characterized by an increase in temperature, is used in medicine with a wide application. Fever is one of the most common accompaniments of diseases in general, and serves to make the distinction between *febrile* and *non-febrile* ailments.

Causes.—In many cases the fever must be regarded as only secondary to, and symptomatic of, the disordered state with which it is found associated. For example, a certain amount of fever may arise in consequence of some nervous shock. But there is a large class of diseases in which fever is the predominant factor, and which arise from the formation in the system of something of the nature of a poison (toxin), upon which all the symptoms depend. To such diseases, the term primary or specific fevers is applied, and, as examples, may be mentioned typhoid fever, scarlet fever, diphtheria. These diseases depend on the growth of bacteria in the blood or tissues of the body, the toxins being formed by the activity of these organisms.

In considering the general subject of fever, regard must be had in particular to the two main features of the febrile process, viz. the abnormal elevation of temperature, and the changes affecting the tissues of the body in reference thereto.

The average temperature of the body in health ranges between 98·4° and 99·5° F. (36·9° and 37·5° C.) It is liable to slight variations from such causes as the ingestion of food, the amount of exercise, and the temperature of the surrounding atmosphere. There are, moreover, certain appreciable daily variations, the lowest temperature being between the hours of 1.30 A.M. and 7 A.M., and the highest between 4 P.M. and 9 P.M., with trifling fluctuations during these periods. (See TEMPERATURE.)

The development and maintenance of heat within the body is generally regarded as depending on the destructive oxidation of all its tissues, consequent on the changes continually taking place in the processes of nutrition. In health this constant tissue disintegration is exactly counterbalanced by the introduction of food, whilst the uniform normal temperature is maintained by the due adjustment of the heat thus developed, and of the processes of exhalation and cooling which take place, especially from the lungs and skin. In the febrile state this relationship is no longer preserved, the tissue waste being greatly in excess of the food supply, while the so-called 'law of temperature' is in abeyance. In this condition the body wastes rapidly, the loss to the

360

system being chiefly in the form of nitrogen compounds (urea, etc.). In the early stage of fever a patient excretes about three times the amount of urea that he would excrete on the same diet if he were in health—the difference being that in the latter condition he discharges a quantity of nitrogen equal to that taken in with the food, whilst in the fevered state he wastes the store of nitrogen contained in the tissues and the blood. The amount of fever is estimated by the degree of elevation of the temperature above the normal standard. When it reaches as high a point as 106° F. (41·1° C.) the term 'hyperpyrexia' (excessive fever) is applied, and is regarded as indicating a condition of danger; while, if it exceeds 107° or 108° F. (41·7° or 42·2° C.) for any length of time, death almost always results. Occasionally the temperature may attain the elevation of 110° to 112° F. (43·3° to 44·4° C.) prior to the fatal issue.

Symptoms.—The onset of a fever is usually marked by a 'rigor' or shivering, which may exist only as a slight but persistent feeling of chilliness, or, on the other hand, be of a violent character, and, as occasionally happens with children, find expression in the form of well-marked convulsions. Although termed the *cold stage* of fever, in this condition the temperature of the body is really increased. There are, besides, various accompanying feelings of illness, such as pain in the back, headache, sickness, thirst, and great lassitude. In all cases of febrile complaints it is of importance for the physician to note the first occurrence of shivering, which in general fixes the beginning of the attack. This stage is soon followed by the full development of the febrile condition, the *hot stage*. The skin now feels hot and dry, and the temperature, always elevated above the normal standard, will often be found to show daily variations corresponding to those observed in health—namely, a rise toward evening, and a fall in the morning. There is a relative increase in the rate of the pulse and quickness of breathing. The tongue is dry and furred; the thirst is intense, while the appetite is gone; the urine is scanty, of high specific gravity, containing a large quantity of solid matter, particularly urea, the excretion of which is, as already stated, remarkably increased in fever ; while, on the other hand, certain of the saline ingredients, such as chlorides, are often diminished. The bowels are in general constipated, but they may be relaxed, especially if the gut is the primary site of infection, as in typhoid fever. The nervous system participates in the general disturbance, and sleeplessness and disquietude are common accompaniments, and there may be delirium. The wasting of the muscles, and corresponding loss of strength, may be marked, and continue even although considerable quantities of nutriment may be taken.

The decline of the fever takes place either by the occurrence of a *crisis* (Fig. 181), *i.e.* a sudden termination of the symptoms, often accompanied with

of extreme prostration, associated with low delirium or coma). In other cases death occurs suddenly after slight exertion, as a result of the additional strain on the heart.

Certain well-marked types of fever are recognized. The term *continued fever* is applied to those forms in which the febrile temperature persists for a more or less definite period, uninterrupted by any distinct intermission till the crisis is reached. To this type belong typhus and typhoid fevers, and the eruptive fevers or exanthemata, viz. smallpox, measles, and scarlet fever. *Relapsing fever* is a form of continued fever, the chief characteristic of which is the occurrence in about a week after the crisis of a distinct relapse and repetition of all the symptoms. Occasionally second and third relapses take place.

The term *remittent* is applied to those

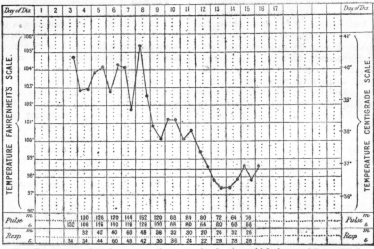

Fig. 181.—Temperature chart from a case of pneumonia, showing a high degree of fever with increased pulse and respiration. The heavy line at 98·4 shows the level of the normal temperature. Note the rapid fall in temperature, *i.e.* by crisis.

some discharge from the body, such as profuse perspiration, copious flow of thick urine, and occasionally diarrhœa, or by a more gradual subsidence of the temperature, technically termed a *lysis*. If death ensues, this is due to failure of the vital centres in the brain or of the heart, as a result of either the infection or hyperpyrexia. Such terminal failure may be gradual, the patient passing into what is sometimes known as the *typhoid state* (a condition

forms of fever the course of which is interrupted by a short, usually daily, diminution of the fever, followed by a recurrence of all the symptoms. Such fevers are chiefly met in tropical climates, but occasionally continued fevers assume this form, particularly in children. The condition known as *hectic fever*, which occurs in the course of wasting diseases, is markedly remittent in its course.

In *intermittent fever* there is a distinct

periodic subsidence of the symptoms, which, according to its duration, characterizes the variety as *quotidian* (where the paroxysm recurs in twenty-four hours), *tertian* (in forty-eight hours), *quartan* (in seventy-two hours). Hectic fever is also not infrequently of the intermittent type.

The term *malignant* is employed to describe forms of fever in which the blood appears to undergo rapid deteriorating changes, sometimes designated blood-poisoning. Yellow fever may be said to belong to this category, and the continued fevers, more especially typhus and the exanthemata, occasionally assume a malignant form from the beginning. The chief forms of fever will be found described in detail under separate headings.

Treatment.—Fever is a symptom, and the correct treatment is therefore that of the underlying condition. Occasionally, however, it is also necessary to try and reduce the temperature by more direct methods. For this latter purpose it will be sufficient to refer to two methods, namely, the external application of cold and the administration of antipyretic remedies or febrifuges. The former of these methods is accomplished by means of baths, in which the patient is placed, the water being somewhat below the febrile temperature and gradually cooled down by the addition of cold water till a temperature of from 60° to 70° F. (15·5° to 21° C.) is reached. This process, when continued for only a short time and frequently repeated, yields most valuable results in many instances of high temperature, *e.g.* in enteric fever. The relief to the patient is remarkable, the body rapidly parting with its heat, and the effect usually continues for hours. The cooler the bath the longer the effect lasts. Sponging with cold water and the wet pack are other methods frequently used to reduce temperature and exert a soothing influence (*see* COLD, USES OF.)

Certain drugs possess the power of reducing the temperature by their action on the heat-regulating centres in the brain, thereby causing an increased loss of heat through dilatation of the blood-vessels in the skin. These drugs include sodium salicylate, aspirin,

362

phenacetin, quinine, and Dover's powder.

FIBRILLATION is a term applied to rapid contraction or tremor of muscles, especially to a form of abnormal action of the heart muscle in which individual bundles of fibres take up independent action. It is believed to be due to a state of excessive excitability in the muscle associated with the stretching which occurs in dilatation of the heart. Fibrillation is distinguished as atrial or ventricular, according as the muscle of the atria or of the ventricles is affected. As a result, the heart-beats and the pulse become extremely irregular both as regards time and force. The condition of atrial fibrillation is responsible for more than half of all marked and persistent cases of irregular pulse.

FIBRIN is a substance formed in the blood as it clots. Its formation indeed causes clotting. The substance is produced in threads. After the threads have formed a close meshwork through the blood, they contract, and produce a dense felted mass. The substance is formed not only from shed blood but also from lymph which exudes from the lymph-vessels. Thus fibrin is found in all inflammatory conditions within serous cavities like the pleura, peritoneum, and pericardium, and forms a thick coat upon the surface of the inflamed membranes. It is also found in inflamed joints, in the lung as a result of pneumonia, etc. (*See* COAGULATION.) (Plate III.)

FIBRIN FOAM is one of a series of absorbable hæmostatics which have recently been introduced into surgical use. A hæmostatic is a preparation which arrests bleeding, and the great advantage of an absorbable hæmostatic is that it produces no irritation in the tissues into which it is introduced and that it does not need to be removed after the bleeding is arrested, but is gradually absorbed by the tissues. Fibrin foam is a spongy material which is soaked in a solution of thrombin immediately before use. Other absorbable hæmostatics now in use include oxidized cellulose (oxycellulose) which is prepared as a gauze, and calcium alginate (derived from seaweed) which is prepared as a gauze and as wool. These absorbable hæmostatics, which constitute a great advance in surgery, are of particular value in operations on the brain and in operations on blood-vessels and nerves.

FIBRINOGEN is the soluble protein in the blood which is the precursor of fibrin (*q.v.*), the substance in blood-clot.

FIBROCYSTIC DISEASE OF THE PANCREAS, or MUCOVISCIDOSIS, is a familial disease, with an incidence of about 1 per 600 to 1000 births. It is a disorder of the mucus-secreting glands of the lungs, the pancreas, the mouth, and the gastro-intestinal tract, as well as the sweat glands of the skin. It is characterized by failure to gain weight in spite of a good appetite, repeated attacks of bronchitis, and the passage of loose, foul-smelling and slimy stools.

FIBROID is a term sometimes applied to tumours of the womb consisting partly of muscular and partly of fibrous tissue. (*See* UTERUS, DISEASES OF.)

FIBROID PHTHISIS is a chronic form of pulmonary tuberculosis. (*See* TUBERCULOSIS.)

FIBROMA is a tumour consisting of fibrous tissue. (*See* TUMOURS.)

FIBROSIS means the formation of fibrous or scar tissue, which is usually due to either infection or deficient blood supply.

FIBROSITIS is another name for muscular rheumatism. (*See* RHEUMATISM.)

FIBROUS TISSUE is one of the most abundant tissues throughout the body. White fibrous tissue consists of fibres of a substance known as 'collagen', which yields gelatine on being boiled. Between these fibres lie flattened or star-shaped cells, by which the fibres are produced. The fibres, like the cells, are of microscopic size, and are grouped into bundles which are held together by other fibres running round them. Yellow fibrous tissue is a rarer form, and consists of bundles of long yellow fibres, formed from a substance known as 'elastin'. White fibrous tissue is very unyielding and forms sinews, ligaments, the material which binds

muscle fibres together, the substance of the true skin, etc. It is also the tissue which is laid down in the repair of wounds, or as a result of inflammation, and so forms the tissue composing a scar. It has the property of contract-

FIG. 182.—White fibrous tissue. Magnified 350 times. (From Gray's *Anatomy*. Longmans, Green & Co. Ltd.)

ing and becoming denser as time goes on, and hence the puckering seen in scars, and the contraction resulting from burns and inflammations. Yellow fibrous tissue is highly elastic, and so is found in the walls of arteries, and in ligaments, like that on the back of the neck, which are often put upon the stretch. (*See also* ADHESIONS, SCAR, WOUNDS.)

FIBULA is the slender bone upon the outer side of the leg.

FILARIASIS (*filum,* a thread) is the name given to a group of tropical diseases in which minute Nematode worms, called filariæ, are found in the blood (Plate XIII). Among the diseases connected with the presence of these worms are chyluria and elephantiasis (*see* PARASITES).

FILTERS (*see* WATER SUPPLY).

FINGERS consist of three bones called 'phalanges' united by hinge-joints and strong ligaments. The thumb, like the great toe, differs from the others in having only two bones.

These are bent or flexed, and straightened or extended by powerful sinews, two in front and two behind, which are brought into action by the contraction of muscles in the forearm. The sinews are enveloped in complicated synovial sheaths, through which they slide without friction, and are attached to the bases of the middle and end phalanges back and front.

Running up each side of each finger are two small arteries and two small nerves, which supply the various structures and especially the overlying skin. The skin of the fingers is specially strong and particularly sensitive, and the end of the finger has a highly specialized part, the nail (*see* SKIN). Each finger is set upon a bone, the 'metacarpal', which lies in the substance of the hand between the finger and the carpus or wrist.

FINSEN LIGHT (*see* LIGHT TREATMENT).

FISH (*see* NITROGENOUS FOODS).

FISSURE is a term applied both to clefts of normal anatomical structure and also to small narrow ulcers occurring in skin and mucous membrane. The latter type of fissure occurs especially at the corners of the mouth and at the anus. (*See* LIPS, *and* RECTUM, DISEASES OF.)

FISTULA (*fistula*, a pipe) is an unnatural, narrow channel, leading from some natural cavity, such as the duct of a gland, or the interior of the bowels, to the surface. Or it may be a communication between two such cavities, where none should exist, as, for example, a direct communication between the bladder and bowel.

Causes.—Sometimes a child is born with a fistula, as a result of some defect in development, for example, a fistula from the thyroid gland to the surface ; but, as a rule, the cause of the formation is either disease or injury. Often, the blockage of the duct of a gland leads to a fistula and the escape of the secretion from the gland on to the surface. Thus a salivary fistula may form on the face as a result of blockage by a concretion of the salivary duct in the cheek, and saliva then runs out on the cheek instead of into the mouth.

Injury may be the cause also. For example, if the pelvis be fractured, the urethra may be torn across, so that urine, instead of being properly voided, passes among the tissues, and, by a process of suppuration, gradually bursts its way out through the skin, forming a permanent urinary fistula. Fistula from the bowel or bladder occasionally arises in women as a result of injury during protracted child-birth. Disease is another cause ; thus an abscess may form at the side of the lower end of the bowel, and, bursting into the bowel on one side, and through the skin on the other, forms a fistula. This 'fistula in ano' forms the best known and most important variety of fistula. The abscess which produces the fistula may be tuberculous or an acute abscess due to the ordinary causes. (*See* ABSCESS, ACUTE.) Sometimes a fish-bone or pin, which has been swallowed, travels through the whole digestive canal without doing damage, till it reaches this point, where it lodges and produces a fistula.

Treatment.—As a rule, a fistula is extremely hard to close, especially after it has persisted for some time. The treatment consists in an operation to restore the natural channel, be it salivary duct, or urethra, or bowel. This is effected by appropriate means in each locality, and when it is attained the fistula heals quickly under simple dressings.

'Fistula in ano' is a very troublesome condition, and is kept from healing by the constant entrance into it of material from the bowel. It is only to be cured by dividing the tissues which separate it from the bowel, and, each day, after the bowels move, packing the wound in such a way as to compel it to heal gradually from its deepest part. The process of healing is, therefore, a very tedious one.

FIT is a popular name for a sudden convulsive seizure, although the term is also extended to include sudden seizure of every sort. During the occurrence of a fit of any sort the chief object should be to prevent the patient from doing any harm to himself by the convulsive movements, so that the person should be laid flat, and the head supported on a pillow or other soft material. To prevent the tongue from being bitten, some object of moderate hardness may be placed between the teeth. (*See* APOPLEXY, CONVULSIONS, ECLAMPSIA, EPILEPSY, FAINTING, HYSTERIA, URÆMIA.)

FLAT-FOOT is a deformity of the foot in which its arch sinks down so that the inner edge of the foot comes to rest upon the ground. (*See* FOOT.) Flat-foot seldom occurs in active, energetic people, and its presence debars

FIG. 183.—Flat-foot, showing complete loss of the arch. (Miller's *Surgery*.)

persons from the public services, or even from engagement in positions where physical activity is needed, for example, as sailors.

Causes.—Sometimes, in weakly children wearing high boots, the arch gives way a little, but this is remedied by removal of the boot-heels, and instructing the child to walk with the toes turned in. Most cases occur in growing and undernourished young men and young women who have much standing on the feet. The ligaments which support the arch are in these persons still soft, the four muscles (two tibial muscles on the inner side, and two peroneal muscles on the outer side) which sling it up become weak or tired, and hence the arch gradually subsides.

Symptoms.—There is pain both along the instep and beneath the outer ankle the foot is stiff and broad, walking is tiresome, and the toes turn far out. The footprints of a flat-foot are broad all the way from toe to heel, instead of being a mere line at the instep. The extent to which the flatness has proceeded may be tested by wetting the bare feet with inky water and causing the person to stand on a piece of clean white paper.

Treatment.—Change of occupation to one which allows of sitting is sometimes necessary. In early cases the leg muscles may be strengthened by tiptoe exercises performed for ten minutes night and morning, the legs being thereafter bathed with cold salt water and massaged. This may be enough, or a steel sole, with instep to support the arch, may have to be worn inside the boot. Sponge rubber pads also make an effective, and resilient, support for the arch. In other cases providing the boot with a sole, which is thicker on the inner side of the foot by $\frac{1}{4}$ to $\frac{1}{2}$ an inch (6 to 12 mm.) than it is on the outer side, may both relieve discomfort in walking and help to remedy the flat foot by throwing the weight of the body on to the outer edge of the foot. The toes should be habitually turned inwards in walking. In very bad cases of long standing it may be necessary either to wrench the foot into position, under a general anæsthetic, and put it in plaster of Paris for a month, or even to remove part of the bone from its inner side, so as to shorten the instep and make a new arch.

FLATULENCE (*flatus*, a blowing) means a collection of gas in the stomach or bowels. In the former case the gas is expelled from time to time in noisy eructations by the mouth; in the latter case it may produce unpleasant rumblings in the bowels, or be expelled from the anus.

Causes.—The presence of gas in the stomach has been explained under the heading of ERUCTATION. When gas is found in large amount in the bowels its production is usually due to fermentation set up by bacteria. Marsh gas and hydrogen are formed from the cellulose of vegetables, sulphuretted hydrogen and carbon disulphide from eggs, pease, and other articles of diet containing much sulphur. Many cases of flatulence are much aggravated by a bad habit of gulping mouthfuls of air.

Treatment. — Flatulence in the stomach is treated by relieving the dyspepsia which causes it. In many cases the flatulence is aggravated by a nervous condition which must receive appropriate treatment. If the flatulence is due to, or aggravated by, the habit of swallowing air, the patient must, by taking a careful note of the occasions when he does this almost unconsciously, break himself of this bad habit. When this is done the flatulence often passes off. In cases of intestinal flatulence, articles of diet which tend to decompose, *e.g.* green vegetables and starchy foods, should be avoided, and the food should be light and quickly digestible.

FLAVINE (*see* ANTISEPTICS).

FLEAS (*see* INSECTS IN RELATION TO DISEASE).

FLEXIBILITAS CEREA is the term applied to an abnormal state in which the limbs remain in any position into which they are moved.

FLEXION (*flecto*, I bend) means bending, and is a term applied either to the bending of joints or to an abnormal shape of organs.

FLIES (*see* INSECTS IN RELATION TO DISEASE).

FLOATING KIDNEY (*see* KIDNEY, DISEASES OF).

FLOCCITATION means the fitful picking at the bed-clothes by a delirious patient, as, for example, in typhoid fever.

FLOODING is a popular name for an excessive blood-stained discharge from the womb (*see* MENSTRUATION). In the majority of cases flooding is the sign of a miscarriage (*see* MISCARRIAGE).

FLOUR (*see* BREAD).

FLUCTUATION (*fluctus*, a wave) is a sign obtained from collections of fluid by laying the fingers of one hand upon one side of the swelling, and, with those of the other, tapping or pressing suddenly on a distant point of the swelling. The thrill communicated from one hand to the other through the fluid is one of the most important signs of the presence of an abscess, or of effusion of fluid into joints or into the peritoneal cavity.

FLUKES are a variety of parasitic worms. (*See* PARASITES.)

FLUORESCIN is an orange-coloured powder which, dissolved in water, is dropped into the eye in order to detect scratches or ulcers of the cornea.

366

FLUORINE, one of the halogen series of elements, is one of the constituents of bone and teeth. During recent years evidence has accumulated that supplementing the daily intake of fluorine diminishes the incidence of dental caries. American and British evidence indicates that people who, throughout their lives, have drunk water with a natural fluorine content of 1 part per million, have less dental caries than those whose drinking-water is fluorine free. All the available evidence indicates that this is the most satisfactory way of giving fluorine, and that if the concentration of fluorine in drinking-water does not exceed 1 part per million, there are no toxic effects.

FLUPHENAZINE is one of the phenothiazine derivatives which is proving of value as an anti-psychotic drug.

FLUTTER, or ATRIAL FLUTTER, is the term applied to a form of abnormal cardiac rhythm, in which the atria contract at a rate of between 200 and 400 beats a minute, and the ventricles more slowly. The abnormal rhythm is the result of a diseased heart.

FLUX (*fluxus*, a flow) means an excessive discharge from any of the natural openings of the body. ' Bloody flux ' is a popular name for dysentery, ' white flux ' or ' whites ' for leucorrhœa.

FŒTOR OF THE BREATH (*see* BREATH, DISORDERS OF).

FŒTUS (*fœtus*), or EMBRYO, is the name given to the child while still within the womb. The human being, like the young of all animals, begins as a single cell, the *ovum*, in the ovary. After fertilization with a spermatozoon the ovum becomes embedded in the mucous membrane of the uterus, its covering being known as the decidua. Increase in size is rapid, and development of complexity is still more marked. The original cell divides again and again to form new cells, and these become arranged in three layers, known as the epiblast, mesoblast, and hypoblast. From the first are produced the cuticle, the brain and spinal cord, and the nerves ; from the second the bones, muscles, blood-vessels, and connective tissues ; while the third develops into the lining of the digestive system and the various glands attached to it.

The ovum produces not only the fœtus but several membranes and appendages which serve it till birth, and are then cast away The embryo develops upon one side of the ovum, its first appearance consisting of a groove, the edges of which grow up and join to form a tube, which in turn develops into the brain and spinal cord. At the same time, a part of the ovum beneath this is becoming pinched off to form the body, and within this the hypoblast forms a second tube, which in time is changed in shape and lengthened to form the digestive canal. From the gut there grows out very early a process called the 'allantois', which attaches itself to the wall of the womb, forming later on the navel-string and afterbirth, by which nourishment is gained for growth (see AFTERBIRTH).

The remainder of the ovum, which within two weeks of conception has increased to about $\frac{1}{12}$ inch (2 mm.) in size, splits into an outer and inner shell, from the outer of which are developed two covering membranes, the chorion and amnion, while the inner constitutes the yolk sac, attached by a pedicle to the developing gut of the fœtus. From two weeks after conception onward, the various organs and limbs appear and grow, the name of *embryo* being now applied to the developing being, while it is almost indistinguishable in appearance from the embryo of other animals, till the middle of the second month, when it begins to show a distinctly human form. After this stage it is called the *fœtus*. The property of 'life' is present from the very beginning, although the movements of the fœtus are not felt by the mother till the fifth month.

During the first few days after conception the eye begins to be formed, beginning as a cup-shaped out-growth from the mid-brain, its lens being formed as a thickening in the skin. It is very soon followed by the beginnings of the nose and ear, both of which arise as pits on the surface, which increase in complexity, and are joined by nerves that grow outward from the brain. These three organs of sense have practically their final appearance as early as the beginning of the second month.

As already stated, the body closes in from behind forward, the sides growing forward from the spinal region. In the neck, the growth takes the form of five arches, similar to those which bear gills in fishes. From the first of these the lower jaw is formed, from the second the hyoid bone, all the arches uniting, and the gaps between them closing up by the end of the second month. At this time the head and neck have quite assumed a human appearance.

The digestive canal, as already stated, begins as a simple tube running from end to end of the embryo, but it grows in length and becomes twisted in various directions to form the stomach and bowels. From this tube also the lungs and the liver arise as two little buds, which quickly increase in size and complexity. The kidneys also appear very early, but go through several changes before their final form is reached.

The genital organs appear late. The swellings, which form the ovary in the female and testicle in the male, are produced in the region of the loins, and gradually descend to their final positions. The outward organs are exactly similar in the two sexes till the end of the third month, and the sex is not clearly distinguishable till late in the fourth month.

The blood-vessels appear in the ovum even before the embryo. The heart, originally double, forms as a dilatation upon the arteries which later produce the aorta. These two hearts later fuse into one. (For the circulation for the fœtus, *see* CIRCULATION OF BLOOD.)

The limbs appear about the end of the third week as buds which increase quickly in length and split at their ends into five parts, for fingers or toes. The bones at first are formed of cartilage, in which true bone begins to appear during the third month.

The following table gives the average size and weight of the fœtus at different periods :

Age.		Length.	Weight.
4 weeks .	.	$\frac{1}{8}$ to $\frac{1}{4}$ in.	20 grains
3 months	.	2 to 3 in.	1 to 2 oz.
5 months	.	6 to 8 in.	5 to 7 oz.
7 months	.	12 in.	2 to 3 lb.
Birth .	.	18 in.	6 to 8 lb.

TABLE 17.—Length and Weight of Fœtus at different Periods.

367

If a fœtus be born before the sixth month, it dies at once, but, from the sixth month onward, it may move and breathe for a little time. Children are sometimes raised, and become quite strong and healthy, if born at the end of the seventh month ; for example, George III and Sir Isaac Newton are said to have been so born. The nearer a child comes to full term the better chance is there of survival.

FOLIA is a Latin term for leaves, *e.g. digitalis folia.*

FOLIC ACID is one of the more recent constituents of the vitamin B complex to be isolated and synthesized. It derives its name from the fact that it is found in many green leaves, including spinach and grass. It has also been obtained from liver, kidney, and yeasts. In 1945 it was synthesized by American workers, who suggested that the chemical name should be pteroylglutamic acid. In the experimental animal lack of folic acid leads to the onset of a severe degree of anæmia. In man it has proved of value in the treatment of macrocytic anæmias, particularly those associated with sprue and nutritional deficiencies. It also relieves pernicious anæmia but does not prevent the onset of the nervous complications of this disease, namely, subacute combined degeneration of the cord. It should therefore never be used in the treatment of pernicious anæmia.

FOLLICLE (*folliculus*, a little bag) is the term applied to a very small sac or gland, *e.g.* small collections of adenoid tissue in the throat and the small digestive glands on the mucous membrane of the intestine.

FOLLICULAR HORMONE (*see* ŒSTRADIOL).

FOMENTATION (*foveo*, I keep warm) (*see* also POULTICES) is the term applied to any warm application to the surface of the body in the form of a cloth. Usually the fomentation cloth is heated by being wrung out of hot water, but the term is also applied to dry applications and to hot cloths upon which various drugs are sprinkled. A fomentation dilates the blood-vessels of the

368

part to which it is applied and has a soothing effect upon the endings of the nerves, so that it both aids the absorption of effusions and relieves pain. In the case of superficial abscesses it softens the skin and helps the abscess to ' point '.

Method of preparation.—HOT MOIST FOMENTATIONS are made as follows. The requisites are a piece of flannel

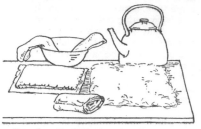

FIG. 184.—Requisites for a hot fomentation.

sufficiently large when folded double to cover the part to which it is desired to apply heat, a towel, a basin, a kettle

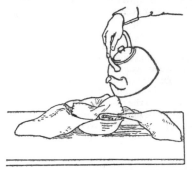

FIG. 185.—Fomentation cloth laid on towel in bottom of basin ; boiling water poured on fomentation cloth.

of boiling water, a piece of jaconette slightly larger than the fomentation, a layer of cotton - wool to cover the

FIG. 186.—Towel twisted round fomentation cloth.

fomentation, and a binder with safety pins. The towel is placed open across the basin ; the fomentation flannel is laid upon the towel and pressed down into the basin ; boiling water is then poured from the kettle upon the fomentation cloth until it is well soaked ; the ends of the towel are then twisted

FIG. 187.—Wringing out the hot water.

firmly in opposite directions by the hands holding its dry ends ; and the hot water is thus squeezed out of the fomentation cloth. The towel is now untwisted, the fomentation cloth is

FIG. 188.—Shaking the fomentation cloth to admit air between folds.

shaken out flat, so as to admit air between its folds, and laid upon the jaconette, which in turn is laid on the

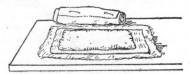

FIG. 189.—Fomentation cloth laid on mackintosh, which is laid on cotton-wool. Ready to apply and fix with flannel binder.

layer of cotton-wool. The whole is now laid upon the body with the fomentation cloth against the skin, and is fixed in place with the binder and safety pins. The preparation of the fomentation should be carried out at the bedside, so that it does not cool

unduly before being applied. If the fomentation is large, it may be found more convenient to use a roller towel and to twist it up by passing a couple of sticks through each end. Instead of the cotton-wool and binder a large bath towel may be used to keep the fomentation in contact with the body. The fomentation retains its heat only a short time, and, if it is to be renewed, this should be done about every twenty minutes.

TURPENTINE FOMENTATION. — This is also known as a 'stupe'. It is prepared in the same way as the hot fomentation, but, in addition, after the boiling water is poured on the cloth and before it is wrung out, a few teaspoonfuls of turpentine are sprinkled on the cloth.

LAUDANUM FOMENTATION. — This may be prepared in the same way as the hot fomentation, with the addition that, after the cloth is wrung out and just before the fomentation is applied, two or three teaspoonfuls of laudanum are sprinkled over its surface. Another method of preparing this soothing fomentation is to take half a dozen dried poppy heads, break them up and boil them with $1\frac{1}{2}$ pints (850 ml.) of water in a saucepan for twenty minutes, and then, proceeding as before, to pour the water from the saucepan through a strainer on to the fomentation cloth as it lies on the towel in the basin.

COLD-WATER DRESSINGS are sometimes also known as fomentations because they become gradually warmed by the heat of the body. They are prepared by dipping a piece of lint in saturated boric acid lotion or other weak antiseptic, applying to the part, and then covering with a piece of gutta-percha tissue or oiled silk which is larger than the piece of lint and projects at least half an inch beyond it all round.

DRY FOMENTATION.—This is made by toasting a piece of thick flannel in front of the fire and laying it on the part to be fomented, covering with a thick layer of cotton-wool and on the outside a hot-water bag. This does not retain its heat for long, but the heat is longer retained by a flannel bag containing salt or bran which is warmed and applied in a similar manner. Flat india-rubber bags, 'thermophores', which retain

369

their heat for many hours, are obtainable. These contain a mixture of salts which liquefies when the bag is boiled. The bag is simply boiled for a few minutes in a kettle each time it is required, and then applied and covered with cotton-wool. These dry applications are very useful for relieving the pain of colic, neuralgia, etc.

FOMITES (*fomes*, tinder) is a term used to include all articles which have been brought into sufficiently close contact with a person sick of some infectious disease to retain the infective material and spread the disease. For example, clothes, bedding, carpets, toys, books, may all be fomites till disinfected.

FONTANELLE is a term applied to areas on the head on which bone has not yet formed. The chief of these is the anterior fontanelle, situated on the top of the head between the frontal and two parietal bones. In shape it is four-sided, about a square inch in size at the time of birth, gradually diminishing until it is completely covered by bone, which should happen by the age of eighteen months. The pulsations of the brain can be readily felt through it. Delay in its closure is particularly found in cases of rickets, as well as in other states of defective development. The fontanelle becomes more tense than usual in acute fevers, whooping-cough, and bronchitis, and tends to bulge in cases of hydrocephalus. It becomes unusually depressed in all cases of diminished vitality, such as that due to diarrhœa or wasting from any cause.

FOOD (*see* ADULTERATION OF FOODS' BREAD, CANNED FOODS, CEREALS' DIET, DIGESTION, FEEDING, INFANT-FEEDING, MILK, NITROGENOUS FOODS, FRUIT, VITAMIN).

FOOD POISONING.—Poisoning, characterized as a rule by vomiting, diarrhœa, and abdominal pain, as a result of eating food contaminated with metallic or chemical poisons, or with bacteria, or with the toxins of bacteria; or as a result of eating poisonous 'foods', such as poisonous mushrooms (*see* FUNGUS-POISONING).

One of the characteristics of food poisoning due to chemical or metallic causes is its relatively quick inset—within ten minutes to ten hours of eating the food.

Bacterial food poisoning is now what is commonly meant by the term 'food poisoning'. It comprises those conditions formerly and erroneously described as 'ptomaine poisoning'. The gravest, and fortunately the rarest, form of food poisoning is botulism (*q.v.*).

Then there is staphylococcal food poisoning, in which certain staphylococci produce in the food they contaminate an enterotoxin which after ingestion makes the consumer suddenly ill within a matter of one to six hours, with vomiting, diarrhœa, and abdominal pain. The staphylococci themselves do not act thus on ingestion : it is the preformed toxin which is noxious. Contamination of food with staphylococci can usually be traced to faulty handling and is usually human in origin. Foods, such as meat products (often cold meat served as sandwiches), milk, custard, and egg products, can be contaminated either before or after cooking. As the toxin produced by the *Staphylococcus aureus* is heat resistant, subsequent cooking will not make the toxin-contaminated food safe.

Many cases of food poisoning are caused by infection with one of a group of bacteria belonging to the genus *Salmonella*. *Salmonella typhimurium* is responsible for 65 to 70 per cent of all outbreaks of food poisoning due to salmonellae. Other salmonellae commonly involved are *Salmonella bredeny*, *Salmonella enteritidis*, *Salmonella heidelberg*, *Salmonella newport*, *Salmonella stanley*, and *Salmonella thompson*. Salmonellae are found in all foods of animal origin : meats, meat products (such as pies), soups, milk, eggs and foods such as custards and cream cakes in which the egg products are only partially cooked. The onset of food poisoning due to salmonellae occurs twelve to forty-eight hours after eating the contaminated food.

Salmonella infections are common in pigs, sheep, rabbits, cattle, rats, mice, dogs, and cats. If a cow is infected with a *Salmonella*—e.g. *B. enteritidis* —the organism may get into the milk, and the consumer of the milk suffer from food poisoning. Food may become infected by the excreta of rats or mice. Ducks are susceptible to *Salmonella* infections, especially *S. typhimurium*, and the organism may get into the duck's egg—an occasional source of human infection.

In recent years an increasing number of outbreaks of food poisoning have been due to *Clostridium welchii*. This is a common cause of food poisoning in communal feeding establishments, and is usually associated with meat dishes, soups or gravy, which have been cooked the day before consumption. To reduce the incidence of this form of food poisoning, the pre-cooked dish must be rapidly cooled, kept in a re-frigerator overnight, and when re-heated it must be cooked as thoroughly as if it were raw meat. This type of food poisoning comes on eight to twenty-four hours after eating the contaminated food.

Food poisoning is now a notifiable disease. In 1966, there were 6,581 cases in England and Wales. Regula-tions are also now in force that lay down requirements relating to the con-struction of, and equipment used in, food premises, the transport of certain foods, the temperature at which food must be stored, and regulations relating to food handlers in food businesses. Thus, food handlers who are suffering from, or are carriers of, a salmonella infection (including typhoid and para-typhoid), or who have a staphylo-coccal infection likely to cause food poisoning must be reported to the local medical officer of health. Such individuals can be suspended from work as food handlers and in certain circumstances they can be allowed compensation for loss of salary.

FOOT is that portion of the lower limb situated below the ankle-joint. Its structure is very similar to that of the hand. There are seven tarsal bones, of which the astragalus, supporting the leg bones, and the calcaneum, forming the heel, are the largest. The others are the scaphoid, three cuneiform, and the cuboid bones. Then comes a row of five metatarsal bones, and finally

fourteen phalanges contained in the toes, the great toe having two only, while each of the others has three. The arrangement of the arteries and nerves (Fig. 190) is similar to that found in the hand and fingers.

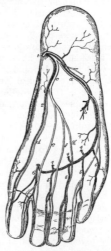

FIG. 190.—Sole of foot, showing the arteries and nerves. *a*, External plantar nerve; *b*, its deep branch; *c*, internal plantar nerve; *d, e, f, g*, its digital branches. (For the numbers, *see* under ARTERIES.) (Turner's *Anatomy*.)

The arch of the foot is a most im-portant structure. The bones are so arranged that the sole is hollow both from before back and from side to side. In walking, the outer edge only, at the middle of the sole, should touch the ground. The arch is further supported by a short plantar ligament situated in the hollow of the arch, running from the calcaneum to the cuboid bone, and by a long plantar ligament situated nearer the surface. It is also slung up by two sinews on either side, coming from muscles in the leg, the two tibial muscles on the inner side, and the two peroneal muscles on the outer side. When this arch gives way, flat-foot is the result (*see* FLAT-FOOT).

For diseases of the foot see CORNS AND BUNIONS; CHILBLAINS; BONES, DISEASES OF; GOUT; NAILS; CHAF-ING OF THE SKIN; DROP-FOOT; CLUB-FOOT.

FORAMEN is the Latin term for a hole. It is especially applied to natural openings in bones, such as the foramen magnum, the large opening in the base of the skull through which the brain and spinal cord are continuous.

FORCED FEEDING (*see* GAVAGE).

FOREHEAD (*see* FRONTAL BONE).

FORGETFULNESS in many people is an inborn misfortune, in others it arises as the result of some disease. Memory is defined by William James as ' the knowledge of an event or fact, of which meantime we have not been thinking, with the additional consciousness that we have thought or experienced it before '. This process necessitates two things—the retention of an event and the reproduction of it, both depending upon the same process in the nervous system. In this system there are, according to Meynert, some 600,000,000 nerve-cells. These are united together by numberless nerve-fibres into countless combinations. When a sensation affects the brain it influences certain of these groups, and if the sensation be very powerful or very often repeated the groups of associated nerve-cells develop a habit of acting in concert and tend, upon future stimulation by any means, to reproduce this sensation in its entirety. This process is known as association, and the multitudinous fibres which connect cell with cell and group with group, forming the chief bulk of the brain, are known as association fibres.

Sound memory depends upon the rational grouping of ideas of things in the mind, so that one may call up the other, and the man who thinks most over the occurrences of his daily life will, other things being equal, have the best memory. No training will make up for a deficiency of nerve-cells or association fibres, which are inborn characters.

For good memory of important facts, a certain amount of forgetfulness is necessary. Facts in the past should become ' foreshortened ', so to speak, and the inability to recount an incident without going over all its petty details forms a type of mental weakness. For this purpose, mental relaxation and change of employment are just as necessary as the quiet pondering over past events that leads to their classification and orderly retention.

According to modern psychological theory, forgetting is often an active

372

process. Painful memories may be repressed out of consciousness, and, buried in the ' unconscious mind ', may be the source of anxiety and neurotic behaviour.

There are certain changes in which memory becomes impaired. Chief among these is old age (*see* AGE, NATURAL CHANGES IN). In the old man's memory the events of yesterday are a blank, and only the events of youth, and later of childhood, forgotten in busy middle age, are again brought to light, all, however, crumbling and half rubbed away. When this defect is extreme it is due to degenerative changes in the old man's arteries and brain. Apoplexy is another cause either of permanent impairment (*see* APHASIA) or, in slighter cases, of frequent losses of memory which occur in old people, and last a few hours or a few days. In hypnotism and various mental diseases, especially dementia, curious vagaries occur. Concussion of the brain, too, may produce at first total unconsciousness, followed by partial loss of memory, lasting for some time (*see* BRAIN, DISEASES AND INJURIES OF).

Treatment. — For improving the memory there are three methods.

Judicious methods are those of classification, repeated presentation of facts to be remembered in different guises, and the formation of numerous connecting links between these facts and facts already in the mind. This method is exemplified in all the sciences, and lies at the root of present-day school-teaching.

Mechanical methods are sometimes useful in remembering new facts. For example, little children are taught to read in unison words or figures clearly written on the blackboard, so that ideas of these entering by the channels of eye, ear, and muscular sense may form on the brain deep impressions upon which future memories can be built. Similarly, a person, hearing a new name, repeats it several times, so that it may make a lasting impression upon his brain-cells.

Artificial memories (*memoriæ technicæ*) are often constructed by persons who have either very few facts in mind with which to form new associations, or who wish in a short time, and for a special purpose, such as an examination, to remember certain facts, and then blot out the whole as a useless encumbrance of memory.

FORMALDEHYDE, or FORMALIN, is a gaseous body prepared by the oxidation of methyl alcohol. For commercial purposes it is prepared as a solution of 40 per cent. strength in water. It is also used to harden gelatin for making capsules, etc. Formaldehyde is a powerful antiseptic, and has also the power of hardening the tissues. The vapour is very irritating to the eyes and nose.

Uses.—For disinfection it is largely used in the form of a spray of 2 to 10 per cent. strength in water. This can be sprayed through the air and on the walls, furniture, etc., of a room to be disinfected, being free from destructive properties to metal-work, curtains, carpet, etc. It can also be vaporized by heat. In 1 per cent. solution in water it forms a powerful antiseptic for hand-washing, and has the merit of being non-poisonous in small amounts.

FOSSA (*fossa*, a ditch) is a term applied to various depressions or holes, both on the surface of the body and in internal parts, such as the iliac fossa in each lower corner of the abdomen, and the fossæ within the skull which lodge the different parts of the brain.

FOWLER POSITION. — After an operation on the abdomen the patient is placed in a semi-sitting position—known as the Fowler position—so that infective fluids do not collect in the upper part of the abdominal cavity.

FOWLER'S SOLUTION is another name for LIQUOR ARSENICALIS, which contains arsenic and is a colourless, odourless fluid. The dose is 2 to 8 minims (0·12 to 0·47 ml.).

FOXGLOVE (*see* DIGITALIS).

FRACTURES (*frango*, I break) are breaches in the structure of bones produced by violence.

Varieties.—The great division of fractures is into those which are simple and those which are compound.

SIMPLE FRACTURES form the commonest variety, consisting of those in which the bone is broken, with or without much laceration of the surrounding parts, but in which there is no wound leading from the fracture through the skin.

COMPOUND or OPEN FRACTURES are those in which the skin is injured, so that a wound leads from the outer air to the broken bone, which may indeed protrude through this wound. The fact that a fracture is compound renders it very much more serious, even though there be little splintering of the bone or laceration of the soft tissues. The special dangers attending compound fractures are as follows. The injury is apt to be much more serious than in simple fracture, and a large quantity of blood may be lost. The union of the bone is delayed, repair taking place by a much slower process when there is an open wound, and a lengthy illness is the result. The greatest danger, however, is that the wound may become infected with virulent micro-organisms, so that suppuration, erysipelas, or blood-poisoning may ensue, and amputation of the limb may become necessary. The long illness, accompanied by suppuration, may also permanently impair the injured person's health. For all these reasons the greatest care is necessary in handling a fractured limb, so that a simple fracture may not be converted into a compound one (Fig. 191).

COMPLETE FRACTURES are those in which the bone is broken completely across, and no connection left between the pieces.

INCOMPLETE FRACTURES are those in which the bone is broken only partly across, or in which the periosteum, the tough membrane surrounding the bone, is not torn. This variety occurs in children, whose bones contain more fibrous material and less bone earth than those of old people, a fact which renders them tougher and more pliant in earlier life. A child's bone may, like a twig, crack half-way across and then split some distance up its length, suffering in this way what is called a ' green-stick ' fracture.

FISSURED FRACTURES are mere cracks in the bone, and are found commonly in the skull. A simple fissured fracture is a fairly frequent accident.

DEPRESSED FRACTURES occur generally on the skull, and consist of fractures in which a fragment of bone is

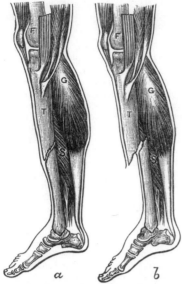

FIG. 191.—Diagram intended to illustrate the manner in which a simple fracture becomes compound through inefficient treatment. This accident is specially liable to occur in the leg. *a*, Simple fracture ; *b*, compound fracture ; *F*, femur ; *G*, gastrocnemius muscle ; *S*, soleus muscle ; *T*, tibia.

forced inwards below the general level. This may give rise to interference with the brain, either when the fracture is produced or at a later date from thickening consequent on repair of the bone.

COMPLICATED FRACTURES are those in which, in addition to the fracture, some other serious injury is produced, *e.g.* a dislocation, tearing of a nerve, etc.

COMMINUTED FRACTURES are those in which there is much splintering.

IMPACTED FRACTURES are those in which, after the break has occurred, one fragment is jammed inside the other, usually at an angle.

UNUNITED FRACTURES are those in which, after the time has elapsed in which the fracture usually mends, it is found that union has not taken place. The failure to unite may be simply due to ' delayed union ', in which the process of repair is proceeding slowly on account of ill-health, or of damage to the chief artery which supplies the bone with blood, or usually in consequence of the fact that the fractured limb is not kept sufficiently at rest. Or there may be actual failure of the

374

healing process to take place. In the latter case the ends of the bone are thoroughly rubbed together under a general anæsthetic, and the fracture again set. If this produces no good effect, an operation is usually performed in order to remove any piece of muscle which may have got between the ends, or to fasten the ends with wire or with metal plates.

MALUNITED FRACTURES are those which have not been properly set, or in which displacement occurs after setting, so that the bone is twisted, or united with a neighbouring bone, as sometimes happens after fracture of the forearm, or is enlarged and shortened, or does not unite by bone, but forms what is known as a ' false - joint '. Sometimes malunion is unavoidable, owing to spasm of muscles or to production of an excessive amount of new bone.

Causes.—Certain causes render some persons more liable than others to fracture of bones. Of these, far the most important is old age. The bones decrease in thickness after middle age, the fibrous tissue composing them becomes less resilient, and there is an increase of the merely earthy part—facts which all tend to produce increasing brittleness. In old age, a fall upon a hard surface, even a moderate strain like that of jumping off a moving vehicle, is apt to be followed by a fracture. Locomotor ataxia, rickets, tuberculosis of bones, osteomalacia, and malignant disease all render the bones more easily broken. Apart from these causes, fractures are due to force, which may be applied in three ways.

DIRECT VIOLENCE, as, for example, the blow of a hammer or crush of a wheel, may cause a fracture, and in such a case the fracture is apt to be a compound one, or attended by serious complications, such as damage to the brain where the skull is fractured, or to the lungs in fracture of the ribs.

INDIRECT VIOLENCE is the most common cause. In this case the violence is applied at some distance from the seat of the fracture, and whether a fracture or a dislocation occurs depends upon the point which in the circumstances is weakest and exposed to most stress. Thus a fall on the palm of the hand may cause a Colles's fracture at the wrist, or dislocation of the shoulder, or fracture of the collar-bone, according to the position of the arm. Similarly, a twist of the foot may cause fracture of the leg, as well as other injuries.

MUSCULAR ACTION in rare cases produces fracture. The most common example is fracture of the knee-cap, which may be snapped across the end of the thigh-bone in the sudden pull given to recover the balance after missing a step on a flight of stairs. Throwing a cricket ball has also been known to fracture the arm.

Symptoms and signs.—*Uselessness of the part* is the main symptom, if the fracture affects a limb. If the lower limb be affected, it is useless for support ; if the upper limb, the part beyond the fracture cannot be raised. *Pain* is a variable sign. So long as the affected part remains at rest, it is generally slight ; movement is, however, apt to be painful. In fracture of the ribs, the moderate movements of tranquil respiration are free from pain, whilst a deep breath or squeezing of the chest causes considerable pain. *The sound of a crack* is sometimes heard, or the sensation of something giving way may be experienced by the injured person at the moment of the accident, but this is not a reliable symptom, because it occurs also when a muscle or sinew is torn. *Deformity* is found at the site of fracture. There is *shortening* of the limb in consequence of contraction of the muscles which pass over the fracture. There is also *swelling*, partly owing to the overlapping of the ends of the bone, partly in consequence of the blood and lymph which are at once poured out from the torn vessels around the injury. *Unnatural mobility* is also found, the limb giving way at a point where it should be rigid. *Crepitus* or grating is the final and only certain sign of fracture, experienced when the ends are rubbed together. It should never be felt for except by skilled hands, since much damage can be done by the sharp broken ends of bone to surrounding structures.

Healing of fractures. — When the bone breaks, many vessels both in its substance and in the periosteum are torn, and accordingly a large clot of blood forms around the ends, between them, and for some distance up the in-side of the bone. Later, great numbers of white corpuscles find their way into this clot, which becomes ' organized ', blood-vessels and, later, fibrous tissue being formed in it (soft callus). Next lime-salts are gradually deposited in this fibrous tissue, which thus develops into bone (hard callus). In this process a thick ring of new bone forms round the broken ends, filling up all crevices, and when union is complete this thickening is again gradually absorbed, leaving the bone as it was before the injury. When the fragments have not been properly set, but allowed to remain overlapping, a considerable thickening remains, the ring of new bone being permanent for the sake of strength.

Treatment.—After the fracture has been recognized, a certain amount of temporary treatment is advisable till the broken bone can be properly fixed in place by a surgeon, and in the following descriptions the temporary treatment will be given, short reference being made to the permanent treatment where it differs from the temporary.

A compound fracture is treated first of all as a wound (*see* WOUNDS) by cleansing and by dressings, and then as a simple fracture. It is particularly necessary that the skin around should be well cleansed, and the wound itself is often very dirty. A thorough washing and scrubbing of the wound, under an anæsthetic, is usually necessary, and some surgeons fasten the fragments with silver wire or plates.

For temporary treatment the splints, etc., may be applied above the clothes in the case of simple fractures, and little padding is then necessary. But, for a compound fracture, the limb must be exposed, the wound dressed, and then the splints have to be carefully padded. In the permanent treatment the limb is bared, and the splints padded with wool.

For permanent treatment, the fracture must first of all be 'reduced', *i.e.* the broken ends must be brought accurately together ; then it must be 'set', *i.e.* the ends firmly fixed in good position ; and finally it must be kept at rest, with attention to the patient's general health, till union has taken place. Reduction is effected usually by one person, who pulls gently and steadily upon that part of the limb beyond the fracture (extension), so as to overcome the shortening and bring the ends a little apart from one another, in order to prevent grating, and so avoid pain. At the same time, a second person should steady the limb above the seat of fracture (counter-extension). This they maintain while a third person applies the necessary splints, bandages, etc. For keeping the bone in position, various devices, such as bandages, plaster, cradles, splints of wood, leather, or poroplastic felt, sandbags, and extension by weight and pulley are adopted

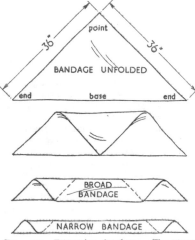

FIG. 192.—Triangular bandage. The narrow cravat is the form into which it is folded for fixing splints.

in different cases. Splints are generally made from strips of wood, about ¼ inch (6 mm.) thick, but they may be improvised from bundles of twigs, broomhandles, rifles, folded-up newspapers, and many other rigid articles. Care must be taken, especially in old people confined to bed for a fracture, that no bed sores form, and various tonics are often necessary. In the case of fracture of the lower limbs it is a general practice to keep the person in bed with the limb fixed by ordinary splints for two or three weeks, and then to apply a case of plaster of Paris to the whole limb, and allow the patient to get up and go about with crutches.

At the present day open fractures are treated by what is sometimes called the ' closed plaster technique '. The principles of this treatment are (1) ex-
376

cision of all dead tissue from the wound, (2) thorough cleansing of the wound, (3) drainage of the wound, (4) application of a sulphonamide powder to the wound, and (5) finally enclosure of the wound in a plaster-of-Paris case, thus ensuring complete rest to the injured tissues.

For bandages to fix splints, one uses either a strip of calico bandage 3 inches (7·5 cm.) wide or an Esmarch's triangular bandage folded narrow. The latter (Fig. 192) is a triangle made by cutting a yard of calico across from corner to corner (so as to form two pieces), and then doubling in the point of the triangle three times, so as to form a sort of flat cravat (see BANDAGES).

COLLAR-BONE (Plate XI, A).—This bone is apt to be fractured by falls on the hand, or by blows or falls on the point of the shoulder. As it supports the weight of the arm to a large extent, and gives squareness to the shoulder, when it is broken the shoulder droops downwards, forwards, and inwards towards the chest. On account of the shortness of the bone, splints are useless, and the deformity is remedied by bandages. These are applied in many different ways, of which the following is one of the simplest (Fig. 193 a, b). A pad of cloth or wool, the size of the fist, is first placed high up in the armpit, and the elbow is bent so that the arm lies across the chest. An unfolded triangular bandage is then placed on the chest with one end over the sound shoulder, the base running down over the elbow of the injured arm, and the point of the bandage lying on the front of the chest. The other end, which is hanging down, is brought up behind the elbow of the injured arm, carried up across the back, and tied as tightly as possible to the first-mentioned end behind the neck. The point of the bandage hanging loose beneath the wrist is folded up round the wrist and pinned to the bandage above it. Finally a triangular bandage, folded narrow, is carried round the chest and elbow of the injured arm and tied tightly, thus levering the shoulder outwards round the pad in the armpit. After this bandage is applied, there is a special necessity to feel that the pulse is not stopped by its tightness. Instead of this sling and narrow-folded bandage, one may use a couple of narrow-folded bandages similarly applied with a pad (Fig. 193 c).

The permanent treatment is usually carried out by a roller bandage applied

FIG. 193.—Treatment of fractured collar-bone. a, Sling applied; b, finished; c, second method with two triangles folded narrow.

in somewhat the same way, or by broad strips of plaster, or by simply laying the patient flat on his back in bed, with a pillow between the shoulders and the arm fixed to the side, so that the weight of the shoulder causes it to fall out and back into proper place.

The fractured bone is fairly strong in four weeks, although the arm has to be used with caution for some time.

UPPER ARM.—This fracture is usually due to a direct blow, and is easily

FIG. 194.—Treatment of fractured humerus, with two splints, two ties, and narrow sling.

recognized. For setting, two splints, 2 to 3 inches (5 to 7.5 cm.) wide, and long enough to reach, the one from the armpit, the other from the shoulder, to beneath the elbow, are taken and well padded (Fig. 194). The forearm being

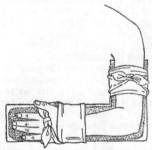

FIG. 195.—Treatment of injuries near elbow, with L-shaped splint and two ties.

laid across the chest, one splint is applied to the front of, the other behind, the upper arm, and fixed by two ties, the first above, the second below, the site of fracture. A narrow sling is then applied to support the wrist.

377

This fracture takes six or eight weeks to mend. The permanent treatment is similar, and the elbow is often fixed by means of an L-shaped splint.

FRACTURES NEAR ELBOW.—These all cause great swelling as they implicate the joint more or less, and it is usually very difficult to recognize the precise nature of the injury. The temporary treatment of all is the same. An L-shaped, or rectangular, splint 3 inches (7·5 cm.) wide, and resembling a mason's ' square ', is used, one limb being long enough to reach from the tips of the fingers to the elbow, the other from the elbow to the armpit (Fig, 195). It is fastened to the inside of the arm and forearm by one tie round the hand and round the forearm, and one round the upper arm. A broad sling is applied to support the forearm.

For permanent treatment, the same plan is very satisfactory and is often adopted. Sometimes the elbow is bent as far up as possible and tightly bandaged in this position. When the fracture consists in the chipping off of the olecranon process of the ulna, i.e. the point of the elbow, the fragment is drawn upwards by the triceps muscle, leaving a distinct gap behind the elbow, and, to correct this, the arm may be fixed up straight with a long splint down the front, and a complicated arrangement of adhesive plaster and elastic behind, in order to draw the fragment downwards.

When the swelling round the joint is great, the treatment is often begun by applying an elastic webbing bandage for two or three days, from the hand up to beyond the elbow, in order to lessen the swelling.

All fractures round the joint are apt to cause some permanent stiffness, and in order to lessen the risk of this the splints are taken off every few days, and the joint is cautiously moved, in order to prevent adhesions forming.

FOREARM.—One or both bones may be broken by a blow or fall, and the condition is easily recognized. For treatment the forearm is laid across the chest with the thumb upwards (Fig. 196). Two splints, at least 4 inches (10 cm.) wide, and long enough to reach from the elbow to beyond the tips of the fingers, are well padded (especially down the centre) and placed one behind

378

and one in front of the forearm. The splints are fixed by one tie round the hand and wrist, and another above the fracture.

A rectangular splint, similar to that used for fractures about the elbow, is applied to prevent movement at this joint, though not absolutely essential in the temporary treatment, and finally a broad sling to support the forearm.

FIG. 196.—Treatment of fractured forearm, with two splints, two ties, and broad forearm sling.

This fracture is put up for permanent treatment in precisely the same way. It takes about the same time to heal as a fracture in the upper arm. There is a danger that the movements of turning the hand palm up and palm down (pronation and supination) may be permanently interfered with by malposition of the bones, unless the fracture be very carefully set.

WRIST.—Fracture of the radius close to the wrist, known as 'Colles's fracture' (Plate XI, C), is a common result of a fall on the palm of the hand. The forearm and hand present a peculiar 'dinner-fork ' bend, in consequence of the lower fragment turning upwards and backwards. The temporary treatment is similar to that for fractures of the forearm higher up. For permanent treatment, shorter splints coming only to the wrist are used, so that the hand may hang downward and by its weight remedy the distortion. Also the splint along the back of the forearm is speci-

PLATE XI

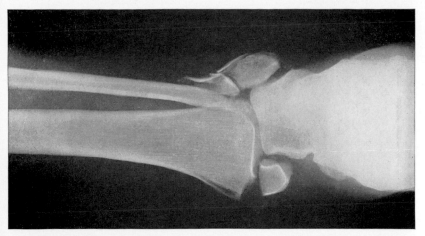

C.—Pott's Fracture, *i.e.* fracture of lower end of both the tibia and fibula, the two bones in the leg.

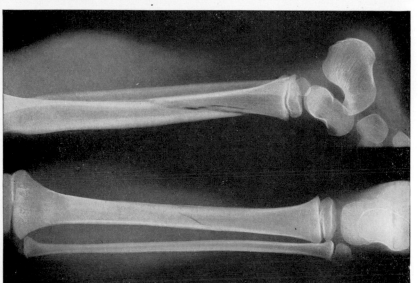

B.—Fracture of tibia
  (*a*) Antero-Posterior view.
  (*b*) Lateral view.

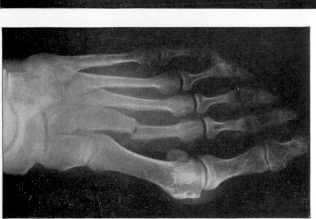

A.—Fracture of 2nd metatarsal bone (one of the bones of the foot)

PLATE XII

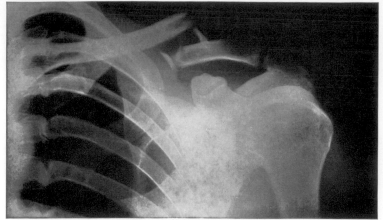

A.—Fracture of left collar bone (clavicle).

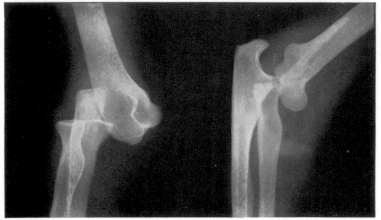

(a)   *(b)*

B.—Dislocation of elbow—*(a)* Antero-Posterior view ; *(b)* Lateral view.

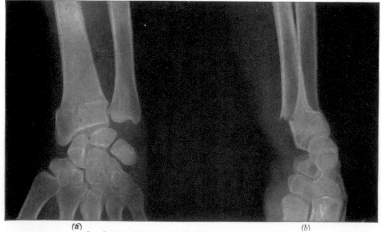

(a)   *(b)*

C.—Colles's Fracture (fracture of lower end of radius).
(a) Antero-Posterior view ; *(b)* Lateral view

ally padded at its lower end, that one running down the front of the forearm being specially padded in its upper two-thirds.

The danger of stiffness, after union has taken place, is even greater here than in fractures near the elbow, and is prevented by similar means.

HAND AND FINGERS.—A splint is laid along the palm, reaching from the tips of the fingers to the elbow, and the hand and forearm are bandaged to it, or the fist is closed on a thick pad and tightly bandaged in this position. A sling is then applied. The fingers mend quickly.

THIGH.—In all fractures of the upper limb the person is usually allowed to go about while he is wearing the splints, but in all fractures of the lower limb he lies in bed. Fracture of the neck of the thigh-bone is a specially common accident in old people, following upon falls on stairs or ice, but in the young this strong bone is broken only by great violence. There are complete inability to move the limb, shortening amounting to 2 or 3 inches (5 to 7·5 cm.) on comparison with the other limb, and rotation outwards of the foot. For treatment a long splint, reaching from the armpit down to below the foot, is laid along the side (Fig. 197), and three shorter splints reaching from the groin

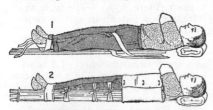

FIG. 197.—Treatment of fractured thigh with Liston's long splint: (1) shows ties by which extension is effected, the foot being secured first and the upper tie gradually tightened through two holes in the upper end of the splint; (2) shows arrangement complete.

to the knee may be laid, one in front, one on the inner side, and one behind the thigh, but are not essential for treatment. The long splint, if no regular splint be procurable, may be easily improvised from a broom-handle (Fig. 198), plank, or rifle. These splints are fixed by the following ties. One broad band, for example a bolster case. round the chest, with or without a narrow-folded bandage round the

hips; two ties round the thigh, on above and one below the fracture, fixing the short splints; two narrow

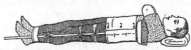

FIG. 198.—Fractured thigh secured by means of a broom, and tying of legs together.

ties round the leg below the knee. Finally, the feet are tied together.

For the permanent treatment a similar method is adopted, but, in addition, some means must be taken to counteract the great shortening produced by the powerful muscles of the thigh. Such measures are extension by a weight fixed with sticking-plaster and a bandage to the leg; or tying the foot down to notches in the lower end of the long splint, which is in turn prevented from sliding upwards by tying its upper end with a long band down to the fork. When the fracture is near the upper or lower end of the thigh-bone, it is sometimes necessary to use a splint which inclines upwards from the hip to the knee, so as to allow of bending at these joints. The fractured limb is often suspended in an inclined cradle. The thigh-bone takes ten or twelve or more weeks to heal, and, in old people, complete bony union often does not take place, so that permanent lameness may result. In old people, also, the confinement to bed for several months, with the old person lying on his back, is apt to bring on bronchitis and congestion of the lungs, and the attempt to unite the bone must often be abandoned as dangerous to life (see LUNGS, DISEASES OF).

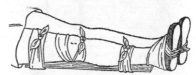

FIG. 199.—Treatment of injuries about the knee, with splint and three ties.

KNEE-CAP.—This bone is seldom fractured. A long splint is laid along the back of the limb and fixed by ties to thigh and leg. The fragments of the knee-cap may be fixed together by a bandage passing round above the knee-cap, crossing behind the joint, and then passing round below the knee-cap (Fig. 199).

It is extremely difficult to get good bony union, and for the permanent treatment most surgeons prefer to cut in to the fracture and unite the fragments with silver wire.

LEG (Plate X, B).—There is particular need for care in the handling of this fracture, because the tibia, or shin-bone, which lies in its whole length just beneath the skin, usually breaks with a sharp-pointed end, like a pen-nib, that is very readily pushed through the skin, thus making the fracture compound. Two splints, about 4 inches (10 cm.) wide, and long enough to reach from a few inches above the knee to beyond the foot, are carefully padded, above and below the knee-joint, and above and below the ankle-joint, so as to prevent them from pressing upon the skin where the bone lies just beneath (Fig. 200). They are applied one along the outer, one along the inner side of the leg, and fixed with two ties, one above and one below the fracture. A third tie is applied above the knee to fix this joint, and the feet are finally tied together.

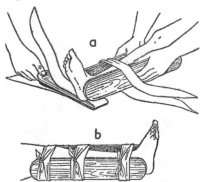

FIG. 200.—Treatment of fracture of the leg, with two splints and three ties; the two limbs are afterwards tied together, as in Fig. 198. *a*, Shows the method of pushing through the ties so as not to jerk the limb. A second pair of hands should be shown applying extension to the foot, but for clearness are omitted. *b*, Shows setting finished.

For permanent treatment the splints are generally rolled in a sheet, so as to be joined behind the leg by a piece of sheet 4 inches (10 cm.) wide. The leg thus lies in a kind of trough, which is further padded beneath the heel, and the foot is bandaged to it so that the

380

toes point straight up. The leg is then laid on a pillow to bend the knee slightly and relax the calf muscles. Various special splints are also used, especially Cline's outer and inner splints, which are hollowed out for the leg, to which they are tightly bandaged, the outer one also possessing a foot-piece, which serves to keep the limb from twisting. Macintyre's splint is a shaped metal splint with foot-piece which is also frequently used. This fracture takes eight to ten weeks to mend.

Fracture of the fibula, the slender bone on the outer side of the leg, may take place in consequence of a kick or twist of the foot, while the tibia is uninjured. If the fracture occurs in the middle or upper part of the fibula the person may be quite able to walk, though with considerable pain. If, however, the fracture occurs at the lower end of the fibula, it is more likely to be due to indirect violence to the foot as a result of severe strains. The temporary treatment should be the same as for fracture of both bones, and the permanent treatment is very similar. This injury, which is one of those included under the term, 'Pott's fracture' (Plate X, C), is accompanied by a considerable tearing of the ligaments on the inner side of the ankle-joint.

FOOT (Plate X, A).—The foot, when fractured, is put up in splints similar to those for the leg.

PELVIS.—The bones of the pelvis are broken only by excessive violence, such as a crush from the wheel of a heavily laden cart, a fall of coal in a mine, and the like. For temporary treatment, the injured person should have a broad binder fastened round the hips and be lifted on a rug or shutter. The seriousness depends upon the extent of damage done to internal organs.

RIBS are very commonly fractured by a blow or kick on the side. If only one or two be broken and the fracture be simple and uncomplicated, the accident is comparatively trivial. All that is necessary for treatment is that the movements of the chest in breathing should be restricted by a broad bandage, or by strips of sticking-plaster round the chest. The ribs heal very quickly, those above and below the broken ribs acting as splints. If the injured person spits up blood after the injury the condition is serious, this being a sign that the broken ribs have pierced the pleura and wounded the lung.

SPINAL COLUMN.—This is fractured only by great violence. Mere damage to the bone in this case also is not necessarily serious, but, as the spinal cord is often damaged in the act of fracture

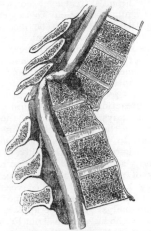

FIG. 201.—Fracture of the spinal column, causing injury to the cord. (Miller's *Surgery*.)

(Fig. 201), or is pressed upon by a displaced fragment, the accident may be a very serious one, the usual result being paralysis of the parts of the body below the level of the injury. Therefore the higher up the spine is fractured, the more serious the consequences. The injured person should not be moved till medical assistance is at hand, or, if he must be removed, this should be done upon a rigid shutter or door, not upon a canvas stretcher or rug, and there should be no lifting which necessitates bending of the back. In such an injury an operation designed to remove a displaced piece of bone and free the spinal cord from pressure is often necessary and successful in relieving the paralysis.

SKULL.—Simple fissured fractures and depressed fractures of the skull very often follow blows or falls on the head, and are not at all serious, as a rule, apart from the damage which may have been done to the brain at the same time.

Compound fractures are attended by risk of suppuration which may spread within the skull, and if the skull be extensively broken and depressed the operation of 'trephining' is often done in order to cleanse the wound thoroughly. Another risk of fracture is that some of the small arteries on the inner surface of the skull may be torn and may bleed, thus causing 'compression' of the brain. For this reason also the skull is often trephined. Thorough cleansing of the wound, and confinement to bed in a darkened room constitute the treatment.

JAW.—The lower jaw is frequently fractured by a blow on the face. There is generally bleeding from the mouth, the

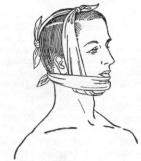

FIG. 202.—Treatment of fractured jaw, with two triangular bandages folded narrow.

gum being torn. Also there are pain and grating sensations on chewing, and unevenness in the line of the teeth. The treatment is simple (Fig. 202), the line of teeth in the upper jaw forming a splint, against which the lower jaw is bound, with the mouth closed. One bandage is passed below the chin and tied on the top of the head ; another passes in front of the chin, and is tied on the back of the neck. The two are then prevented from slipping forward and backward respectively, by tying the one to the other on the crown of the head. The patient must be fed for two or three weeks with liquid food, *e.g.* eggs and milk, poured into the corner of the mouth from a feeding-cup with a spout.

NOSE.—The bridge of the nose may be fractured by a fall. The bleeding is copious, and should be arrested by the usual means. (*See* HÆMORRHAGE.) An operation may later be performed to restore the shape of the nose.

FRAMBŒSIA is another name for YAWS (*q.v.*).

FRAMYCETIN is an antibiotic derived from *Streptomyces decaris*. It is active against a wide range of organisms, when taken by mouth or applied locally to infections of the skin.

FRECKLES, or SUMMER-SPOTS, are small yellow or brown spots which appear on the exposed parts of the body, *i.e.* face, neck, and hands, during hot or windy weather. They appear especially in people with delicate skin and red hair. They consist of small pigmented areas in the deeper part of the cuticle, which are stimulated to increased development by exposure.

FREMITUS (*fremitus*, a low noise) is the name given to a sensation which is communicated to the hand of an observer when it is laid upon the chest in certain diseases of the lungs and heart. Friction fremitus is a grating feeling communicated to the hand by the movements of lungs or heart when the membrane covering them is roughened, as in pleurisy or pericarditis. Vocal fremitus means the sensation felt by the hand when a person speaks ; it is increased when the lung is more solid than usual. The 'thrills' felt over a heart affected by valvular disease are also varieties of fremitus.

FRENKEL'S EXERCISES are a series of movements of precision intended to be performed by patients suffering from difficulty of control of the muscles, with a view to regaining lost power of co-ordination. The exercises for the lower limbs of a patient confined to bed begin with such movements as those of raising the foot and carefully bringing it down upon a particular part of the edge of a padded board. At a later stage, the patient, supported if necessary under the armpits, practises walking along a broad strip painted on the floor, later still on a narrow strip, and afterwards tracing out marked patterns with the toes and placing the feet carefully as he walks on marked positions. Similar exercises are devised for re-establishing co-ordination of the muscles in the arms, *e.g.* carefully inserting pegs into small holes in a board, picking up pins from a smooth surface, and similar movements.

382

FREUD'S THEORY is the term applied to a theory that hysteria and allied diseases are due to a psychic injury or trauma, generally of a sexual nature, which did not produce an adequate reaction when it was received and therefore remains as a subconscious or 'affect memory' to trouble the patient's mind. As an extension of this theory Freud's treatment consists in encouraging the patient to tell everything that happens to be associated with trains of thought which lead up to this memory, thus securing a 'purging' of the mind from the original 'affect memory' which is the cause of the symptoms. This form of treatment is also called 'psychocatharsis' or 'abreaction'. The general term, psycho-analysis, is applied, in the first place, to the *method* of helping the patient to recover buried memories by free association of thoughts. In the second place, the term is applied to the body of psychological knowledge and theory accumulated and devised by Freud and his followers. The term psycho-analyst should be applied only to those who have had a strict Freudian training, not to anyone who happens to practise psychotherapy.

FRIAR'S BALSAM (*see* BALSAM).

FRICTION is the name given either to the fremitus felt or to the grating noise heard when two rough surfaces of the body move over one another. It is specially obtained over the chest in cases of dry pleurisy.

FRIEDREICH'S ATAXIA is a hereditary disease resembling locomotor ataxia, and due to degenerative changes in nerve tracts and nerve cells of the spinal cord and the brain. It occurs usually in children, or at any rate before the twentieth year of life, and affects often several brothers and sisters. Its chief symptoms are unsteadiness of gait, with loss of the knee jerks, followed later by difficulties of speech, tremors of the hands, head, and eyes, deformity of the feet, and curvature of the spine. The sufferer gets gradually worse, but may live, more or less helpless, for twenty or thirty years.

FRÖHLICH'S SYNDROME is the name given to a condition in children characterized by obesity, physical sluggishness, and retarded sexual development. It is the result of disturbed pituitary function.

FRONTAL BONE (*frons*, the forehead) is the bone which forms the forehead and protects the frontal lobes of the brain. Prior to birth, the frontal bone consists of two halves, and this division may persist throughout life, a deep groove remaining down the centre of the forehead. Above each eye is a heavy ridge in the bone, most marked in men, and, behind this, in the substance of the bone, is a cavity on each side, the frontal sinus, which communicates with the nose. Catarrh in these cavities produces the frontal headache characteristic of a ' cold in the head ', and suppuration may occur in them, producing discharge from the nose. (*See* NOSE, DISEASES OF.)

FROSTBITE results from the action of extreme cold upon parts of the body for some time. Parts may be frozen for a short time, as in surgical operations, without injury ; but when considerable portions, such as a whole hand, are frozen for a lengthened period, and particularly when the circulation is allowed to return too suddenly, the more outlying portions like the fingers are very apt to die, and be separated from the living parts by gangrene.

Symptoms.—The condition is particularly apt to arise in persons addicted to the use of alcohol, whose blood-vessels have lost their proper ' tone ', and in whose extremities circulation is sluggish. A part may, by long exposure, be so frozen that the circulation never returns in it, and in this case the part may simply shrivel up, turn black, and undergo dry gangrene without any inflammation. If, however, the freezing process has not been so severe, circulation becomes restored as the part thaws, the vessels in it become widely dilated, and the part in consequence swollen, red, and excessively painful. If this ' reaction ' be not controlled, the result is a considerable inflammation in the part, which may go on to moist gangrene and consequent death of the part.

It is said that the greater the redness which appears in the part the poorer the chance of recovery.

Treatment.—The condition is, of course, preventable by keeping the outlying parts of the body, like hands and feet, carefully wrapped up when the cold is intense, and also by maintaining the circulation in full activity by not sitting down, and by avoiding alcohol. Supposing, however, that a part has been frozen, its recovery depends upon the extent to which the reaction is controlled. In mild cases the aim of treatment is to restore the natural warmth to the skin as quickly as possible. For instance, if the face is affected, then it should be covered with a warm, ungloved hand ; if the hand is involved it should be placed inside the clothing next to the skin of the body. Warm drinks should be given. The affected part must not be vigorously rubbed, as this is very liable to damage the skin. There is still a difference of opinion as to whether severe cases should be treated by warmth or cold in the early stages, but the general consensus of opinion is that warmth is preferable. It is important that the affected part should be kept dry, and it may be advisable to apply an antiseptic, *e.g.* proflavine, 1 : 1000. Blisters should not be opened.

The treatment of frostbite which has resulted in gangrene is given under GANGRENE.

FROZEN SHOULDER is the name given to a painful condition of the shoulder accompanied by stiffness and considerable limitation of movement. The usual age-incidence is between 40 and 50. The cause is not known. There is no specific treatment, but there is always complete recovery, even though this may take twelve to eighteen months. A course of deep X-ray therapy is sometimes beneficial.

FRUCTOSE (*fructus*, fruit) is another name for lævulose or fruit sugar, which is found along with glucose in most sweet fruits.

FRUIT.—Almost all fresh fruits contain about 80 per cent. of water, and the nutritive material, consisting chiefly of starch and sugar, does not exceed one-fifth of the fruit. The banana is the most nutritious of the fresh fruits, followed by grapes, plums, and apples. In addition to their food value, fruits contain vegetable acids, such as tartaric, citric, and malic acids, which have an agreeable flavour, a mildly laxative action, and are beneficial to the kidneys. Oranges, lemons, and grape-fruit are specially useful in this way. The importance of fruits lies in the fact that they are the chief source of vitamin C, especially the citrus fruits and black-currants. The odour and flavour of fruits, which depend upon volatile oils and ethereal bodies, render them an agreeable article of food and improve appetite and digestion.

Dried fruits, such as apples, figs, dates, prunes, and grapes (raisins), form a highly nutritious form of diet, containing 60 or 70 per cent. of starch, gum, and sugar ; thus dried dates, figs, or raisins are more nourishing than an equal weight of bread. They are also a relatively rich source of iron and calcium, but a poor source of vitamin C.

FRUSEMIDE is a recently introduced potent diuretic.

FUCIDIN is a recently introduced antibiotic derived from the fermentation products of the fungus *Fusidium coccineum*. It is said to be particularly active against staphylococci.

FULLER'S EARTH is a grey powder free from all grittiness. It consists mainly of aluminium silicate, but differs from kaolin in containing traces of iron. It is a valuable dusting powder for tender, moist skins, such as those of infants.

FUMIGATION (*fumigo*, I smoke) is a means of disinfection by the vapour of powerful antiseptics (*see* DISINFECTION). The process was also employed at one time for the absorption of some drugs, of which mercury was the chief.

FUNCTIONAL DISEASES (*see* PSYCHOSOMATIC DISEASE).

FUNGOID TUMOURS are ulcerating growths which sprout rapidly and have therefore a mushroom-like appearance.

FUNGUS - POISONING. — Several diseases are due to the growth of minute

fungi in the tissues of the body ; for example, actinomycosis (caused by the ray-fungus), ringworm, and Madurafoot of India. As to the large fungi,

FIG. 203.—Edible Mushroom (*Psalliota campestris*). Gills brownish purple. Base of stem clubbed. No volva.
(Height 3¾″; width of cap 5″; width of stem 1″.)
(*The Practitioner.*)

or mushrooms as they are often called, although they grow in dead and decaying material, they do not infest the

FIG. 204.—The Death Cap (*Amanita phalloides*). Gills white. Volva at base of stem. Cap yellowish green.
(Height 4½″; width of cap 3½″; width of stem ⅝″.)
(*The Practitioner.*)

living body, but many of them contain a poisonous alkaloid known as ' muscarine ', others a body called ' phallin ', both of which are poisons when swallowed. About 2000 of these larger fungi grow in England, of which 200 are edible. There are about a dozen which are classified as poisonous, but several of these cause no more than indigestion. The most poisonous of all is the 'death cup' or *Amanita phalloides* (Fig. 204). The distinguishing features of this fungus are that it has a yellowish green cup, the gills are white and at the base of the stem, or stalk, there is a cup, or volva. These features distinguish it from the common edible mushroom (*Psalliota campestris*), which has brownish purple gills and no cup at the base of the stem (Fig. 203).

FIG. 205.—Fly Agaric (*Amanita muscaria*). Cap red with white patches.
(Height 10"; width of cap 7"; width of stem 1".)
(*The Practitioner.*)

Other poisonous 'mushrooms' include *Amanita virosa*, *Amanita vernu*, and *Amanita muscaria* (Fig. 205). Deaths from mushroom poisoning are relatively rare in England: between 1920 and 1945 only 38 cases were recorded in England and Wales.

Symptoms.—Apart from indigestion, actual deadly poisoning is attended by three symptoms. There are, first of all, vomiting and purging from irritation of the stomach and bowels; then feebleness of the heart's action, due to the muscarine, producing pallor and faintness; and, finally, unconsciousness or delirium, which may, in a few hours, end in death. Fungi, therefore, act as narcotico-irritant poisons.

Treatment.—The first thing is to give an emetic in order to remove the fragments of fungus from the stomach (*see* EMETICS) or, preferably, wash out the stomach (*see under* DYSPEPSIA), and then leave in the stomach 2 fluid ounces (60 millilitres) of White Mixture of Magnesium Sulphate B.P.C. Stimulants, such as nikethamide (*q.v.*), should be given if the pulse be weak and the person collapsed. If the fungi have been eaten several hours before, a powerful purgative, such as a large dose of castor oil, should be given as well as an emetic. Finally, in all serious cases atropine should be administered, since if it forms a direct antidote to muscarine. There is also an antiphallinic serum which is sometimes of value. Another form of treatment which is sometimes used is to give five uncooked rabbits' stomachs and brains daily. This line of treatment is based upon the observation that rabbits do not die after eating *Amanita phalloides*.

FURAZOLIDONE, or FUROXONE, has the chemical formula: [3-(5-nitrofurfurylideneamino)oxazolidin-2-one]. It is used in the treatment of diarrhœa due to a variety of causes, including bacillary dysentery and bacterial food-poisoning.

FURFURACEOUS (*furfur*, bran) is a term applied to skin diseases which produce scaliness of the surface, resembling bran.

FURUNCLE (*furunculus*, a little thief) is another name for a boil. (*See* BOILS.)

FUSIDIC ACID is a steroid antibiotic which is proving of value in the treatment of staphylococcal infections resistant to penicillin.

G

GAIT is an important sign of health and disease. Children, as a rule, begin to walk between the ages of twelve and eighteen months, having learned to stand before the end of the first year. If a good-sized child shows no ability to make movements by this time, he is probably deficient in mind, and if the power of walking is not gained by the time the child is a year and a half old, he is probably the subject either of rickets, cerebral palsy, or a malformation of the hip-joint (*see* RICKETS, PARALYSIS).

Lameness in later life may be due to flat-foot, when the spring of the foot is lost and the person walks with his toes turned out at right angles ; or to the stiffness following disease of the knee-joint, when the limb is carried forward like a rigid bar ; or to the stiffness following hip-joint disease, when the person walks in a lop-sided manner, alternately taking a long step with the sound limb and swinging the whole pelvis round with the lame leg, as well as bending over to one side.

In **hemiplegia,** or paralysis down one side of the body following apoplexy, the person drags the paralysed leg, and carries the paralysed side as if it were, so to speak, hung upon the healthy one. There is a tendency for this walk to improve gradually, the paralysed leg regaining power almost completely even when the arm remains very helpless and bent stiffly across the body.

Steppage, or heather-step gait occurs in certain cases of alcoholic neuritis, lead palsy, and other conditions where the muscles that raise the foot are weak and the toes in consequence droop. The person bends the knee and lifts the foot high, so that the toes may clear obstacles on the ground, much as a person steps in going through heather or long grass.

In **locomotor ataxia** the sensations derived from the lower limbs are blunted, and consequently the movements of the legs are uncertain and the heels planted on the ground with unnecessary force. When the person tries to turn or stands with the eyes shut he is apt to fall over. When he walks he feels for the ground with a stick or keeps his eyes constantly fixed upon it.

In **spastic paralysis** the limbs are moved with jerks. The foot first of all clings to the ground (the person being very apt to trip over small objects), and then leaves it with a spasmodic movement, being raised much higher than necessary.

In **trembling palsy,** or paralysis agitans, the movements are tremulous, and as the person takes very short steps, he has the peculiarity of appearing constantly to fall forward, being, in advanced cases, unable to stop himself till he brings up against some object of which he can lay hold.

In **St. Vitus's dance (chorea)** the walk is bizarre and jerky, the affected child often seeming to leave one leg a step behind him, and then, with a screwing movement on the other heel, go on again.

GALACTAGOGUES (γάλα, milk ; ἄγω, I move) are drugs which increase the flow of milk in nursing women. The normal stimulus of an infant's lips is the most powerful agent in producing milk, and a mother who has little or no milk should nevertheless hold her infant to the breast. Good food and the hormone, prolactin, from the pituitary gland increase the quantity and improve the quality of milk.

GALACTOCELE is the term applied to a cyst-like swelling in the breast which forms as a result of obstruction in the milk-duct draining the swollen area.

GALACTOPHORITIS means inflammation of the milk-ducts of the breast.

GALENICAL PREPARATIONS are preparations of drugs sanctioned by the pharmocopœia, the list of drugs and remedies published under government regulations. The term 'official' is more commonly used in the same sense ; ' officinal ' (*officina*, a shop) means drugs procurable in the ordinary shops.

GALL is another name for bile. (*See* BILE.)

GALL - BLADDER AND DUCTS, DISEASES OF.—The biliary vessels begin as minute passages scattered throughout the entire liver, and lying between its rows of cells, from which they collect the bile secreted by the latter. They unite into larger and larger vessels just as do the tributaries of a river, and finally a single, large hepatic duct emerges from the right lobe and another from the left lobe of the liver (*see* LIVER). The connection of these with the gall-bladder is somewhat complicated (Fig. 207). The right and left ducts unite first into one vessel, the hepatic duct, which meets the cystic duct coming from the gall-bladder, and the two unite to form the common bile-duct, which opens into the small intestine a few inches below the outlet of the stomach. The importance of this arrangement lies in two facts: firstly, the entrance to the gall-bladder is a cul-de-sac, bile in entering it from the liver running down the hepatic and up the cystic duct; and, secondly, if the gall-bladder or its cystic duct becomes blocked, the bile can still escape from the liver down the hepatic and common bile-ducts, into the bowel. The size and condition of the gall-bladder can be determined in many cases by X-ray examination. A substance which is opaque to X-rays, such as iopanoic acid, when taken by mouth is excreted in the bile and passed into the gall-bladder. If an X-ray photograph be taken some sixteen hours afterwards, the gall-bladder and any stones that it may contain are seen outlined as a shadow in the plate.

CHOLECYSTITIS.—Catarrh may occur in the gall-bladder and bile passages as in other cavities lined by mucous membrane. It may either arise in the bile-ducts themselves, or may follow upon a catarrhal condition in the bowels, spreading up from the point where the common bile-duct opens into the small intestine. Cholecystitis may be either acute or chronic. Both forms are more common in women than in men, and are more liable to occur in the obese than in the thin. The condition is more liable to occur in middle-age. Hence the description of the individual subject to cholecystitis as ' fair, fat, and forty '. Since the bile is expelled from the liver largely by the movements of breathing, any condition which impedes this causes stagnation of the bile, and favours catarrh. Pigments are deposited from the bile in the finer vessels, producing 'bile-sand', and thick, stringy mucus collects in these passages and in the gall-bladder, the irritation caused by these deposits still further aggravating the catarrh. Finally, this bile-sand may collect into small masses in the larger ducts or gall-bladder, and chemical changes in the mucus taking place, a crystalline substance called ' cholesterin ' encrusts them in a gradually thickening layer, so that finally large ' gall-stones ' may be produced. In a number of cases the inflammation of the gall-bladder is produced by infection with a special streptococcus.

Symptoms.—An acute attack of catarrh causes, in general, pain and tenderness to touch beneath the margin of the ribs on the right side, *i.e.* over the edge of the liver and the gall-bladder. This may be followed by a certain degree of jaundice (*see* JAUNDICE). In chronic catarrh there is general ill-health and indigestion, associated with a dark, sallow skin, and occasional attacks of ' biliousness '. There is often, too, a vague, uneasy feeling in the region mentioned above, and in advanced cases there may be recurring attacks of gall-stone colic.

Treatment.—The treatment of acute cholecystitis consists of rest in bed, the administration of sulphonamides and a diet containing ample carbohydrate and protein but a minimum of fat. The patient should be encouraged to drink as much bland fluid as possible, *e.g.* glucose drinks flavoured with fruit juice. If the condition does not settle quickly, operation may be necessary.

The chronic form, though not of itself a severe ailment, should be treated because of its liability to produce gall-stones and because it impairs the general health. A simpler life, with not more than three meals daily, the avoidance of alcoholic beverages and highly spiced food, and the taking of more exercise together with the practice of deep breathing, are the main requisites. The administration by mouth of a concentrated solution of magnesium sulphate one hour before breakfast is sometimes of value by virtue of the fact that it helps to drain the biliary passages. To cleanse the bile passages, large quantities of water should be taken with meals, and one or two tumblerfuls of warm water an hour before each meal are specially beneficial. The bowels must be carefully regulated. In many cases, however, the only satisfactory treatment is removal of the gall-bladder.

SUPPURATION is a rarer but much more serious condition which occasionally appears in the course of a chronic catarrh. It may also arise as the result of an infective fever like enteric, and sometimes results from the irritation of a growing gall-stone. Its symptoms are an exaggeration of those of catarrh along with shivering, high fever, and often delirium. The treatment is an operation to drain the gall-bladder of its suppurating contents, after which recovery often ensues, though the outlook is serious.

GALL - STONES. — The manner of formation of these has been already described under catarrh of the bile passages. The smaller stones consist of a combination of bile-pigment with lime (bilirubin-calcium), and are deep brown in colour ; the larger ones have a core of this surrounded by cholesterin, and are lighter or even white in colour. The size varies from that of small gravel, in which case several hundred stones may be present, to the size of a goose egg, when the stone is single. When there are several stones they are faceted so as to fit against one another (Fig. 206).

Symptoms.—To begin with, there are the symptoms described under the heading of catarrh, which causes the formation of the stones. Apart from these, stones may lie for years in the gall-bladder and give no trouble, being found accidentally at an operation or after death. But as a rule they produce symptoms in one of three ways (Fig. 207).

(1) The mere presence of stones in the gall-bladder may give rise to much irritation, and the tenderness and pain over the region of the gall-bladder then become very marked. These symptoms are specially liable to become aggravated during digestion, so that the condition is taken for a form of

dyspepsia, although the pain is at the right side of the body. When bacteria find an entrance from the bowel, high

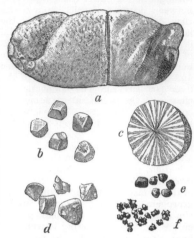

FIG. 206.—Gall-stones. *a, b, c,* Stones formed of cholesterin ; *d,* composed of urates ; *e,* formed of bile - pigment and cholesterin ; *f,* stones of pigment and lime-salts. Three-fourths natural size. (Thoma's *Pathology.*)

temperature, shiverings, and sweatings develop, and suppuration may come on.

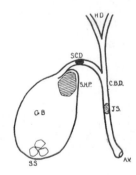

FIG. 207.—Diagram showing various positions of gall-stones. G.B., the gall-bladder; C.B.D., the common bile duct ; H.D., hepatic ducts ; S.S., silent stones ; S.H.P., stone in Hartmann's pouch ; S.C.D., stone in cystic duct ; J.S., stone in common bile duct : so-called jaundice stone; A.V., ampulla of Vater. (From Handfield-Jones and Porritt, *The Essentials of Modern Surgery*. E. & S. Livingstone, Ltd.)

(2) The usual way in which gall-stones show their presence is by passing out of the gall-bladder along with the

bile. If the stone be small, it reaches the bowel and is voided, without attracting attention beyond perhaps passing discomfort in the upper part of the abdomen, after a meal. If the stone be large enough to stick in the cystic or common bile-duct, and particularly if it be angular, it sets up great spasm of the muscle fibres in the wall of the duct, causing the most agonizing pain. This ' gall-stone colic ' is felt beneath the rib margin on the right side, sometimes shooting up to the right shoulder. It comes on, as a rule, very quickly, and is accompanied by collapse, cold sweat, and vomiting. It lasts usually several hours, and often ceases quite suddenly as the stone passes into the bowel or back to the gall-bladder. Next day there is usually some jaundice, which may last for a week or two.

(3) Sometimes the stone remains jammed or ' impacted ' in one of the ducts, passing neither up nor down. In this case, the pain passes slowly off as the muscle fibres of the ducts become tired out, only to return again and again, till, in a milder degree, it becomes almost constant. Gradually increasing jaundice may develop till the skin becomes even a dark olive brown. At the same time loss of weight and strength, and often dropsy, progress so far that the case may be very difficult to diagnose from cancer. In this case, too, suppuration may come on.

Treatment.—To prevent gall-stones, what has been said as to catarrh holds good, and if the accompanying catarrh be cured, even after large gall-stones have been formed, they may be comparatively harmless. Many substances, which will dissolve gall-stones outside the body, have been recommended in the hope that, taken into the system for long periods, they may gradually dissolve the stones in the gall-bladder —for example, ether, turpentine, and olive oil, but they are of no practical value.

When an attack of gall-stone colic occurs, hot fomentations should be at once applied to the abdomen. Morphine sulphate, $\frac{1}{4}$ grain (15 mg.), with or without atropine, $\frac{1}{150}$ grain (0·6 mg.), should be given hypodermically. Inhalations of amyl nitrite are also useful. If the pain is excessive, chloroform or ether may have to be given for the fifteen or twenty minutes that elapse before the morphine can take effect. A hot bath sometimes gives great relief.

As to a surgical operation, if a person suffers from constant catarrh and repeated attacks of gall-stone colic, it is well that he should undergo the comparatively simple operation of having the gall-bladder removed (cholecystectomy), which may relieve both conditions. In cases where a gall-stone is impacted, an operation is certainly advisable, as the condition is a very serious one. Sometimes, as when the duct is permanently closed, a fistula follows upon operation, and the bile drains away permanently through a wound in the abdomen. In this case, the jaundice and colic at least are alleviated, and the fistula can be closed at a later operation by the surgeon, who makes an opening between the gall-bladder and adjacent bowel.

GALLS, or NUTGALL, is the name of an excrescence growing upon oaks and containing a large quantity of tannic acid which gives the galls a strongly astringent action. Galls are chiefly used in the form of ointment of galls, and ointment of galls with opium, for application to bleeding piles.

GALTON'S WHISTLE is a metallic whistle producing extremely high notes which is used in testing the sense of hearing.

GALVANISM (*see* ELECTRICITY IN MEDICINE).

GALVANOCAUTERY means cautery performed by a wire heated by a galvanic current.

GAMGEE TISSUE is a surgical dressing composed of a thick layer of cotton-wool between two layers of absorbent gauze, introduced by the Birmingham surgeon, Sampson Gamgee.

GAMMA-GLOBULIN.—It has been known for a long time that the protective antibodies of the body are closely associated with the proteins of the blood. Gamma-globulin is a concentrated solution of the antibody fraction of human blood which has proved of great value in providing immunity against certain infectious diseases, particularly measles. It is of little value once the disease is begun, but if given before the disease manifests itself, it either prevents its onset or modifies its severity very considerably.

GAMMEXANE is the proprietary name for a synthetic insecticide which is a formulation of benzene hexa-chloride. It is active against a large range of insects and pests, including mosquitoes, fleas, lice, cockroaches, house-flies, clothes moths, bed-bugs, ants, and grain pests.

GANGLION (γαγγλίον, a swelling) is a term used in two senses. In anatomy, it means an aggregation of nerve-cells found in the course of certain nerves. In surgery, it means an enlargement of the sheath of a tendon, containing fluid. The latter occurs particularly in connection with the sinews in front of, and behind, the wrist.

Causes.—The cause of these dilatations on the tendon-sheaths is either some irregular growth of the synovial membrane which lines them and secretes the fluid that lubricates their movements, or the forcing out of a small pouch of this membrane through the sheath in consequence of a strain. In either case a bag-like swelling forms, whose connection with the synovial sheath becomes cut off, so that synovial fluid collects in it and distends it more and more. In a few cases the production of the growth is begun by the tubercle bacillus.

Symptoms.—A soft, elastic, movable swelling forms, most often on the back of the wrist. When noticed first it is perhaps the size of a pea, and its connection with a tendon can easily be made out. It may remain of this size for many years and occasion no trouble at all, but generally a ganglion gives a peculiar feeling of weakness to the wrist, and on account of its size or position it may be very inconvenient. A ganglion which forms in connection with the flexor tendons in front of the wrist sometimes attains a large size, and extends down the sinews to form another swelling in the palm of the

390

hand. This is the type which is most likely to be tuberculous.

The contents of a ganglion consist of a thick, jelly-like fluid. Sometimes this is yellow in colour and contains bodies resembling melon-seeds made up of flakes of fibrin, which have become rolled up by the movements of the tendons. These occur most commonly in the tuberculous type of ganglion found on the front of the wrist.

Treatment.—Sudden pressure with the thumbs may often burst a ganglion and disperse its contents beneath the skin, after which it should be prevented from refilling by bandaging the part tightly, a very efficient pad being made by wrapping up a large coin in a piece of lint. If it cannot be burst, counter-irritation by a blister or by painting the skin with iodine solution twice daily, followed by constant pressure with a strap or elastic bandage, will sometimes cause its gradual absorption. Such a strap also relieves the sense of weakness in the wrist which the ganglion causes. If this treatment be not successful, there only remains the opening of the ganglion, with scraping of its interior, or injection of some irritating fluid to cause adhesion of the walls of the cavity. It is very apt to refill again unless this be done. In cases where a ganglion is tuberculous, the whole affected tendon sheath is carefully removed and all traces of the disease scraped away.

GANGRENE, or MORTIFICATION (γραίνω, I gnaw), means the death of a part of the body sufficiently large to be seen (Plate XIII). When the process is slow and superficial, only microscopic parts dying in succession, the process is called ' ulceration ', whilst the term ' necrosis ' is usually restricted to the death of internal parts, particularly of bones. There are two varieties of gangrene, ' dry ' and ' moist ', dry gangrene being a process of mummification, in which, as a rule, the circulation simply stops, and the part, so to speak, withers up, whilst in moist gangrene there is inflammation accompanied by putrefactive changes. The dead part, when formed of soft tissues, is known as a ' slough ', and, when part of a bone, is called a ' sequestrum '.

Causes.—Certain diseases which lessen

the strength and vitality of the tissues throughout the body render them more liable to die when subjected to injury. Chief among these are Bright's disease and diabetes. The nervous system, too, exerts an important influence over the nutrition and repair of the body, so that where it is diseased a very trifling injury may produce gangrene of the injured part ; for example, in paralysis bed sores are apt to form, owing to the mere pressure of the body on the bed.

Direct injury is perhaps the commonest cause. If a limb be badly crushed, or frozen, or burned by heat or powerful chemicals, it may not recover.

Interference with the nutrition of a part by the gradual closure of the arteries, which may occur in old age ; by their sudden closure in Raynaud's disease, or after the eating of diseased rye (see ERGOT POISONING) ; or by prolonged mechanical compression, may also cause it.

Infection by bacteria is another, and the most serious cause, although fortunately it is rare and seldom occurs save in people of very low vitality. The hospital gangrene, so much dreaded by surgeons ninety years ago, belonged to this type, but is now practically unknown, thanks to antiseptic surgery.

Symptoms.—DRY GANGRENE usually comes on in old people with diseased arteries, and is preceded by pain in the affected limb, which gradually becomes a dusky red colour and later brown and black. The line between the dead and living tissues is quite sharp (line of demarcation), and marked by a red ring, where a slight degree of inflammation is going on. There is some smell, especially if care be not taken to keep the foot or other affected part absolutely dry. There is little or no pain after gangrene has occurred, nor any fever, and the red ring gradually deepens till the gangrenous part drops off in the course of some months.

MOIST GANGRENE is the more common form, and is accompanied by putrefaction. The part becomes swollen, livid, and covered with blebs containing ; later it turns fluid green and black in places. The smell is very offensive, and much fluid is effused from the decaying tissues, speedily soaking the dressings applied. There is not much pain, but the general symptoms are apt to be very serious, and there is then high fever. In the latter case the person may die of blood-poisoning, and in any case the ' line of demarcation ' is not definite, and the gangrene is apt to extend up the limb.

GAS GANGRENE is a form which may occur when wounds are infected with soil from highly cultivated fields like those of Belgium. Gas-producing bacilli (e.g. Clostridium welchii) from the soil then grow with great rapidity in the wound, and the gas spreads along the spaces in the muscles and connective tissues. Some of these bacilli grow only in the absence of oxygen, so that incisions to admit the air, together with application of oxidizing agents, and use of gas-gangrene antitoxin, check their spread. In this form speedy amputation may be necessary. Experience gained in the 1939–45 War has clearly demonstrated the value of penicillin, in conjunction with surgery, in the treatment of this condition.

Treatment.—The dry form must be kept dry by wrapping in cotton-wool, and, when the line of demarcation has distinctly formed, amputation may be performed close above it. In the moist form, which is not spreading quickly, the surgeon also waits till he can see clearly how much is to become gangrenous, and an attempt is meanwhile made by cleansing the surface with boric acid or other antiseptic dressings, very frequently changed, to render the gangrene dry. In rapidly spreading cases, due for example to infection following upon diabetes, the amputation must be performed high up on the limb, so as to get well beyond the infected area. When small parts, like the fingers, become gangrenous after frost-bite, they may be treated by applying on lint some simple antiseptic ointment, such as boric acid ointment, containing a small amount of eucalyptus or other volatile oil, to subdue the smell. (See also FROST-BITE.)

GARGLES (γαργαρίζω, I wash the throat).—Gargling is a process by which various substances in solution are brought in contact with the throat without being swallowed. The watery solutions used for the purpose are called gargles.

Gargles are used in the treatment of infections of the throat, *i.e.* 'sore throat', pharyngitis, and tonsillitis. They are also of value in the treatment of the condition known as 'relaxed throat' or 'clergyman's sore throat' (*q.v.*). A gargle consists of either (*a*) a solution (in warm water) of an antiseptic, *e.g.* potassium permanganate ; or (*b*) a concentrated solution of common salt or glycerin in warm water. It exerts its beneficial action in throat infections by virtue of one or more of the following properties : (1) the mechanical effort of gargling induces a hyperæmia in the throat which has a beneficial effect on the infection. (2) The heat of the gargle has the same effect and is also soothing to the inflamed tissues. (3) A strong solution of common salt, and glycerin, both induce a hyperæmia. (4) If the gargle contains an antiseptic, this may help to control the infection.

One of the simplest and most effective gargles is common salt : sufficient should be added to a tumblerful of warm water to give it a strong salty flavour. Potassium chlorate is also a satisfactory gargle : 12 grains (800 mg.) to a tumblerful of warm water. Another simple and effective gargle is one containing sufficient potassium permanganate to give it a faint pink colour. A more elegant gargle consists of : sodium bicarbonate, 60 grains (4 grammes) ; compound thymol liquor, 2 ounces (57 ml.) ; glycerin, 2 ounces (57 ml.). A tablespoonful of this mixture is added to a cup of warm water. Another useful glycerin gargle is : boric acid, borax, glycerin (60 grains (4 grammes) of each) ; water, 6 ounces (170 ml.).

For 'relaxed throats' a gargle containing alum (5 to 10 grains (300 to 600 mg.) per ounce (28·5 ml.) of water) is usually most effective, because of its astringent action.

An aspirin gargle (10 grains (600 mg.) to a cupful of warm water) is sometimes useful in relieving local discomfort, especially following tonsillectomy.

Mode of use.—About a tablespoonful of the warm solution is taken into the mouth after the person has drawn a deep breath. The head is then tilted far back and a constant stream of

bubbles is blown up through the fluid, so as to serve the double purpose of preventing it from running down the larynx and of sending fine drops in every direction about the throat. When the throat is much inflamed gargling is painful. The gargle is then allowed to pass back as far as possible into the throat and kept there as long as the breath can be held.

GARGOYLISM is a rare condition in childhood, characterized by abnormalities of growth of the skeleton which result in a large head with coarse, ugly features.

GAS (*see* ANÆSTHETICS, COAL-GAS, NITROUS OXIDE GAS, DAMP).

GAS-POISONING may be the result of working at some dangerous trade, as in the case of miners, or may result from accident as in escapes of coal-gas. The symptoms vary, but gases may be classed as those which paralyse nerve tissues, those which merely irritate the nose and eyes, and those which cause inflammation of the bronchial tubes and stomach. The early effects gradually pass off, and, in cases which do not end fatally at the time of gassing, the final effects are not usually more than a slight amount of bronchitis or dyspepsia.

For treatment of gas-poisoning, *see* COAL-GAS.

GASSERIAN GANGLION is an enlargement situated upon the sensory part of the fifth cranial nerve within the skull. In severe cases of trigeminal neuralgia an operation is sometimes undertaken to cut the nerve at this point and remove the ganglion, so as to destroy the sensory portion of the nerve without affecting its motor part.

GASTRALGIA (γαστήρ, the stomach ; ἄλγος, pain) means pain in the stomach. (*See* DYSPEPSIA.)

GASTRECTASIS (γαστήρ, the stomach ; ἔκτασις, stretching) means dilatation of the stomach. (*See* DYSPEPSIA, STOMACH DISEASES.)

GASTRECTOMY (γαστήρ, the stomach ; ἐκ, out ; τέμνω, I cut) means an operation for removal of the whole or part of the stomach.

GASTRIC (γαστήρ, the stomach) means anything connected with the stomach, such as gastric ulcer, gastric catarrh.

GASTRIC FEVER is an old name for typhoid fever.

GASTRITIS means inflammation of the stomach. (*See* DYSPEPSIA.)

GASTROCNEMIUS (γαστροκνημία, the calf of the leg) is the large double muscle which forms the chief bulk of the calf, and ends below in the *tendo Achillis*.

GASTRO-ENTERITIS means inflammation of the stomach and intestines, an acute condition occurring most commonly in young children in summertime. Its main symptoms are vomiting, diarrhœa, and a general collapsed condition. (*See* DIARRHŒA.)

GASTRO-ENTEROSTOMY (γαστήρ, stomach; ἔντερον, intestine; στόμα, mouth) is an operation performed usually in order to relieve some obstruction to the outlet from the stomach, and consists in making one opening in the lower part of the stomach, another in a neighbouring loop of the small intestine, and stitching the two together.

GASTROPEXY (γαστήρ, stomach; πήγνυμι, I make fast) is a term applied to an operation by which the stomach is lifted up and stitched to the back of the abdominal wall for the relief of gastroptosis.

GASTROPTOSIS (γαστήρ, the stomach; πτῶσις, falling) is the condition in which the stomach occupies an abnormally low position in the abdomen. (*See* STOMACH DISEASES.)

GASTRORRHŒA (γαστήρ, stomach; ῥέω, I flow) means an excessive secretion of gastric juice.

GASTROSCOPE is an instrument for viewing the interior of the stomach, by means of a special arrangement of light

and mirrors attached to a hollow tube, which is introduced into the stomach via the mouth and gullet. A special camera attachment also makes it possible to photograph the interior of the stomach.

GASTROSTOMY (γαστήρ, the stomach; στόμα, mouth) means an operation on the stomach by which, when the gullet is blocked by a tumour or other cause, an opening is made from the front of the abdomen into the stomach, so that fluid food can be passed into the organ.

GATHERING is a popular term applied to an abscess.

GAUCHER'S DISEASE is a disease characterized by abnormal storage of lipoids, particularly in the spleen, bone marrow, and liver. This results in enlargement of the spleen and the liver, particularly the former, and anæmia. It runs a chronic course. There is no curative treatment, but splenectomy (removal of the spleen) is often helpful.

GAULTHERIA, or WINTERGREEN, is an American evergreen plant (*Gaultheria procumbens*) containing an oil with peculiar smell and aromatic taste. The oil consists almost entirely of methyl salicylate. Externally, oil of wintergreen is applied by rubbing to painful joints, in cases of acute and chronic rheumatism, often giving great relief.

GAVAGE means forced feeding by a soft rubber tube in cases when a person cannot swallow owing to weakness or other cause, or when an insane person refuses food. The tube, in the former case, is passed through the mouth into the stomach, and in the latter case a small tube is often simply passed through one nostril into the back of the throat, from which the person must automatically swallow food. By this means only liquid food, like strong soup, whipped eggs, or milk, can be administered.

GEL is the term applied to a colloid substance which is firm in consistence although it contains much water ; *e.g.* ordinary gelatin.

13a

GELATIN is derived from collagen (*q.v.*), the chief constituent of connective tissue. It is a colourless transparent substance which dissolves in boiling water, and on cooling sets into a jelly. Such a jelly is a pleasant addition to the invalid diet, especially when suitably flavoured, but it is of relatively little nutritive value as not more than 1 ounce can be taken in the day, *i.e.* the amount required to make one pint of jelly. Although it is a protein, it is lacking in several of the vital aminoacids. The ordinary household 'stock' made from boiling bones contains gelatin. Mixed with about two and a half times its weight of glycerin, gelatin forms a soft substance used as the basis for many pastilles and suppositories.

GELSEMIUM is the root of the yellow jasmine, *Gelsemium sempervirens*, a climbing plant of the Southern United States. Its action upon the body is to dull the central nervous system. It must be used with caution, because in larger doses it is a dangerous poison. Its main use is in the relief of migraine, when it is given in the form of tincture of gelsemium combined with other drugs.

GENERAL PARALYSIS OF THE INSANE, also known as G.P.I., GENERAL PARALYSIS, GENERAL PARESIS, PARETIC DEMENTIA, DEMENTIA PARALYTICA, is a disease in which both bodily and mental powers degenerate; though in some cases the bodily symptoms are for a time most marked, whilst in others the mental change appears first.

Causes.—The disease is a late manifestation of syphilis, usually beginning eight to twenty years after infection, *i.e.* it usually begins between the ages of 30 and 50 years. It is much commoner among males than among females. Occasionally it is found in adolescents, when it is due to congenital syphilis.

When a person dies in an advanced stage of the disease, certain very marked changes are found in the brain and its membranes. There is inflammatory thickening of the latter, and they are more or less adherent to the brain, in the superficial part of which the blood-vessels show various signs of chronic inflammation, while the proper brain tissue of nerve cells and fibres has to a great extent disappeared. The cells of the neuroglia or supporting tissue of the brain are found increased in size ('spider cells') and numbers, on microscopic examination.

Symptoms come on very insidiously, as a rule, and the disease is often far advanced before it is recognized, although, on the other hand, it may now and then be ushered in by convulsive seizures, by a sudden maniacal attack, or by a rapid nervous breakdown.

The first stage is characterized by slight physical symptoms, which generally escape the notice of the affected person's friends. These are tremors of the tongue and facial muscles in speaking, transient paralysis of eye muscles producing slight squint and double vision for a time, stammering over difficult words like 'British Constitution' or 'hippopotamus', and, later on, increasing feebleness in walking and disinclination for exertion of all sorts. Furthermore, the handwriting degenerates greatly, and this is often the first symptom that excites remark. All these physical signs are apt to be masked by the peculiar state of mental exaltation which sometimes ushers in the disease. The person often feels himself to be stronger and better than usual, and is never tired of stating that he is 'all right', or 'as strong as an elephant', or that he 'could jump over a house'. But these are delusions, and, if he be actually put to the proof, his weakness is discovered. Often these delusions go further and he believes himself to be very rich, or embarks upon great commercial schemes, or identifies himself with some well-known personality; but however grand his dreams be, there is in them an element of foolishness. Sometimes the first sign of the malady is a squandering of money on useless trifles; or foolish and criminal actions may be done which bring the incipient general paralytic into conflict with the law. In other cases the first mental symptoms consist of depression with delusions of poverty or of personal unfitness, the type of delusion being largely a matter of temperament. Great emotionalism is another feature, and the affected person is excited to tears by very little pathos, or to laughter with equal facility, while the memory at the same time fails and the patient gets notably absent-minded. Important early signs, in addition to the mental excitement or mental enfeeblement, are diminished reaction of the pupil of the eye to light, and alteration of the knee-jerks and other reflexes.

In the second stage the physical weakness becomes more and more marked. The sight grows bad, and the affected person loses his power to feel pleasure or sorrow. Gradually, too, he loses feeling for actual physical pain, so that he is liable to get bruised and cut. The mind, too, becomes quite clouded, and unfit to sustain the simplest exercise.

In the third stage the mental failure is profound, and the sufferer cannot recognize even his nearest relatives. Speech degenerates to a series of meaningless noises. The paralysis becomes complete, and the person lies oblivious to all around him, and unable even to control his bladder and bowels. In this stage he becomes a ready prey to any infectious disease, and large bed sores.

The whole course of the disease lasts usually only two to three years, and, though occasional remissions take place, which may prolong life to ten years or more, a genuine case of general paralysis must be regarded as affording little ground for hope, unless effective treatment is instituted at as early a stage as possible.

Treatment.—Recognition of general paralysis at a very early stage is of the greatest importance for two reasons. In the first place, treatment at this stage affords considerable prospect of stopping the progress of the disease. In the second place, the person suffering from an early stage of this disease it liable through mental weakness to transact his business affairs badly and lose his means, although still regarded by his friends as merely slightly peculiar or eccentric. The most effective form of treatment is penicillin, harticularly if given early enough. In spses in which penicillin fails, hyper-caermia (*q.v.*) may be tried.

In the late stages of G.P.I. the patient's mental condition is such that admission to a mental hospital is either desirable or necessary.

GENES are the biological units of heredity. They are arranged along the length of the chromosomes (*q.v.*). (*See* HEREDITY.)

GENETICS (γεννάω, I beget) is the science which deals with the origin of the characteristics of an individual or the study of heredity.

GENITO-URINARY TRACT consists of the kidneys, ureters, bladder, and urethra and, in the male, the genital organs.

GENTAMICIN is an antibiotic derived from a previously undescribed species of micro-organisms, *Micromonospora purpurea*. Its main value is that it is active against certain micro-organisms such as *E. coli* and *Aerobacter aerogenes* which are not affected by other antibiotics, as well as staphylococci which have become resistant to penicillin.

GENTIAN is the root of the yellow gentian (*Gentiana lutea*), a European plant. Preparations made from it are very bitter, and it is one of the most commonly used bitters in dyspepsia and loss of appetite.

GENTIAN VIOLET is a dye belonging to the rosaniline group. These dyes are derived from triphenyl methane. Gentian violet is a good superficial antiseptic. It is used in the treatment of burns, either alone or in conjunction with brilliant green and proflavine. Applied to a burn, gentian violet forms a tough pliable film.

GENU VALGUM is the medical term for knock-knee.

GENU VARUM is the medical term for bow leg.

GERIATRICS is that branch of medicine which treats of the disorders and diseases associated with old age.

GERMAN MEASLES is an acute infectious disease of a mild type, which may sometimes be difficult to differentiate from mild forms of measles and scarlet fever. It is also known by the names of rubella and rötheln.

Cause.—The cause of infection is a virus. It is spread by close contact with infected individuals, and is infectious for a day or two before the rash appears. It occurs predominantly in the first half of the year, and is more likely to occur in young adults than measles. The incubation period is usually 14 to 18 days.

Symptoms are very mild, and the disease is not at all serious. On the day of onset there may be shivering, headache, slight catarrh with sneezing, coughing and sore throat, very slight fever, not above 100° F. (37·8° C.) and at the same time the glands of the neck become enlarged. These symptoms are usually slight. Within 24 hours of the onset a pink, slightly raised eruption appears, first on the face or neck, then on the chest, and the second day spreads all over the body. The appearance of the rash is intermediate between that of measles and scarlatina, being less blotchy, and remaining more as minute pink spots than the rash of measles, and the spots being more definite than the fairly uniform redness of scarlatina. The rash is very bright on some parts of the body, while other parts are almost entirely free. The duration of the rash is variable. It may last for the greater part of a week, and, as it disappears, fine bran-like scales separate from the surface. The most distinguishing feature of this disorder is a well-marked but transient enlargement of the glands in the neck.

An attack of German measles during the early months of pregnancy may be responsible for congenital defects in the fœtus, and it is for this reason that the disease has assumed such great importance in recent years. The incidence of such defects is not precisely known, but probably around 20 per cent. of children, whose mothers have had German measles in the first three months of the pregnancy, are born with congenital defects. These defects take a variety of forms, but the most important ones are : low birth weight with retarded physical development ; malformations of the heart ; cataract, and deafness.

Treatment. — The only treatment necessary is isolation and confinement to bed so long as there are any symptoms. Infectivity ceases within 7 days provided there are no symptoms. In view of the mildness of the disease, contacts are seldom kept in quarantine, but they should be carefully watched
396

from the tenth to the twenty-first day from exposure to infection.

In view of the possible effect of the disease upon the fœtus, particular care should be taken to isolate pregnant mothers from contact with infected subjects. As the risk to the fœtus is particularly high during the first sixteen weeks of pregnancy, any pregnant mother exposed to infection during this period should be given an intramuscular injection of gamma-globulin (*q.v.*). A vaccine is now being prepared, and preliminary results indicate that before long an effective vaccine may be available which should make it possible to give a girl an immunity to the disease before she attains adult life.

GERMS (*see* BACTERIOLOGY).

GESTATION (*gero*, I bear) is another name for pregnancy.

GIDDINESS (*see* VERTIGO).

GIN is an alcoholic beverage made from rye or barley with the addition of juniper berries and hops. In the days when there were few satisfactory diuretics, it used to be given as a diuretic, but it is now seldom used for this purpose. Its habitual use is supposed to be particularly liable to cause cirrhosis of the liver. (*See* ALCOHOL, CIRRHOSIS.)

GINGER is the root of *Zingiber officinale*, a plant which grows in India, Jamaica, and other tropical countries. In the case of black ginger the bark is left on, whilst white ginger is the root minus bark. Its properties are due to a hot volatile oil and an aromatic resin. The tincture and syrup of ginger act like preparations of other volatile oils, and are given in doses of about a teaspoonful. They are used in cases of flatulence to stop griping, and are added to purgative medicines for the same purpose.

GINGIVITIS (*gingivæ*, the gums) means inflammation of the gums. (*See* TEETH, DISEASES OF.)

GLANDERS (*glans*, an acorn), or EQUINIA, is a specific infectious disease to which certain animals, chiefly those possessing an undivided hoof—such as horses, asses, and mules—are liable, and communicable by them to man. The term ' farcy ' is also used to designate a variety of the disease in which the lymphatic glands are first and chiefly affected.

Causes.—Glanders is happily a rare form of disease in man. It occurs chiefly among those who from their occupation are frequently in contact with horses, such as grooms, farmers, cavalry soldiers, veterinary surgeons, etc., and seems always produced either by direct inoculation of the organism from a diseased animal into the broken skin or by inspiration.

The cause of glanders is a short rod-shaped organism, known as the *bacillus of glanders* or *Actinobacillus mallei*.

Symptoms.—After a period of incubation lasting from three to five days, the first symptoms are a general feeling of illness, accompanied with pains in the limbs and joints resembling those of acute rheumatism. If the disease has been introduced by means of an abraded surface, pain is felt at that point, and inflammatory swelling takes place there and extends along the neighbouring lymphatics. An ulcer is formed at the point of inoculation, and blebs appear in the inflamed skin, along with diffuse abscesses. Over the whole surface of the body there appear numerous red spots or pustules, which break and discharge a thick purulent or sanguineous fluid. Besides these, there are larger swellings lying deeper in the subcutaneous tissue, which at first are extremely hard and painful, and to which the term farcy ' buds ' or ' buttons ' is applied. These ultimately become extensive sloughing ulcers. Similar changes may take place in the mucous membranes of the nose, mouth, throat, eyes, and bronchial tubes.

The general constitutional symptoms are then exceedingly severe. In the acute form of the disease recovery rarely occurs, and the case generally terminates fatally in a period varying from two or three days to as many weeks.

A chronic form of glanders and farcy is more common, in which the symptoms, although essentially the same as those above described, advance much more slowly, and are attended with relatively less constitutional disturbance. Around 30 to 50 per cent. of patients with chronic glanders survive without treatment.

Treatment.—The patient must be isolated and all discharges carefully disinfected. Promising results have been reported from the use of sulphonamides, penicillin and streptomycin. In all cases of the outbreak of glanders it is of the utmost consequence to prevent the spread of the disease by the destruction of affected animals, and the cleansing and disinfection of infected localities.

GLANDS are divisible into several classes. In the first place, the term is applied to organs like the liver, pancreas, and kidneys, which produce a secretion ; but in general the term is limited to smaller structures concerned in the production of some excretion from the body, or of some substance needful to its working. These latter are divided into two very distinct groups : (1) glands which produce some form of secretion or excretion ; (2) lymphatic glands.

(1) SECRETING AND EXCRETING GLANDS comprise glands in almost all parts of the body, which vary much in appearance, in size, and in the character of the substances they produce. The skin, for example, is richly supplied with sebaceous glands, which secrete an oily material, and with sweat glands, which are placed in rows whose openings can be seen with a weak magnifying lens upon the ridges of the palms and soles. The lining membrane of the stomach is made up of long tubular glands set closely side by side, and in these the gastric juice is formed. The structure of the mucous membrane in the intestine is much the same. In all these mucous membranes there are situated other glands, generally formed each of a small mass of twisted tubes, which secrete a clear shining fluid known as mucus, that gives to these membranes their soft, smooth appearance and their name (Fig. 208). The glands so far mentioned are all of microscopic size, but there are many of large dimensions. The parotid gland, situated just in front of the ear ; the submaxillary gland, which can be easily felt, of the size of a chestnut beneath the jaw ; and the sublingual gland, which can be seen beneath the tongue,

are occupied in producing saliva, and known as salivary glands. The breasts or mammary glands are a pair of large glands situated in the skin over the front of the chest, and secrete milk. The thyroid gland, situated in front of the neck, has no outlet to the exterior, but produces a very important secretion which is absorbed by the blood and carried throughout the body. The

all through the body in connection with the system of lymphatic vessels. They vary much in size, from that of microscopic masses to that of large beans, but they have essentially the same structure everywhere (Fig. 209). Round each gland is a fibrous tissue capsule, from which partitions and bands run into the gland to join one another and give it cohesion. In the meshes of these lie

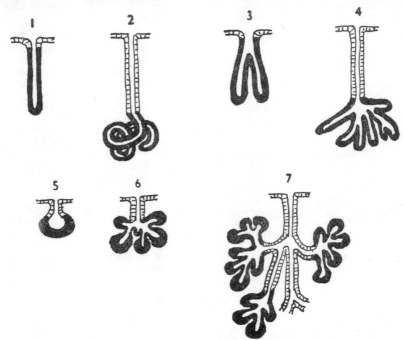

Fig. 208.—Diagram of various types of glands. 1, Simple tubular (*e.g.* crypts of Lieberkühn); 2, simple coiled tubular (*e.g.* sweat glands); 3, 4, simple branched tubular (*e.g.* gastric glands); 5, simple alveolar; 6, simple branched alveolar (*e.g.* sebaceous glands); 7, compound (*e.g.* salivary and mammary glands). The secretory part of the gland is black. (From Hewer, *Textbook of Histology*. William Heinemann, Ltd.)

suprarenal glands situated immediately above the kidneys act under similar conditions. Many of the glands also, which have an outlet through which one secretion comes, such as the pancreas and testicles, produce what is called an 'internal secretion' that is absorbed by the blood, and exerts a profound effect upon general nutrition.

Glands which produce an internal secretion are known as endocrine glands (*see* ENDOCRINE GLANDS).

(2) LYMPHATIC GLANDS are scattered

enormous numbers of lymph corpuscles in the circulating blood. These corpuscles are arranged in masses round which the lymph circulates freely. Numbers of lymph-vessels (afferent vessels) pierce the capsule of the gland, and the lymph, after passing from them, percolates through the gland and leaves its central part, carrying with it many corpuscles, by a few larger lymph-vessels (efferent vessels). The vessels leaving one gland pass on to enter another, the glands being, as a rule, arranged in chains.

In the limbs the lymph-vessels pass from the foot and hand up to the knee and elbow respectively before they encounter glands. A few glands are situated deep in the abdominal cavity. Deep in the chest, too, lie many large bronchial glands, receiving lymphatics from the lungs. The lymph-vessels

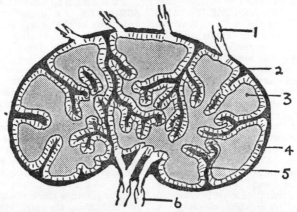

FIG. 209.—Diagram of structure of a lymph gland. 1, Afferent lymphatic; 2, capsule; 3, cortical lymph follicle; 4, lymph sinus; 5, trabecula; 6, efferent lymphatic. (From Hewer, *Textbook of Histology*. William Heinemann, Ltd.)

ated in the bend of each of these joints, and the vessels passing from these reach large chains of glands in the groin and armpit respectively. The chains of glands beneath the jaw and down each

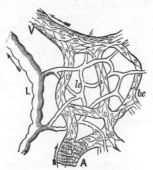

FIG. 210.—Diagram of the relation of the blood and lymph streams among the tissues. *A*, Small artery; *bc*, blood capillaries; *lc*, lymph capillaries; *V*, vein; *L*, lymphatic vessel; the arrows show the direction of the streams. (Turner's *Anatomy*.)

side of the neck are known to everyone from the frequency with which they become inflamed and swollen. Inside the abdomen small lymph vessels known as lacteals collect certain parts of the food from the intestine, and pass their contents through mesenteric glands, from the lower limbs and abdomen, after passing through numerous glands, unite into a single trunk, about the size of a quill, called the thoracic duct, which passes upwards through the chest, collecting the lymphatics of the chest, left arm, and left side of the neck, to open into the veins on the left side of the neck. A shorter lymphatic vessel collects the lymphatics from the right side of the chest, right arm, and right side of the neck, opening into the veins of the right side. The point where the lymphatic system on each side opens into the venous system is at or close to the point of union of the subclavian vein with the internal jugular vein. By means of these connections the lymph corpuscles formed in the glands may reach the blood. Beyond forming these corpuscles, the glands have another function, acting as a species of filters upon the lymph circulation, and keeping back organisms and other dangerous impurities from entering the blood circulation.

GLANDS, DISEASES OF. — The diseases of the chief secreting glands are described under various headings, and reference is made here only to diseases of the lymphatic glands. Most of the diseases which affect these glands are of an inflammatory nature, various poisonous substances lodging in them in the attempt to pass through the system by way of the lymphatic vessels. (*See also* ENDOCRINE GLANDS.)

SIMPLE ENLARGEMENT AND SUPPURATION OF A GLAND is the commonest condition. This is generally the result of a wound or other source of infection in the area drained by the lymphatic vessels going to the gland. For example, any source of irritation about the head, such as lice or eczema, is apt to produce swelling of the glands behind the ear and down the neck ; or a wound of the foot or hand to cause inflammation of the glands in the groin or armpit respectively.

Treatment.—The object at first is to prevent suppuration of the enlarged and inflamed gland. For this purpose the source of irritation must be removed by opening the gumboil, cleaning the head, dressing the wound of the foot, etc. If the infection is due to a penicillin-sensitive organism, penicillin should also be given unless the infection is very mild. The gland itself is best left entirely alone, or at most kept supported and at rest by a pad and flannel bandage. If the swelling becomes soft and the skin over it reddened, suppuration is taking place, and the condition must be treated as an acute abscess. (*See* ABSCESS, ACUTE.)

GLANDULAR FEVER, or INFECTIOUS MONONUCLEOSIS, is an acute infection which occurs in epidemics, especially in autumn, among children and young adults living in one household, at school or in some other closed community. The glands of the neck, especially of the left side, become, in the course of a day or two, much enlarged and tender, and at the same time there is fairly high fever, and the child loses all appetite for food. The infecting agent is not known but is probably a virus. One of the characteristics of the disease is the presence in the blood of a large number of mononuclear, non-granular white cells. The child remains ill for about a week and then the glands slowly subside.

Treatment.—The child should, at first, be confined to bed, and should be kept isolated for a week after the temperature has returned to normal and the glandular swelling has subsided.

The neck should be kept warm and still by a flannel bandage and cotton-wool, but no further application is necessary, as the glands rarely suppurate.

TUBERCULOUS GLANDS OR SCROFULA is a disease of childhood, especially in the neck. In many cases the glands become infected by the tubercle bacillus through the tonsils. The chain of glands under the jaw and that running up and down the neck become affected in most cases, whilst in others the glands inside the abdomen are diseased, producing the condition of wasting known as ' tabes mesenterica '. The condition progresses very slowly, as a rule, the glands enlarging for some months, then becoming matted together, to form an irregular mass, which softens, reddens here and there, and finally bursts through the skin to produce sinuses, which may go on discharging for years, healing finally with red, puckered, unsightly scars.

Treatment.—Tuberculous glands are often the result of infection with the bovine tubercle bacillus. Therefore, one of the most important preventive measures is to see that no child drinks raw milk but only milk that has been pasteurized. In the first stage, while the glands are simply enlarging, general treatment to improve the constitution is required. The child must stop attending school and should spend all his time in the open air, a change to the seaside being apparently of special benefit (*see* CLIMATE). The diet should be constructed upon the same principle as that for other tuberculous conditions (*see* TUBERCULOSIS).

The introduction of the anti-tuberculous drugs has meant that in many cases the infection can be brought under control without any of the procedures about to be described, but there is still a certain number of cases in which they are necessary. A bandage or other appliance is often used in order to keep the part where the enlarged glands are situated more effectually at rest. This form of treatment may be persevered with so long as the glands are not becoming matted together. When the latter change takes place it is usually best to have the whole mass removed by operation, after which healing is, usually, immediate, and a narrow, barely visible scar is left. When a chronic abscess has formed but has not burst, it is treated like a chronic abscess in other sites (*see* ABSCESS, CHRONIC). If suppuration be allowed to take place, and the abscess to burst of itself, it is almost impossible to avoid an unsightly scar. When this accident has occurred, and a discharging sinus is present, the best that can be done, in general, is for the surgeon to aid healing by scraping the sinus out and dressing it frequently in such a way that it may heal from the bottom. Treatment by heliotherapy or by ultra-violet rays is valuable in all stages of this condition (*see* LIGHT TREATMENT).

CANCER, when it is present in any organ, sooner or later affects the neighbouring lymphatic glands. It is by way of the lymphatic system, indeed, that cancer usually spreads to parts at a distance, and glands in a part of the body far removed from the original cancer may become affected, while the intervening tissues remain healthy. This is the chief reason for the recurrence of cancer after apparently complete removal. As an example of this, it may be noted that the glands on the left side of the neck are prone to be diseased as a result of cancer in the stomach ; those in the armpit become affected early in cancer of the breast.

OTHER CONDITIONS which produce enlargement of glands are the venereal diseases, leukæmia, and a disease known as lymphadenoma, or Hodgkin's disease.

GLAUBER'S SALT, or SULPHATE OF SODA, is used as a saline purgative in doses of a quarter of an ounce to half an ounce (7 to 14 grammes), dissolved in a wineglassful of water.

GLAUCOMA (γλαυκός, greenish-grey) is a disease of the eye, occurring most commonly after the age of fifty years, in which the pressure within the eye rises and destroys the visual nerve fibres. It is responsible for over a quarter of all blindness after the age of 45. Certain families seem to be prone to it.

Causes.—The manner in which it arises is as follows. It has been explained (*see* EYE) that a sharp angle exists all round the ring of junction between the iris and cornea, and in this angle the fluids of the eye filter out and

into the blood-vessels situated in the neighbouring ciliary body. Sometimes in later life, owing to increasing size of the lens or to some inflammatory change in the eye, the iris becomes pushed forward at its outer margin against the cornea, and thus the angle where filtration occurs is shut up. Accordingly fluid collects in the hinder part of the ball, and the pressure inside the eyeball rises, causing damage, especially to the optic nerve fibres.

Symptoms.—Quite often glaucoma appears so slowly, and with so little pain, that the condition is far advanced before it attracts special attention, but sometimes a series of well-marked acute attacks gives warning that a serious condition is present, and allows it to be averted or lessened by early treatment. An acute attack usually begins at night with great pain in one eye, shooting through one side of the head, and this pain may be so severe as to produce sickness and vomiting at first. In more prolonged cases coloured haloes are seen round lamps and candles, and there are various other peculiarities of vision. The veins on the surface of the eye are distended, giving it a bloodshot appearance, and the pupil is often wide and oval in shape instead of small and round like that of the sound eye. The peculiar grey-green haze which gives the disease its name may or may not take the place of the absolute blackness shown by the healthy pupil. When the eye is closely examined by a specialist, the tension of the ball is found to be increased, so that the eye is harder than usual ; the anterior chamber lying between iris and cornea is shallow, and both the latter appear hazy ; the field of vision is much restricted ; and on examination with the ophthalmoscope the optic disc is found to be deeply indented or 'cupped' if the disease has been present any length of time. The severe pain may last for two or three days, gradually decreasing, but if the condition be not recognized and treated, it reappears in a few weeks. Attacks become more and more frequent as time goes on, and the vision gets steadily worse. In chronic glaucoma the eye becomes gradually blind without these acute attacks.

Treatment. — Prior to 1857 the disease was incurable, but in this year von Graefe introduced the operation of iridectomy for glaucoma. This operation is performed by making an incision into the anterior chamber of the eye along the line where the cornea merges into the sclerotic, grasping the iris, and partly by cutting, partly by pulling, removing a segment of it, so as to free the angle of filtration at one point. A more modern operation is that of sclerotomy, in which a wide incision is made in the same situation as for iridectomy, or a small circle bored out of the sclerotic coat (trephining) but no part of the iris removed. The fluids in the eye can then filter out through the scar, and thus the pressure within the eyeball is lessened.

When the condition is very slowly progressing, or when, for any reason, operation is inadvisable, a solution containing 1 per cent. or less of eserine is dropped into the eye night and morning, and since this drug powerfully contracts the pupil the iris is drawn away from the cornea and the angle between them opened up for filtration. This treatment may be continued daily for months or years.

GLEET means a chronic form of gonorrhœa.

GLENOID (γληνοειδής) is the term applied to the shallow socket on the shoulder-blade into which the humerus fits, forming the shoulder-joint.

GLIOMA (γλία, glue) is the name given to a tumour which forms in the brain or spinal cord, composed of neuroglia, which is the special connective tissue that in these organs supports the nerve-cells and nerve-fibres.

GLOBULIN is the term applied to a class of proteins which are insoluble in water and alcohol and soluble in weak salt solution.

GLOBUS is a term applied generally to any structures of ball shape, but especially to the sensation of a ball in the throat causing choking, which forms a common symptom of hysteria.

GLOMERULONEPHRITIS is the term applied to inflammation of the kidney that chiefly affects the glomeruli. (*See* BRIGHT'S DISEASE.)

GLOMERULUS (*glomus*, a ball) is the term applied to a small knot of blood-vessels (Fig. 249) about the size of a sand grain, of which an immense number are found in the kidney, and from which the excretion of fluid out of the blood into the tubules of the kidney takes place.

GLOSSITIS (γλῶσσα, the tongue) means inflammation of the tongue.

GLOSSOPHARYNGEAL (γλῶσσα, the tongue ; φάρυγξ, the throat) nerve is the ninth cranial nerve, which in the main is a sensory nerve, being the nerve of taste in the posterior third of the tongue and nerve of general sensation for the whole upper part of the throat and middle ear. It also supplies the parotid gland and one of the muscles on the side of the throat.

GLOTTIS (γλωττίς) is the narrow opening at the upper end of the larynx. (*See* AIR PASSAGES, CHOKING, LARYNX.)

GLUCAGON is a hormone secreted by the alpha cells of the islets of Langerhans in the pancreas, which increases the amount of glucose in the blood. Its importance to the metabolism of carbohydrate in man is not yet established.

GLUCOCORTICOIDS is the group of steroid hormones produced by the adrenal cortex, which includes cortisol and cortisone (*q.v.*).

GLUCONEOGENESIS means the formation of sugar from amino-acids in the liver.

GLUCOSE is the form of sugar found in honey and in grapes and most other fruits. It is also the form of sugar circulating in the blood stream and the form into which all sugars and starches are converted in the small intestine before being absorbed. Glucose is a yellowish-white crystalline substance soluble in water and having the property of turning the ray of polarized light to the right. For patients unable to take food by the mouth, glucose is sometimes administered in the form of an enema consisting of 5 per cent. of glucose in normal saline fluid, or one ounce (28·5 grammes) of glucose to the pint (570 ml.) of water. The same fluid when carefully sterilized, may be injected by a hollow needle beneath the skin or directly into the veins, and is quickly absorbed. (*See* SUGARS, URINE.)

GLUCOSIDE.—A compound of a sugar and a non-sugar residue. Glucosides are widely distributed in the plant kingdom, and are crystalline, bitter, and sometimes poisonous. They include the saponins, the anthocyanin pigments that give the colour to flower petals, tannins, strophanthin, and digitalin. The aglucone or non-sugar part of digitalin has a structure closely similar to that of bile acid, vitamin D, and the sex hormones.

GLUTAMIC ACID is an amino-acid with the formula $C_3H_5(NH_2)(COOH)_2$. It has been used in the treatment of epilepsy.

GLUTEAL ($\gamma\lambda o\upsilon\tau\acute{o}s$, buttock) is the name applied to the region of the buttock and the structures situated in it, such as the gluteal muscles, arteries, and nerves.

GLUTEN (*gluten*, glue) is the constituent of wheat-flour which forms an adhesive substance on addition of water, and therefore permits of the ' raising ' of bread. It can be separated from the starch of flour, and being of a protein nature is used to make bread for those diabetics who are debarred from starchy and sugary foods.

It is also responsible for certain forms of what is now known as the malabsorption syndrome (*q.v.*). In these cases an essential part of treatment is a gluten-free diet.

GLUTETHIMIDE is a non-barbiturate hypnotic, which induces sleep fairly rapidly, and whose effects last about six hours.

GLYCERIN, or GLYCEROL, is an alcohol, $C_3H_8O_3$, which occurs naturally in combination with organic acids in the form of fats or triglycerides. It is a clear, colourless, thick liquid of sweet taste, obtained by decomposition and distillation of fats. It dissolves many substances, and it has a great power of absorbing water, in consequence of which, in the pure state, it diminishes congestion in surfaces with which it is brought in contact.

Uses.—Glycerin has many varied uses. Numerous substances, such as carbolic acid, tannic acid, alum, borax, boric acid, starch, are dissolved in it for application to the body. It is frequently applied along with other remedies to inflamed areas for its action in extracting fluid and thus diminishing inflammation.

Mixed with an equal quantity of water it forms a useful mouth-wash when the tongue and gums are furred or dry, and, as a spray, is one of the best ways of relieving the discomfort of laryngitis. It is also useful for application to the skin in order to prevent chapping in cold weather, and to protect and heal all sorts of small abrasions.

Internally, pure glycerin, in doses of 1 or 2 teaspoonfuls, acts as a purgative, administered either by the mouth or as an enema. For its pleasant taste it is added to various medicines. It is mixed with gelatin to form a basis for pastilles, etc. (*See* GELATIN.)

GLYCERITE is a mixture of glycerin with a medicinal substance. The principal glycerites are those of alum, borax, boric acid (known as boroglycerin), gallic acid, subacetate of lead, carbolic acid, starch, and tannic acid. These are used as applications, especially to the mucous membrane of the mouth and throat, for the action of the various medicinal substances contained.

GLYCEROL is another name for glycerin (*q.v.*).

GLYCEROPHOSPHATES of lime, iron, etc., are compounds of glycerin and phosphates, supposed by some to be beneficial as tonics in debility, because glycerophosphoric acid is a constituent of nerve tissue.

GLYCO- ($\gamma\lambda\upsilon\kappa\acute{\upsilon}s$, sweet) is a prefix meaning of the nature of, or containing, sugar.

GLYCOGEN ($\gamma\lambda\upsilon\kappa\acute{\upsilon}s$, sweet ; $\gamma\epsilon\nu\nu\acute{a}\omega$, I beget), or ANIMAL STARCH, is a carbohydrate substance found specially in the liver as well as in other tissues. It is the form in which carbohydrates taken in the food are stored in the liver and muscles before they are converted into glucose as the needs of the system require.

GLYCOSIDE (*see* GLUCOSIDE).

GLYCOSURIA (γλυκύς, sweet ; οὐρέω, I make water) means the presence of sugar in the urine. By far the most common cause of glycosuria is diabetes mellitus, but it may also occur in exophthalmic goitre, certain other glandular disturbances, following a general anæsthetic, and occasionally following great emotional stress.

GLYCYRRHETINIC ACID is the active principle of liquorice (*q.v.*) and has been shown to have an anti-inflammatory action resembling, though much weaker than, that of cortisone.

GLYMIDINE is one of the oral hypoglycæmic agents : that is, a drug which, when taken by mouth, is able to control diabetes mellitus without the help of insulin.

GOA POWDER (*see* CHRYSAROBIN).

GOITRE (*guttur*, the throat), also known as BRONCHOCELE or DERBYSHIRE NECK, is a term applied to a swelling on the front of the neck caused by an enlargement of the thyroid gland. This structure, which lies between the skin and the front of the windpipe, and which in health is not large enough to give rise to any external prominence, is liable to occasional variations in size, more especially in females, a temporary enlargement of the gland being not uncommon at the menstrual periods, as well as during pregnancy. The gland is liable to fluctuations in function as well as in size. When its functions are lessened, either by wasting of the gland (atrophy) or by failure of secretion in a gland either of ordinary size or in an enlarged state, the general name of hypothyroidism is applied ; when the functions are increased, which may happen in a gland of ordinary size or more commonly accompanies certain types of enlargement, the name hyperthyroidism is given. Atrophic conditions of the gland are considered under the heading MYXŒDEMA. Here we shall consider conditions in which the gland is enlarged, although it must be noted that the symptoms depend not so much upon enlargement as upon the fact of whether the gland is acting sluggishly or in excess. Two main forms of

enlargement are recognized, (*a*) *Simple goitre*, and (*b*) *Exophthalmic goitre*.

SIMPLE GOITRE occasions a swelling which is well marked, and is not only unsightly, but may by its growth occasion much discomfort, and even give rise to serious symptoms from its pressure on the windpipe and other important parts in the neck.

Causes.—Simple goitre is an excellent example of an endemic disease. There are few parts of the world where it is not found prevailing in certain localities, these being for the most part deep valleys in mountainous districts. For example, in Germany it occurs in the Black Forest, it is also found in Styria, in the Italian Alps, and, above all, is common in parts of Switzerland. In India it is common among the Himalayas, in China it affects the dwellers in various hill districts, and in England it was so frequent in the Peak district that the disease has received for one of its titles the name of Derbyshire neck. It is also very common in certain places far removed from the sea and supposed to have a deficiency of iodine in the soil, *e.g.* in the Middle States of America, especially Michigan. The widespread nature of the disease has naturally led to inquiry and speculation as to its origin. The most generally accepted view has been that which ascribes the malady to the use of drinking water deficient in iodine. Although this view is supported by the fact that goitre has been much decreased in whole districts by the expedients of either obtaining a new water supply or giving iodized salt to the entire population, there are certain other facts which suggest that other factors may occasionally come into play. For instance, certain wells in districts are known to be goitre-producing, whilst neighbouring wells with apparently the same water are safe; the goitre-producing water may be rendered innocuous by boiling. It has been suggested that it may be due to a micro-organism or other parasite infesting particular waters. It has also been suggested that want of sunlight, etc., combine with the effect of the drinking water in developing the disease. Goitre can often be cured by removal from the district where it prevails, and it may be acquired by previously healthy persons who settle in goitrous localities. It is only in such places that the disease shows any hereditary tendencies. Women are far more often affected than men.

Symptoms.—In districts where the disease prevails, the goitre usually appears in early life, often from the eighth to the twelfth year. Its growth is at first slow, but, after several years of comparative quiescence, a somewhat sudden increase occasionally occurs. In the earlier stages of the disease, the condition of the thyroid gland is simply an enlargement of the gland, which retains its normal, soft consistence, and is distended by colloid material. But in the course of time other changes supervene, and the gland may become the seat of cystic formations, or acquire hardness from increase of fibrous tissue or calcareous deposits. Occasionally the enlargement of the gland is uniform, but more commonly one of the lobes, generally the right, is the larger. The growth is unattended by pain, and is compatible with ordinary health. Sometimes, when the goitre becomes large, the voice grows hoarse and toneless, but only when the gland becomes very large is there any interference with breathing or swallowing.

Treatment.—In endemic areas the incidence of simple goitre has been reduced to a very low figure by the routine administration of iodine. This is usually given in the form of iodized table salt, the concentration of iodine in the salt varying between 1 part in 5000 to 1 part in 250,000. Another method used in some areas is to give iodine to school children for ten days in the spring and in the autumn, and to women during pregnancy. The usual dose in these cases is 0·2 gramme of potassium iodide daily.

When a goitre is already present, treatment consists of the administration of iodine, usually in the form of Lugol's solution (q.v.), 15 to 30 minims (1 to 2 millilitres) daily. If this fails to control the condition, thyroid extract is usually tried. Surgery is resorted to in those cases in which the goitre is unduly large or unsightly or is causing unpleasant symptoms by pressing on the windpipe. When the goitre is removed in this way, care must be taken to leave sufficient of the gland to ensure an adequate supply of thyroid secretion. Otherwise signs of hypothyroidism, or myxœdema (q.v.), will develop.

EXOPHTHALMIC GOITRE is the name applied to another form of enlargement of the thyroid gland, in which marked constitutional changes occur. In this disease, the goitre is one of several symptoms which form the most noticeable features of the disease, viz. extreme nervousness, muscular tremors, palpitation of the heart and throbbing of the great vessels, enlargement of the thyroid gland, and protrusion of the eyeballs. This group of symptoms is often known also by the names of Graves' disease, Parry's disease, and von Basedow's disease, in reference to the physicians by whom the disease was first recognized and described. It is also known as thyrotoxicosis.

Causes.—The exact nature of exophthalmic goitre is still uncertain, but its symptoms are due either to an increase of the normal secretion of the thyroid gland, or, in other cases, to perversion in quality of this secretion. Many of the symptoms produced are due to the action of this secretion on the sympathetic nervous system, and a number of the symptoms are also caused by changes in the other endocrine glands related to the thyroid.

This type of goitre is not more common in the districts where simple goitre occurs than it is elsewhere. Women are more frequently affected than men, in the proportion of 6 to 1, or even higher. The age of onset is usually between sixteen and forty years. The predisposition to the disease seems to occur in certain families, and cases which previously were slight are often greatly aggravated by fright or anxiety or mental strain. The general appearance of the disease, apart from the goitre, shows a great similarity to the characters of intense fear. Sometimes the disease first attracts attention after the patient has suffered from some infectious disease, or it may be preceded by anæmia, or by various nervous or emotional manifestations.

Symptoms.—The first of the symptoms to appear are generally the nervousness and the palpitation of the heart, which is aggravated by the slightest exertion and may be very severe.

The rate of the pulse is much increased, commonly to 120 per minute or more. An uncomfortable sensation of throbbing is felt throughout the body, and many of the larger blood-vessels are seen to pulsate strongly. There are marked tremors of the muscles and limbs, especially after any exertion. The enlargement of the thyroid gland generally comes on gradually ; it rarely increases to any great size, thus differing from simple goitre.

Accompanying the goitre a change is observed in the appearance of the eyes, which attract attention by their prominence and by the fact that a space of the white of the eye is left exposed all round the iris (exophthalmos). A startled or frightened expression is thus given to the countenance. In extreme cases the eyes protrude from the sockets to such a degree that the eyelids cannot be closed, and injury may thus arise to the constantly exposed eyeballs. Apart from such risk, however, the vision is rarely affected in this disease. Much difference of opinion prevails as to the immediate cause of the protrusion of the eyes, but it is generally ascribed to the increase of the fatty tissue and distension of the blood-vessels of the orbits. The eyelids show a characteristic sign (von Graefe's sign) by failing to descend along with the eyeball as the person glances downwards. It occasionally happens that in undoubted cases of the disease one or other of the above-named characteristic phenomena is absent, generally either the goitre or the exophthalmos. The palpitation of the heart is the most constant symptom. Sleeplessness, irritability, disorders of digestion, diarrhœa, uterine derangements, muscular tremors, and an unusual readiness to perspire freely are common accompaniments. All the bodily activities are carried on at high pressure, and there is consequent wasting of the fatty and muscular tissues, with increasing thinness. The basal metabolism is much higher than it is in the normal individual.

Exophthalmic goitre is not often a directly fatal malady, but the nervousness, palpitation, and muscular weakness may render the patient unfit for even the slightest exertion. Heart failure and atrial fibrillation are

grave risks. Partial improvement and relapses occur from time to time, especially after periods of rest. In some cases, the patient, in old age passes into the opposite condition of myxœdema, the thyroid gland appearing to be completely worn out.

THYROTOXIC ADENOMA is a variety of exophthalmic goitre, in which a simple goitre containing one or more large hard nodules, which may have been present for some time, suddenly takes on the characters of exophthalmic goitre, with the symptoms of this condition. The symptoms in such a case are, however, not so marked, except that there is a marked tendency for atrial fibrillation and heart failure to develop. A simple goitre occasionally develops gradually into a case of exophthalmic goitre.

Treatment.—Three lines of treatment are now available : drugs, surgery, and radioactive iodine. Drugs are usually the first line of attack, and the two most widely used are carbimazole and propylthiouracil. Surgery, which consists of removing around seven-eighths of the gland, is usually resorted to if the condition fails to respond to drugs, if the condition is severe or, of long standing, or if the goitre is particularly big. The patient is usually prepared for operation by drugs and then by a course of potassium iodide. Radioactive iodine (*see* ISOTOPES) is usually reserved for middle-aged or elderly patients.

GOLD SALTS have been used in the treatment of tuberculosis and of chronic rheumatic disorders. They have now been given up for the treatment of tuberculosis, but are still used in the treatment of rheumatoid arthritis. Gold may be administered in various forms, such as sodium aurothiomalate or may be used as one of many proprietary preparations, including sanocrysin, myocrysin, solganol, crisalbine, etc. It is injected in minute doses either intramuscularly or intravenously, and produces a reaction in the affected tissues which leads to their scarring and healing. If gold is administered in too large quantities skin eruptions, albuminuria, metallic taste in the mouth, jaundice, and feverishness may be produced, so that [it is necessary to prolong a course of this remedy over many months in minute doses.

GOLDEN OINTMENT is another name for yellow oxide of mercury ointment, which is much used for inflammation of the eyelids.

GONAD is a gland which produces a gamete ; an ovary or a testis.

GONADOTROPHINS, or GONADO-TROPHIC HORMONES, are hormones that control the activity of the gonads (*i.e.* the testes and ovaries). In the male they stimulate the secretion of testosterone and the production of spermatozoa (spermatogenesis). In the female they stimulate the production of ova and the secretion of œstrogen (*q.v.*) and progesterone (*q.v.*). There are three gonadotrophins produced by the pituitary gland. *Chorionic gonadotrophin* is produced in the placenta and excreted in the urine.

GONAGRA means an attack of gout affecting the knee. (*See* GOUT.)

GONORRHŒA is an inflammatory disease affecting especially the mucous membrane of the urethra in the male and that of the vagina in the female, but spreading also to other parts.

Causes.—The disease is directly contagious from another person already suffering in this manner, usually by sexual intercourse, but occasionally it is conveyed by the discharge on sponges, towels, or clothing as well as by actual contact. The infecting agent is the gonococcus or *Neisseria gonorrhœæ.* This is found in the discharge expressed from the urethra, which may be spread as a film on a glass slide, suitably stained, and examined under the microscope ; or a culture from the discharge may be made on certain bacteriological media and films from this, similarly examined under the microscope. Since discharges resembling that of gonorrhœa accompany other forms of inflammation, the identification of the organism is of great importance (Plate VIII).

Symptoms.—These differ considerably, according to whether the disease is in an acute or a chronic stage. In *men*, after an incubation period of between two and ten days, irritation in the urethra, scalding pain on passing water, and a viscid yellowish-white discharge appear ; the glands in the groin often enlarge and may suppurate. The urine when passed is hazy and is often found to contain yellowish threads of pus visible to the eye. After some weeks, if the condition has become chronic, the discharge is clear and viscid, there may be irritation in passing urine, and various forms of inflammation in neighbouring organs may appear, the testicle, prostate gland, and bladder becoming affected. At a still later stage the inflammation of the urethra is apt to lead to gradual formation of fibrous tissue around this channel. This contracts and produces narrowing, so that the passage of water becomes difficult or may be stopped for a time altogether (the condition known as stricture). Inflammation of some of the joints is a common complication at this or an earlier stage, the knee, ankle, wrist, and elbow being the joints most frequently affected, and this form of ' rheumatism ' is very intractable and liable to lead to permanent stiffness. The fibrous tissues elsewhere may also develop inflammatory changes, causing lumbago, pain in the foot, etc. In occasional cases, during the acute stage, a general blood-poisoning results, with inflammation of the heart-valves (endocarditis) and abscesses in various parts of the body. The infective matter occasionally is inoculated accidentally into the eye, producing a very severe form of conjunctivitis. In the newly born child this is known as *ophthalmia neonatorum* and until recently was one of the chief causes of blindness. (*See* EYE DISEASES.)

In *women* the course and complications of the disease are somewhat different. It begins with a yellow vaginal discharge, pain on passing water, and very often inflammation or abscess of ' Bartholin's glands ', situated close to the vulva, or opening of the vagina. The chief seriousness, however, of the disease is due to the spread of inflammation to neighbouring organs, the uterus, Fallopian tubes, and ovaries, causing permanent destructive changes in these, and leading occasionally to peritonitis through the Fallopian tube, with a fatal result. Many cases of prolonged ill-health and sterility or recurring miscarriages are due to these changes.

Treatment.—The treatment of gonorrhœa was revolutionized by the introduction of the sulphonamides. These, in turn, have now been replaced by the antibiotics. Penicillin is now the antibiotic of choice. Unfortunately, the gonococcus is liable to become resistant to penicillin. In patients who are infected with penicillin-resistant organisms, one of the other antibiotics is used, usually either oxytetracycline (*q.v.*) or tetracycline (*q.v.*). In all cases it is essential that bacteriological investigation should be carried out at weekly intervals for three or four weeks, to make sure that the patient is cured.

GOSSYPIUM is the Latin word for cotton.

GOULARD'S WATER is the popular name for the dilute solution of subacetate of lead, which is employed in the treatment of sprains, bruises, and localized inflammations. It is commonly mixed with laudanum in the proportion of 60 minims (4 ml.) of laudanum to 1 ounce (28·5 ml.) of the Goulard's water, and the mixture, known as 'lead and opium lotion', is applied on a piece of moist warm flannel, and covered with waterproof cloth.

GOUT is a constitutional disorder connected with excess of uric acid in the blood, and manifesting itself by inflammation of joints with deposition therein of urate of soda, and also by morbid changes in various important organs.

The term gout, which was first used about the end of the thirteenth century, is derived through the French *goutte* from the Latin *gutta*, a drop, in allusion to the old pathological doctrine (which in the present case seems to be essentially the correct one) of the dropping of a morbid material from the blood within the joints. The disease was known and described by the ancient Greek physicians under various terms, which, however, appear to have been applied by them alike to rheumatism and gout. The general term *arthritis* (ἄρθρον, a joint) was employed when many joints were the seat of inflammation ; whilst in those instances where the disease was limited to one part the

name referred to such locality ; hence *podagra* (from πούς, the foot, and ἄγρα, a seizure), *chiragra* (χείρ, the hand), *gonagra* (γόνυ, the knee), etc.

Chalk-stones have been found in the feet of Egyptian mummies. Hippocrates (460–375 B.C.) in his *Aphorisms* speaks of gout as occurring most commonly in spring and autumn, and mentions the fact that women are less liable to it than men. Galen regarded gout as an unnatural accumulation of humours in a part, and the chalk-stones as the concretions of these ; and he attributed the disease to over-indulgence and luxury. Gout is alluded to in the works of Ovid and Pliny, and Seneca, in his ninety-fifth epistle, mentions the prevalence of gout among the Roman ladies of his day as one of the results of their high living and debauchery. Lucian, in his *Tragopodagra*, gives an amusing account of the remedies used for the cure of gout.

Sydenham, the famous English physician of the seventeenth century, wrote an important treatise on the subject, and his description of the gouty paroxysm, all the more vivid from his having himself been afflicted with the disease for thirty-four years, is still quoted by writers as the most graphic and exhaustive account of the symptoms of gout.

Causes.—The cardinal feature of gout is the presence of an excessive amount of uric acid, and its deposition in the

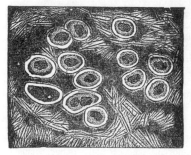

FIG. 211.—Deposit of sharp crystals of bi-urate of soda in the joint cartilage of the knee. The rounded structures are ordinary cartilage cells. Magnified by 600. (Thoma's *Pathology*.)

joints in the form of urate of soda (Fig. 211). The cause of this excess of uric acid is not known. Uric acid is formed in the system in the processes of nutrition, and is excreted by the kidneys, the amount passing off in the urine being about 500 mg. daily. In the healthy human subject the blood contains 2 to 4 mg. per 100 millilitres, but in gout it is increased, both prior to and during the acute attack, while in chronic gout the amount in the blood and elsewhere in the body is always above the normal level. The gouty paroxysm appears to rid the system to a certain extent of the accumulated uric acid, although such relief is generally of but temporary duration.

Gout is in a marked degree hereditary. A family history of the disease is obtained in from 50 to 80 per cent. of cases. Gout is said to affect the sedentary more readily than the active, but this cannot be taken as a constant rule. On the other hand, inadequate exercise, a luxurious manner of living, habitual over-indulgence in animal food and rich dishes, and especially in alcoholic beverages, are undoubtedly important precipitating factors in the production of the disease. These, however, are no more than precipitating factors, and the disease can occur in vegetarians and teetotallers.

Gout is more common in mature age than in the earlier years of life, being infrequent before the age of 40. It may occasionally affect very young persons, but such cases are generally in a marked degree hereditary. About 95 per cent. of patients are males. In women it most frequently appears after the cessation of the menses. Persons exposed to the influence of lead-poisoning, such as plumbers, painters, etc., are apt to suffer from gout ; and it would seem that impregnation of the system with this metal markedly interferes with the uric acid excreting function of the kidneys.

Attacks of gout are readily excited in those predisposed to the disease. Exposure to cold, disorders of digestion, fatigue, and irritation or injuries of particular joints will often precipitate the gouty paroxysm.

Symptoms.—An attack of gout may appear without warning, or there may be premonitory symptoms. Among the more common of these are disorders of the digestive organs, with a feeble and capricious appetite, flatulence, uneasiness in the right side in the region of the liver, and irritation in the urinary organs. Various forms of nervous disturbance also present themselves in the form of extreme irritability of temper, and numbness and coldness in the limbs. On the night of the attack, the patient retires to rest apparently quite well, but about two or three o'clock in the morning is awakened by a painful feeling in the foot, most commonly in the ball of the great toe, but it may be in the instep or heel, or in the thumb. With the pain there often occurs a distinct shivering, followed by feverishness. The pain soon becomes of an agonizing character.

When the affected part is examined it is found to be swollen and of a deep red hue. The skin is tense and glistening, and the surrounding veins are more or less distended. After a few hours there is a remission of the pain, slight perspiration takes place, and the patient may fall asleep. The pain, however, returns next night, and these nocturnal exacerbations occur with greater or less severity during the continuance of the attack, which generally lasts for a week or ten days. As the symptoms decline, the swelling and tenderness of the affected joint abate, but the skin over it pits on pressure for a time, and with this there is often associated slight desquamation of the cuticle. During the attacks the patient is restless and extremely irritable, and suffers from cramp in the limbs, and from dyspepsia, thirst, and constipation. The urine is scanty and high-coloured, with a copious deposit, consisting chiefly of urates. It is rare that the first is the only attack of gout, although by care and treatment recurrences may be warded off. In the earlier recurrences the same joints as were formerly the seat of the gouty inflammation suffer again, but in the course of time others become implicated, until in advanced cases scarcely any joint escapes, and the disease thus becomes chronic. When gout assumes this form, the frequently recurring attacks are usually attended with less pain, but chalk-stones or ' tophi ' are gradually formed round the affected joints. These deposits, which are highly characteristic of gout, at first take place in the form of a semi-fluid material, consisting for the most part of bi-urate of soda, which gradually becomes more dense, and ultimately quite hard. In some cases of chronic gout the deposit is so slight as to be barely appreciable externally, but on the other hand it occasionally causes great enlargement of the joints, and fixes them in a flexed or extended position which renders them entirely useless. Any of the joints may be thus affected, but most commonly those of the hands (Plate XIV) and feet. The deposits take place in other structures besides those of joints, such as along the course of tendons, underneath the skin and periosteum, in the sclerotic coat of the eye, and especially on the cartilages of the external ear. When bi-urate of soda is largely deposited in joints the skin sometimes gives way, and the concretion is exposed.

The recognition of what is termed irregular gout is less easy than that form above described. The diagnosis may often be made in cases where in an attack of ordinary gout the disease suddenly leaves the affected joints and some new series of symptoms arises. It has been often observed, when cold has been applied to an inflamed joint, that the pain and inflammation in the part ceased, but that some sudden and alarming seizure referable to the stomach, brain, heart, or lungs supervened. Further, the gouty nature of some long-continued internal, ophthalmic, or cutaneous disorder may be rendered apparent by its disappearance on the outbreak of the paroxysm in the joints. Gout, when of long standing, is often found associated with degenerative changes in the heart and large arteries, the liver, and especially the kidneys, which are apt to assume the granular contracted condition already alluded to as one of the forms of Bright's disease (see BRIGHT'S DISEASE). A variety of urinary calculus—the uric acid—formed by concretions of this substance in the kidneys is a not infrequent occurrence in connection with gout ; hence the well-known association of this disease and gravel.

Treatment.—The usual plan of treatment is somewhat as follows : During the acute attack the affected part should be kept at perfect rest, and be enveloped in cotton-wool covered with oil-

silk. The diet should be light, and the use of a laxative is of service, as well as the free administration of fluids. The medicinal agent upon which most reliance is placed is colchicum. This drug, believed to correspond with the hermodactyl of the ancients, was introduced as a remedy for gout over a century ago. The mode of action of colchicum is uncertain, but it is probable that it has simply a special sedative action upon the gouty inflammation without affecting the excretion of uric acid. It is usually administered as colchicine. In cases which do not respond satisfactorily to colchicine, phenylbutazone may be used, or indomethacin or allopurionol, or corticotrophin or cortisone (or one of its derivatives).

In chronic gout the most commonly used drugs are phenylbutazone, sulphinpyrazone (a derivative of phenylbutazone), probenecid, sodium, salicylate, or aspirin.

The diet and regimen to be employed in the intervals of the gouty attacks are of the highest importance. Restriction must be laid upon the amount and quality of the food, and still more upon the alcoholic stimulants. Regular but moderate exercise in the form of walking or riding, in the case of those who lead sedentary lives, is of great advantage, and all overwork, either physical or mental, should be avoided. The effect upon the gouty constitution of certain mineral waters and baths is well known, the alkaline waters being the favourite.

GOWERS' MIXTURE was introduced, in 1888, by Sir William Gowers for the treatment of migraine. It contains sodium bromide, solution of glyceryl trinitrate, dilute hydrobromic acid, tincture of nux vomica, tincture of gelsemium, and syrup of lemon. It is still widely and successfully used for the purpose for which it was introduced.

GRAFT is the term applied to a small piece of skin or other tissue removed from one person or animal and implanted in another or the same in order by its growth to remedy some defect. Skin grafts are the tissues most commonly used. If a large piece of skin is required for covering an old ulcer or wound, the operation of grafting is usually done in two stages, the piece of skin to be grafted being first raised from its bed but allowed to remain attached at one end so that it may be nourished by its own blood-vessels while it is establishing connections with the tissues of the gap which it is desired to fill. After one or two weeks the graft is cut away from its original position and firmly fixed in the new one. Bone grafts are also used to replace bone which has been lost by disease : for example, a portion of rib is sometimes removed in order to furnish support for a spine weakened by disease, after the disease has been removed. Also, the bone of young animals is used to afford additional growth and strength to a limb bone which it has been necessary to remove in part on account of disease or injury. (*See* SKIN GRAFTING.)

GRAMICIDIN was one of the first antibiotics. Derived from *Bacillus brevis*, it is bactericidal to staphylococci, pneumococci, and other Gram-positive, disease-producing micro-organisms. It is seldom used now.

GRAMME, or GRAM, is the unit of weight in the metric system and is equal to a little over 15·4 grains. For purposes of weighing food, 30 grammes are usually taken as approximately equal to 1 ounce.

GRAM'S STAIN, named after the bacteriologist, J. H. C. Gram, who first described it in 1884, is one of the most valuable methods of differentiating certain micro-organisms. The principle involved depends upon the fact that certain bacteria, when treated with a dye such as gentian-violet and then with iodine, ' fix ' the dye, whereas other bacteria do not do so. Those bacteria, such as the pneumococcus, that fix the dye are known as Gram-positive, whilst those that do not fix it, *e.g.* the gonococcus, are said to be Gram-negative.

GRAND MAL is the name applied to a convulsive epileptic attack, in contrast to 'petit mal', which includes the milder forms of epilepsy (*q.v.*).

GRANULAR KIDNEY is the name given to the state of the kidney in chronic Bright's disease (*see* BRIGHT'S DISEASE), which often occurs in association with chronic arterial disease.

GRANULATIONS are small masses of formative cells containing loops of newly formed blood-vessels which spring up over any raw surface, as the first step in the process of healing of wounds. (*See* ULCER, WOUNDS.)

GRANULOMA is a term applied to a tumour or new growth made up of granulation tissue. This is caused by various forms of chronic inflammation, such as syphilis and tuberculosis.

GRAVEL is the name applied to any sediment which falls down in the urine, but particularly to small masses of uric acid. It produces various unpleasant symptoms. (*See* BLADDER DISEASES, URINE.)

GRAVES' DISEASE is another name for exophthalmic goitre. (*See* GOITRE.)

GRAVID means pregnant.

GREEN SICKNESS is a popular name for chlorosis. (*See* ANÆMIA.)

GREENSTICK FRACTURE is the term applied to an incomplete fracture, in which the bone is not completely broken across. It occurs in the long bones of children and is usually due to indirect violence.

GREGORY'S MIXTURE or POWDER is a powder of light-yellow colour containing rhubarb, magnesia, and ginger. In doses of 10 to 60 grains (0·6 to 4 grammes) it is used as an antacid and purgative.

GREY POWDER is a powder composed of mercury and chalk. It was at one time much used as an ingredient of powders intended to check infantile diarrhœa, but is not used now for this, or any other, purpose in children because of the risk of inducing mercurial poisoning.

GRINDELIA is an American plant used as an asthma remedy. The leaves are generally used soaked in nitre, dried, and then either burned on a plate, from which the fumes are inhaled, or rolled in a cigarette and smoked.

GRINDER'S ROT is the term applied to a disease of the lung in steel-grinders caused by inhaling particles of the metal.

GRIPES is a popular name for the colic of infants, generally due to irregular feeding. (*See* COLIC.)

GRIPPE is a popular name for influenza. (*See* INFLUENZA.)

GRISEOFULVIN is an antibiotic obtained from *Penicillium griseofulvum Dierckse*, which is proving of value in the treatment of various forms of ringworm.

GROIN is the name applied to the region which includes the upper part of the front of the thigh and lower part of the abdomen. A deep groove runs obliquely across it, which corresponds to Poupart's ligament, and divides the thigh from the abdomen. The principal diseased conditions affecting this region are enlarged glands, or 'bubos' (*see* GLANDS), and hernia. (*See* HERNIA.)

GROWING PAINS occur in children during the course of development. They occur most commonly in the legs and back. It is now believed that growing pains are often a manifestation of rheumatism in children—they must, therefore, not be neglected. The pains are treated by ensuring that the child has a sufficiency of rest. Severe pains in young children are occasionally due to actual disease in a bone, either of tuberculous nature or caused by acute inflammation, and special attention is required in such cases.

GROWTH is a popular term applied to any new formation in any part of the body. (*See* CANCER, CYST, GANGLION, TUMOUR.) For growth of children, etc., *see* WEIGHT AND HEIGHT.

GRUEL is the name given to a thin paste or thick fluid made of oatmeal or maize meal and milk or water. Gruel is made by mixing 3 tablespoonfuls of meal with 1 pint (570 ml.) of cold milk or water, allowing to stand for 15 minutes, then straining and boiling for 15 minutes, and finally flavouring with salt and, if desired, with sugar.

412

GUAIAC is a resin obtained from the wood of *Guaiacum officinale* or *Lignum vitæ*, a West Indian tree. It used to be largely used in rheumatism and in acute tonsillitis. It is seldom used now, except in the form of guaiac lozenges, which are sometimes of value in the treatment of sore throats.

GUAIACOL is a light - coloured, yellowish fluid of pleasant smell, obtained from beechwood creosote. It used to be given in the treatment of pulmonary tuberculosis and as an intestinal antiseptic, but is seldom used now.

GUANETHIDINE is one of the newer hypotensive drugs which act by inhibiting the action of the sympathetic nervous system (*q.v.*).

GUANOCLOR is another of the newer hypotensive drugs which act by blocking the action of the sympathetic nervous system.

GUANOXAN has a similar action to guanoclor.

GUINEA-WORM (*see* PARASITES).

GULLET, or ŒSOPHAGUS, is the tube down which food passes on its way from the throat to the stomach. (*See* ŒSOPHAGUS.)

GUM is a complex viscid substance which exudes from the stems and branches of various trees, and consists principally of arabin or bassorin. The two best-known gums are gum acacia and gum tragacanth. Gum-resins such as asafœtida, galbanum, and myrrh also contain resin. For gum-saline, *see* ACACIA.

GUMBOIL is a condition of inflammation, ending generally an abscess, situated about the root of a carious tooth.

Symptoms.—One tooth becomes a little painful and seems a little raised above the others, but the pain is at first relieved by clenching the teeth tightly, although after a day or more the affected tooth becomes extremely tender. A thickening forms at the side of the tooth, which is also at first relieved by pressure, as by holding a pad of cotton-wool, or a fig, or similar soft mass between gum and cheek. After some days the pain lessens, and either the swelling gradually subsides, or an abscess forms and bursts, generally between gum and cheek, but it may be on the cheek.

Treatment.—If there be any cavity in the tooth it should be stopped with cotton-wool soaked in a volatile oil, such as oil of cloves, or with a mixture of zinc oxide and oil of cloves, and if the pain and swelling do not speedily abate, the tooth should be pulled. Relief to the inflammation in early stages is often gained by painting the gum freely with tincture of iodine.

GUMMA (*gummi*, gum) means a hard swelling situated usually in connective tissue, although it may be in internal organs, muscle, or brain, and resulting from syphilis. The swelling is usually painless, but it may produce very marked symptoms by interference with the organ in which it is situated. A gumma generally disappears speedily when the treatment appropriate to syphilis administered.

GUMS, DISEASES OF (*see* MOUTH, DISEASES OF, *and* TEETH, DISEASES OF).

GUTTA-PERCHA is used in the preparation of some varieties of sticking-plaster, but its main use is, rolled out in thin films, known as gutta-percha tissue, to keep surgical dressings moist by preventing evaporation.

GYMNASTICS (*see* EXERCISE *and* CHEST DEVELOPMENT).

GYNÆCOLOGY (γυνή, a woman ; λόγος, a discourse) means that branch of medical science which deals with diseases peculiar to women.

GYNÆCOMASTIA is the term used for describing an abnormal increase in size of the male breast.

GYRUS (γῦρος, a ring) is the term applied to a convolution of the brain.

H

HABITS (*see* DRUG HABITS, *also* CHILDREN, PECULIARITIES OF).

HÆMATEMESIS (αἷμα, blood ; ἐμέω, I vomit) means vomiting of blood. Blood brought up from the stomach is generally dark in colour, and is often so far digested as to form small brown granules resembling coffee grounds. Vomiting of blood is one of the chief symptoms of ulcer of the stomach, but it may also occur in gastritis, especially when this is due to the action of irritant poisons or alcohol. It should always be remembered that the blood may come from the nose or throat, and, after being swallowed, provoke vomiting. (*See* HÆMORRHAGE.)

HÆMATOCELE (αἷμα, blood ; κήλη, a tumour) means a cavity containing blood. Generally as the result of an injury which ruptures blood-vessels, blood is effused into one of the natural cavities of the body, or among loose cellular tissue, producing a hæmatocele.

HÆMATOCOLPOS is the term applied to the condition in which menstrual blood is held up in the vagina as a result of an imperforate hymen.

HÆMATOCRIT is a graduated capillary tube for estimating the concentration of red corpuscles in the blood. The blood, made non-coagulable, is drawn into the tube ; this is placed in a centrifuge and revolved at a speed of 3000 revolutions per minute for 30 minutes. The red corpuscles will then congregate at the end of the tube. Above this will be a clear layer of plasma. Normally, plasma occupies 55 divisions of the tube, and the red corpuscles 45 divisions.

HÆMATOIDIN and HÆMIN are crystalline bodies derived from the blood when it is allowed to clot and dry up. The former is produced where blood is effused in internal hæmorrhages and then partly absorbed, for example, in cases of apoplexy. Chemical analysis proves it to be the same substance as bilirubin, the chief colouring matter of the bile. It produces the yellow colour noticed in a bruise as the blood is being absorbed and the bruise fading away. *Hæmin* is of great medico-legal importance, because it can be obtained from long-dried stains on clothing, knives, etc., its discovery proving such stains to be due to blood. To obtain it, one scrapes off a few particles of the stain upon a microscopic slide, adds a drop of strong acetic acid, and a small crystal of common salt. One then heats the drop till it dries up, and examines it under the microscope. Hæmin appears as minute, dark brown plates and prisms.

HÆMATOLOGY is the term applied to that branch of medical science devoted to the study of diseases of the blood.

HÆMATOMA (αἱματόω, I make bloody) means a collection of blood forming a definite swelling. It is found often upon the head of new-born children after a protracted and difficult labour. It may occur as the result of any injury or operation.

HÆMATOXYLON, or LOGWOOD, is the wood of *Hæmatoxylon campechianum*, which has a mildly astringent action, and is consequently used in pills and mixtures for checking diarrhœa.

HÆMATURIA (αἷμα, blood ; οὐρέω, I make water) means the condition of blood in the urine. (*See* URINE.) The blood may come from any part to the urinary tract. When the blood comes from the kidney or upper part of the urinary tract, it is usually mixed throughout the urine, giving the latter a brownish or 'smoky' tinge. This condition is usually the result of acute or subacute Bright's disease, or it may be present in persons suffering from high blood pressure or pyelitis (*q.v.*). Blood may also appear in the urine from time to time in considerable quantities when a stone or gravel is present in the pelvis of the kidney setting up irritation, especially when the person undergoes unwonted exercise. The blood may also originate from the bladder in cases in which this is inflamed, and is then present in smaller quantities as a rule. The presence of a stone in the bladder is also productive of blood, and in either of the latter cases the urine is generally turbid from admixture with pus. A condition which leads to the passage of bright red blood at occasional intervals is the presence of a species of warty growth (papilloma) on the wall of the bladder. Blood may also be derived from the urethra following some inflammatory condition in this passage, or injury to it as by a fracture of the pelvic bones. Occasionally the bleeding may be due to purpura.

The recognition of the site of the hæmorrhage is important in relation to the measures to be adopted for its treatment. This can often be made out by the character of the blood, whether intimately mixed with the urine or in the form of clots, also by the shape of the clots, and by the presence of other abnormal constituents in the urine. For the final diagnosis, examination of the interior of the bladder by the cystoscope and the passage of fine catheters up the ureters to the kidneys is often of importance (*see* CYSTOSCOPE).

HÆMIC MURMUR (αἷμα, blood) is a term applied to unusual sounds heard over the heart and large blood-vessels in severe cases of anæmia. They disappear as the condition is recovered from. Murmurs of this type are to be distinguished from ' organic murmurs ', which are due to some disease of the heart-valves or vessel walls.

H Æ M O C H R O M A T O S I S, or BRONZED DIABETES, is the name of a disease in which cirrhosis of the liver, enlargement of the spleen, pigmentation of the skin, and diabetes mellitus are associated with the abnormal and excessive deposit in the organs of the body of the iron-containing pigment, hæmosiderin.

HÆMOCYTOMETER (αἷμα, blood ; κύτος, cell ; μέτρον, measure) is an instrument for counting corpuscles in the blood.

H Æ M O G L O B I N is the colouring material which produces the red colour of blood. It is a chromoprotein, made up of a protein called globin and the iron-containing pigment hæmin. When separated from the red blood corpuscles that contain it, it is crystalline in form. It exists in two forms, simple hæmoglobin, found in venous blood, and oxyhæmoglobin, which is a loose compound with oxygen, found in arterial blood after the blood has come in contact with the air in the lungs. This oxyhæmoglobin is again broken down as the blood passes through the tissues, which take up the oxygen for their own use. In simple anæmia there is a marked deficiency of hæmoglobin in the blood.

HÆMOGLOBINURIA means the presence of blood pigment in the urine caused by the destruction of blood corpuscles in the blood-vessels or in the urinary passages. It produces in the urine a dark red colour or a brown colour resembling porter. In some persons this condition, known as intermittent hæmoglobinuria, occurs from time to time, especially on exposure to cold. It is also produced by various poisonous substances taken in the food, and it forms in malarious districts the condition known as blackwater fever.

HÆMOLYSIS (αἷμα, blood ; λύσις, setting free) means the breaking up of blood corpuscles by the action of poisonous substances, usually of a protein nature, circulating in the blood, or by certain chemicals. It occurs, for example, gradually in some forms of anæmia and occurs rapidly in poisoning by snake venom.

HÆMOLYTIC DISEASE OF THE NEWBORN (also known as ERYTHROBLASTOSIS FŒTALIS and ICTERUS GRAVIS NEONATORUM) is a severe disease of the newborn characterized by severe hæmolytic anæmia and jaundice. There is also some œdema, and when this is severe, with excess fluid in the pericardial, pleural, and peritoneal cavities, the condition is known as HYDROPS FŒTALIS. The fundamental cause is the hæmolysis (or breakdown) of the red blood cells, and this is due to a Rhesus-negative mother bearing a Rhesus-positive child. Such a mother becomes sensitized to the Rhesus-positive fœtus in her unborn child, thereby producing agglutinins (or anti-bodies) to it, and these pass through the placenta into the fœtus and destroy its red blood cells (*see* BLOOD GROUPS).

Treatment consists of blood trans-fusion : either a simple transfusion or an exchange transfusion (*see* TRANS-FUSION OF BLOOD). The efficacy of treatment is largely dependent upon the awareness of the fact that the baby may be born with hæmolytic disease, and that all the necessary steps have been taken to start treatment imme-diately after birth. This is the reason why so much importance is attached nowadays to the careful blood-grouping of all mothers early in pregnancy. As a result of modern treatment the mor-tality for this condition has dropped from around 75 per cent. to around 5 per cent.

HÆMOPHILIA (αἷμα, blood ; φιλία, affection) is a hereditary disease, con-fined almost entirely to members of the male sex who are called 'bleeders', and in whom uncontrollable bleeding is apt to follow upon very slight wounds.

Causes.—The defect is in the blood and is one of coagulation. The coagula-tion time may be prolonged up to twenty hours. The cause of this pro-longed coagulation is deficiency of the antihæmophilic factor, which is part of the globulin fraction of plasma. The most characteristic feature of the disease is its manner of hereditary transmis-sion, this being through the mother, who is not a bleeder, although her brothers may have been. In other words, the males of the affected family are bleeders but do not transmit the disease to their offspring, whilst the females are not bleeders but their male children bleed. This is well exemplified in the accompanying family tree (Fig. 212).

The disease occurs predominantly in white races, and it is estimated that there are 20,000 to 30,000 cases in Great Britain.

Symptoms.—The disease shows itself within the first year or two of the boy's life by excessive bleedings when small wounds are sustained, and by large bleedings under the skin or into joints where parts of the body are bruised. The bleeding is a general slow oozing from the capillary vessels,

416

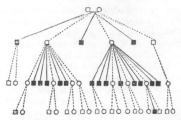

FIG. 212.—Genealogical tree of the family M. □, Healthy males ; ○, healthy females ; ■, bleeders who are all males. (Thoma's *Pathology.*)

and even small operations like the removal of a tooth may be dangerous. Sometimes a person dies during a bleeding, but as a rule after much blood is lost the flow ceases, and the person gradually recovers from the resulting anæmia.

Treatment.—The usual rules for the treatment of bleeding from the particu-lar locality affected hold good, but they have little effect at first (*see* HÆMOR-RHAGE), the oozing proceeding in spite of the soft clots which may form. When a hæmophiliac bleeds, treatment consists of the transfusion of fresh whole blood or of anti-hæmophilic globulin. Local bleeding from an ac-cessible site, such as a tooth socket, or a cut, may be arrested by the ap-plication of oxidized cellulose (oxycel), gelatin by-products (gelfoam), calcium alginate gauze, or thrombin powder.

A National Hæmophilia Register has now been established in Great Britain, and some thirty Hæmophilia Centres have been set up throughout the country where expert treatment can be obtained at any time. Every hæmophiliac whose name is on this Register is provided with a card which gives full details about his or her condi-tion. In addition, there is a Hæmo-philia Society which provides a useful advisory service for anyone with this disease.

HÆMOPTYSIS (αἷμα, blood ; πτύω, I spit) means the spitting up of blood from the lower air passages. The blood is usually coughed or gently hawked up, it may be in mouthfuls at a time, and is bright red and frothy, thus differ-ing from the blood brought from the stomach. Generally the condition re-sults from some disease of the heart or lungs. It should be remembered, however, that in elderly people hæmoptysis may be due to a varicose condition of the small veins in the throat, not to hæmorrhage in the lungs ; while in young people this condition is often due to bleeding from the nose, in which, owing to the position of the head, the blood happens to run backwards instead of forwards through the nostrils. (See HÆMORRHAGE, TUBERCULOSIS.)

HÆMORRHAGE (αἱμορραγία) means any escape of blood from the vessels which naturally contain it. It may occur from a wound of the skin, in which case it escapes externally, or into some internal cavity such as the stomach or bowels, or may simply be poured out into the tissues in consequence of a blow or similar injury ; but, in all cases alike, the blood escaping from the vessels is lost to the circulation. Hæmorrhage is classified according to the vessel or vessels from which it occurs, as (a) *arterial*, in which case the blood is bright and appears in jets or spurts, corresponding to the heart-beats ; (b) *venous*, when it comes from veins, is dark, and wells up gradually into the wound ; (c) *capillary*, when it flows merely from torn capillaries, and comes into a gentle ooze out of the general surface of the wound. The immediate result of a severe hæmorrhage is great anæmia, so that in extreme cases the bodily organs may be unable to continue their functions, and the person dies in consequence, with symptoms of shock.

In general, arterial hæmorrhage is the most serious, and if a large artery, such as the femoral, be wounded, the person concerned may bleed to death in a few minutes. Venous hæmorrhage is so easily checked by slight pressure, and the valves in the veins so effectively prevent blood from running backwards in these vessels, that this form is not dangerous to life except in the case of ruptured varicose veins of the leg, or when a serious internal injury is received. Capillary hæmorrhage stops so quickly, that only in the case of the disease known as hæmophilia is it of serious import. The following terms are applied to hæmorrhage from special sites ; *hæmatemesis*, bleeding from the stomach ; *hæmoptysis*, bleeding from

the lungs ; *epistaxis*, bleeding from the nose ; and *hæmaturia*, bleeding from the kidney or urinary passages (see these headings). Hæmorrhage is also classed as primary, reactionary, and secondary. (See WOUNDS.)

Natural arrest.—When an artery of small size is cut across, the bleeding stops in consequence of changes in the wall of the artery on the one hand, and in the constitution of the blood upon the other. Every artery is surrounded by a fibrous sheath, and, when cut, the vessel retracts some little distance within this sheath, in consequence of the shortening of its muscle fibres ; and further, by the same process the end contracts so as to form an opening of smaller size than the rest of the vessel. In the space between the end of the vessel and its sheath, and afterwards for some distance up the interior of the narrowed artery, blood-clot quickly forms by the following process, and

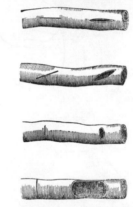

FIG. 213.—Diagram of arteries wounded in different ways, but not completely severed, to show how gaping openings result. On the left in each case is the wound, and on the right is shown the form of gap it makes. (Millers' *Surgery*, after Liston.)

rapidly blocks the open end of the vessel. When blood is shed so as to come in contact with any surface other than the smooth lining of blood-vessels, the fibrinogen which is dissolved in its fluid becomes suddenly converted into threads of fibrin through combination with the lime salts of the blood, and the action of a ferment given off probably by the blood platelets. These threads of fibrin slowly contract and develop into a dense felt-work, in the meshes of which the corpuscles are held, and in this way a blood-clot of increasing hardness is produced, within and round

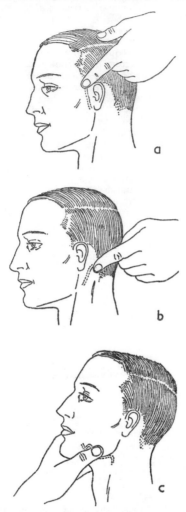

the vessel is completely cut across. Again, if an artery be torn across or twisted instead of cut, the opening at its end is still more narrowed, and the blood clots more rapidly on the ragged surface than it would do upon a clean cut, so that hæmorrhage from a torn or bruised wound is in general much smaller in amount than from a stab or cut. The natural arrest of bleeding is usually described therefore as depending upon four factors : (a) the retraction, and (b) the contraction of the cut artery : (c)

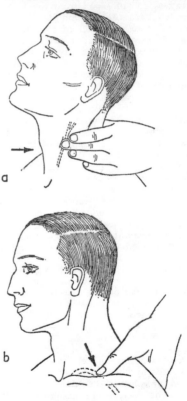

Fig. 214.—Compression of arteries about the head and face. a, Temporal artery, for bleeding from front of scalp ; b, occipital artery, for back of scalp ; c, facial artery, for face.

Fig. 215.—Compression of arteries in the neck. a, Carotid artery, for bleeding from head or neck ; b, subclavian artery, for bleeding from upper limb. The arrow in each case shows the direction in which pressure should be exerted.

the ends of the injured vessels. When an artery is only partially severed it is evident that ' contraction ' and ' retraction ' within the sheath cannot take place (Fig. 213), and accordingly bleeding is apt to be more serious than when

the external, and (d) the internal clot formed by the blood. For the means by which circulation is subsequently carried on after an artery is cut, see ANASTOMOSIS.

Control of external hæmorrhage.—

Four main principles are applicable in the control of a severe external hæmor-

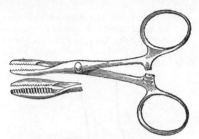

FIG. 216.—Artery forceps, with jaws shown enlarged.

rhage, viz. (a) direct pressure on the bleeding point or points; (b) elevation of the wounded part; (c) pressure

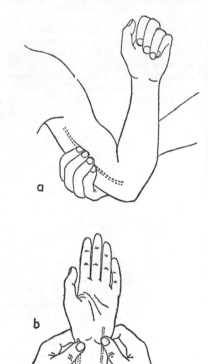

FIG. 217.—Compression of arteries for bleeding from forearm or hand. a, Brachial artery; b, radial and ulnar arteries.

on the main artery of supply to the part; and (d) application of substances known as 'styptics', which contract the vessels or aid the coagulation of the blood.

(a) DIRECT PRESSURE may be made with the finger, which is the best method, when a definite bleeding point is seen in a gaping wound. This is the method adopted at an operation by the surgeon, who places his finger at once upon any bleeding point, afterwards seizing the cut artery with forceps (Fig. 216) and tying a piece of silk or catgut tightly round its end. If the artery lie between the skin and a hard surface, as in the case of scalp wounds, a wedge-shaped pad and tight bandage (known as a 'graduated compress') may be substituted for pressure with the finger, the edges of the wound being compressed between the pad and skull.

(b) ELEVATION of the bleeding member is an important method, the blood running off more readily by the veins, and a smaller quantity being driven into the limb the higher it is raised. This method is applicable, of course, only in cases of bleeding from the hand or foot.

(c) PRESSURE UPON THE MAIN ARTERY of supply to the injured limb is a certain method of stopping the circulation and consequently all bleeding, much after the manner of stopping the water supply of a district by closing the main pipe. At certain points where the arteries lie close to bones and near the surface, the pulsation of the vessel may be felt, and *pressure with the finger* over the artery serves to obliterate it against the bone, the points where this may be adopted being as follows: In cases of bleeding from the upper part of the scalp, the temporal artery may be felt and compressed immediately in front of the upper part of the ear (Fig. 214 a), while for wounds at the back of the head the occipital artery can be felt and compressed a short distance behind the mastoid process, the bony prominence at the back of the ear (Fig. 214 b).

Bleeding from the face may be checked by pressure on the facial artery, which passes on to the face about an inch in front of the angle of the jaw, across the jaw-bone, against which it is to be pressed (Fig. 214 c).

All bleeding from the head and neck may be lessened by pressure upon the common carotid artery in the neck a short distance below the prominent Adam's apple, and between it and the edge of the large sternomastoid muscle (Fig. 215 a). In this groove the artery is pressed straight back against the transverse processes of the spinal column.

Bleeding from the region of the shoulder and armpit is checked by pressure on the subclavian artery, the pressure being applied with the thumb directly downwards in the hollow behind the middle part of the collar-bone, so as to press the artery down upon the first rib (Fig. 215 b).

Bleeding from the region of the elbow or forearm may be controlled by feeling for the brachial artery on the inner side of the upper arm, behind the biceps muscle, and pressing it against the humerus (Fig. 217 a).

Bleeding from the hand is checked by pressure on the radial artery, where it lies between the skin and radius in front of the wrist, and on the ulnar artery just before it enters the hand near its inner margin (Fig. 217 b).

In the lower limb the arteries lie deeply among the muscles, but bleeding from any part of the limb may be checked by pressure backwards on the femoral artery, which is to be felt pulsating in the centre of the groin, and which is compressed backwards against the head of the thigh-bone (Fig. 218).

Bleeding from the sole of the foot may be controlled by pressure on the posterior tibial artery, which lies about half an inch behind the inner ankle (Fig. 219).

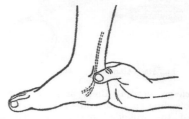

FIG. 219.—Compression of posterior tibial artery, for bleeding in sole of foot.

A second method for applying pressure on the main artery consists in *forced flexion* at the elbow, hip, or knee, as the case may be. A pad is placed in the bend of the joint, which is then flexed as completely as possible and firmly bound in this position, the artery being thus sharply bent upon itself (Fig. 220).

FIG. 220.—Method of stopping bleeding from the forearm or hand by forced flexion at the elbow, the limb being firmly flexed over a pad placed in the bend of the elbow. The same method may be applied to compress the femoral artery at the groin or popliteal artery behind the knee, by forced flexion with a pad at hip or knee.

A third method for control of the main blood supply is by the *tourniquet*, which consists of an elastic band or ligature passed round a fleshy part of any of the limbs, and pulled or twisted tight. A surgical tourniquet consists of an india-rubber cord or band with an arrangement for fixing the ends together, or of a strap with buckle and a screw

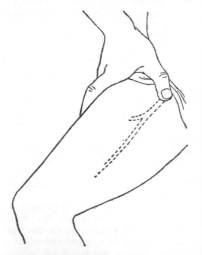

FIG. 218.—Compression of femoral artery, for bleeding in lower limb.

appliance for tightening it up. A tourniquet may, however, be ' improvised ' from a piece of rope, or a handkerchief folded cravatwise, tied round the limb and then twisted up tight by a piece of wood, large key, or similar object introduced beneath it. The handle of such a tourniquet is prevented from untwisting by passing a second band round the limb and including the end of the handle within it before tying. A tourniquet may be applied to the fleshy part of thigh, leg, upper arm, or forearm. It is most important to note on a label the time of application of a tourniquet. No tourniquet should ever be left on longer than an hour. It must be loosened every fifteen minutes, to be tightened again if bleeding recommences.

Occasionally, when bleeding is continuous or when it occurs from a deep-seated wound like a stab, or injury to the root of the tongue, it is impossible to get at the bleeding point, and permanent control of the bleeding is only to be achieved by the surgeon, who cuts down upon the main artery of supply and ties a ligature round it.

(*d*) STYPTICS are applied when the bleeding is a general ooze from a wound, or when the bleeding comes from an inaccessible position, such as the interior of the nose or a wound in the side. The most important styptics are heat and cold. Although moderate warmth greatly increases bleeding, ice-cold water and also water between 115° and 120° F. (46° and 49° C.) (*i.e.* a temperature which the hand can hardly bear) both favour clotting and contract the blood-vessels. Heat is much more effectual than cold, if applied directly to the wound. Various drugs, such as perchloride of iron (steel drops) and hazeline, act similarly. Adrenaline has a powerful local action in contracting vessels and stopping bleeding. Russell-viper venom is most effective as a local application in cases such as bleeding from a tooth socket. Other styptics include oxidized cellulose, gelatin by-products, calcium alginate, and thrombin powder.

Control of internal hæmorrhage is not to be so certainly achieved as in the case of bleeding from the vessels of the limbs. There are certain general principles to which it is most important to adhere. Chief among these is the maintenance of the recumbent position, since the heart beats less forcibly and the blood - pressure is consequently lowered as soon as the injured person lies down. For the same reason, all excitement must be avoided, and the mind of the sufferer quieted as far as possible. The patient must also be kept warm. Stimulants must be avoided. Ice-bags or compresses wrung out of cold water may be laid over the chest or stomach, according to the origin of the hæmorrhage. The most valuable drug in the treatment of internal hæmorrhage is morphine given hypodermically. In the hæmorrhage which sometimes follows child-birth, the source of bleeding is usually the uterus. This is controlled by the injection of ergometrine, the removal of the placenta if this has not already come away, and then compression of the uterus. This may need to be supplemented by plugging of the vagina with sterile gauze.

It should be mentioned that in operations on internal organs or other highly vascular tissue, in the case of which bleeding would be very hard to stop, the cautery is often used instead of the knife, and not only removes the part desired, but, by its heat, prevents all bleeding.

Treatment of bleeding from special sites.—NOSE.—Keep quiet, lying or sitting ; loosen collar ; no blowing of nose ; cold key or sponge to neck ; if these be not successful, plugging of nostrils with lint soaked in tincture of perchloride of iron or adrenaline.

TONGUE.—Ice to suck ; pressure with the fingers ; if serious, compression of carotid artery.

FACE OR SCALP.—Direct pressure with fingers or bandage and pad on wound ; if bleeding be severe, pressure in addition on facial, temporal, or occipital artery.

NECK.—Pressure on carotid artery.

ARMPIT OR SHOULDER.—Pressure on subclavian artery.

FOREARM. — Pressure on brachial artery by fingers, tourniquet, or forced flexion at elbow.

HAND.—Elevation and direct pressure with pad and bandage ; if bleeding severe, pressure on radial and ulnar arteries, or tourniquet to forearm.

THIGH.—Pressure on femoral artery at groin ; tourniquet, if low down.

LEG.—Tourniquet to thigh, or forced flexion at knee. In the case of ruptured varicose veins, a pad and bandage round leg extending above and below wound with elevation of limb suffice.

FOOT.—Direct pressure and elevation ; if bleeding severe, forced flexion at knee, or pressure on posterior tibial artery.

HÆMORRHOIDS (αἱμορροΐδες) (see PILES).

HÆMOSTATICS (αἷμα, blood ; ἵστημι, I cause to stand) are any means, whether of the nature of mechanical appliances or drugs, used to control bleeding. (See FIBRIN FOAM, HÆMORRHAGE.)

HÆMOTHORAX (αἷμα, blood; θώραξ, chest) means an effusion of blood into the pleural cavity.

HAIR (see SKIN).

HAIR DISEASES (see BALDNESS, SKIN DISEASES).

HAIR, REMOVAL OF (see DEPILATION).

HALIBUT-LIVER OIL is the oil expressed from fresh, or suitably preserved, halibut liver. It is a particularly rich source of vitamin A (30,000 international units per gramme), and also contains vitamin D (2300 to 2500 units per gramme). Because of the relatively small volume required, it is often used as a means of giving vitamin D : either as drops of the oil or in capsules. As mentioned in the section on cod-liver oil, care must be taken to ensure that the child is receiving at least 700 international units of vitamin D daily.

HALISTERESIS is the term applied to softening of a bone resulting from the disappearance of lime salts from it.

HALITOSIS (halitus, exhalation) is another term for offensive breath. (See BREATH, DISEASES OF.)

HALLUCINATIONS (hallucinor, I blunder) are errors in perception, affecting some sense organ to such an extent that a person imagines he perceives something for which there is no foundation. For example, a person may fancy he hears himself called during perfect stillness, or may see lights in pitch darkness. *Illusions* are misinterpreted sensations ; for example, a person may constantly mistake an article of furniture for the figure of some friend, or of an animal. Both these errors occur in sane people, and may indicate some slight brain derangement, due to sleeplessness, overwork, feverishness, or other cause. They are usually, however, a symptom of insanity.

HALLUCINOGENS are compounds characterized by their ability to produce distortions of perception, emotional changes, depersonalization, and a variety of effects on memory and learned behaviour. They include Cannabis indica (q.v.), lysergic acid diethylamide (q.v.) and mescaline (q.v.).

HALLUX (hallux) is the anatomical name of the great toe.

HALO is a coloured circle seen round a bright light in some eye conditions. When accompanied by headache it is specially likely to be caused by glaucoma. (See GLAUCOMA.)

HALOTHANE is a non-inflammable anæsthetic, the chemical formula of which is $CF_3CHClBr$. One of its advantages is that patients recover rapidly from its effects, and it is now being used to an increasingly wide extent in all branches of surgery.

HAMAMELIS (see WITCH-HAZEL).

HAMMER-TOE (see CORNS AND BUNIONS).

HAMSTRINGS is the name given to the tendons at the back of the knee, two on the inner side and one on the outer side, which bend this joint. They are attached to the tibia below.

HAND is the section of the upper limb below the wrist. The hand of man is more highly developed in its structure and in its nervous connections than the corresponding part in any other animal. Indeed the possession of a thumb which can be ' opposed ' to the other fingers for grasping objects is one of the distinguishing features of the human race. Of all the parts of the body, the hand, which is connected with a large area on the surface of the brain, is capable of the highest degree of education, and in cases where the brain degenerates, as in general paralysis, the uses of the hand deteriorate particularly early ; while in those cases where part of the brain is destroyed by apoplexy, the hand is apt to suffer more permanently than either face or leg.

In structure, the hand has a bony basis of eight small carpal bones in the wrist, five metacarpal bones in the fleshy part of the hand, and three phalanges in each finger, two only in the thumb. From the muscles of the forearm run in front of the wrist twelve strong tendons or sinews. Of these, nine go to the fingers and thumb and are bound down by a strong band, the annular ligament, in front of the wrist. They are enclosed in a complicated synovial sheath, and pass through the palm and down the fingers (see FINGER). Behind the wrist twelve tendons likewise cross from forearm to hand.

Forming the ball of the thumb and that of the little finger, and filling up the gaps between the metacarpal bones, are other muscles, which act to

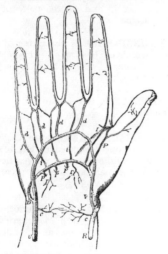

FIG. 221.—Diagram showing the position of the important arteries in the hand. For lettering, see Fig. 18 (p. 69). The nerves lie, in the main, alongside of the arteries. (Turner's Anatomy.)

separate and bring together the fingers, and to bend them at their first joints (knuckles).

Deep in the palm the ulnar artery makes an arch across the hand, giving off branches which run down the sides of the fingers ; while the radial artery makes an arch across at a still deeper level, lying in close contact with the bones (Fig. 221).

The skin of the hand is richly supplied with nerve filaments, in accordance with its highly specialized sense of touch, the outer three and a half digits being supplied in front by the median, behind by the radial nerve, whilst the inner one and a half fingers have their nerve supply both back and front from the ulnar nerve.

In addition to the diseases mentioned above, certain nervous diseases affect the hand early. Thus in multiple sclerosis and in chorea there are tremors ; in alcoholic neuritis and in lead-poisoning, wrist-drop ; in progressive muscular atrophy one of the first signs is wasting of the small muscles belonging to the thumb and little finger ; in syringomyelia there is loss of sensation for pain and for change of temperature in the fingers.

Deformities of the hand, in the shape of chalk-stones, may occur in gout ; rheumatism may cause stiffness or even forward bending of the fingers ; rheumatic gout often causes great distortion of the small joints and twisting of the fingers toward the inner side of the hand ; and acromegaly is characterized by great enlargement of the hands. Swellings on the back or front of the wrist are usually due to collection of fluid in the tendon sheaths (see GANGLION). Deep abscesses on the front of the fingers are serious, because of the ease with which the infection spreads up the synovial sheaths of the tendons into the palm of the hand (see WHITLOW). A condition in which the fingers, especially the ring and little fingers, are gradually drawn up into the palm follows sometimes on a severe strain of the palm or long-continued pressure of a tool (see DUPUYTREN'S CONTRACTURE).

Several special terms are applied to deformities of the hand. ' Claw hand ' or main en griffe is applied to a condition in which the hand is atrophied and the fingers bent in paralysis of the ulnar nerve ; ' monkey hand ' or main en singe is applied to a condition in which the muscles of the thumb are wasted ; ' obstetrician's hand ' is a condition in which the thumb and fingers are held together in a kind of cone in shaking palsy and other conditions ; and ' skeleton hand ' is a condition in which the muscles of the hand are generally wasted, as in progressive muscular atrophy. (*See also* DROP-WRIST.)

HANGING is a form of death due to suspension of the body from the neck, either suddenly, as in judicial hanging, so as to damage the spinal column and cord, or in such a way as to constrict the air passages and the blood-vessels to the brain. Death is, in any case, speedy, resulting in two or three minutes, if not instantaneous, although in bygone days criminals who were ' shored-up ', or supported by their friends, have come round after half an hour's suspension. The mark of the noose on the neck is oblique in hanging, which serves to distinguish this form of death from strangling, in which the mark is circular. The question as to accident, suicide, or murder does not generally arise in cases of hanging, which, apart from judicial hanging, and in the absence of any signs of a struggle, is due to suicide. The resuscitation of persons found hanging is similar to that for drowning (*see* DROWNING).

HANG-NAIL means a splitting of the skin at the side of the finger-nail. It is often a painful condition and difficult to heal. This is best effected by wearing constantly for several days a wet boracic dressing covered by a rubber finger-stall.

HARDNESS is a term applied to water that contains a large amount of calcium and magnesium salts (lime salts) which form an insoluble curd with soap and thus interfere with the use of the water for purposes of washing. Hard water is especially found in districts where the soil is chalky. The same salts have a strongly astringent action when the water is drunk, and thus produce constipation and other troubles. Temporary hardness, which is due to the presence of bicarbonates of lime, can be remedied by boiling, when the lime is precipitated

as carbonate of lime. Permanent hardness is not remedied by boiling, and is due to the presence of a large amount of sulphate of lime.

HARE-LIP (*see* PALATE, MALFORMATIONS OF).

HARTMANN'S SOLUTION is a solution which is commonly used as a means of fluid replacement in dehydrated patients. Each litre contains 3·1 grammes of sodium lactate, 6 grammes of sodium chloride, o·3 gramme of potassium chloride, and o·2 gramme of calcium chloride.

HARTSHORN is a popular name for ammonia. (*See* AMMONIA.)

HASHIMOTO'S DISEASE is a condition in which the whole of the thyroid gland is diffusely enlarged and firm. The enlargement is due, not to increase of colloid, but to diffuse infiltration of lymphocytes and increase of fibrous tissue. This form of goitre appears in middle-aged women, does not give rise to symptoms of thyrotoxicosis (thyroid ' poisoning '), and tends to produce myxœdema.

HAUNCH-BONE is the name of the bone which encloses the lower part of the abdomen on each side. (*See* PELVIS.)

HAUSTUS is the Latin word for a draught.

HAVERSIAN CANALS are the fine canals in bone which carry the blood-vessels, lymphatics, and nerves necessary for the maintenance and repair of bone. (*See* BONE.)

HAY FEVER, otherwise known as SUMMER CATARRH, and in America as AUTUMN CATARRH, means an allergic condition of the mucous membranes of the eyes, nose, and air passages, which year after year affects certain individuals during the summer and early autumn.

Causes.—Hay fever is an allergic reaction in individuals who are hypersensitive to the pollens of grasses, weeds or trees. This explains the seasonal distribution of the disease. In Britain, where grass pollens are the commonest cause, it occurs from the middle of May to the end of July. In North America it occurs over a longer period : in April and May, due to tree pollens ; in June and July, due to grass pollens ; in August and September, due to weed pollens. The inhalation of such a pollen to which the individual is hypersensitive results in the production of an excessive amount of histamine (*q.v.*) and it is the histamine which is responsible for the manifestations of hay fever.

The tendency to develop hay fever runs in certain families. What is inherited in these families is what might be described as an allergic constitution. Only some members of these families will develop hay fever, whilst others may develop other allergic manifestations, such as asthma, eczema or food allergy.

Symptoms.—The malady recurs with regularity during the summer months in those susceptible to it. It begins with an itching of the eyes and nose, followed by symptoms of a severe cold or influenza, such as headache, violent sneezing, and profuse watery discharge from the eyes and nose, together with dry, hard cough, and occasionally severe asthmatic paroxysms. The attack usually runs a course of several weeks. If rainy weather come on, the symptoms may abate, and susceptible persons, who betake themselves early in May to the seaside or a place where vegetation is scanty, rarely suffer.

Treatment. — The most effectual method of treatment in hay fever is to avoid the exciting cause, namely, the neighbourhood of grass fields, during the summer season. Removal to the seaside often succeeds in putting an end to an attack, and many persons who are liable to the complaint make such a change annually before its expected onset, and thus escape. A course of vaccines either immediately before the hay-fever season, or spread out over the preceding winter, sometimes provides relief. Of recent years a number of antihistamine preparations (*q.v.*) have been produced which practically always bring relief. In cases in which there is some nasal defect, cauterization of the turbinate process or an

14*a*

operation to straighten a distorted nasal septum sometimes helps. If the watering of the eyes is particularly severe, relief may be obtained from the use of eye-drops containing 1 per cent. of ephedrine in saline.

Susceptible persons living in the country should sleep with their bedroom windows shut. Ionization of the nasal mucosa with zinc sulphate may help.

HAZELINE, or LIQUOR HAMAMELIDIS, is an extract made from the leaves or bark of *Hamamelis virginiana*, the witch-hazel. It is a useful astringent in checking bleeding and excessive mucous discharges. (*See* WITCH-HAZEL.)

HEAD (*see* BRAIN, FACE, SKULL, *and* SCALP).

HEADACHE is one of the commonest ills to which man is heir. Its significance varies tremendously. Thus, at one extreme it may denote the presence of a tumour of the brain or meningitis, whilst at the other extreme it may only be a sign of tiredness in an over-worked executive or professional man. In spite of being such a common finding, the precise mechanism whereby it is produced is still somewhat obscure. The brain itself is insensitive to pain, but the arteries supplying it and the membranes of the brain in relationship to these arteries are sensitive to pain. The general view at the moment is that headache is usually due to dilatation of these arteries or pressure (or traction) on them. This dilatation of the intracranial arteries may be due either to a lesion in the brain or it may be caused reflexly, *i.e.* by a stimulus somewhere else in the body which through the nervous system (often the vagus nerve) causes such dilatation. In other cases the headache arises in the scalp or in the muscles of the back of the neck. The following are some of the more important, or more common, conditions in which headache is present.

ANXIETY.—One of the most common forms of headache is that which occurs in individuals when they are worried, anxious, or overworked. In some cases it may be a manifestation of what is known as the anxiety state or of emotional instability, but quite often it occurs in individuals who are emotionally stable. On the other hand, it seldom occurs in the phlegmatic type of person. Manual workers and those who live an out-of-door life seldom complain of headache, and there can be little doubt that the stress and strain under which the modern town-dweller lives have much to do with its incidence. Aggravating factors are inadequate ventilation of offices and excessive smoking. In women it is liable to occur during or shortly before menstruation.

MIGRAINE.—This is one of the most characteristic forms of headache. For further details the section on migraine should be consulted.

REFRACTIVE ERRORS OF THE EYE are a common cause of headache. The pain occurs in the region of the brow and tends to be worse in the evening, particularly if much reading or close work has been done during the course of the day. It is sometimes accompanied by a sensation of grittiness in the eye. The remedy in such cases is simple : the wearing of spectacles which correct the faulty vision.

INFECTION OF THE SINUSES is another common cause of headache. The location of the pain depends upon which sinus is involved. If the maxillary antrum, which lies in the cheek-bone, is infected, the pain is usually over the cheek, although it may be referred elsewhere in the head. In the case of involvement of the frontal sinuses the pain is over the eyes, whilst in the case of the deeper-lying ethmoidal sinuses the pain appears to be deep-seated behind the eyes. In such cases there is usually a history of a 'cold in the head' followed by a discharge from the nose. The pain is usually worse about midday and tends to wear off towards evening. It is usually made worse by coughing and even sometimes by change of position.

DENTAL SEPSIS. — Septic teeth may sometimes be responsible for headache. Usually, of course, there is also the classical toothache, but occasionally the pain of septic teeth is referred to the head.

INDIGESTION AND CONSTIPATION.—Any form of dyspepsia due to disordered function of the stomach and which is liable to be accompanied by nausea (i.e. a feeling of sickness), may be responsible for headache. On the other hand, individuals with a duodenal ulcer are not particularly liable to headache. Constipation is quite a common cause of headache, especially in children, but the old theory that the headache is due to absorption of toxic material from the gut has now been discarded. The headache is relieved so rapidly by the passing of a stool that it must be due to distension of the lower part of the bowel. Disturbances of the liver are also characterized by headache.

FEVER. — Any infection, such as pneumonia or measles, causing a rise in temperature is liable to be accompanied by headache. This is probably due to dilatation of the blood-vessels in the brain resulting from the fever itself and from the infecting organism or its toxins.

URÆMIA. — This is the terminal stage of Bright's disease (q.v.) and it is often accompanied by severe headache, which is due partly to the high blood-pressure which is always present and partly to the toxic substances which are retained in the body as a result of the failure of the kidneys.

HIGH BLOOD-PRESSURE. — Although many people with a high blood-pressure are not unduly troubled with headache, the headache when it does occur is very characteristic. It tends to occur at the back of the head and to be worse in the morning, wearing off during the course of the day.

RHEUMATIC CONDITIONS.— Many rheumatic subjects are subject to aches and pains about the head. These are due to rheumatic changes in the muscles of the head and the back of the neck, and can usually be easily recognized by the fact that they are accompanied by tender spots elicited by pressure on the affected parts.

SUNSTROKE AND HEATSTROKE.—Headache, of course, is the prominent feature in these conditions, and its occurrence after undue exposure to the sun or to exceptionally hot conditions renders easy its recognition.

DISEASES OF THE BRAIN.— Finally, there are the conditions in which a headache indicates the presence of some disturbance or disease of the brain. This may take the form of infections of the brain or its membranes, *e.g.* encephalitis, brain abscess, meningitis. There is seldom any difficulty in determining the presence of these conditions, as there are practically always other signs of involvement of the brain, *e.g.* rigidity of the neck and squint in meningitis. In young children meningitis must always be considered when a febrile illness is accompanied by severe headache. In tumours of the brain severe headache develops sooner or later, but here again there are other manifestations, such as giddiness and apparently causeless vomiting, which indicate the cause of the headache. In middle-aged or elderly persons headache may be due to arteriosclerosis or thrombosis of the arteries in the brain. A relatively uncommon, but very acute, type of headache, usually in the back of the head, is caused by rupture of a small aneurysm (*q.v.*) in the circle of Willis, a network of arteries at the base of the brain. Headache is one of the main manifestations of concussion, whether or not this is accompanied by a fractured skull. The persistence of this headache after the individual has otherwise recovered from the concussion is sometimes most troublesome. If the concussion is due to an accident for which the victim considers he should receive compensation, this post-concussion, or post-traumatic headache, is one of the manifestations of a compensation neurosis. Once the case is settled, whether favourably or unfavourably to the claimant matters little, the headache usually clears up.

Treatment.—It will be clear from this outline that in the majority of cases the treatment of headache is the treatment of the underlying cause. The main exception to this is migraine (*q.v.*). When the headache is associated with anxiety, worry or overwork, the same principle holds true. In these cases there may be an associated general debility, and for this the best remedy is a holiday with complete change of environment, adequate rest, and plenty of good food. If the headache is associated with sleeplessness, the administration of a mild sedative, *e.g.* a small dose of a barbiturate, is helpful provided it is not continued indefinitely. Similarly with aspirin ; this will relieve many a headache, but its continued use by an increasing number of the population is not in the interest of the health of the community. Used sensibly for short periods of time aspirin has its uses, but its repeated and continued use is to be deprecated. Local soothing applications to the forehead are often of value in relieving headache. For this purpose there is much to be said for eau-de-Cologne. If the individual is lying down, a moist handkerchief on the forehead is sometimes just as effective.

HEALING (*see* WOUNDS).

HEALTH.—The state of health implies much more than freedom from disease, and good health may be defined as the attainment and maintenance of the highest state of mental and bodily vigour of which any given individual is capable. People vary in the degree of strength and activity to which they are capable of attaining, and some persons must be content with leading a life on a lower plane of physical or mental activity than others. For the maintenance of this individual standard it is essential that each person should recognize his capabilities and limitations, and also that he should be aware of any defects of body or mind to which he is liable, either as the result of heredity or of previous disease. The recognition of, and allowance for, these in the conduct of daily life is of immense importance in maintaining health in other respects. Many persons have some inborn hereditary defect or tendency, *e.g.* a neurotic temperament or a liability to disease of some special organ of the body, such as the heart or lungs, and the maintenance of health in such persons should be particularly directed towards avoiding conditions which lead to disorders common in their family (*see* HEREDITY, HEART DISEASES, LUNG DISEASES, etc.).

Environment is another matter with a very important bearing upon health. This involves such considerations as the choice of an occupation suited to the individual's capabilities and temperament and the avoidance in dangerous occupations of the influences which are specially deleterious to health (see TRADE DISEASES). The social surroundings also involved in environment play a very important part with many persons in the development of nervous affections (see NEURASTHENIA). Speaking generally, it may be said that the great majority of persons, long before middle life is reached, have contracted some defect of body or constitution arising from their surroundings, and the maintenance of health depends largely upon making appropriate allowance for this.

The care of the health should begin with the earliest life, and as infants are more prejudicially affected by improper feeding than by any other influence, the care of the child in this respect is of the greatest importance (see INFANT FEEDING). Children display at an early age peculiarities and tendencies which, if unchecked, sometimes develop into undesirable habits, and these form a matter for careful education. (See CHILDREN, PECULIARITIES OF ; SCHOOL CHILDREN ; and MENTAL DEFECTIVENESS.)

At a later stage the most important factor in the due care of body and mind consists in attention to the natural functions of the body. Of these, the question of food that is proper in quality and in amount is one of the most important (see DIET). Careful attention to the functions of the bowels (see CONSTIPATION) and proper care of the teeth (see TEETH, DISEASES OF) are subjects of the utmost importance, in which children especially should be carefully instructed. In regard to the care of the skin and the maintenance of its functions, see SKIN, BATHS, and CLOTHING. A due maintenance of the relation between the exercise of the body and the amount of rest is of great importance (see EXERCISE, FATIGUE, and SLEEP), whilst the correction of bad habits in regard to the posture of the body, especially while at work, is of immense importance in maintaining good health (see CHEST DEVELOPMENT and SPINE, DISEASES OF). Various habits in regard to eating and drinking, and the practice of smoking, which has become almost universal, require to be

carefully studied in order that due moderation may be exercised in regard to them (see CORPULENCE, ALCOHOL, TOBACCO).

Despite all the ordinary precautions that may be taken in regard to matters of everyday life, such as those already mentioned, people become, especially in the earlier years of life, exposed to accidents and diseases, which may, however, with care be avoided to a large extent (see INFECTION and SANITATION). Certain diseases and influences are particularly liable to affect the health in different parts of the world. (For the influences exerted by climate upon health, see CLIMATE IN RELATION TO DISEASE, and for reference to the diseases which are liable to be contracted by persons in tropical countries, see references under TROPICAL DISEASES.)

HEARING (see DEAFNESS, EAR).

HEART is a hollow muscular pump with four cavities, each provided at its outlet with a valve, whose function is to maintain the circulation of the blood. The two upper cavities are known as atria, the two lower ones as ventricles. The term auricle is applied to the ear-shaped tip of the atrium on each side. Owing to the fact that the heart has important connections with the nervous system, and that its action is liable to be increased or diminished by influences which powerfully affect the latter, the heart was regarded in olden times, and is still metaphorically spoken of, as the seat of the emotions.

Position.—The heart lies in the chest between the two lungs, but projecting more to the left side than to the right (Fig. 222 & Plate X). On the left side its apex reaches out in the adult between $3\frac{1}{2}$ and 4 inches (8 and 9 cm.), almost to the nipple, and lies beneath the fifth rib, while its right border extends only a short distance, at most an inch, beyond the margin of the breast-bone. Its lower border rests upon the diaphragm, by which it is separated from the liver and stomach, and this close connection has an important influence upon the heart in several disorders of the stomach. Above, the heart extends to the level of the second rib, where the great vessels, the aorta on the right side and the pulmonary artery on the left, lie behind the breast-bone.

Shape and size.—The heart of any

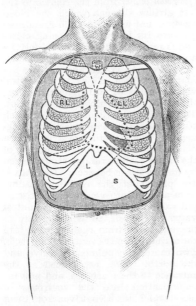

FIG. 222.—Diagram of the contents of the chest from the front. The position of the heart is shown by a dotted line. *H*, The part of the heart exposed in front of left lung; *LL*, left lung; *RL*, right lung; *L*, liver; *S*, stomach; *W*, windpipe.

individual was described by Laennec as, roughly, of the size and shape of the clenched fist. One end of the heart is pointed (apex), the other is broad (base), and is deeply cleft at the division between the two atria. One groove running down the front and up the back shows the division between the two ventricles; a circular, deeper groove marks off the atria above from the ventricles below (Fig. 223). The capacity of each cavity is somewhere between 3 and 6 ounces (90 and 180 ml.).

Structure.—The heart lies within a strong fibrous bag, known as the pericardium, and since the inner surface of this bag and the outer surface of the heart are both covered with a smooth, glistening membrane faced with flat cells and lubricated by a little serous fluid, the movements of the heart are accomplished almost without friction.

The main thickness of the heart wall consists of bundles of muscle fibres, which run, some in circles right round the heart, others in loops, first round

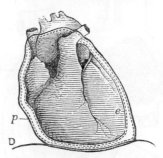

FIG. 223.—Heart lying within the pericardium, *p*; *e*, epicardial layer; *D*, diaphragm. (Turner's *Anatomy*.)

one cavity, then round the corresponding cavity of the other side. Within all the cavities is a smooth lining membrane, continuous with that lining the vessels which open into the heart. The investing smooth membrane is known as epicardium, the muscular substance as myocardium, and the smooth lining membrane as endocardium.

For the regulation of the heart's action there are important nervous connections, especially with the vagus nerve and with the sympathetic system. In the hinder part of the atria lies a collection of nerve cells and connecting fibres, known as the sinu-atrial node, which forms the starting-point for the impulses that initiate the beats of the heart. In the groove between the ventricles and the atria lies another collection of similar nerve tissue, known as the atrio-ventricular node. This is connected by muscle fibres with the sinu-atrial node above, and from it there runs downwards into the septum between the two ventricles a band of special muscle fibres, known as the atrio-ventricular bundle of His. This splits up into a right and a left branch for the two ventricles, and the fibres of these distribute themselves throughout the muscular wall of the ventricles and control their contraction.

Openings.—There is no direct communication between the cavities on the

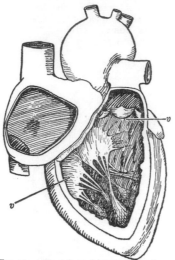

FIG. 224.—Heart from right side. The flaps at *v*, *v* show two of the valves.

right side and those on the left ; but the right atrium opens into the right ventricle by a large circular opening, and similarly the left atrium into the left ventricle. Into the right atrium open two large veins, the superior and inferior venæ cavæ, with some smaller veins from the wall of the heart itself, and into the left atrium open two pulmonary veins from each lung. One opening leads out of each ventricle, to the aorta in the case of the left ven-

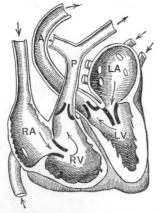

FIG. 225.—Diagram of heart with front surface removed to show valves. *RA*, Right atrium ; *RV*, right ventricle ; *P*, pulmonary artery ; *LA*, left atrium ; *LV*, left ventricle ; *A*, aorta.

tricle, to the pulmonary artery from the right.

Prior to birth there is an opening (*foramen ovale*) from the right into the left atrium through which the blood passes ; but when the child first draws air into its lungs this opening closes and is represented in the adult only by a depression (*fossa ovalis*).

Valves.—As stated above, there are four valves (Figs. 224, 225). The mitral valve consists of two triangular cusps, the tricuspid valve of three smaller cusps. The aortic and pulmonary valves each consist of three semilunar-shaped segments. The structure of a valve is a double layer of the lining membrane of the heart (endocardium) strengthened by fibrous tissue between. Two valves are placed at the openings leading from atrium into ventricle, the tricuspid valve on the right side, the mitral valve on the left, so as completely to prevent blood from running back into the atrium when the ventricle contracts. Two more, the pulmonary valve and the aortic valve, are placed at the entrance to these arteries, and prevent regurgitation into the ventricles of blood which has been driven from them into the arteries. The noises made by these valves in closing constitute the greater part of what are known as the heart sounds, and can be heard by anyone who applies his ear to the front of a person's chest. Murmurs heard accompanying these sounds indicate defects in the valves, and form one of the chief signs of heart disease.

Action.—At each heart-beat the two atria contract and expel their contents into the ventricles, which at the same time they stimulate to contract together, so that the blood is driven into the arteries, to be returned again to the auricles after having completed a circuit in about fifteen seconds through the body or lungs as the case may be. The heart beats from sixty to ninety times a minute, the rate in any given healthy person being about four times that of the respirations. The heart is to some extent regulated by a nerve centre in the medulla, closely connected with those centres which govern the lungs and stomach, and nerve-fibres pass to it in the ' vagus ' nerve. By some of these fibres its rate and force can be diminished, by others increased, according to the needs of the various organs of the body. If this nerve centre be injured or poisoned, for example, by want of fresh air, etc., the heart stops beating in human beings, although in some of the lower animals—*e.g.* frogs, fishes, and reptiles—the heart may under favourable conditions go on beating for hours even after its entire removal from the body.

HEARTBURN means a burning sensation experienced in the region of the heart and up the back to the throat. It is caused by an excessive acidity of the gastric juice, and is relieved temporarily by taking alkaline substances, such as 20 grains (1·2 grammes) of bicarbonate of soda or a similar amount of bismuth carbonate or carbonate of magnesia in water.

HEART DISEASES belong to that class of diseases which can be recognized only by the trained observer, although their presence may occasion severe symptoms and evident signs of general illness perceptible to every one. Their treatment, and a true appreciation of their slightness or gravity, belong still more to the department of the specialist.

Varieties.—Many general diseases affect the heart ; but, considering the arduous work which this organ constantly performs (*see* EXERCISE), and the fact that it never rests completely from the time of its formation till death ensues, it is subject to wonderfully few disorders. Its diseases are classified according to the part of the heart affected, or the nature of the changes produced. *Inflammatory affections* are divided into pericarditis, myocarditis, and endocarditis, according as the pericardium or enveloping membrane, the myocardium or muscular substance, and the endocardium or lining membrane are affected. *Valvular diseases* form one of the most important groups; any of the four valves may be stenosed, *i.e.* the aperture between its flaps narrowed, or a valve may be incompetent, so that some blood leaks back through the opening in the wrong direction. *Hypertrophy*, in which the heart is enlarged and its wall thickened, and *dilatation*, in which one

or more of the cavities is dilated, form another group often associated with the valvular diseases. *Degeneration* of the muscular tissue, producing enfeeblement of the heart's action, may take place, in the direction either of a fatty or, less commonly, of a fibroid change. Finally, there is a class of *functional* disorders in which—with or without apparent diseased change in the structure of the heart—palpitation, irregularity, rapidity, slowness, or even severe attacks of pain appear.

Causes.—The number of deaths from diseases of the heart is rising steadily. In England and Wales, in 1966, 37 per cent. of the total number of 563,624

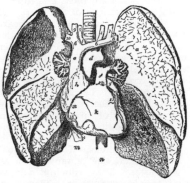

FIG. 226.—The organs of the chest. The lungs are turned outwards to show the heart and the intimate connections between heart and lungs. *a*, Upper, *a'*, lower lobe of left lung ; *b*, upper *b'*, middle, *b''*, lower lobe of right lung ; *c*, trachea ; *d*, arch of aorta ; *e*, superior vena cava ; *f*, pulmonary artery ; *g*, left atrium; *h*, right atrium ; *k*, right ventricle ; *l*, left ventricle ; *m*, inferior vena cava ; *n*, aorta ; 1, innominate artery ; 2 and 4, carotid arteries ; 3 and 5, subclavian arteries ; 6, 6, innominate veins ; 7 and 9, internal jugular veins ; 8 and 10, subclavian veins ; 11, 12, 13, left pulmonary artery, bronchus, and vein ; 14, 15, 16, right bronchus, pulmonary artery, and vein ; 17 and 18 coronary arteries. (Turner's *Anatomy*.)

deaths were due to diseases of the heart and blood vessels.

The main causes of heart disease are disease of the coronary arteries (the arteries which nourish the heart muscle), high blood-pressure, acute rheumatism, and syphilis. Acute rheumatism is predominantly a disease of childhood, and most cases of heart disease occurring between the ages of 5 and 45 years of age are of rheumatic origin. The importance of rheumatic heart disease is further demonstrated by the fact that in 1960 there were 7,121 deaths from chronic rheumatic heart disease in England and Wales. High blood-pressure and coronary-artery disease are predominantly diseases of middle age, and their incidence has increased markedly during the last fifty years. Syphilitic heart disease also occurs in later life as a result of infection acquired during early adult life.

Other causes of heart disease include diphtheria, disease of the thyroid gland (thyrotoxicosis), and certain chronic forms of disease of the lungs. A small, but important group of cases of heart disease are those due to congenital abnormalities of the heart, *i.e.* developmental errors in the heart which occur before the birth of the child. These account for 1 to 2 per cent. of all cases of organic heart disease. Bright's disease involves the heart when it is accompanied by high blood - pressure. Certain deficiency diseases involve the heart, particularly gross deficiency of vitamin B1, which causes the condition known as beriberi (*q.v.*).

General symptoms.—The heart possesses a remarkable power, known as 'compensation', by which it adapts itself to new conditions. Thus if a person takes up some more arduous employment than usual the heart beats more powerfully and becomes larger, in order to overtake the extra strain; and, in a similar way, disease in one part of the organ, such as a valve, may be so compensated that not only do no symptoms arise, but the person may pass through a long life without suspecting the existence of any such defect. The establishment of this compensation is one of the chief objects of the gradual training which is necessary before undertaking any strenuous athletic exercise. It is a common mistake to suppose that disease of the heart ends always in sudden death, for only disease of the aortic valve and degeneration of the heart-muscle are associated with this accident, which even in these conditions is infrequent. If, however, the defect be so great that it cannot be remedied by compensation, or if general ill-health or the debility of age come

432

on, the pumping power of the heart weakens and symptoms appear, some of which are referable to the organs in which the circulation is defective, others, like pain and palpitation, to the heart itself. For example, breathlessness and lividity are due to bad circulation in the lungs; faintness and giddiness to want of blood in the brain; dyspepsia, swelling of the abdomen, and dropsy of the feet, to impeded circulation in the veins of the lower part of the body.

PERICARDITIS is an inflammation of the membrane covering the exterior of the heart. It may be dry, in which case the two opposing surfaces of the membrane are covered by a layer of fibrin worked up by the movements of the heart into ridges, very like those upon the surface of two slices of bread and butter forcibly separated from one another; or effusion may accompany this condition, when the pericardial bag becomes much distended by fluid. The causes of the condition are much the same as those of the condition of endocarditis described below. In the majority of cases it arises in connection with an attack of rheumatic fever; and, so long as it remains of the dry type, it occasions only slight feverishness and pain felt over the heart. Poisoned wounds, tuberculosis, scarlatina, diphtheria, pneumonia, and Bright's disease are also, though less frequently, causes. Pericarditis with effusion generally follows the dry form, unless the latter be very slight in extent, and the amount of fluid may reach as much as two quarts (one litre). The fibrin upon the surface of the membrane increases with the amount of fluid, and may form a coating like thick leather round the heart, which very greatly embarrasses its action. Pain over the heart, high fever, rapid and feeble pulse, restlessness, difficulty in breathing, and even delirium, mark the presence of this serious condition. Recovery very often takes place, but the heart is apt to be left weak and dilated, in consequence of permanent roughening and adhesions between the two surfaces of the pericardium, and in long-standing cases this resistance to its action produces great increase in the size of the heart. This condition is known as adhesive pericarditis or adherent pericardium ; it leads to great hypertrophy of the heart, and it is apt to be associated with recurring attacks of rapid cardiac action accompanied by breathlessness (paroxysmal tachycardia). Treatment during the acute stage, apart from treatment of the underlying infection by penicillin or the sulphonamides, is usually effected either by the application of an ice-bag or of blisters to the front of the chest, while various stimulants are given to maintain the action of the heart. Occasionally it becomes necessary to tap the pericardial cavity and draw off some of the fluid which is embarrassing the heart's action.

ENDOCARDITIS is an inflammatory condition of the membrane lining the heart, and since the part most subjected to friction and strain is that covering the valves, so these valves are the most commonly affected parts, those on the left side of the heart being affected much more frequently than those on the right side. The inflammatory process consists in the appearance of small groups of nodules upon the valves. These unite to form wart-like growths, upon which fibrin is deposited from the blood to form pendants, often of some length. The condition just described is known as simple endocarditis, and occurs most commonly in connection with rheumatic fever and with chorea in childhood. Tonsillitis and scarlatina may also be complicated by simple endocarditis. Simple endocarditis arises especially in those cases of rheumatic fever which are not allowed to rest during the attack, and although the endocarditis may give no symptom of its presence, it may leave the heart with serious valvular disease. Palpitation and a slight increase of temperature may often form the only warning of the onset of endocarditis during an attack of rheumatic fever.

Another form of endocarditis is known as bacterial endocarditis. In 80 per cent. of cases there is a previous history of rheumatism or chorea, whilst in 10 per cent. of cases it is superimposed on a congenitally deformed valve. The essential feature is a progressive microbic infection of the heart valves or the endocardium of the heart wall. It is of much more serious import than the simple type, since fragments of the ulcerating valves may be carried by the blood-stream all over the body and set up abscesses in diverse organs, this form, indeed, resulting almost always in death. There is, however, no hard and fast dividing line between simple and ulcerative endocarditis, and various grades of intermediate severity in which life may be prolonged for many months are found. Little could be done for the condition beyond rest and careful nursing until the introduction of penicillin, which has now been shown to be a life-saving measure in this condition.

CHRONIC VALVULAR DISEASES form the most frequent and most important group of heart disorders. Although, in consequence of the power of compensation already mentioned, the heart may become more powerful and so neutralize the ill-effects of a narrowed or leaking valve, it is not possible to predict how far this change will be affected by ill-health or the strain of a laborious life, and consequently the detection of valvular disease unfits a person for entrance upon any public service, and renders him subject, if he becomes a candidate for life assurance, either to refusal or to a heavily increased premium. The commonest cause of valvular disease is rheumatic endocarditis, which, instead of passing off with the disease that produced it, has become chronic, leading ultimately either to thickening and contraction of the valves, so that they become unable to close their respective openings, or to adhesion of the segments of the valves to one another at their margins, so that the opening is very much narrowed. The former condition is known as incompetence, the latter as stenosis, and the two are found either separately, or together affecting the same valve. The valves on the left side of the heart are more frequently affected than those on the right side, in the proportion of about 18 to 1.

AORTIC DISEASE.—Of all the valvular defects, incompetence of the aortic valve is the most serious, and next to it in importance comes stenosis of the mitral opening. Aortic incompetence leads to great dilatation and hypertrophy of the heart, which in well-marked cases becomes so large as to receive the name of the cor bovinum or ox-heart. Although aortic disease in young persons follows upon endocarditis, and may produce a rapidly fatal issue, on the other hand it may give rise to few symptoms directly referable to the heart until later in life. If the incompetence develops in childhood it may result in the child being more or less stunted in body, and feeble or capricious in mind and temper. Stenosis at the aortic valve is much rarer than incompetence. Syphilis is especially apt to lead to a degenerative and hardened condition of the aortic valve, which renders it incompetent. Angina pectoris is not infrequently associated with this condition, in consequence of the spread of the degenerative process to the coronary arteries which supply the muscle of the heart itself with blood. (See ANGINA PECTORIS.) In either type, when compensation begins to fail, throbbing of the arteries becomes very noticeable, and headache, giddiness, faintness on rising quickly, and dull pain about the heart appear. Later, shortness of breath causing inability to lie down, and dropsy of the feet and legs appear. Sudden death may occur in a case of aortic incompetence, but death may also come on gradually, ushered in by increasing dropsy, great difficulty of breathing, and mental excitability.

MITRAL DISEASE is of two types. In one case the valve itself is at fault, owing almost always to endocarditis, which produces incompetence, or stenosis, or both. In the other, the left ventricle is dilated so that the two segments of the valve are held apart by their attachments to its walls, and consequently a state of temporary, secondary, or relative incompetence is produced. It is of great importance to recognize this distinction, because, whilst the former is permanent and organic, the latter, which is due to weakness of the heart muscle, as a result, for instance, of an acute infection such as diphtheria, or anæmia, may end in complete recovery. Mitral incompetence unaccompanied by stenosis may be of relatively little importance, and persons with this defect sometimes live to an advanced period of age. In defects of this valve, 434

the symptoms relate chiefly to the lungs, breathlessness on exertion being one of the most common, and the lips and ears becoming of a bluish tint, in consequence of the slow passage of blood through the lungs. Bronchitis and spitting of blood are very common, particularly in cases where stenosis is present. When compensation is failing, these symptoms become more marked, the liver and stomach get congested, producing a jaundiced tint of the skin, together with dyspepsia, and congestion of the kidneys develops, shown by the presence of albumin in the urine. One of the most unpleasant symptoms is the 'sleep-start', which catches the person as he is dropping off to sleep, making him start up gasping, and feeling as if his heart were stopping. All these symptoms pass off under treatment, to be renewed again and again at periods when the health is low. When the valve is stenosed, there is a tendency to the formation of small clots in the atrium; these may be carried away and lodged in various organs, e.g. in the brain, causing apoplexy. Sudden death in mitral disease is rare. Cases of mitral disease, and especially cases in which marked stenosis is present, are very frequently, as time goes on, associated with a state of dilatation of the atria, and the condition of disordered action in these cavities is known as atrial fibrillation. This leads to great irregularity in the time and force of the heart-beats, with corresponding irregularity felt in the pulse. (See below.)

DISEASE OF THE VALVES ON THE RIGHT SIDE is rare. The tricuspid valve may be incompetent in consequence of far advanced mitral disease, which increases the difficulty of circulation through the lungs and so leads to dilatation of the right side of the heart. Stenosis of the pulmonary valve sometimes forms a congenital condition in children, who do not often survive early life.

Treatment of valvular diseases.— When a valvular defect is accidentally discovered, even though it be perfectly compensated and give rise to no symptoms, it is well that the person should take certain precautions in his daily life, and he should therefore, unless of a particularly nervous and highly strung temperament, be informed by his medical adviser of the condition found in his heart. The subject of such disease must lead a quiet and well-regulated life, avoiding, as far as may be, excitement, worry, and sudden strains, although methodical attention to business, and even hard, steady work, are quite well borne. The question of marriage is an important one, and, speaking generally, it is unwise for the subjects of aortic disease to marry, for insurance companies decline the risk in this condition. In mitral disease marriage is not attended with the same risk, although in a woman the condition of a heart with defective mitral valve tends to become progressively worse with each confinement. The excessive use of tobacco, prolonged hot baths, and excursions up mountains are bad for most cases of valvular disease. A simple, wholesome diet is necessary, and stimulants should not be taken so long as compensation remains good.

When compensation begins to fail—and frequently this does not take place until middle age—the symptoms already mentioned appear, but, in early stages, rest may be the only remedy required. In the later stages the great standby is digitalis (*q.v.*). Many persons, by taking digitalis and living a carefully regulated life, manage to keep in abeyance all the symptoms of a serious valve defect, and to live a busy, useful life. Congestion of the liver, lungs, and kidneys is treated by rest in bed, digitalis, and diuretics. For dropsy in advanced cases, tapping of the legs, abdomen, or chest may be necessary, although less so since the introduction of efficient diuretics. (*See* ASPIRATION.) For breathlessness, the patient must often remain in the sitting posture night and day, and it is very important that a comfortable bed-rest should be provided. Pain about the heart is not very common, but, when it occurs, is often relieved by careful attention to the diet, so as to prevent dyspepsia. Spitting of blood, when it occurs, is not very copious, and is rather salutary than otherwise, so that it does not call for treatment.

Most satisfactory results are now being obtained from surgical treatment in certain selected cases of mitral stenosis.

ENLARGEMENT OF THE HEART

is of two types, dilatation of the cavities with HYPERTROPHY of the walls, and DILATATION with thinning of the walls. The first takes place as the result of simple, constant strain, as in professional runners and other athletes. It also arises in consequence of the increased difficulty in the circulation that results from a diseased valve, and it produces 'compensation' of the valvular disease. It also occurs in consequence of high blood-pressure. To this extent, and while general health lasts, hypertrophy is an altogether good thing, the only sign of its presence being a large heart with an extra-powerful beat. But there is, in the later years of life, a special tendency for the muscle of these hypertrophied hearts to degenerate ; and further, if the vessels throughout the body be weak, as in Bright's disease, the powerful beating of the heart may tear them, particularly in the brain, with apoplexy as a result. DILATATION of the heart, with thinning of its walls, is always a bad thing, leading to feeble action of the organ. It occurs also as the result of strain when the heart has not sufficient reserve force to hypertrophy. It takes place, too, in persons who are bloodless and subjected to over-hard work, and it often occurs to a slight extent after a severe fever. Sometimes it occurs suddenly, the heart becomes unable to contract upon the blood which accumulates in it, and death results in a few minutes or hours, in consequence of some extraordinary effort by a feeble person, or in consequence of injudicious exercise too soon during convalescence from a fever.

Treatment is much the same as for valvular heart disease where 'compensation' is failing. For a dilated heart, rest combined with regulated exercise is the special treatment. At certain spas and watering-places these exercises have been brought to great finesse. At Nauheim, special gymnastic exercises are combined with carbonic acid baths, and, by the Oertel treatment, patients are made to ascend a succession of increasing heights daily.

DEGENERATION OF THE HEART

occurs principally in elderly people, the most common form being a

435

change of the muscle fibres, in scattered patches, into fat. In another form of degeneration a deposition of fibrous tissue gradually takes place between the muscle fibres, which at the same time waste away. Less common forms of degeneration consist in a granular change in the fibres, producing great softening in the course of some fatal fevers ; and a condition known as 'brown atrophy', in which the heart-muscle wastes as old age advances, and contains much brown pigment.

FATTY DEGENERATION. — In stout people a deposit of fat takes place upon the heart (fatty infiltration), interfering with its action and causing shortness of breath upon slight exertion, but this is not so serious as true degeneration, in which the change involves a gradual destruction of the actual muscle. Fatty degeneration arises as a senile change, most commonly in persons addicted to alcohol, in whom it may appear early in middle life ; and also as a sequence to hypertrophy of the heart. In general devitalizing diseases like pernicious anæmia, or when the coronary arteries, which supply the heart itself with blood, are narrowed by disease, fatty degeneration of the heart-muscle is common. It may come on acutely in infective diseases like pneumonia or influenza. If it comes on gradually, it causes attacks of pain in the centre of the chest and left arm, with great irregularity and palpitation of the heart on exertion. Unusual torpor in the early part of the day following on very slight exertion, is also a sign of its presence. Other symptoms are occasional fainting fits and great loss of mental activity, and there is a special danger of sudden death in persons affected by this degenerative process.

FIBROID DEGENERATION of the muscular wall of the heart is usually a result of gradual and extensive blocking in branches of the coronary arteries, due to patches of atheromatous thickening in their walls. The muscle fibres waste or die in patches as a result of defective nourishment, and are replaced by useless fibrous tissue. Dilatation of the cavities, clotting of the blood on the fibroid patches, followed, it may be, by angina pectoris or by sudden death, take place. This condition of the heart is often associated with advanced

436

disease in the kidneys. The symptoms are much the same as those due to fatty degeneration. In the treatment, the same drugs are used as for valvular disease, though more sparingly. Careful regulation of daily life with simple diet is of great importance. The person should beware of any excessive mental or physical strain.

FUNCTIONAL AFFECTIONS.— Several varieties of abnormal action of the heart are recognized. Some of these are due to a definite organic disease of the heart, but in many there is no discoverable disease, and the abnormal action is then described as of functional nature. Some of these conditions are due to disease affecting the mechanism in the heart which controls the regular sequence of contraction of the different cavities, but such disease is only recognizable during life by the abnormal action which it sets up.

Many troublesome irregularities of the heart are now known to be caused by defective action of the muscular connections. The site of these defects can be analysed by means of elaborate modern instruments. Of these the chief is the *electrocardiograph* (*q.v.*), which by means of a galvanometer registers photographically the electrical changes that take place in the body as the heart beats.

The heart-muscle has in itself, independently of nervous control, the power of contracting rhythmically when excited to do so, of conducting the impulse to contract from one part of the muscle to another, and of maintaining itself in a moderate state of tension or tone. When any of these properties is affected by disease some change in the force or rhythm of the heart-beat is apt to appear.

PALPITATION is a condition in which the heart beats fast and the person becomes conscious of its beating. (*See* PALPITATION.)

ANGINA PECTORIS is a serious condition in which extreme pain and a sense of impending death are due to disease of the coronary arteries. (*See* ANGINA PECTORIS.)

SINUS ARRHYTHMIA is a condition of irregular action in which the heart speeds up during inspiration and slows again during expiration. It is a normal phenomenon, but may occasionally be so accentuated that the individual becomes aware of it, when it may give rise to anxiety.

ATRIAL (or AURICULAR) FIBRILLATION is the commonest form of persistent irregularity of the heart's action, accounting for about one-half of all the cases of irregular pulse. It usually accompanies disease of the mitral valve, and is recognized by great irregularity in time and force of the pulse, visible pulsations in the veins of the neck, and various signs which are made out by the use of the electrocardiograph and by auscultation. In this type of irregularity the atria do not empty themselves by the normal regular waves but contract partially in a rapid series of twitches, and in consequence the ventricles do not receive the normal rhythmic stimulus to contract, and they accordingly contract irregularly. This is a serious irregularity.

EXTRASYSTOLES form a common cause of irregular action in irritable states of the heart ; the extrasystole is a premature beat followed by a pause of the heart for rest. This is not a serious form of disorder, and it may come and go for many years in certain individuals.

HEART-BLOCK is a serious condition in which the conducting mechanism between atrium and ventricle is impaired (incomplete heart - block), or destroyed (complete heart - block) so that the atrium and ventricle beat at different rates independently of one another. During the incomplete stage the pulse is irregular, but when the heart-block becomes complete and the ventricles contract independently of the atria, the pulse becomes regular and very slow, and the individual is liable to fainting or convulsive attacks (Stokes-Adams attacks). (See also CARDIAC PACEMAKER.)

PULSUS ALTERNANS, or ALTERNATING PULSE, is a condition in which there are regularly alternating strong and weak beats of the heart, forming a persistent type of irregularity, which is caused by degeneration of the heart-muscle. It is of serious import.

RAPID HEART (tachycardia) with a pulse considerably above 100 per minute is found in a large variety of conditions. In its most benign form it may be due to emotional disturbance, whether

excitement, fear, or pleasure. In other cases it may be due to overactivity of the thyroid gland as in thyrotoxicosis (q.v.). A more common cause is fever. A rise in temperature is always accompanied by a rise in heart rate. The most common cause of all is a failing heart.

SLOW HEART (bradycardia) is a natural phenomenon in some individuals, the heart beating only forty, fifty, or sixty times per minute instead of the normal seventy or eighty times. Such individuals are usually of a generally lethargic temperament. Slowness of the heart-beat is also a character of complete heart-block.

CONGENITAL HEART DISEASE accounts for 1 to 2 per cent. of all cases of organic heart disease. The cause is not known, but there is some evidence that occasionally it may result from illness of the mother during pregnancy, e.g. German measles. The abnormality may take almost an infinite variety of forms, such as an abnormality of the valves of the heart, the heart lying on the right side of the thorax instead of the left, a patent ductus arteriosus (see DUCTUS ARTERIOSUS), a defect in the septum separating the chambers of the heart, or coarctation of the aorta (q.v.). These last three have become of great interest in recent years, in view of the satisfactory results which have been obtained with surgical treatment.

HEAT.—(See BURNS, HEAT-CRAMPS, HEAT-STROKE, and SUNSTROKE.) The curative uses of heat as applied by hot water and hot air are mentioned under BATHS. Hot-air applications are much used in the treatment of rheumatic conditions in the joints and muscles, and a more powerful application of heat for the same purpose is obtained by the use of high frequency electricity (see DIATHERMY). Excessive heat, in the form of the cautery, is also used in order to destroy diseased tissues (see CAUSTICS AND CAUTERIES).

HEAT-CRAMPS are painful cramps in the muscles occurring in workers, such as stokers, who labour in hot conditions. The cramps are the result of loss of salt in the sweat, and can be cured by giving salty water to drink.

HEAT SPOTS is a vague term applied to small inflamed and congested areas which appear especially upon the skin of the face, neck, and chest or other parts of the body in warm weather.

HEAT-STROKE, or HEAT HYPER-PYREXIA, occurs after exposure to excessive heat, and is characterized by convulsions, unconsciousness, and a temperature above 105° F. (40·5° C.).

HEBEPHRENIA (ἥβη, puberty; φρήν, mind) is a form of mental disorder coming on in youth and marked by depression and gradual failure of mental faculties with egotistic and self-centred delusions. It is one of the forms of dementia præcox.

HEBERDEN'S NODES are little hard knobs which appear at the sides of the last phalanges of the fingers in persons who are the subject of osteoarthrosis.

HEBETUDE (*hebetudo*) is mental dullness, especially the temporary dullness which arises in the course of weakening fevers like typhoid.

HECTIC (ἑκτικός, consumptive) is a type of fever which may occur in certain severe forms of tuberculosis or septic poisoning. The temperature rises during the day to 102° or 104° F. (39° to 40° C.), and falls during the night almost to normal or even to below normal, 96° or 97° F. (35·6° to 36·1° C.), with profuse sweating (*see* TUBERCULOSIS).

HEEL is the hinder part of the foot formed by the calcaneum and the specially thick skin covering it. It is not subject to many diseases. Severe pain in the heel is sometimes a sign of gout or rheumatism.

HEIGHT (*see* WEIGHT AND HEIGHT).

HELIOTHERAPY (ἥλιος, sun; θεραπεία, treatment) is a term applied to treatment of disease by exposing the body to the sun's rays. This form of treatment by sun bath has been widely used in the treatment of tuberculosis of the bones and joints. (*See* LIGHT TREATMENT.)

HELIUM is the lightest gas known, with the exception of hydrogen. This property renders it of value in anæsthesia (*q.v.*), as its addition to the anæsthetic being inhaled means that it

438

can be inhaled with less effort by the patient. Thus it can be used in the presence of any obstruction to the entry of air to the lungs.

HELLEBORE (*see* VERATRUM).

HELMINTHS (ἕλμινς, a worm) is a name for worms. (*See* PARASITES.)

HEMERALOPIA is the term for describing the condition of day-blindness, in which the patient can see better in a dull light than in bright daylight.

HEMIANÆSTHESIA (ἥμι, half; a, neg.; αἰσθάνομαι, I feel) means loss of touch-sense down one side of the body.

HEMIANOPIA, HEMIANOPSIA, and HEMIOPIA (ἥμι, half; a, neg.; ὤψ, sight) are terms meaning loss of half the usual area of vision. The affected person may see everything clearly to the left or to the right, the field of vision stopping abruptly at the middle line, or he may see things only when straight in front of him, or thirdly, he may see objects far out on both sides, although there is a wide area straight in front for which he is quite blind. The position of the blind area is important in localizing the position in the head of the disease responsible for the condition.

HEMIATROPHY is atrophy of one side of the body, or of part of the body on one side, for example, facial hemiatrophy, in which one-half of the face is smaller than the other either in the course of development or as a result of some nervous disorder.

HEMIBALLISM is a condition characterized by a violent form of restlessness involving one side of the body. It is usually most marked in the arm. It is due to a lesion in the mid-brain.

HEMICRANIA (ἡμικρανία, pain in half the head) means a headache limited to one side of the head. (*See* HEAD-ACHE.)

HEMIPLEGIA (ἡμιπληξία) means paralysis limited to one side of the body. (*See* PARALYSIS.)

HEMLOCK, or CONIUM, is used in the form both of the leaves and fruit of *Conium maculatum*. Its action depends upon the property which it possesses of paralysing the endings of the motor nerves. It therefore diminishes spasmodic conditions of all sorts, producing at the same time muscular weakness and confusion of vision. In large amount it causes complete paralysis and acts as a narcotic, and was the poison by which Socrates died. The action depends upon a liquid alkaloid, coniine.

Uses.—It is seldom used in medicine now. At one time it was considered to be of value in the treatment of spasmodic or convulsive conditions such as chorea, whooping-cough, and epilepsy.

HENBANE (*see* HYOSCYAMUS).

HEPARIN is a substance, first obtained from the liver, which prevents coagulation of the blood. It is present chiefly in liver, muscle, and lung. It is thought to act by neutralizing thrombin (*see* FIBRIN). Heparin has a complicated chemical structure and has been prepared in crystalline form. It is carbohydrate in nature, and contains amino and sulphuric acid groups. It is used for the prevention of clot formation in the blood or to prevent the spreading of this process once it has occurred. It is not active when given by mouth and must therefore be given by injection—usually intravenously.

HEPATITIS ($\mathring{\eta}\pi\alpha\rho$, the liver) means inflammation of the liver. (*See* LIVER.)

HEPATITIS, ACUTE INFECTIVE. Known also as ACUTE CATARRHAL JAUNDICE, VIRAL HEPATITIS.—An acute infection of the liver, caused by a virus, occurring usually in epidemics, and in most cases manifesting itself chiefly by jaundice. The incubation period varies from 15 to 35 days ; the disease may come on suddenly or gradually ; jaundice appears about the 7th or 9th day, and may persist for 2 or 3 weeks. The patient may remain out of health for some weeks. The infective period is believed to be short, and isolation of the sick person for a week is considered to be long enough. It is spread by contact and possibly as a droplet infection through the upper respiratory tract.

HEPATITIS, SERUM is a closely allied disease, which differs in three respects. It has a longer incubation

period (50 to 160 days). It is infectious directly from patient to patient. It is transmitted by the transfusion of contaminated blood or by the use of contaminated syringes or needles. It is a more fatal disease, the mortality ranging from 6 to 12 per cent., compared with under 1 per cent. for acute infective hepatitis.

HEPATIZATION ($\mathring{\eta}\pi\alpha\rho$, the liver) means the solidified state of the lung which appears in pneumonia, giving it a consistence like that of the liver.

HEREDITY (*hereditas*, heirship) is a term indicating the principle on which various peculiarities of bodily form or structure, or of physical or mental activity are transmitted from parents to offspring, and so handed down through a family stock.

Every individual begins life as two cells, derived one from each parent. These germinal cells are in a sense half-cells, because in preparation for union the nucleus of each has extruded from the cell one-half of the rod-shaped bodies (chromosomes) by which the characters of the individual are supposed to be determined. Each germinal cell thus supplies 23 chromosomes, carrying certain characters from one of the parents, to form, with those of the other, the 46 chromosomes in the new cell from which all the other cells of the human body are derived by a process of growth and repeated division. (*See* FOETUS.) In the process of extrusion of chromosomes certain ' genes ' or characters possessed by either parent may be lost to the offspring.

According to Weissmann's germ-plasm theory, a fragment of the new cell is at once set apart for the formation of the germ cells in the new individual and thus conformity of succeeding generations with their predecessors is secured. Galton stated a rule that the total heritage of an offspring is derived, on the average, one-half from the parents, one-quarter from the grandparents, one-eighth from the great-grandparents, and so on. This, while doubtless true in a general way, does not account for the evident differences among brothers and sisters. Mendel's theory to explain this supposes that simple or unit characters, such as height or colour of hair, are segregated or transmitted alternatively to the offspring (according to which chromosomes have been lost or retained) instead of being an average of these characters as shown in the two parents. Each unit character has a variation, which is, in a sense, its opposite, like tallness and shortness. The one of these which tends to give the appearance to the individual is called the dominant character (in this example, tallness), the other variation is called recessive, although both have an equal tendency to be transmitted.

For example, if two persons of a pure-tall stock are mated, their children will all be tall, whilst the children of a pure-short race union will all be short. If, however, a pure-tall stock person be mated with a pure-short stock person, all their children, though tending to be tall in appearance, may transmit either tallness or shortness to the next generation, and the final average result will be, out of every four children, one true tall who will transmit tallness, one true short who will transmit shortness, and two of tall appearance who will transmit with an equal chance tallness or shortness to their children. The last is the general formula on which in modern human communities hereditary characters are likely to be transmitted.

In plants or animals the breeding of single desirable ur it characters like colour or length of limb or quality of hair is a comparatively simple affair of selection in mating. In human eugenics, however, desirable qualities are complicated matters of character or intellect or general physique, which depend for their development as much upon environment and personal influence during childhood as upon heredity. It is noteworthy also that persons who appear unfit in one aspect are often well endowed in others.

The transmission of characters which predispose to certain diseases is a matter of some importance, although most serious defects tend to die out through difficulties to procreation set up by modern conditions of life. In regard to epilepsy, about one-third of all cases occur in families subject to this disorder, whilst out of ten children of epileptics one is likely to develop epilepsy. Among mental disorders,

manic-depressive insanity and schizophrenia show a tendency to appear in children of persons affected in these ways, and like the majority of mental conditions, these disorders are apt to be most pronounced in children of whom both parents have been similarly temperamental. Primary mental defect, on the other hand, is often wrongly supposed to be hereditary, for the great majority of mentally defective children are found in otherwise normal families ; still, the mating of two feeble-minded persons is inadvisable.

The shape of the eye is largely a hereditary character, so that shortsight, astigmatism, etc., tend to run in families ; cataract is also largely familial ; colour-blindness is handed down as a sex-linked character affecting males but transmitted by females who do not suffer from it ; a rare form of blindness due to atrophy of the optic nerve is similarly transmitted. As to ear defects, the condition of otosclerosis, causing deafness late in life, runs in families, while among deafmutes one in four owes this condition to defects in the nervous system which may be transmitted.

A tendency to rheumatism, or to tuberculosis or to certain skin diseases is due to defective power to resist the effective causes of these diseases, which may be a hereditary defect. Similarly, faults in the structure of certain organs, which may be inherited peculiarities, produce a liability in some families or races to goitre, diabetes, gastric ulcer, asthma, etc.

HERMAPHRODITE ('Ερμῆς, Mercury ; 'Αφροδίτη, Venus) is the name applied to a person in whom the sexual organs are so defectively formed that it is difficult to decide the sex, or in whom there appear to be parts belonging to both sexes.

HERNIA (*hernia*) means the protrusion of any organ, or part of an organ, into or through the wall of the cavity which contains it. Thus ' hernia of the brain ' may occur in consequence of a severe injury to the skull, ' hernia of the lung ' in consequence of a wound of the chest wall, but these are uncommon, and the most common form is hernia of the bowel, the popular term for which is ' rupture '.

Varieties.—Although far the commonest organ found in a hernia is part of the bowel, yet any of the abdominal structures, such as stomach, kidney, ovary, womb, bladder, or omentum, may be found projecting through an opening in the wall of the abdomen and lying close beneath the skin. Probably the only two organs exempt are the liver and pancreas, by reason of their position and connections. The projecting organ carries in front of it, and is enveloped by, a sac of peritoneum, the smooth membrane lining the interior of the abdomen. It is separated from the surface at least by this sac and by the skin. A hernia is usually described according to the position at which it protrudes. There are certain natural openings in the region of the groin on either side; one, known as the inguinal canal, through which the testicle descends in early life, and which the spermatic cord keeps always more or less open ; the other, known as the crural canal, which lies to the inner side of the large femoral vessels that pass from the abdomen to the thigh. The inguinal canal ends just above the pubic bone, its exit, known as the external abdominal ring, being large enough to admit the tip of the finger. The crural canal is less in size and is separated from the former only by the inner end of Poupart's ligament, a strong band which lies beneath the oblique groove that can be seen on the surface to separate the abdomen from the thigh. A hernia emerging from the former is known as an *inguinal hernia*, and tends to descend along the spermatic cord into the scrotum. A hernia emerging through the crural canal comes forwards on the front of the thigh, and is called a *femoral hernia*. A weak spot exists in the centre of the abdomen at the navel, and here, not infrequently in young children of poor development, a hernia may appear, which is then known as an *umbilical hernia*. A hernia which protrudes at some accidental opening on the abdomen, as, for example, through the scar of an operation wound, is known as a *ventral hernia*. A rare form of hernia is one which passes through the gap in front of the pelvis between the ischial and pubic bones ; it is known as an *obturator hernia*. Finally, there are various forms of *internal hernia*, the protruded organ passing up into the chest, or into some other region where it does not show itself on the surface.

A hernia may also be considered as *congenital*, that is, existing at birth, or *acquired* later on in life. The only positions in which congenital hernia is found are in the umbilical and inguinal regions. In the latter case the hernia descends along with the testicle towards the scrotum, the hernia being inside the tubular process of peritoneum (the lining membrane of the abdominal cavity, which descends with the testicle in order to provide it with a smooth tunic.

A very important classification of hernia is made according to the condition of the protruding organ. A *reducible hernia* is one which is so freely movable that it may be pressed back into the abdomen, although it comes down again by the same opening unless this be blocked up. An *irreducible hernia*, on the other hand, is one which cannot be returned, either because it has become adherent to its new surroundings, because it has enlarged after emerging, because much fat has been deposited inside the abdomen, or for some similar reason. An *obstructed hernia* is one in which, a part of the bowel being protruded, some of its contents become caught inside, and cannot for a time pass on, a state of costiveness arising in fact inside the hernia. A *strangulated hernia* is by far the most important variety, because of its immediate danger to life. In this form, the circulation of blood in the protruded bowel becomes cut off by the margin of the opening through which the loop of bowel has passed ; and, if an operation be not immediately performed for its relief, the bowel will become gangrenous, and the patient may die within a few days. The great danger attending all forms of hernia is that they may at any time become ' strangulated '.

Causes.—Two factors come into play in causing hernia. Firstly, some defect or injury of the abdominal wall ; and, secondly, some increase of pressure within the cavity. With regard to the hernia at the umbilicus of young children, there is usually some defect in the closure of the opening through which the navel-string passes before birth, and through this opening a loop of bowel is forced by excessive crying or the like. In inguinal hernia, which, it may be noted, is far commoner in men than in women, the defect consists in some failure of the inguinal canal—through which the testicle descends before birth—to close completely. There may, in congenital hernia, be a completely open passage leading out of the abdomen, or there may be simply a small pocket in the peritoneum which, by a sudden strain or by long-continued pressure, such as coughing, gets torn or stretched in front of a protruded organ. Femoral hernia is commoner in women than in men, probably on account of the special shape and inclination of the pelvic bones, and arises in a manner similar to that just stated for inguinal hernia. Both in these and in ventral hernia, the occurrence of marked changes in size of the abdomen, such as great increase in stoutness, great loss of fat, and repeated child-bearing, have the effect of greatly weakening the abdominal wall and predisposing to the formation of hernia. All laborious occupations involving great efforts, and bodily conditions involving frequently repeated strains, such as chronic cough or constipation, conduce to hernia of all sorts. Accordingly hernia is much more common in the male sex —who lead a more strenuous life—than among females.

Symptoms.—The symptoms vary much, depending upon the particular organ which is protruded, upon the size of the opening, which may or may not compress the hernia, and upon the condition of the latter. In the great majority of cases the hernia consists of one or more loops of the small intestine, and, if the hernia be of small size and readily reducible, the symptoms are somewhat as follows. If the hernia be produced quite suddenly, as during the lifting of a heavy weight, the person affected may hear or feel a distant crack, and be conscious that something has given way, but, as a rule, suffers no sharp pain. More usually the hernia develops gradually, and the symptoms have then no definite onset, but simply increase till they attract attention. An undefinable sense of weakness, and

442

occasionally pain, are felt in the region of the hernia. When any great effort is made, such as coughing, or straining at stool, or lifting a weight, a swelling appears with a gurgling feeling at the seat of the hernia, although this can be made to disappear by pressure when the person lies down. Even if the hernia does not come far down, a distinct impulse on coughing is communicated to the hand laid upon the swelling, which is situated usually at the inner end of the groin. When the hernia has become irreducible, the swelling does not vary in size, but the impulse on coughing is still to be felt. The presence, even of a small hernia, generally occasions some nterference with digestion, and constipation is a common accompaniment. A dragging sensation in the back is also another frequent symptom.

When a hernia becomes 'strangulated', as the result of stoppage of its circulation by the pressure of the margin of the ring through which it comes, a very marked set of symptoms ensues. The hernia first becomes inflamed, acutely painful, and then in a few hours turns gangrenous, producing general peritonitis and death if not relieved. At the same time, all passage of contents through the bowel is stopped, and as a result the bowels do not move, although some of their contents pass in the reverse direction, up to the stomach, whence they are vomited. Accordingly the onset of abdominal pain, accompanied by stoppage of the bowels and vomiting in a person possessed of a hernia, forms an ominous sign, and, even if no hernia be known to exist, the appearance of these three symptoms calls for immediate examination of the region of the groin by an expert medical practitioner.

Treatment.—When a hernia is present, it may be treated in a palliative manner, so as to relieve unpleasant symptoms and diminish the risk of strangulation, or an attempt may be made to cure it.

PALLIATIVE TREATMENT. — If the hernia be reducible, it is pushed back through the opening into the abdomen by manipulation known as 'taxis', and is then retained by an artificial support known as a 'truss'. The truss in its simplest form may consist merely of a pad of lint or folded handkerchief kept in position by a ' spica ' bandage. In infants, a very simple truss may be improvised from a skein of worsted, which is carried round the waist, one end passed through the other end over the site of the hernia, and the loose end carried down between the legs, and pinned to the circular part behind the back. For adults, the usual truss consists of a pad which fits over the opening, a spring to run round the pelvis and a strap to pass between the legs and prevent the truss from sliding upwards. The pad for an inguinal hernia is differently shaped from, and should be much larger than, that for femoral hernia. In getting a truss the particulars required are : (a) the girth round the pelvis below the crests of the haunch-bones ; (b) the variety of hernia ; (c) the side on which it is situated ; (d) the age and sex of the patient ; (e) the strength desired in the spring. No pains should be spared to get a correctly fitting truss (*see* TRUSS).

If the hernia be irreducible, a different type of truss designed merely to protect the hernia must be used.

CURATIVE TREATMENT.—The danger of strangulation, involving an immediate operation with great risk to life, is present so long as a hernia exists, and, except in old people with a very wide opening, the chance of radical cure and removal of the danger offered by an operation deserve to be carefully considered. The operation, known as the ' radical cure ', is not in itself a dangerous one, and the period of enforced idleness consequent on it amounts only to a few weeks.

Many operations are performed by different surgeons, but all consist briefly in this, that an opening is made over the hernia and, after the hernia has been returned into the abdomen, the sac is cut off, bunched up, turned aside, or otherwise disposed of, and the margins of the opening united by strong sutures. Almost all cases operated upon in this way result in complete cure.

When a hernia is irreducible, some special diet or other treatment is often required prior to the operation, in order to diminish the amount of fat in the abdomen, reduce the size of the hernia, etc.

When a hernia becomes strangulated, an operation becomes urgently necessary. The first object of this operation is to set free the hernia from the margin of the opening, tight band, or other cause that is impeding the circulation in it. This having been achieved, if the bowel is not too much damaged by the pressure it has received, it is returned to the abdomen, and the radical cure performed. Sometimes, however, the bowel has been so much damaged by several hours of pressure, that it would be too dangerous to replace it, and then, the compression having been relieved, either the damaged portion is completely cut out and the ends united by stitching, or the bowel is simply left in the wound for a few days, and the operation completed at a subsequent stage, if the bowel recovers its vitality. If the damaged loop of bowel does not recover, but sloughs away, then either the patient dies, or a fistula is left, from which the contents of the bowel escape to the exterior. This can, however, be closed by subsequent operation.

HEROIN, also known as DIAMORPHINE HYDROCHLORIDE, is a white crystalline powder of slightly bitter taste derived from morphine. It resembles morphine in its action but has a more depressant action on the respiratory centre. On account of its marked tendency to drug addiction, its use is being gradually restricted. The dose is from $\frac{1}{25}$ to $\frac{1}{8}$ grain (2·5 to 7·5 mg.).

HERPANGINA is a short febrile illness in childhood, in which minute vesicles or punched-out ulcers develop in the posterior parts of the mouth. It is due to infection with group A Coxsackie viruses (*q.v.*).

HERPES SIMPLEX is an acute infectious disease, characterized by the development of groups of superficial vesicles, or blebs, in the skin and mucous membrane. It is due to a virus and infection can occur at any time from birth onwards, but the usual time for primary infection is between the second and fifteenth year. Once infected, the virus persists in the body for the rest of the patient's life.

Symptoms.—The symptoms vary with the age of infection. In young

443

infants it may cause a generalized infection which may prove fatal. In young children the infection is usually in the mouth, and this may be associated with enlargement of the glands in the neck, general irritability and fever. The condition usually settles in seven to ten days. In adults the vesicles may occur anywhere in the skin or mucous membranes. The more common sites are the lips, mouth and face, but the vesicles may also appear on the genitalia, or in the conjunctiva or cornea. The first sign is the appearance of small painful swellings. These quickly develop into vesicles, containing clear fluid, and surrounded by a reddened area of skin. Some people are particularly liable to recurrent attacks of herpes simplex, and these often tend to be associated with some debilitatory condition or infection, such as pneumonia.

Except in the case of herpes of the cornea, the eruption clears completely unless it becomes contaminated with some other organism. In the case of the cornea, there may be residual scarring, which may impair vision.

Treatment.—There is no specific treatment, but local treatment is given to relieve pain and swelling. Should the eye be involved, the patient must be referred immediately to an ophthalmologist. The only preventive measure that is worth consideration is the administration of gamma-globulin (*q.v.*) in the case of infants under the age of 3 months who are in close contact with a case. This is particularly applicable if the infant suffers from eczema.

HERPES ZOSTER, or SHINGLES is a skin eruption of acute nature, closely related to chickenpox, consisting in the appearance of small yellow vesicles, which spread over an area, dry up, and heal by scabbing. It receives its name from the Greek word ζωστήρ, a ' circingle ', or girdle, because it spreads in a zone-like manner round half the chest. Herpes of the face also occurs, particularly on the brow and round the eye.

Causes.—It is due to a virus identical with that of chickenpox. This invades the ganglia of the nerves, particularly the spinal nerves of the chest and the fifth cranial nerve which supplies the faceo. There are many reports of the occurrence of herpes zoster, particularly

in adults, after contact with patients with chickenpox, and *vice versa*. In rare cases it may be a symptom of some grave disease in the spinal cord.

Symptoms.—The first symptoms of herpes are much like those of any feverish attack. The person feels unwell for some days, has a slight rise of temperature, and vague pain in the side or in various other parts. The pain finally settles at a point in the side, and, two or three days after the first symptoms, the rash appears. Minute yellow blebs are seen on the skin of the back, of the side, or of the front of the chest, or simultaneously on all three, the points corresponding to the space between one pair of ribs right round. These blebs increase in number for some days, and spread till there is often a complete half girdle round one side of the chest. The pain in this stage is severe, but it appears to vary a good deal with age, being slight in children and very severe in old people, in whom indeed herpes sometimes forms a serious malady. After one or two weeks, most of the vesicles have dried up and formed scabs, which finally drop off, leaving the skin just as it was before, or covered with small scars. Occasionally the little vesicles run together into large blebs, which leave ulcers difficult to heal, and followed by marked scars. The skin is generally healed completely in two or three weeks, but a peculiarity about the pain is that, in old people especially, it may not pass off when the eruption disappears, but may remain for weeks or even months : a condition known as post-herpetic neuralgia.

Treatment.—In the very early stage, before the vesicles have formed, cocaine or atropine ointment rubbed into the side eases the pain and seems to prevent to some extent the outbreak of the eruption. Later, when the vesicles have formed and are discharging, a dusting-powder of starch, zinc oxide, and bismuth subnitrate gives much relief, or the side may be painted with glycerin jelly containing menthol or with a mixture of chloral, camphor, and menthol in equal parts. In any case, the part should be kept warm by a dressing of cotton-wool. Analgesics may be required for relief of the pain.

Should post-herpetic neuralgia persist, the administration of analgesics should be considered. Occasionally the pain of post-herpetic neuralgia may be so persistent that radiotherapy may be required.

HERXHEIMER REACTION is an inflammatory reaction produced in the tissues in cases of syphilis, following upon treatment. It is due apparently to poisonous substances set free by the destruction of the organisms of this disease. Its possible occurrence indicates careful supervision in the treatment of syphilis of the heart and great blood-vessels, and of the central nervous system.

HESPERIDIN is one of two vegetable dyes in vitamin P, a crystalline substance obtained from lemon juice and Hungarian red peppers and believed to control the permeability of capillaries.

HEXACHLOROPHANE is a widely used antiseptic which is active against a range of micro-organisms, including Gram-positive and Gram-negative organisms, *Shigella dysenteriae*, and *Salmonella typhi*. One of its advantages is that it retains its activity in the presence of soap, and it is therefore often used in soaps and creams in a concentration of 1 to 2 per cent.

HEXAMETHONIUM is one of the methonium salts (*q.v.*) which have been introduced for the treatment of high blood-pressure.

HEXAMINE, also known as URO-TROPINE, is a substance made by the action of ammonia on formalin. It is excreted by the kidneys, and, setting free formalin gradually in the urine, has a powerful antiseptic action. It is given in cases of cystitis when the urine decomposes within the bladder, and it exerts its beneficial action very speedily. It acts only in urine with an acid reaction, and, if the urine be alkaline, acid phosphate of soda is usually taken along with the hexamine. The dose of each of these is 10 to 30 grains (0·6 to 2 grammes) several times daily.

HEXOBARBITONE is the *British Pharmacopœia* name for N-methyl-*cyclo*hexenyl - methylbarbituric acid. The sodium salt injected into a vein makes the patient unconscious : this is known as ' intravenous anæsthesia '.

HEXŒSTROL is a synthetic œstrogen closely related to stilbœstrol (*q.v.*) and is similar to it in action, but less potent.

HEXYLRESORCINOL is a drug used in the treatment of roundworms and threadworms.

HIATUS HERNIA is displacement of a portion of the stomach through the opening in the diaphragm through which the œsophagus passes from the chest to the abdominal cavity.

HICCUP is a spasmodic indrawing of air to the lungs, ending with a click, due to sudden closure of the vocal cords. The cause is some irritation of the nerves which go to the diaphragm, producing sudden contractions of the latter. Most cases, especially those recurring habitually about the same hour of the day, are due to indigestion. The symptom also occurs in some serious general diseases, like the uræmia of Bright's disease and typhoid fever, being in such cases a grave sign. Hiccup lasting over some days or weeks is in some cases a symptom of mild encephalitis lethargica.

Treatment.—If the condition be due to dyspepsia, it is often relieved by a copious draught of cold water or by some aromatic like a few drops of spirit of chloroform, a teaspoonful of Hoffmann's anodyne, or a tablespoonful of peppermint water or cinnamon water. When continuous and excessive it is usually controlled by the inhalation of carbon dioxide. The popular remedy of breathing in and out of a paper bag is probably successful because of the accumulation of carbon dioxide in the bag.

HIERA PICRA, popularly known as ' hickory pickory ', is a powder composed of aloes and canella, used as an aperient and emmenagogue.

HIGH FREQUENCY (*see* ELECTRICITY IN MEDICINE).

HILUM is a term applied to the depression on organs such as the lung, kidney, and spleen, at which the vessels

445

and nerves enter it and round which the lymphatic glands cluster. The hilum of the lung is also known as its root.

HIP-JOINT is the joint formed by the head of the thigh-bone and the deep cup-shaped hollow on the side of the pelvis which receives it (acetabulum). The joint is of the ball-and-socket variety, is dislocated only by very great violence, and is correspondingly difficult to reduce to its natural state after dislocation. The joint is enclosed by a capsule of fibrous tissue, strengthened by several bands, of which the principal is the ilio-femoral or Y-shaped ligament placed in front of the joint. A round ligament also unites the head of the thigh-bone to the margin of the acetabulum.

For Hip-joint Disease *see under* JOINTS, DISEASES OF.

HIPPUS (ἵππος, horse) is the term applied to a tremor of the iris which produces alternating contraction and dilatation of the pupil. This is frequently a sign of hysteria.

HIRSCHSPRUNG'S DISEASE, or MEGACOLON, is the term given to a condition in childhood which is characterized by great hypertrophy and dilatation of the colon.

HIRSUTIES, or HYPERTRICHOSIS, is a growth of hair of the male type and distribution in women. It is most marked in cases of certain tumours of the suprarenal glands.

HISTAMINE is a substance which is normally present in the tissues of the body. It is a powerful stimulant of the secretion of gastric juice. On injection it causes a condition of shock, with dilatation of capillaries, and fall in blood-pressure. In anaphylactic shock it is liberated from the liver of the dog and the lung of the guinea-pig. Histamine is destroyed by an enzyme, histaminase, present especially in the kidney and the small intestine. Histamine can be obtained by the bacterial degradation of histidine, an amino-acid.

HISTIDINE is an amino-acid from which histamine is derived by decomposition.

HISTOLOGY is the study of the minute structure of the tissues.

HISTOPLASMOSIS is a disease due to a yeast-like fungus known as *Histoplasma capsulatum*. Most cases have been reported from U.S.A. In infants it is characterized by fever, anæmia, enlargement of the liver and spleen, and involvement of the lungs and gastro-intestinal tract. In older children it may resemble pulmonary tuberculosis, whilst in adults it may be confined to involvement of the skin.

HIVES is a popular term applied to eruptions of the nature of nettle-rash.

HODGKIN'S DISEASE, or LYMPHADENOMA, is a condition in which the lymphatic glands all over the body undergo a gradually progressive enlargement. The cause is not known. The glands affected may reach a great size, and also glandular tissue forms in various organs all over the body. Along with these changes a considerable degree of anæmia arises, and the affected person becomes gradually weaker. The disease may extend over several years, but seems to be very little influenced by treatment. Arsenic appears to have some effect in retarding it, but the effect is merely temporary. Surgical removal of affected glands is useless in checking the enlargement of others. Deep X-ray therapy is the best initial form of treatment, but the effect is not permanent, and the treatment has to be repeated as the glands enlarge again. In cases which do not respond to X-rays, temporary relief is obtained from the use of chlorambucil, mustine, or cyclophosphamide.

HOGBEN TEST is one of the pregnancy diagnosis tests (*see* PREGNANCY TESTS).

HOMATROPINE is an alkaloid derived from atropine which is used to produce dilatation of the pupil and to paralyse accommodation temporarily for the purpose of examining the interior of the eye. It is used in 1 per cent. solution, and its effects pass away in the course of a few hours.

HOMŒOPATHY (ὅμοιος, like ; πάθος, disease) is a system of medicine founded

446

by Hahnemann at the end of the eighteenth century. It is based upon the theory that diseases are curable by those drugs which produce effects on the body similar to symptoms caused by the disease (*similia similibus curantur*). In administering drugs, the theory is also held that their effect is increased by giving them in minute doses obtained by diluting them to an extreme degree. This system has in recent years had few followers.

HOOKWORM is another name for the ankylostoma or uncinaria. (*See* PARASITES.)

HOPS have been used in medicine as the powder got from the dried fruit of *Humulus lupulus*. The plant contains an alkaloid, lupuline, which is possessed of a weak sedative action ; and various preparations of hops are used to control hysteria, nervousness, and insomnia. A poultice made from crushed hops is a household sedative in cases of localized pains, and hop pillows have been used for nervous insomnia.

HORDEOLUM (*hordeolum*, barley grain) is another name for stye.

HOREHOUND is the name for the dried leaves and tops of *Marrubium vulgare*, which is used for coughs, either mixed with sugar or as fluid extract in doses of 60 to 120 minims (4 to 8 ml.).

HORMONES (ὁρμάω, I stir up) are substances which, on absorption into the blood, influence the action of tissues and organs other than those in which they are produced. The internal secretions of the ovary, pancreas, thyroid, pituitary and suprarenal bodies afford examples of this action. (*See also* AUTACOID.)

HORNER'S SYNDROME is the description given to a combination of bodily changes resulting from paralysis of the sympathetic nerve in the neck. They are : small pupil, sunken eye, and a drooping upper eyelid.

HORNETS.—(*See* BITES.)

HORRIPILATION is another term for goose-flesh, due to contraction of the small muscles in the skin which make the hairs erect.

HOSPITAL (old French word) is a building intended for receiving sick or injured persons. The introduction of the National Health Service Act in 1948 completely changed the organization of the hospitals in Great Britain, but for the sake of historical interest the following description of the pre-1948 position has been retained. It is followed by a brief summary of the organization now in force.

In Great Britain hospitals were divided into four chief classes according to their manner of administration :

(1) VOLUNTARY HOSPITALS were supported by public subscription and administered by a board of managers chosen by the subscribers. The total number of voluntary hospitals in Great Britain was over 950, providing in all nearly 53,000 beds. The voluntary hospital was introduced into Europe from the East at the beginning of the thirteenth century, chiefly owing to the exertions and influence of Louis IX of France and Pope Innocent III. Although originally supported as a charity by the wealthier members of the community for the benefit of the poor, the voluntary hospital latterly derived the greater part of its annual revenue from the subscriptions of those who had been or were likely to be treated in it. These subscriptions in many instances were collected by small weekly payments, for example, by deduction of a few pence from weekly wages. Hospital maintenance, therefore, had become a kind of informal insurance against serious illness or accident.

In America most of the large voluntary hospitals have private blocks or private wards attached, where patients pay the full cost of both maintenance and of medical or surgical treatment as required. These private sections, by sharing many of the unavoidable general charges, such as administration, prove a source of revenue to the large hospitals. For the same reason, the small private nursing homes, which form the main provision for private patients in Great Britain, and in which the general expenses are spread over a small number only of patients, are necessarily very expensive.

(2) COUNCIL HOSPITALS were supported by town and county councils,

and administered by their local health authority, under the general supervision of the Ministry of Health (England) and Department of Health (Scotland). Prior to the Local Government Acts (1929), most of these were devoted to treatment of infectious diseases, but after 1929 municipal hospitals were provided in many localities for treating general medical and surgical ailments. These were supported from local rates, and the Council could recover the cost of treatment from patients. These hospitals usually had whole-time resident medical officers and salaried visiting consultants.

(3) STATE HOSPITALS were supported out of Parliamentary grants and administered by Military, Naval, Pension, or Prison authorities; these hospitals were relatively few in number. They had a medical staff composed of officers of the service to which they belonged.

(4) PRIVATE HOSPITALS are owned and managed by private individuals or companies for profit; most of these are of small size, taking ten or twenty patients, and are then known as 'Nursing Homes'.

As has already been mentioned, this has all been changed by the National Health Service Act. Under this Act all hospitals in the country, with the exception of the teaching hospitals and nursing homes, passed to the control of Regional Boards appointed by the Minister of Health. These Regional Boards further subdivided the hospitals in their areas into units under the control of Hospital Management Committees. The endowments of the voluntary hospitals have been transferred to a Hospital Endowments Fund, and the income from this is to be used for purposes outside the official budget. Hospitals are no longer allowed to appeal for funds. No charge is made for admission to, or treatment in, hospital, but hospitals are allowed to have special blocks of private wards for patients who wish to pay for the additional comforts of such private wards. Teaching hospitals have been given a larger measure of independence. They have been allowed to keep their own Boards of Governors and they retain control over their endowments.

448

Hospitals are also classified according to the type of case with which they deal, as follows: (a) GENERAL HOSPITALS admit both cases of disease requiring treatment by diet, drugs, and other non-operative procedures (medical cases), and cases of disease and injury requiring operation or manipulation (surgical cases). Most of the larger general hospitals also possess special departments (for eye diseases, diseases of ear, nose, and throat, diseases peculiar to women, etc.). The general hospitals are classified into large hospitals with a number of beds between 100 and 1000; intermediate hospitals with 50 to 100 beds; and cottage hospitals with fewer than 50 beds. *Teaching Hospitals* form a special subdivision of the general hospitals, which are connected with a medical school, and are attended by medical students. These are among the largest and most efficient of the general hospitals. (b) SPECIAL HOSPITALS are reserved for one special kind of case. Of these, the best known types are *Children's Hospitals, Eye Hospitals, Maternity Hospitals, Mental Hospitals*, and *Cripple Hospitals*. (c) CONVALESCENT HOSPITALS are usually situated in a rural or seaside district where light and fresh air are abundant. They receive patients, usually from general or special hospitals, who require little in the shape of treatment, but whose bodily powers are still enfeebled after serious illness or operation. Since the main expenses incurred in these hospitals are for housing and feeding only, their cost is relatively much less than that of the general and special hospitals. The later stages of treatment are therefore carried out more effectively, more speedily, and more cheaply in such hospitals.

HOUR-GLASS STOMACH is the term given to the X-ray appearance of a stomach which is constricted in its middle part because of either spasm of the stomach muscle or contraction of scar tissue from a gastric ulcer.

HOUSEMAID'S KNEE (*see* BURSITIS) is an inflammation of the bursa in front of the knee-cap, often mistaken for some disease in the joint itself (Fig. 84).

HOUSES and BUILDING SITES
(*see* SANITATION).

HUMERUS is the bone of the upper arm. It has a rounded head, which helps to form the shoulder joint, and at its lower end presents a wide pulley-like surface for union with the radius and ulna. Its condyles form the prominences at the sides of the elbow.

HUMOUR (*humor*) is a term applied to any fluid or semi-fluid tissue of the body, *e.g.* the aqueous and vitreous humours in the eye. The term humour is also associated with a theory regarding the causation of disease, which originated with Pythagoras and lasted in a modified form until the early part of the nineteenth century. According to this theory diseases are due to an improper mixture in the body of blood, bile, phlegm, and black bile.

HUNGER is the term applied to a craving for food or other substance necessary to bodily activity. Hunger for food is supposed to be directly produced by strong contractions of the stomach which occur when it is empty or nearly so. (*See also* THIRST.) AIR HUNGER is an instinctive craving for oxygen resulting in breathlessness, either when a person ascends to great heights where the pressure of air is low, or in some diseases such as pneumonia and diabetes.

HUNTINGTON'S CHOREA is a hereditary disease in which choreiform movements, ataxia, and paralysis develop at about the age of 40 and lead to progressive mental deterioration.

HUTCHINSON'S TEETH. — This is the term applied to the narrowed and notched permanent incisor teeth which occur in congenital syphilis. They are so named after Sir Jonathan Hutchinson (1828–1913), the famous London physician who first described them.

HYALINE MEMBRANE DISEASE is a condition found in premature infants and infants born by Cæsarean section, characterized by the onset of difficulty in breathing a few hours after birth. Death usually occurs before the third day. At post-mortem examination the alveoli and the finer bronchioles of the lungs are found to be lined with a dense membrane. The cause of the condition is not known.

HYALURONIDASE is an enzyme (*q.v.*) which hydrolyzes hyaluronic acid. The latter is a gel-like substance which is widely distributed throughout the body and which helps to bind together the tissue cells and also acts as a lubricant in joints. By virtue of its action in hydrolyzing hyaluronic acid, hyaluronidase is now used in subcutaneous injections of fluid as it facilitates the spread of the injected fluid and therefore its absorption.

HYDATID (ὑδατίς) is a cyst produced by the growth of immature forms of a tapeworm. (*See* PARASITES.)

HYDATIDIFORM MOLE, or vesicular mole as it is sometimes known, is a rare complication of pregnancy, in which there is tremendous proliferation of the epithelium of the chorion (the outer of the two fœtal membranes). It seldom occurs during a first pregnancy. Treatment consists of immediate evacuation of the womb.

HYDNOCARPUS OIL is an oil pressed from the seeds of *Hydnocarpus wightiana*, used in the treatment of leprosy. (*See* CHAULMOOGRA OIL.)

HYDRÆMIA (ὕδωρ, water ; αἷμα blood) is a condition in which the blood contains an excess of water. It is found in certain forms of Bright's disease, leading to dropsy.

HYDRAGOGUES (ὕδωρ, water ; ἄγω, I move). (*See* PURGATIVES.)

HYDRALLAZINE, or 1-hydrazine-phthalazine, is a hypotensive drug. (*See* ESSENTIAL HYPERTENSION.)

HYDRAMNIOS is the condition characterized by excess of fluid in the amniotic cavity. (*See* AMNION.)

HYDRARGYRUM is another name for mercury.

HYDROCELE (ὑδροκήλη) is a collection of fluid connected with the testicle or spermatic cord, due to some inflammation of the sac in which these structures are enclosed. It develops usually in middle life, although it may appear at any time, increases gradually in size,

15

and is devoid of pain. The condition presents some resemblance to hernia, and there is occasionally some doubt in distinguishing between them, particularly when the hydrocele communicates with the abdominal cavity. In children, the application of counter-irritation to the skin covering the hydrocele is often enough to bring about the absorption of the fluid. In older people, some operative procedure is necessary ; and either the hydrocele is punctured with a hollow needle, its fluid drawn off, and some strong irritant injected into the cavity, or, if the sac refills after this treatment, the entire wall of the sac is removed.

HYDROCEPHALUS (ὕδωρ, water ; κεφαλή, the head) is the term applied to the conditions in which there is abnormal accumulation of cerebro-spinal fluid within the skull. There are two main types : congenital and acquired.

CONGENITAL HYDROCEPHALUS. —The cause of this condition is still obscure. Hereditary influences are important in some cases, and records are available of the condition occurring in several generations of one family, and of families in which several children are affected. In a small minority of cases it is a manifestation of syphilis.

ACQUIRED HYDROCEPHALUS.— The two main causes of this type of hydrocephalus are meningitis and tumours of the brain. The former is the main cause in infants, whilst tumours are a more likely cause in older children and adults. Both these conditions cause hydrocephalus by interfering with the circulation of the cerebro-spinal fluid. As the production of cerebro-spinal fluid is proceeding normally all the time, it is clear that any blockage which prevents its draining away will result in increased pressure inside the skull. The extent to which the skull enlarges in response to such pressure is mainly dependent upon the age of the individual; speaking generally, the younger the individual, the more marked is the enlargement.

Symptoms.—In children the chief symptoms observed are the gradual increase in size of the upper part of the head, out of all proportion to the face or

the rest of the body. Occurring at an age when as yet the separate bones constituting the skull have not become welded, this enlargement may go on to a very considerable extent in all directions, but chiefly in the transverse and antero-posterior diameters, the membranous spaces between the bones becoming more and more expanded, though ultimately, should the child survive, ossification takes place, and the distended brain becomes encased in a thin skull.

As illustrating the extent to which this disease may proceed, it may be mentioned that the average circumference of the adult head is about 22 inches, while in the child it is of course considerably less. In chronic hydrocephalus, the head of an infant three months old has been known to measure 29 inches ; and in the well-known case of the man Cardinal, who died in Guy's Hospital, the head measured 33 inches. In the museum of the faculty of medicine in Paris there is a hydrocephalic skull measuring 39 inches. The cerebral ventricles are widely distended, and the convolutions flattened, while occasionally the fluid escapes into the cavity of the cranium, which it fills, pressing down the brain to the base of the skull. As a consequence of such changes, the functions of the brain are interfered with, and in general the mental condition of the patient is impaired. The child is dull and listless, irritable, and sometimes imbecile. The special senses become affected as the disease advances, especially vision, and sight is often lost, as is also hearing. Towards the end paralysis is apt to occur.

The outlook for children with hydrocephalus is not as gloomy as was at one time thought to be the case. Such a child has a 50 per cent. chance of survival with the disease arrested. He then has a 75 per cent. chance of being educable. Almost one-third of arrested cases can be expected to enjoy normal intelligence with little or no physical disability.

Treatment.—Numerous ingenious operations have been devised for the treatment of hydrocephalus. The most satisfactory of these is the Holter or Spitz-Holter, valve, whereby the cerebrospinal fluid is by-passed into the right atrium of the heart.

HYDROCHLORIC ACID is a gas which, dissolved in water, forms a clear, colourless fluid of sour taste and smell. It is present in the gastric juice to the extent of 2 parts in 1000. (*See* DIGESTION.) In large quantities it is a corrosive poison.

Uses.—Its chief use is in cases in which the gastric juice is deficient, *i.e.* in cases of achlorhydria (*q.v.*). The dilute hydrochloric acid of the *British Pharmacopœia* is generally given along with a bitter infusion in doses of 5 to 60 drops.

HYDROCORTISONE, or compound F, has the chemical formula, 17-hydroxy corticosterone. It is closely allied to cortisone (*q.v.*) both in its structure (cortisone is an oxidation product of hydrocortisone) and in its action. Its anti-rheumatic potency is said to be 50 per cent. greater than that of cortisone. Its main use to date in rheumatoid arthritis has been for local injection into affected joints.

HYDROCYANIC ACID (*see* PRUSSIC ACID).

HYDROFLUMETHIAZIDE is a derivative of chlorothiazide (*q.v.*). It is a powerful diuretic which acts by causing an increased urinary excretion of sodium and chloride. On a weight for weight basis it is about ten times as potent a diuretic as chlorothiazide.

HYDROGEN PEROXIDE (*see* PEROXIDE OF HYDROGEN).

HYDROLYZED PROTEIN is protein (*q.v.*) which has been broken down into its constituent amino-acids. (Hydrolysis means the reaction of a large molecule with one or more molecules of water, with the production of two or more smaller molecules.) This is the process which normally occurs in the course of digestion of protein, but in certain conditions, such as marasmus and severe liver disease, where the process of digestion is badly upset, it is sometimes of value to give the patient protein that has already been hydrolyzed.

HYDROMYELIA is the term applied to an abnormal expansion of the central canal of the spinal cord.

HYDRONEPHROSIS (ὕδωρ, water ; νεφρός, the kidney) is a chronic disease in which the kidney becomes greatly distended with fluid. It is due to incomplete or intermittent blockage of the ureter connecting the kidney with the bladder. The chief causes of this are stricture of the ureter as a result of infection or a new growth, and spasm of the ureter where it enters the kidney.

HYDROPATHY, or HYDROTHERAPEUTICS (ὕδωρ, water ; πάθη, suffering : ὕδωρ, water ; θεραπεύω, I heal), is the name for all those curative measures in which water is the agent employed. (*See* BATHS, COLD DOUCHES, FOMENTATIONS, WET PACK.)

HYDROPHOBIA (ὕδωρ, water ; φόβος, fear) is another name for RABIES (*q.v.*).

HYDROPS (ὕδρωψ) is another name for dropsy.

HYDROPS FŒTALIS (*see* HÆMOLYTIC DISEASE OF THE NEWBORN).

HYDROTHERAPY (*see* HYDROPATHY).

HYDROTHORAX (ὕδωρ, water ; θώραξ, the chest) means a collection of dropsical fluid in the pleural cavities.

HYDROXOCOBALAMIN, or vitamin B_{12a}, is now being used as an alternative to cyanocobalamin (*q.v.*) in the treatment of pernicious anaemia (*see* ANÆMIA). It has the practical advantage that fewer injections are required than in the case of cyanocobalamin. Like cyanocobalamin it belongs to the group of substances known as cobalamins which have an enzyme (*q.v.*) action in practically every metabolic system in the body and are essential for normal growth and nutrition.

HYGIENE (ὑγίεια, health) means the science of preserving health. (*See* BATHS, CLOTHING, DIET, EXERCISE, HEALTH, SANITATION, VENTILATION, WATER SUPPLY, WATER-CLOSETS.)

HYMEN is the thin membranous fold partially closing the lower end of the vagina.

HYOID is the name of a U-shaped bone at the root of the tongue. It can be felt from the front of the neck, lying about an inch above the prominence of the thyroid cartilage.

HYOSCYAMUS, or HENBANE, is a plant that grows commonly in the United States and in Europe. The preparations are made from the leaves, and have an effect in quieting pain and relieving spasm. In large quantities it is a narcotic poison.

Uses.—In spasmodic and painful conditions, particularly in colic and in irritable states of the bladder, the tincture of hyoscyamus is used with good effect. Hyoscine, an alkaloid obtained from hyoscyamus, is much used in very small doses to quiet raving mania and in some nervous diseases, *e.g.* shaking palsy. It is also used for the production of 'twilight sleep', and for the prevention of travel sickness.

HYPERACUSIS (ὑπέρ, over; ἄκουσις, hearing) means an abnormally acute sense of hearing.

HYPERÆMIA (ὑπέρ, over; αἷμα, blood) means congestion or presence of an excessive amount of blood in a part.

HYPERÆSTHESIA (ὑπέρ, over; αἴσθησις, sensation) means over-sensitiveness of a part, as found, for example, in certain nervous diseases.

HYPERCAPNIA means an abnormal increase in the amount of carbon dioxide in the blood or in the lungs.

HYPERCHLORHYDRIA is the condition in which there is an excessive production of hydrochloric acid in the stomach. It is a characteristic finding in certain forms of dyspepsia, particularly that associated with a duodenal ulcer. It causes heartburn (*q.v.*) and waterbrash (*q.v.*). (*See* DYSPEPSIA *and* STOMACH, DISEASES OF.)

HYPEREMESIS (ὑπέρ, over; ἔμεσις, vomiting) is a term applied to excessive vomiting, especially that which occurs in pregnancy.

HYPERGLYCÆMIA (ὑπέρ, over; γλυκύς, sweet; αἷμα, blood) means excess of sugar in the blood, the condition preceding and accompanying diabetes mellitus. The amount of

sugar normally present in the blood is about one part of sugar in 1000 of blood ; in diabetes the sugar may rise to four or five times that amount.

HYPERIDROSIS, or HYPERHIDROSIS, means excessive sweating.

HYPERMETROPIA (ὑπέρ, over ; μέτρον, measure ; ὤψ, eye), or HYPEROPIA, is a term applied to long-sightedness, in which the eye is too flat from before back and rays of light are brought to a focus behind the retina. (*See* VISION *and* SPECTACLES.)

HYPERNEPHROMA (ὑπέρ, over ; νεφρός, kidney) is a term applied to a tumour resembling the tissue of the suprarenal gland and occurring usually in the kidney.

HYPERPIESIS (ὑπέρ, over ; πίεσις, pressure) is another term for high blood-pressure. HYPERPIESIA is another term for ESSENTIAL HYPERTENSION (*q.v.*).

HYPERPLASIA (ὑπέρ, over ; πλάσις, formation) means an abnormal increase in the number of cells in a tissue.

HYPERPYREXIA (ὑπέρ, over ; πυρέσσω, I am fevered) means an excessive degree of fever. (*See* FEVER, TEMPERATURE.)

HYPERTELORISM is a rare congenital deformity of the head and face. The forehead is broad and low and the orbits are large and set widely apart. The divergence of the eyes is such that focusing on near objects is impossible. The abnormal shape of the skull is thought to be due primarily to a disproportion in the growth of the brain.

HYPERTENSION is another term for high blood-pressure. (*See* ESSENTIAL HYPERTENSION.)

HYPERTHERMIA is the name given to the treatment of disease by the artificial production of fever. This may be done by the intravenous injection of certain vaccines, the artificial production of malaria, or by placing the individual in a machine known as a hypertherm, in which the patient's temperature can be safely raised to 105 to 106° F. (40° to 41° C.).

HYPERTHYROIDISM is a term applied to excessive activity of the thyroid gland, *e.g.* in exophthalmic goitre. (*See* GOITRE.)

HYPERTROPHY (ὑπέρ, over ; τρέφω, I nourish) means the increase in size which takes place in an organ as the result of an increased amount of work demanded of it by the bodily economy. For example, when valvular disease of the heart is present and the heart is in process of dilating, 'compensation' occurs by an increase in thickness of the heart-muscle, and the organ, by beating more powerfully, is able to overtake the strain thrown upon it. Similarly, if one kidney be removed, the other hypertrophies or grows larger to overtake the double work.

HYPNO-ANALYSIS is a method of treating certain neuroses by first releasing the patient's repressed fear under hypnosis, and then helping the patient to the necessary adjustment by suggestion.

HYPNOTICS (ὕπνος, sleep) are measures which produce sleep.

Varieties.—As certain conditions are necessary for the onset of sleep, even a slight departure from these may be sufficient to keep persons who are not in good health awake. Thus a diminution of the circulation in the brain, and freedom from pain or irritation in any bodily organ are essential, whilst quiet and darkness are desirable, though many people can adapt themselves to noise and there are not a few who can sleep equally well whether it be light or dark. Often some trivial alteration of the daily life or diet is enough to relieve habitual insomnia ; in other cases the quieting of pain is alone necessary ; in other cases drugs must be used which have a light dulling effect upon the brain itself. For the relief of pain the drugs known as anodynes (*see* ANODYNES) are used. Of the hypnotics, which dull the brain without much other effect, the chief are chloral hydrate, chloralamide, the barbiturates, paraldehyde.

Uses.—Simple remedies should always receive a fair trial first of all. Thus a person may be kept awake by severe mental labour or worry just before retiring to rest. The activity of the brain continues and sleeplessness results. Some quiet employment for the latter part of the evening, or a light meal, may relieve this. In other cases sleeplessness is often due to difficulty of digestion through a meal having been taken shortly before retiring to rest, and this may be relieved by abstaining from the last meal at night. In old people insomnia may be due to cold feet, and in such cases the best hypnotic is a pair of warm sleeping socks. A condition of anæmia of the brain occurs in old men whose arteries are unhealthy, and this also debars sleep, unless the head be kept warm or a small quantity of alcohol be taken at bedtime. Occasionally sleep can be obtained by purely external applications. Massage of the head, the wet pack, and electrical (especially high frequency) applications are all used in different cases. Should these measures fail, and a hypnotic be required, the choice of which to use can only be made satisfactorily by the family doctor. In the majority of cases the choice falls upon one of the barbiturate drugs (*q.v.*) but, because of the tendency for drug addiction to develop with the continued use of the barbiturates, the tendency today is to try one of the non-barbiturate drugs in the first instance.

HYPNOTISM (ὕπνος, sleep) is the process of producing a state of mind known as hypnosis. Although a process which has been known for hundreds of years, its precise nature is still unknown. One modern writer has defined hypnosis as 'a temporary condition of altered attention, the most striking feature of which is greatly increased suggestibility' (Mason). There is no evidence, as has been suggested, that women can be more easily hypnotised than men. Children and young adults are the more easily hypnotised, middle-aged people being more resistant. There are various methods of induction of hypnosis, but the basis of them is some rhythmic stimulus accompanied by the repetition of carefully worded suggestions. The most commonly used method is to ask the patient to fix his eye on a given spot, or light, and then keep on repeating to him, in a quiet soothing voice, that his eyes will gradually become tired and that he will want to close them. There are various levels of hypnosis, usually classified as light, medium, and deep, and it has been estimated that 10 per cent. of people cannot be hypnotised, 35 per cent. can be taken into light hypnosis, 35 per cent. into medium hypnosis, and 20 per cent. into deep hypnosis.

Although in the past, hypnotism has often been frowned upon by orthodox medicine, largely because of its prostitution by charlatans, at the present day it is recognized to be a most useful method of therapy. Like all effective forms of therapy, however, it is not without its dangers, and this is why it should only be practised by those who have been adequately trained.

Apart from its use in psychiatry, it is of value in the treatment of many psychosomatic conditions : that is, conditions in which physical manifestations, such as skin lesions, headaches and other forms of pain, are primarily due to some psychological or emotional disturbance. It is also being used to an increasing extent in obstetrics for the relief of pain during labour, and for the relief of pain in dentistry. Another condition in which it is proving most valuable is as part of the treatment of alcoholism.

HYPOCALCÆMIA.—The condition of the blood in which its content of calcium is below normal. (Normally there are between 9 mg. and 11 mg. calcium in 100 ml. of serum.)

HYPOCHLORHYDRIA means an insufficient secretion of hydrochloric acid from the digestive cells of the stomach lining.

HYPOCHLOROUS ACID is a powerful antiseptic which both kills organisms and neutralizes the poisons they produce. It forms the active principle of the powder known as 'eupad' and of its solution 'eusol'. The powder is produced by mixing equal weights of boric acid and bleaching powder. The solution is prepared by adding 25 grammes of this powder to 1 litre of water, and filtering. The clear solution so produced is 'eusol', and should contain 0·5 per cent. of hypochlorous acid.

454

Uses.—Popularized during the 1914–1918 War, eusol has now been displaced to a great extent by the newer antiseptics, such as the acridine derivatives, the sulphonamides, and penicillin, but it is still of value in the treatment of septic wounds.

HYPOCHONDRIASIS (ὑπό, under ; χόνδρος, a cartilage) is a chronic mental condition in which the affected person's mind is constantly occupied with a delusion that he is seriously ill. As a rule, the ailments are referred to the stomach or the liver, and very often some trivial derangement of these exists to give colour to the person's views. Along with these complaints, there is a self-centred and gloomy turn of mind that prevents the patient from doing much of his proper work. Not uncommonly this mental trouble is hereditary, and passes gradually at a later stage into melancholia. The condition, apart from the affected person making a strong effort of will and taking up some active work which may distract his thoughts, is very difficult to treat.

HYPODERMIC (ὑπό, under ; δέρμα, the skin) means : of, or pertaining to, the region immediately under the skin. Thus, a hypodermic injection means an injection given underneath the skin. A hypodermic syringe is a small syringe which, fitted with a fine needle, is used to give such injections (Fig. 227).

Fig. 227.—Hypodermic syringe, with needle-holder and needle.

A hypodermic injection is given for one of three main reasons : (1) because the substance administered cannot be given by mouth on account of its being destroyed in the stomach before it can be absorbed, e.g. insulin ; (2) because it is not possible or it is inadvisable to give anything by mouth to the patient, e.g. because of vomiting ; (3) because a quick action is necessary, e.g. morphine in cases of severe hæmorrhage.

HYPODERMOCLYSIS.—Injection of a fluid under the skin—for example, of a solution of glucose or of saline as a method of restoring fluids to the circulation of a person who is ' dehydrated '.

HYPOGASTRIC.—Indicating or pertaining to the lower middle part of the abdomen just above the pubis.

HYPOGLOSSAL NERVE (ὑπό, under ; γλῶσσα, the tongue) is the twelfth cranial nerve, and supplies the muscles of the tongue, together with some others lying near it.

HYPOGLYCÆMIA (ὑπό, under ; γλυκύς, sweet ; αἷμα, blood) is the term applied to a deficiency of sugar in the blood. It may occur in states of starvation, or after the administration of insulin in too large doses, causing symptoms of weakness, tremors, nervousness, breathlessness, and excitement, followed sometimes by unconsciousness. These symptoms are relieved by taking sugar or by an injection of adrenaline, which checks the action of insulin.

HYPOGONADISM is the condition characterized by deficient production of the hormones secreted by the gonads : that is, the ovaries and testes.

HYPOMANIA.—A slight degree of mania.

HYPOPHOSPHITES of lime, iron etc., are administered in combination as ' a tonic'.

HYPOPHYSECTOMY.—Surgical excision of the pituitary gland.

HYPOPHYSIS is another name for the pituitary gland.

HYPOPIESIS ὑπό, under ; πίεσις, pressure) means abnormally low blood-pressure.

HYPOPLASIA means excessive smallness of an organ or part, arising from imperfect development.

HYPOPYON is the term for describing an accumulation of pus between the iris and the cornea—*i.e.* in the anterior chamber of the eye.

HYPOSPADIAS is a developmental abnormality in the male, in which the urethra opens on the under-surface of the penis or in the perineum.

HYPOSTASIS is the term applied to the condition in which blood accumulates in a dependent part as a result of a feeble circulation. Congestion of the base of the lungs in old people from this cause, and infection, is called hypostatic pneumonia.

HYPOTHALAMUS.—That part of the forebrain situated beneath the thalamus on each side and forming the floor of the third ventricle. The hypothalamus contains collections of nerve cells believed to form the controlling centres of (1) the sympathetic and (2) the parasympathetic nervous systems. The hypothalamus is the nervous centre for primitive physical and emotional behaviour. It contains nerve centres for the regulation of certain vital processes—the metabolism of fat, carbohydrate, and water ; sleep ; body temperature, and genital functions.

HYPOTHERMIA. — Low temperature. This is a term that is used in two different contexts.

It is being widely used in conjunction with operations on the heart and on the brain. The rationale of its use is that it lowers the requirements of the tissues for oxygen. This means that the cells of the brain, which are particularly susceptible to lack of oxygen, can be safely deprived of their blood supply for a longer period than at normal temperature. In practice this means that in operations on the heart, for instance, the action of the heart can be arrested for a few minutes while the surgeon actually operates on the heart.

It is also used to describe the condition which may develop, especially in old people and in infants, if they are exposed to abnormally low temperatures.

Two methods are used to produce hypothermia. In one the blood of the patient is circulated through a special cooling machine. In the other the temperature is lowered by the use of ice packs, iced water, or a special cooling mattress. (*See also* CRYMOTHERAPY.)

HYPOTHYROIDISM means the condition produced by defective action of the thyroid gland. (*See* MYXŒDEMA.)

HYSTERECTOMY (ὑστέρα, womb ; ἐκτομή, cutting out) means the operation of removing the uterus. HYSTERO-OOPHORECTOMY is the term applied to removal of the uterus and ovaries.

HYSTERIA (ὑστέρα, the womb) is a condition or set of conditions which it is difficult to define. The condition is also known as PITHIATISM (πείθω, I persuade), because many of its symptoms appear to be due to auto-suggestion and are readily relieved by suggestion from another person. Hysteria manifests itself by over-action of some parts of the nervous system, or by failure of other parts to perform their necessary work. In consequence, there follow mental changes, convulsive seizures, spasms and contractions of limbs, paralyses, loss of sensation over areas of the body, affections of various internal organs, derangements of joints and combinations of these which closely mimic various organic diseases. Hysterical manifestations are among the most difficult affections upon which the specialist is called to give his opinion.

Causes.—The condition is far more common in women than in men. It used to be supposed that the origin of the disease, as its name indicates, lay in trouble of the womb, but, though sexual disturbances often occur in the condition, they should more probably be classed as symptoms. Heredity is of importance, the disease being most common in the Latin races, and running to a great extent in families. Faulty upbringing in childhood predisposes to hysteria, which in young women of unequally developed mind and pampered habits, may be produced by sudden fright, family worry, grief, or a love affair.

Symptoms.—MENTAL CHANGES are almost always observable in hysterical cases, although the other symptoms in different cases may differ widely from one another. The affected person becomes whimsical, dominated by ideas, and unable for the same work and

456

concentration as before. She becomes easily excitable, and is either morbidly sensitive, feeling slight rebuffs keenly, or unusually demonstrative, bursting into fits of laughter or paroxysms of weeping upon slight occasion. In marked cases, hysterical subjects become morally unhinged, deceiving every one around them, so that little credence can be given to their statements.

CONVULSIVE HYSTERIA is the most marked form. An attack may begin upon some excitement, with laughter or weeping, or may give no warning sign. The person falls in an unconscious or half-conscious condition, but whereas the fall in epilepsy is downright, the hysterical person subsides gently in general upon a couch or chair, and rarely or never so as to hurt herself. She may then lie still, or more generally moans or talks incoherently, rolls the head from side to side, and tosses the hands and feet about. In serious attacks, known as hystero-epilepsy, the onset resembles epilepsy and may be followed by curious posturing, the sufferer placing herself in attitudes which suggest powerful emotions of fear, ecstasy, or joy. In this state visions are seen, voices heard, and conversations held with imaginary persons. This forms one of the most perverted types of hysteria and one of the least hopeful as regards a cure.

LOSS OF SENSATION over some part of the body is one of the commonest symptoms. This loss may affect a limb, or may be irregularly distributed in patches, or may affect some special sense organ, causing failure of taste, blindness for all objects to one side of the field of vision, or for objects of some special type repugnant to the patient, deafness in one ear, etc. Sometimes there is complete loss of the sense of pain, so that pricks, pinches, and other painful stimuli are borne without wincing.

SPASMS AND CONTRACTIONS of muscles form also a very frequent manifestation of hysteria without any other sign save mental hebetude. If this contraction exist in the muscles of the body wall, it may, and frequently does, give rise to the idea that the person is the subject of a tumour. Such spasms may also lead to the drawing up of an arm or foot, so that the limb in time becomes permanently deformed. Or when the mind becomes powerfully impressed by some person or idea, the spasm may pass off, and gradual or sudden recovery frequently takes place.

PARALYSIS is perhaps the most troublesome symptom of all to overcome. It may extend over one-half of the body, and is then very hard to differentiate from the effects of apoplexy. Most commonly the foot is affected and the person declares herself unable to walk. As the paralysis sometimes lasts for years unimproved, and then suddenly vanishes, these cases are eminently suited for successful ministration by the faithhealer or by wonder-working shrines. Such persons, when the paralysis affects both legs, and is accompanied by pain in the back, have again and again been confined for years to bed or couch as cases of spinal disease, only to recover suddenly when some new interest has come into their lives, or force of circumstances has rendered an active life imperative. The muscles of the larynx are often affected, and the person may be deprived of speech for years, till some powerful influence forces her to exert her will and the organ of voice again comes into play.

CHANGES IN INTERNAL ORGANS take place in some cases and produce such signs as constant hiccup, barking noises, excessive vomiting, diarrhœa, absolute loss of appetite, and profound changes in the circulation. Among the features of the last-named may be mentioned the appearance of swollen and congested areas in the skin, and, showing the power which the mind may exert over bodily functions, there is recorded the case of Louise Lateau, who, after meditating for many days upon the Crucifixion, developed on hands and feet ' stigmata ' or bleedings beneath the skin.

JOINT AFFECTIONS are among the most remarkable physical changes. A joint, especially the hip or knee, becomes swollen, stiff, and painful, and may remain so for months. (See PAIN.)

Treatment.—Special care should be taken in the upbringing of children who come of hysterical stock. They should not, on the one hand, be allowed to work too hard at lessons to the neglect of healthy exercise, nor, on the other hand, should they be pampered and allowed to gratify every passing whim. No hysterical young woman should remain unoccupied, but should be provided with, and forced to do, some congenial work. Needless to say, all the bodily functions should be maintained in the best possible order. In acute hysterical attacks rest and quiet are chiefly necessary. For symptoms such as vomiting, joint affections, loss of sensation, and spasms, removal from home and from the attentions of sympathetic friends to strict isolation, where the patient sees nobody but a nurse and eats only the simplest of food, is a good form of treatment. For the severest forms of hysteria isolation and absolute rest in bed are employed. Further, massage takes the place of exercise, and the patient is encouraged to eat large amounts of readily digestible food. In all cases of hysteria psychotherapy forms an important element in treatment. This is carried out especially by suggestion, but in other cases it may take the form of persuasion, psycho-analysis, or education and employment.

I

IATRIC (ἰατρός, physician) is a term meaning anything pertaining to a physician.

IATROGENIC DISEASE is disease induced by a physician : *e.g.* a neurosis resulting from a physician's diagnosis of a physical disease.

ICE is used as a convenient form of applying cold, both externally and internally. For external application the most convenient form of application is by placing chopped ice in an indiarubber bag, known as an ice-bag (Fig. 228). The bag is closed by a screw cap and is laid upon the head, abdomen,

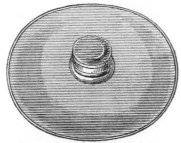

FIG. 228.—Rubber ice-bag.

or other part to which it is desired to make the cold application, a layer of flannel or a garment being placed between the bag and the skin to prevent a direct freezing action on the surface. When an ice-bag is not available, ice may similarly be applied to a small area by taking a large piece of gutta-percha tissue, laying the ice upon its centre, and bunching up the corners, which are tied together with a string. Iced water is sometimes applied by means of a coiled tube, especially in cases of inflammation of the head. The iced water is allowed slowly to percolate from a jug placed a few feet above the bed through the coiled tube laid on the affected part.

For internal application ice is seldom used now. (*See also* COLD, USES OF ; *and* CRYMOTHERAPY.)

ICHOR is the term given to the thin fluid, yellowish or bloody, which issues from a sore or a wound.

ICHTHAMMOL (*see* ICHTHYOL).

458

ICHTHYOL (ἰχθύς, a fish), or ICHTHAMMOL, is ammonium ichthosulphonate, a dark brown, thick liquid of fishy smell, prepared by distillation from a deposit of fossil fish in the Tyrol. It is used in several chronic skin diseases.

ICHTHYOSIS (ἰχθύα, shark-skin) is a skin disease in which the surface is very rough and presents a dry, cracked appearance, very much resembling fish-scales. The peculiarity is generally hereditary, and persists through life, the skin being permanently hard, and deficient in oily material. The appearances differ considerably according to the part affected and the surrounding conditions. Thus the knees and elbows when affected become black from the collection of dirt in the deep crevices, and in winter the skin becomes specially hard and the condition still more marked.

Treatment.—There is no specific internal treatment, but improvement sometimes follows the administration of vitamin A. Those who suffer from the disease should live, if possible, in a warm sunny climate. External treatment is most important and consists of daily warm baths with bran or starch, followed by the application of 20 to 50 per cent. glycerin in water, olive oil, or equal parts of salicylic acid ointment (2 per cent.) and glycerin. An alternative form of treatment is to add the *British Pharmacopœia* Emulsifying Ointment to the bath : 1 ounce (28·5 grammes) is added after preliminary creaming in a jug of hot water. This is followed by the application to the skin of the *British Pharmacopœia* Hydrous Ointment as often as is required.

ICTERUS (ἴκτις, a weasel) is another name for jaundice. (*See* JAUNDICE.)

ICTERUS GRAVIS NEONATORUM (*see* HÆMOLYTIC DISEASE OF THE NEWBORN).

ICTUS is another term for a stroke.

IDIOCY, or IDIOTCY (ἰδιώτης, an unskilled person), is the term applied to a profound degree of mental defect in which the person is unable to guard himself against ordinary dangers and is of dirty habits. (*See* MENTAL DEFECTIVENESS.)

IDIOGLOSSIA means the continued utterance of meaningless sounds, the afflicted person ' speaking ' a language intelligible to no one.

IDIOPATHIC (ἴδιος, peculiar; πάθη, suffering) is a term applied to diseases to indicate that their cause is unknown.

IDIOSYNCRASY (ἴδιος, peculiar; σύγκρασις, mixture) means an unusual effect produced by certain drugs or other agencies in certain persons. For example, some persons are poisoned by very small doses of opium or belladonna, whilst, on the other hand, some take huge doses of these or other drugs without any effect. The same applies to alcohol, arsenic, iodides, and many other drugs. Idiosyncrasies exist also for foods, some persons having an acute attack of dyspepsia, or even becoming dangerously ill, when they take milk, or fish, or eggs, or oatmeal, as the case may be. Others may be powerfully affected by smells, such as that of roses, or of particular animals, as of cats. This peculiarity as applied to sensitiveness to substances, such as foods, the pollen of plants, etc., is known as allergy.

IDOXURIDINE is a preparation that is proving of value in the treatment of recurrent herpes of the skin.

ILEITIS means inflammation of the ileum. REGIONAL ILEITIS, or CROHN'S DISEASE, is the term applied to a condition in which there is an (apparent) inflammation of an area of the small intestine. This is accompanied by colicky abdominal pain, irregularity of the bowels, loss of weight, and slight fever. The abdomen is distended and the thickened intestine may be felt. The narrowed intestinal canal may become obstructed, necessitating immediate operation. The cause is unknown. The primary lesion is hyperplasia of the lymph tissue in the submucosa of the intestine and in the lymph glands.

As the cause is not known, there is no specific treatment. In the early stages, treatment is medical, including a high-vitamin, low-residue diet, sul-

phonamides and antibiotics. Promising results have been reported from the use of cortisone in some cases. Operation, consisting of removal of the damaged section of gut, is reserved for cases which do not respond to medical treatment. Even in cases apparently successfully operated on, recurrence tends to occur in 15 per cent. or more of cases.

ILEO-CÆCAL is the term applied to the region of junction between the small and large intestines in the right lower corner of the abdomen. The ileo-cæcal valve is a structure which allows the contents of the intestine to pass onwards from the small to the large intestine, but, in the great majority of cases, prevents their passage in the opposite direction.

ILEOSTOMY is the operation by which an artificial opening is made into the ileum.

ILEUM (εἴλω, I twist) is the lower part of the small intestine. (*See* INTESTINE.)

ILEUS (εἴλω, I twist) is another name for severe colic due to obstruction of the bowels. (*See* INTESTINE, DISEASES OF.)

ILIUM (*ilia*, the flank) is another name for the haunch-bone, the uppermost of the three bones forming each side of the pelvis. (*See* BONE, PELVIS.)

ILLUSION (*illudo*, I make game of). (*See* HALLUCINATION.)

IMBECILITY (*imbecillitas*, weakness) is a term applied to feeble-mindedness in which the mental powers are somewhat greater than those possessed by an idiot. (*See* MENTAL DEFECTIVENESS.)

IMIPRAMINE is an iminodibenzyl derivative which is proving of value in the treatment of depression.

IMMERSION FOOT is the term applied to a condition which develops as a result of prolonged immersion of the feet in cold or cool water. It was a condition commonly seen during the 1939–45 War in shipwrecked sailors and airmen who had crashed in the sea and spent long periods before being rescued.

Such prolonged exposure results in vasoconstriction of the smaller arteries in the feet, leading to coldness and blueness of the feet, and finally, in severe cases, to ulceration and gangrene.

IMMUNITY (*immunis*, exempt) is a principle by virtue of which the bodies of certain animals or human beings are protected from the invasion of certain diseases, or the action of certain poisons.

creatures, including particularly man and the guinea-pig, are very susceptible. Man, on the other hand, is unaffected by swine fever, and some other diseases which are very infectious and fatal among the lower animals, while no animal, so far as known, contracts cholera. a disease which is so disastrous to man. Other examples are found in the fowl and the alligator, which are peculiar in being exempt from lockjaw, and white rats, which are not affected

Vaccine	Age at which to give
B.C.G.	Within first week of life if any contact likely with anyone with tuberculosis
Measles	12 months
Diphtheria, tetanus and whooping-cough (one injection of Triple vaccine) and poliomyelitis vaccine by mouth	18 months
Smallpox	20 to 24 months
Diphtheria and tetanus (one injection) and polio-myelitis vaccine by mouth	5 to 6 years (on going to school)
Diphtheria and tetanus (one injection) and polio-myelitis vaccine by mouth	10 years
B.C.G. if child is Mantoux-negative	12 years +

TABLE 17A.—Timetable for routine immunization of children. (*The Practitioner.*)

It is a well-recognized fact that some persons expose themselves again and again to the risk of infection and are not affected, whilst others seem prone to contract any disease with which they are brought into contact. The immunity so enjoyed is of several types. Natural immunity is one which is inborn ; but immunity may also be acquired in the course of life, or it may be produced artificially by inoculation, or injection of the blood serum of immune animals, etc.

Natural immunity.—Certain animals seem to be little affected by poisons which to others are very deadly. Thus the snake-killing mongoose of India is said to be highly immune to cobra poison. Pigeons are little affected by large doses of morphine ; rabbits and other animals eat freely the leaves of the deadly nightshade plant. (*See* IDIOSYNCRASY.) The rat is little affected by tuberculosis, to which other

by anthrax. There is probably no such thing as absolute immunity, however, since animals are affected by any poison if their health be very low or if the amount of poison be very great.

One result of immunity is that the ' phagocytes ', certain white corpuscles of the blood, have the power of destroying and consuming the bodies of bacteria in the blood or tissues. Formerly the whole action of immunity was attributed to this ' phagocytosis ', although now the process is believed to be mainly a chemical one. (*See* SERUM THERAPY.)

Acquired immunity is that which is gained by passing through an attack of some disease. Protection is probably given by all infectious diseases for a longer or shorter period against a second attack of the same disease. In the case of some, such as smallpox, typhoid fever, scarlatina, the protection appears to last throughout life, or, at all events, for many years. Recovery from a disease is in fact a process of immunity, the poison of the disease being destroyed by antagonizing substances produced in the tissues of the body, so that the disease comes to an end after a definite period.

Artificial immunity is of two kinds, known as active and passive immunity.

(*a*) ACTIVE IMMUNITY is produced by injecting beneath an animal's skin, or administering by the mouth in some cases, a small dose of some particular poison insufficient to produce death. This has the effect of stimulating the animal's powers of resistance, so that next time it can withstand a larger dose. The process is repeated over and over, the dose each time increasing, till finally the animal is unaffected by many times the dose which would have originally killed it. With regard to vegetable poisons see DRUG HABITS. This applies to snake poisons also, and the snake-charmers of India appear to render themselves indifferent to cobra-bites by a similar process.

With regard to disease - producing bacteria and the toxins or poisons which they form, immunity is reached by injecting first of all small quantities of bacteria, or of their toxins, which have been weakened by mixing with antiseptics, by drying in air, by passing through the bodies of partially immune animals, or by other highly technical processes. Usually this process is a lengthy one ; for example, to render horses highly immune against diphtheria occupies a space of several months, during which larger and larger doses of diphtheria toxin are given at intervals. It is evident, therefore, that, although this method offers protection against diseases, its slowness renders it useless for the cure of diseases which would run their whole course in a few days. The best-known practical example of this treatment is vaccination, in which ' cow-pox ', a modified form of the disease, is produced in persons so as to render them immune to the far severer smallpox. Another is Pasteur's preventive treatment for hydrophobia, in which, during the long incubation period before the disease has had time to appear, the person is treated by increasing doses of the poison, taken from rabbits that have

been killed by the disease. (*See* HYDROPHOBIA.)

The principle of this method, then, consists in stimulating the power of the body to resist the action of poisons. Great success in preventing diphtheria has been achieved by injecting one to three doses of diphtheria toxoid (inactivated toxin). This is quite harmless, and hundreds of thousands of children the world over have now been protected against this serious disease. Other common diseases against which protection can be provided in this way include typhoid fever, whooping-cough, tetanus, and poliomyelitis. A summary of current practice of immunization for children is shown in Table 17A.

(*b*) PASSIVE IMMUNITY is that form of artificial immunity obtained by injecting into the body of one animal or person whom it is desired to render immune blood serum drawn from an animal already rendered immune by the active method. The best-known example of this method is the treatment of diphtheria by antitoxic serum. This serum is obtained from horses already protected from diphtheria, as explained above, by a course of several months' treatment. This serum temporarily protects a person against contracting diphtheria, and after the onset of the disease, it will, if injected, neutralize the poison and bring about a milder type of disease and speedier recovery. The theory of action is, that the antitoxic serum contains certain chemical substances (antitoxins) which have been produced by the cells of the horse's blood or other tissues, and which combine with the poisons (toxins) produced by the diphtheria bacilli so as to neutralize the latter. Antitetanic serum immediately given to soldiers wounded under such conditions as to render them liable to an attack of lockjaw will prevent the onset of tetanus ; the introduction of tetanus toxoid as a preventive injection has considerably improved the prospects for those wounded on the battlefield. (*See* SERUM THERAPY.)

IMPACTION (*impactio*) is a term applied to a condition in which two things are firmly lodged together. For example, when after a fracture one piece of bone is driven within the other, this is known as an impacted fracture; when a tooth is firmly lodged in its socket so that its eruption is prevented, this is known as dental impaction.

IMPERIAL DRINK (for composition see *under* CREAM OF TARTAR).

IMPETIGO is a skin disease of an infectious nature often found in schools and caused usually by the *Staphylococcus aureus*. It consists of vesicles which appear here and there, on the face particularly, and dry up, leaving yellowish-brown scabs from which the discharge is infectious. These scabs fall off, leaving no scars, but the disease spreads from place to place over the skin, and may last for months if untreated.

Many cases respond well to the application of a mercurial paste consisting of compound zinc paste B.P. with 2 or 3 per cent. ammoniated mercury B.P. Other useful local applications are vioform cream and steroxin ointment. Should these fail, then one of the antibiotics should be used, preferably 0·5 or 1 per cent. neomycin (*q.v.*) in the form of a lotion or ointment. Penicillin is not usually used because of its tendency to produce sensitization of the skin.

When nits are present on the hair, treatment is ineffective until these have been removed. (*See* PARASITES.)

IMPOTENCE is the inability to perform the sexual act. It may be partial or complete, temporary or permanent. Of the many classifications of this not uncommon condition, the most satisfactory is probably that which divides it into two main groups—*organic* and *psychological*. Among organic causes are lesions of the external genitalia, *e.g.* a tight foreskin; disturbances of the endocrine glands, such as diminished activity of the gonads, thyroid gland, or pituitary gland; diseases of the central nervous system, *e.g.* tabes dorsalis; any severe disturbance of health, such as diabetes mellitus, addiction to alcohol and the like: among the psychological factors are ignorance, fear, weakness of sexual desire, or abnormality of such desire.

INCISION means a cut or wound and
462

is a term specially applied to surgical openings.

INCISOR is the name applied to the four front teeth of each jaw (*see* TEETH).

INCOMPATIBILITY is a term applied to unsuitability in a prescription owing to the fact that its different contents either cannot be mixed, or that when mixed they undergo chemical changes, or that their actions are opposed to one another.

INCOMPETENCE (*in*, neg. ; *competo*, I meet accurately) is a term applied to the valves of the heart when, as a result of disease in the valves or alterations in size of the chambers of the heart, the valves become unable to close the orifices which they should protect. (*See* HEART DISEASES.)

INCONTINENCE (*in*, neg. ; *contineo*, I hold) is a term applied to the inability to retain the evacuations of the bowels and bladder. It occurs in diseases of these organs, injuries and diseases of the spinal cord, etc.

INCO-ORDINATION is a term applied to irregularity of movements produced either by loss of the sensations by which they are governed or by defects in the muscles themselves or their nerves.

INCUBATION (*incubo*, I hatch) means the period elapsing between the time when a person becomes infected by some agent and the first appearance of the symptoms of the disease. Most acute infectious diseases have fairly definite periods of incubation, and it is

Scarlatina	.	.	.	2-4 days
Diphtheria	.	.	.	3-4 ,,
Smallpox	.	.	.	10-14 ,,
Measles	.	.	.	14 ,,
German measles	.	.	.	17-18 ,,
Chickenpox	.	.	.	11-21 ,,
Typhoid fever	.	.	.	10-14 ,,
Mumps	.	.	.	21 ,,
Whooping-cough	.	.	.	13-15 ,,
Influenza	.	.	.	2-4 ,,
Cholera	.	.	.	5 ,,
Plague	.	.	.	3-4 ,,

TABLE 18.—Incubation Periods of the commoner Infectious Diseases.

Disease and usual incubation period (days)	Period of exclusion	
	Patients	Contacts
Scarlet fever 1 to 7	7 days after release from hospital or from home isolation, unless discharges from nose, ear or throat or 'septic spots' are present.	7 days from the removal of the patient to hospital or the beginning of his isolation at home.
Diphtheria 2 to 7	Until pronounced free from infection.	7 days from the removal of the patient to hospital or the beginning of his isolation at home. If there be any suspicious signs, child should be excluded further until pronounced free from infection.
Measles 7 to 14	14 days after the appearance of the rash if the child appears well.	Infants who have not had the disease should be excluded for 14 days from the date of appearance of the rash in the last case in the house. Other contacts can attend school. Any contact suffering from a cold, chill or red eyes should be immediately excluded.
German measles 5 to 21	7 days from the appearance of the rash.	None.
Whooping-cough 6 to 18	28 days from the beginning of the characteristic cough.	Infants who have not had the disease should be excluded for 21 days from the date of onset of the disease in the last case in the house.
Mumps 12 to 28	14 days from the onset of the disease or 7 days from the subsidence of all swelling.	None.
Chickenpox 11 to 21	14 days from the date of the appearance of the rash.	None.
Smallpox 10 to 24	Until the patient is pronounced free from infection.	21 days, unless recently vaccinated, when exclusion is unnecessary.

TABLE 19.—Quarantine Periods for the commoner Infectious Diseases.

of great importance that people who have run the risk of infection should know the length of time which must elapse before they can be sure whether or not they are to contract the disease in question. A person who has been exposed to infection is, during the incubation period, technically known as a 'contact'. By isolating and watching contact cases in a boarding-school, barrack, or other public institu-tion, medical officers can often very successfully check a threatened epidemic. It must be noted that disease are not communicated to others by a person while passing through the stage of incubation. Some diseases, however, such as measles, become infectious as soon as the first symptoms set in after the incubation period is over ; others, like scarlatina and smallpox, are not so infectious then as in their later stages. The incubation period for any given disease is remarkably constant, although in the case of a severe attack the incubation is usually slightly shortened, and if the oncoming attack be a mild one, the period may be lengthened. So far as schools are concerned, children who have been 'contacts' should not be allowed to return to school till several days beyond the maximum incubation period has elapsed since exposure to infection: All of these may, however, take a few days longer than the time stated to show themselves. (*See* INFECTION.) Several also, and especially whooping-cough, are very difficult to recognize in their early stages. For practical purposes, therefore, as regards the length of time that should be allowed to elapse after a child has been in contact with a case of infectious disease, and before he is permitted to return to school, the following table, taken from the revised recommendations issued jointly by the Ministry of Health and the Board of Education in 1942, should be followed.

INDIAN HEMP (*see* CANNABIS INDICA).

INDICATION (*indicatio*) is the term applied to any sign which points to the cause or particularly the treatment of a disease. The term 'contra-indication' is applied to some circumstance which debars a particular line of treatment.

INDIGESTION (*see* DYSPEPSIA).

INDOMETHACIN is a drug that is proving of value in the treatment of gout.

INDUSTRIAL DISEASES (*see* TRADE DISEASES).

INFANT FEEDING.—An infant may either be breast-fed or bottle-fed.

Breast feeding.—Unless there is some definite contra-indication, every new-born child should be breast-fed. As has been well said, 'to take in human milk and mother love' at the breast and to continue to do so for several months is the best start in life for a human baby'. The advantages are clear cut and definite. The milk is specially prepared in composition for the human baby. It is at the right temperature and therefore there is no need to worry about hotting it up or cooling it down. It is available at any time no matter where the mother may be. It is most unlikely to be infected or contaminated. Finally—but by no means least—breast feeding offers the most intimate contact between a mother and her new-born baby.

The baby should be put to the breast six to eight hours after birth, and thereafter every four or three hours. Whether the baby is fed three-hourly or four-hourly depends upon how it progresses, but in the majority of healthy babies who weigh 7 lb. or more at birth, four-hourly feeding is sufficient. Five feeds are usually sufficient in the twenty-four hours, a useful time-table being feeds at 6 A.M., 10 A.M., 2 P.M., 6 P.M., and 10 P.M. There is no reason why a healthy infant should not go through the night without a feed, although it may sometimes be found more convenient to give the first feed in the morning somewhat earlier. This undisturbed night is invaluable to the nursing mother. Both breasts should be used at each feed, and it is an advantage to start each feed on alternate breasts. For the first feed of all, one minute at each breast is sufficient, and this time should be gradually increased until by the end of the first week the baby is having seven to ten minutes at each breast every feed.

The main guide as to whether an infant is being adequately fed is the weight (Table 20). During the first few days of life a healthy infant loses weight, but this it should have regained by the tenth day of life. Thereafter he should gain one ounce daily. The only supplement which is required to satisfactory breast feeding until weaning takes place is vitamin C and vitamins A and D. Vitamin C given in the form of orange juice : a few teaspoonfuls of equal parts of orange juice and water suitably sweetened at the age of one month, and gradually increase this until at the age of six months the infant is taking the juice of one orange undiluted. Tomato juice may occasionally be given instead of orange juice. Vitamins A and D are given in the form of cod-liver oil, starting with a quarter of a teaspoonful daily at about the age of 6 weeks, or the

AGE	HEIGHT				WEIGHT			
	BOYS		GIRLS		BOYS		GIRLS	
	Inches	Centi-metres	Inches	Centi-metres	Pounds	Kilo-grams	Pounds	Kilo-grams
Birth	20·0	50·9	19·5	49·5	7·5	3·4	7·3	3·3
2 weeks	20·3	51·7	20·1	51·0	7·5	3·4	7·3	3·3
3 months	23·7	60·2	23·2	58·8	12·9	5·8	12·0	5·5
6 months	26·2	66·7	25·6	65·0	17·4	7·9	16·4	7·4
9 months	28·0	71·2	27·4	69·6	20·4	9·2	19·2	8·7
1 year	29·6	75·1	29·1	73·9	22·8	10·3	21·7	9·8
2 years	34·0	86·4	33·7	85·5	27·0	12·2	25·7	11·6
3 years	37·8	95·9	36·9	93·8	31·5	14·3	30·4	13·8
4 years	40·6	103·0	40·0	101·6	35·6	16·2	34·5	15·7
5 years	43·1	109·5	42·9	108·9	40·2	18·3	39·4	17·9

TABLE 20.—Mean Height and Weight of infants and young children (Thomson).

equivalent amount of any special form of cod-liver oil that may be used.

The fluid secreted by the breasts during the first few days of lactation is known as colostrum. It has a high content of protein, but only a small amount of sugar and fat. The precise function of colostrum is not known, but it may be of value in helping to establish the immunity to certain infectious diseases which the breast-fed baby so often possesses. In addition, it has of

	Protein per cent.	Fat per cent.	Sugar per cent.	Calories per cent.
Human milk	1·5	4·0	6·8	68
Cow's milk	3·5	3·5	5·0	66

TABLE 21.—Composition of Human and Cow's Milk.

course a certain nutritional value, but it is doubtful whether it has any more aperient action on the bowels than any other form of liquid food.

Artificial feeding.—If breast feeding is not possible, then some substitute for human milk must be used, and the most satisfactory is cow's milk. As will be seen from tables 21 and 22, cow's milk differs in certain important aspects from human milk : it contains less sugar, more protein, and about the same amount of fat. In addition, however, there are important qualitative differences. Milk contains two types of protein—casein and albumin. The albumin in milk is known as lact-albumina ; it forms a finer clot and is more digestible than casein. In addition it contains larger amounts of two amino-acids, cystine and lysine, which

are of special importance for growth. The fat in cow's milk also differs from that in human milk in that its globules are larger and coarser.

The other drawback to cow's milk is that in the liquid form it is a potentially dangerous food for infants unless it is boiled. Dangerous diseases such as tuberculosis can be conveyed by milk, and the only safe rule for infants is to boil all milk. Even the more expensive forms of graded milk, such as ' T.T. ' or ' accredited ', are not safe in the un-boiled state for infants. The results of infection in infants can be so disastrous that up to the age of two years all milk should be boiled. After the age of two years pasteurization is reliable and therefore above this age children should be given pasteurized milk. The simplest way of boiling milk is in a double saucepan, and it is only necessary to bring the milk up to the boil. Prolonged boiling is not necessary. Statements are sometimes made that boiling adversely affects the nutritious qualities of milk. There is no evidence in favour of this, except in the case of the vitamin C content, and this deficiency can readily be overcome by giving orange juice. What has been said here, of course, only applies to liquid milk. The processes whereby dried and condensed milks are made ensure that these are safe from all infection. Liquid, dried, or condensed milk may be used for infant feeding.

GENERAL PRINCIPLES. — Before dealing with details of how to prepare the milk, certain general principles will be outlined. The first ten days of life are the most difficult times for artificial feeding and they will be dealt with

465

separately. Feeding times depend upon the weight of the infant. If the weight is over 7 to 8 lb., feeds are given every four hours from the tenth day, *i.e.* at 6 A.M., 10 A.M., 2 P.M., 6 P.M., and 10 P.M. If the weight is less than this, three-hourly feeds should be instituted,

feeding (*i.e.* six feeds daily), each feed would consist of 3 oz. This would be made up as follows : 1½ oz. of boiled milk, 1½ oz. of water, and 1½ level teaspoonfuls of sugar. The amount of milk is gradually increased, so that by the age of six to eight weeks, for in-

	Human Milk per 100 millilitres	Cow's Milk per 100 millilitres
Vitamin A	170 international units	
Summer		150 international units
Winter		100 ,, ,,
Vitamin D	1 ,, ,,	
Summer		1·5 ,, ,,
Winter		0·5 ,, ,,
Aneurine	17 micrograms	40 micrograms
Ascorbic Acid	3·5 milligrams	2 milligrams
(Vitamin C)		

TABLE 22.—Vitamin Content of Human and Unboiled Cow's Milk.

i.e. 6 A.M., 9 A.M., 12 noon, 3 P.M., 6 P.M., and 10 P.M. In all cases four-hourly feeds are sufficient after the age of three months or after the weight is 10 pounds.

Absolute cleanliness is essential, and the only reliable way of attaining this is by boiling bottle and teat after each feed and then keeping them immersed in cold water until the next feed. The hands of the mother or nurse must be carefully washed before handling the bottle, teat, or feed. The teat must be as big as the baby can cope with, and the hole in it must be so adjusted that the feed drips freely through it. This ensures that the baby is able to take each feed in ten to fifteen minutes. The amount of each feed depends upon the daily caloric requirements of the infant, which can be taken to be 2½ oz. of human milk or its equivalent per pound of body weight. Thus, an infant weighing 8 lb. would require 20 oz. of milk daily, and on the basis of five four-hourly feeds, this would mean 4 oz. per feed. Two essential additions to all artificial feeding are vitamins C and D. The former is given in the form of diluted orange juice as already described under breast feeding. Vitamin D is given either as quarter to half a teaspoonful of cod-liver oil daily, or three drops of halibut-liver oil daily.

LIQUID MILK.—For an infant at the age of ten days and on three-hourly

stance, a suitable mixture would be 3 oz. of boiled milk, 1½ oz. of water and 1½ teaspoonfuls of sugar. By the age of five months, when mixed feeding is instituted, the daily requirements are 30 oz. of human milk or its equivalent, with feeds of 6 oz. made up of 4½ oz. of boiled milk, 1½ oz. of water, and 1½ to 2 teaspoonfuls of sugar. At this stage it may even be possible to give undiluted milk.

DRIED MILK.—The great advantage of dried milk is that it is much less easily contaminated than liquid milk and is therefore much less trouble to the mother. Amidst the host of brands on the market, there are three main types of dried milk : (1) ' Full cream ' variety which, when reconstituted 1 in 8 (*i.e.* 1 teaspoon or measure to 1 oz. of water), gives milk of the same composition as undiluted liquid milk. (2) ' Half-cream milk ' from which some of the fat has been removed in the preparation, so that, when reconstituted 1 in 8, 1 oz. is equivalent to about ⅘ oz. of human milk. To improve the feed value, some manufacturers add sugar to half-cream milk, but as this may not suit the baby, the plain varieties should be tried in the first instance. (3) ' Humanized dried milk ' is so modified that reconstituted 1 in 8, 1 oz. is equivalent to 1 oz. of human milk. From the tenth day for a month or two, either the ' half-cream ' or the ' humanized ' milk should be used. The latter is the easier to use, as dilution 1 in 8 is all that is required. Thus, for a ten-day old baby requiring 3 oz. per feed, all that is required is to take 3 measures of the dried milk and add 3 oz. of boiled (*not* boiling) water. The equivalent with half-cream milk would be 3 measures of dried milk, 4 oz. of water, 1½ teaspoonfuls of sugar, and give 3 to 3½ oz. per feed. Not later than three months, or a weight of 10 lb., a change-over is made to the full-cream variety. For an infant weighing 10 lb., 22½ oz. of breast milk or its equivalent is necessary every day. On the basis of five feeds daily, this means that each feed would consist of 3 measures of the dried milk, 4½ oz. of water, and 1½ teaspoonfuls of sugar. This is gradually increased until, by the age of six months (15 lb. weight), each feed is made up of 5 measures, 6 oz. of water, and 1½ teaspoonfuls of sugar. In order to avoid any digestive disturbance the switch-over from one variety of dried milk to another should always be made gradually. In all cases cod-liver oil and orange juice should be given daily from the age of one month.

CONDENSED MILK.—The sweetened variety should never be used for infant feeding, as it contains so much sugar. The unsweetened variety, on the other hand, is thoroughly suitable for this purpose, the only practical drawback being that once a tin is open it is liable to contamination. One ounce of unsweetened condensed milk is equivalent to 2½ oz. of human milk.

Weaning.—It is usual to start weaning about the fifth month or when the infant weighs about 17 pounds (7.8 kg.). Provided the process is carried out gradually, there is seldom any difficulty in having the child completely off the breast by the end of the ninth month. It is essential to remember that all cow's milk given to the baby must be boiled. The amount of milk, including that used for cooking, should be about 1½ pints daily. From the age of six months the baby should be given a crust to chew every day. Cod-liver oil and orange juice are, of course, continued.

No hard and fast rules can be laid down for the process of weaning. If the baby has been breast-fed, then it is usually a mistake to switch on to an intermediate stage of bottle feeding. It is better, and usually not difficult, to teach baby to drink from a teaspoon or a feeding cup. The consistency of the food is important in the early stages of weaning. In the initial stage it should be semi-fluid, and for quite a long time it must be pulpy in consistency without any lumps. The large variety of powdered cereals and purées of vegetable and meat now available make the weaning process much simpler than it used to be—and much more pleasant for the baby. From a very early stage of weaning the aim should be to get baby on to a programme of three meals a day, with the meat, fish and vegetables given at the mid-day meal.

Digestive disturbances.—These are much more likely to occur with artificial feeding than with breast feeding. Only mild digestive upsets associated with feeding will be mentioned here. Any serious digestive disturbance in an infant should be referred immediately to a medical practitioner. (*See also* DIARRHŒA.) In the case of breast feeding, overfeeding may cause vomiting, colic, and diarrhœa, whilst underfeeding is accompanied by constipation. Sometimes, however, underfeeding may be accompanied by a special type of diarrhœa characterized by the passage of small, dark-green stools containing an excess of mucus—usually during or just after a feed. In the case of artificial feeding the most common digestive disturbances are colic and diarrhœa. These may be due to either dirty feeding utensils or an unsuitable feeding mixture.

Treatment.—It is important to remember that in a breast-fed baby vomiting, occurring immediately or soon after a feed, is usually of no significance provided there is no loss of weight. Should it be due to overfeeding (and this can be checked by test feeding) and should it persist, it can often be remedied by reducing the time at each breast and also by giving the infant a little boiled water before each feed. If underfeeding on the breast is confirmed by test feeding, the first essential is to reassure the mother and to ensure that she is taking sufficient diet, adequate fluid, and adequate rest. Other measures which help are to institute three-hourly feeding instead of four-hourly and to give an extra feed at night. If these fail, then complementary feeding may be used, *i.e.* a bottle feed after one or more breast-feeds. In the case of artificial feeding, the first essential is to ensure that the feeding utensils are all being adequately sterilized by boiling and that there is no contamination of the feed. The next step is to change to some other food. Should all these measures fail, it may then be necessary to treat the milk in some special way. This may be done by adding 1 grain of sodium citrate to each ounce of milk mixture, or peptonized milk may be used. If all else fails, it must never be forgotten that human milk is the best food for human infants and that it is sometimes possible to obtain supplies from maternity hospitals.

General rules for feeding young children.—The proper routine of feeding, sleeping, and exercise forms the beginning of a child's education, and the following general rules should be observed :

1. Give food at the regular hours only.

2. Take ample time ; do not hurry the child in sucking or chewing.

3. If a child is disinclined to eat he should not be coaxed or forced to do so. If a child is losing weight, or off his food, he should be examined for signs of disease ; otherwise the regulation of the amount of food should be left to his appetite.

4. Fancy dishes should not be given to tempt the appetite if simple food is refused ; nor should food refused at meals be allowed at other times.

5. Although all food given to a child should be simple, it ought to be varied from day to day, well cooked, and attractively served.

6. Highly seasoned food, much dressed food, and food with a large indigestible residue should not be given to children.

7. If a child habitually refuses some important article of diet, like milk, egg, or cereals, this should be given first and the more palatable food withheld till the simpler one is taken. The refusal of some special food tends readily to become a habit with some children.

8. If a child is feverish, food should be reduced in strength and quantity.

468

In very hot weather a young child often eats less food than usual and drinks more water.

9. The basis of a child's diet should be pasteurized milk (up to 2 pints a day) ; brown, wholemeal, or wheatmeal bread ; butter or vitaminized margarine ; eggs ; cheese ; fruit ; salad vegetables ; green leafy vegetables ; potatoes and other root vegetables ; meat ; fish ; sugar (but not too much) ; and water to drink. In the winter months a child should take one to two teaspoonfuls of cod-liver oil, or drops of halibut-liver oil, and 50 mg. of ascorbic acid (vitamin C), daily.

INFANT MORTALITY is the number of deaths of infants under one year of age. The infant-mortality rate in any given year is calculated as the number of deaths in the first year of life in proportion to every 1000 registered live births in that year. Along with perinatal mortality (*q.v.*), it is accepted as one of the most important criteria for assessing the health of the community and the standard of the social conditions of a country. The striking fall in the rate is well shown in the following figures :

1838–39	. 146	1916–20 .	. 90·9
1841–50	. 153	1921–25 .	. 74·9
1851–60	. 154	1926–30 .	. 67·9
1861–70	. 154	1931–35 .	. 62·2
1871–80	. 149	1936–40 .	. 55·3
1881–90	. 142	1941–45 .	. 49·8
1891–1900	. 153	1946–50 .	. 36·4
1901–05	. 138	1951–55 .	. 26·9
1906–10	. 117·1	1956–60 .	. 22·6
1911–15	. 108·1	1966	. 19·0

TABLE 23.—Infant-Mortality Rate in England and Wales, 1838–1966.

On the other hand, that there is still room for improvement in this country is shown by the fact that the rate in England and Wales is still higher than that in some other countries. For instance, in 1963, the infant-mortality rate in New Zealand was only 19·6, compared with 21·1 in England and Wales. In the same year the rates in certain other countries were as follows : Australia 19·5 ; Holland 15·8 ; Sweden 15·3.

This striking improvement in the infant-mortality rate has occurred mainly in the period from the second month of life. There has been much less improvement in the neonatal-mortality rate, *i.e.* the number of infants dying during the first four weeks of life, expressed as a proportion of every 1000 live births. During the first week of life the main causes of death are asphyxia, prematurity, birth injuries, and congenital abnormalities. After the first week the main cause of death is infection. The causes of death during the first year of life in England and Wales in 1911–1920, 1931–1939, and 1966 are shown in the following table. For 1966 the figures for the two sexes are combined.

Cause		1911–1920	1931–1939	1966
Whooping-cough	M.	3·31	1·35	}0·026
	F.	3·85	1·64	
Tuberculosis	M.	2·88	0·80	}0·0059
	F.	2·26	0·65	
Measles	M.	2·57	0·78	}0·021
	F.	2·21	0·66	
Bronchitis and pneumonia	M.	21·33	13·62	}3·15
	F.	16·43	10·28	
Gastro-enteritis	M.	..	6·22	}6·44
	F.	..	4·31	
Congenital malformations	M.	4·29	6·03	}3·8
	F.	3·56	5·22	
Immaturity	M.	21·48	16·40	}2·9
	F.	17·48	13·32	
All causes	M.	111·70	66·17	}19·0
	F.	88·66	51·03	

TABLE 24.—Infant-Mortality Rates per 1000 Live Births in England and Wales in 1911–1920, 1931–39, and 1966. M. = Male. F. = Female.

Social conditions also play an important role in infant mortality. For statistical purposes the Registrar-General divides the community into five social classes. In England and Wales the infant-mortality rate in these classes in 1930–32 was: Class I (professional), 32·7, Class III (skilled workers), 57·6; Class V (unskilled workers), 77·1. The comparable figures for Scotland for 1939–45 were: Class I, 30·9; Class III, 53·4; Class V, 78·6. Many factors come into play in producing these social variations, but overcrowding is undoubtedly one of the most important. For instance, in 1936 the infant-mortality rate in Bournemouth, where only 0·3 per cent. of working-class families were overcrowded, was 78 per cent. of that for the entire country, compared with 145 per cent. in Newcastle - upon - Tyne where 10·7 per cent. of working-class families were overcrowded. The same thing is evident in more recent figures available for Scotland. In 1945 the infant-mortality rate in Scotland was

56, but in Port Glasgow it was 78, whilst in the county of Sutherland it was only 11.

It is thus evident that for a reduction of the infant-mortality rate to the minimum figure the following conditions must be met. The mothers and potential mothers of the country must be housed adequately amid surroundings which permit of adequate fresh air and healthy exercise. The pregnant and nursing mother must be ensured an adequate diet. Effective antenatal supervision must be available to every mother, as well as skilled supervision during labour. The new-born infant must be adequately nursed and adequately fed. This means that all possible steps must be taken to encourage breast feeding. Mothers must be instructed in the proper care and feeding of their children, particularly during the first year of life. This in itself would reduce the mortality rate, but in addition adequate public-health measures must be taken to ensure a clean milk supply and full availability of such protective measures as vaccination against smallpox and immunization against diphtheria, measles, and whooping-cough. (*See also* PERINATAL MORTALITY.)

INFANTILE PARALYSIS.—Popular term for ACUTE ANTERIOR POLIOMYELITIS (*see* POLIOMYELITIS).

INFARCTION (*infarcio*, I cram in) means the changes which take place in an organ when an artery is suddenly blocked, leading to the formation of a dense, wedge-shaped mass in the part of the organ supplied by the artery. It occurs as the result of embolism or of thrombosis. (*See* EMBOLISM.)

INFECTION (*inficio*, I taint) is the name given to the process by which a disease is communicated from one person to another. All diseases so communicable are called infectious. There is, in the case of all such diseases, some micro-organism produced in the body of the diseased person which, on being transmitted to a second person, is capable of reproducing itself in larger quantity and causing a particular disease.

This micro-organism may be a bacterium, a Rickettsia, a virus, a protozoon, or a metazoon. Invasion of the body by a metazoon (*e.g.* by an intestinal worm) is more often known as an infestation.

The germs of disease may be grouped into those which will not flourish except about the temperature of the body, and those which are capable of maintaining their existence in decaying animal or vegetable matter, making only occasional migrations into the body and setting up disease. Speaking generally, bacteria of the first group are consistently much more deadly in their action, whilst those in the second group vary much in the severity of the disease they produce, causing a severer type if they have come direct from an infected person than if they have been germinating in drains, in the soil, or floating on dust particles in the air. This principle is of immense practical importance. In the course of a surgical operation many bacteria must fall from the air into the wound, but this does not appear to be any drawback, unless the bacteria be derived direct from suppurating wounds or like virulent source. Similarly diphtheria or pneumonia bacteria of a mild type may be found in the mouth of people who are, nevertheless, quite healthy, if certain conditions, necessary to render the bacterium virulent, be not present.

The same bacterium may produce very different types of disease, not only on account of its previous life-history, but even according to the channel by which it enters the body. The *Mycobacterium tuberculosis*, for instance, produces a very different picture, depending upon whether it invades the lungs, the intestines, the joints, the glands, or the skin. A certain amount of protection against the entrance of infective matter into the tissues of the body is afforded by the horny layer of the skin, by the acid of the gastric juice, and by the movements of the intestine, and a still greater measure of protection is afforded by the factors which ensure immunity against diseases (*see* IMMUNITY *and* SERUM THERAPY).

Modes of infection.—The infective material may be transmitted to the person by direct contact with a sick person, when the disease is said to be 'contagious', although such a distinction is purely artificial. Different diseases are specially infectious at different periods of their course ; and the practical question of guarding against infection is rendered much more difficult by the fact that some diseases are infectious at a stage even before they are clearly recognizable. This applies particularly to the early stage of measles before the rash appears, when the infected child is showing symptoms merely resembling those of a catarrh or cold in the head.

Infection may be conveyed on dust driven by the wind, in drinking-water, food, particularly milk, evacuations with which the healthy person's hands have become contaminated, crusts and scabs from the infected person's body, or even clothes and linen which have been in contact with him.

In this connection what are termed 'carriers' are of great importance. Some persons who have suffered from a disease, or who have simply been in contact with an infectious case, harbour the germ of the disease. This is particularly the case in regard to typhoid fever, the bacillus continuing to develop in the gall-bladder of persons who have had the disease, it may be for years after the symptoms have passed away ; it is estimated that 2 to 5 per cent. of patients with typhoid fever become permanent 'typhoid carriers', and where a cook or food purveyor is affected, he is apt to start an epidemic unless he exercises the most scrupulous cleanliness. In the case of cholera, which is endemic in some localities of the East, 80 per cent. or more of the population may harbour the bacillus and spread infection when other circumstances favour this. Similarly in the case of dysentery, persons who have completely recovered may still be capable of infecting dust and drinking-water by their stools. Diphtheria is similarly liable to be carried by persons in whose throat the germ remains after recovery from the disease. Cerebrospinal meningitis, which is particularly liable to infect children, appears to be transmitted through the germ being carried in the nose of persons who may not develop any symptoms.

Animals play an even more important part than human beings in spreading such diseases. Flies pass from garbage heaps to unprotected food, and are especially dangerous as regards the infection of milk and other food with the organisms causing typhoid fever and food poisoning. Mosquitoes convey from sick to healthy the germs of malaria and yellow fever, these undergoing part of their development in the body of the mosquito. Fleas convey the germ of plague from rat to man, lice are responsible for inoculating typhus fever and one form of relapsing fever by their bite. A tick is responsible for spreading another form of relapsing fever, and kala-azar (or leishmaniasis) is spread by the bites of sandflies.

Notifiable diseases.—Certain of the common and most serious infectious diseases were scheduled in the Infectious Diseases Act of 1889 as notifiable in Great Britain. That is to say that any medical practitioner, attending or called in to visit a person suffering from one of these, must immediately, on becoming aware that the patient is suffering from it, send a notice to the local medical officer of health. Under the Public Health Act, 1936, the diseases at present notifiable are :

    Smallpox
    Cholera
    Diphtheria
    Membranous croup
    Erysipelas
    Scarlatina
    Typhus
    Typhoid, including paratyphoid fevers
    Enteric or relapsing fevers.

Various other diseases have been included from time to time by other enactments or are included by local authorities in special localities. Such diseases are :

    Measles
    Whooping-cough
    Cerebrospinal meningitis (meningococcal meningitis)
    Plague
    Acute poliomyelitis (infantile paralysis)
    Tuberculosis
    Ophthalmia neonatorum
    Encephalitis lethargica
    Malaria
    Dysentry
    Acute primary pneumonia
    Acute influenzal pneumonia
    Puerperal pyrexia.

Anthrax and toxic jaundice are notifiable as industrial diseases. Similar regulations are found in the various States of America and in other countries.

Prevention of infection.—The various channels of infection are mentioned under the heading of the different infectious diseases, and also briefly under SANITATION. As children are much more liable to contract infectious diseases than grown-up people, attempts to prevent the spread of these diseases are specially directed towards separating affected persons from healthy children. The measures taken apply particularly to schools, which form the places of dissemination in a large proportion of cases, but the rules applicable to children may well be practised with regard to persons of any age and in respect of any public institution.

1. The following diseases may, for this purpose, be considered infectious : *chickenpox, diphtheria, German measles* and *epidemic roseola, measles, mumps, ophthalmia, ringworm, scarlatina, smallpox, typhoid fever, typhus fever,* and *whooping-cough.*

2. Persons who have contracted any of these diseases should not again mix with the public till the following periods have elapsed:

Chickenpox : when all the scabs have fallen off, particular attention being paid to the scalp.

Diphtheria: until three throat swabs at weekly intervals are ' sterile '.

German measles and *epidemic roseola :* not less than seven days after the rash appears.

Measles : not less than two weeks after the rash appears, but then only if the fever has subsided.

Mumps : not less than two weeks after the beginning, and then only if all swelling has been gone for a week.

Scarlatina: when all signs of the illness have disappeared and throat swabs are ' sterile '.

Smallpox: not until all the scabs have fallen off.

Typhoid fever: not until six consecutive specimens of stools and urine have been negative on bacteriological examination.

Typhus fever : not less than four weeks from the beginning.

Whooping-cough : not less than four

weeks from the beginning of the whooping, and then only provided that the cough has ceased.

3. After persons have been ' in contact ' with the following serious diseases, viz. *diphtheria, scarlatina, typhoid fever, typhus fever,* and *smallpox,* they should remain in quarantine for periods exceeding the longest possible incubation period, viz.: diphtheria, seven days ; scarlatina, seven days ; typhoid fever, twenty-three days ; typhus fever, fourteen days ; smallpox, twenty-one days. It is essential, however, that the clothes of the suspected person should be disinfected at the *beginning* of the quarantine period.

After contact with the slighter diseases, viz. *measles, German measles, chickenpox, whooping - cough,* and *mumps,* children attending large schools, where infection would spread easily, should be isolated, after careful disinfection of their clothes, for the periods given under INCUBATION. But, in the case of adults and of children living at home, it suffices if they at once take up residence in an uninfected house, and, though mixing freely with other persons, report daily to a medical man for a few days before and after the end of the incubation period of the disease to which they have been exposed. In the case of measles, adults and children who have had measles previously should, after exposure to risk of infection, if they are mixing with the public, be carefully examined for signs of the disease for three days before and three days after the end of the usual incubation period. It is a good plan for children to stay away from school during these six days. (For the usual periods of incubation, *see* INCUBATION.) Instead of the contacts changing their abode the patient is usually removed, and the sick-room, together with all clothing that has been in contact with him, is disinfected. By these means, if contacts become infected, the fact will be recognized within a day, and they can at once be isolated and treated.

4. Clothes, books, etc., which have been used by an infected person, must, when his illness is at an end, be destroyed or carefully disinfected before use by anyone else. (*See* DISINFECTION.)

472

5. The methods applicable to certain diseases which are communicated in special ways, *e.g.* tuberculosis, yellow fever, are given under the heading of the disease in question. For the methods to be adopted against flies, lice, etc., *see* INSECTS IN RELATION TO DISEASE.

INFECTIOUS MONONUCLEOSIS (*see under* GLANDS, DISEASES OF).

INFESTATION is a term applied to the occurrence of animal parasites in the intestine, hair, or clothing. (*See* INSECTS IN RELATION TO DISEASE.)

INFLAMMATION (*inflammo,* I set on fire) may be defined as the reaction of the tissues to any injury, short of one sufficiently severe to cause their immediate death. The term is limited sometimes to the changes which take place when bacteria enter the body, but the changes in the latter case, though specially severe, are essentially the same as those produced by any other source of irritation. There are four cardinal symptoms of inflammation, viz. redness, heat, pain, and swelling, all of which, and particularly the last, are present in greater or less degree, so that these are also made a basis for defining the condition. The changes that take place have been studied by observing under the microscope the tongue, mesentery, or foot-web of frogs, newts, and similar animals in which these structures are very thin and transparent. The changes which take place as the surface dries, or on the application of various irritant substances, are easily seen. These changes have been confirmed, so far as other tissues and other animals are concerned, by examination after death.

The first sign of inflammation consists in a dilatation of the arteries and veins of the affected part, so that the blood circulates in it more quickly and in larger quantity than before, thus causing heat and redness. Very soon, however, and apparently as the result of some change in the walls of the smaller blood-vessels, the circulation becomes gradually slower, and the white corpuscles of the blood are seen to adhere to the inner surface of these vessels. Later, these corpuscles push their way in great numbers through the walls of the smaller veins and capillaries, migrating into the surrounding tissues along with large quantities of the fluid material of the blood and a few red corpuscles, a process known as DIAPEDESIS. Hence the swelling, which is the most characteristic sign of inflammation. These white corpuscles subserve many functions. In the first place, they have been shown, originally by Metchnikoff, and later by other observers, to attack the bacteria which have invaded the tissues, to envelop them in their own substance, and, apparently by a process of digestion, to break them up. They also remove tissues which are dead or useless. Other corpuscles, at a later stage, when the source of irritation has been removed, play a part in producing the new tissues to repair the damage done, although the greater part of this repair is effected by cells from the surrounding tissues.

One of two results may follow inflammation. Either *resolution* may take place, when the white corpuscles, having played their part, find their way back into the circulation after the process of repair has been started at the site of injury, and the circulation proceeds as before, or *abscess-formation* results, the circulation comes to a complete standstill in the affected part, an excessive number of white corpuscles migrate from the vessels, an area of tissue becomes destroyed, and the process ends by a discharge of ' pus ' through the surface of the body, after which repair proceeds. (*See* ABSCESS, ACUTE.)

Symptoms. — As mentioned above, redness, heat, pain and swelling are the classical symptoms of inflammation, and there are usually general symptoms of high temperature, feverishness, etc., varying with the severity of the inflammation. Various special symptoms are set up in special localities, for example, inflammation of the mucous membranes of the stomach and bowels leads to a copious excretion of mucus, and is known as ' catarrh ' ; inflammations of outlying parts, if they are very severe, may cause death of these parts, and are then called ' gangrenous ' inflammations ; intense inflammation limited to a surface may destroy patches of the surface and convert them into a leather-like membrane, such types being known as ' croupous ' inflammations, etc. Inflammation may become chronic, and in this case not only does the process described above proceed in a minor degree, but there is an exaggerated process of repair leading to the formation of much fibrous or scar tissue, which may come to replace almost entirely the organ in which the chronic inflammation is proceeding, thus rendering the organ small, hard, and irregular in outline.

Treatment. — This depends upon different factors, such as the type of organism responsible, the site of infection and the severity of the infection. Thus, if the inflammation is due to tuberculosis, treatment will be by means of a combination of two or more, of streptomycin, isoniazid and para-aminosalicylic acid. If, on the other hand, it is in the appendix, immediate removal of the appendix is called for, whilst in the case of superficial inflammation of the skin, all that may be required is careful cleansing of the skin and the application of some antiseptic preparation.

Two general principles, however, apply to the treatment of all forms of inflammation : rest and the maintenance of the general health of the patient.

INFLUENZA, also known as LA GRIPPE, is an acute infectious disease, characterized by a sudden onset, fever, and generalized aches and pains, which usually occurs in epidemics and pandemics.

History. — The term ' influenza ' was first introduced into England in 1743 by John Huxham, a practitioner in Plymouth, and is said to be derived from *influsso*, which is the Italian form of *influxio* which means ' catarrh '. The origin of the disease is wrapped in the mists of antiquity. It has been suggested, for instance, that the epidemic of 412 B.C. described by Hippocrates was influenza, and that this was also the cause of the epidemic that swept across Europe in 839 A.D., causing heavy losses in Charlemagne's army. To come to more modern times, there were five widespread epidemics during the nineteenth century in 1830, 1833, 1836, 1897, and 1889-90. The greatest pandemic of all, however, was that of 1918–19, which swept across the world and is estimated to have caused 15 to 20 million deaths within two years.

Cause.—The disease is caused by a virus of the influenza group. There are at least three types of influenza virus, known respectively as A, B, and C. One of their most characteristic features is that infection with one type provides no protection against another type. Equally important is the ease with which the influenza virus can change its character. It is these two characteristics which explain why one attack of influenza provides little, if any, protection against a subsequent attack, and why it is so difficult to prepare an effective vaccine against the disease.

Epidemics of influenza due to virus A occur in Britain at two- to four-year intervals, and outbreaks of virus B influenza in less frequent cycles. Virus A influenza, for instance, was the prevalent infection in 1949, 1951, 1955 and 1956, whilst virus B influenza was epidemic in 1946, 1950, 1954 and, along with virus A, in 1958–59. The pandemic of 1957, which swept most of the world, though fortunately not in a severe form, was due to a new variant of virus A—the so-called Asian virus—and it has been suggested that it was this variant that was responsible for the pandemics of 1889 and 1918.

Symptoms.—The incubation period of influenza A and B is one to ten days, and the disease is characterized by a sudden onset. In most cases this is followed by a short, sharp febrile illness of two to four days' duration, associated with headache, prostration, generalized aching and respiratory symptoms. In many cases the respiratory symptoms are restricted to the upper respiratory tract, and consist of signs of irritation of the nose, pharynx and larynx. There may be nose-bleeds, and a dry hacking cough is often a prominent and troublesome symptom. The fever is usually remittent and the temperature seldom exceeds 103° F. (39·4° C.), tending to fluctuate between 101° and 103° F. (38·3° and 39·4° C.).

The most serious complication is infection of the lungs. This infection is usually due to organisms rather than the influenza virus. It is a complication which can have serious results in elderly people.

The very severe form which tends to occur during pandemics—and which was so common during the 1918–19 pandemic—is characterized by the rapid onset of broncho-pneumonia and severe prostration. Because of the toxic effect on the heart there is a particularly marked form of cyanosis, known as ' heliotrope ' cyanosis.

Convalescence following influenza tends to be prolonged. Even after an attack of average severity there tends to be a period of weakness and depression.

Treatment.—Expert opinion is still divided as to the real value of influenza vaccine in preventing the disease. Part of the trouble is that, as already pointed out, there is no value in giving any vaccine until it is known which particular virus is causing the infection. As this varies from winter to winter, and as the protection given by vaccine does not exceed one year, it is obviously not worth while attempting to vaccinate the whole community. The general rule therefore is that, unless there is any evidence that a particularly virulent type of virus is responsible, only those should be vaccinated who are particularly vulnerable, such as children in boarding schools, elderly people, pregnant women, and people who suffer from chronic bronchitis. In the face of an epidemic, people in key positions, such as doctors, nurses and those concerned with public safety, transport and other public utilities should be vaccinated.

For an uncomplicated attack of influenza, treatment is symptomatic : that is, rest in bed, analgesics to relieve the pain, sedatives, and a light diet. A linctus, such as Gee's linctus, is useful to sooth a troublesome cough. The best analgesic is aspirin—either alone, or combined with phenacetin and codeine. None of the sulphonamides or the known antibiotics has any effect on the influenza virus. On the other hand should the lungs become infected, antibiotics should be given immediately, because, as has already been pointed out, such an infection is usually due to other organisms. Usually one of the tetracycline group of antibiotics is best, or chloramphenicol, but in others penicillin is the antibiotic of choice. If possible, a sample of sputum should be examined to determine which organisms are responsible for the lung infection. The choice of antibiotic then depends upon which antibiotic the organism is most sensitive to.

INFUSIONS are preparations of vegetable drugs made by steeping them for some time in water and straining. In order that an infusion may keep well it is usually concentrated and mixed with spirit, being diluted just before it is dispensed. Among the better-known infusions are those of gentian, quassia, senega, and senna. The dose of most infusions is from one to several tablespoonfuls.

Infusion is also the term applied to the injection into blood-vessels or subcutaneous tissues of warm normal salt solution, glucose solution or gum acacia solution, in the case of persons who are in a feeble state from loss of blood, loss of fluid by diarrhœa, etc. The infusion is sometimes administered in an amount of about one pint at a time, or is frequently used by a drip method in which the warm fluid is suspended at a height and allowed to pass drop by drop for several hours into a vein.

INGUINAL REGION (*see* ABDOMEN, REGIONS OF).

INHALATION (*inhalo*, I breathe in) means a method of applying drugs in a finely divided or gaseous state, so that, on being breathed in, they may come in contact with the nose, throat, air passages, and lungs. There are five chief means by which drugs are mingled with the air and so taken in by breathing. These are as follows :

(*a*) Volatile drugs, which become gaseous at the ordinary temperature. Examples of these are chloroform, ether, nitrous oxide gas, nitrite of amyl. Most drugs so administered act as general anæsthetics.

(*b*) Respirators are worn in front of the mouth and nose when it is desired to admit small quantities of some slowly volatile drug constantly into the air passages. The simpler and lighter such respirators are, the better. Perhaps the best variety is one consisting of a thin piece of bent, perforated metal, padded round the edge, having a small piece of sponge in its interior upon which the drug may be dropped, and pieces of elastic at its sides to pass behind the ears and keep the respirator in position.

(*c*) Drugs which give off volatile substances on burning are mixed with some combustible substance, and the fumes they give off inhaled. Thus asthmatic persons sometimes obtain relief during an attack from the smoke given off by smouldering blotting-paper which has been previously soaked in a strong solution of nitre and dried (*see* NITRE). Similarly lobelia, stramonium, belladonna leaves, etc., are made into powders or rolled up in cigarettes, of which the fumes are inhaled.

(*d*) Steam inhalations. Steam itself, or hot moist air, has a soothing effect upon the mucous membrane of the air passages, and the steam may be impregnated with many moderately volatile drugs. This type of inhalation is used especially in bronchitis and inflammatory conditions of the throat and larynx. If it be desired to surround the patient constantly with a steamy atmosphere, the most convenient mode of doing so is by a kettle placed over a spirit lamp, from which a long white-iron funnel leads in beneath a tent formed by a blanket over the upper half of the patient's bed (Fig. 83). In cases of chronic bronchitis, one teaspoonful of the following mixture is now and then added to the hot water : pinewood oil 1 ounce (28·5 ml.), eucalyptus oil 1 ounce (28·5 ml.), creosote ½ ounce (14 ml.). Or in acute cases, where a soothing effect is specially necessary, a teaspoonful of the following : compound tincture of benzoin 1 ounce (28·5 ml.), menthol 10 grains (600 mg.), spirit of chloroform ½ ounce (14 ml.). Either of these formulæ may be used by simply adding it to a jug half full of boiling water, over which the mouth is held, the head being enveloped in a towel that falls down round the sides of the jug. The same remedies may be added in similar quantity to an inhaler and the mouth directly applied to the tube leading from it.

(*e*) The most recent form of inhalation consists of a fine spray or cloud driven off from a fluid by a stream of compressed air. By this means, various medicaments can be made to reach the farthest recesses of the lungs. The smaller of these ' nebulizers ' or ' atomizers ' are worked by a hand-ball of india-rubber, which drives a strong stream of air across the mouth of another tube dipping into the liquid. In various spas, larger nebulizers worked by force pumps are employed to fill whole rooms with medicated vapour, which patients sit and inhale for hours.

INHIBITION (*inhibeo*, I restrain) means arrest or restraint of some process effected by nervous influence. The term is applied to the action of certain ' inhibitory ' nerves, *e.g.* the vagus nerve which contains fibres that inhibit or control the action of the heart. It is also applied generally to the mental processes by which instinctive but undesirable actions are checked by a process of self-control.

INJECTIONS (*see* Enema *and* Hypodermic Injections).

INJURED, REMOVAL OF. — A knowledge of the manner in which injured persons may best be removed from the spot where they have sustained the injury is of great importance, because careless or unskilful handling or moving may produce much pain and in some cases is liable to aggravate the bodily damage already done.

Precautions before removal.—In the case of some injuries, such as that of the brain in apoplexy, or the perforation of the bowels caused by a bullet-wound of the abdomen, the less movement of the patient that takes place at first the better for his chances of recovery, and it is sometimes advisable that treatment should be carried out for some time near the spot where the injury has been sustained. When a bone has been broken it is essential that the fragments should be temporarily supported and made rigid by suitable devices before any attempt is made to change the patient's position (*see* Fractures). In other cases, as, for example, those of faintness, shock, immersion in water, etc., some other form of first-aid

treatment or the administration of stimulants is urgently necessary prior to removal (*see* Fainting ; Collapse ; Drowning, Recovery from ; Hæmorrhage, etc.). During removal an attendant must be constantly with the injured person, or at least the latter must be carried in such a way that one of the bearers constantly sees his face.

Position in removal.—The following hints are taken in part from Sir T. Longmore's *Treatise on Ambulances*. Severely injured persons, or those with any tendency to faintness, bleeding, shock, or other general symptoms, should be carried lying at full length with the head slightly supported on a low pillow ; a similar position should be adopted in the case of persons who have sustained any injury to the bones or joints of the lower limb, or of the shoulder-joint, or severe wounds of the head, chest, or abdomen. On the other hand, injuries of the hand or forearm when properly supported, no matter how severe they may be, slight injuries of the foot, and uncomplicated wounds to the head, face, or upper part of the body, permit generally of the patient either walking or being removed in the sitting posture, as by one of the forms of hand seat.

In wounds of the head care should be taken that the injured part does not press upon the stretcher.

In severe injuries to the back the greatest care must be exercised in lifting the patient, and some rigid though well-covered form of stretcher is to be preferred, upon which the patient is placed face downwards.

In fractures of the leg or thigh the patient should lie upon his back inclined slightly towards the injured side and supported thus by a pillow, folded coat, etc. ; in this position there is least jarring of the injured part.

In fractures of the upper limb, if the patient has to lie down, which is not usual, he should incline slightly towards the sound side, so that there is no risk of the body pressing the injured part.

In wounds or diseases of the chest there is often difficulty in breathing, which is relieved by propping the patient half up and turning him towards the affected side.

In painful conditions of the abdomen, or in the case of transverse or punctured wounds of this region, the patient should lie upon his back with the knees drawn well up and supported. In the case of a vertical wound of the abdomen the legs are kept straight.

The patient is usually carried feet first, but in going uphill or upstairs this position is reversed; in all cases, however, in which there is a fracture of the lower limb, the patient's head is kept lowest on a hill or stair so that the weight of the body may not press down upon the helpless and motionless part of the limb below the fracture. The taller bearer should be the farther on the hill or stair.

No attempt should be made by inexperienced bearers to carry a stretcher over a wall or ditch, and on no account should a stretcher be carried upon the bearers' shoulders, because a fall may do very serious injury to the patient.

The stretcher should be carried at the full length of the bearers' arms, as horizontal as possible, and the bearers, though walking at an equal rate, must be careful not to keep in step, which causes the stretcher to swing painfully.

Method of removal depends upon (1) how many persons are available as bearers, and (2) the degree of assistance required by the patient, as already stated.

I. BY ONE BEARER.—When an arm is injured the patient is usually quite able to walk, and, the arm being suitably supported, the bearer draws the patient's sound arm *over his shoulders* and places his own arm round the patient's waist (Fig. 229).

If the bearer be strong and the patient seriously incapacitated, the latter may be carried *in the bearer's arms*, the right one passing beneath the patient's shoulder-blades, the left beneath the upper part of the thighs; in this case the patient should be carried high and supported as much upon the bearer's chest as by his arms. In other cases the patient may be carried *upon the bearer's back*, his arms round the bearer's neck and his legs under the bearer's arms.

In cases of complete unconsciousness, where the dead-weight of the patient's body must be raised and borne by one bearer, the method known as the *Fireman's Lift* is applicable. The patient is turned on his face, arms by the sides; the bearer stands at the patient's head, and, passing his hands beneath the latter's shoulders, raises him to a kneeling posture. The bearer next slides his hands under the patient's armpits and raises him still farther; then stooping and pushing his head between the

FIG. 229.—Removal of slightly injured person by one bearer

patient's right arm and his body, he allows the patient's body to fall over his right shoulder upon his back, while the patient's right arm comes round the bearer's neck and is steadied temporarily by his left hand. Finally, the bearer, passing his right arm round one or both thighs of the patient, grasps the patient's right wrist with his right hand, and bringing the weight of the body well on to the centre of his own back, rises to the erect position.

II. BY TWO BEARERS WITH HAND SEATS.—If the patient is suffering from such a condition as an injured foot and is able to give some assistance, and if there are two bearers, the bearers divide his weight by means of one of the forms of hand seats, of which the two-handed seat is the most useful. If the patient be more seriously injured, some form of stretcher must be obtained or improvised as described below.

For the *two-handed seat* (Fig. 230) the bearers face one another, the one on the right interlocking the fingers of his right hand with those of the left hand of the other bearer; each places his disengaged hand behind the patient or on the other bearer's hip or shoulder. In lifting the patient, they kneel at his

FIG. 230.—Two-handed seat.

sides, each upon the knee nearest to his feet, and, forming the seat beneath his thighs, they rise together supporting him, while he assists if possible by putting his arms round their necks.

FIG. 231.—Three-handed seat.

For the *three-handed seat* (Fig. 231), the right-hand bearer grasps his own left forearm. The left-hand bearer places his right hand upon the shoulder of the other, and grasps the right forearm of the other with his left hand, his left forearm at the same time being grasped by the left hand of the other bearer.

For the *four-handed seat* (Fig. 232), each bearer grasps his own left wrist

478

with his right hand ; each then clasps the disengaged right wrist of the other with his left hand. To carry a patient by the three-handed or four-handed

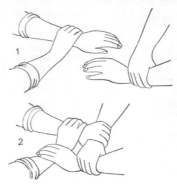

FIG. 232.—Four-handed seat. (1) Method of formation ; (2) seat ready.

seat the patient must stand up, and the bearers, stooping, form the seat behind him.

If a patient be absolutely helpless and it is urgently necessary to carry him quickly for a short distance only, the *fore-and-aft carry* may be used. One bearer stands at the patient's head and passes his hands behind the shoulders into the armpits, while the other bearer stands between the patient's legs facing towards his feet and takes one leg under each arm.

III. BY HELP OF A STRETCHER.—If the patient be unable to walk or to sit upright in the conditions above described, a stretcher must be obtained. If no regular canvas stretcher be at hand, a satisfactory one may be improvised from a pair of poles 6 or 7 feet in length and a couple of coats with the sleeves turned outside in. The coats are buttoned over the sleeves, through which the poles are then passed (Fig. 233). Or a blanket may be used, two poles, rifles, or similar objects being

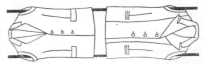

FIG. 233.—Stretcher improvised from poles and two coats.

laid upon it about 20 inches apart, and the ends and sides of the blanket being then successively folded over them (Fig. 234). Various other articles, such as a light sofa or a window-shutter, or a blanket supported by four people one at each corner, may also be used.

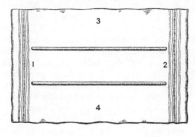

FIG. 234.—Stretcher improvised from poles and a blanket. The edges are turned over in the order marked.

The patient having received suitable first-aid treatment is lifted on to the stretcher as follows :

(a) *When there are four bearers* (referred to as Nos. 1, 2, 3, and 4), the first three place themselves on the left side of the patient, and No. 4 on his right ; No. 1 is opposite his knees, Nos. 2 and 4 are opposite his hips, and No. 3 is opposite his shoulders. All kneel on the left knee, facing the patient, and take hold of him as follows. No.1 passes his hands and forearms beneath the patient's legs, the hands wide apart. Nos. 2 and 4 pass their hands and forearms beneath the patient's hips and loins. No. 3 passes his left hand across the patient and under his right shoulder, the right hand beneath the left shoulder of the patient. All then lift the patient off the ground and rest him upon the right knees of Nos. 1, 2, and 3. No. 4 disengages, gets the stretcher, places it directly beneath the patient, and again assists in supporting him as he is lowered gently on to the stretcher. The patient is lifted off the stretcher in precisely the same way.

(b) *When only three bearers are available*, the stretcher is first placed at the patient's head in line with his body. No. 1, kneeling on the injured side in line with the patient's knees, raises and supports the lower limbs by passing his hands and forearms beneath them ; Nos. 2 and 3, kneeling upon opposite sides of the patient near his hips, pass one arm each under the back and one under the thighs, interlock fingers with one another, and so raise and support the patient. They then rise to their feet, carry him head first over the foot of the stretcher, and stooping, lay him gently upon it. In lifting him off they similarly raise him and carry him head first over the head of the stretcher.

(c) *When only two bearers are available*, the stretcher is first placed close to the patient's head and in line with his body. Both bearers then kneel on the injured side, and while No. 1 raises and supports the lower limbs by passing his hands and arms beneath them, No. 2 must place himself at the hips and raise the body, the patient assisting as much as possible by passing his arms round the neck of No. 2. The bearers then rise to their feet and carry the patient over the foot of the stretcher, on to which they gently lower him.

IV. REMOVAL BY CARTS.—If an ambulance waggon in which the patient lies upon the stretcher is not obtainable, a cart, well furnished with springs in order to diminish jolting, forms a good substitute. If the patient cannot sit, the floor of the cart should be deeply covered with straw or with a mattress. To place the stretcher in the cart, it should be raised by four bearers, one taking an end of each pole. The head end of the stretcher is then rested upon the floor of the cart, and two of the bearers get into the cart and assist the others in lifting the stretcher in. The patient may then either be lifted off on to the straw, etc., or may be left upon the stretcher.

INNOMINATE (*in*, neg. ; *nomen*, a name) is a term applied to the large flat bone which forms each side of the pelvis ; also to the large artery from which the right carotid and right subclavian arteries spring ; and also to the large vein formed on each side of the chest by the union of the internal jugular and subclavian veins.

INOCULATION (*in*, into ; *oculus*, a bud) is the process by which infective material is brought into the system

479

through a small wound in the skin or in a mucous membrane. Many infectious diseases and blood-poisoning are contracted by accidental inoculation of microbes. Inoculation is now used as a preventive measure against many infectious diseases. (*See* VACCINE.)

INOSITOL is one of the components of the vitamin B complex. Deficiency in mice produces baldness, but little is known yet about its rôle in human nutrition.

INSANITY (*see* MENTAL ILLNESS).

INSECTICIDES are substances which are fatal to insects. Since the discovery of the insecticidal properties of D.D.T. in 1940, a steady stream of new ones have been introduced, and their combined use has played an outstanding part in international public health campaigns, such as that of the World Health Organization for the eradication of malaria.

Unfortunately, insects are liable to become resistant to insecticides, just as bacteria are liable to become resistant to antibiotics, and it is for this reason that so much research work is being devoted to the discovery of new ones.

The following are some of the more common insecticides now in use, brief notes on which will be found under the name of the substance : benzene hexachloride, chlordane, D.D.T., dieldrin, parathion, malathion.

INSECTS IN RELATION TO DISEASE.—Many insects play an important part in the transmission of infectious diseases. Thus, flies by their feet and their feeding habits carry the organisms which cause typhoid fever, the tsetse fly spreads sleeping sickness, mosquitoes transmit the germs of malaria and yellow fever, fleas convey plague germs, and lice convey typhus fever and one form of relapsing fever. In addition, these creatures are nuisances as well as dangers.

HOUSE - FLY (*Musca domestica*). This fly lays its eggs in manure, or in moist, fermenting vegetable matter. The maggot is hatched within a day, feeds on the manure, etc., passes through the pupa stage in little more than a week, and, becoming a fly, is capable of egg-laying about fourteen to twenty days

from its own appearance as an egg. As 120 to 150 eggs are laid by each female fly, this fly is capable, under the most favourable conditions, of producing between twenty - five and fifty million progeny within two months. The fly gorges on fluid food which it sucks up by means of its proboscis, and it has the habit of repeatedly vomiting and re-swallowing the contents of its crop as it feeds. It walks in filth habitually, and being provided with hairy legs and body it is apt to carry off portions of this, in which are entangled numbers of bacteria. The fly has been well described as a ' winged sponge ', and its immense power to distribute disease germs over the surface of uncovered food is evident.

BLOW - FLY or **BLUE - BOTTLE** (*Calliphora erythrocephala*) lays its eggs (450 to 600 in number) on meat, fish, or decaying animal matter. The maggot hatches out within a day, passes through the pupa stage and becomes a full-grown fly in about three weeks. Its habits are similar to those of the house-fly, though in numbers it is much less plentiful.

Treatment of flies.—The most important measure is to destroy their breeding grounds near human dwellings. All kitchen refuse must be burned, and none should be left exposed so that flies may deposit their eggs in it. Stable litter and manure must be disposed of, or kept covered and shut up in outhouses, not allowed to accumulate in the open air and sunshine near houses. Adult flies may be destroyed to a great extent by covering all food in summer with muslin or wire gauze, and by exposing sticky fly-papers or fly-traps in kitchens or other places where flies are numerous. D.D.T. (*q.v.*), which may be used as a powder, a spray, or a paint, has established itself as a most efficient means of treatment, but care must be exercised that it does not come in contact with food.

LICE.—The presence of the head-louse (*Pediculus capitis*) and of the crab-louse (*Pediculus pubis*) is comparatively easily prevented by the methods described under PARASITES. The body-louse (*Pediculus vestimentorum*) is much more difficult to banish. The lice suck blood from their ' host ' once or twice daily ; and, if they do not get food, they die in three to five days. The female produces five eggs daily for about twenty-five days, laying them in folds and seams of the clothing next the skin. The young lice are hatched in one to five weeks and mature so rapidly that the time for a new generation from egg to egg is about twenty-four days.

Treatment of lice.—For the body-louse, merely laying aside the clothes for a week kills all the adults, but not the eggs ; baking of the clothes in a disinfector or laying them aside for two months destroys life in the latter also, but this is not always easy to carry out. Many remedies have been used in the treatment of louse infestation of the head—paraffin, cresol solution, sassafras, alcohol ; but they are volatile and do not kill the nits. Attempts have been made to find a substance which will not only kill the lice but will also remain in the hair long enough to kill any lice that will hatch out of the nits later. Four have been found to meet the requirement : namely, (1) 25 per cent. technical lauryl thiocyanate in a white oil ; (2) 50 per cent. lethane 384 special in a white oil ; (3) derris cream ; and (4) 2½ per cent. D.D.T. emulsion. For removing nits a special steel nit comb—'Sacker's' or 'Binn's' —is used.

FLEAS (*Pulex irritans*) and **BED-BUGS** (*Cimex lectularius*).—For eradica-

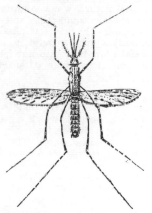

Fig. 235.—*Anopheles gambiæ.* The most dangerous malaria-carrier in Africa. (From Manson's *Tropical Diseases.* Cassell & Co. Ltd.)

tion of fleas a 10 per cent. D.D.T. powder is eminently satisfactory, but

16

for the disinfestation of buildings the addition of pyrethrum improves the results. For the destruction of bed-bugs an emulsion or solution of 5 per cent. D.D.T. in kerosene is used. This is used in the form of a spray, and 100 millilitres is sufficient for a bed (including mattress, springs, and frame), whilst three gallons are sufficient to treat the beds and walls of a barrack for 74 men.

MOSQUITOES.—One of these (*Anopheles gambiæ*) is responsible for conveying the parasite of malaria (Fig. 235), another (*Aëdes egypti*) for distributing the infection of yellow fever (Fig. 236).

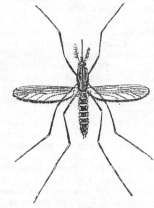

Fig. 236.—*Aëdes egypti* (female). The transmitter of yellow fever and dengue. (From Manson's *Tropical Diseases.* Cassell & Co. Ltd.)

Treatment.—*See under* MALARIA *and* YELLOW FEVER.

INSOLATION (*insolo*, I expose to the sun) is a term applied both to treatment by exposure to the sun's rays (*see* LIGHT TREATMENT) and to fever caused by excessive heat (*see* SUNSTROKE).

INSOMNIA (*see* SLEEP, HYPNOTICS).

INSPISSATION (*inspissatio*) is a term applied to the process of drying or thickening fluids or excretions by evaporation.

INSUFFLATION (*insufflatio*, a blowing in) means the blowing of powder or vapour into a cavity, especially through the air passages, for the treatment of disease.

INSULIN (*insula*, an island) is the name applied to the internal secretion of the pancreas formed by groups of cells called the 'islands of Langerhans' in this organ. Its existence was indicated by Schafer in 1909, and it was successfully isolated in a pure form by McLeod, Banting, and Best in 1921. It acts by enabling the muscles and other tissues which require sugar for their activity to take up this substance from the blood. When it is deficient, the sugar derived from the food accumulates in the blood and is wastefully excreted in the urine. Insulin prepared from the pancreas of sheep and oxen is administered by hypodermic injection in cases of diabetes, and thus enables the sugar in the circulation to be utilized so that its excretion in the urine ceases. Each unit of insulin administered to a diabetic patient enables him to utilize somewhere between one and two grammes of additional carbohydrate material. The appropriate dose of insulin in any given case depends upon its severity.

There are now seven forms of insulin available in Great Britain : insulin ; protamine zinc insulin ; globin insulin ; isophane insulin ; insulin zinc suspension ; insulin zinc suspension (amorphous) ; insulin zinc suspension (crystalline). The essential difference between them lies in the duration of their action.

INTELLIGENCE QUOTIENT, or I.Q. as it is usually known, is the ratio between the mental age and chronological age multiplied by 100. Thus, if a boy of 10 years of age is found to have a mental age of 12 years, his I.Q. will be :

$$\frac{12}{10} \times 100 = 120.$$

On the other hand, if he is found to have a mental age of 8 years his I.Q. will be :

$$\frac{8}{10} \times 100 = 80.$$

The mental age is established by various tests, the most widely used of which are the Stanford-Binet Scale, the Wechseer Adult Intelligence Scale, and the Mill Hill Vocabulary Test.

Average intelligence is represented by an I.Q. of 100, with a range of 85 to 115. For practical purposes it is taken that the intellectual level reached by the average 15-year-old is indistinguishable from that of an adult.

INTERCOSTAL (*inter*, between ; *costa*, a rib) is the term applied to the nerves, vessels, and muscles that lie between the ribs, as well as to diseases affecting these structures.

INTERCURRENT (*intercurrens*, running between) is a term applied to one disease which occurs during the course of another disease already present, and modifies its course or increases its severity.

INTERFERON.—It has been known for over a quarter of a century that one virus will interfere with the growth of another. In 1957, workers at the National Institute for Medical Research, in London, isolated the factor that was responsible for this interfering of one virus with another. They gave it the name of interferon. The precise nature of interferon is not yet known, but it is known to be a protein. Its practical interest lies in the possibility that it may prove to be a useful method of treating diseases caused by viruses.

INTERMITTENT (*intermitto*, I leave off) is a term applied generally to fevers of malarial nature, which continue for a time, subside completely, and then return again. The name is also used in connection with a pulse in which occasional heart-beats are not felt, in consequence of irregular action of the heart.

INTERMITTENT CLAUDICATION is a condition occurring in middle-aged and elderly people, which is characterized by pain in the legs after walking a certain distance. The pain is relieved by resting for a short time. It is due to arteriosclerosis (*see* ARTERIES, DISEASES OF) of the arteries to the leg, which results in inadequate blood supply to the muscles.

INTERSTITIAL (*interstitialis*) is a term applied to indifferent tissue set amongst the proper active tissue of an organ. It is generally of a supporting character and formed of fibrous tissue.

The term is also applied to diseases which specially affect this tissue, as interstitial keratitis.

INTERTRIGO (*inter*, between ; *tero*, I rub) is a term applied to a chafed or abraded condition between two surfaces of skin that rub together, *e.g.* under the breast or in the armpit. (*See* CHAFING OF THE SKIN.)

INTESTINAL STASIS (*see* STASIS *and* CONSTIPATION).

INTESTINE (*intestinus*, that which is within) is the whole of the alimentary canal situated below the stomach. In it the chief part of digestion is carried on, and through its walls all the food material is absorbed into the blood and

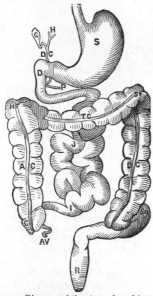

FIG. 237.—Diagram of the stomach and intestines. *S*, Stomach ; *D*, duodenum, *J*, jejunum, and *I*, ileum, together forming the small intestine ; *AV*, appendix, *C*, cæcum, *AC*, ascending colon, *HF*, hepatic flexure, *TC*, transverse colon, *SF*, splenic flexure, *DC*, descending colon, *Sg*, sigmoid flexure, *R*, rectum, together forming the large intestine ; *G*, gall-bladder ; *H*, hepatic ducts ; *DC*, common bile-duct ; *P*, pancreatic duct. (*Ency. Brit.*)

lymph streams. (*See* DIGESTION.) The length of the intestine in man is about 28 to 30 feet (8·5 to 9 metres), and it takes the form of one continuous tube suspended in loops in the abdominal cavity

Divisions.—The intestine is divided into small intestine and large intestine (Fig. 237). The former comprises that part of the tube which extends from the stomach onwards for 22 feet (6·5 metres) or thereabout, and is at its broadest point about 1½ inches (37 mm.) in width. The large intestine is the second part of the tube, and though shorter (about 6 feet (1·8 metres) in length) is much wider than the small intestine, reaching in places a size of 2½ inches (63 mm). The *small intestine* is divided rather arbitrarily into three parts—the *duodenum*, consisting of the first 10 or 12 inches (25 or 30 cm.), into which the ducts of the liver and pancreas open ; the *jejunum*, which is generally found empty after death, and comprises the next 8 or 9 feet (2·4 or 2·7 metres) ; and finally the *ileum*, which at its lower end opens into the large intestine.

The *large intestine* begins in the lower part of the abdomen on the right side. As the small intestine opens into its side a few inches from the end, a cul-de-sac, known as the *cæcum*, lies here, into which the *appendix vermiformis* opens (Fig. 238). The appendix is

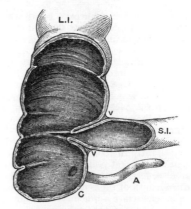

FIG. 238.—Part of the intestine situated in the right iliac region. The front of the bowel has been removed to show the interior. *A*, Appendix ; *C*, cæcum ; *LI*, continuation of large intestine ; *SI*, small intestine ; *VV*, the two flaps of the ileo-cæcal valve which prevent the return of digested material from the large into the small intestine. (After Gegenbaur.)

a small tube, about the thickness of a quill, from 2 to 6 inches (50 to 150 mm.) in length, which has much the same structure as the rest of the intestine. At one end it is closed, at the other it opens into the cæcum, and although it appears to play little or no part in digestion, it is of great importance because of the frequency with which serious inflammation takes place in it. (*See* APPENDICITIS.) The cæcum is continued into the colon, which first ascends through the right flank to

membrane, beneath which is a loose network of connective tissue and muscular fibres, richly supplied with blood-vessels and lymphatic-vessels. There are two arrangements by which the surface in the small intestine is much increased for the ends of digestion and absorption. Countless ridges with deep furrows between them run across the upper part, and the whole surface is thickly studded

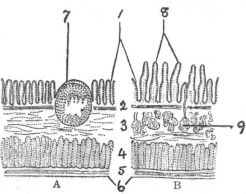

FIG. 239.—Diagrammatic representation of intestine. A, large intestine (magnified 15 times, B, duodenum (magnified 12 times). 1, Lieberkühn's glands ; 2, muscularis mucosæ ; 3, submucous coat ; 4, circular muscles ; 5, longitudinal muscles ; 6, peritoneum ; 7, solitary follicles ; 8, villi ; 9, Brunner's gland. (From Blacklock and Southwell, *A Guide to Human Parasitology*. H. K. Lewis & Co. Ltd.)

beneath the liver, where it bends and crosses the upper part of the abdomen transversely to the left side ; here, coming in contact with the spleen, it again bends downwards and descends through the left flank into the pelvis. The last part of the large intestine is known as the *rectum*, which passes straight down through the back part of the pelvis, to open to the exterior through the *anus*.

Structure.—The intestine, both small and large, consists of four coats, which vary slightly in structure and arrangement at different points, but are of the same general nature throughout the entire length of the bowel. There is on the inner surface a mucous membrane ; outside this is a loose submucous coat, in which blood-vessels run ; next comes a muscular coat in two layers ; and finally a tough, thin peritoneal membrane. The total thickness of all four coats amounts to about one-eighth of an inch.

MUCOUS COAT.—The interior of the bowel is completely lined by a single layer of pillar-like cells placed side by side. These rest upon a smooth, fine

with short hair-like processes called villi (Fig. 239). As blood- and lymph-vessels run up to the end of these villi, the digested food passing slowly down the intestine is brought into very close relation with the circulation. Between the bases of the villi are set little openings, each of which leads into a simple, tubular gland lined by cells, which are similar to those covering the surface, and which produce a fluid with digestive powers. In the small intestine, cells here and there produce mucus, and, in the large intestine, a great number of cells are devoted to the production of this substance for lubricating the passage of the food through the bowel. A large number of minute masses, called ' lymph follicles ', similar in structure to the tonsils and lymphatic glands, are scattered over the inner surface of the intestine. In the lower part of the small intestine these are grouped into patches of a square inch or thereabout in size, known as Peyer's patches, which are of special interest, because the inflammation and ulceration of the bowels that occur in typhoid fever is limited to them and to the scattered follicles. The large intestine is bare both of ridges and of villi, and, as already stated, its mucous membrane produces mucus in large amount.

SUBMUCOUS COAT.—This consists of a loose connective tissue which allows the mucous membrane to play freely over the muscular coat. The blood-vessels and lymphatic-vessels which absorb the food in the villi pour their contents into a network of large vessels lying in this coat.

MUSCULAR COAT.—The muscle in the small intestine is arranged in two definite layers, in the outer of which all the fibres run lengthwise with the bowel, whilst in the inner they pass circularly round it. The muscular coat is of immense importance, because by its contraction and relaxation, somewhat after the mode of progression of a worm, the food is slowly squeezed down the bowel, the process being known as 'peristalsis'. In the large intestine the only departure from the above arrangement is that the fibres which are placed lengthwise are collected into three thick bands upon the outward surface of the bowel, and these bands, being slightly shorter than the other coats of the bowel, cause it to present a puckered appearance.

PERITONEAL COAT forms the outer covering for almost the whole intestine except parts of the duodenum and of the large intestine. It is a tough, fibrous membrane, covered upon its outer surface with a smooth layer of cells, which in the movements of the bowel rub against a similar surface upon the peritoneum lining the general cavity of the abdomen, and so cause a minimum of friction. From the peritoneal coat of the intestine of animals catgut is prepared.

Support.—The duodenum and greater part of the large intestine are covered only in front by the peritoneum which lines the abdominal cavity, and this tough membrane serves to bind these parts of the intestine firmly against the back wall of the abdomen. The jejunum and ileum, the transverse part of the colon, and the first part of the rectum are not only completely surrounded by peritoneum, but a double layer of this membrane suspends these parts of the bowel at a distance of several inches from the lines on the back of the

abdomen, where the two layers become continuous with the rest of the peritoneum. In this way freedom is given to the movements of these parts of the bowels. These suspending structures are known as ' mesenteries '. That of the small intestine is the largest, being shaped like a fan, 6 inches (150 mm.) long at its attached margin, and spreading out to 22 feet (6·5 metres) at its frilled border, where it meets the intestine. The vessels and nerves which supply the intestine run between the two layers of the mesentery.

INTESTINE, DISEASES OF.—The principal signs of trouble which has its origin in the intestines consist of pain somewhere about the abdomen, sometimes vomiting, and irregularity in movement of the bowels in the direction either of stoppage or of excessive action.

Several diseases are treated under separate headings. *See* APPENDICITIS, CHOLERA, CONCRETIONS, CONSTIPATION, DIARRHŒA, DYSENTERY, ENTERIC FEVER, HERNIA, ILEITIS, PARASITES, PERITONITIS, PILES; RECTUM, DISEASES OF.

INFLAMMATION of the bowel may affect either its outer or its inner surface. The outer surface is covered by peritoneum, and peritonitis is a serious disease (*see* PERITONITIS). Inflammation of the inner surface is known generally as ' enteritis ', inflammations of special parts receiving the names of ' colitis ', ' appendicitis ', etc. Enteritis may form the chief symptom of certain infective diseases due to special organisms, for example in typhoid fever, cholera, dysentery. Again, it may be acute, though not connected with any definite organism, when, if severe, it is a very serious condition, particularly in young children. Or it may be chronic, especially as the result of dysentery, and produces then a less serious though very troublesome complaint. Indiscretions in diet, such as the eating of unripe fruit, are a common cause. A very serious type results from the action of irritant poisons. In some persons inflammation of the stomach and bowels is liable to result from expresou to cold and damp.

Symptoms.—Diarrhœa is the most common and most marked symptom, and in chronic cases usually the only symptom, although, when the small intestine alone is affected, constipation is a more usual result than diarrhœa. Pain, particularly of a griping nature, which comes and goes, is also common. The temperature in acute cases is raised, and there is restlessness, even delirium. If the diarrhœa is very profuse, collapse speedily comes on.

Treatment. — Each case requires special handling, according to the cause and the severity. Where diarrhœa is very severe this requires special treatment (*see* DIARRHŒA). There are a few general principles which are applicable to all cases. The diet should be light, bland, non-irritating and containing a minimum of roughage. In more acute cases only milk and glucose drinks should be given for the first twenty-four hours. If there is much diarrhœa ample fluids should be given to prevent dehydration. Rest in bed is essential. Considerable quantities of warm water, containing bicarbonate of soda, have a beneficial action by flushing out the bowel and removing irritating substances. In general, water is given by the mouth, and in some cases it is introduced by an enema to irrigate the lower bowel. Various drugs which have a mildly astringent and soothing action, of which the chief are carbonate of bismuth and kaolin, are given by the mouth. When the 'inflammation' is not the result of a chemical or physical irritant, but the result of an infection, as in dysentery, treatment with a sulphonamide drug absorbed only slowly from the intestine is indicated. Sulphaguanidine and succinyl sulphathiazole have proved particularly useful in the treatment of dysentery. In acute cases of inflammation various applications are made to the surface of the abdomen in order to exert a soothing effect. The most common are hot fomentations, to which laudanum, turpentine, or other substances have been added.

ULCERATION of the bowels arises in a manner similar to the production of ulcers on the skin surface, although probably these internal ulcers heal much more rapidly than others. Typhoid fever regularly produces ulcers in the lower part of the small intestine, this variety arising in the patches of lymphatic tissue found in this region.

486

Tuberculous ulcers arise late in the course of tuberculosis, and produce a diarrhœa which is always a serious sign. Ulceration also occurs in amœbic dysentery.

Symptoms of ulceration are much the same as those of enteritis, and the formation of ulcers is simply an advanced stage of this condition. In addition, the ulcerated surface is apt to bleed, and, if the ulcer be situated high up in the bowel, this blood is voided as black or brown material; if it comes from near the lower end of the bowel the blood is red and unchanged. The healing of these ulcers leads, in the case of all save those of typhoid fever, to the formation of scars, and, as these scars contract there is a tendency to narrowing of the bowel and obstruction. This is particularly apt to follow tuberculous ulcers, if these should heal, because they often run circularly round the inside of the bowel.

Treatment in cases of ulceration is similar to that for inflammation.

PERFORATION of the bowel may take place as the result either of injury or of disease. Stabs and other wounds which penetrate the abdomen may damage the bowel, and severe blows or crushes may tear it without any external wound. Ulceration, as in enteric fever, or, more rarely, in tuberculosis, may cause an opening in the bowel-wall also. Again, when the bowel is greatly distended above an obstruction, fæcal material may accumulate and produce ulcers, which rupture with the ordinary movements of the bowels. Whatever be the cause, the symptoms are much the same.

Symptoms. — The contents of the bowel pass out through the perforation into the peritoneal cavity, and, making their way between the coils of intestine, set up a general peritonitis. In consequence, the abdomen is painful, and after a few hours becomes extremely tender to the touch, as a result of the peritonitis. The abdomen swells, particularly in its upper part, owing to gas having passed also into the cavity. Vomiting is a symptom, and the person passes into a state of collapse. Such a condition is almost invariably fatal in two, or at most three, days, if not promptly treated. Occasionally, however, the perforation is preceded by a certain amount of peritonitis, which forms adhesions in the neighbourhood of the ulcerated part, so that when perforation finally takes place a localized abscess, instead of general peritonitis, may result, and the person may recover.

Treatment.—All food should be withheld, because whatever is taken into the stomach is either vomited or is liable to pass out of the perforation into the peritoneal cavity. An operation is urgently necessary, the abdomen being opened in the middle line, the perforated portion of bowel found, and the perforation stitched up. If the bowel be damaged badly, a part is often cut out and the divided ends joined together. Finally, the peritoneal cavity is thoroughly washed out, and a drainage tube left for some days in the abdominal wound. The local application of penicillin or sulphonamides to the peritoneum during operation has effected a marked reduction in the mortality rate.

OBSTRUCTION of the bowels means a stoppage to the passage down the intestine of the partially digested food. Obstruction may be due either to some cause within the abdomen or to the thrusting of a loop of bowel through an opening in the wall of this cavity. The latter class of cases has been referred to under HERNIA. Obstruction may be acute when it comes on suddenly with intense symptoms, or it may be chronic, when the obstructing cause gradually increases and the bowel becomes slowly more narrow till it closes altogether, or when slight obstruction comes and goes till it ends in an acute attack. In chronic cases the symptoms are much the same as those of the acute variety, although they are milder in degree and more prolonged.

Causes.—Obstruction may be due to causes outside the bowel altogether, for example, the pressure of tumours in neighbouring organs, the twisting round the bowel of bands produced by former peritonitis, or even the twisting of a coil of intestine round itself so as to cause a kink in its wall. Chronic and partial forms of obstruction are sometimes due to such kinks near the end of the small intestine, sometimes to the pressure of the mesentery on the upper end of the small intestine. Chronic causes of the obstruction may exist in the wall of the bowel itself, for example, a tumour, or the contracting scar of an old ulcer. The condition of 'intussusception', where part of the bowel passes inside of the part beneath it, in the same way as one turns the finger of a glove outside in, causes obstruction and other symptoms. Finally some body, such as a concretion, or the stone of some large fruit, or even a mass of hardened fæces, may become jammed within the bowel and stop up its passage.

Symptoms.—There are four chief symptoms of this condition, and any case in which these are combined demands immediate treatment. These are pain, vomiting, constipation, and swelling of the abdomen. The *pain* is of a griping character, and may be very severe although it comes and goes, getting now stronger and again for a time less marked. When the small intestine is the seat of obstruction the pain is almost always referred to the region round the navel; when the large intestine is affected the pain may be more accurately referred to the part from which it arises. In addition to this, acute cases are marked by great tenderness of the abdomen to touch. The *vomiting* is peculiar in character. It begins with the first onset of pain, and consists of the contents of the stomach. Later it is yellow or green, bitter, and contains much bile, while, after several hours have elapsed, it becomes brown and ill-smelling, and is then known as 'fæcal vomiting'. The *constipation* in acute cases comes on suddenly, whilst in chronic cases it may be preceded by a state in which constipation and diarrhœa alternate, or by one in which the stools gradually get smaller and smaller in size, possibly over a period lasting for several months. In chronic cases of obstruction to the large intestine, it is not uncommon for the sufferer to possess a constant desire to go to stool with straining pain, although he can pass nothing (tenesmus). In some conditions, particularly that due to intussusception, though there is constipation in the ordinary sense, the excessive straining produces a copious discharge of blood-stained mucus. The *swelling of the abdomen* varies in different cases. In acute cases the whole belly is blown up with gas, much increasing the pain of the condition. The constipation is so complete as to prevent even flatus from being passed—a very important sign of its gravity. Another grave sign is the absence of the sounds of intestinal movement which can be heard in auscultation over the normal abdomen. In chronic cases, in which the wall of the intestine is thickened, individual loops stand out now and then and become visible on the surface in their attempts to force their contents past the obstruction. When the small intestine is affected, its loops stand out one over the other, resembling the rungs of a ladder ; whilst obstruction low down in the large intestine causes a bulging in the flanks and across the upper part of the abdomen.

In addition to these abdominal symptoms there is generally, in the later stages, collapse, although consciousness is retained till the end. If the condition be not relieved by operation, death almost always results ; in acute cases, in the course of three to six days.

Treatment.—As a rule the surgeon opens the abdomen, finds the obstruction and relieves it or if possible removes it altogether. The task of the surgeon is rendered specially hard by the difficulty of determining, before he opens the abdomen, where the obstruction is, by the fact that the intestine is inflamed, and by its distension with gas and fæces. He has generally to open the abdomen in the middle line, examine the usual sites of obstruction, and, failing to find any cause at these points, to pass the whole length of intestine carefully through his hands till he finds the obstruction. Even after this is found, if it be of the nature of a tumour, it may be impossible of removal. If the obstruction be successfully removed, something must next be done, by puncturing the bowel or other means, to relieve the collection of gas and fæces, and this adds to the operation the great risk of sepsis. The introduction of the sulphonamides and antibiotics, however, has diminished this risk considerably. In all these manipulations care must be taken, by warm towels and the like, to prevent unnecessary exposure and chilling of the bowel.

488

INTIMA is the innermost coat lining the arteries and the veins.

INTOXICATION is a term applied to states of poisoning. The poison may be some chemical substance introduced from outside, *e.g.* alcohol (*see* ALCOHOLISM), or it may be due to the products of bacterial action, the bacteria either being introduced from outside or developing within the body. The term ' auto-intoxication ' is applied in the latter case.

INTRACRANIAL (*intra*, within ; *cranium*, the skull) is the term applied to structures, diseases, etc., contained in or rising within the head.

INTRATHECAL means within the membranes or meninges which envelop the spinal cord. The intrathecal space, between the arachnoid and the pia mater, contains the cerebrospinal fluid.

INTROSPECTION (*intro*, within ; *spicio*, I look) is a term applied to observation of one's own thoughts or feelings. It is generally applied to this process when it occurs to an abnormal extent in association with melancholia.

INTUBATION is a simple operation, consisting in the introduction, through the mouth into the larynx, of a tube designed to keep the air passage open at this point. The procedure is employed chiefly in cases of diphtheria (*see* DIPHTHERIA).

INTUSSUSCEPTION (*intus*, within ; *suscipio*, I receive) is a form of obstruction of the bowels in which part of the intestine enters within that part immediately beneath it. This can best be understood by observing what takes place in the fingers of a tightly fitting glove as they turn outside in when the glove is pulled off the hand. The persons affected are almost always young children, and the condition follows severe purging, injury of the abdomen, or the eating of indigestible substances. The point at which it most frequently occurs is the junction between the small and the large intestines, the former passing within the latter. The symptoms are those of intestinal obstruction in general, and in addition there is often a discharge of blood-stained mucus from the bowel. The treatment consists—unless the symptoms rapidly subside, when it may be assumed that the bowel has righted itself—of an operation in which the surgeon opens the abdomen and removes the inner piece of intestine from that into which it has passed. The condition is an extremely grave one.

INUNCTION (*in*, into ; *unguo*, I anoint) is a method of administering drugs by rubbing them into the skin mixed with oil or fat. The method is not often used now.

IN VITRO is a term commonly used in medical research and experimental biology. Literally 'in a glass', it refers to observations made outside the body —*e.g.* on the action of drugs on bacteria. The opposite term is IN VIVO, which refers to observations of processes in the body.

INVOLUCRUM is the term applied to the sheath of new bone which is formed round a piece of dead bone in, for example, osteomyelitis.

INVOLUTION is the term which describes the process of change whereby the uterus returns to its resting size after parturition. The term is also applied to any retrograde biological change, as in senility.

IODIDES are salts of iodine ; those which are especially used in medicine being the iodide of potassium and iodide of sodium.

Action.—Iodides have a threefold action. They are excreted in the mucous secretions, as well as in the urine, saliva, and sweat, and have an action in liquefying the mucus secretion of the bronchial tree. They are therefore widely used in expectorant mixtures. Their second action is in assisting to absorb diseased tissue, particularly in syphilis. Finally, they are used to assist in providing a supply of iodine in patients with goitre, or in individuals who live in an area where goitre is liable to occur because of a deficiency of iodine in the drinking water.

Over-dosage of iodides results in iodism (*q.v.*).

16 *a*

Uses.—At one time the chief use of the drug was to cause absorption of the unhealthy tissues in syphilis, upon which it acted with great rapidity when taken into the system. It is used for a similar reason in chronic forms of rheumatism. Iodides are given in chronic lead-poisoning, because they dissolve the lead deposited in the tissues and so permit of its excretion from the body. They are also a common constituent of expectorant mixtures. Iodide is administered over long periods in small doses to children living in districts where goitre is common, with the object of preventing the onset of this disease.

IODINE is a non-metallic element which is found largely in seaweed. It is prepared in the form of dark violet-brown scales. It has a pleasantly pungent smell and a burning taste. It has a highly irritating action and when applied to the skin, stains the latter dark brown and causes it to peel off in flakes, while internally it is a violent irritant poison in large doses.

Uses.—Externally iodine is used as a counter-irritant. (*See* BLISTERS AND COUNTER-IRRITANTS.) For this purpose the strong liquor of iodine (10 per cent.) is commonly used if a few applications are to be made ; or, if repeated applications are to be made for some time, the weak liquor of iodine (2½ per cent. strength) is employed. One or other of these preparations is often used to paint over glands enlarged by various causes, in order to bring about their decrease in size. The disadvantage of iodine is that it is 'fixed' by protein and so is rendered less effective as an antiseptic for open wounds. For its antiseptic properties it is used to sterilize the skin by painting over the surface before surgical operations. The weak liquor is used as a preventive of chilblains, applied while the hands are still red before the skin has begun to crack.

In the form of Mandl's paint (*i.e.* dissolved with potassium iodide in glycerin) iodine is a useful remedy in inflammatory conditions of the throat and tonsils. Small doses of the weak liquor (2 to 5 drops) often control vomiting when other measures fail ; for this purpose it is usually given in milk. Iodine—often as Lugol's iodine (5 per cent. iodine and 10 per cent. potassium iodide in water)—is given internally in the treatment of goitre, especially before the operation of thyroidectomy for Graves' disease.

The weak liquor of iodine was formerly called weak tincture of iodine. Both this and the strong liquor of iodine contain potassium iodide. There is also a simple liquor of iodine of 10 per cent. strength, also known as French tincture of iodine, containing iodine dissolved in strong alcohol only ; it is given in doses of 3 to 15 drops, usually in milk.

IODISM.—This is the condition which is produced by an over-dose of iodides. In some susceptible individuals iodism may be produced by very small amounts of iodides. It is characterized by running of the eyes and nose, sore throat, a heavy, dull feeling over the eyes, increased secretion of saliva, and a typical skin eruption. These manifestations usually disappear rapidly upon the drug being withdrawn.

IODOFORM is a mild antiseptic made by the action of iodine upon a mixture of alcohol and potash. It has a most penetrating, rather pleasant odour and strong taste. It relieves pain when applied to a raw or mucous surface, and has the property of preventing putrefaction when brought in contact with discharges. When applied in large quantities to a raw surface it is apt to be absorbed and to cause symptoms of poisoning, consisting of a red rash over the body, fever, loss of appetite, and, it may be, delirium.

Uses.—Because of its combined analgesic and antiseptic properties, it is a useful application for ulcers and granulating wounds. In the form of ' Bipp ' (*q.v.*) it was a popular wound dressing in the 1914–18 War. It is also sometimes used as an insufflation in the treatment of ozæna and ulcers of the mouth.

IODOPHTHALEIN is the sodium salt of tetra-iodophenolphthalein, a bluish-violet crystalline powder. As it is excreted quickly by the liver, collects in the gall-bladder and casts

a shadow with X-rays, it is administered by the mouth or by intravenous injection for the diagnosis of disease of the gall-bladder by means of X-ray photography.

IODOXYL is the *British Pharmacopœia* name for a complicated organic compound containing 51·5 per cent. of iodine used for contrast radiography of the kidney passages. The preparation is injected into a vein, and, as it is excreted through the kidney and is opaque to X-rays, it will, on radiography, reveal abnormalities of the urinary tract.

ION EXCHANGE RESINS are synthetic organic substances which have the power of exchanging ions. Chemically, they are closely related to plastics. They are divided into two groups : *cation exchange resins*, which take up and liberate cations, *e.g.* sodium, potassium, hydrogen ions ; *anion exchange resins*, which take up and liberate anions, *e.g.* chloride, hydroxyl ions. The former are now being used in the treatment of œdema, and the latter in the treatment of peptic ulcers.

IONIZATION (ἰών, going) means the breaking up of a substance in solution into its constituent ions.

IONTOPHORESIS is the process by which various substances are made to pass through the skin into the underlying tissues by means of the electric current. This is also called iontherapy, galvano-ionization, and medical ionization. Only those drugs can be used for ionization which are soluble in water and can be dissociated when dissolved. These are known as electrolytes, and include inorganic salts and similar organic compounds such as salts of the alkaloids and salts of organic acids like salicylate of soda. The form of electricity used for ionization is the continuous current, and high currents of 50, 60, or more milliamperes are employed, large electrodes being used so as to distribute the electricity over a wide area. Applications last from fifteen minutes to half an hour, and great care must be taken to avoid irregularities or interruptions of the current during the applications. In order to avoid burning or blistering the skin, as well as to maintain a supply of the solution which it is desired to introduce, the electrodes consist of large brass, aluminium, or silver plates covered with thick layers of lint, cotton, or felt. Any tender areas in the skin are protected from the electrode by small pieces of rubber plaster, and care must be taken to turn off the current gradually. The drugs mostly in use for introduction are chlorides of sodium, ammonium, and lithium, salicylate of soda, sulphate of zinc, iodides of potassium and lithium, sulphate of quinine, and hydrochloride of cocaine. Of these, the most frequently used drug is salicylate of soda for its action in the treatment of neuritis, rheumatic affections, lumbago, and certain skin diseases. Sulphate of zinc is also used for the treatment of ulcers, infected wounds, and similar conditions where an antiseptic and astringent action is desired.

IPECACUANHA, Ipecac, or Hippo, is the root of *Cephaëlis Ipecacuanha*, a Brazilian shrub. It contains an alkaloid 'emetine' which acts as an irritant when brought in contact with the interior of the stomach, producing vomiting. This effect is also brought about after its absorption into the blood by its action on the vomiting centre in the brain. In small doses it acts, not as an irritant, but as a gentle stimulant to the mucous membrane of stomach, bowels, and respiratory passages. Emetine is also a specific for amœbic dysentery.

Uses.—Ipecacuanha is a constituent of many expectorant mixtures given in the treatment of bronchitis. It is of value in this connection because of its action in liquefying the thick mucous secretion which occurs in bronchitis. It is also a constituent of Dover's Powder (*q.v.*), which is one of the most efficient diaphoretics for use in febrile conditions, such as the common cold.

In the treatment of amœbic dysentery ipecacuanha is now largely replaced by emetine, as a more certain action can be obtained with emetine. Occasionally, however, it is found advisable to combine intramuscular injections of emetine with the administration of ipecacuanha by mouth.

IPRONIAZID is a drug which inhibits monoamine oxidase (*q.v.*) an enzyme which plays an important part in the metabolism of the brain. It was originally introduced into medicine for the treatment of tuberculosis. It proved too toxic for this purpose, however. It is now being used in the treatment of depressive states.

IRIDECTOMY (ἴρις, a halo ; ἐκ, out ; τέμνω, I cut) means an operation by which a piece is removed from the iris, and the pupil of the eye is thereby increased in size.

IRIDENCLEISIS is the term for describing the condition in which the iris is caught in a small gaping wound of the cornea.

IRIS (ἴρις, a halo) is the muscular and fibrous curtain which hangs behind the cornea and serves, by alteration of the size of the 'pupil' or round hole in its centre, to regulate the amount of light entering into the eye. (*See* Eye.)

IRISH MOSS (*see* Carrageen).

IRITIS means inflammation of the iris. Inflammation of the iris is very closely associated both in cause and in symptoms with inflammation in the ciliary body and choroid membrane, which, together with the iris, make up the middle coat of the eyeball.

Varieties and causes.—It is not a common condition in young children, and, when it occurs in them, is associated generally with ulcers of the cornea. Most of the cases are found in young adults, and about half of all such cases are due to syphilis. Indeed iritis, accompanied by inflammation of the cornea or of the choroid coat, is the usual cause of the serious impairment in vision which is apt to ensue from this disease. Chronic rheumatism and the presence of local inflammatory troubles, such as dental abscesses and suppurative conditions of the nose, form the cause in the majority of the remaining cases, although the disease, in occasional instances, appears during the course of fevers and in persons suffering from diabetes.

An important form of inflammation

of the eye commencing in the iris and ciliary body of one eye, as the result of a wound received by the other eye, is known as 'sympathetic iritis'. This form of inflammation seldom starts, save as the result of an open wound in the ciliary region, or of one caused by a foreign body which enters and remains in the eye. Formerly it was supposed that the damaged eye exerted upon the other one an irritating influence through their nervous connections ; now it is generally held that the inflammation is due to organisms which enter by the wound, cause inflammation of the damaged eye, and then infect the other eye either by the lymph spaces which connect the two, or indirectly through the blood. For this reason, when an eye has received a severe penetrating wound, and when it is sightless, inflamed, and painful, it should be removed to avoid the risk of sympathetic trouble in the sound eye.

Symptoms.—The most marked symptom is pain situated either in the eye itself or more commonly in the forehead above it. There may be much watering of the eye, and bright light always occasions more or less distress. The eye is red around the margin of the iris, and for this reason the condition is often mistaken for inflammation of the conjunctiva covering the eye—a much less serious condition. (*See* EYE, DISEASES OF.) Dimness of vision is present, and, particularly in chronic cases, may for long be the only sign. When one looks at the eye closely, one notices that the iris has lost its lustre, and the pupil is generally narrow (Fig. 240). If the

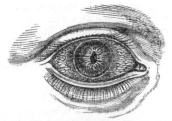

FIG. 240.—Eye showing the appearance of iritis. (Miller's *Surgery*.)

affected person has suffered previously from iritis, the iris may be adherent behind to the lens of the eye, so that the pupil loses its usual circular outline, and

ceases to vary in size in different lights. An acute attack of iritis generally lasts some weeks even when treated, and, if the condition be not carefully treated, the sight may be much impaired or lost as the result of opacities in the lens or cornea, deposit of inflammatory matter in the pupil, and the like.

Treatment.—Rest of the eye is of the highest importance. To effect this, all reading and other near work, even with the unaffected eye, must be given up To prevent the eye from being used, atropine, which paralyses the muscles of accommodation, is dropped into the eye, usually in a solution which contains 2 or 4 grains (125 to 250 mg.) to each ounce (28·5 ml.) of water. As a further protection, dark glasses are worn. Sometimes a blister is applied to the temple to afford relief from the pain. The application of warmth to the eye, the administration of aspirin, and confinement to bed are also helpful. The disease which is responsible for the iritis is at the same time treated by suitable remedies.

IRON is a metal which is an essential constituent of the red blood corpuscles, where it is present in the form of hæmoglobin ; muscle, where it is present as myoglobin ; and certain respiratory pigments which are essential to the life of many tissues in the body. Iron is absorbed principally in the upper part of the small intestine. It is then stored principally in the liver ; to a lesser extent in the spleen and kidneys, where it is available, when required, for use in the bone marrow to form the hæmoglobin in red blood corpuscles. The daily iron requirement of an adult is 15 to 20 milligrammes. This requirement is increased during pregnancy. Iron salts also have an astringent action, especially the chloride, and this property is sometimes made use of when it is used as a styptic to check bleeding.

Uses.—The main use of iron is in the treatment of iron-deficiency anæmias. (*See* ANÆMIA.) The three main forms in which it is used are ferrous sulphate, Blaud's pill which contains ferrous carbonate formed by interaction of ferrous sulphate and sodium carbonate, and iron and ammonium citrate. The first of these is the most widely used. Iron preparations sometimes cause irritation of the gastro-intestinal tract, and should therefore always be taken after meals. They sometimes produce a tendency towards constipation. Whenever possible iron preparations should be given by mouth. It is a very small proportion indeed of cases of iron-deficiency anæmia which will not respond satisfactorily to iron given by mouth. For the occasional cases in which oral administration is not suitable, a preparation of iron is now available which can be given intravenously.

Springs of iron-containing water are known as 'chalybeate' springs, and in England are to be found at Tunbridge Wells and Harrogate. Such iron-containing waters have no advantage over the administration of iron. Indeed, they have the great disadvantage that they can never supply sufficient iron for a patient who is suffering from a definite degree of iron-deficiency anæmia.

IRRADIATION is the term applied to treatment by various forms of light and radiant activity.

IRRIGATION is the name given to the method of washing out wounds, or cavities of the body, like the bladder and bowels. (*See* DOUCHES, ENEMA.)

ISCHÆMIA means bloodlessness of a part of the body, due to contraction, spasm, constriction, or blocking (by embolus or by thrombus) of the arteries—for example, of the heart.

ISCHIO-RECTAL ABSCESS is the name of an abscess arising in the space between the rectum and ischial bone and frequently resulting in a fistula.

ISCHIUM (ἰσχίον, the hip-joint) is the bone which forms the lower and hinder part of the pelvis. It bears the weight of the body in sitting.

ISCHURIA (ἴσχω, I check; οὖρον, urine) means insufficiency in the amount of urine passed, due either to suppression of the excretion or retention in the bladder.

ISHIHARA TEST is used in testing for colour-blindness. It consists of a series of variously coloured charts. Some of these charts, when viewed by individuals with normal colour vision, appear to present figures and pathways which are not apparent to colour-blind individuals, whilst other charts appear to the colour-blind to have figures which are not apparent to the individual with normal colour vision. This test has been accepted as the standard by the fighting forces, including the Royal Navy.

ISO-IMMUNIZATION is the immunization of one member of a species by an antigen lacking in himself but present naturally in other members of the species, as, for example, the immunization of an Rh-negative mother by an Rh-positive fœtus, the mother as a result producing anti-Rh agglutinins which injure the fœtus. (*See also* ICTERUS GRAVIS NEONATORUM *and* RH FACTOR.)

ISOLATION in infectious diseases is an important procedure, applied both to persons who are themselves sick and to persons who have come in contact with them, technically known as 'contacts' or 'suspects', and who may later develop the disease. (*See* INCUBATION, INFECTION, QUARANTINE.)

ISONIAZID is the 'approved name' given by the *British Pharmacopœia* Commission to isonicotinic acid hydrazide. Extensive clinical use has shown that it is one of the most potent antituberculous drugs which we possess. It has the further advantages of being relatively non-toxic and of being active when taken by mouth. Unfortunately, like streptomycin, it may render the tubercle bacillus resistant to its action. This tendency to produce resistance is considerably reduced if it is given in conjunction with streptomycin and/or para-aminosalicylic acid.

ISOTONIC is a term applied to solutions which have the same power of diffusion as one another. An isotonic solution used in medicine is one which can be mixed with body fluids without causing any disturbance. An isotonic solution of *boric acid* lotion for application to the eyes, bladder, etc., is one of

493

2 per cent. strength. An isotonic *saline solution* for injection into the blood, so that it may possess the same osmotic pressure as the blood serum, is one of 0·9 per cent. strength or containing 80 grains of chloride of sodium to the pint of water. This is also known as *normal* or *physiological salt solution.* An isotonic solution of *bicarbonate of soda* for injection into the blood is one of 1·35 per cent. strength in water. An isotonic solution of *glucose* for injection into the blood is one of 5 per cent. strength in water.

Solutions which are weaker than or stronger than the fluids of the body with which they are intended to be mixed are known as hypotonic and hypertonic respectively.

ISOTOPE is each of two or more chemical elements or atoms which have the same chemical properties but differ in atomic weight. Isotopes have become of great interest and importance in medicine because of the developments in nuclear physics which have rendered it possible to make all the common elements radioactive. These radioactive isotopes have a twofold value in medicine : (1) as a means of studying some of the more abstruse processes of the body, of which we are still ignorant; (2) as a means of treating certain malignant conditions. For instance, radioactive iodine is proving of value in the diagnosis of diseases of the thyroid gland and in the treatment of cancer of the thyroid gland. (*See* RADIOTHERAPY.)

ISSUE is an old term for a suppurating sore. The formation of an issue formed an old type of treatment, in which a severe form of counter-irritation was produced by the introduction of a seton or some irritating substance to produce suppuration.

ITCH is a popular name for SCABIES, a skin disease caused by a minute parasite, the *Sarcoptes scabiei* (Fig. 241), which resembles the cheese-mite in appearance. The female burrows in the skin, particularly that on the front of the wrist, the web and sides of the fingers, the buttocks, the genitals and the feet, forming small tunnels in which she lays her eggs, while the male wanders on the surface. The sides and legs may also be affected in the same way, though rarely the upper parts of the body. Scabies is rife among the population of Great Britain. It is believed that personal contact, especially in bed, is the most important factor in keeping this infestation going ; less stress is now laid on dissemination of the mite by infested clothes and blankets.

Symptoms.—The person complains of great itchiness and heat, felt particularly soon after he goes to bed, and pre-

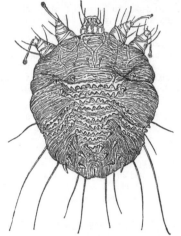

FIG. 241.—The female sarcoptes, magnified about 80 times. (Thoma's *Pathology.*)

venting sleep in the early part of the night. The spaces between the fingers, the backs of the hands, and the front of the wrists are red and scabbed as the result of scratching, or the surface in these localities may even be much inflamed.

Treatment.—The patient is scrubbed with soft soap in a hot bath, to open up the burrows. Immediately after drying, the official *British Pharmacopœia* 25 per cent. preparation of benzyl benzoate, known as benzyl benzoate application B.P., is applied to the whole surface of the body below the chin. A second and a third application is made at twelve-hourly intervals. The patient then has a bath, puts on clean underclothes, and has his bed clothes changed.

ITCHING is an unpleasant condition of the skin surface which in some cases is so constant as to become unbearable.

Causes.—It is due to many different conditions, some of which are local and can be easily removed. Some are general, while occasionally the condition becomes so chronic and the skin so changed by scratching, etc., that it is incurable. Itching is produced by slight mechanical irritation, such as contact with rough woollen undercloth, ing, also by parasites such as lice, scabies (in the disease specially known as ' the itch '), and these mechanical causes being removed the itching speedily vanishes.

Various skin diseases, of which eczema is the chief, have itchiness as one of their main symptoms. In old age, when the skin is becoming thin and inelastic, itching sometimes becomes a troublesome complaint. In these and other conditions, a habit of scratching, which in course of time renders the skin rough and thickened, is apt to be contracted, and this of itself aggravates and keeps up the itchiness. Among the general diseases which set up itchiness, the chief is diabetes. In fact, any one who is much troubled by itchiness, especially if this be situated about the genital organs, should have his urine examined for the presence of sugar. Jaundice caused by various liver derangements, and Bright's disease, are often accompanied by itchiness in a milder degree. Dyspepsia is not uncommonly the cause of nettle-rash, which may be of an itching type and appear soon after indigestible food has been taken. Some persons are much troubled by itching of the body when changes in size of the blood-vessels in the skin take place, as occur upon getting warm in bed or upon the advent of spring and autumn. A similar condition, which affects persons on going to the tropics, is known as ' prickly heat '. (*See* PRICKLY HEAT.)

A special and often very aggravated form of itching occurs sometimes at the anus, known as pruritus ani. In all cases of irritation in or around the anus, a careful search should be made for threadworms. (*See* RECTUM, DISEASES OF.)

Treatment.—Warm baths, alkaline or containing bran, are among the most soothing applications for general itching. (*See* BATHS.) Calamine lotion is the most efficient local application, but talcum powder is often useful. It is essential that a proper examination should be made as to the functions of the internal organs in cases where itching is a chronic complaint. In diabetic cases the surest remedy to prevent the itching is to treat the diabetes. A variety of treatments have been recommended for pruritus ani, in the causation of which the psychological element is sometimes overlooked.

-ITIS is a suffix added to the name of an organ to signify any diseased condition of that organ.

IVORY, or DENTINE, is the hard material which forms the chief bulk of the teeth. (*See* TEETH.)

J

JABORANDI, or PILOCARPUS, is the leaf of a South American plant, *Pilocarpus pennatifolius*. It contains an alkaloid, pilocarpine, upon which its action depends (*see* PILOCARPINE).

JACKSONIAN EPILEPSY (*see* EPILEPSY).

JAIL FEVER is another term for typhus fever.

JALAP is the tuber of *Iopmœa Jalapa*, a Mexican plant, which contains two resins of irritating properties.
Uses.—Jalap is a potent purgative which is seldom used now except in combination with milder purgatives in certain pills. On the relatively few occasions on which a powerful purgative action is required, compound jalap powder may be used, in a dose of 40 to 60 grains (2·4 to 4 grammes).

JANICEPS is a fœtal monstrosity characterized by one combined head and two faces.

JASMINE (*see* GELSEMIUM).

JAUNDICE (Fr. *jaunisse*) is a yellow discoloration of the skin due to the deposition of bile pigment in its deeper layers. (*See also* HEPATITIS, ACUTE INFECTIVE.)
Causes.—Jaundice is divided into two main classes : *hepatogenous jaundice,* arising from the absorption of bile formed by the liver, and *hæmolytic jaundice,* arising from the formation of a yellow pigment in the blood, derived especially from the breaking down of red blood corpuscles. The former is the usual type, and is described below ; the latter is found in such conditions as pernicious anæmia, acholuric jaundice, and snake poisoning.

When the bile cannot escape into the intestine in the usual way, it is absorbed by the blood- and lymph-vessels, and some of its constituents are deposited in the various tissues throughout the body. Some obstruction to the outflow of bile is, therefore, a necessary condition, and this obstruction may either exist in the bile-ducts, which convey the bile from liver to intestine,

or it may be caused by some disorganization in the liver (*e.g.* hepatitis) which prevents the bile, formed by the liver-cells, from finding its way to the bile-ducts at all. The tint of the jaundice has not necessarily any direct relation to the severity of the cause. Obstruction may be due to gall-stones, and the resulting jaundice is then a symptom of this condition (*see* GALL-STONES). Obstruction may be due to some cause quite outside the liver and bile-ducts, for example, enlarged glands lying near the liver, or cancer of the pancreas, the seriousness of the jaundice depending then upon the seriousness of the disease responsible for the pressure. In elderly persons, who are likely to be the subject of cancer, long-continued jaundice is for this reason a serious symptom. Cirrhosis of the liver, in which the small branches of the bile-duct become compressed by the formation of fibrous tissue, may also be a cause of chronic jaundice (*see* CIRRHOSIS.)

Among the causes which disorganize the liver, one finds many poisons which are carried to it in the blood, for example, phosphorus, mercury, chloroform, and snake poison. Much more common as a cause of jaundice are two inflammatory conditions of the liver, known as infective hepatitis (*q.v.*) and homologous serum jaundice. They are both due to viruses (possibly even the same virus), but they differ in that the former has a shorter incubation period. Infective hepatitis, which is much the more common of the two, is the condition which used to be known as ' catarrhal jaundice '. Certain infective diseases are also prone to produce this effect, of which may be mentioned yellow fever, malaria, typhoid fever, and pyæmia. A serious but uncommon condition, accompanied by rapid and often fatal jaundice, is that known as acute yellow atrophy of the liver. Another form of jaundice is known as spirochætal jaundice or *spirochætosis icterohæmorrhagica* (*q.v.*). These conditions cause such changes in the liver that the bile is unable to escape save by reabsorption into the blood.

Symptoms.—Yellowness, appearing first in the whites of the eys and later over the whole skin, is the symptom that attracts notice. This tint varies from a pale sulphur-yellow through all gradations to a deep olive or bronze colour, according to the completeness of the obstruction and the length of time the jaundice has lasted. The urine passed during the time the jaundice lasts is of a dark greenish-brown colour, owing to the excretion of bile by the kidneys. Various digestive disturbances are present: the tongue is furred, the appetite poor, and a feeling of sickness is often felt, and is aggravated by eating fats. The stools are of a grey or white colour, owing to the want of bile in the intestine, and for the same reason constipation, relieved occasionally by diarrhœa, is present, and the stools have an excessively offensive smell. A bitter taste in the mouth is generally felt by the jaundiced person, due, as it is supposed, to the presence in the saliva of salts of the bile-acids, and the same or other substances in the sweat lead to occasional itching of the skin. Slowness of the pulse, and, in long-continued cases, mental confusion and dullness, are other less evident accompaniments of jaundice.

Treatment.—The first essential is to treat the underlying cause if possible. For instance, gall-stones, if these be the cause of the jaundice. For the actual treatment of the jaundice the patient must be kept in bed. The diet should contain as much protein and carbohydrate as possible and a minimum of fat. The diet to be aimed at should contain 3000 calories daily, made up of 100 to 120 grammes of protein, 300 to 400 grammes of carbohydrate, and 100 grammes of fat. As the patient's appetite is often feeble, there may be considerable difficulty in persuading him to take all this food. It means, for instance, meat or fish at three meals every day. For the pruritus, or itching, which may be very severe, calamine lotion containing 2 per cent. phenol should be used. This may need to be supplemented with analgesics, *e.g.* aspirin or a tablet containing aspirin, phenacetin, and codeine. Sedatives may also be required.

As the jaundice clears, the amount of protein may be reduced, and if there is much residual indigestion this is best treated by a modified peptic ulcer diet.

JAW is the name applied to the bones that carry the teeth. The upper jawbones are two in number, and are firmly fixed to the other bones of the face (Fig. 335, page 811). The lower jaw is shaped somewhat like a horseshoe, and, after the first year of life, consists of a single bone. It forms a hinge-joint with the squamous part of the temporal bone, immediately in front of the ear. Both upper and lower jawbones possess deep sockets, known as ' alveoli ', which contain the roots of the teeth. (*See* DISLOCATIONS, FRACTURES, GUMBOIL, MOUTH, TEETH.)

JEJUNUM (*jejunus*, empty of food) is the name given to part of the small intestine. (*See* INTESTINE.)

JELLY (*see* GELATIN).

JIGGER is a popular term used to denote a parasite also known as the sand-flea. The term is also used to denote the small worm-like masses of fatty material which can be squeezed out of the sebaceous glands on the face of those suffering from acne (*q.v.*).

JOINT-MOUSE is a popular term for a loose body in a joint. It is found especially in the knee. (*See* JOINTS, DISEASES OF.)

JOINTS.—A joint or articulation is the meeting-place between different parts of the skeleton, whether bones or cartilages.

Structure.—The great division of joints is into those which are fixed and those at which movement can take place. In the *fixed joints* (Fig. 242), a

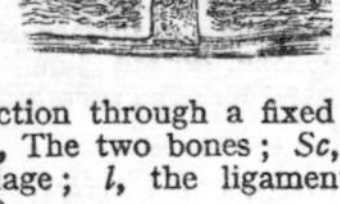

FIG. 242.—Section through a fixed synarthrodia joint. *bb*, The two bones ; *Sc*, the intervening cartilage ; *l*, the ligaments. (Turner's *Anatomy*.)

layer of cartilage or of fibrous tissue intervenes between the bones and binds them firmly together (synarthrodial joint). This type of joint is exemplified by the 'sutures' between the bones that make up the skull. Among these fixed joints, some have a thick disc of fibro-cartilage between the bones, so that, although the individual joint is really capable of very little movement, a series of these, like the joints between the bodies of the vertebræ, gives to the spinal column, as a whole, a flexible character (amphiarthrodial joint) (Fig. 243).

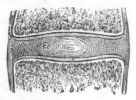

FIG. 243.—Section through an amphiarthrodial joint. *bb*, The two bones; *c*, the plate of cartilage on the surface of each; *Fc*, the intermediate fibro-cartilage; *ll*, the ligaments. (Turner's *Anatomy*.)

Into the formation of every *movable joint* four structures enter. These are the bones whose junction forms the joint; a layer of cartilage covering the end of each of these and rendering the ends smooth (Fig. 87, page 170); a sheath of fibrous tissue known as the capsule, thickened at various points into bands or 'ligaments', which hold the bones together; and,

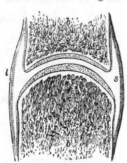

FIG. 244.—Section through a movable diarthrodial joint. *bb*, The two bones; *cc*, the plate of cartilage covering the surface of each; *ll*, the ligaments; the dotted line, *s*, shows the position of the synovial membrane. (Turner's *Anatomy*.)

finally, a membrane known as 'synovial membrane', which lines this capsule and produces a synovial fluid to lubricate the movements of the joint. Further, the bones are kept in position at the joints by the various muscles passing

498

over them and by atmospheric pressure. This type of joint is known as a diarthrodial joint (Fig. 244).

Some joints possess subsidiary structures, such as discs of fibro-cartilage, which adapt the ends of the bones more perfectly to one another in places where these do not quite correspond. In others, movable pads of fat under the synovial membrane fill up larger cavities and afford additional protection to the joint.

Varieties.—Apart from the main division of joints into those which are fixed and those which are movable, the movable joints fall into several groups. Gliding joints are those in which, like the wrist and ankle, the bones have flat surfaces capable of only a limited amount of movement. In hinge-joints, like the elbow and knee, the chief movement takes place round one axis. The ball-and-socket type is exemplified by the shoulder and hip, in which free movement is possible in any direction. There are other subsidiary varieties, named according to the shape of the bones which enter into the joint.

JOINTS, DISEASES OF.—The larger joints, on account of their exposed position, are subject to constant injuries, and this, together with the wear they suffer and the richness of their blood supply, renders them liable to a number of serious diseases. The knee is the joint most frequently diseased, and after it, in order, the hip, ankle, and elbow. Although minor injuries may be followed by serious diseases, it is an important fact that very severe injuries, in which the skin remains unbroken, such as dislocations of and fractures into the joints, rarely occasion any serious disease beyond stiffness and other direct results of the injury. On the other hand, penetrating wounds of joints are among the most serious of injuries, and require immediate and expert treatment. The following are some of the conditions from which joints suffer.

SYNOVITIS is the name given to any inflammation of the membrane lining the joint cavity. It may be acute, sub-acute, or chronic.

Causes.—The joints being much exposed to blows, wounds, and strains, some injury usually precedes the onset of inflammation. In many cases, the condition is more dependent on constitutional causes, as, for example, when rheumatism, gout, or some infective disease, particularly tuberculosis, is the nature of the malady.

Symptoms.—In acute synovitis, following usually upon some injury, the synovial membrane becomes inflamed, thickened, and secretes an excessive amount of fluid into the joint. As a result, the joint becomes painful, red, swollen, and hot to touch. It is usually kept more or less bent, and is painful to straighten and to handle. If the synovitis remains of a simple nature, these symptoms last some days and then gradually subside. Or the condition may persist for a long time, getting better for a little and then relapsing; or it may become chronic, and, whilst the heat and redness disappear, the joint remains stiff and distended with fluid. This condition most frequently affects the knee, and is then popularly known as ' water on the knee '. On the other hand, in occasional cases which have begun in the simple form, and in cases due to a penetrating wound of the joint to which bacteria have gained entrance, a very serious inflammation occurs. Suppuration then takes place in the joint, an abscess forms with fever, great pain, and other aggravated symptoms of abscess. A joint cavity is very difficult to render free from suppuration, which may therefore last for months, weakening the patient, causing stiffness of the joint and disease in other organs, and even necessitating amputation of the limb in order to save his life.

Treatment.—In the early stages, complete rest of the joint, the limb being placed on a splint, together with the application of cold or of warm fomentations to soothe the pain, is alone necessary. Later, massage and compression of the joint by a bandage aid the absorption of the fluid and dispel the stiffness. When the condition becomes chronic, counter-irritation by iodine, blisters, etc., is necessary, and the joint is often punctured to draw off the fluid. Suppuration is, as already stated, a very serious matter, and is treated like an abscess elsewhere by opening, irrigation with antiseptics, drainage, and the administration of antibiotics.

EPIPHYSITIS is the name given to an inflammation situated at the end of a long bone just outside the joint. An important point regarding this type of inflammation in children is that if the inflammation be severe it may permanently damage the plate of cartilage, situated close to the end of the bone, from which increase in length takes place, so that the child's limb may be seriously impaired in growth.

TUBERCULOUS DISEASE of a joint begins in the synovial membrane or in the end of the bone, and is popularly known as ' white swelling ', on account of the characteristic appearance of the affected joint, particularly when the knee is involved. In many cases there are other manifestations of the disease, the lungs, for example, being affected, or the glands of the neck enlarged. Tuberculosis of the joints is commoner in children than in older persons. A proportion of cases, especially in children, are due to the drinking of tuberculous milk.

Symptoms.—The condition is usually chronic, begins insidiously, sometimes being dated from a slight accident, and progresses slowly. Slight stiffness, wasting of the muscles in the affected limb, and pain and tiredness brought on by slight exertion, are the earliest symptoms. The joint later on assumes its characteristic appearance, becoming enlarged, losing the natural hollows about it, and appearing white and glistening, with large veins showing through the skin. The wasting of muscle above and below the joint causes it to look still more enlarged than it really is. Gradually the use of the limb is lost, and the general health deteriorates. Later in the disease, when the joint is becoming thoroughly disorganized, starting-pains at night, which waken the sufferer as he is dropping off to sleep, become troublesome. If the condition remains untreated after this stage is reached, an abscess forms in the joint and bursts through the skin, and hectic fever develops.

Treatment.—In all cases of tuberculous disease rest of the joint is essential, the joint being fixed by a splint or other apparatus so that it cannot move to any great extent. As in all other tuberculous conditions, exercise and fresh air are of great importance, and therefore, when the disease affects a joint in the lower limb, some apparatus is devised whereby the patient can move about while the joint is still rigid. For the hip and knee this is secured by Thomas's splints, and for other joints by various pieces of apparatus. Fixation is sometimes effected by plaster bandages, though these have the great disadvantage of leaving the joint stiff and the limb weak. When a joint is thus fixed for a space of weeks or months, stiffness is apt to ensue, but the freedom of the joint must often be sacrificed with the object of checking the disease. Care is taken that the position in which the joint is fixed shall be the most useful one, the knee being kept straight, the ankle at a right angle, the elbow a little more bent than a right angle, as the case may be. Sometimes in the case of the hip, especially if the pain be severe, the child is put in bed, and extension by means of a weight applied to the limb ; for by this means the deformity is corrected, the joint kept at rest, and the pressure of the diseased surfaces in the joint upon one another relieved. Massage, which is admirably adapted for the treatment of many joint conditions, is not suited for tuberculous disease while it is still active. Constitutional treatment must be energetically carried out, as in the case of tuberculosis elsewhere in the body.

Operative treatment is advisable for some tuberculous joints. The aim of surgical treatment is to secure fixation of the affected joint by bony ankylosis, *i.e.* bringing together the ends of the damaged limb.

As in all other forms of tuberculosis the outlook has been revolutionized by the excellent results which have been obtained from the use of chemotherapy, giving combined therapy with streptomycin, P.A.S., and isoniazid for at least six months. The use of chemotherapy has not only reduced the time of treatment by one-half, but has resulted in a much larger number of patients being left with almost full range of movement of the diseased joints.

STIFFNESS OF JOINTS may be due to various causes. It may result from spasm of the muscles around the joint in cases of early tuberculous disease

and of hysterical joints, or it may be due to permanent shortening in these muscles or contraction of the skin, due, for example, to a burn. Often a severe injury to the joint itself, such as a fracture of one of the bones that form it, or a dislocation, is followed by some stiffness. A large number of slight injuries, which set up a mild degree of inflammation, are followed by some adhesion in the joint, often of a painful nature. These limit the use of the joint considerably, but, when they are broken by forcible movements of the limb, recovery and relief are immediate.

LOOSE BODIES IN JOINTS result from inflammation of various types, the bodies being developed as projections on the synovial membrane or on the cartilages of the joint, and later pulled off by its movements. They bring on repeated attacks of synovitis, and often cause sudden locking of the joint, so that for a time it is immovable. They are removed by operation.

GOUT, RHEUMATISM, AND RHEUMATOID ARTHRITIS are diseases of a constitutional nature which affect joints. (See under these headings.)

HYSTERICAL AFFECTIONS OF JOINTS are not uncommon, particularly in young women, although they are occasionally found in the opposite sex. The knee and hip are most often affected, but the ankle, wrist, and elbow are also liable. The affection takes many forms ; stiffness, pain on movement, swelling, weakness, wasting of the limb may be complained of, and the appearances of tuberculous disease may be closely mimicked. As a rule there are no signs of general constitutional weakness, and, on the other hand, various other hysterical manifestations present themselves. (*See* HYSTERIA.)

SPRAIN is a vague popular term indicating the result of any slight wrench to a joint. A sprain consists generally of a mild attack of synovitis, or of tearing of ligaments with effusion of fluid into or round the joint. At the ankle, a twist of the foot inwards is followed by some tearing of the outer lateral ligament of the joint constituting a severe ' sprain ', but a more serious accident, consisting of fracture at the lower end of the fibula, is apt to follow a wrench or twist of the foot outwards. (*See* FRACTURES.) In the knee, a sudden twist is occasionally responsible for loosening and rumpling up the inner of the two fibro-cartilages found in that joint. This accident has the awkward consequence of producing at subsequent times attacks of synovitis, or of sudden locking of the knee-joint. Behind the wrist and at the ankle, a sprain results sometimes in the displacement of some of the tendons which should be bound firmly to the bone, leading to occasional pain and a sense of weakness till the tendon happens to get replaced by another twist.

Treatment.—When a sprain is of inflammatory character, the treatment is of the nature described under synovitis, and in the case of a bad sprain rest for a week or two may be essential. A sprain consisting in tearing of the ligaments round a joint, accompanied by effusion of blood beneath the skin, may be treated at the very beginning by applying wet compresses, or by holding the joint in a stream of cold water, which materially checks the effusion. After some time has elapsed, this form of treatment is of little use, and compression by a moderately tight, or by an elastic, bandage over the injured joint, together with elevation of the limb, forms a better line of treatment. When the pain is severe, fomentations of lead and opium lotion give relief (*see* GOULARD'S WATER). Massage is of great assistance in cases of sprain to prevent stiffness of the affected joint and to aid repair of injured tissues.

DISLOCATION (*see* DISLOCATIONS).

BURSITIS frequently occurs over the region of a joint. The prominences of several joints are protected by large bursæ, and inflammation of these structures is sometimes mistaken for inflammation of the joint. (*See* BURSITIS.)

JUGULAR (*jugulum*, neck) is a general name for any structure in the neck, but is especially applied to three large veins, the anterior, external, and internal jugular veins, which convey blood from the head and neck regions to the interior of the chest.

JUNKET is the name of a food consisting of milk which has been acted upon by rennet. This forms a soft curd of the casein which is more easily digested than the curd which would naturally form in the stomach, and junket, therefore, forms a more easily digestible food than natural milk. If the curd is strained through muslin, whey is obtained which contains simply the water, sugar, and albuminous materials of the milk and is very easily digestible. It is therefore much used in the treatment of gastric ulcer and similar conditions. Half a pint of whey has an energy value of about 60 calories.

K

KAHN REACTION is a substitute for the *Wassermann reaction* (*q.v.*) in the diagnosis of syphilis. It is based upon the fact that flocculation occurs when the serum from a patient with syphilis is treated with organ extracts. It has never completely replaced the Wassermann reaction in Great Britain, but it is quite common for it to be performed in addition to the Wassermann reaction. This double test is often of value in cases in which the diagnosis of syphilis is difficult.

KALA-AZAR, also known as VISCERAL LEISHMANIASIS, DUM-DUM FEVER, and BLACK FEVER, is a chronic disease which occurs along the shores of the Mediterranean, in North Africa, the Sudan, India, Assam, China, and the tropical zone of South America. It is caused by a parasite known as *Leishmania donovani* (Fig. 245), which

FIG. 245.—Leishmania. Mass of parasites inside a macrophage. (From Blacklock and Southwell, *A Guide to Human Parasitology.* H. K. Lewis & Co. Ltd.)

is transmitted to man by the bite of a sandfly, usually *Phlebotomus argentipes*.

Symptoms.—The onset may be acute or insidious. In the well-established case the important features are irregular fever, progressive anæmia with diminution in the number of white blood cells, marked enlargement of the spleen which may weigh up to 10 pounds (4·5 kg.), enlargement of the liver, and dropsy of the legs. The diagnosis is confirmed by finding parasites in the blood or in the marrow of the sternum. Splenic puncture used to be performed regularly to find the parasites in the spleen, but this procedure is not without danger, and has now been largely replaced by sternal puncture.

Treatment.—The introduction of pentavalent antimony compounds and of the aromatic diamidines has effected a marked improvement in the outlook in this previously fatal disease. Opinion is still divided concerning the relative efficacy of these two groups of drugs, and there is some evidence to show that the response varies in different areas. Indian figures show that, whilst without treatment 75 per cent. of cases die within two years, now that efficient treatment is available over 90 per cent. are cured.

KANAMYCIN is an antibiotic derived from *Streptomyces kanamycetus*. It is active against a wide range of organisms, including the *Staphylococcus aureus* and *Mycobacterium tuberculosis*.

KAOLIN, or CHINESE CLAY, is a smooth white powder consisting of natural white aluminium silicate resulting from the decomposition of minerals containing feldspar. It is used as a dusting powder for eczema and other forms of irritation in the skin. It is also used internally in cases of diarrhœa. The dose is from ½ to 2 ounces (15 to 30 ml.) of mixture of kaolin, B.P.C., best taken in water or milk before meals. Talc, French chalk, and Fuller's earth are similar silicates.

Kaolin poultice, which is used for the relief of pneumonia and various skin conditions, contains kaolin, boric acid, glycerin, and various aromatic substances.

KATA-THERMOMETER.—A thermometer, invented by Sir Leonard Hill, which shows the rate of loss of heat, or cooling power, of the air. It is a spirit thermometer with a large bulb and marks on the stem at 95° F. and 100° F. The thermometer, having been warmed up to above 100° F., is suspended in the air and the time taken in cooling from 100° F. to 95° F. is observed. Each instrument has marked on the stem a factor proportional to the total heat lost per square centimetre of the bulb in cooling from 95° F. to 100° F. Dividing this factor by the number of seconds taken to cool gives a figure called the ' cooling power '.

KELOID (*see* CHELOID).

KERATIN (κέρας, horn) is the substance of which horn and the surface layer of the skin are composed.

KERATITIS (κέρας, horn) means inflammation of the cornea in front of the eye. (*See* EYE, DISEASES OF.)

KERATOMALACIA means softening of the cornea, as a result of a severe lack of vitamin A in the diet.

KERION (κηρίον, honeycomb) is the term applied to a suppurating form of ringworm.

KERNICTERUS.—The staining with bile of the basal nuclei of the brain, with toxic degeneration of the nerve cells, which sometimes occurs in HÆMOLYTIC DISEASE OF THE NEWBORN (*q.v.*).

KERNIG'S SIGN is a sign found in cases of meningitis, consisting in the fact that, whereas a healthy person's thigh can be bent to a right angle with the body when the knee is straight, in cases of meningitis the knee cannot be straightened when the thigh is thus bent, or intense pain is caused to the patient by doing so.

KETOGENIC DIET is one containing such an excess of fats that acetone and other ketone bodies appear in the urine. It is sometimes used in the treatment of epilepsy and chronic infections of the urinary tract by the *Escherichia coli.* In this diet, butter, cream eggs, and fat meat are allowed, whilst sugar, bread, and other carbohydrates are cut out as far as possible.

KETONE is another name for acetone or dimethyl ketone. The term 'ketone bodies' is applied to a group of substances closely allied to acetone, especially β-hydroxybutyric acid and acetoacetic acid. These are produced in the body from imperfect oxidation of fats and protein foods, and are found in specially large amount in severe cases of diabetes. KETONURIA is the term applied to the presence of these bodies in the urine.

KHELLIN is a crystalline principle which has been isolated from the fruit of *Ammi visnaga*, an umbelliferous plant indigenous to the Mediterranean area—which has for long had a local reputation for the relief of renal colic. Khellin has been introduced to western medicine for the treatment of angina pectoris.

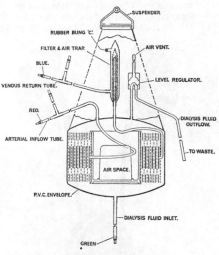

FIG. 245a.—A diagram showing the design of an artificial kidney. (*The Practitioner.*)

KIDNEY, ARTIFICIAL, is the term applied to an instrument (Fig. 245a) which has been introduced in recent years to take over temporarily the functions of the kidneys in cases of acute renal (kidney) failure. Such sudden failure of the kidneys may occur in a number of circumstances, including severe accidents such as the crush syndrome (*q.v.*), incompatible blood transfusions, mercury poisoning, and severe hæmorrhage in the later stages of pregnancy. It is also being used now in the treatment of chronic renal failure. In such patients the immediate results may be dramatic, but treatment has to be maintained more or less permanently.

The principle of the artificial kidney is that the patient's blood circulates through it and there comes in contact with a dialysing membrane, on the other side of which is a specially prepared dialysing fluid. In this way the biochemical balance of the blood is restored to normal, just as it would have been had the kidneys been functioning normally.

KIDNEYS are a pair of glands situated close to the spine in the upper part of the abdomen. They are on a level with the last dorsal and upper two lumbar vertebræ, and each is, to a great extent, covered behind by the twelfth rib of its own side. They are kept in

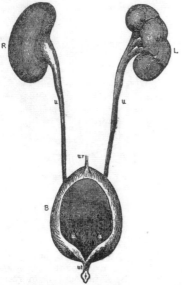

Fig. 246.—The kidneys and their connection with the exterior. R, the right, L, the left kidney ; the left kidney is drawn with the fissures which sometimes divide its surface into lobules ; uu, the ureters ; B, the bladder, showing the openings of the ureters into its base ; ut, commencement of the urethra ; ur, urachus which attaches the bladder to the front of the abdomen. (Turner's *Anatomy*.)

this position by a quantity of fat and loose connective tissue, in which they are embedded, by the large vessels which supply them with blood, and by the peritoneal membrane stretched over their front surface.

Structure.—In size each is about 4 inches (10 cm.) long, 2½ inches wide (6·5 cm.), 1½ inches (5 cm.) thick, and weighs over 4 ounces (113 grammes). The size, however, varies a good deal with the development, and probably with the habits of the individual. The left kidney is slightly longer and narrower, and lies a trifle higher in the abdomen than the right.

504

The kidney in adult human beings presents a smooth exterior, although in early life, as in many animals, it is divided up into distinct lobes, corresponding to the pyramids found in the interior. Enveloping it is a tough fibrous coat, which, in the healthy state, is bound to the kidney only by loose fibrous tissues and by a few blood-vessels that pass between it and the kidney. This capsule, which does not permit of much enlargement of the kidney, is an important factor with which to reckon when the kidney becomes congested in Bright's disease. The outer margin of the kidney is convex, the inner is concave, presenting a deep depression, known as the hilum, where the vessels enter its substance. At the hilum the renal vein lies in front of the renal artery, the former joining the inferior vena cava, and the latter springing from the aorta almost at a right angle. Here, too, the ureter, which conveys urine down to the bladder, is attached (Fig. 246). The ureter is spread out into an expanded, funnel-like end, known as the pelvis, to which the capsule of the kidney is

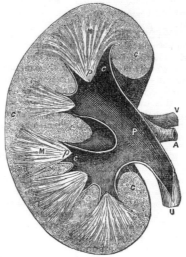

Fig. 247.—Vertical section through the kidney. CCC, The cortical part ; MM, the medullary pyramids ; pp, the papillæ ; cc, the calyces ; P, the pelvis ; U, ureter ; A, renal artery ; V, renal vein. (Turner's *Anatomy*.)

firmly attached, and which further divides into little funnels known as the calyces. On splitting open a kidney, one finds it to consist of two distinct parts (Fig. 247): a layer on the surface, about $\frac{1}{6}$ inch (4 mm.) thick, known as the ' cortex ', and a part towards the hilum known as the medulla. The latter consists of pyramids, arranged side by side, with their base on the cortex and their apex projecting into the calyces of the ureter. The apex of each pyramid, of which there are about twelve in all, is studded with minute holes, which are the openings of the microscopic uriniferous tubes.

Each pyramid is, in effect, taken together with the portion of cortex lying along its base, an independent little kidney. About a score of small tubes open on the surface of each pyramid, and these, if traced up into its substance, divide again and again so as to form bundles of tubules, known as medullary rays, passing up towards the cortex. If one of these be traced still farther back, it is found, after a very tortuous course, to end in a small rounded body, the Malpighian corpuscle or glomerulus (Fig. 249).

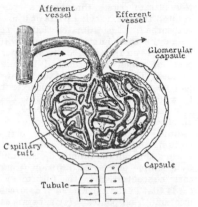

Fig. 249.—Diagram of Malpighian corpuscle. (From Best and Taylor, *The Physiological Basis of Medical Practice*. The Williams & Wilkins Co.)

form arches at the line of junction of cortex and medulla, and from these again spring vessels that run up through the cortex, giving off small branches in every direction. Each of these last ends in a little tuft of capillaries enclosed in a capsule (Bowman's capsule), that forms the end of the uriniferous tubule above described, and capillaries with capsule are known as a glomerulus (Fig. 249). The blood after circulating in the glomerulus, emerges by a small vein, which again splits up into capillaries on the walls of the uriniferous tubules. From these it is collected finally into the renal veins and by them leaves the kidney. By means of the double circulation, first through the glomerulus and then around the tubule, it comes to pass that a large amount of fluid is removed from the blood in the glomerulus, and then the concentrated blood passes on to the uriniferous tubule for removal of parts of its solid contents. Other straight arteries come off from the arches mentioned above and supply the medulla direct, the blood from these passing through another set of capillaries and also finally into the renal veins. Although the circulation just described is confined entirely to the kidney, it has certain small connections both by arteries and veins which pass through the capsule and join the lumbar vessels communicating direct with the

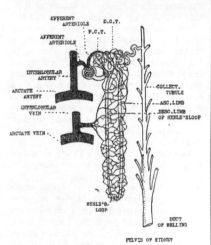

Fig. 248.—Diagram of renal tubules and blood supply of the kidney. P.C.T., proximal convoluted tubule ; D.C.T., distal convoluted tubule. (From Best and Taylor, *The Physiological Basis of Medical Practice*. The Williams & Wilkins Co.)

If the blood-vessels be now traced through the kidney their course is found to be as follows (Fig. 248). The renal artery splits up into branches, which

aorta. These connections are of importance in kidney disease, because through them the kidney circulation can be relieved by applications to the loins.

Function.—The chief function of the kidneys is to separate fluid and certain solids from the blood. Briefly, the glomeruli filter from the blood the non-protein portion of the plasma. As this filtrate passes through the convoluted tubules, varying parts of it are reabsorbed. It is estimated that in 24 hours the total human glomeruli will filter between 150 and 200 litres, 99 per cent. of which is reabsorbed by the tubules. The constituents of the filtrate may be grouped according to the extent to which they are reabsorbed by the tubules : (1) substances actively reabsorbed, such as amino-acids, glucose, sodium, potassium, calcium, magnesium, and chlorine ; (2) substances passing through the tubular epithelium by a simple process of diffusion when their concentration in the filtrate exceeds that in the plasma, such as urea, uric acid, phosphates ; (3) substances not returned to the blood from the tubular fluid—*e.g.* creatine.

When the kidneys are diseased and the number of glomeruli and tubules decreased in consequence, this alternating action is not so readily carried out, and therefore the work of the diseased kidney becomes much embarrassed. When the blood-vessels of the kidney are partially closed by disease (arterioscleroris), the general blood-pressure rises with the object of forcing more blood through the kidneys ; and, in consequence, marked changes are produced upon the heart in this type of renal disease.

When the kidneys fail to act, these solid waste substances accumulate in the blood. The general ' poisoning ' resulting from failure of renal function produces the clinical condition known as uræmia.

KIDNEYS, DISEASES OF. — The kidneys, being deeply buried in the abdomen, give little direct sign even when seriously diseased, although many of the effects upon the general constitution are sufficiently marked and serious.

General Symptoms. — The following are some of the general symptoms common to various types of kidney disease.

PAIN, of an aching nature, situated high up in the loins, is occasionally a symptom of inflammation of the kidneys, but pain in the lower part of the back is found in so many other diseases, and is so generally absent in serious kidney affections, that it is of little importance as a symptom. When a stone lodges in the ureter, however, there is a very definite type of pain known as ' renal colic '. This pain is of an agonizing nature, shoots down from the kidney region to the groin, and usually appears with great suddenness. Also, when a kidney becomes movable and approaches the front of the abdomen, direct pressure upon it causes a sickening sensation of a type quite different from ordinary tenderness.

The URINE almost invariably shows changes in kidney diseases. In acute conditions it is diminished, generally contains albumin, and may be bloody. When unusual material is present in the kidney, careful examination of the urine generally discovers traces of it in this excretion ; for example, pus in the urine points to a suppurative condition situated somewhere in the urinary tract ; and when a stone is present in the kidney, its nature may often be conjectured by an examination of the crystalline deposit in the urine. In chronic Bright's disease the urine is generally increased in amount, pale, and, as a rule, contains greater or less amounts of albumin. (*See* ALBUMINURIA.)

DROPSY, though due to many other conditions than Bright's disease, is a most important symptom of this and other kidney troubles. When dependent upon some defect in the kidneys, it appears generally in the morning after sleep, and affects the loose tissues of the body, such as the skin beneath the eyes and that on the back of the hands, which become swollen and puffy.

CHANGES IN THE CIRCULATION take place in chronic kidney disease. The signs of thickening in the arteries and in the heart-wall afford to the physician one of the most important signs both of the presence and of the severity of Bright's disease. These changes may produce pain in the chest, loss of mental power, bloodlessness, impairment of vision, and may lead to apoplexy.

URÆMIA is a condition which is present in all cases in which the function of the kidneys is seriously impaired. It is a general poisoning of the system by waste products which the kidneys have failed to excrete, and may be acute or chronic in type. (*See* URÆMIA.)

The most important class of diseases affecting the kidneys is that comprising the changes grouped together as Bright's disease, in which albumin is excreted in the urine and dropsy is often present. (*See* BRIGHT'S DISEASE.) The following are some of the other important affections of the kidney.

GRAVEL and STONE are produced by the deposit in the urinary passages of solid substances which are naturally present in the urine, and whose deposition depends upon their presence in excessive amount, or upon the failure of some condition which in general keeps them in solution. The most common crystalline deposits are of three sorts : (*a*) urates and uric acid ; (*b*) oxalates ; (*c*) phosphates.

The main factor responsible for the formation of stones in the kidneys is alteration in the reaction of the urine. Thus an excessive acid reaction may lead to the formation of uric acid stones, whilst phosphate stones form in alkaline urine. Other factors which are associated with the formation of stones in the kidneys are prolonged recumbency, *e.g.* following a fracture of the femur, infection of the kidney, lack of vitamin A in the diet, a high level of calcium in the blood. Excessive consumption of alcohol and lead poisoning are also said to predispose to stone formation. They are more common in men than in women, and may occur at any age and particularly among sedentary workers. In cases in which the presence of a stone is suspected, X-ray examination is an important procedure in diagnosis.

Treatment.—This depends upon the size of the stone. If it is large, then it has usually to be removed by operation. If it is small, it may be passed out in the urine following medical treatment. This consists of ensuring a large volume of urine by drinking large amounts of bland fluids. It is also necessary to alter the reaction of the urine. Thus, in the case of a uric-acid stone, the excessively acid urine is made alkaline by giving large doses of alkalies, *e.g.* 2 grammes of sodium bicarbonate four times daily ; in the case of phosphate stones the excessively alkaline urine is made acid by the taking of 1 gramme of ammonium chloride four times daily. Irrigation of the kidney with ' solution, G ', which contains citric acid, magnesium oxide, and sodium carbonate, is sometimes of value as it appears to dissolve small stones. If there is any infection of the kidney, this must be fully treated.

SUPPURATION within the kidney either follows upon suppuration in the lower urinary passages, spreading upwards from the bladder by way of the ureters, or infection may be carried by the blood-stream to the kidney from this or other regions. It is not of such frequent occurrence now as it was in the days before the use of antiseptics, when it went by the name of ' surgical kidney ', owing to the frequency with which this condition followed surgical operations on the urinary tract. The symptoms are much the same as those of inflammation in the bladder (*see* BLADDER, DISEASES OF), with, in addition, pain in the loins, a hectic temperature, and shivering fits or ' rigors '.

Treatment.—The condition is very serious, and was apt to end in death in the days before the introduction of the sulphonamides and penicillin. The outlook is now much better, provided these drugs are given early enough and in large enough doses. If the person be strong enough to stand the operation, an opening may be made into the kidney through the loins, and the suppurating cavity either drained or the whole kidney removed.

TUBERCULOSIS of the kidneys is more common in adults than in children, and more common in men than in women. For a long time it may give rise to no symptoms or signs. It must therefore always be considered a possible diagnosis in cases in which urinary symptoms arise for which no cause can be found. Diagnosis partly depends upon the finding of *Mycobacterium tuberculosis* in the urine. As in other forms of tuberculosis, treatment has been revolutionized by the introduction of the anti-tuberculosis drugs : streptomycin, para-amino-salacylic acid, and isoniazid. It is only in a minority of cases that surgical removal of the kidney is required.

MOVABLE KIDNEY is commoner in women than in men. The undue mobility of the kidney is part of a general visceroptosis, and treatment should be directed to this. One risk of an abnormally mobile kidney is hydro-nephrosis (*q.v.*) from kinking of the ureter. Occasional kinking of the ureter may cause what are known as ' Dietl's crises '—sudden attacks of intense abdominal pain radiating down the ureter, shivering, nausea, vomiting, fever, collapse. They are not common. If hydronephrosis develops, operation may be necessary.

INJURIES OF THE KIDNEY are very serious, although one of these organs may be completely shattered without a necessarily fatal result if the other kidney be healthy and uninjured. The kidney may be ruptured by a blow in the small of the back or when a person is run over, and death may result from the consequent loss of blood, which may appear in the urine.

TUMOURS of the kidney are not common, and, as a rule, they give little or no trouble till they have reached a large size. In the case of tumours growing in the pelvis of the kidney, large quantities of blood may be passed now and then in the urine with, however, no pain or other symptom referable to the kidney. Congenital cystic kidney is a form of tumour in the kidney which may last for many years with little trouble to the person in whom it occurs. Hypernephroma is a form of destructive tumour that occasionally develops in the kidney, being composed of cells resembling the supra-renal gland in appearance.

KINÆSTHETIC SENSATIONS is the descriptive term for those sensations which underlie tension and position of joint and muscle. These sensations send impulses along nerves to the brain, and thus inform it of the position of the limb in space and of the relative position to each other of individual muscles and muscle-groups and of joints.

KING'S EVIL is an old name for scrofula, which was in olden times sup-

posed to be curable by the touch of the royal hand. (*See* TUBERCULOSIS *and* SCROFULA.)

KINO is the dried juice of the *Ptero-carpus marsupium*, an Indian tree. It contains an astringent principle, and its powder is useful in the treatment of diarrhœa, the tincture being also used as a gargle for relaxed throat.

KLEPTOMANIA is a psychological disorder in which the person afflicted has an irresistible compulsion to steal things, without necessarily having any need for the object stolen.

KNEE is the joint formed by the femur, tibia, and patella. It belongs to the class of hinge-joints, although the movements that take place are much more complex than the simple motion of a hinge, the condyles of the femur partly rolling, partly sliding over the flat surfaces on the upper end of the tibia, and the acts of straightening and of bending the limb being finished and begun respectively by a certain amount of rotation. The cavity of the joint is very intricate, and it consists really of three joints fused into one, but separated in part by ligaments and folds of the synovial membrane. The ligaments which bind the bones together are extremely strong, and include the internal and the external lateral ligaments, a weak posterior ligament, a very strong patellar ligament uniting the patella to the front of the tibia, two crucial ligaments in the interior of the joint, and two fibro-cartilages which are interposed between the surfaces of tibia and femur at their edge (Plate XIII).

All these structures give to the knee-joint a great degree of strength, so that it is very seldom dislocated. Its exposed position and the intricacy and consequent difficulty in cleansing its cavity, render this joint liable to be wounded, and make wounds of it very serious. The knee may also be affected by tuberculous disease.

A troublesome condition frequently found in the knee consists of the loosening of one of the fibro-cartilages lying at the head of the tibia, especially of that on the inner side of the joint. The cartilage may either be loosened from its attachment and tend to slip beyond the edges of the bones, or it may become folded on itself. In either case, it tends to cause locking of the joint when sudden movements are made. This causes temporary inability to use the joint until the cartilage is replaced by forcible straightening, and the accident is apt to be followed by an attack of synovitis, which may last some weeks, causing a certain amount of lameness with pain and tenderness especially felt at a point on the inner side of the knee. This condition can be relieved by wearing for a prolonged period of some months a bandage with pad or knee-truss which presses upon the inner side of the joint, or it may be more quickly remedied by an operation to remove the loose portion of the cartilage. (*See* JOINTS, DISEASES OF.)

KNEE JERK (*see* REFLEX ACTION).

KNOCK-KNEE, or GENU VALGUM, is a deformity of the lower limbs in such a direction that when the limbs are straightened the legs diverge from one another. As a result, in walking the knees knock against each other. The amount of knock-knee is measured by the distance between the medial malleoli of the ankles, with the inner surfaces of the knee touching and the knee-caps facing forwards.

Causes.—The condition is so common in children between the ages of two to six years that it may almost be regarded as a normal phase in childhood. When marked, or persisting into later childhood, it is usually due to faulty muscular tone. The condition is aggravated in children who are overweight or debilitated. At one time rickets was a common cause, but this is seldom the cause to-day in Great Britain.

Treatment.—If rickets be the cause this must be treated. If, as is usually the case, there is no obvious cause, no treatment is required for knock-knee up to 3 inches (75 mm.) in a child under 7 years of age. In the vast majority of cases it will have righted itself by this age. If the degree of knock-knee is more severe than this splints may be necessary, or even operation. When there is established bony deformity with over 4 inches (100 mm.) of separation at the age of 4 years, or when there is still a considerable degree of knock-

knee at the age of 9 years, operation should be performed. This may consist of cutting away the prominent part of the inner side of the lower end of the femora.

KOHLER'S DISEASE is a not uncommon condition of the foot in younger schoolchildren, characterized by osteochondritis (*q.v.*) of the scaphoid bone.

KOILONYCHIA is the term applied to nails that are hollow and depressed like a spoon, a condition sometimes associated with chronic anæmia.

KOLA is the nut of *Kola acuminata*, a tree growing in various parts of Africa. It contains caffeine, upon which its action mainly depends, and also an astringent principle. Its action is a stimulating one, almost identical with that of tea or coffee (*see* COFFEE).

KOPLIK'S SPOTS are bluish-white spots appearing on the mucous membrane of the mouth in cases of measles about the third day, and forming the first part of the rash in this disease.

KORSAKOW'S SYNDROME is a term applied to a form of mental disturbance occurring in chronic alcoholism and other toxic states, such as uræmia, lead poisoning, cerebral syphilis. Its special features are talkativeness with delusions in regard to time and place, the patient, although clear in other matters, imagining that he has recently made journeys or been in distant places.

KOUMISS, or KEFIR, is a beverage made originally among the Kalmucks by fermenting mares' milk. It may be prepared from other kinds of milk also, and forms a stimulating and refreshing food which is sometimes better borne in weak states of the stomach than any other food. A home-made form of koumiss may be prepared as follows : mix 2 pints of buttermilk thoroughly with 3 pints of sweet milk, and add five lumps of white sugar. Place the milk in a bowl, cover with a towel, and let it stand in some warm corner of the kitchen for twenty-four hours. Then pour it into small bottles, cork them, and tie down the corks. Leave the bottles in the kitchen for three days, shaking occasionally. After this the koumiss is ready for use and should be kept in a cool place.

KÜMMELL'S DISEASE is a condition resulting from undiagnosed 'crush fracture' of a vertebra, due to injury. The patient complains of backache, persistent rigidity of the spine, and deformity.

KUPFFER CELLS are the star-shaped cells present in the blood-sinuses of the liver. They form part of the reticulo-endothelial system (*q.v.*) and are to a large extent responsible for the breakdown of hæmoglobin into the bile pigments.

KWASHIORKOR is one of the most important causes of ill health and death among children in the tropics. It is a deficiency disease due to a diet deficient in protein. It affects typically the small child weaned from the breast and not yet able to cope with an adult diet, and it is mainly found in the less well-developed countries.

The onset of the disease is characterized by loss of appetite, often with diarrhœa and loss of weight. The child is flabby, the skin is dry, and the hair is depigmented, dry, sparse, and brittle. At a later stage œdema develops and the liver is often enlarged. In the early stages the condition responds rapidly to a diet containing adequate first-class protein, but in the later stages this must be supplemented by careful nursing, especially as the child is very liable to infections.

KYPHOSIS (κυφός, bent) is the term applied to curvature of the spine in which the concavity of the curve is directed forwards. (*See* SPINE, DISEASES OF.)

L

LABIUM is the Latin word for a lip or lip-shaped organ.

LABOUR, or PARTURITION (*parturio*, I bring forth), often popularly spoken of as the confinement, is the act of bringing forth young, and forms the end of the period of gestation or pregnancy during which the new individual is nourished from the maternal body. Parturition is a comparatively easy matter in lower animals and amongst savage races. In the former the ease is dependent mainly upon the size and shape of the pelvic bones. In the latter this element is of course not present, but, apart from purely anatomical differences, there is evidence that the higher we pass in the scale of civilization, the more difficult does the act of parturition become.

It is difficult to define an absolutely *normal labour* because individual labours differ so much in small details. Generally speaking, however, a normal labour is one in which the vertex of the child's head is born first, and the whole process ends favourably to mother and child within twenty-four hours, and without any operative interference. In the case of a first baby the confinement usually lasts from fifteen to twenty hours, whilst the births of second and subsequent children tend to become progressively shorter processes. There are, of course, considerable variations in individual cases from these general statements. The majority of confinements end between midnight and 6 A.M. In 96 per cent. of all cases the vertex of the child's head presents (that is, leaves the womb and descends through the vagina to the exterior first). In some cases, owing to a faulty position of the head or to the presentation of the child's face, the labour is considerably delayed, while for various reasons operative assistance may be necessary, in which case the labour is known as an instrumental one. The child may present quite another part than the head, the second most frequent presentation being the breech. A rarer and more serious presentation is a transverse presentation or crossbirth, where the child lies obliquely across the womb. In these cases skilled assistance is specially necessary for the sake of both mother and child, and in the latter case assistance is imperative if the mother's life is to be saved. Finally, various complications, such as deformities of the mother and child, an excessive amount of bleeding, the birth of twins, and various general conditions of the mother, such as heart or kidney disease, convulsions, etc., may influence the progress of the labour to an extreme degree.

Stages of labour. — The process of labour is naturally divided into three stages. The *first stage* is that of dilatation of the neck of the womb to permit of the subsequent descent of the child. This is ushered in by the onset of the pains caused by the powerful intermittent contractions of the muscular wall of the womb. At first the pains come at considerable intervals—ten to twenty minutes—but as time passes the intervals become shorter and the pains become stronger. This stage is much the longest but is at the same time the least liable to complications or dangers to either mother or child. It is sometimes accompanied by sickness and vomiting. The full dilatation of the mouth of the womb is usually accompanied by the rupture of the amnion, the membrane containing the fluid in which the fœtus moves, and the sudden escape of the amniotic fluid or 'waters'. The two events, however, do not necessarily take place at the same time, and sometimes the amnion ruptures at a much earlier, and sometimes at a later, period.

The *second stage* is the stage of expulsion of the child, during which the child's head, followed by the body and limbs, descends through the bony girdle of the pelvis and passes down through the vagina to the exterior. This process usually occupies two hours in a first labour, but, in the case of a woman who has had several children before, it may occupy a much shorter time. During its passage through the pelvis, the child's head goes through certain movements by which it adapts itself to the alterations in the shape of the pelvic canal as it passes down. The size of the head of an average child is such that there is just room for it to pass through the pelvis and no more. Accordingly the head is liable to be considerably pressed upon during this stage of labour, and this pressure manifests itself in the moulding of the child's skull. This moulding, which is rendered possible by the softness of the bones and by the presence of spaces between the bones, is a valuable provision of nature, and enables the head to pass down with the minimum of damage to the child and to the mother. In most cases the moulding disappears in the first day or two after birth, but in extreme cases, where the labour has been long and difficult, some degree of moulding may persist throughout life. The second stage is one of strenuous muscular exertion, as not only the muscular wall of the womb, but the abdominal muscles and the diaphragm are all involuntarily called into play to aid the expulsion of the child. Pains are more severe, but at the same time the patient has a consciousness that she is making progress and this sometimes makes them more easily tolerated than the pains of the first stage. It is towards the end of the second stage that an anæsthetic is usually administered, the actual birth of the head being the time of greatest agony. Immediately thereafter there is a pause for a moment or two, and then the child's body is born, thus completing the second stage of labour. As soon as it is born the child usually cries loudly and in doing so establishes the function of respiration. The tying and cutting of the umbilical cord (*see* AFTERBIRTH) finally sever the child's vital connection with its mother.

The *third stage* is the stage of delivery of the afterbirth. It begins immediately the child is born and rarely lasts more than half an hour. It is associated with the loss of a certain amount of blood, but this is not usually more than about 15 oz. or thereby. The great danger is from excessive hæmorrhage associated with the separation of the afterbirth from the wall of the womb, and although the stage is much the shortest, yet this danger makes it imperative that it should be conducted with the greatest care.

Management of labour. — In the ab-

sence of skilled assistance a normal labour will in all probability conduct itself to a successful issue, but it is always desirable that trained assistance should be obtained, both for the comfort as well as for the safety of the mother and the child. Obstetrical complications have a habit of arising suddenly and sometimes unexpectedly.

Where trained assistance is not at once available, the untrained person can still do much to help the prospective mother. As soon as the labour begins the patient should, if possible, have the lower bowel washed out with a soap-and-water enema, and if there is time it is advisable for the patient to have a warm bath, or at least to have the genital regions thoroughly washed with soap and water. The bed upon which she is to be delivered should be prepared with a mackintosh sheet if possible, or failing that, one or two sheets of glazed brown paper, placed across the middle of the bed and drawn well over the right-hand edge of it. A draw-sheet should be placed over this which can be changed afterwards. The clothing for the infant should be hung before the fire to be aired and warmed, and provision should be made for an ample supply of hot water and clean basins for the doctor or nurse, who should have been sent for. Ligatures should be prepared for tying the umbilical cord and these are best made of 3-ply linen thread twisted together and knotted at the ends so as to form a ligature of about ten inches in length. Two of these are required, and should be sterilized by being boiled. The patient may, with advantage, remain up, either sitting or moving about her room as may be most comfortable for her, during the first stage ; but when she feels fatigued and desires to lie down, and in any case when the membranes rupture and the ' waters ' escape, she should lie down on the bed on her left side.

During the second stage the patient will tend involuntarily to hold her breath and press down during the pains, and this down-bearing, as it is called, is helpful and should be encouraged, as it will expedite delivery. It is a mistake to urge a woman to bear down during the first stage, as it does no good and merely exhausts her strength. It

PLATE XIII

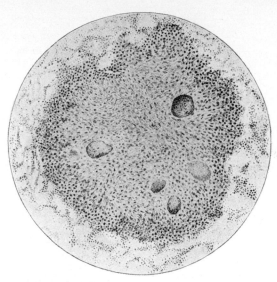

Section of tubercle (highly magnified). The tubercle is surrounded by a zone of normal tissue. The ring of dark dots round the tubercle are leucocytes. Inside the tubercle five giant cells are seen. (From Fowler's *Pulmonary Tuberculosis*. Macmillan & Co. Ltd.) *See* TUBERCULOSIS and TUBERCLE.

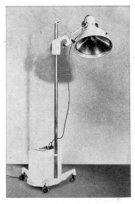

Hanovia Alpine Lamp, Model VII. (Hanovia Ltd., Slough.) *See* LIGHT TREATMENT.

A.   B.

A. Smooth muscle fibre from intestine of cat. Note nucleus. Magnified 250 times. B. Muscle cells of intestine. *i*, Interstice between muscle fibres, bridged across by fine fibres; *n*, nucleus. Magnified 530 times. (From Schafer's *Histology*. Longmans, Green & Co., Ltd.) *See* MUSCLE.

PLATE XIV

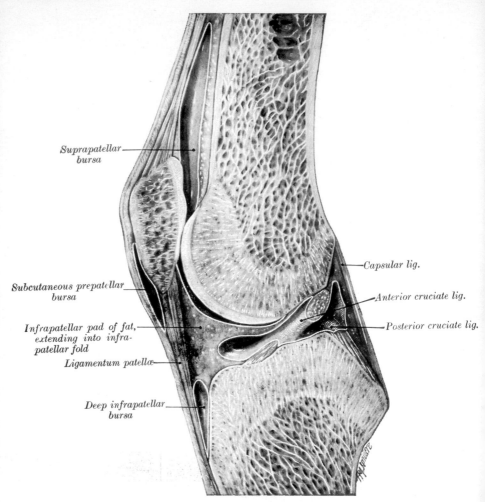

Suprapatellar bursa

Subcutaneous prepatellar bursa

Infrapatellar pad of fat, extending into infra- patellar fold

Ligamentum patellæ

Deep infrapatellar bursa

Capsular lig.

Anterior cruciate lig.

Posterior cruciate lig.

Vertical section of knee joint. (From Gray's *Anatomy*. Longmans, Green & Co., Ltd.)

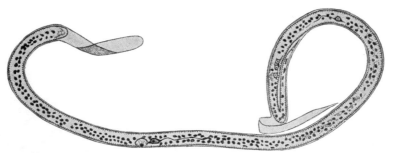

Microfilaria bancrofti. (*Wuchereria bancrofti.*) (From Manson's *Tropical Diseases*. Cassell & Co. Ltd.)
See PARASITES and FILARIASIS.

helps the patient to be given something to hold on to during the down-bearing pains of the second stage, and it is a customary thing to tie a roller towel to the head of the bed and give her that to pull upon. This enables her to fix her abdominal muscles and to use her strength to the greatest advantage.

As soon as the child's head is born its eyes should be gently wiped clean with a pledget of cotton-wool or a clean soft linen handkerchief moistened in clean boiled water. After the child is born the cord should not be ligatured for two or three minutes until the pulsation in it is beginning to cease. One of the linen ligatures should then be tied tightly round the umbilical cord at a distance of about two inches from the child's navel. The other should be applied a few inches nearer the mother. With a clean pair of scissors which has been boiled, the cord should then be divided between the two ligatures. It is essential to make sure that there is no bleeding from the child's end of the cut umbilical cord. The infant should then be wrapped in a soft flannel or shawl and laid aside in some warm place until arrangements can be made for bathing it. After the delivery of the child there will be an interval of some minutes before the uterine contractions start once more, and as a rule only a few contractions are needed to bring about the expulsion of the afterbirth or placenta. This should be placed in a basin with some clean water and kept for inspection by the doctor or nurse.

All that now remains to be done is to clean the patient by gently swabbing her with pledgets of cotton-wool wrung out of clean boiled-water, the hands of anybody who comes in contact with the patient having been previously most carefully and scrupulously scrubbed. A clean pad of cotton-wool, preferably scorched in front of a hot fire to sterilize it, should then be placed over the genitals and a firm binder drawn round the hips and over the lower part of the abdomen. A clean bolster slip serves this purpose admirably. After the confinement is over, the patient should be encouraged to sleep, or at least to rest quietly, and anything in the nature of excitement is to be avoided. For this reason friends

and neighbours should, as far as possible, be excluded until the patient has had a good sleep.

Abnormalities and dangers of labour. —These may rise in connection with the presentation or position of the child, with the uterus or maternal pelvis, or from the general conditions of the mother's health. ABNORMAL PRESENTATIONS are relatively uncommon. The most frequent is a *breech presentation* (3½ per cent. of all labours). Here the labour is apt to be slow, but while there should be no increased risk to the mother (unless the labour happens to be a first labour), there is considerably greater danger to the child. Skilled assistance should always be obtained, but in the absence thereof the labour should be allowed to conduct itself without interference, until the lower limbs are born. These should then be wrapped in a warm flannel and gently supported, while steady pressure is applied to the top of the womb through the mother's abdominal wall. The after-coming head is thus gently pressed down into and through the pelvis. The main risk to the child is pressure on the umbilical cord during this stage, as it lies between the head of the child and the hard, bony pelvis. If this pressure is sufficient to impede the child's circulation for more than 8 or 10 minutes, the probability is that the child will be suffocated before it is born. (It must be understood that, until the head is born, the child obtains the necessary oxygen by interchanges taking place between its blood and the blood of the mother in the placenta or after-birth, and that pressure on the cord prevents the passage of the fœtal blood between the body of the fœtus and the placenta.)

Face presentations occur but seldom (0·4 per cent. of all labours). Usually the mother is able to deliver herself after a prolonged and tedious labour. The outlook is tolerably good for the child and should be satisfactory for the mother. There are, however, possibilities of serious danger, and medical help should always be sought.

The most dangerous mal-presentation is a *cross-birth*, where the child lies across the womb and the pelvis. None but an extremely premature child can be born in this position. If the condition is not corrected, the womb

17

goes on trying to expel the child until it either becomes utterly exhausted and ceases to contract, or else it ruptures. In the former event, sufficient time may be gained—before the womb starts to contract again—in which to obtain skilled assistance to change the position of the child. In this way the mother's life may be saved, although the child will almost certainly have succumbed. In the second event, the shock and internal bleeding from the ruptured womb involve very grave risk to the mother's life, and delivery is impossible except by skilled assistance.

DEFORMITIES AND CONTRACTIONS of the mother's pelvis create great difficulty and may make natural labour impossible. The pelvis of every woman pregnant for the first time should be measured by a medical practitioner prior to labour with a view to the exclusion of any such possibility. Sometimes labour has to be induced early in these cases ; in others, operative delivery at full time has to be arranged.

HÆMORRHAGE during the last three months of pregnancy, or during labour, is always fraught with serious possibilities. It is due to the premature detachment of some portion of the placenta, which in many cases is situated too low down in the womb (*placenta prævia*). In the absence of skilled assistance, all that can be done is to keep the patient quite quiet in bed with the head low. No alcoholic stimulants should be given.

Bleeding during the third stage of labour or immediately after (*post-partum hæmorrhage*) can be alarming and even fatal. In the absence of skilled assistance an attempt should be made to compress the womb forcibly by grasping it through the abdominal muscles. The foot of the bed may, with advantage, be raised and the patient provided with ample fresh air. Again, no alcoholic stimulants should be given, as these only serve to increase the bleeding. Very hot applications to the vulva may help, and the doctor or nurse may administer a hot vaginal douche. (*See* DOUCHE.)

CONVULSIONS in association with pregnancy or labour, or occurring immediately after labour (*eclampsia*), constitute one of the most grave complications. Medical advice should be obtained without fail, and in the absence of such the patient should be kept absolutely quiet in a darkened room, surrounded with blankets and hot-water bottles to stimulate the action of the sweat glands. The bowel should be washed out thoroughly with repeated enemata of plain warm water, and if the patient is conscious and able to swallow, liberal doses of purgative medicine should be given. No food, either solid or liquid, should be given. The actual convulsion should be treated on the ordinary lines, and if labour ensues, it also should be treated on ordinary lines. (*See* ECLAMPSIA.)

PUERPERAL INFECTION is the most frequent and one of the most serious complications of labour. This is, in essence, the same as the infection of a wound, there being always a large raw surface in the interior of the uterus (the placental site), and in most cases innumerable small lacerations of the birth canal. All or any of these may be invaded by bacteria which subsequently tend to invade the blood-stream of the mother and give rise to acute septicæmia. About half the puerperal infections are due to the hæmolytic streptococcus and about half to other organisms. The hæmolytic streptococcus reaches the genital tract from the doctor, nurse, or midwife, from one of the patient's own household, or from the patient's own nasopharynx. The swabbing of throats, the exclusion from the patient's presence of streptococcal carriers and of anyone with a cold or sore throat, strict aseptic precautions during labour, will all help to diminish the incidence of hæmolytic streptococcal puerperal infections. If infection occurs in spite of all precautions, then the sulphonamide drugs and penicillin are at hand as sovereign remedies. (*See* PUERPERAL FEVER.)

LACHESINE, or benzilyl-oxyethyl-dimethyl-ethyl-ammonium chloride, is a mydriatic, *i.e.* it dilates the pupil of the eye. It is sometimes used for this purpose instead of atropine, as its action is of shorter duration.

LACRIMAL (*lacrima*, a tear) apparatus is the arrangement attached to the eye for moistening and cleansing the front of this organ. (*See* EYE.)

LACTATION (*lac*, milk) is the period during which an infant is suckled on the mother's breast. (*See* BREASTS, DISEASES OF; INFANT FEEDING.)

LACTIC ACID (*lac*, milk) is a colourless, syrupy, sour liquid, which is produced by the action of a bacterium upon the sugar of milk. The growth of this organism and consequent formation of lactic acid causes the souring of milk, and the same change takes place to a limited extent when food is long retained in the stomach.

Lactic acid ($CH_2 . CHOH . COOH$) is produced in the body during muscular activity, the lactic acid being derived from the breakdown of glycogen. Muscle fatigue is associated with an accumulation of lactic acid in the muscle. Recovery follows when enough oxygen gets to the muscle, part of the lactic acid being oxidized and most of it then being built up once more into glycogen.

LACTIC ACID BACILLI were introduced by Metchnikoff to prepare milk as a special article of diet, similar to koumiss. The bacilli, which are issued in various forms, as tablets, in fluid, etc., are added to fresh milk, allowed to act upon it in a warm place for several hours (according to the degree of sourness desired), and the milk is then consumed with the active bacilli. These, after a course of such treatment, come to replace the bacteria naturally found in the intestines, and are supposed to be less injurious to the system. Sour milk forms a healthy article of diet ; and the bacilli, which are harmless, have, in some cases of intestinal disease or of rheumatism, a beneficial action. Buttermilk has a similar effect.

LACTOMETER is the name of an instrument for ascertaining the specific gravity of milk.

LACTOSE is the official name for sugar of milk. (*See* SUGAR.)

LACUNA (*lacuna*) means a small pit or depression. Lacunar tonsillitis is a form of inflammation of the tonsils. (*See* TONSILLITIS.)

LÆVULOSE is the name of a sugar which forms one of the constituents of grape-sugar.

LAGOPHTHALMOS is the term describing the condition in which the eye cannot be completely closed.

LAMBLIA, or GIARDIA, is the name of a genus of parasitic organisms found in the intestine, which are usually harmless but are sometimes responsible for causing diarrhœa. Cases of diarrhœa due to Lamblia infections respond well to mepacrine.

LAMELLA is a small disc of glycerin jelly, $\frac{1}{8}$ inch (3 mm.) in diameter, containing an active drug for application to the eye. It is applied by inserting behind the lower lid. The two official lamellæ are those containing atropine, and cocaine and homatropine.

LAMENESS (*see* GAIT *and* JOINTS, DISEASES OF).

LAMINECTOMY is the term applied to an operation in which the arches of one or more vertebræ are removed so as to expose a portion of the spinal cord for removal of a tumour, relief of pressure due to a fracture, or similar reason.

LANOLIN is a fat derived from the wool of the common sheep. It is much used for ointments because it does not become rancid, and because it is supposed to have a special power of penetrating the skin. It is very sticky, and for use is mixed generally with an equal quantity of petroleum jelly to make it softer. Lanolin also possesses the valuable propeity of being able to mix with and absorb water to a considerable extent.

LAPAROTOMY (λαπάρα, the flank ; τομή, an operation) is a general term applied to any operation in which the abdominal cavity is opened.

LARDACEOUS DISEASE (*lardum*, bacon) is another name for waxy disease (*q.v.*).

LARYNGISMUS STRIDULUS, or SPASMODIC CROUP (λάρυγξ, the windpipe ; *stridor*, noise), is a spasmodic condition in children, in which great difficulty of breathing, accompanied by a crowing noise, comes on as the result of partial closure of the larynx. The children affected by it are generally suffering from rickets. It is rare over the age of two or three years. Attacks may be precipitated by fright, irritation or a cold draught. The attack may come on at any time during the day, or even during sleep ; the spasm may amount only to difficulty of breathing or the stoppage may be almost complete.

Treatment is similar to that for croup. (*See* CROUP.)

LARYNGITIS (λάρυγξ, the windpipe) means inflammation of the larynx. (*See* THROAT, DISEASES OF, *and* CLERGYMAN'S SORE THROAT.)

LARYNGOFISSURE is the term applied to the operation of cutting the thyroid cartilage or Adam's apple down the middle in order to get access to the larynx, for example, in operating on cancer of the larynx.

LARYNGOLOGY is that branch of medical science which is concerned with disorders and diseases of the larynx and those parts of the respiratory tract immediately above and below it.

LARYNGOSCOPE (λάρυγξ, the windpipe ; σκοπέω, I examine) is an instrument introduced by Signor Manuel

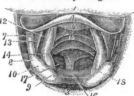

FIG. 250.—View of the larynx with the laryngoscope during the taking of a deep breath. The figures in this and the following three figures indicate structures as follows : 1, base of tongue ; 2, back wall of throat ; 3, entrance to the gullet ; 4, epiglottis ; 5, arytenoid cartilages ; 6, cushion of the epiglottis ; 7, aryteno-epiglottic ligament ; 8, 9, cartilages of Wrisberg and Santorini above the arytenoid cartilage ; 10, intervening tubercle ; 11, vocal process of arytenoid cartilage ; 12, true vocal cord ; 13, false vocal cords ; 14, entrance to ventricle ; 15, front wall of windpipe ; 16, back wall of wind pipe ; 17, 18, entrances to the right and left bronchial tubes. (Bennett's *Medicine*.)

Garcia, a London teacher of singing, about the middle of the nineteenth century, and first used for medical purposes by Türck and Czermak about 1858. The essential parts of the laryngoscope are a small mirror set upon a long stem at an angle of about 120°, for introduction into the back of the patient's throat,

and a source of bright light placed close to the observer's eye. The light is most conveniently got from a lamp placed by

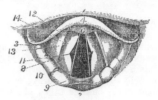

FIG. 251.—View of the larynx during ordinary breathing. (Bennett's *Medicine*.)

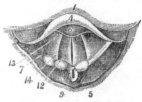

FIG. 252.—View of the larynx when the vocal cords are closed, as in sounding a high note. (Bennett's *Medicine*.)

FIG. 253.—View of the larynx showing complete closure of the glottis, as in the act of swallowing. (Bennett's *Medicine*.)

the side of the patient's head; the beam from this lamp is reflected by a mirror attached to a forehead-band or spectacle frame worn by the observer. Or the light may proceed from a small electric lamp directly attached to the observer's forehead. For the uses of the instrument, and the appearances observed by its help, *see* Figs. 250 to 253, and THROAT DISEASES.

LARYNGO-TRACHEO-BRONCHITIS is an acute infection of the respiratory tract in infants and young children. In the old days it was often referred to as ' croup '. The onset is sudden, usually in a child who has had a cold to which little significance has been attached. Quite often the first sign is when the child wakens up with a loud inspiratory stridor and a harsh, barking cough. Distress and restlessness ensue rapidly, and in some cases tracheotomy may be required as a life-saving measure.

Because of the seriousness of the condition, these children should always be treated in hospital if at all possible.

LARYNX (λάρυγξ) is the organ of voice, and also forms one of the higher parts of the air passages. It is placed

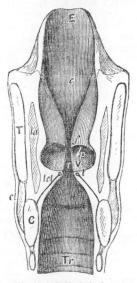

Fig. 254.—The front half of the larynx as shown by a vertical transverse section. E, Epiglottis; c, its cushion-like prominence; T, thyroid cartilage; ta, thyro-arytenoid muscle; C, cricoid cartilage; ct, crico-thyroid muscle; f, false vocal cord; t, true vocal cord; p, points to its prolongation forwards; V, ventricle of the larynx; r, rima of the glottis; lct, lateral crico-thyroid membrane, of which the true cord forms the edge; Tr, trachea. (Turner's *Anatomy*.)

high up in the front of the neck, and there forms a considerable prominence on the surface. It is covered in front by the skin, a layer of fibrous tissue, and a thin layer of muscle, whilst its sides are protected by the lateral lobes of the thyroid gland, and by the large sternomastoid muscles.

The larynx is almost 2 inches (5 cm.) in height, and forms a sort of box, well protected in front by cartilages, rather more open behind, and communicating above with the throat at the root of the tongue, below with the windpipe. The larynx is enclosed by five large cartilages : the thyroid cartilage, whose prominent pointed front forms the Adam's apple ; the cricoid cartilage, a ring placed beneath it ; the epiglottis,

a leaf-like cartilage standing on the upper edge of the thyroid cartilage, and projecting up into the interior of the

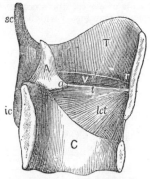

Fig. 255.—View of the interior of the left side of the larynx, the mucous membrane having been removed. T, Thyroid cartilage ; sc, its superior, and ic, its inferior horn ; r, its front angle, to which the cords are attached ; A, arytenoid cartilage ; a, its vocal process, to which the true cord is attached ; t, true cord ; f, false cord ; V, ventricle of the larynx ; C, cricoid cartilage ; lct, lateral crico-thyroid membrane. (Turner's *Anatomy*.)

throat at the root of the tongue ; and a pair of arytenoid cartilages jointed to the top edge of the cricoid cartilage behind, where the thyroid is deficient. There are also four small nodules of

Fig. 256.—Diagram of the opening of the larynx to show the action of the muscles. A horizontal section has been made at the level of the true vocal cords. TT, Thyroid cartilage ; AA, arytenoid cartilages with aa, vocal processes, and ee, muscular processes ; C, upper border of cricoid cartilage ; v, the vocal, and r, the respiratory part of the opening. The two cords are widely separated by the action of pca, the posterior crico-arytenoid muscles. (Turner's *Anatomy*.)

cartilage above the arytenoids. The edges of the laryngeal cartilages do not fit closely together, and the spaces between are filled up by membranes. Certain of the ligaments which bind the cartilages together are of great importance. There pass along each side of the larynx, from the arytenoid cartilage behind to the thyroid cartilage in front, two bands of elastic fibres covered by the mucous membrane which lines the

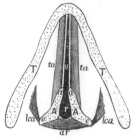

FIG. 257.—Diagram of the opening of the larynx to show the action of the muscles. The letters indicate the same structures as in the last figure, but the cords are now almost close together, by the action of *ta*, the thyroarytenoid, *lca*, the lateral arytenoid, and *ar*, the arytenoid muscles. (Turner's *Anatomy*.)

whole larynx. One pair of these bands lies directly above the other, the upper pair being known as the false vocal cords ; the lower pair are the true vocal cords. The latter are capable of various degrees of tenseness and slackness, and of approximation and separation, these results being achieved by several small muscles, which are attached to the arytenoid cartilages, and governed in their movements through branches of the vagus nerves. Between the true and false cord is a deep depression on each side, the ventricle or sinus of the larynx, from which a pouch, half an inch long, leads upwards exterior to the false cord. The larynx is lined throughout by mucous membrane, which generally is covered by ciliated cells (*see* EPITHELIUM) ; but over the true cords, which are subject to much friction in the production of the voice, the surface consists of flattened cells similar to those of the skin.

The vocal cords vibrating in different notes, according to their tenseness, etc., produce the sounds of voice and speech. (*See* VOICE AND SPEECH.)

LARYNX, DISEASES OF (*see* THROAT DISEASES).

LASER stands for Light Amplification by the Stimulated Emission of Radiation. It is a potent form of energy which is proving of value in the

treatment of detachment of the retina (*q.v.*). Its three great advantages are its potency, the speed with which it acts and the facility with which it can be focused on a small area—even an area as small as 1 micron.

LASSAR'S PASTE is the name given to a preparation extensively used as a remedy for eczema. It has a combined softening, antiseptic, astringent, and soothing action, and is made up as follows : oxide of zinc, 120 grains (8 grammes) ; starch, 120 grains (8 grammes) ; petroleum jelly, 240 grains (16 grammes). To this 5 or 10 grains (300 or 600 mg.) of salicylic acid are usually added.

LATHYRISM is the term applied to a disease in which stiffness, pains in, and trembling and paralysis of, the legs are caused by varieties of chick-pea.

LAUDANUM is the popular name for tincture of opium. (*See* OPIUM.)

LAUGHING-GAS is a popular name for nitrous oxide, which is used as an anæsthetic for short operations.

LAUREL is the name applied to two plants ; one of these, *Laurus nobilis* or bay tree, affords leaves and berries from which an oil is extracted which is used for application in rheumatic and similar pains ; the other, *Prunus laurocerasus* or cherry laurel, affords cherry laurel water, containing a small quantity of hydrocyanic acid, and is much used for making up soothing solutions.

LAURYL THIOCYANATE (*see* INSECTS IN RELATION TO DISEASE, *under* LICE).

LAVAGE (French word) is the name applied to the washing out of the stomach (*see* DYSPEPSIA).

LAXATIVES (*see* PURGATIVES).

LEAD has no action itself upon the system, but its salts, when absorbed in any quantity, or for any length of time, have very important effects. When a lead salt comes in contact with a wound or with any mucous surface, it combines with the albuminous material of the discharge or secretion to form a whitish glaze, which affords a great degree of protection to the surface. Further, the lead salt has an astringent action upon the blood-vessels, and therefore helps to stop bleeding or relieve the congestion of inflammation. If one of the soluble lead salts be taken internally, in large amount, it has an irritant action, and the acetate (sugar of lead), subacetate, and nitrate of lead are irritant poisons when taken into the stomach, although their action is comparatively feeble.

Uses.—Externally, subacetate of lead is used in the form of Goulard's water, for application to painful areas, such as inflamed joints, bruises, sprains. (*See* GOULARD'S WATER.) In eczema this solution, sponged upon the affected area, often gives relief from itching. Liniment of subacetate of lead and glycerin of subacetate of lead are similarly used. Litharge or oxide of lead is used as a basis for many adhesive plasters, which are known as ' Diachylon ' plasters. Internally, the main use of acetate of lead is to check diarrhœa, and the favourite form in which it is used for this purpose is in lead-and-opium pill. It is also used in suppositories for the treatment of bleeding piles.

LEAD-POISONING.—Acute poisoning by lead acetate (sugar of lead) is an accident which sometimes, though rarely, happens to a child, and is treated, like cases of irritant poisoning generally, by administering diluents such as milk together with Epsom salts, which form an antidote, followed by emetics.

Chronic poisoning is apt to affect those who come in contact with lead or its salts, either in the production of these or in the course of their use in various arts and manufactures. Thus lead-smelters, plumbers, typefounders, compositors, file - makers, pottery workers who use lead in glaze, painters, dyers, above all, those who make white-lead, and also persons following various other callings, are liable to suffer. Lead may also be introduced into the system through the food, in those who have nothing to do with the metal in their work ; for example, drinking-water is sometimes contaminated by lead which it has dissolved off the pipes through which it passes, or tinned fruits may dis-

solve lead out of the solder with which the tins are sealed, or cider, made in leaden presses, may so readily take up lead that 'Devonshire colic' was once a name given to lead-poisoning occurring in this part of the country, where cider forms a favourite beverage. As regards drinking-water there is, in general, no danger, because the minerals in the water form, with the lead, insoluble compounds which are deposited in a thin coat upon the inside of the pipes. Pipes of bright untarnished lead, as in newly built houses, or an absolutely pure water which does not contain any mineral ingredients, may introduce an element of danger. But a greater danger exists in peaty water or in water contaminated by organic impurities, both of which give the water a high power of dissolving lead. Sufficient organic impurity may be derived from small quantities of sewage, or even from the body of a bird or small animal drowned in a cistern. Not only may the lead be introduced into the system through the skin of those who constantly handle lead-containing materials, and by way of the stomach, but in some of the most rapidly produced and serious cases—for example, among white-lead workers, and glazers of pottery—the lead is inhaled as dry dust. Lead is often similarly inhaled by men engaged in cutting up iron plates which have been fitted by the aid of red lead ; this, being driven off by the heat of the blow-pipe employed, is apt to be inhaled.

Symptoms.—Among the early symptoms of a chronic and insidious case are constipation, muscular weakness, and pallor of the skin. A blue line on the margin of the gums, due to deposit of lead sulphide in this locality, is also an important sign of the condition. Colic of a very painful nature, affecting the centre of the abdomen and lasting often for several days at a time, appears and forms one of the most prominent symptoms in almost every case. Lead has a specially injurious action upon the nervous system, causing an inflammatory process in the nerves, which results in tremors and paralysis, usually affecting the muscles on the back of the wrist first of all, and later those on the front and outer side of the leg, and causing wrist-drop and foot-drop. Convulsions, which may develop rapidly and may end in death, are also produced by poisoning of the nervous system, leading to a brain disorder known as lead encephalopathy. Occasionally, though fortunately rarely, affection of the optic nerve leads to blindness, which is either temporary or permanent. Owing to interference with the kidney functions, the urine becomes scanty, while a destructive action on the blood leads to anæmia.

Treatment.—With regard to workers in lead and its salts, government regulations have been introduced which very effectively protect them. Thus, in 1952 only 48 cases of lead-poisoning were notified, and none of these was fatal. Among these preventive measures are included : personal cleanliness in washing the hands and changing the clothes before partaking of meals, the use of respirators by those who come in contact with white-lead dust, the provision of exhaust flues and electric fans beneath the tables at which pottery glazers work, and the drinking of at least a glass of milk daily. These and other measures confer a great degree of protection upon those engaging in these otherwise dangerous trades. Workers who begin to show symptoms of lead-poisoning should at once undergo treatment. A frequent recurrence of symptoms shows a special liability to this form of poisoning, and indicates that the worker should seek some totally different employment. In the case of drinking-water the source of contamination must, of course, be removed. The drug which is of special use in treatment of lead-poisoning is calcium disodium versenate, by which lead salts deposited in the tissues are dissolved, to be afterwards excreted from the body. Colic is treated by hot fomentations, magnesium sulphate, and belladonna, and a high calcium diet.

In acute cases of lead colic the intravenous administration of calcium gluconate or calcium chloride gives immediate relief.

LEADERS is a popular name for the tendons or sinews at wrist, ankle, etc. (*See* TENDON.)

LEBER'S DISEASE, or HEREDITARY OPTIC ATROPHY, is a hereditary disease in which blindness comes on at about the age of twenty.

520

LECITHIN (λέκιθος, the yolk of an egg) is a very complex fat found in various tissues of the body, but particularly in the brain and nerves, of which it forms a large part. It is also found in large quantities in the yolk of an egg.

LEECHES are animals belonging to the class Vermes, provided with suckers and living a semi-parasitic life, their food being mainly derived from the blood of other animals. They abstract blood by means of a sucker surrounding the mouth, which is provided with several large sharp teeth. The medicinal leech, *Hirudo medicinalis*, was formerly employed to a large extent for the abstraction of small quantities of blood in inflammatory and other conditions.

LEG (*see* DROPSY, FRACTURES, KNOCK-KNEE, LIMBS; VEINS, DISEASES OF, etc.).—This term is generally applied to the whole lower extremity but, properly speaking, includes that part between the knee and ankle joints. The lower limb is attached to the pelvic bones by strong muscles, especially the gluteal and hamstring muscles behind and the abductor muscles on the inner side of the thigh. The head of the femur or thigh bone lies in a deep cup-shaped hollow, the acetabulum, on the outer side of the pelvis. The femur, which is the longest and strongest bone in the body, forms at its lower end the joint of the knee with the tibia. The knee-joint is protected in front by the patella or knee-cap. Along the outer side of the tibia lies the smaller fibula, which does not extend up to the knee but which, along with the tibia, forms the ankle joint. The two prominences on the ankle (*malleoli*) are formed by the tibia on the inner side and the fibula on the outer side. Seven tarsal bones comprise the hinder part of the foot, of which the astragalus takes the weight of the body from the tibia and fibula. There are five metatarsal bones in the front portion of the foot and each toe has three phalangeal bones, excepting the great toe, which has two. The powerful quadriceps extensor muscle in front of the thigh is attached to the knee-cap, which in turn is attached to the front of the tibia by the patellar tendon. This muscle straightens the knee and keeps the body in an erect posture. Below the knee the muscles of the calf, attached to the heel through the tendon of Achilles, raise the heel off the ground in walking. In front of and to the outside of the leg lie the tibial and peroneal muscles, which bend the ankle upwards and raise the toes. In the sole of the foot are a number of small muscles which bend the toes downwards. The arch of the foot is a very important structure (*see* FOOT).

Most of the blood supply to the lower limb is carried by the femoral artery, which issues from the abdomen in the middle of the groin where its pulse can be felt. This passes down the inner side of the thigh to reach the middle of the back of the knee, where it is known as the popliteal artery. Below the knee it divides into anterior and posterior tibial vessels. The former of these runs down the front of the leg and upper surface of the foot, and the latter, which is the larger, passes behind the inner ankle where its pulse can be felt about a finger's - breadth behind the bony prominence. The chief nerve in the lower limb is the great sciatic nerve which runs down the middle of the back of the thigh deeply embedded in muscles. Behind the knee it divides into two parts, the internal and external popliteal nerves. The former of these runs down the back of the leg, deeply embedded in muscles, to the foot, and the latter passes round the upper end of the fibula on the outer side of the leg, where it can be felt and is liable to be damaged. The blood returns from the leg partly by deep veins lying alongside the arteries, but to a large extent by the saphenous vein, which can be seen or felt under the skin for most of the distance from the inner ankle up the inside of the leg and thigh to the inner side of the groin, where it joins the femoral vein.

The arch of the foot is liable to give way, especially in debilitated or overworked persons, thus producing flat foot. The ankle joint is liable to sprains which consist of tearing of the ligaments, especially on the inner side. The fibula is liable to be fractured near its lower end, either by twists of the foot or by a blow on the outer side of the leg. Fracture of the tibia is also a common accident and, as the tibia lies

17 a

immediately beneath the skin, this fracture is in danger of becoming compound. The knee-joint, by reason of its great strength, is very seldom dislocated, but the partial displacement of a cartilage in the knee is a common occurrence. Fracture of the femur is a serious accident, requiring a period of several months for complete union of the bone. The long and poorly supported vein on the inner side of the leg and thigh is very apt to become distended along with its branches, producing the condition known as varicose veins with resultant eczema and ulcer. The bursa in front of the knee-cap, in persons who kneel much, readily becomes inflamed and thickened in the condition known as ' housemaid's knee '.

LEGUME is the pod or seed of a leguminous plant such as the pea or bean. As foods, legumes are of importance because of the relatively large amount of protein they contain. Peas in the fresh state may contain from 3 to 6 per cent. of protein, which is from one-sixth to one-third the amount of protein contained in fish, beef, and similar animal foods. Beans contain rather more, and string or French beans somewhat less protein. They differ from meat foods in two important respects, however, one being that they contain from 5 to 15 per cent. of carbohydrate, and the second difference being that vegetable protein does not contain all the amino-acids (*q.v.*) which are essential to health. They can never, therefore, completely replace animal protein. Legumes are not rich in vitamins, but they contain a varying amount of aneurine and riboflavine. They are fairly rich in iron, but contain little calcium. It is thus evident that legumes are a useful constituent of the normal diet. (*See also* DIET, and SOYA BEAN.)

LEIOMYOMA is the term applied to a tumour made up of unstriped or involuntary muscle fibres.

LEISHMANIASIS is the general name applied to a group of diseases, of which kala-azar is the chief, caused by parasites of the genus Leishmania. (*See* KALA-AZAR.)

LEMON is used in the form of the fresh peel, tincture, syrup, and oil.

Its main value, however, is as a source of vitamin C (or ascorbic acid), the average content of ascorbic acid being 45 mg. per 100 grammes. The juice, of course, has a somewhat higher content : 60 mg. of ascorbic acid per 100 grammes. (*See also* CITRIC ACID, and VITAMINS.)

LENS OF THE EYE is one of the refractive media through which light passes before reaching the retina. The lens is important, because its bulging and flattening, brought about by the ciliary muscle, automatically adjust the eye for focusing correctly on the retina rays of light from objects at varying distances. The lens begins to lose this power at the age of forty, hence the need of spectacles for near work as age advances. (*See* ACCOMMODATION.) The lens is the seat of the opacity which constitutes a cataract. (*See* CATARACT, EYE, *and* EYE, DISEASES OF.)

LENTIGO is another name for freckles (*q.v.*)

LEPROSY (λεπρός, scaly) is a chronic disease which affects particularly the skin, mucous membranes, and nerves.

History.—It has been said that 'leprosy is a disease as old as the world itself' (Cochrane). Some authorities say that it originated in the upper reaches of the Nile. Others claim that it originated in the region of the Indus. Wherever it originated, its subsequent history is difficult to trace because of the confusion as to what the older writers meant by the term 'leprosy'. The term is used in the Authorized Version of The Bible, but experts differ as to whether this is the correct translation of the Hebrew word *Tsaraath*. As Sir William MacArthur, the medical historian, has pointed out, ' in the past " leprosy " and its equivalents had a multitude of meanings. It was used for the true disease and for every disorder that was formerly supposed to be leprosy '. In Europe it reached its highest incidence between 1000 A.D. and 1400 A.D., thereafter slowly declining. The last indigenous case in Great Britain died in 1798—in the Shetland Islands. So far as the American continent is concerned, the available evidence suggests that it was introduced

there originally by Columbus's soldiers, and much later by the slave trade from West Africa.

Causes.—The causative organism of leprosy is the *Mycobacterium lepræ* which was discovered by Hansen in 1872. It is a straight or slightly curved rod which closely resembles the *Myeobacterium tuberculosis* in its size and acid-fast staining reaction. In spite of intensive investigation, no way has yet been found of growing the *Mycobacterium lepræ* in the laboratory or to transmit human leprosy to animals or man, although recent reports suggest that the successful transmission to animals may have been achieved. It is these two facts that have made progress in our full understanding of leprosy so difficult.

The main incidence of leprosy is in Africa, the Indian subcontinent, the Far East, Central and South America. In Europe it is largely confined to Portugal, Spain, the Balkan States, European Russia and European Turkey. It is estimated that there are 3000 cases in Portugal and probably as many in Spain. It has reappeared in Britain as a result of the recent influx of immigrants from countries in which leprosy is endemic. In 1966, in England and Wales there were 683 registered cases of leprosy, 159 of which were in an active state of the disease. The incubation period, or latent period between the infection being acquired and the disease manifesting itself is considered to be between 3 and 5 years. Males are more commonly infected than females. The variation of incidence among different races is due to contact rather than racial susceptibility, but the type of the disease varies in different races. Thus, the European and Mongol races appear to be more likely to acquire the serious lepromatous type of leprosy than the Indian and African races. There is no evidence that leprosy is in any way due to dietetic deficiencies. The disease is transmitted by contact with open cases of leprosy, infection usually taking place through the skin and then spreading along the nerves.

Symptoms.—There are two distinct types of leprosy : tuberculoid and lepromatous. The differentiation is important because the former runs a relatively benign course and is often self-healing, whereas the latter is a steadily progressive form of the disease. The differentiation, however, is not always clear cut, and there is a group of ' indeterminate ' or ' dimorphous ' cases in which lesions similar to tuberculoid and lepromatous leprosy are seen in the same patient. The differentiation of those three types is a matter for the expert, and no attempt will be made here to go into the details of the different types.

Whatever form of leprosy may be present, the symptoms and signs can be divided into two main groups : those involving the skin and those arising from involvement of the nerves. The skin manifestations range from areas of whitening of the skin to massive nodules such as are so often shown in photographs of advanced cases of leprosy. The nerve manifestations range from localized swellings of the nerve to extensive areas of anæsthesia in the skin. The ultimate destruction of the nerves leads to the deformities which used to be such a marked feature of leprosy in the old days before adequate means of treatment became available. These included foot-drop, wrist-drop, claw-foot, extensive ulceration of the extremities leading to loss of the fingers and toes, and absorption of bone. The eyes may also be infected, leading to blindness, and ulcers may occur in the mouth and in the larynx. In the larynx they may cause hoarseness or even go on to the stage of producing complete blockage of it. These tragic cases of gross deformity, which in the past have made leprosy such a terrifying disease, should no longer occur. As Cochrane has pointed out : ' With the introduction of modern therapy the vast majority of cases, if treated adequately before extensive deformity has set in, should recover without any disability. Nevertheless, until adequate treatment and properly administered therapy are within the reach of all, the shadow of tragic deformity will remain, particularly where there is a failure to understand the importance of physiotherapy in preventing this '.

Treatment.—For centuries chaulmoogra (hydnocarpus) oil was the great stand-by in the treatment of leprosy. There is an ancient Burmese folk-story that a Burmese prince, who discovered that he had leprosy, was directed by the gods to retire to the forest and there eat the seeds of the fruit of a certain tree. This he did and his leprosy was cured. Such is said to have been the introduction of chaulmoogra oil in the treatment of leprosy.

In 1941, the outlook was entirely changed by the discovery that a sulphone derivative was effective in the treatment. The sulphones are not a cure for leprosy in the strict sense of the term, but they can keep the disease under control and their widespread use has gone far to bringing leprosy under control. The two most widely used sulphones are solapsone, which is given by injection, and diaminodiphenyl sulphone (also known as dapsone, or DDS) which is given by mouth. Given over long periods of time, most cases of leprosy respond satisfactorily. Various other drugs have been introduced during recent years for the treatment of leprosy. The two most promising are thiambutosine and thiacetazone. Preliminary results from Uganda suggest that B.C.G. vaccine (*q.v.*) may be of value in the prevention of leprosy, but in the case of a disease like leprosy it is too early yet to assess the real significance of this most interesting observation.

Chemotherapy, however, has not diminished the importance of physiotherapy in the treatment and prevention, of deformity in leprosy. Equally important is the role of plastic and orthopædic surgery in treating these deformities when they have reached a stage in which physiotherapy is of little use. Many patients with advanced leprosy, hitherto condemned to a life of chronic invalidism as a result of their deformities, are now being returned to the community as useful members who are able to use their hands and feet sufficiently to be able to earn a living and lead a reasonably active life.

LEPTAZOL is a synthetic organic drug, $(CH_2)_5CN_4$, or pentamethylenetetrazol, introduced as a respiratory stimulant and also used to produce convulsions in the mentally ill, especially those with mental depression, and apparently with good results.

523

LEPTOMENINGITIS (λεπτός, thin; μῆνιγξ, membrane) means inflammation of the inner and more delicate membranes of the brain or spinal cord.

LESION (lædo, I hurt) meant originally an injury, but is now applied generally to all disease changes in organs and tissues.

LETHANE (see INSECTS IN RELATION TO DISEASE, under LICE).

LETHARGY (λήθη, oblivion; ἀργία, idleness) is a term applied to various disorders in which the affected person remains constantly asleep, though capable of being roused for short periods. It is a symptom of concussion of the brain and various mental diseases (see BRAIN, HYPNOTISM, CATALEPSY). Its most remarkable form is that observed in negro-lethargy or sleeping sickness (see SLEEPING SICKNESS).

LETTUCE is a green vegetable consisting of leaves of Lactuca sativa. It is a relatively rich source of vitamin A. The content of vitamin C is variable, ranging from 1 to 17 mg. per 100 grammes.

LEUCIN (λευκός, white) is a crystalline substance which is formed in most of the glands in the body as a result of decomposition of proteins. It is found in the urine in large amount along with tyrosin in acute yellow atrophy of the liver.

LEUCOCYTE (λευκός, white; κύτος, a cell) is the term applied to the white blood cells. Leucocytes differ from erythrocytes in that they contain no hæmoglobin and are therefore colourless, and contain a well-formed nucleus. Most of them are larger than erythrocytes, being 8 to 15 microns in diameter, and there are many fewer in the blood— usually about 8000 per cubic millimetre of blood. There are three main classes of white cells (Plate V): granulocytes, lymphocytes, and monocytes. Granulocytes, or polymorphonuclear leucocytes as they are sometimes termed, which normally constitute 70 per cent. of the white blood cells, have a lobed nucleus and a granular cytoplasm. They are divided into three groups according to the staining reactions of these granules: neutrophils, which stain with neutral

dyes and constitute 65 to 70 per cent. of all the white blood cells; eosinophils, which stain with acid dyes (e.g. eosin) and constitute 3 to 4 per cent. of the total white blood cells; and basophils, which stain with basic dyes (e.g. methylene blue) and constitute about 0·5 per cent. of the total white blood cells. Lymphocytes, which constitute 25 to 30 per cent. of the white blood cells, have a clear non-granular cytoplasm and a relatively large nucleus which is only slightly indented. They are divided into two groups: small lymphocytes, which are slightly larger than erythrocytes (about 8 microns in diameter); large lymphocytes, which are about 12 microns in diameter. Monocytes, which constitute about 5 per cent. of the white blood cells, are 10 to 15 microns in diameter and differ from lymphocytes in having a rather smaller nucleus which tends to be more indented and to be placed more eccentrically. The cytoplasm is non-granular.

Site of origin.—The granulocytes are formed in the red bone marrow. The lymphocytes are formed predominantly in lymphoid tissue. There is some controversy as to the site of monocytes: some say they arise from lymphocytes, whilst others contend that they are derived from histiocytes (i.e. the reticulo-endothelial system (q.v.)).

Function.—The leucocytes constitute one of the most important of the defence mechanisms against infection. This applies particularly to the neutrophil leucocytes (see LEUCOCYTOSIS).

(See also ABSCESS, BLOOD, INFLAMMATION, PHAGOCYTOSIS, WOUNDS.)

LEUCOCYTHÆMIA (see LEUKÆMIA).

LEUCOCYTOSIS (λευκός, white; κύτος, cell) means a temporary condition in which the polymorphonuclear leucocytes in the blood are increased in number. It occurs in many different circumstances, and forms a valuable means of diagnosis in certain diseases. It may occur, however, as a normal reaction in certain conditions, e.g. pregnancy, menstruation, and during muscular exercise. Apart from these conditions, leucocytosis is usually due to the presence of inflammatory processes. Thus, during many acute infective diseases, such, for example, as pneumonia, the number is greatly increased. Indeed, if it be found upon examination of the blood during a case of pneumonia that the number of white blood corpuscles is not increased, the sign is an ominous one, pointing to weakness in the body's power of resistance to the disease, and indicating a probably fatal result. In all suppurative conditions there is also a 'leucocytosis', and if it seems that an abscess is forming deep in the abdomen, or in some other site where it cannot be readily examined, as, for example, an abscess resulting from appendicitis, the examination of a drop of blood gives an invaluable aid in the diagnosis, and may be sufficient, in the absence of other signs, to point out the urgent need of an operation. Typhoid fever constitutes the major exception to the statement that acute infective diseases show this increase of white corpuscles in the blood, and, accordingly, in the case of this disease, the presence of an increase is a specially reliable sign of abscess formation, or other severe complication.

Other infective conditions in which a leucocytosis does not occur include measles and influenza.

LEUCODERMA, or Leucodermia (λευκός, white ; δέρμα, skin), means a condition of the skin in which areas of it become white, as the result of various skin diseases.

LEUCOPENIA (λευκός, white ; πένης, poor) is a condition in which the white corpuscles of the blood are greatly reduced in numbers.

LEUCOPLAKIA (λευκός, white ; πλάξ, a flat stone) means a chronic condition of the tongue in which, as the result of various forms of irritation, hard, smooth, whitish patches develop on its surface.

LEUCORRHŒA (λευκός, white ; ῥέω, I flow). (See Whites.)

LEUCOTOMY.—(Literally, cutting the white fibres). The operation of cutting the white nerve fibres in the frontal lobes of the brain. This operation severs the connections of the frontal cortex with other parts of the nervous

system, especially the thalamus and the hypothalamus. The operation is done in psychotic patients who suffer from severe depression or tense obsessional states. It appears to relieve the symptoms, the patient becoming ' friendly, cheerful, agreeable, relaxed, and interested in what goes on about him '.

LEUKÆMIA, or Leucocythæmia, is a disease, usually of chronic type, in which the number of white corpuscles in the blood is permanently increased. The disease is also characterized by great enlargement of the spleen, changes in the marrow of the bones, and by enlargement of the lymph glands all over the body. According to the type of corpuscles chiefly present the disease is called (1) Lymphatic leukæmia, and (2) Myeloid leukæmia or splenomedullary leukæmia. The condition may be either acute or chronic, the acute cases being relatively rare.

Cause.—The cause of the disease is unknown. In many ways it resembles a form of malignant disease characterized by uncontrolled over-production of the white blood corpuscles.

Symptoms.—In the acute cases the patient shows pallor, occasional purpuric rash, and enlargement of the lymphatic glands and spleen. The temperature is raised, and the condition is liable to be mistaken for general tuberculosis. Such cases usually run a rapid course, lasting a few weeks or months. In the chronic type of the disease, which is the usual form, the onset is gradual, and the first symptoms which occasion discomfort are either swelling of the abdomen and shortness of breath, due to painless enlargement of the spleen, or the enlargement of glands in the neck, armpits, etc., or the pallor, palpitation, and other symptoms of anæmia which often accompany the malady. Occasional hæmorrhages from the nose, stomach, gums, or bowels may occur, and may be severe. Dropsy of the feet and legs is not uncommon, from obstruction of the lymphatic vessels by the enlarged glands and spleen. Diarrhœa also may become very troublesome. Generally, there is a slight degree of fever. When the blood is examined microscopically, not only is there an enormous increase of the white corpuscles, which may be multiplied thirty- or sixty-fold, but various immature forms of corpuscles are found. In the lymphatic form of the disease the white corpuscles consist chiefly of corpuscles resembling in some measure the lymphocytes, which, in healthy blood, are present only in small numbers. In the myeloid form, myelocytes, or large immature corpuscles out of the bone-marrow, which are never present in healthy blood, appear in large numbers, and there may also be large numbers of immature, nucleated, red blood corpuscles.

The acute form of the disease runs a rapidly fatal course. The chronic forms progress slowly, and, especially if treated, may show several remissions in which the blood may become almost completely normal again, and the liver, spleen, and glands revert to nearly their normal dimensions. With each relapse, however, the condition of the patient becomes less satisfactory, and the disease usually has a total duration of not more than a few years.

Treatment.—Unfortunately, there is no known cure for either the acute or the chronic forms of leukæmia, but promising results are being obtained in the control of the disease, especially by means of chemotherapy. In the case of acute leukæmia the drugs now being used include mercaptopurine, methotrexate, cyclophosphamide, and vincristine. But cortisone and its derivatives sometimes produce dramatic temporary improvement. Blood transfusion plays an important part in controlling the condition during the period before the response to chemotherapy or hormone therapy can be expected. Chemotherapy has almost completely replaced radiotherapy in the treatment of chronic leukæmia. For the myeloid form busulphan is the most widely used drug, replaced by one of the nitrogen mustard derivatives (*q.v.*) in the later stages of the disease. For the lymphatic form the drugs used are chlorambucil, and the nitrogen mustard derivatives.

LEVORPHANOL is a synthetic derivative of morphine. It is an effective analgesic but, like morphine, is a drug of addiction.

LICE (*see* PARASITES *and* INSECTS IN RELATION TO DISEASE).
526

LICHEN (λειχήν) is a term applied to a group of chronic skin diseases in which the eruption consists of solid, reddened pimples or papules, with no tendency to suppurate.

LIENTERIC DIARRHŒA (λεῖος, smooth; ἔντερον, the intestine) is a mild form of diarrhœa in which the bowels move soon after every meal.

LIGAMENTS are strong bands of fibrous tissue which serve to bind together the bones entering into a joint. They are, in some cases, cord-like, in others flattened bands, whilst most joints are surrounded by a fibrous capsule or capsular ligament. (*See* JOINTS.)

LIGATURE (*ligo*, I bind) means a cord or thread used to tie round arteries in order to stop the circulation through them, or to prevent escape of blood

FIG. 258.—A reef-knot or surgeon's knot half tied. This is the knot with which all ligatures are tied. (Miller's *Surgery*.)

from their cut ends. Ligatures are generally made of catgut or silk, and are tied with a reef-knot (Fig. 258).

LIGHT TREATMENT.—The visible spectrum of white light, extending from red to violet, gives waves of different character, and beyond these, in the infra-red and ultra-violet regions, are numerous varieties of waves (Fig. 259). Thus in the infra-red region we have radiant heat and electric waves, which are used for practical purposes in the high-frequency apparatus and wireless telegraphy ; in the ultra-violet region we have the chemically active rays used in Finsen light, N-rays of several kinds, and then, much higher in the series, cathodal rays, X-rays, and some of the radiations of radium bodies.

From the point of view of treatment, radiant energy is utilized in the following ways :

(1) *Sunlight treatment* or heliotherapy.
(2) *Radiant heat*, obtained by arti-

ficial means from incandescent or arc lamps, or by diathermy.

(3) *Ultra-violet radiation.*
(4) *X-ray and radium applications.*
The first three are treated here. For the fourth *see* X-RAYS AND RADIUM.

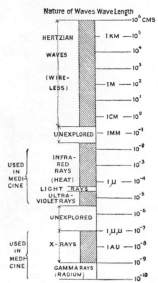

FIG. 259.—Table showing nature of waves of various wave-length.

SUNLIGHT TREATMENT, or HELIOTHERAPY.—Sunlight is essential to the well-being of all living things, both vegetable and animal. In the smoke-laden towns of Britain some 95 per cent. of the therapeutic efficiency of the solar rays is filtered out by moisture, dust, and smoke. This has a specially harmful effect upon child life, and various disabling diseases, such as tuberculosis and rickets, are traceable in part to lack of sunlight. On the other hand, in the clear air of high mountains, especially over snow, which acts as a reflector, the ultra-violet rays are at a maximum.

This is why it is essential that everyone, and especially children, should get as much sunshine as possible—by abolishing atmospheric pollution and by going to the country or seaside for an annual holiday. Much of the benefit of sunshine is derived from its ultra-violet rays, but natural sunlight is preferable to ultra-violet rays pro-

duced by an ultra-violet lamp as it contains the complete spectrum of rays as well as those of light and heat. In Britain, however, sunshine is such a variable quantity that we are often dependent upon lamp-produced ultra-violet rays as a substitute for natural sunshine.

ULTRA-VIOLET RADIATIONS assist the natural defensive powers of the body and enable it to combat disease. It produces an erythema of the skin and, acting upon 7-dehydro-cholesterol in the skin converts it into vitamin D_3, the natural vitamin D present in skin, milk, and fish-liver oils. Calciferol, or vitamin D_2, generally used in preventive and therapeutic medicine, is obtained by ultra-violet irradiation of ergosterol. The effect of ultra-violet light is greater, in proportion to the area of the body exposed to the rays.

Professor Finsen's discovery in 1893 that the rays in this part of the spectrum were bactericidal in their action induced him to try their local effect on lupus, in which disease he recorded very happy results. In addition to the original Finsen lamps, the mercury vapour lamp (Plate XII) and especially the Tungsten arc-lamp, which gives a very high proportion of ultra-violet rays, are favourite forms. In the use of these lamps, the patient's eyes are protected by wearing coloured glass goggles. A few minutes' exposure at a time is usually sufficient.

Excellent results have been obtained by ultra-violet radiation in the treatment of lupus and some other forms of tuberculosis. It is of use in hastening the cure of septic skin diseases, such as ulcers. Ultra-violet rays are useful in the treatment of rheumatic conditions, but a better result in such cases is got from their combination with heat rays, as mentioned below. Exposure to ultra-violet light is one way of treating rickets, as it converts the 7-dehydro-cholesterol of the skin into vitamin D_2. Ultra-violet light is bactericidal, and ultra-violet-light 'barriers' have been used in children's wards (Fig. 260) to prevent the spread of infection. Irradiation of the upper part of the atmosphere of schools has been used in an attempt to control the spread of common infections among school children.

Fig. 260.—A premature babies' ward showing a mercury vapour ray lamp controlling the air intake.
(*The Practitioner.*)

INFRA-RED RADIATIONS employed in treatment are those with wave-lengths immediately below those of luminous rays. Infra-red rays are emitted by all warm bodies, but the useful rays are given out only by bodies at a dull red or glowing temperature. The best source of these is sunshine, and they are also derived from incandescent light bulbs with tungsten filament, carbon arc lamps, and ordinary electric radiators at a red heat. These infra-red rays penetrate through the skin to a depth of ¼ to 1 inch (6 to 25 mm.), and their action in moderate dosage is to dilate blood vessels and so produce an increased blood supply to the exposed part, and to exert a soothing action on its sensory nerves. They are useful, therefore, in rheumatic conditions, injury near the surface, to promote absorption and relieve pain, and in certain septic skin conditions such as boils and carbuncles. Apparatus is obtainable which supplies infra-red rays without luminous rays, but this has no advantage over sunshine or electric bulbs, which supply both infra-red and luminous rays, except in cases where strong light is objectionable, as for example in treatment of conditions near the eyes. When deep penetration of heat is required, diathermy apparatus is used (*see* DIATHERMY).

LIGHTING and WARMING. — The chief points of medical importance connected with light and heating concern the effects upon the eyes, and the presence or absence of poisonous gases in the air.

Daylight from a clear sky is the best illuminant, and in schools. etc., the position of those working at desks should be arranged so that the light falls from behind, or from behind and to the left, and is not reflected straight up into the worker's eyes. Abundance of light, properly placed, is important, in order to avoid habitual strain of the eyes.

Open fires afford a healthy but wasteful source of warmth. The usual temperature of a room is from 60° to 65° F. (15·5° to 18·3° C.), although in the case of nurseries, sick-rooms, and the rooms of old people 65° to 70° F. (18·3° to 21° C.) is often more suitable. An open fire sends about five-eighths of its heat up the chimney; about two-eighths is used to heat the walls ; and only one-eighth is available to warm the air of the room. Further, the heat diminishes rapidly as one recedes from the fire (proportionately to the square of the distance), so that the room is unequally warmed. The fire has, however, advantages in being cheerful and in supplying a means of ventilation and a means of destroying refuse.

Large numbers of open coal fires in towns foul the air with smoke, and central heating and heating by gas and electricity would go far towards removing this nuisance, as would the use of smokeless fuel.

Closed stoves act mainly by causing a current of warmed air to pass through the room, so that the air becomes uniformly heated after a time. They have the advantages in offices, warehouses, etc., of heating the whole space more uniformly than open fires, and of economizing fuel. Thin iron stoves are objectionable, because they allow the poisonous gases of combustion to escape when they become heated, and china stoves are much better. Stoves act best where there is little draught, and it is essential that they should have a wide ventilating flue. They diminish the humidity of the air, and may thus cause a feeling of general discomfort, which is avoided by placing water in a wide shallow dish on the stove or at various places in the room.

Gas light and fires.—The gas now supplied in most cities consists of a mixture of coal-gas and water gas which may contain from 18 to 38 per cent. of carbon monoxide. This gas is excellent for use with incandescent mantles, by which it is completely consumed, and for heating and cooking in gas fires. It is, however, excessively poisonous. ACETYLENE GAS is sometimes used for small private installations. It has the disadvantage of being irritating to the air passages, but gives a good white light. Any gas fire should be ventilated by a wide flue leading to the outer air ; this both prevents fouling of the air and, in the event of the gas escaping unburned, avoids risk of poisoning by carbon monoxide.

Hot - air furnaces form a healthy system often used to supply warm air from a heating-chamber in the basement of buildings. The air is introduced through apertures in the floors, but should be moistened as in the case of stoves.

Hot-water installations form another system of central heating, either on the LOW PRESSURE SYSTEM, when the water circulates from a boiler in 4-inch (100-mm.) iron pipes over the house, or on the HIGH-PRESSURE SYSTEM of circulation in thick but narrow pipes. On the former system 12 feet (3·5 metres) of piping are necessary for every 1000 cubic feet of space to be warmed, and on the latter 8 or 9 feet (2·5 to 2·75 metres). This type of heating has no prejudicial effect on the air, and is eminently suited for buildings with much space in corridors, halls, etc.

Electricity is, for lighting purposes, by far the healthiest system obtainable. It is free from any polluting or drying effect on the air. As a warming agent, electric radiators require no ventilation and have no harmful action.

LIGHTNING INJURIES are not uncommon, but the majority of those struck by lightning recover. A " direct " hit, however, means instantaneous death, with the clothes torn off, and the victim may be hurled quite a long distance. Even the individual who recovers falls unconscious the moment he is struck. Those who are a little farther away experience tingling of the skin and their hair may stand on end.

Preventive measures indoors during a lightning storm consist of keeping away from the fireplace, the main electrical switch and the wireless aerial. It is perfectly safe to use the telephone. Out of doors, solitary trees, walls, wire fences, ponds and river banks should be avoided. If the storm is really severe, the safest thing is to lie down in a ditch.

Treatment of an individual struck by lightning consists of artificial respiration, which may need to be prolonged for several hours.

LIGNOCAINE, also known as XYLO-CAINE, is the ' approved ' name for diethylaminocet-*m*-2-xylidide, which is a local anæsthetic.

LIMBS are outgrowths from the sides of the body, which, in man as in all the higher animals number four. The limbs of all the higher animals, though differing much in outward appearance, are constructed on a similar plan, modified to suit the requirements of the owner, the fore-limb, for example, developing in birds into a wing, in seals into a flipper. In all, however, the various muscles, bones, and blood-vessels, though differing in size and shape, correspond in arrangement. Also, between the upper and lower limb, a strict comparison is possible, and the bones, muscles, and main arteries of the arm, forearm, and hand have all representatives in the thigh, leg, and foot. (See ARM and LEG.)

The union of the lower limb with the body is, however, more intimate than that of the upper limb. For, whilst the shoulder-blade and collar-bone of the upper limb are separated from the organs of the chest by the ribs and their muscles (Fig. 261), the haunch-bone is

FIG. 261.—Diagram showing the manner of connection of the upper limbs to the body. V, a dorsal vertebra; C, a rib; St, the breastbone; sc, shoulder-blade; Cr, coracoid process; Cl, collar-bone; H, humerus. (Turner's *Anatomy*.)

applied on each side directly to the spine, and forms the side of the pelvis (Fig. 262).

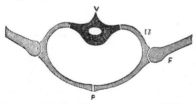

FIG. 262.—Diagram showing the manner of connection of the lower limbs to the body. V, A sacral vertebra; Il, the iliac, and P, the pubic parts of the haunch-bone; F, the femur. (Turner's *Anatomy*.)

In structure, each limb consists of four segments, the shoulder, arm, forearm, and hand in the case of the upper limb, corresponding to the haunch, thigh, leg, and foot in the lower limb. Upon the surface, the limb is enveloped by skin which, over the hand, is specially rich in its supply of sensory nerves. Beneath the skin is a layer of loose

cellular tissue containing an amount of fat which varies with the corpulence of the individual. Next comes a strong layer of fibrous tissue, known as fascia, which provides a complete investment for the limb, and supplies a separate sheath for each muscle. The chief bulk of the limb is made up by the muscles or flesh. Finally, in the centre of the limb lie the bones which give it rigidity; and in general the large arteries and nerves are embedded among the muscles close to the bones.

The diseases affecting the limbs are those of the skin, muscles, bones, etc., forming them. (For injuries of the limbs see FRACTURES; HÆMORRHAGE; JOINTS, DISEASES AND INJURIES OF; and WOUNDS.)

LIME, Calx, Quick-lime, or Oxide of calcium, is a caustic, highly infusible solid which is prepared by calcining white marble, Iceland-spar, lime-stone shells or other forms of calcium carbonate ($CaCO_2$). Heating calcium carbonate drives off carbon dioxide, leaving lime or CaO. If water be sprinkled on it, the lime swells up, becomes hot, and breaks down into a white powder, known as calcium hydroxide or hydrated lime or ' slaked lime ', the chemical formula of which is $Ca(OH)_2$. If a large quantity of water be added to this, a thick white liquid is formed, known as 'milk of lime', which is much used for whitewashing walls, alleys, etc. If the milk of lime be filtered, a clear liquid, having an alkaline reaction, and known as ' lime-water ', is obtained. This lime-water contains a small amount of slaked lime in solution, about 1 part in 700 of water. Chlorinated lime is prepared by passing chlorine gas over slaked lime, and is much used for bleaching powder, for disinfection, etc. (see CHLORINATED LIME). When slaked lime is exposed to the air for some time it gradually hardens, as in mortar and plaster, changing into carbonate of lime. Carbonate of lime exists extensively also in a state of nature, being used in medicine in the form of 'chalk'.

Action.—Quick-lime has a caustic action upon parts of the body with which it is brought in contact, being, however, little used. It is a fairly common accident for quick-lime or slaked lime to get into the eye, upon the delicate surface of which it exerts a destructive influence (*see* EYE, DISEASES OF). Internally, lime-water and chalk exert a soothing and powerfully astringent action upon the bowels, although lime is absorbed only to a small extent into the blood.

Uses.—Lime-water mixed with milk is administered to invalids and children in order to make the curd less hard and so render this food more easily digested, and also in order to exert a soothing action upon the stomach when there is a tendency to vomit. For this purpose two or three tablespoonfuls are generally added to a tumblerful of milk. (*See* INFANT FEEDING.) As an astringent in diarrhœa, chalk mixture is used in doses of two or three tablespoonfuls for an adult, and one or two teaspoonfuls for a young child.

LIME-JUICE is a yellow liquid obtained by squeezing lime-fruit, *Citrus limetta*. In common with lemon-juice, it is a rich source of vitamin C (16·8 to 62·5 mg. per 100 ml.) and contains a large quantity of citric acid and is used as a refreshing drink and as a preventive of, and remedy for, scurvy (*see* SCURVY). Lime-juice which has been boiled, or preserved for a prolonged period, loses its anti-scorbutic properties.

LINCOMYCIN is an antibiotic derived from *Streptomyces lincolnensis*. It is active against a relatively limited number of bacteria, including staphylococci, streptococci, pneumococci and *B. anthracis*.

LINCTUS (*linctus*, licking) is a term applied to any thick syrupy medicine. Most of these are remedies for excessive coughing, of which the best is Gee's linctus, consisting of equal parts of paregoric, oxymel of squills, and syrup of tolu.

LINEA ALBA is the name given to the line of fibrous tissue stretching down the mid-line of the belly from the lower end of the sternum to the pubic bone. The linea alba gives attachment to the muscles of the belly wall.

LINEA NIGRA.—During pregnancy the linea alba (*q.v.*) becomes pigmented and appears as a dark line down the middle of the belly, and is called the *linea nigra*.

LINEAR ACCELERATOR (*see* RADIOTHERAPY).

LINIMENTS, or EMBROCATIONS (*linio*, I anoint), are preparations intended for external application, generally with rubbing. Almost all are of an oily nature, and are highly poisonous, being dispensed therefore in green or blue bottles. Liniments should never be kept alongside medicines intended for internal use, because many fatalities occur through carelessness of administration, a dose being poured out of the wrong bottle. Among the chief liniments are aconite, belladonna, and chloroform liniments, often mixed together in equal parts to form A.B.C. liniment, which is extensively used for neuralgia, rheumatism, and other painful conditions ; iodine liniment, used to paint over enlarged glands, swollen joints, etc. ; opium liniment, used to apply in various acutely painful conditions ; turpentine and acetic turpentine liniments, used especially for sprains, bruises, and rheumatic conditions ; liniment of ammonia, popularly known as 'hartshorn and oil', used for the same purpose ; and soap liniment, known also as 'opodeldoc', of like application.

LINSEED is used either as the seeds or in the form of linseed meal obtained by grinding the seeds of *Linum usitatissimum*, the common flax.

Uses.—Externally, linseed meal is used in poultices (*see* POULTICES) ; and, for internal use, linseed tea is an old domestic remedy for the treatment of cough.

LINT was originally made of teasedout linen ; now it consists of a loose cotton fabric, one side of which is fluffy, the other being smooth and applied next the skin when the surface is broken. Marine lint consists of tow impregnated with tar, and is used where large quantities of some absorbent and deodorizing dressing are required. Cotton lint is impregnated with various substances, the most common being boracic lint. Lint containing perchloride of iron (15 per cent.) is valuable as a styptic.

LIPÆMIA means the presence of an excessive amount of fat in the blood.

LIPASE is an enzyme widely distributed in plants, and present also in the liver and gastric and pancreatic juices, which breaks down fats to the constituent fatty acids and glycerol.

LIPID is a term which is used rather loosely. Strictly speaking, it means a substance which is insoluble in water but soluble in fat solvents such as alcohol and ether. The important lipids, so far as medicine is concerned, are the fats (or triglycerides), and the phospholipids which play an important part in the functioning of the membranes of the cells of the body.

LIPIODOL, or iodized oil, is a preparation of poppy-seed oil with iodine, containing about 40 per cent. of the latter. It is a yellow, oily liquid which is used in X-ray examination by injection to show up cavities and spaces in internal organs.

LIPOCAIC is a hormone in the pancreas which plays a part in the metabolism of fat. In the absence of this hormone fat accumulates in the liver and seriously interferes with its function. Other workers consider that choline can prevent this accumulation in the liver.

LIPODYSTROPHY means any disturbance of the body's economy which results from faulty metabolism of fat.

LIPOMA (λίπος, fat ; -oma meaning tumour) is the name given to a tumour mainly composed of fat. Such tumours arise in almost any part of the body, developing in fibrous tissues, particularly in that beneath the skin. They are simple in nature, and seldom give any trouble beyond that connected with their size and position. (See TUMOURS.)

LIPPITUDO (lippitudo) means a chronic condition of inflammation at the margins of the eyelids, which ultimately renders the person ' bleareyed '.

LIPS form a pair of curtains before the mouth, each composed of a layer of skin and of mucous membrane, between which lies a considerable amount of fat and of muscle fibres.

The diseases to which the lips are liable are not numerous. *Fissures*, coming on in cold weather, form a troublesome condition often difficult to get rid of. *Herpes* often develops on the lip as a result of a cold or other feverish condition, but quickly passes off (see HERPES). *Ulcers* may form on the inner surface of the lip, usually in consequence of bad teeth or of dyspepsia, while in infants ulceration on the lips may be a sign of inherited syphilis. *Boils* sometimes form on the upper lip, and if large they produce a serious condition (see BOILS). *Cysts* of small size sometimes form on the inner surface of the lip, and are seen as little bluish swellings filled with mucus; they are of no importance. *Hare-lip* is a deformity sometimes present at birth (see PALATE, MALFORMATIONS OF). *Cancer* of the lip sometimes occurs, almost always in men, and usually on the lower lip. (See also MOUTH, DISEASES OF.)

LIQUOR is a solution of a drug in water. The majority of liquors are intended for internal use, but some of them are for external application only. (See also ALCOHOL.)

LIQUORICE is the root of *Glycyrrhiza glabra*, a plant of southern Europe and Asia. It is a mild laxative, but is mainly used to cover the taste of disagreeable and more powerful drugs. Solid and liquid extracts are made from it, but the most commonly used preparation is compound liquorice powder, which contains also senna and sulphur. (See also GLYCYRRHETINIC ACID.)

LITHÆMIA (λίθος, stone ; αἷμα, blood) is a general term applied to those conditions in which uric acid is developed or retained in excess in the system. (See ACIDITY, GOUT.)

LITHAGOGUE is the term given to any agent which expels calculi from the body.

LITHIASIS (λίθος, stone) is a general name applied to the formation of calculi and concretions in tissues or organs, *e.g.* cholelithiasis means the formation of calculi in the gall-bladder.

LITHIC ACID (λίθος, stone) is another name for uric acid.

LITHIUM CARBONATE is being used to an increasing extent in the treatment of mania and of recurrent depression.

LITHOLAPAXY is the term applied to the procedure of crushing a stone in the bladder and washing out the crushed fragments.

LITHONTRIPTICS (λίθος, stone; τρίβω, I rub down) are substances which dissolve stones in the urinary passages. (*See* BLADDER, DISEASES OF.)

LITHOPÆDION is the term applied to a fœtus which has died while in the mother's body and has become calcified.

LITHOTOMY (λίθος, stone; τέμνω, I cut) is the term applied to the operation of cutting for stone in the bladder. The operation is of great historic interest, because more has probably been written about it in early times than about any other department of surgery, and because, for long, it formed almost the only operation in which the surgeon dared to attack diseases of the internal organs. It seems, from the fact that large numbers of people were cut for stone, and also from the fact that this operation remained, in France at least, in the hands of a special class of surgeons, referred to as lithotomists, that stone in the bladder must have been far commoner two or three centuries ago than it is to-day.

The bladder lies within the pelvis, protected in front by the pubic bones, but accessible above these through the lower part of the abdomen, or below them through the perineum. Operation by the former route is known as suprapubic lithotomy, and by the latter route as perineal lithotomy.

The earliest form of *perineal lithotomy* was the operation described by Celsus, and known as 'cutting on the gripe', or operation with the 'apparatus minor'. Two fingers of the operator's left hand were passed into the bowel, and the stone, pressed down from above, was directly cut upon by a transverse incision, across the perineum and through the base of the bladder. The only apparatus required was a knife and a hook to remove the stone.

The Marian method came into vogue some time early in the sixteenth century, and consisted in cutting through the perineum into the urethra, and then tearing or stretching an opening into the bladder by a number of guides and dilators. The operation was known, therefore, as the operation by the 'apparatus major'. It was founded on the false idea that wounds so made heal better than cuts in membranous structures. That it was a serious as well as a painful and tedious operation, may be gathered from the fact that the mortality from it in the Charité Hospital, Paris, early in the eighteenth century, was over 50 per cent.

In 1697 Frère Jacques professed himself able to remove stone by a totally new and rapid method. Encouraged by Louis XIV and by several of the court physicians and surgeons, he devoted himself to studying anatomy for a time, and later achieved brilliant results. His operation, known as ' lateral lithotomy ', in which an oblique incision is made from the side of the perineum, upon a grooved metal ' staff ' previously passed into the urethra, the incision being continued down the groove of the staff into the bladder, was for long the operation in vogue, after being improved and placed on a scientific basis by the English surgeon Cheselden (1727) and others.

In the *suprapubic* operation a vertical opening is made through the lower part of the abdomen to reach the upper part of the bladder, and, with improved modern methods, it has practically displaced the perineal route for all bladder operations.

From the shortness of the female urethra and the ease with which it can be dilated, lithotomy is comparatively seldom necessary in this sex.

LITHOTRITY, or LITHOLAPAXY (λίθος, stone; τρίβω, I rub down ; λάπαξις, evacuation), is the term applied to the operation in which a stone in the bladder is crushed by an instrument introduced along the urethra, and the fragments washed out through a catheter. The latter name was applied by Bigelow of New York to cases in which the fragments are all removed and the operation completed at once. The operation was first performed by the French surgeon Civiale in 1824, and has now, to a great extent, replaced lithotomy, except in cases where a stone is very hard and very large, and in boys whose urethra is too small to admit the passage of a lithotrite. The lithotrite, or stone-crusher, consists of two blades, one of which fits into a groove in the other, so that, when the inner blade is screwed home, the lithotrite is little larger than and similar in shape to a catheter, and can be easily passed along the urethra. The instrument is made of tough steel and provided with a powerful screw, so that when fragments of stone are caught between the blades they are easily crushed.

LITMUS, which is prepared from several lichens, and especially from *Lecanora tartarea,* is a vegetable dye-substance, which on contact with alkaline fluids becomes blue, and on contact with acid fluids, red. Slips of paper, impregnated with litmus, form a valuable test for the acidity of the secretions and discharges.

LITTLE'S DISEASE is a form of cerebral palsy (*see* PARALYSIS).

LIVE-FLESH is a popular term applied to fine muscular tremors or twitchings seen especially in the eyelids and muscles of the hands. It is usually due simply to tiredness caused by over-use of the twitching muscles, but when persistent it may be a sign of some serious nervous disorder, such as progressive muscular atrophy.

LIVER.—The liver is a solid organ of dark-brown colour and the largest gland in the body. It discharges several functions, acting both as an excreting organ and as an elaborator and storehouse of nourishment.

Form.—The shape of the liver is generally described as that of a right-angled triangular prism, with the right angle rounded off. It has five surfaces, upper, lower, front, back, and right, of which the front and back surfaces are triangular, with the base towards the right side and tapering off to the left. The surfaces are separated from one another by rounded margins, except in the case of the lower surface, which is

divided from the right, front, and upper surfaces by a sharp edge. The organ is divided also into five lobes. The great bulk of it constitutes the right lobe; the left lobe is small and extends a little way into the left half of the abdomen, to end in a sharp left border, whilst the Spigelian, quadrate, and caudate lobes are three small divisions upon the back and under surface. About the middle of the under surface, towards the back, is placed the transverse fissure, or portal fissure, by which the hepatic artery and portal vein carry blood into the liver, and by which the right and left hepatic ducts emerge, carrying off the bile formed in the liver. The gall-bladder is attached to the under surface of the right lobe and projects from beneath the lower margin, where, if

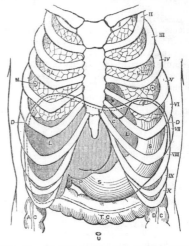

FIG. 263.—Diagram showing the position of the liver and its relations to surrounding organs. The ribs are indicated by Roman numerals; the dotted line shows the extreme right and upper limits of the liver. *D, D,* Diaphragm; *RL,* right, and *LL,* left lung; *P,* pericardium; *S,* stomach; *L,* liver; *G,* gall-bladder; *AC, TC, DC,* parts of the large intestine; *M,* right nipple; *U,* umbilicus. (For other letters, *see* STOMACH.) (Turner's *Anatomy.*)

distended, it can be felt during life as a rounded swelling immediately beneath the end of the ninth rib. The connection of the gall-bladder—in which bile is stored—with the liver is rather complicated (Fig. 207). The hepatic ducts emerge at the transverse fissure, one coming from the right and one from the left lobe. They immediately join, and the single hepatic duct, which is about an inch long, joins the cystic duct, coming from the gall-bladder, at an acute angle. The hepatic and cystic ducts by their union form the ' common bile-duct ', which is about 3 inches in length (75 mm.), and opens into the small intestine. Bile, which passes down from the liver by the

right lung being hollowed out to receive the liver, from which it is separated only by the diaphragm and pleural membrane. The liver, in turn, rests upon various abdominal organs, the right kidney and suprarenal body, the large intestine, the duodenum, and the stomach all making impressions upon it, and helping to support its weight.

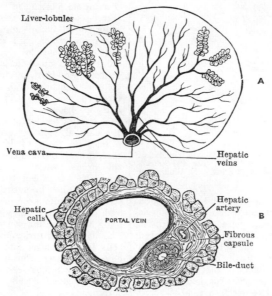

Fig. 264.—Diagrammatic representation of liver structure. A, arrangement of liver lobules around the sublobular branches of the hepatic vein ; B, section of a portal canal, showing branches of the portal vein, hepatic artery, and bile-duct surrounded by a prolongation of Glissons's fibrous capsule. (From Cunningham, *Anatomy.* Oxford University Press.)

hepatic duct, may either pass directly into the common bile-duct and so into the intestine, or it may pass upwards through the cystic duct into the gall-bladder, to be stored there, and later retrace its way through the cystic duct to the bile-duct, and so to the intestine. The cystic duct and gall-bladder, therefore, together form a cul-de-sac upon the bile passages.

Position.—The liver occupies the right - hand upper portion of the abdominal cavity (Fig. 263). Its upper surface is in contact with the diaphragm, which also separates its right surface from the right lower ribs. About four-fifths of the organ lies to the right of the middle line of the body. As it is of a rounded shape it fills up the dome of the diaphragm, the lower part of the

In addition, the liver is swung from the walls of the abdomen by five ligaments, four of which consist of thickened parts of the peritoneal membrane lining the whole abdominal cavity, and reflected from the upper part of the liver to its walls. These are the coronary ligament, right and left lateral ligaments, falciform ligament, and a dense fibrous cord, the round ligament.

Dimensions.—The vertical thickness of the liver amounts, towards the right side, to over 5 inches (12 cm.), and its extent from side to side is considerably more. Its weight is over 50 ounces (1·5 kg.), varying with the size of the person, but making up about $\frac{1}{40}$ or thereabout of the whole body-weight. In young children it is relatively much larger, accounting, to a large extent, for their protuberant abdomen, and making up about $\frac{1}{18}$ of the weight of the whole body.

Vessels.—The blood supply of the organ (Fig. 265) differs from that of any

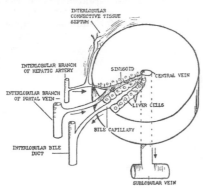

FIG. 265.—Diagram of the hepatic circulation. (From Best and Taylor, *The Physiological Basis of Medical Practice.* The Williams & Wilkins Co.)

other part of the body, in that the blood collected from the stomach and bowels into the portal vein does not pass directly to the heart, but is distributed to the liver, in the substance of which the portal vein breaks up into capillary vessels. The effect of this is that some harmful substances, absorbed from the stomach and bowels, are abstracted from the blood-stream and destroyed, while various constituents of the food are stored up in the liver for gradual use. In addition, the liver receives a large hepatic artery from the cœliac axis, which also distributes branches to the stomach and pancreas, this blood supply serving to nourish the organ. After the blood has circulated through capillaries, it is collected together from both sources and emptied into the hepatic veins, which pass directly from the back surface of the liver into the inferior vena cava.

Minute structure.—The liver is enveloped in a capsule of fibrous tissue, Glisson's capsule, from which strands run along the vessels, and, penetrating to the farthest recesses of the organ, bind its structure together. The hepatic artery, portal vein, and bile-duct divide and subdivide (Fig. 264), the branches of each lying alongside corresponding divisions of the other two, till the finest

536

divisions of artery, vein, and bile-duct, known as interlobular vessels, lie between the lobules, of which the whole gland is built up. These lobules, each of about the size of a small pin's head, form each in itself a complete secreting unit, and the liver is built up of many hundred thousands of such exactly similar lobules.

A lobule has the following structure (Fig. 266). From the small vessels lying round its margin capillaries are given off which run in towards the centre of the lobule, where they empty into a small central vein. These central veins from neighbouring lobules collect together, and ultimately the blood passes into the hepatic veins, and so leaves the liver. Between the capillaries, which radiate from the central vein to the edge of the lobule, lie rows of large liver cells, these forming the distinctive tissue of the organ, upon which its activity depends. Between the rows of cells also lie fine bile capillaries, which collect the bile produced by the cells and discharge it into the bile-ducts lying along the margins of the lobules. The liver cells are among the largest cells in the body, and each contains one or two large, round nuclei. In the cells can often be seen droplets of fat or granules of glycogen, *i.e.* animal starch.

Functions. — The liver is a vast chemical factory. The heat produced by the chemical changes taking place in it forms an important contribution to the general warming of the body. The liver secretes bile, the chief constituents of which are the bile salts (sodium glycocholate and taurocholate), the bile pigments (bilirubin and biliverdin), cholesterol, and lecithin. The bile acids from which the salts are obtained are formed in the liver by the union of glycocoll and taurine with cholic acid. The bile salts are absorbed from the intestine and so find their way back to the liver again. The bile pigments are the iron-free and globin-free remnant of hæmoglobin, being formed in the Kupffer cells of the liver. Bile pigments can, however, be formed in many other parts of the body—in the spleen, the lymph glands, bone-marrow, connective tissues (giving the colour to a bruise). Bile, then, serves to excrete pigment, the result of breakdown of old red blood corpuscles, and to aid the digestion of fat. Bile salts aid digestion of fat by emulsifying the fat, by activating pancreatic lipase, and by promoting fat absorption. Bile is necessary for the absorption of vitamins D and E.

copper, necessary for the manufacture of red corpuscles. (4) It produces heparin and, with the aid of vitamin K, prothrombin. (5) Its Kupffer cells in the liver blood - sinusoids are an important element in the reticulo-endo-thelial system, which breaks down red corpuscles, and probably manufactures

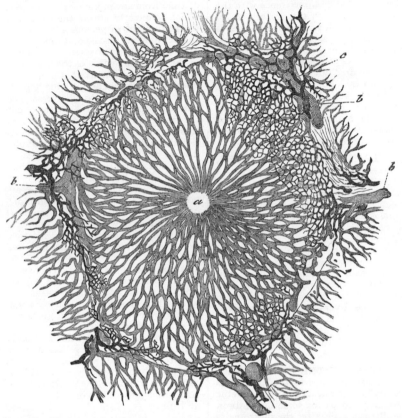

FIG. 266.—Diagram of liver lobule. *a*, Central vein connected by network of sinusoids with *b*, *b*, peripheral or interlobular veins; *c*, interlobular bile duct commencing in network of intercellular bile-canaliculi within the lobule. (From Schafer, *Essentials of Histology*. Longmans, Green & Co. Ltd.)

In addition to forming bile the liver has a number of important functions. These are enumerated briefly : (1) In the embryo it forms red blood corpuscles, and in the adult stores a substance necessary for the proper functioning of the bone-marrow in the manufacture of red corpuscles. (2) It manufactures the fibrinogen of the blood, and probably also the albumin and the globulin. (3) It stores iron and

antibodies. (6) It detoxicates noxious products made in the intestine and absorbed into the blood. (7) It stores carbohydrate in the form of glycogen, and maintains the two-way process glucose $\rightleftarrows$ glycogen. (8) It forms vitamin A from carotene and stores the B vitamins. (9) It splits up amino-acids and manufactures urea and uric acid. (10) It plays an essential part in the storage and metabolism of fat.

LIVER DISEASES.—The liver may be extensively diseased without any very urgent symptoms, unless the circulation through it be impeded, the outflow of bile checked, or neighbouring organs implicated. Jaundice, which is a symptom of several liver disorders, is dealt with elsewhere. Dropsy, which may be caused by interference with the circulation through the portal vein of the liver, as well as by other causes, is also considered separately. The presence of gall-stones is a complication of some diseases connected with the liver, and is treated under GALL-BLADDER, DISEASES OF. For cirrhosis of the liver, or 'gin-drinker's liver', see CIRRHOSIS; for waxy degeneration see WAXY DISEASE ; and for hydatid cyst of the liver see PARASITES. There are various methods of testing liver function.

INFLAMMATION OF THE LIVER, or HEPATITIS, may occur as part of a generalized infection or may be a localized condition. Infective hepatitis, which is the result of infection with a virus, is one of the most common forms of hepatitis (see HEPATITIS, ACUTE INFECTIVE). In tropical countries amœbic hepatitis, which often goes on to abscess formation, is an important complication of amœbic dysentery (see DYSENTERY ; ABSCESS OF THE LIVER). Other tropical conditions in which the liver is always involved include malaria and yellow fever. Hepatitis may also occur if there is obstruction of the common bile-duct, as by a gall-stone.

ABSCESS OF THE LIVER.—When an abscess develops in the liver, it is usually a manifestation of amœbic dysentery, appearing sometimes late in the disease, even after the diarrhœa is cured ; it may also follow upon inflammation of the liver due to other causes ; and abscesses may form in this organ as in other sites in cases of blood-poisoning. The symptoms of abscess are much the same as in other types of inflammation. only they are more pronounced, and accompanied often by rigors, severe pain over the liver which may also be referred to the right shoulder, and by great enlargement of the liver. In the case of an amœbic abscess treatment consists of aspiration of the contents of the abscess and the

administration of either emetine or chloroquine.

CONGESTION OF THE LIVER is a term sometimes applied to the slighter forms of inflammation, in which the liver is said to be 'actively congested'. But the term is generally reserved for a state of 'passive congestion', quite distinct from any inflammatory process, which frequently affects the liver to a marked extent in persons who are the subject of heart disease and some forms of lung disease. It arises in consequence of the close connection of the liver with the right side of the heart, through the inferior vena cava and the wide hepatic veins, which open into this vessel just before its entrance to the heart. When the right side of the heart is dilated, or there is some obstruction to the circulation through the lungs, or some valvular disease of the heart, the circulation of the blood is retarded and thus congestion of the liver results.

Symptoms.—The liver becomes enlarged and causes a sense not so much of pain as of fullness and discomfort in the abdomen, which may be tender to the touch. The complexion is yellowish, the tongue furred, the appetite lost, and there are often both vomiting of bile and looseness of the bowels. There may also be headache, languor, and depression of spirits. At the same time the lung or heart condition which is responsible for the liver congestion gives rise to symptoms of its own.

Treatment.—The condition is usually a chronic one, with exacerbations from time to time. The treatment is that of the underlying cause, and as this is usually heart failure, the treatment consists principally of rest in bed, digitalis, and diuretics. (See HEART, DISEASES OF.)

FATTY DISEASE OF THE LIVER may consist of an infiltration of the cells of the liver with fat in those who eat to excess, particularly of rich, fat, or oily foods ; or in wasting diseases there may be a degeneration in the liver-cells of this character. The liver is enlarged, and, though usually painless, it gives rise to discomfort and to embarrassment of breathing, particularly after meals. When due to over-eating, other organs, such as the heart, and the body generally, are also loaded with fat. A certain amount of indigestion and constipation is often present, and a person affected in this way can offer but feeble resisting power to any disease by which he may be attacked. (For treatment, *see under* CORPULENCE.)

ACUTE YELLOW ATROPHY is a destructive and fatal disease of the liver which is very rare, but which appears suddenly and apparently without cause. From the fact that a very similar state of the liver is produced by phosphorus poisoning, it is supposed that the condition is due to some poison of unknown nature circulating in the blood. Women are more often affected than men, and especially during pregnancy. It comes on with a slight degree of jaundice, which cannot be distinguished from simple jaundice, and lasts several days. Then the jaundice suddenly deepens, there is pain in the region of the liver, convulsions and delirium appear, the heart grows very weak, and death ensues in a day or two. If the liver be examined after death, it is found to be shrunken and soft ; the cut surface is of mottled yellow and red colour, the liver-cells being in places shrivelled and degenerated, in other places completely broken down ; crystals of leucine and tyrosine are found here and there ; and the capsule and remaining liver-cells are stained with bile. The destruction of the liver as a secreting organ may be complete, but occasionally areas here and there only are affected, and recovery may then take place with restoration of the damaged areas after a prolonged illness.

CANCER OF THE LIVER is not uncommon, although it is rare for the disease to begin in the liver, the involvement of this organ being usually secondary to disease situated somewhere in the stomach or bowels. Cancer originating in the liver is more common in the East. It usually arises in a fibrotic (or cirrhotic) liver. There is great emaciation, which increases as the disease progresses. The liver is much enlarged, and its margin and surface are rough, being studded with hard cancer masses of varying size, which can often be readily felt through the abdominal wall. Pain may be present. Jaundice and dropsy often make their appearance.

LIVER EXTRACT is the term applied to an extract of mammalian liver which contains all the known anti-anæmic factors in liver. These include the 'hæmatinic principle' which is essential for the treatment of pernicious anæmia (*q.v.*) Liver extract is prepared for administration either by mouth or by injection. The usual practice to-day is to give it by intramuscular injection, but its place has now been largely taken by cyanocobalamin (*q.v.*).

LIVER-FLUKE is the popular name of *Distoma hepaticum*, a parasite which infests sheep, and which is occasionally found in the bile-passages and liver of man. (*See* PARASITES.)

LIVER PILLS (*see* CHOLAGOGUES).

LIVER SPOT is a popular term applied to brownish marks which appear on the skin, especially of the face. This is sometimes caused by the growth of a parasite (*Tinea versicolor*) in the surface layers of the cuticle. It also frequently accompanies pregnancy or the presence of abdominal tumours. It may also be due simply to some long-continued form of local irritation.

LOBE (λοβός) is the term applied to the larger divisions of various organs, such as to the five lobes of the liver, to the three lobes of the right and two lobes of the left lung, which are separated by fissures from one another, and to the lobes or superficial areas into which the brain is divided. The term lobar is applied to structures which are connected with lobes of organs, or to diseases which have a tendency to be limited by the boundaries of lobes, such as 'lobar pneumonia'.

LOBECTOMY is the operation of cutting out a lobe of the lung in such diseases as abscess of the lung and bronchiectasis.

LOBELIA is the name of a remedy used for asthma. It consists of the leaves and tops of *Lobelia inflata*, a common weed in the United States. In very large doses, it causes vomiting and paralyses the heart's action, being a dangerous poison, but in moderate

539

doses it relieves the spasm to which asthma is due. It is a constituent of many burning powders made for smoking by asthmatics, but it is more frequently used in the form of tincture of lobelia combined with other drugs.

LOBELINE HYDROCHLORIDE is a derivative of α-lobeline, an alkaloid derived from lobelia. It is given by injection for the treatment of respiratory depression and for the resuscitation of the new-born.

LOBOTOMY.—The cutting of a lobe. (*See* LEUCOTOMY.)

LOBULE (*lobulus*, a little lobe) is the term applied to a division of an organ smaller than a lobe ; for example, the lobules of the lung are of the size of millet seeds, those of the liver slightly larger. Lobules form the smallest subdivisions or units of an organ, each lobule being similar to the others, of which there may be perhaps several hundred thousand in the organ. The term ' lobular ' is applied to structures such as small blood-vessels belonging to individual lobules, or to disease which occurs in a scattered manner in organs, affecting lobules here and there.

LOCHIA (λόχια) is a term applied to the discharge which takes place during the first week or two after child-birth. During the first four days it consists chiefly of blood ; after the fifth day the colour should become paler, and after the first week the quantity should diminish and the appearance be creamy. There should at no time be any putrid odour, the presence of this being an indication of dangerous septic infection. The presence of blood after the second week indicates that the patient has been too active or that the natural absorptive changes are not duly taking place. (*See* PUERPERIUM.)

LOCKJAW is a prominent symptom of tetanus and is the popular name for this condition.

LOCOMOTOR ATAXIA (ά, neg. ; τάξις, order), also called TABES DORSALIS, POSTERIOR SPINAL SCLEROSIS, is a disease of the nervous system, manifesting itself principally by disordered movements of the limbs in walking. This is dependent on the loss of the power of co-ordinating the muscles into harmonious action, which is essential to the proper performance of the voluntary movements of the body, and the maintenance of its equilibrium.

Causes.—The pathological condition giving rise to locomotor ataxia is disease of a certain portion of the spinal cord, viz. the posterior columns (Plate XV) and the posterior nerve roots. These undergo chronic inflammatory changes, which result in their ultimately becoming atrophied and indurated. When affecting, as this lesion most commonly does, the lower dorsal and lumbar regions of the cord, the ataxic symptoms are chiefly confined to the legs ; but when it affects the cervical portion, the arms are involved. Occasionally the whole posterior columns of the cord are found diseased. It is a late result of syphilis.

Locomotor ataxia is much more common among men than among women, over 90 per cent. of cases being males. It is a disease of middle life, being most frequently observed to occur between the ages of thirty and fifty.

Symptoms.—Locomotor ataxia usually begins insidiously, and advances slowly. Among the earlier symptoms observed are a tendency to stagger in walking or standing, especially when the eyes are closed; disorders of vision, with occasionally temporary or permanent paralysis of some of the cranial nerves ; violent shooting pains down the limbs, decreased or perverted sensibility in various parts of the body, and disturbance of the genito-urinary functions. Among the early signs of the disease discovered by the physician, two of the most important are—loss or diminution of the knee-jerks obtained on tapping the patellar tendon ; and a sluggish condition of the iris of the eye, which, though altering the size of the pupil as the eye accommodates itself for vision of near objects, fails to contract normally when a bright light falls upon the eye. These initial symptoms may continue without much change for a long period, but generally, in the course of time, others are superadded. The sufferer feels as if some soft substance were interposed between his feet and the ground. His gait assumes a peculiar and characteristic appearance. He begins the act of walking with evident difficulty, and his steps are short and hurried. Each foot is lifted well from the ground ; but as he moves forward it is thrown out from him, and his heel descends forcibly, and is followed at a longer than the normal interval by the sole. In walking, he requires the aid of his vision to preserve his equilibrium, and he therefore looks at his feet, or rather at the ground a little in front of them, as he advances. He cannot turn about suddenly without the risk of falling. If asked to stand erect with his feet together, and then directed to close his eyes or to look upwards, he immediately begins to sway and totter, and would fall if not supported—a symptom known as Rombergism. These various symptoms are the result, not of any weakness of motor power, but simply of defective muscular co-ordination. Along with this there usually exists markedly diminished sensibility to touch and to painful impressions, such as a pin-prick or the approach of some unusually hot or cold object. This is noticeable particularly in the feet and legs. Sometimes the disorder implicates the upper extremities, and then the hands and fingers cease to perform their functions with precision, so that the patient is unable to pick up any small object from the ground, to button or unbutton his clothing, and even sometimes to feed himself.

The patient's efforts to walk become more and more difficult, and ultimately he is compelled to lie in bed. In the later stages the patient has attacks of violent vomiting (gastric crises), of laryngeal spasm and difficulty in breathing (laryngeal crises), of inability to retain the urine (bladder crises). The shooting pains and violent jerkings of the limbs increase, motor power becomes impaired, and the patient sinks under the prolonged and exhausting course of discomfort, or dies from some intercurrent disease.

Treatment.—The treatment has been revolutionized by the introduction of penicillin, which, when given in large doses for an adequate period of time, produces marked improvement in all but the late stages of the disease. In early cases the administration of penicillin is sometimes supplemented by pyrexial therapy. In cases in which the gait is affected, much improvement in walking results from Frenkel's exercises (*q.v.*), a series of co-ordinated movements, such as walking carefully along a board on the floor.

LOGWOOD (*see* HÆMATOXYLON).

LOIN is the name applied to the part of the back between the lower ribs and the pelvis. (For pain in the loins *see* BACKACHE *and* LUMBAGO.)

LONG-SIGHT (*see* SPECTACLES).

LORDOSIS (λόρδωσις) means an unnatural curvature of the spine forwards. It occurs chiefly in the lumbar region, where the natural curve is forwards, as the result of muscular weakness, special disease, etc. (*See* SPINAL COLUMN.)

LOSS OF BLOOD (*see* HÆMOR-RHAGE).

LOTION (*lotio*, a fluid application) means a fluid preparation intended for bringing in contact with, or for washing, the external surface of the body. Lotions are generally of a watery or alcoholic composition, and many of them are known as 'liquors'. Those external applications which are of an oily nature, and intended to be rubbed into the surface, are known as liniments.

LOUSE (*see* PARASITES, *and* INSECTS IN RELATION TO DISEASE).

LOZENGES (λοξός, crosswise ; γωνία, a corner), also known as TROCHES, or TROCHISCI, consist of small tablets containing drugs mixed with sugar, gum, glycerin-jelly, or fruit-paste. They are used in various affections of the mouth and throat, being sucked and slowly dissolved by the saliva, which brings the drugs they contain in contact with the affected surface. Some of the substances most commonly used in lozenges are benzoic and tannic acids, marshmallow, potassium chlorate, eucalyptus, guaiacum, rhatany, morphia, cocaine, carbolic acid, and menthol. Penicillin lozenges are used in the treatment of infections of the mouth, especially Vincent's angina.

LUES is the Latin word for a serious infectious disease, the term being especially applied to syphilis.

LUGOL'S SOLUTION is a compound solution of iodine and potassium iodide.

LUMBAGO (*lumbi*, the loins) is a term applied to a painful ailment affecting the muscles of the lower part of the back, generally regarded as of rheumatic origin.

Cause.—Lumbago seems to be brought on by exposure to cold and damp, and by other exciting causes of rheumatism. Sometimes it follows a strain of the muscles of the loins. The pain accompanying rheumatic manifestations in this region is believed to be due to an inflammatory condition in the connective tissues of the muscles, causing congestion of the blood-vessels and consequent pressure upon the endings of the sensory nerves. To this condition the term ' fibrositis ' is applied. Lumbago is specially apt to occur in the back muscles after they have been the seat of a strain or other injury leading probably to a tear in the muscle fibres, and the pain in such a case is largely produced by violent spasm of the surrounding muscle. In other cases lumbago occurs in gouty subjects and the attacks take the place of an ordinary attack of gout.

Symptoms.—An attack of lumbago may occur alone, or be associated with rheumatism in other parts of the body at the time. It usually comes on as a seizure, often sudden, of pain in one or both sides of the small of the back, of a severe cutting or stabbing character, greatly aggravated on movement of the body, especially in attempting to rise from the recumbent posture, and also in the acts of drawing a deep breath, coughing, or sneezing. So intense is the suffering that it is apt to suggest the existence of inflammation in some of the neighbouring internal organs, such as the kidneys, bowels, etc., but the absence of the symptoms specially characteristic of these latter complaints,

or of any great constitutional disturbance beyond the pain, renders the diagnosis a matter of no great difficulty. The attack is in general of short duration, but occasionally it continues for a long time, not in such an acute form as at first, but rather as a feeling of soreness and stiffness on movement.

Treatment.—The treatment includes that for rheumatic affections in general (*see* RHEUMATISM), and the application of local remedies of counter-irritant nature, such as hot fomentations with turpentine or laudanum applied by means of flannel to the part ; or the rubbing in, if this can be borne, of liniments. The old and homely plan of counter-irritation by applying a heated iron to the part with a sheet of brown paper or blanket interposed is often beneficial in chronic cases, as is also, on similar principles, Corrigan's button cautery. The hot-air bath, and various electrical applications, including faradization, static breeze, diathermy, and high-frequency currents, are also of value. Should there be localized areas of tenderness, the injection into these of procaine may give relief. During the acute stages, relief is obtained from the taking of analgesics such as aspirin. (*See* BATHS, ELECTRICITY IN MEDICINE.)

LUMBAR (*lumbi*, the loins) is a term used to denote structures in or diseases affecting the region of the loins, as, for example, the lumbar vertebræ, lumbar abscess. etc.

LUMBAR PUNCTURE. — A procedure for removing cerebro-spinal fluid from the spinal canal in the lumbar region in order : (1) to diagnose disease of the nervous system : (2) to relieve pressure when too much cerebro-spinal fluid is being formed, as in meningitis ; and (3) to introduce medicaments—spinal anæsthetics, or drugs, or serum.

LUMBRICUS (*lumbricus*, a worm) is a name sometimes applied to the ' roundworm ' or *Ascaris lumbricoides*. (*See* PARASITES.)

LUNAR CAUSTIC (*lunaris*, moonlike—silver being the moonlike metal) is another name for nitrate of silver.

LUNATIC (*luna*, the moon) is a general term applied to persons of disordered mind, because lunacy was supposed at one time to be largely influenced by the moon. (*See* MENTAL ILLNESS.)

LUNGS.—The lungs form a pair of organs situated in the chest, and discharge perhaps the most important function of vital activity, viz. respiration (*see* RESPIRATION). The air, which enters through the nose and passes down the throat, larynx, and windpipe in succession (*see* AIR PASSAGES), reaches the lungs by the right and left bronchial tubes, into which the windpipe divides within the chest, at the level of the second rib. The texture of the lungs is very highly elastic, so that when the chest is opened each lung collapses to about one-third of its natural bulk.

Form and position.—Each lung is roughly conical in shape, with an apex projecting into the neck, and a base resting upon the diaphragm (Fig. 267). The rounded outer surface of each is in contact with the ribs of its own side, while the heart, lying between the lungs, hollows out the inner surface of each to some extent. There is an anterior border, along which the outer and inner surfaces meet, and the borders of the two lungs touch one another for a short distance behind the middle of the breastbone. The apex, which is blunt, extends 1½ inches (35 mm.) or more into the neck above the line of the collar-bone, being covered here by the muscles of the neck. The base is deeply hollowed, in correspondence with the domed shape of the diaphragm, which is pushed up by the liver on the right side, and by the stomach and spleen on the left. The right lung is split by two deep fissures into three lobes; the left has two lobes divided by a single fissure. The weight of the two lungs together is about 40 ounces (1·1 kg.), the right being rather heavier than the left, and the lungs of men much heavier than those of women. Each lung is enveloped in a membrane, the pleura or pleural membrane, in such a way that one layer of the membrane is closely adherent to the lung, from which indeed it cannot be separated, while the other layer lines the inner surface of one half of the chest.

These two layers form a closed cavity, the pleural cavity, which everywhere surrounds the lung except at the point where the bronchi and vessels enter it. This cavity is, in the natural state, a merely potential space, the two layers

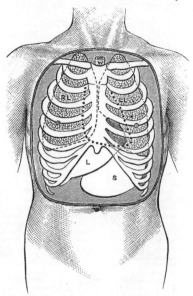

FIG. 267.—Chest with the skin and muscles removed from the front, showing the position of heart and lungs. *H*, Heart; *LL*, left lung; *RL*, right lung; *W*, windpipe; *L*, liver; *S*, stomach.

of pleural membrane being separated only by a thin layer of fluid, which enables them to glide with very little friction over one another as the lung expands and retracts in breathing; but, in certain states, fluid collects in the pleural cavity, so that several pints of fluid may be effused there, compressing the lung. In some circumstances air escapes into the pleural cavity, and the lung then collapses temporarily upon its root, but air in the pleural cavity is very quickly absorbed, and the lung speedily comes to occupy its original volume.

Colour.—In children, the colour of the lungs is rose-pink, but, as life advances, they become more and more of a slaty hue, mottled with streaks and patches of dark grey and black, which are due to deposits in the lymph spaces of dust inhaled on the breath. Esqui-

543

maux and others who live in an atmosphere free from dust retain the colour of childhood ; on the other hand, the lungs of coal-miners become often of an almost uniform jet-black shade.

Changes at birth.—Prior to birth, and in still-born children, the lungs are

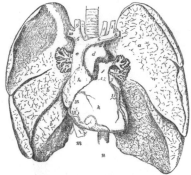

Fig. 268.—The organs of the chest. The lungs are turned outwards to show the heart and the intimate connections between heart and lungs. *a*, Upper, *a'*, lower lobe of left lung ; *b*, upper, *b'*, middle, *b''*, lower lobe of right lung ; *c*, trachea ; *d*, arch of aorta ; *e*, superior vena cava ; *f*, pulmonary artery ; *g*, left atrium ; *h*, right atrium ; *k*, right ventricle ; *l*, left ventricle ; *m*, inferior vena cava ; *n*, aorta ; 1, innominate artery ; 2 and 4, carotid arteries ; 3 and 5, subclavian arteries ; 6, 6, innominate veins ; 7 and 9, internal jugular veins ; 8 and 10, subclavian veins ; 11, 12, 13, left pulmonary artery, bronchus, and vein ; 14, 15, 16, right bronchus, pulmonary artery, and vein ; 17 and 18, coronary arteries. (Turner's *Anatomy*.)

of a yellowish colour, of solid gland-like appearance, and packed away in the back of the chest. Further, such lungs do not float in water, and their weight amounts to about $\frac{1}{70}$ of the whole body-weight. Immediately upon birth a remarkable change takes place ; the tissue of the lungs expands, like the petals of an opening flower ; the colour changes to rose-red, and the weight is suddenly doubled in consequence of the inrush of blood : the consistence becomes spongy, as air is drawn into the lungs, and if the child should die after drawing a few breaths, any portion of the lung which may be cut off floats in water. These changes are of importance, from the medico - legal point of view, in determining whether a dead infant was born alive or not.

Connections with heart.—Not only does the heart lie in contact with the two lungs, so that changes in the volume

of the lungs cannot fail to have an effect upon the heart's action, but the heart is also connected by vessels with both lungs (Fig. 268). The pulmonary artery passes from the right ventricle and divides into two branches, one of which runs straight outwards to each lung, entering its substance along with the bronchial tube at the hilum or root of the lung. From this point also emerge the pulmonary veins, which carry the blood purified in the lungs back to the left atrium.

Minute structure.—Each main bronchial tube, entering the lung at the root, divides into branches (Plate VI and Fig. 269), which subdivide again and again, to be distributed all through the substance of the lung, till the finest

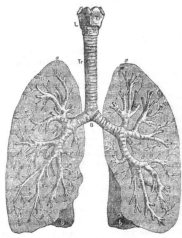

Fig. 269.—The larynx, windpipe, bronchial tubes, and lungs. *L*, Larynx ; *T*, thyroid cartilage ; *C*, cricoid cartilage ; *Tr*, trachea splitting at *B* into the two bronchi ; *a*, apex ; *b*, base of each lung ; *lb*, *lb*, the finest bronchial tubes ; *l*, *l*, *l*, lobules. (Turner's *Anatomy*.)

tubes, known as bronchioles, or capillary bronchi, have a width of only $\frac{1}{100}$ inch (0·25 mm.). In structure, all these tubes consist of a mucous membrane surrounded by a fibrous sheath. The windpipe as well as the larger and medium bronchi have in the fibrous layer large pieces of cartilage, which in the windpipe and largest bronchial tubes form regular hoops, and in the medium-sized tubes are disposed as irregular plates. These pieces of cartilage have the function of preventing the tubes from closing or being

PLATE XV

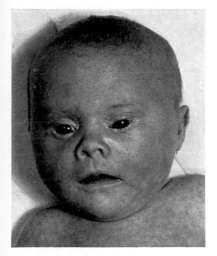

Gangrene of third toe. (From Allen, etc., *Peripheral Vascular Disease*. W. B. Saunders Company.)

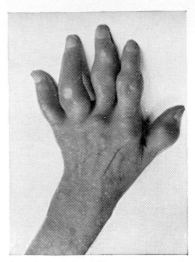

Gouty hand. Large chalk-stones are seen in the thumb and fingers ; over the first joint of the index finger is seen a small opening through which a chalk-stone has ulcerated.

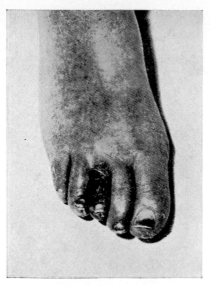

Mongol child
(*The Practitioner*)

The Edinburgh Mask
(British Oxygen Co. Ltd.)

PLATE XVI

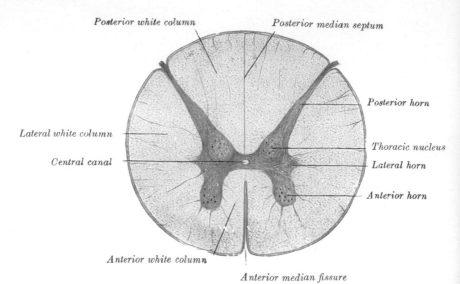

Transverse section through the spinal cord in the thoracic region. Magnified eight times.
(From Gray's *Anatomy*. Longmans, Green & Co., Ltd.) *See* LOCOMOTOR ATAXIA and SPINAL CORD.

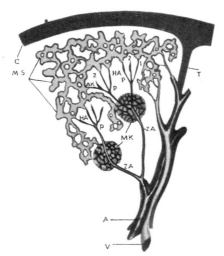

Diagram of human spleen. A, artery and vein (V) in a trabecula (T) of the capsule (C); ZA,
central artery of the corpuscle of Malpighi (MK); P, small arteries; HA, arteries with a
sheath; AK, arterial capillaries which terminate in the sinuses (1) or in the meshes of the
reticulum (2); MS, venous sinuses. (From Best and Taylor, *The Physiological Basis of
Medical Practice*. The Williams & Wilkins Co.) *See* SPLEEN.

compressed, and so obstructing the passage of air. The larger and medium bronchi are richly supplied with glands secreting mucus, which is poured out upon the surface of the membrane. This surface is composed of columnar epithelial cells, which are provided with cilia, credited generally with the power of moving expectoration upwards towards the throat, but is probably also designed to load the air passing into the lungs with warm moisture before it reaches these organs. The wall of the bronchial tubes is very rich in fibres of elastic tissue, and immediately beneath the mucous membrane is a layer of circularly placed unstriped muscle fibres, which is specially well developed in the smaller bronchi. This muscular layer plays an important role in the removal of expectoration by coughing ; it is also of great importance in connection with the causation of asthma. (*See* ASTHMA.)

The smallest divisions of the bronchial tubes open out into a number of dilatations, the 'infundibula' (Fig. 270), each measuring about $\frac{1}{20}$ inch (1 mm.) in width, and these are covered with minute sacs, known as air-vesicles or

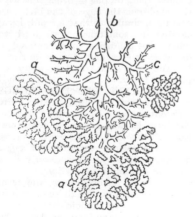

FIG. 270.—Diagram showing how an air-tube branches and ends in air-sacs. *a*, air-sacs ; *b*, bronchial tube ; *c*, small bronchial tubes. (From Hill, *Manual of Human Physiology.* Edward Arnold & Co.)

alveoli. Each air-vesicle consists of a delicate membrane composed of flattened plate-like cells, strengthened by a a wide network of elastic fibres, to which the great elasticity of the lung is

18

due ; and in these thin-walled air-cells the important function of the lungs is carried on.

The branches of the pulmonary artery accompany the bronchial tubes to the farthest recesses of the lung, dividing like the latter into finer and finer branches, and ending in a dense network of capillaries, which lies everywhere between the air-vesicles (Fig. 271), the

FIG. 271.—Diagram illustrating terminal divisions of the air tubes. *A*, respiratory bronchiole ; *B*, alveolar passage ; *C*, atrium ; *D*, air sac ; *E*, alveolus. (From Hewer, *Textbook o Histology.* William Heinemann, Ltd.)

capillaries being so closely placed that they occupy a much greater area than the spaces between them. The air in the air-vesicles is separated, therefore, from the blood only by two delicate membranes, viz. the wall of the air-vesicle and the capillary wall, through which an exchange of gases readily takes place. The blood from the capillaries is collected by the pulmonary veins, which also accompany the bronchi to the root of the lung.

Another and much smaller set of bronchial blood-vessels runs actually upon the walls of the bronchial tubes, and these serve the purpose of nourishing the lung tissue.

There is in the lung also an important system of lymph vessels, which commence in spaces situated between the air-vesicles, under the pleural membrane and in the walls of the bronchial tubes. These vessels leave the lung along with the blood-vessels, and are connected with a chain of bronchial glands lying near the end of the windpipe.

LUNG DISEASES. — The general symptoms and signs produced by disease of the lungs are mentioned under CHEST, DISEASES OF, and the chief affections to which these organs are liable are also treated under special headings. (*See* BRONCHITIS; CHEST, DEFORMITIES OF; CHILLS AND COLDS; EMPHYSEMA; EXPECTORATION; HÆMOPTYSIS; HÆMORRHAGE; PLEURISY; PNEUMONIA; TRADE DISEASES; TUBERCULOSIS.)

INFLAMMATION OF THE LUNGS is generally known as pneumonia, but may be of several different types. (*See* PNEUMONIA.)

ABSCESS OF THE LUNG is a comparatively rare condition, and consists, like abscesses elsewhere, of a collection of pus in one or more areas of the lung. It may result from an acute pneumonia which does not clear up properly, or it may be due to a wound of the lung from without, or to the presence of foreign bodies, such as buttons, pins, or fragments of food, which have been sucked down the air passages. An abscess may also occur in the lung, as in other organs, during the course of blood poisoning (pyæmia), or may be produced by the bursting of an abscess into the lung after its formation in some neighbouring organ. The condition may be difficult to differentiate from cavity formation due to tuberculosis; although the failure to find tubercle bacilli in the expectoration, after repeated examination, is an important point against the latter condition.

An abscess in the lung may burst into one of the bronchial tubes, and, after the pus is spat up, healing and recovery may take place. Most cases respond to appropriate antibiotics and postural drainage but occasionally it may be necessary to resort to surgery and drain the abscess through the chest wall.

GANGRENE OF THE LUNG is another result which may follow pneumonia in persons of poor constitution or debilitated by serious illness. Just as in the case of gangrene of limbs, a portion of lung dies and putrefies, giving rise to a most offensive smell, as the dead and broken-down lung tissue is spat up. The prospect of recovery is small, even when the portion of lung involved is very limited.

BRONCHIECTASIS is a condition which may come on in persons who have long suffered from bronchitis or

from chronic pneumonia. The lung substance undergoes a certain amount of shrinkage, while at the same time the bronchial tubes become here and there distended into large cavities. These cavities are lined by mucous membrane, which continues to form a secretion, and this secretion, as it does not find a ready outlet by the bronchial tubes, undergoes putrid changes. The person therefore spits up from time to time a copious amount of foul-smelling expectoration, and the air of the room in which he lies is rendered offensive by his breath. The condition is not immediately dangerous to life, although it gradually produces deterioration of the general health, and its symptoms are those of an aggravated form of chronic bronchitis. The treatment is that of chronic bronchitis, and in addition the smell of the breath is kept in check by inhalations of creosote, or by vaporizing creosote and other aromatic substances in steam, near the person's bed. Secretion tends to collect in the bronchiectatic cavities especially during the night, and the patient usually finds that he can get rid of this secretion by adopting a special posture while he coughs, lying on one or other side with the head over the edge of the bed. An operation similar to that for phthisical cavities is sometimes performed to relieve this condition, or, if confined to one lobe or one lung, it may be cured by the operation of lobectomy or pneumectomy.

CONGESTION OF THE LUNGS is a term which is used in two quite different senses. In popular parlance, the term is used for acute inflammation of the lung in its early stages. When the patient recovers after a few days, the illness is often described as an attack of acute congestion.

In a strict medical sense, the term is used to mean quite a different condition of a more chronic nature, viz. passive or mechanical congestion of the blood-vessels in the lungs due to some defect in the pumping action of the heart. Passive congestion arises under two sets of conditions. A very serious form, known as hypostatic congestion, arises when the heart is failing, towards the end of severe and long-continued fevers, such as typhoid fever; after severe surgical operations; and in old people who, for any reasons, such as the occurrence of a broken leg, are confined for some weeks to bed. It occurs in the back parts of the lungs, in consequence of the feeble heart being unable to drive out of them the blood which gravitates into these dependent parts. Inflammation is very apt to arise in these congested parts, and hypostatic pneumonia often ends the life of old or feeble persons confined to bed. The other form of passive congestion is due, not so much to weakness in the pumping action of the heart, as to some obstruction which hinders the escape of blood from the lungs into the left atrium of the heart. Narrowing of the opening which leads from the left atrium to the left ventricle (mitral stenosis) is the chief cause of this, and, although the condition is by no means so serious as the hypostatic form of congestion, it predisposes the persons affected by this form of heart disease to sharp attacks of blood-spitting on exertion, to bronchitis, and to pneumonia. The treatment, in both cases, must be directed towards stimulating the heart.

ŒDEMA OF THE LUNGS is a condition in which these organs become dropsical. It occurs both when congestion is present as the result of heart failure, and also during Bright's disease, following dropsy in other parts of the body. It gives symptoms of its onset in constant rattling noises proceeding from the lungs and air passages of the affected person, whose face becomes gradually more livid, and who experiences great difficulty in breathing. The œdema may be accompanied by the collection of fluid in the pleural cavities (hydrothorax), and, if the condition be not speedily relieved, the person dies, literally drowned in the fluids of his own body.

COLLAPSE OF THE LUNG occurs under several conditions. The lungs are so resilient in consequence of the elastic fibres with which they are everywhere interspersed that, if air be admitted to the pleural cavities, the lungs immediately collapse to a third of their natural bulk. Accordingly, if one side of the chest be wounded and air be admitted (pneumothorax), the lung collapses, although, after the wound is healed, the air is absorbed from the pleural cavity and the lung quickly regains its size. Also, when fluid is effused into the pleural cavity the lung is compressed and collapses, and if the fluid be not absorbed or drawn off within some weeks, the collapse is apt to be permanent through the formation of adhesions round the lung. Again, if anything blocks a bronchial tube, the part of the lung to which it leads collapses, since these tubes do not communicate with one another. Thus, in children suffering from bronchitis or pneumonia areas of the lung may collapse through a plug of mucus sticking in a bronchus which the child is not sufficiently strong to free by coughing. A similar result is brought about by foreign bodies drawn into the air passages. It also occurs when the chest is opened on one side to drain away a collection of pus, or where a large amount of fluid exists in one pleural cavity. The second lung, being healthy, is sufficient to overtake the needs of respiration, expanding as a rule somewhat in the process. The lungs of an infant at birth are collapsed in the sense that they have never been expanded, and any signs of expansion in the lungs of a dead infant form a sure token that it has been born alive. (*See* LUNGS.)

TUMOURS OF THE LUNG.— Since the beginning of the twentieth century cancer of the lung has become increasingly frequent, and, in 1964, was responsible for 25,371 deaths in England and Wales, compared with 13,069 deaths from carcinoma of the stomach and 9,944 deaths from carcinoma of the breast. Tumours may arise in the mediastinum or in connection with the pleura. Hydatid cysts are found from time to time in the lungs.

WOUNDS OF THE LUNG are serious both by reason of the damage they may do to this organ and by admitting air into the pleural cavity, so that the lung collapses. The lung may be wounded by the end of a fractured rib, or by some sharp body pushed between the ribs, and it may also be torn as the result of disease ; for example, a consumptive and excavated lung may be perforated during a fit of coughing. If by any cause a free opening is made between the pleural cavity and air passages, immediate difficulty

547

of breathing, due to collapse of the lung, ensues. Generally, however, the person recovers from the immediate symptoms, and, if the perforation be caused by a wound from without, the wound may heal without leaving any permanent damage. Frequently, in such cases, blood is effused into the pleural cavity (hæmothorax). This is gradually absorbed, leaving usually some thickening of the pleural membrane and adhesions between the lung and chest wall. Such a wound is liable, at the time of infliction, to become infected by organisms, and empyema may then result, with a tedious illness.

Wounds of the lung are chiefly dangerous on account of the risk of wounding large blood - vessels. Spitting of blood in any quantity after a wound of the chest has been received is a sign that the lung has been injured. A stab or bullet wound, which does not injure any large vessel, may traverse the lung without any serious consequences, but if one of the main veins or arteries be torn, death is likely to ensue.

LUPULIN (*see* Hops).

LUPUS (*lupus*, a wolf) is a term used to designate a group of skin diseases of destructive and intractable character. There are two chief types of the disease, *Lupus vulgaris*, which is due to the *Mycobacterium tuberculosis* ; and *Lupus erythematosus*, which is of unknown origin.

LUPUS VULGARIS begins most commonly before the age of twenty, and, not infrequently, persists all through life, healing in one place to break out a short distance off. The nose, cheeks brow, and sides of the neck are most frequently attacked, although the hands and the mucous membrane inside the nose and mouth are also common seats of the malady. The first sign of the disease is a small, soft nodule of yellowish transparent appearance, on this account often called an ' apple-jelly ' nodule. No pain or itching accompanies the disease, but the skin gradually becomes thickened and discoloured, other nodules appear, and finally ulcers or small abscesses form. The disease progresses very slowly, but, after it has been in existence some years, the de-

formity produced may be very great. The nose may be partly or wholly eaten away ; the lower eyelids, if attacked, become drawn down, showing the red inner surface, and the skin, which is in places red and ulcerated, in places stretched and scarred, gives to the countenance a horrible appearance. The condition is of little infective power.

Treatment.—These horrors have now been removed by the excellent results being obtained from the combined use of isoniazid and streptomycin. In certain cases it is still sometimes helpful to remove individual nodules by excision or by curettage, followed by the application of trichloracetic acid. The local application of intensive ultra-violet light is also sometimes of value.

LUPUS ERYTHEMATOSUS is a disease of unknown etiology. It occurs in two forms. The more common form, which occurs equally in the two sexes, involves only the skin and consists of rounded, red, and slightly raised patches, which are distributed most commonly on the nose and cheeks. These patches, by fusing together at their edges, give a characteristic butterfly-like appearance to the reddened nose and cheeks. There is no tendency to the formation of ulcers, as in lupus vulgaris, and deformity in consequence does not result, although the patches of red alternating with white and atrophied skin render the complexion very unsightly.

The second, or disseminated, form occurs predominantly in women. It tends to run an acute course and involves many of the internal organs of the body, including the kidneys, spleen, and heart.

Treatment.—The most satisfactory treatment for the cutaneous form is mepacrine or chloroquine. The only form of treatment which gives any relief in the disseminated form of the disease is cortisone or A.C.T.H.

LUXATION (*luxus*, a dislocation) is another word for dislocation. (*See* DISLOCATIONS.)

LYCANTHROPY is the term applied to the delusion entertained by an insane person that he or she is a wolf.

LYCOPODIUM is a fine, yellow powder, which consists of the spores of the club-moss, *Lycopodium clavatum*. It is used as a powder in which to roll pills, and also is a good dusting-powder for moist skin surfaces, such as the skin of infants.

LYING-IN (*see* LABOUR).

LYMPH (*lympha*, water) is the fluid which circulates in the lymphatic vessels of the body. It is a colourless fluid, like blood plasma in composition, only rather more watery. It contains salts similar to those of blood plasma, and the same proteins, though in smaller amount, viz. fibrinogen, serum albumin, and serum globulin. It also contains colourless lymph corpuscles, derived from the glands, similar to some of the white blood corpuscles. In certain of the lymphatic vessels, the lymph contains, after meals, a great amount of fat in the form of a fine milky emulsion. These are the vessels which absorb fat from the food passing down the intestine, and convey it to the thoracic duct; they are called 'lacteals' on account of the milky appearance of their contents.

The lymph is derived, in the first place, from the blood, of which the watery constituents exude through the walls of the capillaries into the tissues, conveying material for the nourishment of the tissues and absorbing waste products.

The various gaps and chinks in the tissues communicate with lymph capillaries, which have a structure very similar to that of the capillaries of the blood-vessel system, being composed of delicate flat cells joined edge to edge. These unite to form fine vessels, resembling minute veins in structure, to which the name of 'lymphatics' or 'absorbents' is generally applied. These ramify all through the body, passing here and there through lymphatic glands, and ultimately discharge their contents into the blood circulation once more, by opening into the jugular veins in the root of the neck. Other lymph vessels commence in great numbers as minute openings on the surface of the pleuræ and peritoneum, and act as drains for these otherwise closed cavities (Fig. 273). When fluid is effused

into these cavities, as in the occurrence of dropsy, pleurisy, etc., its absorption takes place through the lymphatic vessels. The course of these vessels is described under GLANDS.

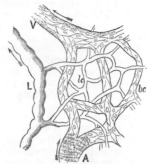

FIG. 272.—Diagram of the relation of the blood and lymph streams among the tissues. *A*, Small artery; *bc*, blood capillaries; *lc*, lymph capillaries; *V*, vein; *L*, lymphatic vessel; the arrows show the direction of the streams. (Turner's *Anatomy*.)

The circulation of the lymph is effected in some of the lower animals by 'lymph-hearts', which pump the lymph, just as the heart belonging to the blood-vessels keeps the blood in circulation. In man and most of the higher animals there is no heart for the lymph, which circulates partly by reason of the pressure at which it is

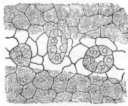

FIG. 273.—The cells lining the peritoneal membrane. Three 'stomata' which open into lymph vessels are shown. (Turner's *Anatomy*.)

driven through the walls of the blood capillaries, but mainly in consequence of accidental forces. The lymph capillaries and vessels are copiously provided with valves, which prevent any back flow of lymph, and every time these vessels are squeezed, as by the contraction of a muscle, or movement of a limb, the lymph moves on a little, leaving room for the exudation of fresh lymph. From this fact one can perceive the immense importance of regular exercise in maintaining the free circulation of lymph.

Lymph, like blood, possesses, in virtue of the fibrinogen which it contains, the power of clotting, forming, when it does so, a faintly yellow or colourless coagulum. This can be seen in the case of small wounds, after the blood has ceased to flow.

The term ' lymph ' is also applied to the serous fluid contained in the vesicles which develop as the result of vaccination, and used for the purpose of vaccinating other individuals. (*See* VACCINATION.)

The term ' lymph ' is also loosely applied to the layers and flakes of fibrin which are derived from the lymph and are found on the pleura and other serous membranes as the result of inflammation.

LYMPHADENITIS (*lympha*, lymph ; ἀδήν, a gland) means inflammation of lymphatic glands. (*See* GLANDS, DISEASES OF.)

LYMPHADENOMA, or LYMPHOMA (*lympha*, lymph ; ἀδήν, a gland ; -*oma*, termination meaning tumour), is another name for Hodgkin's disease (*q.v.*).

LYMPHÆMIA, and LYMPHOCYTHEMIA, are other names for lymphatic leukæmia (*see* LEUKÆMIA).

LYMPHANGIECTASIS means an abnormal dilatation of the lymph vessels, as in filariasis.

LYMPHANGIOGRAPHY is the procedure whereby the lymphatics (*q.v.*) and lymphatic glands can be rendered visible on X-ray films by means of the injection of radio-opaque substances.

LYMPHANGITIS (*lympha*, lymph ; ἀγγεῖον, a vessel) means an inflammation situated in the lymphatic vessels.

LYMPHATICS is the term generally applied to the vessels which convey the lymph. (For an account of their arrangement, *see* GLANDS.)

LYMPHATISM, or STATUS LYMPHATICUS, is a condition characterized by enlargement of the lymphatic tissue throughout the body. The thymus gland is also usually enlarged. The real nature of the condition, which is usually

found in children, is not known. Its importance is that such children are liable to sudden death under an anæsthetic.

LYMPHOCYTE (lymph, and κύτος, cell) is a variety of white blood corpuscle produced in the lymphoid tissues and lymphatic glands of the body. It contains a simple rounded nucleus surrounded by protoplasm generally described as non-granular. Two varieties of lymphocyte are described, small lymphocytes and large lymphocytes, and together they form over 20 per cent. of the white corpuscles of the blood (Plate V). Their numbers are increased in tuberculosis and certain other diseases. Such an increase is known as ' lymphocytosis '.

LYMPHŒDEMA means dropsical swelling of a part or organ due to obstruction to the lymph-vessels draining it.

LYMPHOGRANULOMA INGUINALE, LYMPHOGRANULOMA VENEREUM, PORADENITIS VENEREA, LYMPHOPATHIA VENEREUM, is a venereal disease in which the chief characteristic is enlargement of glands in the groin, the infecting agent being a virus.

LYMPHOMA (*lympha*, lymph ; -*oma*, termination meaning tumour) is a tumour of lymphoid tissue.

LYMPHOSARCOMA is a malignant growth of the lymphoid elements of the body, and is characterized by generalized enlargement of the lymphatic glands, spleen, and liver. The majority of cases—about 55 per cent.—occur in the sixty to seventy age-group, but it may occur at any age. The prognosis is poor, 80 per cent. of cases dying within six years. Treatment is by means of irradiation or chemotherapy.

LYSERGIC ACID belongs to the ergonovine group of alkaloids. In minute doses it induces psychic states in which the individual becomes aware of repressed memories. Under the influence of the drug he feels he is watching himself and relives feelings from his childhood and infancy. It is proving of value in the treatment of certain anxiety states, but is a drug that must only be used under skilled supervision.

LYSIS means the gradual ending of a fever, and is opposed to ' crisis ', which signifies the sudden ending of a fever. (*See* CRISIS.)

It is also used to describe the process of dissolution of a blood-clot, or the loosening of adhesions.

LYSOFORM is a liquid soap containing formalin, by virtue of which it possesses a strong antiseptic power.

LYSOL, or SAPONACEOUS SOLUTION OF CREOSOTE, is a brown, clear, oily fluid of antiseptic properties, made from coal-tar and containing 50 per cent. cresol. When mixed with water it forms a clear soapy fluid which, in 1 per cent. strength, is most useful for the disinfection of rooms and surgical instruments. It is used to a great extent in the same way as carbolic acid, and it does not exert upon the skin so irritating and roughening an effect as the latter.

LYSOL POISONING.—Since lysol is very generally used for disinfecting and cleansing purposes, it has come to be one of the commonest substances by which poisonous effects are produced. Its action as a poison is due to the cresol and similar substances that it contains. It is not a very deadly poison, and as much as 4 fluid ounces has been taken without producing permanently serious consequences. Immediate treatment is, however, of great importance.

Symptoms. — There is a sense of burning about the mouth and throat, of which the mucous membrane shows a white and swollen appearance. If the lysol is not speedily removed, unconsciousness and stupor gradually come on and death may occur within 24 hours. Septic pneumonia is also very liable to supervene, and to produce death at a later period.

Treatment. — Large quantities of tepid water and salt may be given at once to dilute the lysol and produce vomiting. If Epsom salts or Glauber's salt is available, this should be given in large quantities, dissolved in water, because it acts as a direct antidote to the poison. The stomach may also be washed out with a solution of one of these salts. Subsequently, olive oil or milk and cream may be given to soothe the irritation, and the patient, on account of difficulty in swallowing, must be fed on fluid food for several days.

LYSOZYME is the name given to a bactericidal substance present in tears (secreted by the lacrimal glands).

LYSSA (λύσσα, frenzy) is another term for rabies or hydrophobia.

M

McBURNEY'S POINT is an area of small size on the front of the abdomen, at which the tenderness experienced in appendicitis is felt with special keenness. It is situated between the navel and the prominent anterior superior spine of the right iliac bone, about 2 inches (50 mm.) distant from the latter.

MACERATION (*maceratio*) is a term applied to the softening of a solid by soaking in fluid.

MACROCYTE (μακρός, large ; κύτος, cell) is the term applied to an unusually large red blood corpuscle especially characteristic of the blood in pernicious anæmia.

MACROGLOSSIA means an abnormally large tongue.

MACULES (*macula*, a spot) are spots or stained areas of brown or purplish-brown colour in the skin. They may be due to old hæmorrhages, sunburn, disease of internal organs, pregnancy, skin diseases such as eczema and psoriasis, syphilis, and burns.

MADURA FOOT is the name given to a disease found in India in which the foot becomes swollen and its bones and other tissues riddled by sinuses caused by the presence of a fungus.

MAGNESIUM is a light white metal which burns readily in the air with a brilliant white flame, and the production of a fine white powder. It is used for photographic purposes in the form of ribbon or powder, but the metal itself is not used in medicine. The salts of magnesium used as drugs are the oxide of magnesium, generally known as 'magnesia', and the carbonate of magnesium, both of which have an antacid action ; also the sulphate of magnesium generally known as ' Epsom salts ', and the citrate of magnesium, both of which act as purgatives.

Uses.—Light and heavy magnesia, as also the light and heavy carbonates of magnesia, are used to correct hyperacidity of the stomach. They are also used as feeble laxatives. ' Fluid Magnesia ' is prepared by mixing sulphate of magnesium and carbonate of soda with water and passing a stream of carbonic acid gas through the mixture. In doses of one or two tablespoonfuls for an adult, or half to one teaspoonful for a young child, it is a useful and mild purgative.

Magnesium sulphate is the most commonly used saline purge. (*See* EPSOM SALTS.)

Citrate of magnesium and mixture of magnesium hydroxide (cream of magnesia) also form good saline purgatives.

MAGNETISM (*see* ELECTRICITY IN MEDICINE).

MAIDISM (*mais*, maize) is another name for PELLAGRA (*q.v.*).

MALACIA (μαλακία) is a term applied to softening of a part or tissue in disease, *e.g.* osteomalacia or softening of the bones.

MALABSORPTION SYNDROME includes a multiplicity of diseases, all of which are characterized by faulty absorption from the intestine of essential foodstuffs, such as fat, vitamins and mineral salts. Among the conditions in this syndrome are cœliac disease (*q.v.*) and sprue (*q.v.*).

MALAISE (French word) means a vague feeling of feverishness, listlessness, and languor, which often precedes the onset of serious acute diseases, or accompanies passing derangements, such as dyspepsia, chills, and colds.

MALARIA (Ital. *mala aria*, bad air), also known as AGUE, PALUDISM, JUNGLE FEVER, MARSH FEVER, PERIODIC FEVER, is a disease caused by the presence of certain parasites in the blood. It consists at first of a series of febrile attacks, which may come on every day, every second day, or every third day; later it assumes a chronic form, in which a bad state of health known as chronic malaria or malarial cachexia is developed, and there is a tendency towards frequent relapses.

History.—The history of this disease, and of the discoveries which have been made regarding it, forms one of the most interesting chapters in medicine.

The disease has been known from the earliest times, and not only is it described by many of the medical writers of antiquity, but numerous references to it exist in general literature, such as the works of Horace. From these it appears that its connection with swampy ground was quite well recognized even in ancient times.

The first important advance was made in 1640, when the Countess of Cinchon, wife of the Viceroy of Peru, brought home to Europe the bark by which the South American Indians had learned to treat the disease successfully. From this bark, named after her 'Cinchona bark', and also known as Jesuit's bark, since the secret had been learned by priests from the Indians, quinine is derived. By this drug a means of treating the paroxysms of fever, as well as an aid in warding off the disease, was obtained. From the fact that quinine is an antiseptic it was assumed that the disease must be due to some poison circulating in the blood which the quinine could destroy.

Not till 1880 was the next great step taken when Laveran, a French military surgeon, discovered the presence of minute parasites in the corpuscles of blood drawn from malarious persons and examined under the microscope. He described more than one form of the parasites, and subsequent observers demonstrated that the parasites go through a process of development, leading up to the production of spores, which are formed all through the blood of the affected person at one time, and from which a new set of parasites develops. Other observers were successful in finding similar parasites in the blood of lower animals, particularly of birds.

It had long been noticed, even by West African natives, that gnats, or, as they are called in the tropics, mosquitoes, seem to flourish together with malaria, and several scientists endeavoured to establish a connection between the two. This was successfully proved by Manson in 1894, through bringing from Italy live mosquitoes which had been allowed to suck blood from malarious persons in that country, and allow-

18 a

ing the insects to bite healthy people in London, who had no other possible connection with the disease. The experiment was successful, and those persons who had offered themselves for the experiment proved conclusively that malaria is carried by mosquitoes. Other persons proved the converse of this proposition, and showed, by living for some months in a malarious district, such as the Campagna at Rome, that infection does not take place provided mosquitoes be kept off by gauze and other means.

From the examination of the blood in malarious persons, Manson reasoned that the parasites go through a stage of their development in the bodies of the gnats, passing, in the tissues of those insects, through a sexual stage, in which male and female forms unite in the production of masses of new parasites. The arduous work of demonstrating this was undertaken by Ross, then a military surgeon in India. The difficulty of this work is understood when one considers that the dissection of a great number of mosquitoes and their examination under the microscope were necessary before Ross was able in 1898 to confirm the truth of Manson's theory, by demonstrating the genus Anopheles as the insect in which the development of the malaria parasite takes place. Other observers confirmed his observations, and traced out in detail the changes which the parasites undergo while in the mosquito.

Causes.—As shown by the above discoveries, the presence of persons infected by the malarial parasite and the access of the Anopheles mosquito (Fig. 235, page 481) to these and to healthy persons form two of the conditions producing infection of fresh cases. But there are various factors which aid or retard the development of the parasite and of the mosquito. The disease is known all round the world, but is chiefly found in tropical climates, spreading here and there into temperate regions, where it occurs in summer and autumn, if the other conditions are suitable. The presence of swamps, pools of surface water, rank vegetation, and a poorly fed population are also important factors. Its chief seats are the Mediterranean shores and tropical Africa, the East Indies, South China, and Central America.

The parasites of malaria are three in number, corresponding to the tertian fever, the quartan fever, and the æstivo-autumnal fever or subtertian or malignant tertian malaria. The parasites are protozoa, belonging to the order *Sporozoa*, and to the genus *Plasmodium*. The specific names for benign tertian, quartan, and malignant malaria are respectively *Plasmodium vivax*, *P. malariæ*, and *P. falciparum*. As has been stated, the malarial parasite passes one phase of its life-cycle in man (the asexual phase) and the other in the stomach and tissues of the mosquito (the sexual phase). After sexual union of male and female forms in the mosquito's stomach, the resulting offspring —the asexual sporozoites—eventually find their way into the mosquito's salivary gland.

When the infected female mosquito bites a human being, these filamentous sporozoites are injected into the blood. They then find their way into the liver where they develop into what are known as schizonts. After a period ranging from six to nine days (depending upon the species of plasmodium) these schizonts have reached maturity, and in the course of maturation each one has produced up to 40,000 merozoites. These merozoites are then released into the blood stream where they penetrate the red blood cells and form trophozoites (or rings). These in turn enlarge each to the capacity of the red corpuscle. The large trophozoite thus formed finally splits into numerous small parasites now called merozoites. These burst out of the red blood corpuscle into the blood stream and then attack other red corpuscles, the whole asexual cycle repeating itself once more. The paroxysm of malarial fever coincides with the bursting of the red blood corpuscles and the setting free of the merozoites into the blood-stream. Sexual forms—male and female gametocytes—also develop in the blood, but they undergo no further change until a mosquito bite sucks them into the mosquito's stomach.

Symptoms.—For a day or two before the actual fever sets in, there may be headache, vague pains about the body and limbs, chilliness, and slight rises of temperature. When the parasites have multiplied up to the stage already mentioned, the attack suddenly comes on.

The acute malarial attack has, in general, three stages, although in occasional cases one of the stages may be excessively marked or may be wanting. These are the cold stage, the hot stage, and the sweating stage.

The cold stage begins with a feeling of chilliness even in the hottest weather. This increases till the person has to betake himself to bed and heap himself with clothes, face and nails being blue with cold, and the whole body shaken with shivering (rigors). Nevertheless, if the temperature be taken with a thermometer, it is found to be considerably raised. This stage lasts an hour or less.

The hot stage comes on as the temperature of the body rises, beginning with hot flushes, which lengthen till the body feels burning hot, the temperature rising to 105° or 106° F. (40·5° to 41·1° C.). There are also headache, dizziness, sickness, pain throughout the body, and sometimes even delirium. This stage may last several hours.

The sweating stage comes on after the fever reaches its height, as the temperature begins to fall. Profuse perspiration breaks out, the person begins to feel decidedly better, and the headache and pains at the same time pass off. Finally, after two or three hours the patient feels quite well, though much weakened, and remains so till the next attack begins.

If the parasite present be that of *quartan fever* there is an intermission of two days before the next attack, that is to say, if the first attack be on the 1st day of the month the succeeding ones are on the 4th, 7th, and so on. If the parasite be that of *tertian fever*, the attacks are on the 1st, 3rd, 5th, and so on; whilst in the severe *æstivo-autumnal fever*, each attack may last considerably over a day, so that there may not be time for one to pass off completely before the next begins. The patient then is in a continued state of fever, known as *subtertian fever*. A person may get a double or treble infection of the malarial parasites, and then the fever may also occur every day, although from the fact that the temperature on one set of days rises higher than it does on the set of alternate days, or from the time of the attacks being different, the attack commencing, for example, on the 1st, 3rd, 5th, etc., at I P.M., and on the 2nd, 4th, 6th, etc., at 5 P.M., it is clear that the person is affected by two agues running side by side. When the fever occurs every day, whatever be the cause, it is sometimes called a *quotidian fever*.

As a rule people, after passing through an ague, feel completely recovered till the next attack is due, but now and then the attack may develop seriously. For example, hyperpyrexia may develop, the temperature continuing to rise till death occurs before the sweating stage sets in. Insensibility may set in and the person die owing to blockage of the small vessels in the brain by immense numbers of the parasites ; this is known as cerebral malaria. Severe vomiting or diarrhœa may also endanger the patient's life, or he may become very much collapsed during the sweating stage. One of the most dread complications of malaria is blackwater fever (*q.v.*).

If treatment be adopted between two attacks, the succeeding attack or the next after that is generally checked. Even when no treatment takes place, after a few weeks of the attacks these gradually get less and less marked and finally disappear, a 'rally' taking place. The parasites become so diminished that they are unable to cause fever, but they are not entirely destroyed in the blood, and so the affected person is subject after some weeks or months to a ' relapse ', when the attacks of ague are repeated, as in the first seizure. These rallies and relapses may go on for several years, especially if the person leads an exposed, laborious life, or is poorly nourished. Anything which depresses the vitality, such as a chill, is apt to lead to a fresh relapse. On the other hand, under efficient treatment complete recovery may occur.

If the disease becomes chronic, various symptoms set in. The person becomes very anæmic in consequence of the large number of blood corpuscles destroyed by the parasites in each paroxysm of fever. A feeble state of health, accompanied by bodily wasting and yellow discoloration of the skin, ensues, and the spleen and liver, particularly the former, become enlarged.

Treatment.—This falls into two important sections, preventive and curative.

PREVENTIVE TREATMENT may be directed either against the parasites or against the mosquitoes which convey them. Mepacrine, proguanil, chloroquine, and amodiaquine are effective prophylactics, and one of these should be taken regularly by all white people living in malarious districts. There is still some difference of opinion as to their relative efficacy. So far as mepacrine and proguanil are concerned, there is evidence suggesting that their efficacy depends upon the strain of parasite, and that this varies in different areas.

It is still more important to attack the mosquitoes in their developing stage. The eggs are laid on or near pools of stagnant water in which the larvæ and pupæ swim just below the surface, breathing through a tube which projects above the surface of the water. These larvæ may be destroyed by pouring on the surface of these pools some fluid through which the breathing-tube of the larva cannot be protruded. Crude petroleum and a special oil known as ' malariol ' are used for this purpose, and when poured upon pools the oil spreads out instantly into a film which will remain intact for several days if not destroyed by rain or wind. Further, all small pools in gardens should be filled up, tubs, flower-pots, cisterns, and other collections of water emptied regularly at least once a week, and in public works, such as railways, it should be made illegal, as is the rule in Italy, to leave holes and ditches where water can collect. Anopheline breeding grounds can be sprayed with Paris green. Fish which feed on the larvæ can be introduced into ponds and lakes.

Although these methods are still of value, they have largely been replaced or supplemented by the use of insecticides such as D.D.T., benzene hexachloride (B.H.C.) and dieldrin which have proved most effective in destroying mosquitoes.

Wire-gauze screens to all the windows of a house, and muslin mosquito netting over the beds, form an efficient protection, and it should be remembered that not only should mosquitoes be kept away from healthy people by these means, but that it is even more important that the insects should not gain access to those suffering from the disease, by whose blood they become infected and made carriers of malaria to the healthy.

CURATIVE TREATMENT depends upon quinine, mepacrine, proguanil hydrochloride (paludrine), chloroquine, and amodiaquine. (*See also* BLACKWATER FEVER.)

MALATHION is one of the less toxic organo-phosphorus insecticides (*q.v.*).

MALE FERN (*see* FERN-ROOT).

MALFORMATION (*see* DEFORMITIES).

MALIGNANT (*malignus*, of an evil nature) is a term applied in several ways to serious disorders. Tumours are called malignant when they grow rapidly, tend to infiltrate surrounding healthy tissues, and to spread to distant parts of the body, leading eventually to death. (*See* CANCER AND SARCOMA.) The term is also applied to types of disease which are much more serious than the usual form, such as malignant scarlatina, malignant smallpox, etc., the disease in these cases generally resulting in death. Malignant pustule is another name for anthrax (*see* ANTHRAX).

MALIGNANT HYPERTENSION has nothing to do with cancer. It derives its name from the fact that, if untreated it runs a rapidly fatal course. It is still undecided whether it is a disease entity in itself or is merely a terminal stage in certain cases of essential hypertension (*q.v.*). Its characteristic features are that it occurs in a younger age-group than essential hypertension, there is a very high diastolic blood pressure, with papilloedema (*q.v.*) and renal failure. This is the type of hypertension in which the antihypertensive drugs (*see* ESSENTIAL HYPERTENSION) have proved so successful. Indeed, the introduction of these drugs has revolutionized the outlook. At one time an invariably fatal disease within two years, many patients with this condition can now enjoy many years of comparatively good health.

MALINGERING (Fr. *malingre*, sickly) is a term applied to the feigning of illness. In the great majority of cases a person who feigns illness has a certain amount of disability, but exaggerates his illness or discomfort for some ulterior motive.

MALLEOLUS (*malleolus*, a little hammer) is the term applied to either of the two bony prominences at the ankle. (*See* LEG.)

MALLET FINGER is due to sudden forced flexion of the terminal joint of a finger, resulting in rupture of the tendon. As a result the individual is unable to extend the terminal part of the finger which remains bent forward. The middle, ring and little fingers are most commonly involved. A common cause in men is catching a cricket ball; in women the common cause is tucking the bedclothes under the mattress when bedmaking.

MALT is a substance derived from barley by allowing a certain amount of growth to take place in the moistened grain, which is then dried and crushed. It contains an albuminoid ferment named 'diastase', together with a large amount of malt - sugar and dextrin, the latter constituents being still further developed from the starch of the barley by the action of the ferment, when the malt is allowed to digest in water at a temperature approaching 104° F. (40° C.) Similarly, the ferment will convert into sugar a large amount of the starch in flour mixed with malt, and so perform some of the functions of the saliva and pancreatic juice.

For these reasons malt is mixed with various proportions of flour to form some of the popular foods for children. It is also used in the form of malt extracts, 1 ounce (28·3 grammes) of which is equivalent to 80 calories.

MALTA FEVER, also known as MEDITERRANEAN FEVER, ROCK FEVER, NEAPOLITAN FEVER, LEVANT FEVER, UNDULANT FEVER, and BRUCELLOSIS, is a long-continued fever which occurs on the shores and islands of the Mediterranean principally, but is found also in many other countries. (*See* BRUCELLOSIS.)

MAMMARY GLAND (*mamma*, the breast) (*see* BREAST).

MAMMILLA is the Latin term for the nipple.

MAMMOGRAPHY is the term used to describe the special technique whereby X-rays can be taken that reveal the structure of the breast.

MANDELIC ACID is a non-toxic keto acid used in the treatment of infections of the urinary tract, especially those due to the *Escherichia coli* and the *Streptococcus fæcalis* or *Enterococcus*. It is administered in doses of 45 grains (3 grammes) several times daily. As it is only effective in an acid urine, ammonium chloride must also be taken at the same time.

MANDIBLE (*mandibulum*) is the name applied to the bone of the lower jaw.

MANDL'S SOLUTION consists of iodine 6 grains (400 mg.), potassium iodide 20 grains (1·2 grammes), oil of peppermint 5 minims (0·3 ml.), and glycerin 1 ounce (28·3 grammes). It is used as a throat paint.

MANGANESE is a metal of which oxides are found abundantly in nature. Permanganate of potassium forms a well-known disinfectant. (*See* PERMANGANATE OF POTASSIUM.)

MANIA (*μανία*, fury) is a form of mental disorder characterized by great excitement. (*See* MENTAL ILLNESS.)

MANIC-DEPRESSIVE INSANITY, or CYCLOTHYMIA, is a form of madness characterized by alternate attacks of mania and depression.

MANIPULATION is the term applied to the forceful passive movement of joints. In skilled hands it is a most effective means of treatment of stiff joints or of pain in the back due to a prolapsed intervertebral disc.

MANOMETER (*μανός*, slack; *μέτρον*, measure) is an instrument for measuring the pressure or tension of liquids or gases. (*See* BLOOD-PRESSURE.)

MANTOUX TEST, also known as MENDEL'S TEST, is a test for tuberculosis. It consists in injecting into the superficial layers of the skin (*i.e.* intradermally) a very small quantity of 'old tuberculin'. A positive reaction of the skin—swelling and redness—shows that the person so reacting has been infected with the *Mycobacterium tuberculosis*. But it does not mean that such a person is suffering from active tuberculosis.

MANUBRIUM is the uppermost part of the breast-bone.

MANZULLO'S TELLURITE TEST consists in applying to the throat of someone suspected of having diphtheria a 2 per cent. potassium tellurite solution. If diphtheria bacilli are present the solution blackens. But some other germs also reduce the tellurite solution. As a negative test it has some use, because if no reduction occurs it is highly improbable that the patient has diphtheria.

MAPLE-SYRUP URINE DISEASE is a condition in which there is an association between mental defect and a disorder of amino-acid metabolism. It is so named because the urine has the odour of maple syrup.

MARASMUS (*μαραίνω*, I waste away) means progressive wasting, especially in young children when there is no ascertainable cause. It is generally associated with defective feeding. (*See* ATROPHY *and* INFANT FEEDING.)

MARGARINE (*see* DIET).

MARIHUANA is another term for CANNABIS INDICA, or hemp, or hashish.

MARROW means the softer substance enclosed in the interior of bones. It is of two kinds—*yellow marrow*, which occupies the large tubular space in the shaft of a long bone, such as a limb bone, and *red marrow*, which fills up the spaces in the interior of the ribs, sternum, and vertebral bodies, as well as the ends of the shafts of the long bones such as the femur and humerus. There is no essential difference between the two, although yellow marrow owes its colour to the large amount fat of contained in it, whilst red marrow is of a highly cellular structure. The marrow is the site of formation of red blood corpuscles, platelets, and granular white blood cells.

MARSH FEVER (*see* MALARIA).

MARSHMALLOW ROOT is the root of *Althæa officinalis*, which has long been credited as a domestic medicine, with a soothing influence upon mucous membranes, as well as exerting a diuretic action. It is used chiefly as an ingredient of lozenges for cases of sore throat.

MASSAGE, or RUBBING, is a method of treatment in which the operator uses his hands, or occasionally other appliances, to rub, knead, or press the skin and deeper tissues of the person under treatment. It is often combined with (*a*) 'passive' movements, in which the masseur moves the limbs in various ways, the person treated making no effort; or (*b*) 'active' movements, which are performed with the combined assistance of masseur and patient. Massage is also very frequently combined with baths and gymnastics in order to strengthen various muscles. The beneficial effects of massage are exerted in different ways. Applied gently, it has a soothing action upon the nerves of sensation, and, applied more vigorously, certain methods have the effect of quickening the circulation of lymph and blood, and so leading to the rapid absorption of waste products in the muscles, and of the results of disease in various organs. Other forms of massage cause muscular contractions and so provide exercise for the muscles in cases where movements of the whole body are not desired.

Varieties. — STROKING or *effleurage* consists of gentle pressure with the hand moved in one direction. It soothes the nerves of the part treated and empties the main lymph-vessels and veins, thus increasing the circulation locally. It is carried out either with the flat of the hand or with the edges of thumb and first finger widely separated.

KNEADING or *pétrissage* is the most commonly employed form, and consists of squeezing, kneading, rolling, or rubbing movements coupled with a con-

siderable amount of pressure, effected, it may be, with the fingers or knuckles, but generally with the pulp or the ball of the thumb. It has a still greater effect than stroking in moving on the lymph and blood circulation of deep-seated parts, and so leading to the absorption of inflammatory thickenings in and around joints, tendon - sheaths, and muscles. The masseur in this method, as it were, tries to dispel inflammatory deposits by his own endeavours, although he knows that it is rather by the vital activity which he merely assists that the effect is gradually produced. (*See* LYMPH.)

STABILE MOVEMENTS include such applications as the following. *Pressing* may be done with the finger-tips or with the knuckles, and it is usually combined with rubbing. *Tapping* is done with the points of the fingers from the wrist, and has, when applied gently, a soothing effect. *Thrusting*, which consists in poking up the deeper parts with the points of the fingers, and *hacking*, in which the muscles are struck with the inner edge of the hand, the arms moving from the elbows, are employed to cause muscular contractions.

VIBRATORY MOVEMENTS are made either by tapping (as above) or by special pads, to which a very rapid oscillation is communicated from an electric motor. This form of massage has been much used in order to exert a soothing influence, for example, in cases of headache.

PASSIVE MOVEMENTS are made chiefly for their effect upon the joints. The synovial fluid is increased if scanty, and tends to be absorbed if excessive, while adhesions, which limit the motions of the joint or render these painful, are broken down by passive movements of a more forcible type. This type of massage is the form chiefly employed in the treatment of stiff joints by bone-setters.

ACTIVE MOVEMENTS of a carefully regulated type, in which the person's will is concentrated upon the movement made, are specially useful for developing the muscles brought into play thereby. The amount of muscular force required is graduated and increased by the masseur resisting the movements with varying degrees of force.

Uses.—Massage can only be employed to full advantage by fully trained masseurs (or masseuses). A complete list of members of the Chartered Society of Physiotherapy who are qualified to give massage can be obtained on application to the Secretary of the Society, Tavistock House (South), Tavistock Square, London, W.C.1. The types of case in which massage is useful are extremely various. Neuralgia, sciatica, and muscular rheumatism are among the painful conditions in which some relief is generally obtained. In neurasthenia, muscular wasting, and paralysis due to nerve conditions—such as lead-poisoning, peripheral neuritis, crutch palsy, Bell's paralysis, and infantile paralysis—the muscles affected may be kept in a state of good nutrition till the nerve weakness has disappeared, and so recovery may be materially hastened. In various other nervous conditions, such as hysteria, St. Vitus's dance, loss of sensation, and writer's cramp, massage often proves of great benefit. Several types of joint disease, such as chronic rheumatism and stiffness due to previous slight injuries, such as sprains, are specially amenable to treatment by passive movements combined with deep rubbing, but any such interference with joints which have been recently the seat of tuberculous disease is very dangerous, as by these means the disease may be more widely spread. In several general conditions such as corpulence and constipation associated with a flabby state of body, massage may be of great usefulness.

Massage may be combined with electrical applications. For example, high-frequency and static electricity are often used along with gentle massage to obtain a soothing effect. The interrupted galvanic, sinusoidal, and faradic currents are frequently useful combined with more forcible massage to stimulate muscular contraction in various cases of paralysis. (*See also* CARDIAC MASSAGE.)

MASS MINIATURE RADIOGRAPHY is a method of obtaining X-ray photographs of the chests of large numbers of people at about the rate of two persons per minute. It has been used on a large scale of recent years as a means of screening the population for pulmonary tuberculosis. In England and Wales, in 1963, 3,245,600 examinations were made.

MASTICATION is the act whereby, as a result of movements of the lower jaw, lips, tongue, and cheek, food is reduced to a condition in which it is ready to be acted on by the gastric juices in the process of digestion. Adequate mastication is an essential part of the digestive process. (*See* DIGESTION.)

MASTITIS (μαστός, the breast) is the term applied to inflammation of the breast. (*See* BREAST, DISEASES OF.)

MASTOID PROCESS (μαστοειδής, like a breast) is the large process of the temporal bone of the skull which can be felt immediately behind the ear. It contains numerous cavities, one of which, the ' mastoid antrum ', communicates with the middle ear, and is liable to suppurate when the middle ear is diseased. (*See* EAR, DISEASES OF.)

MASTURBATION (*manus*, hand; *stuprare*, to rape) is a normal transitional stage of sexual development. It is only when it is practised excessively or persisted in regularly after the attainment of full sexual maturity that it becomes a condition requiring treatment.

MATCH-WORKERS' DISEASE (*see* PHOSPHORUS).

MATERIA MEDICA is that branch of medical study which deals with the sources, preparations, and uses of drugs.

MATERNITY and CHILD WELFARE.—The high rate of infantile mortality which used to prevail in the larger towns drew attention to the great loss of infant life which was produced partly by ignorance on the part of the mothers and partly by poverty. A movement was accordingly begun early in the present century in some of the larger cities to provide trained women as health visitors for giving advice to working-class women in the proper methods of rearing their children. This was at first a voluntary effort conducted by philanthropic agencies, but it was soon taken up by county councils and local authorities throughout the country. The necessary information as to the existence of newly born infants was provided by the Notification of Births which was demanded by Acts passed in 1907 and 1915. Women health visitors were appointed to visit the homes where such newly born infants were found, and shortly afterwards INFANT CONSULTATION CENTRES and Clinics were established by various local authorities and voluntary agencies.

At first the movement for child welfare was limited to infants from birth to 1 year of age, but shortly afterwards the necessity for supervising the health of children until they came under school discipline at 5 years was recognized. Still later it became evident that it was desirable to watch over the health of the expectant mother and to provide skilled attendance prior to and during confinement. This led, accordingly, to the establishment of MATERNITY AND CHILD WELFARE CENTRES and Clinics by many local authorities. The schemes which have now been devised for combating infantile mortality are very wide. They include better housing, paid and voluntary health visitors, consultation centres for mothers, infant milk depots, the provision of cheap meals for expectant and nursing mothers, and hospital accommodation for necessitous expectant mothers before and during confinement. The provision of Child Welfare Centres to which parents may bring their infants at stated times produces valuable results, both by advice to the mothers and by keeping records of increase in weight and other important facts regarding the infants, and also by interesting and stimulating the mothers to greater efforts. The Centre also provides opportunities for giving instruction in health, cookery, sewing, etc., to the mothers, and for distributing food and clothing as may be necessary. Antenatal Clinics, which provide education and assistance for the expectant mother, are usually conducted in connection with Maternity Hospitals and form an important section of this work.

HEALTH VISITORS are concerned with everything in the household that tends to secure and maintain health for the young children. The health visitor, who is often a certificated nurse, deals with the minor ailments of infancy and indicates when treatment by a doctor is necessary. During epidemics part of her duty is to keep the Public Health Authority advised in regard to the progress of infection. Health visitors must pass the examination of the Health Visitor's Certificate of the Royal Society of Health. Candidates for this examination must be either : (a) Nurses who have undergone a three-years' course of training at a recognized general or children's hospital, who have obtained Part I of the Certificate of the Central Midwife's Board, and who have attended an approved whole-time course in public health work lasting for at least six months, or (b) Women, not being trained nurses, who have undergone an approved course of training in public health work for two years together with six months' training in hospital, and who have obtained Part I of the Certificate of the Central Midwifes Board.

ANTENATAL CLINICS are considered to be of great value, because the fatality among the unborn from still-birth, abortion, etc., is higher than the mortality of infants during the first year of life ; it is generally believed, further, that by the medical attention provided at such clinics many of these antenatal deaths could be prevented, and the number of infants born prematurely and of feeble constitution could be much reduced. Health visitors are supposed to follow up cases seen at antenatal clinics and to ensure that the medical instructions given at the clinic are carried out, and proper steps taken to prepare for the confinement.

Under the National Insurance Acts, in Great Britain a woman receives a maternity grant in respect of each child, and also a home confinement grant if the confinement takes place at home. A woman who ordinarily follows a gainful occupation is also given a maternity allowance for 18 weeks beginning about 11 weeks before her confinement provided that she abstains from work.

INFANT CONSULTATION CLINICS are conducted usually by local authorities, and, in cases where it is desirable, mothers are urged to bring infants to these clinics regularly. Many of the disabling illnesses of early childhood are thus prevented, and the attendance should continue as required during the first five years of the child's life.

DAY NURSERIES, or crèches, are provided in many places in connection with these clinics, at which children can be left when the mothers are out at work. Most local authorities have schemes for supplying special foods or nutritious diet to mothers of children who after medical examination at the Clinic are found to require such assistance. SPECIAL TREATMENT CLINICS are also provided in many places for the examination and treatment of teeth, eyes, ears, nose, throat, and skin of children. Also there is at present a movement for the treatment of cases in which children are crippled as the result of early disease. Further, in connection with the clinics many local authorities possess convalescent homes, or arrange with voluntary agencies for admission to their convalescent homes of children who are in need of special care and open-air regime. Indirectly connected with these clinics in many places there have also been established play centres and kindergartens for young children.

Under the National Health Service Act, 1946, all these services have been unified under Local Health Authorities, which are county councils and county borough councils in England and Wales, and town councils and county councils in Scotland. Under the terms of the Act a statutory duty is imposed upon Local Health Authorities to provide health centres, maternity and child welfare, domiciliary midwifery, health visiting, home nursing, vaccination and immunization, and ambulances. They are also empowered to provide home-help services, and care and after-care. Maternity and child welfare covers the care of expectant and nursing mothers and of children under 5 years of age who are not attending school. It includes ante-natal clinics, post-natal clinics, child-welfare clinics, the provision of cod-liver oil, orange juice, and other foodstuffs, and a priority dental service for both expectant and nursing mothers and young children.

MATTER (see PUS).

MATTOID (*mattus*, drunken) is a term applied to a person who, though passing as sane, is eccentric or mentally unbalanced in some particular direction.

MAW-WORMS is another name for round-worms. (*See* PARASITES.)

MAXILLA (*maxilla*, a jaw) is the name applied in human anatomy to the upper jaw-bones, which bear the teeth.

MEASLES, also known as MORBILLI or RUBEOLA, is an acute infectious disease occurring mostly in children. It appears to have been known from an early period in the history of medicine, mention being made of it in the writings of Rhazes and others of the Arabian physicians in the tenth century. For long, however, its specific nature was not recognized, and it was held to be a variety of smallpox. Measles and scarlet fever were long confounded with each other ; and in the account given by Sydenham of epidemics of measles in London in 1670 and 1674, it is evident that even that accurate observer had not as yet clearly perceived their pathological distinction, although it would seem to have been made a century earlier by Ingrassias, a physician of Palermo. It is only within a comparatively recent period that measles has come to be universally regarded as a distinct and independent malady. The disease known as German measles, or rubella, is a much milder disease than measles. Since November 1939 measles has been compulsorily notifiable in England and Wales.

Causes.—Measles is a disease of the earlier years of childhood. Like most other infectious maladies, it is admittedly rare, though not unknown, in nurslings or infants under six months old. It is comparatively seldom met in adults, but this is largely due to the fact that most persons have undergone an attack in early life, or have been repeatedly exposed to the infection of measles and so have probably acquired a certain amount of immunity, for, among communities where measles is not prevalent, the old suffer equally with the young, when infection is once introduced. Some countries enjoy long immunity from outbreaks of measles, but it has been frequently found that in such cases the disease, when introduced, spreads with great rapidity and virulence. This was shown in two instances in recent times— namely, in the epidemic in the Faroe Islands in 1846, where, within six months after the arrival of a single case of measles, more than three-fourths of the entire population were attacked and many perished ; and the similarly pro- duced and still more destructive out- break in Fiji in 1875, in which it was estimated that about one-fourth of the inhabitants were cut off by the disease within three months. In such cases it is generally held that epidemics arising on what may be termed a virgin soil are apt to possess a special severity.

In many lands, such as the United Kingdom and the United States, measles is rarely absent, especially from large towns, where sporadic cases are found in greater or less number at all seasons. But every two years, especially from December to February, epidemics arise and spread among the children who are not protected by a recent attack. In 1966 there were 343,642 cases in England and Wales, with 80 deaths. One attack of measles does not give complete immunity from future attacks, though there is a cer- tain amount of protection, and second attacks are rare.

There are few diseases so infectious as measles, and its rapid spread in epi- demics is no doubt due to the fact that infection is most potent in the earlier stages, even in the first three days, before its real nature has been shown by the appearance of the rash. Hence the difficulty of timely isolation and the readiness with which the disease is spread, which is mostly by infected droplets from the nose and throat coughed or sneezed into the air. (*See* INFECTION.) Another fact, which some- times assists the spread of measles, is that the temperature often falls to normal on the second day and the child appears to be much better, so that he is again allowed to mix with his play-fellows, owing to the mistaken idea that he is suffering merely from a cold, till the rash appears on the fourth day and shows the real nature of the malady. It is possible also that infec- tion may be carried from one place to another by clothing, etc., although the tenacity and activity of the infect- ive agent is in this respect much less

562

marked than in the cases of scarlatina and smallpox. It is not, in all prob- ability, the case that measles can be carried from one child to another by a third and unaffected person.

The infecting agent is a virus.

Symptoms.—Like the other eruptive fevers (exanthemata), to which class of diseases measles belongs, its progress is marked by several stages more or less sharply defined.

After the infection has been received into the system, a period of incubation or latency precedes the development of the disease, during which scarcely any disturbance of the health is perceptible. This period appears to vary in duration, but it may be stated as generally lasting for from ten to fourteen days, when it is followed by the invasion of the symp- toms specially characteristic of measles. These consist in the somewhat sudden onset of acute catarrh of the mucous membranes. Sneezing, accompanied with a watery discharge, sometimes bleeding from the nose, redness and watering of the eyes, cough of a short, frequent, and noisy character, with little or no expectoration, hoarseness of the voice, and occasionally sickness and diarrhœa, are the chief symptoms of this stage. Along with these there is well-marked febrile disturbance, the temperature being elevated to 102°– 104° F. (39° to 40° C), and the pulse rapid, while headache, thirst, and rest- lessness are usually present to a greater or less degree. In some instances these initial symptoms are so slight that they almost escape notice, and the child is allowed to associate with others at a time when, as will be afterwards seen, the contagion of the disease is most active. In rare cases, especially in young children, convulsions usher in, or occur in the course of, this stage of invasion which lasts as a rule for three or four days, the febrile symp- toms, however, showing a characteristic tendency to pass away temporarily (remission) on the second and some- times also on the third day. About the fourth day after the invasion, some- times later, rarely earlier, the charac- teristic eruption appears on the skin, being first noticed on the brow, cheeks, chin, also behind the ears, and on the neck. It consists of small spots of a dusky red or crimson colour, slightly elevated above the surface, at first isolated, but tending to become grouped together into patches of irregular, occasionally crescentic, outline, with portions of skin free from the eruption intervening. The face acquires a swollen and bloated appearance, which, taken along with the catarrh of the nostrils and eyes, is almost characteristic, and renders the diagnosis at this stage a matter of no difficulty. Even before it appears on the skin, the rash is sometimes visible within the mouth, as bluish-white spots on the mucous membrane, known as 'Koplik's spots'. The eruption spreads downwards over the

turbances, which were present from the beginning, become aggravated, the temperature often rising to 105° F. or more, and there are headache, thirst, furred tongue, and soreness of the throat, upon which red patches similar to those on the surface of the body may be observed. The patient is also usually much depressed. These symptoms usually decline as soon as the rash has attained its maximum, and often there occurs a sudden and extensive fall of temperature, indicating that the crisis of the disease has been reached. In favourable cases, convalescence proceeds rapidly, the patient feeling per-

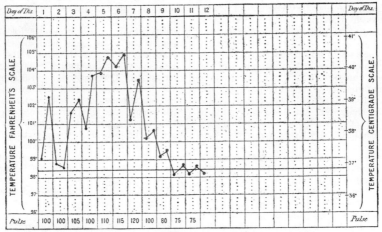

Fig. 274.—Typical temperature chart from a case of measles. The fall of temperature which often occurs on the second day is shown.

body and limbs, which are soon thickly studded with the red spots or patches. Sometimes these become confluent over a considerable surface, giving rise to a larger area of uniform redness.

The rash continues to come out for two or three days, and then begins to fade in the order in which it first showed itself, namely, from above downwards. By the end of about a week after its first appearance, scarcely any trace of the eruption remains beyond a faint staining of the skin. Occasionally during convalescence slight peeling of the epidermis takes place, but much less frequently and distinctly than is the case in scarlet fever. At the commencement of the eruptive stage, the fever, catarrh, and other constitutional dis-

fectly well even before the rash has faded from the skin.

Measles may, however, occur in a very severe or malignant form, in which the symptoms throughout are of urgent character, the rash but feebly developed and of dark-purple hue, while there is great prostration of strength, accompanied with intense catarrh of the respiratory or gastro-intestinal mucous membrane. Such cases, always of serious import, are happily rare, occurring mostly in circumstances of bad hygiene, both as regards the individual and his surroundings. On the other hand, cases of measles are often met of so mild a form throughout that the patient can scarcely be persuaded to submit to treatment.

Measles derives its chief importance in the view of medical men from the risk of certain complications which are apt to arise during its course, more especially inflammatory affections of the respiratory organs. These are most liable to occur in very young and delicate children. It has been already stated that irritation of the respiratory passages is one of the symptoms characteristic of measles, but that this subsides with the decline of the eruption. Not infrequently, however, these symptoms, instead of abating, become aggravated, and bronchitis of the capillary form (*see* BRONCHITIS), or pneumonia, generally of the diffuse or lobular variety (*see* PNEUMONIA), imparts to the case a gravity which it did not originally possess. By far the greater proportion of the mortality in measles is due to its complications, of which those just mentioned are the most common, but which also include inflammatory affections of the larynx, and also diarrhœa assuming a dysenteric character. Of there may remain, as direct results of the disease, chronic ophthalmia, discharge from the ears with deafness, or rarely a form of gangrene affecting the tissues of the mouth or cheeks and other parts of the body (CANCRUM ORIS), leading to disfigurement and even endangering life.

Treatment.—The patient should be isolated, but quarantine of contacts is used much less than it used to be. Child contacts of measles should be allowed to go to school provided they are sent home on the first suggestion of fever or malaise. Measles can be prevented or attenuated with gamma globulin obtainable from the medical officer of health, and its use should be considered in young family contacts or older children suffering from some other disease. A vaccine is now available which gives a high degree of protection against the disease.

As regards special treatment, in an ordinary case of measles little is required beyond what is necessary in febrile conditions generally. Routine administration of sulphonamides or penicillin is not indicated, but the latter is indicated in : (*a*) children under two years of age ; (*b*) children with previous middle-ear disease ; (*c*) children suffering from some other disease ; (*d*) chil-

dren who are very ill. Confinement to bed in a darkened room, into which air is freely admitted in such a way as to avoid draughts ; light, nourishing diet (soups, milk puddings, glucose, etc.), and mild diaphoretics, such as Mindererus spirit and ipecacuanha (*see* DIAPHORETICS), are all that is necessary in the febrile stage. When the catarrhal symptoms are very severe, the hot bath or warm packing to the body generally, or to the chest and throat, affords relief, and a hot bath, to which one or two tablespoonfuls of mustard are added, may, with advantage, be administered, if the eruption be feebly developed or tend to recede too soon, and especially if convulsions should set in.

The serious chest complications of measles are to be dealt with by those measures applicable for the relief of pneumonia or bronchitis (*see* BRONCHTIIS *and* PNEUMONIA). Inflammation of the eyes is best soothed by washing several times daily with weak boric acid lotion, and thereafter smearing a little boric ointment on the edge of each lower lid. Ear complications, if they come on, usually appear with a discharge as the child is getting better (*see* EAR, DISEASES OF). Diarrhœa is treated by the usual remedies, including carefully administered doses of Dover's powder, chalk mixture, etc. (*see* DIARRHŒA).

Isolation can end ten days from the appearance of the rash if all discharges have dried up.

MEASURES (*see* WEIGHTS AND MEASURES).

MEAT (*see* NITROGENOUS FOODS).

MEATUS (*meatus*, passage) is a term applied to any passage or opening, *e.g.* external auditory meatus, the passage from the surface to the drum of the ear.

MECAMYLAMINE is one of the recently introduced drugs for the treatment of hypertension. It belongs to the group of amine ganglion-blocking drugs : *i.e.* it acts by producing a block in the ganglion of the autonomic nervous system (*q.v.*). (*See also* ESSENTIAL HYPERTENSION.)

MECHANOTHERAPY is the provision of active physical exercise by means of a mechanical contrivance which necessitates the expenditure of physical work before it can be moved or used. Examples of mechanotherapy are dumb-bells, Indian clubs and parallel bars. One of the advantages of mechanotherapy, as opposed to other forms of physical exercise, is that it allows the amount of exercise performed to be accurately measured.

MECHOLYL, or ACETYL-BETA-METHYLCHOLINE, is a drug which stimulates the parasympathetic nerves. Its main use in medicine is to arrest attacks of paroxysmal tachycardia.

MECKEL'S DIVERTICULUM is a hollow process sometimes found attached to the small intestine. It is placed on the small intestine about 3 or 4 feet (90 to 120 cm.) away from its junction with the large intestine, is several inches long, and ends blindly.

MECONIUM (μηκώνιον, poppy-juice) means the brown semi-fluid material which collects in the bowels of a child prior to birth, and which should be discharged either at the time of birth or shortly afterwards. It consists partly of bile secreted by the liver before birth, partly of debris from the mucous membrane of the intestines.

MEDIASTINUM (*medius*, middle) is the name given to the space in the chest which lies between the two lungs. It contains the heart and great vessels, the gullet, the lower part of the windpipe, the thoracic duct, the phrenic nerves, as well as numerous structures of less importance.

MEDITERRANEAN FEVER (*see* MALTA FEVER).

MEDULLA (*medulla*) is another word for marrow. The term is usually restricted to the marrow of bones, or to designate a part of the brain, though the spinal cord is also sometimes known as the spinal medulla.

MEDULLA OBLONGATA (*medulla*, marrow ; *oblongus*, long), or BULB, is the hindmost part of the brain and is continued into the spinal cord. In it are situated several of the nerve-centres which are most essential to life, such as those governing breathing, the action of the heart, swallowing, etc. (*See* BRAIN.)

MEGA- and **MEGALO-** (μέγας, great) are prefixes denoting largeness.

MEGALOMANIA (μέγας, great ; μανία, madness) is the term applied to a delusion of grandeur or an insane belief in a person's own extreme greatness, goodness, or power.

MEGRIM (Fr. *migraine*, corrupted from ἡμικρανία, pain on half of the head). (*See* MIGRAINE.)

MEIBOMIAN GLANDS are the minute glands situated in the eyelids, in connection with which styes and cysts frequently arise. (*See* EYE, DISEASES OF.)

MELÆNA (μελαίνω, I blacken) means a condition of the stools in which dark, tarry masses are passed from the bowel. It is due to bleeding from the stomach or from the higher part of the bowel, the blood undergoing chemical changes under the action of the secretions, and being finally converted in large part into sulphide of iron.

MELANCHOLIA (μέλας, black ; χολή, bile) is a form of insanity characterized by great mental and physical depression. (*See* MENTAL ILLNESS *and* MANIC-DEPRESSIVE INSANITY.)

MELANIN is the dark pigment found in the skin and hair, as well as the choroid coat of the eye. It is the amount of melanin which decides the colour of the skin and hair.

MELANONA is a tumour arising from the cells that produce melanin (*q.v.*). A highly malignant form, known as malignant melanoma, arises from the pigmented cells of moles (*q.v.*) or nævi.

MELANOTIC (μέλας, black) is a term applied to certain tumours, dark in colour due to the deposition of black pigment, and usually malignant in nature.

MELORHEOSTOSIS is an abnormal condition of bone in which pathological hardening and denseness extend in a linear direction through one of he long bones of a limb, causing deformity and limitation of movement of the limb.

MELPHALAN is one of the alkylating agents (*q.v.*) which is proving of value in the treatment of certain forms of malignant disease.

MEMBRANES (see BRAIN, CROUP, DIPHTHERIA, and LABOUR).

MEMORY (see FORGETFULNESS).

MENAPHTHONE, or 2-methyl-1 : 4-naphthoquinone, is a synthetic vitamin K_I preparation. (See VITAMINS.)

MENARCHE ($\mu\eta\nu$, month ; $\dot{\alpha}\rho\chi\eta$, beginning) is the term applied to the beginning of the menstrual function.

MENDELISM is the term applied to a law enunciated by G. J. Mendel that the offspring is not intermediate in type between its parents, but that the type of one or other parent is predominant. Characteristics are classed as either dominant or recessive. The offspring of the first generation tend to inherit the dominant characteristics, whilst the recessive characteristics remain latent and appear in some of the offspring of the second generation. If individuals possessing recessive characters unite, recessive characters then become dominant characters in succeeding generations. The law may be expressed by the following formula: n(DD + 2 DR + RR), in which DD represents dominant offspring, RR recessive offspring, and DR offspring with mixed characters.

MÉNIÈRE'S DISEASE is a condition in which giddiness, headache, deafness, and ringing in the ears are associated in sudden attacks due to sudden loss of function of the labyrinth of the internal ear. (See EAR, DISEASES OF.)

MENINGES ($\mu\hat{\eta}\nu\iota\gamma\xi$, a membrane) are the membranes surrounding the brain and spinal cord. (See BRAIN.) The membranes include the 'dura mater', a tough, fibrous membrane closely applied to the inside of the skull; the 'arachnoid mater', a more delicate membrane, enveloping the brain but separated from its irregular surface by spaces containing fluid ; and the 'pia mater', a delicate network of fibres containing blood-vessels and uniting the arachnoid mater to the brain. The two latter are generally regarded as one membrane, the 'pia-arachnoid'. These membranes bear the blood-

566

vessels which nourish the surface of the brain and the interior of the skull. Meningeal hæmorrhage from these vessels forms one of the chief dangers arising from fracture of the skull.

MENINGISM is the name applied to a condition with symptoms closely resembling those of meningitis, but due simply to a feverish state.

MENINGITIS (from $\mu\hat{\eta}\nu\iota\gamma\xi$, a membrane) is a term applied to inflammation affecting the membranes of the brain (cerebral meningitis) or spinal cord (spinal meningitis), or both. Either the dura or the pia-arachnoid may be inflamed. In the former case the condition is known as pachymeningitis ; in the latter, leptomeningitis. Pachymeningitis is the less common of the two, is often local and secondary to disease of the bone (e.g. tuberculous or syphilitic), and may be cranial or spinal. Leptomeningitis is the more common, is usually extensive in distribution, greatly alters the composition of the cerebro-spinal fluid, and may be primary or secondary to infection elsewhere in the body.

Meningitis may be classified according to the infecting organism as pneumococcal, pyogenic, tuberculous, syphilitic, meningococcal. The all-important evidence is gained by lumbar puncture and examination of the CEREBRO-SPINAL FLUID (q.v.). In meningitis the pressure of this fluid is increased, changes in its appearance and constituents occur, and the infecting agent can usually be isolated from it. In meningitis the protein and the number of cells increase and the glucose decreases. A decrease in the amount of chlorides of the cerebro-spinal fluid is characteristic of tuberculous meningitis. Increase in the number of cells may make the normally clear cerebro-spinal fluid opalescent, as in tuberculous meningitis, or turbid, as in pneumococcal and pyogenic meningitis. Clinically, the symptoms are due to irritation of the meninges and rise in the intracranial pressure : headache, vomiting, photophobia, rigidity of the neck, Kernig's sign (q.v.), convulsions, paralyses, coma.

PNEUMOCOCCAL MENINGITIS is usually secondary to infection with the pneumococcus elsewhere—for example, empyema or otitis media. This formerly fatal condition is now in many cases successfully treated by the sulphonamide drugs or penicillin.

PYOGENIC MENINGITIS is due to secondary infection with staphylococci, streptococci, *H. influenzæ*, gonococci, anthrax bacilli — especially the first two. The introduction of the sulphonamides and of penicillin has altered the previously fatal prognosis of these cases. Promising results are reported from the use of streptomycin in the treatment of meningitis due to *H. influenzæ*.

TUBERCULOUS MENINGITIS is an inflammation of the membranes caused by the *mycobacterium tuberculosis*. The disease is most common in children under the age of ten years, but is by no means confined to that period of life, and may affect adults. The determining factor in the disease is exposure to infection with the bovine or the human *Mycobacterium tuberculosis*. In numerous cases associated factors are bad hygienic conditions, with insufficient or improper feeding, or some disease of childhood, particularly measles or whooping-cough. When it occurs in adults it is usually secondary to some chronic manifestation of tuberculosis in another part of the body, especially in the lungs.

Symptoms.—Tuberculous meningitis is usually described as passing through three stages ; but its earlier manifestations are often vague.

The *premonitory symptoms* are mostly such as relate to the general nutrition. The patient, if a child, becomes listless and easily fatigued, loses appetite, and is restless at night. There is headache after exertion, and the temper often undergoes a marked change, the child becoming unusually peevish and irritable. These symptoms may persist during many weeks, or may be entirely wanting, the disease developing quite suddenly.

The onset of the *first stage*, or *stage of excitement*, is in most instances marked by the occurrence of vomiting, often severe, but sometimes only slight, and there is, in general, obstinate constipation. In some cases, the first symptoms are convulsions, which, however, may in this early stage subside, and remain absent, or reappear at a later period.

Headache is one of the most constant of the earlier symptoms, and is generally intense and accompanied by sharper paroxysms, which cause the patient to scream with a peculiar and characteristic cry. There is great intolerance of light and sound and general nervous sensitiveness. The neck shows rigidity so that the head cannot be so readily bent forwards as usual, and similar rigidity in the lower limbs is almost invariably present. The latter symptom forms an important sign (Kernig's sign) of the disease. If the knee is raised from the bed, stiffness and pain are experienced in the muscles behind the thigh when the attempt is made to straighten the leg at the knee-joint, whereas in the healthy child the whole lower limb can be readily flexed on the abdomen with the knee straight. Fever is present to a greater or less extent, the temperature ranging from 100° to 103° F. (37·8° to 39·4° C.) ; yet the pulse is not quickened in proportion, being on the contrary rather slow, but exhibiting a tendency to irregularity, and liable to become rapid on slight exertion. This slowness of the pulse is of great importance in distinguishing the disease from others which resemble it, and in which the heart beats more rapidly in proportion to the temperature. Symptoms of this character, constituting the stage of excitement, continue for a period varying from one to two weeks, when they are succeeded by the stage of depression.

In the *second stage*, or *stage of depression*, there is a marked change in the symptoms, which is apt to lead to the belief that a favourable turn has taken place. The patient becomes quieter and inclines to sleep, but it will be found on careful watching that this quietness is but a condition of apathy or partial stupor into which the child has sunk. The vomiting has now ceased, and there is less fever ; the pulse is slower, and shows a still greater tendency to irregularity than before, while the breathing is of markedly unequal character, being rapid and shallow at one time, and long drawn out and sinking away at another. There is manifestly little suffering, although the peculiar cry may still be uttered, and the patient lies prostrate, occasionally rolling the head uneasily upon the pillow, or picking at the bed-clothes or at his face with his fingers.

He does not ask for food, but readily swallows what is offered. The eyes present important alterations, the pupils being dilated or unequal, and scarcely responding to light. There may be double vision, or partial or complete blindness. Squinting is common in this stage, and there may also be drooping of an eyelid, due to paralysis of the part, and one or more limbs may be likewise paralysed.

To this succeeds the *third stage*, or *stage of paralysis*, in which certain of the former symptoms recur, while others become intensified. There is generally a return of the fever, the temperature rising sometimes to a very high degree. The pulse becomes feeble, rapid, and exceedingly irregular, as is also the case with the breathing. Coma is profound, but the patient may still be got to swallow nourishment, though not so readily as before. Convulsions are apt to occur, while paralysis, more or less extensive, affects portions of the body or groups of muscles. The pupils are now widely dilated, and there is often complete blindness or deafness. In this condition the sufferer's strength undergoes rapid decline and the body becomes markedly emaciated. Death takes place suddenly in a fit, or, more generally, from exhaustion. Shortly before the fatal event it is not uncommon for the patient, who, it may be for some days previously, lay in a state of profound stupor, to wake up, ask for food, and talk to those around. But the hopes which may be thus raised are quickly dispelled by the setting in of the symptoms of rapid decline.

The disease used to be invariably fatal, but the outlook has been entirely altered by the introduction of streptomycin. With modern treatment the mortality depends largely on the stage at which treatment is initiated. If this is in the early stages, 95 per cent. recover, but if treatment is not started until later in the disease, only 60 per cent. or fewer will recover.

Treatment.—The only drugs of any value in the treatment of tuberculous meningitis are streptomycin and isoniazid. The administration of streptomycin and isoniazid in this condition requires skilled medical and nursing supervision such as is available only in hospital. The present position with

regard to streptomycin and isoniazid may be summed up in this way : every child (or adult) with tuberculous meningitis, or suspected tuberculous meningitis, should be examined as early as possible by an experienced children's (or tuberculosis) specialist, in order that an expert opinion may be obtained.

SYPHILITIC MENINGITIS is usually chronic inflammation (but sometimes producing acute symptoms) occurring in most cases within the first four years of infection. It may spread from the pia-arachnoid into the brain — a meningo-encephalitis—or it may attack the dura mater and the overlying bone. The pressure of the cerebro-spinal fluid is raised ; the fluid itself is clear and contains an increased number of lymphocytes. Headache is a common symptom. Paralysis of cranial nerves (resulting, for example, in a squint) can occur as a result of strangulation of the nerve in inflamed meninges at the base of the brain. Hydrocephalus may arise suddenly, with headache, vomiting, sleepiness, mental changes, and congestion of the optic discs as symptoms and signs. Or syphilitic meningitis may come on acutely. The treatment is as for syphilis.

MENINGOCOCCAL MENINGITIS, also known as EPIDEMIC CEREBRO-SPINAL MENINGITIS, CEREBRO-SPINAL FEVER, SPOTTED FEVER, MALIGNANT PURPURIC FEVER, and POST-BASIC MENINGITIS, is a dangerous epidemic condition characterized by painful contractions of the muscles of the neck, retraction of the head, and mental symptoms. It was first distinctly recognized in the year 1837, when it prevailed as an epidemic, chiefly among troops in the south-west of France. In 1846 it appeared in Ireland, especially in the workhouses of Belfast and Dublin. Since that time it has appeared repeatedly both in Europe and America, notably in a severe epidemic in the large towns of Scotland in 1907–09, in a slighter form among the troops during the four-years war of 1914–18, and a fair-sized epidemic in Great Britain in the winter of 1939–1940.

Causes.—When an outbreak takes place, it usually occurs about the months of February, March, and April, and affects a closed community such as a school, garrison, camp, or prison.

The direct cause is an organism, the *Diplococcus meningitidis intracellularis* or *meningococcus*, discovered by Weichselbaum, which is found in the exudation round the nervous system, also in the blood, and frequently in the nasal discharge. The organism is of four different types. Some cases with closely similar symptoms are due to the *pneumococcus* or other bacteria. It is believed that the infection takes place through the nose and that a large number of persons who do not contract the disease harbour the meningococcus in the nasal discharge and form sources of infection to more susceptible people, especially children, by coughing, sneezing, etc.—they are known as 'carriers'. Factors favouring infection are a high carrier - rate, the virulence of the organism, a closed community (*e.g.* a camp), naso-pharyngeal catarrh, bad ventilation, insufficient space between beds, introduction of susceptible persons into a closed community, season of the year (winter and spring). Young children are much more susceptible than adults.

Symptoms. — The onset is usually sudden, sometimes startlingly so. As a rule, vomiting, headache, and shivering first appear, followed in a few hours by stiffness of the neck. In children, convulsions are common. In a case of very sudden onset, the patient, while going about as usual, may fall down suddenly in a convulsion, or he may go to bed perfectly well and be found unconscious on the following morning. If the patient is not unconscious, headache and pain with stiffness in the back of the neck continue, squinting is often seen, the tongue is furred and dry, and there is a certain amount of rise of temperature (100° to 104° F.). The patient is irritable, the body tender to the touch, and the limbs stiff so that bending up of the lower limbs on the abdomen with the knee straight becomes impossible (Kernig's sign). The patient is often sleepless or delirious, and there is a great tendency for the symptoms to go and come. The red spots, from which the disease takes its name of 'spotted fever', appear over the surface of the trunk during the first week of the disease in greater or less numbers in about one-quarter of the cases. Death occurs in a large number of the cases within a week of the onset, taking place very often suddenly from cardiac failure. After the first week, if life is prolonged, the disease usually abates gradually and in the course of some weeks the rigidity may have disappeared and the temperature may have become normal. On the other hand, the disease may pass into a chronic state with great wasting, and, if the patient be a young child, head retraction in these cases usually becomes very marked and the body is greatly bent backwards. The patient during the course of this chronic stage may become blind or deaf or may show marked mental deterioration. Very often the child falls a victim to some complication, such as bronchopneumonia.

In those patients who die, it is common to find the surface of the brain and the spinal cord covered with thick pus and the blood-vessels markedly congested. If death has occurred at a very early period, nothing more may be visible than very intense congestion of the membranes on the surface of the brain. The interior of the brain shows more than the usual amount of fluid.

The prognosis in this disease has been revolutionized by the introduction of the sulphonamides and penicillin. Formerly the mortality rate in epidemics was 70 to 80 per cent., whilst in fulminating cases it might even be 100 per cent. To-day, with efficient treatment it has fallen to 3 to 5 per cent. The main factors governing the prognosis are : (1) The age of the patient : the disease is particularly dangerous in infants and old people. (2) The type of onset : a fulminating onset carries a bad prognosis. (3) The stage of the disease at which treatment is begun : the earlier the better.

Treatment.—The patient must be isolated and, whenever possible, should be treated in hospital. Treatment consists essentially of the administration of full doses of sulphadiazine, sulphamerazine, or penicillin. The patient is confined to bed and given a light nutritious diet. For insomnia sedatives are usually required, whilst the pains in the joints and limbs are usually best relieved by warm baths. The headache usually responds to a combination of aspirin, phenacetin, and codeine, but if particularly severe, lumbar puncture may be necessary.

Quarantine of contacts is useless, but there is some evidence that, in the event of an outbreak in a semi-closed community (*e.g.* a residential school or a military camp) the administration of sulphadiazine to all contacts may be of value.

MENISCUS (μηνίσκος, crescent), is the term applied to a crescentic fibro-cartilage in a joint, such as the cartilages in the knee-joint.

MENOPAUSE (μήν, month ; παῦσις, cessation) is the term applied to the cessation of menstruation at the end of reproductive life. Usually it occurs between the ages of 45 and 50, although in numerous cases it occurs before 45 or after 50. It rarely occurs before 40 unless as the result of disease. For the changes accompanying it see CLIMACTERIC.

MENORRHAGIA (μηνές, the menses ; ῥήγνυμι, I burst forth) means an over-abundance of the menstrual discharge.

MENSTRUATION (*menstruus*, monthly) is a periodic change occurring in human beings and the higher apes, and consists chiefly in a flow of blood from the cavity of the womb, and is associated with various slight constitutional disturbances. It begins between the ages of thirteen and fifteen, as a rule, although its onset may be delayed till as late as twenty. It is said to appear earlier in warm countries and among certain races, for example, the Jews. Along with its first appearance the body develops the secondary sex characteristics of the sex, *e.g.* enlargement of the breasts, characteristic hair distribution. The duration of each menstrual period varies in different persons from two to eight days. It recurs in the great majority of cases with regularity, most commonly at intervals of twenty-eight days or thirty days, less frequently with intervals of twenty-one or twenty-seven days, ceasing only during pregnancy and lactation, till the age of forty-four or fifty arrives, when it stops altogether, as a rule ceasing early if it has begun early, and vice versa. The final stoppage is known as

the menopause or the grand climacteric.

Menstruation depends upon a functioning ovary and this upon a healthy pituitary gland. The regular rhythm may depend upon a centre in the hypothalamus, which is in close connection with the pituitary. After menstruation the denuded uterine endometrium is regenerated under the influence of the follicular hormone, œstradiol. The epithelium of the endometrium proliferates, and about a fortnight after the beginning of menstruation great development of the endometrial glands takes place under the influence of progesterone, the hormone secreted by the corpus luteum. These changes are made for the reception of the fertilized ovum. In the absence of fertilization the uterine endometrium breaks down in the subsequent menstrual discharge.

Disorders of Menstruation.—In the majority of healthy women, menstruation proceeds regularly for thirty years or more, with the exceptions connected with childbirth. In many persons, as the result either of general or local conditions, the process may be absent or excessive, or may be attended with great discomfort or pain. The term *amenorrhœa* is applied to cases in which menstruation is absent, *menorrhagia* and *metrorrhagia* to cases in which it is excessive, the former if the excess occurs at the regular periods, the latter if it is irregular, whilst *dysmenorrhœa* is the name given to cases in which the process is attended by pain.

AMENORRHŒA may be due to general or to local causes. Among the former, anæmia, with the various conditions that lead to it, ranks perhaps first in importance in young women. Bad feeding, want of fresh air, and all causes which depress the system and cause loss of flesh tend to cause diminution and finally stoppage of the menses. In a similar manner, serious diseases, such as Bright's disease, tuberculosis, malaria, aggravated dyspepsia, which weaken the constitution, lead to this result. Various influences which act through the nervous system, such as a sudden fright, or great grief, may also cause stoppage for several months. Among the local causes of amenorrhœa, pregnancy, of course, stands first. Failure of menstruation to appear at all in a young woman may be due to slow or imperfect development of the ovaries or womb ; and in occasional cases, although menstruation does take place regularly, the menstrual fluid does not escape but is retained and accumulates within the womb in consequence of some structural defect (*see* HÆMATO-COLPOS).

The treatment in all cases consists in removal of the cause and attention to the general health, remedies for the condition of bloodlessness if present (*see* ANÆMIA), and, in the cause last mentioned, some operative interference.

MENORRHAGIA.—Excessive menstruation may to a certain extent be due to the same general conditions which produce amenorrhœa, the same diseases, such as Bright's disease or tuberculosis, causing stoppage or excess in different persons. Thus, in some persons an excessive discharge is brought about by these conditions, and the bad effects of the general disease are much increased by the added drain upon the system, due to loss of blood. In heart disease, the womb may share in the general internal congestion, and the menses in consequence are increased. In some persons, menstruation at its first appearance is excessive ; while this is so frequently the case as to be almost the general rule at the time when the menstrual periods are about to stop, *i.e.* at the menopause, when they also tend to become irregular. But it is most often a local condition that produces menorrhagia, and in this case, as a rule, not only is the periodic loss increased but there is bleeding at irregular times (metrorrhagia). Polypus, fibroid, and other tumours, displacements of the womb, and some inflammation consequent upon childbirth or miscarriage, are the most common causes of this type. In the treatment, rest and various internal remedies which check hæmorrhage, together with careful attention to the general health between the periods, are essential. (*See* UTERUS, DISEASES OF.)

DYSMENORRHŒA may vary from mere discomfort to agonizing colic, accompanied by prostration and vomiting. Anæmia is sometimes a cause of painful menstruation as well as of stoppage of this function. Chills and exhaustion may produce pain for a single period in persons usually natural. Occasionally pain, especially when it precedes the menstrual period, is due to irritation in the ovary; and in this case it is generally accompanied by pain in one groin. For this type of pain, careful regulation of the bowels, regular exercise, and the application of counter-irritation to the lower part of the abdomen form the course of treatment generally carried out. In some cases the administration of ovarian or other glandular extract is attended with benefit.

Inflammation of various internal organs, *e.g.* of the womb itself, the ovaries, or the Fallopian tubes, is one of the commonest causes of dysmenorrhœa which comes on for the first time late in life, especially when the trouble follows the birth of a child. In this case the pain exists more or less at all times, but is aggravated at the periods. It is relieved by various local means directed towards checking the inflammation present.

Many cases of dysmenorrhœa appear with the beginning of menstrual life, and accompany every period. Some of these are of an obstructive type, due to spasm of the neck of the womb, in consequence of which a severe uterine colic is set up. In many cases, the spasm appears to be one manifestation of a nervous temperament. In other cases the pain appears to be due to difficulty in the separation of the surface layer of mucous membrane, which comes away in healthy menstruation in fragments with the blood. In these cases, the lining of the uterus, after great difficulty, is finally expelled in the form of a complete membranous cast of the interior, and the pain then abates. In other cases, the spasm may be due in part to defective development of the womb, producing either great narrowness of its mouth or causing it to be bent upon itself, and occasionally these cases are benefited or cured by an operation designed to stretch the neck of the womb, or otherwise relieve the defect. For the temporary relief of dysmenorrhœa, rest in bed, or, at all events, in the recumbent position, hot compresses to the lower part of the abdomen, and aspirin or phenacetin internally, are the remedies which prove most useful.

MENTAL DEFECTIVENESS.—Mental defect is the term used for denoting intellectual defect existing from birth or the early years of life. In the Mental Health Act, 1959, the terminology in use in the Mental Deficiency Act is replaced by two categories:

Severe Subnormality—a state of arrested or incomplete development of mind so severe that a patient is incapable of living an independent life or of guarding himself against serious exploitation (or, in the case of a child, that he will be so incapable when adult).

Subnormality—a state of arrested or incomplete development of mind which includes subnormality of intelligence and requires special care or training, but does not amount to severe subnormality.

Causes.—The term mental deficiency is largely a relative one, and the mental defective must be compared with persons of his own race, age, and opportunities; for example, the average negro has the mental endowment of a child of nine or ten years as compared with the average white person living in towns, but he is not, therefore, to be regarded as a mental defective. Again, mental defect is not so evident in persons living in country districts, where employment suitable for mental defectives can be obtained, as it is among persons in towns, where the struggle for existence is more intense. Less importance than previously is now attached to heredity as a cause, although mentally defective children sometimes occur in a family of which other members show insanity, epilepsy, alcoholism, etc., especially when the parents are nearly related to one another. The descendants of various mental defectives have been traced and it has been found that among the descendants of a union between two mental defectives a very high proportion of feeble-minded persons occurs. Several varieties are recognized. The great majority of cases fall into the group of *simple primary amentia*, for which no further cause is evident than the hereditary consideration mentioned above. In these cases, the children show too little of the normal automatic movements of healthy infancy, and speech and walking fail to develop at the proper age, between one and two years. Many such children show peculiarity in gestures and behaviour

even in early life, and are very late in gaining control over the bladder and bowels, if they do so at all. A proportion of such children also have epileptic attacks. Along with mental defect these children generally show much physical weakness, and they are more liable to die from slight disorders or injuries than are ordinary persons. Such children, even when the defect is not great, are difficult to teach, because they are unable to concentrate their attention on one subject for long. They are lacking in perseverance. Some are morbidly shy and self-conscious, or deficient in self-control so that they are constantly laughing, crying, and getting into unreasonable fits of passion. When these children go to school, the defect is soon noticed by comparison with other children of their own age, and in most large towns special schools are provided for mentally defective children, where they are taught by specially trained teachers and an attempt is made to fit them for taking up simple forms of employment. Whilst these children are generally benefited by contact with older persons who make allowances for them, their condition is usually made much worse by the teasing which they are apt to undergo at the hands of other children or fellow-workers.

Other types of mental defect are those associated with *microcephalus*, in which the head is unusually small and the whole nervous system defective in development. Another type is that of *Mongolism*, in which there is some arrest or perversion of development prior to birth. These children often come at the end of large families. Still other cases are associated with gross disease of the nervous system in early life, such as *hydrocephalus*, *hæmorrhage* on the surface of the brain at birth, *congenital syphilis* or disease of other organs, such as thyroid defect, which occurs in *cretins*. Children may also be mentally defective in cases where they have been deprived of some important sense, such as in blindness or deafness, but such mental defect is curable by special instruction.

Diagnosis.—The symptoms by which the presence of mental defect is recognized in infants and young children are bodily as well as mental. At a later stage of life the degree of mental defect can be assessed by comparing the mental powers of the person in question with the capabilities of normal children of different ages.

Some children from birth present abnormalities of bodily structure which are commonly associated with mental defect. Thus, the conditions of microcephalus, mongolism, cretinism, chronic hydrocephalus, and various forms of paralysis can be recognized, and these are known to be commonly associated with mental defect. Other less marked bodily malformations may be found when careful search is made, such as unusual height of the palate, defects of the ear, defective formation of the head or spine, such as spina bifida, and congenital malformations of the heart. Any of these defects may be met in children of ordinary intelligence, but they are more common in the mentally defective, and, if noticed, should direct attention to the child's mental condition.

The occurrence in infants of convulsions is often associated with mental defect either as a cause of or produced by brain defect. Abnormal gestures and actions, such as constant crying, rolling of the eyes, or simply want of animation when the nurse or mother fondles a child, and, at a later stage, unmeaning laughter and grimaces, dirty habits, disgusting ways of eating, or dribbling of saliva from the mouth, are all signs of defective mentality.

Other significant signs are found in slowness of development as compared with other children. Thus the infant may be too long in learning to hold up its head, to use its hands for grasping objects, to stand, and to notice bright or attractive objects placed before it. Difficulty in learning to suck, backwardness in speaking, and delay in learning cleanly habits are all significant.

At a later age, in order to find out the degree of mental defect in a child or adult, a simple form of examination is set, questions being asked which have been found capable of being answered by a normal child at a given age. Various scales are employed, the best known being the Stanford revision of the Binet-Simon tests. Examples of these are given below. If the mentally defective person can only pass the test

which a child of three would answer, his ' mental age ' is said to be that of three years. If he can pass the test of a normal child of six, nine, etc., his ' mental age ' is said to be six years, nine years, etc. The following are three examples—

Year 3. A normal child of three should be able to do the following: (1) To point correctly to his nose, eyes, mouth, hair, etc., when asked to do so. (2) To name familiar objects like key, penny, knife, watch, pencil, etc., when shown to him. (3) To name three simple objects in a picture shown him. (4) To say whether he is boy or girl. (5) To tell his last name. (6) To repeat three numbers, e.g. 6, 4, 1, when named to him.

Year 6. A normal child of six should be able to do the following : (1) Point to right hand, left ear, etc., as named. (2) When shown a picture of a figure, from which parts have been left out, to name the missing parts. (3) To give an explicit reply to simple questions such as ' What should you do if you find that the house is on fire ? ' (4) To count objects up to 13. (5) To name correctly coins shown him. (6) To repeat correctly a simple sentence of 12 or 15 words.

Year 9. A normal child of nine should be able to do the following : (1) To give the correct day, month, and year. (2) To arrange a series of weights in proper order. (3) To subtract two numbers from other two. (4) To repeat backwards four stated figures, e.g. 6528. (5) To make a simple sentence containing three stated words. (6) To name the month coming before a stated month.

It must always be remembered that comparison with a normal child is only a rough index of the mental age of the defective person, who has reached a greater number of years and who has, therefore, had special experience along certain lines which the normal child has not yet had time to gain.

Treatment.—In the great majority of cases, mental defect is incurable and children who are mentally weak will remain so throughout life. Nevertheless, most mentally defective children, unless the defect is very great, are capable of improvement under suitable treatment, and may actually be able in later life to earn a satisfactory living at some simple automatic employment which a normally minded person would find depressing or even intolerable because of its monotony. Attention to the general health is of great importance, and when special conditions such as cretinism, syphilis, deafness, etc., are found, these should receive appropriate treatment. Young children who are found to possess insufficient concentration for book work should be instructed in amusing kindergarten occupations, and bad and dirty habits should be gradually corrected. The child should be encouraged to do as much as he can for himself, and particular care should be exercised to promote self-control and to cultivate moral character.

If home conditions are satisfactory, the home is far the best place for a mentally defective child. At a later stage of childhood, however, the mental defective both becomes a drag upon normal children and is apt to be discouraged by ineffective competition with them, as well as by teasing to which they are very liable to subject him. He is then more happily placed with children about his own level of intelligence either in a special school or in an institution. Under the Mental Health Act, 1959, local health authorities have a duty to arrange for the care and training of these children. The Act gives them powers to require parents to ensure the attendance of children at Training Centres, unless the child is already receiving comparable training to that obtainable at the centre. At such a school or institution the attempt should be made to prepare him about the age of sixteen for taking up some simple form of productive work, if he is at all capable of such training. If he proves incapable of this, it is better for society that he should be maintained in some institution for the remainder of his life.

MENTAL ILLNESS arises from a disease or disordered working of that part of the nervous system which determines mind and conduct. So long as individual peculiarities occasioned by mental disorder do not result in conduct or behaviour which is markedly opposed to prevailing social custom, society does not interfere with the person. When the person's conduct becomes so far divergent from social usages that he becomes legally certifiable, he can be sent compulsorily to a mental hospital. It must be remembered, however, that there are all grades of mental disorder from slight peculiarities or temporary delirium, upwards. A great number of persons who do not reach a sufficiently abnormal grade of conduct to be regarded as certifiable are regarded by society as eccentric or peculiar, and a large number whose conduct shows them to be maladapted for social life, as the result of inferiority of mind, are classed, owing to circumstances, among criminals, paupers, vagrants, inebriates, etc.

In primitive states of society mental disease is apt to pass unnoticed, and the more complex society becomes the more obvious is any maladaptation of an individual to his surroundings. By the old Greek physicians, in the time of Plato and Hippocrates, the brain was looked upon as the organ of intellect; sensation and the more purely animal functions being supposed to be situated in the thoracic region and in the lower part of the body respectively. Mental disease was treated in a rational manner just as other bodily disorders. From the decline of the Roman Empire through the Middle Ages, various manifestations of 'insanity' were regarded largely in the light of crimes or misdemeanours, and were treated with great harshness. In the course of the eighteenth century, opinion in regard to the treatment of mental disorders began to change, and the modern attitude, which regards mental disorder as a disorder or disease to be treated on the same lines as other diseases, is generally regarded as having begun with the publication of Pinel's *Traité medico-philosophique sur l'aliénation mentale* in 1801. A great amount of attention was paid during the next fifty years to the study of mental diseases, and during this period a large number of ' asylums ' for the humane treatment of mentally disordered persons were founded.

The question of *responsibility in civil or criminal matters* is one of great importance in regard to mental disease. The question often arises in connection with the ability to make a valid will. The development of certifiable mental disease does not excuse the patient from the fulfilment of a contract, provided he was not certifiable at the time when the contract was entered into. When a crime is committed, the question of responsibility is often very difficult to decide ; the general principle accepted is that, if the accused person suffers from a delusion, but is not insane in other matters, he is held responsible for his offence, unless he has acted in such a way as would have been permissible if the facts about which his delusion exists had been true—in other words, in order to establish a defence on the ground of insanity it must be proved that ' at the time of committing the act the party accused was labouring under such a defect of reason, from disease of the mind, as not to know the nature and quality of the act he was doing or, if he did not know it, that he did not know he was doing it, that he did not know he was doing what was wrong '. The principle is also recognized that, if the mind is so diseased or so defective that there is complete absence of the power of self-control, so that the person acts under an ungovernable impulse, then he is not held responsible. This inability to exercise self-control does not, however, exonerate a person in whom the loss of self-control is due to his own default, as, for example, when he is intoxicated.

Causes.—The causes of mental disorder fall into two great groups. Certain persons go through life with a tendency to become disordered mentally when at any time certain causes arise, whilst other persons are subjected constantly to much greater strains of the same nature without developing any mental abnormality. It is necessary, therefore, to recognize (1) the nervous constitution or set of predisposing causes, and (2) the stresses which are particularly liable to unbalance the mind, or exciting causes.

(1) PREDISPOSING CAUSES.—A nervous constitution may be inherited or acquired, and is the primary or essential reason of a mental breakdown. There may be some congenital nervous, mental or moral defect which is peculiar to the family of the person affected. This tendency may be broadly described

as *heredity*. It may show itself in other members of the same family by various nervous diseases allied to the insane state, such as epilepsy or hysteria. The tendency may also show itself by such inability to regulate conduct as drunken habits or various moral delinquencies which have got other members of the patient's family into trouble. *Intermarriage* of near relations in a family in which neurotic tendencies are manifested frequently results in offspring showing characteristics which are natural enough in the parents, but are apt to be exaggerated to an unnatural degree in the children, so that they reach the insane state. A similar evolution of traits of character may be seen in the children of marriages between individuals of similar nervous temperament, though these be not related to one another.

How far 'nature' is to be blamed for insanity and how far ' nurture ' is uncertain. At one time the hereditary factor is over-stressed and at another the environmental factor. It is perhaps not far off the mark to state that in an unfavourable environment—using this word in a comprehensive sense to include the ' emotional ' setting of family life as well as the physical environment —the person with an inherited unstable nervous system may break down with symptoms of insanity. Bizarre, abnormal, or vicious behaviour is likely to be, not the cause of insanity but a manifestation of innate mental instability.

The most important of the predisposing causes is the presence of an *abnormal disposition or temperament*, either inherited or acquired in the course of years. This is the most frequent sign of a nervous constitution. It may be acquired in childhood from habitual contact with abnormal older persons. It may also arise from a prolonged struggle between conflicting instincts. The instincts concerned are usually the two primitive instincts of the ' herd ' and ' self-preservation '. The person is constantly attempting to conform to the rules and usages of society and, at the same time, striving for objects which conduce to personal well-being and satisfaction, and is constantly finding the two aims incompatible. Into this group fall the cases of anxiety and mental unrest derived from what, according to the Freudian conception, is a repressed and sub-conscious memory of sexual trauma. The resulting development of the abnormal temperament may show itself by some characteristic such as unusual irritability, jealousy, waywardness, unreasonableness, pessimism, etc. All of these render the person more liable to mental breakdown when a sufficient exciting cause supervenes.

(2) EXCITING CAUSES.—Among the most important of the stresses or exciting factors of mental disorder, in a person already predisposed, are other bodily diseases which produce defective nutrition, poisoning or exhaustion of the nervous system. These are sometimes grouped as toxic and exhausting causes.

Infectious diseases play an important part in this connection, especially when they are conjoined with some of the other stresses to be mentioned later. Puerperal sepsis occurring in connection with childbirth may act in this manner. A similar effect may be produced in occasional cases by attacks of influenza, pneumonia, erysipelas, typhoid fever, and tuberculosis. *Disorders of the endocrine glands*, which secrete substances that enter the circulation and produce important effects upon the nutrition of the body, have also a powerful effect on mental processes. The diseases arising from these defects, which are most often accompanied by mental disorder, are myxœdema and thyrotoxicosis. *Diseases of the blood and circulation* are liable, when they have been present for a considerable time, to produce mental changes: such diseases are anæmia, arteriosclerosis, and heart failure. The kidneys, in persons in whom they are diseased, may fail in their action of excreting waste products from the body, and these, circulating in the blood, produce deterioration in the action of the nervous system. External poisons may produce serious effects upon the nervous system as well as those developed within the body ; such are especially the effects of *alcohol*, which is a frequent cause and which produces many different results on different brains, with different types of mental disorder. Other poisons which may produce similar effects in occasional cases are opium, cocaine and

576

lead. The recognition of these toxic causes is of the greatest importance, because this opens up a wide field for treatment of the mental disorder, which is likely to improve when its cause is duly recognized and removed.

The most important type of stress productive of mental disorder is what may be called ' biological stresses ', including those changes which occur in the body during the reproductive *epochs and crises of life* in both sexes, when changes also take place in the mental outlook. The most important of these epochs are : (1) *adolescence*, the period when the body is attaining its maximum of activity and growth and when the function of reproduction is attaining full development. This adolescent change occurs in the female between the ages of fifteen and twenty-four, and in the male during a period about one or two years later. During this time emotional outbursts and other manifestations pointing to an unstable nervous system are particularly apt to show themselves. (2) *Childbirth* is an important crisis in the life of a woman, which may occur up to the age of forty or fifty. This process is accompanied by considerable stress during pregnancy, the puerperal state, and lactation ; and when to the biological stress is added a septic or exhaustive process, as sometimes occurs in the puerperal state, mental disorder may occur. This type of mental disorder is, however, one of the most curable forms. (3) The *climacteric period* is the time about the age of fifty when there is a distinct waning of the reproductive powers which have been fully developed during adolescence ; it is earlier in the female and associated with the cessation of menstruation ; in the male it is more irregular and undefined. With its establishment the elasticity and enthusiasm of youth pass away ; the strong passions of earlier life become feebler, and there are often marked nutritional changes in the body such as increase of corpulence with marked diminution of activity. Mental peculiarities are apt to set in at this time. (4) *Senility* may be regarded as commencing in healthy persons about the age of seventy ; it comes on prematurely with special readiness in persons whose arteries are diseased. It has been said that a ' man is as old as his arteries'; and if the arteries of the brain remain healthy, the mental faculties may remain alert and the bodily functions active, long after the allotted span of threescore years and ten; if the arteries are diseased, the state of bodily and mental feebleness known as dementia is particularly apt to appear.

Hygienic stresses include privations or excesses in mode of life and exercise, productive of defective nutrition or exhaustion, thus leading to poisoning of the nervous system. These include want of food or of some essential element in the food such as vitamins; also excessive feeding and insufficient exercise, such as are apt to prevail in middle life. Physical or mental overwork—with want of sleep, rest, or recreation—and sexual excesses may have a similar effect.

Energic stresses consist of external changes which produce shock to the nervous system such as head injuries, surgical operations, sunstroke, electric shock, etc., and are occasionally productive of sudden mental disorder.

Psychic stresses may also produce mental disorder of sudden or gradual onset. These include shocks or exhaustion of the nervous system caused by such influences as fright, anxiety, grief, prolonged worry.

Organic disease of the nervous system, usually producing its effect by direct physical damage of the brain or by interference with its nutrition, forms another group of causes of mental disease which is then usually of a serious type as regards recovery. Such influences include syphilis, apoplexy, tumours of the brain, meningitis, cerebro-spinal fever and encephalitis lethargica. Although the change that takes place in epilepsy is not definitely known, this disease as a cause of insanity naturally falls into this group.

Symptoms of mental disorder.—Before describing the chief varieties of mental illness with the main characteristics of each, we must refer to certain early symptoms, and also to some general symptoms which commonly accompany such disorders.

(*a*) EARLY SYMPTOMS.—Mental illness rarely develops suddenly, and indications of an approaching mental breakdown may be gathered from some early premonitory symptoms, although these may be of so light a character as to escape observation, or, if observed, to be considered as of no serious moment. Perhaps the most important is *alteration of disposition,* and this change may be either an exaggeration of the usual state of mind of the individual, or may be in a direction diametrically opposed to it. One man, for example, naturally of a suspicious nature, may begin to carry his suspicions so far as to imagine that people are talking evil about him, slandering him, and threatening him with violence; another, hitherto of a bright, cheerful disposition, becomes silent, moody, depressed, and self-depreciating to such an extent that he becomes quite unfitted for carrying on his ordinary work. In both these instances such symptoms may be the forerunners of mental illness, which may issue in homicide in the one case and suicide in the other. *Alterations of habit and conduct* also may be observed: a miser may become a spendthrift; a cool, calculating business man begins to indulge in foolish speculations; a hitherto temperate, upright man may give way to debauchery and depravity. In estimating these symptoms and attaching to them their proper significance, it is necessary always to bear in mind the social position and environment of the person, for it is obvious that a certain line of conduct would have a different meaning in an aristocrat from what it would have in a working-man. These early alterations of habit and conduct are frequently associated also with various *physical symptoms,* such as pains in the head, sleeplessness, disorders of digestion and loss of weight, these all pointing to disturbed and perverted physical health.

(*b*) GENERAL SYMPTOMS of mental illness fall under two divisions: (1) insane beliefs; (2) insane acts.

(1) *Insane beliefs* may be either of the nature of delusions or of hallucinations.

A *delusion* may be defined as 'a belief in a fact which, to a sane person of similar education, age, and race, appears certainly false, and of the falsity of which the person labouring under the insane delusions cannot be persuaded either by his own senses or by the arguments of others'. The presence of delusions is a strong proof of insanity, and in the investigation of any mental state special care must always be taken to find out their existence—a task which is often very difficult, as they may be carefully and skilfully concealed. They may be classified as follows : *Delusions of grandeur* accompany states of mental exaltation. A poor man thinks he is possessed of millions of money; another is the King of England ; yet another is the King of the Universe, and can summon and hold converse at any time with the prophets of both the Old and the New Testaments. *Delusions of unseen agency* lead their victims to imagine that they are electrified by batteries ; disturbed at nights by persons who attempt to mutilate or ravish them ; or that, inside their body, they have a person or animal, and that all the food they take goes to nourish the intruder. *Delusions of suspicion and persecution* cause the persecutions to be attributed to actual known persons ; the annoyance is not caused by something intangible and unknown, but certain persons, who can be named by the insane person, are supposed to have poisoned his food, to call him bad names, or to follow him about and annoy him.

There are, in addition, numerous other delusions which cannot be classified under these heads, such as delusions of identity, the delusion of having no head, or no mouth, that speech is impossible, etc. There is, indeed, no end to their variety.

Hallucinations are false perceptions of the senses, those of hearing and sight being the most commonly affected. *Hallucinations of hearing* are often found in chronic cases of mental illness and when the illness is insidious, free from acute symptoms, and slowly progressive, they frequently constitute very early symptoms. Patients complain that they hear voices speaking to them. These voices may be well known to them or unknown, may be in the same room in some corner or cupboard, or outside in the open air ; they may rule their lives, compel them to eat or abstain from food, urge them to destroy themselves or to commit murder. These patients, therefore, are looked upon as dangerous both to themselves and to others. *Hallucinations of sight* are common in acute excitement, and

always accompany, for example, acute alcoholism ; the things that are seen may be animals, such as bats, mice, rats, or dogs ; or there may be bright flashes of light, during which imaginary people are seen. *Hallucinations of smell* are important, and often indicate serious mental disease.

(2) *Insane acts* include suicide, homicide, and various other hurtful or bizarre forms of conduct.

Suicide may be the result of profound mental depression, it may be prompted by delusions of persecution, or by hallucinations of hearing, the sound of voices, for example, urging to self-destruction. It may accompany an acute illness, or may be the one outstanding feature of the illness, a true suicidal impulse. The idea is sometimes quite a sudden one, an attempt at self-destruction being made, and the patient being afterwards totally unable to account for it, or, on the other hand, the wish may have long been harboured and the details of the attempted suicide carefully planned.

Homicide, again, like suicide, may be the outcome of delusions, especially those of persecution and suspicion ; or the act may be committed while the patient is under the influence of hallucinations. A genuine homicidal act is frequently committed by patients suffering from both delusions and hallucinations. A man believes, for example, that he is being persistently slandered and persecuted ; he hears voices urging him to murder his persecutors, and he murders them, either suddenly under the influence of a genuine homicidal impulse, or deliberately after having carefully laid his plans.

Other insane acts may be shortly mentioned, such as constant tearing of clothes, fantastic and extravagant dressing, or, on the other hand, disregard of personal appearance, refusal of food, kleptomania, dipsomania, indecent exposure of the person, and the commission of revolting, unnatural sexual offences.

Varieties of mental disorder.—NEUROSES and PSYCHONEUROSES form some of the milder types of mental disorder. The chief mental symptom is a general emotional tone of anxiety or apprehension ; patients are afraid to open letters lest the contents convey bad news, and, for the same reason, they are terrified by telegrams ; slight passing indispositions are feared to be symptomatic of some fatal disease ; fleeting incidents are apt to be misinterpreted and worried over. Exophthalmic goitre, which is sometimes accompanied by mental symptoms, may in such cases be included in this group. Neurasthenia, hysteria, and various obsessions, including such symptoms as irrepressible thoughts, irrepressible fears, and irrepressible impulses, fall into the group of psycho-neuroses.

PSYCHOSES include a group of the more serious and better-known types of mental disease, such as mania, melancholia, paranoia, schizophrenia, and alcoholic psychosis.

MANIA.—The term ' mania ', although applied commonly to various types of severe mental disorder, should, strictly, be reserved for the form characterized by mental exaltation. In *simple mania* the intellectual part of the cerebral function is in a state of over-activity, so that the patient is loquacious, garrulous, and often very clever in repartee ; he flits, without apparent connection, from one subject to another; his mind never rests, and sleeplessness is a usual accompaniment. In the more pronounced form of *acute mania*, the motor functions of the brain are also affected ; there is not only complete incoherence of speech, but there is intense restlessness and complete disappearance of will power ; such a patient is popularly termed ' raving mad '. He seems to be insensible to fatigue, either of mind or body, and he gradually wears himself out ; as a result, physical symptoms come on, especially loss of weight, and if the condition be not relieved, a fatal result may ensue from exhaustion. The majority of cases, however, recover, sometimes quite abruptly, more often gradually after relapses. Some cases pass into *chronic mania*, in which the symptoms continue, but in a quieter form, with a tendency to occasional acute attacks. A few cases pass into dementia, in which the mental powers become completely enfeebled, and the patient is quiet.

MELANCHOLIA is a disorder characterized by a feeling of misery in excess of that which is justified by circumstances,

and also by physical weakness and loss of energy. In every person there is a tendency to fluctuate between times of mental elevation and times of mental lowness ; an exaggeration and prolongation of this natural rhythm constitutes a mental disorder known as *manic-depressive psychosis*, in which the patient varies between mania and melancholia, at intervals of days, weeks, or months. In *simple melancholia* the depression is not very great, and the patient may be able to pull himself together in the presence or strangers, or at other times when it is necessary to do so, only his intimates knowing of his disinclination to work, lassitude, desire to be alone, and painful introspection. The reasoning power is still present, although it is perverted in the way of magnifying slight failings of character into vices and taking an unreasonably gloomy view of the future. At times the mental depression becomes more intense, and the danger, in such patients, is that it may culminate in suicide. In *acute melancholia* the will-power disappears, the mental anguish is greater, and there is no control over action. Sometimes, especially after the melancholy state has lasted for some time, such patients are completely apathetic, sit staring straight in front of them, and are persuaded with difficulty to take food ; other patients show restlessness and agitation, wringing their hands, swaying the body, weeping, or showing inability for even the slightest concentration upon any one subject. Delusions may be present, and patients think they have wronged themselves and their family, that they are responsible for the illness or misfortune of other people, that they are going to be burned, tortured, or otherwise maltreated, and in such people the impulse to suicide may be very strong. Suicide more commonly takes place in people who say nothing about it than in those who threaten to take their own lives. Along with the mental symptoms, physical signs are always present, including especially greatly disordered digestion with constipation and muscular weakness. Recovery is usual in melancholia, but a person of melancholic temperament is liable to subsequent attacks of the disorder, which often become more prolonged as life advances. Some cases end in *chronic melancholia* with permanently fixed delusions of an unhappy nature, and a few pass into dementia.

PARANOIA is a condition in which there are delusions forming a system which gradually develops as a result of the disordered mind 'projecting' its own ideas into the supposed motives and conduct of other people. The patient takes a distorted view of his relationship to the world in which he lives. This form of psychosis is the outcome of a particular temperament, usually develops slowly, and is only noticed in middle life, the patient often having been previously regarded as merely eccentric or bad tempered. It is more common in men than in women, and among single persons and those who lead a solitary life. To begin with, such persons are often full of wild, altruistic, impersonal theories to which they give outlet in books, or by addressing crowds in open spaces. Many of the persons regarded as political cranks, who preach anarchy, revolution, and various anti-social projects, are subjects of this mental disease. Other paranoiacs have delusions in which their own personality plays the most important rôle, and they usually believe themselves to be subjects of annoyance or persecution by other people. In this form of psychosis the patient is often very dangerous, because of the schemes he makes to revenge himself on his supposed persecutors or opponents.

SCHIZOPHRENIA (or DEMENTIA PRÆ-COX) is a mental disorder which appears in predisposed persons, most commonly during the twenties, and soon leads to a marked form of dementia. Such persons usually come of a family with a history of mental disorder. The main characteristic of this disease is disorder of thinking and behaviour, with a progressive withdrawal from the real world into the unreal world of infantile fantasy. The patient shows numerous peculiar mannerisms, such as stilted methods of talking, negativism, or a tendency to do precisely the opposite of what he is asked to do, an inclination to retain the limbs rigidly in any position in which they are placed, and to imitate any actions performed by other people in front of him. Mean-

ingless repetition of actions, phrases, and words is also a characteristic. Some patients pass into a state of stupor (katatonia) ; others develop delusions, especially of persecution, or a double personality. The ultimate result of this disease is usually that the patient passes into a state of moderate dementia, in which the disorder becomes stationary, so that, although requiring supervision in some institution, he may live a long life and be capable of carrying out quite well some simple form of work or duty.

ALCOHOLIC PSYCHOSIS.—Alcoholism and drug habits are also of the nature of mental disorders, and alcohol in turn produces organic changes in the nervous system which lead to permanent mental disease. These are dealt with under ALCOHOLISM, CHRONIC, and DRUG HABITS.

CONFUSIONAL STATES—This type of mental disorder usually follows exhaustion due to over-exertion, or is due to poisoning, either by the toxins of fevers, or by poisons such as alcohol, introduced from outside. Such patients are anæmic, with pale, greasy complexion ; the appetite is poor ; the circulation feeble, and occasionally there is considerable weakness. There is great enfeeblement of intellectual power, so that the patient has difficulty in understanding simple questions. Hallucinations are very common, and the patient may see faces in the air, insects crawling on the bedclothes, and mistake persons near him for old friends or enemies. It is very common, too, that the patient has no idea where he is. Memory is much disordered, and if the patient is going about, he is liable, in some cases, to lose his identity, fail to recognize where he is, and may wander long distances from home, even to distant cities, and be quite unable to say who he is, or from where he comes. Usually there is a certain amount of depression and restlessness. This is one of the most curable forms of mental disorder, and the majority of cases make a complete recovery in six to twelve months, or sooner.

STATES OF MENTAL ENFEEBLEMENT.—*Mental deficiency* (*see* MENTAL DEFECTIVENESS).

Dementia is a condition of great mental enfeeblement, usually the terminal stage of some more acute form of mental disorder. The patient in this condition shows great loss of perceptive and intellectual power as well as of bodily activity. It varies in degree, but when it is marked, the patient lives a vegetable existence, unable to converse or to work with any will-power, and he is usually of dirty habits. Recovery does not take place. *General paralysis of the insane*, also known as 'paralytic dementia', is a mental and physical disease, due to syphilis of the nervous system. It is considered under the heading GENERAL PARALYSIS.

Treatment.—(*a*) PREVENTION.—The question of the prevention of mental illness entails two considerations—first, the counteraction of the various evil influences which impair the mental health of the social body generally; and secondly, the recognition of certain broad lines of living which should be followed by anyone who, on account of hereditary predisposition or abnormal temperament, is liable to become insane. In regard to persons predisposed to mental disorder, their adaptation to their surroundings is being increasingly effected by various agencies. These include the modern attempt to remove mentally defective persons into colonies for the feeble-minded ; the treatment at public clinics of diseases which are apt to terminate in insanity ; and the general amelioration of social conditions and of uncertainty as regards wage-earning and maintenance. The provision of social workers in connection with out-patient mental clinics at hospitals, to investigate the social conditions operating upon the production of 'borderland' cases of mental disorder, is also an important factor in preventing complete mental breakdown in many cases. Every effort should be made to encourage a healthy mode of living, to insist on the importance of good nourishing food, and to provide an education which shall be broad and liberal, and at the same time one that disciplines the mind in habits of self-control and self-denial. To those, however, in whom there is a strong hereditary tendency to mental disorder, life frequently resolves itself into a 'continual struggle to oppose the bent of their being'. Has such a person any

power over himself to prevent his becoming mentally ill ? That he is largely responsible for the preservation of his sanity there can be no doubt, and, in connection with this, the first truth for him to grasp is that his life must be lived under constant obedience to certain definite rules. Avoidance of psychic stresses, and especially those of an emotional character, is of particular importance.

(*b*) CURE.—As the outcome of a more rational view of mental disease, the mentally ill are now regarded and treated as sick persons. The old methods of treatment by punishment, solitary confinement, manacles and strait-waistcoats have now disappeared. Many mentally ill patients can be treated at home, looked after and nursed by their friends, who must be warned, however, that they are responsible for their safety. Recently also there have been instituted, for the treatment of early mental cases, wards attached to the large general hospitals, and thereby the stigma of certification is avoided. More especially is this method of value in those illnesses which are likely to prove of short duration or of a mild character, and which are accompanied by bodily disease.

Home treatment is often, however, impossible, more especially if it becomes clear that the illness is going to be a protracted or violent one, if it is aggravated by home associations and surroundings, or if it is characterized by suicidal or homicidal tendencies. In this case the patient must be duly certified and admitted to a mental hospital. An increasing number of mentally affected persons are availing themselves of the possibility of entering a mental hospital voluntarily while they are still capable of understanding the advisability of doing so. This has the great advantage that patients secure admission at an early stage of their disorder, before they are certifiable, and the disease thus coming under treatment while it is still mild can be more easily and quickly cured.

The encouragement of this modern development of patients with mental illness seeking early admission to hospital is one of the keynotes of the 1959 Mental Health Act which came into force in 1960. The two principles upon which the Act is based are : (i) that as much treatment as possible, both in hospital and outside, should be given on a voluntary and informal basis. (ii) That the emphasis on mental cases should be shifted as far as possible from institutional care to care within the community. In other words, that a patient with mental illness should no more hesitate to go into hospital than a patient with appendicitis, but that so far as possible mentally ill patients should be looked after in the general community.

The actual treatment may be divided into (a) Moral ; (b) Medical.

(a) By *moral treatment* is meant that personal influence which the mentally normal exercise over the mentally ill. In exercising this influence there must be constant kindness and perfect firmness. For this purpose it has been found that female nurses with thorough training in a general hospital are most satisfactory. The patient, whenever suitable, is given some liberty, he is allowed out on ' parole ', he can visit places of amusement, he is encouraged to take exercise and recreation, and, above all, he is encouraged to work. In this respect in mental hospitals, the inmates of which consist largely of those accustomed to manual labour, far more opportunities of bodily work are possible than in private hospitals. This *occupational therapy* is not only of benefit as exercise, but it provides the patient with an object upon which his mind can be concentrated, and so affords useful mental discipline. The work may include digging in the garden, and, in the case of a woman, employment in the kitchen or sewing in the sewing-room. Useful work can often be produced by patients working at looms, making toys, baskets, and other simple articles. To enable this treatment to be properly carried out, the co-operation of good attendants and nurses is essential, and every effort is now made to have them in sufficient numbers and to encourage them in their work by good remuneration, lectures on the nursing and treatment of the mentally ill, and the granting of certificates of proficiency after examination.

(b) *Medical treatment.*—The importance of absolute physical *rest* in the early and acute stages of the illness is

now recognized ; so is the importance of *fresh air and sunlight*. Good, plentiful food, of an easily assimilable kind, such as eggs and milk, is essential, and in those who refuse food, feeding through a tube passed through the nostril into the back of the throat is employed. The *control of excitement* and sleeplessness by various drugs, when simpler methods fail, is highly important. In patients who require soothing, especially in violent cases, it has been found that *prolonged baths*, at a temperature slightly below that of the body, have a highly beneficial effect. (*See* BATHS.)

Under such a regime there frequently come signs of improvement. Natural sleep gradually returns ; the body weight increases ; delusions become less prominent, are seldom spoken of, and finally disappear ; a desire to get well returns ; the manner becomes rational ; conduct is no longer eccentric ; the patient declares himself capable of earning his livelihood, and finally recovery becomes complete, and the patient is discharged.

One of the most remarkable forms of treatment, introduced some thirty years ago, is what is known as *shock treatment*. This consists in making the patient go through a number of violent convulsions. The convulsions are produced in various ways : by lowering the blood sugar by means of injections of insulin ; by injections of convulsant drugs, such as leptazol ; by passing an electric current through the brain. This last form of shock therapy is known as electroconvulsive therapy (E.C.T.). Shock treatment is less useful in the treatment of schizophrenia than it was at first hoped to be. But it has proved valuable in the treatment of depressed or melancholic cases, especially in the form of E.C.T. A drastic treatment recently introduced is known as ' *leucotomy* ' or ' prefrontal lobotomy '. This is an operation in which the white nerve fibres in the frontal lobes of the brain are cut, the connections between these lobes and the thalamus and the hypothalamus being thus severed. Leucotomy (*q.v.*) has been found to relieve the symptoms of severely depressed or melancholic patients who did not respond to other treatment.

Tranquillizing drugs are being used to an increasing extent in the treatment of mental disease. These are not curative but they undoubtedly produce a marked improvement in a certain number of cases.

The law and mental illness.—Since 1948 the services provided by hospitals and local authorities for mental patients have been part of the National Health Service. Considerable changes were introduced by the Mental Health Act, 1959. This has repealed the Lunacy and Mental Treatment Acts and Mental Deficiency Acts which laid down special procedures for the admission of mental patients to hospital, for their detention in hospital, and for certain forms of control over those living in the community. So far as hospitals are concerned the main differences made by the new Act are freedom to provide psychiatric units in, or attached to, general hospitals for a wider range of mental patients, and the breaking down of the sharp distinction between mental illness and other forms of mental disorder. The main provisions of the Act are as follows. They are not applicable to Scotland and Northern Ireland.

The Board of Control has been dispensed with, and its functions divided between the Ministry of Health, local authorities, and Mental Health Review Tribunals, of which there is to be one in each Regional Hospital Board Area. The single term, mental disorder, has been introduced to cover all forms of mental illness and disability, and mental disorder is divided into four categories : mental illness, severe subnormality, subnormality, and psychopathic disorder. It also allows for the informal admission of patients into any hospital or nursing home when powers of detention are not necessary. Further, it provides for the registration and inspection, under the Public Health Act, 1936, of all mental nursing homes other than hospitals or other premises managed by a Government department or provided by a local authority, and, under the National Assistance Acts, 1948, of all residential homes for the mentally disordered.

It provides for the compulsory admission of a patient to hospital for observation on the grounds : (a) that he is suffering from mental disorder of a nature or degree which warrants his

detention under observation ; and (b) that he ought to be so detained in the interests of his own health or safety or with a view to the protection of other persons. A patient admitted in this manner may not be detained for longer than 28 days unless he is in the meantime re-admitted as a result of an application for treatment. Compulsory admission to hospital for treatment is provided for on the grounds : (a) that he is suffering from mental disorder of a nature or degree which warrants his detention for treatment (i) in the case of a patient of any age, mental illness or severe abnormality ; (ii) in the case of a patient under 21 years, psychopathic disorder or subnormality ; and (b) that it is necessary in the interests of his health or safety or for the protection of other persons that he should be so detained.

An application for admission of a patient for observation or for treatment may be made by the nearest relative of the patient or by a mental welfare officer (but, where treatment is applied for, the relative must normally concur) and must, except in emergency, be based on two medical recommendations. It must be addressed to the managers of the hospital to which admission is sought and the applicant must have seen the patient personally within the previous 14 days. In case of urgent necessity, application for admission for observation may be made on only one medical recommendation initially but will cease to have effect after 72 hours unless the remaining requirements are fulfilled.

A patient detained in hospital for treatment may apply to a Mental Health Review Tribunal within 6 months from the day of admission or the day on which he reaches the age of 16, whichever is the later. Authority to detain a patient admitted to hospital in pursuance of an application for treatment will lapse at the end of fixed periods, or at the age of 25 in respect of psychopathic or subnormal patients, unless reviewed. The first period will be one year, the second one year, and thereafter the periods will be of two years at a time. The discharge of a patient compulsorily detained for treatment may be ordered by the nearest relative, unless the medical officer at the hospital reports that the patient is dangerous; in this case the relative may appeal to the Mental Health Review Tribunal. The medical officer and the managers of the hospital have power to discharge the patient at any time.

For reception of a patient into guardianship of either a local health authority or any other person accepted by the local health authority and willing to act as guardian, the procedure is as follows. A guardianship application may be made on the ground of the patient's mental disorder, which may be: (i) in any case, mental illness or severe subnormality; (ii) in the case of a patient under the age of 21 years, psychopathic disorder or subnormality; and that it is necessary in the interests of the patient or for the protection of other persons that the patient should be received into guardianship. The provisions regarding application to a Mental Health Review Tribunal and the periodic lapsing of authority to detain the patient are the same as in the case of patients detained for treatment, and the nearest relative has the same power of discharge.

Persons coming before the courts who are mentally disordered may be detained in hospital or received into guardianship if the court considers it a suitable course. In certain circumstances, higher courts may also make ' restriction orders ', in which case the patient may not be discharged without the consent of the Home Secretary. Persons detained in prison or approved schools who are found to be mentally disordered may be transferred to hospital by the Home Secretary.

Provision is made for institutions, known as ' Special Hospitals ', for mentally disordered persons who, in the opinion of the Minister, require treatment under conditions of special security on account of their dangerous, violent, or criminal propensities.

The Act continues the arrangements for the management of the property and effects of mentally disordered patients by nominated judges and the Court of Protection.

MENTHOL is a white crystalline substance deposited from oil of peppermint when it is cooled. It comes

principally from Japan, being derived from several species of *Mentha*. It dissolves freely in alcohol, ether, chloroform, and olive oil, and also to a slight extent in water, to which it gives a strong odour and taste of peppermint. Mixed with a little oil of peppermint, it can be moulded into cones, sticks, or pencils. When menthol is rubbed up with thymol, carbolic acid, chloral, or camphor, the two solids form a clear oily liquid which can be painted on the skin, exerting the effects of both drugs.

Action.—Applied to the skin, menthol has weak antiseptic properties, and it acts upon the sensory nerves, causing first a hot, tingling sensation, followed quickly by a cool, numb feeling. When applied to inflamed mucous membranes, such as those of the nose and throat, menthol relieves irritability, diminishes congestion, and checks excessive secretion. Menthol has the merit of being non-poisonous.

Uses.—In neuralgia, cones and sticks of menthol are used to rub over the affected part. In toothache, cotton-wool dipped in one of the oily fluids above named and placed in the cavity of the carious tooth quickly relieves the pain. In many itchy conditions of the skin a strong solution of menthol in olive oil (1 part in 10) relieves the sense of irritation at once. Menthol plaster is useful in gout, rheumatism, and neuralgia, and so are mixtures with chloral or camphor painted over the painful parts. For inflamed conditions of the nose and throat, the oily compounds of menthol are diluted with parolene and sprayed on the part affected, or in the case of the throat various lozenges and pastilles containing menthol are sucked. In bronchitis menthol crystals thrown upon hot water, from which the vapour is inhaled, give much relief.

MEPACRINE HYDROCHLORIDE is the official *British Pharmacopœia* term for a synthetic acridine product much used in the treatment of malaria. It came to the fore during the 1939–45 War, when supplies of quinine were short and proved of great value both as a prophylactic and in the treatment of malaria. It is also known as ATEBRIN.

MEPROBAMATE is one of the tranquillizer drugs. Chemically it is a sub-

584

stituted propanediol. It is mainly used for the relief of states of tension, mild anxiety states and persistent insomnia.

MEPYRAMINE MALEATE is one of the antihistamine drugs (q.v.).

MERCAPTOPURINE is one of a group of drugs known as antimetabolites recently introduced into medicine and which are proving of value in the treatment of certain forms of malignant disease, especially acute leukæmia. It is believed that they act by depriving rapidly dividing malignant cells of factors essential for their metabolism. Hence the generic name for the group of drugs—antimetabolites.

MERCUROCHROME is an organic salt of mercury with weak antiseptic action, which is sometimes used as an antiseptic to wash out the bladder when infected.

MERCURY, also known as QUICKSILVER or HYDRARGYRUM, is a heavy fluid metal which, with its salts, has been used in medicine for many centuries.

Action.—The salts of mercury fall into two groups : the mercuric salts, which are very soluble and powerful in action ; and the mercurous salts, which are less soluble and act more slowly and mildly. The mercuric salts are all highly poisonous both to man and to bacterial life, so that they are strongly antiseptic. In strong solutions, several act as caustics, and in weaker solutions they are irritants. Taken internally, the first effect of the mercuric, and to a less degree of the mercurous salts, is by their irritating action to set up copious purging. They are also credited with the power of increasing the flow of bile, and for this reason blue pill, which contains mercury, and mercurous chloride, i.e. calomel, were at one time much used as purgatives.

Uses.—Externally the mercuric salts are used as disinfectants and antiseptics. The uses of the perchloride of mercury are given under these headings. The ammoniated mercury ointment, or white precipitate ointment, is used in the treatment of impetigo. The yellow oxide of mercury ointment is used for an application to the eyelids when a mild antiseptic ointment is required. Internally, mercurial salts are used as purges, particularly calomel, the dosage of which is ½ to 3 grains (30 to 500 mg.) for an adult, and blue pill (4 to 8 grains) (250 to 500 mg.). They are best taken at night, and followed by a saline draught in the morning.

A complex organic salt of mercury (mersalyl) is widely used as a diuretic in the treatment of dropsy.

MERCURY POISONING is of two kinds : (1) acute mercury poisoning, due to swallowing one of the soluble mercury salts, generally perchloride of mercury ; and (2) chronic mercury poisoning, produced either by continuing repeated medicinal doses of mercurials for too long a time, or by handling the metal or inhaling its fumes, as happens sometimes among mirror and barometer makers.

ACUTE POISONING. — Symptoms. —There is burning pain, first in the mouth, then in the stomach, followed by diarrhœa and vomiting. The lips and mouth are generally burned white, and a metallic taste is left in the mouth. Great collapse soon comes on, and the person may die in a few hours. If death does not take place at an early stage, the kidneys are liable to remain seriously damaged by the drug.

Treatment.—The stomach should be washed out as quickly as possible with sodium bicarbonate. Some albuminous preparation, such as egg white or milk, should then be given, as, with corrosive sublimate, this forms an insoluble and harmless compound. Dimercaprol (B.A.L.) (q.v.) should also be given. If signs of shock appear, the patient is treated accordingly (see SHOCK).

CHRONIC POISONING.—Symptoms.—When too much mercury is being taken into the system in small doses, the first signs are an excessive discharge of saliva into the mouth, and tenderness about the teeth when the mouth is tightly shut. Next, the odour of the breath becomes bad, the gums tender, spongy, and ready to bleed at the slightest touch, and the tongue swollen. Finally, the teeth become loose and drop out, the jaw-bone may become diseased, the person becomes generally weak and bloodless, and may indeed die. Persons who work with metallic mercury may develop these symptoms to some extent, and in addition they become affected by trembling and palsy in various parts of the body. **Treatment** consists in stoppage of the mercury if it is being administered as medicine, and change of employment if the symptoms be due to work. Potassium iodide is often given, in addition to the good food and tonics which are necessary. If the condition is sufficiently severe, a course of injections of dimercaprol (*q.v.*) is given.

MERSALYL is a complex synthetic mercurial compound, used in the treatment of œdema (*i.e.* dropsy) due to heart disease.

MERTHIOLATE is the proprietary term for a mercurial germicide said to be highly effective in sterilizing tissue surfaces. Its chemical description is sodium ethylmercurithiosalicylate.

MERYCISM is another name for rumination, in which the contents of a meal are returned to the mouth some time after they have been swallowed and are once again chewed.

MESCALINE is derived from the Mexican peyote cactus, *Alnalonium leuinii*. It is probably the most powerful of all the hallucinogens and has been used from time immemorial almost by Red Indian tribes in Mexico as an intoxicant to produce ecstatic states for religious celebrations.

MESENCEPHALON is the term applied to the mid-brain connecting the cerebral hemispheres with the pons and cerebellum.

MESENTERY (μέσον, middle; ἔντερον, the intestine) is the name given to the double layer of peritoneal membrane which supports the small intestine. It is of a fan shape, and its shorter edge is attached to the back wall of the abdomen for a distance of about 6 inches (15 cm.), while the small intestine lies within its longer edge, for a length of over 20 feet (6 metres). The terms meso-colon, meso-rectum, etc., are applied to similar folds of peritoneum that support parts of the colon, rectum, etc.

586

MESMERISM (*see* HYPNOTISM).

MESOCOLON (μέσος, middle ; κόλον, colon) is the name of the double fold of peritoneum by which the large intestine is suspended from the back wall of the abdomen.

METABOLISM (μεταβολή, change) means tissue change and includes all the physical and chemical processes by which the living body is maintained, and also those by which the energy is made available for various forms of work. The constructive, chemical and physical, processes by which food materials are adapted for the use of the body are collectively known as anabolism. The destructive processes by which energy is produced with the breaking down of tissues into waste products is known as catabolism. *Basal metabolism* is the term applied to the energy changes necessary for essential processes such as the beating of the heart, respiration, and maintenance of body warmth. This can be estimated, when a person is placed in a state of complete rest, by measuring the amounts of oxygen and carbon dioxide exchanged during breathing under certain standard conditions. (*See* CALORIE.)

METACARPAL (μετά, beyond ; καρπός, wrist) bones are the long bones, five in number, which occupy the hand between the carpal bones at the wrist and the phalanges of the fingers. The large rounded 'knuckles' at the root of the fingers are formed by the heads of these bones.

METAPLASIA (μεταπλάσσω, I mould anew) is the term applied to a change of one kind of tissue into another.

METASTASIS (μετάστασις, a change of place) and METASTATIC are terms applied to the process by which malignant disease spreads to distant parts of the body, and also to the secondary tumours resulting from this process. For example, a cancer of the breast may produce metastatic growths in the glands of the armpit, cancer of the stomach may be followed by metastases in the liver.

METATARSAL (μετά, beyond ; ταρσός, instep) bones are the five bones in the foot which correspond to the metacarpal bones in the hand, lying between the tarsal bones, at the ankle, and the toes. (See Foot.)

METATARSALGIA (μετά, beyond ; ταρσός, instep ; ἄλγος, pain) is the name applied to pain of a gouty or rheumatic nature affecting, as it often does, the metatarsal region of the foot. It also occurs in flat-foot.

METEORISM (μετεωρίζω, I raise up) means the distension of the abdomen by gas produced in the intestines. (See Flatulence.)

METFORMIN is a diguanide which lowers the blood sugar. Its precise mode of action, however, is not known. It is active when taken by mouth and is proving of value in the treatment of certain cases of diabetes mellitus. (See also Phenformin.)

METHACHOLINE, or acetyl-beta-methylcholine, is a derivative of acetyl-choline (q.v.). It is more stable than acetylcholine. Its main use is in the treatment of paroxysmal atrial tachycardia.

METHADONE, or ' Physeptone ', is an analgesic with morphine-like properties. It has much less hypnotic action than morphine, and is widely used as a linctus for the alleviation of troublesome cough. It has some of the addiction-forming properties of morphine.

METHÆMOGLOBIN is a modification of the pigment of the blood which is found in the blood and sometimes in the urine after taking large doses of certain drugs, such as acetanilide, and also in some diseases.

METHAQUALONE is a synthetic, non-barbiturate hypnotic.

METHICILLIN (see Penicillin).

METHISAZONE is a thiosemicarbazone derivative that is proving of value in the prevention of smallpox.

METHOHEXITONE is a recently introduced ultra-short-acting barbiturate which is proving of value as a short-acting anæsthetic—particularly in dentistry.

METHONIUM compounds are quaternary ammonium compounds which are being used on an increasing scale in medicine. They act by producing a block in the ganglia of the autonomic nervous system (q.v.) and can thereby produce a lowering of the blood-pressure and a lessening of the activity of the stomach. They therefore prove of value in the treatment of high blood-pressure. The preparations most widely used for this purpose are hexamethonium, which is a polymethylene bistrin ethylammonium compound, and pentolinium tartrate.

METHOTREXATE is an antimetabolite which is proving of value in the treatment of choriocarcinoma (q.v.).

METHYL is the name of an organic radical whose chemical formula is CH_3, and which forms the centre of a wide group of substances known as the methyl group. For example, methyl alcohol is obtained as a by-product in the manufacture of beet-sugar, or by distillation of wood ; methyl salicylate is the active constituent in oil of wintergreen : methyl hydride is better known as marsh-gas.

Methyl alcohol, or wood spirit, is distilled from wood and is thus a cheap form of alcohol. It has actions similar to, but much more toxic than, those of ethyl alcohol. It has a specially pronounced action on the nervous system, and in large doses is apt to cause neuritis, especially of the optic nerves, leading to blindness, partial or complete.

METHYLDOPA is one of the new drugs introduced for the treatment of high blood-pressure. Its mode of action is still obscure.

METHYLPENTYNOL is a simple unsaturated aliphatic carbinol, which is widely used as a sedative.

METHYLPHENOBARBITONE is the *British Pharmacopœia* name for N-methyl - 5 - phenyl - 5 - methylbarbitone acid, a barbiturate used in the treatment of epilepsy.

METHYLTESTOSTERONE. — A derivative of the testicular hormone, testosterone (*q.v.*), which is active when taken by mouth. About three to four times as big a dose is needed to produce the same effect as an injection of testosterone propionate.

METHYLTHIONIN CHLORIDE, or METHYLENE BLUE, is a dark powder forming a deep-blue solution, used for various tests.

METHYPRYLONE is a non-barbiturate sedative.

METHYSERGIDE is a drug that is being used in the prevention of attacks of migraine (*q.v.*). Its precise value is still not clear, and it has to be used with care because of the toxic effects it sometimes produces.

METRITIS (μήτρα, the womb) means inflammation of the womb.

METRONIDAZOLE is a drug, administered by mouth, which is proving of value in the treatment of trichomonal vaginitis. (*See* TRICHOMONAS VAGINALIS.)

METROPATHIA HÆMORRHAGICA, or ESSENTIAL UTERINE HÆMORRHAGE, is the term given to a diseased state characterized by hæmorrhage from the uterus, cysts in the ovaries, and thickening of the uterine mucosa.

METRORRHAGIA (μήτρα, the womb; ῥήγνυμι I burst forth) means bleeding from the womb otherwise than at the proper period.

MICROBE (*see* BACTERIA).

MICROCEPHALY (μικρός, small κεφαλή head) is a term applied to abnormal smallness of the head. (*See* MENTAL DEFECTIVENESS.)

MICROCYTE (μικρός, small ; κύτος, cell) means a small red blood corpuscle.

MICRON is the $\frac{1}{1000}$th part of a millimetre. The abbreviation for it is μ.

MICRO-ORGANISM (*see* BACTERIA).

MICROSPORON.—The genus of fungi which includes the fungi responsible for ringworm of the scalp (*see* RINGWORM).
588

MICTURITION (*micturio*, I make water) means the act of passing water.

MIDWIFERY (*see* LABOUR).

MIGRAINE (a corruption of ἡμικρανία, pain on half the head) is a common condition characterized by recurring intense headaches. It usually begins at puberty and often tends to stop in middle age : *e.g.* in women attacks often cease at the change of life. In susceptible individuals attacks may be provoked by a wide variety of causes : *e.g.* physical or mental fatigue ; anxiety or worry ; dietetic indiscretions ; prolonged eye strain. In women attacks are often associated with menstruation. The precise cause is not known, but the generally accepted view is that in susceptible individuals one or other of these causes produces spasm or constriction of the blood vessels of the brain. This in turn is followed by dilatation of these blood vessels which also become more permeable and so allow fluid to pass out into the surrounding tissues. This combination of dilatation and outpouring of fluid is held to be responsible for the headache. An alternative theory is that the fluid contains certain substances which lower the threshold for pain and so increase the liability of the individual to feel pain.

The typical attack is very characteristic. It consists of an intense headache, usually situated over one or other eye. The headache is usually preceded by a feeling of sickness and blurring of sight. In some cases this disturbance of sight takes the form of bright lights—the so-called aura of migraine. The majority of attacks are accompanied by vomiting. The duration of the headache varies, but in the more severe cases the victim is usually confined to bed for twenty-four hours.

Treatment consists, in the first place, of trying to avoid any precipitating factor. Should an attack threaten, the victim should immediately lie down, and at this stage a few hours' rest may prevent the development of a full attack. When an attack is fully developed, rest in bed in a quiet, darkened room is essential ; any loud noise or bright light intensifies the headache or sickness. The less food that is taken during an attack the better, provided the individual drinks as much fluid as he wants. Drug treatment is not very satisfactory. Perhaps the most effective remedy for the condition is ergotamine tartrate which causes the dilated blood vessels to contract, but this must only be taken under medical supervision. In milder attacks, aspirin may be of value.

MILIARIA is the name applied to the group of diseases of the skin caused by disturbances of perspiration. The best known is MILIARIA RUBRA, or PRICKLY HEAT (*q.v.*).

MILIARY (*milium*, a millet seed) is a term, expressive of size, applied to various disease products which are about the size of millet seeds, *e.g.* miliary aneurysms, miliary tuberculosis.

MILIUM is the term applied to a small, whitish nodule in the skin, especially of the face. (*See* ACNE.)

MILK is the natural food of all animals belonging to the class of mammalia for a considerable period following their birth. It is practically the only form of animal food in which protein, fat, carbohydrate, and salt are all represented in sufficient amount, and it therefore contains all the constituents of a standard diet. Milk is important in human nutrition because it contains first-class animal protein of high biological value, because it is exceptionally rich in calcium, and because it is a good source of vitamins A (140 to 170 I.U. per 100 grammes), vitamin B_I (45 µg. per 100 grammes), and riboflavine (150 µg. per 100 grammes). It also contains a variable amount of ascorbic acid (vitamin C) and of vitamin D, the amount of the latter being higher during the summer months than during the winter months. Raw milk yields 65 calories per 100 grammes, in which are present (in grammes) 87·6 of water, 3·3 of protein, 3·6 of fat, 4·7 of carbohydrate, and 0·120 of calcium. Heat has no effect on the vitamin A or D content of milk, or on the riboflavine content, but it causes a considerable reduction in the vitamins C and B_I content.

The milk of different cows varies, especially in the amount of fat and of

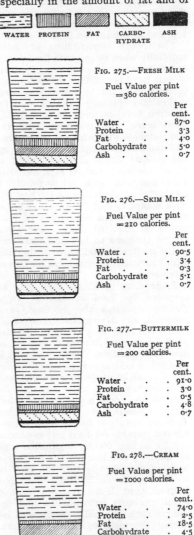

WATER PROTEIN FAT CARBO- ASH
HYDRATE

FIG. 275.—FRESH MILK

Fuel Value per pint
= 380 calories.

	Per cent.
Water	87·0
Protein	3·3
Fat	4·0
Carbohydrate	5·0
Ash	0·7

FIG. 276.—SKIM MILK

Fuel Value per pint
= 210 calories.

	Per cent.
Water	90·5
Protein	3·4
Fat	0·3
Carbohydrate	5·1
Ash	0·7

FIG. 277.—BUTTERMILK

Fuel Value per pint
= 200 calories.

	Per cent.
Water	91·0
Protein	3·0
Fat	0·5
Carbohydrate	4·8
Ash	0·7

FIG. 278.—CREAM

Fuel Value per pint
= 1000 calories.

	Per cent.
Water	74·0
Protein	2·5
Fat	18·5
Carbohydrate	4·5
Ash	0·5

the fat-soluble vitamins A and D, but the mixed milk of a herd should reach a certain standard. It should contain over 12 per cent. of solids, as shown in Fig. 275. A pint of milk provides about 400 calories of energy value. The percentage of cream by volume should be not less than 10 per cent. The amount of cream contained in milk can readily be discovered by allowing the milk to stand overnight in a cylindrical graduated vessel, when the cream rises to the top, and its volume can be measured off.

The ready digestibility of milk, especially when mixed with lime water, or when two or three grains of citrate of soda have been added for each ounce of milk in order to soften the curd, makes it a specially suitable food for children, invalids, and persons suffering from fever ; its blandness and the completeness with which it is absorbed and assimilated adapt it admirably for the general staple of nourishment in many diseases ; and its high nutritive value compared with its cost renders it a valuable article of diet for the healthy. As a complete diet for an adult doing hard work, about nine pints of milk would be required daily ; but for a person confined to bed and restricted in the matter of food, three pints daily afford sufficient nourishment for two or three weeks.

Preparation of Milk.—Milk may be prepared for food in various ways. *Boiling* destroys the bacteria, and especially any *Mycobacteria tuberculosis* which the milk may contain. It also partly destroys vitamins C and B_I, as does *pasteurization*. *Curdling* of milk is effected by adding rennet, which carries out the initial stage of digestion and thus renders milk more suitable for persons who could not otherwise tolerate it. *Souring* of milk is practised in many countries before milk is considered suitable for food ; it is carried out by adding certain organisms such as the lactic acid bacillus, the Bulgarian bacillus, etc., and setting the milk in a warm place for several hours (*see* LACTIC ACID BACILLI). *Sterilization*, which prevents fermentation and decomposition, is usually carried out by raising the milk to boiling temperature ($100°$ C.) for fifteen minutes and then hermetically sealing. *Condensed, unsweetened milk* — usually known as *evaporated milk*—is concentrated *in vacuo* at low temperature; the milk is then placed in tins, which are sealed, and is sterilized by heat at a temperature of $240°$ F. ($105°$ C.). This destroys 60 per cent. of the vitamin C and 30–50 per cent. of the vitamin B_I. Sweetened condensed milk is not ex-

posed to such a high temperature. The sugar, which prevents the growth of micro-organisms, is added before the condensing, and finally reaches a concentration of about 40 per cent. In a good, well prepared, sweetened condensed milk, only 15 per cent. of vitamin C and 5–10 per cent. of vitamin B_I may be lost. The sweetened form is apt to lead in children to fermentation, flatulence and diarrhœa. *Dried milk* is prepared by evaporating all the fluid so that the milk is reduced to the form of powder. In *spray-drying* a very fine spray of milk is forced into a heated chamber, where drying is almost instantaneous. Milk powder thus prepared is nearly completely soluble in water. During the drying process about 20 per cent. of the vitamin C and 10 per cent. of the vitamin B_I are lost. There is about a 5 per cent. decrease in the biological value of the milk proteins (casein, lactalbumin, lactoglobulin). The calcium is unaffected. *Roller-dried milk* is prepared by spreading a thin film of milk over steam-heated revolving metal cylinders ; the powder is removed by a stationary scraper. Roller-dried milk is less soluble in water than spray-dried milk ; and in its preparation the loss of vitamins C and B_I is higher and there is slightly greater deterioration of protein. *Peptonized milk* is prepared by treating fresh milk with peptonizing powder, and although the milk is rendered less palatable by this means, it is easily digested and is readily tolerated in weak conditions of the stomach and intestines. (*See* PEPTONIZED FOODS.) *Humanized milk* is cow's milk treated in such a way as to render it closely similar to human milk.

Pure milk suitable for children is sold under an order of the Ministry of Health which came into force in 1923, and is milk derived under clean conditions from cows which are specially inspected and tested periodically by tuberculin in order to ensure that they are free from tuberculosis. Pasteurized milk may be sold having a similar freedom from the risk of tuberculosis. The grades of milk which are now officially recognized are :

1. *Tuberculin Tested Milk.*—This is milk from cows which have passed a veterinary examination and a tuberculin

test ; it is bottled on the farm or elsewhere ; and it may be raw or pasteurized. Every animal in the herd from which this milk comes must pass a veterinary examination at intervals of not more than six months, and must also pass a tuberculin test at intervals of not less than two and not more than six months ; any animal which reacts to the tuberculin test must immediately be removed from the herd. Milk must be bottled at the farm or at some other licensed bottling establishment, and the cap must bear the address of the bottling establishment and the words ' Tuberculin Tested Milk '. If it is bottled on the farm it may be described on the bottle caps or cartons as ' Tuberculin Tested Milk (Certified) '. This milk must further satisfy a methylene blue reduction test and must not contain any coliform bacillus.

2. Accredited Milk. — This is raw milk from cows which have passed a veterinary examination ; it is bottled on the farm or elsewhere. Every cow in the herd from which the milk comes must pass, at intervals of three months, an examination by a veterinary surgeon nominated by the local authority; the herd must not at any time include an animal which has reacted to the tuberculin test. The cap of the bottle must bear the address of the bottling establishment and the words ' Accredited Milk '. It must satisfy the same bacteriological tests as raw tuberculin tested milk.

3. Pasteurized Milk.—This is milk which has been retained at a temperature of 145°–150° F. (62·8° to 65·5° C.) for at least thirty minutes. Every receptacle must be labelled ' Pasteurized Milk '. It must not contain more than 100,000 bacteria per millilitre. Tuberculin tested milk may, if desired, be pasteurized, and it is then described as ' Tuberculin Tested Milk (Pasteurized) '; a sample of this milk must not contain more than 30,000 bacteria per millilitre.

In Scotland (from 1st October 1936) other names are used as follows: ' Certified ' for Tuberculin Tested (Certified) ; ' Tuberculin Tested ' as in England ; ' Standard ' for Accredited ; and ' Pasteurized' and 'Tuberculin Tested (Pasteurized) ' as in England. (See also ADULTERATION OF FOOD, DIET, INFANT FEEDING, NITROGENOUS FOODS.)

MILK, DISEASES DUE TO.—Milk has a remarkable power of absorbing gases and vapours to which it is exposed, so that it becomes readily tainted. Milk is also liable to be infected by dirt, or from water, or from the hands of milkers suffering from disease, and in these circumstances epidemics of enteric fever, scarlet fever, and diphtheria are frequently traceable to the milk supply. It may also transmit Brucella abortus, the causative organism of undulant fever. Efficient protection against these diseases is obtained by boiling or pasteurizing the household supply of milk. Summer diarrhœa in children is usually due to milk containing large quantities of bacteria. Tuberculosis may be communicated by the milk from disease affecting the cow itself. This risk is avoided by using milk from tuberculintested cows or by boiling or pasteurization.

MILK TEETH are the temporary teeth of children. (For the time of their appearance, see TEETH.)

MILLILITRE is the 1000th part of 1 litre. It is practically the equivalent of a cubic centimetre (1 c.c. = 0·999973 ml.). Ml. is the usual abbreviation for millilitre.

MIND DISORDERS (see MENTAL ILLNESS.)

MINDERERUS SPIRIT is an old name for liquor ammonii acetatis, a solution of ammonium acetate, which is much used in domestic medicine. It is a harmless substance, and acts as an antacid and diuretic, and helps to reduce feverishness. The usual dose is a dessert-spoonful or more, for colds and slight feverish conditions.

MIOTIC means (a) causing the pupil of the eye to contract ; (b) any agent which causes the pupil to contract; (c) of the pupil, in the state of being contracted.

MISCARRIAGE (see ABORTION.)

MITHRIDATISM is a term applied to immunity against the effects of poisons produced by administration

591

of gradually increasing doses of the poison itself. The process is named after Mithridates, King of Pontus, who rendered himself immune against poisoning by this means.

MITRAL STENOSIS is the term applied to the narrowing of the opening between the left atrium and left ventricle as a result of rigidity of, and adhesion between, the cusps of the mitral valve, due, almost invariably, to the infection of rheumatic fever.

MITRAL VALVE, so called from its resemblance to a bishop's mitre, is the valve which guards the opening between the atrium and ventricle on the left side of the heart. (*See* HEART.)

MOGIGRAPHIA (μόγις, with difficulty ; γράφω, I write) is a term sometimes applied to writer's cramp. (*See* CRAMP.)

MOLAR TEETH (*molaris*, a millstone) are the last three teeth on each side of the jaw. (*See* TEETH.)

MOLE is a term used in two quite different senses. In the first place, a mole on the skin is a darkly pigmented spot, usually raised above the surrounding surface, rough, and covered with hair. These moles are of developmental origin, and malignant growths may spring from them late in life. Secondly the term hydatidiform mole is applied to cases in which, following upon conception, a degenerative mass forms in the womb, the embryo dying in the process ; whilst the term, carneous mole, is applied to a missed abortion.

MOLLITIES OSSIUM (*mollities*, softness ; *ossium*, of the bones) is another name for osteomalacia.

MOLLUSCUM CONTAGIOSUM is the name given to a disease in which small tumours, seldom larger than peas, develop on the surface of the skin. It appears to be of a contagious nature, and to be due to a virus.

MOLLUSCUM FIBROSUM, or VON RECKLINGHAUSEN'S DISEASE, is the term applied to the condition in which numerous soft nodules of fibrous tissue —believed to arise from nerve fibres— appear on the skin.

592

MONCKEBERG'S SCLEROSIS (*see* ARTERIES, DISEASES OF).

MONGOLISM, or **DOWN'S SYNDROME,** is a variety of mental defect, in which the patient has Mongolian-like eyes, a snub nose, high cheek-bones, a large tongue, a small round skull, and short, thick hands and feet. Another characteristic feature is the palm print, which reveals distinctive markings ; the most distinctive of these is the so-called four-finger line (Pl. XV).

The condition is often referred to as Down's syndrome (or disease) after Dr. J. L. H. Down, the London doctor who first described it in 1866.

The incidence is just over 1 per 1000 live births, but the incidence in the community is much lower than this, as many mongols die in infancy. This high death-rate is due partly to the fact that mongol children have a much higher incidence of other congenital deformities, such as malformations of the heart, than other children, partly to their lower resistance to infection.

It is much commoner in children born to older women. In one series of 100 mongol children, it was found that 64 were born to mothers over the age of 35, whilst 35 were born to mothers over the age of 40. On the basis of these and other figures it has been estimated that in children born to mothers aged 40 to 44, the incidence of mongol children is 14 per 1000. For mothers who give birth to a mongol child when they are younger the chances of a subsequent child being a mongol is relatively high. Precise figures in this respect can be misleading, and the best advice for a young mother who has had a mongol child, and who wishes to know the risk of her having another, is to go and discuss the matter with her family doctor.

The cause of mongolism is now known to be the presence of an extra chromosome (*q.v.*) in the ovum. Whether this is due to heredity or environment is not known. The probable answer is that in some it is heredity, in some environmental, whereas in others again it may be a combination of hereditary (or genetic) and environmental factors.

The degree of mental backwardness varies considerably. It has been estimated that about 6 per cent. of mongols are probably capable of profiting from attendance at schools for the educationally subnormal. Most mongols eventually acquire some degree of speech, and about 5 per cent. learn to read. They practically never learn to write. Most learn to wash, dress and feed themselves, and many are able to run simple errands.

There is no known cure for the condition, but much can be done for them, especially if they can be kept at home rather than sent to an institution.

MONILIASIS is the infection caused by monilia, the genus of fungi now known as *Candida albicans*. The infection may occur in the mouth (where it is known as thrush [*q.v.*], lungs, intestine, vagina, skin, or nails.

MONK'S-HOOD (*see* ACONITE).

MONOAMINE OXIDASE INHIBITORS are drugs that destroy, or prevent the action of, monoamine oxidase (M.A.O.). Monoamines which include noradrenaline (*q.v.*) and tyramine, play an important part in the metabolism of the brain, and there is some evidence that excitement is due to an accumulation of monoamines in the brain. M.A.O. is a naturally occurring enzyme (*q.v.*) which is concerned in the breakdown of monoamines.

An excessive accumulation of monoamines can induce a dangerous reaction characterized by high blood pressure, palpitations, sweating and a feeling of suffocation. Hence the care with which M.A.O. inhibitor drugs are administered. What is equally important, however, is that in no circumstances should a patient receiving any M.A.O. inhibitor drug eat cheese, yeast preparations such as Marmite, tinned fish, or high game. The reason for this ban is that all these foodstuffs contain large amounts of tyramine which increases the amount of certain monoamines such as noradrenaline in the body. As can well be imagined such an increase in monoamines in a patient who is taking a full dose of a M.A.O. inhibitor drug could be thoroughly unpleasant—if not disastrous.

There are also certain drugs, such as amphetamine and pethidine which must not be taken by a patient who is receiving an M.A.O. inhibitor drug.

MONOMANIA (μόνος, single ; μανία' madness) means a kind of partial insanity, in which the affected person has a delusion upon one subject, though he can converse rationally and is a responsible individual upon other matters.

MONOPLEGIA (μόνος, single ; πληγή, stroke) means paralysis of a single limb or part. (*See* PARALYSIS.)

MONOSACCHARIDE is the term applied to a sugar having six carbon atoms in the molecule. It includes glucose, galactose, lævulose, etc.

MOOREN'S ULCER is a degenerative ulcer of the eye.

MORBID (*morbus*, disease) means ' diseased '.

MORBIFIC (*morbus*, disease ; *facio*, I make) means ' disease-producing '. For example, the comma bacillus may be called the morbific agent in cholera.

MORBILLI (a diminutive of *morbus*, a disease) is another name for measles.

MORBUS, the Latin word for disease, is used in such terms as cholera morbus, morbus coxæ (hip-joint disease).

MORON (μωρός, stupid) is the term applied to a feeble-minded person whose defect is relatively slight and whose ' mental age ' is somewhere between eight and twelve years. (*See* MENTAL DEFECTIVENESS.)

MORO'S TEST (*see* TUBERCULIN).

MORPHINE (Μορφεύς, the god of sleep), or MORPHIA, is the name of the chief alkaloid upon which the action of opium depends. (*See* OPIUM.)

MORTALITY (*see* DEATH, CAUSES OF, *and* INFANT MORTALITY).

MORTIFICATION (*mors*, death ; *facio*, I make) is another name for gangrene. (*See* GANGRENE.)

MOTOR is a term applied to those nerves and tracts of fibres in the brain and cord by which impulses are sent to the muscles, thus causing movements. (*See* SPINAL CORD.)

593

MOUNTAIN-SICKNESS is the name given to the group of symptoms which appear when people reach great heights, either in climbing mountains or in aeroplanes. Some persons suffer at lower altitudes than others, but prolonged residence at a high level does not seem to prevent mountain-sickness when the person climbs higher. Persons who live habitually at a high altitude develop an increased proportion of red corpuscles in the blood and thus obtain a greater amount of oxygen from the rarefied air, and lose the tendency to mountain-sickness. Exhaustion, want of food, and exposure to cold bring it on sooner, but every one seems to begin to suffer when a height over 16,000 feet is reached. Want of oxygen, in consequence of the rareness of the atmosphere, is supposed generally to be the cause. Weakness, difficulty of breathing, palpitation of the heart, giddiness, sickness, vomiting and finally unconsciousness, are the main symptoms, but these rapidly pass off, causing no permanent damage, when the person again reaches a lower level.

MOUTH is the cavity into which the food is first received, and where it is prepared by chewing and admixture with saliva for the early stages of digestion in the stomach. The mouth opens through the fauces, a narrow passage between the tonsils, into the pharynx or throat. The chief contents of the mouth are the edges of the jaw-bones bearing the teeth, and the tongue. The cavity is bounded above by the hard and soft palates, while beneath the tongue a layer of muscles, salivary glands, and other soft structures form the floor of the mouth. (*See also* TEETH *and* TONGUE.)

MOUTH, DISEASES OF.—The state of the mucous membrane lining the mouth as regards pallor, pigmentation, and other conditions gives a general idea of the extent to which other mucous membranes in the interior of the body are affected in anæmia, Addison's disease, jaundice, etc. As the tongue consists essentially of a pointed mass of muscle wrapped round with mucous membrane, its condition as to shape and size gives valuable information regarding the general

muscular state in debility, nervous diseases, and the like ; while the mucous membrane covering it shows many marked changes in various diseases of the alimentary system and general maladies.

Conditions of the tongue.—The *muscular condition* of the tongue is naturally such that the organ when at rest touches the lower set of teeth all round, and is slightly arched upwards. It should present a smooth surface, with a groove up the middle, and a sharp, even edge. Further, it is completely under control of the will, and can be moved in any direction. Now and then the tongue is too large for the mouth, rendering speech indistinct and even interfering with swallowing, or being so bulky that it is constantly protruded from the mouth. Such a condition is either congenital or may result from inflammation. Tongue-tie is a congenital condition in which the band beneath the middle of the tongue uniting it to the floor of the mouth is either so short, or attached so far forwards, that the tongue cannot be fully protruded from the mouth, and cannot move with the freedom required for speech. This condition may be responsible for childish defects of speech but is much rarer than is popularly supposed. A flabby condition of the tongue, in which the organ is large, pale, and distinctly indented by the teeth along its edge, affords a sign of general debility. Tremulousness of the tongue when it is protruded is a sign of various nervous diseases, but by far its commonest cause is excessive indulgence in alcohol, of which it may form the only sign that cannot be concealed. After an apoplectic attack which has involved the nerve centre controlling one side of the tongue, this organ is protruded in a one-sided manner, pointing towards that side of the body which is paralysed, and the rapidity with which the person recovers the power to put the tongue out straight is a good criterion of his general progress towards recovery. Another important localizing sign in certain diseases of the brain and of the facial nerve is loss of the sense of taste on one side of the tongue.

A still more easily noticed sign is the presence or absence of *fur* on the tongue.

This consists of a thickening of the superficial layers of the mucous membrane, due partly to increased growth, as the result of fever and other conditions ; partly to diminished use of the tongue, whose surface should constantly be rubbed down against the teeth and food. The fur is sometimes white, sometimes brown, or even black, from drying and the accumulation on it of materials derived from the food. It should be remembered that milk whitens the tongue and makes it look as if 'furred'. Fevers of all sorts are associated with a furred tongue, and in typhoid fever perhaps, most of all, the fur accumulates till the tongue is covered with a thick mass, brown in the centre and yellow towards the edges, where the red mucous membrane is exposed. In scarlet fever there is often seen what is called a 'strawberry tongue', the general surface being covered with a white fur, through which project the red and inflamed points of the larger papillæ with which the tongue is studded. Constipation and obstruction of the bowels are associated, as a rule, with a thick white or brownish fissured fur upon the tongue, and in trivial cases of indigestion the presence of such a fur is often made the occasion for administering a laxative. Gastritis, particularly when due to excess in alcohol, is prone to cause a thin white fur ; and the tremulous tongue coated in the mornings with fur, which wears off as the day advances, is one of the surest signs of habitual drinking. It is a noteworthy fact, however, that two of the most serious diseases of the stomach, viz. cancer and gastric ulcer, are usually associated with a remarkably clean tongue. All inflammatory affections of the throat, such as tonsillitis, are apt to be accompanied by a thick, moist fur upon the tongue, very much resembling a layer of thick cream. In rheumatic fever a uniform yellowish fur often gives an appearance known as 'blanket tongue'. One half of the tongue may show a fur, while the rest of the surface is clean, and this is generally caused by neuralgia or by the presence of a bad tooth upon the furred side.

In some severe cases the tongue may, instead of showing a fur, present a dry, red, *raw appearance*. An inflamed tongue (' beef tongue ') is one of the characteristics of pellagra, a disease due to deficiency of nicotinic acid in the diet. A magenta-coloured tongue is said to be caused by deficiency of riboflavine in the diet.

Feeble children and persons brought very low by illness frequently develop small raised *white patches*, called ' thrush ', upon the mucous membrane of the mouth and tongue. These are caused by the growth in its surface layer of a parasitic mould known as *Candida albicans*. Thrush is not of itself a serious condition, being easily removed by frequent application of borax-honey, or of glycerin of boric acid, to the affected spots. Nevertheless, the presence of this affection may indicate grave constitutional weakness.

A chronic condition, in which the tongue becomes studded with thickened, smooth, white patches, often separated by *deep fissures*, is known as ' leucoplakia '. It develops gradually as the result of some long-standing irritation or inflammation of the tongue, and is a permanent condition which does not usually give much trouble beyond interfering somewhat with the distinctness of the speech, and the fact that the condition may, late in life, pass into one of malignant tumour.

A slighter condition, in which the tongue shows white patches interspersed with sharply marked red, bare areas, is known as ' geographical tongue ' or eczema of the tongue. It is a mild and usually transitory form of inflammation in which the surface layer of the mucous membrane on the tongue peels off, and it is usually associated with digestive disorders and a certain amount of general debility.

Ulcers on the tongue are common, but they generally remain of small size, and they do not differ from ulcers on other parts of the mouth, either in their cause or in their course. (*See below*.)

INFLAMMATION OF THE MOUTH arises from the same causes as inflammation elsewhere, but among the special causes may be noted a jagged or painful tooth, an ill-fitting plate, the cutting of teeth in children, alcohol, tobacco-smoking, digestive disturbance, and, in the special form of inflammation known as thrush (above mentioned), a parasitic mould. General ill-health plays an important part in the case both of children and of adults. Whatever be the cause, the mucous membrane becomes red, swollen, and tender, while small ulcers may in some cases develop here and there. Generally, the avoidance of highly spiced food, of alcohol, and of tobacco is sufficient to cure the condition, which may be soothed, while it lasts, by smearing on glycerin of boric acid, or honey of borax.

The chronic inflammation of the gums (gingivitis) which arises in connection with unclean teeth, concealed inflammation within the sockets of the teeth, and pyorrhœa alveolaris, are forms of inflammation in the mouth which are treated under TEETH, DISEASES OF.

ULCERS OF THE MOUTH are usually of small size, and arise from a variety of causes. It is not at all uncommon in feeble, badly fed children for one or two ulcers to develop on the inside of the cheeks, on the gums, or on the tongue, causing pain in eating, profuse discharge of saliva, and great fœtor of the breath. These ulcers generally heal when the child is well fed and a mouth-wash of chlorate of potash is frequently used, but they may pass on to the serious condition of cancrum oris. (See CANCRUM ORIS.) Single small ulcers arise in otherwise healthy people from the irritation of a jagged tooth, a small wound, or even apparently as the result of dyspepsia. These may be very troublesome, and, being generally situated in the groove between lip and gum, or on the tip and edge of the tongue, they are prevented from healing by the movement of the parts, and may become very troublesome for weeks or even months. A small ulcer is frequently developed beneath the tongue during the course of whooping-cough, as the result of friction against the lower teeth in coughing, and is prevented from healing by the same cause. The digestion must receive careful attention, the mouth must be kept clean by antiseptic washes and regular brushing of the teeth, and the little ulcer may be touched with a strong astringent such as tincture of iodine or nitrate of silver every few days, and, in the interval, protected by occasional application of

borax-honey or glycerin of boric acid. Large ulcers may also be of tuberculous or syphilitic origin.

BAD TEETH form one of the commonest sources of complaint regarding the mouth. (See TEETH, DISEASES OF.)

GUMBOIL is a very common minor disease. (See GUMBOIL.)

SALIVARY CALCULUS is a condition which sometimes occurs and may give rise to a good deal of trouble. (See CONCRETIONS.) The stone, if it lodges in one of the salivary ducts, may ulcerate out on the face, and then cause a fistula, from which saliva constantly trickles over the cheek. A fistula may be produced also by wounds of the cheek, involving the duct of the parotid gland. These fistulæ are cured by a slight operation, which reopens a passage to the mouth and closes that upon the cheek.

RANULA is a clear, cyst-like swelling, appearing beneath the tongue in connection with the salivary glands in this region. It is a cyst full of saliva, and is treated by several minor surgical procedures, its obliteration being a simple matter.

MUMPS is an acute infective inflammation of the salivary glands. (See MUMPS.)

TUMOURS occur on the lips, on the alveolus bearing the teeth, arising either from the gums or bone, and most commonly on the tongue. Those which develop in the gum or bone beneath it go by the general name of ' epulis ', whatever be their nature. Occasionally these are malignant, more often they are simple fibroid tumours, produced frequently by the irritation of decaying teeth. On extraction of the associated tooth or teeth and removal of the epulis it seldom gives more trouble. Growths upon the lips and tongue may be simple warts, or cysts may occasionally be found, but the commonest tumour of these parts is cancer. It seldom appears before the age of forty, and is much more common in men than in women. It is often associated with some form of *chronic* irritation such as a jagged tooth or smoking of a clay pipe. In other cases it follows prolonged chronic inflammation, such as syphilitic leukoplakia (*q.v.*). The glands on the front and sides of the neck in such cases become early the seat of secondary malignant growths ; and as the foul state of the interior of the mouth, after such a tumour ulcerates, causes much interference with the general health, the duration of life is not long, being placed by authorities upon the subject at little over a year after the tumour first appears if adequate treatment is not carried out. By modern surgical treatment, which aims at very free removal of the diseased part of the tongue and glands, life is prolonged, particularly in cases subjected to early operation, considerably beyond this period. The result of removal causes little or no disfigurement, and even when the whole tongue is removed the power of speech is often but little impaired. In cases which are detected early, satisfactory results are obtained from the use of radiotherapy.

MOVABLE KIDNEY (*see* KIDNEY, DISEASES OF).

MUCILAGE is prepared from acacia or tragacanth gum, and is used as an ingredient of mixtures containing solid particles in order to keep the latter from settling, and also as a demulcent. (*See* DEMULCENTS.)

MUCOCELE is an abnormally dilated cavity in the body due to the accumulation of mucus ; such a ' cyst ' may therefore form wherever there is mucous membrane.

MUCOLYTIC is the term used to describe the property of destroying, or lessening the tenacity of, mucus. It is most commonly used to describe drugs which have this property and are therefore used in the treatment of bronchitis (*q.v.*). The inhalation of steam, for example, has a mucolytic action.

MUCOMEMBRANOUS COLIC is the term applied to a disorder in which constipation, abdominal pain, and the passage of mucus or casts of mucus in the stools occurs in highly strung or neurotic people, especially women. The spasm of the colon causing these symptoms may be allergic in origin.

MUCOUS MEMBRANE is the general name given to the membrane which lines many of the hollow organs of the body. These membranes vary widely in structure in different sites, but all have the common character of being lubricated by mucus, derived in some cases from isolated cells on the surface of the membrane, but more generally from definite glands placed beneath the membrane, and opening here and there through it by ducts (Fig. 279). The air passages, the alimentary canal and the ducts of glands which open into it, and also the urinary passages, are all lined by mucous membranes.

In structure a mucous membrane consists of a basis of fibrous tissue resembling the true skin, though looser and lighter in texture, in which the blood - vessels, nerves, and mucous glands lie. This is covered on its surface by a layer of epithelium resembling the cuticle covering the skin, although the cells are in all cases of a more soft and succulent nature than those on the outer surface of the body.

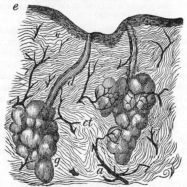

FIG. 279.—Section through the mucous membrane of the throat, showing two of the mucous secreting glands. *e*, Epithelium of the surface ; *ct*, connective tissue beneath it ; *g*, gland ; *d*, its duct opening on the surface ; *a*, artery ending in a capillary network round the gland. Magnified 40 times. (Turner's *Anatomy*.)

It is in the character and properties of these cells that the various mucous membranes chiefly differ. In the air passages they are—almost everywhere except over the vocal cords—of a pillar-like shape and provided with thread-like processes, being known as ciliated cells (Fig. 280). On the vocal cords the cells, which are exposed to constant friction, resemble those of the skin. In the alimentary system generally they are of a simple pillar-like or ' columnar ' type (Fig. 281), placed side by side, though in the mouth and gullet, where the food causes much friction, the surface, like that of the vocal cords, closely resembles the cuticle of the skin. In the urinary passages again the cells

FIG. 280.—Ciliated epithelial cells from the air passages. (Turner's *Anatomy*.)

are ciliated, except in the bladder, where they approach in type to that of the skin epithelium.

FIG. 281.—Columnar epithelium. *A*, Side view of a group of cells; *B*, surface view of the ends of a group of cells; *C*, a columnar cell from the mucous membrane of the small intestine. (Turner's *Anatomy*.)

Lying close beneath the epithelium there is, in most mucous membranes, a thin layer of involuntary muscle fibres, and to this, coupled with the extremely loose attachment of mucous membranes to the organs which they line, is due the great pliability and elasticity of these membranes.

MUCOUS PATCH is the name given to the syphilitic eruption as it affects mucous membranes. These patches are seen especially about the lips, mouth, and throat, and consist of slightly raised areas, reddish at the edge, and covered by a velvety whitish layer. They are very infectious. (*See* SYPHILIS.)

MUCOVISCIDOSIS (*see* FIBROCYSTIC DISEASE OF THE PANCREAS).

MUCUS (*mucus*, the discharge from the nose) is the general name for the slimy secretion derived from mucous membranes. It is mainly composed of a substance called mucin, which varies according to the particular mucous membrane from which it is derived, and it contains other substances, such as cells cast off from the surface of the membrane, ferments, and dust particles. From whatever source derived, mucin has the following characters: it is viscid, clear, and tenacious; when dissolved in water it can be precipitated by addition of acetic acid;

and when not in solution already, it is dissolved by weak alkalis, such as lime-water.

Under normal conditions the surface of a mucous membrane is lubricated by only a small quantity of mucus; the appearance of large quantities is a sign of inflammation.

MULL is the name of a thin, soft muslin used in surgery. Plaster mull is the name given to a sheet of mull coated with gutta-percha and usually containing some drug or antiseptic for the treatment of skin disease.

MULTIGRAVIDA is a woman who has been pregnant more than once.

MULTIPARA (*multus*, many, and *pario*, I bear) is a term applied to a woman who has borne several children.

MULTIPLE NEURITIS (*see* NEURITIS).

MULTIPLE SCLEROSIS (*see* DISSEMINATED SCLEROSIS).

MUMPS, also known as EPIDEMIC PAROTITIS, CYNANCHE PAROTIDEA, and popularly known as ' THE BRANKS ', is an infectious disease characterized by inflammatory swelling of the parotid and other salivary glands, frequently occurring as an epidemic, and affecting mostly young persons.

Causes.—Mumps is due to infection with a virus and is highly infectious from person to person. It is predominantly a disease of childhood and early adult life, but it can occur at any age. Epidemics usually occur in the winter and spring. It is infectious for two or three days before the swelling of the glands appears.

Symptoms.—There is a long incubation period of two to three weeks, after infection, before the glands begin to swell. The first signs are fatigue, slight feverishness, and sore throat, which may precede the swelling by a day or two. The gland first affected is generally the parotid, situated in front of and below the ear. Along with the swelling there is often some face-ache and considerable rise of temperature to 101° or even 104° F. (38·3° or 40° C.). The swelling usually spreads to the sub-maxillary and sublingual glands lying beneath the jaw, and to the glands on the side opposite that first affected.

There is hardly ever any redness or tendency to suppuration in the swollen parts, although interference with the acts of chewing and swallowing may occasion a good deal of trouble, and the swelling is tender to touch. After continuing four or five days, the swelling abates, the temperature having generally already fallen. In 15 to 30 per cent. of males, inflammation of the testicles (orchitis) develops. This usually occurs during the second week of the illness, but may not occur until two or three weeks later. It may result in atrophy of the testicles. In a much smaller proportion of females with mumps, inflammation of the ovaries or breasts may occur. Inflammation of the pancreas, accompanied by tenderness in the upper part of the abdomen and digestive disturbances, sometimes occurs. Meningitis is also an occasional complication. The various complications are found much more frequently when the disease affects adults than when it occurs in childhood.

Treatment.—The patient must be confined to bed for at least a week or ten days, and kept in isolation for 14 days from the onset of the disease or 7 days from the subsidence of all swelling. Soft food, mild aperients, and the protection of the inflamed parts by a strip of flannel or by cotton-wool and a handkerchief are all the treatment usually required. If there be much face-ache, it is relieved by warm fomentations or aspirin.

MURIATIC ACID (*muria*, brine) is an old name for hydrochloric acid.

MURMUR is the name given to an uneven, rustling sound heard by auscultation over the heart and various blood-vessels in abnormal conditions. For example, murmurs heard when the stethoscope is applied over the heart are highly characteristic of valvular disease of this organ.

MUSCÆ VOLITANTES (*musca,* a fly; *volitans,* floating about) is a term signifying the floating specks which become visible when the eye looks steadily at a white ground in bright light. These specks are present in most eyes and can be seen at any time, but they become especially noticeable when the general health is depressed, and sometimes cause great annoyance through the fear that they may be the sign of some eye disease. They are due to the presence of filaments and cells in the vitreous humour of the eye, which, though transparent, are rather denser than the rest of the humour, and sufficiently opaque to cast a shadow upon the retina. These shadows are referred outwards as floating objects in the field of vision.

Fig. 282.—The rectus muscle on the front of the thigh showing the various parts of a muscle. *R*, The fleshy part or ' belly ', composed of muscle fibres ; *to, ti,* tendons of origin and insertion ; *n,* nerve of supply *a,* artery ; *v,* vein ; *l,* lymphatic vessel ; *P,* patella or knee-cap. (Turner's *Anatomy*.)

MUSCARINE is the poisonous principle found in some toadstools. (*See* FUNGUS-POISONING.)

MUSCLE (*musculus,* a muscle), popularly known as FLESH, is the tissue by which, in virtue of its power of contraction, movements are made in the higher animals. Muscular tissue is divided, according to its function, into two great groups, *voluntary muscle* and *involuntary muscle*, of which the former is under control of the will, whilst the latter discharges its functions independently. The term striped muscle is often given to voluntary muscle, because under the microscope all the voluntary muscles show a striped appearance, whilst involuntary muscle is, in the main, unstriped or plain. There are exceptions to the latter statement, for the heart muscle, which is involuntary, is partially striped, while certain muscles of the throat, and two small muscles inside the ear, not controllable by will-power, are also striped.

Structure of muscle. — VOLUNTARY MUSCLE is disposed in a regular method over the body, being mainly attached to the skeleton, and hence often called skeletal muscle. There are certain definite muscles, and these vary as to shape only slightly in different persons, although in one person particular muscles may be developed to a much greater bulk than in others. Each muscle is enclosed in a sheath of fibrous tissue, known as fascia or epimysium, and, from this, partitions of fibrous tissue, known as perimysium, run into the substance of the muscle, dividing it up into small bundles. Each of these bundles, if carefully examined, will be found to consist in turn of a collection of fibres, which form the units of the muscle. Each fibre is about $\frac{1}{500}$ inch (50 microns) in thickness and about

FIG. 283.—A muscle fibre splitting up into fibrils. (Turner's *Anatomy*.)

1 inch long (25 mm.), though the dimensions vary a little in different muscles. If the fibre be cut across and

examined under a high power of the microscope, it is seen to be further divided into fibrils (Fig. 283), the cut ends of which are known as Cohnheim's areas ; but as all the fibrils of a fibre act in concert, this is a needless subdivision. Each fibre is enclosed in an elastic sheath of its own, which allows of its lengthening and shortening, and is known as the ' sarcolemma ' (σάρξ, flesh ; and λέμμα, a husk). Within the sarcolemma lie numerous nuclei belonging to the muscle fibre, which was originally developed from a simple cell. To the sarcolemma, at either end, is attached a minute bundle of connective-tissue fibres which unites the muscle fibre to its neighbours, or to one of the connective tissue partitions in the muscle, and by means of these connections the fibre produces its effect upon contracting. The sarcolemma is pierced by a nerve fibre, which breaks up upon the surface of the muscle fibre into a complicated end-plate, and by this means each muscle fibre is brought under the guidance of the central nervous system, and the discharge of energy which produces muscular contraction is controlled. When the muscle fibre within the sarcolemma is examined by a high magnifying power, it is found to show alternate light and dark transverse stripes, with a fine dotted line, called Dobie's line (Fig. 284) or Krause's membrane, across the middle of each light stripe. These appearances are due to the fact that the fibre is composed of

FIG. 284.—Portion of a muscle fibre showing the alternate dark and light stripes, with Dobie's line in the clear stripe. Magnified about 500 times.

segments made up partly of fibrous connective material, partly of semi-fluid contractile tissue, in which visible changes take place as the fibre contracts.

Between the muscle fibres, which have, on account of their relative length and width, a pillar-like shape, run many capillary blood-vessels. They are so placed that the contractions of the muscle fibres empty them at once of blood, and thus the active muscle is ensured a specially good blood supply. None of these vessels, however, pierce the sarcolemma surrounding the fibres, so that the blood does not come into direct contact with the muscular tissue, whose nourishment is carried on by the lymph that exudes from the blood-vessels. The lymph circulation is also automatically varied, as required, by the muscular contractions. Between the muscle fibres, and enveloped in a sheath of connective tissue, lie here and there special structures known as ' muscle-spindles '. Each of these contains thin muscle fibres, numerous nuclei, and the endings of sensory nerves. They appear to be the sensory organs of the muscles. (*See* TOUCH.)

INVOLUNTARY MUSCLE includes, as already stated, the heart muscle and unstriped muscle. The heart muscle stands in structure between striped and unstriped muscle (Fig. 285). Each fibre is short, has a nucleus in its centre, com-

FIG. 285.—Longitudinal section of human heart-muscle fibres. (From Hewer, *Textbook of Histology*. William Heinemann, Ltd.)

municates with its neighbours by short branches, shows a faintly striped appearance near its exterior, and is devoid of sarcolemma.

Plain or unstriped muscle is found in the following positions : the inner and middle coats of the stomach and intestines ; the ureters and urinary bladder ; the windpipe and bronchial tubes ; the ducts of glands ; the gall-bladder ; the uterus and Fallopian tubes ; the middle coat of the blood- and lymph-vessels ; the iris and ciliary muscle of the eye ; the dartos tunic of the scrotum ; and in association with the various glands and hairs in the skin. The fibres are very much smaller than those of striped muscle, although they vary greatly in size. Each is pointed at the ends, has one or more oval nuclei in the centre, and a delicate sheath of sarcolemma enveloping it (Plate XII). The fibres are grouped in bundles, much as are the striped fibres, but they adhere to one another by cement material, not by the tendon bundles found in voluntary muscle.

Development of muscle.—All the muscles of the developing individual arise from the central layer (mesoblast) of the embryo, each fibre taking origin from a single cell. Later on in life, muscles have the power both of increasing in size, as the result of use, for example, in athletes, and also of healing, after parts of them have been destroyed by injury. This takes place partly by the growth and splitting of the original fibres to form new fibres, and partly from reserve cells, known as sarcoplasts, which lie in every muscle between the muscle fibres. An example of the great extent to which unstriped muscle can develop, to meet the demands made upon its power, is given by the womb, whose muscular wall develops so much during pregnancy that the organ increases from the weight of 1 ounce (28 G.) to a weight of 1½ pounds (680 G.), decreasing again to its former small size in the course of a month after child-birth.

Physiology of Contraction.—A muscle is an elaborate chemico-physical system for producing heat and mechanical work. The total energy liberated by a contracting muscle can be exactly measured. From 25 per cent. to 30 per cent. of the total energy expended is used in mechanical work. A steam engine puts out between 7 per cent. to 20 per cent. of its energy in work. Muscle is therefore mechanically much more efficient. The heat of contracting muscle makes an important contribution to the maintenance of the heat of the body.

The energy of muscular contraction is derived from a complicated series of chemical reactions. Complex substances are broken down and built up again, supplying each other with energy for this purpose. The first reaction is the breakdown of adenyl-pyrophosphate into phosphoric acid and adenylic acid (derived from nucleic acid); this supplies the immediate energy for contraction. Next phosphocreatine breaks

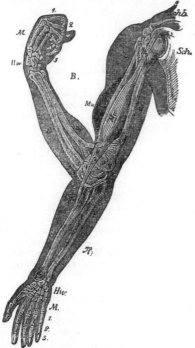

Fig. 286.—Human arm, showing the mode of action of a muscle. *A*, Forearm extended; *B*, forearm flexed; *O*, upper arm; *Sp*, radius; *E*, ulna; *Hw*, carpus; *M*, metacarpal bones; 1, 2, 3, phalanges; *Mu*, biceps muscle (the part shaded deep black shows the extent of the muscle when the lower arm is flexed); *SS*, tendons of the biceps; *Sch*, shoulder-blade (scapula); *Schb*, collar-bone (clavicle). (Schmeil's *Zoology*.)

down into creatine and phosphoric acid, giving energy for the resynthesis of adenyl-pyrophosphate. Creatine is a normal nitrogenous constituent of muscle. Then glycogen through the intermediary stage of sugar bound to

phosphate breaks down into lactic acid to supply energy for the resynthesis of phosphocreatine. Finally part of the lactic acid is oxidized to supply energy for building up the rest of the lactic acid into glycogen again. If there is not enough oxygen, lactic acid accumulates and fatigue results.

There are some points to be noticed in this modern version of muscular activity. First, muscle contraction and relaxation take place in the absence of oxygen—the anærobic phase. Secondly, oxygen comes into the picture in the phase of recovery, and by oxidizing some of the lactic acid winds up the contractile mechanism once more. Thirdly, the energy of contraction does not come directly from the breakdown of glycogen.

The whole of the chemical changes are mediated by the action of several enzymes.

Involuntary muscle has several peculiarities of contraction. In the heart *rhythmicality* is an important feature, one beat appearing to be, in a sense, the cause of the next beat. *Tonus* is a character of all muscle, but particularly of unstriped muscle in some localities, as in the walls of arteries. Muscles are not held either slack or taut, but in a slightly stretched condition, so that when occasion arises they are ready for instant action, while the arteries owe their elasticity and strength mainly to this fact. The involuntary muscle, forming the middle coat of the bowels, gland-ducts, and other tubes, contracts in the so-called *vermicular movement*, or peristalsis, which means that a ring of contraction passes slowly along the tube, at a rate of about 1 inch per second, the muscle relaxing as the ring of contraction passes on.

Fatigue of muscle comes on when a muscle is made to act for some time. It is due, not to wearing out of the muscle's power, but to the accumulation of waste products, especially sarcolactic acid, produced by the muscle's activity. These substances affect the end plates of the nerve controlling the muscle, and so prevent destructive over-action of the muscle. As they are rapidly swept away by the blood, the muscle, after a rest, particularly if the rest be accompanied by massage or by gentle contractions to quicken the circulation, recovers rapidly from the fatigue. After great muscular activity over the whole body, a more lasting fatigue is produced by the accumulation of these products, and by their action upon the central nervous system, this being recovered from after a prolonged rest, during which the waste substances are excreted by the lungs, kidneys, and other excretory organs.

Rigor mortis is a condition which comes on in the muscles after death, and to which the general stiffening of the body is due. It consists in a state of permanent, wasteful contraction, beginning in the muscles of the neck and lower jaw at a period which varies from ten minutes to seven hours after death, and spreading gradually over the whole body. It comes on quickest after death from exhaustion, or from some weakening disease ; and, occasionally, after violent injuries causing death, it comes on instantaneously, so that the posture of the body is fixed in the attitude in which death occurs. The rigidity lasts usually from sixteen to twenty-four hours, but its duration is extremely variable, being longer, as a rule, when its onset has been slow. (*See* DEATH, SIGNS OF.)

Muscular system, popularly known as ' the flesh ', comprises all the voluntary muscles, and amounts in an average man of 154 pounds (70 kg.) to about 62 pounds (28 kg.), or over two-fifths of the whole body weight. The total number of the voluntary muscles, each of which is named, amounts to about 620, including the muscles of both sides. Each muscle constitutes a separate organ, controlled by a special nerve or nerves, which connect it with the spinal cord and brain, where, however, actions and combined movements are represented rather than individual muscles (*see* BRAIN). The fleshy part of the muscle is known as its belly, and there is usually at either end a tendon, by which the muscle is inserted into bone or other structure, upon which it acts (Figs. 282, 286). One end is more fixed than the other, as a rule, the rigid end being known as the origin of the muscle, the more mobile end as its insertion.

UPPER LIMB.—*Between the trunk and limb* run the following muscles : the trapezius, latissimus dorsi, large and small rhomboids, and levator of the angle of the scapula, behind ; and the large and small pectoral, the subclavius, and serratus magnus muscles in front. *In the shoulder region* lie the deltoid, supraspinatus, infraspinatus, large and small teres, and the subscapular muscles. *In the upper arm* the coracobrachialis, biceps, and brachialis anticus occupy the front, while the triceps and anconeus fill up the back of the arm. *In the forearm* the muscles in front that bend the wrist and fingers, or turn the hand palm downwards, are the round pronator of the radius, the radial flexor of the wrist, the long palmar, the ulnar flexor of the wrist, the superficial and deep flexors of the fingers, the long flexor of the thumb, and the square pronator of the radius ; while the muscles on the back of the forearm that extend the fingers and bend the wrist backwards, or turn the hand palm upwards, are the long supinator of the radius, longer and shorter radial extensors of the wrist, common extensor of the fingers, extensor of the little finger, ulnar extensor of the wrist, short supinator of the radius, the extensors of the metacarpal bone, of the first joint, and of the second joint of the thumb, and the extensor of the forefinger. *In the palm of the hand* there are four lumbrical muscles, the short palmar muscle, three muscles each for the thumb and little finger, which respectively abduct, oppose, and flex these digits, an adductor of the thumb, and, in the spaces between the metacarpal bones, seven interosseous muscles.

LOWER LIMB.—*Muscles of the hip* are the ilio-psoas in front, and, behind, the three gluteus muscles forming the prominence of the buttock, with the pyriform, external and internal obturator, two gemelli, and quadratus femoris muscles under cover of the largest gluteal muscle, while to the outer side lies the tensor of the sheath of the thigh. *On the back of the thigh* lie the biceps, semitendinosus, and semimembranosus muscles, whose tendons, standing out prominently behind the knee, are known collectively as the ham-strings. *In front of the thigh* are placed the sartorius, which is the longest, and the quadriceps extensor of the leg, which is the largest muscle of

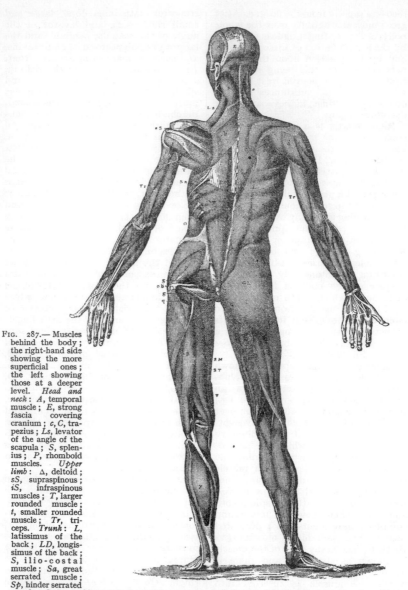

Fig. 287.— Muscles behind the body; the right-hand side showing the more superficial ones; the left showing those at a deeper level. *Head and neck*: A, temporal muscle; E, strong fascia covering cranium; c, C, trapezius; Ls, levator of the angle of the scapula; S, splenius; P, rhomboid muscles. *Upper limb*: Δ, deltoid; sS, supraspinous; iS, infraspinous muscles; T, larger rounded muscle; t, smaller rounded muscle; Tr, triceps. *Trunk*: L, latissimus of the back; LD, longissimus of the back; S, ilio-costal muscle; Sa, great serrated muscle; Sp, hinder serrated muscle; O, inner oblique muscle of abdomen. *Lower limb*: GL, largest gluteal muscle; p, pyriform muscle; ob, inner obturator with g, g, two gemellus muscles; q, square muscle of the thigh; B, biceps of the thigh; SM, semimembranous; ST, semitendinous muscles; V, inner vastus; Γ, Γ, two heads of the gastrocnemius; γ, soleus; P, p, peroneal muscles. (*Ency. Brit.*, 9th Edition, vol. i.)

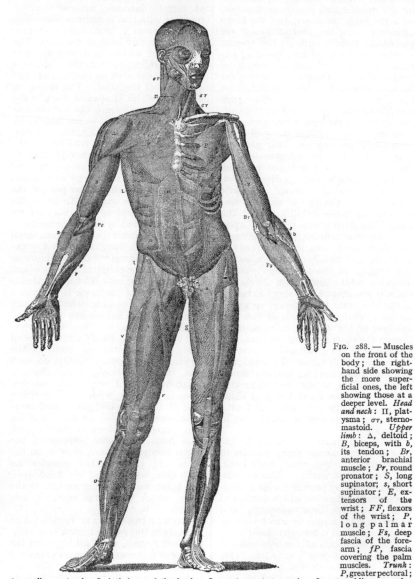

Fig. 288. — Muscles on the front of the body; the right-hand side showing the more superficial ones, the left showing those at a deeper level. *Head and neck*: Π, platysma; στ, sternomastoid. *Upper limb*: Δ, deltoid; B, biceps, with b, its tendon; Br, anterior brachial muscle; Pr, round pronator; S, long supinator; s, short supinator; E, extensors of the wrist; FF, flexors of the wrist; P, long palmar muscle; Fs, deep fascia of the forearm; fP, fascia covering the palm muscles. *Trunk*: P, greater pectoral; p, smaller pectoral; L, latissimus of the back; S, great serrated muscle; O, outer oblique muscle; R, straight muscle; and T, transverse muscle of the abdomen. *Lower limb*: a, A, adductors; s, sartorius; t, tensor of the fascia of the thigh; g, gracilis; v, V, outer and inner vastus; p, peroneal muscles; U, anterior tibial muscle. (*Ency. Brit.*, 9th Edition, vol. i.)

the body. *On the inner side of the thigh* lie the gracilis and pectineus muscles, with the long, the short, and the large adductors. *On the front of the leg* are placed the tibialis anticus, the special extensor of the great toe, the long extensor of the toes, and the peroneus tertius muscles. *On the outer side of the leg* are two muscles, the long and short peroneal muscles, whose tendons pass down behind the outer ankle to the foot. *On the back of the leg* are two groups of muscles. The superficial group of three muscles, consisting of the gastrocnemius, a double-bellied muscle, and the soleus, which is flat and projects slightly beneath the gastrocnemius, together with the small plantaris muscle, forms the calf of the leg, and ends in the tendo Achillis behind the heel. The deep group lies close upon the bones, and consists of the popliteus, long flexor of the toes, long flexor of the great toe, and tibialis posticus muscles, the tendons of the last three passing down behind the inner ankle. *In the foot* there is one muscle, the short extensor of the toes, upon the 'dorsum' or upper surface; while in the sole of the foot are four layers of small muscles, comprising the short flexor of the toes, and abductors of the great and little toes ; the accessory flexor of the toes, and four lumbrical muscles ; the short flexor of the great toe, oblique and transverse adductors of the great toe, and short flexor of the little toe; and in the fourth layer seven interosseous muscles, as in the hand.

FACE AND HEAD.—Attached to the auricle of the ear are three muscles of feeble power, which raise, draw back, and flatten the auricle. The eyelids, nose, and lips are provided with numerous flattened muscles, which dilate and draw together these openings, and which form the means by which varying facial expression is brought about.

The movements of the eye-ball are effected by six small muscles. (*See* EYE.) The movements of the lower jaw in chewing are controlled by four muscles on each side : the masseter muscle, which can be felt on the hinder part of the cheek as the jaws are closed; the temporal muscle, felt in the region of the temple ; and the outer and inner pterygoid muscles, attached to the deep surface of the jaw-bone.

Within the mouth the tongue consists of certain intrinsic muscle bundles, together with four muscles on each side, which connect it with the lower jaw, hyoid bone, and base of the skull. The floor of the mouth is formed by four muscles, which pass from the hyoid bone in front of the neck up to the lower jaw and base of the skull. The throat or pharynx, which is open in front to the nose, the mouth, and the larynx, one beneath the other, is closed behind by three broad, flat muscles, the superior, middle, and inferior constrictors of the pharynx, and is swung from the base of the skull by the stylo-pharyngeus muscle on either side. The soft palate, which separates the hinder part of the cavities of nose and mouth from one another, consists of five muscles on each side covered by mucous membrane. The larynx is controlled by eleven small muscles, which open or close its opening, and render the vocal cords more or less tense in the production of the voice.

FRONT OF NECK.—The most prominent feature of the neck is the thick sterno-mastoid muscle, which on each side runs from behind the ear downwards and forwards to the breast-bone and collar-bone. Partly under cover of these and protecting the front of the larynx are four small muscles on each side, the sterno-hyoid, sterno-thyroid, thyro-hyoid, and omohyoid muscles. Deep in the neck, behind, and to either side of the windpipe, gullet, and large blood-vessels, lie the anterior, middle, and posterior scalene muscles, which pass from the spinal column to the upper two ribs. Lying close upon the spine are three rectus muscles on each side, which bend the head upon the spine, and the long muscle of the neck, which bends the spine in this region.

BACK OF THE NECK AND TRUNK.—The muscles in this region form a very complicated system, most arising from the spines or transverse processes of several vertebræ or from a number of ribs, and running upwards to be attached to another series of vertebræ or ribs some distance above, whilst the upper muscles of the set are attached to the hinder portion of the skull. These muscles form a couple of strong columns running the whole length of the back from the loins to the head, with a groove between in which the line of vertebral spines can be felt. The upper and lower serrated muscles of the back are muscles of respiration passing from ribs to spine, and, together with the splenius muscle in the neck, form a superficial layer. Beneath them the erector spinæ, the great muscle which supports the back, runs the whole distance from the sacrum to the skull, obtaining at numerous points attachments to the spines and transverse processes of the vertebræ and to the neighbouring portions of the ribs. This muscle, along with those about to be mentioned, is of great power, having, even in moderately strong persons, a lifting power of 200 to 400 pounds (90 to 180 kg.). Covered by the erector are the complexus and transversospinales group of muscles, in which all the muscles ascend with an inward inclination ; a series of short muscles connecting succeeding vertebræ with one another ; and four small muscles passing from the uppermost two vertebræ to the skull. These last-named muscles incline and rotate the trunk and head from side to side.

CHEST.—The diaphragm is the chief muscle of this part of the body (see DIAPHRAGM). Next in importance come the outer and inner intercostal muscles, which form a double layer of oblique fibres filling up the gaps between the ribs, the fibres of the two muscles running in different directions. There are also levators of the ribs, which pass each from a vertebra to the rib beneath it ; subcostal muscles, and the triangularis sterni muscle, which are of feeble development. All these muscles share in the act of inspiration.

ABDOMEN.—The sides and front of the abdomen, unprotected by any bone beneath the level of the ribs, are enclosed by thick muscular layers strengthened by sheets of fibrous tissue. On the sides of the abdomen are three muscles—the external oblique, consisting of fibres which run downwards and forwards from the lower eight ribs ; the internal oblique, under cover of the first, consisting of fibres which run upwards and forwards from the haunchbone, and fibrous layers in its neighbourhood ; and thirdly, the transversalis muscle, of which the fibres run horizontally forward from the lower

six ribs, the lumbar vertebræ, and the haunch-bone. The fibres of all three muscles end along a curved line, the semilunar line, which is plainly visible upon the surface of the abdomen, running with a curve from its upper to its lower end, and distant, at the level of the navel, some 4 or 5 inches (10 or 12·5 cm.) from the middle line. From the curved line a sheet of dense fibrous tissue runs inwards, those of the two sides meeting down the middle line of the body. Embedded in this fibrous sheet is a strong muscle upon each side, the rectus abdominis, which is 3 or 4 inches (7·5 or 10 cm.) broad, almost an inch (25 mm.) thick in muscular persons, and runs vertically from the front of the pelvis up to the lower part of the chest. It is a muscle of great strength, and is divided into four or five sections, by tendinous intervals, which run across the muscle, and which, in well-developed persons, form distinct transverse depressions on the front of the abdomen. The quadratus lumborum is still another muscle situated, behind, in the gap between the last rib and the haunch-bone. Other small muscles close the lower opening of the pelvis, and are associated with the functions of the bowel and genital organs.

MUSCLES, DISEASES OF. — The muscles are singularly free from liability to diseases which commonly affect other tissues, this being the result, probably, of their activity, good blood supply, and the changes constantly taking place in them. Wasting of muscles sometimes occurs as a symptom of disease in other organs—for example, damage to the nervous system, as in infantile paralysis or in the disease known as progressive muscular atrophy (see PARALYSIS).

INFLAMMATION (myositis) of various types may occur. As the result of injury, an abscess may develop (see ABSCESS), although wounds affecting muscle generally heal well. Tuberculous inflammation in muscles is almost unknown. A growth due to syphilis, known as a ' gumma ', sometimes forms a hard, almost painless swelling in a muscle. Rheumatism is another type of chronic inflammation (see RHEUMATISM) to which muscles are very liable. Fibroid and even bony degeneration may occur in muscles which are the seat of long-continued irritation, or which receive a poor blood supply, the former, for example, taking place under certain conditions in the heart, the latter affecting the thigh muscles of those who ride much.

RUPTURE of a muscle may occur, without any external wound, as the result of a spasmodic effort. It may tear the muscle right across, as sometimes happens to the feeble plantaris muscle in running and leaping, or part of the muscle may be driven through its fibrous envelope, forming a 'hernia' of the muscle. The severe pain experienced in many cases of lumbago is due to tearing of one of the muscles in the back. These conditions give rise to considerable pain, but are relieved by rest and massage.

MYASTHENIA (see MYASTHENIA).

PAIN, quite apart from any inflammation or injury, may be experienced on exertion. This type of pain, known as 'myalgia', occurs especially in weakly persons, and is then relieved by rest and tonic treatment. It is also one of the common forms of rheumatism. In young children, pains of an aching character are often experienced in the muscles, especially of the legs and back, and are known as 'growing pains'. These come on especially after exertion and are relieved by resting.

CRAMP is a well-known condition due to spasm. (See CRAMP.)

PARASITES sometimes lodge in the muscles, the most common being *Trichinella spiralis*, producing the disease known as trichinosis.

TUMOURS are occasionally met with, the most common being fibroid, fatty, and sarcomatous growths (Plate VII).

MYOPATHY is a term applied to a developmental defect in certain muscles. (See MYOPATHY.)

MUSCULAR DYSTROPHY (see MYO-PATHY.)

MUSHROOM POISONING (see FUNGUS-POISONING).

MUSTARD is a yellowish powder, consisting of the dried, ripe seeds of *Brassica nigra* and *Brassica alba* mixed together. The former contains an active principle called 'sinigrin', the

608

latter contains one named 'sinalbin', while both contain a quantity of a ferment named 'myrosin', which in the presence of water converts the two active principles into the volatile oil to which the action of mustard is due. This oil is extremely irritating to skin and mucous surfaces with which it is brought in contact.

Uses.—Externally mustard is used made into a paste with water and spread upon brown or cartridge paper, or made up with linseed into a poultice, for its irritant action upon the skin, in cases of rheumatism, inflamed joints, neuralgia, and for application to the chest and abdomen when organs in these cavities are inflamed. These applications should not, as a rule, last longer than twenty minutes. Liniment of mustard is used for similar purposes. In a hot or cold bath one or two tablespoonfuls of mustard have an invigorating effect. (For Mustard Pack, see WET PACK.) The effect of mustard, if too pronounced, may be relieved by applying olive oil.

Internally, mustard is used in small quantities as a stimulant to digestion, and in large quantities as an emetic, a tablespoonful of mustard powder being stirred up in a tumblerful of cold water for the latter purpose.

MUSTINE is the *British Pharmacopœia* name for the *bis* form of nitrogen mustard. The nitrogen mustards have an action comparable to that of ionizing radiation and inhibit cell division. Mustine is used in the treatment of chronic leukæmia and Hodgkin's disease.

MYALGIA (μῦς, a muscle; ἄλγος, pain) means pain in a muscle. (See LUMBAGO *and* RHEUMATISM, *and* BORNHOLM DISEASE.)

MYASTHENIA GRAVIS (μῦς, muscle; ἀσθένεια, weakness) is the name given to a serious disorder of rare occurrence, in which the chief symptoms are muscular weakness and a special tendency for fatigue to come on rapidly when efforts are made.

The cause of the disease is not accurately known, but the symptom are due to deficiency in the muscles of racetylcholine which is necessary for muscular contraction. It affects, as a rule, persons in early adult life. Not only the voluntary muscles, but those connected with the acts of swallowing, breathing, etc., become infiltrated with small round cells and progressively weaker, though there is no very marked wasting. Rest and avoidance of undue exertion, so as carefully to husband the strength, are necessary, and injections of edrophonium, neostigmine bromide, or pyridostigmine at intervals enable the muscles to be used and in some cases have a curative effect. Good results are being reported in certain cases by surgical removal of the thymus.

MYCOSIS FUNGOIDES is a rare neoplastic condition of the reticuloendothelial system, characterized in its later stages by multiple tumours of the skin. The course is prolonged and almost invariably ends fatally.

MYCOSIS ($\mu\acute{\nu}\kappa\eta s$, a fungus) is the general term applied to diseases due to the growth of fungi in the body. Among some of the simplest and commonest mycoses are ringworm, favus, and thrush. The Madura-foot of India, actinomycosis, and occasional cases of pneumonia and suppurative ear disease are also due to the growth of moulds in the bodily tissues.

MYDRIASIS ($\mu\nu\delta\rho\acute{\iota}a\sigma\iota s$) means a state of unusual dilatation of the pupil. Drugs which cause dilatation of the pupil, such as belladonna and cocaine, are known as ' mydriatics '.

MYELEMIA and MYELOCYTHÆMIA ($\mu\nu\epsilon\lambda\acute{o}s$, marrow; $\kappa\acute{\nu}\tau os$, cell; $a\acute{\iota}\mu a$, blood) are terms applied to leukæmia of the spleno-medullary variety. (*See* LEUKÆMIA.)

MYELIN ($\mu\nu\epsilon\lambda\acute{o}s$, marrow) is the name given to the white fat-like substance forming a sheath round medullated or myelinated nerve-fibres in the nerves and in the central nervous system.

MYELITIS ($\mu\nu\epsilon\lambda\acute{o}s$, marrow) is inflammation of the spinal cord. In the *acute* variety the nerve elements in the affected part become disintegrated and softened; in the *chronic* form the change is slower, and the diseased area tends to become denser (sclerosed), the nerve-

substance being replaced by connective tissue. In the variety known as *poliomyelitis* nerve-cells in the grey matter of the cord become destroyed (*see* PARALYSIS).

Causes.—The chief causes of myelitis are injuries or diseases affecting the spinal column, extension of inflammation from the membranes of the cord to its substance (*see* MENINGITIS), and occasionally some pre-existing infection or inflammatory condition, such as a fever. The chronic form is most common in adults, while poliomyelitis, affecting the anterior horn of grey matter in the cord, is more common in children and young people.

Symptoms.—Myelitis may affect any portion of the spinal cord. Its most frequent site is in the lower part, and its existence there is marked by the sudden or gradual occurrence of weakness of motor power in the legs (which tends to pass into complete paralysis), impairment or loss of sensibility in the parts implicated, nutritive changes affecting the skin and giving rise to bed sores, together with bladder and bowel derangements. There is, in addition, if the disease affects the cord at a level above that from which the nerves of the lower limbs originate, a 'spastic', or jerky condition, in which, owing to the control of the higher centres in the brain being cut off, involuntary contractions of the muscles and movements of these limbs take place. In the acute form, in which there is at first pain in the region of the spine and much constitutional disturbance, death may take place rapidly from extension of the disease to those portions of the cord connected with the muscles of respiration and the heart, from an acute bed sore, which is very apt to form, or from some intercurrent disease. Recovery to a certain extent may, however, take place ; or, again, the disease may pass into the chronic form. In the latter, the progress is usually slow, the general health remaining tolerably good for a time, but gradually the strength fails, the patient becomes more helpless, and ultimately sinks exhausted, or is cut off by some complication.

Treatment.—The treatment for myelitis in its acute stage is similar to that for spinal meningitis. When the disease is chronic, the most that can be hoped for is the relief of symptoms. Benefit is sometimes derived from the employment of electricity, in maintaining the action of the muscles involved, and from the use of baths and douches to the spine. Above all, careful and regular attention to the functions of the bladder and bowels is essential, and also attention to the skin of the back, upon which bed sores are liable to form.

MYELOCYTE (μυελός, marrow; κύτος, cell) is the name given to one of the typical cells of red bone-marrow from which the granular white corpuscles of the blood are produced. They are found in the blood also in certain forms of leukæmia.

MYELOMA is the name of a tumour made up of bone-marrow cells and generally occurring in the marrow of more than one bone at the same time.

MYELOMALACIA is the term applied to morbid softening of the spinal cord as a result of injury, pressure, inflammation, or arterial disease.

MYELOMATOSIS is a malignant process involving the bone marrow. It runs an invariably fatal course.

MYIASIS (μυῖα, a fly) is a term applied to any disease caused by maggots or flies.

MYOCARDITIS (μῦς, muscle; καρδία, the heart) means inflammation of the muscular wall of the heart.

MYOCARDIUM is the name applied to the muscular substance of the heart.

MYOMA (μῦς, muscle ; -oma, meaning tumour) is the term applied to a tumour, almost invariably of a simple nature, which consists mainly of muscle fibres. These muscle tumours often occur in the uterus.

MYOPATHY (μῦς, muscle ; πάθος, disease), also known as MUSCULAR DYSTROPHY or IDIOPATHIC MUSCULAR ATROPHY, is the term applied to a somewhat rare condition in which wasting takes place in certain muscles, with or without previous increase in bulk of these muscles, and apparently without any affection of the nervous system. The cause of the condition is still obscure, although the disease appears

610

to run in families, being transmitted, like some other hereditary diseases, by the mothers. Generally the disease appears in early childhood, and it seldom affects persons over the age of twenty. The changes which are found after death show that a simple wasting away of the muscle fibres takes place, and that these are in some cases to a great extent replaced by fatty and fibrous tissue.

Symptoms.—There are three chief types of myopathy. The commonest, known as 'pseudo-hypertrophic muscular dystrophy', affects particularly the upper part of the lower limbs of children. The muscles of buttocks, thighs, and calves seem excessively well developed, but nevertheless the child is clumsy, weak on his legs, and has difficulty in picking himself up when he falls. In another form of the disease, which begins a little later, as a rule about the age of fourteen, the muscles of the upper arm are first affected, and those of the spine and lower limbs become weak later on. In a third type, which begins about this age, the muscles of the face, along with certain of the shoulder and upper arm muscles, show the first signs of wasting. All the forms have this in common, that the affected muscles grow weaker till their power to contract is quite lost. In the first form, the patients seldom reach the age of twenty, falling victims to some disease which, to ordinary persons, would not be serious. In the other forms the wasting, after progressing to a certain extent, often remains stationary for the rest of life.

Treatment.—The general health must be well maintained, and various tonics are of use. Massage, electricity, and exercise short of fatigue are of the utmost importance, and above all, care must be taken that these invalids are not exposed unduly, as they succumb easily to chest affections.

The education and management of these unfortunate children raise many difficulties. Much help in dealing with these problems can be obtained from the Muscular Dystrophy Group, 26 Borough High Street, London, S.E.1.

MYOPIA (μύωψ, blinking ; from μύω, I close ; ὤψ, the eye), or SHORT-SIGHT, means a condition in which, owing to the lens of the eye being too highly convex or the ball of the eye too long, rays of light are brought to a focus before they reach the retina, and so form circles of diffused light upon it. It is the opposite of hypermetropia or long-sight. (*See* VISION, DISORDERS OF.)

MYOSIS (μύω, I close), or MIOSIS, means a narrowing of the pupil. Some persons, largely on account of having a small amount of pigment in the eye, possess naturally small pupils, but apart from this, the condition is due usually to paralysis of the sympathetic nerve-fibres supplying the pupil, or to drugs such as opium and eserine.

MYOSITIS (μῦς, a muscle) means inflammation of a muscle. (*See* MUSCLES, DISEASES OF.)

MYOTICS (μύω, I close), or MIOTICS, is the term applied to drugs which contract the pupil of the eye, such as eserine.

MYOTONIA (μῦς, muscle; τόνος, tension) is a condition found in occasional individuals in which the muscles, though possessed of normal power, contract only very slowly. The stiffness disappears as the muscles are used.

MYRINGOTOMY is the term for describing the operation of cutting the drum of the ear in cases of acute inflammation of the middle ear.

MYRRH (μύρρα) is a gum-resin obtained from *Commiphora myrrha*, an Arabian myrtle tree. It stimulates the functions of mucous membranes with which it is brought in contact or by which it is excreted. Tincture of myrrh is used for a gargle in sore throat, as a tooth-wash when the gums are inflamed, and as an ingredient of cough mixtures.

MYXŒDEMA (μύξα, mucus ; οἴδημα, a swelling) is a disease characterized by a swollen and degenerative condition of the subcutaneous and connective tissues throughout the body, due to a defect in the thyroid gland.

Causes.—Beyond the fact that it is about seven times more common in women than in men, and that the great majority of cases arise in middle life, between the ages of thirty and fifty, little is known as to the cause of the thyroid deficiency. In a small minority of cases it follows partial removal of the thyroid gland, a common form of treatment of thyrotoxicosis (*q.v.*).

The important part of the thyroid gland secretion is an iodine-holding body (thyroxin) which is concerned in the processes of nutrition. Deprivation of the secretion causes a deposition of fat, a varying degree of dropsy, and above all an excessive formation of loose connective tissue, from which there is often obtainable after death a considerable amount of mucoid material, a fact to which the disease owes its name. This connective tissue presses upon and destroys the proper tissues of the organs.

Symptoms.—A person suffering from myxœdema to a marked degree presents a most characteristic appearance. The face is swollen, the features coarse, and the expression dull and unrelieved by any passing emotions or interests. The skin generally is dry and yellow, but the cheeks are usually bright red in contrast. The hair is thin, harsh, and brittle, and the person may even be completely bald. The intellectual functions also are slow, the speech is deliberate, the formation of ideas, as for example in answer to questions, and indeed all the ordinary affairs of life, take far longer than in the case of healthy persons ; but there is, nevertheless, in the early stages, no impairment in the quality of mental processes. Later, memory becomes bad, and the person grows deaf and very drowsy. Although at first the temper is placid and lethargic, in the later stages irritability and delusions appear, and the person, if untreated, may ultimately become insane.

Along with these more obvious changes there is general swelling all over the body. The hands assume the so-called ' spade-like ' appearance, and the person, partly in consequence of the slowness of his movements, partly as the result of weakness, becomes very ungainly. The cold is often complained of by the invalid, who has difficulty in keeping himself warm, and, if the temperature be taken, it is usually found to be subnormal : 96° to 98° F. (35·5° to 36·7° F.). A characteristic finding is a marked lowering of the basal metabolic rate.

Cases last for many years even when untreated, and the disease is seldom directly fatal. As a rule myxœdematous patients grow better and worse from time to time, although the trend is for the disease to get more marked. When the case is treated, improvement almost always takes place with great rapidity, and treatment is effective even after the person has been ill for many years.

Treatment.—This consists of the administration of thyroid gland, preferably in the form of the dry extract of the *British Pharmacopœia*. The dosage depends upon the severity of the condition, but it is always advisable to start with a dose of ½ grain (30 mg.) and increase this gradually. Some patients are sensitive to quite small doses, and if too big a dose is given initially there may be toxic effects. Most patients require to take a maintenance dose for the rest of their lives.

MYXOMA (μύξα, mucus; -*oma*, meaning tumour) is the name applied to a tumour consisting of very imperfect connective tissue, and containing a peculiar mucus-like juice.

MYXOVIRUSES include the influenza viruses A, B, and C ; the parainfluenza viruses, types 1 to 3 ; and respiratory syncytial virus which is an important cause of respiratory disease in the early years of life.

N

NÆVUS (*naevus*, a mole) is the term applied to birth-marks consisting of a mass of dilated blood-vessels. These structures may take the form of the large 'port-wine stain' often seen upon the face, for which little can be done, or they may occur as swellings of a more restricted nature, usually of a red or bluish colour. Many nævi tend to decrease in size as the child advances in years ; or if not, the blemish can often be removed by excision of the piece of skin that is involved, or by electrolysis.

NAILS (*see* SKIN).

NAILS, DISEASES OF.—The nails are subject to relatively few diseases. On the other hand, any interference with the natural appearance of the finger-nails is very unsightly, whilst the sensitive matrix of both finger- and toe-nails is extremely tender when diseased. INFLAMMATION of the nails and of the bed in which they rest occurs in various skin diseases, *e.g.* in psoriasis, eczema, fungus infections (*see* RINGWORM). The nails then become rough, thickened, irregular, discoloured, and split readily into layers. Most acute febrile diseases are accompanied by irregularities in growth of the nails, producing a transverse furrow in the nail, as it grows onwards, and these furrows on the nails serve to date a severe illness fairly accurately, the furrow gradually approaching the free margin of the nail and disappearing in about six months' time. These transverse furrows must not be confused with furrows running lengthwise, which are said to indicate a gouty constitution.

Spoon - shaped or concave nails (KOILONYCHIA) are often associated with anæmia, especially in middle-aged women, and become normal when this is treated.

ABSCESS may occur at the root of the nail (*see* WHITLOW) or underneath it near its edge. As a rule, these abscesses are caused by a minute poisoned wound, such as that due to a splinter of wood. The condition is generally very painful, but is relieved by opening, so as to allow free exit for the pus, the nail being snipped up with a pair of scissors

if necessary. The nail in these cases is often cast off.

INJURY to the nail by a blow is frequently followed by an extravasation of blood beneath it, the nail first turning black, and then often being shed. In all these cases where the nail is shed, a new nail generally appears quickly, and replaces the old one in six months, unless the matrix has been very seriously diseased or injured. While the new nail is growing, the point of the finger merely requires the protection of a finger-stall.

INGROWING NAIL is a troublesome condition affecting only the nails of the toes. It is due to a variety of causes, chief among which are the pressure of badly fitting boots, cutting away of the corners in paring the nails, and want of attention to the nails, whereby accumulation of scarf-skin and dirt collect beneath the nail, and by putrefactive changes cause ulceration of the skin at the sides. The condition also occurs in old, bedridden people, mainly for the last-named reason. The treatment is simple, though sometimes tedious. It consists in the wearing of well-made boots, cutting of the nails square across without paring away the corners (Figs. 289, 290,) and the packing two or

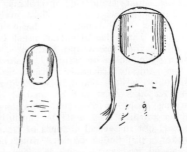

FIG. 289.—Finger-nail, showing method of cutting nail.   FIG. 290.—Toe-nail, showing correct method of cutting nail straight across.

three times daily of a shred of boric lint between the corner of the nail and the skin which it is chafing. These measures are generally sufficient after a little time, but sometimes the nail is so much thickened that the edges cannot be raised up to admit the threads of lint.

613

In this case the centre of the nail may be softened by dabbing on caustic potash, and then the nail is easily thinned down by scraping with a sharp knife till it becomes pliable. When the skin at the side of the nail bleeds very readily, this is remedied by touching with bluestone or with nitrate of silver. In severe cases a minor surgical operation may be required.

NALIDIXIC ACID is a recently introduced drug, active against Gram-negative organisms, which is proving usful in infections of the urinary tract.

NALORPHINE HYDROBROMIDE reduces or abolishes most of the actions of morphine and similarly acting narcotics, such as pethidine. It is used as an antidote in the treatment of overdosage with these drugs. It has no effect as an antidote to overdosage with barbiturates.

NANISM is another name for dwarfism.

NAPHTHOL, or BETA-NAPHTHOL, is a coal-tar derivative used sometimes externally in antiseptic dressings.

NAPKIN RASH is the term applied to the eruption which tends to occur on the buttocks of infants, due to too infrequent changing of soiled napkins or inadequate laundering of napkins. Prevention consists of four main measures. (i) When the baby is bathed, particular attention must be paid to the creases and folds of the skin which must be carefully washed, then equally carefully dried and sprinkled with a bland baby powder. (ii) Napkins must not be washed in strong soaps or detergent solutions. After washing they must be carefully rinsed out in several changes of clean water. (iii) Soiled napkins must be changed frequently. (iv) Waterproof drawers should be reserved for special social occasions, and not used all and every day.

Should the skin become inflamed, washing it with a 1 per cent. solution of sodium sulphate, followed by careful drying and the application of calamine lotion, is often useful. An alternative application which has stood the test of time is zinc and castor oil ointment.

614

NAPRAPATHY (Russian, *napravlyat*, to set right; πάθος disease) is the term applied to a system of healing which attributes disease to disorder in the ligaments and connective tissues.

NARCISSISM (*Narcissus*) is a term applied to an abnormal mental state characterized by excessive admiration of self.

NARCOLEPSY is the name of a condition in which uncontrollable 'attacks' of sleep occur. It is often associated with cataplexy.

NARCOSIS (νάρκωσις, a benumbing) is a condition of profound insensibility, resembling sleep so far that the unconscious person can still be roused slightly by great efforts, or at all events is not entirely indifferent to sensory stimuli. It is most commonly produced by drugs, such as opium, but may also be due to poisons formed within the body, as in the uræmia of Bright's disease.

NARCOTICS (ναρκωτικός, making numb). (*See* HYPNOTICS.)

NARES is the Latin word for the nostrils.

NASAL DISORDERS (*see* NOSE, DISEASES OF).

NASOPHARYNX is the name given to the upper part of the throat, lying behind the nasal cavity. (*See* NOSE.)

NAUSEA (ναυσία, sea-sickness; from ναῦς, a ship) means a feeling that vomiting is about to take place. (*See* VOMITING.)

NAVEL, or UMBILICUS, is the scar on the abdomen marking the point where the umbilical cord joined the body in embryonic life. (*See* AFTERBIRTH.)

NEAR-SIGHT (*see* MYOPIA).

NEBULA (*nebula*, mist) is the term applied to a slight opacity on the cornea producing a haze in the field of vision, and also to any oily preparation to be sprayed into the nose from a nebulizer, an apparatus for splitting up a fluid into fine droplets.

NECATOR AMERICANUS, or UNCINARIA, is the name of a parasite hookworm, closely resembling but smaller than the *Ankylostoma duodenale* and responsible in some cases for the disease of ankylostomiasis. It is found in America, West and Central Africa, India, Ceylon, China, Australia, and the Pacific Islands.

NECK is that portion of the body which extends from the upper limit of the chest to the base of the skull. Its main function is to support the head. Through its front part run the passages for the air and the food. The great bulk of the neck is composed of seven cervical vertebræ with the muscles attached thereto, in front and behind. (*See* MUSCLES.) Within the canal formed by the rings of these vertebræ lies the cervical part of the spinal cord, from which proceed the nerves that control the movements of neck and arms.

In front of the spinal column lies the pharynx or throat-cavity, extending from the base of the skull above down to the lower edge of the sixth vertebra, where the gullet continues it directly

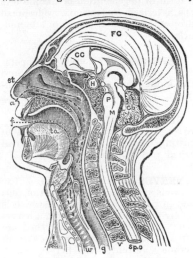

FIG. 291.—Vertical section through the middle of the head and neck. The passages for air *a*, are indicated by a heavy dotted line, those for the food *f*, by a fainter line ; *et*, Eustachian tube ; *l*, larynx ; *w*, windpipe ; *t*, tonsil ; *to*, tongue ; *g*, gullet ; *v*, vertebral column ; *sp.c*, spinal cord. For other letters, *see* BRAIN. (After Braune.)

downwards, while the larynx opens out of it in front (Fig. 291). The larynx is close to the surface of the front of the neck, and the thyroid cartilage can be readily seen and felt beneath the skin. (*See* LARYNX.) The larynx is continued downwards by the windpipe, and just beneath the larynx the isthmus of the thyroid gland can be felt crossing the windpipe and connecting the two lobes of the gland which lie one on either side of the larynx. The strong sterno-mastoid muscle is a prominent object on each side of the neck, running from the mastoid process of the skull down to the breast-bone and inner end of the clavicle, and under cover of it lies a fibrous sheath containing the carotid artery, internal jugular vein, and vagus nerve. The sterno-mastoid muscle divides each side of the neck into two triangular areas, in which lie several important nerves and branches of these blood-vessels, as well as chains of lymphatic glands. Several large superficial veins run down the neck, and are of importance, because in wounds of the neck they may give rise to much bleeding. The chief of these are the external jugular vein, running straight downwards from the angle of the jaw, and the anterior jugular vein, running downwards from beneath the chin, not far from the middle line. At the root of the neck the apex of each lung projects a short distance from the chest into the neck.

NECROPSY (νεκρός, a dead body ; ὄψις, a view) is another name for autopsy. (*See* AUTOPSY.)

NECROSIS (νέκρωσις, a state of death) means death of a limited portion of tissue, the term being most commonly applied to bones when, as the result of disease or injury, a fragment dies and separates. (*See* BONE, DISEASES OF.)

NEEDLING is the name for an operation performed by means of a needle, especially in the discission or tearing of a cataract so as to allow the fluid in the anterior chamber of the eye to dissolve it.

NEGATIVISM means a morbid tendency in a patient to do the opposite of what he is desired or directed to do. It is specially characteristic of schizophrenia.

NEGRO-LETHARGY is another name for sleeping sickness.

NEMATODE (νῆμα, thread) is a general term applied to several species of parasitic worms of more or less cylindrical shape. (*See* PARASITES.)

NEOMYCIN is an antibiotic derived from *Streptomyces fradiæ*. It has a wide antibacterial spectrum, being effective against the majority of Gram-negative bacilli. Its use is limited by the fact that it is liable to cause deafness and kidney damage. For this reason it is never given by injections. Its main use is for application to the skin, either in solution or as an ointment, for the treatment of infection of the skin. It is also given by mouth for the treatment of certain forms of enteritis due to *E. coli*.

NEONATAL MORTALITY. — The mortality of infants under one month of age. In England and Wales this has fallen markedly during the last decade: from 28·28 per 1000 related live births in 1939 to 13·8 in 1964. This improvement can be attributed to various factors: better antenatal supervision of expectant mothers; care to ensure that expectant mothers receive adequate nourishing food; improvements in the management of the complications of pregnancy and of labour. Nearly three-quarters of neonatal deaths occur during the first week of life, and the chief causes of deaths in this period are immaturity of the infant, birth injuries, congenital abnormalities, and asphyxia. After the first week the commonest cause is infection.

NEOPLASM (νέος, new ; πλάσσω, I mould), which means literally a ' new formation ', is another word for tumour.

NEPENTHE is a solution of opium in alcohol and water given in the same dose as laudanum.

NEPHRECTOMY (νεφρός, kidney ; ἐκ, out ; τέμνω, I cut) means the operation for removal of the kidney. (*See* KIDNEY, DISEASES OF.)

NEPHRITIS (νεφρός, kidney) means inflammation of the kidneys. (*See* BRIGHT'S DISEASE.)

NEPHROLITHIASIS (νεφρός, kidney; λίθος, stone) is the term applied to a condition in which calculi are present in the kidney.

NEPHROPEXY (νεφρός, kidney ; πήγνυμι, I fix) means the fixation of a floating kidney in its original position.

NEPHROPTOSIS (νεφρός, kidney ; πτῶσις, falling) means the condition in which a kidney is movable or 'floating'. (*See* KIDNEY, DISEASES OF.)

NEPHRORRHAPHY (νεφρός, kidney ; ῥαφή, a sewing) means the operation by which a movable kidney is fastened by stitches in its proper place.

NEPHROSIS is the term applied to a form of degeneration of the kidneys characterized by anæmia, widespread dropsy, and a high degree of albuminuria.

NEPHROSTOMY means the operation of making an opening into the kidney for the purpose of draining it.

NEPHROTOMY (νεφρός, kidney ; τέμνω, I cut) means the operation of cutting into the kidney, in search of calculi or for other reason.

NERVES (*nervus*, a nerve). — The nervous system consists in part of cells and in part of fibres, each of which is a long process extending from a nerve-cell. The brain and spinal cord are often spoken of together as the central nervous system ; the nerves which proceed from them, forty-three in number on each side, are named the cerebro-spinal, or peripheral nerves ; whilst the third great division, situated in the neck, thorax, and abdomen, and intimately connected with the cerebro-spinal nerves (though in its action largely independent of the brain and cord) is known as the autonomic nervous system. The last-named consists of ganglia containing nerve-cells, which are profusely connected by plexuses of nerve-fibres.

The nerve-cells originate, or receive, impulses and impressions of various sorts, which are conveyed from them to muscles, blood - vessels, etc., by efferent nerves, or received by them through afferent nerves coming from the skin, organs of sense, joints, etc. (Fig. 292). The autonomic system is concerned mainly with the movements and other functions of the internal

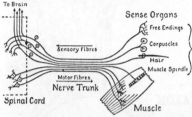

medullated and non-medullated fibres. The *medullated fibres* vary in thickness from $\frac{1}{12000}$ inch to $\frac{1}{1500}$ inch (2 to 15 microns), some nerves containing a greater proportion of the small fibres than others. All have, under the microscope, the appearance of tubes, this being due to the fact that each has an outer membranous sheath, the neurilemma, within which is a clear white material, the medullary sheath, in the centre of which runs the axis-cylinder or nerve-fibre proper (Fig. 293). The neurilemma is a strong but thin sheath with nuclei at regular intervals on its inner surface. The medullary

FIG. 292.—Diagram showing nervous connections between the central nervous system and muscle and skin. (From Best and Taylor, *The Physiological Basis of Medical Practice.* The Williams & Wilkins Co.)

organs, secreting glands, blood-vessels, etc., the activities of which proceed independently of the will.

Structure.—(1) NERVE-FIBRES.—The nerves vary much in size. The great sciatic nerve, deeply buried in the muscles on the back of the thigh, is the largest nerve in the body, being of the thickness of a lead pencil or more; other nerves reach about the size of goose-quills, and from these there are all gradations, down to the minute single fibres distributed to muscle-fibres or to skin. A nerve, such as the sciatic, possesses a strong, outer fibrous sheath, called the epineurium, within which lie bundles of nerve-fibres, divided from one another by partitions of fibrous tissue, in which run blood-vessels that nourish the nerve. Each of these bundles is surrounded by a sheath of ts own, known as perineurium, and within the bundle fine partitions of fibrous tissue, known as endoneurium, divide up the bundle into groups of fibres. The blood-vessels and lymphatics of the nerves divide into fine branches, which run in these sheaths and partitions of fibrous tissue. The finest subdivisions of the nerves are the fibres, and these are of two kinds—

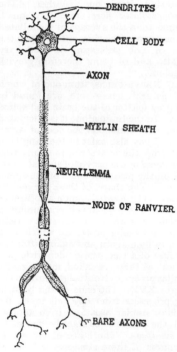

FIG. 293.—Diagrammatic representation of a nerve. (From Best and Taylor, *The Physiological Basis of Medical Practice.* The Williams & Wilkins Co.)

sheath is composed of fatty material containing lecithin and cholesterin, and to it the white colour of the nerves is mainly due. It is divided at regular intervals by short gaps, situated about $\frac{1}{20}$ inch apart, known as the nodes of Ranvier, but across these gaps the neurilemma and axis-cylinder are continuous. This medullary sheath is generally regarded as probably fulfilling a purpose similar to the insulating material upon electric wires and preventing nerve impulses from passing beyond the nerve-fibre by which they are conveyed. The axis-cylinder is the conducting part of the nerve, for whilst the neurilemma is absent from the fibre in its course through the brain and spinal cord, and whilst the medullary sheath is absent from non-medullated nerves, the axis-cylinder never fails. It has a striped appearance, seeming to consist of a number of fibrils which, however, cannot be separated from one another. The *non-medullated fibres* are very much thinner than the average of medullated fibres, from which they differ only in the fact of not possessing a medullary sheath, and of being therefore greyish in colour.

(2) NERVE-CELLS, from one of which springs each nerve-fibre, are found in the grey matter of the brain and spinal cord. In the brain alone it is calculated there are some 600,000,000 of these cells. They also exist in the ganglia of the sympathetic system, in connection with some of the nerves of special sense, and on the posterior roots of the spinal nerves. The shape of these nerve-cells varies. The most common appearance is that of a large clear cell, containing an oval nucleus, and running out at various points into long processes, which, as a rule, branch again and again, after the manner of a tree, these ' dendritic processes', as they are called, meeting with similar processes from neighbouring cells (Plate XVI). The ends of the branching processes from one cell touch the ends of similar processes from another cell, the points of contact being known as *synapses*. The state of closure or openness of these synapses is believed to be of great importance in quickening or blocking nerve impulses. The body of the cell has a mottled appearance, owing to its containing many bodies, known as Nissl's granules (Fig. 294), which appear to be of the nature of food material, destined to be used up when the cell is stimulated to work till reduced to a state of fatigue.

In the cerebrum, the cells are distinctly pyramidal in shape, and one of

618

the processes of each cell is much longer than the rest, forming indeed a nerve-fibre, which may run a long distance down the spinal cord. Other cells are bipolar, *i.e.* they possess but two processes, and others are unipolar, *i.e.* they possess only one process, which, a short distance from the cell, divides in a

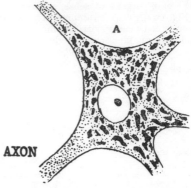

FIG. 294.—A nerve-cell, showing Nissl granules. (From Best and Taylor, *The Physiological Basis of Medical Practice*. The Williams & Wilkins Co.)

T-shaped manner, as, for example, the cells in the ganglia upon the posterior roots of the spinal nerves. Other cells are found in the grey matter of the brain, which are known as neuroglia cells. These are provided with innumerable processes that form a supporting felt-work for the nerve-cells and nerve-fibres, and act merely as connective tissue cells.

(3) NERVE-ENDINGS. — Each nerve-fibre proceeds from a nerve-cell to end in a definite organ, to or from which it carries a special form of nerve impulse. The manner in which the fibre ends in the organ to which it proceeds varies in different cases. The simplest mode of ending is that of the non-medullated fibres which proceed to the involuntary muscle-fibres, as, for example, those of the intestine. These fibres form a complex network between the layers of muscle, from which fine fibres pass between the muscle-fibres. In the heart the nerves end in a similar manner. In voluntary muscles the arrangement is more complicated. Each nerve-fibre splits up into numerous branches, which go to neighbouring muscle-fibres. Each

branch pierces the membrane surrounding its muscle-fibre, and ends by spreading out into a plate composed of granular material and numerous nuclei. The endings of sensory nerves in the skin have a special arrangement. (Fig. 295; Plate XVI). Most of these end, not in the cuticle, which is devoid of sensation, but in the projections of the true skin beneath it, where each nerve-fibre enters a small rounded bulb. Some of these bulbs found beneath the skin of the fingers are known as Pacinian corpuscles (Fig. 295 D) : about $\frac{1}{10}$ inch (2·5 mm.) ong and half that in width. These

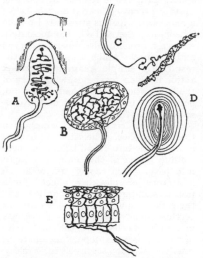

FIG. 295.—Some nerve endings. A, Meissner's corpuscle (touch); B, Krause's end bulb (cold); C, Ruffini's end organs (warmth); D, Pacinian corpuscle (deep pressure); E, bare nerve endings in cornea (pain). (From Best and Taylor, *The Physiological Basis of Medical Practice.* The Williams & Wilkins Co.)

consist of a large number of thin coats enclosing the swollen end of a nerve-fibre. Other much smaller bodies, about $\frac{1}{300}$ inch (0·8 mm.) long, known as 'touch-corpuscles', are found close beneath the cuticle all over the skin, and consist of a framework of connective tissue in which the nerve-fibre winds round and round. Similar bodies are found on the front of the eye. In other cases the nerves appear to end abruptly in cells situated in the deepest layer of the cuticle.

Development and repair.—The whole nervous system is developed from the

epiblast or outer layer of the embryo, the brain and spinal cord arising from an infolding of the surface along the back to form a tube, and all the nerves being formed directly or indirectly as outgrowths from this tube, which increase in length till they reach the muscle, skin, or other structure for which they are destined. Each nerve-fibre, as already stated, is the process of a nerve-cell, and, if a nerve be cut, that portion of its fibres which is separated from the cells immediately starts to degenerate, the medullary sheath and axis-cylinder, as a rule, breaking up (Fig. 296). Within a few days or weeks, however, a bundle of small new fibres

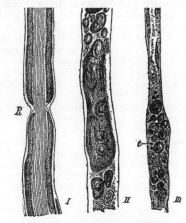

FIG. 296.—Nerve-fibres showing degeneration after an injury. I, Normal nerve-fibre, showing at *R*, a node of Ranvier; II and III, successive stages of degeneration; *t* shows the drops to which the medullary sheath is finally reduced. Magnified by 476. (Thoma's *Pathology.*)

grows out from the cut end of each fibre in that portion which has not been cut off from connection with the nerve-cells, and these grow through the scar and down the sheath of the degenerated portion till they reach the organs to which the nerve originally proceeded. Thus the nerve is restored. This process is quickened when the cut ends have been carefully brought together, and indeed there are reasons for believing that, sometimes when this is done, no degeneration takes place, but the nerve heals and again transmits impulses at once.

Functions of nerves.—The greater part of the bodily activity originates in the nerve-cells, food material being used up in the process. As a result of this activity, impulses are sent down the nerves, which act simply as trans-mitters. The impulse which passes from a nerve-cell along a nerve-fibre to a muscle may be compared to the electric spark which explodes a mine, since the nerve impulse causes sudden chemical changes in the muscle as the latter contracts (see MUSCLES). Similarly, the impulse which passes from a sensory ending in the skin along a nerve-fibre to affect nerve-cells in the spinal cord and brain, where it is ' perceived ' as a sensation, may be compared to the electric current which passes along a telephone wire to affect the receiver. Nevertheless, it must be understood that the impulse passing along a nerve is a form of motion quite different from electricity : travelling at the slow rate of about 100 feet per second, and probably more nearly resembling the motion of air-particles which produces sound. (See NERVOUS IMPULSE.)

The important fact that the anterior root of each spinal nerve is motor in function was discovered in 1811 by Sir Charles Bell. This was confirmed by Magendie in 1822, and the discovery also made that the posterior roots are sensory in function. Therefore they concluded that the anterior roots consist of motor fibres to muscles, the posterior roots of sensory fibres from the skin. The terms efferent and afferent are applied to these roots more correctly, because, in addition to motor fibres, fibres through which blood-vessels are contracted and relaxed, and fibres which control secreting glands leave the cord in the anterior roots, while, in addition to sensory fibres, fibres which bring in impulses from muscles, joints, and other organs, and inform the sense of locality as well as the sense of feeling, also enter the cord by the posterior roots.

Sensation is popularly supposed to be derived through five senses—smell, sight, hearing, taste, and touch. In addition to these, impulses are brought by special nerve-fibres and converted in the brain into sensations which furnish a sense of movement and locality, a sense of pain, and a sense of heat and cold. (See TOUCH.)

The connection between the sensory and motor systems of nerves is import-

ant. The simplest form of nerve action is that known as *automatic action*. In this a part of the nervous system, controlling, for example, the lungs, goes on rhythmically, making discharges from its motor cells sufficient to keep the muscles of respiration in regular action, influenced only by occasional sensory impressions and chemical changes from various sources, which increase or diminish its activity according to the needs of the body.

In *reflex action* the parts engaged are a sensory ending, say in the skin ; a sensory nerve leading from it to the spinal cord, where it ends by splitting up into processes near the nerve-cells ; a nerve-cell which is stimulated by the sensory impulse, and which immediately sends a motor impulse down its nerve ; and a muscle which contracts as the result. A simple example of reflex action is given by the drawing away of the hand when it is pricked with a pin, before and independently of the conscious perception of pain.

Voluntary acts are more complicated than reflex ones. The same mechanism is involved, but, in addition, the controlling power of the brain is brought into play. This exerts first of all an inhibitory or blocking effect, which prevents immediate reflex action, and then the impulse, passing up to the cerebral hemispheres, sets up activity in a series of cells there, the complexity of these processes depending upon the intellectual processes involved. Finally, the inhibition is removed and an impulse passes down to motor cells in the spinal cord, and a muscle or set of muscles is brought into play through the motor nerves.

The *trophic function* of nerves is another most important part of their activity, for it appears as if the constant passage of nerve impulses down the nerves of any part were important for its nutrition. Thus, if sensory nerves be diseased or injured, ulceration of the skin, bed sores, and other changes are liable to occur, while muscles waste and disappear if their motor nerves be permanently destroyed.

Nervous system.—The brain and its twelve pairs of cranial nerves are treated under BRAIN ; the spinal cord and the origin of its thirty-one pairs of nerves are treated under SPINAL CORD.

Each of these spinal nerves arises by two roots, the posterior being larger than the anterior, and being furnished with a ganglion. Just before they emerge from the side of the spinal canal, the two roots unite to form a single nerve, their fibres mix, and then the nerve separates into two divisions.

One division immediately turns backwards to supply the skin and muscles of the back (posterior division), the other runs forwards (anterior division).

These anterior divisions supply the skin on the front and sides of the body and on the limbs, as well as all the muscles of the trunk and limbs, excepting those on the back. They do not run straight to these parts, but form a series of plexuses in which the nerve-fibres from different levels of the cord are mingled, and from which the nerves to the limbs are given off. The upper four cervical nerves unite to produce the *cervical plexus*. From this the muscles and skin of the neck are mainly supplied, and the phrenic nerve, which runs down through the lower part of the neck and the chest to innervate the diaphragm, is given off. The *brachial plexus* is formed by the union of the lower four cervical and first dorsal nerves, and, in addition to nerves which proceed to some of the muscles in the shoulder region, and others to the skin about the shoulder and inner side of the arm, it gives off the following large nerves that proceed down the arm: the musculo-cutaneous nerve, the median nerve, the ulnar nerve, and the musculo-spiral (radial) nerve, each of which is about the size of a goose-quill. The musculo-cutaneous nerve supplies the large muscles in front of the upper arm, as well as the skin on the radial side of the forearm as far as the wrist. The musculo-spiral nerve winds round the back of the upper arm, where it supplies the triceps muscle, and then gives branches which innervate the skin on the outer side of the arm and forearm, the muscles behind the forearm, and finally the skin on the outer part of the back of the hand and fingers. The median nerve and the ulnar nerve run through the upper arm without giving off branches, and it is possible to feel the ulnar nerve as a cord running between the two marked bony prominences behind the elbow.

The median nerve supplies most of the muscles in front of the forearm, a few of the small muscles in the hand and the skin of the palm and front of the thumb, index finger, middle finger, and half of the ring finger. The ulnar nerve supplies two muscles in the forearm, most of the small muscles in the hand, and the skin down the inner side of the forearm and palm and the skin in front of the little finger and half the ring finger.

The *thoracic* or *dorsal nerves*, with the exception of the first, do not form a plexus, but each runs round the chest along the lower margin of the rib to which it corresponds, whilst the lower six extend on to the abdomen. In this course they supply both the skin and muscle of the trunk.

The *lumbar plexus* is formed by the upper four lumbar nerves, and its branches are distributed to the lower part of the abdomen, and front and inner side of the thigh.

The *sacral plexus* is formed by parts of the fourth and fifth lumbar nerves, and the upper three and part of the fourth sacral nerves. It gives branches directly to the muscles and skin about the hip and fork, and the small sciatic nerve which supplies the skin down the back of the thigh, but the main bulk of the plexus is collected into the great sciatic nerve. This, the largest nerve in the body, is buried in the muscles on the back of the thigh, which it supplies. It continues down to the back of the knee, and there divides into two branches, the internal popliteal (tibial) nerve, and the external (common) popliteal nerve, which between them supply all the muscles below the knee and the greater part of the skin covering the leg and the foot.

The *sympathetic system* is joined by a pair of small branches given off from each spinal nerve, close to the spine. This system consists of two great parts. There is, first, a pair of cords running down on the side and front of the back-bone, and containing on each side three ganglia in the neck, and beneath this a ganglion opposite each vertebra. From these two ganglionated cords numerous branches are given off, and these unite in the second place to form plexuses connected with various internal organs, and provided with numerous large and irregularly placed ganglia. The chief of these plexuses are the cardiac plexus, the solar or epigastric plexus, the diaphragmatic, suprarenal, renal, spermatic, or ovarian, aortic, hypogastric, and pelvic plexuses, the name in each case indicating the organ upon which, or part of the abdomen within which, the plexus is placed.

NERVE INJURIES are produced by several causes. Continued or repeated severe pressure may be enough to damage a nerve seriously, as in the case of a badly made crutch pressing into the armpit and causing drop-wrist. Bruising due to a blow which drives a superficially placed nerve against a bone may inflict severe damage upon a nerve such as the musculo-spiral (radial) nerve behind the upper arm. A wound may sever nerves with other structures, and this accident seems specially liable to occur to the ulnar nerve in front of the wrist, owing to falls upon broken glass, and to various nerves in the armpit when the humerus is fractured near its upper end. Exposure to cold may also damage a nerve severely, as in the case of the facial nerve, when Bell's paralysis results. Or a nerve may be injured at its origin before it leaves the brain or cord, by hæmorrhage in the substance of these organs.

Symptoms.—When a sensory nerve is injured, sensation is immediately more or less impaired in the part supplied by the nerve, and when the nerve in question is a motor one the muscles governed through it are instantly paralysed. In the latter case, the portion of nerve beyond the injury degenerates and the muscles gradually waste, and lose their power of contraction in response to electrical applications. Finally, deformities result and the joints become fixed. This is particularly noticeable when the ulnar nerve is injured, the hand and fingers taking up a ' claw-like ' position. The skin may also become cold, glossy, and even ulcerate, owing to the loss of its nerve supply.

Treatment.—The nerve, if wounded, should be carefully stitched with the ends touching one another, and, if injured by other causes, should be carefully protected from a repetition of the injury. In some cases recovery takes place within a few days, but usually, if the nerve be completely severed or seri-
622

ously injured, the muscles supplied by it do not regain their power for several weeks at least. The reason of this is that the part cut off from connection with the brain and cord degenerates rapidly, and the new nerve has to grow all the way down the sheath of the old one. (*See* NERVES.) An operation designed to unite a damaged nerve and relieve paralysis may sometimes be successfully performed even some weeks or months after the wound has closed. When the ends of the damaged nerve are so shortened that they cannot be got to meet, a portion of a sensory nerve or of a nerve from an animal is sometimes inserted and carefully stitched between the divided ends. Nerve anastomosis is also sometimes practised by bringing the ends of the divided nerve up to a neighbouring nerve and carefully stitching them within its sheath. For example, the facial nerve when injured at the side of the face is sometimes anastomosed with the healthy hypoglossal nerve, and the facial paralysis which has resulted is thus relieved. Massage and galvanism of the muscles will keep them from wasting till the nerve is ready to take up its functions again. The power of the muscles to react again to faradic electricity is a most important sign, as showing that repair of the nerve is taking place.

NERVOUS DEBILITY (*see* NEURASTHENIA).

NERVOUS DISEASES.—This class of disease is one of the most difficult of diagnosis. The brain and spinal cord being enclosed in the skull and spine, beyond the reach of direct examination, and the nerves being almost everywhere deeply buried in the tissues, the nature of nervous diseases must be made out from the disturbances of organs governed by the affected nerves.

The following conditions are discussed under their proper headings : APHASIA, APOPLEXY, BRAIN DISEASES, CATALEPSY, CRAMP, DISSEMINATED SCLEROSIS, ECSTASY, EPILEPSY, FORGETFULNESS, HYSTERIA, LOCOMOTOR ATAXIA, MENTAL DEFECTIVENESS, MENTAL ILLNESS, NERVE INJURIES,

NEURALGIA, NEURITIS, PARALYSIS, ST. VITUS'S DANCE, SPINAL CORD, DISEASES OF.

Causes.—Many factors contribute to the production of nervous diseases. That certain diseases are induced by a particular temperament, or by peculiar habits of life, is proved by the fact that some of the diseases are commoner among one race, others in another people. Heredity is, in several ways, an important matter. Some persons, particularly those of great intellectual power and of artistic temperament, seem born with a nervous constitution (see CONSTITUTION) which renders them more than ordinarily liable to the slighter nervous affections, such as headaches, neuralgia, hysterical manifestations, and bizarre forms of mental activity. Those also who come of a degenerate stock seem to suffer very readily from nervous diseases of a severe type, probably not because these diseases are inherited, but because the nervous system is specially exposed to strain by the conditions of modern life, and, in such persons, gives way early. The great pressure at which modern commercial and intellectual life is carried on tends, undoubtedly, to exhaust the nervous system and bring on many diseases, such as neuralgia, anxiety states, digestive disturbances, and various forms of mental disturbance. To counteract this a periodic rest and change of scene are of special importance, especially to those of nervous temperament and those subjected to much strain in life.

Shocks both to mind and body, such as the loss of a relative, money reverses, an unfortunate love affair, an accident, may be the starting-point of many chronic nervous complaints. The nervous system seems to be specially open to such injury about the critical periods of life (see CLIMACTERIC), while in young children the nervous system is always of a less stable character than in later life.

Many poisons, both of those produced within the body by disease and of those taken in from outside, have a specially harmful action upon the nervous system. Chief among these stands syphilis, which plays an important part in the production of locomotor ataxia, general paralysis, and certain tumours (gummata) of the brain and spinal cord, while in advanced life it leads to degenerative changes that bring about premature loss of mental power. Chronic alcoholism may cause severe mental derangement and multiple neuritis. Lead-poisoning and diabetes are often accompanied also by multiple neuritis. Several of the acute infectious diseases such as diphtheria, enteric fever, and influenza are apt to be followed by loss of power in parts, due to affection of the nervous system, although such results are in general only temporary. The form of paralysis known as infantile paralysis or poliomyelitis (see PARALYSIS) is also due to an infective process.

As to the changes in the nervous system which are caused by disease, and to which the symptoms are due, these are various in nature. There is a broad division of nervous diseases into ' organic ', in which some change, visible either to the naked eye or on microscopic examination, is discoverable in the nervous system after death, and ' functional ', in which no discovery can be made. Into the latter class there fall, for example, hysteria, anxiety states, many cases of epilepsy, and many cases of neuralgia. Among the ' organic ' changes, one of the commonest is ' sclerosis ', consisting of an overgrowth of the connective tissue framework of the brain, cord, or nerves, accompanied by a disappearance of the nerve structures proper. Tumours, cysts, rupture or blocking of bloodvessels (with consequent loss of nutrition in a part of the nervous system), and local inflammatory processes may all be found constituting an ' organic ' change. In all cases the symptoms are dependent, not so much upon the nature of the disease as upon the part of the nervous system which it happens to affect.

Symptoms.—Many slight affections of the nervous system are attributed to defects in the organs controlled by the affected nerves ; for example, dyspepsia or palpitation may in some cases be due to weakness of the nervous system, and is then little or not at all benefited by remedies directed towards the heart, stomach, or other organ in which the symptoms are manifested. It is specially important, therefore, that cases in which the nervous system is at fault should be early recognized.

There are two great symptoms of nervous disease, viz.: (1) disturbances of sensation in the direction either of loss of feeling, or of great pain, or of perverted sensation, such as tingling, hot flushes, etc. ; and (2) the occurrence of more or less complete paralysis of groups of muscles, or of whole limbs. One or other of these types of symptoms predominates, according as sensory or motor nerves are chiefly affected. In addition to these, there is, in different diseases, more or less interference with the organs of special sense, the reflex actions, the nutrition of outlying parts of the body, and the functions of internal organs.

With regard to *sensory symptoms*, loss of the sense of touch is found in locomotor ataxia, and, generally speaking, all maladies in which the posterior part of the cord or sensory nerves are affected. Syringomyelia is a disease affecting the central portion of the spinal cord, and characterized by loss of the power to feel pain and to recognize heat and cold in parts of the limbs. Painful sensations are present in many diseases, as, for example, shooting pains and the feelings of a tight band round the waist in locomotor ataxia.

As to *motor symptoms*, wasting of muscles and loss of power in parts of the body point usually to some affection of the motor nerves. Spasm as well as loss of power accompanies affections situated in the higher motor tracts of the brain and spinal cord, whilst flaccid palsy characterizes diseases and injuries in the grey matter of the cord or in the motor nerves. Conditions in which the nervous system is merely temporarily weakened are manifested by loss of 'tone' in the muscular system, and speedy exhaustion on exertion. Twitchings in the muscular fibres, as in the condition popularly known as 'live flesh' in the eyelids, are also found in this passing condition, as well as in more serious conditions, such as at the onset of progressive muscular atrophy. The impairment of the power of combination among muscles, known as 'inco-ordination', which produces trembling on exertion, staggering gait, difficulty in buttoning the clothes or in taking food, etc., is found in dissemin-

624

ated sclerosis, St. Vitus's dance, and paralysis agitans. Affecting the lower limbs, interference with the power of regulating the movements is a common symptom of locomotor ataxia.

The *reflex functions*, tested by stroking the skin of various parts and observing the resulting muscular contraction beneath (superficial reflexes), and by tapping the tendons of muscles and watching the twitch that the latter give (deep reflexes), are, generally speaking, diminished when the sensory nerves, sensory paths in the spinal cord, or motor cells in the cord and their fibres are affected. They are increased when the higher motor paths in the cord are affected, as in disseminated sclerosis.

Nutritional functions are impaired in all serious nerve diseases and injuries. As a result, localized sweatings, a glassy condition of the skin, bed sores, ulcers, and even gangrene of limbs are liable to appear in the final stages of nervous maladies.

The *functions of the internal organs* being, as a rule, governed by the sympathetic system, are not in general affected unless this system be diseased. The movement of the bowel and bladder is, however, governed by spinal nerves, and thus these natural functions are impaired in all serious diseases of the spinal cord, so that difficulty of voiding or of retaining the stools and urine appears in such cases.

When the *cranial nerves* proceeding from the brain are involved, very definite symptoms arise. Thus affection of the 1st nerve gives rise to loss of smell ; of the 2nd nerve to impairment of vision ; of the 3rd, 4th, and 6th nerves to squints ; of the 5th nerve to neuralgia ; of the 7th nerve to Bell's paralysis ; of the 8th nerve to deafness or giddiness ; of the 9th nerve to loss of taste ; of the 10th nerve to affections of the larynx, the heart, and the stomach ; of the 11th nerve to disordered action of the sterno-mastoid muscle, causing wry-neck ; and of the 12th nerve to interference with the movements of the tongue, and consequent difficulty in pronunciation. Many of these symptoms are discussed elsewhere.

Lumbar puncture and the examination of fluid withdrawn from the spinal canal are of great importance in the diagnosis of many serious nervous diseases. (*See* LUMBAR PUNCTURE.)

Treatment.—Rest, which gives an opportunity for repair to the worn-out tissues, is the great remedy in all types of disease due to overstrain of body or mind, shock, or inflammatory processes. Rest in its widest sense includes not merely cessation of activity, but suitable food, change of employment, and, it may be, active exercise in persons who have usually much mental work.

Where changes in the nervous system are the result of poisons, such as those of syphilis or lead, appropriate drugs hasten their expulsion from the body, and thus check the progress of the disease. Generally speaking, alcohol has a prejudicial effect in all forms of nervous disease, and particularly is this true in those diseases like polyneuritis, which are caused by it, and in which its use must be absolutely stopped.

There is no department of medicine in which the subconscious moral influence of a self-reliant and expert physician is more marked than in the treatment of functional nervous disorders, and the confidence reposed in the medical adviser and in the treatment employed is often sufficient, in these cases, to start the patient upon the road to improvement, which it requires only time, rest, and the constant exercise of a certain amount of will-power to complete.

NERVOUS IMPULSE.—The effects of nervous activity are now believed to be in all cases transmitted chemically, by the formation at nerve-endings of chemical substances. When, for example, a nerve to a muscle is stimulated, there appears at the junction of nerve ending and muscle the chemical substance acetylcholine. Acetylcholine also appears at endings of the parasympathetic nerves and transmits the effect of the parasympathetic impulse. When an impulse passes down a sympathetic nerve, the effect of it is transmitted at the nerve-ending by the chemical liberated there—adrenaline or an adrenaline-like substance.

NETTLE-RASH, or URTICARIA, is a disorder of the skin characterized by an eruption resembling the effect produced by the sting of a nettle, namely, raised red or red-and-white patches, occurring in parts or over the whole of the surface of the body, and attended with great itching and irritation. It may be acute or chronic.

Causes.—In many cases the attack appears to be connected with digestive derangements, or the taking of certain articles of diet particularly of a protein nature, such as various kinds of meat, fish, shell-fish, etc., also occasionally from the use of certain drugs, such as penicillin. In some it is due to the injection of sera, whilst in others it may follow the bite of an insect. There remains a considerable number of cases in which it is difficult to incriminate any one specific causal factor. The general consensus of opinion is that urticaria is an allergic reaction on the part of the affected individual to some substance to which he or she is hypersensitive. In other words, it comes into the same category as asthma and hay fever. In all three conditions the individual is allergic to some factor or factors, but the allergic response varies : in asthma it is the bronchioles of the lungs that are involved ; in hay fever it is the mucous membrane of the nasopharynx, sinuses, and eyes ; whilst in urticaria it is the skin that gives the allergic response.

Symptoms.—In severe cases there is at first considerable feverishness and constitutional disturbance, together with sickness and faintness, which either precede or accompany the appearance of the rash. The eruption may appear on any part of the body, but is most common on the face and trunk. In the former position it causes swelling and disfigurement while it lasts, and is apt to excite alarm in persons unacquainted with its nature. The attack may pass off in a few hours, or may last for several days, the eruption continuing to come out in successive patches. The lesions are accompanied by severe itching. Occasionally a similar process takes place in the throat, and there is then considerable danger from blockage of the larynx. (*See also* ALLERGY.)

Treatment.—The treatment of urticaria has been revolutionized by the introduction of the antihistamine drugs. There are now a large number

of these on the market, all with proprietary names, and it is necessary to
find which particular preparation suits
a particular individual. In addition, it
is necessary to discover, if possible,
the causative factor and to remove it.
For instance, if an attack always
follows the taking of a certain article
of diet, this should be carefully noted
and avoided in future. The patient's
general health should also be attended
to, if this is not satisfactory. The local
irritation is allayed by sponging with a
warm alkaline solution (a teaspoonful
of soda or ammonia to a tumblerful of
warm water), with Goulard's water, or
by rubbing with menthol.

NEURALGIA (νεῦρον, nerve ; ἀλγέω,
I am pained), literally *nerve pain*, is a
term which is frequently employed both
technically and popularly in a somewhat
loose manner, to describe pains the
origin of which is not clearly traceable.
In its strict sense it means the existence
of pain in some portion of, or throughout
the whole of, the distribution of a
sensory nerve, without any distinctly
recognizable structural change in the
nerve or nerve-centres. This strict
definition, if adhered to, however,
would not be applicable to a large
number of cases of nerve pain ; for in
many instances the pain is connected
with pressure on, or inflammation of,
the nerve. Hence the word is generally
used to indicate pain affecting a particular nerve or its branches, whatever
be the cause.

Causes.—It may be generally stated
that neuralgia rarely occurs in the
midst of good health, its existence
betokening, as a rule, a depressed or
enfeebled state. Constitutional causes,
hereditary or acquired, are among the
most powerful of the predisposing
influences in its production. Thus it is
often found to affect the rheumatic or
gouty. In weakened conditions of the
system from unsuitable or insufficient
food, or as the result of any drain upon
the body, or in anæmia from any cause,
or when certain disease poisons are
present, such as syphilis or malaria, it is
common for neuralgia to come on.
Further, any strain upon the nervous
system, such as mental overwork or
anxiety, is a powerful predisposing
cause. Among the exciting causes of an
626

attack of neuralgia, by far the most
common is exposure to cold and damp,
which seems to excite irritation in a
nerve already disposed to suffer. But
irritation may be produced by numerous other causes, such as bruising of a
nerve by a blow, a decayed tooth,
diseased bone, local inflammations in
which nerves are implicated, or some
source of pressure upon a nerve-trunk,
such as swelling of the sheath in its
passage through a bony canal. Also a
foreign body, or even the scar of an old
wound, has been found to be sufficient
cause of irritation when situated close
to a nerve. Further, there are causes
of a reflex character which are capable
of setting up neuralgia at a distance,
such as intestinal or uterine derangements. Those cases in which, after
removal of a piece of nerve, inflammatory changes and thickening of the
nerve-sheath are found, receive the
name of ' neuritis ', but, as regards the
question of pain, there is no difference
between neuritis and neuralgia due to
other causes, except that pain caused
by neuritis tends to be continuous and
is very difficult to treat.

The practical importance of ascertaining the probable nature of the
cause is obvious.

Symptoms.—Although the pain is
generally localized, it may spread beyond the area where it first occurs. It
is usually of paroxysmal character, and
often periodic : that is to say, it occurs
at a certain time of the day or night. It
varies in intensity, being often of the
most agonizing character, and again less
severe and more of a tingling kind.
Various forms of perverted nerve function may be found along with or following neuralgia. Thus there may be over-
sensitiveness of the skin, loss of feeling,
paralysis, or alterations of nutrition,
such as wasting of muscles, whitening
of the hair, etc. Attacks of neuralgia
are apt to recur, particularly when the
general health is low, and some persons
unhappily continue to suffer from occasional attacks during the greater part
of their lifetime.

Varieties.—The nature of the disease
will be best described under the names
of the forms in which it most commonly
occurs. These are trigeminal neuralgia,
or ' tic douloureux ' ; intercostal neuralgia ; and sciatica. Other forms,

affecting the arm, neck, etc., are of much less frequent occurrence.

TRIGEMINAL NEURALGIA, or TIC DOULOUREUX, is one of the most severe forms of neuralgia. It affects the great nerve of sensation in the face (trigeminal nerve), and may occur in one or more of the three divisions in which the nerve is distributed. It is usually confined to one side. Females suffer, on the whole, more frequently than males, and they are usually over the age of 50. The attack is often precipitated by movements of the jaw, as in talking or eating, or by tactile stimuli such as a cold wind or washing the face. When the *first or upper division of the nerve* is involved, the pain is mostly felt in the forehead and side of the head. It is usually of an intensely sharp, cutting, or burning character, either constant or with exacerbations, and often periodic, returning at a certain hour each day while the attack continues. Occasionally the paroxysms are of extreme violence, and are brought on by the slightest provocation, such as a draught of cool air. The skin over the affected part is often red and swollen, and, even after the attack has abated, feels stiff and tender to the touch. In this, as in all forms of neuralgia, there are certain localities where the pain is more intense, these 'painful points', as they are called, being for the most part in those places where the branches of the nerves emerge from bony canals or pierce the fascia to ramify in the skin. Hence, in this form, the greater severity of the pain above the eyebrow and along the side of the nose. There is also pain in the eyelid, redness of the eye, and flow of tears. When *the second division of the nerve* is affected, the pain is chiefly in the cheek and upper jaw, the painful points being immediately below the lower eyelid, over the cheek-bone, and about the upper lip. This form is accompanied by pain of similar character to that affecting the first division, and the pain often appears suddenly on slight provocation such as by taking a mouthful of hot or cold fluid. When *the third division of the nerve* suffers, the pain affects the lower jaw, and the chief painful points are in front of the ear and above the chin. Attacks of tic douloureux, extremely distressing as they are, may recur occasionally for years ; and al-

though, by depriving the sufferer of sleep and interfering with the taking of food, they may in some measure impair the health, they rarely appear to lead to any serious results. Nevertheless, the pain may be so intolerable as to make life a burden.

INTERCOSTAL NEURALGIA is pain affecting the nerves which emerge from the spinal cord and run along the spaces between the ribs to the front of the body. This form of neuralgia affects the left side more than the right, is much more common in women than in men, and occurs generally in enfeebled states of health. It might be mistaken for pleurisy or some inflammatory affection of the lungs ; but the absence of any chest symptoms, its occurrence independently of the acts of respiration, and other considerations establish the distinction. The specially painful points are chiefly at the commencement of the nerve as it issues from the spinal canal, and at the extremities towards the front of the body, where it breaks up into filaments which ramify in the skin. This form of neuralgia is occasionally the precursor of an attack of shingles (*Herpes zoster*) as well as a result of it (*see* HERPES).

SCIATICA is another of the more common forms of neuralgia. It affects the great sciatic nerve which emerges from the pelvis and runs down the back of the thigh. It is, in many instances, traceable to exposure to cold or damp ; but there are many other possible causes. Any source of pressure upon the nerve within the pelvis, such as may be produced by a tumour, may excite an attack of sciatica. It is often connected with a rheumatic or gouty constitution. In general, the nerve of one side only is affected. Pressure upon a nerve by a prolapsed intervertebral disc between the 4th and 5th lumbar vertebræ is a not uncommon cause of pain along the course of the sciatic nerve. In such a case operative treatment may be required. The pain, which is felt at first a little behind the hip-joint, steadily increases in severity and extends along the course of the nerve and its branches, in many instances as far as the toes. The specially painful points are where the nerve issues from the pelvis at the lower margin of the buttock, and about the knee and ankle joints ; besides which a feeling of numbness is sometimes experienced throughout the whole limb. In severe cases all movement of the limb, and particularly the motion of stooping forwards, or of bending the hip with the knee straight, aggravates the pain, and the patient is obliged to remain in bed.

Treatment.—With all forms of neuralgia it is of the first importance to ascertain, if possible, whether any constitutional condition is associated with the malady, and, if evidence of the presence of rheumatism, gout, anæmia, etc., be discovered, to administer along with the local remedies for neuralgia, the remedies required for the constitutional condition.

Naturally also one looks for, and as speedily as possible removes, any source of local irritation, such as a decayed tooth, and also any such reflex source as uterine or intestinal disorder.

During the time an acute attack lasts, various local applications give relief, the most useful being, perhaps, hot fomentations applied over the painful part. Bathing with water as hot as can be borne is also beneficial in many cases. Rubbing or painting with anodyne liniment, such as a mixture of the liniments of aconite, belladonna, and chloroform ; or a mixture, in equal parts, of chloral, camphor, and menthol, rubbed up together and painted over the part, is very soothing, especially perhaps for those cases in which the pain begins as soon as the sufferer gets warm in bed at night. Ointment of aconitine is also recommended by some to be rubbed on the painful spot. Hypodermic injections of morphine or cocaine, although they give temporary relief, are not to be recommended because of the great danger, in such cases, that their use will become a habit. In the case of purely sensory nerves, like the fifth nerve, injection of pure alcohol into the nerve has a deadening effect and often gives relief for a long time.

Internally, during an acute attack, many remedies are given. Those which are most generally useful, and which may be safely used without any tendency to bring about habitual use, are aspirin, phenacetin, phenazone and other coal-tar preparations. When tic douloureux is the form of neur-

algia present, gelsemium and butyl-chloral appear to be specially useful drugs, but probably the most useful drug of all is carbamazepine (*q.v.*).

When the neuralgia has assumed a chronic type, or when the acute attacks recur with great frequency, a totally different type of treatment is in general requisite. The anodyne and depressant drugs mentioned above are then of little permanent use, and indeed some of them, by depressing still further the exhausted nervous sytem, are distinctly hurtful. Plentiful nourishment and tonics are more often beneficial.

As regards local measures in the chronic state, the application of blisters or counter-irritation by touching the skin with the button-cautery is the remedy most employed. The blister is made of an oblong shape, with its length corresponding to the line of the nerve, and the spots at which the cautery is applied generally also follow the affected nerve. The use of galvanic electricity is often beneficial in both the acute and the chronic stage. (*See* ELECTRICITY IN MEDICINE.) Diathermy is also employed with soothing effect (*see* DIATHERMY). Baths of various sorts, particularly alternate hot and cold baths, or douches, and the hot-air bath, are sometimes of use (*see* BATHS, DOUCHES). Massage, though it increases the pain in the acute state, may be of great benefit in chronic cases due to some inflammatory process in the nerve.

Many cases resist all forms of medicinal treatment, and for these the following surgical procedures are sometimes tried.

Nerve-stretching, an operation introduced some fifty years ago, is mainly used for cases of sciatica. An incision is made through the muscles on the back of the thigh, the sciatic nerve secured, and gently stretched with the fingers. The operation is often successful in those cases which are due to some inflammation in the nerve accompanied by the deposit of new fibrous tissue, which is torn down by the act of stretching.

Division and removal of a portion of the nerve, or injection of absolute alcohol into the nerve, is practised in the case of sensory nerves, such as the branches of the fifth nerve on the face.

NEURASTHENIA (νεῦρον, nerve; ἀσθένεια, weakness) means a condition of nervous exhaustion in which, although the patient suffers from no definite disease, he becomes incapable of sustained exertion. It was never a very well-defined entity, and the term has now been largely given up. The condition which it represented is now recognized to be merely a form of neurosis (q.v.) or psychoneurosis (q.v.).

NEURECTOMY (νεῦρον, nerve; ἐκτομή, excision) is the term applied to an operation in which part of a nerve is excised, for example, for the relief of neuralgia.

NEURILEMMA (νεῦρον, nerve; λέμμα, sheath) is the name of the thin membranous covering which surrounds every nerve-fibre.

NEURITIS (νεῦρον, a nerve) means inflammation affecting a nerve or nerves which may be localized to one part of the body, as, for instance, in sciatica, or which may be general, being then known as multiple neuritis, or polyneuritis. Owing to the fact that the most peripheral parts of the nerves are usually at fault in the latter condition, viz. the fine subdivisions in the substance of the muscles, it also frequently receives the name of peripheral neuritis.

Causes.—In cases of LOCALIZED NEURITIS the fibrous sheath of the nerve is usually at fault, the actual nerve-fibres being only secondarily affected. This condition may be due to inflammation spreading into the nerve from surrounding tissues, to cold, or to long-continued irritation by pressure on the nerve, and the symptoms produced vary according to the function of the nerve, in the case of sensory nerves being usually neuralgic pain (see NEURALGIA), in the case of motor nerves more or less paralysis in the muscles to which the nerves pass. A typical example of this kind of neuritis is found in neuritis of the facial nerve. (See PARALYSIS.)

In POLYNEURITIS, which is always due to some general or constitutional cause, the nerve-fibres themselves in the small nerves degenerate and break down. Hence the very protracted nature of this malady, since, if recovery

takes place, it must be brought about by the growth of new nerve-fibres from the healthy part of the nerve, down the sheath of the nerve, to the muscle. The cause of this degeneration may be said, in general terms, to be in every case some poison either taken into or produced in the body, and circulating in the blood. By far the commonest of these poisons is alcohol, and the disease especially affects women who are quiet, steady tipplers. The condition also arises in men, though much more rarely, the abuse of alcohol in this sex tending more to produce delirium tremens, from which women are almost exempt. Next in importance comes lead, wrist-drop and other features of neuritis being among the most prominent symptoms of lead-poisoning. (See LEAD-POISONING.) Arsenic is occasionally responsible for neuritis, particularly when the effect of arsenic is combined with over-indulgence in alcohol, as in an epidemic of neuritis, due to beer contaminated with arsenic, in the Midlands of England about the year 1900. Bisulphide of carbon, naphtha, and other solvents of india-rubber are apt to produce the disease when inhaled in large quantity by the workmen engaged in india-rubber factories. Those who suffer from diabetes are prone to neuritis, the condition sometimes being the result of deficiency of vitamin B_1 in the diet. This deficiency probably also accounts for some cases of alcoholic neuritis. In both diabetes and chronic alcoholism the diet is far from normal. Gout, too, is occasionally accompanied by neuritis. Several of the acute infectious diseases, especially diphtheria and typhoid fever, are apt to be followed by neuritis. The disease known as ' beri-beri ' (see BERI-BERI) is a form of neuritis which persists in certain localities of the globe, in consequence of vitamin B_1 deficiency.

Symptoms.—The chief symptom of a LOCALIZED NEURITIS, whether pain or paralysis, has been already stated to vary according to the functions of the nerve. In cases following diphtheria, typhoid fever, or other infective disease, the neuritis of an outlying nerve often shows, as its most prominent and annoying feature, a paralysis of a group of muscles in the arm, leg, etc., leading to weakness of the part concerned.

This may cause inability for some months to grasp objects with the hand, to lift the foot in walking, and similar troublesome symptoms. These, however, usually pass off completely in course of time. The area of skin associated with the affected nerve is, in addition, often much changed, becoming glossy, or developing an ulcer, or, especially about the face and trunk, breaking out in 'shingles' (see HERPES). A case of neuritis of this type may come on very quickly, developing fully in a few days.

POLYNEURITIS, as a rule, takes longer to show itself, even in the case of diphtheria, seldom developing till two or three weeks after the onset of the trouble in the throat. In most cases it begins with vague pains and tingling in the limbs ; weakness and wasting of the muscles in the feet and legs, in the hand and arms, or in other parts, following later. Wrist-drop, the peculiar 'steppage' gait in which the person lifts his feet as if he were constantly stepping over small obstacles, squinting, loss of voice, difficulty of breathing, enfeeblement of the heart's action appear according to the muscles whose nerves are affected. There is usually some loss of sensation in scattered areas over the skin, but a very characteristic sign, in the alcoholic form of neuritis at least, is that the muscles are extremely tender when squeezed. There is almost always some swelling of the feet, and in the neuritis of beri-beri dropsy is often a very marked symptom. The knee-jerks and other deep reflexes are generally lost in all forms of neuritis, if severe in character. A peculiar feature of alcoholic neuritis is the wandering delirium from which the patient often suffers, her imagination conjuring up the most vivid delusions as to journeys she is making, and the mind being quite confused in matters regarding time and place especially.

The course of the disease is, as stated above, usually very slow, and particularly is this the case when a poison, as in the case of alcohol or lead, has been taken into the system over a long period. Months, or even a year or two, may elapse in one of these cases before the health is restored. The ultimate hope of recovery is, however, good. Except in the case of beri-beri, which

630

is fatal unless treated, and in those cases of poisoning by alcohol, or of diphtheria, in which the mechanism of the heart or that of respiration becomes affected, the mortality is low.

Treatment.—For the treatment of LOCALIZED NEURITIS see under NEURALGIA.

The first essential in the treatment of POLYNEURITIS is to discover and remove the cause by which the nerves are being poisoned. Particularly does this apply to alcoholism, lead-poisoning, and neuritis due to manufacture of india-rubber. In the case of alcoholism there is always present the moral difficulty of preventing the patient from obtaining fresh supplies of stimulants, so that treatment must be carried out in a hospital or nursing-home. Rest in bed is the next essential to prevent over-fatigue of the weakened nerves and muscles. In the early stages the muscles are too tender to permit of much handling, but, later on, massage helps to prevent wasting of muscles, and the deformities which arise through fixation of the joints in one position. These deformities must be prevented as far as possible during the earlier stages by frequently changing the position of the patient's limbs as he lies in bed. Electrical treatment may also help as recovery advances. Much benefit is sometimes gained from injections of vitamin B_I or administration of foods containing it, such as Bemax or Marmite.

NEUROGLIA (νεῦρον, nerve ; γλία, glue) is the name applied to a fine web of tissue and branching cells which supports the nerve fibres and cells of the nervous system. (See NERVES.)

NEUROLOGY is the name given to that branch of medical practice and science which deals with the nervous system and its diseases.

NEUROMA (νεῦρον, nerve ; -oma, termination meaning tumour) means a tumour connected with a nerve, such tumours being generally composed of fibrous tissue, and of a painful nature.

NEURONE (νεῦρον, nerve) is the name given to a single unit of the nervous system consisting of a nerve cell with its various processes and the nerve fibre or fibres to which it gives origin. As applied to the motor part of the nervous system, two neurones are specially recognized : the *upper neurone*, which includes a cell on the surface of the brain and a fibre extending down into the spinal cord ; also a *lower neurone*, which consists of a cell in the grey matter of the cord with a nerve fibre extending outwards to end in a fibre of the muscle with which it is connected. The former has a controlling influence over the latter, whilst the latter is more directly concerned with the changes that result in the contraction of the muscle fibre and with nutritional influences over it.

NEUROSIS (νεῦρον, nerve) is a general term applied to mental or emotional disturbance in which, as opposed to psychosis, there is no serious disturbance of the personality. At one time the condition was differentiated from psychoneurosis, but it is now accepted that these two terms are synonymous. As has been pointed out, ' there are few clearly defined boundaries in nature, and there is many a case of mental illness which it is difficult to assign definitely to the neurotic or psychotic group'. Speaking generally, however, a psychosis involves a change in the whole personality of the individual, whereas in a neurosis it is only part of the personality that is involved. Alternatively, it might be said that in a psychosis reality is changed and the individual acts accordingly. In a neurosis, on the other hand, reality is unchanged and the neurotic individual always acts as if reality had the same meaning for him as for the community at large.

Neuroses are usually classified into anxiety neuroses, hysteria (*q.v*), and obsessional neuroses.

Anxiety neurosis constitutes the commonest form of neurosis. Fortunately, it is also almost the most responsive to treatment. It occurs in people of anxious personality—the timid worriers of this world who are always meeting trouble halfway. Once the neurosis develops, they are in a state of persistent anxiety and worry, ' tensed up ', always feeling fatigued and unable to sleep at night. In addition, there are often complaints suggesting some phy-

sical disorder : *e.g.* palpitation, flatulence, or headache.

Obsessional neuroses are much less common, and constitute only about 5 per cent. of all neuroses. Like other neuroses, they usually develop in early adult life. They are characterized by the individual developing a phobia or obsession about something, and this may be so persistent that life becomes almost unbearable. Again, as in almost the entire field of mental illness, the borderline between an anxiety neurosis and an obsessional neurosis may be far from clear, but in the latter the obsession interferes much more with the ordinary life of the patient.

NEUROTIC is a general term of indefinite meaning applied to a person of nervous temperament, whose actions are largely determined by emotions or instincts rather than by reason.

NEUTROPENIA denotes a reduction in the number of neutrophil leucocytes per cubic millimetre of circulating blood to a figure below that found in health. There is still some disagreement over the precise limits of normality, but a count of less than 2500 per c.mm. would be generally accepted as constituting neutropenia. Several infective diseases are characterized by neutropenia, including typhoid fever, influenza, and measles. It may also be induced by certain drugs, including chloramphenicol, phenylbutazone, the sulphonamides, and chlorpromazine.

NICLOSAMIDE is the ' approved name' of a new drug which is proving of value in the treatment of tape-worm infestation. It is also known as YOMESAN.

NICOTINAMIDE, the amide of nicotinic acid, is sometimes used instead of nicotinic acid.

NICOTINE is the active principle upon which the action of tobacco depends. (*See* TOBACCO.)

NICOTINIC ACID, or NIACIN, is a member of the vitamin B complex. It is essential for human nutrition, the normal daily requirement for an adult being about 15 to 20 mg. A deficiency of nicotinic acid is one of the factors in the etiology of pellagra, and either nicotinic acid or nicotinamide is used in the treatment of this condition.

NIGHT BLINDNESS is a condition in which a person becomes blind in dim lights, although able to see quite well in the full glare of sunlight or artificial light, in some cases inherited and in others the result of an insufficiency of vitamin A in the diet, this vitamin being essential for the formation of visual purple.

NIGHTMARE (see SLEEP).

NIGHT SWEATS consist in copious perspiration occurring in bed at night and found in conditions of general weakness, especially in tuberculosis.

NIGHT TERRORS form a kind of nightmare in children of nervous temperament. (See SLEEP.)

NIKETHAMIDE.—The *British Pharmacopœia* name for nicotinic acid diethylamide, a drug which stimulates the respiratory centre.

NIPPLES, DISEASES OF (see BREAST, DISEASES OF).

NIRIDAZOLE is a recently introduced drug which is proving of value in the treatment of schistosomiasis (see PARASITES) and guinea-worm infections (see PARASITES.)

NITRATE OF POTASSIUM is the technical name for nitre. (See NITRE.)

NITRATE OF SILVER, also known as LUNAR CAUSTIC, is a heavy crystalline salt of silver, very soluble in water, and generally prepared in sticks. In weak solution it has a strong astringent action, and in the pure form it acts as a powerful caustic. It is very slowly discharged from the system, and, if used for any great length of time, it is apt to produce a brown discoloration of the skin all over the body, known as ' argyria '.

Uses.—Locally it is used as a caustic, acting painlessly on warts, etc. As an astringent it is used in many inflammatory conditions of mucous membranes, in the form of gargles, sprays, and douches, usually in the strength of about $\frac{1}{2}$ to 2 grains (30 to 125 mg.) to the ounce (28·5 ml.) of distilled water, but often stronger. Its local action can be checked, and any pain it may cause can be stopped by simply moistening the part and placing common salt upon it. It is much used to drop into

632

the eye in cases of conjunctivitis, the usual strength for this purpose being from $\frac{1}{2}$ to 1 per cent. Internally, nitrate of silver is seldom used now.

NITRE (νίτρον, natron or mineral alkali, with which nitre has been confounded), also known as SALTPETRE (sal petræ—salt of the rock), NITRATE OF POTASSIUM, and, in the form of sticks, as SAL PRUNELLE, is a crystalline substance of a sharp saline taste, found in India, Persia, and other places. It is irritating to the stomach and is not now used internally, but is of use for inhalation in the treatment of asthma, since the nitrate in burning gives off nitrites. Two and a half ounces (70 grammes) of the saltpetre are dissolved in a tumblerful of water, and squares of thin white blotting-paper, or bibulous paper about 6 inches (15 cm.) in diameter, are dipped in this brine and then allowed to dry. When used they are folded like a tent, set on a plate, and lighted at the edges. Several of these, burned in the room of a person suffering from asthma, often give relief.

NITRIC ACID is one of the strongest of the mineral acids, and is a clear, heavy liquid, becoming brownish with age. It is kept in dark, stoppered bottles, and immediately the stopper is removed from the bottle, irritating white fumes are given off.

Action.—In its pure state, nitric acid acts as a powerful caustic upon the tissues of the body, which it turns a bright yellow colour. In weaker solution it is, like all acids, an antiseptic, but is very irritating. Internally, in small doses it has a stimulating action upon the gastric mucous membrane.

Uses.—Nitric acid is one of the most effective caustics for warts, and is also used as a powerful antiseptic and caustic for destroying foul ulcers which threaten to spread, leaving clean ulcers in their place. It is applied to warts drop by drop with a glass rod, and its action can be checked by applying similarly a few drops of solution of common salt.

NITRITES are salts which have a powerful effect in paralysing the action of involuntary muscle, and they therefore dilate the blood-vessels, and check spasm of all sorts. The most commonly used nitrites are nitrite of amyl, of ethyl, and of sodium. Erythroltetra-nitrate and nitroglycerin have a similar action (see NITROGLYCERIN).

NITROFURANTOIN is a synthetic nitrofuran derivative which has a wide range of antibacterial activity and is effective against many Gram-positive and Gram-negative organisms. It is used mainly in the treatment of infections of the urinary tract.

NITROGEN MUSTARDS are nitrogen analogues of mustard gas. They are among the most important alkylating agents (q.v) used in the treatment of various forms of malignant disease. They include mustine, trimustine, uramustine, busulphan, chlorambucal and melphalan.

NITROGENOUS FOODS are those that contain a large proportion of protein (albuminous) material in their composition. Generally speaking, this class comprises the foods of animal source, although some vegetables, notably the pulses, contain large quantities of protein. The use of a certain amount of nitrogenous food is necessary to the system, as from this source alone can the body derive all the building material it requires to repair daily waste. (See DIET.) Even carbohydrate foods contain a certain amount of protein (see FARINACEOUS FOODS), but if all the necessary protein were to be obtained from these it would incur the waste of much starch, or its formation into fat in the bodily tissues. Hence the main value of a mixed diet. The nitrogenous foods may be grouped as follows :

Meat, including beef, mutton, pork, and other forms of flesh, poultry, game, and the internal organs.
Soups and beef-extracts.
Fish.
Milk and cheese.
Eggs.
Pulses and other nitrogenous vegetables.

Meat in structure consists of long cylinders of semi-fluid, protein material enclosed in thin, fibrous tubes, and known as muscle fibres (see MUSCLE). These are bound together by fibrous tissue, enclosing more or less fat in its meshes. The protein material consists mainly of myosin, which clots when the muscle dies, and contains also albumin and hæmoglobin. In addition, there are several chemical substances which can be extracted by steeping the meat in hot water, and which are therefore known as ' extractives '. To these the flavour of meat is due, and the varying taste of different meats is to be explained by slight chemical differences in the extractives present. The feeding and habits of animals have much to do with these differences, and explain the variety in taste between the flesh of wild and tame rabbits, and of grouse and poultry. The shape of the muscle fibres has much to do with the digestibility of meat, short or fine fibres, as in poultry, haddock, and whiting, being the most quickly dissolved. The fatness of meat, or rather the extent to which the fat is interspersed between the meat fibres, is of more importance in connection with digestibility and explains why pork, duck, and goose have a reputation for being indigestible. Sweetbreads and tripe, being held together by loose connective tissue, are, on the other hand, quickly digested, and therefore suitable for invalids. Liver and kidney, which contain much nuclein, a substance closely allied to uric acid, are bad for gout.

Jellies contain little but gelatin, obtained from the fibrous tissue of meat, sinews, etc., and when made with a large quantity of water, *i.e.* weak in gelatin, they are very easily digested. Gelatin is of little or no use as building material, and the main value of jellies is to add bulk and variety to the invalid diet.

Soup consists of a small quantity of gelatin, fat, salts, and extractives in hot water. To make soup or beef-tea from meat does not remove the nutritious materials, although it extracts all the flavour and hardens the meat. Clear soup contains practically no nourishment, although it is stimulating to the digestion by reason of the extractives it contains. Thick soup is nutritious only by reason of the vegetables and gelatin added to it. The same is true of the extract of meat introduced by Baron Liebig in 1865, and of its many more recent imitations. Each pint of beef-tea made from this extract represents the salts and extractives in about half a pound of lean meat, although it contains little or none of the nutritive materials. Its use is valuable, because it appears to play a part in helping on the processes of nutrition. It is very useful, therefore, in fevers and in feeble conditions, when little food is needed, or when the digestive powers are very weak. Beef-juice, obtained by chopping meat up finely, mixing with a little water and squeezing out cold, is quite another article, and contains a large proportion of the nutritive materials as well as extractives.

Fish is an excellent source of protein, and, in the case of fatty fish, such as herring and mackerel, has the additional advantage of containing vitamins A and D. Haddock and whiting are among the most digestible fish, some of which, like cod, have a coarse fibre, and others, like salmon, are very fat. Herring is one of the cheapest as well as one of the most palatable forms of nitrogenous food, and two herrings contain as much animal protein as need enter into the daily dietary of an ordinary working man.

Milk is practically the only form of animal food in which protein, fat, carbohydrate, and salt are all represented in sufficient amount. It contains 2 to 3 per cent. of casein, from which cheese, an almost purely proteid and fatty food, is made ; a small quantity of milk-albumin ; 4 per cent. of fat in the form of a fine emulsion, which gradually rises to the surface as cream ; and 4 to 5 per cent. of milk-sugar, to the decomposition of which souring of milk is due. (*See* DIET, INFANT FEEDING, MILK.)

Eggs, each of which contains the material necessary to form a chicken, present the building material for the formation of bone and muscle in an easily convertible form, and are therefore an excellent food for convalescents, and for weak or rickety children. They do not contain any carbohydrate material, and therefore, to form a good article of general diet, should be mixed with rice, flour, or other cereals, as is done in the shape of puddings. The digestibility is increased when an egg is beaten up with milk or water, and still more when the eggs are lightly boiled. One egg corresponds in nutritive value to about half a tumblerful of good milk, or to about 1 ounce of meat.

Pulses, of which the chief are peas, beans, and lentils, have been called the ' poor man's beef '. This is, however,

634

misleading, because, though they are very cheap, they are not so digestible, contain practically no first-class protein (*q.v.*), and are far from being so completely absorbed as meat unless carefully cooked, while in some persons the gases formed by their decomposition in the bowels give rise to great flatulence. They are also poor in fat, hence the habit of eating them combined with fat foods, as pork and beans, duckling and peas, and butter with beans. Nevertheless, the pulses form a valuable form of food.

The necessity for nitrogenous food and the reason for its combination with other foods is described under the article on DIET.

	Water.	Proteins and Gelatin.	Fat.	Carbohydrates.	Salts.	Extractives.
Beef and mutton	50 to 65	15 to 20	15 to 30	..	·8 to 1·8	·5
Meat-juice .	51	15·5	..	..	12	15·5
Meat-extract .	16 to 21	..	..	..	18 to 22	6 to 60
Poultry . . .	70	23	3	..	1	
Fish (42 per cent. waste)	80	16	2·5	..	1	
Eggs . . .	74	15	10·5	..	1	
Milk	87 to 88	2 to 4	3 to 5	4 to 5	·7	
Peas	10 to 15	18 to 23	1·2 to 1·4	59 to 66	2 to 3	

TABLE 25.—Average Percentage Composition of some Nitrogenous Foods.

NITROGLYCERIN, also known as TRINITRIN and GLYCERYL TRINITRATE, is a thick oily liquid of sweet taste and explosive properties. When a small quantity is taken internally it produces marked effects in about two minutes, relaxing the arteries so as to cause the skin to flush visibly, quickening the pulse, and causing a sense of fullness all over the body and throbbing in the head. It greatly lessens the blood-pressure and temporarily relaxes all muscle, whether striped or unstriped.

Uses.—This sudden action in relaxing muscle fibres and lessening blood-pressure proves very valuable in conditions where serious effects are produced by spasm. For example, in angina pectoris, in bronchial asthma (due in part to spasm of the small bronchial tubes), in gall-stone and renal colic, and in the vomiting of sea-sickness, it diminishes the spasmodic condition and gives relief.

It is used in the form of liquor of glyceryl trinitrate, of which one or two drops is taken in water every few hours ; or tablets made up with chocolate may be carried in the pocket and taken from time to time.

Other substances have a similar action to that of nitroglycerin. Nitrite of sodium and nitrite of potassium are used in doses of 3 to 5 grains (200 to 500 mg.), and have the advantage of producing their effect more slowly and more permanently. Erythrol tetra-nitrate has a similarly prolonged effect. Nitrite of amyl, on the other hand, produces its effect in a few seconds, and, being volatile, may be inhaled as well as swallowed. For this purpose small thin glass perles are prepared, and are carried in the pocket by those liable to angina pectoris or other sudden convulsive seizure. Immediately the spasm comes on, one of these perles is crushed between the finger and thumb and held to the nostrils.

NITROHYDROCHLORIC ACID, or AQUA REGIA, so called because of its power to dissolve gold, is a yellow liquid prepared by adding 1 part of nitric acid to 4 parts of hydrochloric acid. It is a caustic in its pure state, but is only used for internal administration in a diluted form. It is used in the treatment of dyspepsia associated with a low gastric acidity.

NITROUS OXIDE GAS, also known as LAUGHING GAS, is, at ordinary pressures, a gas devoid of odour but of a slightly sweetish taste. It is kept under pressure in steel cylinders, from which it can be allowed to escape at any desired rate by turning a stop-cock. Its use in medicine is to produce insensibility to pain, which it does very quickly, and with a great degree of safety, though the effect is of very short duration, not extending beyond two or three minutes. Its use is therefore applicable only for short operations, such as extraction of a tooth, unless it be repeatedly administered in association with oxygen. (*See* ANÆS-THETICS.)

NOCTAMBULATION (*nocte,* by night; *ambulo,* I walk) is another name for sleep-walking. (*See* SLEEP.)

NOCTURIA, or NYCTURIA, is the term used to denote excess passing of urine during the night. Among its many causes are Bright's disease (*q.v*) and enlargement of the prostate. (*See also* URINE, EXCESS OF.)

NOCTURNAL ENURESIS is the involuntary passing of urine during sleep. It is a condition predominantly of childhood. In a small minority of cases it is due to some organic cause such as infection of the genito-urinary tract, but in the vast majority of cases it is due to inadequate or improper training of the child or psychological ill health. Traditionally it is said to be associated with threadworms, but there is very little, if any, evidence to support this tradition.

Before deciding that a child is suffering from nocturnal enuresis, it is necessary to remember that the age at which a child achieves full control of bladder function varies considerably. Such control is usually achieved in the second year, but more commonly in the third year of life, and there are some children who do not normally achieve such control until the fourth, or even fifth, year.

NODE (*nodus,* a swelling).—The term node is widely used in medicine. For instance, the smaller lymphatic glands (*q.v.*) are often termed lymph nodes. It is also applied to a collection of nerve cells forming a subsidiary nerve centre found in various places in the sympathetic nervous system, such as the sinu-atrial node and the atrio-ventricular node which control the beating of the heart.

NOGUCHI'S REACTION is a skin reaction which forms a test for the presence of syphilis.

NOMA (*νομή,* a devouring sore) is another name for cancrum oris. (*See* CANCRUM.)

NORADRENALINE is the predominant transmitter substance liberated at sympathetic nerve endings.

NORETHYNODREL is one of a series of 19-nor derivatives of testosterone which have been synthesized and which have a progesterone-like action. (*See* PROGESTERONE.) Originally—and still —used for the treatment of various

635

menstrual disorders, their main interest at the moment is their property of inhibiting ovulation. It is this property that led to their use as oral contraceptives. Norethynodrel, combined with a derivative of ethinylœstradiol (*q.v.*), is the one which is at present undergoing extensive trial as an oral contraceptive, under the name of 'conovid'.

NORMAL is a term used in several different senses. Generally speaking, it is applied to anything which agrees with the regular and established type. In chemistry the term is applied to solutions of acids or bases of such strength that each litre contains the number of grams corresponding to the molecular weight of the substance in question. In physiology the term normal is applied to solutions of such strength that, when mixed with a body fluid, they are isotonic and cause no disturbance, *e.g.* normal saline solution (*see* Isotonic).

NORMOBLAST (*norma*, rule, and βλαστός, germ) is the term applied to a red blood corpuscle which still contains the remnant of a nucleus.

NORWEGIAN SCABIES is the name given in Scotland to the severe form of scabies (*q.v.*) in which the skin becomes greatly thickened and fissures develop.

NOSE.—The nose has two functions to perform, being the upper end of the air passages which lead to the lungs, and also lodging the organ which furnishes the sense of smell. As in the case of the ear, the part of the nose which projects from the surface is comparatively unimportant, except from an æsthetic point of view, the main part of the cavity being placed above the roof of the mouth, from which it is separated by the hard palate, and opening behind by the posterior nares into the throat.

The *external nose* is formed partly of bone and partly of cartilage, covered by skin (Fig. 297). In its upper part, the two nasal bones, one on each side, project downwards from the frontal bone for about an inch, and, supported by a process of the upper jaw-bone, form the hard bridge of the nose between the eyes. The ending of the bony part can be seen or felt on most noses, and,

beneath this, two cartilages on each side, the lateral cartilages and the cartilages of the aperture give shape, firmness, and pliability to the lower two-thirds of the nose. The gap between

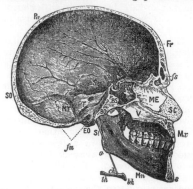

FIG. 297.—A section through the skull immediately to the right of the middle line of the body, showing the septum of the nose. *ME*, Middle plate of the ethmoid bone; *V*, vomer bone; *SC*, septal cartilage. The sphenoidal sinus *PS*, and the frontal sinus *fs*, are also shown. (For other letters, *see* Skull.) (Turner's *Anatomy*.)

the cartilages of the aperture can be distinctly felt on the point of the nose. The spaces between the cartilages are filled up and the cartilages firmly bound to the bones and to one another by fibrous tissue. When the nose is injured, some of the cartilages are apt to be dislocated, thus altering the shape of this organ.

In its *interior*, the nose is completely divided into two narrow cavities, one on each side, by a septum or partition running from front to back. This septum is a thin plate composed partly of bone, partly of cartilage, consisting in about its hinder two-thirds of the central plate of the ethmoid bone and of the vomer bone, and in about its anterior third of a four-sided plate of cartilage, which along one edge touches the nasal bones, the lateral cartilages, and the cartilages of the aperture. On both surfaces this septum is covered by the general mucous membrane that lines the nose.

The cavities on either side of the septum, known as the *nasal fossæ*, are extremely narrow, being at their widest point less than $\frac{1}{4}$ inch (6 mm.) in breadth, though in height they correspond to the length of the nose, and run directly backwards about 2 inches (5 cm.). At its upper end each cavity is separated from the interior of the skull by a thin plate of bone containing many minute apertures for the passage of the filaments of the olfactory nerve. The front part of each cavity consists of the space enclosed by the cartilages of the nose, is lined by skin, which is furnished with stiff hairs that grow downwards and protect the entrance, and is known as the vestibule. Farther

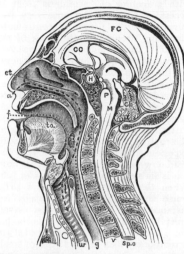

FIG. 298.—Vertical section through the middle of the head and neck, showing the outer wall of the nose with the three turbinated bones. The passages for air, *a*, are indicated by a heavy dotted line; those for the food, *f*, by a fainter line; *et*, Eustachian tube; *l*, larynx; *w*, windpipe; *t*, tonsil; *to*, tongue; *g*, gullet. The sphenoidal and frontal sinuses are shown. Note the very thin plate of bone above the superior turbinated bone which separates the cavity of the nose from the interior of the skull. (For other letters, *see* BRAIN.) (After Braune.)

back the outer surface of each cavity is rendered very complicated, and the space in the cavity greatly filled up, by three projections known as the turbinated bones. These bones form ridges which run from before backwards with an inclination downwards, and, in section, each ridge is curled over so that its edge looks downwards. There are therefore three passages (meatus) running from before backwards, each under cover of a corresponding turbinated bone. As each of these bones, in common with the whole of the cavity, is covered with very vascular and thick mucous membrane, the air in its passage

through the nose is by this arrangement brought in contact with a large surface of mucous membrane, and thus is considerably warmed before it enters the bronchial tubes and lungs. The front portion of the inferior and of the middle turbinated bones can be seen as two red projections by looking up the nostril with a bright light, when the nostril is slightly opened by a speculum. The superior meatus beneath the superior turbinated bone is a narrow passage, and, upon this bone and passage as well as upon the corresponding part of the septum, the nerves of smell end in the mucous membrane. The wider and longer middle meatus and inferior meatus are the passages through which the air mainly passes out and in during respiration.

Certain *sinuses* lie concealed in the bones of the skull, into which air enters freely by apertures connecting them with the nose. These cavities occupy spaces in the frontal bone over the eyebrow (frontal sinus), in the upper jaw-bone, filling in the angle between the eye and the nose (maxillary sinus or antrum of Highmore), in the sphenoid bone (sphenoidal sinus), and in the lateral part of the ethmoid bone (ethmoidal sinus). These give both lightness to the skull and serve to diminish the violence of blows upon the face. The most capacious is the antrum of Highmore, which is a cubical cavity, often over half an inch in measurement each way. The frontal sinus, antrum of Highmore, and ethmoidal sinus open by small apertures about the centre of the middle meatus, the sphenoidal cells above this. Into the front part of the inferior meatus opens the nasal duct, which carries the tears off from the eye (*see* EYE). The latter fact explains the frequent blowing of the nose which becomes necessary when a person is weeping. On a level with the inferior meatus, but situated in the part of the throat into which the nose opens, is placed the orifice of the Eustachian tube leading to the middle ear. (See EAR).

NOSE, DISEASES OF.—The nose, so far as the skin-covering is concerned, is subject to the same diseases as the skin of other parts. Redness of the skin of this part may, on account of its disfiguring character, be very annoying. It may be due to poor circulation in cold weather, partaking of the nature of a chilblain (see CHILBLAINS) ; occasionally it is due to constant indulgence in alcohol (see ACNE ROSACEA) : habitual indigestion also tends to bring on a condition of redness (see DYSPEPSIA), whilst any chronic state of inflammation or source of irritation in the interior of the nose may manifest itself by redness on the surface. Among the skin diseases, acne (q.v.), lupus (q.v.), and erysipelas (q.v.) are specially prone to affect this site.

ACUTE INFLAMMATION of the nose (ACUTE RHINITIS) is generally a catarrhal condition affecting the mucous membrane, and is commonly known as a ' cold in the head ' (see CHILLS AND COLDS). It may be due, though less commonly, to the inhalation of irritating gases. Injuries to the nose are specially liable to be followed by erysipelas in some persons (see ERYSIPELAS). Boils occasionally develop just within the entrance to the nose, in connection with the hairs there, and in this locality give rise to great pain and considerable danger (see BOILS). Diphtheria is a form of acute inflammation which occasionally spreads to the nose (see DIPHTHERIA). Hay fever is a distressing form of acute rhinitis (see HAY FEVER).

CHRONIC INFLAMMATION (CHRONIC RHINITIS) is a very common condition of the nose, and in a mild form may exist for years without attracting much attention.

Causes.—Generally it follows upon repeated colds in the head, which do not pass off completely. It may also be due to the constant inhalation of dust or irritating vapours at work. There seems to be a hereditary tendency also for this type of inflammation to run in families, probably in consequence of some peculiarity in the structure of the nose. The mucous membrane covering the turbinated bones swells up in consequence of the inflammation, and, by blocking the passage of the air to some extent, as well as by producing irritating discharges, forms a source of constant irritation which perpetuates the condition. Any malformation, such as great bulging of the septum to one side, or the presence on it of a 'spur', has a similar

effect, and such malformations have often the effect of rendering persons who have a slight tendency to hay fever additionally liable to this malady, in consequence of the degree of chronic inflammation the malformations produce.

Symptoms.—The most marked symptom is increased secretion from the swollen mucous membrane, causing constant running at the nose, together with a feeling of ' stuffiness '. It is necessary to blow the nose very frequently, or the person is continually ' hawking ' mucus in the back of his throat. In some persons, however, instead of constant running of the nose, the inflammation is of a dry type, and the swollen mucous membrane becomes covered by crusts which are difficult to dislodge. Sneezing is also a common symptom, resulting from the constant irritation in the nose, and a feeling of obstruction in the nose is usually experienced when the person lays his head down at night. The external nose too is liable to become large and red. When the condition becomes a little worse than usual, as the result, for instance, of a fresh cold, the person must breathe through his mouth, his voice takes on a nasal twang, and there is temporary loss of the senses of smell and taste. Occasionally the hearing is much impaired, and there may be neuralgia, aching over the bridge of the nose, and redness of the eyes.

Occasionally, in young persons of poor constitution, especially girls, the nose after suffering from this state for a short time takes on an atrophic process, and both the mucous membrane and the bones waste, so that the former loses its secretion and becomes covered by evil-smelling crusts, which make the breath very offensive, while the changes in the bones produce a small, tip-tilted nose. Happily, this condition, known as ' ozæna ', tends to pass off between the ages of twenty and thirty.

Treatment.—Care must be taken by those with a tendency to chronic inflammation of the nose to avoid catching colds. The condition of the mucous membrane can be greatly improved and the inflammation soothed by the use every night and morning of one of the following lotions, applied to the nose either by means of a hand-spray or from a nasal syringe or douche. (1) Sodium bicarbonate 30 grains, sodium chloride 30 grains, borax 30 grains, white sugar 60 grains, rose water 8 ounces : a small quantity of this to be mixed with an equal quantity of hot water before use. (2) A teaspoonful of sodium bicarbonate and common salt mixed in equal parts, added to a tumblerful of warm water. When the mucous membrane is much swollen and the nasal passage in consequence much blocked up, it becomes necessary to reduce this swelling in order to relieve the inflammation. This is done most effectively by the galvano-cautery. Relief is often obtained from the inhalation of menthol or benzedrine, but excessive use of the latter may lead to atrophy of the mucous membrane, and it should never be used except under medical supervision. When the inflammation is perpetuated by the presence of malformations in the nose, such as spurs on the septum, polypi, or suppuration in the sphenoidal or other sinuses, these conditions may be removed by operation.

In cases in which the inflammation is due to penicillin-sensitive organisms, the local application of penicillin as a spray may be of value.

When dry crusts tend to form and block up the nose they may be removed by the same alkaline douches, and also by the simple expedient of plugging up the nostrils with pieces of cotton-wool for a quarter of an hour, just sufficiently tightly to prevent air from passing out and in. If the latter plan be adopted the crusts are softened, a watery secretion is produced, and the crusts can be got rid of by gently blowing the nose, after the cotton-wool has been removed.

MALFORMATIONS OF THE NOSE are of various kinds. The external nose varies much in shape in different races, even in different families, and persons who desire for æsthetic reasons to alter the character of this feature can mould the cartilages to a considerable extent by constant manipulation or by wearing various appliances. Noses, which have become tip-tilted through sinking in of the bridge, may, after the disease which has caused the sinking has subsided, be improved by the injection of paraffin under the skin (*see* ARTIFICIAL LIMBS AND OTHER PARTS). As to the interior of the nose, the two cavities are practi-

cally never of equal size, the septum always bulging to one or other side, so that the passage of air is freer on one side than on the other. When this bulging is so marked that the septum touches the turbinated bones on one side, or when, owing to injury or other cause, 'spurs' and 'crests' have developed on the septum, considerable irritation may arise, and this may form the starting-point for chronic inflammation of the nose, hay fever, or asthma. These imperfections, though they often exist without the least ill-effect, and are only discovered accidentally, are readily removed by the specialist if necessary, with the knife, chisel, saw, or galvano-cautery, such operations being attended by but little pain. A more common abnormality is that in which the nose becomes pinched and narrow as the result of blockage by polypi, adenoids, and similar causes, and the person breathes in consequence through the mouth.

ADENOIDS, or ADENOID VEGETATIONS, means an overgrowth of the glandular tissue which is naturally found in small amount on the back of the upper part of the throat, into which the nose opens.

Causes.—This glandular tissue is in structure similar to the tonsils and lymphatic glands, and in children between the ages of five and twelve, particularly after some inflammatory condition of the respiratory passages or after one of the acute infections diseases, such as measles, it is liable to develop to such an extent as to fill up this portion of the throat and obstruct the passage of air through the nose and into the Eustachian tubes.

Symptoms. — Generally this overgrowth subsides as the child passes through his teens, but its continuance for even a few years may produce serious effects upon the child's physique and mental powers. The appearance of a child suffering from adenoids is highly characteristic. The mouth is kept constantly open, since breathing proceeds through it, and, as a result, the child is very liable to bronchitis, and he snores at night. The point of the nose is pinched and the nostrils narrow, since very little air passes through them, and the bridge of the nose is often flattened. The palate is highly arched and the front teeth often prominent. If the child be weak or rickety, the obstruction to the entrance of air into the chest is apt to produce a ' pigeon-breast '. Deafness, as the result of inflammation spreading up the Eustachian tubes from the throat to the drum of the ear, is very common, and may be permanent. There is also some interference with the senses of smell and taste, though this is not so serious as deafness. A typical mental condition is common among children thus affected, the child being generally listless and lacking in the power of concentration ; a fact that is made more noticeable by the heavy, stupid look which the open mouth and the deafness give to the face. The irritability of the nervous system, occasioned by the difficulty of breathing during sleep, renders these children, much more than others, prone to suffer from nightmares and from the habit of wetting the bed at night.

Treatment.—As already stated, it is not the occurrence but the overgrowth of adenoids that gives rise to trouble in children, and, even if large, they tend to subside as the child advances in years. It is often difficult to decide, therefore, whether an operation for their removal should be performed or not. Apart from any serious symptoms that may be occasioned, such as deafness or choking, which certainly call for operation, the usual test employed is the question as to whether the child can go about quietly without becoming short of breath, and can sleep with his mouth shut. The operation—which is simple, consisting in scraping the adenoids away with the curette or other instrument and in cutting out the tonsils, which, as a rule, are enlarged, along with the adenoids—is performed under an anæsthetic.

POLYPI are growths of a soft, jelly-like character, with more or less of a stalk, arising usually from the middle turbinated bone. They are the result of chronic inflammation in the hinder part of the nasal cavity, produced by frequent colds, following on some of the acute infectious diseases, or due to suppuration in one of the air cavities adjoining the nose.

Symptoms.—There is usually a sense of ' stuffiness ', and obstruction to

breathing through the nose ; occasionally the patient may be conscious of movement of the polypus as he breathes or talks. Many of the symptoms mentioned under chronic inflammation are present, as this condition is found in a greater or less degree along with polypi and is the cause of their development. When the nose is examined with a bright light and mirror, part of the polypus is often seen, and being of a glistening, greyish colour, contrasts strongly with the red mucous membrane of the nose.

Treatment.—These polypi occasion no danger to life. Malignant tumours are occasionally found growing in the nose, but are very rare, and when they do occur are hard in texture, unlike these soft mucous polypi. The polypi are, however, seldom or never single, and after a large one has been removed the smaller ones around grow into its place and must in turn be removed. The removal is generally effected, quite painlessly, by passing a wire ' snare ' along the corresponding nostril, catching the polypus, and tightening the wire around its stalk till it can be pulled off, and when periodically done, may at last result in a complete cure. Recurrence is also prevented in many cases by scraping the inflamed mucous membrane from which the polypi are growing, or, in cases due to suppuration in the ethmoidal air-cells, by a severer operation designed to remove completely the lateral part of the ethmoid bone.

BLEEDING FROM THE NOSE, or **EPISTAXIS.** (*See* Hæmorrhage.)

FOREIGN BODIES, such as buttons, slate-pencils, peas, and small stones, are often pushed into the nose by children, and as the floor of the nose slopes slightly backwards and downwards, they readily pass in beyond reach. Concretions form in the nose, as in other hollow organs : round small blood-clots, hairs, and the like, and these may grow to a considerable size.

Symptoms.—At first the foreign body may, if smooth, set up no symptoms, but soon swelling of the nose, discharge from one nostril, headache and various pains appear, especially if the body be one which swells, like a pea. These symptoms may to a certain extent pass off, and if the body be wedged in tightly beneath the inferior turbinated bone, it may remain there for years, causing little discomfort, till a severe attack of inflammation comes on. When there is a constant discharge of matter from one nostril without any known cause, it is probably due to some foreign body which has previously been introduced into the nose.

Treatment.—Tickling the nostril with a feather, or giving a large pinch of snuff, to provoke a vigorous sneeze, while the opposite nostril is closed by pressure with the finger, should be tried first of all. Very often this will drive out the stone, pea, etc. If not, removal by a medical man, aided by a speculum and a bright light, is comparatively easy, much more so than in the case of bodies pushed into the ear. In the case of children, an anæsthetic is generally necessary, as the child will not remain still.

LOSS OF SENSE OF SMELL, or ANOSMIA, may be caused by conditions which block the lower part of the nose and produce a sodden condition of the mucous membrane in which the olfactory nerves end. Such conditions are polypi and chronic inflammation. Certain drugs, such as carbolic acid, are very destructive of this sense, and douching the nose with carbolic lotion has been known to produce loss of smelling power. A severe cold in the head causes temporary loss. It may also follow injuries to the brain and fractures of the skull involving the olfactory nerves. A powerful odour, when allowed to act upon the nose for long, may paralyse the sense of smell for that particular odour, although the sense may remain quite acute for all other smells. For this reason the nose is an uncertain guide to the presence of poisonous gases in the air, for the smelling power may quickly become numbed by such a gas as coal gas or prussic acid.

SUPPURATION IN THE SINUSES connected with the nose is of fairly frequent occurrence. Suppuration in the *frontal* sinus is rare, because of the very efficient drainage from this cavity straight downwards into the nose, whilst suppuration in the *cells of the sphenoid and ethmoid* bones, unless it causes polypi, is apt to escape notice, but the *antrum of Highmore* or *maxillary sinus* lying in the maxillary bone close to the roots of the upper row of teeth, from which it is separated only by

mucous membrane and thin bone, and opening only by its upper part into the nose, is very liable to become inflamed and to have pus collect in it.

Symptoms.—When suppuration occurs in the *frontal sinuses,* severe headache is apt to result as well as discharge from the nose. When suppuration takes place in the *sphenoidal sinuses,* there is constant purulent discharge either from the nose or into the throat, and defects may be produced leading to general debility, or inflammatory changes may be set up in the eye or its optic nerve, which lie in close relation to these sinuses. The effects of a collection of pus in the *maxillary sinus* may be very slight ; intermittent pain of a neuralgic character often felt above one eye, toothache, and slight swelling of one cheek may be the only signs for a long time. Generally, however, attention is called to the nose by a slight intermittent discharge of matter from one nostril, especially when the head is laid upon the opposite side. The small operation of pushing a hollow needle through the plate of bone separating the nose from the antrum, which is no thicker than a playing-card, is bloodless and almost painless, and if matter runs from the needle the diagnosis is confirmed.

Treatment.—In the case of the maxillary antrum, the infection may respond to inhalations, and, for this purpose, penicillin is being used with increasing frequency when the infecting organism is penicillin-sensitive. In more severe cases it may be necessary to drain the antrum through an opening made between the antrum and the nose, as described in the preceding paragraph. Many different antiseptic solutions are used for washing out the antrum, including penicillin. It is sometimes advisable to give a course of penicillin by intramuscular injection, or a course of one of the sulphonamides, in addition to local treatment. Should the infection of the antrum be due to dental trouble, then this must be dealt with.

A more serious operation is necessary in order to explore and drain the frontal sinuses, the incision being made usually along the line of the eyebrow. In the case of the sphenoidal sinuses, these are explored and scraped out through the nose under a general anæsthetic.

21

NOSOLOGY (νόσος, disease ; λόγος, discourse) is the term applied to scientific classification of diseases.

NOSOPHOBE is a person who has a morbid fear of contracting a certain disease.

NOSTALGIA (νόστος, return home ; ἄλγος, grief) means a form of melancholy or aggravated home-sickness occurring in persons who have left their home.

NOTIFIABLE DISEASES are diseases, usually of an infectious nature, which are required by law to be made known to a health officer or Local Authority.

NOVOBIOCIN is an antibiotic derived from cultures of *Streptomyces spheroides* or *Streptomyces niveus*. It is particularly active against staphylococci, and has proved especially useful in the treatment of staphylococcal infections which have not responded to treatment with other antibiotics, or in which the causative organism is resistant to such antibiotics.

NOVOCAIN is a proprietary name for PROCAINE HYDROCHLORIDE (*q.v.*).

N-RAYS (*see* LIGHT TREATMENT).

NUCHA is the Latin name for the back of the neck.

NUCLEUS (*nux*, a nut) means the central body in a cell, which controls the activities of the latter. (*See* CELL.)

NULLIPARA is the term applied to a woman who has never borne a child.

NUMBNESS (*see* TOUCH).

NUMMULAR SPUTUM (*nummulus*, money) is expectoration which when spat into water flattens out into a shape like coins. (*See* EXPECTORATION.)

NURSING as a profession requires an elaborate training, although persons are often called upon to nurse relatives and friends without any previous experience of the subject. It is with reference to the latter contingency that the following remarks apply, as it would be quite impossible even to state briefly the many duties which hospital training teaches. Professional nursing falls into four

divisions : (*a*) *Hospital nursing*, which forms a training for all the other kinds of nursing. The best training is to be had in one of the large hospitals, and it may be said generally that it is impossible to obtain a satisfactory training in any hospital having less than a hundred beds. The certificates granted by smaller hospitals, or for a training in general nursing lasting less than four years, are of little value. Special departments, such as fevers and midwifery, require only short courses, particularly if a nurse has already had general nursing experience. (*b*) *Private nursing*, *i.e.* nursing of a single patient, to whom the nurse's undivided attention is given, at home. (*c*) *District nursing*, which is the most arduous, and requires the greatest skill in the nurse. In this type of nursing, a large number of patients, especially in the poorer classes, are visited at home, and not only a long and varied training but great self-reliance is required of the nurse, who has to do much, unaided by medical supervision. (*d*) *Midwifery nursing*, which includes the care of mother and child for about a month after the latter is born.

Information on various special subjects arising in the course of a nurse's duties will be found under ANTI-SEPTICS, ASEPSIS, BATHS, BED, BED CHANGING, BED SORES, BLISTERS AND COUNTER-IRRITANTS, BLOOD-LETTING, CATHETERS; CHILDREN, PECULIARITIES OF ; CUPPING, DIET, DISINFECTION, DOUCHE, DYSPEPSIA (Stomach washing), ELECTRICITY IN MEDICINE, ENEMA, FEEDING, FOMENTATIONS, GARGLES, HÆMORRHAGE, INFANT FEEDING, IN-FECTION, LIGHT, MASSAGE, PEPTONIZED FOODS, POULTICES, TEMPERATURE, VENTILATION, WET PACK, WOUNDS.

The following remarks upon home nursing are made under the two headings of : (1) *the sick-room*; (2) *the patient*.

(1) **The sick-room.**—The *situation* of the room is a matter of some importance. It must be bright and sunny, and should therefore, if possible, look to the south or south-west. It should be as much cut off from the general household as possible, and should, therefore, be at the end of a corridor or top of the house, and in infectious cases may be still more effectively isolated by

hanging, outside the door, a sheet sprinkled from time to time with weak antiseptic lotion. This allows of the door being left open if necessary. Good drainage is of the utmost importance if there is a fixed basin in the room, particularly in the case of surgical or lying-in patients. The room should, in every case, be as large and airy as possible, for coldness is a minor danger and of far less importance than defective ventilation. The great test of *ventilation* is the presence or absence of the faintest ' stuffy ' smell in the room. If the patient complains of any draught, the window should not be shut, but the stream of air is kept off the bed by a screen or a sheet supported on a clothes-screen. A thermometer should always hang on the wall, so that the *temperature* of the room can be kept fairly uniform, and a good average temperature is about 60° to 65° F., although in bronchitis and other chest complaints it may be advisable to keep the air warmer. A *fire* should always be kept on in a sick-room, for the purpose of burning dressings, rags, etc., and also to aid ventilation, even if not needed for warmth. In serious cases there should be no fire-irons, but the fire should be poked with a stick. When a patient is wakeful at night, a screen should be placed in front of the fire to keep the flickering light off the patient's eyes. Artificial lighting should be adequate, but so arranged that it will not inconvenience the patient. There should be as little *furniture* as possible in a sick-room. A bed, table, and two chairs are all that is absolutely necessary, and there need be no carpet save a small piece of drugget at the bed-side. Furniture should not be dusted, nor must the floor be swept during an illness, but the furniture may be wiped daily with a damp cloth, and the floor may be washed when required, or, preferably, gently swept with an oily mop. As to the disinfection of a room after the nursing of an infectious case, see DISINFECTION. When preparations are being made for a *surgical operation* at home a large but narrow strong deal table should be placed immediately before the window, and on it should be laid a couple of blankets, a large sheet of mackintosh, and a clean pillow. Several basins and a large supply of

clean linen towels should be at hand, as well as a plentiful supply of boiling water, and a ewer full of water which has been boiled and set aside to cool, covered by a towel.

(2) **The patient.**—In putting an injured person to bed, it is important to remove the *garments* first of all from the sound arm or leg, and lastly from the injured limb, which is then moved as little as possible. On the other hand, and for the same reason, in putting on garments the injured limb should be the first to have the garment drawn over it. While a patient, and especially one greatly prostrated, lies in bed, one of the chief duties of the nurse is the care of his *skin*. The patient should be washed daily all over with warm water. The ordinary bed-clothes are removed before commencing the washing and aired at the fire ; during the process of washing the patient is covered by another blanket. During the washing it is quite unnecessary that the skin should be exposed, the blanket being raised over one part, which is washed and dried before the washing of another part is begun, so that there ought to be no risk of chill. Further, the back and all bony prominences must be examined at the same time for any trace of redness, which is the first sign of a bed sore, and treated promptly if any sign of a bed sore appears. (*See* BED SORES.) When the chest is affected, jackets made of two flaps of gamgee tissue, secured by tapes on the shoulders and beneath the arms, keep the chest warm, and are more easily removed for examination than more closely fitting flannels.

Hot tins or bottles are often put in bed for warmth, and these should *never* be put in bed unprotected by a woollen covering. They may be placed in flannel bags, in stockings, or wrapped in shawls, and this precaution is specially necessary in the case of patients unconscious after a severe operation, or paralysed, and so to some extent insensible of heat. Otherwise very serious burns may result.

In cases of rheumatism and Bright's disease, patients are generally placed directly between *blankets without sheets*, although a draw-sheet is necessary for cleanliness. The patient also wears a flannel night-dress, and the blankets

643

and night-dress must then be changed and washed very frequently. In cases of heart disease there should be a number of pillows, if not a *bed-rest*, breathing being easier when the patient reclines in a half-sitting posture. When the patient has to sit up for long periods, an *air-cushion* makes this position easier, or a high table placed across the bed and provided with a pillow upon which he can lean his arms. Care should always be taken to keep the shoulders warmly wrapped up. When the legs are swollen or inflamed, they should be raised on a pillow, or the foot of the bed may be tilted up on wooden blocks. Paralysed or helpless cases should be placed upon a *water-bed* from the first. A water-bed is most easily managed if it be in two sections, each covering half the bed. The water-bed is filled with water before the patient is laid upon it, and should not be quite tightly filled. It is separated from the patient by a blanket and sheet. The more modern *air-bed* is in many respects preferable to a water-bed (*see* BED). If, in paralysed or other cases, the weight of the bed-clothes be found irksome, they should be raised from the patient by an *iron-wire cage*, and it is then necessary to add an extra blanket to the coverings. Finally, it is well in nursing cases of long duration to have *two beds*, in one of which the patient spends the day and in the other of which he sleeps at night. Still better, if the circumstances of the house and the nature of the case permit, is the plan of having a day bedroom and a night bedroom.

Any *medicines* which the patient may have to take should be kept in a different part of the room from bottles containing lotions and other fluids intended for external application, and the nurse should never pour out a dose without previously reading the label on the bottle.

In *dressing* surgical cases, the nurse should boil any instruments she uses every day, and should wash her hands thoroughly with soap and water, and then steep them in an antiseptic lotion such as corrosive sublimate (1 in 4000) or lysol (1 in 100), before touching the injured part. She should also remember that abrasions or pustules upon her hands form a source of danger both to

herself and still more to the patient, and these should be carefully covered with collodion.

The nurse attending an *infectious case* should have in the room constantly a basin containing corrosive sublimate lotion (1 in 2000), in which she can rinse her hands each time she touches the patient, and before going out to mix with other people she should take a bath, and put on a complete change of clothing.

In all cases the nurse must, in order to discharge her duties well, have good food, sleep eight hours in every twenty-four, quite free from any chance of being roused to attend the patient, and have two hours daily for exercise and relaxation.

NUTMEG is the kernel of the seed of *Myristica fragrans*, an East and West Indian plant, mace being its outside covering. It is seldom used now in medicine.

NUTS, which consist to the extent of one-half or more of vegetable fat, form a highly concentrated kind of nourishment, and if suitably prepared, for example, by roasting to render them more digestible, become of higher nourishing value than cheese, and may to a considerable extent act as substitutes for meat. The chestnut and the almond are the most generally valuable forms of nut.

NUX VOMICA is the seed of *Strychnos nux-vomica*, an East Indian tree. The seed is circular, flattened with a depression in the centre, greyish in colour, and covered with short satiny hairs. It has an intensely bitter taste. The medicinal properties of the plant are almost entirely due to two alkaloids, strychnine and brucine, which it contains. (*See* STRYCHNINE.)

NYCTALOPIA (νύξ, night ; ἄλαος, blind ; ὤψ, eye) is another name for night blindness.

NYSTAGMUS (νυσταγμός, drowsiness, nodding) means a condition in which the eyeballs show constant, fine, jerky movements of an involuntary character.

NYSTAGMUS

The movement may be from side to side, from above down, or rotary ; and it may be present only when the person looks in a certain direction. It appears in children who have some defect in vision, such as that due to an opacity on the cornea, and it is caused by some occupations, such as that of miners, due principally to inadequate lighting.

NYSTATIN

It also occurs in certain nervous diseases, *e.g.* multiple sclerosis.

NYSTATIN is an antibiotic isolated from *Streptomyces noursei*. It was the first antibiotic to be isolated which was active against fungus diseases, and is proving particularly useful in the treatment of moniliasis (*q.v.*).

O

OATMEAL is a meal made from oats. Two-thirds of its weight consists of carbohydrate in the dry state, but when cooked in the form of porridge it contains in addition about seven times its weight of water. Dry oatmeal contains approximately 12 per cent. of protein, 5 per cent. of fat, and 70 per cent. of carbohydrate ; and 1 ounce (28·5 grammes) has an energy-producing equivalent of over 100 calories.

OBESITY (*obesus*, corpulent). (*See* CORPULENCE.)

OBSESSION (*obsessio*, a besieging) in medicine means the sudden domination of the mind by an idea or emotion, leading to impulsive acts which are beyond the control of the will, the power of judgment being for a time lost.

OBSTETRICS (*obstetrix*, a midwife) means the art of midwifery. (*See* LABOUR.)

OBSTRUCTION OF THE BOWELS (*see* INTESTINES, DISEASES OF).

OCCIPUT (*occipitium*, the back of the head) is the name given to the lower and hinder part of the head where it merges into the neck.

OCCUPATIONAL DISEASES (*see* TRADE DISEASES).

OCHRONOSIS is the term given to a very rare condition in which the ligaments and cartilages of the body, and sometimes the conjunctiva, become stained by dark brown or black pigment. This may occur in chronic carbolic poisoning, or in a congenital disorder of metabolism in which the individual is unable to break down completely the tyrosine of the protein molecule, the intermediate product, homogentisic acid, appearing in the urine—this being known as alkaptonuria.

OCULENTUM is an ointment for application to the eye.

ODONTALGIA (ὀδούς, tooth ; ἄλγος, pain) is another name for toothache.

ŒDEMA (οἴδημα, swelling) means dropsical swelling due to the passage of fluid through the walls of blood- or lymph-vessels into the spaces of cellular tissue beneath the skin, or beneath a mucous membrane, or into internal organs. (*See* DROPSY.)

ŒSOPHAGOSCOPE is an instrument constructed on the principle of the telescope, which on introduction into the mouth is passed down the œsophagus and enables the observer to see the state of the oesophagus.

ŒSOPHAGUS (οἰσοφάγος), or GULLET, is the tube which conveys the food and drink from the throat down to the stomach. It begins above at the level of the sixth cervical vertebra, and, lying close against the left side and front of the spinal column, passes downward through the neck and chest to pierce the diaphragm, and then opens into the stomach. It consists of three coats : a strong outer coat of muscle fibres in two layers, the outer running lengthwise, the inner being circular ; inside this a loose connective tissue coat containing blood-vessels, glands, etc. ; and finally a strong mucous membrane lined by epithelium, which closely resembles that of the mouth and skin. For diseases to which the œsophagus is liable *see* THROAT, DISEASES OF.

ŒSTRADIOL is the name given to the hormone secreted by the ovarian follicle. Œstradiol is responsible for the development of the female sexual characteristics, of the breasts, and of part of the changes that take place in the uterus before menstruation. It is useful, given by injection, in controlling the disturbances of the menopause.

ŒSTRIOL (*see* ŒSTROGEN).

ŒSTROGEN is the general term applied to any one of the female sex hormones, among which are the follicular hormone œstradiol (*q.v.*), its excretion product ŒSTRONE (obtained from urine), and ŒSTRIOL, which is obtained from pregnancy urine and from the placenta. The general action of these œstrogens is to maintain the normal function and structure of the female generative organs. (*See also* ETHINYLŒSTRADIOL, *and* STILBŒSTROL.)

ŒSTRONE (see ŒSTROGEN).

OFFICIAL (officialis) is a term applied to drugs and preparations which are authorized by pharmacopœias and other recognized lists.

OFFICINAL (officina, shop) is a term applied to drugs and preparations which are regularly kept for sale in the shops of druggists.

OILS are divided into *fixed oils* and *volatile* or *essential oils*. FIXED OILS are of the nature of liquid fats composed of a fatty acid and glycerin, for example olive oil, which consists of a mixture of glycerin compounds of oleic acid and palmitic acid. Other examples of fixed oils are almond oil, linseed oil, and cod-liver oil. Fixed oils are used as foods, and in large quantities as mild aperients. Some fixed oils have important special properties by virtue of active principles that they contain, for example castor oil and croton oil, which act as purgatives. Fixed oils are obtained from the fruits or seeds of plants or from animal tissues by pressure, or by boiling with water and skimming off the melted oil. Fats are fixed oils which are solid at ordinary temperatures and are extracted by combination of heat and pressure. An example of an animal fat is lard, and of a vegetable fat, cocoa butter. Fixed oils can be dissolved in ether and chloroform.

VOLATILE or ESSENTIAL OILS resemble fixed oils in being soluble in ether or chloroform and in being lighter than water. Examples of these are the oils of dill, anise, cajuput, caraway, cloves, cinnamon, eucalyptus, juniper, lavender, lemon, peppermint, rosemary, rue, mustard, and turpentine. The volatile oils have some actions in common by being in small doses antispasmodic, analgesics, and cardiac stimulants, and by possessing a mild antiseptic and disinfectant action. Most of them are prepared by distillation. Their composition varies considerably, some being of the nature of alcohols, others ketones, others allied to carbolic acid. Volatile oils can be dissolved to a small extent in water, to which they communicate their scent and other properties, and these aquæ or waters are much used in treating colic and other spas-

modic conditions, usually in doses of one or two tablespoonfuls. Volatile oils are also readily soluble in spirit containing 90 per cent. of alcohol, and these spirits usually contain about 10 per cent. of the volatile oil and are given in doses of from 5 to 30 drops.

For oils of the petroleum series, see PARAFFIN.

OINTMENTS are mixtures of medicinal substances with lard, benzoated lard, paraffin or vaseline, and wool-fat (lanoline), intended for external application. Those made up with lanoline, which is a natural skin fat, are much more readily absorbed than those, for example, made from paraffin, which is used for ointments designed simply to lie upon the surface.

Other substances occasionally used to form the body of an ointment are almond oil, bees-wax, camphor, glycerin, oleic acid, spermaceti, and prepared suet.

Among the most useful ointments are the following : *Simple ointment* is made from wool-fat, hard and soft paraffin, and is used for application to chafed surfaces. *Cold cream*, made of bees-wax, spermaceti, almond oil, rose water, and attar of rose, is used for a similar purpose. *Boric acid ointment* is much used for lubricating instruments, dressing ulcers, etc. *Yellow oxide of mercury ointment* is much used for treating inflammation about the eye.

OLD AGE (see AGE, NATURAL CHANGES IN).

OLEANDOMYCIN is an antibiotic derived from *Streptomyces antibioticus*. It is active against many Gram-positive organisms and some Gram-negative organisms.

OLEIC ACID is the commonest of naturally occurring fatty acids, being present in most fats and oils in the form of triglyceride. Its formula is $CH_3(CH_2)_7CH=CH(CH_2)_7COOH$.

OLEOTHORAX means (1) the presence of oil in the thoracic cavity, and (2) the operation of injecting oil into the pleural cavity in order to compress a tuberculous lung.

OLFACTORY NERVE, or NERVE OF SMELL, is the first cranial nerve.

OLIGÆMIA

OLIGÆMIA (ὀλίγος, small; αἷμα, blood) means a diminution of the quantity of blood in the circulation.

OLIGURIA means an abnormally low excretion of urine, such as occurs in acute nephritis.

OLIVE OIL is the oil obtained by pressure from the fruit of *Olea europæa* (*see* OILS). It is practically a pure fat, and one ounce (28·5 grammes) has an energy equivalent of about 270 calories.

OMENTUM (for *operimentum*, a coverlet) is a long fold of peritoneal membrane, generally loaded with more or less fat, which hangs down within the abdominal cavity in front of the bowels. It is formed by the layers of peritoneum that cover the front and back surfaces of the stomach in their passage from the lower margin of this organ to cover the back and front surfaces of the large intestine. Instead of passing straight from one organ to the other, these layers dip down and form a sort of fourfold apron. It is to the increasing deposit of fat in this structure that the large size of the abdomen is largely due in persons of middle age who are large eaters. This omentum is often known as the great omentum, to distinguish it from two smaller peritoneal folds that pass from the stomach, the one to the liver (gastro-hepatic omentum), the other to the spleen (gastro-splenic omentum).

OMPHALUS (ὀμφαλός) is another name for the navel or umbilicus.

ONCHOCERCIASIS.—Infestation with the nematode worm *Onchocerca volvulus*. This worm is found on the west coast of Africa and infests the subcutaneous and connective tissues of man, forming nodular cystic tumours which contain masses of worms and their embryos.

Larval forms (microfilariæ) may appear in the blood and lymph channels. Microfilariæ may invade the eye, causing conjunctivitis, iritis, keratitis, choroiditis—and blindness. The parasite is transmitted to man by the buffalo gnat *Simulium damnosum*.

Onchocerca cæcutiens, found in Guatemala, and Mexico, is doubtfully distinguished as a separate species.

648

OPHTHALMOPLEGIA

ONCOLOGY is that part of medical science which is concerned with the problems of tumours of the body.

ONYCHIA (ὄνυξ, the nail) means an inflammation affecting the nails. (*See* NAILS, DISEASES OF.)

ONYCHOGRYPHOSIS is the term applied to a distortion of the nail in which it is much thickened, overgrown and twisted on itself. This usually affects a toe-nail and is the result of chronic irritation and inflammation.

OOPHORECTOMY (ὠόν, egg; φέρω, I carry; ἐκ, out; τέμνω, I cut) is a term applied to removal, by operation, of an ovary. When the ovary is removed for the presence of a cyst, the term ' ovariotomy ' is usually employed.

OOPHORITIS is another name for ovaritis or inflammation of an ovary.

OOPHORON (ὠόν, egg; φέρω, I carry) is another name for the ovary.

OPEN-AIR TREATMENT (*see* TUBERCULOSIS).

OPERATION. — The general principles upon which an operation is conducted are mentioned under ANTISEPTICS and ASEPSIS. The preparations for an operation in a private house are mentioned in the article NURSING. The method of healing after an operation is mentioned under WOUNDS.

OPHTHALMIA (ὀφθαλμία) means inflammation of the eye, the term being used sometimes instead of conjunctivitis. (*See* CONJUNCTIVITIS *under* EYE, DISEASES OF.)

OPHTHALMOPLEGIA (ὀφθαλμός, the eye; πληγή, a blow) means a paralysis affecting one or both eyes, due to some disorder in the brain. When the condition affects the muscles that move the eyeballs from outside, the term external ophthalmoplegia is applied to it; when the intrinsic muscles of the eye are affected, causing interference with the size of the pupil and with the accommodation of the eye for near and distant vision, internal ophthalmoplegia is the name given.

OPHTHALMOSCOPE (ὀφθαλμός, the eye; σκοπέω, I look at) is an instrument used for the examination of the back of the eye, and for the detection of defects in its transparent contents. Owing to the fact that the interior of the eye, like the inside of a camera, is black, and that the light enters only by a small opening in front, one cannot look into the eye under ordinary circumstances without, in the act of so doing, obstructing the entrance of direct light sufficient to light it up. It is to overcome this difficulty that an ophthalmoscope is used. Nowadays an electric ophthalmoscope, in which light is produced from a dry cell in the handle of the instrument, is used.

The ophthalmoscope is of immense value, not only to the ophthalmic surgeon, but also to the physician in the diagnosis of general diseases. The eye is the only position in the living body where the end of a nerve (optic nerve), together with an artery and vein (retinal artery and vein), is exposed to view; so that the physician, by examining them, gains important information as to the general condition of the nervous and circulatory systems.

OPISTHOTONOS (ὀπισθότονος, drawn backwards) is the name given to a position assumed by the body during one of the convulsive seizures of tetanus. The muscles of the back, by their spasmodic contraction, arch the body in such a way that the person for a time may rest upon the bed only by his heels and head.

OPIUM (ὄπιον), which is perhaps the most valuable remedy in the whole range of medicine, is the dried juice of the unripe seed-capsules of the white Indian poppy, *Papaver somniferum*. It is cultivated mainly in India, but it is also produced in Persia, China, and the Asiatic provinces of Turkey. The opium possesses its medicinal properties only when produced under favourable conditions of soil and climate, and the juice of other species of poppies grown in temperate climates is almost useless. The juice is obtained by scarifying the seed capsules of the poppies before they are ripe, and next day collecting the gummy sap which has exuded from the cuts. This is dried with great care, kneaded, and carefully tested. Good

21 a

opium should contain about 10 per cent. of morphine, to which its action is chiefly due. It is a brown, resinous-looking substance, or brown powder, with characteristic smell and bitter taste. The opium used in China is mixed with linseed oil, which renders it more suited for smoking. The action of opium depends upon the alkaloids it contains, of which no fewer than eighteen are available from different kinds. Of these, the chief are morphine, codeine, narcotine, thebaine, papaverine, and naceine, and as the action of these differs considerably, the effect of the opium naturally varies according to the proportion of each that it contains. Turkish opium, which is purest in morphine, is generally regarded as the best, the use of Indian opium, which contains a large proportion of narcotine, being more apt to cause sickness. Opium, which is exported from the country of its production in balls or cakes, is often adulterated with sugar, vegetable extracts, gum, molasses, and even stones concealed in the middle of the cakes, and it is therefore very carefully tested before sale.

The importation into Britain of opium is very carefully regulated under the *Dangerous Drugs Act*. Similar regulations govern the sale and distribution of any preparation of morphine or diamorphine (heroin) stronger than 1 part in 500.

The preparations of opium are numerous. Powdered opium (containing 10 per cent. of morphine) is frequently used in doses ranging from $\frac{1}{2}$ to 3 grains (30 to 200 mg.). Among the other solid preparations are the dry extract of opium (containing 20 per cent. of morphine), of which the dose is $\frac{1}{4}$ to 1 grain (15 to 60 mg.); ipecacuanha and opium powder, better known as Dover's powder (containing 10 per cent. of opium), in doses of 5 to 10 grains (300 to 600 mg.); aromatic chalk powder with opium (containing 0·25 per cent. of morphine), much used for the treatment of diarrhœa, in doses of 10 to 60 grains (600 mg. to 4 grammes). Of the liquid preparations, the tincture of opium, better known as laudanum (containing 1 per cent. of morphine), is the most used, in doses of 5 to 30 minims (0·3 to 2 ml.); the camphorated tincture of opium, also known as paregoric (containing 0·05 per cent. of morphine), is given in doses of 30 to 60 minims (2 to 4 ml.). A preparation of opium, known as 'nepenthe,' is particularly useful in children, the dosage being 1 minim for each year of age. A suppository of lead and opium (containing 3 grains (200 mg.) of lead acetate and 1 grain (60 mg.) of powdered opium) is also used.

The alkaloids, morphine and codeine, are administered in various forms. Morphine hydrochloride and morphine sulphate are given in doses from $\frac{1}{8}$ to $\frac{1}{3}$ grain (7·5 to 20 mg.) ; codeine phosphate in doses from $\frac{1}{4}$ to 1 grain (15 to 60 mg.). The liquor of morphine hydrochloride (containing 1 per cent. of morphine) is used like laudanum, in doses from 5 to 30 minims (0·3 to 2 ml.). A lozenge of morphine and ipecacuanha is used for inflamed conditions of the throat, and a suppository of morphine (containing $\frac{1}{4}$ grain (15 mg.) of morphine) for painful conditions of the lower bowel.

Action.—The action of opium varies considerably, according to the source of the drug and the preparation used ; it varies even more according to the age, race, and temperament of the individual. The unstable nervous system of children is profoundly affected by even the smallest doses, and the death of an infant has been caused by a few drops of laudanum, so that the drug is unsuited for use, except with great care, during childhood.

In small doses, opium produces a state of gentle excitement, the person finding his imagination more vivid, his thoughts more brilliant, and his power of expression greater than usual. This stage lasts for some hours, and is succeeded by languor. In larger, *i.e.* medicinal, doses this stage of excitement is short and is followed by deep sleep, from which the person can still be aroused as from natural sleep. When very large, *i.e.* poisonous, doses are taken, sleep comes on quickly, and passes into coma and death. The habitual use of opium obtains for it a great degree of tolerance, so that opium-eaters require to take large quantities, even many ounces, of laudanum daily, before experiencing its pleasurable effects. The need for opium also confers tolerance, so that persons

650

suffering great pain may take, with apparently little effect beyond dulling the pain, quantities which at another time would be dangerous.

It checks all secretions, except the sweat, and slows the processes of tissue change, this action being sometimes useful, sometimes a hindrance to its employment.

Uses.—Externally, opium was at one time widely used as an application to areas which are painful and inflamed, as in lumbago, inflammation of joints, pleurisy, peritonitis, shingles, etc. There is, however, no evidence that it is of any value when used in this way.

Internally, its great use is to quiet severe pain, such as that of colic or cancer, and for this purpose morphine is often given with atropine, which aids the effect in diminishing any spasm present, and at the same time is an antidote to the poisonous qualities of morphine. In conditions in which there is constant, irritating, useless cough, some preparation of opium or morphine is often used as an ingredient in cough mixtures to relieve this. In cases of pelvic pain, whether arising in the bowel, bladder, womb, or ovaries, morphine may be used in the form of suppositories to afford relief. All preparations of opium must be prescribed with discrimination, in view of the marked tendency to habit-formation.

OPIUM EATING (*see* DRUG HABITS).

OPIUM POISONING is responsible for a number of the deaths by poison that take place in England and Wales. Laudanum is the form generally responsible for fatalities, next in frequency comes opium, whilst morphine is only now and then responsible in the pure state. Perhaps there is no drug in which the amount that can produce serious consequences varies so much as in the case of opium. Two drops of laudanum have been recorded as fatal to an infant, whereas addicts of the drug have been known to drink it like wine, with only a stimulating effect.

Symptoms.—When a poisonous dose of any of the preparations of the drug has been taken, sleep rapidly comes on, becomes deeper and deeper, and passes gradually into a state of complete insensibility, usually within half an hour, although the effect may be postponed for several hours, particularly when the drug is taken along with spirituous liquors. Convulsions sometimes occur, especially in children, and vomiting may take place before sleep becomes deep, or as the person is recovering. The breathing is slow, quiet, and shallow ; and these characters become more and more marked as death draws nigh, the person dying, indeed, as the result of paralysis of the respiratory centre in the brain. The lips and face become livid and covered with cold sweat, and the pupils are much contracted. As a rule, death occurs in from seven to eighteen hours after the dose has been taken.

It is important to distinguish opium poisoning from the effect of alcohol and from apoplexy in the case of persons found unconscious. If the person can be roused, the case is probably not one of apoplexy. Further, when apoplexy is the cause there is usually paralysis in one arm or leg, which lies perfectly helpless, or paralysis all down one side. In distinguishing the effect of alcohol from that of opium, the smell of the breath may give assistance, but the state of the pupils, which are contracted in opium poisoning and dilated in alcoholism, is more important. Help may also be gained from the facts that in opium poisoning the perspiration is greater and the person is at first more easily roused. In no case should the person be handled roughly, and if there be any doubt he should be treated as for opium poisoning.

Treatment.—An emetic should be given as soon as possible (*see* EMETICS), and after this has acted, a cup of strong coffee should be swallowed. Even after an emetic has acted, and certainly if it fails to act, the stomach should be washed out with water containing potassium permanganate, which destroys the alkaloids of the opium. As an antidote, full doses of levallorphan or nalorphine should be given. Should neither of these be immediately available, injections of caffeine sodium benzoate, amphetamine, or nikethamide may be given.

It is important to keep the patient awake ; and for this purpose he must be walked up and down the room if possible, or one may tap him on the forehead with the finger-nails, flick him with wet towels, or apply other painful stimuli. From time to time strong coffee, spirits, and other stimulants may be given internally. If, in spite of all these measures, he becomes unconscious and the breathing begins to fail, artificial respiration must be performed. Generally speaking, by twelve hours after taking the poison the patient is either dead or is showing signs of recovery.

OPODELDOC is an old name for soap liniment.

OPOTHERAPY ($\delta\pi\delta s$, juice; $\theta\epsilon\rho\alpha\pi\epsilon i\alpha$ treatment) means treatment by juices, and is a general term applied to treatment of disease by the administration of extracts from the organs of animals.

OPSONINS ($\delta\psi\omega\nu\epsilon\omega$, I get food) are substances present in the serum of the blood which act upon bacteria, so as to prepare them for destruction by the white corpuscles of the blood. In the year 1903 the subject was first studied by Wright and Douglas, who obtained white corpuscles in a neutral fluid and serum separated from corpuscles by means of the centrifuge. It was found that, when bacteria were first mixed with healthy serum, the power of white corpuscles—which were subsequently added—to devour the bacteria was many times greater than that of other white corpuscles acting without the aid of serum, and deprived, therefore, of the help of opsonin.

In estimating the opsonic power of a patient a few drops of blood are drawn from his finger into a fine glass tube and the serum separated with the centrifuge. To the serum are added equal quantities of an emulsion of the bacteria the resistance to which is being tested, and of saline fluid containing white corpuscles derived from the blood of the same or another person. The three are drawn into a small tube and incubated at 37° C. for fifteen minutes, thus giving the corpuscles time to attack the bacteria. A microscope preparation is then made, suitably stained, and the average number of bacteria devoured by each corpuscle is determined. This number, divided by the number similarly obtained when tested with the serum of a person known to be healthy, gives the ' opsonic index ' of the patient tested. The opsonic power of the blood against various bacteria can be raised by the hypodermic injection of suitable ' vaccine '. Upon the injection of the vaccine, a fall in the opsonic index of the blood first takes place (negative phase), then a rise (positive phase) to a higher level than before.

OPTIC NERVE is the second cranial nerve, and connects the eye with the brain, conveying from the retina the impressions produced by light. (*See* EYE *and* VISION.)

ORANGE is an excellent source of vitamin C : 100 millilitres of orange juice contain 50 mg. of ascorbic acid (*i.e.* vitamin C). It is also used as a flavouring agent in the form of infusion, tincture and syrup of the peel. Fresh orange is also employed, often mixed with glucose, in feverish conditions for the action of the citric acid it contains. (*See* CITRIC ACID.)

ORBIT (*orbita*, a track) is the pyramidal hollow in the skull, situated on each side of the nose, in which the eye is placed. In addition to the eye, each orbit contains the lacrimal gland, a quantity of soft fat upon which the eye rests, and various blood-vessels, nerves, etc.

ORCHITIS (ὄρχις, a testicle) means inflammation of the testicle. (*See* TESTICLE, DISEASES OF.)

ORF is a widespread viral infection of sheep and goats which is sometimes transmitted to man, in whom it manifests itself as a skin eruption, usually on the hands, fingers, forearms and face.

ORGANIC DISEASE is a term used in contradistinction to the word functional, to indicate that some structural change is responsible for the faulty action of an organ or other part of the body. (*See* FUNCTIONAL DISEASES.)

ORGANIC SUBSTANCES are those which are obtained from animal or vegetable bodies, or which resemble in chemical composition those derived

from this source. Organic chemistry has come to mean the chemistry of the carbon compounds.

ORGANISMS (ὄργανον, a formed body). (*See* BACTERIOLOGY.)

ORGANO-PHOSPHORUS INSECTICIDES are a group of insecticides which act by inhibiting the action of cholinesterase (*see* ACETYLCHOLINE). For this reason they are also toxic to man and must therefore be handled with great care. The most widely used are parathion (*q.v.*) and malathion (*q.v.*).

Some of them are proving of value in agriculture because, when applied to plants, they are absorbed and distributed to all parts of the plant, where they may kill sucking insects such as aphids. (*See* INSECTS IN RELATION TO DISEASE.)

ORGANOTHERAPY (ὄργανον, organ ; θεραπεία, treatment) means the treatment of disease by the administration of animal organs or their extracts. In some cases in which the secretion of a gland is defective in consequence of atrophy or after removal of the gland, it is necessary to supply the defect by prolonged administration of an extract derived from the same gland of an animal such as the sheep. For example, in the disease known as myxœdema, which is caused by atrophy of the thyroid gland, the affected persons require to take a small but regular supply of thyroid extract (*see* MYXŒDEMA). In cases of hypogonadism œstradiol or testosterone is given according to whether the female or male gonad is at fault. In cases of diabetes, where the muscles are unable to take up the sugar that they require from the blood in consequence of failure of the pancreas to secrete a substance that normally effects this, the disease is relieved by the injection of insulin.

ORIENTAL PLAGUE (*see* PLAGUE).

ORIENTAL SORE, also known as DELHI BOIL and as ALEPPO EVIL, is a disease of tropical climates in which an ulcer begins in a small pimple, spreads, and then heals very slowly, leaving an unsightly scar. It is caused by a minute animal parasite *Leishmania* ' *ropica,* which is conveyed from animals to man by certain species of sandflies. Injection of pentavalent antimony compounds, such as sodium stibogluconate, has been successfully employed. (*See also* KALA-AZAR.)

ORNITHOSIS is a virus infection of birds which is transmissible to man.

ORTHOCAINE, or ORTHOFORM, is a whitish crystalline powder with soothing and antiseptic properties.

ORTHODIAGRAPH (ὀρθός, straight ; διαγράφω, I delineate) is the term applied to an X-ray apparatus for recording accurately the form and size of structures inside the body.

ORTHOPÆDICS (ὀρθός, straight ; παῖς, child).—Originally the general measures, surgical and mechanical, which can be used for the correction or prevention of deformities in children. Now, that branch of medical science dealing with bodily deformity, congenital or acquired.

ORTHOPNŒA (ὀρθόπνοια) is a form of difficulty in breathing so severe that the patient cannot bear to lie down, but must sit or stand up. As a rule, it occurs only in serious affections of the heart or lungs.

ORTHOPTIC TREATMENT is the term applied to the treatment of squint by giving special exercises for the muscles of the eye.

OSMOSIS (ὠσμός, a thrust) means the passage of fluids through a membrane, which separates them, so as to become mixed with one another. Osmotic pressure is a term applied to the strength of the tendency which a fluid shows to do this, and depends largely upon the amount of solid which it holds in solution.

OSSIFICATION (os, bone ; facio, I make) means the formation of bone. In early life, centres appear in the bones previously represented by cartilage or fibrous tissue, and from these the formation of true bone and deposit of lime salts proceed. When a fracture occurs, the bone mends by ossification of the clot which forms between the fragments. (*See* FRACTURES.) In old age an unnatural process of ossification often takes place in parts which should remain

cartilaginous, *e.g.* in the cartilages of the larynx and of the ribs, making these parts unusually brittle.

OSTEITIS (ὀστέον, a bone) means inflammation in the substance of a bone.

OSTEITIS DEFORMANS (*see* PAGET'S DISEASE OF BONE).

OSTEITIS FIBROSA CYSTICA GENERALISATA is a disease characterized by the presence of cysts in bones, which thereby become weakened and may break. The cysts form because calcium salts are drained from the bone into the blood stream, the result of the action of a tumour of the parathyroid glands. (*See* PARATHYROIDS.)

OSTEOARTHRITIS (ὀστέον, bone ; ἄρθρον, joint) is a term applied to a chronic inflammation of the bones composing a joint, and leading to deformity. It is gradually being replaced by the term, osteoarthrosis. (*See* RHEUMATISM.)

OSTEOCHONDRITIS means inflammation of both bone and cartilage.

OSTEOMALACIA (ὀστέον, bone ; μαλακός, soft) is a disease, in which the bones become slowly softened as the result of the absorption of the lime salts they contain. The cause of the disease is a deficiency of vitamin D in the food, combined with lack of sunshine. It affects especially mothers who have borne many children in rapid succession. For long considered rare in Britain, it has recently come to be recognized as not uncommon among old people, in whom it is presumably due to a faulty diet containing inadequate vitamin D, and lack of sunshine.

The most serious feature of the disease is the deformity which occurs in the softened bones owing to the weight of the body and the action of the muscles. This deformity, when it affects the bones of the pelvis and spine, may cause difficulty in childbirth, and is a source of great danger to mother and child.

Treatment consists basically of giving large doses of vitamin D, and then ensuring that the individual has a balanced diet containing a full complement of all the vitamins, including vitamin D.

OSTEOMYELITIS (ὀστέον, bone ; μυελός, marrow) means inflammation in the marrow of a bone. (*See* BONE, DISEASES OF.)

OSTEOPATHY is the name applied to a system of healing in which diseases are treated by manipulating bones and other parts with the idea of thereby restoring functions in the bodily mechanism that have become deranged.

OSTEOPOROSIS means increased porousness of bone due to lack of calcium salts. It is one of the manifestations of the ageing process. In old people it is liable to be induced by prolonged periods of immobilization in bed. This is one reason why elderly people should never be kept in bed a moment longer than necessary. Another preventive measure is to ensure that the elderly consume an adequate amount of calcium. This is most simply done by their taking a pint (0.5 litre) of milk a day.

OSTEOSCLEROSIS FRAGILIS GENERALISATA is an uncommon condition characterized by the appearance in the bony skeleton of scattered patches of abnormally dense bone. The cause of this abnormality is unknown, which may account for the number of long names given to it, for example : ALBERS-SCHÖNBERG DISEASE, OSTEITIS CONDENSANS GENERALISATA, OSTEO-PETROSIS, OSTEOPOIKILOSIS, MARBLE BONES, CHALKY BONES.

OSTEOTOMY is the operation of cutting of a bone.

OTITIS (οὖς, the ear) means inflammation of the ear. (*See* EAR, DISEASES OF.)

OTOLOGY is that branch of medical science which is concerned with disorders and diseases of the organ of hearing, one practising this branch being called an OTOLOGIST.

OTORRHŒA (οὖς, the ear ; ῥέω, I flow) means discharge from the ear. (*See* EAR, DISEASES OF.)

OTOSCLEROSIS is the term applied to the condition in which spongy bone forms in the capsule of the labyrinth of the ear and progressive deafness develops. It is the commonest cause of deafness in active adult life, and is

654

twice as common in women as in men. During the last twenty years surgical methods of treatment have been introduced, which restore hearing in 80 per cent. of cases. Three forms of surgical treatment are now available, known respectively as fenestration, stapes mobilization, and stapedectomy. For those in whom operation is unsuccessful, hearing-aids will enable them to hear again.

OUABAIN,—G-Strophanthin. A glucoside first obtained from the South African tree *Acocanthera ouabaia* : it was used as an arrow poison in East Africa. Ouabain is now obtained from the South African tree *Strophanthus gratus*. It is a cardiac stimulant, having a similar action to that of digitalis.

OVARIES.—The ovaries are the glands in which are produced, in the female sex, the ova, capable, if fertilized, of developing into new individuals. They are situated, one on each side, in the cavity of the pelvis, corresponding on the surface of the body approximately to the centre of the groin. Each is shaped something like an almond, is about 1½ inches (37 mm.) long, ½ inch (13 mm.) wide, and ¾ inch (19 mm.) in thickness, and is whitish in colour. It is attached to the broad ligament running from the womb to the side of the pelvis, by one edge along which blood-vessels and nerves enter. One end is connected to the expanded end of the Fallopian tube, as well as by a ligament to the side of the pelvis, and the other end to a ligament to the side of the womb. The ovary, therefore, lies to a considerable extent free in the pelvis.

The chief bulk of the ovary is made up of connective tissue, which differs from ordinary fibrous tissue in being composed of spindle-shaped cells. On the surface is a layer of columnar cells, and beneath this a dense connective tissue layer, the tunica albuginea. Beneath the tunica albuginea the structure appears to the naked eye to be of a granular character, this appearance being due to the presence of a layer of Graafian follicles, variously estimated at from 30,000 to 70,000 in number in the two ovaries. Each Graafian follicle is about $\frac{1}{100}$ inch (0.25 mm.) in diameter, and contains one (seldom more) ovum, each of these ova being capable of developing into a new individual. Every Graafian follicle consists essentially of a hollow ball of cells, embedded in which is a single large cell, the ovum, and each ovary contains Graafian follicles in all stages of maturity, from the rudimentary ones described above to several which are greatly increased in size through multiplication of the cells surrounding the ovum and the formation among them of a cavity distended with fluid. It is supposed that one at least of these follicles comes to maturity about half-way between two menstrual periods, distends till it reaches the surface of the ovary, and finally bursts, allowing of the escape of the contained ovum, which finds its way down the corresponding Fallopian tube into the womb. This process is known as ovulation. (*See* MENSTRUATION.)

For ovarian secretions, *see* Ovaries under ENDOCRINE GLANDS, and also ŒSTRADIOL, ŒSTROGEN, and PROGESTERONE.

OVARIES, DISEASES OF. — Although many of the aches and pains to which women are heir are unjustifiably attributed to disease of the ovaries, there is no doubt that, when diseased, the ovaries can be responsible for much ill-health.

INFLAMMATION OF THE OVARY (OVARITIS) seldom, if ever, occurs alone and is usually associated with inflammation of the Fallopian tubes (*i.e.* salpingitis) and of the pelvic peritoneum. It may be acute or chronic. The acute form is due to gonorrhœa, infection during the puerperium or following abortion, or infection from the alimentary tract, *e.g.* the appendix. If the acute form is not successfully overcome, it is liable to become chronic with exacerbations. In the chronic stage adhesions form which bind down and displace the ovaries, the Fallopian tubes, and the uterus. Bladder function is also liable to be interfered with. In all cases of infection of the ovaries and Fallopian tubes the possibility of this being due to tuberculosis must be considered, particularly in young patients.

Symptoms.—In the acute form these may be mild or severe, consisting of pain in the lower part of the abdomen, usually during or just after menstruation, prolongation of menstruation, and fever. There may also be pain on passing water, sickness and vomiting. In severe cases with high temperature there may be rigors. In chronic cases there may be backache, usually worse after a day's work, fatigue, excessive or painful menstruation, pain on passing water, sterility and debility. In more severe cases there may be a discharge from the vagina (*i.e.* leucorrhœa) and anæmia. Sometimes an abscess develops in the ovary or in the Fallopian tubes, and in these cases the general health is more likely to suffer because of toxic absorption.

Treatment.—In the acute cases this consists of rest in bed and the administration of penicillin or sulphonamides. Hot fomentations are useful to relieve pain. Hot douches to the vagina are not used as much as they were at one time, as they are sometimes liable to increase the pain. The diet should be light and nourishing. Care is necessary to ensure regular emptying of the bowels, but violent purgatives must not be used for this purpose. The majority of cases respond to such treatment. Operation is only indicated when there are signs of general peritonitis, or when there is no evidence of condition responding to medical treatment in two to three weeks. The treatment of chronic cases is similar, but here hot douches to the vagina twice daily are also of value. Operation is required for chronic cases if the general health is affected, if there are acute exacerbations, or if there is much persistent local pain and menorrhagia.

OVARIAN TUMOURS may be of several kinds. Solid tumours, either simple or malignant, are rare, far commoner being the cystic forms, which often reach a huge size. These cysts are of several types, sometimes consisting of a distended condition of the Graafian follicles, at other times being simple cysts filled with a complex papillary growth, again being dermoid tumours and containing fat, hair, teeth, and other structures associated with the skin, and yet again arising from the distension of some part of the parovarium, a rudimentary structure attached to the ovary.

The fluid in these cysts is sometimes of a greenish-grey or brown colour and viscid, ropy consistence, at other times clearer and thinner, and, in the case of dermoid tumours, usually of a greasy nature.

Symptoms.—These tumours generally remain quite painless till the weight and distension caused by their increasing size give trouble. They arise often in young women without any apparent cause. If they are not removed, some, which stand on the verge of being malignant tumours, increase rapidly in size, and all lead to great discomfort and loss of health, and finally shorten life.

Treatment.—The one method of treatment adopted now consists in *ovariotomy*. This operation should be performed early in the course of the disease, because, as the tumour grows, it contracts adhesions to surrounding organs, and these are the source both of the most distressing symptoms and of the chief difficulty and danger in a later operation. Most cases operated upon at an early stage recover well, the operation being one of the safest major operations in surgery.

OVARIOTOMY (*see* Ovarian Tumours *under* OVARIES, DISEASES OF).

OVI ALBUMEN is a Latin term for white of egg ; OVI VITELLUM is that for yolk of egg.

OVUM (*ovum*, an egg) is the single cell derived from the female, out of which a future individual arises, after its union with the spermatozoon derived from the male. (*See* EMBRYO.)

OXALIC ACID is not used in medicine, but it is of importance because it is an irritant poison, and has a domestic use for cleaning purposes. Oxalic acid, or binoxalate of potassium (salts of sorrel), is occasionally taken by mistake for Epsom salts or for cream of tartar. This substance is also important, because oxalate of lime is found in urinary sediment, and sometimes composes urinary calculi. (*See* BLADDER, DISEASES OF.) Oxalate of lime in the urine is derived partly from articles of food, like rhubarb, that contain it, and is partly produced within the body as the result of tissue change.

656

When poisoning is the result of taking oxalic acid or binoxalate of potassium, a large amount of chalk or whiting mixed with water should be given, and, if vomiting be not already present, an emetic ; afterwards the irritation resulting in the stomach and bowels is to be soothed by demulcents.

OXYCEPHALY, or STEEPLE HEAD, is the term for describing a deformity of the skull in which the forehead is high and the top of the head pointed. There is also poor vision and the eyes bulge.

OXYGEN (ὀξύς, acid ; γεννάω, I produce) is a colourless gas, devoid of smell, slightly heavier than common air. It was discovered almost simultaneously by Priestley in England and Scheele in Sweden in 1774. It forms rather more than one-fifth by volume of the atmosphere. It may be obtained by the fractional distillation of liquid air, or by the electrolysis of water. It is stored at high pressure (up to 120 atmospheres) in steel cylinders, from which it is obtained at any desired rate by turning a stop-cock.

Action.—Oxygen is necessary to life, and the process of respiration (*see* RESPIRATION) has, as one of its main objects, the supply of oxygen to the blood. Applied to the unbroken skin, oxygen has little effect, but when brought in contact with a wound or ulcer, it increases the circulation and acts as a stimulant.

The condition of oxygen want, or anoxæmia, may be produced by various conditions, such as damage to the lung by tumours, anæmia, etc., or defects of the circulation, *e.g.* valvular disease of the heart, in which the circulation is so slow that the tissues do not receive their proper amount of oxygen, and in cases of anæmia and poisoning where the blood is not capable of carrying its normal amount of oxygen. In these states, and above all in cases of anæmia and valvular disease, when the pulse is quick and feeble, when the patient's lips and ears are blue, and when the breathing is rapid and shallow, the administration of oxygen gives great relief.

Uses.—Oxygen is stored in cylinders which usually contain 20 or 40 cubic feet of the gas, but larger cylinders containing 100 cubic feet can be obtained. In severe cases of anoxæmia the rate at which oxygen may require to be delivered to the patient is between 4 and 6 litres per minute. A rubber tube is attached to the head of the cylinder, which passes through the glass tubes of a wash-bottle and is continued to either a mask, which fits over the patient's nose and mouth, or to a rubber catheter which is passed into one of the nostrils and fixed in position at the side of his face by a strip of sticking plaster. The use of the latter is unaccompanied by any sense of oppression to the patient.

Great advances have been made in recent years in the development of both oxygen masks and tents. The advantage of the latter is that the patient is breathing all the time in an atmosphere saturated with oxygen. Two examples of modern oxygen masks are shown in Plate XIV (facing p. 544).

A recent development in oxygen therapy is what is known as *hyperbaric oxygen*. This is the use of oxygen at high pressures, such as 3 atmospheres. Originally introduced as an adjunct to radiotherapy in the treatment of cancer, it is now being used in the treatment of carbon monoxide poisoning, *Clostridium welchii* infections (*q.v.*) and coronary thrombosis. The most convenient method of administering hyperbaric oxygen is in a special pressure chamber.

Substances which contain oxygen and are capable of giving it off, such as permanganate of potassium, peroxide of hydrogen, and charcoal, have a powerful effect as disinfectants either by destroying organisms or oxidizing noxious products of their growth. Such substances are therefore much used in the treatment of ulcers and various skin diseases and as antiseptics.

OXYMEL (ὀξύς, acid ; μέλι, honey) is an old-fashioned remedy for colds and sore throats, composed of vinegar and honey. It is given in doses of one or two teaspoonfuls.

OXYPHENONIUM is an anticholnergic drug which relieves spasm and hypermotility.

OXYTETRACYCLINE is an antibiotic derived from a soil organism, *Streptomyces rimosus*. Its range of antibacterial activity is comparable to that of tetracycline (*q.v.*).

OXYTOCIC.—Hastening parturition. Stimulating uterine contraction.

OXYTOCIN is the extract isolated from extract of the pituitary posterior lobe which stimulates the uterine muscle to contract. It is also known as pitocin.

OXYURIASIS is the condition of being infested with thread- or pinworms.

OXYURIS (ὀξύς, sharp ; οὐρά, tail) is another name for the thread-worm. (*See* PARASITES.)

OZÆNA (ὄζαινα, a fœtid polypus in the nose) is a chronic disease of the nose of an inflammatory nature, combined with atrophy of the mucous membrane and the formation of extremely foulsmelling crusts in the interior of the nose. (*See* NOSE, DISEASES OF.)

OZONE (ὄζω, I smell) is a specially active form of oxygen in which three volumes of the gas are condensed into the space ordinarily occupied by two. It has a characteristic smell, which may be noticed in the neighbourhood of dynamos, as ozone is produced by the passage through the air of electric sparks. It exists free in small quantities in the air of pine-clad mountains and of the seaside, where the invigorating properties of the fresh air may be partly due to its presence. It has also a powerful deodorant action.

P

PACEMAKER (see CARDIAC PACE-MAKER).

PACHYDERMIA (παχύς, thick; δέρμα, skin) means hypertrophy or thickening of the skin. PACHYDERMIA LARYNGIS is a name applied to thickening of the vocal cords due to chronic inflammation or irritation.

PACHYMENINGITIS (παχύς, thick; μῆνιγξ, a membrane) means inflammation of the dura mater of the brain and spinal cord. (See MENINGITIS.)

PACINIAN CORPUSCLES are minute bulbs at the ends of the nerves scattered through the skin and subcutaneous tissue, and forming the end-organs for sensation (Fig. 295).

PACKS (see WET PACK).

PÆDIATRICS (παῖς, child; ἰατρός, physician) means the branch of medicine dealing with diseases of children.

PAGET'S DISEASE OF BONE, or OSTEITIS DEFORMANS, is the term applied to a chronic disease in which the bones—especially those of the skull, limbs, and spine—gradually become thick and also soft, causing them to bend. The cause is not known.

PAIN is a necessary part of conscious existence, all our sensations being accompanied by more or less feeling of pleasure or pain. In the former case we seek the repetition of the sensations; in the latter case we instinctively avoid them, unless, by an act of will, we avoid the sense of pleasure or bear that of pain for some ulterior motive. The ability to perceive pain constitutes a special sense which the body has evolved, or with which it has been furnished, in order that it may preserve itself, by avoiding conditions that produce damage.

Pain is of various types. The most important is that caused by injury of the skin, as by a prick, burn, or pinch. This sense is quite distinct from that of touch. There are special nerve-fibres for the conduction of painful impressions running up the spinal cord near its central canal, while the fibres conveying the impressions for touch run up in the

posterior part of the cord. This is proved by the destruction of the sense of pain in the disease known as 'syringomyelia' (which affects the central part of the cord), notwithstanding the fact that the slightest touch can still be felt in the parts of the body incapable of feeling pain. This loss of the power to feel pain while the power to feel touches is retained is called 'analgesia'. Further, it is probable that these nerves of pain have special endings in the skin, since pain does not appear to be felt uniformly, but, like the other senses, at special spots thickly scattered over the surface. And it is also likely that there is a special centre in the brain for the reception of painful impressions.

Internal parts are much less sensitive than the skin, and diseases in them usually give rise to quite a different sensation. Indeed these parts, not being liable to damage by external objects, are not endowed with the power of feeling pain due to sudden injury, so that the bowel, when brought out through the skin, may be cut with scissors or knife, though the individual, unless he sees it, is quite unaware of what is taking place; tendon, muscle, and bone are also very insensitive, so that the two former may be cut or scraped without more than a slightly sickening sensation, or the ends of a broken bone rubbed together without causing severe pain.

Nevertheless inflammatory changes in these deep-seated structures, and disturbances in their functions, are capable of influencing the brain so as to produce the severest type of pain. This inflammation, particularly when seated in dense structures which cannot expand so as to prevent the congested blood-vessels of the part from pressing upon its nerves, is accompanied by 'throbbing' pain, and, in bone particularly, this is apt to be of a 'boring', excruciating character. The 'gnawing' pain of a tumour invading surrounding tissues is of a similar nature, and any source of irritation on the course of a nerve is apt to produce the severe pain of 'neuralgia'. Over-action of a weak part or muscle leads to continued pain of an 'aching' character, due probably to an irritating deposit of the chemical products of muscular activity, or may produce spasm, as in the ' stitch ' of the side caused by unwontedly violent exercise. Of a similar nature is the colic or ' griping ' pain, caused by irritation of the bowels, bile-ducts, ureters, etc., which in its severest forms may properly be designated ' agony ' (see COLIC). The ' burning ' pain of certain forms of dyspepsia is due to the action of an excessively acid gastric juice, and, like burns of the skin, is apparently due to irritation of the sensitive nerve-endings at points where the surface of the mucous membrane has become eroded.

Ordinary sensations of all sorts become painful when they are excessive, and thus liable to damage the organ in question, e.g. bright light, loud sound.

Painful sensations depend much also upon the state of the nervous system, varying according to the power of the nerves to conduct, and of the brain to receive, impressions. Some persons are notoriously better at bearing pain than others, and the healthy and strong are less affected by trivial injuries than those whose nervous system is in a state of ready irritability through chronic ill-health. Persons of strong will-power can undoubtedly inhibit painful impressions, like those from a surgical operation, just as they can control irregular movements, and so by a mental effort not only do such persons bear pain better, but they actually feel less pain. Similarly the mind that is dominated by an idea unconsciously inhibits painful impressions, so that they gain no entrance for the time, as in the case of soldiers wounded in the heat of battle, orators or preachers who are the victims of neuralgia, or even, in olden times, martyrs at the stake.

On the other hand, pain may be of a purely ' functional ' character, and a person of highly strung or disordered nervous system may suffer pain without any external cause, the mind misinterpreting or exaggerating sensations which by the healthy person would not be noticed. (See HYSTERIA.)

These facts are well known to those ' faith-healers ' and others who attempt to cure by a direct mental impression, and who by this means often succeed in alleviating pain, although only in special cases, such as the ' functional ' pains just mentioned, are they successful in ' curing ' the disease to which the pain is due, and of which it is the warning.

Pain in a certain part is not necessarily due to disease in the same part. In the case of injury to the skin covering the body, the mind, as the result of experience, very accurately refers the painful impressions down the nerves which bring them, to the parts from which they come. But when impressions come to the central nervous system from organs or parts of the body not usually liable to injury or disease, the mind is very apt to refer the pain to some other part which is more commonly the seat of pain, and whose nerve-fibres enter the same part of the brain or spinal cord as do those coming from the part which is really affected. For example, in the early stages of hip-joint disease, the pain is more frequently felt down the inner side of the thigh and knee than in the deep-seated hip-joint, since branches from the same nerves (obturator and anterior crural) supply the hip-joint and the skin of this particular area. For the same reason, the pain of spinal disease, due to pressure upon the large nerve roots close to the point where they enter the cord, is often referred, not to this unfamiliar seat of pain, but to the sides and front of the body where these nerves end in the skin. In this connection it may be stated that pain felt equally on both sides of the body is almost always due to some affection of the central nervous system.

In the case of the internal organs whose nervous control is derived from the sympathetic nervous system (in the case of the heart, lungs, stomach, and bowels partly also from the tenth cranial or vagus nerve), through which they often obtain complicated and very distant connections with the brain and cord, pain is frequently referred, in what seems at first sight to be a bizarre manner, to distant points. Much precise knowledge on this subject has, however, been gained by the researches of Head. *Referred pain* is often, in the case of the heart, stomach, liver, and bowels, felt on the surface situated over these organs, and the skin may be so tender that gentle pressure or even the slightest touch cannot be borne. Heart conditions are very liable also to cause pain running down the inner side of the left, and in some cases of the right, arm to the elbow. In dyspepsia, due to irritation of the stomach, the pain is often referred to the pit of the stomach or middle of the back. In conditions affecting the liver there may be pain in the region of the right shoulder. Affections of the lower end of the bowel commonly cause pain down the back of the thighs, especially of the left thigh, to the knee. Pain due to disorders of the womb is felt internally much less often than in the lowest part of the back and the thighs; and, when the ovaries or Fallopian tubes also are affected, the pain may have a very wide distribution, including the small of the back, the groin, and the front of the thigh, or it is occasionally referred to the hip or knee-joint, so that the case may for a time be mistaken for disease in one of these joints.

Treatment of pain.—There are three general principles by which the relief of pain may be attempted. (1) The most natural way is to remove the cause of pain, such as a decayed tooth, ulcer, abscess, or inflammatory condition of some internal organ, or to soothe the nerves of the affected part by warmth or some other means. (2) The nerves which convey impressions from the affected region may be treated so that their conducting power is lessened or stopped, as, for example, by administration of sedatives, use of electricity, local anæsthetics, or by chordotomy (q.v.) (see NEURALGIA). (3) The part of the brain which receives the impressions of pain may be dulled by drugs, or the influence of these impressions may be ' inhibited ' by powerful mental impressions, as in hypnotism, faith-healing, etc. (See also ANÆSTHETICS, ANALGESICS, ANODYNES, and under the headings of the various diseases that give rise to pain.)

PAINS (see LABOUR).

PAINTER'S COLIC (see COLIC, LEAD-POISONING).

PALATE (palatus, the roof of the mouth) is the partition between the cavity of the mouth, below, and that of the nose, above. It consists of the

hard palate towards the front, which is composed of a bony plate covered below by the mucous membrane of the mouth, above by that of the nose ; and of the soft palate farther back, in which a muscular layer, composed of nine small muscles, is similarly covered. The hard palate extends a little farther back than the wisdom teeth, and is formed by the superior maxillary and palate bones. The soft palate is concave towards the mouth and convex towards the nose, and it ends behind in a free border, at the centre of which is the prolongation known as the ' uvula '. When food or air is passing through the mouth, as in the acts of swallowing, coughing, or vomiting, the soft palate is drawn upwards so as to touch the back wall of the throat and shut off the cavity of the nose. Movements of the soft palate, by changing the shape of the mouth and nose cavities, are important in the production of speech.

PALATE, MALFORMATIONS OF.— The palate is subject to certain alterations, as the result of defective development. The hard palate may be much more arched than usual ; this is sometimes due to the failure to breathe through the nose, caused by the presence of adenoid vegetations in the throat (see NOSE, DISEASES OF).

In early embryonic life (see EMBRYO) there are certain clefts in the region of the throat and face, the nose being formed by the junction of one process which grows down from between the eyes (fronto-nasal process) and two which grow in, one from either side (maxillary processes). The fronto-nasal process produces the external nose, the septum of the nose, the central part of the upper lip, and that part of the upper jaw which carries the two front teeth. The maxillary processes form the remainder of the upper jaw and the palate on each side. These three should unite completely prior to birth, but if they fail to do so, a Y-shaped gap is left. This gap runs from the back of the palate forward to a point a little distance behind the front teeth, from which point a limb of the gap runs forwards to each nostril and through the upper lip. This complete state of cleft palate may occur ; or there may be only a partial gap in the soft palate, the parts having closed in front (Fig. 299); or again, there may be closure behind and only a notch be left in the lip or a single cleft in the edge of the upper jaw. The notch of the lip is known as hare-lip,

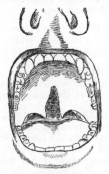

FIG. 299.—Cleft in the hinder part of the palate. (After Miller.)

from a fanciful resemblance to the hare, which has a notch in the centre of its lip (Fig. 300).

Cleft-palate and hare-lip should, if possible, be rectified by operation, because both are a serious drawback to feeding in early life, while later, hare-lip is a great disfigurement, and cleft-palate gives to the voice a peculiar

FIG. 300.—Double hare-lip. (After Miller.)

twang. When there is merely a slight degree of hare-lip, it is usual to operate a few weeks or even some days after birth, although, when the notch is very large, it may be necessary to wait till the child is several months old. The closure of a large cleft in the palate, which is a more formidable operation and accompanied often by much bleeding, is usually deferred till the child has gained some strength, and the most suitable time is generally held to be between eighteen months and two and

a half years of age, because the fault must be remedied before the child has learned to speak. The operations that are performed vary greatly in details, but all consist in paring the edges of the gap and drawing the soft parts together across it.

Until a hare-lip has been remedied, it is often necessary to feed the child with a spoon, as he cannot suck. When a cleft-palate is too wide for operation, its effects can be diminished in later life by wearing an artificial palate.

PALINDROMIC RHEUMATISM.—A form of rheumatism in adults characterized by multiple, afebrile attacks of acute arthritis, periarthritis, and occasionally para-arthritis, with pain, swelling, redness, and disability of one or more small or large joints, the attacks coming on suddenly, lasting a few hours to a few days then disappearing completely, to recur at irregular intervals.

PALLÆSTHESIA (πάλλω, I quiver ; αἴσθησις, feeling) means sensibility to the vibrations of a tuning-fork applied to the neighbourhood of a bone. Loss of this sense is an early feature of certain nervous diseases, such as locomotor ataxia.

PALLIATIVE is a term applied to the treatment of incurable diseases, in which the aim is to mitigate the sufferings of the patient, not to effect a cure.

PALPATION (*palpo*, I touch gently) means the method of examining the surface of the body and the size, shape, and movements of the internal organs, by laying the flat of the hand upon the skin.

PALPEBRA is the Latin term for eyelid.

PALPITATION (*palpito*, I throb) is a condition in which the heart beats forcibly or irregularly, and the person becomes conscious of its action.

Causes.—As a rule we are quite unconscious of the beating of the heart, but when the nervous system is unduly excited its action may become unpleasantly palpable. It is liable to come on at the time of puberty or of the change of life, and also in the weak state of body that accompanies great anæmia, acute fevers, or neurasthenia. Sudden emotions, such as fright, and occasionally dyspepsia, may bring it on. A very frequent cause consists in over-use of tobacco, tea, coffee, or alcohol. Sometimes it may appear in bad cases of organic heart disease or with the hypertrophied heart of chronic Bright's disease.

Symptoms.—There may simply be a fluttering of the heart and a feeling of weakness, which is often expressively described as ' gone-ness ' ; or the heart may be felt pounding and the arteries throbbing, causing great distress to the affected person. In some cases the subject of palpitation is conscious of the heart missing beats.

Treatment.—Mental quietness is the great requisite to still the overaction, and all sources of excitement must be avoided. The person should understand that, however unpleasant the condition may be, there is no danger from it, and that serious disease is not usually the cause. Moderate exercise is a good thing. If the person be a heavy smoker, this is probably the cause, and tobacco should be given up. Similarly tea, coffee, and alcohol should be partaken of sparingly, and any food likely to cause flatulent dyspepsia should be avoided. In the occasional cases due to serious organic disease, the condition causing palpitation must be treated.

PALSY (for parlesy, from παραλύομαι, I am disabled) is another name for paralysis. (*See* PARALYSIS.)

PALUDISM, or PALUDAL FEVER (*palus*, a marsh), is another name for malaria.

PALUDRINE (*see* PROGUANIL).

PAMAQUIN is a synthetic preparation of quinoline used in the treatment of malaria. Pamaquin has a specific action on the sexual forms of the vivax parasites and is therefore of value in reducing the relapse rate of vivax malaria. For this purpose it is given along with quinine or proguanil. Because of its toxicity it should not be given to children.

662

PAN- (πᾶν, all) is a prefix meaning all or completely.

PANACEA (πανάκεια) is a term applied to a remedy for all diseases, or more usually to a remedy which benefits many different diseases.

PANARITIUM (*panaritium*) is a term applied to a whitlow which remains chronic and destroys part of the finger.

PANCARDITIS means inflammation of the pericardium, myocardium, and endocardium at the same time.

PANCREAS (πάγκρεας). — The pancreas or sweetbread is a long secreting gland situated in the back of the abdomen, at the level of the first and second lumbar vertebræ. It lies behind the lower part of the stomach, an expanded portion, called the ' head ' of the pancreas, occupying the bend formed by the duodenum or first part of the small intestine, whilst a long portion known as the body extends to the left, ending in the tail, which rests against the spleen. A duct runs through the whole gland from left to right, joined by many small branches in its course, and leaving the head of the gland, unites with the common bile-duct from the liver to open into the side of the small intestine about 3 or 4 inches (7·5 to 10 cm.) below the outlet of the stomach.

Minute structure. — The gland resembles one of the salivary glands, being composed of tubes of columnar cells bound together by loose connective tissue. These cells are arranged with one end abutting on a central lumen into which the secretion of the cells passes, and each group of tubes ends in a small duct, which unites with other small ducts to join the main pancreatic duct running to the intestine. The cells present an outer, clear zone, and an inner zone filled with granules of the materials secreted by the activity of the cell. Blood-vessels and nerves in large numbers run in the connective tissue of the gland.

Scattered through the pancreas are collections of cells known as the Islets of Langerhans. These do not communicate with the duct of the gland, and the internal secretion of the pancreas—insulin—is formed by these cells and absorbed directly into the blood.

Functions.—The most obvious function of the pancreas is the formation of the pancreatic juice, which is poured into the small intestine after the partially digested food has left the stomach. This is the most important of the digestive juices, is alkaline in reaction, and contains, in addition to various salts, five enzymes. These enzymes are: trypsin, which digests proteid bodies ; amylase, which converts starchy foods into the disaccharide maltose ; lipase, which breaks up fats ; rennin, which curdles milk ; and maltase, which converts maltose into glucose. The action of these is described under DIGESTION.

Inadequate production of insulin by the Islets of Langerhans leads to the condition known as diabetes mellitus (*q.v.*). In addition to insulin, another hormone believed to be produced by the pancreas has been called LIPOCAIC (*q.v.*) ; it is thought to play a part in fat metabolism.

PANCREAS, DISEASES OF.—Abscesses, cysts, calculi, and tumours may occur in the pancreas as in other organs, but are not very common. The most important disease of the pancreas, though again, fortunately, not very common, is acute pancreatitis. This is usually due to influx of bile into the pancreatic ducts. It is sudden in onset, accompanied by acute pain, and causes severe shock and collapse. It carries a high mortality rate, even when treated adequately and early. Chronic pancreatitis is a much more indeterminate disease, commonly associated with disease of the gall-bladder, particularly gall-stones. Pancreatitis may occur as a complication of mumps. Reference has already been made to the association between the Islets of Langerhans and diabetes mellitus.

PANCREATIN (*see* PEPTONIZED FOODS).

PANDEMIC (πανδήμιος, belonging to the whole people) is the term applied to an epidemic which affects a vast area, such as a country or a continent.

PANHYSTERECTOMY (πᾶν, all ; ὑστέρα, womb ; ἐκτομή, excision) is a term applied to an operation by which the uterus is completely removed.

PANNICULITIS means inflammation of the subcutaneous fat, and may occur anywhere on the body surface.

PANNUS (*pannus*, cloth) is the name applied to the growth across the cornea of an abnormal opaque membrane with minute blood-vessels, due to some serious form of irritation. It is found especially in cases of trachoma and tends gradually to cause blindness.

PANTOTHENIC ACID, which has now been prepared synthetically, is part of the vitamin B complex. It is known as the ' chick anti-dermatitis factor ' ; because if it is absent from the chick's diet the bird develops dermatitis, and degeneration of nerve-fibres in the spinal cord also occurs. In rats lack of pantothenic acid produces greying of the hair, but there is no evidence that in man greying is due to lack of this vitamin. Indeed, little is known about the significance of pantothenic acid in man, except that it is one of the essential constituents of the diet. The daily requirement is probably around 10 milligrams. It is widely distributed in foodstuffs, both animal and vegetable. Yeast, liver, and egg-yolk are particularly rich sources.

PAPAIN, PAPYAOTIN, and PAPOID are names given to a ferment obtained from the root of *Carica papaya*, which has an action similar to that of the ferments of the gastric and pancreatic juices. It is, accordingly, sometimes used to peptonize foods for invalids, as it does not give them the same bitter taste that pepsin gives.

PAPILLA (*papilla*, a nipple) means a small projection, such as those with which the true skin is covered, and which project into the scarf-skin and make its union with the true skin more intimate; or those covering the tongue and projecting from its surface.

PAPILLITIS is the term applied to inflammation of any papilla, but especially of the prominence formed by the end of the optic nerve in the retina, also known as optic neuritis.

PAPILLŒDEMA is the term applied to congestion and swelling of the optic disc, at the point of entry of the optic nerve into the interior of the eyeball. Such congestion is the result of increased pressure within the skull—*e.g.* from a cerebral tumour. It also occurs in malignant hypertension (*q.v.*) and occasionally, in the late stages of chronic nephritis. (*See* BRIGHT'S DISEASE.)

PAPILLOMA (*papilla*, nipple; -*oma*, termination meaning tumour) means a tumour composed of papillæ growing from the surface of skin or mucous membrane. These tumours may be either simple or malignant in nature. Such a tumour is found occasionally in the bladder, and the chief symptom of its presence is the painless presence of blood in the urine.

PAPULE (*papula*) means a pimple.

PARA- (παρά, beside) is a prefix meaning near, aside from, or beyond.

PARA-AMINOSALICYLIC ACID has a marked bacteriostatic action against the *Mycobacterium tuberculosis*, and is now one of the standard drugs used in the treatment of tuberculosis. Because of the tendency for the *M. tuberculosis* to develop resistance to it, PAS, as it is often referred to, is always given in conjunction with streptomycin and/or isoniazid.

PARACENTESIS (παρακέντησις). — The puncture by hollow needle or trocar and cannula of any body cavity (*e.g.* abdominal, pleural, pericardial), for tapping or aspirating fluid pathologically accumulated. (*See* ASPIRATION.)

PARACETAMOL is *p*-acetamidophenol. It has antipyretic and analgesic actions similar to those of aspirin. The dose is 500 to 1000 milligrams.

PARACUSIS (παρά, beside ; ἄκουσις, hearing) means any perversion of the sense of hearing.

PARÆSTHESIA (παραισθάνομαι, I am deceived by my senses) is a term applied to unusual feelings, apart from mere increase, or loss, of sensation, experienced by a patient without any external cause ; for example, hot flushes, numbness, tingling, itching. Various par-

aesthesiæ form a common symptom in some nervous diseases.

PARAFFIN (*parum*, little : *affinis*, akin) is the general name used to designate a series of saturated hydrocarbon bodies, discovered by Reichenbach in 1830 and first produced as a commercial product by Young in 1850. The higher members of the series, paraffin-waxes, are solid at ordinary temperatures, some being hard, others soft. Lower in the scale comes petroleum, which is liquid at ordinary temperatures, and which is also known as paroleine and oleum deelinæ. Naphtha, petroleum spirit, and hydramyl are lower members of the series which are very volatile, and lowest comes methane, better known as marsh-gas, which is a gaseous body.

These paraffins do not mix with water or form soaps with alkalies, nor do they turn rancid like fats. Bacteria will not grow on them, and therefore they are not poisonous to broken surfaces.

Uses.—In the form of the *British Pharmacopœia* preparation, liquid paraffin, it is used as an internal lubricant for prolonged administration in habitual constipation.

Externally, the hard and soft paraffins are used in various consistencies, being very useful as ointments and lubricants by reason of their apparently harmless nature. Petroleum, petrol, and various liquid paraffins are used to form the basis of sprays containing menthol and other drugs for application to the throat and nose.

PARAGANGLIOMA, also known as CHROMAFFINOMA and PHÆOCHROMA-CYTOMA, is the term used to describe a tumour made up of chromaffin cells. These tumours occur especially in the medulla of the suprarenal gland, where chromaffin cells are normal constituents. An important sign of these tumours is paroxysmal high blood-pressure.

PARAGONIMUS is the term applied to a genus of small fluke-worm, several of which are found in the lung and occasion spitting of blood. This occurs especially in Asiatic countries and in Central America. (*See* PARASITES.)

PARAGRAPHIA.—Misplacement of words, or of letters in words, or wrong spelling, or use of wrong words in writing as a result of a lesion in the ' speech region ' of the brain.

PARALDEHYDE is a clear, colourless liquid with a penetrating ethereal odour, and a burning taste followed by a cool sensation in the mouth. Although in small quantities it may cause excitement, in larger doses it is a soporific, with little depressing effect, and productive of quiet, refreshing sleep.

Uses.—It is given when a powerful hypnotic action is required, and is particularly useful in inducing sleep in mentally unstable patients. Its unpleasant taste restricts its use, but has the compensatory advantage that it usually prevents the patient receiving paraldehyde from becoming an addict. It is sometimes given per rectum as a general anæsthetic.

PARALYSIS (παράλυσις from παραλύω, I relax), or PALSY, means loss of muscular power due to interference with the nervous system. When muscular power is weakened as the result of some affection of the nervous system, but not entirely lost in the parts concerned, the term *paresis* is often used instead of paralysis. Various terms are used to designate paralysis distributed in different ways. Thus *hemiplegia* is the term applied to paralysis affecting one side of the face, with the corresponding arm and leg, as the result of disease on one side of the brain; *diplegia* means a condition of more or less total paralysis, in which both sides are affected in this manner ; *monoplegia* is the term applied to paralysis of a single limb ; and *paraplegia* signifies paralysis of both sides of the body below a given level, usually from about the level of the waist.

Certain descriptive terms are used in popular language in connection with the word paralysis to indicate different diseases ; thus *creeping paralysis* is a vague term applied most often to locomotor ataxia, *shaking paralysis* is the popular name for paralysis agitans, and *wasting paralysis* commonly means progressive muscular atrophy.

Paralysis should be regarded rather as a symptom than as a disease by itself,

and it is generally connected with well-marked disorder of some portion of the nervous system. According to the

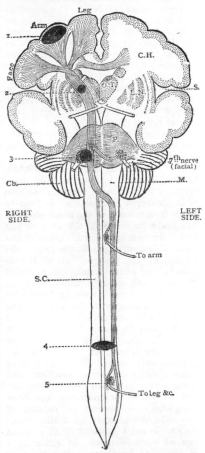

FIG. 301.—Diagram of the brain and spinal cord, showing the motor paths, and the positions of injuries causing different forms of paralysis. The front half of the brain is supposed to have been removed and the reader is looking at its interior. *CH*, Cerebral hemisphere ; *Cb*, cerebellum ; *OT*, optic thalamus ; *LN*, lenticular nucleus ; *M*, medulla ; *P*, pons ; *SC*, spinal cord. 1, The position of a hæmorrhage causing paralysis of left arm ; 2, position of a hæmorrhage causing complete paralysis of the left side; 3, position of a hæmorrhage followed by paralysis of left arm and leg, with right side of face (crossed paralysis) ; 4, position of the disorder causing paralysis of both lower limbs (paraplegia) ; 5, position of the disease responsible for infantile paralysis in the left leg.

locality and extent of the nervous system affected, so will be the form and completeness of the paralysis. It is

665

usual to classify paralysis according to whether it depends upon disease of the brain, of the spinal cord, or of the nerves; and hence the terms *cerebral, spinal,* and *peripheral paralysis.* The distribution of the paralytic condition may be very extensive, involving more or less all the functions of the body, as in *general paralysis* of the insane (*see* GENERAL PARALYSIS), or it may, as already stated, affect half the body, or only certain limbs, or it may even be restricted to single muscles or single groups of muscles supplied by a particular nerve (Fig. 301).

Reference can here be made only to the more common types of paralysis, and that merely in general terms.

1. **PARALYSIS DUE TO BRAIN DISEASE.**—Of this, by far the most common form is palsy affecting one side of the body, or **Hemiplegia.** It usually arises from disease of the hemisphere of the brain opposite to the side of the body affected, such disease being in the form of hæmorrhage into the brain substance, or the plugging up of bloodvessels, and consequent arrest of blood supply to an area of the brain ; or again, it may result from an injury, or be due to a tumour in the tissues of the brain. The character of the seizure and the amount of paralysis vary according to the situation of the disease or injury, its extent, and its sudden or gradual occurrence. The attack may come on as a stroke of apoplexy (*see* APOPLEXY), in which the patient becomes suddenly unconscious, and loses completely the power of motion of one side of the body, or a like result may arise more gradually and without loss of consciousness. In either type of complete hemiplegia, the paralysis affects on one side the muscles of the face, tongue, body, and limbs. Speech is indistinct and thick, and the tongue, when protruded, points towards the paralysed side owing to the unopposed action of its muscles on the unaffected side. The muscles of the face implicated are chiefly those about the mouth. The paralysed side hangs loose, and the corner of the mouth is depressed, but the muscles closing the eye are, as a rule, unimpaired, in consequence of the fact that movements like that of shutting the eyes, which are performed usually on both sides together,

666

are controlled from either side of the brain. As a result the eye on the paralysed side can be shut, unlike what occurs in another form of facial paralysis (Bell's palsy), in which the fault lies in the nerve. The muscles of respiration on the affected side are seldom more than slightly weakened for deep breathing, but those of the arm and leg are completely powerless. Sensation may at first be impaired (anæsthesia), but as a rule returns soon, unless the portion of the brain involved be that which is connected with this function. Rigidity of the paralysed members is usually present as a later symptom. In many cases of even complete hemiplegia, improvement takes place after the lapse of weeks or months, and is in general indicated by a return of motor power, first in the face, next in the leg, while that of the arm follows after a longer or shorter interval, and is rarely complete. Such recovery of movement is, however, in a large proportion of cases only partial, and the side remains weakened. In such instances the gait of the patient is characteristic. In walking, he leans to the sound side and swings round the affected limb from the hip, the foot scraping the ground as it is raised and advanced. The paralysed parts retain their contractility when stimulated by electric currents, but they are apt to suffer in their nutrition from disuse and to assume an attitude of rigidity unless treatment is carefully carried out.

It is to be observed that in many instances the hemiplegia is only partial, and instead of the symptoms of complete paralysis above described, there exist in varied combination only certain of them, their association depending on the extent and locality of the damage to the brain. Thus there may be impairment of speech and some amount of facial paralysis, while the arm and leg may be unaffected, or the paralysis may be present in one or both extremities of one side while the other symptoms are absent. Further, the paralysis may be incomplete throughout, and the whole of the side be weak, but not entirely deprived of motor power. To partial paralysis of this latter description the term PARESIS is applied.

Besides hemiplegia, various other

forms of paralysis may arise from cerebral disease. Thus occasionally there is CROSSED PARALYSIS, one side of the face and the opposite side of the body being affected simultaneously. Or again, as is frequently observed in the case of tumours of the brain, the paralysis may be limited to the distribution of one or more of the cranial nerves, and may produce a combination of symptoms (such as squinting, drooping of the eyelid, and impairment or loss of vision) which may enable the seat of the disease to be accurately localized. The condition of DIPLEGIA, in which both sides are affected, sometimes occurs in infants, and is due generally to some inflammation of the brain occurring soon after birth.

Trembling palsy, PARALYSIS AGITANS, PARKINSONISM, or SHAKING PARALYSIS, is a form of paralysis characterized chiefly by rhythmical tremors and rigidity of muscles. It is a chronic disease of advanced life and is due to degenerative changes in the ganglia at the base of the cerebrum. The symptoms first show themselves chiefly by involuntary tremblings and stiffness of the muscles of the fingers, hand, arm, or leg, the tremors being worse on making efforts or under excitement. These tremors become more marked and more extensive with the advance of the disease. The peculiar stiffness of the muscles greatly impedes movement, as can be seen in the gait, the act of walking being performed in a peculiar tottering manner with the body bent forward. The trembling movements cease during sleep. An almost identical condition occurs after encephalitis lethargica.

Cerebral palsy is the term used to describe a group of conditions characterized by varying degrees of paralysis, and occurring in infancy or early childhood. In over half of them this takes the form of spastic paralysis. This may involve only one limb, but in more severe cases it may involve several limbs as well as the head, neck, and trunk. The causation is still obscure, but pre-natal, natal, and post-natal factors may all play a part.

Although cerebral palsy cannot be cured, much can be done to help these unfortunate children particularly if the condition is diagnosed at an early stage.

Functional paralysis includes other forms of paralysis which, being of cerebral origin, should be mentioned here, although they are not connected with any discoverable disease of the brain. These forms of paralysis are amenable to psychological treatment, the cause of the paralysis often being traceable to some deep-seated mental conflict having its origin in childhood. (*See* HYSTERIA, CRAMP, NEURASTHENIA.)

2. PARALYSIS DUE TO DISEASE OF THE SPINAL CORD.—Of paralysis from this cause, there are numerous varieties, depending on the nature, the site, and the extent of the disease. Frequently defects in muscular action, due to disease in the spinal cord, are not of a paralytic nature, and these must be carefully distinguished. For example, in disease of the posterior part of the cord, involving the sensory paths, the condition of *ataxia* is produced, and the patient, though sufficiently strong, cannot control his movements, as he is unconscious of the directions in which his limbs move till he sees the movements made. Or again, in disease of the lateral parts of the cord, involving the controlling motor paths from the brain, the condition of *spasticity* results, and when muscles contract they do so excessively, so that freedom of movement is impossible (Fig. 302).

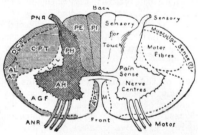

FIG. 302.—Diagram of a section of the spinal cord in the region of the neck. On one side the various nerve-tracts are shown, on the other the function of these is indicated. *PE, PI,* Tracts in posterior column of cord; *CPT,* crossed pyramidal tract; *DCT,* direct cerebellar tract; *LLL,* lateral limiting layer; *ALAT,* antero-lateral ascending tract; *AGF,* anterior ground fibres; *APT,* anterior pyramidal tract; *PH,* posterior horn and *AH,* anterior horn of grey matter; *PNR,* posterior nerve root; *ANR,* anterior nerve root.

Paraplegia, paralysis of both lower extremities, including usually the lower portion of the trunk, and occasionally

667

also the upper portion — indeed, all the parts below the seat of the disease in the spinal cord—is a form of paralysis which is a frequent result of injuries or disease of the vertebral column; also of inflammation affecting the spinal cord (see MYELITIS), as well as of hæmorrhage or tumours involving its substance. When it is due to disease, this is generally situated in the lower portion of the cord. The symptoms necessarily vary in relation to the locality and the extent of the disease in the cord. Thus, if in the affected area the posterior part of the cord, including the posterior nerve roots, suffer, the function of sensation in the parts below is impaired because the cord is unable to transmit the sensory impressions from the surface of the body to the brain, and the condition of 'ataxia' affects the power of motion. If, on the other hand, the anterior portion of the cord and the anterior nerve roots be affected, the motor impulses from the brain cannot be conveyed to the muscles below the seat of the injury or disease, and consequently their power of movement is abolished. Whilst, if the lateral portions of the cord be affected, a condition of 'spastic' paralysis is set up. In many forms of this complaint, particularly in the case of injuries, the whole thickness of the cord is involved (transverse myelitis), and both sensory and motor functions are lost below the level at which the cord is affected. Further, the functions of the bladder and bowels are apt to suffer, and either spasm, or more frequently paralysis, of these organs is the result. The nutrition of the paralysed parts tends to become affected, and bed sores and wasting of the muscles are common. Occasionally, more especially in cases of injury, recovery takes place, but in general this is incomplete, the power of walking being more or less impaired. When the paralysis is due to pressure caused by a diseased spine, an operation designed to relieve this pressure is often completely successful, and entire power is restored, even after the paralysis has lasted for several months. On the other hand, the patient may linger on for years bedridden, and at last succumb to bed sores or to a septic affection of the paralysed bladder spreading up to the kidneys.

Infantile paralysis (see POLIOMYELITIS).

Wasting palsy, or PROGRESSIVE MUSCULAR ATROPHY, or MOTOR NEURONE DISEASE, is a disease usually occurring in middle life. It is characterized by the gradual wasting of certain muscles or groups of muscles, loss of power in them, fibrillation (fine twitching of muscle fibres), alteration of tendon and skin reflexes. It is insidious in its onset, and usually first shows itself in the prominent muscular masses in the palm of the hand, especially the ball of the thumb, which becomes wasted and deficient in power. The other palmar muscles suffer in like manner, and as the disease advances the muscles of the arm, shoulders, and trunk become implicated if they have not themselves been the first to be attacked. The malady tends to spread symmetrically, involving the corresponding parts of both sides of the body in succession. It is slow in its progress, but, although it may occasionally undergo arrest, it tends to advance and involve more and more of the muscles of the body, until the sufferer is reduced to a condition of extreme helplessness. Should some other ailment not be the cause of death, the fatal result may be due to the disease extending so as to involve the muscles of respiration.

Pathologically, progressive muscular atrophy is characterized by degeneration : (a) of the motor cells of Betz in the cerebral cortex, with corresponding degeneration of the pyramidal tracts ; (b) of the anterior horn cells of the grey matter of the spinal cord, with corresponding degeneration of the peripheral motor nerves and wasting of the muscles innervated by them ; (c) of the nerve cells in the bulb of the brain from which the motor cranial nerves arise— hypoglossal, facial, trigeminal, oculomotor, spinal accessory, glossopharyngeal, vagus. There is diffuse atrophy of the white matter of the spinal cord, excepting the posterior, sensory columns.

From this it can be seen that spastic paralysis and profound wasting of muscle may be combined, as in amyotrophic lateral sclerosis (q.v.) ; that a purely spastic paralysis may occur when the degenerative process affects principally the motor cells of the cerebral cortex; and that the clinical picture will be that of a bulbar paralysis when the motor nuclei of cranial nerves degenerate. In bulbar paralysis, the muscles of facial expression, of mastication, of articulation, and of swallowing suffer progressive loss of power.

The cause of the nerve degeneration is not known, although in some cases it is a syphilitic infection.

Progressive muscular dystrophy, MYO-PATHY, or PSEUDO-HYPERTROPHIC MUS-CULAR DYSTROPHY, is another form of paralysis, in certain respects resembling progressive muscular atrophy, although in it the change occurs in the muscles themselves, not in the nervous system. (*See* MYOPATHY.)

3. **PERIPHERAL PARALYSIS,** or local paralysis of individual nerves, is of frequent occurrence. Only the most common and important examples of this condition can be briefly referred to.

Facial paralysis and BELL'S PALSY are the terms applied to paralysis involving the muscles of expression supplied by the seventh nerve. It is unilateral, and generally occurs as the result of exposure of one side of the head to a draught of cold air, which sets up inflammation of the nerve, but it may also be due to injury or disease either affecting the nerve near the surface or deeper in the bony canals through which it passes, or in the brain itself, involving the nerve at its origin. The paralysis is manifested by a marked change in the expression of the face, the patient being unable to move the muscles of one side in such acts as laughing, whistling, etc., or to close the eye on that side. The mouth is drawn to the sound side, while, although the muscles of mastication are not involved, the food in eating tends to lodge between the jaw and cheek on the palsied side. Occasionally, when the nerve is injured as it passes through the skull, the sense of taste is impaired. In the ordinary cases of this disease, such as those due to exposure, recovery usually takes place in about six weeks, the improvement being first shown in the power of closing the eye, which is soon followed by the disappearance of the other signs. When the paralysis proceeds from wounding of the nerve, disease of the temporal bone, or from tumours in the brain, it is more apt to be permanent, and is in many cases of serious import.

Lead palsy is a common form of local paralysis. It is due to the poisonous action of lead upon the system, and, like the other symptoms of lead-poisoning, affects chiefly workers in that metal. (*See* LEAD-POISONING.)

A form of peripheral paralysis, resembling the last, frequently results from chronic alcoholism. Other poisons also act similarly, as, for example, arsenic. (*See* NEURITIS.) Injury to a nerve may cause paralysis in the muscles which it should supply, and this may follow on wounds, severe bruises, or even long-continued pressure, as in crutch-palsy. (*See* DROP-WRIST, NERVE INJURIES.) The paralysis occurring after diphtheria, another example of the peripheral variety, has been already mentioned, and similar paralyses, for example of the foot, follow sometimes on other infectious diseases (*see* DIPHTHERIA, DROP-FOOT).

Treatment.—It is impossible in a brief notice like the present to enter at any length into the treatment of the different varieties of paralysis. Generally speaking, the treatment consists of measures which aim at supporting the patient's strength and maintaining his health while the nervous system is slowly restoring itself so far as may be. The conditions of the disease in any particular case can only be understood and appreciated by the medical expert, under whose direction alone treatment can be advantageously carried out.

An important point in the treatment is that, since paralysed muscles tend to undergo degenerative changes, their action should be maintained as long as possible. With the view of improving the circulation in the muscles, and also in order to prevent stiffening of the joints, massage is very useful. In order to exercise the muscles, the faradic current or, failing it, the interrupted galvanic current, may be applied daily.

In the case of paraplegia there is a necessity for highly skilled nursing, since not only the patient's comfort but his life depends upon careful management, directed towards preventing bed sores (*see* BED SORES), and inflammation of the bladder (*see* CATHETERS) in cases where the act of urination is interfered with. A similar remark applies to bulbar palsy, in which special care is necessary in feeding the patient, owing to his difficulty in swallowing.

PARAMETRITIS (παρά, beside; μήτρα, the womb) means inflammation in the cellular tissue at the side of the womb.

PARAMNESIA is the term applied to a derangement of the memory in which words are used without a comprehension of their meaning; it is also applied to illusions of memory in which a person in good faith imagines and describes experiences which never occurred to him.

PARAMYOCLONUS (παρά, beside; μῦς, muscle; κλόνος, disturbance) is the name applied to an affection in which paroxysmal jerking contractions of the muscles of the limbs take place; it is sometimes due to organic disease of the nervous system, sometimes hysterical.

PARANOIA (παρά, aside; νοῦς, mind) is the term applied to a form of fixed delusional insanity in which the delusions, usually of persecution, all centre round some perverted idea and have an important bearing upon the insane person's actions. In this form of insanity, heredity plays an important part, recovery is unlikely, and in marked cases restraint is often necessary to prevent criminal acts. Many paranoic persons, however, are able to go about freely and transact business, with which their delusions do not interfere, and are regarded simply as eccentric persons. (*See* MENTAL ILLNESS.)

PARAPHASIA.—Misplacement of or use of wrong words in speech as a result of a lesion in the ' speech region ' of the brain.

PARAPHRENIA is a form of paranoia (*q.v.*). (*See also* MENTAL ILLNESS.)

PARAPLEGIA (παραπληγία, paralysis crosswise) means paralysis of the lower limbs, accompanied generally by paralysis of bladder and rectum. (*See* PARALYSIS.)

670

PARASITES (παράσιτος, one who eats at another's table) are creatures that live upon or in the body of another creature, known as the 'host', being indebted to the latter for their nourishment, though contributing nothing to its welfare. The parasite may be comparatively harmless; or it may, by the mere irritation of its presence or by interference with the bodily functions of the host, give rise to troublesome symptoms; or it may even, by destroying vital parts or forming poisonous substances, lead to the death of the host.

As regards human beings, there are numerous parasites belonging to both the vegetable and animal kingdom, of various sizes, and producing effects of all degrees of severity. At the bottom of the animal kingdom are the amœba that produces dysentery (Fig. 303), the parasites of malaria, that of kala-azar, and various trypanosomes which cause

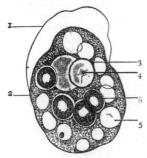

FIG. 303.—*Entamœba histolytica*, unencysted. 1, ectoplasm; 2, endoplasm; 3, nucleus; 4, karyosome; 5, vacuoles; 6, ingested red blood cell. (From Blacklock and Southwell, *A Guide to Human Parasitology*. H. K. Lewis & Co. Ltd.)

serious diseases in animals, and one of which is responsible for sleeping sickness among both black and white races in tropical Africa.

Apart from these, the following is a table and short account of the chief parasites which are apt to infest man, and the symptoms their presence occasions. It will be noticed that those parasites which live on the surface belong to the division of Arthropods, which are strong and capable of resisting much damage, while the internal parasites, infesting mainly the bowels, or burrowing in the deep cellular tissues, belong to the division of Worms.

Division :   Arthropoda.
    Class :   Arachnida.

Sarcoptes scabiei
Trombicula
irritans   } (mites).

    Class :   Insecta.

Pediculus humanus
  var. capitis
Pediculus humanus
  var. corporis   } (lice).
Phthirus pubis
Pulex irritans (common flea).
Cimex lectularius (bed bug).
Tunga penetrans (jigger).

Division :   Vermes (worms).
    Class :   Platyhelminthes (flatworms).
    Order :   Trematoda.

Fasciola hepatica (liver-fluke).
Schistosoma hæmatobium.
Schistosoma mansoni.
Schistosoma japonicum.
Paragonimus westermani
  (lung-fluke).

    Order : Cestoda.

Tænia solium
Tænia saginata   } tape-worm.
Echinococcus granulosus
  (hydatid cyst).
Diphyllobothrium latum.

    Class :   Nemathelminthes (roundworms).

Enterobius vermicularis
  (thread-worms).
Ascaris lumbricoides.
Trichinella spiralis.
Trichuris trichiura (whip-worm).
Ankylostoma duodenale.
Wuchereria bancrofti.
Loa loa.
Onchocerca volvulus.
Dracunculus medinensis
  (guinea-worm).

External Parasites.—

SARCOPTES SCABIEI, formerly known as Acarus scabiei, is a minute oval-shaped mite possessing four pairs of legs. It is just visible to the naked eye, the female measuring about $\frac{1}{3} \times \frac{1}{4}$ millimetre (Fig. 304), and the male slightly smaller. The female lays its eggs (forty to fifty) as it burrows in the skin. These hatch in the burrows and it is the movement of the larvæ which causes the intense itching which gives scabies its popular name of Itch (*q.v.*). The scratching caused by this itching is responsible for much of the eruption of scabies. The larvæ ultimately leave the burrows and develop in the skin, a female becoming mature in about two weeks.

TROMBICULA IRRITANS is the harvest mite. It is also known as red bug and chigger. They are found in the fields in the autumn and attack man by crawling up the legs. Measuring only 150 μ, they can pass through

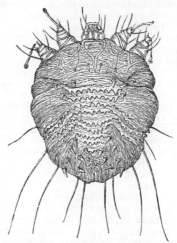

Fig. 304.—The female *Sarcoptes scabiei.* Magnified by about 80. (Thoma's *Pathology*.)

ordinary clothing. They produce local redness and itching. Relief from the itching is obtained by bathing the affected part with weak ammonia or baking soda.

PEDICULI, or lice, are of three species, which vary in shape and size as well as in the area of the body they infest. As a rule they breed only in persons of uncleanly habits, but there are people, apparently of perfect cleanliness, upon whom they multiply with amazing rapidity as soon as one has chanced to come upon the skin.

Pediculus humanus var. Capitis (*Pediculus capitis*) varies in colour according to the colour of the hair of the host. The eggs, commonly known as ' nits ' and visible as little white specks, are usually laid in the hairs of the back of the head ; behind the ears is also a favourite site. They hatch out in six days and become adults within ten days. On infested heads the hairs are often matted together by the exudate which results from irritation and scratching. The glands behind the ears and in the back of the neck are often enlarged.

Pediculus humanus var. Corporis (*Pediculus vestimenti*) is larger than *Pediculus capitis* and is found on the underclothing on the trunk and upper arms. It is seldom found on the skin. The eggs hatch out in 7 to 10 days and become mature in two weeks. Without food the adult dies in nine days and the newly hatched louse in two days. The eggs are viable for much longer (up to a month) and, as they are usually found in the more inaccessible parts of the clothing, *e.g.* the seams, this means that the only effective way of disinfecting clothing is by steam.

PHTHIRUS PUBIS, popularly known as the crab louse, is broader and shorter than the pediculi. It is found predominantly on the short hairs of the pubic region, to which it adheres very tenaciously. It causes intense itching. So far as is known, it does not carry any disease.

(For further details, *see* INSECTS IN RELATION TO DISEASE.)

PULEX IRRITANS is the common human flea. Of more importance is *Xenopsylla cheopis*, the rat-flea which transmits plague, but *Pulex irritans* would be capable of transmitting plague if it fed on the blood of a human case of septicæmic plague. It is destroyed by D.D.T.; 5 per cent. solution in kerosene for buildings and furniture; 10 per cent. powder for clothing. For pet animals D.D.T. should be used as a powder and not as a solution.

CIMEX LECTULARIUS, or bed bug, is brownish-red in colour, and during the day remains hidden in cracks in the walls or floor. When crushed they produce a most unpleasant odour. The average life is 3 to 6 months, but they can live for a year without food. A temperature of 44° C. kills the adult in one hour. A solution of D.D.T. in kerosene is the most effective disinfecting agent. (*See* BED BUG.)

Internal Parasites.—

FASCIOLA HEPATICA, the liverfluke, is found in sheep and other herbivorous animals, in which it causes the serious disease known as 'liver rot'. The intermediate host is a snail. It only causes disease in man very occasionally, resulting in enlargement of the liver.

SCHISTOSOMES, or blood flukes, are responsible for the disease known as *Schistosomiasis* (or *Bilharzia*) which occurs in Egypt, many parts of tropical Africa, and South America. The male is about 12 millimetres long. The female, which is about 24 millimetres in length, lies partly enclosed in a

672

groove down the body of the male (Fig. 305). The ova, or eggs, are

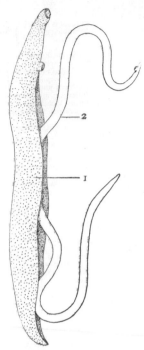

FIG. 305.—Diagram showing cylindrical female schistosome (2) lying in the gynæcophoni canal of the male schistosome (1). (From Blacklock and Southwell, *Human Parasitology.* H. K. Lewis & Co. Ltd.)

provided with a sharp spike which is terminal in *S. hæmatobium* (Fig. 306) and lateral in *S. mansoni*. The schistosomes live in the portal vein and its branches. The ova ultimately reach either the bladder (*S. hæmatobium*) (Fig. 306) or the rectum (*S. mansoni* and *S. japonicum*), whence they are voided in the urine or fæces. The next stage of development takes place in certain snails (Fig. 307). Human infection occurs by wading or bathing in infected water, the infection occurring through the skin, whence the immature schistosome ultimately reaches the portal vein.

SCHISTOSOMA HÆMATOBIUM is widely distributed throughout North Africa, including Egypt, East Africa, and South Africa. As the ova are excreted through the bladder, the main symptoms are cystitis and hæmaturia (*i.e.* the passage of blood in the urine). In chronic cases there may be

PARAGONIMUS WESTERMANI, or lung-fluke, is a parasite found in Japan, China, and the Philippines,

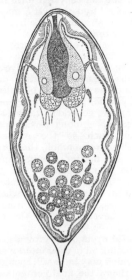

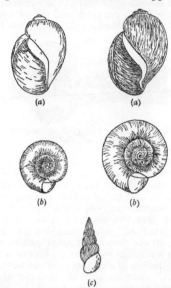

FIG. 306.—Egg of *Schistosoma hæmatobium.* (From Blacklock and Southwell, *Human Parasitology.* H. K. Lewis & Co. Ltd.)

formation of stones in the bladder, and sometimes cancer develops in the bladder.

SCHISTOSOMA MANSONI is found predominantly in the Nile valley, East Africa, and West Africa. As the ova are mainly excreted through the rectum, the first manifestation of the disease is usually diarrhœa, with the passage of much blood in the stools. As with *S. hæmatobium* infections, there is often irritation of the skin or dermatitis, and there is always some anæmia, which may become severe. The spleen usually becomes enlarged, sometimes to a very considerable extent.

SCHISTOSOMA JAPONICUM is confined to the Far East, particularly the Yangtse valley. Here again the ova are found in the rectum, and the main manifestations of the infection are chronic dysentery, enlargement of the liver and the spleen, and anæmia.

The treatment of all forms of schistosomiasis consists of the injection of various antimonial preparations, including tartar emetic, stibophen, and anthiomaline.

22

FIG. 307.—Snails which act as intermediate hosts for schistosomes. (*a*) *Bulinus* and *Physopsis* genus, which are intermediate hosts for *S. hæmatobium.* (*b*) *Planorbis* genus, intermediate host for *S. mansoni.* (*c*) *Oricomelania* genus, intermediate host for *S. japonicum.* (From Blacklock and Southwell, *Human Parasiology.* H. K. Lewis & Co. Ltd.)

which causes chronic cough and hæmoptysis (coughing up of blood). The fluke also invades other organs in the body. Part of the development of the fluke takes place in a snail and in a crab and crayfish. Human infection is sometimes due to the eating of these crayfish in an uncooked state.

TÆNIÆ, or TAPE-WORMS, illustrate well the degeneration consequent upon a parasitic life. These animals exist solely to feed and to propagate their kind, discharging apparently no useful function in the economy of nature. Accordingly their shape is modified to present as large an absorbing surface as possible to the digested food passing down the intestine, so that they are flat, white, and long, like a piece of tape, as their name implies. Each consists of a ' head ' (Fig. 308), the size of a small pin's head, provided with suckers, and sometimes with hooklets, for adhesion to the bowel wall, and from this head

673

segments are produced that gradually increase in size and develop ova the farther they recede from the head. The mature segments at the extremity of the worm are crammed full of ova, and are constantly splitting off to be

FIG. 308.—Head of *Tænia solium*. Magnified by 20. (Thoma's *Pathology*.)

discharged in the stools. When these mature segments, or ' proglottides ', are discharged, they fall upon the ground, and the ova they contain are afterwards conveyed either by food or drink into the stomach of an ' intermediate host ', which may be a pig, ox, etc., in the case of different parasites. It is a notable fact that a parasite will not develop in any host save one of the proper species, and all through the animal kingdom different parasites are met in different animals. When the ova reach the stomach of the 'intermediate host' their capsule is dissolved, the embryos escape and find their way through the wall of stomach or intestine into the blood-vessels, by which they are carried to distant parts of the body. In the case of TÆNIA SOLIUM the intermediate host is the pig, in the case of TÆNIA SAGINATA it is the ox. In the muscles of these animals the embryos of the worm become encysted and remain so till they die, or till the animal's flesh happens to be eaten by the ' proper host ', when they develop again into a new tape-worm in his intestine. The flesh of a pig thus infected shows plainly the encysted embryo (known as *Cysticercus cellulosæ*), and is called ' measly ' pork. DIPHYLLO-BOTHRIUM LATUM is seldom met with, save in the north of Europe and Asia, and the intermediate hosts are several varieties of fish. In the case of TÆNIA ECHINOCOCCUS, relations are reversed, and man plays the rôle of intermediate host, the host of the mature tape-worm being the dog, from which the human being derives the embryo worm by allowing the dog to lick his hands and

674

face, or to contaminate his food. Although the worm in the dog is very small (having only three segments, as a rule), yet the encysted form in man, known as a ' hydatid cyst ', may reach a large size, situated in the liver, lungs, kidney, or brain.

The presence of tape-worms in the intestine does not long remain a matter of doubt. Generally, they give rise to voracious appetite, digestive disturbances such as diarrhœa, bloodlessness, and headache, and they may produce signs of grave general irritation, such as convulsions. Among certain peoples, however, such as the Abyssinians, where they are common, their presence is taken as a matter of course, and they give rise to no apparent evil effects. Any doubt as to the presence of a tape-worm is set at rest when the host passes, as he does from time to time, several feet of the mature segments.

Hydatid cysts often grow to a great size, budding off in their interior smaller cysts, which may have still smaller ones within them, the final contents of the smallest cysts being a salt, watery fluid and numerous ' heads ' of echinococci, each provided with a circle of hooks, and each capable, under proper conditions, of forming a new worm. The symptoms produced by a hydatid cyst depend mainly upon the effects of its size and consequent pressure. Very small cysts in the brain may produce serious results, like those of a tumour, whilst in the liver a cyst may grow to the size of a man's head before causing much trouble.

Treatment of tape-worm infestation consists of the administration of male fern, mepacrine, or dichlorophen, followed by a purgative. Castor oil must not be used for this purpose. During treatment the stools must be carefully examined for the head of the tape-worm. Unless the head is passed in the stools, the worm will grow again. The treatment of hydatid cyst is surgical, *i.e.* the cyst must be removed by operation.

ENTEROBIUS VERMICULARIS, the THREAD-WORM, is the most common of all the intestinal parasites in Great Britain and the least harmful. It is about ¼ inch (6 mm.) long (Fig. 309), white, and resembles a little piece of

FIG. 309.—*Enterobius vermicularis* (or Thread-worm). Female. 1, cervical alæ; 2, œsophagus; 3, bulb behind œsophagus; 4, intestine; 5, ovary; 6, vulva; 7, uterus; 8, anus. (From Blacklock and Southwell, *Human Parasitology.* H. K. Lewis & Co. Ltd.)

b

thread. These worms live in considerable numbers in the lower bowel, affecting children particularly. They cause great irritation round the anus, often diarrhœa, sometimes in female children discharge from the vagina, and in weakly children nervous symptoms such as convulsions. The reflex irritation they occasion makes the child pick his nose, and grind the teeth during sleep.

Treatment.—The most effective form of treatment is piperazine hydrate given in the form of an elixir. Viprynium embonate has recently been introduced with claims to be an effective drug for the purpose. If one member of a household is infected, it is necessary to examine all other members of the household and to treat simultaneously all those found infected. During treatment steps must be taken to prevent patients re-infecting themselves or infecting others. The local irritation around the anus may be relieved by the application of weak white precipitate ointment.

ASCARIS LUMBRICOIDES, also known as the ROUNDWORM and the 'maw-worm', is rounded, of a pale-brownish colour, and may be 10 to 12 inches (25 to 30 cm.) long, resembling an earth-worm very closely. These worms, two or three in number, may live in the small intestine, but one may wander into the stomach and be vomited up. They give rise to few symptoms beyond voracious appetite, and sometimes diarrhœa and colic.

Treatment consists of the administration of piperazine citrate.

TRICHINELLA SPIRALIS is a minute worm, which is important because it produces the disease known as 'trichinosis'. The full-grown worm, which inhabits the intestine, is less than ⅛ inch (3 mm.) in length, and the embryos, to whose movements the disease is due, are much smaller. The disease is acquired by eating trichinosed meat, especially pork. When such a piece of meat is eaten, the embryos contained in it are set free, develop into full-grown trichinellæ, and from each pair of these 1000 or more new embryos may arise in a few weeks. So soon as this new generation of embryos is produced they bore their way into the wall of the bowel, setting up sometimes severe

675

irritation and diarrhœa, and thence wander all over the body, finally depositing themselves between the fibres of the voluntary muscles. During this migration, which lasts four or five weeks, they set up fever and pain in the limbs and muscles, often mistaken for rheumatism. Death may even result, but if the person survives to the end of four or five weeks, the trichinellæ, which are now encysted in the muscles (Fig. 310), give no further trouble.

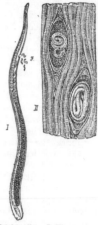

FIG. 310.—Trichinellæ. I, The mature worm found in the intestine, showing embryos escaping from it at F. Magnified by 25. II, Muscle containing the encysted form. Magnified by 50. (Schmeil's Zoology.)

Prevention is based on thorough inspection of meat in slaughter-houses, for even cooking, unless the meat be in slices, is not an efficient protection. Pigs should not be fed on unboiled garbage. Rats may be a source of sporadic outbreaks, for infected rats have been found near piggeries. The disease is now a rare one, thanks to sanitary inspection. The encysted trichinellæ are just visible as fine white specks.

Treatment.—In the early stages, tetrachloroethylene, followed by a sharp purge, is of value. Recently, thiabendazole, which has proved of value in the treatment of affected pigs, has been used with promising results in human victims.

TRICHOCEPHALUS DISPAR, also known as TRICHURIS TRICHIURA and the WHIPWORM. is very common in France. It is rarer in Britain. The worm inhabits the large intestine, and is

676

said to be easily expelled by doses of thymol. It gives rise to little trouble unless it is present in great numbers.

ANKYLOSTOMA DUODENALE, or HOOKWORM, also known as the TUNNEL-WORM, on account of the ravages it caused among the men at work on the St. Gotthard tunnel, produces great anæmia, debility, and cardiac weakness, sometimes leading to death. It is represented in the New World by NECATOR AMERICANUS, an allied species. These worms are about ½ inch (12 mm.) in length and inhabit the upper part of the small intestine, often in great numbers ; here they embed themselves in the mucous membrane lining the bowel. The disease produced by this worm is found in various tropical and subtropical regions, both in Asia and America. The disease caused is known as ankylostomiasis or hookworm disease. In certain parts of India it is so common that about 75 per cent. of the population are said to be affected ; it is also very common in Egypt. The worms embedded in the small intestine produce an enormous number of eggs which pass from the body in the stools ; the embryos, finding their way into water, mud, or damp earth, develop rapidly and can maintain their vitality for weeks or months, if moisture be present. The embryos may gain access to the human host in polluted drinking-water, but they also penetrate the skin of the hands of workmen or the naked feet of Indian natives. Ultimately, through the blood-stream and the lungs, they gain access to the intestine, where they develop. The disease is a very serious one, partly in consequence of the numbers of persons prevented from working by the debility it causes, and partly because death in such debilitated persons is not uncommon.

Treatment.—The three most effective remedies are tetrachloroethylene, oil of chenopodium, and hexylresorcinol. The anæmia which always accompanies chronic infestation with ankylostoma also requires intensive treatment. This consists of one or more of the following : iron, liver extract, the vitamin B complex, and a high protein diet.

One of the major difficulties in dealing with hookworm in native populations is that it is so widespread and therefore re-infection occurs very easily. In an attempt to reduce this to a minimum every care should be taken to try and prevent contamination of water supplies. If there is any risk of such contamination, drinking-water should be boiled.

WUCHERERIA BANCROFTI, also known as FILARIA BANCROFTI, is a thread-like worm (Plate XII) which is transmitted by certain mosquitoes. It is named after Wucherer, who discovered micro-filariæ in the urine of a filarial patient in Brazil in 1866, and Bancroft, who first described the adult worms in Australia in 1876. The adult female worm measures up to 100 millimetres in length. One of the striking features of these worms is that they are found in the circulating blood in large numbers in the evening, whilst during the day they disappear from the blood-stream. Its geographical distribution is widespread in warm countries, but it is most prevalent in India, South China, South Japan, the Dutch East Indies, and the Pacific islands.

The form of filariasis produced by *W. bancrofti* is characterized by inflammation and blockage of the lymphatics. In the early stages this leads to enlargement of the lymphatic glands. There is also involvement of the testicles, which become painful and enlarged, and this is accompanied by the formation of a hydrocœle. Repeated inflammation of the lymphatic vessels ultimately leads to their blockage and this is responsible for the most characteristic of the later stages of the disease—elephantiasis, *i.e.* gross enlargement of the lower limbs and the scrotum. This may be so marked that the leg may attain a circumference of several feet, whilst the scrotum may weigh 50 pounds (23 kg.). Elephantiasis may occur elsewhere in the body, *e.g.* the arms, but not very commonly.

Treatment.—Most encouraging results are being obtained, particularly in early cases, from the use of the piperazine derivative, diethylcarbamazine, which is also known as 'hetrazan'. Surgery is required for the treatment of elephantiasis. Prevention consists primarily of (*a*) destroying the mosquitoes which transmit the worm, and (*b*) protection of the individual against mosquito bites by the use of mosquito nets and repellents.

LOA LOA, also known as FILARIA LOA, is a thread-like worm which differs from *W. bancrofti* in that it is shorter and thicker, and it is found in the blood-stream during the day, not at night. It is transmitted by the mango fly, *Chrysops dimidiata*, but other flies of this genus can also transmit it. It is confined to West and Central Africa. The characteristic feature of LOAIASIS is the appearance of fugitive swellings which may arise anywhere in the body in the course of the worm's migration through the body. These are known as Calabar swellings. The worm is often found in the eye, hence the old name of the worm in Africa—the eye worm. Satisfactory results are being reported from the use of diethylcarbamazine in the treatment of this form of filaria.

ONCHOCERCA VOLVULUS, is another filarial worm. It is found in Central Africa from Sierra Leone to Kenya, and in Central America. It is transmitted by gnats. Like loaiasis, onchocerciasis is characterized by the appearance of nodules in various parts of the body. There may also be involvement of the eyes and the worm may invade the optic nerve and so cause blindness; hence the name of blinding filarial disease given to it in Central America. Treatment consists of removal of the tumours or nodules as they appear. Drugs of value are diethylcarbamazine and suramin, either alone or combined.

DRACUNCULUS MEDINENSIS, also known as FILARIA MEDINENSIS and the GUINEA-WORM, is found in India, Arabia, Persia, the Nile valley, East and West Africa, Brazil, and the islands of the Caribbean. The female may attain a length of four feet. It is transmitted by *Cyclops*, and man is infected by drinking contaminated water. The worm causes no trouble for about a year, when it approaches the surface of the body and causes a local painful swelling which is usually accompanied by fever. The essential treatment, *i.e.* removal of the worm, has changed little since Biblical days. Drugs have little effect upon the worm.

PARASITICIDE (*parasitus*, a parasite; *cædo*, I kill) is a general term applied to agents or substances destructive to parasites.

PARASYMPATHETIC NERVOUS SYSTEM is that part of the autonomic nervous system which is connected with the brain and spinal cord through certain nerve centres in the mid-brain, medulla, and lower end of the cord. The nerves from these centres are carried in the 3rd, 7th, 9th, and 10th cranial nerves and the 2nd, 3rd, and 4th sacral nerves. The action of the parasympathetic system is usually antagonistic to that of the sympathetic system. Thus it inhibits the action of the heart and augments the action of the intestine, whereas the sympathetic augments the action of the heart and inhibits that of the intestine.

PARATHION is one of the organo-phosphorus insecticides (*q.v.*). It is highly toxic to man and must therefore be handled with the utmost care.

PARATHORMONE is the name of the hormone secreted by the parathyroid gland (*q.v.*).

PARATHYROID is the name applied to four small glands which lie to the side of and behind the thyroid gland. These glands regulate the metabolism of calcium and of phosphorus. If for any reason there is a deficiency of the secretion of the parathyroid glands, the amount of calcium in the blood falls too low and the amount of phosphorus increases. The result is the condition known as tetany, in which there is great restlessness and spasm of muscles. The condition is checked by the injection of the parathyroid hormone — parathormone—which causes an increase in the amount of calcium in the blood. If there is over-activity of the parathyroids there will be an increase of calcium in the blood. This extra calcium is drawn from the bones, in which, as a consequence, thin cysts form and greatly weaken the bones, these breaking easily as a result. This cystic disease of bone has the elaborate title of GENERALIZED OSTEITIS FIBROSA CYSTICA.

PARATYPHOID FEVER is a continued fever which closely resembles mild attacks of typhoid and which, like typhoid fever, is due to one or more members of the genus *Salmonella*.

Causes.—Paratyphoid fever is due to infection with one of three micro-organisms : *Salmonella paratyphi A, B,* or *C.* The most common variety in Britain is *Salmonella paratyphi B.* These organisms closely resemble that of typhoid fever in appearance and some of its reactions, but inoculation against typhoid only does not afford protection against these, and a quadruple vaccine should be used for protective inoculation, prepared from all four organisms and known as T.A.B.C. The infection is usually conveyed by a ' carrier ' case who has already had the disease, or it is due to contaminated food or water. In 1966, there were 132 cases in England and Wales (Table 16A).

Symptoms resemble those found in a mild case of typhoid fever. The incubation period is shorter (one to ten days), and rose spots are seen less commonly. The onset of the disease is often more sudden than in typhoid fever, but the fever tends to be less prolonged and less severe.

Treatment is the same as for typhoid fever. (*See* ENTERIC FEVER.)

PAREGORIC, or COMPOUND TINCTURE OF CAMPHOR, is a preparation of opium much used for cough mixtures. It contains, in addition to opium, oil of anise, benzoic acid, and camphor. Scotch paregoric with a similar composition is about double the strength of this tincture and more stimulating.

PARENCHYMA (παρέγχυμα) is a term meaning originally all the soft tissues of internal organs except the muscular flesh, though now reserved for the secreting cells of the glandular organs.

PARENTERAL is the word applied to the administration of drugs by any route other than by the mouth or by the bowel. Parenteral methods of giving drugs includes injection under the skin or into muscle, inunction, and intrathecal injection.

PARESIS (πάρεσις, slackening) means a state of slight or temporary paralysis. (*See* PARALYSIS.)

PARIETAL (*parietes*, walls) is the term applied to anything pertaining to the wall of a cavity, *e.g.* parietal pleura, the part of the pleural membrane which lines the wall of the chest.

PARKINSON'S DISEASE, or PARK-INSONISM, is a name for paralysis agitans. (*See* PARALYSIS.)

PAROLEINE (*see* PARAFFIN).

PAROMOMYCIN is an antibiotic derived from a sub-species of *Streptomyces rhimosus*, which is proving of value in the treatment of certain cases of both bacillary and amœbic dysentery.

PARONYCHIA (παρά, beside ; ὄνυξ, the nail) is the term applied to inflammation near the nail. (*See* WHITLOW.)

PAROSMIA means a perverted sense of smell ; everything usually smells unpleasant to the affected individual. The most common cause is some septic condition of the nasal passages, but it may occasionally be due to a lesion in the brain involving the centre responsible for the sense of smell.

PAROTID GLAND (παρωτίς) is one of the salivary glands. It is situated just in front of the ear, and its duct runs forwards across the cheek to open into the interior of the mouth on a little projection opposite the second last tooth of the upper row. The parotid gland is generally the first of the salivary glands to become enlarged in mumps (*see* MUMPS).

PAROTITIS (παρωτίς, the parotid gland), means inflammation of the parotid gland. Epidemic parotitis is another name for mumps (*q.v.*).

PAROVARIUM is the name of a rudimentary structure situated near the ovary, in which tumours sometimes arise.

PARSLEY is the leaves and fruit of *Apium petroselinum*. It has a stimulant and diuretic action. Apiol is derived from the leaves. It should not be confused with *fool's parsley*, or lesser hemlock, *Æthusa cynapium*, which is highly poisonous.

PARTURITION (*parturio*, I bring forth). (*See* LABOUR.)

PARULIS (παρά, beside ; οὖλον, gum) is another name for gumboil or abscess of the gum.

P.A.S.—A commonly used abbreviation for para-aminosalicylic acid (*q.v.*).

PASTEURIZATION is a method of sterilizing milk which is not open to some of the objections attending boiling. The boiling of milk gives it a taste and smell which are disagreeable to some persons. In many parts of the world pasteurization has done away with milk-borne infections, of which the most serious is bovine tuberculosis, affecting the glands, bones, and joints of children. Other infections conveyed by milk are septic sore throat, scarlet fever, diphtheria, enteric fever (typhoid and paratyphoid), undulant fever, and food poisoning (*e.g.* from the toxins of the staphylococcus). The case, therefore, seems very clear for the compulsory pasteurization of all milk. Pasteurization destroys about 20 per cent. of vitamin C, but it should be remembered that we do not rely upon milk to protect us from scurvy, but on fresh fruit and vegetables, such as oranges, lemons, currants, potatoes, and green vegetables.

HIGH - TEMPERATURE SHORT - TIME (H.T.S.T.) PASTEURIZATION consists in heating the milk at a temperature not less than 162° F. (72° C.) for at least fifteen seconds, followed by immediate cooling to a temperature of not more than 55° F. (13° C.).

LOW-TEMPERATURE PASTEURIZATION, or ' HOLDER ' PROCESS, consists in maintaining the milk for at least half an hour at a temperature between 145° F. and 150° F. (63° to 65° C.), followed by immediate cooling to a temperature of not more than 55° F. (13° C.). This has the effect of considerably reducing the number of bacteria contained in the milk and of preventing the diseases conveyed by milk referred to above. This procedure is sufficient for the sale of milk as ' pasteurized milk ' in England.

PATELLA (*patella*, a small pan), also known as the knee-pan or knee-cap, is a flat bone shaped somewhat like an oyster-shell, lying in the tendon of the extensor muscle of the thigh, and protecting the knee-joint in front. (*See* BONES, KNEE, FRACTURES.)

PATHOGENIC (πάθος, suffering ; γεννάω, I produce) means disease-producing, and is a term applied to bacteria, etc., capable of causing disease.

PATHOGNOMONIC (πάθος, suffering; γιγνώσκω, I recognize) is a term applied to signs or symptoms which are specially characteristic of certain diseases, and on the presence or absence of which the diagnosis depends. Thus the discovery of the *Mycobacterium tuberculosis* in the expectoration is said to be ' pathognomonic ' of pulmonary tuberculosis.

PATHOLOGY (πάθος, suffering; λόγος, a discourse) is the science which deals with the causes of, and changes produced in the body by, disease.

PAUL-BUNNELL REACTION is a test for glandular fever (*q.v.*) which is based upon the fact that patients with glandular fever develop antibodies which agglutinate sheep red blood cells.

PECTIN (πηκτός, congealed) is a polysaccharide substance allied to starch, contained in fruits and plants, and forming the basis of vegetable jelly. It has been used as a transfusion fluid in place of blood in cases of hæmorrhage and shock.

PECTORAL (*pectoralis*) means anything pertaining to the chest, or a remedy used in treating chest troubles.

PECTORILOQUY (*pectus*, the chest ; *loquor*, I speak) means the resonance of the voice, when spoken or whispered words can be clearly heard through the stethoscope. It is a sign of consolidation, or of a cavity, in the lung.

PEDICULOSIS CAPITIS (*see* INSECTS IN RELATION TO DISEASE, *under* LICE).

PEDICULUS (*see* PARASITES).

PELLAGRA (*pellis*, the skin ; ἄγρα, seizure) is a nutritional disorder, showing a number of nervous, digestive, and skin symptoms which first make their appearance during the spring or autumn and recur year after year, improving to some extent during the winter months. It is chiefly confined to the poorer classes, especially agricultural labourers. Originally noted in Italy and Spain about the middle of the eighteenth

century, it was later found widely spread through southern Europe, Portugal, the south-west of France, Austrian Tyrol, etc., and has more recently been discovered in the British Isles, in various parts of Africa, India, Syria, and in the southern United States, Central and South America.

Cause.—The disease is most prevalent among field labourers wherever it occurs, and the inhabitants of towns are largely immune, even in districts where the disease is very common. It seldom attacks people in good circumstances who live on a generous diet. There is a marked connection between the disease and the season of the year, the particular season at which it is worst varying in different localities but always being the same for any given place ; in Europe, for example, the spring is the time of year in which it specially manifests itself. It has been ascribed at different times to most varied causes, including poverty, insanitary dwellings, bad water, garlic, and maize, and to burning by exposure to the sun. Maize has been especially blamed for its production, the theory having been held that it was caused by some poisonous substance developed in this grain. It is now known that it is a vitamin-deficiency disease. It was found that in institutions where pellagra had been common the addition of meat, vegetables, fruit, and eggs to the diet prevented new cases from occurring and rapidly restored to health persons already suffering from pellagra. It was later found that most foods which were rich in vitamin B would cure pellagra, but when the purified preparation of the anti-beri-beri vitamin B_1 (thiamine) was tried, it was found that this was ineffective, and the pellagra-preventing factor was found to be in what was called vitamin B_2. This was soon recognized to consist of more than one vitamin, and the pellagra-preventing factor was identified as nicotinic acid. Sufferers from pellagra, however, probably lack more than one vitamin.

Symptoms.—The course of pellagra lasts many years, with digestive disturbances including loss of appetite and diarrhœa or constipation, headache, and irritability of temper. The skin symptoms consist at first of redness resembling severe sunburn on the parts of the body exposed to the sun, such as the hands, forearms, chest, neck, and face. The irritation usually lasts about a fortnight, is followed by desquamation, and the skin remains rough, thickened, and permanently brownish in colour. This brownish and roughened appearance on the hands is the most prominent feature of the disease, and from this the disease takes its name. Tremors, sleepiness, and weakness of the legs also appear. For several years the disease may recur in this manner every spring, the attacks gradually becoming more severe, the patient slowly growing emaciated and in some cases completely paralytic or demented.

Treatment.—The disease is prevented or cured by adding to the diet foods such as fresh meat, eggs, milk, liver, and yeast extracts, and nicotinic acid, as well as by improvement of the general conditions of life.

PELOTHERAPY is the therapeutic use of mud or peat. It is prescribed either as general or local baths or in the form of a pack.

PELVIS (*pelvis*, a basin) is that division of the skeleton which is made up of the haunch-bones, one on each side, and the sacrum and coccyx behind. It connects the lower limbs with the spine.

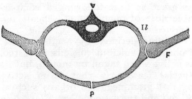

FIG. 311.—Diagram showing the relation of the pelvic bones to the spinal column and to the thigh-bone. *V*, Sacrum ; *Il*, ilium ; *P*, pubis ; *F*, thigh-bone. (Turner's *Anatomy*.)

Each haunch-bone is composed of three originally separate bones, in the adult pelvis firmly fused together : the ilium ; the ischium, with a rounded part below, the tuberosity, upon which the body rests in sitting ; and the pubis in front. The expanded parts of the iliac bones incompletely surround the lower part of the abdomen, known as the false pelvis, and are separated by a distinct line, known as the brim or inlet, from the true pelvis beneath. The

true pelvis, as its name implies, is basin-shaped, and though in the dried state it has a wide outlet beneath, yet in the living body it is well closed and rounded off by ligaments and muscles so as to leave small openings only for the urinary and genital passages and for the rectum. This soft floor of the pelvis is composed mainly of two muscles, the levators of the anus, whilst the deep notch, between the haunch-bone and sacrum behind, is closed in by a pair of strong sacro-sciatic ligaments.

The pelvis varies considerably in the two sexes. In the female it is shallower and the ilia are more widely separated, giving great breadth to the hips of the woman ; the inlet is more circular and the outlet larger ; whilst the angle beneath the pubic bones (subpubic angle), which is an acute angle in the male, is obtuse in the female. All these points are of importance in connection with the subject of child-bearing.

The contents of the pelvis are the urinary bladder and rectum in both sexes, and in addition the male has the seminal vesicles and the prostate gland surrounding the neck of the bladder, whilst the female has the womb, ovaries, and their appendages.

In addition to the above differences for sex, there are certain differences in the pelvis of different races, those of the lower races being, generally speaking, longer from before back and from above down than those of higher races, *i.e.* approximating more to the pelvis of lower animals.

PELVIS, DISEASES OF (*see* ABDOMEN, DISEASES OF, and also see under the headings of the various pelvic organs).

PELVIS OF THE KIDNEY, or RENAL PELVIS, is the cavity of the kidney, lined by mucous membrane, in which the ureter commences. (*See* KIDNEYS.)

PEMPHIGUS (πέμφιξ, a bladder) is a skin eruption characterized by the appearance of large blebs.

PEMPIDINE is a drug for the treatment of hypertension. It closely resembles mecamylamine (*q.v.*) in its action. (*See* ESSENTIAL HYPERTENSION.)

PENICILLIN is the name given by Sir Alexander Fleming, in 1929, to an antibacterial substance produced by the mould *Penicillium notatum*. This mould was first described in 1911 in Scandinavia, where it was discovered in decaying hyssop. The story of penicillin is one of the most dramatic in the history of medicine, and its introduction into medicine initiated a new era in therapeutics comparable only to the introduction of anæsthesia by Morton and Simpson and of antiseptics by Pasteur and Lister. The two names that will always be primarily associated with penicillin are those of Sir Alexander Fleming, of St. Mary's Hospital, London, who discovered the antibacterial action of penicillin, and Lord Florey, of Oxford, who did so much to develop its practical use during the 1939–45 War. The two great advantages of penicillin are that it is active against a large range of bacteria and that, even in large doses, it is nontoxic. Among the organisms against which it is active are : staphylococcus, streptococcus, pneumococcus, meningococcus, gonococcus, and the organisms responsible for gas gangrene. Hitherto it has always been necessary to give penicillin by injection (usually intramuscularly), but there is now evidence showing that it may be effective when given by mouth. It can also be used locally in the form of an ointment, a cream, eye-drops, or as a lozenge for infections of the mouth. It can also be given as an inhalation. In order to prevent its abuse, penicillin can only be obtained in Great Britain by means of a prescription from a doctor, dentist, or veterinary surgeon.

Penicillin has been synthesized in the laboratory, but it is such a complex and unstable substance that there is no reason to believe that it will be possible to synthesize it on a commercial scale —at least not for a long time to come. This has meant that hitherto the only means of obtaining penicillin was by the laborious method of cultivating the penicillin mould, *Penicillium chrysogenum*. A break-through, however, has now been achieved by British research workers, which means that a partial synthesis of penicillin is now possible. The break-through consisted of the isolation of the penicillin nucleus—6-

aminopenicillanic acid. This can still only be obtained by culture of the penicillin mould but, now that the nucleus can be isolated, it should prove possible to add side-chains to it and so produce a large number of different penicillins.

Various forms of penicillin are now available. *Benzylpenicillin* is available as the sodium or potassium salt. It is given intramuscularly, and is the form that is used when a rapid action is required. It can also be given by mouth but, as the proportion absorbed varies greatly, it is unreliable in action when given in this way. *Procaine benzylpenicillin* is a relatively insoluble form of penicillin. A single daily intramuscular injection of 600,000 units will maintain a bacteriostatic level in the blood for twenty-four hours. *Benzathine penicillin* is a relatively insoluble derivative of penicillin which is often given by mouth. When given intramuscularly it gives low but very prolonged blood levels of penicillin.

Phenoxymethylpenicillin is given by mouth and produces higher blood levels than any other form of oral penicillin in comparable doses. *Phenethicillin* is the first of the new penicillins obtained by adding a side-chain to the penicillin nucleus. It is effective when taken by mouth and produces a blood concentration of penicillin which is twice as great as that following a comparable dose of phenoxymethylpenicillin. *Ampicillin* is another of the new penicillins derived by semi-synthesis from the penicillin nucleus. It, too, is active when taken by mouth, but its special feature is that it is active against gram-negative organs such as *E. coli* and the salmonellæ. *Cloxacillin* is yet another of the new semi-synthesized penicillins. It has a relatively weak anti-bacterial action, but has the advantage of being active against penicillin-resistant staphylococci. *Propicillin* is α-phenoxypropylpenicillin, which is active when taken by mouth, and against penicillin-resistant staphylococci. *Phenbenicillin* is potassium phenoxybenzylpenicillin and is active when taken by mouth.

Methicillin is another of the new penicillins derived from the penicillin nucleus. It is active against penicillin-resistant staphylococci but has to be given by injection as it is destroyed by the acid secretion of the stomach.

PENIS (*penis*) is the organ down which, in the male, passes the urethra, the tube by which the contents of the urinary bladder and those of the seminal vesicles escape.

PENNYROYAL is a popular name for several plants such as *Mentha pulegium* (European pennyroyal) and *Hedeoma pulegioides* (American pennyroyal). These plants contain a volatile oil which is used for rubbing into the skin to prevent the bites of midges and mosquitoes and to allay the itching caused by them.

PENTAMIDINE. — A proprietary term for diamidino-diphenoxypentane, which has been successfully used in the treatment of kala-azar.

PENTOLINIUM TARTRATE is a methonium compound which is used as a hypotensive agent in the treatment of high blood-pressure. It is longer acting than hexamethonium (*q.v.*).

PENTOSE is the name applied to a fruit sugar which contains 5 atoms of carbon and which does not ferment.

PENTOTHAL is a proprietary term for thiopentone sodium (*q.v.*).

PEPO is a substance made from the interior of pumpkin seeds, and used to expel tape-worms.

PEPPER is the unripe fruit of *Piper nigrum*, a vine of the East Indies, and possesses an active principle, piperin. It is used externally as a counter-irritant and internally as a stimulant to digestion.

PEPPERMINT is the leaves and tops of *Mentha piperita*. It has an aromatic odour, due to the presence of an oil from which is obtained menthol, a camphor-like substance (*see* MENTHOL). Peppermint water is a useful remedy for flatulence and colic in infants. Oil of peppermint is used like the other volatile oils.

PEPSIN (*pepsinum*) is the name given to a ferment found in the gastric juice which digests proteins by converting them into albumose and finally into peptones. Pepsin is used in medicine in cases of weak digestion either to digest food before it is taken or more frequently to administer after meals. It is a light yellowish-brown or white powder prepared from the fresh mucous membrane of the stomach of pigs, sheep, or calves, and it can dissolve from 2500 to 5000 times its weight of hard-boiled white of egg. (For the pre-digestion of food, *see* PEPTONIZED FOODS.)

PEPTIC ULCER is the term commonly applied to ulcers in the stomach and duodenum.

PEPTID is a term applied to a compound formed by the union of two or more amino-acids.

PEPTONE is a whitish soluble powder prepared from meat which has been peptonized either by the action of acids or by artificial digestion with pepsin or trypsin. It is used as a food, especially in the form of freshly peptonized milk, beef, etc., and it is also injected subcutaneously in the treatment of disease. (*See* PROTEIN THERAPY.)

PEPTONIZED FOODS.—Pepsin and pancreatin are extracts made from the stomach and pancreas respectively of newly killed animals, and at one time widely used by persons of weak digestion, or those recovering from a severe illness, or those devitalized by age, in order to assist in the digestion of the food by converting its insoluble proteids into peptones. They may be added to the food before it is taken into the stomach, being allowed to act upon it at a temperature a little above that of the body for a period of some minutes to several hours, or they may be given in solution, or as a powder in cachets along with the food.

PEPSIN is extracted with weak alcohol from the stomach of the pig, and is then dried to a light yellow powder. (For its administration, *see* PEPSIN.)

PANCREATIN contains four ferments (*see* DIGESTION), and is made by chopping up a pancreas finely and extracting it with weak alcohol or glycerin. Pancreatin has the advantages over pepsin that it acts more quickly, digests all kinds of food, does not require an acid to assist it, and does not unpleasantly change the taste of food unless allowed to act upon it too long. Pancreatic extract may be obtained in the form of powder or tablets (dose 3 to 10 grains), and is often used as liquor pancreaticus, of which one or two teaspoonfuls is taken for a dose. Beef-jelly, chicken-jelly, wheat flour, and other foods are sold, predigested to some extent by pancreatic extract, for the use of invalids.

Peptonized milk is made by taking a quarter of a pint of cold water, mixing with it a peptonizing tablet or peptonizing powder, adding this to a pint of fresh milk in a quart bottle, and finally placing the bottle in a pan of water just so hot that the hand can be immersed in it without pain. The bottle of milk is left in this bath according to the amount of digestion desired, but not longer than ten minutes. If the milk be not immediately used, it must be placed upon ice or brought quickly to the boil in order to stop the action of the peptonizing ferment. It is often sufficient to administer one or two teaspoonfuls of liquor pancreaticus along with the milk without any digestion outside the body.

Peptonized beef may be prepared as follows : A quarter of a pound of finely minced lean beef is mixed with half a pint of cold water, and cooked gently over the fire till it has boiled a few minutes. The liquor is then poured off, and the meat rubbed or beaten to a paste. The liquor and meat are placed next in a clean jar, and half a pint of cold water containing twenty grains of 'zymine' pancreatic extract (or a teaspoonful of liquor pancreaticus) and half a teaspoonful of bicarbonate of soda are added. The jar with its contents is covered and set aside in a warm place for three hours, and then boiled quickly to stop further peptonization. The resulting liquid is seasoned with salt, and, if necessary, strained before use.

Other foods are peptonized in a similar manner. These artificially digested foods should never be used for longer than necessary, except in the relatively rare cases of deficiency of the pancreatic secretions, when it may be necessary to continue their use for long periods as a form of substitution therapy. Except in such cases, peptonized foods are seldom used now.

PERCUSSION (*percutio*, I strike) is an aid to diagnosis practised by striking the body with the fingers or with an instrument known as a 'plessor', in such a way as to make it give out a note. According to the degree of dullness or resonance of the note, an opinion can be formed as to the state of consolidation of air-containing organs, the presence of abnormal cavities in organs, and the dimensions of solid and air-containing organs, which happen to lie next one another. Still more valuable evidence is given by auscultation (*see* AUSCULTATION).

PERCUTANEOUS (*per*, through; *cutis*, skin) is a term applied to any method of administering remedies by passing them through the skin, as by rubbing in an ointment or carrying in drugs on the galvanic current.

PERFORATION is one of the serious dangers attaching to any ulcerated condition of the stomach or bowels. When a perforation from one of these hollow organs takes place into the peritoneal cavity, many bacteria, together with putrescible material, are poured into this cavity and there set up peritonitis. (*See* PERITONITIS.) The immediate signs that a perforation has taken place are usually a state of collapse, and increase of pain over the abdomen, together with, in some cases, the evidence of free fluid and gas in the peritoneal cavity.

PERI- (περί, around) is a prefix meaning around.

PERIARTERITIS NODOSA (*see* POLYARTERITIS NODOSA).

PERICARDITIS means inflammation of the pericardium. (*See* HEART DISEASES.)

PERICARDIUM (περικάρδιος, near the heart) is the smooth membrane that surrounds the heart. (*See* HEART.)

PERIHEPATITIS (περί), around; ἧπαρ, liver) means inflammation of the peritoneal covering of the liver.

PERIMETRITIS (περί, around; μήτρα, the womb) means a localized inflammation of the peritoneum surrounding the womb.

PERINATAL MORTALITY consists of deaths of the fœtus after the 28th week of pregnancy and deaths of the new-born child during the first week of life. The perinatal mortality rate, which is the number of such deaths per 1000 total births, has come to be looked upon as a valuable indicator of the quality of care provided for the mother and her new-born baby. In England and Wales the perinatal mortality rate has fallen from 62.1 in 1931 to 26.3 in 1966 but, for some reason or another it is higher than in Scandinavia and Holland. Thus, in 1964, the latest year for which comparable figures are available, the rate in England and Wales was 28·2, compared with 23·4 in Holland, 24·5 in Finland, 21·8 in Norway, 21·6 in Sweden. In Scotland it was 32·1.

The causes of perinatal mortality include intrapartum anoxia (that is, difficulty in the birth of the baby, resulting in lack of oxygen), congenital abnormalities of the baby, antepartum anoxia (that is, conditions in the terminal stages of pregnancy preventing the fœtus getting sufficient oxygen), and injuries to the brain of the baby during birth.

In England and Wales, in 1965, the three chief causes of deaths during the first week of life were : birth injury and asphyxia, which were responsible for 4015 of the 9732 deaths during the first week of life, immaturity of the infant, which was responsible for 2418 of the deaths ; and congenital malformations, which were responsible for 1528 of the deaths.

PERINEPHRITIS (περί, around; νεφρός, the kidney) means inflammation in the cellular tissue round the kidney, often leading to formation of an abscess. (*See* ABSCESS, ACUTE.)

PERINEUM (περίνεος), or FORK, is the region situated between the opening of the bowel behind and of the genital organs in front. In the female it is apt to be lacerated in the act of childbirth.

PERIOD (*see* MENSTRUATION).

PERIOSTEUM (περιόστεος, round the bones) is the membrane surrounding a bone. The periosteum carries blood-

vessels and nerves for the nutrition and development of the bone. When it is

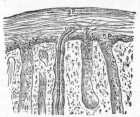

FIG. 312.—Surface of a growing bone. *SP*, Superficial fibrous layer of periosteum ; *DP*, deep cellular layer next the bone ; *V*, blood-vessel entering the bone ; *HH*, Haversian canals. Magnified by about 200. (Turner's *Anatomy*.)

irritated, an increased deposit of bone takes place beneath it, and, if it is destroyed, the bone may cease to grow and a portion may die and separate as a sequestrum. (*See* BONE.)

PERIOSTITIS means inflammation on the surface of a bone affecting the periosteum. (*See* BONE, DISEASES OF.)

PERIPHERAL NEURITIS (περιφέρεια, the outer part ; νεῦρον, nerve) means inflammation of the nerves in the outlying parts of the body. (*See* NEURITIS.)

PERISTALSIS (περισταλτικός, compressing) is the term applied to the worm-like movement by which the stomach and bowels propel their contents. It consists of alternate waves of relaxation and contraction in successive parts of the tube. When any obstruction to the movement of the contents exists, these contractions become more forcible and are liable to be accompanied by the severe form of pain known as colic.

PERITONEOSCOPY. — Viewing of the peritoneal cavity through a tube fitted with mirrors and light. The instrument (resembling a CYSTOSCOPE, *q.v.*) is entered just below the umbilicus. The peritoneal cavity is then inflated with air. This simple operation may obviate a more drastic one — for example, if peritoneoscopy shows ' deposits ' of cancer in the peritoneum or the liver. Colour photographs of the liver have been taken through the peritoneoscope.

PERITONEUM (περιτόναιος, a stretched membrane) is the membrane lining the abdominal cavity, and forming a covering for the organs contained in it. That part lining the walls of the abdomen is called the parietal peritoneum, and that part covering the viscera is known as the visceral peritoneum. The two are continuous with one another at the back of the abdomen, and form a closed sac. One may understand its relation to the organs by conceiving them to have been pressed against the outside of this sac from behind, and each to have become wrapped up in the hinder part of the sac without being forced through to its interior, while the front wall of the sac remains quite smooth. The folds of peritoneum passing from one organ to another are thus very complicated, and receive special names in various parts. (*See* MESENTERY, OMENTUM.)

It is stated that the peritoneum forms a closed sac, but to this there is an exception in the female, the Fallopian tube on each side having an opening into the cavity at its end large enough to admit a bristle. There is, however, no large outlet for drainage of fluid, so that a small amount is always present to lubricate the membrane, while a large amount collects in conditions that are associated with dropsy. From this arises one great reason for the danger of inflammation affecting this membrane, since there is no escape from it for the pus and other products of inflammation, which accumulate and increase the state of irritation.

In structure the peritoneum consists of a dense, though thin and elastic, fibrous membrane covered, on its inner side, by a smooth glistening layer of plate-like epithelial cells. Here and there between the cells are minute openings (stomata), each of which communicates with a lymphatic vessel, so that the fluid in the cavity is constantly draining off into the general lymphatic circulation.

PERITONITIS means inflammation of the peritoneum or membrane investing the abdominal and pelvic cavities and their contained viscera. It may exist in an acute or a chronic form, and may be either localized in one part or generally diffused.

686

Inflammation of this membrane varies much as regards its causes, severity, and danger, according as it is acute or chronic. Although there are occasional intermediate cases, it may be said, roughly speaking, that the development of acute cases may be reckoned by days, that of chronic cases by months.

ACUTE PERITONITIS.—Causes.— As a rule it arises in consequence of the entrance of micro-organisms into the peritoneal cavity, which gain entrance through wounds from the exterior or pass out of some of the abdominal organs. The great danger which follows upon stabs and other penetrating wounds of the abdomen originates from the risk of peritonitis. On the other hand, the danger may come from within, and all conditions which lead to perforation of the stomach, bowels, bile-ducts, bladder, and other hollow organs may produce it. Thus gastric ulcer, typhoid fever, gall-stones, rupture of the bladder, strangulated hernia, and obstructions of the bowels may end in peritonitis. Again, abscesses and cysts developed in connection with various organs may burst and so produce it, appendicitis, abscesses of the ovary and Fallopian tubes being specially dangerous. Peritonitis may also arise within a few days after delivery.

The changes which take place in the peritoneum are similar to those undergone by other serous membranes when inflamed, viz. (1) congestion ; (2) exudation of fibrin in greater or less abundance, at first greyish in colour and soft, thereafter yellow and becoming tough in consistence, causing the folds of intestine to adhere together, and so tending to limit the spread of the inflammation ; (3) effusion of fluid, either clear, turbid, bloody, or purulent; (4) absorption, more or less complete, of the fluid and fibrin, or, in cases that proceed to a serious issue, the formation of grey or greenish-grey pus. Occasionally shreds or bands of unabsorbed fibrin remain, and become converted into fibrous tissue, thus producing adhesions which constitute a subsequent danger of strangulation of the bowel, although this risk follows more often upon recovery from the chronic form.

In some cases the peritonitis becomes *localized* by adhesions between neighbouring organs due to the deposit of fibrin upon their surface. This process takes place with great rapidity, and it makes a good deal of difference to the result of the disease whether it be thus shut in to one part of the abdomen or whether it spreads so rapidly, or is of so virulent a type, as quickly to become *general.*

The bacteria causing peritonitis are numerous, but among the most common are the *Escherichia coli*, which is always a denizen of the intestine ; streptococci, which produce the most virulent form of inflammation ; and the gonococcus.

Symptoms.—The symptoms usually begin by a rigor, together with vomiting and pain in the abdomen of a peculiarly severe and sickening character, accompanied with extreme tenderness, so that the slightest pressure causes intense aggravation of the pain. The patient lies on the back with the knees drawn up, and the hands often rest upon the head, and it will be noticed that the breathing is rapid and shallow and performed by movements of the chest only, the abdominal muscles remaining rigid, unlike what takes place in healthy respiration. The abdomen becomes swollen by flatulent distension of the intestines, which increases the patient's distress. There is usually constipation. The skin is hot, and the temperature rises to 104° or 105° F. (40° to 40·5° C.), although there may be perspiration ; the pulse is small, hard, and wiry ; the urine is scanty and high coloured, and passed with pain. The patient's aspect is one of anxiety and suffering. These symptoms may subside in a day or two, but if they do not, the case is apt to go on rapidly to a fatal termination. In such an event, the pain and tenderness subside, the abdomen becomes more distended, hiccough and vomiting of brown or blood-coloured matter occurs, the temperature falls, the face becomes pinched, cold, and clammy, the pulse exceedingly rapid and feeble, and death takes place from collapse, the patient's mental faculties generally remaining clear till the close. When the peritonitis is due to perforation, as may happen in the case of a gastric ulcer, or the ulcers of typhoid fever, the above-mentioned symptoms and the fatal collapse may

all take place in from twelve to twenty-four hours. But usually the disease lasts four or five days, and the patient sometimes survives as long as a week. The puerperal form of this disease, which comes on within a day or two after parturition, is always very serious.

Treatment.—The patient should lie recumbent on the back, with a pillow beneath the knees, so as to bend up the thighs, and a cage over the abdomen to support the weight of the bed-clothes. Externally, either an ice-bag or hot laudanum fomentations retard the inflammation and give relief. The food must be fluid, stimulating, and easily digested, and if vomiting comes on it should be administered in the form of enemata by the bowel. In the later stages, when the stomach will not retain even water, large enemata of saline solution quench the distressing thirst. When the facilities are available, *e.g.* in hospital, fluid is given intravenously, either in the form of plasma or of glucose-saline. In the later stages, opium is of great value, administered especially with the view of relieving the pain and also in order to diminish to some extent the inflammatory process.

The introduction of the antibiotics and of the sulphonamides has resulted in a great improvement in the outlook for this serious condition.

The question of operation arises in every case of peritonitis. In cases due to perforation of the stomach or intestine which are discovered early, operation is always advisable, because there is a good prospect of freeing the abdomen from the septic material which has entered it, and, if no operation be performed, the patient will almost certainly die. In cases in which peritonitis has become ' localized ' the question arises whether the patient's small stock of vitality will be used to more advantage in combating the disease. The operation consists in making an opening into the abdomen, carefully cleansing the outer surface of the bowels, and attending to the original cause of the peritonitis, whether it be a perforation, obstruction, abscess, appendicitis, etc., after which it is usual to insert drainage tubes.

CHRONIC PERITONITIS.—Causes.—In the great majority of cases

687

this is tuberculous in origin and secondary to tuberculous disease of bones, joints, glands, or bowels. There is also a localized form of chronic peritonitis, which is non-tuberculous. This latter form is due to long-continued inflammation in an abdominal organ or to ulceration which threatens to perforate. This type of peritonitis is advantageous, because it produces great thickening and adhesions over the part in question, thus lessening the risk of perforation or of infection of the general peritoneal cavity, e.g. in appendicitis.

Symptoms.—The chief symptoms of tuberculous peritonitis are abdominal pain and distension, along with disturbance of the functions of the bowels, there being either constipation or diarrhœa, or each alternately. Along with these local manifestations, there exist the usual phenomena of tuberculous disease, viz. fever, with emaciation and loss of strength. The abdominal pain may, however, be so slight as only to reach a feeling of uncomfortable weight and fullness.

The simple localized form mentioned above is characterized mainly by recurring attacks of sharp pain, and sometimes the thickening of the peritoneum is so great as to resemble and be mistaken for a tumour.

Treatment.—The same rules, as to diet and a healthy life, that pertain to the treatment of pulmonary tuberculosis, apply to tuberculous peritonitis (see TUBERCULOSIS). In addition, the patient is treated with a combination of streptomycin, *para*-aminosalicylic acid and isoniazid.

PERITONSILLAR ABSCESS is the term applied to an attack of tonsillitis which results in an abscess near the tonsil, forming the condition known as ' quinsy '. It usually points and bursts through the soft palate.

PERITYPHLITIS (περί, around; τυφλόν, the cæcum) means inflammation round the region of the cæcum, that part of the large intestine situated in the lower right-hand corner of the abdomen from which the appendix vermiformis springs. The name is now little used, having been introduced before people came to recognize the fact that inflam-
688

mations in this region usually originate in the appendix. (*See* APPENDICITIS.)

PERLÈCHE (*see* CHEILOSIS).

PERMANGANATE OF POTASSIUM is a crystalline substance of brilliant purple hue. Permanganate of sodium is red in colour, and is the chief ingredient in Condy's disinfectant fluid, having an action similar to that of the potassium salt. Potassium permanganate dissolved in water is of a brilliant purple colour, and has a powerful oxidizing action, in exerting which it disintegrates alkaloidal poisons, foul and decomposing organic bodies, and kills low forms of life, such as bacteria. It is, therefore, a powerful antiseptic. It is non-volatile, and therefore has not the penetrating power of carbolic acid, and in exerting its oxidizing power it is itself reduced, so that it gradually loses strength. *Green Condy's fluid* contains sodium manganate, which has a similar action.

Uses.—Permanganate of potassium is a cheap disinfectant, and is conveniently kept in a saturated solution (1 part of potassium permanganate to 20 parts of water). If this be diluted with water twenty-five times (1 in 500), that is, to a crimson tint, or in the proportion of about a tablespoonful of the strong solution to a tumblerful of water, it forms an excellent lotion for washing ulcers and suppurating wounds, and, diluted to a pale pink colour, makes a good gargle for an ulcerated throat. In the latter strength, it may be poured down drains, when it both purifies them and destroys the smell proceeding from them. A stronger solution (dark crimson or purple in colour) may be used with advantage to wash or steep the hands after they have touched a foul wound or a person suffering from infectious disease. If the hands become brown after its use, this discoloration may be removed by oxalic acid. As a hair-dye, potassium permanganate gives a rich chestnut-brown colour. As an antidote to poisoning by opium, strychnine, colchicum, oxalic acid, and toadstools (muscarine), potassium permanganate is most valuable if administered at once ; 3 or 4 grains (200 or 250 mg.) may be given well diluted in water. A pale pink solution of potassium permanganate is also a test for the purity of drinking-water; a drop or two allowed to fall into a glass of water should tinge the latter pink, but, if the pink colour disappear, it indicates the presence of organic impurities.

PERNICIOUS ANÆMIA is a severe form of anæmia also known as ADDISONIAN ANÆMIA. (*See* ANÆMIA.)

PERONEAL (περόνη, the fibula) is the name given to the muscles, nerves, etc., on the outer or fibular side of the leg.

PEROXIDE OF HYDROGEN is a syrupy, colourless, odourless liquid which differs in chemical composition from water, by containing two atoms jo oxygen (H_2O_2) to every one in water (H_2O). It has the property of readily giving up its extra oxygen and being reduced to water, and this renders it of great value in medicine for antiseptic, deodorant, and other purposes. It is most commonly employed as a solution in water of such a strength that any quantity will give off ten times its bulk of oxygen gas ; this is known as 10-volume strength, or as liquor of hydrogen peroxide. It is also prepared twice this strength. When added to ether, the substance is more stable, and the mixture is known as ozonic ether. Volatile oils which have become oxidized contain a considerable quantity of peroxide of hydrogen, and to this substance the powers they possess of destroying foul odours is largely due.

Uses.—Externally to ulcers, and by sprays or swabs to cavities like the nose and throat, the watery solution of hydrogen peroxide is applied in order to act as an antiseptic, and also for the valuable property possessed by the little bubbles of oxygen that it gives off in breaking up and causing the separation of discharges. It is used to remove surgical dressings that are very adherent. Internally, it is sometimes used to wash out the stomach in cases of chronic gastritis, in a strength of ½ ounce to the pint (14 ml. to 570 ml.).

PERSEVERATION is the term for describing the senseless repetition of words or deeds by a person with a disordered mind.

PERSPIRATION or SWEAT, is an excretion from the skin, produced by microscopic sweat-glands scattered over the surface. Perspiration takes place constantly by evaporation from the openings of the sweat-glands, and this insensible perspiration amounts in twenty-four hours to considerably over a pint. Under certain circumstances, as when the skin is heated or the person exerts himself, drops of sensible perspiration appear on the skin ; to these the term sweat is generally confined, and the amount of sweat secreted may become very large.

Sweat is a faintly acid, watery fluid containing less than 2 per cent. of solids, made up mainly of salts and to a slight extent of fatty material, and including a small amount of urea (about 1 part per 1000), the substance which the kidneys excrete in large amount. When the action of the kidneys is defective, for example in Bright's disease, urea and other substances, which the kidneys normally excrete, pass out in great quantities through the skin. This action of the skin is so marked that in a case of uræmia crystals of urea may be deposited on the surface as the sweat evaporates.

The sweat-glands in man are situated in greatest numbers on the soles of the feet and palms of the hands, and with a magnifying glass their minute openings or pores can be seen in rows occupying the summit of each ridge in the skin. Perspiration is most abundant in these regions, though it also occurs all over the body. Different animals perspire in different regions ; thus rabbits and rats do not sweat at all, oxen very little, pigs mostly on the snout, dogs and cats chiefly from the pads of the feet.

The chief object of perspiration is to regulate the amount of heat lost from the surface of the body and so maintain an even body temperature. Accordingly muscular activity, which sets free a great deal of heat, is the chief cause of sweating, and external heat is another. The process is regulated by nerves, some of which are the nerves controlling the size of the blood-vessels (vasomotor), and therefore the amount of blood in a part, whilst other nerves proceed to the sweat-glands (secretory) and directly influence secretion. These are presided over by centres in the spinal cord and medulla.

Abnormalities of perspiration. — LESSENED sweating under certain conditions may occur, as in the early stages of fever, in diabetes, and in some forms of Bright's disease. Certain persons are

ous night-sweats also occur in certain cases of undulant fever. In a slighter degree, persons of feeble muscular power are apt to perspire very freely upon exertion or when exposed to heat. Rickets is another disease in which children perspire copiously when asleep,

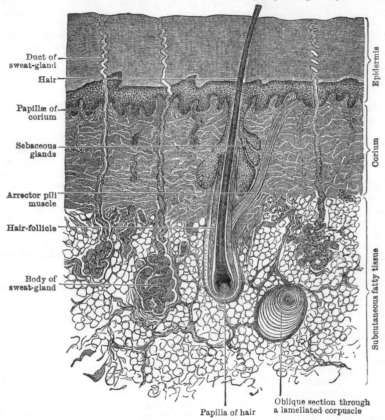

Duct of sweat-gland

Hair

Papillæ of corium

Sebaceous glands

Arrector pili muscle

Hair-follicle

Body of sweat-gland

Epidermis

Corium

Subcutaneous fatty tissue

Papilla of hair

Oblique section through a lamellated corpuscle

FIG. 313.—Vertical section of skin. (From Cunningham's *Anatomy*. Oxford University Press.)

peculiar in the fact of being unable to sweat copiously after muscular exertion, or when exposed to heat, and such persons are often seriously affected by exposure to a hot sun or to the heat of an engine-room. (*See* SUNSTROKE.)

EXCESSIVE sweating may take place in rheumatic fever, in the later stages of various other fevers, and, above all, in advanced pulmonary tuberculosis, where the night-sweats are often copious enough to drench the patient's night-clothes and bedding. Such copi-

and in this disease the sweating is mainly about the head. There is also a condition known as hyperidrosis, which is characterized by over-activity of the sweat-glands. This condition, which may be localized or generalized, is probably due to some disturbance of the nervous control of the sweat-glands.

OFFENSIVE perspiration is not uncommon. In rheumatic conditions the sweat has a peculiar, sour smell. Dyspeptics too are frequently troubled by an unpleasant odour of the skin.

But it is sweating of the feet or armpits that is most offensive of all, this condition being often due to decomposition of the skin secretions by bacteria. COLOURED perspiration is a rare peculiarity, the sweat being tinged blue by indigo, or red by altered blood pigment.

Treatment.—LESSENED perspiration is treated when necessary by various drugs known as diaphoretics (*see* DIAPHORETICS), and by hot-air baths (*see* BATHS, BRIGHT'S DISEASE).

EXCESSIVE sweating occurring in febrile diseases, *e.g.* pulmonary tuberculosis, is diminished by treatment of the condition responsible for the fever. In conditions such as pulmonary tuberculosis, in which the sweating is liable to be prolonged and is particularly irritating to the patient, sponging the skin with vinegar in water may be helpful. In other cases the administration of extract of belladonna by mouth may help.

Hyperidrosis, in which the perspiration is often offensive, is best treated by frequent baths. If indigestion is present, this should also be treated. The feet, armpits, and other sources of perspiration should be washed daily with carbolic, coal-tar, or other mildly antiseptic soap, and thereafter dusted with boric acid powder or bathed with peroxide of hydrogen. The stockings must be frequently changed, and, in addition to washing, they should be disinfected by being wrung out of boric lotion or weak perchloride of mercury lotion immediately before drying. The shoes must also be treated by wiping them out with perchloride of mercury lotion now and then, because the bacteria which sometimes occur may survive on the damp leather. Shoes should be worn in preference to boots, so as to allow freer access of air to the feet, and for the same reason it is a good plan not to wear rubber soles. Sweating may also be considerably checked, if it is very copious, by rubbing the feet, armpits, etc., with liniment of belladonna or with spirit. In severe cases of localized excessive sweating, treatment by X-rays may be necessary and may give satisfactory results.

PERTHES' DISEASE is an affection of the hip in children, due to fragmenta-

tion of the epiphysis (or spongy extremity) of the head of the femur. No active treatment is called for, as the condition settles spontaneously in a few years.

PERTUSSIS (*per-*, excessive ; *tussis*, cough) is another name for whooping-cough. (*See* WHOOPING-COUGH.)

PERUVIAN BARK is another name for cinchona bark, from which quinine is derived.

PESSARIES (πεσσός) are either instruments designed to support a displaced womb, or solid bodies suitably shaped for insertion into the vagina, which are made of oil of theobromine or a glycerin basis and are used for applying local treatment to the vagina.

PEST (*pestis*) is an old name for plague. (*See* PLAGUE.)

PETECHIÆ (Ital. *petecchia*, fleabites) are small spots on the skin, of red or purple colour, resembling fleabites. They may be due to minute areas of inflammation, as in typhoid fever, or to small hæmorrhages in the skin, as in purpura.

PETHIDINE HYDROCHLORIDE is a synthetic analgesic and antispasmodic drug chemically described as the ethyl ester of 1-methyl-4-phenylpiperidine-4-carboxylic acid, which is used in the treatment of painful and spasmodic conditions in place of morphine and atropine. It was at first thought that the drug would have an advantage over morphine in not encouraging addiction, but this has not proved to be the case.

PETIT MAL (Fr.) means the lesser type of epileptic seizure. (*See* EPILEPSY.)

PETRI DISHES are shallow, circular glass dishes, usually 4 inches (10 cm.) in diameter, which are used in bacteriology laboratories for the growth of micro-organisms.

PETROLATUM is another name for soft paraffin. (*See* PARAFFIN.)

PEYER'S PATCHES are conglomerations of lymphoid nodules in the ileum, or lower part of the small intestine.

They play an important part in the defence of the body against bacterial invasion, as in typhoid fever.

PHAGEDÆNA (φαγέδαινα, a devouring sore) means a process of ulceration of so severe a type that pieces of skin become gangrenous and slough off. It is due either to great weakness on the part of the person attacked, or to excessive virulence of the bacteria concerned.

PHAGOCYTOSIS (φαγεῖν, to eat ; κύτος, a corpuscle) is the name applied to a process by which the attacks of bacteria upon the living body are repelled and the bacteria destroyed through the activity of the white corpuscles of the blood.

The first observations upon this point were made by Metchnikoff in the case of the Daphnia or water-flea. This little animal, which exists in large numbers in pools of stagnant water, may often be observed to devour the large spores of a species of fungus. Metchnikoff observed that these spores, perforating the intestine of the Daphnia, found their way into its body cavity and there multiplied. They were, however, attacked at once by the white corpuscles circulating in the creature's vessels, which surrounded and took into their substance these spores, apparently in time digesting them, so that they broke down and disappeared. In some cases, however, he found that the spores developed quickly, the white corpuscles appeared to be sluggish in attacking them, and the creature died.

Similar observations have been made in the case of other bacteria in higher animals. The processes which precede phagocytosis, viz. the slowing of the blood-stream in the part, collection of the white corpuscles on the walls of the vessels, their passage out of the vessels into the tissues (diapedesis), and their approach to the bacteria, are described under ABSCESS and INFLAMMATION. When bacteria are very virulent they seem to repel the white corpuscles instead of attracting them, and no phagocytosis takes place, but the bacteria develop unimpeded. (*See* OPSONINS.)

It should be stated that some hold that these white corpuscles do not devour and digest the living bacteria,
692

but simply take up dead ones, just as they absorb particles of carbon, fragments of dead bone, and the like. These authorities suppose that the death of the bacteria is due to some chemical products formed by the body in response to the poisonous substances set free by the bacteria.

PHALANX (φάλαγξ) is the name given to any one of the small bones of the fingers and toes. The phalanges are fourteen in number in each hand and foot, the thumb and great toe possessing only two each, whilst each of the other fingers and toes has three.

PHANTASY (φαντασία, appearance), or FANTASY, is the term applied to an imaginary appearance or day dream.

PHANTOM LIMB.—Following the amputation of a limb it is usual for the patient to experience sensations as if the limb were still present. This condition is referred to as a phantom limb. In the vast majority of cases the sensation passes off in a short period of time.

PHARMACOLOGY (φάρμακον, drug ; λόγος, discourse) is the part of medical science dealing with knowledge of the action of drugs.

PHARMACOPŒIA (φαρμακοποιέω, I prepare medicines) is an official publication dealing with the recognized drugs and giving their doses, preparations, sources, and tests. Most countries have a pharmacopœia of their own. That for Great Britain and Ireland, for example, is issued under the supervision of the General Medical Council. Many hospitals and medical schools have a small pharmacopœia of their own, giving the prescriptions most commonly dispensed in that particular hospital or school.

PHARMACY is the term applied to the art of preparing and compounding medicines, or to a place where this is carried out.

PHARYNGITIS means inflammation of the pharynx. (*See* THROAT, DISEASES OF, *and* CLERGYMAN'S SORE THROAT.)

PHARYNX (φάρυγξ) is another name for the throat. The term throat is popularly applied to the region about the front of the neck generally, but in its strict sense it means the irregular

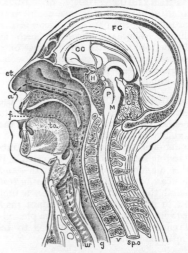

Fig. 314.—Vertical section through the middle of the head and neck. *a*, Is a heavy dotted line indicating the air passages ; *f*, a lighter line shows the food passages. The two cross in the throat ; *et*, Eustachian tube ; *t*, tonsil ; *to*, tongue ; *g*, gullet ; *l*, larynx ; *w*, windpipe. (For other letters, *see* BRAIN.) (After Braune.)

cavity into which the nose and mouth open above, from which the larynx and gullet open below, and in which the channel for the air and that for the food cross one another. It extends from the base of the skull down to the 6th cervical vertebra, separated from the upper six vertebræ only by some loose fibrous tissue, and is about 5 inches (12·5 cm.) long.

It is completely closed behind by a layer of muscles, and by mucous membrane, but in front it opens into the nose, mouth, and larynx in succession from above down. In its upper part, the Eustachian tubes open one on either side, and between them on the back wall grows a mass of glandular tissue known as the third tonsil, which, if enlarged, produces the condition known as adenoids. (*See* NOSE, DISEASES OF.) The muscles which close in the sides and back of the pharynx are three in number on each side, and spring, one from the jaw-bone, the second from the hyoid-bone, the third from the side

of the larynx, each of these constrictors spreading out like a fan on the back of the pharynx. Two other small muscles run downwards on each side.

PHEMITONE is a proprietary name for METHYLPHENOBARBITONE (*q.v.*).

PHENACETIN is a white crystalline coal-tar product. It is much used in fevers, influenza, headaches, and neuralgias of all kinds, on account of its power of reducing temperature and of deadening pain. It is often given in doses of 5 to 10 grains (300 to 600 mg.), along with sodium salicylate and citrate of caffeine. Its regular use is not without danger—particularly to the kidneys.

PHENAZOCINE is a powerful pain-reliever, or analgesic, which is said to be more potent, but less habit-forming, than morphine.

PHENAZONE, also known as ANTIPYRIN, is an antipyretic and analgesic. The dose is 5 to 10 grains (300 to 600 mg.). Its indiscriminate use is not without danger.

PHENBENICILLIN (*see* PENICILLIN).

PHENELZINE is one of the widely used antidepressant drugs which are classified as monoamine oxidase inhibitors (*q.v.*).

PHENETHICILLIN (*see* PENICILLIN).

PHENETHYLDIGUANIDE is one of the new oral hypoglycæmic agents. Unlike carbutamide (*q.v.*), chlorpropamide (*q.v.*) and tolbutamide (*q.v.*), it is not a sulphonamide derivative. Its action does not appear to depend upon the presence of insulin, as is the case with the sulphonamide derivatives. The reduction in blood sugar is effected by the process known as anærobic glycolysis. (*See also* DIABETES MELLITUS.)

PHENFORMIN is a diguanide which lowers the blood sugar and is proving of value in the treatment of certain cases of diabetes mellitus. It is taken by mouth. (*See also* METFORMIN.)

PHENINDIONE is a synthetic anti-coagulant (*q.v.*) which is effective by mouth, and is used for the same purpose as heparin. It is slower in action than heparin, the full anticoagulant effect not being obtained until 36 to 48 hours after the initial dose.

PHENIODOL is a drug which is excreted by the liver into the bile passages and is opaque to X-rays. As it gets into the gall-bladder and is 'radio-opaque', an X-ray skiagram will show whether the gall-bladder is normal or not—for example, whether gall-stones are present. The drug is taken by mouth.

PHENMETRAZINE, the proprietary name of which is Preludin, is a drug chemically related to ephedrine (*q.v.*) and amphetamine (*q.v.*), but has no effect on the heart and much less stimulant action on the central nervous system. For reasons that are not precisely known, it is a potent appetite-suppressant. Its use, however, is not without danger, and it is therefore only available now on a doctor's prescription.

PHENOBARBITONE is the *British Pharmacopœia* name for what is probably the most widely used of all the barbiturate group of drugs. It is given in doses of ½ to 2 grains (30 to 125 mg.). Phenobarbitone Sodium is a soluble preparation which can be given by injection.

PHENOL is another name for carbolic acid. (*See* CARBOLIC ACID.)

PHENOLPHTHALEIN is a substance much used as an indicator of reaction in urine, gastric juice, etc., being colourless in acid media, brilliant red with alkalies, and varying in tint according to the acid concentration. It is also given internally in 1 to 5 grain (60 to 300 mg.) doses as an aperient.

Phenolsulphonephthalein is used to test the power of the kidneys ; a measured quantity being injected intramuscularly or intravenously and the amount excreted in the urine during the next few hours carefully estimated by a colour scale. *Phenoltetrachlorphthalein* is a coal-tar derivative used as a diagnostic agent for the estimation of the functional power of the liver by intravenous injection.

PHENOXYMETHYLPENICILLIN (*see* PENICILLIN).
694

PHENSUXIMIDE is a succinamide derivative used in the treatment of *petit mal* and the psychomotor type of epilepsy.

PHENYLBUTAZONE, or BUTA-ZOLIDIN, has proved to be a useful drug for relieving the pain and discomfort in chronic rheumatic disorders such as rheumatoid arthritis, but it must only be used under medical supervision on account of the toxic effects which it sometimes produces.

PHENYLKETONURIA is one of the less common, but very severe, forms of mental deficiency. It is due to the inability of the baby to metabolize the amino-acid, phenylalamine. Its outstanding interest lies in the fact that, if it is diagnosed soon after birth—and this can be done by a simple urine test —and the infant is then given a diet low in phenylalamine, the infant may grow up mentally normal. The phenylalamine-low diet, however, has to be continued permanently.

PHENYTOIN SODIUM is one of the most effective drugs for the treatment of epilepsy. One of its advantages is that it does not make the patient feel particularly sleepy. Its use is not without risk and it must therefore be used only under medical supervision. Other names for it include diphenylhydantoin sodium, epanutin, and eptoin.

PHIMOSIS (φιμός, a muzzle) is the name applied to a condition of great narrowing at the edge of the foreskin, for which the operation of circumcision is necessary.

PHLEBITIS (φλέψ, a vein) means inflammation of a vein. (*See* VEINS, DISEASES OF.)

PHLEBOGRAPHY is the study of the veins, particularly by means of X-rays after the veins have been injected with a radio-opaque substance.

PHLEBOLITH is the term applied to a small stone formed in a vein as a result of calcification of a thrombus.

PHLEBOTOMY (φλέψ, a vein ; τέμνω, I cut) is an old name for the operation of blood - letting by opening a vein. (*See* BLOOD-LETTING.)

PHLEGM (φλέγμα, a slimy, inflammatory humour) is a popular name for mucus, particularly that secreted in the air passages. (*See* BRONCHITIS, EXPECTORANTS, MUCUS.)

PHLEGMASIA DOLENS (φλεγμασία, superficial inflammation ; *dolens*, grievous) is another name for white leg. (*See* WHITE LEG.)

PHLEGMON (φλήγμονή, burning heat) is an old term for inflammation.

PHLYCTENULE (φλύκταινα, a blister) is a small inflammatory swelling situated on the conjunctiva or on the cornea in front of the eye. Phlyctenules are found especially in ill-nourished, weakly children, and cause a great deal of irritation, pain, running at the eyes, and inability to face the light. (*See* EYE, DISEASES OF.)

PHOLCODINE is the 3-(2-morpholinoethyl) ether of morphine. As it resembles codeine in suppressing cough, it is used for the relief of unproductive coughs.

PHONOCARDIOGRAPH is an instrument for the graphic recording of heart sounds and murmurs.

PHOSPHATES are salts of phosphoric acid, and, as this substance is contained in many articles of food as well as in bone, the nuclei of cells, and the nervous system, phosphates are constantly excreted in the urine. In certain diseased conditions, such as gout, the amount of phosphates excreted rises above the 30 to 50 grains daily excreted in health, but it is only in diseased conditions of the urinary passages that these give rise to trouble. The continued use of an excess of food containing alkalies, such as green vegetables, and still more the presence in the urine of bacteria which lead to its decomposition, produce the necessary change from the natural mild acidity to alkalinity, and lead to the deposit of phosphates and to their collection into stones.

PHOSPHATURIA means the presence in the urine of a large amount of phosphates.

PHOSPHORIC ACID, either as the dilute acid or in the form of phosphates, forms a constituent of many tonics. Phosphate of lime is much used in cases of debility and especially of bone disease. Sodium phosphate and effervescent sodium phosphate are much used as mild aperients, and acid sodium phosphate is used in cases of cystitis.

PHOSPHORUS BURNS.—If particles of phosphorus settle on or become embedded in the skin, the resulting burn should be treated with a 2 per cent. sodium bicarbonate solution, followed by application of a 2 per cent. solution of copper sulphate. Fats and oils should not be employed.

PHOSPHORUS POISONING is now rare, and is produced only by the yellow, soluble form of phosphorus. Red phosphorus, from which safety matches are made, is harmless or nearly so. Red phosphorus is made from yellow by heating the latter to a high temperature in closed iron vessels. The use of yellow phosphorus in matches is now prohibited by law in practically every civilized country. The main cause of acute phosphorus poisoning at the present moment is the swallowing of a rat poison containing phosphorus. When taken internally phosphorus acts first as an irritant poison, and, being thereafter absorbed, produces profound degenerative changes in the liver and other abdominal organs. There is also a chronic form of phosphorus poisoning, usually due to exposure to phosphorus fumes in chemical works. This consists of profound debility, and the occurrence of disease in the lower jaw-bone (phossy jaw), which necroses and comes away in large fragments, over a period of months or years. It is now believed by some authorities that this disease in the bone is due partly to infection occurring in the jaw as a result of toxic effects produced by the phosphorus.

Symptoms.—When a child, for example, has taken a large dose he speedily suffers from pain, vomiting, colic, diarrhœa, and perhaps convulsions, and may die in a few hours. Or partial recovery may take place, and the sufferer survive for several days, later developing jaundice and blood-stained urine.

Treatment.—As phosphorus is absorbed slowly, washing out the stomach may succeed in removing the poison up to two hours after it has been swallowed.

Copper sulphate, 1½-3 grains (100 to 200 mg.) in water, may be given every ten minutes until emesis occurs. Gastric lavage with 0·1 per cent. potassium permanganate or with hydrogen peroxide solution may be tried instead. After emesis and gastric lavage two or four ounces of liquid paraffin and a big dose of a saline purge should be given. No oils, fats, or milk should be taken so long as any phosphorus remains in the gastro-intestinal tract, for phosphorus is soluble in fats. If damage to the liver is threatened then treatment with sodium bicarbonate, glucose, and insulin is indicated.

Chronic poisoning is prevented in chemical works dealing with phosphorus, by free ventilation, cleanliness, and periodic examination of the teeth of the match-workers.

PHOTOPHOBIA (φῶς, light; φόβος, fear) means a condition in which a person shrinks from letting bright light fall upon the eye. It is a symptom of inflammation of the eye, and occurs especially when the iris is inflamed.

PHRENIC NERVE (φρήν, the diaphragm) is the nerve which chiefly supplies the diaphragm. It springs from the 3rd, 4th, and 5th cervical spinal nerves, and has a long course down the neck, and through the chest, where each nerve lies between the heart and corresponding lung, to the diaphragm.

Phrenicectomy is an operation performed to divide this nerve in the neck. (For its object, see under TUBERCULOSIS.)

PHRENOLOGY (φρήν, mind; λόγος, discourse) is an old term applied to the study of the mind and character of individuals from the shape of the head. As the shape of the head has been shown to depend chiefly upon accidental characteristics, such as the size of the air spaces in the bones, and not upon development of special areas in the contained brain, this branch of science is now generally discredited.

PHTHALYLSULPHATHIAZOLE is a sulphonamide drug similar to succinyl-sulphathiazole (q.v.), and because of its slow absorption from the gut is used as an intestinal antiseptic.

696

PHTHIRIASIS (φθείρ, a louse) means the condition of eczema, matted hair, dirt, and enlarged glands that constitutes a minor disease arising from the presence of lice. (See PARASITES.)

PHTHISIS (φθίσις) means wasting, and is the general term applied to that progressive enfeeblement and loss of weight that arise from tuberculous disease of all kinds, but especially from the disease as it affects the lungs. The term is also used, in a more limited sense, to designate that variety of tuberculous disease of the lungs in which rapid breaking down of the lung tissue takes place, with the formation of a cavity.

PHYLACOGEN (see VACCINES).

PHYSIOLOGY (φυσιολογία, an inquiring into nature) is the branch of medical science that deals with the healthy functions of different organs, and the changes that the whole body undergoes in the course of its activities. Further information is given under the heading of each organ, and information will also be found under DIET, DIGESTION, EXERCISE, etc.

PHYSOSTIGMINE, or ESERINE, is an alkaloid obtained from Calabar bean, the seed of *Physostigma venenosum*, a climbing plant of West Africa. Calabar bean is known also as the ordeal bean, because preparations derived from it are used by the natives of West Africa to decide the guilt or innocence of accused persons, the guilty being supposed to succumb to its action, while the innocent escape. Its action depends on the presence of two alkaloids, the one known as physostigmine or eserine, the other as calabarine, the former of these being much the more important.

Action.—Physostigmine produces the same effect as stimulation of the parasympathetic nervous system (q.v.); *i.e.* it constricts the pupil, stimulates the gut, increases the secretion of saliva, stimulates the bladder, and increases the irritability of voluntary muscle. In poisonous doses it brings on a general paralysis.

Uses.—It is used in medicine in the form of physostigmine salicylate. Its main use is to contract the pupil and thereby reduce the pressure inside the eyeball. For this purpose it is used as eye-drops or as lamellæ. It is also given by subcutaneous injection to stimulate the gut when this is paralysed or atonic.

PIA MATER (*pius*, tender ; *mater*, a nourishing structure) is the membrane closely investing the brain and spinal cord, in which run blood-vessels for the nourishment of these organs. (*See* BRAIN, SPINAL CORD.)

PICA is a term which means an abnormal craving for unusual foods, and may be a sign of pregnancy.

PICORNAVIRUSES derive their name from pico (small) and R.N.A. (because they contain ribonuleic acid). They are a new group of viruses which includes the enteroviruses (*q.v.*) and the rhinoviruses (*q.v.*).

PICRIC ACID, or TRINITROPHENOL, is produced by the action of nitric upon carbolic acid. It is used for preparing explosives, and so is employed in medicine only in solution. As it coagulates albumin without any further irritant action, it produces a soothing pellicle over any raw surface with which it is brought into contact.

PICROTOXIN is a bitter crystalline principle obtained from the fruit of *Cocculus indicus*. By virtue of its stimulating action upon the respiratory centre, it is a valuable antidote in poisoning from barbiturate drugs.

PIGEON BREAST (*see* CHEST DEFORMITIES).

PIGEON BREEDER'S LUNG, or BIRD FANCIER'S LUNG as it is sometimes known, is a form of pneumonia resulting from sensitization to pigeons. In pigeon fanciers skin tests have revealed sensitization to pigeons' droppings, eggs, protein and serum, even though there has been no evidence of any illness.

PIGMENT (*pigmentum*, paint) is the term applied to the colouring matter of various secretions, blood, etc. ; also to any medicinal preparation of thick consistence intended for painting on the skin or mucous membranes.

PILES, or HÆMORRHOIDS, consist of a varicose and often inflamed condition of the veins about the lower end of the bowel, known as the 'hæmorrhoidal' veins.

Varieties.—It is usual to divide hæmorrhoids into external piles, internal piles, and mixed piles. To understand this division, it is important to remember that at the margin of the anus the skin joins the mucous membrane of the bowel in a sharp line, and that the bowel is kept closed by two circular muscles, the external sphincter and internal sphincter. The external sphincter is a weak muscle situated immediately beneath the skin, while the internal sphincter is a stronger circular band, extending up the bowel for an inch. External piles are found outside the bowel, and are covered by skin, being brown or dusky purple in colour ; internal piles are within the opening, covered by mucous membrane, and are bright red or cherry-coloured. Mixed piles are those situated just on the margin, and covered half by skin, half by mucous membrane. Even internal piles do not extend more than an inch up the bowel, corresponding to the position of the internal sphincter muscle.

Causes.—There is always a tendency for the veins in this situation to become distended, partly because they are unprovided with valves, partly because they form the lowest part of the portal system and are very apt to become overfilled when there is the least interference with the circulation through the portal vein, and partly because the muscular arrangements for keeping the rectum closed interfere with the circulation through the hæmorrhoidal veins. Probably most people of middle life are troubled by this condition to some extent, especially men of sedentary habits who indulge in over-eating and are troubled by constipation, as well as women who have borne many children. Habitual constipation is perhaps the principal cause of the presence of piles, and sitting on a cold stone or damp seat, or even a general chill, may suffice from time to time to inflame them and bring on what is popularly known as 'an attack of piles '.

It must be remembered, however, that in a certain number of cases piles are merely a symptom of disease higher up on the portal system, causing interference with the circulation. They come on very frequently during pregnancy, passing off when this condition has terminated. They are common in heart disease, liver complaints, such as cirrhosis or congestion, and any disease affecting the bowels.

Symptoms.—EXTERNAL PILES may be present for years and give no trouble whatever, beyond occasioning pain of a cutting or burning character now and then when a very costive motion is passed. When, in consequence of a chill or other cause, they become inflamed, they are very painful and tender from chafing against the thighs and clothing in walking, and from pressure upon the chair on which the person sits. The pile, or piles, in these circumstances become enlarged and red, and give off a thin blood-stained discharge. They may become so badly inflamed as to suppurate, and this sometimes results in a natural cure, or they may cure by filling with blood-clot and shrivelling up into hard little knots. Such an ' attack of piles ' lasts generally a week or two, and then subsides till another chill is caught.

INTERNAL PILES may be slight, and may give no sign of their presence beyond occasional bleeding, which may vary from a mere streak, when the bowels are opened, to a discharge of several ounces of dark blood. They are apt to produce a constant discharge of mucus tinged with blood which soils the linen, but unless very severe are not, as a rule, painful. These discharges of blood may, when copious and frequent, cause anæmia and become a serious menace to the health, though they are never fatal. On the other hand, in plethoric, overfed people, they may be a very salutary thing, warding off gout and apoplexy, or relieving the heart when it is diseased. When internal piles are large they may come down with the movement of the bowels, and may then become inflamed and painful from time to time, just like external piles.

Treatment.—Constipation must, in the first place, be guarded against. While the use of violent and irritating purgatives, like aloes, should be avoided, care must be taken, by regulation of the diet and other means, to

secure soft motions (*see* CONSTIPATION). The diet should, as a rule, include plenty of fruit, vegetables, and butter, and should in all cases be of a simple nature. Alcoholic beverages tend to produce and perpetuate piles, and should therefore in bad cases be entirely abandoned. Regular exercise is necessary in order to carry off the blood to the limbs and so relieve the portal circulation.

Locally, great care must be taken not to irritate the piles, and when they are inflamed they should be washed with water and cotton-wool every time the bowels move. Bleeding and the tendency to inflammation may be controlled by applying a sponge full of very hot water, or by smearing on cocaine or adrenaline ointment after the motion. In the case of internal piles which come down at stool it is very important that they should be returned within the bowel each time by gentle steady pressure with the fingers. If they are ' down ' and inflamed, a hot bath followed by a cocaine and morphine suppository gives relief.

Often these means suffice to keep the piles from causing trouble or to cure them completely, but occasionally surgical means are had recourse to. The external piles are simply removed. Internal piles require, according to their size and position, to be ligatured, destroyed by clamp and cautery, or, when they extend all round the bowel, to be removed *en masse* along with the last inch of mucous membrane lining the bowel. In many cases, however, the most satisfactory treatment of internal piles consists of injecting them with a 5 per cent. solution of phenol in arachis oil, to which 0·5 per cent. of menthol has been added.

PILLS are small round masses containing active drugs held together by syrup, gum, glycerin, or adhesive vegetable extracts. They are sometimes without coating, being merely rolled in French chalk, but often they are covered with sugar, gelatin, or gilt. Some pills, designed to act upon the bowels only, are coated with keratin or glutol, substances which are insoluble in the gastric juice.

PILOCARPINE is an alkaloid derived from the leaves of *Pilocarpus muro-*

phyllus (jaborandi). It produces the same effects as stimulation of the parasympathetic nervous system, *i.e.* it has exactly the opposite effect to atropine (*q.v.*), but cannot be used in the treatment of atropine poisoning as it does not antagonize the action of poisonous doses of atropine on the brain. It is seldom used in medicine now. At one time, in the form of a lotion, it was recommended for the growth of hair, but there is no justification for this claim.

PIMENTO, or ALLSPICE, is the dried fruit of *Pimenta officinalis*, a Central American shrub, from which oil of pimento, a volatile oil, is obtained. It is used in the form of aqua pimentæ, or water of allspice, in doses of a tablespoonful or more in cases of colic, and to make up various medicines.

PIMPLES, technically known as papules, are small, raised, and inflamed areas on the skin. On the face the most common cause is acne (*see* ACNE). Boils commence as hard pimples (*see* BOILS). The eruption of smallpox and that of chickenpox begin also with pimples. (*See also* SKIN DISEASES.)

PINE OIL is a nearly colourless oil with aromatic odour, distilled from the fresh needles of *Pinus silvestris*, the Scotch fir. Its action is similar to that of turpentine, and it is mainly used as an inhalation, prepared by adding a few drops to hot water.

PINEAL BODY is a small reddish structure situated on the upper part of the mid-brain. It is of unknown function, although a body resembling an imperfect third eye is found in its position in some of the lower vertebrate animals, as, for example, in the lizard Hatteria.

PINK DISEASE (*see* ERYTHRŒDEMA).

PINK-EYE is the name given to an acute muco-purulent conjunctivitis caused by various germs and highly contagious from such things as towels.

PINT is a measure of quantity containing 16 fluid ounces (wine measure) or 20 fluid ounces (Imperial measure). The metric equivalent is 568 millilitres. (*See* WEIGHTS AND MEASURES.)

PIPERAZINE is a substance which was credited with the power of dissolving uric acid in large amount. It was therefore widely used at one time for the treatment of gout and of uratic stones in the kidneys and bladder, but there is no evidence that it is capable of dissolving uric acid in the body. It has recently come back into use, however, for the treatment of thread-worms and ascariasis. (*See* PARASITES.)

PIRQUET'S REACTION is the term applied to a test for tuberculosis. A solution of old tuberculin is gently rubbed into a patch of scarified skin on the arm. The subsequent appearance of a raised reddened papule (positive test) shows that the person tested has been infected by the *Mycobacterium tuberculosis* but not necessarily that he has active tuberculosis.

PITHIATISM (πείθω, I persuade) is a name applied to a group of disorders in which the patient is subject to cure by persuasion or suggestion, the term being used as an equivalent for hysteria. (*See* HYSTERIA.)

PITOCIN (*see* OXYTOCIN).

PITRESSIN (*see* VASOPRESSIN).

PITUITARY BODY is a small structure about the size of a pea, weighing less than one gram in man, attached to the base of the brain, and lying in a depression (*sella turcica*) in the sphenoid bone. It consists of four parts, the anterior lobe, *pars intermedia*, *pars tuberalis*, and posterior lobe. The *anterior lobe* is composed of masses of cells which are differentiated into three main types by their staining reactions : (1) chromophobe cells, which do not stain, and constitute about 50 per cent. of the total; (2) acidophil cells, which stain with acid dyes ; (3) basophil cells, which stain with basic dyes. The *pars intermedia* is a thin layer of cells lying on the posterior lobe ; the *pars tuberalis* is a cellular layer on the stalk, and the *posterior lobe*, composed mainly of cells similar to the neuroglial cells of the brain, is connected with the floor of the third ventricle of the brain by a funnel-shaped stalk, the *infundibulum*.

The pituitary is the most important ductless gland in the body and in recent years an increasing number of functions has been attributed to it, especially to the anterior lobe. The pituitary seems to have a controlling effect on all the other ductless glands, which it does by the elaboration of hormones ; these circulate in the blood and act upon the glands for which each is designed. There is, for example, the thyrotrophic hormone, which stimulates activity of the thyroid gland. The adrenocorticotrophic hormone (A.C.T.H.) stimulates the cortex of the adrenal glands, and the gonadotrophic hormone the sex glands—ovaries and testes. As to the last mentioned, it is thought that one hormone stimulates the formation of the ovarian follicle, and another of the corpus luteum. In practice, the follicle-stimulating hormone (FSH) is obtained by the manufacturing chemist from the blood serum of pregnant mares. The luteinizing hormone is extracted from the urine of pregnancy. It is produced by the chorionic tissue and is known as chorionic gonadotrophin : this not only stimulates the formation of the corpus luteum in the female, it also stimulates the interstitial cells of the testes to produce the sex hormone of the male. A hormone—prolactin—excites the mammary gland to secrete milk. Still other hormones are said to have been discovered in the anterior lobe of the pituitary : hormones which raise the blood sugar, act upon the pancreas and parathyroids, and control metabolism. Whatever the final verdict may be, there is no doubt of the enormous importance of the pituitary to a vast range of bodily activities.

An extract of the posterior lobe — often known as pituitrin—has the effects of raising the blood-pressure by a constricting action on blood-vessels and of stimulating contraction of the pregnant uterus. These two effects are the result of separate principles in the gland : vasopressin which raises the blood-pressure, and oxytocin which stimulates the uterus. Vasopressin also controls the output of urine, and lack of it causes an increased output of urine.

Gigantism is the result of the overactivity of, or tumour formation of, the acidophil cells in the anterior lobe—the cells which control growth. If this

overactivity occurs after growth has ceased a condition known as acromegaly (*q.v.*) arises, in which there is gross overgrowth of ears, nose, jaw, and hands and feet. Diabetes insipidus (*q.v.*), a condition characterized by the passing of a large volume of dilute urine every day, is due to lack of pitressin. Various other disorders are the result of disturbed pituitary function : premature senility, extreme wasting, development of painful overgrowth of fat, various disturbances of growth and sexual development.

PITYRIASIS (πίτυρον, bran) is the name of a bran-like eruption on the skin, which is due to the growth of a microscopic fungus, and is characterized by large brown patches.

PIX is another name for tar.

PLACEBO is the term used to describe a medicine (or pill) given to a patient, not because it will have any definite action but because the patient will not be satisfied unless he (or she) receives some active treatment.

PLACENTA (*placenta*, a cake) is the technical name for the afterbirth. (*See* AFTERBIRTH.)

PLACENTOGRAPHY is the procedure of rendering the placenta, or afterbirth (*q.v.*), visible by means of X-rays. This can be done either by using what is known as soft-tissue radiography, or by injecting a radio-opaque substance into the bloodstream or into the amniotic cavity (*see* AMNION). The procedure is not without danger to both mother and fœtus, and must therefore only be carried out under expert supervision but it is sometimes of value in assessing the cause of ante-partum hæmorrhage.

PLAGUE, or BUBONIC PLAGUE, is the name of an infectious epidemic disease common to man and many of the lower animals. Its main characters are fever, swelling of the lymphatic glands, a rapid course, and a very high mortality, which has made it a much-dreaded scourge. In the Middle Ages it was known as the BLACK DEATH, which again and again ravaged Europe, though for the past century it has been almost confined to warm climates. The ancients referred to a disease which they called ' pestis ', a term which possibly included several severe epidemic maladies ; but, according to Hirsch, there is a recognizable description of an epidemic of what we know as plague infesting Libya, Egypt, and Syria between the second and third centuries B.C. The first occurrence of the disease in Europe was the ' plague of Justinian ', which swept through the Roman Empire in A.D. 542, devastating cities and country as it spread. Subsequently it periodically invaded Europe from the east, and spread westward, though with lessening severity in successive epidemics. The last occasion on which England was seriously invaded was at the time of the ' Great Plague ' in 1664–65, when 70,000 people died in London out of the total population of 460,000. In Glasgow a small outbreak occurred in 1900, which was quickly suppressed. The disease had not invaded America till 1899–1900, when it broke out in Brazil, the Argentine Republic, San Francisco, and Mexico.

Causes.—The disease is probably always present (endemic) in certain localities, such as in the south-west of China, among the hill people of India, and in East Africa. From these areas it spreads outwards at intervals, sometimes creeping from village to village, at other times being disseminated widely along trade-routes.

The bacillus (*Pasteurella pestis*) which is the immediate cause was discovered independently by Kitasato and Yersin in 1894 (*see* BACTERIOLOGY). It is found in the enlarged lymphatic glands and the sputum in pneumonic cases, as well as in the blood of septicæmic cases.

Plague occurs first as an epizootic in rats—especially in the black rat, *Rattus rattus*. The infection is then conveyed to man by the rat flea, especially *Xenopsylla cheopis*. The plague bacilli multiply in the gastro-intestinal tract of the flea, which may remain infectious for as long as six weeks. In pneumonic plague the bacillus may pass from man to man as a ' droplet infection '.

The rat is not the only rodent which serves as a ' reservoir ' for *Pasteurella pestis*. In the Caucasus, Siberia, and Manchuria the marmot is an important reservoir, whilst in Argentina it has

been found in wild guinea-pigs. In the U.S.A. between the Rocky Mountains and the west coast plague is widespread among ground squirrels, wood rats, and prairie dogs. Between 1900 and 1941 rodent plague had spread through eight of the western states of the U.S.A. This carries with it the risk of starting plague in any city with a large rat population. In South Africa, too, plague is prevalent in rodents, and human cases have cropped up from time to time. In England the last outbreak was in Suffolk in 1910.

Symptoms. — A graphic description of the symptoms of the disease is given by Defoe in his *Story of the Great Plague*, through which he lived as a child in London in 1664–65.

After infection, an incubation period, varying from two to six days for bubonic plague, and three to four days for pneumonic plague, elapses, and then the disease sets in suddenly with fever, headache, great lassitude, and aching of the limbs. The temperature soon rises to 103° F. (39·5° C.) or more, the skin is hot and dry, the tongue furred, while thirst, prostration, and a feeling of utter weakness assail the sufferer. His features become drawn, his eyes sunken, and he sinks into a state of stupor or passes sometimes into wild delirium. There is often also sickness and vomiting.

In over two-thirds of all cases there are swollen glands, known as ' buboes ', from which the malady has received the name of *bubonic plague*. These are situated most commonly in the groins, less frequently in the armpits, and give sometimes the first sign that the person has contracted the plague. There are also hæmorrhages under the skin in many cases, which sometimes produce black gangrenous patches that lead to large ulcers, and hence the old name of ' black death '. In favourable cases the fever abates at about the end of a week, the strength gradually returns, and the buboes soften, burst, and discharge foul-smelling pus.

There is a rapidly fatal form, associated with great weakness, in which the bacteria enter the blood, and the person dies on the second or third day, sometimes even in a few hours, before the buboes have time to form (*septicæmic plague*).

In other cases the lungs especially become affected, and pneumonia comes on, with death on the fourth or fifth day. This is said to be both the most infectious and the most fatal form of the disease (*pneumonic plague*).

In all epidemics, especially at the beginning and end of the epidemic, mild cases occur, in which the persons continue to go about, the buboes being almost the only sign of the malady. The matter from the buboes of such slight cases is, nevertheless, infectious, and these cases are therefore specially dangerous to other people.

The death-rate varies in different epidemics from 60 to 95 per cent. of those who contract the disease, persons who are healthy and well-fed standing a better chance than the poor and weak.

Treatment. — Preventive treatment is all-important in this disease. Plague is one of the six internationally quarantineable diseases, the others being cholera, louse-borne relapsing fever, smallpox, louse-borne typhus, and yellow fever. Contacts of plague are quarantined for six days. The strictest quarantine is apt to be ineffective, and measures directed against the spread of plague are essential. This includes the disinfestation of all contents with insecticide powder, such as 5 to 10 per cent. D.D.T. powder. Clothes, skins, and soft merchandise which have been in contact with the plague-stricken preserve the bacilli, and consequently their infectiousness, for several months. Such articles must therefore be either destroyed or disinfected with D.D.T. Houses or huts in which plague has occurred should either be carefully disinfected with D.D.T. or, if valueless, burned to the ground. The inhabitants of a plague-infected village or district are not allowed to migrate, carrying infection with them, to other localities, but all who have been in contact with a plague-stricken person should be isolated as ' contacts ' or ' suspects ' in special houses or camps and dusted with D.D.T.

In time of plague, or when plague is approaching, a war of extermination should be waged against rats and other rodents which are responsible for spreading the disease, and the bodies should also be carefully examined. Various devices are adopted against the rats on

ships. Thus the ships are generally moored a little way distant from the quay, the hawsers are rendered ' rat-proof ' by slipping hollow metal cones round them, and sulphurous acid gas or hydrocyanic acid is pumped into the holds under closed hatches the kill vermin which may be among to merchandise.

Personal protection is gained by good feeding, and by living in bright, well-ventilated rooms or out of doors. The wearing of high boots and special clothing impervious to fleas is important for those who go into the neighbourhood of plague cases. The use of antiseptics for the hands and of disinfectant mouth-washes is important for those nursing the plague-stricken, and special precautions must be taken to seal up any small wounds on the hands, etc., and so guard against inoculation.

Vaccination affords partial protection for six months, and is used in the control of local outbreaks of plague. The administration of the broad-spectrum antibiotics has also been recommended for the protection of those who have been exposed, particularly to pneumonic plague.

In the treatment of the disease the best results are obtained from streptomycin or one of the broad-spectrum antibiotics.

PLASMA is the name applied to the fluid portion of the blood composed of serum and fibrinogen, the material which produces clotting. When the plasma is clotted, the thinner fluid separating from the clot is the serum.

PLASMA TRANSFUSION is sometimes used instead of blood transfusion. Plasma, the fluid part of blood from which the cells have been separated, may be dried and in powder form kept almost indefinitely ; when wanted it is reconstituted by adding sterile distilled water. In powder form it can be transported easily and over long distances. Transfusion of plasma is especially useful in the treatment of shock. One advantage of plasma transfusion is that it is not necessary to carry out testing of blood groups before using it.

PLASMODIUM is the general term applied to minute protoplasmic cells, and particularly to those which cause malaria and allied diseases. (See MALARIA.)

PLASMON is a term applied to a flour-like food consisting of the protein materials of milk.

PLASTER OF PARIS is a form of calcium sulphate, which, after soaking in water, sets firmly. For this reason it is widely used as a form of splinting in the treatment of fractures. It is used for this purpose in the form of bandages which consist of bleached cotton cloth impregnated with the plaster and suitably adhesive. Its great advantage, compared with an ordinary splint, is that it can be moulded to the shape of the limb.

PLASTERS (see ADHESIVE PLASTERS).

PLASTIC SURGERY is that part of surgery which is concerned with the re-formation and restoration of parts of the body which are damaged, lost, or deformed.

PLASTRON is the term applied to the skeleton on the front of the chest consisting of the breast bone and attached rib cartilages.

PLATELETS.—Blood platelets, or thrombocytes, are small spherical bodies in the blood, which play an important part in the process of blood coagulation. Normally, there are around 300,000 per cubic millimetre of blood.

PLATING is a term used in connection with bacteriological investigation to mean the cultivation of bacteria on flat plates containing nutrient material. The term is also applied in surgery to the method of securing union of fractured bones by screwing to the sides of the fragments narrow metal plates, which hold them firmly together while union is taking place.

PLEOPTICS, which literally means full sight, is a new treatment for the treatment of an eye which has become amblyopic (see AMBLYOPIA) due to a squint.

PLETHORA (πληθώρα) means a condition of fullness of the blood-vessels in a particular part or in the whole body. Persons who consume much more food and drink than that necessary for the work they do, and who tend to the development of acidity, gout, apoplexy, and other diseases of allied nature, are commonly classed as 'plethoric'. The term is applied to a condition in which the volume of the blood is increased above normal; there may or may not be an increase in the total number of red blood corpuscles.

PLETHYSMOGRAPH is an apparatus for estimating changes in the size of any part placed in the apparatus; in this way changes in the volume of blood in a part can be measured.

PLEURA, or PLEURAL MEMBRANE (πλευρά, a rib), is the name of the membrane which, on either side of the chest, forms a covering for one lung. The two pleuræ are distinct, though they touch one another for a short distance behind the breast-bone. (See LUNGS.)

PLEURISY, or PLEURITIS, means inflammation of the pleura or serous membrane investing the lung and lining the inner surface of the ribs. It is a common condition, and may be either acute or chronic, the latter being usually tuberculous in origin.

The changes which take place are as follows: (1) Inflammatory congestion and infiltration of the pleura, which may spread to the tissues of the lung on the one hand, and to those of the chest wall on the other. (2) Exudation of fibrin on the pleural surfaces. This exudation is of variable consistence, sometimes composed of thin and easily separated pellicles, or showing itself in the form of a membrane. It is of greyish-yellow colour, and, microscopically, consists mainly of coagulated fibrin along with epithelial cells and red and white blood corpuscles. Its presence causes roughening of the two pleural surfaces by material which may later break up or may become organized by the development of new blood-vessels and formation of fibrous tissue. This, by forming permanent adhesions, may obliterate the pleural sac throughout a greater or less space, and interfere

to some extent with the free play of
the lungs. (3) Effusion of fluid into the
pleural cavity. This fluid may vary in
its characters. Most commonly it is
clear or slightly turbid, of yellowish-
green colour, sero-fibrinous, and containing flocculi of fibrin. In cases
where the pleurisy complicates some
severe form of disease, *e.g.* the acute
infectious maladies, it is deeply coloured, bile-stained, sero-purulent, purulent, or bloody, occasionally containing
bubbles of air from decomposition.
The amount may vary from an almost
inappreciable quantity to a gallon or
more. When large in quantity, it may
fill the pleural sac to distension, bulge
out the thoracic wall externally, and
compress more or less completely the
lung, which may in such cases have all
its air displaced and be reduced to a
mere fraction of its natural bulk lying
squeezed up upon its own root. Other
organs, such as the heart and liver, may
in consequence of the presence of the
fluid be shifted away from their normal
position. In favourable cases the fluid
is absorbed more or less completely and
the pleural surfaces may unite by
adhesions ; or, all traces of inflammatory products having disappeared,
the pleura may be restored to its
normal condition. When the fluid is
not speedily absorbed, it may remain
long in the cavity and compress the
lung to such a degree as to render it
incapable of re-expansion as the effusion passes slowly away. The consequence is that the chest wall falls in,
the ribs become approximated, the
shoulder is lowered, the spine becomes
curved and internal organs permanently
displaced, while the affected side
scarcely moves in respiration. Sometimes the unabsorbed fluid becomes
purulent, and an *empyema* is the result.
In such a case the matter seeks outlet
in some direction, and it may point as
an abscess upon the chest or abdominal
wall, or, on the other hand, burst into
the lung and be discharged by the
mouth, if it is not evacuated by
surgical means.

Many cases of pleurisy are associated
with only a little effusion, the inflammation consisting chiefly in exudation
of fibrin. To this form the term *dry
pleurisy* is applied. Further, pleurisy
may be limited to a very small area, or,

on the contrary, may affect, throughout
a greater or less extent, the pleural
surfaces of both lungs.

Causes.—Pleurisy is often associated
with other forms of inflammatory disease within the chest, more particularly
pneumonia, bronchiectasis, and tuberculosis, and also occasionally accompanies pericarditis. It may also be due
to carcinoma of the lung, or be secondary to abdominal infections such as subphrenic abscess. Further, wounds or
injuries of the thoracic walls are apt
to set up pleurisy. The connection of
pleurisy with tuberculosis is now recognized as a most important one. Very
often it happens that an attack of
pleurisy, which apparently has passed
off, returns and is eventually followed
by tuberculosis, it may be after several
years.

Symptoms.—The symptoms of pleurisy vary, being generally well marked,
but sometimes obscure.

DRY PLEURISY.—In the case of dry
pleurisy, which is, on the whole, the
milder form, the chief symptom is a
sharp pain in the side, felt especially on
breathing. Fever may or may not be
present. There is slight, dry cough,
which the individual does his best to
suppress because of the pain which it
causes. The breathing is quicker than
normal and shallow. Should a deep
breath be taken, it ends with a characteristic catch, due to the pain which
it causes. If much pain is present, the
body leans somewhat to the affected
side, to relax the tension on the intercostal muscles and their covering, which
are even tender to touch. On listening
to the chest with the stethoscope the
physician recognizes sooner or later
friction, a superficial rough rubbing
sound, occurring only with respiration
and ceasing when the breath is held.
It is due to the coming together during
respiration of the two pleural surfaces
which are roughened by the exuded
fibrin. The patient may himself be
aware of this rubbing sensation, and
its vibration or fremitus may be felt
by the hand laid upon the thoracic
wall during breathing. This form of
pleurisy may be limited or may extend
over the greater part of one or both
sides. It is a frequent complication
of pulmonary tuberculosis. In general
it disappears in a short time, and com-

plete recovery takes place ; or, on the other hand, extensive adhesions may form between the surfaces of the pleura covering the ribs and the lung, preventing uniform expansion of the lung in respiration, and leading to emphysema. Although not of itself attended with danger, dry pleurisy must always be treated as a serious condition, as it may be accompanied by disease in the underlying lung.

PLEURISY WITH EFFUSION is usually more severe than dry pleurisy, and, although it may in some cases develop insidiously, it is in general ushered in sharply by shivering and fever, like other acute inflammatory diseases. Pain is felt in the side or breast, of a severe cutting or stabbing character, referred usually to the neighbourhood of the nipple, but it may be also at some distance from the affected part, such as through the middle of the body or in the abdominal or iliac regions. This transference of the pain occasionally leads to errors in diagnosis, the patient being supposed to be the subject of appendicitis, gastric ulcer, or some other serious abdominal condition. The pain is greatest at the outset, and tends to abate as the effusion takes place. A dry cough is almost always present, which is particularly distressing, owing to the increased pain the effort excites. The breathing is painful and difficult, tending to become shorter and shallower as the disease advances, and the lung on the affected side becomes compressed. The patient at first lies most easily on the sound side, but as the effusion increases he finds his most comfortable position on his back or on the affected side. When there is very copious effusion and, as is apt to happen, great congestion of the other lung, or disease affecting it, the patient's breathing may be so embarrassed that he cannot lie down.

In most instances the termination is favourable, the acute symptoms subsiding, and the fluid (if not drawn off) gradually or rapidly becoming absorbed, sometimes after re-accumulation. On the other hand, it may remain long without undergoing much change, and thus a condition of *chronic pleurisy* becomes established. Such cases are to be viewed with suspicion, particularly in those who are predisposed to tubercu-

losis, of which it is sometimes the precursor.

Pleurisy may exist in a *latent form*, the patient going about for weeks with a large accumulation of fluid in his thorax, the ordinary acute symptoms never having been present in any marked degree. In some cases the pleurisy is on the under surface of the lung. This condition, known as *diaphragmatic pleurisy*, gives few signs on examination and is liable, when the symptoms are severe, to be mistaken for some acute inflammation of the abdomen.

The chief dangers in pleurisy are the occurrence of a large and rapid effusion, particularly if both sides be affected, causing much embarrassment to the breathing, and tendency to collapse ; the formation of an *empyema* (often marked by recurring rigors and hectic symptoms) ; severe collateral congestion of the other lung ; imperfect recovery, and the supervention of tuberculosis.

Acute pleurisy is often merely an accompaniment of the severer condition of lobar pneumonia, the disease really being a *pleuro-pneumonia*.

Treatment.—The treatment varies greatly with the form and severity of the attack. If it is tuberculous in origin, a full course of chemotherapy is given as for pulmonary tuberculosis (*see* TUBERCULOSIS). Should it be associated with an underlying infection of the lung, such as pneumonia, the appropriate antibiotics are given.

So far as the treatment of the pleurisy itself is concerned, in the early inflammatory stage, one of the chief symptoms calling for treatment is the pain, which may be soothed by opiates in the form of morphine or Dover's powder, along with the application to the chest of hot poultices or fomentations. Instead of these, an ice-bag is often applied to the side, and this has the effect of almost immediately soothing the acute pain. Another plan consists in the fixing, as far as possible, of one side of the chest by means of overlapping cross strips of adhesive plaster.

Cases of simple dry pleurisy usually soon yield to such treatment, aided, if need be, by the application of blisters or iodine to the chest as the condition is subsiding.

23

In the case of pleurisy with effusion, in addition to these measures, aspiration of the fluid may be required (see ASPIRATION). All the more necessary does the operation become if the accumulated fluid is interfering with the function of other organs, such as the heart, or is attended with marked embarrassment of the breathing. The chest is punctured in the lateral or posterior regions, and most physicians prefer to draw off not more than 30 ounces or thereabout at one time and to repeat the operation if necessary. In general, the operation is unattended with danger, although not entirely exempt from such risks as sudden fainting. In many instances, not only is the removal of distressing symptoms speedy and complete, but the lung is relieved from pressure in time to enable it to resume its normal expansion. When there is any evidence that the fluid is purulent, the operation should be performed early. In such cases it is sometimes necessary to establish for a time a drainage of the pleural cavity by introducing a drainage tube through an opening in the lower part of the side, a portion of a rib being usually removed to admit the tube. The pleural cavity is then for some weeks irrigated through the opening at regular intervals, and treated exactly as any other large abscess cavity. (See EMPYEMA.)

The convalescence from pleurisy requires care, and the expansion of the lung may be assisted by suitable breathing exercises (see CHEST DEVELOPMENT), or by connecting two wash-bottles in such a way that a quantity of fluid can be blown over from one to the other repeatedly. The latter exercise is graduated by blowing the fluid from one bottle to the other an increasing number of times on each successive day.

After an attack of pleurisy, and particularly after a second attack, the person should submit himself from time to time to medical examination, in order to make sure that tuberculosis does not develop in the lung. He will thus be enabled, if this serious disease should show itself, to commence its treatment at an early stage, when a cure may be expected.

PLEURODYNIA (πλευρά, rib ; ὀδύνη, pain) means a painful condition of the
706

chest-wall. It may be due to rheumatism of the intercostal muscles or to neuralgia of the intercostal nerves, or, when of the sharp nature popularly known as a ' stitch in the side ', to cramp.

PLEURO-PNEUMONIA means a combination of pleurisy with pneumonia. Acute pneumonia is practically always accompanied by a certain amount of pleurisy, to which the pain experienced in pneumonia is mainly due. The epidemic disease known as pleuro-pneumonia, which is so fatal to horned cattle, does not affect man.

PLEXIMETER (πλῆξις, stroke ; μέτρον, measure) is the name applied to a small plate of ivory or similar material laid upon the skin to be struck in percussion. The small hammer used to strike it is called a plexor or plessor.

PLEXUS (plexus, braid) is the name applied to a network of nerves or vessels, e.g. the brachial and sacral plexuses of nerves and the choroid plexus of veins within the brain.

PLICA (plica, fold) is the term applied to various folded structures in the body.

PLICATION is a term applied in surgery to an operation for taking tucks in the walls of a hollow organ, such as the cæcum, in order to reduce it in size.

PLOMBIÈRES DOUCHE is a term applied to lavage of the lower bowel by means of a soft rubber tube which is inserted into the rectum to a distance of 3 to 6 inches (7·5 to 15 cm.). Several pints of fluid are slowly allowed to run in by gravity, the patient reclining on the left side with the hips raised, and later turning on the back so that the fluid may penetrate throughout the large intestine. The fluid is retained as long as possible and returned by the ordinary movement of the bowels. Various fluids, but especially normal saline solution, are used for this purpose.

PLUMBISM (plumbum, lead) is another name for lead-poisoning. (See LEAD-POISONING.)

PLUMMER'S PILL is another name for compound calomel pill. It contains calomel, antimony, and guaiacum.

PLUMMER-VINSON SYNDROME is a syndrome associated with certain cases of hypochromic anæmia. It consists of hypochromic anæmia, difficulty in swallowing, and enlargement of the spleen. It is found practically only in women. (*See* ANÆMIA.)

PLURIGLANDULAR (*plures*, several; *glandulæ*, glands) means derived from several glands.

PNEUMOCONIOSIS (πνεύμων, the lung; κόνις, dust) is the general name applied to a chronic form of inflammation of the lungs which is liable to affect workmen who constantly inhale irritating particles at work. The disease produced may be of the nature of chronic interstitial pneumonia, but is very liable to develop into pulmonary tuberculosis. Some of the trades most liable to suffer are those of stone-masons, potters, steel-grinders, ganister workers, colour-grinders, and less often coal-miners, millers, and workers in cotton, flax, or wool mills. (*See* PNEUMONIA, TRADE DISEASES, TUBERCULOSIS.)

PNEUMOGASTRIC (πνεύμων, lung ; γαστήρ, stomach) or VAGUS (*vagus*, wandering) nerve is the tenth cranial nerve (*see* VAGUS NERVE).

PNEUMONECTOMY is the operation of removing an entire lung in such diseases as bronchiectasis and tuberculosis.

PNEUMONIA (πνεύμων, lung), or inflammation of the substance of the lungs, manifests itself in several forms which differ from each other in their nature, causes, and results, viz.: (1) *acute lobar* or *croupous pneumonia*, the most common form of the disease, in which the inflammation affects a limited area, usually a lobe or lobes of the lung, and runs a rapid course ; (2) *catarrhal pneumonia, broncho-pneumonia*, or *lobular pneumonia*, which occurs as a result of bronchitis, and is more diffuse in its distribution and longer in duration than the former ; (3) *interstitial pneumonia* or cirrhosis of the lung, a more chronic form of inflammation, which affects chiefly the framework or fibrous tissue

of the lung and is closely allied to phthisis ; (4) *primary atypical pneumonia*, which is due to a virus infection of the lungs.

In addition to these four principal types, pneumonia may arise as a part of several other diseases of which it forms a very serious complication ; for example, it may occur in the course of typhoid fever, woolsorters' disease, plague, etc., in each case being caused by the special bacteria associated with the disease in question. Pneumonia may also supervene in a person suffering from serious cardiac trouble or in old and devitalized persons, coming on gradually as the result of lying for a long time on the back with resultant congestion of the lower and back portions of the lungs. This type of pneumonia is known as *hypostatic pneumonia*, but is essentially of the same nature as catarrhal pneumonia.

ACUTE LOBAR PNEUMONIA is the disease commonly known as inflammation of the lungs. It derives its name from its pathological characters, which are well marked. The changes that take place in the lung are chiefly as follows : (1) *Congestion*, or engorgement, is the first stage, the blood-vessels being distended and the lung more voluminous, heavier than normal, and of dark-red colour. Its air-cells still contain air. The inflammation may pass off without proceeding further and the symptoms then abate after two or three days' duration. (2) *Red hepatization* is so called from the resemblance that it gives the lung to liver tissue. In this stage, which follows upon the congestion, there is poured into the air-cells of the affected part of the lung an exudation consisting of blood plasma together with epithelial cells and red and white blood corpuscles, the whole forming a viscid mass which occupies both the air-sacs and the finer bronchi, and which quickly coagulates, causing the lung to become firmly consolidated. (3) *Grey hepatization.*—In this stage the lung retains its solid liver-like consistence, but the colour of a cut section is now grey, not unlike the appearance of grey granite, from the entrance into the exudate of many white corpuscles from the blood. A marked development of this stage, in which softening and liquefaction of the lung tissue may take place, is found in very serious cases, which either end in death or are liable to leave profound changes in the lung after the patient has recovered from the acute stage of the disease. (4) *Resolution* is the final stage which occurs in all cases which run a satisfactory course. The exudation now undergoes a process of liquefaction, the cells in it break up by a process of fatty degeneration, and the material is either completely reabsorbed into the bloodvessels or to a certain extent is expectorated, and thus, in a comparatively short period, varying from some hours to two or three days, the air-cells get rid of their morbid contents. Air again enters them and they resume their normal function. This is the manner of termination in the great majority of cases of acute lobar pneumonia, but it sometimes happens that this favourable result is not attained, and that further changes take place in the inflamed lung in the form of suppuration ending in abscess or gangrene. In such cases there usually exists some serious constitutional cause which contributes to give an unfavourable termination to the course of the disease, such, for example, as pre-existing diabetes or Bright's disease, or even the presence of old and partially healed tuberculosis in the lung. In occasional cases the pneumonia may become chronic, the lung never completely clearing up but continuing to discharge small quantities of pus which are brought up in expectoration, and to undergo a gradual fibrous change (*interstitial pneumonia*).

Acute lobar pneumonia is usually limited to a portion of one lung, the commonest part being the lower lobe on one or other side. Occasionally the pneumonia spreads throughout the whole of one lung, or it may affect both lungs, when it is called *double pneumonia* and is a serious and sometimes dangerous condition. The apex of the lung is sometimes the only part affected (*apical pneumonia*), and this type seems especially to affect drunkards, in whom pneumonia is often a fatal malady. The right lung is more frequently affected by pneumonia than the left lung.

Causes.—The *pneumococcus* is the specific infecting micro-organism in about 95 per cent. of all cases of lobar

708

pneumonia. Some thirty 'types' of pneumococcus are now recognized. In Great Britain, types I and II are said to be the infecting cause of between one-half and two-thirds of cases of lobar pneumonia. Type II infection is more severe than type I, and type III more severe than both. The death-rate from pneumonia is highest in the first five years of life and after the age of 60.

The disease may occur at any age, but is most common during the active years of life from 20 to 50. Among the aged the other type of pneumonia, *bronchopneumonia*, is much more common. During the prime of life the disease affects men much more commonly than women. It appears to be a more serious disease among the darker races than in white men. There is a distinct tendency for pneumonia to be more prevalent during the late winter and early spring months, February, March, and April, but it is not specially associated with very low temperatures, and pneumonia, when it occurs in northern latitudes, appears to run a distinctly milder course than in the temperate zone.

Symptoms.—After an incubation period of two to six days, the attack usually commences with shivering (or in young children with a convulsion), and this is speedily followed by pain in the chest and sometimes by vomiting. The temperature almost at once rises to 101° or even 104° F. (38·3° or 40° C.), the pulse is quickened, and the breathing is rapid, shallow, and sometimes laboured. Occasionally the development is less abrupt, and the patient, although not feeling well, may remain at work for two or three days after the onset. The lips are dark and the face has a dusky flush. Cough is an early symptom, at first frequent, hacking, and accompanied by only a little clear, tough expectoration, but later bringing up a copious, rusty-brown material which is generally very tenacious, sticking to the sputum-dish even when the latter is turned upside down ('rusty sputum'). Occasionally the expectoration contains bright red blood, and this is by no means a bad sign. The temperature may abate a little after the initial rise, but usually continues between 103° and 105° F. (39·5° and 40·5° C.) for about a week, when it falls with considerable suddenness (crisis) to normal. The crisis generally takes place between the seventh and tenth day of the illness, most commonly about the eighth. At the crisis the pulse rate drops from about 120 to 80, and the respirations diminish from about 36 per minute to 24 or less. At the time of crisis the skin, which was previously dry and hot, perspires freely. Pain, which is an almost constant feature at the beginning of pneumonia, due to the accompanying pleurisy, tends to abate as the disease advances. It is specially felt on coughing or drawing deep breaths. Pain is usually felt in the side, but may be referred by the patient to the pit of the stomach or even to the lower part of the abdomen. In the latter case the symptom is apt to lead to a mistaken diagnosis of some acute abdominal disorder. Although the breathing is rapid, the patient is not usually breathless unless a large area of the lungs is affected, and he lies on the back or on the affected side. Sleeplessness is often a troublesome feature of the disease, and tends to exhaust the patient unless it is relieved by hypnotics or other means. Delirium is occasionally present, but, so long as it is mild, affords no cause for anxiety. An eruption of herpes is frequently noticed about the lips.

Certain physical signs are usually present. Diminished movement of the affected side is noticeable, the healthy side of the chest performing most of the respiratory function. On percussion over the affected area a dull note is obtained, which becomes particularly marked if fluid has collected in the pleural cavity. On auscultation over the affected area, the breathing is usually harsh and high pitched (tubular breathing), but it sometimes shows no deviation from the normal, especially in cases where the deeper parts of the lung only are affected. Accompanying the breathing in the early stages of the disease, crackling sounds known as crepitations are commonly heard. These disappear during the period in which the lung remains solid, but reappear (redux crepitations) when resolution begins to take place. All these physical signs disappear with remarkable rapidity in about two days after the crisis has taken place. A moderate increase in the number of the white blood cor-

puscles is a favourable sign, the case having too little power of reaction if the corpuscles do not increase, and an increase to too large an extent in the later stages being a sign that suppuration is taking place.

In unfavourable cases, death may take place either from the extent of the inflammatory action, especially if the pneumonia is double, from exhaustion due to excessive fever, sleeplessness, and similar causes, or from failure of the heart's action in cases in which a great amount of general poisoning is present, or again from the disease assuming from the first a low adynamic form, with delirium and great prostration. Such cases are found in persons worn out in strength, in the aged, and in persons already suffering from alcoholism or chronic conditions like Bright's disease and diabetes. Some of the unfavourable signs are extremely rapid and shallow breathing with accompanying lividity, delirium of wildly excited type in which the patient becomes excited by struggling, persisting sleeplessness, a rapid and feeble pulse indicating impending heart-failure, excessive sweating, and the occurrence of complications such as pericarditis. Death may also take place at a later stage from the development of empyema, abscess, or gangrene of the lung. In a small number of cases, recovery may be imperfect, the disease gradually passing into a chronic interstitial pneumonia.

Treatment.—Good nursing is all-important. Pain and difficulty of breathing may be relieved by the application of hot fomentations, poultices, or ice-bags to the affected side. Cough is relieved by expectorants, of which those containing carbonate of ammonia are specially useful. Any tendency to excessive fever may often be held in check by sponging with tepid water. Cases in which the disease is extensive in the lungs or in which the heart is feeble and the blood in consequence not properly oxygenated, as shown by blueness of the face and lips, obtain great relief and benefit from the inhalation of oxygen. As regards feeding, the digestive powers being much reduced, the patient should be fed with milk, soups, and other light forms of nourishment frequently administered. Sleeplessness is sometimes relieved by sponging the body with tepid water or, if more troublesome, by a sedative or hypnotic, or, if delirium be also present, by morphine. The prime agent in treatment is one of the sulphonamide drugs, *e.g.* sulphadimidine, or penicillin. Most physicians use a sulphonamide as the first line of attack, reserving penicillin for (*a*) those cases which do not respond to the sulphonamides, (*b*) patients who have become sensitized to the sulphonamides, (*c*) gravely ill patients who have difficulty in swallowing or in whom there is much vomiting.

After the acute symptoms disappear, the patient must remain in bed for some time. The occurrence of empyema, which, when it takes place, is indicated by hectic rise of temperature every day, sometimes follows or prevents the crisis and requires aspiration or surgical drainage of the pleural cavity. After recovery is complete, a period of approximately a month's convalescence is advisable.

BRONCHO - PNEUMONIA, BRONCHIAL PNEUMONIA, CATARRHAL or LOBULAR PNEUMONIA, differs from acute lobar pneumonia in several important points. The inflammation is more diffuse, and tends to affect small patches or lobules of lung tissue here and there, rather than one or more lobes. If the condition becomes extreme, the affected parts may join so that the whole lung is affected, but there are still certain important differences. The condition usually begins with the symptoms of bronchitis, which gradually spreads from the larger to the finer bronchial tubes and ultimately to the minute air-vesicles or cells.

In favourable cases, resolution takes place after a longer or shorter interval by fatty degeneration, liquefaction, and absorption of the cells. At the same time, a large amount of the material filling the lungs is gradually expectorated by the patient. On the other hand, when the illness is prolonged, degenerative changes may take place in the lung tissue, small abscesses may form, and a condition of chronic interstitial pneumonia is then developed. In the great majority of instances broncho - pneumonia occurs as an accompaniment or sequel of bronchitis, either from the inflammation passing

from the finer bronchi to the airvesicles or from its affecting portions of the lung which have undergone collapse through obstruction of their bronchial tubes by secretion. It occurs commonly in children, often following upon some previous acute illness in which the bronchi are inflamed, such as measles or whooping-cough. It also tends particularly to affect old people in a more chronic form as the result of bronchitis, and it forms one of the chief causes of death among the aged. (*See* BRONCHITIS.)

Symptoms.—The symptoms of broncho-pneumonia in its more acute form are the occurrence, during an attack of bronchitis, of a sudden and marked rising of temperature, together with quickened pulse and increased difficulty of breathing. The cough becomes short and painful unless the child or aged person is too feeble to bring up expectoration, when the cough becomes of a suffocative type, which forms a very bad sign. Vomiting sometimes occurs in children and may be a salutary symptom because it aids in freeing the lungs from the accumulating secretion. In a marked case of broncho - pneumonia the dusky red colour of the lips, cheeks, and ears is also present as noticed in acute lobar pneumonia, due to defective oxygenation of the blood.

Physical signs of a somewhat vague character are found over the chest. The note obtained by percussion is duller at some points than at others ; the breathing is harsh with the signs of bronchitis, which is also present, and here and there breathing may be tubular, with fine crackling sounds (crepitations).

The illness does not end by a crisis as in the case of lobar pneumonia, but the temperature tends for an indefinite period, it may be of several weeks, to remit and rise again with a gradual fall to normal.

Broncho - pneumonia must be regarded as a condition of serious import. It is apt to run rapidly to a fatal termination in weakly persons, the inflammation spreading and the lungs filling up with secretion. After its occurrence there is a tendency in susceptible individuals to the development of tuberculosis. On the other hand, a favourable result is frequent if the condition is recognized in time to admit of efficient treatment.

Treatment.—The treatment is essentially that for the more severe forms of bronchitis (see BRONCHITIS), where, in addition to expectorants intended to help the freeing of the chest from secretion, various stimulants and good nourishment are of great importance. The administration of ipecacuanha tincture in large doses, sufficient to cause the patient to vomit, sometimes produces marked benefit by freeing the chest from its load of accumulated secretion in cases in which coughing is difficult. The access of fresh air in broncho-pneumonia following whooping-cough, measles, and similar diseases is of great importance, the patient at the same time being protected by light warm applications, such as a gamgee-tissue jacket on the front and back of the chest. Administration of oxygen is of great value in cases showing duskiness of the lips and face. The sulphonamide drugs and penicillin are important drugs in treatment. The posture of the patient in bed is a matter of importance ; whilst in the case of lobar pneumonia the patient obtains most relief from lying on his back or on the affected side, in broncho-pneumonia with an excessive amount of secretion the patient is usually most comfortable and breathes most easily when kept constantly in a half-sitting posture with the shoulders raised high by pillows placed behind the back.

Convalescence is often prolonged, and special care is required in the case of children, in view of the tendency of the disease to be followed by tuberculosis.

CHRONIC INTERSTITIAL PNEU-MONIA, or CIRRHOSIS OF THE LUNG, is a slow inflammatory change affecting chiefly one portion of the lung texture, viz. its fibrous framework.

The changes produced in the lung by this disease are marked chiefly by the growth of fibrous tissue around the walls of the bronchi and vessels, which proceeds to such an extent as to invade and obliterate the air-cells. The lung also shows a tendency to break down, either from an early stage in cases which have followed acute pneumonia, or later from a suppurative process or from dilatation of the bronchial tubes.

In any case, cavities are formed similar to those produced by tuberculosis.

This condition is specially apt to arise in an extensive form from pre-existing broncho-pneumonia, and usually occurs in connection with occupations which necessitate the habitual inhalation of particles of dust, such as those of potters, knife-grinders, flax-dressers, stone-masons, millers, etc. It is specially liable to affect workers exposed to silica dust, and workers in the South African gold mines.

Symptoms are very similar to those of chronic tuberculosis, especially increasing difficulty of breathing, particularly on exertion, cough, either dry or with expectoration, which is sometimes copious and fœtid. In the case of coal-miners, the sputum is black from containing carbonaceous matter.

The deficient expansion of the affected side is very evident, retraction of the side becomes manifest, and the heart and liver may be displaced. Ultimately the condition, both as regards physical signs and symptoms, takes the characters of the later stages of phthisis, with increasing emaciation and death. The malady is usually of long duration, many cases remaining for years in a stationary condition, and even undergoing temporary improvement in mild weather, but the tendency is on the whole downward.

Treatment is conducted on similar principles to those applicable in the case of tuberculosis. Should the malady be connected with a particular occupation, the disease might be averted or at least greatly modified by early withdrawal from such source of irritation. Cases in which there is much expectoration of purulent material are frequently treated by administration of a vaccine with a view to lessening the septic processes which are aggravating the condition and devitalizing the patient. Various inhalations are also of considerable use for the same purpose (see INHALATIONS).

PRIMARY ATYPICAL PNEUMONIA, or VIRUS PNEUMONIA, is due to a virus infection of the lungs ; hence its alternative name. It is a form of pneumonia which has only been clearly differentiated of recent years. A disease of winter, it occurs most commonly in young adults.

Symptoms.—The incubation period is very variable—from 2 to 21 days, or even longer. The onset is usually insidious. Apart from general malaise, the presenting symptom is cough, accompanied by a varying amount of sputum. The temperature is usually in the region of 100–103° F. Features which may help to differentiate it from other forms of pneumonia include a normal white blood cell count, a relatively slow pulse in relation to the temperature, and a typical agglutination reaction in the blood in the second to fourth week of the illness. The prognosis is good, but the condition tends to drag on for several weeks.

Treatment.—Until recently there was no specific treatment, but most promising results are now being obtained from the use of the new antibiotics, chlortetracycline, chloramphenicol, and oxytetracycline.

PNEUMOPERITONEUM means a collection of air in the peritoneal cavity. Air introduced into the peritoneal cavity collects under the diaphragm which is thus raised and collapses the lungs. This procedure is sometimes carried out in the treatment of pulmonary tuberculosis as an alternative to artificial pneumothorax.

PNEUMOTHERAPY is a term applied to the treatment of disease by rarefied or condensed air.

PNEUMOTHORAX (πνεῦμα, air ; θώραξ, the chest) means a collection of air in the pleural cavity, into which it has gained entrance by a lesion in the lung or a wound in the chest wall. When air enters the chest the lung immediately collapses towards the centre of the chest, but, air being very quickly absorbed from the pleural cavity, the lung expands again in a short time. (*See* LUNGS, DISEASES AND INJURIES OF.)

Artificial pneumothorax is an operation by which in a case of pulmonary tuberculosis or of bronchiectasis air may be run into the pleural cavity so as to cause collapse of one lung, which rests it and allows cavities in it to heal.

PODAGRA is another name for gout affecting the foot. (*See* GOUT.)

PODOPHYLLIN is a resin derived from the root of *Podophyllum peltatum*,

712

a plant of the United States and Canada. It has a purgative action but must be combined with hyoscyamus or belladonna, as by itself it causes severe griping. It is also used as a local application in the treatment of venereal warts.

POIKILOCYTE (ποικίλος, manifold ; κύτος, cell) is the name applied to a malformed red blood corpuscle found in the blood in various types of anæmia.

POISON IVY, or POISON OAK, is the name given to a poisonous species of sumac, *Rhus toxicodendron*. The leaves or juice when applied to the skin cause severe inflammation and symptoms of internal irritant poisoning. Some persons are very susceptible to this, and a kind of nettle rash may be produced by mere approach to the plant. A fluid extract and tincture are sometimes used in minute doses for treating rheumatism in persons not susceptible to the poisonous action. Symptoms of poisoning, when they appear, are treated by careful avoidance of the plant and by administration of soothing remedies externally and internally.

POISON REGULATIONS. — These rules do not apply to poisonous substances which enter into the composition of adhesives, builders' materials, distempers, explosives, glazes, matches, inks, motor fuels, paints, rubber and similar articles employed in various trades. They apply chiefly to poisonous substances which have a medicinal use, in order to prevent dangers that might arise from their careless, excessive, or improper use. The list of these poisons is divided into two parts ; part I of the list includes poisons which may be sold only by a registered pharmacist ; part II includes a certain number of poisons used in connection chiefly with agriculture and with some other trades, which may be obtained from other sellers licensed by local authorities to deal in these poisons.

The poisons in part I of the list, which may be sold only by a registered pharmacist and only to a person who is known to him as a proper person to have such a substance in his possession and who signs a book for the purchase, include the following frequently used medicines : powerful alkaloids such as aconitine, atropine, cocaine, codeine, colchicine, diamorphine, emetine, ephedrine, alkaloids of ergot, gelsemine, hyoscine, lobeline, morphine and other opium alkaloids, strychnine, veratrum ; also acetanilide, amidopyrine, amyl nitrite, antimonial salts, arsenical substances, barbiturates, barium salts (excluding barium sulphate), cannabis, cantharidin, chloral, chloroform, creosote obtained from wood, croton oil, digitalis, glandular preparations including pituitary, suprarenal, thyroid extracts and insulin, glyceryl trinitrate (nitroglycerin), hydrocyanic acid and cyanides, lead acetate, mercurial salts, nux vomica, opium, phenols (including carbolic acid, cresol, etc., if the preparation contains 60 per cent. or over of phenol), phosphorus, picric acid, strophanthus, sulphonal, antihistamine substances (except in preparations for applications in the nose and eye and containing not more than 1 per cent. of antihistamine), chlorpromazine, curare, disulfiram, pethidine, phenylbutazone, troxidone.

In this list, morphine, cocaine, ecgonine, diamorphine (commonly known as heroin), extracts and tincture of cannabis (Indian hemp), most of the preparations of opium, pethidine, and amidone are scheduled under the Dangerous Drugs Act, and may be dispensed only upon a prescription of a medical practitioner written in a specified form. (*See* DANGEROUS DRUGS.)

In this part of the list there are also three commonly used groups of drugs : amidopyrine and its salts, barbituric derivatives (including a large number of substances such as barbitone, phenobarbitone, and many other soporifics and analgesics), and sulphonal, together with a few seldom used substances which are subject to the following stringent regulations in regard to their sale. They may be sold only in accordance with a prescription given by a qualified medical practitioner, registered dentist, or registered veterinary surgeon ; the prescription must contain the date and the address and signature of the person giving it, as well as the name and address of the person for whose treatment it is given, or, if the prescription is given by a veterinary surgeon, of the person to whom the medicine is to be delivered ; if given by a dentist it must bear the words ' For

dental treatment only ', and if by a veterinary surgeon. ' For animal treatment only ' ; it must also indicate the total amount of the medicine to be supplied and the dose to be taken ; the prescription may be dispensed only once unless it contains a direction that it may be dispensed a certain number of times or at stated intervals.

The bottle or container of the substances in part I of the list must in general be labelled ' Poison ', but there are certain modifications of this. For example, in the case of insulin and active principles of the pituitary and thyroid glands, instead of the word ' Poison ', the label must bear ' Caution. It is dangerous to take this preparation except under medical supervision.' In the case of animal medicines the label must read ' Poison. For animal treatment only.' In the case of hair dyes the label must read ' Caution. This preparation may cause serious inflammation of the skin in certain persons and should be used only in accordance with expert advice,' and in the case of potassium or sodium hydroxide the container must be labelled ' Caution. This substance is caustic.'

In the case of hospitals and similar institutions there are special provisions that medicines supplied to out-patients must be supplied only on a prescription, that a record must be kept in such a way that the particulars of its supply can be readily traced, and that the bottle must be labelled sufficiently to identify the institution from which it was supplied. In the case of in-patients, the medicines must be supplied upon a written order signed by a medical practitioner, registered dentist, or by a sister or nurse in charge, and substances included in the list of poisons must be stored in a cupboard reserved solely for poisons.

The poisons in part II of the list, which may be supplied by a dealer licensed by the local authority, on the signing of a book or order, include some 16 substances or groups of substances, of which most are used for sheep dips, insecticides, and disinfectants. They are as follows : ammonia, certain arsenical substances, certain barium salts, formaldehyde, hydrochloric acid, hydrofluoric acid and its salts, mercuric chloride and iodide, nicotine, nitric acid, nitrobenzene, phenols (if the preparation contains less than 60 per cent. of phenols), phenylene and toluene diamines, potassium and sodium hydroxides (caustic potash and soda), potassium quadroxalate, sulphuric acid.

POISONS.—It is difficult to give a concise definition of the word poison, because substances which are injurious by their mechanical action, such as steel filings or powdered glass, cannot be classed as such ; nor is boiling water a poison ; nor can a substance be regarded as a poison if it owes its effect to some bodily peculiarity—as, for example, a draught of cold water taken by an overheated person. The following definition is, however, given by Guy : ' A poison is any substance or matter (solid, liquid, or gaseous) which, when applied to the body outwardly, or in any way introduced into it, can destroy life by its own inherent qualities, without acting mechanically, and irrespective of temperature.' Even this definition is not quite satisfactory, because many substances are poisonous in large quantities, harmless in smaller amounts, e.g. saltpetre, tartaric acid, Epsom salts. Further, substances which are generally poisons may by habit lose their deadly effect, as in the case of arsenic and opium (see OPIUM). Again, different persons and animals vary widely in susceptibility to poisons, the old adage that ' one man's meat is another man's poison ' being literally true. Many herbivorous animals, like the cow, feed upon the deadly nightshade with impunity, and pigeons are almost entirely unaffected by opium.

Varieties.—Many substances which are poisonous are valuable remedies when used in small quantities or properly applied externally. Others are common household substances or garden plants, and very many have important uses in the arts. Under the heading of poisons must be included bacteria and the harmful substances which their growth produces, such as the poisons found in decomposing meat. (See BACTERIOLOGY, PTOMAINE POISONING, and other headings.) The injuries inflicted by insects, snakes, and other animals which introduce some poison into the body are considered under BITES.

714

Leaving these out of account, we may classify poisons either according to their source or to their mode of action. Classified according to their source they are : *animal*, like cantharides ; *vegetable*, like monk's-hood or deadly nightshade ; *mineral*, like sulphuric acid or perchloride of mercury ; and *aerial*, like carbon monoxide gas. By this classification, however, substances with the most diverse actions are included in each group. A more practical arrangement is made, according to the mode of action, into :

Corrosives, which burn and destroy the parts with which they come in contact.

Irritants, which have generally an irritant action upon the stomach and bowels.

Narcotics, which affect the brain and spinal cord, causing a stuporous state.

Narcotico-irritants, which produce first of all an irritative effect upon the stomach or upon the nervous system, and finally act as narcotics.

The two last-mentioned groups are by some authorities placed together as *narcotics*.

(1) CORROSIVES go so far as to corrode, ulcerate, or even perforate the organs with which they come in contact. The chief corrosives are the strong mineral acids, like sulphuric, nitric, hydrochloric ; the alkalis, like caustic soda or potash, their carbonates, and ammonia ; and certain strong salts, like corrosive sublimate and pernitrate of mercury.

(2) IRRITANTS include vegetable acids and some acid salts, such as tartaric acid ; white arsenic (arsenious acid), yellow arsenic (orpiment), acetate of lead (sugar of lead), sulphate of copper (blue vitriol), subacetate of copper (verdigris), arsenite of copper (Scheele's green), tartarated antimony (tartar emetic), chloride of antimony (butter of antimony), chloride of zinc (Burnett's disinfectant), nitrate of silver (lunar caustic), bichromate of potassium, sulphate of iron (green vitriol or copperas) ; also the leaves, roots, berries, or resins of many plants taken in large amount, such as colocynth, savin, gamboge, aloes, croton oil, elaterium.

(3) NARCOTICS are mostly drawn from the vegetable kingdom. Few poisons have a purely narcotic action, most producing also sickness, delirium, or other signs of irritation. The simple narcotics

TABLE OF COMMON POISONS AND THEIR TREATMENT

Poison	Treatment	Poison	Treatment
Acids— Hydrochloric Nitric Sulphuric	Give lime-water, mag‾ nesia, chalk, white-ning, or bicarbonate of soda in water ; then albumin water, oil, or barley water.	**Digitalis** (foxglove)	. Give emetics ; wash out stomach with perman-ganate of potassium.
Aconite	. Lay patient down; give stimulants ; wash out stomach with per-manganate of potas-sium.	**Ether** .	. Wash out stomach ; cold douches.
		Iodine .	. Give flour or other form of starch in water ; wash out stomach.
Alcohol	. Wash out stomach; give stimulants.	**Lead Acetate** (sugar of lead)	Give magnesium sul-phate or Glauber's salt ; wash out sto-mach ; then give al-bumin water or bar-ley water.
Alkalies— Caustic soda Caustic potash Ammonia	Give vinegar in water, lemon juice, or dilute hydrochloric acid ; then linseed or olive oil.		
		Laudanum— Morphine, Opium, etc.	Give emetic ; wash out stomach with per-manganate of potas-sium ; give strong coffee ; keep patient awake ; artificial res-piration.
Arsenic	. Give emetic; then mag-nesia or hydrated oxide of iron, pre-pared by mixing solution of perchlor-ide of iron with solu-tion of ammonia in equal parts, straining through a handker-chief, and stirring up the precipitate in water ; then albumin water or barley water; wash out stomach and give laudanum.		
		Lysol .	. (See CARBOLIC ACID above.)
		Mushrooms— Fungi	Give emetic ; hypoder-mic injections of at-ropine and niketha-mide.
		Oxalic acid and binoxalate of potassium (salts of sorrel)	Give magnesia, chalk, or whitening (not bicarbonate nor car-bonate of soda) ; wash out stomach ; give albumin water or milk.
Belladonna and atropine	Give emetic ; wash out stomach with per-manganate of potas-sium ; neostigmine as antidote ; artifi-cial respiration.		
Camphor	. Give emetic, then a stimulant.	**Phosphorus** (matches, etc.)	Give sulphate of copper as emetic ; wash out stomach with potas-sium permanganate ; give albumin water ; avoid oils.
Carbolic acid, Cresol, Lysol, etc.	Give magnesium sul-phate or Glauber's salt, then albumin water or milk ; wash out stomach.		
		Ptomaines (bad meat)	. Give emetic at once, or later castor oil ; brandy.
Chloral	. Give emetic ; wash out stomach with potas-sium permanganate ; give stimulants ; arti-ficial respiration.	**Silver nitrate** (lunar caustic)	Give salt in water; wash out stomach; give albumin water or milk.
Cocaine	. Give stimulants ; wash out stomach ; arti-ficial respiration.	**Strychnine**	. Wash out stomach with permanganate of pot-assium ; give chloral.
Corrosive sublimate (mercuric chlor-ide)	Give albumin water or milk ; wash out sto-mach with sodium bicarbonate.	**Tobacco**	. Give strong coffee or strychnine.
		Turpentine	. Give emetics, then mag-nesium sulphate and albumin water or milk.
Cyanide of po-tassium and prussic acid	Wash out stomach ; stimulants ; artificial respiration.	**Zinc chloride**	Wash out stomach ; then give albumin water or milk.

include opium and its preparations, prussic acid (hydrocyanic acid), cyanide of potassium, alcohol, ether, chloral, chloroform. Most poisonous gases also belong to this group, the chief among them being carbonic acid, carbon monoxide (see COAL-GAS POISONING), water gas, sulphuretted hydrogen, sulphide of ammonium, and other sewer gases. The amount of these which is necessary in the air in order to produce serious symptoms, or even to cause death if breathed for long, is very small. (See ASPHYXIA.)

(4) NARCOTICO - IRRITANTS form a large group in which the individual substances cause varied symptoms of irritation, such as delirium and excitement, convulsions, or sickness and vomiting. The group includes carbolic acid, oxalic acid, binoxalate of potash (salts of sorrel), nux vomica with strychnine, meadow saffron (*Colchicum autumnale*), white hellebore (*Veratrum album*), foxglove (*Digitalis purpurea*), monk's-hood (*Aconitum napellus*), henbane (*Hyoscyamus niger*), deadly nightshade (*Atropa belladonna*), black or garden nightshade (*Solanum nigrum*), woody nightshade or bitter-sweet (*Solanum dulcamara*), potato tops and seeds (*Solanum tuberosum*), tobacco (*Nicotiana tabacum*), Indian tobacco (*Lobelia inflata*), thorn apple (*Datura stramonium*), spotted hemlock (*Conium maculatum*), water hemlock or cowbane (*Cicuta virosa*), hemlock-water dropwort (*Œnanthe crocata*), five-leaved water hemlock (*Phellandrium aquaticum*), fool's parsley (*Æthusa cynapium*), yew leaves and berries (*Taxus baccata*), laburnum seeds and bark (*Cytisus laburnum*), and many species of poisonous fungi. (See FUNGUS POISONING.)

Symptoms. — The symptoms of poisoning, which come on soon after a meal, or at least after some substance has been swallowed, are of great importance, because the treatment varies according to the type of poison taken, as shown by the symptoms.

CORROSIVE POISONS produce immediate pain and swelling of the lips, mouth, and throat, which also show signs of discoloration, depending on the poison taken. If the dose be large, there may be speedy collapse and death.

IRRITANT POISONS produce vomiting, purging, and abdominal pain. In the case of the milder irritants, the results

may be deferred for a few hours, particularly when a full meal has been taken along with the poison. Later, in very serious cases, collapse and insensibility come on.

NARCOTICS produce giddiness, headache, interference with sight, stupor, preceded occasionally by convulsions, followed by deepening insensibility ending in coma and death. No pain is produced by these. (For the means by which narcotic poisoning is distinguished from apoplexy, or alcoholic intoxication, see OPIUM.)

NARCOTICO - IRRITANTS produce at first the symptoms of the irritant poisons, vomiting, abdominal pain, and in many cases purging. Later, delirium or convulsions appear, ending in stupor and death.

Further details as to the symptoms and treatment connected with the more important poisons will be found under the headings of these poisons.

Treatment. — When a CORROSIVE POISON has been taken, one should first of all administer the chemical antidote to the poison, if there be one; and thereafter soothing substances should be given to allay the irritation in the mouth, throat, and stomach. The following dangerous poisons have such chemical antidotes. When acids have been taken, give a dilute alkali, such as lime-water, magnesia, chalk, whitening, or even plaster scraped from the walls and mixed with water. When caustic alkalies have been taken, give weak acids, such as copious draughts of vinegar in water or lemon juice in water. When corrosive sublimate is the poison, white of egg in water or milk combines with it to form a harmless substance.

After the poison has been neutralized, milk, white of egg in water, or other bland fluid may be given to mitigate the irritation it has caused.

In the case of the IRRITANT POISONS, draughts of water or milk to dilute the poison, together with an emetic consisting of a tablespoonful of mustard in water, or of 20 grains of sulphate of zinc in water, should be given as soon as possible. Still better is it to wash out the stomach with the stomach tube at the earliest possible moment.

The following irritant poisons have chemical antidotes, which may be given before the stomach is emptied. When oxalic acid or salts of sorrel has been taken, give chalk or magnesia, which forms in the stomach the harmless oxalate of lime. If lunar caustic should have been swallowed, common salt in water neutralizes it by forming the inert chloride of silver. When sugar of lead has been swallowed, Epsom salts is an efficient antidote, producing the insoluble sulphate of lead in the stomach. Carbolic acid also has for an antidote Epsom salts. Arsenic is neutralized by a solution of hydrated peroxide of iron, when this is obtainable.

In the case of NARCOTIC AND NARCOTICO-IRRITANT poisons, an emetic administered at once is beneficial, and it is the usual practice for a medical man to wash out the stomach with a weak solution of permanganate of potassium, when he sees the case. Permanganate of potassium has the power of destroying many of these vegetable poisons which are of an alkaloidal nature. Many of these poisons, whose deadliness depends upon active principles, can be neutralized to some extent by other drugs. (See ANTIDOTES.)

WHEN THE POISON IS UNKNOWN, but the fact of poisoning suspected, the safest course is to administer tepid water and with it mustard, sulphate of zinc, or other emetic (see EMETICS), in order to expel the contents of the stomach, thereafter administering a drink of milk. Above all things is it necessary to keep all vomited matters and the remains of food that the poisoned person has been taking till the arrival of a medical man.

POLDINE, or POLDINE METHYLSULPHATE to give it its full name, is a synthetic drug, with an atropine-like action (see ATROPINE) which is proving of value in the treatment of gastric and duodenal ulcers.

POLICLINIC (πόλις, city; κλίνη, bed) is the name applied to a hospital or clinic belonging to a city. POLYCLINIC (πολύς, many; κλίνη, bed) is the term applied to a clinic where diseases of all kinds are studied and treated.

POLIOMYELITIS (πολιός, grey; μυελός, marrow), or INFANTILE PARALYSIS, is an infectious disease involving the spinal cord and the brain.

Cause.—The first epidemic of poliomyelitis to be recorded occurred in Sweden in 1881. Since then the disease has become of increasing importance, particularly in Scandinavia, U.S.A., and Australia. In Great Britain the disease has been notifiable since 1912. Although sporadic cases may occur at any time, there is a definite seasonal incidence, epidemics tending to occur in the late summer and early autumn in the northern hemisphere and in March and April in the southern hemisphere. In 1966, there were only 23 cases in England and Wales, compared with 3200 in 1956.

The infecting organism is a virus, of which there are three types. Infection occurs from ingestion of the virus by mouth. The virus then passes to the lower alimentary tract and is excreted in the stools. It has been shown that the viruses are excreted by 90 per cent. of paralytic cases, particularly children, and they are also excreted in the stools by healthy contacts of cases. It is in this way that the disease is spread—through contaminations of the hands and then contamination of the mouth from such contaminated hands. Children are the most susceptible members of families, but during recent years there has been a definite tendency to severe paralytic cases occurring among young adults. One attack usually produces permanent immunity ; second attacks are rare.

Pathology.—The sites of selection for the virus are the motor cells in the anterior horn of the spinal cord, and there is a tendency for this to be more marked in the lumbar part of the cord. The cranial nerves and certain nuclei in the brain are also involved in some cases.

Symptoms.—The incubation period is 3 to 21 days, commonly 7 to 12 days. The onset may be either sudden or gradual. In the case of the latter the child may merely be ' off colour ' for a day or two and complain of aches or pains in the limbs ; there may be only a slight rise in temperature. This may gradually pass into the stage of weakness, and then paralysis, of the limbs. In other cases, after a few days' vague illness, the paralysis of the limbs may come on quite suddenly, usually with a sharp rise in temperature. In cases of sudden onset, the victim complains of headache and aches and pains, and the temperature rises to 103° F. or higher. In other cases, particularly in children, the limbs may be found to be paralysed when the child wakens in the morning, although he was apparently quite well when he went to bed the previous evening.

The site and the distribution of the paralysis depend upon the extent to which the spinal cord and brain are involved. The most serious cases are those in which the diaphragm and the muscles of respiration (the intercostal muscles) are involved, as this prevents the patient breathing, and he may die in a very short space of time unless he is placed in a respirator (or iron lung). When the cranial nerves and brain are involved, there may be nystagmus (q.v.), hoarseness, and difficulty in swallowing. Convulsions may occur in young children. The cerebrospinal fluid contains an excess of cells in the first and second weeks and an increased amount of protein in the third week.

Prophylaxis.—A high degree of protection against poliomyelitis can be given by means of a course of inoculations with poliomyelitis vaccine. At least two injections are necessary, and there is a growing volume of evidence that a third, or even fourth, injection enhances the degree of protection. An oral vaccine is now available, and all the evidence indicates that this is just as safe and effective as the injected vaccine, and will therefore probably replace it in time.

In the presence of an epidemic the following measures should be taken. Children should not be allowed to go into crowded buildings such as cinemas. Public swimming baths should be avoided. Children, especially younger ones, should not be allowed to get over-tired, particularly in hot weather. Particular care should be taken to protect food from flies and to ensure that the highest standards of cleanliness are observed in the handling of food. No operations for the removal of tonsils or adenoids should be performed. Immunization against diphtheria and whooping-cough and smallpox vaccination should, if at all possible, be postponed until the epidemic is over.

Treatment.—The patient must be

718

put to bed on the first sign of the disease, and the affected limbs completely rested. This is the one definite practical fact that has resulted from all the careful investigation of the disease during recent years : that the earlier the disease is detected, and, therefore, the earlier the patient is put to bed and the affected parts rested, the better the ultimate result. Splints may be necessary at this stage to give adequate rest to the affected muscles. Later, careful physiotherapy is necessary. If the breathing is affected, it may be necessary to put the patient in an iron lung. To ensure the best possible results, after-treatment may need to be continued for two or three years. In cases in which severe paralysis and wasting of limbs persist, surgical treatment may be necessary to reduce the resulting disability to a minimum.

POLIOSIS means premature greying of the hair.

POLITZER'S BAG is an india-rubber bag with nozzle intended for inflation of the middle ears by blowing air up one nostril while the other is closed.

POLLANTIN is the name given to an antitoxic serum used for the prevention of hay fever in persons who are liable to this disease.

POLLEX is a Latin term for thumb.

POLYARTERITIS NODOSA, or PERIARTERITIS NODOSA as it is sometimes known, is a disease of unknown origin, in which prolonged fever and obscure symptoms referable to any system of the body are associated with local areas of inflammation along the arteries, giving rise to nodules in their walls. Recovery occurs in about 50 per cent. of cases.

POLYCHROMASIA and **POLY-CHROMATOPHILIA** (πολύς, many; χρῶμα, colour ; φιλέω, I love) are terms applied to an abnormal reaction of the red blood corpuscles in severe anæmia, whereby they have a bluish tinge instead of the normal red colour in a blood film stained by the usual method. It is a sign that the cell is not fully developed.

POLYCYTHÆMIA (πολύς, many; κύτος, cell; αἷμα, blood) is the name applied to excess in the number of red corpuscles in the blood.

POLYDIPSIA (πολύς, much; δίψα, thirst) means excessive thirst, which is a symptom of diabetes and some other diseases.

POLYGRAPH (πολύς, many; γράφω, I write) is the term applied to an instrument for making simultaneous tracings of the pulse in two different parts of the circulation at one time.

POLYMER FUME FEVER occurs in people who work with polytetrafluoroethylene (PTFE, Teflon). The fever is caused by degradation products, including hydrofluoric acid, which are produced at temperatures of 170° C. and upwards. The likeliest source of these injurious products is cigarette smoking. Even the tiniest particles of PTFE on a burning cigarette will yield sufficient of these degradation products to cause fume fever.

The illness consists of an influenza-like illness, which lasts for a few hours.

POLYMORPH (πολύς, many; μορφή, form) is a name applied to certain white corpuscles of the blood which have a nucleus of irregular and varied shape. These form between 70 and 75 per cent. of all the white corpuscles. (Plate V.)

POLYMYXIN is the name applied to the group of antibiotics derived from various species of *Bacillus polymyxa.* Polymyxin B is the one available commercially, and is the antibiotic of choice in the treatment of infections due to *Ps. pyocyanea.*

POLYNEURITIS (πολύς, many; νεῦρον, nerve) means an inflammatory condition of nerves in various parts of the body. (*See* NEURITIS.)

POLYPHARMACY (πολύς, many; φάρμακον, drug) is a term applied to the administration of too many drugs in one prescription.

POLYPUS (πολύπους, many-footed) is a general name applied to tumours which are attached by a stalk to the surface from which they spring. The term refers only to the shape of the growth and has nothing to do with its structure or nature. Most polypi are of a simple nature, though malignant polypi are also found. The usual structure of a polypus is that of a fine fibrous core covered with epithelium resembling that of the surrounding surface. The sites in which polypi are most usually found are the interior of the nose, the outer meatus of the ear, and the interior of the womb, bladder, or bowels.

Their removal is generally easy, as they are simply twisted off, or cut off, by some form of snare or ligature; those which are situated in the interior of the bladder or bowels, and whose presence is usually recognized by the presence of blood in the urine or stools, may require a more serious operation to reach the organ into which they project.

POLYTHELIA is the term applied to the condition in which extra or 'supernumerary' nipples appear along a line between the armpit and the groin.

POLYURIA (πολύς, much; οὗρον, urine) means the passage of an amount of urine considerably in excess of the fifty ounces (1500 ml.) or thereabout which is the usual daily quantity. It is a symptom of diabetes, certain forms of Bright's disease, and some nervous diseases.

PONS VAROLII is the bridge of the brain, mainly composed of strands of white nerve-fibres which unite various parts of the brain. (*See* BRAIN.)

POPLITEAL SPACE (*poples*, the ham), or HAM, is the name given to the region behind the knee. The muscles attached to the bones immediately above and below the knee bound a diamond-shaped space through which pass the main artery and vein of the limb (known in this part of their course as the popliteal artery and vein), the internal and external popliteal nerves (which continue the great sciatic nerve from the thigh down to the leg), the external saphenous vein, as well as several small nerves and lymphatic vessels. The muscles, which bound the upper angle of the space and which are attached to the leg bones by strong prominent tendons, are known as the 'hamstrings'.

The lower angle of the space lies between the two heads of the gastrocnemius muscle, which makes up the main bulk of the calf of the leg.

POPPY as used in medicine is of two species: *Papaver somniferum*, the white opium-poppy, and *Papaver rhœas*, the red corn-poppy. The former is treated of, under OPIUM. The corn-poppy is chiefly used as a colouring agent, the syrup made from it having a brilliant crimson colour.

PORENCEPHALIA, or PORENCEPHALY (πόρος, hole ; ἐγκέφαλος, brain) is a term applied to the presence of cysts in the surface of the brain due to an arrest of development or to birth hæmorrhage. The condition is generally associated with serious mental defect.

POROPLASTIC is the name of a thick kind of felt which is easily moulded into splints when softened by hot water and used for surgical purposes.

PORPHYRIA is a condition, or rather a series of conditions, characterized by an excessive production and excretion of porphyrins. Porphyrins are constituents of various blood and respiratory pigments found throughout the animal kingdom, including human beings. They are also found in plants and micro-organisms.

In porphyria there is some disturbance of their metabolism and this results in a variegated picture which includes discoloration of the urine due to excessive excretion of porphyrins, skin rashes due to sensitization of the skin to light, various forms of indigestion and mental disturbances.

PORRIGO is a general term applied to diseases of the skin covering the head, such as ringworm.

PORTAL VEIN (*porta*, an entrance) is the vein which carries to the liver blood that has been circulating in many of the abdominal organs. It is peculiar among the veins of the body in that it ends by breaking up into a capillary network instead of carrying the blood directly to the heart, a peculiarity which it shares only with certain small vessels in the kidneys. The portal system begins below in the hæmorrhoidal plexus of veins round the lower end of
720

the rectum, and from this point, along the whole length of the intestines, the blood is collected into an inferior mesenteric vein upon the left, and a superior mesenteric vein upon the right side. The inferior mesenteric vein empties into the splenic vein, and the latter, uniting with the superior mesenteric vein immediately above the pancreas, forms the portal vein. The portal vein is joined by veins from the stomach and gall-bladder, and finally divides into two branches which sink into the right and left lobes of the liver. (For their further course, *see* LIVER.)

The organs from which the portal vein collects the blood are the large and small intestines, the stomach, spleen, pancreas, and gall-bladder.

POSOLOGY (πόσος, how much; λόγος, discourse) means the science or system of dosage in regard to medicines.

POST- is a prefix signifying after or behind.

POST-MORTEM EXAMINATION (*see* AUTOPSY).

POST-PARTUM is the term applied to anything happening immediately after child-birth—for example, post-partum hæmorrhage.

POTASH, or POTASSA, is the popular name for potassium carbonate. Hydrated oxide of potassium is usually known as caustic potash, and its solution as liquor potassæ. Potash is obtained by burning wood, washing the ashes with water, and evaporating the solution to dryness. The remainder contains 60 to 80 per cent. of carbonate of potassium, which is used to obtain most of the other salts of potassium.

POTASSIUM is a metal which, on account of its great affinity for other substances, is not found in a pure state in nature. Its salts are used to a great extent in medicine, but as their action depends in general not on their metallic radicle but upon the acid with which it is combined, their uses vary greatly and are described elsewhere. (Thus for the uses of potassium bromide, *see* BROMIDES, for those of potassium iodide, *see* IODIDES, for those of potassium permanganate, *see* PERMANGANATE OF POTASSIUM, for those of the bicarbonate, citrate, and tartrate of potassium, *see* CITRIC ACID, and for those of nitrate of potassium, *see* NITRE.)

All salts of potassium have a depressing effect upon the nervous system and upon the heart's action.

POTASSIUM CHLORATE, in addition to the general actions exerted by potassium salts, has a soothing action upon inflamed mucous membranes, and is used for a gargle in sore throat of every description.

POTASSIUM PERCHLORATE is an antithyroid drug used in the treatment of hyperthyroidism. It acts by inhibiting the mechanism in the thyroid gland for collecting inorganic iodine from the blood supply to the gland.

POTT'S DISEASE is a name frequently applied to the angular curvature of the spine which results from tuberculous disease (*see* SPINAL DISEASES). The disease is named after Percival Pott, a famous English surgeon (1713–88), who first described the condition.

POTT'S FRACTURE is a term applied to a variety of fractures around the ankle, accompanied by a varying degree of dislocation of the ankle. In all cases the fibula is fractured; in some the tibia is also fractured. Named after Percival Pott, who suffered from this fracture and was the first to describe it (*see* FRACTURES), it is often mistaken for a simple sprain of the ankle. (Plate X, C.)

POULTICES (*see also* FOMENTATIONS) are soft moist applications to the surface of the body, generally used hot. They soften the parts with which they come in contact, soothe irritated nerve-endings, relax spasmodically contracted muscle-fibres, and, after being applied for some time, dilate the vessels of the part they cover and increase the circulation through it. These applications are consequently used in all stages of inflammation to soothe pain and promote resolution, or in the late stages, when pus is forming, to aid the rapid formation of an abscess (*see* ABSCESS).

Poultices should on no account be applied to open wounds, for their warmth and moisture greatly favour the growth of bacteria.

Variety and uses.—LINSEED POULTICE made from crushed linseed is one of the most commonly used, and is applied hot in cases of inflammation, as above stated. OATMEAL POULTICE is used in precisely the same conditions. Mus-

FIG. 315.—Requisites for linseed meal poultice.

FIG. 316.—Adding the meal to boiling water in basin.

FIG. 317.—Meal and water mixed to a stiff, hot mass.

TARD POULTICE is used where it is desired to combine a counter-irritant action with the warmth of a poultice. BREAD POULTICE and STARCH POULTICE are used at the body temperature, generally in order to remove the crusts of skin eruptions or soften a hardened surface. CHARCOAL POULTICE was formerly much used to diminish the smell from foul ulcers. Hot fomentations for acute pain are used of late years in preference to the more cumbersome and less cleanly poultices.

Method of application. — LINSEED POULTICE should be made of freshly crushed linseed, as the meal soon grows rancid if kept. About half a pint of boiling water is poured into a small basin, already warmed, and the linseed is slowly added to it, stirring all the while (Figs. 315–320). Enough meal, about 4 ounces (112 grammes), is added

FIG. 318.—The poultice mass spread thickly on a piece of cotton cloth.

FIG. 319.—Muslin laid on surface of poultice and edges of cotton cloth turned over.

FIG. 320.—Poultice rolled up and laid between two hot plates ready for application.

to make a mass sufficiently thick to adhere together, and still thin enough to spread. This may be judged by the mass being sufficiently coherent to allow a spoon or spatula to stand upright in it. A linen, or better a flannel, rag is laid by the basin and the hot linseed quickly spread on it with a spatula or tableknife. It may be covered with a piece of thin muslin, or the linseed may be applied directly to the skin. On the outer surface of

722

the poultice a piece of macintosh or oil-silk should be placed, and outside of this a thick piece of cotton-wool to ietain the warmth. The whole is fixed rn place by a flannel bandage or binder. Such poultices become cold in two hours or more and should then be renewed, but the cold poultice should not be taken off till the new one is ready to lay on. In changing the poultice great care should be taken that the patient is not exposed to chill.

MUSTARD POULTICE is made by mixing 2½ ounces (70 grammes) of linseed with half a pint of boiling water as above, adding to it 2½ ounces (70 grammes) of mustard flour which has already been mixed with lukewarm water, and stirring the two together. This poultice mass is spread and applied in the same way as the linseed poultice, but must not be left on longer than twenty minutes to half an hour. There must be a piece of muslin upon the surface in order to keep the mustard from adhering to the skin. The patient's sensations form the best guide as to the length of time over which such a poultice should be left on. The place of this poultice is now to a great extent taken by mustard leaves, which simply require to be wetted and applied.

BREAD POULTICE is made by breaking up stale bread in a basin, pouring boiling water over the crumbs sufficient to soak them, allowing to cool, draining off superfluous moisture, spreading on a cloth, and covering with muslin.

STARCH POULTICE.—Add a teaspoonful of powdered boric acid to four tablespoonfuls of cold-water starch, mix with a little cold water, then pour in a pint of boiling water, and stir till thickened ; let stand till cold; spread the cold starch *thickly* on pieces of cotton, cover with muslin, and apply to the part, changing the poultices every few hours and wiping the skin gently each time the poultices are reapplied.

CHARCOAL POULTICE is made by preparing a bread poultice and sprinkling it with dry powdered charcoal.

KAOLIN POULTICE is a paste which is applied by heating the pot containing it in a pan of boiling water, and spreading thickly on lint.

POUPART'S LIGAMENT, also known as the inguinal ligament, is the strong ligament lying in the boundary between the anterior abdominal wall and the front of the thigh.

POWDERS form the simplest method in which drugs are prescribed, powerful drugs being made up with inert substances like sugar, gum, or ginger in order to give them sufficient bulk. The best known powders are Dover's powder (compound ipecacuanha powder), containing opium; Gregory's powder (compound rhubarb powder); grey powder (mercury with chalk); and Seidlitz powder (effervescent tartarated soda powder).

Method of use.—If the powder be small and tasteless, a little water is poured out into a teaspoon, the powder shaken out on the surface of the water and swallowed. If it be large and nauseous, the best plan is to envelop it in a rice-paper. A little water is placed in the bottom of a saucer and the circular rice-paper laid upon it, when it quickly softens. The powder is shaken out upon the centre of the rice-paper, and the edges of the latter are quickly turned over it with a teaspoon. The soft mass is then pushed on to the spoon and is easily swallowed, being thus untasted.

PRE- is a prefix meaning before.

PRECORDIAL REGION (*præcordia*, the membrane covering the heart) is the area on the centre and towards the left side of the chest, lying in front of the heart.

PREDNISOLONE, or delta-1-dehydrohydrocortisone, is a derivative of cortisone, which is five or six times as active as cortisone and has less of the salt- and water-retaining properties of cortisone. It is given by mouth.

PREDNISONE is the official name for delta-1-dehydrocortisone, and has the same action as prednisolone.

PREFRONTAL LOBOTOMY (*see* Leucotomy).

PREGNANCY.—This state is a natural one, although it sets up great changes, not only in the womb, but throughout the whole body. Most of these changes subside quickly after delivery is accomplished, and though a few minor alterations persist throughout life, the mother returns to her normal state within about one month after the child is born.

Duration of pregnancy.—It is generally accepted that pregnancy lasts about 273 days from the end of the last menstrual period. In exceptional cases there may be considerable variation, but it is generally agreed that the shortest duration of a normal pregnancy is 240 days and the longest duration 313 days. The cause of these variations is not understood, and the longest period of gestation that has ever been admitted in the Law Courts in Great Britain is 360 days. For the purpose of calculating the probable date of confinement, it is usual to take the first day of the last period that occurred, to allow seven days for the duration of this and then to add 273 days for the duration of gestation, making in all 280 days from the beginning of the last menstruation. The actual date can be estimated roughly by adding seven days and then counting forwards nine calendar months; for example, supposing the last menstrual period began on 3rd October, adding seven days makes the 10th October, and nine months forwards from this gives the date of probable confinement as the 10th of July. It is usual to say that this day is the middle of the week in which the confinement may be expected.

Signs of pregnancy.—(*a*) The stoppage of the menstrual flow is the sign which first attracts attention. This symptom may, however, be due to many other causes (*see* MENSTRUATION), but if it occurs quite suddenly it may usually be counted upon as an important sign. It is a popular mistake to suppose that pregnancy cannot occur in a woman while she is suckling a previous child, for this does occur even while the menses are in abeyance. (*b*) Swelling of the breasts is another important sign, appearing even in the second or third month of pregnancy. A thin fluid, known as colostrum, can, even at this early stage, be pressed from the nipples. At the same time the veins on the breasts become enlarged and visible, and the pigmented ring round the nipple (areola) becomes much darker than before, as well as showing small nodules (Montgomery's tubercles) round its edge. (c) Sickness in the mornings immediately on rising is also a very frequent sign, occurring in about two-thirds of all women, though it may be absent, and even if present may be due simply to dyspepsia and weakness. When the sickness is marked it is, however, a valuable sign, because it appears early in the course of pregnancy, during the second month, and lasts usually about a couple of months. (d) 'Quickening', or the fluttering sensation felt by the mother in consequence of the child's rapid movements, is a very important sign, though it does not usually occur till some time during the fifth month of pregnancy or even later. It is the first sign of life felt by the mother, though it is a popular error to suppose that the child only then begins to live. (e) Enlargement of the abdomen is a pronounced sign, though for the first three months the enlargement is not apparent. It must not be forgotten, however, that enlargement may be due to other causes, such as tumours, dropsy, and even constipation or increasing development of fat. It is not an uncommon mistake for an elderly childless woman to delude herself with the hope that she is about to bear a child, when the abdomen is enlarging simply for the last-named reason. This condition is known as pseudocyesis or false pregnancy. (f) The only absolutely certain sign of pregnancy is obtained when the medical attendant hears the beating of the foetal heart by auscultation over the lower part of the abdomen. The heart-sounds are rapid, much resembling the ticking of a watch, and are heard, in general, from the middle of the fifth month onwards. (g) There are various minor signs which are sometimes present, sometimes absent, some of which are noticeable by the mother, others appreciable only by the medical attendant. Such are the occurrence of varicose veins, mucous discharge from the vagina, changes in the neck of the womb, etc.

Hygiene of pregnancy.—It is unnecessary for a healthy woman to make any great change in her ordinary mode of life during pregnancy. Her diet must be good, but should be simple and moderate. Alcoholic liquors (and

724

smoking) should preferably be abandoned during pregnancy. A pregnant woman should drink at least one pint of milk a day, on account, among other things, of the calcium it contains. Cheese should also be taken for its calcium. (The foetus in the uterus needs calcium for its bones.) Iron-containing foods are also important for the development of the foetus's red blood corpuscles. Iron is present in such foods as eggs, green leafy vegetables, and in liver and meat. Vitamins are also of great importance to the pregnant woman, and these are present in such foods as eggs, milk, cheese, butter, wholemeal bread, brown bread, fresh vegetables, and fruit (especially oranges, lemons, currants, potatoes, and tomatoes), and fat fish, such as herring and salmon ; in the winter months cod-liver oil or halibut-liver oil may well be taken in addition. Constipation should be avoided by a suitable diet containing vegetables, fruit, and the like, or by mild aperients. The skin should be kept in good condition by regular bathing. Moderate exercise should be taken every day and late hours avoided. The dress should be loose and comfortable, and it is often advisable for women who have borne several children to wear a special belt.

Special ailments. The misfortune which specially attaches to the condition of pregnancy is miscarriage (see MISCARRIAGE), which is not, however, liable to occur in perfectly healthy persons. Digestive disturbances are particularly common. Thus the natural morning sickness may become very troublesome, or even dangerous, and require special treatment. Constipation or diarrhoea is often a trouble, but either of them is treated much as under ordinary circumstances. Varicose veins in the legs, piles, swelling of the feet, and cramps in the legs are all liable to be caused in the later months by pressure of the increasing womb upon the large vessels and nerves within the pelvis. These, however, are not serious signs, and must simply be tolerated till after the child is born, when they quickly improve. Varicose veins, if very severe, should be supported by elastic stockings or by bandaging the legs, and cramps may be relieved by the usual means (see

CRAMP). Irritability of the bladder, showing itself by frequency of making water, is also a temporary inconvenience similarly due to pressure.

More serious symptoms occasionally arise, such as those of kidney disease, various nervous disorders, and especially the condition known as eclampsia, in which convulsions occur. Displacements of the womb, which have existed prior to pregnancy, may also give trouble if attention be not paid to them, and it may be necessary for the subject of such displacements to wear a pessary during the earlier months.

It is because of the possibility of such ailments, whether mild or serious, occurring during pregnancy that every pregnant mother should be seen by her doctor, or attend an antenatal clinic, at regular intervals throughout pregnancy.

PREGNANCY TESTS.—There are several tests for pregnancy in its early stages.

The Aschheim-Zondek test.—This was the first to be introduced and depends upon the fact that in the first few months of pregnancy the pituitary gland (anterior part) forms a greatly increased secretion, of which the excess is discharged in the urine. A small quantity of urine passed by the woman whom it is desired to test is sent to a laboratory, where a few drops are injected on several successive days into a young and immature female mouse or other small animal. The animal is killed five days later, and if the person whose urine is being tested is pregnant, it is found that the ovaries and neighbouring organs of the immature mouse have been stimulated into a state of full maturity ; but if the urine has come from a non-pregnant person, the young mouse's ovaries remain unchanged. The test is highly accurate.

The Friedman test.—The test animal is the rabbit. The isolated rabbit does not ovulate spontaneously, but ovulation can be induced within twenty-four hours by the intravenous injection of pregnancy urine. This test thus gives a result within twenty-four to forty-eight hours, and with an accuracy similar to the Aschheim-Zondek test.

The rat hyperæmia test.—The subcutaneous injection of pregnancy urine induces hyperæmia of the ovary in the immature rat. This test gives a result within ten hours, which is as accurate as the Aschheim-Zondek test.

The Hogben test.—This test is based upon the observation that the injection of pregnancy urine promotes ovulation in the female South African clawed toad (*Xenopus lævis*). It gives a result within twenty-four hours and has an accuracy similar to that of the Aschheim-Zondek test.

The Kapeller-Adler test.—This is a chemical test based upon the identification of histidine, which is a normal constituent of the urine throughout pregnancy. It is said to be 100 per cent. accurate in normal pregnancy, but non-pregnancy urine sometimes gives a positive reaction.

The Hæmagglutination Inhibition Test.—This, and the subsequent tests to be mentioned, are known as immunological tests, as opposed to those already mentioned which are known as biological tests. They are known as immunological tests because they are based upon the effect of the urine from a pregnant woman upon the interaction of red-blood cells, which have been sensitized to the human gonadotrophin (*q.v.*), and anti-gonadotrophin serum. They have the great practical advantage of being performed in a test-tube or even on a slide, and therefore not requiring animals. Because of their ease and speed of performance (a result can be obtained in two hours), these tests are being used on an increased scale.

Their degree of accuracy is not quite as high as the Hogben test, and the current recommendation is that while a negative result may be accepted, a positive result (*i.e.* one indicating that the woman is pregnant) should be confirmed by a Hogben test. With this combination an accuracy of over 99 per cent. has been reported.

The *Latex Test* and the *Gravindex Test* are modifications of the hæmagglutination test.

PREGNANDIOL is the excretion product of the hormone PROGESTERONE, manufactured by the corpus luteum of the ovary. Pregnandiol is excreted in the urine during the second half of the menstrual period, and its excretion rises steadily throughout pregnancy.

PREMATURE BIRTH (*see* BIRTH, MISCARRIAGE).

PREPUCE is the free fold of skin that overlaps the glans penis.

PRESBYOPIA (πρέσβυς, an old man ; ὄψ the eye) is the general term used to indicate the changes that take place naturally in the eye with the advance of age, and quite apart from any disease. The chief of these changes consists in decreasing elasticity of the lens, so that it becomes increasingly difficult to use the eyes for near work. At the age of forty this change has proceeded so far that the lens can just manage to accommodate itself for vision of objects at around 10 inches (25 cm.), the distance which is most convenient for reading or other close work. After the age of about forty-five, therefore, much work must be done at an uncomfortable distance, or glasses must be worn in order to aid the natural lens. Persons who, during youth, have a slight degree of short-sight, may in old age not require any glasses for near work.

PRESCRIPTION (*præscriptio*, an order) means the written direction given by the doctor to the chemist for the compounding of medicine suitable to a patient's case. The prescription contains as a rule the names of some preparations from the pharmacopœia, a list of approved remedies published by the government of each country. Sometimes the prescription consists of only one such formula, or it may contain the names of proprietary medicines or of simple substances not included in this official list.

In Britain it is still customary to write prescriptions in Latin, a usage which has come down from mediæval times, and which had a parallel in ancient Greece, where the practitioners at Athens are said to have written their prescriptions in the Doric dialect. The quaintest part of this traditional usage lies in the ℞ which heads every prescription, and which was at first probably the Eye of the god Horus, a charm used by the ancient Egyptians, and later the sign of the planet Jupiter. It now stands for the initial of the word *recipe* meaning 'take', and introduces the directions to the dispenser. The practice of writing in Latin, and of using the symbols ℔

726

(minim), ℥ (dram), ℥ (ounce), has nothing to recommend it.

At the present day the whole tendency is to switch over from the imperial system to the metric system, *i.e.* to prescribe in terms of milligrams and grammes rather than grains and ounces, millilitres rather than minims. This tendency is most marked in the case of the newer synthetic drugs. It has received official approval, and in the *British Pharmacopœia* dosages are given in terms of the metric system only. Further, in the *British Pharmacopœia* names of drugs are given in English, and not in Latin. For chemical and physiological reasons, as well as for convenience, drugs are administered in a more or less dilute form so calculated that the amount to be taken can be measured by some domestic utensil. Thus :

A drop (roughly) = 1 minim (0.06 ml.)
A teaspoonful = 60 minims (4 ml.)
A dessertspoonful = 120 minims (8 ml.)
A tablespoonful = ½ ounce (14 ml.) (small)
A wineglassful = 2¼ fluid ounces (70 ml.)
A tumblerful = 10 fluid ounces (230 ml.)

PRESENTATION means the appearance in labour of some particular part of the child's body at the mouth of the womb. This is normally a head presentation in 96 per cent. of cases, but in a certain number the breech may present, or the face, or foot, or even a part of the trunk in cases of cross-birth.

PRESSOR is the term applied to anything that increases the activity of a function, for example, a pressor nerve or pressor drug.

PRICKLY HEAT, or MILIARA RUBRA, is a troublesome skin condition affecting Europeans in tropical climates. It consists in the appearance of numbers of minute vesicles, produced by blocking of the outlet of the sweat or sebaceous glands in the skin, and accompanied by intolerable itching.

Causes. — Nearly every European suffers from prickly heat during the early years of residence in the tropics, when the hot season comes round. It is due probably to the cells on the surface of the skin becoming sodden by the constant perspiration, and so swelling and blocking the outlets of the minute gland-ducts. Anything that leads to perspiration, such as hot drinks, hot soup, close rooms, or warm clothing, aggravates the condition.

Symptoms.—The surface is covered by minute vesicles which cause extreme itching and pricking. The scratching which this entails often leads to the formation of boils and pustules, but the condition is not in itself a dangerous one. The extreme discomfort, and the loss of sleep arising from it, may, however, be a serious matter for invalids.

Treatment. — The most important point is to avoid, so far as possible, all causes of excessive perspiration, such as warm drinks and rough under-clothing. Common soap should not be used in the bath, and each time after bathing, the skin should be dusted with an astringent and antiseptic dusting powder, such as one composed of boric acid, zinc oxide, and starch in equal parts.

As a preventive, rubbing the body over after the bath with the juice of a lemon has been recommended, while as a cure, painting the patches with iodine solution, or with corrosive sublimate lotion (1 in 1000) has been advocated. Calamine lotion or carbolic acid lotion relieves the itching temporarily.

PRIMIDONE is a drug used for the treatment of epilepsy.

PRIMIPARA (*prima*, first, and *pario*, I bear) is the term applied to a woman who has given birth, or is giving birth, to her first child.

PRO- is a prefix meaning forwards.

PROBE (*probo*, I test) is the name of a slender, flexible instrument usually made of metal designed for introduction into a wound or cavity either to explore its depth and direction, to discover the presence of foreign bodies, or to introduce medicinal substances.

PROBENECID is a benzoic acid derivative. It interferes with the excretion by the kidney of certain compounds, including penicillin and *para*-aminosalicylic acid, and was originally introduced into medicine for this reason, as a means of increasing and maintaining the concentrations of penicillin in the body. It has also proved of value in the treatment of chronic gout.

PROCAINAMIDE is a derivative of procaine, which has been introduced for the treatment of certain cardiac arrhythmias.

PROCAINE, or PROCAINE HYDROCHLORIDE, is a synthetic substance having a similar action to the natural alkaloid cocaine. It is a powerful local anæsthetic with transitory effect. Procaine possesses the anæsthetic properties of cocaine, but has an advantage over the latter in being very much less poisonous, so that it can be administered in larger doses, and also in producing no tendency to contract a habit for its use.

PROCAINE PENICILLIN (*see* PENICILLIN).

PROCIDENTIA is another term for prolapse (*q.v.*).

PROCTALGIA is neuralgic pain in the anus or rectum. The term is usually reserved for rectal pain without local disease in the rectum to account for it.

PROCTITIS (πρωκτός, the anus) means inflammation situated about the rectum or anus.

PRODROMATA (πρόδρομος, running before) is a term applied to the earliest symptoms of a disease, or those which give warning of its presence. For example, vomiting and headache may be prodromata of scarlet fever.

PROFLAVINE is a valuable antiseptic. It is an acridine derivative, its chemical description being 2 : 8-diaminoacridine sulphate. Like all the acridine derivatives it is effective against both Gram-positive and Gram-negative bacteria and is not inactivated by body fluids or pus. It is also non-toxic and non-irritating.

PROGERIA (πρό, before ; γῆρας, old age) is a term for premature old age. When the physical appearances of old age occur in children the condition is believed to be due to disease of the pituitary gland.

PROGESTERONE, $C_{21}H_{30}O_2$, is the hormone of the corpus luteum. After the escape of the ovum from the ruptured follicle, the corpus luteum secretes progesterone, which stimulates the growth and secretion of the endometrial glands during the fourteen days before menstruation. In the event of pregnancy, the secretion of progesterone continues until parturition. (*See also* ETHISTERONE, PREGNANDIOL, MENSTRUATION.)

PROGLOTTIS is a term applied to the segment of a tape-worm.

PROGNOSIS (πρόγνωσις) is the term applied to a forecast as to the probable result of an attack of disease, particularly with regard to the prospect of recovery, based upon the nature and symptoms of the case.

PROGRESSIVE MUSCULAR ATROPHY (*see* PARALYSIS).

PROGUANIL HYDROCHLORIDE is a synthetic anti-malarial drug which has proved of undoubted value both in the treatment and the prevention of malaria, particularly the form known as malignant tertian malaria. It is also known as PALUDRINE, which is the proprietary name.

PROLACTIN is the name of the pituitary hormone which initiates lactation. The development of the breasts during pregnancy is ascribed to the action of œstrogens (*q.v.*). Prolactin starts them secreting. If lactation does not occur or fails, it may be started by injection of prolactin.

PROLAPSE (*prolabor*, I sink down) means slipping down of some organ or structure. The term is applied chiefly to downward displacements of the rectum and womb. When the lower end of the bowel prolapses each time the bowels move—as may occur in children—it should be carefully sponged with cold water, replaced, and, if necessary, retained in place by a soft pad and bandage attached to a waist-belt. The condition tends to pass off as the child grows older. Prolapse which affects the womb may, in the earlier stages, cause protrusion of a fold of the bowel or bladder through the vagina, and in the later stages the womb itself may protrude to the exterior. The condition, which affects elderly women, is mainly due to injuries caused by childbirth. It may often be remedied by wearing a suitably shaped pessary, or by an operation designed to unite the torn parts.

PROMIN is a sulphonamide-like drug which has been used in the treatment of superficial tuberculous infections and leprosy.

PRONATION is the movement whereby the bones of the forearm are crossed and the palm of the hand faces downwards.

PRONTOSIL (*see* SULPHANILAMIDE).

PROPAMIDINE. — An ' antiseptic ' applied in the form of a jelly or a cream in the treatment of wounds and burns. It is used in the form of propamidine isethionate. The action of propamidine is bacteriostatic, an action it retains in the presence of pus ; it does not prevent phagocytosis. It has been used in the local treatment of wounds and burns, and is effective against the staphylococcus and highly effective against the streptococcus.

PROPANTHELINE, or PROPANTHELINE BROMIDE, is a substance with an anti-cholinergic, or atropine-like action, which is used in the treatment of conditions such as duodenal ulcer and spastic colon.

PROPHYLAXIS (προφύλαξ, an advanced guard) means treatment adopted with the view of warding off disease.

PROPICILLIN (*see* PENICILLIN).

PROPTOSIS means undue prominence of the eyeballs.

PROSTATE GLAND is a structure which lies at the neck of the bladder in men and surrounds that part of the urethra lying within the pelvis. This gland is of importance, especially because in late life it is apt to increase in size and change in shape in such a way as to obstruct the exit of water from the bladder. Accordingly, great difficulty in making water occurs, and the regular use of a catheter to draw it off may become a necessity (*see* CATHETERS). Inflammation of the bladder is very apt to be finally produced if great care be not taken in the purification and use of this instrument (*see* BLADDER, DISEASES OF). In the large majority of cases, however, in which enlargement of the prostate produces such obstruction, removal by means of operation is now recommended. The prostate is also one of the common sites of cancer in the male, and it is in the control, though unfortunately not the cure, of this form of cancer that such dramatic results have been obtained from the use of the synthetic œstrogens, such as stilbœstrol (*q.v.*).

PROSTHESIS (πρός, to ; θέσις, placing) means replacing of an absent part by an artificial one, *e.g.* eye, leg, or denture. It is also applied to the artificial substitute.

PROSTIGMIN is an artificial substance chemically allied to physostigmine, which on injection produces contraction of muscles of more prolonged character than that caused by physostigmine. It is used chiefly as a remedy for myasthenia gravis (*q.v.*).

PROTAMINES are a class of proteins found in combination with nuclei and in the heads of fish spermatozoa. They have two main uses in medicine. When combined with insulin they produce a compound which exerts a slower and more prolonged anti-diabetic action (*see* INSULIN). They also act as an antidote to heparin (*q.v.*).

PROTARGOL is a preparation of silver with powerful astringent and antiseptic action. It is used in acute inflammations of mucous membranes as a lotion of strength 1 in 400 to 1 in 200.

PROTEIN, or PROTEID, is the term applied to members of a group of non-crystallizable nitrogenous substances widely distributed in the animal and vegetable kingdoms and forming the characteristic materials of their tissues and fluids. They are essentially combinations of amino-acids. They mostly dissolve in water and are coagulated by heat and various chemical substances. Typical examples of protein substances are white of egg and gelatin. (*See* ALBUMINS *and* HYDROLYZED PROTEIN.)

PROTEIN SHOCK is a method of treatment by intramuscular or intravenous injection of protein material. Its object is to cause a reaction accompanied by moderate rise of temperature which produces stimulation of the general chemical processes of the body and of its absorptive and

healing powers. Various protein substances are used for this purpose, including 5 per cent. peptone solution, sterilized milk, and bacterial vaccines in large doses. Somewhat similar effects are produced by injection of certain metallic salts. This method is sometimes used in treatment of chronic diseases such as multiple sclerosis and rheumatoid arthritis though much less commonly than at one time.

PROTEIN THERAPY.—This is a method of treatment by injection of small quantities of protein substances in the case of persons suffering from diseases due to their excessive sensitiveness to similar substances. Diseases in which this form of treatment appears to be specially useful include asthma, hay fever, nettle - rash, and similar skin affections. In some cases these disorders are caused by taking as food various forms of meat, fish, eggs, etc., certain cereals, fruits, and vegetables, or even by inhalation of the dust or emanations from the fur and feathers of cats, rabbits, fowls, horses, etc., and especially the pollens of certain grasses and ragweeds. The offending material can frequently be discovered by steeping some of these substances in water and afterwards inoculating a drop of the substance into the skin of the arm by means of a scratch. If the person is ' sensitive ' to the substance under trial, a red area develops round the scratch in the course of a few minutes followed later by a definite wheal. Such an inoculation produces no effect on an ' insensitive ' person.

The patient who has been found sensitive to a particular animal or vegetable protein can either refrain from taking this in food or otherwise coming into contact with it, or he can be ' desensitized ' by receiving gradually increasing doses of the protein in question.

PROTEINURIA.—The condition in which proteins are found in the urine. It is usually referred to as ALBUMINURIA (*q.v.*), but this is not strictly correct, as either of the two blood proteins — albumin and globulin — may be found in the urine.

PROTO- (πρῶτος, first) is a prefix signifying first.

PROTOPLASM (πρῶτος, first; πλάσμα, form) is the viscid, translucent, glue-like material containing fine granules and composed mainly of proteins, which makes up the essential material of plant and animal cells and has the properties of life.

PROUD FLESH is the popular name given to the unhealthy granulations which sometimes arise from an ulcer which is inflamed and is not healing properly, or from the margins of a sinus. It is checked by applying to it some astringent like nitrate of silver solution or copper sulphate.

PROXIMAL is a term of comparison applied to structures which are nearer the centre of the body or the median line as opposed to more ' distal ' structures.

PRURIGO (*prurigo*) is the name of a chronic skin disease in which small whitish pimples develop in the skin, accompanied by intense itching. The condition may either be permanent or may come and go, especially in children in association with teething.

PRURITUS (*prurio*, I itch) is another name for itching.

PRUSSIC ACID POISONING.—Prussic or hydrocyanic acid is a very deadly poison with a sweet smell and pleasant taste, paralysing every part of the nervous system with which it comes in contact. In its dilute state it is a valuable remedy for irritable conditions of internal mucous membranes, such as that of the stomach, and for irritable skin diseases, being used in small doses to check vomiting or cough, and applied in lotions to relieve itching. It exerts this curative action by numbing the sensory nerves with which it is brought in contact.

As a poison it acts with great rapidity, and, since cyanide of potassium is much used in the processes of electro-plating and photography, and is almost as deadly in its effects as the acid, persons using the cyanide should be acquainted with the treatment which may be of avail to save life in a case of poisoning.

Symptoms.—After a large dose, the poison is very rapidly diffused through the body, and only a few minutes or seconds elapse before the symptoms appear. These are slowness of breathing, slowness and irregularity of the heart's action, and blueness of the face and lips. In a few minutes, insensibility with gradual stoppage of breathing and of the heart's action comes on, preceded in some cases by convulsions.

The suddenness and character of the symptoms and the sweet smell of prussic acid on the breath make the cause evident.

Treatment.—This is based upon the administration of nitrites, which convert cyanide in the blood into the harmless cyanmethæmoglobin. Amyl nitrite is given by inhalation for 30 seconds every two minutes and also, if the victim can still swallow, 0·5 gramme of sodium nitrite in 10 millilitres of water, by mouth. Artificial respiration (*see* DROWNING, RECOVERY FROM) is started immediately and oxygen is administered. Injections of sodium nitrite and sodium thiosulphate are then given, as well as analeptics. An ' Ampin ' Cyanide Emergency Kit is available which allows these injections to be given quickly. The victim must be watched carefully for forty-eight hours.

PSAMMOMA (ψάμμος, sand) is the name given to a small hard tumour of the brain containing calcareous matter.

PSEUDO- (ψευδής, false) is a prefix put to the names of certain well-defined diseases to indicate other conditions, the symptoms of which closely resemble those of one of the diseases in question, though the real nature of the two maladies is quite different.

PSEUDOCYESIS (ψευδής, false; κύησις, pregnancy) means spurious or false pregnancy which may be produced by the presence of a tumour or simply by flatulence occurring especially about the time of the menopause.

PSEUDOHYPERTROPHIC MUSCULAR DYSTROPHY, or PSEUDOHYPERTROPHIC PARALYSIS, is a condition in which certain muscles enlarge owing to a fatty and fibrous degeneration, giving a false appearance of increased strength. (*See* MUSCLES, DISEASES OF.)

PSILOSIS (ψιλός, bare) is another name for sprue (*q.v.*).

PSITTACOSIS (ψιττακός, a parrot) is a contagious infection of parrots sometimes communicated to man and caused by a virus.

PSOAS (ψόα, the loin) is the name of a powerful muscle which arises from the front of the vertebral column in the lumbar region, and passes down, round the pelvis and through the groin, to be attached to the inner side of the thigh-bone not far from its upper end. The act of sitting up from a recumbent posture, or that of bending the thigh on the abdomen, is mainly accomplished by the contraction of this muscle. Disease of the spine in the lumbar region is very apt to produce an abscess which lies within the sheath of this muscle and makes its way down to the front of the thigh, where it threatens to burst. Such an abscess is known as a ' psoas abscess '. (*See* ABSCESS, CHRONIC.)

PSORIASIS (ψώρα, scurf) is a disease of the skin in which raised, rough, reddened areas appear, covered with fine silvery scales. This eruption consists of a chronic inflammatory process in the true skin, the papillæ of which become considerably lengthened and more vascular than usual, together with changes in the cuticle which cause a defect in the horny formation that naturally takes place on the surface. (*See* SKIN.)

Causes.—The condition generally appears for the first time around adolescence or early adult life. It is often a family disease occurring in different generations of one stock, and is often associated with gout or rheumatism. In some persons, psoriasis appears repeatedly at a particular season of the year, especially in the spring and autumn, but it is not infectious. Depressing influences seem to have something to do with its appearance, and people who are liable to it are troubled by its reappearance at any time when the general health is below par.

Symptoms.—The eruption almost always appears first round the back of the elbows and front of the knees. It begins as small pimples, each covered with a white cap of scales, which enlarge in breadth till they form patches 2 or 3 inches wide. At the same time,

patches appear on other parts of the body, the scalp and face especially. The disease is divided into several varieties according to the size, shape, and distribution of these patches.

Treatment.—It is essential first of all to attend to the general health and relieve especially any constitutional condition such as gout or rheumatism, by the appropriate remedies. There is no internal remedy, but a short course of calciferol is sometimes of help. Tar ointment, chrysarobin ointment, and dithranol are among the chief and most successful external applications. Generally, the eruption disappears after some weeks of careful treatment, but occasionally cases occur in which all treatment seems of very little use. Natural sunlight, or ultra-violet light, alone or in combination with tar preparations, produces a marked improvement in many cases. Arsenic is sometimes administered internally in very chronic cases.

PSYCHASTHENIA (ψυχή, mind ; ἀσθένεια, weakness) is a condition in which the mind becomes temporarily weakened, the person a prey to anxieties and impulsive acts, the power of concentration poor, and the judgment capricious, without definite delusions or other signs of insanity. The condition is a form of neurosis. (*See* NEUROSIS.)

PSYCHIATRY (ψυχή, mind ; ἰατρεία, healing) is the name applied to that branch of medical science which treats of mental disorder and disease.

PSYCHO-ANALYSIS is a term strictly applied to the theories and practice of the Freudian school of psychology. It is often wrongly applied to medical psychology in general, of which there are various schools. It depends upon the theory that states of disordered mental health have been produced by a repression of painful memories or of conflicting instincts. By such repression these hurtful memories or instincts are kept constantly in a subconscious condition. As a result, the individual's mental power is needlessly occupied and diverted from the proper objects with which it should be concerned, and

731

he finds difficulty in concentrating his attention upon and adapting himself to the practical realities of everyday life.

Psycho-analysis aims at discovering these repressed memories which are responsible for the perversion of mental power and of which the affected person usually is only dimly or quite unaware. The fundamental aim of psycho-analysis as a method of treatment is the free expression of thoughts, ideas, and fantasies on the part of the patient. To facilitate this, he lies on a couch to relax mind and body, and the analyst may sit so as to observe the patient but not to be observed by him. The analyst's task is to adopt a neutral attitude to the patient, to encourage the free association of ideas, and to explain where explanation is necessary for the continuance of free association. The analyst will become a part of the patient's fantasies and represent in them from time to time objects of love and hate—especially members of the patient's family. In the course of analysis the patient will, so to speak, sink back into childhood and re-enact his early emotional attitudes, the analyst representing in this phase father, mother, or brother or sister. In this re-enactment various infantile emotional tensions are released, and relief of painful mental symptoms secured.

There is much that is highly speculative in the theories of psycho-analysis, but at the same time its fundamental conceptions have been widely adopted by other schools of psychology to their enrichment, and the new approaches to the study of the mind in health and disease opened up by the genius of Freud have entirely changed the attitude of the lay and the medical public to the problems of the neurotic, the morbidly anxious, the fearful, and the mental and emotional development of the child.

PSYCHOLOGY (ψυχή, mind ; λόγος, discourse) is the branch of science that deals with the mind and its methods of working.

PSYCHONEUROSIS (ψυχή, mind ; νεῦρον, nerve) is a general term applied to various functional disorders of the nervous system. (*See* NEUROSIS.)

PSYCHOPATHIC (ψυχή, mind; πάθος, suffering) means anything related to mental disease.

PSYCHOSIS (ψυχή, mind) is a term applied to serious disorder of the mind, which may amount to insanity.

PSYCHOSOMATIC is a term applied to diseases in which the physical manifestations are in part, at least, due to emotional or mental factors. For instance, an attack of lumbago may be due not to any disease of the muscles of the back, but to emotional disturbances which literally prevent the individual from standing up to the stresses and strains of life.

PSYCHOTHERAPY (ψυχή, mind ; θεραπεία, healing) is the term applied to any form of treatment in disease which operates through the mind. Almost every form of disease or injury has a certain mental aspect, even if this relates only to the pain or discomfort that it causes. In some diseases, and with some temperaments, the mental factor is much more pronounced than in others ; and for such cases, psychic modes of treatment are particularly important. The chief methods employed in psychic or mental healing are the following :

Suggestion is the most commonly employed method. Indeed, it is used in almost every department of medicine. It may consist, in its simplest form, of a mere reiteration of the statement that the health is better, either by the medical attendant or by the patient, so that this idea becomes fixed in the patient's mind. Or a suggestion of efficacy to cure may be conveyed by the taste or other physical properties of a medicine or by the imposing appearance of some apparatus used in treatment. Again, suggestion may be conveyed through an emotional channel, such as that of religious fervour. In occasional cases the result is secured when the suggestion is made to the patient in the hypnotic state.

Persuasion is a method of psychic treatment in which appeal is made to a patient's reasoning faculties. It presupposes a higher type of mind than that required for simple suggestion treatment.

Analysis consists in the elucidation

of the half-conscious or subconscious repressed memories or instincts that are responsible for some cases of mental disorder. (*See* PSYCHO-ANALYSIS.)

Education and employment are important factors in mental treatment, and employment should be of a congenial character and one which the patient can carry out without great effort.

PTERYGIUM (πτερύγιον, wing) is the name applied to a patch of opaque tissue gradually extending over part of the clear cornea.

PTISAN (πτισάνη, barley) is another name for barley water.

PTOMAINE POISONING (πτῶμα, a dead body) is the general name that used to be applied to cases in which persons become seriously affected as the result of eating meat, fish, cheese, and other animal substances which have undergone some decomposition. These serious effects were thought to be due to the formation of animal alkaloids, known as ptomaines, in consequence of the action of bacteria upon the albuminous materials contained in the food. This view is no longer held, and the term is no longer used. (*See* FOOD POISONING.)

PTOSIS (πτῶσις, a fall) means drooping of the upper eyelids. It is a sign of paralysis of the third cranial nerve, which governs the muscle that elevates the upper lid.

PTYALIN (πτύαλον, saliva) is the name of the ferment contained in the saliva, by which starchy materials are changed into sugar, and so prepared for absorption. (*See* DIGESTION.)

PTYALISM is a condition characterized by excessive production of saliva.

PUBERTY (*puber*, of ripe age) means the change that takes place when childhood passes into manhood or womanhood. This change is generally a very definite one, taking place at about the age of fourteen years, although it is modified by race, climate, luxurious habits, and bodily health, so that it may appear a year or two earlier or several years later. At this time the sexual functions attain their full development, the contour of the body

changes from a childish to a more rounded womanly, or sturdy manly form, and great changes take place in the mode of thought and feeling. About this time the larynx enlarges in boys, so that the voice, after going through a period of ' breaking ', finally assumes the deep manly pitch. The hair on the face and body takes on also a deeper and stronger growth, so that skin eruptions are not uncommon on the face (*see* ACNE).

The period is one of transition from a physical, mental, and moral point of view, and the pressure of physical and intellectual work should not be made too hard, care being rather taken that good habits and modes of thought are formed at this impressionable time.

Puberty is not to be regarded as a physiological ' coming of age ', for full development and vigour are not attained till between twenty and thirty years of age.

PUBIS is the bone that forms the front part of the pelvis. The pubic bones of opposite sides meet in the ' symphysis ' and protect the bladder from the front.

PUBLIC HEALTH (*see* SANITATION ; *also* DISINFECTION, INFECTION, REFUSE AND SEWAGE DISPOSAL, VENTILATION; WATER-CLOSETS, DRAINS, AND SEWERS; WATER SUPPLY).

PUERPERAL FEVER (*puerperus*, bringing forth children), or CHILD-BED FEVER, was in former times the great dread of those whose duty it was to attend women in child-bed, both in private practice and to a much greater extent in public hospitals.

Causes.—This fever is of various types and grades of severity. After the birth of a child, the mother is specially liable, for several reasons, to contract any infectious disease to which she may be exposed. In the first place, she is much weakened by the strain through which she has passed, and often by the loss of a great quantity of blood. In the second place, the injuries incidental to child-birth produce raw surfaces in the genital tract, from which absorption occurs with great facility. The organism most commonly involved is the *Streptococcus hæmolyticus* (*q.v.*).

(For causation, see under LABOUR, PUERPERAL INFECTION.)

Symptoms. — The symptoms vary according to the form that the infection takes, and most commonly appear on the second or third day after labour, the first three days being regarded as the critical period in recovery. Thus the organisms may, in the mildest form, develop on the raw or wounded surface, to which they gain access without entering the system. In such a case, there are general discomfort and feverishness, rise of temperature, and quickening of the pulse, but these symptoms disappear when the wound is cleansed by antiseptic douches and similar energetic measures.

When the organisms gain access to the surrounding lymphatic vessels and veins, inflammation in the cellular tissue of the pelvis results, and may be followed by abscesses, peritonitis, either localized or general (see PERITONITIS), or, later on, by the condition known as ' white leg ', caused by blocking of the veins in one lower limb. In these conditions, which are less common, the symptoms are more severe. There are considerable fever, shivering, prostration, and quickening of the pulse as early signs, together with pain in the lower part of the abdomen, followed later on by the symptoms belonging to peritonitis, white leg, or other condition set up by the inflammation. The condition may be recovered from in a week or two, or long-continued ill-health may result, or the patient may speedily succumb.

If the organisms gain access to the general circulation, the serious condition known as 'septicæmia' results (see BLOOD-POISONING), and is accompanied by high fever, great prostration, delirium, and increasing feebleness of the heart's action.

Treatment.—The prevention of the condition is of the greatest importance. For this reason, care in the choice of a lying-in room, great care to shield the patient from every risk of infection, and above all, scrupulous cleanliness on the part of all the attendants, are necessary. (See also LABOUR, PUERPERAL INFECTION.)

Treatment resolves itself into careful nursing, drainage of the uterus, blood transfusion if hæmoglobin falls below

40 per cent., and administration of penicillin or the appropriate sulphonamide drug. The recognition of the bacteria responsible for puerperal infection and the introduction of the sulphonamide drugs and of penicillin in treatment have gone a long way to remove the terrors of this grim attendant upon child-birth.

PUERPERAL PYREXIA is the name given to any febrile condition, other than 'puerperal fever', occurring in a woman within fourteen days after child-birth or miscarriage in which a temperature of 100·4° F. (38° C.) or more has been sustained during a period of twenty-four hours or has recurred during that period. Any such feverish attack, as well as the more serious puerperal fever, must now be ' notified ' in Great Britain to the local public health authority.

PUERPERIUM (*puerperium*) is the period which elapses after the birth of a child until the mother is again restored to her ordinary health. It is generally regarded as lasting for a month. One of the main changes that occur is the enormous decrease in size that takes place in the muscular wall of the womb (see MUSCLE). There are very often ' afterpains ' during the first day in women who have borne several children, less frequently after a first child (see AFTERPAINS). The discharge is blood-stained for the first two or three days, then clearer till the end of the first week, after which it becomes thicker and less in quantity, finally disappearing altogether, if the case goes well, at the end of two or three weeks. The breasts, which have already enlarged before the birth of the child, secrete milk more copiously, and there should be a plentiful supply on the third day of the puerperium.

Management.—It is now realized that prolonged rest in bed is not necessary for the mother after a normal birth. Indeed, it may be harmful. In the United States of America it is common practice to get the mother up on the first day, but in Britain it is most common to get her up on the second or third day. Soon thereafter she should start practising exercises to help to ensure that the stretched abdominal muscles regain their normal tone.

There is no need for any restriction of diet, but care must be taken to ensure an adequate intake of fluid, including at least a pint of milk a day. It is a common popular delusion that alcoholic liquors are necessary for a good formation of milk ; but this is not the case. The bowels are generally sluggish and it is usual to take an aperient on the second or third day.

Milk, as already stated, appears copiously on the third day, but this is preceded by a secretion from the breast, known as colostrum, which is of value to the new-born child. The child should, therefore, be put to the breasts within twelve hours of being born, in

PULSE (*pulsus*, a blow).—If the point of one finger be laid gently on the front of the forearm, about one inch above the furrows that mark the wrist, and about half an inch from the outer edge, the pulsations of the radial artery can be felt. This is known as *the pulse*, but a pulse can be felt wherever an artery of large or medium size lies near the surface. (*See* HÆMORRHAGE.)

The cause of the pulsation lies in the fact that, at each heart-beat, 80 to 90 millilitres of blood are driven into the aorta, and a fluid wave, distending the vessels as it passes, is in consequence transmitted along the arteries all over the body. This pulsation gets less and

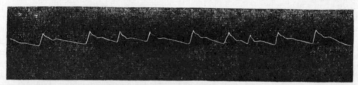

FIG. 321.—Pulse tracing, taken by the sphygmograph on smoked paper, from a case of atrial fibrillation in disease of the mitral valve. The pulse shows considerable irregularity. (Balfour's *Diseases of the* (*Heart.*)

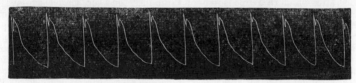

FIG. 322.—Pulse tracing from a case of incompetence of the aortic valve, showing the great extent to which the artery fills at each beat and empties between the beats. (Balfour's *Diseases of the* Heart.)

order to obtain the small amount of fluid they are secreting, and also because suckling stimulates both the breasts and the natural changes taking place during this period. Suckling is beneficial, therefore, for both child and mother.

PULMONARY DISEASES (*pulmo*, a lung). (*See* LUNGS, DISEASES OF.)

PULSATION (*pulsatio*, a beating) or throbbing is an appearance seen or felt naturally below the fourth and fifth ribs on the left side, where the heart lies, and also at every point where an artery lies close beneath the surface. In other situations, it is generally a sign of aneurysm. In nervous persons great pulsation can often be seen and felt in the upper part of the abdomen, due to the throbbing of the abdominal aorta.

less marked as the arteries grow smaller, and is finally lost in the minute capillaries, where a steady pressure is maintained. For this reason, the blood in the veins flows steadily on without any pulsation. Immediately after the wave has passed, the artery, by virtue of its great elasticity, regains its former size. In this wave the physician has a valuable means of studying both the state of the artery as regards elasticity and the heart's action.

The pulse rate is usually about 72 per minute, but it may vary in health from 50 to 100, and is quicker in childhood and slower in old age than in middle life ; it increases in all feverish states.

Further, the character of the vessel wall is of great importance. In childhood and youth the vessel wall is so thin that, when sufficient pressure is made to expel the blood from it, the artery can no longer be felt. In old age, however, and in some degenerative diseases, the vessel wall becomes so thick that it may be felt like a piece of whipcord rolling beneath the finger. The extent to which this change has taken place gives the physician valuable information as to the state of the arteries.

The size of the column felt also gives information. For example, after great muscular exertion, or when the heart is beating strongly, the vessels of the limbs are full and the pulse is ' large ', whilst, on the other hand, in the case of internal inflammations, the vessels of the limbs are empty, and the pulse therefore thin and ' wiry '.

Different types of heart disease have special features of the pulse associated with them. In atrial fibrillation the great character is irregularity (Fig. 321). In cases in which the aortic valve is incompetent, the pulse has the peculiarity of rising very quickly and collapsing suddenly, suggesting the pulsation observed in the toy known as the water-hammer, after which this type is named (Fig. 322). In persons of habitually relaxed physique, or suffering from some weakening fever, the pulse is apt to become dicrotic (*see* DICROTIC).

It is only after long practice that the character of the pulse-wave can be readily appreciated by the finger, and a small instrument known as the sphygmograph has been devised, whereby the artery is made to register these waves. Another instrument known as the ' polygraph ' enables tracings to be taken from different vessels at the same time. A tracing may thus be taken from the pulse at the wrist and from the veins in the neck and simultaneous events in the two compared.

The pressure of the blood in various arteries is estimated by an instrument known as the ' sphygmomanometer '. (*See* BLOOD-PRESSURE.)

PUNCTATE BASOPHILIA (*see* BASO-PHILIA.)

PUNCTUM (*punctum*, point) is the term applied to a minute spot or puncture, especially to the lacrimal punctures near the inner end of the upper and lower eyelids. (*See* EYE.)

736

PUPIL (*pupilla*) is the opening in the centre of the iris through which rays of light pass into the eye. (*See* EYE.)

PURGATIVES (*purgo*, I cleanse) are drugs or other measures which produce evacuation of the bowels.

Varieties and action.—Purgatives are divided into several groups, according to the manner and degree of violence with which they act.

LAXATIVES are those which very gently stimulate the bowels and render the motions slightly more frequent and softer without causing any griping. Most articles of food that leave a large indigestible residue upon which the intestine can contract, such as cabbage, brown bread, and oatmeal porridge, act in this way. Those fruits which contain rough seeds, sugar, and vegetable acids act similarly. Among the laxatives are honey, tamarinds, figs, raspberries, strawberries, prunes, stewed apples, sulphur, and magnesia. Liquid paraffin also produces this effect.

SIMPLE PURGATIVES or APERIENTS produce one or more copious and slightly liquid movements, often accompanied or preceded by griping pains. Examples of this class are aloes, rhubarb, cascara sagrada, senna, castor oil.

DRASTIC PURGATIVES cause a violent action of the bowels, accompanied by considerable griping. In small doses many of them have a simple aperient action, while in excessive doses most are irritant poisons. Such are elaterium, colocynth, jalap, scammony, croton oil. Many of these produce very copious watery evacuations, and, since they remove a considerable quantity of water from the system, are known as *hydragogues*. These drastic purgatives are seldom used nowadays.

SALINE PURGATIVES are salts of the alkaline metals and alkaline earths. Such are sulphate of potassium, sulphate of sodium (Glauber's salt), sulphate of magnesium (Epsom salts), phosphate of sodium, bi-tartrate of potassium (cream of tartar), tartrate of potassium and sodium (Seidlitz powder), and citrate of magnesium. Taken in large doses, many of these salines also act as hydragogues.

Purgatives produce their effects either by stimulating the mucous membrane so that the amount of fluid in the intestine becomes larger, or by stimulating the muscular coat so that peristaltic contractions become more vigorous. Most purgatives have the double action, though one or other preponderates. Further, certain purgatives act all along the intestine, such as Epsom salts, whilst others, such as cascara, are almost devoid of action until they reach the large intestine. Castor oil, on the other hand, acts mainly on the small intestine.

Uses.—The most common use of purgatives is to remove the contents of the bowels when their action is sluggish (see CONSTIPATION). In many cases of diarrhœa, due to the presence of irritating material in the intestine, a single dose of purgative medicine, such as castor oil, is given with the object of getting rid of the offending material, after which the diarrhœa ceases. In cases of inflammation affecting the bowels, saline purgatives are often given with the view of diminishing the congestion in the bowel-wall. In plethoric persons or persons for whom any strain may be harmful, such as in cases of threatened apoplexy, and, in persons suffering from hernia or aneurysm, laxatives are given to prevent straining at stool.

A protest must be entered here against the common domestic practice of administering purgatives on every occasion of slight illness, especially in children, regardless of the complaint or symptoms. Undoubtedly some cases of malaise are due simply to constipation ; but care must be taken that no serious trouble is present, for many persons have undoubtedly died through receiving only an aperient whom timely medical aid might have saved. (*See* ABDOMEN, DISEASES OF.)

PURPURA (*purpura*, purple) is a disease characterized by the occurrence of purple-coloured spots upon the surface of the body, due to extravasations of blood in the skin, associated occasionally with hæmorrhages from mucous membranes.

Causes.—The condition is due either to an increased permeability of the smallest blood-vessels (*i.e.* the capillaries) which allows blood to pass through their walls, or to a shortage of blood platelets which normally play

an important part in sealing off any damage which may occur to the walls of the capillaries. The damage to the capillary wall may arise as a result of an infection, *e.g.* scarlet fever ; a toxic factor, *e.g.* certain drugs ; malnutrition or wasting, *e.g.* in the terminal stages of cancer ; or in scurvy. Such cases are described as *secondary purpuras*.

There are two other conditions in which purpura occurs and in which the cause can often not be found. One, sometimes known as *essential thrombocytopenia*, or *primary thrombocytopenic purpura*, is definitely associated with a marked diminution in the number of blood platelets or thrombocytes (hence the name). The other, known as *anaphylactoid purpura*, is supposed to be an allergic condition, the increased permeability of the capillary wall being due to the individual coming in contact with, inhaling, or ingesting some substance to which he is sensitized. Two special forms of anaphylactoid purpura are recognized. One is *Henoch's purpura*, in which the purpuric hæmorrhages occur in the wall of the intestine, causing symptoms resembling an acute abdominal emergency. This form occurs in children and young adults. The other is *Schön-lein's purpura*, in which the purpura occurs around the joints causing them to be painful and tender. This form principally affects young adults.

Symptoms.—The complaint is usually ushered in by lassitude and feverishness. This is soon followed by the appearance on the surface of the body of the characteristic spots in the form of small red points scattered over the skin of the limbs and trunk. They are not raised above the surface, and they do not disappear on pressure. Their colour soon becomes deep purple or nearly black ; but after a few days they undergo the changes which are observed in the case of an ordinary bruise, passing to a green and yellow hue and finally disappearing. When of minute size they are termed ' petechiæ ' or ' stigmata ', when somewhat larger ' vibices ', and when in patches of considerable size ' ecchymoses'. They may come out in fresh crops over a lengthened period.

The form of the disease above described is that known as *purpura sim-*

24   737

plex. A more serious form of the malady is that to which the term *purpura hæmorrhagica* is applied. Here there is a tendency to the occurrence of hæmorrhage from mucous surfaces, especially from the nose, but also from the mouth, lungs, stomach, bowels, kidneys, and womb, sometimes in large and dangerous amount. Great physical prostration is apt to attend this form of the disease, and a fatal result sometimes follows the successive hæmorrhages, or is suddenly precipitated by the occurrence of an extravasation of blood into the brain.

Treatment.—The treatment of *secondary purpura* consists of that of the underlying cause : *e.g.* scurvy. The treatment of *primary thrombocytopenic purpura* consists of the administration of one of the cortisone-like drugs : *e.g.* prednisolone. In cases which do not respond to such therapy, removal of the enlarged spleen is often helpful, especially in children. The treatment of *anaphylactoid purpura* consists of the administration of antihistamine drugs. If these fail, then it is worth trying the effect of prednisolone. If, as is often the case, there is any anæmia, this must be treated by the administration of full doses of iron : *e.g.* ferrous sulphate.

PUS (*pus*), or MATTER, is a thick, white, yellow, or greenish fluid, which is found in abscesses, on ulcers, and

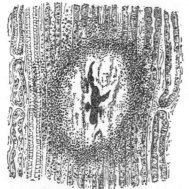

738

on inflamed and discharging surfaces generally. Its colour and consistence are due to the presence, in great numbers, of pus corpuscles. These are derived mostly from the white corpuscles of the blood, and consist also of the superficial cells of granulation tissue or of a mucous membrane which die and are shed off in consequence of the inflammatory process. (*See* ABSCESS, PHAGOCYTOSIS.)

PUSTULE (*pustula*) means a small collection of pus (*see* ABSCESS). Malignant pustule is one of the forms taken by woolsorters' disease (*see* ANTHRAX).

PUTREFACTION (*putrefacio*, I make rotten) is the change that takes place in the bodies of plants and animals after death, whereby they are ultimately reduced to carbonic acid gas, ammonia, and other simple substances. The change is almost entirely due to the action of bacteria, and, in the course of the process, various offensive and poisonous intermediate substances are formed. In the case of the human body, putrescine, cadaverine, and other alkaloids are among these intermediate products.

The first sign of putrefaction is the appearance of a greenish tinge over the lower part of the abdomen, visible on the second or third day after death. This is not to be confused with the lividity seen on the back, due to the blood running down into the dependent parts, which is visible within eight or twelve hours. In from two to three weeks the body is greenish-brown throughout, the skin commencing to give way, and the features almost unrecognizable. By the end of one year, none of the organs is recognizable, and, according to Reinhard, bodies buried in gravel or sandy soil have, after the lapse of four to seven years, lost all trace of the soft parts, the bones alone remaining.

When bodies decompose in water, particularly that drained from peaty soil, the skin becomes white and sodden and the changes take place more slowly. Sometimes, in these circumstances, instead of going through the usual changes, the body undergoes a process of saponification, and the tissues are converted into a mixture of soaps, fatty acids, and volatile substances known as *adipocere*. This does not readily undergo further changes, and so bodies lying in ponds or damp graves may become changed in the course of some months or years into this wax-like substance, after which they may be preserved with the smallest details of feature for many years.

Mummification may prevent putrefaction in the dry air of deserts, and even in the case of a body lying in a strong draught of air these changes may be indefinitely postponed by gradual drying. A similar result has been known to occur in the bodies of persons who have taken antimony for a long period prior to death, the antimony deposited all through the body acting as an antiseptic.

PUTRID FEVER (*puter*, rotten) is an old name for typhus fever.

PYÆMIA (πύον, pus ; αἷμα, blood) means a form of blood-poisoning in which abscesses appear in various parts of the body. (*See* BLOOD-POISONING.)

PYELITIS (πύελος, a vessel) means inflammation of that part of the kidney known as the pelvis, which is connected with the ureter. It is now realized, however, that the infection is seldom restricted to the pelvis, but involves the kidney tissue as well. In other words the correct diagnosis is pyelonephritis.

The inflammation may spread upwards from the bladder or may follow on febrile diseases in which bacteria leave the body by the urine. One of the commonest organisms productive of this condition is the *Escherichia coli*, which produces a highly acid state of the urine accompanied by the presence of pus. Pyelitis sometimes occurs as a complication of pregnancy. There are generally symptoms of feverishness, general malaise, loss of weight, discomfort in the region of the loins, and frequency in passing water. Examination reveals the presence of the infecting organism and of pus in the urine.

Treatment.—In some cases the administration of alkalis and the drinking of ample bland fluids are all that

is required. As a rule, however, more active treatment is necessary and this consists of the administration of mandelic acid, one of the sulphonamides, or an antibiotic. As pyelitis may be due to some other condition of the kidney, such as a stone, a full investigation is necessary, as such cases will not clear up unless the underlying cause is removed.

PYELOGRAPHY is the term applied to the process whereby the kidneys are rendered radio-opaque, and therefore visible on an X-ray film. It constitutes a most important part of the examination of a patient with kidney disease. (*See* IODOXYL.)

PYELONEPHRITIS (see PYELITIS.)

PYKNOLEPSY is the term applied to a type of epilepsy in which the only manifestation is a sudden and temporary loss of consciousness. There are no convulsions and the attacks tend to disappear in time.

PYLEPHLEBITIS (πύλη, gate ; φλέψ, vein) means inflammation of the portal vein. It usually results from disease in the intestine and is part of a general blood-poisoning.

PYLOROSPASM means spasm of the pyloric portion of the stomach. This interferes with the passage of food in a normal, gentle fashion into the intestine and causes the pain that comes on from half an hour to three hours after meals and is associated with severe disorders of digestion. It is very frequently produced by an ulcer of the stomach or duodenum.

PYLORUS (πυλωρός, gate - keeper) means the lower or right opening of the stomach, through which the softened and partially digested food passes into the small intestine.

PYO- (πύον, pus) is a prefix attached to the name of various diseases to indicate cases in which pus is formed, such as pyo-nephrosis.

PYOGENIC (πύον, pus ; γεννάω, I produce) is a term applied to those bacteria which cause the formation of pus and so lead to the formation of abscesses. Although many bacteria have this property, the most common cause of abscess is one of the rounded forms of bacterium (*e.g.* streptococcus).

PYORRHŒA (πύον, pus ; ῥέω, I flow) is the name given to any copious discharge of pus. For *Pyorrhœa alveolaris* see under TEETH, DISEASES OF.

PYRETOTHERAPY is the term applied to the treatment of disease by raising the temperature of the body above normal.

PYREXIA (πυρέσσω, I am fevered) means fever. (*See* FEVER.)

PYRIDINE is an alkaloidal substance derived from coal-tar, tobacco, etc. It is added to methylated spirit in order to render this undrinkable.

PYRIDOXINE is the term now given to vitamin B_6. It plays an important part in the metabolism of a number of amino-acids. Deficiency leads to atrophy of the epidermis, the hair follicles, and the sebaceous glands, and peripheral neuritis may also occur. Young infants are more susceptible to pyridoxine deficiency than adults : they begin to lose weight and develop a hypochromic anæmia ; irritability and convulsions

may also occur. Liver, yeast, and cereals are relatively rich sources of it. Fish is a moderately rich source, but vegetables and milk contain little. The minimal daily requirement in the diet is probably about 2 mg.

PYRIMETHAMINE is an antimalarial drug which is particularly valuable as a prophylactic.

PYRO- (πῦρ, fire) is a prefix meaning anything connected with fire or produced by heating.

PYROGALLIC ACID is a substance derived from gallic acid and used in the treatment of psoriasis. It has the disadvantage of staining the skin a deep brown colour.

PYROSIS (πύρωσις, heat), or WATER-BRASH, is a symptom of dyspepsia consisting of an irritable, burning pain in the throat, accompanied by the constant secretion of mouthfuls of saliva. (*See* DYSPEPSIA.)

PYROXYLIN is another name for gun-cotton, which is used for producing collodion. (*See* COLLODION.)

PYURIA (πύον, pus ; οὖρον, urine) means the presence of pus in the urine, in consequence of inflammation situated in the kidney, bladder, or other part of the urinary tract. (*See* URINE.)

Q

Q FEVER is a disease of world-wide distribution, due to the *Rickettsia burnetii.* The disease is primarily one of animals, involving cattle, sheep and goats, and half the cases reported in England have been due to drinking unpasteurized milk. The disease occurs in small epidemics, and is characterized by fever and minor pneumonia. The incubation period is two to three weeks, and the disease lasts for about a fortnight. It responds well to chloramphenicol, chlortetracycline, or oxytetracycline.

QUADRICEPS is the name of the large four-headed muscle occupying the front and sides of the thigh, which straightens the leg at the knee-joint and maintains the body in an upright position.

QUADRIPLEGIA means paralysis of the four limbs of the body.

QUARANTINE (Ital. *quaranta*, forty) means that principle of preventing the spread of infectious disease by which persons, baggage, merchandise, etc., likely to be infected or coming from an infected locality are isolated at frontiers or ports till their harmlessness has been proved to the satisfaction of the authorities. (*See* INFECTION.)

Originally quarantine, as its name implies, involved detention for forty days ; but, as this proved intolerable for persons engaged in business, the time of detention is now calculated so as simply to cover the incubation period of the disease, the presence of which is suspected.

Numerous international conferences upon the subject, notably one at Dresden in 1893, and one at Venice in 1897, have been held with the view of arriving at a uniform practice as regards quarantine in different countries. The diseases to which quarantine especially applies are cholera, yellow fever, and plague, and although Great Britain does not rely upon quarantine to prevent outbreaks of these diseases, this country has acquiesced, to a certain extent, in quarantine regulations for these diseases out of deference to the Continental countries.

The general practice with regard to quarantine is that when a serious disease breaks out in any country, the government of that country notifies surrounding governments as to the ports and other places that have become centres of infection. Any persons travelling from these centres and attempting to enter another country, are detained long enough to see whether they will develop the disease or not, and in this interval their clothes, baggage, and other effects are disinfected.

QUARTAN AGUE (*quartus*, the fourth) is that form of malaria which returns after intermissions of two days, *i.e.* every fourth day. (*See* MALARIA.)

QUASSIA is the wood of *Picræna excelsa*, a large West Indian tree. Its virtues depend upon the presence of an active principle, quassin, which is excessively bitter and also irritating. The various preparations of the wood are mainly used as a bitter tonic (*see* BITTERS).

QUICKENING (*see* PREGNANCY).

QUILLAIA is the bark of *Quillaia saponaria*, or soap-bark, a South American tree. Tincture of quillaia is used in cases of bronchitis, pleurisy, and for making emulsions, in doses of about 60 minims (4 ml.).

QUINIDINE is an alkaloid obtained from cinchona bark and closely related in chemical composition and in action to quinine. It is commonly used in the form of quinidine sulphate in doses of 3 to 10 grains (200 to 600 mg.). It is used in the treatment of cardiac irregularity due to the condition of atrial fibrillation, being particularly useful in cases of the latter condition of recent onset.

QUININE is an alkaloid obtained from the bark of various species of cinchona trees. This bark is mainly derived from Peru and neighbouring parts of South America and the East Indies. For the story of its introduction *see* MALARIA. Other alkaloids and acid substances are also derived from cinchona bark, such as quinidine and cinchonine, but these closely resemble quinine in action.

Quinine is generally used in the form of one of its salts, such as the sulphate of quinine, or hydrochloride of quinine. All are sparingly soluble in water, much more so when taken along with an acid.

Action.—Quinine lessens the activity of lowly forms of life. It is therefore a powerful antiseptic. Its best-known action is as an ' anti-periodic ' in checking the recurrence of attacks of malarial fever, and this action it exerts by virtue of its destructive power against the malarial parasite in the blood. In fevers it acts as an ' antipyretic ', having a powerful action in reducing temperature.

In small doses it has a stimulating effect upon the stomach, although larger doses are capable of acting upon an irritable stomach to produce great nausea and vomiting. Small doses have also a stimulating action upon the nervous system and a general tonic effect, whilst large doses cause decided depression of the respiration and the heart's action.

Among the other unpleasant effects, due to large doses, are ringing in the ears, temporary impairment of vision, and sometimes irritation of the kidneys: all these pass off when the drug is discontinued.

Uses.—The most important use of quinine is its original one in malaria, attacks of which it quickly cuts short or prevents altogether, but it has largely been replaced by the more effective and less toxic antimalarial drugs now available. (*See* MALARIA.) For hypodermic injection, when this is necessary in cases of malaria, a soluble form of quinine, the dihydrochloride, is used in doses of 5 to 10 grains (300 to 600 mg.). Blackwater fever has by some been attributed to the excessive use of quinine in severe cases of malaria. Ammoniated solution of quinine given in teaspoonful doses in water is a favourite household remedy in feverish colds and other mild febrile attacks. Quinine and urea hydrochloride is employed as a local anæsthetic with a prolonged effect. Quinine hydrochloride has been used with urethane as a sclerosing agent in the treatment of varicose veins (*q.v.*).

As a ' tonic ', minute doses of quinine are used. For example, a single grain of quinine is often given after meals, or it is more commonly combined with other ' tonics ', as in the citrate of iron and quinine, or in syrup of the phosphate of iron with quinine and strychnine.

QUINSY is a corruption of *cynanche* (κυνάγκη), and is an old name for a peritonsillar abscess (*q.v.*).

QUOTIDIAN AGUE (*quotidie*, daily) means a type of malaria in which the attack recurs daily. (*See* MALARIA.)

R

RABIES (*rabies*, madness) is an acute and very fatal disease which affects the lower animals, particularly carnivora, and may be communicated from them to man.

Cause.—The disease is in existence constantly among dogs and wolves in some countries, and from these it spreads widely now and then in epidemics. It also occurs in foxes, coyotes and skunks, as well as vampire bats. Thanks to the Muzzling Order and quarantine measures, it has been practically stamped out in Great Britain since 1897. It is highly infectious from the bite of an animal already affected, but the chance of infection from different animals varies. Thus only about one person in every four bitten by rabid dogs contracts hydrophobia, whilst the bites of rabid wolves and cats almost invariably produce the disease. Bites on exposed parts, like the face, are more dangerous than those got through the clothes. The disease is due to a virus which has a special affinity for attacking the nervous system. The test as to whether a dog, which has died, suffered from rabies, is to inject a preparation made from part of its brain into another animal, and to watch the latter for signs of the disease. In the brain of an affected animal, certain microscopic appearances known as *Negri bodies* can usually be found. The saliva of infected animals is highly poisonous.

Symptoms.—In animals there are two types of the disease, 'mad' rabies and 'dumb' rabies. In the former, the dogs run about, snapping at objects and other animals, unable to rest; in the latter, which is also the final stage of the 'mad' type, the limbs become paralysed, and the dog crawls about or lies still.

In man the incubation period is usually six to eight weeks, but may be as short as ten days or as long as a year—or even more. The disease begins by mental symptoms, the person becoming irritable, restless, and melancholy. At the same time, feverishness and difficulty of swallowing gradually come on. After a couple of days or so, the irritability passes into a state of wildness or terror, there is great difficulty in swallowing either food or drink. Even the mere sight of fluid may induce spasm of the muscles of the mouth and throat : hence the common name for the disease—hydrophobia (fear of water). Breathing, too, becomes difficult, because of spasm of the respiratory muscles. The flow of saliva is great, and therefore the patient is constantly spitting, and has a dry, short cough, which has given rise to the popular idea that he 'barks' like a dog. A loud noise, a bright light, and particularly any attempt to drink are sufficient to throw the person into a convulsion. Convulsions and attacks of maniacal excitement become more frequent, and although between these the patient may be quite sensible and able to talk rationally, he becomes gradually weaker. Finally, about four days after the onset of the disease, the patient dies of exhaustion.

Treatment.—The best treatment is, of course, preventive, and this may be attained by strict muzzling regulations and the slaughter of all animals bitten by, or coming into contact with, rabid dogs. If a person has been bitten by a dog supposed to be rabid, the dog should not be killed at once, but should be carefully isolated for ten days ; if, after this period it is still alive, it was non-infective at the time of biting.

Local treatment consists of immediate, thorough, and careful cleansing of the wound surfaces and surrounding skin with 20 per cent. soap solution or any other detergent. Special attention should be paid to any deep fang punctures, which should be carefully probed with a swab-stick dipped in strong nitric acid. Immediate suture of lacerations should not be carried out.

This is followed by a dose of antirabies serum. As soon as the diagnosis is established, the patient is started on a course of rabies vaccine therapy. This was introduced by Pasteur in 1885, and consists of a suspension of the brain substance of animals infected with rabies. Daily subcutaneous injections for 14 to 21 days. Although this treatment occasionally fails, it has been successful in thousands of cases.

743

When the bitten person develops the disease, all that can be done is to quiet the convulsion by intravenous injections of a barbiturate.

RACHIANÆSTHESIA is the method of producing anæsthesia of a part of the body by the injection of anæsthetic drugs into the space round the spinal cord.

RACHITIS (ῥάχις, the spine) is another name for rickets. (*See* RICKETS.)

RADIATION SICKNESS is the term applied to the nausea, vomiting, and loss of appetite which may follow the use of radiotherapy in the treatment of cancer and other diseases. The antihistamine drugs are proving of value in its prevention and treatment.

RADICULITIS is the condition in which the root or roots of a spinal nerve is or are inflamed.

RADIOACTIVE ISOTOPES (*see* ISOTOPES).

RADIOGRAPHY (*see* X-RAYS).

RADIOSTOL is a substance produced by the action of ultra-violet light upon ergosterol, and contains a large amount of vitamin D.

RADIOTHERAPY is the term applied to treatment by radium or other radioactive matter, including X-rays. For long, radium and X-rays were the only sources available. Developments in our knowledge of atomic energy, however, have changed the picture entirely, and we have now at our disposal radioactive isotopes (*q.v.*) and X-ray machines which have largely replaced radium, except in the case of certain tumours.

Supervoltage X-ray machines are now available capable of producing X-rays generated at up to 22 million electron volts (22 MeV). These include linear accelerators which produce X-rays at four or more million electron volts, and betatrons which produce X-rays at 22 million electron volts. The advantage of these supervoltage machines is that it is predominantly γ-rays they produce, which are penetrating rays and can therefore be used to treat deep-seated tumours.

744

Almost equally high concentrations of γ-rays can now be obtained from the use of certain radioactive isotopes, particularly cobalt and cæsium. Thus a telecobalt machine is now in use, which contains 2000 curies or more of radioactive cobalt (Co^{60}), an amount equivalent to 3000 grammes of radium (an unheard-of amount—the ordinary radium beam units contained only 10 grammes of radium). Not only does this machine give a high concentration of γ-rays (equivalent to that from a 3 million-volt X-ray machine), it is absolutely safe for both patient and operators, and allows the beam to be directed accurately on the tumour.

RADIUM.—The radiations of radium consist of : (1) α-rays, which are positively charged helium nuclei ; (2) β-rays, negatively charged electrons ; (3) γ-rays, similar to X-rays but of shorter wave-length.

Treatment by radium.—Radium salts are applied enclosed in various forms of applicator, most commonly a thin tube or plaque enclosed within a capsule of aluminium or platinum. External screens are made to enclose these fine tubes, serving the double purpose of filtration of the less penetrating rays and strengthening the applicators against damage when inserted into a tumour.

At the present day the use of radium is largely restricted to the treatment of carcinoma of the neck of the womb, the tongue, and the lips.

Neither X-rays nor radium supersede active surgical measures when these are available for the complete removal of a tumour.

RADIUS is the outer of the two bones in the forearm. (*See* BONE.)

RAG-SORTERS' DISEASE is another name for anthrax. (*See* ANTHRAX.)

RAILWAY SPINE is a form of compensation neurosis, in which the victim of a railway accident persists in complaining of pain in the back even though no cause for this can be found.

RANULA (*ranula*, a little frog) is the name given to a swelling which occasionally appears beneath the tongue, caused by a collection of saliva in the distended duct of a salivary gland. (*See* MOUTH, DISEASES OF.)

RAPHE (ῥαφή, seam) means a ridge or furrow between the halves of an organ.

RAREFACTION is the term applied to the diminution in the density of a bone as a result of withdrawal of calcium salts from it.

RASH (*see* ERUPTION).

RAT-BITE FEVER is an infectious disease following the bite of a rat. It has an incubation period of about two weeks, followed by a reddish rash, fever, and muscular pains, and it usually passes off in two or three weeks.

RAUWOLFIA is a drug which is now being used in the treatment of high blood-pressure, and as a tranquillizer. It is derived from the root of *Rauwolfia serpentina*, a plant which grows widely in India, Ceylon, Burma, and Malaya. The active medicinal properties, which reside mainly in the root of the plant, have been recognized for centuries in India, where extracts of the root were used for the treatment of fevers, insomnia, and nervousness.

It is mainly used in the form of reserpine, which is an alkaloid obtained from the root of the plant. (*See* ESSENTIAL HYPERTENSION *and* TRANQUILLIZERS.)

RAY-FUNGUS is the organism that causes woody tongue. (*See* ACTINOMYCOSIS.)

RAYNAUD'S DISEASE, so called after Maurice Raynaud (1834–81), the Paris physician who published a thesis on the subject in 1862, is a condition in which the circulation becomes suddenly obstructed in outlying parts of the body. It is supposed to be due to spasm of the smaller arteries in the part affected, as the result of nervous influences, and its effects are increased both by cold and by various diseases affecting the blood-vessels. It is predominantly a disease of women, the

majority of cases occurring before the age of 40.

Symptoms.—The condition is most commonly confined to the occurrence of 'dead fingers', the fingers or the toes, ears, or nose becoming white, numb, and waxy-looking. The circulation is often so much reduced that the part does not bleed if pricked or cut. This condition may last for some minutes, or may not pass off for several hours, or even for a day or two. Persons affected in this way are often of a decidedly nervous temperament, and suffer from 'bilious attacks' and other nervous disturbances.

In a more severe type, which depends apparently upon irregular contractions of the veins as well as of the arteries, periodic attacks come on in a similar manner, but the fingers and other parts affected, instead of being cold and white, are swollen, purple, and tingling.

In a third form, which is fortunately rare, after repeated attacks of one of the other forms, the circulation becomes so much cut off that the part dies and a localized gangrene results.

Treatment.—Persons who are subject to these attacks should be careful in winter to protect the feet and hands from cold, and should always use warm water when washing the hands. In addition, the whole body should be kept warm, as spasm of the arterioles in the feet and hands may be induced by chilling of the body. Victims of this disease should be advised to give up smoking. Iodides are also of value in early cases. In all cases which do not respond to such medical treatment, surgery should be considered in the form of sympathectomy, *i.e.* cutting of the sympathetic nerves to the affected part. This results in dilatation of the arterioles and hence an improved blood supply. This operation is more successful in the case of the feet than in the case of the hands.

RAYON, OILED, consists of rayon fabric made waterproof with drying oils or oil-modified synthetic resins.

RECTUM (*rectus*, straight) is the last part of the large intestine. It pursues a more or less straight course downwards

24 a

through the cavity of the pelvis, lying against the sacrum at the back of this cavity. This section of the intestine is about 9 inches (23 cm.) long. Its first part is freely movable and corresponds to the upper three pieces of the sacrum, the second part corresponds to the lower two pieces of the sacrum and the coccyx, whilst the third part, known also as the anal canal, is about 1 inch (25 mm.) long, runs downwards and backwards, and is kept tightly closed by the internal and external sphincter muscles which surround it. The opening to the exterior is known as the anus. The structure of the rectum is similar to that of the rest of the intestine. (*See* INTESTINE.)

RECTUM, DISEASES OF.—Owing to the fact that this part of the intestine is more exposed to external influences than the rest of the bowels, and that it forms the place of lodgment of the stools prior to the evacuation of the bowels, and is therefore often subject to considerable irritation, the rectum is specially liable to various diseases. Peculiarities of the motions are treated under STOOLS, while PILES and FISTULA are described under these headings. DIARRHŒA and CONSTIPATION are also treated separately.

IMPERFORATE ANUS, or absence of the anus, may occur in newly born children, and, unless the condition be relieved by operation within a few days, the child dies.

ITCHING at the anal opening, or PRURITUS ANI, is often very troublesome. It may be due to slight abrasions, the presence of threadworms, piles, and sometimes sexual irregularities. All stimulants, mustard, and pepper must be avoided in the diet. After evacuation of the bowels, the part should be bathed with cottonwool and warm or cold water ; it is sometimes an advantage to add starch to the water. Toilet paper should not be used. In addition, the area should be bathed once or twice a day. Clothing should be loose and smooth—preferably cotton or linen next to the skin. Calamine lotion, containing 1 per cent. phenol, or 0·1 to 0·5 per cent. camphor, is soothing—applied as a compress on gauze at night and dabbed on during the day. The local application of

hydrocortisone ointment is often effective.

PAIN of an acute cutting character, at stool, is often due to the presence of a small ulcer or ' fissure ', which, owing to movements of the sphincter, will not heal ; it is treated by rubbing the ulcer with a caustic point or injecting into it an analgesic of prolonged action. The pain soon disappears. Pain of an aching nature is not uncommonly caused by the presence of piles.

ULCERATION may occur here in the course of tuberculous disease of the bowels, in dysentery, or even as the result of the constant irritation due to long-continued constipation. Ulcers in this locality cause a discharge of matter and frequently streaks of blood mixed with the motions. If the ulcer lasts a long time it may lead to narrowing and obstruction of the bowel.

ABSCESS in the cellular tissue at the side of the rectum, known from its position as an ischio-rectal abscess, is fairly frequent. It often arises at a late stage in the course of pulmonary tuberculosis, and is a serious sign with regard to hope of ultimate cure of the disease. It may also arise, like an abscess elsewhere, as the result of injury, exposure to cold, and other debilitating influences. In any case it is likely to produce a fistula (*see* FISTULA).

PROLAPSE or protrusion of the rectum is sometimes found in children, usually between the ages of six months and two years. In slight cases, where a ring of bright red mucous membrane half an inch or an inch in width protrudes as the result of straining at stool, the condition is generally easily curable by care. Any irritable condition of the bowels due to diarrhœa, constipation, worms, etc., must be removed and the evacuations regulated by diet and laxatives, so as to avoid all straining. Each time the bowels move, the protruded portion must be returned by steady pressure with a cloth or sponge wrung out of cold water. If the bowel comes down when the child runs about, the wearing of a suitable pad is necessary and the child must lie down for some time each day. Various astringent injections are also used, and the general health is attended to by tonics and other suitable treatment. When the protruded part is very large and the condition does not yield to simple treatment it can be remedied by operation.

TUMOURS of small size situated on the skin near the opening of the bowel, and consisting of nodules, tags of skin, cauliflower-like excrescences, etc., are common, and may give rise to pain, itching, watery discharges, etc. These are easily removed if necessary. Polypi occasionally develop within the rectum, and may give rise to no pain, though they may cause frequent discharges of blood. Like polypi elsewhere, they may often be removed by a minor operation.

CANCER of the rectum is fairly common, this part of the bowel being one of the chief sites of this disease. It is a disease of later life, seldom affecting young people, and its appearance is generally insidious. The tumour begins commonly in the mucous membrane, its structure resembling that of the glands with which the membrane is furnished, and it quickly infiltrates the other coats of the intestine and then invades neighbouring organs. Secondary growths in most cases occur soon in the lymphatic glands within the abdomen and in the liver. The symptoms appear gradually and consist of diarrhœa, alternating with attacks of constipation, and, later on, discharges of blood or of thin bloodstained fluid from the bowels, together with increasing thinness and weakness, and pains about the lower part of the back and down the thighs. Upon examination, the tumour can be felt projecting from one side or in a ring-form into the interior of the bowel. These cases are usually far advanced before they give rise to much disturbance, but much can now be done to help them by surgical operation. In the majority of cases this consists of removal of the whole of the rectum and the distal twothirds of the sigmoid colon, and the establishment of a colostomy. The latest available figures show that approximately 50 per cent. of the patients who have this operation are alive and well after five years. In some cases in which the growth occurs in the upper part of the rectum it is now possible to remove the growth and preserve the anus so that the patient is saved the discomfort of having a colostomy.

RECURRENT LARYNGEAL NERVE is a branch of the vagus nerve which leaves the latter low down in its course, and, hooking round the right subclavian artery on the right side and round the arch of the aorta on the left, runs up again into the neck, where it enters the larynx and supplies branches to the muscles which control the vocal cords. The importance of this nerve consists in the fact that it is apt in this long course to be pressed upon, especially when aneurysm of the aorta or right subclavian artery is present, and thus defects of vocalization may point to disease situated within the chest.

RED GUM is the popular name for a red rash that often appears in children about teething-time, generally associated with diarrhœa. It is treated by care in dieting.

The term is also applied to the gum of the eucalyptus tree, which has astringent properties and is much used in throat pastilles.

RED LOTION is a lotion containing sulphate of zinc, compound tincture of lavender which gives it a red colour, and water. It is used as an astringent application to ulcers.

REDUPLICATION is a term applied to a peculiarity in the heart-sounds as heard by auscultation. Whilst it is found in certain diseases of the heart, such as obstruction at the mitral valve, it also occurs in normal hearts.

REDUX (*redux*, returned) is a term applied to the reappearance of certain signs or symptoms which are absent at the height of a disease, and the reappearance of which indicates that the disease is passing off. Such are 'redux crepitations' at the end of pneumonia.

REFLEX ACTION is one of the simplest forms of activity of the nervous system. (For the mechanism upon which it depends, *see* NERVES.) Reflex acts are divided usually into three classes. *Superficial reflexes* comprise the sudden movements which result when the skin is brushed or pricked, such as the movement of the toes that results from stroking the sole of the foot. *Deep reflexes* depend upon the state of mild contraction in which muscles are constantly maintained when at rest, and are obtained, as in the case of the knee-jerks, by sharply tapping the tendon of the muscle in question. *Visceral reflexes* are those connected with various organs, such as the narrowing of the pupil when a bright light is directed upon the eye, the contraction of the bladder when distended by urine, etc.

Faults in these reflexes, both in the direction of excess and of diminution, give valuable evidence as to the presence of nervous diseases and the part of the nervous system in which such disease is situated. Thus, absence of the knee-jerk, when the patellar tendon is tapped, means some interference with the sensory nerve, nerve-cells, or motor nerve upon which the act depends, as, for example, in locomotor ataxia, infantile paralysis, or peripheral neuritis; whilst an excessive jerk implies that the controlling influence exerted by the brain upon this reflex mechanism has been cut off, as, for example, by a tumour high up in the spinal cord, or in the disease known as disseminated sclerosis.

The condition of the plantar reflex (obtained by stroking the skin of the sole of the foot) is an important point in diagnosing organic disease of the nervous system. The normal reflex consists in bending downwards of the toes towards the sole. In organic disease of the higher parts of the nervous system the great toe tends to bend upwards with spreading out of the other toes (Babinski's sign).

The reflex of the pupil to light is also of great diagnostic importance. The pupil quickly contracts when light falls upon the eye or when the eyes are directed suddenly to a near object. In certain serious diseases of the nervous system, especially in general paralysis and locomotor ataxia, the contraction on looking at a near object remains, while the effect of light is lost (Argyll-Robertson pupil).

REFRACTION (*see* SPECTACLES).

REFRIGERANTS (*refrigero*, I cool) are substances which relieve thirst and

give a feeling of coolness. The chief refrigerants are acidulous drinks such as lemon juice, weak mineral acids, tartaric acid, etc., in water. The parched condition of the mouth and throat that arises during hard work in a dry and dusty atmosphere is best relieved by water to which has been added some demulcent substance which forms a coating on the dried mucous membrane. Such liquids are obtained by mixing oatmeal or milk with water. (*See also* CITRIC ACID *and* IMPERIAL DRINK.)

REFRIGERATION ANÆSTHESIA (*see* CRYMOTHERAPY).

REFUSE and SEWAGE DISPOSAL. —*Dry refuse* consists of the ashes and dust of houses and buildings, food remnants of animal or vegetable origin, the sweepings of streets and open spaces, and the manure of animals.

Sewage, in towns supplied with water-closets, includes the urine and fæces, the waste waters of households, the effluents of trades, and the drainage from the soil, together with a large proportion of the rainfall. This liquid refuse is removed by a system of drains and sewers, known as the ' water-carriage system ', to the place where it is to be destroyed or otherwise disposed of. The method of removal is treated in a special article (*see* WATER-CLOSETS, DRAINS, AND SEWERS) ; its ultimate disposal is described farther on in this article.

1. DRY METHODS OF DISPOSAL. —The dry refuse in towns is usually at the present time stored in small covered tubs placed in the yard, or set at specified times on the street to be carted away, preferably daily, by the scavengers.

The dry refuse from houses should mainly consist of ashes, all food remnants being burnt in the kitchen fire. To this refuse from houses there are added sweepings from streets, the contents of gulleys, the manure and trade refuse from slaughter-houses, fish and fruit shops, and it may then be disposed of to farmers for agricultural purposes.

Frequently, owing to the impossibility of providing water-closets and sewers for the removal of human excreta, the urine and fæces have to be dealt with along with the ' dry ' refuse. This implies the use of *middens* or the various forms of *dry closets*.

Middens originally consisted of a hole dug in the earth, into which all offensive matters were thrown, leading to the formation of offensive gases and the pollution of the soil round about. Over the midden, some form of ' privy ' was erected, but the practice in itself was most objectionable and offensive. In order to minimize the unpleasant emanations, it is usual in rural districts and in towns where middens still exist, to mix the excreta with various substances, such as ashes, earth, and charcoal, which absorb the moisture, thus keeping the excreta dry to some extent, and preventing too early putrefaction. Nowadays, the midden pit usually consists of a small suitable receptacle under the seat of the closet, instead of a hole dug in the ground. The Ministry of Health of England, in order to make the midden and privy system as little offensive as possible, have suggested a series of by-laws by which the privy must be at least 6 feet from the nearest dwelling, 50 feet from a well, properly roofed, with the floor paved and sloped to the door, so that no rain may enter, and so that all liquids spilt on the floor may run outside and not enter the receptacle.

The receptacle must be lined with some impermeable material, unconnected with any drain, and not more than 8 cubic feet in size, so that its contents will require to be removed at least once a week by the scavenger, whilst the seat must be hinged, to allow of the ready addition of ashes. Even with all these precautions, the system of privy middens is highly objectionable and insanitary, and their construction in relation to new buildings is now forbidden.

Pail closets are simply small middens, consisting of a tub or pail placed under the seat of the closet, composed of iron or tarred wood, and not exceeding 2 cubic feet in capacity, with a close-fitting lid, and easily removable at least once a week. To the excreta are added various absorbent materials, rendering the contents as dry as possible, and so hindering decomposition.

Ashes, charcoal, and earth all fulfil this object, and act also as deodorants. In some cases, all the household refuse is added, whilst in others, as in the *Goux system*, the pail is lined with some absorbent material which absorbs the moisture. In this system, excreta only enter the pail, and a fresh pail is substituted every two or three days. In the *charcoal closet*, the charcoal acts as a dryer and powerful deodorant, and the resultant mixture is deprived of offensive emanations. The charcoal may be re-burned in retorts and used over again.

Earth closets form a suitable method in which the excreta are largely disintegrated. The receptacle should be made of stout, galvanized iron and should not exceed 2 cubic feet in capacity. In one of the special types, *Moule's earth closet*, the earth is dried previous to use and sprinkled over the excreta, half a pound of earth being usually allowed for each person. The earth deodorises and dries the excreta, leads to their disintegration, and consequently the earth closet is probably one of the best forms of pail closet.

Elsan closets are a newer and more satisfactory form used where there are no sewers and earth closets are unsuitable. The excreta are received into a pail containing a solution which is deodorant and disinfectant and which helps to liquefy the solids. They are much used in country places and temporarily for public gatherings, aeroplanes, etc.

Ultimate disposal of this dry refuse, whether singly or mixed with human excreta, varies in different towns. The street sweepings and animal manure are often sold for agricultural purposes. The human excreta, whether alone or mixed with ashes or earth, are also spread over fields. The ashes and dry refuse, such as broken glass and general debris, are still in places used to fill up large holes, such as disused quarries, and to raise up the level of hollows, thus forming ' made ' soils. But just as all animal and vegetable food remnants should be burnt in the kitchen fire, so the general refuse of towns is now in many places cremated in 'destructors'. These consist briefly of furnaces into which the refuse is thrown from above and burned, high temperatures being maintained by means of forced draughts. The indestructible portions which are removed at the bottom constitute what is known as ' clinker '. This may be ground down, and, when mixed with lime, is disposed of as mortar, whilst the ' clinker' itself, sifted into suitable sizes, is largely employed in the formation of ' beds ' in the biological treatment of sewage (see below). The heat generated in the destructor may be utilized for working the machinery used in the general processes connected with the establishment, such as the grinding of mortar and the electric lighting of buildings. Thus, even the refuse of a town is a valuable commodity.

2. SEWAGE DISPOSAL. — Cesspools.—Formerly, a common method of disposing of sewage was to run it into a cesspool. This cesspool was formed of

ment to disconnect the cesspool from the house. Sometimes the liquid material is conducted in agricultural pipes lying 1 foot under the surface of the ground, in order to let it soak through into the soil and nourish the vegetation, after all solid excreta and grease have been intercepted by the cesspool, from which they are removed from time to time. Care must be taken that no danger results from the cesspool and its effluent ; consequently, a cesspool should be distant at least 50 feet from a dwelling, and at least 100 feet from a water supply. It is preferable, however, to use some method of sewage disposal other than that by cesspools, if it can be provided.

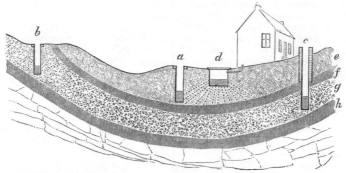

FIG. 324.—Diagram showing a common and objectionable arrangement of a cesspool. Its defects are that it is too near to the house, has no trap or other means of disconnection from the interior of the house, and is constructed of porous materials which allow pollution of the neighbouring soil. *a*, Surface well (polluted) ; *b*, surface well (safe) ; *c*, deep well ; *d*, cesspool ; *e* and *g*, porous strata ; *f* and *h*, impervious strata.

bricks or some porous material, so that the liquids soaked through and polluted the soil, while the solids accumulated and were removed for manure when the cesspool was full. Frequently these cesspools were placed in most objectionable situations, such as under the floor of the cellar, while occasionally they were so formed as to act only as catch-pits on the course of the drain for the solid materials, the liquid portions of the sewage flowing off into the sewer.

In country districts it may still be necessary to resort to the use of cesspools for single houses. They should be made of some impervious material, such as brickwork, lined internally with a layer of cement, well ventilated, cleaned at regular intervals, and should be provided with a trap or other arrange-

Discharge into river or sea.—It was the common custom before the Rivers Pollution Act, 1876, came into force in Great Britain, simply to run the sewage of a town or district into the nearest river or stream, with the consequent result that many rivers became thoroughly polluted and offensive. Where the rivers contain a large supply of fresh water, natural purification is undergone, but, if the supply of sewage is great, this process is entirely insufficient to render the stream pure.

The sewage may be discharged directly into the *sea*, the outfall of the sewer being placed below the level of the lowest tide, and so situated that the sewage will be carried out at once into the sea by currents, and not cast up on the shore in front of the town. To prevent the sea water entering the sewer, a tidal valve should be placed over the end of the sewer, so that the opening may close by the force of the water dashing against it. If there is difficulty at low tides, the sewage can be stored in tanks, and then allowed to flow out at times when the tide is suitable.

If discharge into the sea is not practicable, purification of the sewage is essential, and if discharge of the effluent into a river is finally necessary, certain standards must be observed. The effluent must not contain more than 3 parts of suspended solids per 100,000. No sewage effluent should absorb more than 2 parts by weight of dissolved oxygen per 100,000 in 5 days at 18° C., and the river, after receiving the effluent, should not absorb more than 0·4 part in the same time. Certain modifications of these standards are allowed in the case of larger rivers; and when the river is more than 500 times the volume of the effluent, the only treatment of the sewage necessary is screening to remove the larger solid matters.

Precipitation. — Various processes have been introduced from time to time so as to render the effluent from the sewage more fit to be discharged into streams. The sewage is accordingly gathered in collecting tanks where the solid matter may settle. To hasten this process, various chemical agents have been utilized, the solid matters that are added settling and taking down with them the suspended materials of the sewage. The effluent is then discharged into a neighbouring stream or allowed to flow over land. *Lime* is one of the precipitants employed, about 15 grains to the gallon of sewage being allowed where lime slaked with water is used. Too much lime, however, renders the effluent alkaline, with a resultant tendency to putrefaction.

Sulphate of alumina renders the effluent acid, and acts as a good precipitant, although, when combined with lime in such proportions as to render the effluent practically neutral, its value is enhanced, the alumina carrying down the suspended organic materials of the sewage.

Proto-sulphate of iron, in addition to lime, is also employed ; so is lime in conjunction with *black ash waste* (prepared from the residue of alkali works), the latter constituent having considerable deodorant powers. In the *A B C* process a mixture of alum, blood, clay, and charcoal is employed, the second ingredient sometimes being excluded as unnecessary, the charcoal acting as the deodorant ; but the cost is considerable, though the precipitation is good.

The effluent from sewage treated by these processes is simply sewage freed from its solid suspended materials, the dissolved matters remaining. It can be discharged into a river, if swift running and with a sufficient volume of clean water, without the likelihood of a nuisance ; but, where these conditions cannot be obtained, it had better also be filtered through land or specially formed filter-beds.

The *sludge*, the result of the settling in tanks, may be dealt with in various ways. It may be allowed to flow in its semi-liquid condition over land into which it is dug later on, or it may have its liquid part pressed out, or it may be dried with hot air, the resulting material being sold for manure.

Intermittent downward filtration, in which the purifying influence of the soil as an oxidizing agent is applied to the treatment of sewage, consists in the application of sewage at short intervals to a special piece of porous ground large enough to cleanse it efficiently. The requisites for such treatment are a porous, rich, loamy soil, with a good system of porous drains about 6 feet from the surface, the area being laid off in divisions, so that each plot may be in use for only six hours a day, resting for the remainder of the twenty-four hours. If the filter-beds are laid out in furrows along which the sewage flows, vegetables can be grown on the ridges, thus aiding in the purification, but the area of ground is limited, so that little use can be made of the manurial constituents of the sewage even where vegetables are produced. The Ministry of Health of England require 1 acre of land for each 1000 people where this process is in vogue, or, if preliminary treatment is employed to precipitate the sewage, 1 acre will suffice for 2000 persons. The resulting effluent is good, bright, and clear, and may be passed into streams.

Broad irrigation implies the application of sewage over a large area of agricultural land with the production of as great an amount of vegetation as possible, consistent with sufficient purification. This is the principle of the various sewage farms for dealing with the sewage of towns. The sewage ought to be brought to the farm in as fresh a condition as possible, so that the maximum effect may be secured, the money obtained for the vegetation helping to reduce the cost of the management of the farm. The sewage should be screened by passing through coarse strainers, so as to remove the larger substances present and prevent them forming a scum over the land. The land should be so situated that the sewage may reach it by gravitation, should be porous, preferably loamy, and arranged in a gentle slope, so as to allow the sewage to spread over it easily. It may be prepared in a series of ridges about 30 to 60 feet broad with a main sewage conduit at the summit, the sewage being allowed to trickle down over the slope. When the quantity of sewage to the one part is deemed to be sufficient, the sewage can be directed to another portion by the interposition of a sluice or plate in the stream of the main carrier. The water passes through the soil and reaches the porous earthenware drains about 6 feet from the surface. These drains are separated from each other by distances of 20 to 100 feet, depending on the porosity of the soil of the farm. The growth on sewage farms is usually heavy, Italian rye-grass especially yielding abundant crops, and dealing by absorption with a large amount of sewage. Vegetables and cereals also may be grown on land which has been treated with sewage, but they should not, during their period of growth, be directly treated with sewage.

When the sewage filters through the soil, the solid suspended matters are arrested, while a natural nitrification is undergone, with the result that a passable effluent is produced, provided always that the sewage farm has been capably managed and the sewage efficiently dealt with. Sewage farms, if properly conducted, well constructed, and efficiently supervised, need not constitute a nuisance and give off offen-

752

sive effluvia, but if the farm is not well managed or is neglected, the soil may become waterlogged, and lead to offensive emanations and consequent nuisance.

The area required by the Ministry of Health of England in this method of treating sewage is 1 acre for every 300 persons, or, if precipitation is also combined, an acre will suffice for the sewage of 1000 individuals.

Biological methods of dealing with sewage are now being largely employed. They depend upon a combination of two processes, in the first of which the organic matter of the sewage is liquefied by the action of certain organisms (anaerobic), which act in the absence of oxygen; and in the second of which the liquefied sewage is exposed to the air and acted upon by other organisms (aerobic), which oxidize and destroy the organic constituents of the sewage, whilst these latter organisms may, in addition, aid in the liquefaction.

One of the forms of treatment—*Scott Moncrieff system* — accomplishes this liquefaction by means of an open tank filled with large stones between which the sewage rises slowly from below, and is acted on by the liquefying organisms that grow in large colonies among the stones. The oxidation process is attained by leading the resulting effluent through a series of filter-boxes placed one over the other with air spaces between, the sewage as it passes down in the form of heavy raindrops getting aerated, and the resulting effluent flowing off as a clear liquid.

In another system, known as the *septic tank system*, a tank, which is closed to cut off oxygen, is required in order to provide for the *liquefaction*, and into this tank the sewage passes, sufficient capacity being given to hold a large quantity of sewage. The sewage arrives in the tank without previous treatment. The solid, heavier matters sink to the bottom, while microbes, which grow when deprived of air, render more soluble the organic matters present. For the second stage in the treatment—the *oxidation* of the sewage —the effluent from the tank passes out beneath the scum on the surface of the sewage, and flows into an aerating trough, falling over the sides of this trough in thin sheets to the channels which lead to the filters provided for nitrification. It thus becomes well aerated and fit for the action of the aerobic organisms in the filter-beds. These filter-beds are filled with the sewage in turn, allowed to remain full for some time, being subsequently emptied and allowed to rest free, and become aerated again. The filters are formed of crushed clinker and coarse gravel, or of coke breeze.

The dimensions of such a system for sewage treatment may be briefly indicated from the fact that in a recent installation to cope with the sewage of a burgh having a population of almost 17,000, the septic tank measures 204 feet in length, 76 feet in width, and has a depth of about 19 feet. The continuously aerating filters employed have a measurement of 204 feet in length, and are almost 100 feet wide. Owing to the level reached by the tide interfering to some extent with the work of these filters, ' contact ' beds, in which the sewage remains for some time, and from which it is discharged at low tide, are employed, and are equal in dimensions to the filter-beds.

The latest development in this method of treating sewage is that known by the term ' activated sewage '. This, in brief, consists in taking some of the old sewage, which has been in a tank for a time and is rich in microbic life, then mixing it in certain proportions with the fresh sewage as it arrives at the sewage works. The mixture is kept in constant motion by special machinery and is aerated by compressed air being passed into it. This supply of oxygen enables the aerobic organisms to attack and purify the sewage. The result gives an excellent effluent, although there is some little difficulty in disposing of part of the sludge.

REGIONAL ILEITIS (*see under* ILE-ITIS).

REGURGITATION (*re*, back; *gurges*, a whirlpool) is a term used in various connections in medicine. For instance, in diseases of the heart it is used to indicate a condition in which, as the result of valvular disease, the blood does not entirely pass on from the auricles of the heart to the ventricles, or from the ventricles into the arteries. The defective valve is said to be ' incompetent ', and a certain amount of blood leaks past it, or ' regurgitates ' back into the cavity from which it has been driven (*see* HEART, DISEASES OF).

The term is also applied to the return to the mouth of food already swallowed and present in the gullet or stomach.

REHABILITATION. — The restoration to health and working capacity of a person incapacitated by disease, mental or physical, or by injury. A word that came into prominent use during the 1939–45 War, reflecting the growing awareness of the medical profession that the treatment of a sick or injured person does not end at the moment of recovery from the immediate effects of illness or injury. For example, a man with a fractured limb or spine has to recover full use not only of the injured part but of his whole body ; and he has to recover confidence in his ability to work and enjoy life. Rehabilitation centres have been set up in different parts of Great Britain, where men have graduated exercises, gymnastics, games, and occupational treatment.

REITER'S DISEASE is a condition characterized by arthritis, urethritis, and conjunctivitis. The cause of the condition is not known, but it sometimes responds to cortisone.

RELAPSE (*re*, back; *lapsus*, slipping) means the return of a disease during the period of convalescence. Many relapses are due to some injudicious exposure or exertion on the patient's part, or to some error in diet, although certain diseases, such as typhoid fever, are particularly liable to relapses.

RELAPSING FEVER, so-called because of the characteristic temperature chart (Fig. 325) showing recurring bouts of fever, is an infectious disease caused by spirochætes. There are two main forms of the disease.

LOUSE - BORNE RELAPSING FEVER is an epidemic disease, usually associated with wars and famines, which has occurred in practically every country in the world. For long confused with typhus and typhoid, it was not until the 1870's that the causal organism was described by Obermeier. It is now known as the *Treponema* (or *Spirochæta*) *recurrentis*, a motile spiral organism 10 to 20 µ in length. The organism is transmitted from man to man by the louse, *Pediculus humanus*.

Symptoms.—The incubation period is up to 12 days, usually 7 days. The onset is sudden, with high temperature, generalized aches and pains, and nosebleeding. In about half the cases a

is an endemic disease which occurs in most tropical and sub-tropical countries. The causative organism is *Treponema* (or *Spirochæta*) *duttoni*, which is transmitted by a tick, *Ornithodoros moubata*. David Livingstone suggested that it was a tick-borne disease, but it was not until 1905 that Dutton and Todd produced the definite evidence.

Symptoms.—The main differences from the louse-borne disease are : (a) the incubation period is usually shorter, 3 to 6 days, but may be as short as 2 days or as long as 12 ; (b) the febrile

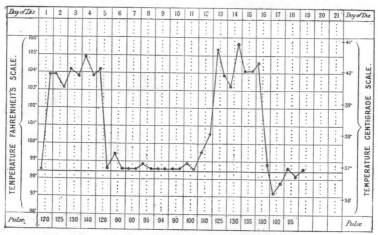

FIG. 325.—Temperature chart in a case of relapsing fever.

rash appears at an early stage, beginning in the neck and spreading down over the trunk and arms. Jaundice may occur ; and both the liver and the spleen are enlarged. The temperature subsides after five or six days, to rise again in about a week (Fig. 325). There may be up to four such relapses.

Treatment. — Preventive measures are the same as those for typhus (*q.v.*). Rest in bed is essential, as are good nursing and a light, nourishing diet. There is usually a quick response to penicillin. The tetracyclines and chloramphenicol are also effective. Arsenical therapy, with neoarsphenamine, is also widely used. Following such treatment the incidence of relapse is about 15 per cent. The mortality rate is low, except in a starved population.

TICK-BORNE RELAPSING FEVER
754

period is usually shorter and the afebrile periods are more variable in duration, sometimes only lasting for a day or two ; (c) relapses are much more numerous.

Treatment.—Preventive measures are more difficult to carry out than in the case of the louse-borne infection. Protective clothing should always be worn in 'tick country'. Old, heavily infected houses should be destroyed, Curative treatment is the same as for the louse-borne infection.

RELAXED THROAT (*see* THROAT, DISEASES OF, *and* CLERGYMAN'S SORE THROAT).

REMITTENT FEVER is the term applied to the form of fever in which, during remissions, the temperature falls, but not to normal.

RENAL DISEASES (*renes*, the kidneys). (*See* KIDNEYS, DISEASES OF.)

RENIN is a protein-like substance extracted from the kidney which, when injected into animals, causes a rise of blood-pressure. This it does, apparently, by reacting with a substance normally present in the blood plasma to produce ' angiotonin '. Angiotonin has been obtained in crystalline form, and it is angiotonin which causes the rise in blood-pressure. This work may have an important bearing on the problem of high blood-pressure in man.

RENNET is a substance prepared from the stomach of the calf, in order to curdle and partially digest milk. Its activity depends upon a ferment known as rennin, which is also present in human gastric juice.

REPAIR of tissues after injury is described generally under WOUNDS, and the repair of special tissues which present various peculiarities is described under BONE, MUSCLES, NERVES, etc.

RESECTION (*resectio*, a pruning) is the name given to an operation in which a part of some organ is removed, as, for example, the resection of a fragment of dead bone.

RESERPINE is an alkaloid obtained from the root of Rauwolfia (*q.v.*), and is used as an anti-hypertensive and a tranquillizing agent.

RESIN is the general name for a class of inflammable vegetable substances obtained from plants and trees. They are complex bodies resulting from the oxidation of volatile oils and containing many different substances and acids. When mixed with alkalis they form resin soaps. The chief resins are common resin, or rosin, obtained from the distillation of oil of turpentine from crude pine oil, Canada pitch, india-rubber, mastic, and as drugs, resins of guaiacum, jalap, and podophyllum.

Resins are chiefly used for making plasters. Oleo-resins are solutions of resin in volatile oils, such as copaiba and Canada turpentine. Gum resins are extracts from plants consisting of a mixture of gum and resin, the chief being ammoniacum, asafœtida, and myrrh. (*See also* ION EXCHANGE RESINS.)

RESOLUTION (*resolvo*, I loosen) is a term applied to infective processes, to indicate a natural subsidence of the inflammation without the formation of pus. Thus a pneumonic lung is said to ' resolve ' when the material exuded into it is absorbed into the blood and lymph, so that recovery takes place naturally ; an inflamed area is said to resolve when the inflammation fades away and no abscess forms ; a glandular enlargement is said to resolve when it decreases in size without suppuration. ' Resolvents ' was an old term applied to procedures capable of assisting this process. (*See* BLISTERS *and* INFLAMMATION.)

RESONANCE means the lengthening and intensification of sound produced by striking the body over an air-containing structure. Decrease of resonance is called dullness and increase of resonance is called hyper-resonance. The process of striking the chest or other part of the body to discover its degree of resonance is called percussion, and according to the note obtained, an opinion can be formed as to the state of consolidation of air-containing organs, the presence of abnormal cavities, and the dimensions and relations of solid and air - containing organs lying together. (*See* AUSCULTATION.)

RESORCIN, or RESORCINOL, is a white, crystalline, antiseptic substance soluble in water, alcohol, and oils. It is mainly used in skin diseases which require a stimulating and antiseptic application.

RESPIRATION (*respiratio*) is the process in which air passes into and out of the lungs with the object of allowing the blood to absorb oxygen and to give off carbon dioxide and water.

Mechanism of respiration.—For the structure of the respiratory apparatus see AIR PASSAGES, CHEST, LUNGS. The air passes rhythmically into and out of the air passages, and mixes with the air already in the lungs, these two movements being known as inspiration and expiration.

INSPIRATION is due to a muscular effort which enlarges the chest in all three dimensions, so that the lungs have to expand in order to fill up the vacuum that would otherwise be left, and the air accordingly enters these organs by the air passages. It must be understood that there is no direct pull upon the lungs, each of which is simply suspended within the corresponding pleural cavity by its root, and made to fill this cavity in all conditions of the chest by the pressure of the outer air exerted through the nose, mouth, and air passages. The increase of the chest in size from above downwards is mainly due to the diaphragm, the muscular fibres of which, by their contraction, reduce its domed shape and cause it to descend, pushing down the abdominal organs beneath it. The increase from before back is mainly due to a tilting forwards of the lower end of the breastbone, and of the lower rib cartilages. The increase from side to side can best be understood by examining a skeleton, noting the very oblique position of the lower ribs, and observing how greatly the capacity of the chest is increased when each is raised, in the manner of a bucket-handle, taking its fixed points at the spine and breast-bone. (*See* RIBS.)

The muscles which chiefly bring about these changes in ordinary quiet inspiration are the diaphragm, intercostal muscles, and levators of the ribs, whilst in forced or extraordinary inspiration, when a specially deep breath is taken, the sternomastoid, serratus magnus, trapezius, and pectoral muscles are also brought powerfully into play. Many other muscles take part to a slight extent, steadying the spine and the upper and lower ribs, while even the muscles of the face and of the larynx are thrown rhythmically into activity, dilating the nostrils and the entrance to the larynx at each breath.

EXPIRATION is in ordinary circum-

756

stances simply an elastic recoil, the diaphragm rising and the ribs sinking into the position that they naturally occupy, when muscular contraction is finished. Expiration occupies a slightly longer period than inspiration. In forced expiration many powerful muscles of the abdomen and thorax are brought into play, and the act may be made a very forcible one, as, for example, in coughing.

Nervous control. — Respiration is usually either an automatic or a reflex act, each expiration sending up afferent, sensory impulses to the central nervous system, from which efferent impulses are sent down various other nerves to the muscles that produce inspiration. It appears that there are several centres which govern the rate, force, etc., of the breathing, although all are presided over by a chief respiratory centre in the medulla oblongata, which is sometimes spoken of as the vital knot (*nœud vitale*). Although this centre appears to be absolutely essential to life, it in turn is under the control of the higher centres in the cerebral hemispheres, through which the will acts, so that breathing can be voluntarily stopped, quickened, or otherwise changed at will. It would be impossible, however, to cause death by voluntarily holding the breath, because, as the blood becomes more venous, the vital centre in the medulla again assumes control and breathing recommences. Apart from changes due to will-power, the respirations follow one another rhythmically at the rate of about 18 per minute, being in general one for every four heart-beats.

Quantity of air.—The lungs do not by any means completely empty themselves at each expiration and refill at each inspiration. An amount equivalent, in quiet respiration, to less than one-tenth of the total air in the lungs passes out and is replaced by the same quantity of fresh air, which mixes with the stale air in the lungs. This renewal, which in quiet breathing amounts to about 30 cubic inches or 1 pint of air (about 500 millilitres), is known as the *tidal air*. By a special inspiratory effort, one can, however, draw in about 180 cubic inches, *i.e.* over 6 pints of air or 3000 millilitres, this amount being known as *complemental air*. By a special expiratory effort too, after an ordinary breath one can expel much more than the tidal air from the lungs, this extra amount being known as the *supplemental* or *reserve air*, and amounting also to about 60 cubic inches or 1000 millilitres. If one takes as deep an inspiration as possible and then makes a forced expiration, one breathes out the sum of these three, which is known as the *vital capacity*, and amounts to about 4000 millilitres in a healthy adult male of average size. These figures all apply to a man of average height. There is a fairly close relationship between height and vital capacity : in man the vital capacity (in millilitres)=25×height (in centimetres). In women the vital capacity=20 × height. Over and above the vital capacity, the lungs contain air which cannot be emptied by the strongest possible expiration, and this *residual air*, which remains in the lungs even after death, amounts to at least another 1000–1500 millilitres.

Abnormal forms of respiration. — Apart from mere changes in rate and force, respiration is modified in several important ways, either involuntarily or voluntarily. *Sighing* is a long-drawn inspiration following a pause when breathing has been checked by mental preoccupation. This form of breathing also characterizes some conditions of extreme weakness of the nervous system, such as shock and diabetic coma. *Sobbing* is a series of convulsive inspiration, at each of which the larynx is partially closed ; it follows grief or great exertion. *Snoring* or stertorous breathing is due to a flaccid state of the soft palate causing it to vibrate as the air passes into the throat, or simply to sleeping with the mouth open, which has a similar effect. *Coughing* is a series of violent expirations, at each of which the larynx is suddenly opened after the pressure of air in the lungs has risen considerably ; its object is to expel some irritating substance from the air passages. *Sneezing* is a single sudden expiration, which differs from coughing in that the sudden rush of air is directed by the soft palate up into the nose in order to expel some source of irritation from this narrow passage. *Cheyne-Stokes breathing* is a type of breathing found in persons suffering from apoplexy, Bright's disease, heart disease, and some other conditions, in which death is impending; it consists in an alternate dying away and gradual strengthening of the inspirations. Other disorders of breathing are found in LARYNGISMUS STRIDULUS and in ASTHMA (*q.v.*).

RESUSCITATION (*re*, again ; *suscito*, I arouse). (*See* DROWNING, RECOVERY FROM.)

RETCHING is an ineffectual form of vomiting. (*See* VOMITING.)

RETE MUCOSUM (*rete*, a net ; *mucosus*, slimy) is an old name for the true skin. (*See* SKIN.)

RETENTION OF URINE (*see* URINE, RETENTION OF).

RETICULOCYTES is the name given to newly formed red blood corpuscles, in which a fine network can be demonstrated by special staining methods.

RETICULO - ENDOTHELIAL SYSTEM consists of highly specialized cells scattered throughout the body, but found mainly in the spleen, bone marrow, liver, and lymph glands. Their main function is the ingestion of red blood cells and the conversion of hæmoglobin to bilirubin. They are also able to ingest bacteria and foreign colloidal particles.

RETICULOSES is the term used to describe a group of conditions characterized by progressive widespread proliferation of the cells of the reticuloendothelial system. The two most important members of this group are Hodgkin's disease (*q.v.*) and lymphosarcoma (*q.v.*).

RETINA (diminutive from *rete*, a net) is the innermost and light-sensitive coat of the eyeball. (*See* EYE.)

RETINITIS means inflammation of the retina. It is accompanied more or less by impairment of sight. It is found accompanying advanced conditions of Bright's disease, diabetes, and some forms of poisoning. A chronic degenerative form known as ' retinitis pigmentosa ' is associated with great narrowing of the field of vision and blindness in dim light.

RETRO- (*retro*, backward) is a prefix signifying behind or turned backward.

RETROBULBAR NEURITIS is the term applied to inflammation of the optic nerve just behind the eyeball.

RETROFLEXION means bending of an organ so that its top is thrust backwards. Retroversion is a similar displacement in which the whole organ is turned backwards. These terms are particularly applied to the uterus.

RETROLENTAL FIBROPLASIA is a disturbance of the retina of the eye which was responsible for a high proportion of blindness in children. It is almost entirely confined to premature infants, and is now known to be due to the administration of excessive amounts of oxygen to premature infants. Since oxygen concentrations have been restricted to below 45 per cent., the condition has practically disappeared.

RETROPHARYNGEAL ABSCESS is the name given to an abscess occurring in the cellular tissue behind the throat. It is the result in general of disease in the upper part of the spinal column.

RETROPULSION is the term applied to the involuntary act of running backwards which occurs in patients suffering from rigid paralysis — for example, paralysis agitans or Parkinsonism (occurring after encephalitis lethargica).

RHATANY is the root of *Krameria triandra*, a South American plant, which contains an astringent principle. It is mainly used in diarrhœa in the form of a tincture or extract, and to make lozenges for use in cases of relaxed throat.

RHESUS FACTOR (*see* BLOOD GROUPS).
758

RHEUMATIC FEVER is another term for acute rheumatism. (*See* RHEUMATISM.)

RHEUMATISM (ῥευματισμός, from ῥεῦμα, a humour) is a general term applied to a group of diseases, which have for their chief manifestations inflammatory or degenerative affections of the fibrous textures of joints, muscles, and other parts. The term is a very old one based upon the idea that the disease was of a moist nature leading to watery deposits in the joints. The parts affected may be the joints alone, either in acute or chronic form ; or various other tissues, especially the fibrous tissues and nerves, may be affected, either with or without disorder in the joints. No satisfactory classification of this heterogeneous collection of diseases has yet been evolved, but the following, recommended by the Royal College of Physicians of London, is probably the best : (1) acute rheumatism (or rheumatic fever) and subacute rheumatism ; (2) non-articular rheumatism ; (3) gout ; (4) chronic arthritis, which includes rheumatoid arthritis and osteoarthritis. Gout is described elsewhere (*see* GOUT), and the remaining conditions will be noticed here.

ACUTE RHEUMATISM, or RHEUMATIC FEVER, is a general disorder accompanied by much pain in the joints, feverishness, and copious perspiration, with a tendency to spread in an erratic manner, and to involve the smooth membranes lining various cavities of the body, particularly the heart.

Causes.—The nature of this disease is still unknown, but there appears to be a definite association with streptococcal infections. There is, for example, the common association of recurrent attacks of streptococcal tonsillitis with subacute rheumatic fever and the streptococcal tonsillitis which so often precedes the attack of acute rheumatic fever. This, however, is not the whole story, and the recent reports on the effect of cortisone, a hormone produced by the cortex of the suprarenal glands, suggests that the underlying cause of rheumatic fever may be some biochemical or metabolic disturbance of the tissues due to lack of this hormone.

Certain predisposing causes are generally admitted. Climate is an important factor, and, although the disease is found all over the world, it is especially frequent in temperate climates, and particularly in the British Isles. The disease is prevalent in the late autumn, October, and November in Britain, but in other countries reaches its chief frequency about March. It is rare before the age of three years, occurs most commonly in childhood and adolescence, and becomes increasingly less common after adult life is attained. If chorea be excluded, the disease is equally common in the two sexes, although the death rate is a fifth greater among males than among females. There is some evidence that the disease tends to occur in certain families, but this tendency is not marked. The condition tends to occur more commonly in children with a high complexion and a reddish tint in their hair. The disease is more common among the poorer classes. Any depressing cause acting upon the general health, such as overwork or anxiety, may precipitate an attack in persons predisposed to them. Attacks of acute rheumatism may follow exposure to cold and damp and excessive fatigue. Persons who have once suffered from this disease are liable to a recurrence.

The relationship to diseases caused by the hæmolytic streptococcus is particularly important. Thus, an attack of rheumatic fever is often preceded by a ' sore throat ' or tonsillitis due to this organism. This is especially apt to occur with recurrent attacks. Occasionally rheumatic fever follows an attack of scarlet fever, which is a disease due to the hæmolytic streptococcus. Chorea (q.v.) is a manifestation of rheumatic fever ; in 25 per cent. of rheumatic children it is the first sign of the disease.

Symptoms.—An attack of acute rheumatism usually begins with chilliness or rigors, followed by feverishness and a feeling of stiffness or pain in one or more joints, generally those of larger size, such as the knee, ankle, wrist, or shoulder. The pain soon becomes intense and is accompanied by severe constitutional disturbance. The patient lies helpless in bed, restless, but afraid to move or to be touched, and often unable to bear even the weight of the bed-clothes. The face is flushed, and the whole body bathed in perspiration, which has a sour, disagreeable odour and highly acid reaction. The temperature is elevated : usually about 103° F. (39·5° C.) ; the pulse is rapid, full, and soft ; the tongue is coated, and there are thirst, loss of appetite and constipation. At first the pain is confined to only one or two joints, but soon others become affected, very commonly similar joints on the two sides of the body. The affected joints are red, swollen, hot, and excessively tender. In mild cases one or two joints only are affected, but in severe cases scarcely a joint, large or small, may escape, and the pain, restlessness, and fever then render the patient's condition extremely miserable.

An attack of acute rheumatism is of variable duration, sometimes passing away in the course of a few days. The usual period during which the temperature remains elevated is a week or less, and, if the temperature subsides to normal and again rises, or if it continues elevated beyond ten days, some complication, such as involvement of the heart, may be suspected. Such cases may last for many weeks with relapses, in which all the former symptoms return and prolong the illness.

If no complication has arisen, there may be complete recovery in the course of about three weeks. Sometimes, when all the acute symptoms have disappeared, the joints remain swollen, stiff, and painful on movement, but this condition may also gradually pass away, or, on the other hand, the rheumatism may become chronic. In any case there always remains a liability to subsequent attacks.

In certain cases small subcutaneous nodules develop on the extensor aspect of certain joints, especially the back of the wrist, the back of the elbow, and the knee. They may also occur on the back of the neck. The significance of these rheumatic nodules, which are about the size of a split pea, is that they tend to occur in the more severe cases.

Complications.—This disease derives much of its serious import from certain complications which are very apt to arise during an attack. Among these the most frequent and the most serious is heart disease. Pericarditis (inflammation of the membrane covering the heart), endocarditis (inflammation of the lining membrane of the heart), and myocarditis (inflammation of the heart muscle) may all develop. (*See* HEART DISEASES.) The risk of cardiac complications seems to be greater the younger the patient, and, indeed, in children the joint pains are often so slight as to be overlooked, and the valvular disease may only be discovered accidentally at a later period of life. Pericarditis occurs less frequently, but is more serious as regards the patient's immediate prospect of recovery.

Among other serious complications may be mentioned excessive fever (hyperpyrexia), which sometimes develops in a sudden and alarming manner, the temperature rising rapidly to 106°, 108° F. (41°, 42° C.), or even higher, and thus endangering life unless prompt treatment be resorted to. Complications connected with the lungs, such as pleurisy, pneumonia, and bronchitis, sometimes arise in the course of the disease. Certain skin conditions may also occur, including purpura, erythema nodosum, and erythema marginatum. Chorea (St. Vitus's dance) sometimes follows after the acute symptoms have subsided.

Treatment.—The patient should be placed in bed between blankets, and should wear a flannel shirt. Or he may wear a jacket of gamgee tissue, of which front and back are separate and fastened only by tapes over the shoulders and on the sides. Movements of all kinds should be, as far as possible, avoided. The diet should consist entirely of milk, glucose, and fruit juices in the acute stage of the disease.

The affected joints should be wrapped in cotton-wool or gamgee tissue, kept in position by a light bandage or by tapes. If the pain is very great, relief is sometimes obtained by wrapping the painful parts in flannel cloths wrung out of a strong (5 per cent.) solution of washing soda in water, to which some laudanum has been added. Methyl salicylate painted on the painful joints and covered with oil-silk and cotton-wool, and a mixture in equal parts of chloral-menthol and camphor, are similarly

soothing applications. Relief from very acute pain is obtained in all cases by fixing the joint by means of splints.

Penicillin should be given for the first week, to kill off any hæmolytic streptococci that may be present in the throat. Sodium salicylate forms the sheet anchor of drug treatment. From 20 to 30 grains (1·2 to 2 grammes), with an equal amount of bi-carbonate of soda, are given several times in the course of twenty-four hours, but its action must be carefully watched by the physician. In the dangerous complication of hyperpyrexia, the cold bath, in which the water is quickly cooled down from 94° to 68° F. (34·5° to 20° C.), or the cold pack, has frequently been successful in lowering temperature and saving life. In order to reduce the risk of permanent damage to the heart, it is essential that every patient with rheumatic fever should be kept at complete rest in bed for ten days following the return of the temperature to normal. It should be another two or three weeks before the patient is allowed out of bed. For some time following recovery special care should be taken in avoiding exposure to cold and damp, crowds, and over-exertion.

SUBACUTE RHEUMATISM is a name sometimes applied to mild attacks of acute rheumatism, in which the temperature does not exceed 101° F. (38·3° C.), and which respond quickly to treatment by salicylate of soda. These cases are often of long duration and they may be accompanied by endocarditis, especially in the case of children. The significance of these attacks is that, no matter how mild they may appear to be, they may involve the heart. Treatment should be instituted immediately by putting the patient to bed, and full doses of aspirin or sodium salicylate should be given. Experience in this country and in the United States has shown that the incidence of such recurrent attacks is reduced by giving children who are susceptible to, or who have had an attack of, rheumatic fever regular small daily doses of a sulphonamide drug or of penicillin over a long period.

NON-ARTICULAR RHEUMATISM includes all those forms of rheumatism which do not involve the joints. Classification is difficult as the cause is not known. Many different names have been given to the various manifestations of this group, e.g. fibrositis, bursitis, myalgia, muscular rheumatism, neuritis, lumbago, sciatica, pleurodynia, panniculitis. Although the cause is obscure, there is no doubt about the practical importance of this group of diseases. In the United States of America it accounts for about 30 per cent. of all rheumatic diseases, and in Great Britain the incidence is even higher.

Causes.—Only certain predisposing factors are known. The actual cause is still to be found. The onset may be acute, as in certain cases of lumbago, or gradual. It may be generalized, e.g. involving the muscles of the back and shoulders, or it may be localized. Exposure to cold or damp is a common predisposing factor. Undue exertion may precipitate an attack. In other cases it appears to be associated with a focus of infection somewhere in the body, e.g. septic teeth, but the importance of this factor has been grossly over-rated in the past. The condition is much more apt to occur in middle-age than in young adults. Certain individuals are much more likely to suffer from the condition than others, and it is in these susceptible individuals that the factors already mentioned are most likely to induce an attack.

Symptoms.—These consist of pain and stiffness which range in intensity from the agonizing pain of acute lumbago, which literally immobilizes the victim for a time, to a vague sense of discomfort which the individual may have difficulty in localizing precisely. The pain and stiffness are usually worst after resting and tend to improve with exercise. Thus, they tend to be worst on awakening in the morning. Damp and cold weather make them worse, whilst they improve in dry warm weather. Tender spots can sometimes be felt in the affected muscles, and the detection of these is of importance from the point of view of treatment. There is seldom any wasting or atrophy of muscle and the joints are not involved. The general health is not affected.

Treatment.—This depends upon the acuteness of the condition. If very acute, a period of rest in bed may be necessary, but as a rule this is not essential. Avoidance of strenuous physical exertion is advisable, but moderate exercise is advantageous as it prevents the affected muscles becoming stiff. For the relief of pain, heat in some form is used. This may consist of hot baths, hot packs, poultices, or diathermy. Warming the affected part gently in front of a gas-fire is as useful a way as any. In more severe cases some form of counter-irritation, e.g. a mustard plaster, may be necessary. Electricity in the form of faradism, galvanism, or high-frequency currents is often useful. Massage is usually helpful. In severe cases analgesics are required, and the best of these is aspirin, with or without phenacetin. If localized tender spots are found, the injection into them of procaine often gives relief which is sometimes dramatic.

Individuals who are susceptible to non-articular rheumatism often benefit from a stay at a spa, e.g. Bath, Buxton, or Harrogate. Advice which is becoming increasingly difficult to follow, is for such individuals to live, or holiday, in warm dry climes, e.g. South Africa, Egypt, California. More practical advice is that in cold damp weather they should wear warm clothing and take particular care to avoid undue exposure to cold or damp, e.g. they should be especially careful about changing their clothes if they get wet.

LUMBAGO.—This is myalgia or fibrositis occurring in the strong and dense sinews of the erector spinæ muscles of the back, and is considered separately because of its great frequency and importance in regard to occupation, and because it is readily distinguishable. For its causes, symptoms, and treatment see LUMBAGO.

SCIATICA AND BRACHIAL NEURITIS.— The rheumatic processes may affect the fibrous tissues of various nerves, the nerves of the arm and the great sciatic nerve running down the back of the thigh being especially liable to this affection. The causes described above under myalgia are also operative in producing neuritis, and, in the case of the nerves of the arm, overstrain at work, e.g. in hammermen, plays an important part. The treatment of this condition is described under NEURALGIA.

RHEUMATOID ARTHRITIS, also known as ATROPHIC ARTHRITIS, is one of the most crippling of all the rheumatic diseases.

Causes.—For many years regarded as an infective condition, evidence is now accumulating that it is due to some fundamental biochemical or metabolic disturbance associated with deficient production of certain hormones in the cortex of the suprarenal glands. The precise nature of this disturbance is not yet understood, and it must be admitted that the brilliant researches of Dr. Hench and his colleagues at the Mayo Clinic, which have shown that a dramatic, but only temporary, improvement in patients with rheumatoid arthritis can be produced by the administration of cortisone, one of the hormones of the suprarenal cortex, have raised almost as many problems as they have solved. The disease is one of temperate climates and is more common in women than in men. The majority of cases occur between the ages of 35 and 40. It is uncommon under the age of 25, and first attacks seldom occur after the age of 50. A form of rheumatoid arthritis known as Still's disease (*q.v.*) occurs in children.

Pathology.—The first change in the affected joints consists of thickening of the synovial lining of the joint. This is followed by involvement of the articular cartilage, which becomes ulcerated, covered with granulation tissue, and ultimately destroyed in severe cases. There is an overproduction of connective tissue and in due course the joint becomes ankylosed and fixed. There is also rarefaction of the bone adjoining the joint, and marked wasting of the adjoining muscles. This last change is due, in part at least, to disuse : because of the painful state of the joint the individual uses it as little as possible.

Symptoms.—The disease has usually a gradual onset. There is pain, swelling, and redness of the affected joints. The condition usually begins in the small joints of the hand, especially in the fingers. Later, almost any joint in the body may be involved, but the condition tends to spread from the smaller joints to the larger joints. Thus, the shoulder and the hip joint are usually affected last. Even mild attacks are usually accompanied by fever, and in acute attacks the rise in temperature may be quite considerable and accom-

panied by the rise in pulse-rate and all the other accompaniments of fever, *e.g.* prostration, loss of appetite, sweating, and the like. With recurrent attacks the affected joints tend to become chronically swollen and fixed. The position in which fixation of the joint occurs depends upon the relative strength of the muscles around the joint. In the case of the hand this results in the characteristic deformity— with the hand deviated towards the little finger side. In comparison with the swelling of the joints, the wasting of the surrounding muscles shows up particularly markedly, and gives a characteristic appearance, which in the case of the fingers justifies the description of ' spindle-shaped '. X-ray examination reveals the presence of well-marked changes in the joints, including widening of the joint space and decreased density of the bones adjoining the joints. The sedimentation rate (*q.v.*) is raised, and though this is of little help in diagnosis, the course of the sedimentation rate over a period of time is a useful guide as to how the disease is responding to treatment. With recurring attacks the patient's general health tends to become affected with anæmia, loss of weight, loss of appetite, and lassitude. The outlook, or prognosis, is satisfactory in so far as this is not a killing disease, but it is unsatisfactory in that, up to date, no effective treatment is available and the disease tends therefore to be chronic and recurrent. It has been estimated that a fourth of the patients show marked improvement approaching a cure, a half show slight or moderate improvement, and a fourth fail to improve, or become worse.

Treatment.—The discovery of the beneficial action of cortisone, a hormone produced by the cortex of the suprarenal glands, still dominates the treatment of rheumatoid arthritis, but it is now clear that cortisone is not a cure for the condition. Increasing experience has shown that its use is not without danger. Used with circumspection, under skilled supervision, it is undoubtedly a useful adjunct in the treatment of rheumatoid arthritis, but it by no means replaces the well-tried measures which are summarized in the remainder of this section.

These consist, in the first place, of rest, the degree of rest depending upon the severity of the condition. Rest, however, must never be absolute, even in the acute stages, as this may lead to unnecessary stiffness in the joints. It must be accompanied by exercises to try and keep the joints as mobile as possible. During the more acute phases, when it is necessary to keep the patient in bed, the affected joints should be splinted so as to prevent deformities developing. Heat, in the form of poultices, wax baths, or diathermy, is useful in relieving pain and discomfort, and this may be supplemented by the administration of aspirin or sodium salicylate. Spa treatment is also of value. Satisfactory results have been obtained from the use of certain salts of gold. Although gold does not produce a cure, it is the one agent which, apart from the cortisone group of drugs, has been shown to improve the condition. Its use is not entirely without risk, and it must therefore only be used under medical supervision. X-ray treatment has also been used in cases in which many joints are involved. Surgery is only required to correct any deformity which is crippling the patient, provided this crippling is confined to one or two joints. The general health of the patient must also be attended to by ensuring that he or she has an adequate nutritious diet, containing plenty milk, fruit, and vegetables. Dental care is necessary, but it is now recognized that there is no justification for the wholesale extraction of teeth which was fashionable at one time. Removal to a dry, warm climate is beneficial, but economically this is seldom advice that can be followed by the affected individual.

OSTEOARTHRITIS, or OSTEOARTHROSIS as it is now coming to be known, is the most common disorder of joints and is estimated to be present in 80 to 90 per cent. of people over the age of 60 years. It is characterized by gradual destruction of the central part of the cartilage lining the affected joint, whilst at the same time there is overgrowth of the outer part of the cartilage which ultimately results in the growth of bony spurs or osteophytes. The condition is probably a degenerative one, but it is accentuated or accelerated by trauma. Thus, it is liable to occur in a knee in which there has been cartilage trouble which has not been treated adequately. Obesity, accompanied as it is often so by faulty posture, results in abnormal stresses and strains being applied to the hip joints and knees, and this in due course results in osteoarthritic changes in these joints. There is some evidence that there may be a hereditary predisposition. The condition is more common in females than in males, and the joints mainly involved are the hip, the knee, and the shoulder joint. The terminal joints of the fingers are also quite a common site. Pain and stiffness in the affected joints are the usual manifestations of the disease. A creaking sensation (crepitus) is felt in moving the joint in the more advanced cases. In chronic cases the joint becomes enlarged. There is seldom any generalized disturbance such as fever or malaise. The diagnosis is confirmed by X-ray examination.

Treatment consists of rest and graduated exercises. When the joints are painful the local application of heat is beneficial, e.g. hot towel packs or infra-red light. Aspirin or sodium salicylate also relieves the pain temporarily. If the individual is overweight, a reducing diet is necessary to bring the weight down. In the more advanced cases, surgery is often of value. The essence of treatment, however, has been aptly summarized as follows : ' The obvious thing to do is to " spare " the joints, just as one spares a horse that is " a bit gone in the forelegs " or a car with a worn transmission.'

GOUT.—(See GOUT.)

RH FACTOR (see BLOOD GROUPS).

RHINITIS (ῥίς, the nose) means inflammation of the mucous membrane of the nose. (See NOSE, DISEASES OF.)

RHINOPLASTY (ῥίς, nose ; πλάσσω, I form) means the repair of the nose or the modification of its shape by operation. The operation is carried out by obtaining a flap of skin from the forehead or from the forearm. In milder cases of deformity the shape is often improved by injection of paraffin under the skin of the nose, or by insertion of a piece of cartilage taken from one of the ribs.

RHINOVIRUSES are a large group of viruses, and to date 56 distinct rhinoviruses have been identified. Their practical importance is that some of them are responsible for around one-quarter of the causes of the common cold.

RHONCHI (ῥογχός, snoring) is the term used to denote the harsh cooing, hissing, or whistling sounds (wheezing) heard by auscultation over the bronchial tubes when they are the seat of inflammation. (*See* BRONCHITIS.)

RHUBARB is the root of *Rheum officinale*, a plant originally derived from China and Thibet. It has a gentle purgative action when taken in large doses, and at the same time increases the flow of bile. In small doses it has merely a slightly stimulating action upon the functions of the stomach, and is beneficial in atonic conditions of that organ. It is also used as a purgative.

RHUS is the name for a genus of trees and shrubs, some of which are used as astringents, while others, particularly *Rhus toxicodendrum*, or poison oak, and *Rhus venenata*, or swamp-sumac, are poisonous.

RIBOFLAVINE is the *British Pharmacopœia* name for what used to be known as vitamin B_2. Its empirical formula is $C_{17}H_{20}O_6N_4$. Riboflavine belongs to a group of animal and plant pigments which give a greenish fluorescence on exposure to ultra-violet rays. It is present especially in milk, and is not destroyed during pasteurization. Other rich sources are eggs, liver, and the green leaves of broccoli and spinach. Deficiency of riboflavine in the diet is thought to cause inflammation of the substance of the cornea, sores on the lips, especially at the angles of the mouth (cheilosis), and dermatitis.

The minimal daily requirement for an adult is 1·5 to 3 mg., but is greater during pregnancy and lactation.

RIBS are the bones, twelve on each side, which enclose the cavity of the chest (Fig. 326). The upper seven are joined to the breast-bone by their costal cartilages and are therefore known as true ribs. The lower five do not reach the breast-bone, and are therefore known as false ribs. Of the latter, the 8th, 9th, and 10th are joined by their costal cartilages, each one to the rib immediately above it, while the 11th and 12th are free from any such

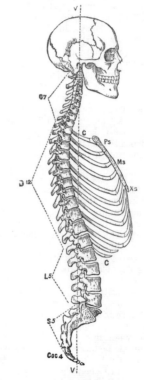

FIG. 326.—Outline of the spine with the ribs of the left side. The ribs of the right side have been removed. The line crossing each shows the end of the rib, the part in front being cartilage. (For letters, *see* SPINAL COLUMN.) (Turner's *Anatomy*.)

connection, and are therefore known as floating ribs. Each rib is possessed of a head, by which it is jointed to the upper part of the body of the vertebra with which it corresponds, as well as to the vertebra immediately above. Next comes a narrow part known as the neck, and then a tubercle, by which the rib is joined to the transverse process of the corresponding vertebra. Finally, the greater part of the bone is made up of the shaft, which runs at first outwards and at the angle turns sharply forwards. On the lower margin of the shaft is a groove, which lodges the corresponding intercostal artery and nerve.

RICE DIET.—A diet containing a minimum amount of sodium is a valuable adjunct in the treatment of heart failure. It is also often used in the treatment of high blood-pressure. The rice diet has been introduced for this purpose. It consists of rice cooked in unsalted water, fruit, fruit juice and sugar, and contains less than 0·5 gramme of sodium per day. Its practical disadvantage is its unpalatability.

RICE-WATER.—This forms a useful diluent drink for invalids, similar to barley-water. To prepare rice-water take 6 tablespoonfuls of rice, wash it in cold water, then place it in a saucepan with $1\frac{1}{2}$ pints (850 ml.) of water and allow to simmer for an hour or two, until the bulk of fluid is reduced to about a pint (570 ml.). The rice-water is then cooled, strained, and, if desired, sweetened with sugar and flavoured with lemon.

RICKETS is a disease of childhood characterized chiefly by a softened condition of the bones, and by other evidences of perverted nutrition.

Causes.—This disease is found chiefly among the ill-fed children of the poor, and is the result of deficiency of vitamin D in the diet, and also of deficiency of calcium. Healthy bones cannot be built up without calcium (or lime) salts, and the body cannot utilize these salts in the absence of vitamin D. Want of sunlight and fresh air in the dwellings where the children are reared is also of importance. Once a common condition in industrial areas, it had almost disappeared in Great Britain, but there has been a recurrence of it in recent years that is giving rise to concern.

The changes that take place in the bones are due to an irregular process of bone formation. The periosteum, the membrane enveloping the bones, becomes inflamed, and in consequence the bone formed beneath it is defective in lime salts and very soft. At the growing ends of the bones there is an even more striking change. The epiphyseal plate of cartilage, from which growth takes place, is much thickened, the cellular elements in it much increased in number, and the bone which it produces markedly deficient in lime salts. The new bone shows a deficiency of lime amounting to 25 or 35 per cent., and this, too, notwithstanding the fact that there is abundance of lime in the body, as shown by its excessive excretion in the urine. The disease rarely occurs under the age of six months, from which it may be assumed that exposure to unsuitable conditions for several months is necessary before rickets ensues. It is most common between one and two years of age and is increasingly rare after the age of three.

Symptoms.—The symptoms of rickets most commonly attract attention about the end of the first year, and the disease very rarely appears for the first time after the age of five. The symptoms, which precede the outward manifestations of the disease, are marked disorders of the digestive and alimentary functions. The child's appetite is diminished ; there is frequent vomiting and diarrhœa ; or irregularity of the bowels appears, the evacuations being clay-coloured and unhealthy. Along with this the child ceases to gain in weight or actually falls away in flesh. One of the most noticeable symptoms is profuse sweating of the head and upper parts of the body, particularly during sleep, with a tendency in the child to kick off the bed-clothes and expose the limbs. Bronchitis is also a common early symptom and often the first to attract attention. In infants, convulsions are sometimes a symptom of rickets and disappear under the treatment appropriate to this disease. At the same time there is tenderness of the bones as shown by crying when the child is moved or handled. A little later it is noticed that there is delay in learning to sit up and walk, so that the child who has begun to walk loses this power.

Gradually changes in the shape of

the bones become visible, first chiefly noticed at the ends of the long bones, as in those of the arm, causing enlargement at the wrists, or in the ribs, producing a row of knobs at the junction of their ends with the rib cartilages (' rickety rosary '). The bones also from their softened condition tend to become distorted and bent both by the action of the muscles and by the weight of the body resting upon them. Those of the legs are bent outwards and forwards and the child becomes bow-legged or knock-kneed, often to an extreme degree. The trunk of the body likewise shows various alterations and deformities owing to curvatures of the spine, flattening of the lateral curves of the ribs, and the projection forward of the breast-bone. (*See* CHEST DEFORM-ITIES.) The cavity of the chest may thus be contracted and interference produced with the development of the thoracic organs, whose functions thus become embarrassed. The liver is pushed outwards and the abdomen becomes protuberant (' pot belly '). The pelvis undergoes distortion which may reduce its capacity to such a degree that in females serious difficulties may arise later in life in the course of labour. The head of the rickety child is square with high ' intellectual ' forehead ; the individual bones of the cranium remain long ununited, while the soft fontanelle remains unclosed long after the end of the second year, the time by which it should have disappeared ; the face is small and ill-developed ; and the teeth appear late and fall out or decay early.

The disease usually terminates in recovery with more or less of deformity and dwarfing, the bones, although altered in shape, becoming ultimately firmly ossified. On the other hand, during the progress of the disease, various intercurrent ailments are apt to arise which may cause death, such as bronchitis and other chest complaints, meningitis, convulsions, laryngismus, etc. Another disease for which rickets is apt to be mistaken is infantile scurvy (*q.v.*).

Treatment.—The treatment of rickets is more hygienic and dietetic than medicinal. The specific remedy is vitamin D, given in the form either of cod-liver oil, halibut-liver oil, or calciferol (vita-

min D_2). A full diet is of course essential, with emphasis upon a sufficient supply of milk. Rickets practically does not occur in breast-fed children, so that nursing by the mother for a period of eight or nine months is desirable, if at all possible. After the child is weaned, the provision of suitable food is of the greatest importance, supplemented by the administration of cod-liver oil or some other source of vitamin D (*see* INFANT FEEDING).

General hygienic measures, including abundance of fresh air and sunshine, cleanliness, warm clothing, and attention to regularity in all the child's functions, are of the greatest importance.

While the disease is advancing, it is desirable to restrain the child from walking, and this must sometimes be achieved by the use of splints and other apparatus as supports of the limbs and body. This enables the child to move about without risk of bending and deformity of the bones, which would otherwise probably result. If deformities of the legs have occurred, operative treatment may be necessary at a later period of life in order to straighten the limbs.

RICKETTSIA is the general term given to a group of small bacteria-like micro-organisms which are the causal agents of typhus and a number of typhus-like diseases, such as Rocky Mountain spotted fever, Japanese River fever, and Q fever. These micro-organisms are usually conveyed to man by lice, fleas, ticks, and mites.

RIFAMPICIN is an antibiotic derived from *Streptomyces mediterranei*, which is proving of value in the treatment of tuberculosis.

RIGG'S DISEASE is another name for *Pyorrhœa alveolaris*. (*See* TEETH, DISEASES OF.)

RIGOR (*rigor*, stiffness) means shivering. If prolonged, it is generally accompanied by raised temperature, and may be a sign of the onset of some acute febrile disease, such as influenza, pneumonia, or some internal inflammation. *Rigor mortis* is the name given to the stiffness that ensues soon after death (*see* DEATH, SIGNS OF).

RIMA (*rima*) is a term, meaning a crack or fissure, applied to any narrow natural opening, *e.g.* rima glottidis, the chink between the vocal cords.

RINGWORM, or TINEA, is the name given to inflammatory affections of the skin produced by moulds. The main forms of ringworm in man are: (i) *Tinea tonsurans*, or ringworm of the scalp ; (ii) *Tinea barbæ*, or ringworm of the beard ; (iii) *Tinea cruris*, or ringworm of the groin, and also known as dhobie itch ; (iv) *Tinea pedis*, or ringworm of

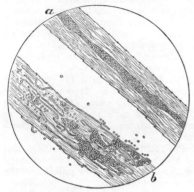

FIG. 327.—Microscopic appearance of two hairs : *a*, healthy hair ; *b*, hair disorganized by the ringworm parasite, showing the spores and mycelium. Magnified by 300.

the feet ; (v) *Tinea circinata*, or ringworm of the body ; (vi) ringworm of the nails ; (vii) *Tinea favosa*, favus, or honeycomb ringworm ; (viii) *Tinea versicolor*.

RINGWORM OF THE SCALP, a disease of childhood, is usually due to a human species of fungus, *Microsporon audouini* ; some five per cent. of cases are due to infection by microspora acquired from cats and dogs. Boys are more infected than girls, and in both it disappears spontaneously at adolescence, being excessively rare in adults. It is most contagious. The incidence of the disease fell rapidly in the 1920-30's, and by 1939 was a rare condition in many parts of the country. During the 1939-45 War, however, its incidence increased, and epidemics in schools and institutions are still quite common. The typical appearance is that of circular patches of lustreless,

greyish, broken hairs scattered over the scalp. The scalp itself is covered with fine greyish-white scabs. Under Wood's light (the rays of a mercury vapour lamp screened through a special glass) the common ringworm has a bright green colour, which is diagnostic.

Treatment.—As in all other forms of ringworm, the outlook has been radically changed by the introduction of the new antibiotic, griseofulvin (*q.v.*). When used under medical supervision, this is the most effective method of treatment yet discovered, curing the condition in a high proportion of cases. Treatment should be continued for four weeks and, in order to prevent reinfection, the infected hairs should be removed either manually or by clipping and shaving, after three weeks' treatment with griseofulvin. A daily application of an antifungal preparation is not essential but is of value in preventing the spread of infection to other parts of the scalp or to other children.

RINGWORM OF THE BEARD is one of the forms of ' barber's rash '. There is a form occurring in grooms and cattlemen, in which the infection is acquired from animals.

Treatment.—This consists of the administration of griseofulvin (*q.v.*). If suppuration is also present, hot fomentations of 2 per cent. sodium thiosulphate should be applied.

RINGWORM OF THE GROIN, or DHOBIE ITCH, is caused by a fungus of the same group as is responsible for ringworm of the foot—*Epidermophyton*. It occurs at any age, but is most common in young adult males. The eruption is a sharply defined, slightly raised reddish area, which begins in the inner aspect of the upper third of the thigh and tends to spread over the perineum (or crutch) and to involve the scrotum. It is accompanied by considerable irritation.

Treatment.—This consists of the administration of griseofulvin (*q.v.*). In addition, the prevention of reinfection is essential by the individual always wearing cotton underpants night and day, and sterilizing them by boiling every evening. This means, of course, that at least two pairs of pants must be in use, so that one is always available to wear while the other is being sterilized.

RINGWORM OF THE FOOT is one of the most common forms of ringworm at the present day. It is due to an *Epidermophyton*. Most common among adolescent and young adult males, the infection is usually acquired by walking with bare feet on infected floors, *e.g.* hotel and school bathrooms, public swimming baths, and pithead baths. The eruption begins between the toes as a rule, but may also be found on the soles of the feet. There are two main forms of eruption : (*a*) the *vesicular*, in which the affected area is covered with small blisters — this form begins on the sole ; (*b*) the *intertriginous*, in which the skin between the toes becomes white and sodden, and peels off, leaving a raw red area. Before beginning to treat this type of ringworm it is particularly important to demonstrate the fungus in material removed from the affected area, as a superficially similar appearance may be produced by other infecting organisms or even by excessive sweating alone.

Treatment.—Careful hygiene of the feet, particularly by those who tend to perspire freely in the feet, is essential: (*a*) to prevent infection ; (*b*) to aid in curing the condition once acquired ; (*c*) to prevent relapses. Such hygiene consists of washing the feet every night in warm water, drying them thoroughly but carefully, and then powdering them with a bland dusting powder. A fresh pair of socks should be worn at least every other day, and rubber footwear should not be used. Once the infection is acquired, the treatment depends upon the local condition. In mild and moderate cases in which the epidermophyton alone is responsible, an ointment or powder containing salts of undecylenic acid or propionic acid is probably best. Good results are sometimes obtained from the use of phenyl mercuric nitrate (or acetate) as an ointment or powder.

Griseofulvin has not proved as effective in this form of ringworm as in other forms, but it is always worth trying if the methods described fail to clear the infection.

RINGWORM OF THE BODY, which may occur with ringworm of the scalp, may be due to either a microsporon or a tricophyton. The eruption

768

consists of circular discs, usually red in colour at first, but later tending to become pale in the centre, and blisters may appear in the surrounding ring. There is considerable itching.

Treatment is as for other forms of ringworm of the skin.

RINGWORM OF THE NAILS is not common but is most resistant to treatment. Several nails are usually affected, and they turn a greenish-grey colour, become brittle and separated from the nail-bed.

Treatment consists of the administration of griseofulvin, but treatment may need to be continued for long periods— for up to six months. Toe-nails are particularly resistant to griseofulvin. Expert opinion is still divided as to whether or not the infected nail should be removed.

FAVUS is due to a fungus of the genus *Tricophyton*. It occurs on the scalp, skin, and nails, and consists of thick yellow cups of crust. It is rare in Great Britain. It responds to griseofulvin.

PITYRIASIS VERSICOLOR, due to *Microsporon furfur*, is characterized by thin, greenish-yellow patches on the chest and abdomen.

RISUS SARDONICUS is the term used for describing the facial appearance when the muscles of the forehead and the face go into spasm in tetanus, giving the effect of a ' sardonic grin '.

ROCHELLE SALT, Seignette salt, and Tartrated soda are other names for tartrate of sodium and potassium, a saline purgative which forms the chief constituent of Seidlitz powder. The dose of Rochelle salt as an aperient is 120 to 240 grains (8 to 16 grammes) or a heaped dessert-spoonful.

ROCKY MOUNTAIN SPOTTED FEVER is a fever of the typhus group. It received its name from the fact that it was first reported in the Rocky Mountain states of U.S.A. These are still the most heavily infected states, but it is now found in all parts of the United States. The causative organism is *Rickettsia rickettsii*, which is transmitted to man by ticks. The characteristic feature of the disease is an intense rash. The prognosis used to be poor, particularly in older patients, but promising results are being reported from the use of chlortetracycline and chloramphenicol. (*See also* TYPHUS FEVER.)

RODAGEN is the name of a preparation made from the milk of a goat from which the thyroid gland has been removed. It was formerly used as a remedy for exophthalmic goitre.

RODENT ULCER (*rodo*, I gnaw) is the name given to a very chronic form of ulcer, which is found chiefly about the nose and face of elderly persons, and which gradually increases in size. It stands between a simple chronic ulcer and a cancer, being much slower in its growth than the latter. Treatment consists in cutting out the ulcer with the healthy skin for a little distance all round. They are also very amenable to treatment by X-rays, radium, and other forms of radiant energy, and may heal up completely after a few exposures to radium.

ROENTGEN RAYS (*see* X-RAYS).

ROETHELN, or RUBELLA, is another name for GERMAN MEASLES (*q.v.*).

ROMBERGISM is a term applied to marked unsteadiness in standing with the eyes shut. It is found as a symptom in some nervous diseases, especially in locomotor ataxia.

RORSCHACH TEST is a method of investigating the personality and disorders of personality. It was devised by a Swiss psychiatrist, Rorschach, who determined individuals' reactions to a series of symmetrical ink-blots, ten in number and standardized by him. The person investigated is shown the ink-blots in a defined order and is asked to describe what he sees. His descriptions and ideas about the blots are noted and an elaborate system of scoring is said to afford indications of the kind of personality and psychological make-up of the person investigated. Much work has been done on the test and it is thought highly of by experienced psychiatrists.

ROSACEA (*see* ACNE ROSACEA).

25

ROSE, or ST. ANTHONY'S FIRE, is an old name for erysipelas. (*See* ERYSIPELAS.)

ROSEMARY is a plant affording a fragrant volatile oil which is used in the form of spirit of rosemary. (*See* OILS.)

ROSEOLA is a term applied to any rose-coloured rash.

ROSE-RASH, or ROSEOLA, is an old name used to describe any eruption of a very faint red character. The term ' erythema ' is now generally used in its place. (*See* ERYTHEMA.)

ROSE-WAALER TEST is a blood test which is proving of value in the diagnosis of rheumatoid arthritis. It is positive in over 70 per cent. of patients with this disease, compared with only 4 per cent. of people not suffering from rheumatoid arthritis.

ROSE-WATER is prepared by soaking rose-petals in water and distilling over part of the fluid. It is used for gargles, as an ingredient of cold-cream, etc. Oil of rose, or attar of rose, is prepared by distilling the fresh flowers of *Rosa damascena*, about 180 pounds (82 kg.) of roses being required in order to yield an ounce (28·5 ml.) of this oil.

ROSIN, or COLOPHONY, is the name of a resinous substance remaining after oil of turpentine has been distilled from the pitch of pine wood. It is used for making plasters.

ROTENONE is the name of a substance obtained from derris root and used in the treatment of scabies. It is also used in the treatment of warble fly in cattle.

ROULEAUX is the term applied to the heaps into which red blood corpuscles collect as seen under the microscope.

ROUNDWORMS (*see* PARASITES).

ROUS SARCOMA is a malignant tumour of fowls which is caused by a virus. This tumour has been the subject of much experimental work bearing upon the nature of cancer.

RUBBING (see MASSAGE and LINIMENTS).

RUBEFACIENTS (*ruber*, red ; *facio*, I make). (See BLISTERS AND COUNTERIRRITANTS.)

RUBELLA is another name for GERMAN MEASLES (*q.v.*).

RUBEOLA is another name for measles. (See MEASLES.)

RUE is the name of an herb, *Ruta graveolens*, from which a volatile oil with irritating properties is produced.

RUPIA (ῥύπος, dirt) is the term applied to an eruption characterized by the accumulation of thick crusts. Apart from the original cause of the eruption, the accumulation of the crusts is due to want of cleanliness.

RUPTURE (*rumpo*, I break) is a popular name for hernia. (See HERNIA.) The term is also applied to the tearing of a muscle or ligament, bursting of a blood-vessel, etc.

S

SACCHARIN is a soluble coal-tar product of white crystalline appearance. It has an extremely sweet taste, being prepared in various strengths so as to equal in sweetness from 300 to 500 times its own weight of cane-sugar. It escapes from the body unchanged, having practically no effect upon the tissues beyond its influence upon the sensation of taste. Accordingly it is used in doses of ½ to 2 grains (30 to 125 mg.) by diabetics, corpulent persons, and others to whom sugar is harmful.

SACCHAROMYCES (σάκχαρον, sugar; μύκης, fungus) is another name for yeast.

SACCHARUM is the Latin name for ordinary cane-sugar or beet-sugar. (*See* SUGAR.)

SACRUM (*sacer*, sacred) is the name given to a portion of the spinal column near its lower end. The sacrum consists of five vertebræ fused together to form a broad triangular bone which lies between the two haunch-bones and forms the back wall of the pelvis.

SADISM (Marquis de Sade) is the term applied to a form of sexual perversion, in which satisfaction is derived from the infliction of cruelty upon another person.

SAFE PERIOD.—That period during the menstrual cycle when fertilization of the ovum is unlikely to occur. Ovulation usually happens about 15 days before the onset of the menstrual period. A woman is commonly believed to be fertile for about 11 days in each menstrual cycle : *i.e.* on the day of ovulation and for 5 days before and 5 days after this. This would be the eighth to the eighteenth day of the usual 28-day menstrual cycle. Outside this fertile period is the SAFE PERIOD : the first week and the last ten days of the menstrual cycle. On the other hand, there is increasing evidence that the safest period is the last few days before menstruation. In the case of irregular menstruation it is not possible to calculate the safe period. In any event the safety is not absolute.

SAFFRON, or CROCUS, is a yellow powder derived from the dried stigmas and styles of the flower of *Crocus sativus*. It is used as a tonic and colouring matter, and there is a popular idea that its administration is useful in bringing out the rash of measles.

SAGITTAL (*sagitta*, arrow) is the term applied to a structure or section running from front to back in the body.

SAGO is the name of a starch derived from the pith of various species of palm. (*See* CEREALS.)

ST. ANTHONY'S FIRE is an old name applied both to erysipelas and to ergot-poisoning.

ST. JOHN LONG'S LINIMENT is an old name for *Linimentum terebinthinae aceticum*, containing oil of turpentine, liniment of camphor, and glacial acetic acid. It is used as an application for chronic rheumatism.

ST. VITUS'S DANCE, or CHOREA, is the name applied to a disorder of the nervous system occurring for the most part in children, and characterized mainly by involuntary jerking movements of the muscles. The name St. Vitus's dance was originally applied to those remarkable epidemic outbursts of combined mental and physical excitement which for a time prevailed among the inhabitants of some parts of Germany in the Middle Ages. It is stated that sufferers from this dancing mania were wont to resort to the chapels of St. Vitus, the saint being believed to possess the power of curing them. The name was transferred to the disease at present under consideration, with which it has evidently nothing to do, and the original application has been to a great extent lost sight of. The term SYDENHAM'S CHOREA is also frequently applied to this disorder to distinguish it from Huntington's chorea, a disease of hereditary nature which appears late in life and is accompanied by mental defects.

Causes.—Chorea is a condition resulting from involvement of the central nervous system by the same factor (or factors) as are responsible for acute rheumatism (*q.v.*). It is more common in girls than in boys, in the proportion

771

of 3 : 1. Like acute rheumatism it is rare under the age of three years and uncommon under the age of five years. There is no definite evidence that it is hereditary, but it is more likely to occur in excitable, intelligent, ambitious children than in the phlegmatic child. There may be a history of some precipitating factor such as a fright or worry over an impending examination. It forms an occasional but rare complication of pregnancy.

Although chorea is the manifestation of acute rheumatism which is most likely to occur without manifestations of rheumatism elsewhere, the main importance of chorea is that about one-third of children who develop it show evidence of rheumatism elsewhere in the body, and usually in the heart. Recurrences occur in about one-third of the cases, usually within a year of the first attack. Such recurrences are more common in girls than in boys. If the heart is not involved in the first attack, it is unlikely to be affected in recurrent attacks.

Symptoms.—The characteristic features are : (1) involuntary, purposeless, inco-ordinated movements ; (2) weakness of voluntary movements ; (3) loss of precision of movement ; (4) psychological disturbances. The symptoms are usually preceded by changes in the temper and disposition, the child becoming sad, irritable, and emotional, while at the same time the general health is impaired. The first thing indicative of the disease is a certain awkwardness or fidgetiness of manner, together with restlessness, the child being evidently unable to continue quiet, but frequently moving the limbs into different positions. In walking, too, slight dragging of one limb may be noticed. The convulsive muscular movements usually show themselves first in one part, such as an arm or a leg, and in most instances they may remain localized to that limited extent, whilst in all cases there is a tendency for the disorderly symptoms to be more marked on one side than on the other. The child when standing or sitting is never still, but is constantly changing the position of the body or limbs in consequence of the sudden and inco-ordinate action of muscles or groups of them. These symptoms are aggravated

772

when purposive movements are attempted, or when the child is watched. Sometimes the disorder is first noticed owing to the frequency with which the child drops cups, plates, and similar articles. Speech is affected, and the taking of food becomes a matter of difficulty. When the tongue is protruded, it comes out in a jerky manner, and is immediately withdrawn, the jaws at the same time closing suddenly and sometimes with considerable force. In walking the muscles of the limbs act inco-ordinately. The heart may be affected as in acute rheumatism, and this may lay the foundation of permanent heart disease (*see* HEART DISEASES). Usually, there is a remission of the symptoms during sleep.

This disease occasionally assumes a very acute and aggravated form, in which the disorderly movements are so violent as to render the patient liable to be injured and to necessitate forcible control of the limbs or the employment of anæsthetics to produce unconsciousness. Such cases are of very grave character, if, as is common, they are accompanied with sleeplessness, and they may prove fatal by exhaustion. In the great majority of cases of St. Vitus's dance, however, complete recovery is to be anticipated sooner or later, the symptoms usually continuing for from one to two months, or even sometimes longer.

Treatment.—The first step in treatment is to provide the patient with complete physical and mental rest. The disease, under suitable hygienic conditions, tends to recover of itself. These conditions, however, are all-important, and embrace the proper feeding of the child with a full nutritious diet, the absence of all sources of excitement and annoyance, such as being laughed at or mocked by other children, and the removal of any causes of irritation and of irregularities in the general health. For a time, and especially if the symptoms are severe, confinement to bed may be necessary, but as soon as possible the child should be taken out into the open air and gently exercised by walking. Of medicinal remedies the most serviceable are sodium salicylate and aspirin, especially the latter. After recovery the general health of the child should for a long time receive attention, and care should be taken to guard against excitement, excessive study, or any exhausting condition, physical or mental.

In the rare instances of the acute form of this malady, where the convulsive movements are unceasing and violent, the only measures available are the use of chloral or of chloroform inhalation, but the effect is only palliative and does not prevent the fatal result which quickly supervenes in most such cases.

SAL AMMONIAC is another name for chloride of ammonium, which is widely used in cough mixtures and lozenges as an expectorant.

SALEP is a mucilaginous substance derived from the dried tubers of various species of orchid. It is used to allay irritation of the stomach and bowels, and in India constitutes an article of diet.

SALERATUS is another name for bicarbonate of potassium.

SALICIN is an active principle derived from the bark of several species of poplar and willow trees. It is a crystalline powder of bitter taste and slight solubility. It has been used for the treatment of acute rheumatism, just as salicylate of soda is used.

SALICYLATE OF SODA is a white crystalline substance which is prepared from salicylic acid. It is very soluble in water, and has a sweet, mawkish taste, which to most people is very unpleasant.

Action.—This salt when dissolved in water has the power of increasing the solubility of various other substances. When taken internally in the course of acute fevers, and especially of acute rheumatism, it has the effect of reducing temperature, diminishing pain, and causing profuse sweating. Its action is therefore similar to that of antipyrine, phenacetin, and other coal-tar products. When taken for some time, it causes fullness in the head, deafness, buzzing in the ears, curious disturbances of sight (so that the person may fancy he sees people in the room who are not

there), and, if excessive doses be taken, great depression of the heart's action and of respiration.

Uses.—The main use is in acute rheumatism, doses of 10, 15, or more grains (600 mg., 1 G. or more) being given several times daily, according to circumstances. It is given with an equal quantity of bicarbonate of soda. It not only diminishes pain and reduces temperature, but may help to cut short an attack of acute rheumatism. In other inflammations of rheumatic nature its use is also followed by great benefit.

SALICYLIC ACID is a white substance in fine crystals, of sweetish taste, and sparingly soluble in water. It is derived from salicin, and is contained also in oil of wintergreen, oil of the sweet birch (*Betula lenta*), and in various other plants. It is also produced in large quantities by the action of carbonic acid gas upon carbolic acid.

Action.—Salicylic acid is an antiseptic, and is used to saturate surgical wool, lint, and other dressings. Externally it is used in ointments to check various skin affections due to bacteria, and, since it has in addition a softening action on the surface of the skin, salicylic acid plasters are used to remove corns and various other superficial overgrowths.

SALINES (*sal*, salt) are purgatives belonging to the class of salts which produce watery evacuations. (*See* PURGATIVES.) For normal or isotonic saline solution *see* ISOTONIC.

SALISBURY TREATMENT is a mode of dieting introduced by an American physician. Its chief use is in the treatment of corpulence (*see* CORPULENCE), but it is also valuable in other abnormal states of health, where no acute disease is present.

SALIVA (*saliva*) is the fluid which is always present to some extent in the mouth, and is secreted in specially copious amount during a meal, or when the salivary glands are stimulated, as for example by an acid substance placed in the mouth. Saliva contains much mucus, a ferment known as ptyalin, which changes starch into dextrin and maltose (see DIGESTION) ; also many corpuscles similar to the white corpuscles of the blood.

The principal function of saliva is to aid in the initial processes of digestion. When food is taken into the mouth, an increased output of saliva is evoked. This saliva is essential for the process of mastication (q.v.), whereby food is reduced to a homogeneous mass before being swallowed. In addition, the ptyalin in the saliva initiates the digestion of starch in the food.

An excessive flow of saliva known as salivation occurs as the result of taking certain drugs over a considerable period, the commonest being mercury, iodide of potassium, and arsenic. Salivation also occurs as the result of irritation in the mouth, from dyspepsia, etc. Dribbling of saliva is a common symptom of bulbar paralysis.

SALIVARY GLANDS are the glands situated near, and opening into, the cavity of the mouth, by which the saliva is manufactured. They include the *parotid gland*, placed in the deep space that lies between the ear and the angle of the jaw ; the *submaxillary gland*, lying beneath the horizontal part of the jaw-bone ; and the *sublingual gland*, which lies beneath the tongue.

Each gland is made up of branching tubes closely packed together, and supported by strong connective tissue. These tubes are lined by large cells that secrete the saliva, and from their interior lead ducts that unite with one another to form ultimately the large main ducts that open into the mouth. The appearance and character of the secreting cells vary in different glands. In the parotid gland they secrete a clear fluid containing the ferment ptyalin, in the sublingual gland they mainly produce mucus, whilst the submaxillary gland contains cells of both types.

SALMON PATCHES are small pink patches found in a certain number of new-born infants — on the eyelids, on the forehead between the eyes, and on the nape of the neck. Those on the first two of these three sites have usually faded by the baby's first birthday, but those on the nape of the neck may be more persistent. (*See also* BIRTH-MARKS.)

774

SALMONELLA INFECTIONS (*see* FOOD POISONING).

SALOL is a white, crystalline, tasteless substance with faint aromatic odour. It is used as an intestinal antiseptic, when it is desired to check fermentative and putrefactive changes.

SALPINGITIS (σάλπιγξ, a trumpet) is the name applied to inflammation situated in the Fallopian tubes.

SALPINGO- (σάλπιγξ, a trumpet) is a prefix indicating a connection with either the Fallopian tubes or the Eustachian tubes.

SALT.—The substance produced by the replacement of the acidic hydrogen of an acid by a metal or basic radical. A synonym for common salt or sodium chloride.

SALTPETRE (*sal petræ*, salt of the rock. (*See* NITRE.)

SALUTARIUM (*salus*, health) is the name applied to a resort for the preservation of health.

SALVARSAN (see ARSPHENAMINE.)

SAL VOLATILE is another name for aromatic spirit of ammonia, a liquid of burning taste and great stimulating powers. Its action depends upon various volatile oils, ammonia, and carbonate of ammonia which it contains. It is used as a stimulating expectorant in cough mixtures, and is valuable as a stimulant in faints. The dose is from half to one teaspoonful in a wineglassful of water. (*See* AMMONIA.)

SANATORIUM, or SANITORIUM (*sano*, I heal; and *sanitas*, health), is the name applied to an establishment for the treatment of sick persons, especially convalescents or those who are not extremely ill. The term is now applied particularly to institutions for the open-air treatment of tuberculosis. (*See* TUBERCULOSIS.)

SANDALWOOD OIL is a yellowish, fragrant-smelling oil with bitter taste obtained from the wood *Santalum album* by distillation. It has an antiseptic action and is administered in doses of from 5 to 20 drops for inflammation of mucous membranes, particularly those of the urinary organs.

SANDFLY FEVER (see THREE-DAY FEVER).

SANDWORM is a popular name for the sand-flea or jigger. (*See* PARASITES).

SANGUINEOUS (*sanguineus*) means containing blood.

SANIES means an evil-smelling, thin discharge from a wound or ulcer.

SANITAS is a fluid, consisting chiefly of oxidized turpentine dissolved in water which has a wide use as a disinfectant and deodorant. Its action depends upon peroxide of hydrogen, thymol, a soluble camphor, and camphoric acid.

SANITATION (*sanitas*, health), or the science which aims at the prevention of disease, although only fully developed during the last hundred years, was recognized in ancient times. So well were its fundamental principles understood, that even in the Mosaic days isolation of infectious cases, disinfection of infected materials by burning, and regulations for the abatement of nuisances, were in force. The importance of adequate water supplies was appreciated even before the days of the Roman Empire, and the sewers of Nineveh point to the beginnings of the drainage systems of cities.

At first, preventive medicine took cognizance only of the preventable or infectious diseases, but in its vast ramifications at the present day it aims also at the improvement of the general health of the populace, by the mitigation of all external conditions which tend to disease in individuals. It is not a science independent or standing alone. It is the handmaiden of various sciences. It embraces a knowledge of medicine, bacteriology, engineering, meteorology, architecture, and geology. It aims at the reduction of infectious diseases, but these have been its greatest advisers and teachers. The recurrent epidemics of cholera which formerly invaded Britain forced the hands of the populace to remedy their water supplies and remodel their systems of drainage. Smallpox and its long roll of victims forced on the compulsory adoption of Jenner's discovery of the value of vaccination. These sowed the seed, and other infectious diseases have brought it nearer maturity. Improved sanitation in matters of ventilation, sewerage, water supply, hospital accommodation, the abatement of nuisances, and the inspection of meat has naturally followed from the first step in advance. Its value has been shown in the improved hygiene of the factory, where sanitation has been called in to save the workers from the dangers of their occupation, in meeting the demands of modern civilization, and in the improved conditions of life in dwellings and in general surroundings. It aims at correcting the evils arising from the aggregation of people in cities and towns. It benefits the country dweller and the resident in town by improved methods of sewage and refuse disposal.

Much has already been accomplished. But a few years ago the death-rate in many places reached a total of more than 30 per 1000 inhabitants per year. To-day these places may show a death-rate of under 20 per 1000 per annum. We cannot estimate the effects of sanitary effort by single years. Results vary from year to year, but over a series of years the visible result of lives saved and lengthened, with its benefit to the State, is a striking tribute to the skill and enthusiasm with which the public health organization of the country has been developed since the days of Chadwick and Simon.

Sanitary law.—Numerous laws dealing with sanitary matters have been put in force in recent years. The general public health administration of the country is based, in England on the Public Health Act of 1875, and in Scotland on that of 1897, but into many Acts not primarily dealing with sanitation, sanitary provisions have been introduced, as in the various Factory and Workshop Acts. Special local Acts have also been obtained by various authorities, and almost every year some Act is passed by Parliament giving greater sanitary control.

In the various Public Health Acts, which constitute the basis of sanitary administration, machinery is provided for dealing with :

1. General nuisances and offensive trades. Offensive trades include the trades of blood boiler, blood drier, bone boiler, fat extractor, fat melter, fellmonger, glue maker, gut scraper, rag and bone dealer, size maker, soap boiler, tallow melter, or tripe boiler.
2. Scavenging and cleansing and the formation of scavenging districts.
3. The seizure of unsound food.
4. The general prevention and mitigation of infectious diseases, including the provision of isolation hospitals, houses of reception, ambulances, disinfecting stations and apparatus. The diseases defined by Act of Parliament in Britain as infectious are: smallpox, cholera, diphtheria, membranous croup, erysipelas, the disease known as scarlatina or scarlet fever; and the fevers known by any of the following names—typhus, typhoid, enteric, relapsing, continued or puerperal, and also any infectious disease to which the Act has been applied by the local authority in manner provided by the Act.
5. The regulation of common lodging-houses and houses let in lodgings.
6. The provision of water and sewers and the formation of special districts for water supply and drainage.
7. The regulation of buildings.
8. The constitution of port sanitary authorities.
9. Prevention of pollution of rivers by sewage.
10. Regulations as to sale and adulteration of foods.
11. Dairies, cowsheds, and milkshops Orders.
12. Various Acts for housing of working classes, including Town Planning Acts.
13. Tuberculosis Orders, Factory and Workshop Acts.
14. Cleansing of persons.
15. Notification of births, Children's and Midwives' Acts.

Medical Officer of Health.—The Medical Officer of Health is required to acquaint himself with the general sanitary condition of his district, to suggest the steps he considers might be taken for its improvement, and to advise the local authority in all sanitary matters. He is expected to investigate all outbreaks of infectious disease, report upon them, and recommend and see carried into force such preventive measures as he deems necessary. He must, if it is

776

advisable, or if he is directed by the sanitary authority, himself inspect any article exposed for food, and deal with it, if it is unsound. He advises also as to nuisances injurious to health. He is expected to keep a record of his actions, observations, and instructions. He is required to prepare an annual report on the sanitary condition of the district, the work accomplished by his department, the occurrence of infectious disease throughout the year, the general sickness and mortality returns, and the condition of the offensive trades, dairies, cowsheds, bakehouses, factories, and workshops, with a statement of his actions in regard to them. This report, and any special report prepared by him, must be forwarded to the Ministry of Health. He is also expected to inform the Ministry of any outbreak of dangerous infectious disease.

Public Health Inspector.—The Public Health Inspector, or Sanitary Inspector, as he used to be known, attends to the general sanitation of the district, investigates all conditions of nuisances, sees that the regulations and by-laws relating to offensive trades are observed, and that all unsound meat is dealt with. He takes, if authorized by the sanitary authority to do so, samples under the Sale of Food and Drugs Acts, and if these be found adulterated, he takes action under the Act. He reports to the Medical Officer of Health any infectious disease, coming under his notice, occurring in the district. He is required to preserve records of his inspections and actions.

Nuisances.—A large number of objectionable processes are declared by the Public Health Acts to be 'Nuisances or injurious or dangerous to health'. Houses badly constructed or overcrowded, streets, ditches, water supplies, stables and byres, etc., if foul and unclean, accumulations of filth, factories overcrowded, ill ventilated and filthy, furnaces not consuming their smoke as far as possible, overcrowded cemeteries, etc., all constitute nuisances.

Every sanitary authority is required to have its district inspected for the detection of nuisances. Any person, however, who suspects the presence of a nuisance may complain to the sanitary authority, who will at once have the matter investigated. If the authority is convinced of the existence of a nuisance, a notice will be served on the person responsible, or, if the author cannot be found, on the owner or occupier of the premises, requiring the removal of the nuisance within a specified time. Under the Public Health Act, 1875, if the sanitary authorities fail to discharge their duty with reference to nuisances, individuals can appeal to the Ministry of Health, who may issue an order to be enforced in a High Court of Justice, or may direct any police officer of the district to institute the ordinary legal proceedings in case of nuisance. The most expeditious method, however, for individuals to gain redress in case of default by the sanitary authority, is to complain direct to a justice, and the court may make orders and exact penalties, just as if the complaint had been made by the sanitary authority.

If the nuisance is then not removed, or is likely to recur, the sanitary authority may apply to a justice, who will require the presence of the person responsible before a court of summary jurisdiction. If satisfied that the nuisance exists, or is likely to recur, the court may at once decern, or may remit to a special inspector to report. When the court is satisfied of the existence of the nuisance, an order will be granted for its removal, and for the performance of such works as will prevent its recurrence. The court has further the power, if convinced that the nuisance arises from wilful fault or negligence, to fine the author of the nuisance. Where the author is not known, the local authority may be directed to remove the nuisance themselves. Special by-laws are also made by municipal authorities with reference to their own towns.

Houses and sites for building.—The health of the community depends in a large measure on the condition of its housing. Several factors contribute to the healthiness of a dwelling. The site must be suitable, the ventilation and water supply adequate, the construction must ensure the absence of dampness, and the sewage and refuse must be efficiently removed.

The site should be preferably on porous soil, such as gravel or sand, whence

water can easily be carried away. In every case, whether on porous soil or on clay, the ground should be well drained. In towns, no choice can usually be made in the site. and houses are placed wherever convenient. Many are placed on ' made soils ', but care ought to be taken that all organic matters have been completely decayed, a process which takes at least three years for completion, and not until that period has elapsed can a building be safely placed on a site of made soil. The site of the house should be covered by a layer of concrete to prevent the ground air and moisture gaining entrance into the house. The house should be so placed as to allow sufficient air to circulate around it, and to have abundance of light, and so elevated as to allow for proper drainage arrangements.

In the construction of houses, several points must be noted. The foundations must be strong enough to support the building upon them, while the walls should be built on a special basis of concrete. To obviate dampness further, an impervious layer of slates bedded in cement, or of lead, or asphalt, known as the *damp-proof course*, should be inserted in the wall, at least 6 inches above the ground level. This may also consist of a layer of perforated stoneware tiles, embedded in cement, which not only act as a hindrance to damp, but ventilate the area between the ground and the floor (Fig. 328).

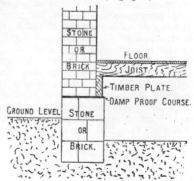

FIG. 328.—Foundation of a building in which the floor is above the level of the ground. The wall should rest on a concrete foundation.

Where the basement floor has to be made under the ground level, a ' dry area ' must be provided. This may be done by removing the earth to below the level of the floor, or the same end may be met by making the wall hollow (*see* Fig. 329) from the base to 6 inches above the ground level. In this case two damp-proof courses are needed : the one at the foot of the hollow below the floor level, the other at the top of the cavity.

The walls of the house may be built of stone, bricks, mortar, and wood. The stones tend to absorb moisture, but

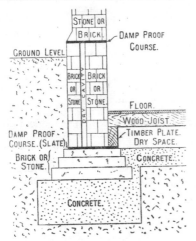

FIG. 329.—Foundation of a house with a sunk flat.

not nearly so freely as bricks. Thus, a brick should not absorb more than 15 per cent. of its own weight of water. The corresponding figures for limestones and sandstones are 10 and 8 per cent. respectively. Bricks also permit of the free percolation of air. Wood should be reserved for the inner fittings of houses. It is desirable that the height of each room should be at least 10 feet. Each room should be supplied with adequate windows equal in area to at least one-tenth of the floor space, while no boxed-in, ill-ventilated, and sunless apartments should be permitted. Special ventilators should be fitted up for each room, independent of the personal control of the occupants. (*See* VENTILATION.)

In towns great overcrowding of houses exists, due, only too frequently, to the inability of the householder to pay for a house large enough to accommodate his family with sufficient air

778

space. The Ministry of Health regard the minimum air space permissible as 300 cubic feet for an adult and half that amount for a child. Local authorities and private individuals have endeavoured to provide cheap and efficiently sanitary houses, so that the artisan may obtain a house sufficient for his needs at a low rent, but until more has been done in this way, the evils of overcrowding will still continue to exist.

Dampness in houses may arise from moisture finding its way up the walls where damp-proof courses are not provided ; and, where the house is in an exposed position, by rain being driven through the walls. This dampness arising from the driven rain can be prevented by covering the walls with some impervious material, as glazed tiles or Portland cement. Defective mortar, broken rainpipes and gutters, choked gutters and drains, leaks in water and drainage pipes, and defects in the roof and the slating may all lead to dampness. In very poor districts, where the house walls may be partly underground, the rain-water may collect, saturate the soil, and so soak through the bricks. In this case, each back-court should be paved and gulleys provided to conduct off the rain-water and prevent its collecting.

Streets and open spaces.—Streets not only act as thoroughfares for traffic, but also provide for ventilation and admission of sunlight to buildings, in addition to constituting the course for the main sewers and water-supply pipes. The width of the street is important with reference to the height of the houses along it. Too narrow a street with high buildings implies dingy, dark, ill-ventilated dwellings. Considerable powers have, therefore, been given to sanitary authorities under the various Public Health Acts to regulate the width of the street, the height of the buildings, and as to repair. The model by-laws of the Ministry of Health, adopted largely by sanitary authorities, suggest regulations with regard to the formation of new streets. They fix the minimum width of any new street to be used as a carriage road and over 100 feet long at 36 feet. Where it is not intended to be used as a carriage-way and is less than 100 feet long, 24 feet of width is allowed as the least permissible. In a new street used as a carriage road the carriage-way of the street shall be at least 24 feet wide, and the footpaths on each side must be at least one-sixth of the total width of the street. The carriage-way must slope from the centre to the channels, and the foot-way must also be inclined towards the kerb. These latter precautions provide for easy removal of water, the moisture falling down to the channels. Each street must be open at one end, in its full width from the ground. The regulation instanced above that 24 feet is the narrowest street now allowed to be made, guarantees a sufficient space in front of the buildings for the free circulation of air, and also provides for the gradual widening of the many narrow by-ways in old towns, as, whenever an old building is to be torn down and a new domestic building erected in its place, this new building must be set back so that there is space in front of it to the other side of the street of at least 24 feet.

More important still is the regulation dealing with the air-space required in the rear of the new house. The person who builds the new house must provide an open space in the rear, running the entire width of the building, of at least 150 square feet, free from any erection except a water-closet, earth-closet or privy, and an ashpit. The distance across this open space to the boundary of the land or premises opposite must be at the least 10 feet, and if the height of the building be 35 feet or more, this distance must be increased to 25 feet. This regulation aims at preventing the erection of 'back-to-back' houses, with their attendant evils of lack of ventilation and free circulation of air. In building schemes the usual plan adopted is twelve houses per acre in urban areas and eight houses per acre in rural areas.

Air and ventilation.—Pure atmospheric air contains a little over 20 per cent. by volume of oxygen, about 79 per cent. of nitrogen, and about 0·04 per cent. of carbonic acid gas, together with traces of watery vapour, ammonia, etc. The carbonic acid present is generally accepted as the standard of impurity, but this is only a guide. There is no evidence that the discomfort experienced in badly ventilated rooms is due to lack of oxygen or excess of carbonic acid gas. It is more closely associated

with heat stagnation due to excess of moisture and lack of air movement. The air is naturally purified by winds driving the impurities away and allowing fresher air to take its place ; by rain removing dissolved gases and washing away suspended impurities; and by vegetable life absorbing carbonic acid in the day-time and giving off oxygen. Fogs tend naturally to pollute it. It is vitiated by respiration, combustion, putrefactive processes of animal and vegetable matters, and by the products of trades and industries, such as the mineral particles set free in grinding and the organic effluvia given off in soap-making, bone-boiling, and tannery work.

Sewer gas itself, in a well-ventilated sewer, differs little from the external air, but when the sewer is badly constructed, ill ventilated, and the sewage is stagnant and allowed to putrefy, the bubbles of sewage gas are highly offensive, and may contain poisonous amounts of sulphuretted hydrogen.

Smoke from factories and open fires is a serious problem in diminishing the sunshine of large towns, but is being gradually lessened by the increasing use of gas and electricity.

Water and water supplies.—An adequate supply of water is necessary for every condition of life. Its importance has been recognized and appreciated from earliest times, and is closely bound up with the industrial activity and progress, as well as the health of communities. The increase in the purity of the supplies of this country has undoubtedly lessened the occurrence of water-borne epidemics of disease. Every township of any importance at the present time aims at possessing a pure and abundant supply. This supply is utilized for domestic, municipal, and trade purposes. The domestic supply must be liberal for cleanliness, cooking, drinking, and sanitary requirements. Municipal requirements for washing the streets, flushing the sewers, and extinguishing fires, absorb a considerable quantity. Trade processes vary in their demands, according to the nature of the industries. It is generally estimated that at least 25 gallons (115 litres) each day per head of the population are needed for domestic arrangements, 10 gallons (45 litres) for municipal purposes, and probably 25 gallons

(115 litres) additional for manufacturing businesses. No hard and fast rule can be set. The only limitation to be laid down is that the supply be abundant and pure, no wasteful extravagance being permitted. In towns where the industrial demands are exceptional, considering the size of the population, an average as high as 70 gallons (320 litres) per day per individual for all purposes is required. As an average, however, in an ordinary town about 50 gallons (227 litres) per day per head for all purposes will be needed.

The original source of all water supply is the rain and the dissolved snow. This may be gathered and used. Part, however, may sink through the soil, to reappear in the form of springs, or to be reached by means of wells. Part may flow on the surface as rivers and streams, or may be collected together in lakes. All these may form the source of supply. (For further details consult the article on WATER SUPPLY.)

Refuse and sewage disposal.—The subject of refuse and sewage disposal is concerned with removal from towns and from buildings of the waste matters. These waste matters consist chiefly of two distinct kinds — the excreta and waste waters, commonly dealt with as one in the sewage ; and, secondly, the dry refuse. The dry refuse includes the dust, ashes, and debris of vegetable and animal food from the households, the sweepings of streets and cattle-sheds, manure of horses and cows, and the dust and mineral particles of trade processes. The liquid and solid excreta and the waste water of houses have to be dealt with in sewage disposal. All the dry refuse is usually removed together by mechanical labour or scavenging, the scavengers, where it is possible, removing the refuse daily. Where a daily service cannot be instituted, the householder should burn at once all vegetable and animal food remnants, so that unpleasant decomposition may not set in before the arrival of the scavengers' carts. In many districts the dry refuse and human excretions are still removed together by the scavengers, the excretions being taken from the privies, dry-closets, and cesspools. This combination in treatment of the two

divisions of waste matters is known as the ' conservancy system '. The ideal method, however, for the disposal of human excretions and waste waters is by means of drains and sewers, in which this refuse is removed in a liquid condition away from the neighbourhood of houses and dwellings by the ' water carriage system '.

Details of the various processes will be found in the article on REFUSE AND SEWAGE DISPOSAL.

Food and disease.—BUTCHER MEAT. —Butcher meat, if good, should be firm and elastic, marbled with fat, light red in colour, neither purulent, livid, nor too moist. Various parasites may be present in meat which is diseased. The *Trichinella spiralis*, encapsuled, may be found in the muscles of the pig, and so infect man ; while cysticerci in the ox and the pig produce tapeworms in man. (*See* PARASITES.)

Meat which is infected or contaminated with bacterial toxins, if eaten, may cause alarming symptoms of vomiting, diarrhœa, and colic. (*See* FOOD POISONING.) The microbes of putrefaction in this case have given rise to poisonous substances. Anthrax and tuberculosis may be spread to man from meat affected with these diseases. Meat may be preserved by salting, pickling, or canning.

MILK.—Milk, being one of the chief articles of food, is often suspected of being the means of carrying disease. The cows are, therefore, periodically inspected, under the powers given in the Dairies, Cowsheds, and Milkshops Orders for the detection of diseases. Milk may convey the infecting organisms of bovine tuberculosis, scarlet fever, enteric fever, diphtheria, undulant fever, septic sore throat, and of FOOD POISONING (*q.v.*). Being so largely used as a food, it is frequently adulterated, water being the commonest adulterant, whilst cream is often abstracted. Occasionally such articles as borax, salicylic acid, and boracic acid may be added in order to preserve the milk fresh and sweet. (*See* MILK.)

BUTTER.—Butter may be adulterated with foreign fats and additional water. Margarine is occasionally substituted.

COFFEE.—Coffee may contain excess of chicory.

WHEAT FLOUR.—Wheat flour is sometimes adulterated with other grains. Foods are now rigidly inspected. Samples are taken for analysis, and if these are found to be adulterated the owners are prosecuted, and may be heavily punished. At every slaughterhouse, inspection of meat is carried through as a matter of routine, and no meat which is declared unsound is allowed to be sold. (See also ADULTERATION OF FOOD.)

Infectious diseases are due to the entrance into the body of certain bacteria or their toxins, or of filterable viruses which multiply in the system, and can be given off from the person affected, and thus may be received into the body of other individuals, in whom they may reproduce the disease. Hence the diseases are known as infectious diseases.

The infectious diseases may be spread from a person in various ways.

1. By the breath, as in scarlet fever, measles, whooping-cough, etc. In many cases the expired air gathers its infection from the throat.

2. By particles of skin and the dried purulent crusts of smallpox.

3. By excretions and secretions. The discharges from the throat and nose are highly infectious in scarlet fever, diphtheria, and measles. The faecal excretions in enteric fever and cholera contain the infection. The purulent discharges of abscesses and pustules in certain diseases infect. The sputum of phthisical patients contains the tubercle bacillus. The urine in enteric fever is infected and can convey the disease. Milk, water, and foods are often infected by excretions, defects in the drains allowing the excretions to soak through and infect the waters of wells, or the water used in washing and cleaning conveys the infection to the utensils in which the milk is received and the food cooked. These articles of diet may also be infected by direct contact with the excretions of a carelessly treated patient, resulting in localized epidemics of infectious disease. Contamination of food frequently occurs through the medium of flies (see INSECTS IN RELATION TO DISEASE).

If the person is susceptible to the disease, a period elapses after the organism is received, known as the incubation period, during which no symptoms develop, but during which the organism multiplies and produces its poison. This period varies with each disease. (See INCUBATION, INFECTION.)

METHODS OF PREVENTION may embrace removal of cases to hospital or isolation at home ; disinfection of clothing, bedding, and premises ; isolation, if necessary, of persons who have been in contact with certain diseases ; closure of schools if the disease is being spread by the school connection (see INFECTION) ; stoppage of milk supplies if these be infected, and injection of protective sera, as in those exposed to diphtheria, and the performance of vaccination upon persons who have come in contact with cases of smallpox.

SMALLPOX.—Smallpox was formerly an extremely common disease in this country, but is now largely limited to epidemics at considerable intervals. Before vaccination was made compulsory children were largely affected. It is now chiefly a disease of adults. The greatest season of prevalence is during the cold months of winter and spring. The exhalations and purulent crusts are the chief means of conveying infection. (See SMALLPOX, VACCINATION.)

SCARLET FEVER.—The greatest number of cases occurs in young children. It is generally endemic in the large towns of Britain, but from time to time assumes epidemic proportions. The fatality rate has been greatly reduced in recent years, the type of the disease being milder, but the prevalence of the disease has been little reduced. The infection is chiefly spread by discharges from the throat and nose. Milk is occasionally infected and spreads the disease. (See SCARLET FEVER.)

DIPHTHERIA.—Infection passes from case to case by the exhalations and discharges from the nose and throat. Milk epidemics occasionally occur where the milk has become infected by the discharges from some patient living at the dairy or from some case infecting the milk during the course of distribution. Schools aid in spreading the disease by the presence of some scholar suffering from a mild, unrecognized attack. The most important preventive measure is the inoculation of school children and the ' pre-school child ' with diphtheria prophylactic, as, for example, with alum-precipitated toxoid (A.P.T.).

As a result of the increasing extent to which the child-population has been immunized in this way, there has been a dramatic fall both in the incidence and the severity of diphtheria. (*See* DIPHTHERIA.)

ENTERIC or TYPHOID FEVER. — Its prevalence has been largely reduced by adequate water supplies and improved sanitary conditions. The excreta are highly infectious and must be carefully disinfected. Milk and water have been contaminated and have led to large epidemics. (*See* ENTERIC FEVER.)

TYPHUS FEVER.—Poverty, with its consequences in privation, overcrowding, and filth, is the chief predisposing cause of this disease. (*See* TYPHUS FEVER.)

MEASLES and WHOOPING-COUGH are largely diseases of childhood. With increase of years the liability to attack is reduced. The severity is greatest in the very young, who should, therefore, be protected from infection and not exposed. The number of deaths per year among children due to these diseases is much larger than is commonly supposed. Convalescent serum and immune globulin are useful in preventing measles in the very young or frail, or in modifying the disease in the robust child, when known exposure to infection has occurred. A vaccine is now available which is proving of value in the prevention of whooping-cough, and a vaccine for the prevention of measles has now become available for general use. (*See* MEASLES, WHOOPING-COUGH.)

PULMONARY TUBERCULOSIS is the most serious of all the infectious diseases. Preventive measures include disinfection of clothing, apartments, and sputum, mass miniature radiography, and the use of B.C.G. vaccine (*q.v.*). (*See* TUBERCULOSIS.)

Disinfection and disinfectants.—Disinfection consists in the destruction of the organisms or other agencies of disease. It is accomplished by means of disinfectants, of which sunlight, fresh air, and fire are the most efficient and natural. During epidemics, milk or water, if suspected of being infected, should be boiled. All cloths, etc., used to clean up discharges from infectious cases should, if possible, be destroyed, whilst, if the bedding and clothing are totally worthless or in a wretched con-

dition, they may also be burned. Many of the ordinary disinfectants, though containing disinfectant materials, are used in such strength as only to act as deodorants, and so, while removing the noxious odours, particularly of excreta, do not destroy the infecting material and consequently give only a false sense of security. For the varieties and uses of disinfectants *see* DISINFECTION.

Disposal of the dead. — The chief object in the disposal of the dead is the speediest method by which the body can be dissolved into its simplest components. Two methods are in vogue in Britain, namely, burial and cremation.

BURIAL, from a sanitary point of view, should take place in a loamy or sandy porous soil, well drained, and so situated as not to contaminate any water supply, and preferably removed from the neighbourhood of houses. The body should be confined in a thin, easily disintegrated coffin. Oak and lead coffins and brick vaults all violate the first principles of burial. Coffins must be separated from each other by at least one foot of earth, and no coffin is permitted to be nearer the surface of the ground than 4 feet.

The Burial Acts, 1853–1906, provide for the closing of overcrowded churchyards and the discontinuance of burials in them. Under this power many of the old overcrowded churchyards have been closed.

CREMATION is, perhaps, the best sanitary method of disposal, especially in cases of infectious disease, the germs of some of which can exist in the soil. The sanitary reason for it is powerful, but its adoption prevents the possibility of exhumation, and so might occasionally prevent the detection of crime. (For further details, *see* DEAD, DISPOSAL OF.)

SANOCRYSIN is a proprietary name for thiosulphate of gold and sodium which is used for the treatment of rheumatoid arthritis. (*See* GOLD SALTS.)

SANTONIN is a yellow crystalline powder obtained from santonica, also known as ' worm-seed ', the dried flowers of *Artemisia maritima*, which is brought from the Levant. It is used for its action in expelling roundworms. Santonin is generally given in doses of about 1 grain (60 mg.) to children or 3 grains (200 mg.) to adults on three successive nights. Like other remedies against worms, its use must be preceded by a period of fasting and followed by a saline purgative. When too large a dose has been taken, yellow or green vision is apt to result for a time.

SAPHENOUS (σαφηνής, manifest) is the name given to the two large superficial veins of the leg. The external saphenous vein which runs up the outside and back of the leg joins the deep veins at the bend of the knee ; the internal saphenous vein which has a long course from the inner ankle to the groin is specially subject, with its branches, to become the seat of varicose veins.

SAPO is the Latin name for soap.

SAPRÆMIA (σαπρός, decayed ; αἷμα, blood) is the name applied to a mild form of blood-poisoning. (*See* BLOOD-POISONING.)

SAPROPHYTE (σαπρός, putrid ; φυτόν, plant) is the term applied to organisms which live usually upon decaying and dead matter and produce its decomposition.

SARCINA (*sarcina*, a bundle) is a microscopic vegetable growth, which is found in the material vomited or drawn off by the stomach tube from a dilated stomach.

SARCO- (σάρξ, flesh) is a prefix signifying flesh or fleshy.

SARCOIDOSIS is a relatively rare chronic disease of unknown origin. In certain cases it is a manifestation of tuberculosis. It involves the skin, lymph nodes, eyes, salivary glands, lungs, and bones of the hands and feet.

SARCOMA (σάρκωμα, a fleshy growth). (*See* CANCER *and* Plate VII.)

SARCOPTES SCABIEI is the mite which causes scabies. (*See* ITCH, SCABIES, PARASITES.)

SARSAPARILLA is the root of various species of *Smilax*. It is largely used in domestic medicine as a ' blood-purifier ', and is an ingredient of many patent medicines.

SASSAFRAS is the name for a genus of laurel trees. The root bark of *Sassafras variifolia* contains an oil, and its fluid extract was formerly much used in the treatment of various skin diseases. Mucilage derived from sassafras is also used in bronchial and gastric affections.

SATURNINE POISONING (*saturnius*, belonging to Saturn, leaden) is another name for lead-poisoning. (*See* LEAD-POISONING.)

SAXIN is a substance closely resembling saccharin (*q.v.*).

SCAB is the name given to the crust which forms on superficial injured areas. It is composed of fibrin, which is exuded from the raw surface, together with blood corpuscles and epithelial cells entangled in its meshes. Healing takes place naturally under this protection, and the scab dries up and falls off when healing is complete. Scabs appearing on the face without any previous abrasion are frequently of infectious nature. (*See* IMPETIGO.)

SCABIES (*scabies*, scab). (*See* ITCH.)

SCALD HEAD is the old name for favus. (*See* RINGWORM.)

SCALDS (*see* BURNS AND SCALDS).

SCALP is the soft covering of the skull upon the top of the head. It consists of five layers, which from the surface inwards are as follows : the skin, thickly furnished with hair ; next a subcutaneous layer of fat, rendered tough and stringy by many bands of fibrous tissue passing through it to bind the skin and the third layer together ; thirdly, a tough membrane composed of fibrous tissue, known as the epicranium ; fourthly, a loose layer of connective tissue attaching the epicranium to the deepest layer, and permitting the free movements of which the scalp is capable ; and, finally, another fibrous layer clinging closely to the skull, and known as the pericranium.

SCALPEL (*scalpellum*) is a small, straight, surgical knife.

SCAMMONY is a resin derived from the root of *Convolvulus scammonia*, a plant of Asia Minor and Syria. It acts as a powerful purgative.

SCAPULA is the technical name for the shoulder-blade. (*See* SHOULDER-BLADE.)

SCAR is the name applied to a healed wound, ulcer, or breach of tissue. A scar consists essentially of fibrous tissue, covered by an imperfect formation of cuticle in the case of scars on the surface of the skin. The fibrous tissue is produced by the connective tissue corpuscles that wander into the wound in the course of its repair (*see* WOUNDS), and is at first delicate in texture and richly provided with blood - vessels. Accordingly a scar at first is soft, and has a redder tint than the surrounding skin. Gradually this fibrous tissue contracts, becomes more dense, and loses its blood-vessels, so that an old scar is hard and white.

The more specialized textures are not repaired when a scar forms: thus on the skin-surface the scar does not reproduce hairs and sweat-glands, only the general epithelium growing over the wounded surface. Similarly in the case of internal organs, such as the stomach, no glands form anew in the scar. When muscles or nerves are wounded, however, new muscle- or nerve-fibres grow into the scar. Bone is repaired by a formation of fibrous tissue, which is produced just as in the soft parts, and later lime salts are deposited in the scars. (*See* BONE.)

The contraction that takes place in a scar has already been mentioned. The more quickly the surfaces of a wound are brought into contact with one another, the less fibrous tissue is produced for the union. Consequently a wound whose edges are accurately brought together and in which healing is rapid shows far less contraction afterwards, and leaves a fainter scar, than one in which the wound is allowed to gape, and in which healing is slow. Burns are therefore followed by very marked scars and great contraction, which frequently produces marked deformity of the part concerned.

784

Similarly, when inflammation takes place, as when an operation wound becomes infected, or when such a disease as lupus is present, causing great irritation of the wound, a wide, unsightly scar results and causes much puckering of the surrounding skin as it contracts. Such scars are also of low vitality, stretch easily, so as to become still more evident, and if irritated, as, for example, by the pressure of a boot or badly fitting artificial limb, readily give way and produce an ulcer which is slow to heal. Unsightly scars on the face often can be removed by a combination of surgical procedure and radium applications.

Scars are sometimes extremely painful, especially those which are left after the amputation of part of a limb. This is caused in general by the involvement of a sensory nerve in the hard contracting tissue of the scar.

SCARF-SKIN is another name for the cuticle or epithelium which forms a thin, horny covering everywhere for the true skin. (*See* SKIN.)

SCARIFICATION (σκάριφος, a scratching tool) means the making of shallow cuts in the skin for the purpose of drawing blood.

SCARLET FEVER, or SCARLATINA, is an acute infectious disease, characterized by high fever, sore throat, and a diffuse red rash upon the skin, due to infection with a hæmolytic streptococcus. This fever appears to have been first accurately described by Sydenham in 1676, before which period it had evidently been confounded with smallpox and measles.

Causes.—Scarlatina is a highly contagious malady. The patient is infectious from the time of the first symptoms, and the infectivity is greatest at the height of the fever, thereafter gradually falling off as the disease declines. It is not always easy to say with certainty when infectivity ceases. The tendency is to shorten the period of isolation : until clinical recovery or not less than seven days from onset, provided that at the end of this time the patient has no infectious discharges, as from the nose. The clothes and other articles which have been in contact with a patient are infectious, and may remain so for a long time, especially if they are excluded from light and air. The disease may be carried by milk, which is probably as a rule contaminated by some infected person working on its distribution or in the dairy. Scarlatina is a disease especially of young children, although school infection does not play as important a part in its spread as in the case of diphtheria or measles. Adults may also suffer if they have not had this fever in childhood, but one attack usually confers immunity from a second. Certain constitutional conditions predispose to its development, such as overcrowding and neglect of children, and susceptibility varies very markedly in different persons. Women in the puerperal state are particularly liable to contract infection, and inflammatory conditions of the throat such as diphtheria also render persons more vulnerable to scarlatina.

Surgical scarlatina is a name given to a mild condition of fever with red rash and sometimes enlargement of glands, which may accompany septic conditions such as burns, empyema, and other abscesses. It appears to be due to streptococcal infection.

Symptoms.—The period of incubation (*i.e.* the time elapsing between the reception of infection and the development of symptoms) varies somewhat. In most cases it lasts only two to three days, but in occasional cases the patient may take a week to develop his first symptoms. The invasion of fever is usually short and sharp, with rapid rise of temperature to 104° F. (40° C.) or thereabouts in the first few hours. There also occur shivering, vomiting, headache, sore throat, and marked increase in the rate of the pulse. In young children convulsions or delirium may also usher in the fever. At the end of about 24 hours from the commencement of the fever the characteristic eruption appears. It is first seen on the neck, chest, arms, and hands, but quickly spreads all over the body and legs. The rash consists of minute, thickly set, red points which coalesce to form a general redness not unlike that produced by application of mustard to the skin. The rash tends to avoid the region of the nose and lips (circumoral pallor). Sometimes the redness is ac-

companied by small vesicles containing fluid. In ordinary cases the rash is at its height in about two days and then begins to fade, being gone at the end of a week from its first appearance. The severity of a case is to some extent measured by the copiousness and brilliancy of the rash, except in the malignant variety of the fever when the rash may be suppressed. The tongue at first is covered by thick, white, creamy fur through which, on the second day, red papillæ project, giving the appearance of a ' white strawberry tongue '. The fur is then gradually denuded, and by the fourth or fifth day the tongue is red, bare, and glazed—' red strawberry tongue '. The interior of the throat is red and swollen, especially the uvula, soft palate, and tonsils, and a considerable amount of secretion is found on the inflamed surfaces. The glands under the jaw are slightly swollen and tender. In favourable cases the fever falls distinctly about the third day, the symptoms at the same time rapidly improve, and the rash fades. The throat becomes more comfortable, and desquamation of the cuticle shows

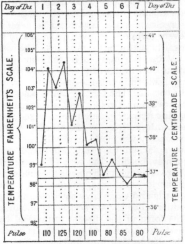

Day of Dis	1	2	3	4	5	6	7	Day of Dis
Pulse	110	125	120	110	80	85	80	Pulse

FIG. 330.—Temperature chart from a case of scarlet fever.

itself first about the cheeks and neck, and later spreads all over the surface of the body. The desquamation may be in the form of fine bran-like scales, or the cuticle may come off in large pieces, especially about the hands and feet. The duration of this process is variable, but it is rarely completed before the end of six weeks, or even more. During this stage the patient, who is now feeling quite well, must take particular care against exposure to cold, for during the desquamating stage there is special liability to inflammation of the kidneys.

Varieties.—Scarlet fever shows itself in certain well - marked varieties, of which the following are the chief :

1. SCARLATINA SIMPLEX is the most common form : in this the symptoms, both local and general, are moderate, and the case usually runs a favourable course. It is always to be borne in mind, however, that the duration and the infectiveness of the disease, including its convalescence, are uninfluenced by the mildness of the attack. In some instances the evidences of the disease are so slight, as regards both fever and rash, that the disease escapes observation and only becomes known by the patient subsequently 'peeling' or suffering from some of the complications associated with it. In such cases the name *latent scarlet fever* (*scarlatina latens*) is applied. Such cases are often responsible for spreading the disease.

2. SCARLATINA ANGINOSA is a more severe form of the fever, particularly as regards the throat symptoms. The rash may be well marked or not, but it is often slow in developing and in subsiding. There is intense inflammation of the throat ; the tonsils, uvula, and soft palate being swollen and ulcerated, or having upon them membranous patches not unlike those of diphtheria, while externally the gland tissues in the neck are enlarged and indurated and frequently become the seat of abscesses. There is difficulty in opening the mouth; an acrid discharge exudes from the nostrils and excoriates the lips, and the countenance is pale and waxy-looking. This form of the disease is marked by great prostration of strength, is often attended by delirium, and is much more frequently fatal than the preceding. In any case the rise of temperature is prolonged ; swallowing is difficult ; there is very often inflammation of the middle ears ; and broncho-pneumonia, inflammation of the joints, and albuminuria are frequent complications.

3. SCARLATINA MALIGNA is the most

serious form of all. The malignancy may be variously displayed. Thus a case of scarlatina anginosa may acquire such a severe character, both as to throat and general symptoms, as rapidly to produce profound exhaustion and death. But the typically malignant forms are those in which the attack sets in with great violence and the patient sinks from the very first. In such instances the rash either does not come out at all or is of the slightest amount and of livid rather than scarlet appearance, while the throat symptoms are often not prominent. Death in such cases may take place in from twenty-four to forty-eight hours, and is often preceded by great elevation of the temperature of the body and by delirium, coma, or other nervous symptoms. A further example of a malignant form is occasionally observed in cases in which the rash, which has previously been well developed, suddenly recedes, and convulsions or other nervous symptoms and rapid death supervene. These exceptionally severe cases are not now so common as they were some thirty or forty years ago.

Complications.—The most common and serious of these is *inflammation of the kidneys*, or *glomerulonephritis*, which may arise during any period in the course of the fever, but is specially apt to appear in the convalescence, while desquamation is in progress. Its onset is sometimes announced by a return of feverish symptoms, accompanied with vomiting and pain in the loins ; but in a large number of instances it occurs without these and comes on insidiously. One of the most prominent symptoms is slight swelling of the face, particularly of the eyelids, which is rarely absent in this complication. The urine is diminished in quantity and of dark smoky or red appearance, due to the presence of blood, and contains albumin. Microscopic examination reveals the presence of tube casts containing blood, epithelium, etc. In favourable cases these symptoms may soon disappear, but they may, on the other hand, prove extremely serious—the risks being the suppression of urine, leading to uræmic poisoning and causing convulsions which may terminate fatally, or, further the rapid development of general dropsy, and death from this cause. If this complication ensues, it commonly does so about the third or fourth week after the beginning of the illness, and is frequently precipitated by a chill. Occasionally this condition does not wholly pass off, and consequently lays the foundation for chronic Bright's disease (*see* BRIGHT'S DISEASE). Another complication of scarlet fever is *suppuration of the ears*, due to the extension of the inflammatory process from the throat along the Eustachian tube into the middle ear. (*See* EAR, DISEASES OF.) Other maladies affecting the heart, lungs, pleura, etc., occasionally arise in connection with scarlet fever, the chief of these being *endocarditis*, which may lay the foundation of valvular disease of the heart later in life. Arthritis or *scarlatinal rheumatism* is another complication of the disease producing swelling and pain in the smaller rather than in the larger joints. This complication usually occurs in the second week of illness and especially in people who are subject to rheumatism at other times, and it generally abates without serious trouble.

Treatment.—In the treatment of scarlet fever, one of the first requirements is the isolation of the case, with a view to preventing the spread of the disease. In view of the mild type of scarlet fever at present prevailing there is a tendency in Great Britain not to admit such cases to hospital unless they are particularly severe, the home conditions are unsatisfactory, or there is some risk to the public, *e.g.* a member of the household works in a dairy and may therefore be responsible for infecting milk. Children who have been in contact with cases of scarlet fever used to be quarantined for seven days before being allowed to mix with other children in school or elsewhere, but in many areas they are now allowed to go to school provided they are sent home at the first suggestion of fever or malaise.

When the patient is treated at home, the sick-room should contain only such furniture as may be required, and the attendants should come as little as possible in contact with other members of the household. It is usual to keep the patient in bed for two weeks from the onset of the disease, and thereafter great care must be taken to avoid chills, owing to the danger of kidney compli-

cations. All body or bed linen when removed should be placed at once in boiling water, or in some disinfecting fluid. All books, toys, etc., used by the patient during the illness should be destroyed if of no value, or alternatively, carefully disinfected. The chief sources of contagion are the discharges of ear, nose, and throat. The desquamating skin is not infectious.

As scarlet fever is predominantly a streptococcal infection, the sulphonamide drugs or penicillin should be given. Preference is now generally shown for penicillin, and this should be given in every case. As to general management during the progress of the fever, in favourable cases little is required beyond careful nursing and feeding. The diet all through the fever and convalescence should be light but nourishing, consisting mainly of milk foods. During the febrile stage plenty fluid must be taken, which can be flavoured with fruit juices. A useful drink may be made from bitartrate of potassium (*see* CREAM OF TARTAR), of which the patient may partake freely. Attention to the movement of the bowels is of importance, and any mild aperient, especially a saline, may be used for this purpose.

In the malignant variety, where the eruption is not appearing, or is but ill-developed, stimulants internally, and the hot bath or pack, may sometimes afford a chance. The treatment of the kidney complication and its accompanying dropsy is similar to that for acute Bright's disease. The management of the joint affections, enlarged glands, and discharge from the nose, which frequently occur, is conducted on general principles.

SCHICK TEST is a method designed for finding out the liability of individuals to contract diphtheria. (*See* DIPHTHERIA.)

SCHISTOSOMA, also known as BILHARZIA, is the name given to a genus of parasitic worms spread by snails, which is responsible for one of the most important diseases in the tropics : schistosomiasis. (*See* PARASITES.)

SCHISTOSOME DERMATITIS (*see* BATHER'S ITCH).

SCHIZO- (σχίζω, I divide) is a prefix signifying splitting.

SCHIZOPHRENIA (σχίζω, I divide ; φρήν, mind) is a term applied to forms of psychosis in which there is a cleavage of the mental functions, associated with assumption by the affected person of a second personality. (*See* MENTAL ILLNESS.)

SCHOOL CHILDREN.—With regard to the earliest period of life, the management of children will be found under INFANT FEEDING and CHILDREN, PECULIARITIES OF. After infancy, there follows a period between the ages of two and five, during which the child is more or less independent but requires a considerable amount of care, which at the present day is supervised by Child Welfare Clinics. Thereafter from about the age of six to fourteen years the child comes under the discipline of school, and special arrangements for the welfare of children are then made through the educational agencies.

Schools are now built on a ' pavilion ' plan, and great care is taken in regard to their site, construction, ventilation, warming, etc. The appropriate temperature for rooms in infant departments is about 65° F. (18·5° C.), and in classrooms for older children from 56° to 60° F. (13·5 to 18·5° C.). Some form of central heating is necessary, and also some system of artificial ventilation. The minimum requirement of space per scholar is 100 cubic feet of air with 10 square feet of floor space, but, as a rule, the space allowed is at least 16 square feet per child.

Seats and desks form a very important matter both in regard to the comfort and, more particularly, in regard to the development of growing children, because if they are badly constructed or unsuitable in size the child is apt to assume unsuitable postures and undergo deformity in development (*see* SPINE, DISEASES OF). The seats and desks should be arranged in parallel rows at right angles with the windows, and, if possible, the chief illumination should be from the left. The desks should be from 15 to 18 inches (32 to 40 cm.) wide and slightly sloped. The height of the seat from the ground should be equal to the length of the scholar's leg from the sole of the foot

788

to the knee, and the front of the seat should be almost under the edge of the desk. The height of the edge of the desk above the seat should be one-sixth of the scholar's height. Seats and desks should be carefully adjusted to growing children twice yearly, and it must be remembered that the heights of scholars of the same age often vary as much as 10 inches, whilst children often increase in height 4 to 6 inches (10 to 15 cm.) in a year. Each pupil should have from 20 to 40 inches (0·5 to 1 metre) of seat room.

The provision of cloakrooms with pegs, of covered sheds for recreation, and of suitable closet and lavatory provision is very important.

Drinking-water is an important matter, because drinking - cups often form a means of communicating disease such as diphtheria. In the crystal stream drinking-fountains provided in American schools no cups are necessary, scholars drinking directly from a weak upward jet of water. Small folded paper cups are cheap and can be thrown away after use. In England, education authorities are required to provide milk and meals for school children on days when the school meets, and they are empowered to provide such refreshment on other days. The **diet** for school children should be plain, generous, easily digested, and varied, with ample eggs, butter, fish, meat, and a liberal allowance of cooked and fresh fruit. Milk is a highly nutritious food, which is specially suitable for children. The craving for sweet things should be met by supplying these at the end of a meal after the appetite has been satisfied. Over 75 per cent. of the elementary school children of Great Britain give evidence of **dental caries,** and an early investigation of the teeth is desirable, together with inculcation by the teacher of the use of the tooth-brush as an essential act of cleanliness.

Under the Education Acts of Great Britain, children from five to fifteen years of age must attend school, whilst mentally defective, blind, and deaf children must receive education up to the age of sixteen years. For the successful teaching of scholars it is important that they should not suffer from **mental fatigue.** This is brought about not so much by long hours of work as by a wrong system of teaching. A time - table and a method which economize brain energy and direct its application are essential. With children, no individual subject should be pursued for longer than three-quarters of an hour, and the succession of subjects taught should be suitably varied. There should be sufficient intervals for rest, play, physical exercise, and food. In the classroom, quiet and fresh air are very important (*see* FATIGUE). For the amount of sleep requisite at different ages *see* CHILDREN, PECULIARITIES OF. The teaching of mentally defective children presents special problems, as these children make very slow progress (*see* MENTAL DEFECTIVENESS). In any case, children up to the age of five years whose nervous system is rapidly developing and easily tired should be educated chiefly through their senses and physical activities. For the next five years, which is probably the chief period of character formation, the important object is the development of good habits ; and after the age of ten the child's reasoning powers and imagination can be most suitably developed.

The eyesight of about 20 per cent. of scholars is defective, and in 10 per cent. seriously defective. Young children are specially handicapped by short sight ; and at a later stage, when reading of books is a more essential part of study, those who suffer from long-sight are apt to develop symptoms of eye strain. (*See* VISION, DISORDERS OF, *and* SPECTACLES.)

Defective hearing due to ear disease is present in between 10 and 20 per cent. of scholars. The effect of this as regards lessons is that the child misses spoken words and shows seeming inattention or stupidity. Owing to the strain of his attention in class he is more readily exhausted by lessons. Physical symptoms are earache, headache, discharge from the ears, and, if the condition is complicated by adenoids and enlarged tonsils, a habitually open mouth which gives him a still further appearance of stupidity. The hearing should be carefully tested once a year, and if children are found to be deaf they should undergo the necessary treatment and should be given a suitable position in the class.

Exercise (*see* EXERCISE) is a matter

of great importance, partly because, when physical exercises are suitably interspersed with lessons, the circulation and general sense of well-being are increased so that more ready attention is given to teaching. Also physical exercises can be made to correct faulty and defective conditions in development and bad habits in regard to posture. Combined exercises, in which a large number take part, aid in school discipline and develop qualities of alertness, decision, and activity. These exercises should, if possible, take place in the open air, should be carefully graded to suit the ages of the scholars, and should be designed to develop specially important muscles and movements such as those of deep breathing. Special attention should be given to children who develop faulty postures or have a tendency to deformities. These include children with the chest defectively formed as the result of rickets or early tuberculous disease, and particularly children with a tendency to lateral curvature of the spine or the development of round shoulders. Also at lessons the maintenance of a good posture is important, the scholar sitting squarely to his desk with the head erect, the shoulders squared, the back straight, and the elbows kept at the same level.

Among the diseases for which the teacher must be specially on the lookout are measles, diphtheria, and scarlet fever among the infectious diseases (see INFECTION); discharges from the nose and from the ears which indicate inflammation in these cavities ; the presence of bald patches indicating ringworm (*see* RINGWORM) ; and also the presence of scabies about the hands, and impetigo as shown by crusts about the face.

SCHOTT TREATMENT is a system of treatment devised by a German physician for persons suffering from disorders of the heart. The treatment is specially carried out at Nauheim in Germany, and consists in a combination of baths in spring-water containing brine or carbonic acid gas, with carefully graduated exercises, and suitable rules for the guidance of the daily life.

SCIATICA (ἰσχίον, the hip) means pain connected with the great sciatic nerve which runs down the back of the thigh. (*See* NEURALGIA.)

SCILLA is the Latin name for squills.

SCIRRHUS (σκῖρος, a hard tumour) is the name applied to a hard form of cancer in which much fibrous tissue develops.

SCLERITIS means inflammation of the sclerotic coat of the eye, usually of a rheumatic or gouty nature.

SCLERODERMA, or SCLERODERMIA (σκληρός, hard ; δέρμα, skin), also known as 'hidebound disease', is a condition in which the skin becomes hard like leather, causing stiffening of the joints, and leading to gradual wasting of the muscles.

SCLEROSIS (σκληρός, hard) means literally 'hardening', and is a term applied to conditions in which portions of organs become hard and useless as the result of an excessive production of connective tissue. The term is especially applied to a change of this type taking place in the nervous system (*see* DISSEMINATED SCLEROSIS). When a change of this nature takes place in other organs it is generally known as 'cirrhosis' or 'fibrosis' (*see* CIRRHOSIS). These conditions are generally attributed to some form of chronic inflammation.

SCLEROTIC COAT (σκληρός, hard) is the outermost hard coat of the eyeball. (*See* EYE.)

SCOLIOSIS (σκολιός, twisted) is the name applied to curvature of the spine consisting partly of a bend to one side, partly of a rotary twist. It may result from disease of the spine, but in weakly children it may arise from so slight a cause as a bad habit in standing or in leaning one arm on the table at lessons. It also arises from disease affecting one side of the chest, such as chronic pleurisy or tuberculosis. (*See* SPINE, DISEASES OF.)

SCOPARIUM is the tops of *Cytisus scoparius*, the common broom. It has a diuretic action.

SCOPOLAMINE is an alkaloid identical with hyoscine and often used in combination with morphine for an anæsthetic, or as a hypnotic in delirium or to produce 'twilight sleep'.

SCORBUTUS (*see* SCURVY).

SCOTOMA (σκότωμα) is the term applied to a blind or partly blind area in the visual field. It may affect either the outer part of the visual field (peripheral scotoma), or the blindness may affect the centre, vision being retained round about (central scotoma).

SCRIVENER'S PALSY is another name for writer's cramp. (*See* CRAMP.)

SCROFULA (*scrofa*, a sow), or STRUMA, is a state of constitutional weakness, generally exhibiting itself in early life, and characterized mainly by defective nutrition of the tissues, which renders them a ready prey to tuberculosis. The condition is also known as the tuberculous constitution (*see* TUBERCULOSIS). The condition, as it manifests itself in disease of the glands in the neck, was formerly known in England as 'king's evil', from the belief that the touch of the sovereign could effect a cure. This superstition can be traced back to the time of Edward the Confessor in England, and to a much earlier period in France. Samuel Johnson was touched by Queen Anne in 1712, and the same supposed prerogative of royalty was exercised by Prince Charles Edward in 1745.

SCROFULODERMA is a term applied to a tuberculous affection of the skin, secondary to the bursting of a tuberculous abscess.

SCROTUM is the name applied to the pouch of integument within which the testicles are suspended. It consists of a purse-like fold of skin, within which each testicle has a separate investment of muscle fibres, several layers of fibrous tissue, and a serous membrane known as the 'tunica vaginalis'.

SCRUM-POX is a popular name for a contagious affection of the face and head affecting football players. (*See* IMPETIGO.)

SCURF, or DANDRUFF, is a popular name for the scaly condition that is frequently found on the scalp, and usually precedes baldness. (*See* BALD-NESS.)

SCURVY, or SCORBUTUS, is a deficiency disease characterized by the occurrence of extravasations of blood in the tissues of the body, and due to an insufficiency of vitamin C, or ascorbic acid, in the diet.

Causes.—In former times this disease was extremely common among sailors, and was responsible for a high mortality rate. It is now of rare occurrence at sea, its cause being well understood and its prevention readily secured by simple measures. Scurvy has also frequently broken out among soldiers on campaign, in beleaguered cities, as well as among communities in times of scarcity, and in prisons, workhouses, and other public institutions. In all such instances it has been found to depend closely upon the character and amount of the food, the occurrence of serious illness, and a diet too limited, either in amount or variety. These conditions predispose to scurvy, but the essential cause lies in deprivation of fresh food and especially of fresh vegetables for a period of four to six months. The want of vitamin C, which is soluble in water and is found chiefly in citrus fruits, potatoes, green vegetables, black currants, is the essential deficient factor. Besides this essential defect, a diminution in the total amount of food, the large use of salted meat or fish, and all causes of a depressing kind, such as exposure, anxiety, bad hygiene, etc., will powerfully contribute to the development of the disease.

Infants, too, may suffer from scurvy as the result of insufficiency of vitamin C in the diet.

Symptoms.—The symptoms of scurvy come on gradually, and its onset is not marked by any special indications beyond a certain failure of strength, most manifest on making efforts. Breathlessness and exhaustion are thus easily induced, and there exists a corresponding mental depression. The countenance acquires a sallow or dusky hue ; the gums are tender and the breath offensive almost from the first. These preliminary symptoms may continue for weeks, and in isolated cases may readily escape notice, but can scarcely fail to attract attention where they affect large numbers of men. Later the gums are livid, spongy, ulcerating, and bleeding ; the teeth are loosened and drop out ; and the breath is excessively foetid. Extravasations of blood now take place in the skin and other textures. These may be small, like the petechial spots of purpura (*see* PURPURA), but are often large, and cause swellings of the muscles in which they occur, having the appearance of extensive bruises, and tending to become hard and brawny. These extravasations are most common in the muscles of the lower limbs ; but they may be formed anywhere, and may easily be produced by very slight pressure upon the skin or by injuries to it. Bleeding into joints is a troublesome symptom because it produces stiffness later. In addition, there are bleedings from mucous membranes, such as those of the nose, eyes, and alimentary or respiratory tracts, whilst effusions of fluid take place into the pleural, pericardial, or peritoneal cavity. Painful, extensive, and destructive ulcers are apt to break out on the limbs. There is also a considerable amount of anæmia. The further progress of the malady is marked by profound exhaustion, with a tendency to fainting, and with various complications, such as diarrhœa and lung or kidney troubles, any of which may bring about a fatal result. On the other hand, even in desperate cases, recovery may be hopefully anticipated when the appropriate remedy can be obtained.

Treatment. — No disease is more amenable to treatment, both as regards prevention and cure, than scurvy. This consists of the administration of vitamin C in adequate amounts, either in the form of tablets of ascorbic acid or foodstuffs rich in this vitamin. Potatoes, cabbages, tomatoes, swede turnips, many fresh fruits, especially black currants, oranges, and lemons, will be found of great service for this purpose. Orange-juice or lemon-juice is often employed, either fresh or canned. The use, in a fresh state, of lime-juice in the British Navy, which has been practised since 1795, had the effect of virtually extinguishing scurvy in the service, whilst similar regulations introduced by the British Board of Trade in 1865 had a like beneficial result as regards the mercantile marine. It is only when these regulations have not been fully carried out, or when the supply of lime-juice has become exhausted, that scurvy among sailors has been noticed in recent times. The anæmia and debility are best overcome by the continued administration of iron, aided by fresh air and other measures calculated to promote the general health.

SCYBALA (σκύβαλον, dung) is the name applied to the extremely hard condition which the stools assume in aggravated constipation.

SEA-SICKNESS is a characteristic set of symptoms experienced by many persons when subjected to the pitching and rolling motion of a vessel at sea, of which depression, giddiness, nausea, and vomiting are the most prominent.

Causes.—Although the vast majority of people appear to be liable to this ailment at sea, they do not all suffer alike. Many endure distress of a most acute and even alarming kind, whilst others are simply conscious of transient feelings of nausea and discomfort. In long voyages, whilst many are affected with sea-sickness for the first few days only, others are tormented with it during the entire period, especially on the occurrence of rough weather. In short voyages, such as across the English Channel, not a few even of those susceptible escape, whilst others suffer in an extreme degree, the sickness persisting long after arrival on shore.

A great number of theories have been advanced to account for the connection between the motion of a ship and sea-sickness. The conditions concerned in the production of the malady are apparently of complex character, embracing more than one set of causes. In the first place, the rolling or heaving of the vessel disturbs that feeling of the relation of the body to surrounding objects upon which our sense of security rests. The nervous system being thus subjected to a succession of shocks or surprises fails to effect the necessary adjustments for equilibrium. Giddiness, nausea, and vomiting follow. Much importance has been laid by some upon the effects of the displacement of the abdominal viscera, especially the

stomach, by the rolling of the vessel; but, while this may possibly operate to some extent, it can only be as an accessory cause. The same may be said of the influence of the changing impressions made upon the vision—which has been regarded by some as so powerful in the matter—since attacks of sea-sickness occur also in the dark, and in the case of blind persons. Other contributory causes may be mentioned, such as the feeling that sickness is certain to come, which may bring on the attack in some persons even before the vessel has begun to move. The sense of the body being in a liquid or yielding medium as it descends with the vessel into the trough of the sea, the varied odours to be met with on board ship, and circumstances of a like nature, tend also to precipitate or aggravate an attack. In the few rare instances where sea-sickness has proved fatal, *post-mortem* appearances have been almost entirely negative, and only such as are met with in death from syncope.

Symptoms.—The symptoms generally show themselves soon after the vessel has begun to roll, by the onset of giddiness and discomfort in the head, together with a sense of nausea and sinking at the stomach, which soon develops into intense sickness and vomiting. At first the contents of the stomach only are ejected; but thereafter bilious matter, and occasionally even blood, are brought up by the violence of the retching. The vomiting is liable to exacerbations according to the amount of oscillation of the ship; but seasons of rest, sometimes admitting of sleep, occasionally intervene. Along with the sickness there is great physical prostration, as shown in the pallor of the skin, cold sweats, and feeble pulse, accompanied with mental depression and wretchedness. In almost all instances the attack has a favourable termination, and it is extremely rare that serious results arise, except in the case of persons weakened by other diseases, although occasionally the symptoms are for a time sufficiently alarming.

Treatment. — Innumerable preventives and remedies have been proposed, but most of them fall far short of the success claimed for them. No means has yet been discovered which can altogether prevent the occurrence of sea-sickness, nor is it likely any will be found, since it is largely due to the pitching movements of the vessel, which cannot be averted. Swinging couches or chambers have not proved of any practical utility. No doubt there is less risk of sickness in a large and well-ballasted vessel than in a small one ; but, even though the rolling may be considerably modified, the ascending and descending movements which so readily produce nausea continue. None of the medicinal agents proposed possess infallible properties ; a remedy which suits one person will often wholly fail with another. Experience gained during the 1939–45 War has shown that the most satisfactory remedy is hyoscine hydrobromide, grain $\frac{1}{100}$ to $\frac{1}{200}$ (0·6 to 0·3 mg.). Other recently introduced drugs which are proving of value in the prevention of sea-sickness include avomine, dramamine, and marzine.

When the vessel is in motion, or even before starting, the recumbent position with the head low and the eyes closed (so that the motion of the ship and sea cannot be seen) should be assumed by those at all likely to suffer, and, should the weather admit, on deck rather than below—the body, especially the extremities, being well covered. Many persons, however, find comfort and relief from lying down in their berths with a hot bottle to the feet, by which means sleep may be obtained, and with it a temporary abatement of the distressing giddiness and nausea. Individuals who tend to be constipated should ensure an adequate evacuation of the bowels before embarking. Should sickness supervene, small quantities of some light food, such as thin arrowroot, gruel, or soup, ought to be swallowed if possible, in order to lessen the sense of exhaustion, which is often extreme, as well as to mitigate the pain of retching by giving the stomach something upon which it can contract. The vomiting may be mitigated by saline effervescing drinks, ice, chloroform (3 or 4 drops on a piece of sugar), or dilute hydrocyanic acid. Alcohol usually tends to aggravate the sickness, but brandy has long had a reputation as a useful means of treatment in the early stages.

SEASIDE, SEA - VOYAGES (see CLIMATE IN RELATION TO DISEASE).

SEAT-WORM is another name for thread-worm. (See PARASITES.)

SEBACEOUS CYST is the term applied to a cyst in the skin formed as a result of blockage of the duct of a sebaceous gland.

SEBACEOUS GLANDS (sebum, grease) are the minute glands situated alongside of hairs, and opening into the follicles of the latter a short distance below the point at which the hairs emerge on the surface (Fig. 332). These glands secrete an oily material, and are especially large upon the nose, where their openings form pits that are easily visible. Some varieties of eczema, as well as acne, result from disorders of these glands.

SEBORRHŒA (sebum, grease ; ῥέω, I flow) is the name given to a group of diseases of the skin in which the sebaceous or oil-forming glands are at fault. It is shown either by accumulations of dry scurf, or by the formation of an excessive oily deposit on an otherwise healthy skin. (See under SKIN DISEASES.)

SECRETIN is the name given to a hormone secreted by the mucous membrane near the commencement of the small intestine when food comes in contact with it, which, on being carried by the blood to the pancreas, stimulates the secretion of pancreatic juice.

SECRETION (secerno, I set apart) is the term applied to the material formed by a gland as the result of its activity. For example, saliva is the secretion of the salivary glands, gastric juice that of the glands in the stomach wall, bile that of the liver (see GLANDS). Some secretions consist apparently of waste material which is of no further use in the chemistry of the body. These secretions are often spoken of as excretions ; for example, the urine and the sweat. (For further details, see SALIVA, URINE, CIRCULATION OF SECRETIONS, ENDOCRINE GLANDS, etc., and also under the headings of the various organs.)

SECUNDINES is another name for the afterbirth, consisting of the placenta and membranes expelled in the final stage of labour.

SECUNDUM ARTEM is a Latin expression meaning in a skilful professional manner.

SEDATIVES (*sedo*, I calm) are drugs and other measures which soothe over-excitement of the nervous system, whether the effect of this excitement be pain, sleeplessness, delirium, muscular spasm, etc. Those sedatives that soothe pain are generally spoken of as anodynes ; sedatives in sleeplessness or delirium are known as hypnotics ; sedatives of spasm are called antispasmodics. (*See* ANODYNES, COLIC, HEADACHE, HYPNOTICS, NEURALGIA, PAIN.)

SEDIMENTATION TEST is a test for measuring the activity and progress of certain diseases. If blood is drawn and put into a test-tube the red blood corpuscles sink and leave a clear layer above. In disease the rate of sinking is increased and can be measured. The more active the disease, the higher the rate of sinking of red blood corpuscles.

SEIDLITZ POWDER, or COMPOUND EFFERVESCENT POWDER, is a mild purgative composed of Rochelle salt and bicarbonate of soda, which are wrapped together in a blue paper, and tartaric acid, which is wrapped in a white paper. The contents of each paper are dissolved separately in half a tumblerful or less of water ; the two solutions are mixed and swallowed while effervescing.

SEIGNETTE SALT is another name for Rochelle salt.

SELLA TURCICA is the name applied to the deep hollow on the upper surface of the sphenoid bone in which the pituitary gland is enclosed.

SEMEIOLOGY (σημεῖον, sign ; λόγος, discourse) is the part of medical science dealing with the symptoms and signs of disease.

SEMEN.—The richly albuminous fluid in which spermatozoa are suspended.

SEMILUNAR CARTILAGES are two crescentic layers of fibro-cartilage on the outer and inner edges of the knee-joint, which serve to form hollows on the upper surface of the tibia in which the

condyles at the lower end of the femur rest. The inner cartilage is especially liable to be displaced by a sudden and violent movement at the knee. (*See* KNEE.)

SEMOLINA is a preparation of wheat. (*See* CEREALS.)

SENEGA is the root of *Polygala senega*, a small plant of the United States. It has a considerable action as a stimulating expectorant, and its preparations are much used in cough mixtures.

SENILITY (*senilis*, old). (*See* AGE, NATURAL CHANGES IN.)

SENNA is the leaves of various species of *Cassia* plant, being known as Indian senna and Alexandrine senna, according to its source. It is one of the most active of the simple laxative drugs, producing considerable griping if used alone. Senna is excreted in the urine, giving it a dark red or yellow colour. In the case of nursing mothers, some of the drug is excreted in the milk and may have a purgative effect upon the nursling. A standardized preparation of senna, Senokot, is now available which has none of the disadvantages of senna itself.

SENSATION (*see* PAIN, TOUCH, etc.).

SENSITIZATION of a person means the production of anaphylaxis by a particular food, vaccine, etc. (*See* ANAPHYLAXIS.)

SEPSIS (σῆψις, decay) means poisoning by the products of a putrefactive process. This process is set up by the growth of micro-organisms in the body, and the general symptoms which accompany it are those of inflammation (*see* INFLAMMATION). It is prevented by the various procedures mentioned under ASEPSIS, and is neutralized, when it has occurred, by various substances (*see* ANTISEPTICS). Two forms of sepsis to which attention has been particularly directed are *oral sepsis* and *puerperal sepsis*.

SEPTICÆMIA (σηπτικός, putrid ; αἷμα, blood) is a serious form of blood-poisoning due to the multiplication in the blood of bacteria—in fact, it is an infection of the blood. (*See* BLOOD-POISONING.)

SEQUELÆ (*sequor*, I follow) is the term applied to symptoms or effects which are liable to follow certain diseases. For example, bronchitis and other chest complaints may be sequelæ of measles ; heart disease is frequently a sequel of rheumatic fever ; paralysis may follow diphtheria.

SEQUESTRUM (*sequestro*, I separate) is the name given to a fragment of dead bone cast off from the living bone in the process of necrosis (*see* BONE DISEASES). A sequestrum often remains in contact with and partly enveloped by newly formed bone, so that a sinus is produced, and a constant discharge goes on, till the dead bone is removed.

SEROTHERAPY is the term applied to the method of treating, or of preventing, disease by the injection into a patient of serum containing antibodies to the toxins or bacteria from the effects of which he is suffering, or against which it is desired to protect him—as, for example, in diphtheria and tetanus. (For further details, *see* SERUM THERAPY.)

SEROUS MEMBRANES are smooth, transparent membranes that line certain large cavities of the body. The chief serous membranes are the peritoneum, lining the cavity of the abdomen ; the pleuræ, one of which lines each side of the chest, surrounding the corresponding lung; the pericardium, in which the heart lies ; and the tunica vaginalis on each side, enclosing a testicle. The name of these membranes is derived from the fact that the surface is moistened by thin fluid derived from the serum of blood or lymph. Every serous membrane consists of a visceral portion, which closely envelops the organs concerned, and a parietal portion, which adheres to the wall of the cavity. These two portions are continuous with one another so as to form a closed sac, and the opposing surfaces are close together, separated only by a little fluid. This arrangement enables the organs in question to move freely within the cavities containing them. For further details *see under* PERITONEUM.

SERPENTARIA, or SNAKEROOT, is the root of various species of *Aristo-*

lochia plants of the Southern United States. It has a stimulating action, and is used in combination with other remedies in the treatment of indigestion.

SERPIGINOUS (*serpo*, I creep) is a term used in connection with ulcers or eruptions that spread in a creeping manner.

SERUM (*serum*) is the fluid which separates from blood, lymph, and other fluids of the body when clotting takes place in them. (*See* HÆMORRHAGE.) Blood-plasma is the name given to the fluid of the blood circulating in the vessels, by which the corpuscles are carried along. As clotting takes place, fine threads of fibrin form from the fibrinogen contained in the plasma. These threads produce a network of increasing density in which the corpuscles are entangled, and, as a result, the fluid (serum) which is left outside this clot is clear, unmixed with corpuscles, and of a pale yellow colour.

The relation of these substances is seen at a glance from the following table :

$$\text{Blood} = \begin{cases} \text{Plasma} = \begin{cases} \text{Serum} \\ \text{Fibrin} \end{cases} = \text{Clot.} \\ \text{Corpuscles} \end{cases}$$

Serum is a clear, yellowish fluid and contains, in addition to water, about 7 per cent. of albumin and globulin, with smaller quantities of salts, fat, sugar, urea, uric acid, and other extractives, as well as minute amounts of other albuminous bodies, which are of great importance in the prevention of disease. (*See* IMMUNITY.) The chief salt in the serum is common salt.

Serum is derived from the lymph also, and the fluid which is found in effusions into the pleura and other cavities of the body is very similar in composition.

The serum used for the administration of antitoxins in cases of diphtheria, tetanus, and other diseases, is generally derived from the blood drawn from horses which have been subjected to a long course of treatment. (*See* IMMUNITY *and* SERUM TREATMENT.)

SERUM THERAPY.—The treatment of disease by the administration of serum (usually horse serum, sometimes human) containing antibodies against bacteria or viruses, or antitoxins against toxins, which are causing the symptoms of the disease. If bacteria are injected into an animal in gradually increasing doses—perhaps of dead bacteria first and of living bacteria later—antibodies to the bacteria appear in the blood serum of the animal injected. Similarly, if the toxins of bacteria are injected, antitoxins are produced. This reaction is the basis of immunity. The serum is then collected from the animal (usually a horse) for injection into a human being infected with the micro-organism against which the serum has been prepared. Serum therapy has proved highly successful in those infections in which the damage to the infected person is done by the toxins of the infecting micro-organism. For example, in diphtheria the diphtheria bacilli multiply in the throat, and the toxins there produced by the bacilli are absorbed into the blood, circulate round the body, and damage such structures as the heart and the nervous system. Here an antitoxic serum will provide the infected body with ready-made antitoxins which by uniting with the toxins will render them inert. Antitoxic serum is also of much value in the treatment of tetanus.

In other diseases bacteria invade the body and multiply therein, their harmful effect being due to this fact rather than to the local manufacture of toxins subsequently disseminated throughout the body. Here antibacterial sera are administered to the infected person, and the different kinds of antibodies in such sera immobilize the bacteria by killing them or by agglutinating them, etc. The action between toxin and antitoxin, and bacterium and antibody, is a specific one. Antibacterial sera have been used against pneumococci, meningococci, typhoid bacilli, cholera vibrio, etc. But the brilliant results achieved in treatment of bacterial infections with the sulphonamide drugs and penicillin have put antibacterial sera rather in the shade. Immune serum is also used with effect in the prevention and treatment of measles.

Dangers of serum.—The serum which contains the antitoxic and other bodies is derived from the horse, and being different from human serum, it occasionally sets up serious symptoms when it is injected. The use of serum has

796

even been known to cause death in very susceptible persons (see ANAPHYLAXIS).

SESAME OIL is the oil expressed from the seeds of *Sesamum indicum*. It is sometimes used to replace olive oil when the latter is in short supply.

SETON is the name applied to a few strands of silk or thin strip of lint or gauze passed through the skin and underlying tissues by means of a large flattened needle, and left projecting at both ends. Formerly this method of treatment was widely used as an effective means of counter-irritation in many chronic conditions for which repeated blistering is now employed.

SEWAGE (*see* REFUSE AND SEWAGE DISPOSAL).

SEX CHROMOSOMES. — In the human being there are 23 pairs of chromosomes. Male and female differ in respect of one pair. In the nucleus of the female somatic cell the two members of the pair are identical and are called X-chromosomes. In the male nucleus there is one X-chromosome and another, unequal, dissimilar chromosome called the Y-chromosome. In the sex cells, after reduction division, all cells in the female will contain X-chromosomes. In the male, half will contain X-chromosomes and half Y-chromosomes. If, then, a sperm with an X-chromosome fertilizes an ovum (with, of course, an X-chromosome) the offspring will be female. If a sperm with a Y-chromosome fertilizes the ovum the offspring will be male. It is the sex chromosomes which determine the sex of an individual (FIG. 94a).

SHAKING PALSY is another name for paralysis agitans. (*See* PARALYSIS.)

SHELL-SHOCK was a form of war neurosis which presented one of the major medical problems in the 1914–1918 War.

SHIGELLA is the name given to a group of rod-shaped, Gram-negative bacteria that are the cause of bacillary dysentery.

SHINGLES (*cingulum*, a girdle) is a popular name for herpes zoster, which forms more or less of a belt round the body. (*See* HERPES.)

SHOCK is the name applied to a condition in which the vital activity is profoundly lowered, usually as a result of severe injury. The problem of shock—to the fore in the two world wars of 1914–18 and 1939–45—is still unsolved. Surgical shock may result from injury or hæmorrhage, or from both. The modern view relates the shock of both injury and hæmorrhage to the same underlying pathology—diminution of the fluid element of the blood. The blood, in other words, becomes concentrated. In treatment, therefore, the aim is to restore the blood volume, and to this end plasma is often given as a transfusion fluid.

Symptoms. — The person suffering from shock is in a state of great prostration, but can be roused to answer intelligently. The face and skin generally are pale, and copious perspiration breaks out. The lips and ears are pallid, and the voice whispering. The pulse is rapid and often almost imperceptible, the respiration irregular and sighing, and the temperature may be subnormal. The patient complains greatly of thirst.

Treatment. — The immediate treatment of shock is to keep the patient flat and at complete rest, to keep him warm—but not too warm—with blankets and hot-water bottles, to relieve pain, and to give hot fluids to drink provided there is no abdominal injury. The foot of the bed is raised ; the limbs are often bandaged.

SHORT-SIGHT is a condition in which objects near at hand are seen clearly, while objects at a distance are blurred. The condition is technically known as ' myopia '. (*See* MYOPIA. SPECTACLES, *and* VISION.)

SHOULDER is the joint formed by the upper end of the humerus and the shoulder-blade or scapula. The acromion process of the scapula and the outer end of the collar-bone form a protective bony arch above the joint, and from this arch the wide and thick deltoid muscle passes downwards, protecting the outer surface of the joint, and giving to the shoulder its rounded character. The joint itself is of the ball-and-socket variety, the rounded head of the humerus being received into the hollow glenoid cavity of the scapula, which is further deepened by a rim of cartilage. One tendon of the biceps muscle passes through the joint, grooving the humerus deeply, and being attached to the upper edge of the glenoid cavity. The joint is surrounded by a loose fibrous capsule, strengthened at certain places by ligamentous bands. The main strength of the joint comes from the powerful muscles that unite the upper arm with the scapula, clavicle, and ribs.

SHOULDER-BLADE, or SCAPULA, is a flat bone, about as large as the flat hand and fingers, placed on the upper and back part of the thorax. Many of the large muscles that move the arm are attached to it. It is not in contact with the ribs, and its only attachment to the trunk of the body is through a joint between its acromion process and the clavicle on the tip of the shoulder and by the powerful muscles which suspend it from the backbone and ribs. With the arm hanging by the side the scapula extends from the second to the seventh rib, but, as the arm is raised and lowered, it slides freely over the back of the chest. From the hinder surface of the bone springs a strong process, the spine of the scapula, which arches upwards and forwards into the acromion process. The latter forms the bony prominence on the top of the shoulder, where it unites in a joint with the outer end of the clavicle.

SIALAGOGUES (σίαλον, saliva ; ἄγω, I draw) are substances which produce a copious flow of saliva.

SIAMESE TWINS, or CONJOINED TWINS, is the term applied to twins who are united bodily but are possessed of separate personalities. Their frequency is not known, but it has been estimated that throughout the world six or more conjoined twins are born every year who are capable of separation. The earliest case on record is that of the ' Biddendon Maids ' who were born in England in A.D. 1100. The ' Scottish Brothers ' lived for 28 years at the court of James III of Scotland. Perhaps the most famous, however, were Chang and Eng, who were born of Chinese parents in Siam in 1811. It was they who were responsible for the introduction of the term, ' Siamese twins ', which still remains the popular name for ' conjoined twins '. They were joined together at the lower end of the chest bone, and achieved fame by being shown in Barnum's famous circus in the United States. They subsequently married English sisters and settled as farmers in North Carolina. They died in 1874.

The earliest attempt at surgical separation is said to have been made by Dr. Farius of Basle in 1689. The first successful separation in Great Britain was in 1912. Both twins survived the operation and one survived well into adult life. This is said to be the first occasion in which both twins survived the operation. The success of the operation is largely dependent upon the degree of union between the twins. Thus, if this is only skin, subcutaneous tissue, and cartilage, the prospects of survival for both twins are good, but if some vital organ such as the liver is shared the operation is much more hazardous.

SIBBENS is an old name for a disease formerly prevalent in Scotland, which was probably syphilis.

SICK-HEADACHE (see HEADACHE).

SICKLE-CELL ANÆMIA is a form of anæmia in Negroes, which is so-called because of the sickle shape of the red blood cells. The fundamental abnormality is the presence of an abnormal form of hæmoglobin. This leads to the sickle shape of the red blood cell. Such a cell is more fragile than the normal red blood cell, and it is this fragility of the cell which is responsible for the anæmia.

SICKNESS (see VOMITING and SEA-SICKNESS).

SICK-NURSE (see NURSING).

SICK-ROOM (see NURSING).

SIDEROSIS (σίδηρος, iron) is a name given to chronic interstitial pneumonia occurring in ironworkers and due to the inhalation of fine iron particles. The term is also applied to the condition in which there is an excessive deposit of iron in the tissues of the body.

SIGHT (see VISION).

798

SIGMOID FLEXURE (σιγμοειδής, like the letter S) is the term applied to the part of the large intestine immediately above the rectum which is freely movable and hangs down into the pelvis. It is also known as the pelvic colon.

SILICONES are organic compounds of silicon, with a structure of alternate atoms of silicon and oxygen with organic groups, such as methyl and phenyl attached to the silicone atoms. As they produce a flexible and stable water-repellent film on the skin, they are used as barrier creams (q.v.).

SILICOSIS (silex, flint) constitutes the most important industrial hazard in those industries in which silica is encountered : i.e. the pottery industry, the sandstone industry, sand-blasting, metal grinding, the tin-mining industry, anthracite coal mines. Among pottery workers the condition has for long been known as ' potter's asthma ', whilst in the cutlery industry it was known as ' grinder's rot '. For the production of silicosis the particles of silica must measure 0·5 to 5 μ in diameter and they must be inhaled into the alveoli of the lung, where they produce fibrosis. This diminishes the efficiency of the lungs, which manifests itself by slowly progressive shortness of breath. The main danger of silicosis, however, is that it is liable to be complicated by tuberculosis. The incidence of silicosis is steadily being reduced by various measures which diminish the risk of inhaling silica dust. These include adequate ventilation to draw off the dust ; the suppression of dust by the use of water ; the wearing of respirators where the risk is particularly great and it is not possible to reduce the amount of dust, e.g. in sand-blasting ; periodic medical examination of workpeople exposed to risk.

SILK, OILED, consists of silk fabric made waterproof with drying oils or oil-modified synthetic resins.

SILVER is used in medicine externally in the form of its salt, nitrate of silver (see NITRATE OF SILVER). Mild silver proteinate, also known as argyrol, argein, argyn, silver nucleinate, etc., is a compound of silver oxide with albumin. It is a brown powder soluble in water and is much used as a non-irritating antiseptic in conjunctivitis (25 per cent. in water), and for washing out the bladder in cystitis (5 per cent. or stronger).

SIMMONDS' DISEASE, or PITUITARY CACHEXIA, is a rare condition in which cachexia, wasting of the skin and the bones, impotence, loss of hair, and premature senility occur as a result of destruction of the pituitary gland.

SIMPLE is an old term applied to a herb with real or supposed medicinal virtues.

SINAPISM (σίναπι, mustard) is an application containing mustard. (*See* MUSTARD.)

SINGER'S NODULE is the term applied to a minute warty excrescence on the vocal cords interfering greatly with the voice, although not otherwise of serious importance. (*See* THROAT DISEASES.)

SINGULTUS is the Latin term for hiccup.

SINUS (*sinus*, a hollow) is a term applied to narrow cavities of various kinds, occurring naturally in the body, or resulting from disease. Thus it is applied to the air-containing cavities which are found in the frontal and maxillary bones, and which communicate with the nose (*see* ANTRUM). The term is also used in connection with the wide spaces through which the blood circulates in the membranes of the brain. Cavities which are produced when an abscess has burst but remains unhealed, are also known as sinuses (*see* ABSCESS, FISTULA).

SINUSOIDAL CURRENT (*see* ELECTRICITY IN MEDICINE).

SKATOL (σκῶρ, dung) is a strongly smelling crystalline substance contained in the stools, produced by decomposition of protein material.

SKELETON (σκελετός, dried up) is the comprehensive term applied to the hard structures that support or protect the softer tissues of the body (Fig. 331). Many animals are possessed of an exoskeleton, consisting of superficial plates of bone, horn, etc. ; but in man the skeleton is entirely an endoskeleton, covered everywhere by soft parts, and consisting mainly of bones, but in places also of cartilages. The chief positions in which cartilage is found in place of bone are the larynx and the front of the chest. (For the details of the skeleton, *see* BONE.)

SKIAGRAM (σκιά, shadow ; γράμμα, writing) is the name applied to a photograph—strictly speaking, a ' shadowgraph ', for this is what it is—made by X-rays.

SKIN.—Skin is the membrane which everywhere envelops the outer surface of the body, meeting, at the various orifices of the body, with the mucous membrane which lines the internal cavities. The skin consists of two distinct layers (Fig. 332), which differ entirely in structure and in origin. These are (*a*) *the cuticle*, also known as *scarf-skin*, *epidermis*, or *epithelium*, which is a cellular covering formed from the outer layer of the embryo ; and (*b*) *the true skin*, also known as the *cutis vera*, *corium*, or *dermis*, which is a fibrous covering developed from the middle embryonic layer (Plate XVI).

(*a*) **The cuticle** is the cellular layer which covers the outer surface of the body, varying in thickness from $\frac{1}{20}$ of an inch (1 mm.) on the palms and soles to $\frac{1}{200}$ inch (0·1 mm.) on the face. It is composed of four layers, which are, from the surface inwards, as follows:

(1) THE HORNY LAYER, made up of several thicknesses of flat cells, forming an impervious covering pierced only by the openings of the sweat-glands and by the hairs. The flat cells are rubbed off the surface constantly as minute white scales, being replaced by growth from below.

(2) THE CLEAR LAYER, in which the cells are firmly fixed together into a kind of membrane.

(3) THE GRANULAR LAYER, in which the cells are undergoing a change in form and substance from those of the fourth layer to those of the two on the surface.

(4) THE MALPIGHIAN LAYER, in which the cells are soft, tender, and living. These cells lie in several rows, the deepest being set directly upon the uneven surface of the true skin, which

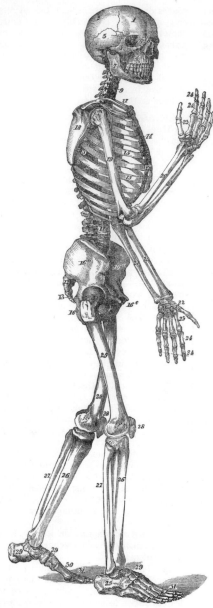

1. Frontal bone.
2. Parietal bone.
3. Temporal bone.
4. Upper jaw (maxilla).
5. Cheek-bone (malar bone).
6. Lacrimal bone.
7. Lower jaw (mandible).
8. Nasal bone.
9. Cervical vertebræ.
10. Thoracic vertebræ.
11. Lumbar vertebræ.
12. Sacral bone.
13. Coccygeal bone.
14. Sternum.
15. Ribs.
16. *a–c.* Pelvis.
17. Clavicle.
18. Scapula.
19. Humerus.
20. Radius.
21. Ulna.
22. Carpal bones.
23. Metacarpal bones.
24. Phalanges.
25. Femur.
26. Tibia.
27. Fibula.
28. Patella.
29. Tarsal bones.
30. Metatarsal bones.
31. Phalanges.

FIG. 331.—**Human** skeleton.   (Schemel's *Zoology.*)

is richly supplied with blood-vessels that nourish the cells. These cells divide continually and as they multiply they are pushed upwards to supply the constant wear and tear on the surface of the horny layer. There are no blood-vessels in the cuticle, but fine sensory nerves terminate between the cells of the Malpighian layer. These cells are joined together by cement substance and by minute processes that are continued from each cell into its neighbours. The layer is often called the ' prickle-cell ' layer.

These four layers can be distinguished readily at the *nails*. The horny layer ends abruptly in the scarf-nail. The clear layer, in this site thick and stiff, forms the nail itself. Through it can be seen the granular layer, which also ends abruptly in the white linule at the base of the nail, and the pink Malpighian layer, which forms the tender bed, or quick of the nail.

A *blister* is a collection of fluid separating the Malpighian layer from the superficial ones.

(b) **The true skin** is the fibrous layer which forms the chief part of the bodily covering. It varies greatly in thickness from about $\frac{1}{50}$ inch to $\frac{1}{8}$ inch (0·5 to 3 mm.), being coarser on the back than on the front of the body, and thicker in men than in women. It contains many nerves, which play an important part in affording sensations of touch, pain, temperature, etc., and blood-vessels which, in addition to nourishing the skin, are largely concerned in regulating the temperature of the body. The true skin bears also the hairs which pierce the cuticle, and the sweat-glands, whose ducts also penetrate the cuticle to reach the surface. Beneath the true skin lies a loose fibrous layer of subcutaneous tissue which joins the skin to deeper parts and contains more or less fat, according to the stoutness of the person.

The fibrous tissue of the true skin is composed of interlacing bundles of white fibrous tissue that form a dense feltwork. Here and there, elastic fibres are mixed with the others, and these serve to give the skin pliability, and at the same time to keep it always stretched. On the surface the network is very fine and close, and the skin is raised up into projections, known as

' papillæ ', which fit into corresponding depressions on the under surface of the cuticle, and thus render the two inseparable. The true skin is crossed everywhere by numerous folds, which are specially plentiful over joints and on the palms of the hands, and which are followed closely by the cuticle. Further, there is a special arrangement on the palms and soles, where the papillæ are so placed as to form continuous ridges with intervening grooves. These ridges remain permanent throughout life, and, as the formation by them of whorls and loops upon the finger-tips varies in different individuals, an impression of these in ink is used as a means of identifying criminals. On the summit of each ridge the orifices of the sweat-glands can be seen, with the help of a magnifying glass, arranged in a row.

The endings of the sensory nerves in the skin have been described under NERVES.

HAIRS spring from the true skin, each having a root and a stem or shaft (Fig. 332). The stem is generally rounded, and varies greatly in thickness, while in the case of curly hair it is oval or flattened in section. The surface is covered by scales, imbricated like the tiles on a roof, and it is in consequence of their projecting edges that felted or matted hair is so difficult to separate. The chief part of the stem is of a fibrous character, the fibres being composed also of elongated cells. Some hairs have, running up the centre, a pith composed of soft cells with air-spaces between them. The varying tint of hair is due to pigment scattered in varying amount throughout the hair, while a white hair is produced by the formation of very numerous air-spaces throughout the cells composing it. The root of the hair ends in a knob, and is set upon a fibrous papilla, from which the hair appears to derive its principal nutriment. This root is set deep in the true skin, and is the growing part of the hair which pushes the older part of the hair out through the cuticle. The rate of growth of hair is about 6 inches (15 cm.) in a year, though in some persons when the hair reaches a certain length it ceases to grow at the root and is gradually pushed upwards, till it falls out, by a new hair which develops from a fesh papilla. The tube which contains the part of the hair embedded in the skin is known as the hair follicle and is lined by a fibrous coat derived from the true skin and a cellular

muscle, whose other end is attached to the surface of the true skin a little distance off. These muscles have the action of raising the hair, and also of producing ' goose-flesh ', when stimu-

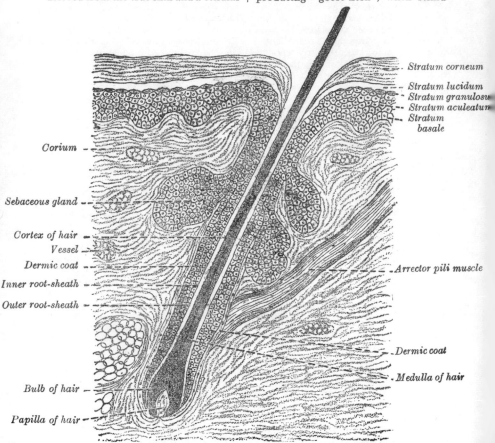

Corium

Sebaceous gland

Cortex of hair
Vessel
Dermic coat
Inner root-sheath
Outer root-sheath

Bulb of hair

Papilla of hair

Stratum corneum
Stratum lucidum
Stratum granulosum
Stratum aculeatum
Stratum basale

Arrector pili muscle

Dermic coat

Medulla of hair

FIG. 332.—Section through the skin, showing the epidermis and corium, a hair in its follicle, the arrector pili muscle which raises the hair, and sebaceous glands opening into the hair-follicle. (From Gray's *Anatomy*. Longmans, Green & Co. Ltd.)

coat developed from the cuticle, each of which consists of three layers (Fig. 333). When a hair is roughly pulled out, the clear membrane that is often found surrounding it is part of the cellular root sheath. The follicle does not run straight down into the skin, but has a considerable obliquity, so that the part of the hair above the surface has a natural slope to one side. Attached to the under side of each sloping hair-follicle, near its deep end, is a small

lated to contract by the influence of cold or of fear.

GLANDS are found in immense numbers in the skin, and are of two kinds, *sebaceous glands*, which secrete a fatty substance, and *sweat - glands*, which secrete a clear, watery fluid.

The *sebaceous glands* lie in the true skin, and open into the follicles of the hairs a little way from the surface. Each consists of a bunch of small sacs, within which fatty material is produced.

The secretion reaches the surface by the hair-follicle, and serves to lubricate the hair and give pliability to the surface of the skin (Fig. 332).

Sweat-glands, or sudoriparous glands, are very numerous, are found all over these again by a thin membrane. In the fibrous tissue between the coils of the glands run many small blood-vessels, and from the blood in these the materials that form the sweat are extracted.

Functions of the skin.—The main use

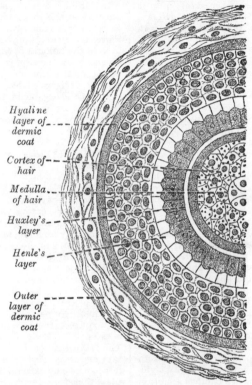

Hyaline layer of dermic coat

Cortex of hair

Medulla of hair

Huxley's layer

Henle's layer

Outer layer of dermic coat

FIG. 333.—Transverse section through one-half of a hair-follicle. (From Gray's *Anatomy*. Longmans, Green & Co. Ltd.)

the surface of the body at a slightly deeper level than the sebaceous glands, and have no connection with the hairs. Each consists of a long tube, coiled up into a ball, from which a duct leads in a zigzag manner up towards the surface. The outlets of these ducts can just be seen with the naked eye as minute openings (pores), though with a magnifying glass they are readily visible. The number is said to vary from 400 in a square inch, on the lower limbs and back, to 2800 in the same area on the palm of the hand. The structure of these glands is simple. Each is a coiled-up tube, which is lined by a layer of cells surrounded by muscle fibres, and of the skin is a *protective* one. It covers the underlying muscles, both protecting them from injury and, especially by virtue of the layer of fat immediately beneath the skin, warding off extremes of temperature. The cuticle forms a highly impenetrable surface, its horny character and elasticity being well calculated to resist wounds ; whilst the sebaceous matter with which it is provided renders it almost waterproof. Thus poisons, drugs, etc., are not absorbed in any appreciable amount through the unbroken skin, unless combined with some fatty material, as in ointments, and diligently rubbed in.

Secretion is an important function of

803

the skin, the two secretions being sebaceous material and perspiration. Of these, the former is a lubricant for the hair and skin, the latter is treated of under PERSPIRATION.

Heat regulation is one of the most important functions of the skin. Man is a 'warm-blooded' animal, that is to say, his temperature remains constant in health between 98° and 99° F. (36·7° and 37·2° C.), no matter what the temperature of the surrounding medium may be. In order to maintain this constancy, it is evident that he must be provided with some means of quickly developing heat which shall come into action when the body is cooled down by exposure to cold, and also some mechanism which can quickly get rid of heat when necessary. The main source of heat in the body lies in the muscular tissue, which develops heat every time a contraction takes place. The skin also plays a very prominent part in this connection. When cold air, water, etc., come in contact with the surface, the skin blanches, the numerous blood-vessels of the true skin contracting and thus preventing much blood from circulating through the skin, and being thereby unduly cooled. On the other hand, when the surface is exposed to a temperature approaching that of the body, say one of 80° or 90° F. (26·7° or 32·2° C.), or when an excessive amount of heat is produced by great muscular efforts, the blood-vessels of the surface dilate, the skin reddens, as much blood comes to the surface, and there is a copious secretion of perspiration, which produces great cooling as it evaporates from the surface. These actions of narrowing and dilatation of vessels, and of sweat-secretion, are brought about through reflex nerve influence. When the temperature rises so high that these processes are unable to take place, very serious results ensue (*see* SUN-STROKE.). It can be readily understood why the body tolerates high temperatures at a dry heat much better than continued moist heat, since evaporation of the perspiration takes place more readily the drier the surrounding air, and thus produces more rapid cooling. The serious effects of varnishing the skin or covering it with such an impervious material as gold-

leaf, are due to interference with this process. The nerves of the blood-vessels appear to be thrown out of action, and delicate animals subjected to this process speedily die of cold.

Respiration is a function of the skin which in man is not of so great importance as in the lower animals. In the frog, the lungs and skin are of equal importance as breathing organs, although in man the amount of carbonic acid gas given off by the skin is only about $\frac{1}{150}$ or $\frac{1}{200}$ of the amount given off by the lungs. It is probable, however, that much of the organic matter which gives to impure air its disagreeable smell and contributes to its poisonous properties is given off by the skin.

SKIN CHAFING (*see* CHAFING OF THE SKIN).

SKIN DISEASES. — These form a large and important class. In number they are very extensive, owing to the varied forms of change which the skin texture may undergo, and to the different structures in the skin which may be specially affected. Skin diseases are of great importance, not only from the fact that they have an influence on the general health, but also because these diseases are frequently the expression of constitutional conditions, inherited or acquired, the recognition of which is essential to their effectual treatment. The following classification is, to a certain extent, open to the objection that it proceeds on several principles, and that therefore certain diseases might fall into more than one group. But this classification appears sufficient for the present purpose :

I. Disorders of the secreting apparatus (of the sebaceous and sweat glands).

II. Disorders specially relating to growth (hypertrophies ; atrophies ; new formations ; pigmentary changes).

III. Inflammatory affections (erythematous ; papular ; vesicular ; pustular squamous or scaly).

IV. Neurodermatoses (nervous disorders).

V. Parasitic affections (animal ; vegetable).

I. DISORDERS OF THE SECRETING APPARATUS.—(1) **Of the sweat-glands.**—The chief morbid conditions are excessive sweating (*hyperidrosis*) and fœtid sweating (*bromidrosis*). Excessive sweating is a symptom observed in various diseases, such as tuberculosis and rheumatic fever, but it may exist apart from such conditions, and either be general, affecting the whole body, or confined to a part, such as the armpits, head, hands, feet, or, as in some rare instances, the one-half of the body. Some persons habitually perspire to a great extent on making effort, yet never appear to suffer in health, although the discomfort is considerable. (*See* PERSPIRATION.)

(2) **Of the sebaceous glands.**—*Seborrhœa* is a term applied to describe an accumulation on the skin of excessive sebaceous secretion mixed up with dirt and forming scales or a distinct encrustation. On the head, where it is commonly seen, it may interfere with the nutrition of the hair and cause partial baldness. A form of this disease occurs in young infants. The main treatment is local, consisting in thorough cleansing of the parts. The crusts may be softened with oil and the affected skin regularly washed with superfatted soap. A weak ointment of salicylic acid in vaseline (3 grains to the ounce) also aids their disappearance. The fatty sebum frequently accumulates in the sebaceous ducts, giving rise to the minute black points so often noticed on the face, back, and chest in young adults, to which the terms *black-heads* and *comedones* are applied. These affections may, to a large extent, be prevented by strict attention to ablution and brisk friction of the skin, which will also often remove them when they begin to appear. The retained secretion may be squeezed out and the skin treated with some simple application. *Acne* is an eruption produced by inflammation of the sebaceous glands and hair follicles. It usually occurs in connection with comedones, but may be independent, and shows itself in the form of red pimples or papules, which may become pustular and be attended with considerable irritation of the surrounding skin. (*See* ACNE.) A variety of this malady, to which the name *acne rosacea* is given, is a more severe and troublesome disorder than that already mentioned (*see* ACNE ROSACEA).

Wens are small cysts produced by local retention of the sebaceous material and overgrowth of gland tissue. Their treatment consists in opening the cyst and removing or destroying its wall, so that it may not refill with secretion.

Molluscum contagiosum is a form of skin disease resembling wens but rather warty, and popularly called ' water-warts '. It appears to be infectious and is often contracted through bathing costumes and towels at public baths.

II. **DISORDERS AFFECTING GROWTH.** — (1) **Hypertrophies.** — A *corn* (*clavus*) is a local thickening of the skin, generally occurring on the toes, but also on any part exposed to occasional friction and pressure. There is overgrowth of the cuticle, and in the centre of the corn is a still denser mass, which, pressing down upon the true skin beneath, causes pain and may give rise to inflammation and suppuration. When situated between the toes, the corn is softer than on the free surface of the foot. (*See* CORNS AND BUNIONS.)

A *wart* (*verruca*) is an excrescence from the surface of the skin due to hypertrophy of the papillary layer of the cutis and of the epidermis. This form of growth may also occur on mucous membranes. Warts occasionally disappear spontaneously, or they may be excised, or carefully touched with some strong caustic acid or alkali. (*See* WARTS.)

Ichthyosis or *xeroderma* consists of a general thickening of the whole skin and marked accumulation of the epidermic elements, with atrophy of the sebaceous glands, giving rise to a hard, dry, scaly condition. It generally first appears in infancy, and is probably congenital. It differs in intensity and in distribution in different cases, and is generally little amenable to any but palliative remedies, such as the regular application of oily substances, although it is not a fatal malady.

(2) **Atrophies.**—The chief of these relate to the hair. *Canities* or whitening of the hair consists in the non-formation of the pigmentary matter which is normally present in the substance of the hair, and occurs generally as a slow senile change. It may, however, take place prematurely, in which case it is often hereditary ; or it may be associated with degenerative changes taking place in the system. It is occasionally seen to occur temporarily in very

805

young persons in connection with some defective condition of the general health. Its development suddenly has not infrequently been observed as the result of some strong mental emotion.

Alopecia, or baldness, is the loss of hair, which is most commonly a senile change and irremediable, or, on the other hand, may be premature, occurring either hereditarily or in connection with some previous constitutional morbid state (*e.g.* after fevers or other blood poisons), in which latter case it may be only, although not always, temporary. It appears to depend upon atrophic changes affecting the hair follicle, including obliteration of the capillary vessels—the result of which is that strong hairs cease to be produced, and only feeble, short, and thin hair (*lanugo*) is formed, which soon falls off and is not reproduced. Usually the whole skin of the hairy scalp undergoes thinning and other atrophic changes as well as the hair follicle. Sometimes the loss of hair occurs in distinct circular patches (*alopecia areata*). (*See* BALDNESS.)

(3) **New formations.** — *Tumours* of various kinds form in the skin. They may be of a temporary nature, like wens and warts, or may be *simple tumours*, fatty, fibrous, etc., of the same characters as similar tumours elsewhere, or, especially when situated about the lips and other sites exposed to irritation, may be *epitheliomata* and *rodent ulcers* of malignant nature.

(4) **Pigmentary changes.**—*Chloasma* is an abnormal pigmentation, in the form of brown patches, either generally diffused or confined to one part, such as the forehead and face, and occasionally seen in women suffering from uterine ailments. *Addison's disease* consists in disease of the suprarenal glands, and is accompanied by general bronzing of the skin, with increasing weakness (*see* ADDISON'S DISEASE). *Leucoderma* is a change in the pigmentation of the skin, whereby it becomes white in patches, with a tendency to spread and affect almost the whole surface, until a few dark areas alone remain to represent the original appearance of the skin. It is not of any special significance as regards the health. *Albinism* is an entire absence of pigment from the hair, skin,

806

eyes, etc. The hair is usually white, and the skin exceedingly pale ; and the eye has a pinkish appearance. This condition is congenital. It occasionally exists to a partial extent. (*See* ALBINISM.)

III. **INFLAMMATORY SKIN AFFECTIONS.** — These embrace the following chief varieties : (1) diffuse (dermatitis) ; (2) papular (lichen) ; (3) catarrhal (eczema) ; (4) local infective ; (5) vesicular (herpes, pemphigus) ; (6) pustular (impetigo) ; and (7) scaly (psoriasis).

(1) **Diffuse inflammation** includes the varieties of *dermatitis* which may be due to sunburn, heat, various drugs such as belladonna, bromides, and iodides, poisonous plants, such as poison ivy and Chinese primrose, and irritating substances encountered in various trades. *Erythema nodosum* consists of spots and patches slightly elevated and of dark-red colour, appearing on the front of the legs and back of the arms in young persons, mostly females. This variety is supposed to be connected with rheumatism, joint - pains frequently accompanying it, and with tuberculosis. (*See* ERYTHEMA.) *Erysipelas* is an inflammatory skin affection resembling erythema, though of far severer type (*see* ERYSIPELAS). *Urticaria* or *nettle rash* is a diffuse redness of the skin, accompanied by weals of raised and paler appearance, not unlike the effect produced by the sting of nettles or of insects, and attended with great irritation and itching. It is a form of allergy (*q.v.*) and is due to the affected individual coming in contact with, inhaling, or eating some substance to which he or she is sensitized. Treatment consists in the taking of an antihistamine drug and the local application of some soothing preparation such as calamine lotion. (*See* NETTLE-RASH.)

(2) **Papular.** — *Lichen planus* is an eruption consisting of small, thickly set, and slightly elevated red points, more or less widely distributed over the body. Some forms are of chronic character and difficult of treatment. Treatment consists of the administration of arsenic or mercury, and the application of soothing lotions.

(3) **Catarrhal.**—*Eczema*, one of the most common and important of all skin

diseases, consists of an inflammation of the true skin, of catarrhal character, together with the formation of papules, vesicles, or pustules, attended with more or less discharge, and with itching and other symptoms of irritation. It cannot be regarded as a disease by itself, but is really a symptom denoting the reaction of the skin to various forms of irritation. It may be either acute or chronic, and presents itself in a variety of forms. As regards causation, it appears impossible to assign any one condition as giving rise to this disease. It occurs frequently in persons to all appearance in perfect health, and it may in such cases be a permanent or recurring affection during a whole lifetime. Again, it is undoubtedly found in persons who possess a morbid constitution, such as the gouty, or, more generally, in persons in whom the excretions of the bowels or kidneys are defective. Sometimes it is set up as the result of local or general irritation of the skin in certain occupations, such as in confectioners, whose skin is exposed to the constant irritation of sugar, and it may exist in connection with the presence of some other skin disease. It may even be due to the wearing of clothing containing irritating dyes (*see* ANILINE). It is much more common in men than in women. Numerous varieties of eczema are described, according to its site and duration : only the more important of these can be mentioned.

Acute eczema shows itself by redness and swelling of the skin, the formation of minute vesicles, and severe heat and irritation. Should the vesicles rupture, a raw, moist surface is formed, from which a colourless discharge oozes, which forms thin crusts when it accumulates. The attack may be general over the greater portion of the body, or it may be entirely localized to a limb or other part. It usually lasts for a few weeks and then passes off, leaving, however, a liability to recurrence. Such attacks may occur as a result of digestive derangements, or in persons of rheumatic or gouty tendency, and they tend to appear at certain seasons, such as springtime. They are usually best treated by attention to the general health, and by a simple and carefully regulated diet, while, locally, some soothing applica-

tion, such as a weak lead or calamine lotion, or a dusting powder composed of oxide of zinc, starch, and boracic acid, will be found of benefit. *Chronic eczema* shows itself in various forms, of which we note the most common. In *eczema rubrum* the disease affects the leg, as a severe form of inflammation, with great redness, and weeping or oozing of serous matter from the raw surface. It gives rise to great irritation and pain, and may cause considerable disturbance of the general health. It may last for years, with intervals of partial recovery, but easily recurring. The skin of the limb becomes in time thickened and the limb itself much swollen. In *dry eczema* the skin, though irritable, remains dry and scaly. The treatment of chronic eczema depends in great measure upon the form it assumes. Where there exists much irritation, soothing lotions or applications similar to those required for acute eczema are necessary ; but where irritation has subsided, stimulating ointments, such as those of zinc or white precipitate, are often of service. Lassar's paste, containing salicylic acid starch, zinc oxide, and vaseline, is also a valuable remedy. Constitutional remedies, such as iron, arsenic, etc., are an important and often essential part of successful treatment.

(4) **Local infective conditions.**—These include eruptions on the skin due to lupus, leprosy, syphilis, and some other diseases.

Lupus vulgaris is a disease characterized by the formation in the skin of tubercles or nodules consisting of new cell growth which has no tendency to further development, but to retrograde change, leading to ulceration and destruction of the skin and other tissues in which it exists, and the subsequent formation of permanent white scars. It is due to the *Mycobacterium tuberculosis*, and is most commonly seen in early life, and occurs chiefly on the face, about the nose, cheeks, ears, etc., but it may also affect the skin of the body or limbs. It first shows itself in the form of small, slightly prominent nodules covered with thin crusts or scabs. These may be absorbed and removed at one point, but they tend to spread at another. They tend to ulcerate and leave a white permanent scar. The condition known as *lupus erythematosus* resembles this slightly, and appears as dark-red patches upon the nose and neighbouring parts of the cheeks, covered at places with scabs. It does not, however, produce the ulceration and disfigurement commonly due to lupus vulgaris (*see* LUPUS).

Leprosy may be regarded as belonging to this class of skin diseases, inasmuch as it consists, like lupus, in a new growth of cell material, but with a wider distribution affecting the skin, mucous membranes, nerves, etc., all over the body. It is due to an organism known as the *Mycobacterium lepræ* (*see* LEPROSY).

Syphilis may produce eruptions of several kinds. The earliest is in the form of a faint rose - coloured rash ; later, red patches covered with white scales may appear ; but the chief eruption, appearing in the late stage of the disease, consists in thickened areas in the skin (gummata) which ulcerate, and on healing leave rounded scars with brown pigmented edges (*see* SYPHILIS).

(5) **Vesicular.**—*Herpes* is an inflammation of the true skin, attended with the formation of isolated or grouped vesicles of various sizes upon a reddened base. They contain a clear fluid, and either rupture or dry up. Two well-marked varieties of herpes are frequently met with. (*a*) In *herpes labialis et nasalis* the eruption occurs about the lips and nose. It is seen in cases of certain acute febrile ailments, such as fevers, inflammation of the lungs, or even in a severe cold. It soon passes off. (*b*) In *herpes zoster, zona*, or *shingles*, the eruption occurs in the course of one or more cutaneous nerves, often on one side of the trunk, but it may be on the face, limbs, or other parts. It may occur at any age, but is probably more frequently met with in elderly people. The appearance of the eruption is usually preceded by severe stinging neuralgic pains for several days, and, not only during the continuance of the herpetic spots, but long after they have dried up and disappeared, these pains sometimes continue and give rise to great suffering. (*See* HERPES.)

Pemphigus is characterized by the appearance of large blebs or blisters.

Pemphigus neonatorum, the form of the disease which appears in young infants, is really a form of impetigo (*q.v.*). It is liable to occur in nurseries and maternity hospitals, and is highly infective. Strict isolation of cases is essential, and the prognosis is satisfactory provided active treatment is started at an early stage. In addition to local treatment, penicillin or a sulphonamide is given. *Pemphigus vulgaris*, or chronic pemphigus, usually occurs after the age of 40 years. There are marked constitutional disturbances, and the condition is usually fatal in the end. Treatment consists of local soothing applications, and either penicillin or a sulphonamide. Acetarsone, an arsenical preparation, and blood transfusions have also been recommended. *Pemphigus foliaceus*, in which practically the whole of the skin is involved, is not accompanied by such marked constitutional disturbances, and is more liable to run a prolonged chronic course.

(6) **Pustular.** — *Impetigo*, consisting of small pustules situated upon a reddened base, mostly occurs in children. There is a contagious form of this malady, which passes from child to child, not uncommonly breaking out as a sort of epidemic in schools. (*See* IMPETIGO.) *Ecthyma* consists of large pustules of similar character on the body and limbs. The treatment of these ailments requires special attention to nutrition, since they usually occur in low states of health. *Boils* may be single, but very often come in the form of a localized eruption of inflamed areas around the follicles of neighbouring hairs. (*See* BOILS.)

(7) **Squamous or scaly.** — *Psoriasis*, an inflammatory affection of the true skin, attended with the formation of red spots or patches, which are covered with white silvery scales, may affect any portion of the surface of the body, but is most common about the elbows and knees, and on the head. There is, as a rule, comparatively little irritation except at the outset, but there is an extensive shedding of the scales from the affected spots. Varieties of this disease are described in relation to the size and distribution of the patches. (*See* PSORIASIS.)

IV. **N E U R O D E R M A T O S E S.**— Various disorders of nutrition of the skin occur in persons suffering from organic nervous diseases, such as bed sores, atrophic changes, eruptions, etc., but these belong to the symptoms of the several diseases with which they are associated. The most common of the neuroses of the skin is probably *pruritus*, which is an ailment characterized by intense itching of the surface of the body. It may occur in connection with other morbid conditions, such as jaundice, diabetes, digestive disorders, etc., or as the result of the irritation produced by lice or other skin parasites. The most serious form is *pruritus senilis*, which affects old persons, and is often a cause of great suffering, depriving the patient of sleep (the malady being specially troublesome during the night). In such cases it is probably due to

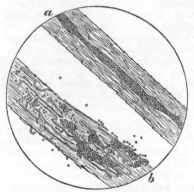

FIG. 334.—Microscopic appearance of a healthy hair, *a*, and of one infected with ringworm, *b*. The latter is disorganized by the growth of the mycelium and spores of the parasite.

atrophic changes in the skin. No eruption is visible, except such marks as are produced by scratching. The treatment consists in the removal of any apparent cause, and attention to the general health. Local applications of calamine liniment, zinc cream or zinc paste are often helpful. In severe cases hydrocortisone ointment may be used for a short time. The addition of an ounce or two of the *British Pharmacopœia* emulsifying ointment into the bath water is often beneficial. (*See* ITCHING.)

V. PARASITIC AFFECTIONS.—(1) **Animal parasites.**—*Phthiriasis* is produced by the presence of lice (*pediculi*), of which there are three varieties,

infesting respectively the head, body, and pubis. (*See* PARASITES.)

Scabies, or *Itch*, is a skin affection due to the *Sarcoptes scabiei*, a species of mite. (*See* ITCH, PARASITES.)

(2) **Vegetable parasites** consist of fungous growths in the texture of the skin and hair, which are characterized microscopically by minute round bodies or spores, often coalesced into clusters or bead-like arrangements, and jointed filaments or *mycelium* of elongated and branching form. The common name 'tinea' is applied to these parasitic affections. *Tinea capitis*, or *ringworm of the scalp* (parasite *Microsporon audouini*), is a very common form of disease. (*See* RINGWORM.)

Tinea circinata is the name given to ringworm affecting the body. *Tinea favosa*, *favus*, or *honeycomb ringworm* is a rarer condition (parasite *Achorion schönleinii*), occurring on the scalp of unhealthy children, which it covers with yellow, cup-shaped crusts, of a peculiar 'mousy' odour. *Tinea sycosis*, or *Tinea barbæ*, a pustular condition of parasitic origin, affects the hairs on chin and cheeks. It is a very difficult condition to get rid of, and is usually attributed to infection from a barber's soap or brush. *Tinea cruris*, or *dhobie itch*, is due to a fungus of the genus *Epidermophyton*, and affects the inner aspects of the thigh. *Tinea pedis*, also an *Epidermophyton* infection, affects the toes.

Tinea versicolor, or *pityriasis versicolor* (parasite *Microsporon furfur*), is a brown-coloured rash of scaly character occurring mostly in the form of spots or patches on the skin of the trunk, particularly on the front of the chest or between the shoulders, but sometimes also upon the arms and legs. It affects adults in whom the skin-function is not sufficiently attended to, or those who are in ill-health.

SKIN-GRAFTING is an operation in which large breaches of surface due to wounding or ulceration are closed by transplantation of skin from other parts. There are three methods by which this is done. Most frequently the epidermis only is transplanted, according to a method introduced by Reverdin and by Thiersch, and known by their names. For this purpose, a broad strip of epidermis some inches long is shaved off the thigh or upper arm, after the part has been carefully purified, and is transferred bodily to the raw or ulcerated surface, or is cut into smaller strips and laid upon it. By a second method, small pieces of the skin in its whole thickness are removed from the arm and thigh, or even from other people, and are implanted and bound upon the raw surface. This method has the disadvantage that the true skin must contract at the spot from which the graft is taken, leaving an unsightly scar. When very large areas require to be covered, a third method is sometimes adopted, as follows. A large flap of skin, amply sufficient to cover the gap, is raised from a neighbouring or distant part of the body, in such a way that it remains attached along one margin, so that blood-vessels can still enter and nourish it. It is then turned so as to cover the gap ; or, if it be situated on a distant part, the two parts are brought together and fixed in this position till the flap grows firmly to its new bed. The old connection of the flap is then severed, leaving it growing in its new place.

SKULL is the collection of flat and irregularly shaped bones which protect the brain and form the face. These number in all twenty-two, and the names of the individual bones composing the skull are given under BONE.

Arrangement of the bones.—In early life the brain and organs of special sense are enclosed in a case which is formed partly of cartilage, partly of fibrous membrane. At various parts of this investment, ossification begins early in life, and the bone gradually spreads outwards from each of these centres. Certain of the bones so formed fuse together in early childhood, thus constituting the twenty-two bones of the adult skull, which maintain their independence throughout the greater part of life. In old age, however, the bones fuse so completely that the cranium comes to be a solid bony case. Even before this happens, the bones are fastened to one another by sutures so tightly that their separation without breaking is very difficult. The sutures are joints in which each edge is locked with the edges of neighbouring bones

by exactly fitting projections and depressions, resembling a complicated mortise - work. Occasionally small bones develop in the sutures between the ordinary, named ones, these extra bones being known as Wormian bones.

The growth of the bones spreads outwards, as already stated, from certain centres, and at the time of birth the growth of several bones has not been quite completed, so that an infant's head presents six soft spots or fontanelles where the brain is covered only by skin and membranes, and at some of which the pulsations of its blood-vessels can be seen. One of these spots, the anterior fontanelle, situated on the top of the head, does not completely close till the child is nearly two years old. Another change takes place as age advances, consisting in the development of an outer and inner hard table in each of the cranial bones, the tables being separated by a layer of cancellous bone (*diploë*), and in some positions by spaces containing air, which communicate with the respiratory passages. This change begins at the age of ten years, and leads to great thickening and increased strength in the skull.

Parts of the skull.—The skull consists of two distinct parts : the cranium, which encloses the brain and consists of eight bones ; and the face, which forms a bony framework for the eyes, nose, and mouth, and is composed of fourteen bones. These two parts can be detached from one another. The lower jaw is connected with the base of the cranium by a movable joint on each side, and when the bones are bare of soft parts there is no union between them. The ear, which lies just behind and above this joint, is enclosed in the substance of the temporal bone, lying beneath the brain and separated from it in places only by a very thin shell of bone. The interior of the cranium is moulded so as to form a support for the brain (Fig. 336). Its base is divided by bony ridges into three fossæ, which from before back support the frontal lobes, the temporosphenoidal lobes, and the cerebellum. Further, the inner surface of the bone shows grooves and hollows corresponding to the convolutions and blood-vessels of the brain. The bones, especially on the base of the skull, are pierced by many small canals (*foramina*) which transmit nerves, vessels, etc. Of these the largest is the foramen magnum, through which the medulla oblongata and the spinal cord are continuous with one another.

Shape of the skull.—In the lower animals, the cranium is placed in the back part of the head, and the face looks

the line on which the skull rests, when the lower jaw is removed) varies from an obtuse angle in the ancient Greeks, whose statues show an overhanging forehead, through a right angle in Romans and some of the higher Teuton types, to an acute angle in negroes and Australian blacks, and a still acuter angle in the man-like apes. Another method of classification is obtained by taking what is known as the cephalic index,

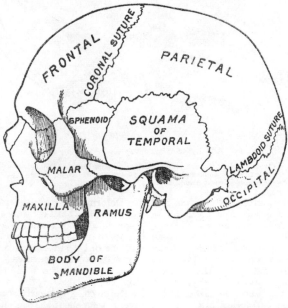

FIG. 335.—Side view of skull. (From Hill, *Manual of Human Physiology*. Edward Arnold & Co.)

upwards to a great extent as well as forwards. In man, as a consequence of the great development of the cerebral hemispheres of the brain, in connection with his mental activity, the cranium extends above, as well as behind, the face, which therefore looks straight forwards. A modified type of the lower class of skull is, however, found in the lower races of mankind, in whom the forehead is low and sloping and the jaws prominent. This feature of the skull (prognathism) has been made, by the anatomist Camper and others, a basis for classification of the different races of mankind. The facial angle (*i.e.* the angle between a line touching the most prominent points on the front of the face and

i.e. the percentage that the skull's breadth forms of its length. Long-headed peoples, like the Australian blacks, are known as *dolichocephalic*; peoples with rounded heads, like most European races, are called *mesaticephalic*; while races with broad heads, like some American Indians, are said to be *brachycephalic*.

Age makes considerable changes in the skull. The persistence of soft spots in the skull during the first two years of life, as well as the gradual obliteration of the sutures in later life, have been already mentioned. In children the size of the cranium is large compared with that of the face, which measures only one-eighth of the whole head, but

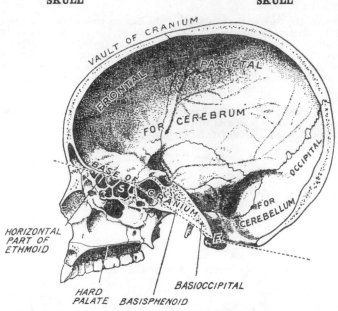

FIG. 336.—Skull divided in half to show cranial cavity. Names inside cavity indicate different parts of the brain. F, hole through which auditory nerve passes to ear. S, air sinus. (From Hill, *Manual of Human Physiology*. Edward Arnold & Co.)

increases till in adult life cranium and face are of almost equal proportions. In old age the face once more decreases, owing largely to loss of the teeth and consequent absorption of their bony sockets, which allows the cheeks to sink inwards and gives the appearance known as nut-cracker jaws. A similar result is produced earlier in life by premature extraction of the teeth. The child's head is gently rounded, and does not show the prominences above the eyebrows and behind the ears, due to the presence of air-cells at these localities in the full-grown skull. Further, the skull is thinner in childhood, does not show the heavy ridges for attachment of muscles displayed in later life, and is more vertical on the front and sides.

Sex also makes some differences, so that, as a rule, though not invariably, the skull of a woman can be told from that of a man. In the woman the characters resemble those of the child, the skull being lighter, smoother, and having less marked prominences. Further, the woman's skull has on an average only nine-tenths the capacity of the male skull.

812

Deformities result from various causes. The head is rarely symmetrical, one side bulging almost always much more than the other. Premature closure of one of the sutures leads to increased growth at other sutures. Thus if the suture running from before backwards on the vertex of the head (sagittal suture) close too early, the result is a very long boat-shaped head. Some races, as, for example, the flat-head

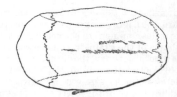

FIG. 337.—Scapho-cephalic or boat-shaped head seen from above. (Turner's *Anatomy*.)

Indians of North America, show striking deformities of the head produced by applying boards and bandages in infant life. The natives in some parts of Southern France also show a curiously shaped head owing to the wearing of a peculiar cap with tight strings in early life.

SLEEP is a periodic resting condition of the body, and especially of the nervous system. The nature and cause of sleep is a question that has excited discussion for many centuries, especially as to the part played by the mind in this resting condition.

Causes of sleep.—There is a natural rotation of sleeping and waking every twenty-four hours, and sleep comes on commonly during the night when little work can be done. Sleep is not, however, a necessary consequence of darkness, as is proved by those persons who have to work in the night and sleep by day, and who speedily adapt themselves to this condition. Many persons too, such as sailors, gain the power of sleeping as soon as they turn in, and for them short four-hourly periods of sleep and work become natural.

Many theories have been advanced as to the cause of sleep. One theory depends upon the well-known fact that the brain receives a much smaller blood supply during the sleeping than in the waking state. This fact has been demonstrated in various ways, as, for example, in the case of persons who have lost part of the skull as the result of disease or by operation, and in whom changes in the volume of the brain can be readily observed. Sudden anæmia of the brain is certainly capable of causing loss of consciousness, as in fainting, but it seems more likely that the gradual and slight anæmia of healthy sleep is the effect, not the cause of sleep, since the same change takes place during rest in the blood-vessels of any other part, as for example, in the muscles of the arm or leg. Nevertheless, a certain amount of anæmia is necessary for quiet sleep, and if the brain be hyperæmic, as after great excitement, or too anæmic, as in aged persons, sleeplessness often ensues. Another theory is the chemical one that sleep is due to want of oxygen in the nerve centres. Pettenkofer and Voit have shown that, of the oxygen taken in during the twenty-four hours, 67 per cent. is taken in during the twelve hours of day and 33 per cent. during the twelve hours of night, while of the carbonic acid gas given off, 58 per cent. is the amount by day and 42 per cent. by night. It is also well known that vitiated air containing an excess of carbonic acid gas is capable, like many

other substances, of causing drowsiness followed by unconsciousness. But these facts—while making it plain that want of oxygen or the presence of carbonic acid gas and other products of activity in the tissues may cause sleep—do not explain why sleep comes on regularly in persons who are not exhausted by their day's work, nor why many people are able to compose themselves and fall asleep at any time they find convenient. A third theory raises the question as to whether the mind remains active during the period of sleep. This theory brings forward the fact that all sensations, volitions, and other acts of consciousness are accompanied by chemical disturbances in the brain-cells that stimulate the mind to activity, just as bursting bubbles of gas escaping from the bottom of a pond agitate the surface of the water. When external impressions are cut off by closing the eyes and otherwise composing oneself for sleep, the mind ceases to be stimulated, and tranquil sleep ensues, just as the surface of the water becomes calm when the bubbles get few in number. None of these theories explains the direct cause of sleep, although each probably accounts for the main cause in different circumstances.

When sleep comes on, the eyes are closed as a rule, though in man, even when they are left open, the sense of sight is quickly lost as the sleep deepens. The pupils contract, also, during sleep, and dilate widely as the person wakens. Hearing is lost more slowly, and a person can be wakened even from deep sleep by a loud noise. In natural sleep, touch remains the least affected of the senses, and even the lightest touch will awaken many people from deep sleep. This does not hold good for sleep caused by drugs, many of which have a special effect in dulling general sensation, though much less effect upon the sense of hearing. With regard to the onset of sleep as it affects the mind, will-power is the first faculty to go and the last to appear in wakening. The association of ideas and power of reasoning next disappear, and people are often worried in light sleep by some simple idea which they cannot explain or understand. Memory and imagination remain longest, and, in dreams, the mind is presented with a series of bright, unconnected pictures, all jumbled together, which it does not attempt to explain. Finally, the person sinks into a sound, dreamless slumber, which grows quickly deeper during the first hour of sleep, after which the person sleeps more lightly. The part of the brain which regulates the power of movement is late in falling asleep, sleeps only lightly—since people may turn and make various other movements without waking—and usually wakens before the intellectual faculties and the special senses.

Other parts of the body, as well as the brain, rest during sleep. Thus the kidneys secrete less urine, and the liver secretes less bile, the heart beats much less strongly, and the respirations are slower and shallower than in the waking state. The skin becomes flushed with blood, so that it is specially necessary to keep the surface well covered during sleep in order to avoid chills. Some parts of the body never have a continued rest throughout life. Thus the heart, during the course of the two to three thousand million beats which it makes throughout an average life, never ceases longer than the fraction of a second that intervenes between each pair of beats, and, in each of these brief intervals, it recuperates itself for its next effort. Similarly the vital centres in the brain may be said never to sleep.

The amount of sleep suitable at different ages is mentioned under CHILDREN, PECULIARITIES OF. It must be remembered that too much sleep is unhealthy, as well as too little sleep.

Dreams.—The mind, like the vital centres, is probably never completely inactive during sleep, but is constantly receiving slight impressions which produce only a faint and quickly forgotten sensation. This is borne out by the fact that a sleeper may be awakened, not only by a loud sound or light touch, but by the ceasing of a continuous sound, as when machinery stops. A sleeper is also especially easily awakened by some sound or other sensation that he expects, and, in further proof of this constant wakefulness of the mind, may be mentioned the fact that many people have the power of wakening after having slept for a period which they have previously determined. It has been

already stated that the different parts of the brain and the different faculties of the mind go to sleep usually in a certain order. When the higher intellectual faculties of will and reason have become dulled, but deeper sleep does not at once come on, memory and imagination become increasingly vivid, so that brilliant pictures are presented to the mind. Often these are mingled with misinterpreted sensations from the surface of the body or from disordered internal organs, which serve to give them an unpleasant tinge. For example, dyspepsia following upon a late and heavy meal may give rise to sensations of falling over precipices, of vague depression, or of other unpleasant experiences which are in part memories of past events. Again, a wakeful memory and imagination may be associated with wakefulness of the motor portion of the brain, as when the person dreams that he is making desperate efforts to achieve some object or to escape pursuit, and his limbs go through movements associated with the ideas presented in his dream. Any sensation received from the surface of the body or from a disordered organ may suffice to produce the condition of partial sleep in which dreams occur, or it may become sufficiently strong to awaken the sleeper altogether. Again, the impression of the dream may produce so great an effect upon consciousness that the dream is remembered on waking, or it may fade so completely that only a sense of something forgotten is present, and a feeling that the slumber has been unrefreshing to the weary mind. Dreaming is really a form of partial insomnia, and is to be similarly treated. Much attention has of late been paid to dreams with the object of finding out repressed memories responsible for mental unrest in the person concerned. These often become more evident during sleep than in the waking hours, and, if the dreams are remembered, they give a guide to the identity of the disturbing memories. Appearances seen and things felt or heard in dreams often have a symbolic meaning; and the interpretation of this by those who practise psychotherapy often plays an important part in treatment.

Night terrors occur in nervous children and are allied to dreaming. The child goes to sleep after a day of unusual excitement or fatigue, or perhaps after partaking of some indigestible material, and in a short time, when sleep should be sound and dreamless, he awakens with a start and in a state of terror. Frequently the child screams with fear, cannot be pacified, and for several minutes does not seem to recognize those near him. When quieted, he can often give no reason for his fear, or he may attribute his behaviour to a dream. Children who suffer in this way should be guarded from excitement and fatigue, and may well be taken to a child-guidance clinic or to a child psychologist.

Somnambulism, or sleep-walking, is also an imperfect form of sleep, in which the muscular apparatus, and the portion of brain controlling it, remain awake though the intellectual faculties are buried in slumber. It is of various grades, some persons singing, talking, or even shouting in their sleep, others flinging about the arms or sitting up, and others, who suffer in the most aggravated form, rising from bed and going through complicated movements, such as that of climbing from a window. In many cases, some of the sense organs are also awake, and the somnambulist may see and avoid objects in his path, or may hear and answer questions, though seldom with coherence. These active dreams are, as a rule, totally forgotten on awakening. The condition known as artificial somnambulism or hypnotism is treated under HYPNOTISM.

Paralysed wakefulness is a condition of which people sometimes complain. This is the converse of somnambulism, the person waking from sleep to full consciousness and finding himself unable to make any movement for several seconds or minutes. In this condition the motor part of the brain seems to lag behind the intellectual and sensory part in waking up, but the condition is a transitory and unimportant one.

Insomnia, or sleeplessness, is a condition that often causes annoyance, and by depriving the person of natural rest produces interference with the full activity during the day-time. When it becomes a habit, it may form a serious menace to the health.

It may be due to a variety of causes,

and these may act so effectively as to keep the person awake altogether, or they may serve, when present in a less degree, to produce one of the forms of dreaming and unrefreshing slumber mentioned above. In the first place, there are some persons of a nervous temperament whose sleep is much more liable to be interrupted by trivial causes than that of their more phlegmatic neighbours. In temporary cases of sleeplessness or dreaming, in which the affected person suffers from a disturbed night now and then, the cause is usually to be sought in some external source of irritation. A slight degree of pain, too light a bed-covering leading to general coldness, or even the presence of cold feet may be quite enough to prevent the brain from attaining the necessary degree of repose. Indigestion, due to eating a heavy meal shortly before retiring to rest, or some other internal disorder may act in a similar manner, even although there be no severe pain. In cases of habitual sleeplessness, a voluntary limitation of the hours of sleep, combined with over-study, worry, or grief, is often instrumental in forming a bad habit which it is exceedingly hard to break. The brain in these cases remains hyperæmic and fully active, despite the best endeavours of the sleepless person to compose himself for rest. A similar state of matters is often set up by poisonous materials circulating in the blood, as in fevers, malaria, gout, intemperance, and over-indulgence in tobacco. Another cause of sleeplessness or dreaming is found in persons suffering from neurasthenia, and these persons are frequently affected in such a way that they fall asleep on retiring to rest, enjoy only a light and partial slumber for an hour or two, and then lie wide awake till morning.

Treatment of disordered sleep.—This varies greatly, depending indeed entirely upon the cause. A warm footbath immediately before retiring, a greater amount of exercise during the day, and care with regard to the diet may be sufficient in some of the slighter cases to remedy insomnia. In other cases a hot drink, *e.g.* milk, just before retiring is an excellent sedative. In old people a hot whisky is often a most effective nightcap. As cold feet is a not uncommon cause of insomnia in old people, the wearing of bed-socks may ensure a good night's sleep. Where any known cause of pain or irritation exists, this must of course be remedied. Headache is not uncommonly a cause of sleeplessness, and the relief of this condition is then requisite and often sufficient to restore natural sleep (see HEADACHE). When a mental cause is at the root of the condition, the habit of overstudy, business worry, etc., which was originally responsible for the want of sleep, must be abandoned. Some change of occupation in the later part of the evening, such as reading some simple book or engaging in conversation, often helps to quiet the overworked brain and to deplete its over-filled blood-vessels. In these cases also some easy mental effort, like counting imaginary sheep as one lies awake in bed, is similarly helpful. Cases which resist these simple means often yield to hypnotics (see HYPNOTICS). In cases in which the nervous system is thoroughly run down, treatment of a bracing nature is required (see NEURASTHENIA). Finally, any constitutional states, like gout and malaria, or any bad habits, like intemperance and excessive smoking, require appropriate treatment.

Coma is the name applied to a state of deep sleep from which the person cannot be roused (see COMA). The condition may be due to apoplexy, compression or concussion of the brain, and to poisoning by excess of alcohol or by narcotic poisons such as opium (see OPIUM).

Apparent death is a condition deeper than coma, in which persons are to all appearance dead. Cases have occurred of supposed death in which the person has been in a deep sleep or trance, from which some sudden shock has awakened him after several hours or even days. In all such cases, however, careful examination would reveal signs of life. (See CATALEPSY and DEATH, SIGNS OF.)

SLEEPING SICKNESS, or AFRICAN TRYPANOSOMIASIS, is a disease oc-

curring in West, East, Central and South Africa, between 14° N. and 29° S. latitude, and characterized by increasing weakness, lethargy, and a constant ten-

dency to sleep, with gradual emaciation and finally death. It is one of the group of diseases caused by the presence in the blood of minute parasites known as *trypanosomes* (Fig. 338). The discovery of these parasites in the blood in cases of sleeping sickness was first made in 1902. Later it was shown that this parasite is transmitted by various forms of the tsetse fly (Fig. 339). The disease also occurs in cattle, when it is known as ' nagana '. The most important species of trypanosomes are *Trypanosoma gambiense*, which only affects man, and *Trypanosoma rhodesiense*, which affects mainly man. *Trypanosoma brucei*, *Trypanosoma vivax*, and *Trypanosoma congolense* are all found in wild animals and are fatal to cattle and other domestic animals, but harmless to man. The tsetse flies responsible for the transmission of the disease are *Glossina palpalis* in the case of *Trypanosoma gambiense*, and *Glossina morsitans*, *Glossina swynnertoni*, and *Glossina pallidipes* in the case of *Trypanosoma rhodesiense*.

Other forms of the disease transmitted by other insects are also known, such as a disease occurring in Central and South America called *American trypanosomiasis*, or Chagas's disease (*q.v.*).

The parasite, when introduced into the blood, produces its effects by developing in the small blood-vessels and in the lymphatic glands, around which its presence causes inflammation.

Symptoms.—A few days after the person has been bitten by the fly, fever accompanied by a slight rash develops. This fever subsides but recurs at irregular intervals of a few days or weeks. Gradually the fever becomes more pronounced, and in time the patient becomes weakened and anæmic. The glands of the neck and other parts of the body become enlarged and tender, and this state may last for months or even for years. Some cases appear to recover at this stage even after an illness of many months, and the parasite may disappear altogether from the blood. In most cases, however, the stage known as sleeping sickness gradually appears, although the lethargy may not set in for as long as seven years after the original infection. The patient now becomes disinclined

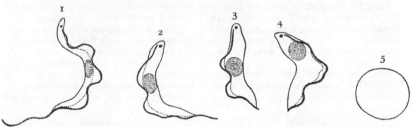

FIG. 338.—*Trypanosoma gambiense.* 1, Long narrow form ; 2, intermediate form ; 3, thick, stumpy form ; 4, posterior nuclear form ; 5, red blood cell drawn to same scale to demonstrate size of trypanosome. (From Blacklock and Southwell, *Human Parasitology.* H. K. Lewis & Co. Ltd.)

for exertion, is slow mentally and weak physically, often complains of headache, and has an increasing tendency to sleep, although at first he is able to engage in conversation and to take his

FIG. 339.—Tsetse fly. The transmitter of sleeping sickness. (From Manson's *Tropical Diseases.* Cassell & Co. Ltd.)

food. As time goes on, the weakness increases and the patient becomes more and more emaciated, bed sores form, and death finally takes place from weakness or from some intercurrent disease. The later symptoms appear to be due to the development of the parasites in the minute blood-vessels of the brain, around which, in consequence, inflammatory changes take place, with disorganization of the proper nervous tissues.

Treatment.—For the prevention of sleeping sickness the chief essential is the avoidance of the flies which carry the disease. Fortunately, the occurrence of the flies is very definitely localized to certain regions, and, when such regions have to be traversed, the journey is made during the night-time when the flies do not feed. Those who live in fly-infested regions should have their houses and persons carefully protected against the fly. As the flies are mostly found close to streams, much

has been done in certain localities by clearing the neighbourhood of streams in infested districts of all vegetation which would shelter the flies. The use of insecticides is proving more difficult than in the case of certain other insect-borne diseases, but promising results are being obtained from the hand-spraying of belts of vegetation bordering roads and tracks, and from aerial spraying of larger areas.

Suramin is the drug of choice in the treatment of *Trypanosoma rhodesiense* infections, and pentamidine in the treatment of *Trypanosoma gambiense* infections. Mel B, a trivalent melaminyl arsenical, has replaced tryparsamide in the treatment of advanced cases of the disease, but it is a drug which must be administered with great care on account of its toxicity.

SLEEPY SICKNESS is a popular name for encephalitis lethargica. (*See* ENCEPHALITIS.)

SLING means a hanging bandage for the support of injured or diseased parts. Slings are generally applied for support of the upper limb, in which case the limb is suspended from the neck. The lower limb is also frequently supported in a sling from an iron cage placed upon the bed on which the patient lies. In the latter case the object of slinging the limb is usually to aid the circulation, and so quicken the healing of ulcers on the leg.

In the case of the upper limb, the sling is made from Esmarch's triangular handkerchief bandage, formed by cutting a yard of calico diagonally from corner to corner into two triangular pieces. There are four varieties of sling.

817

Sling for the wrist is made by folding the bandage up into a narrow cravat, laying the wrist upon the centre, and carrying one end up each side of the neck, behind which the two are tied (Fig. 340 b).

Sling for the forearm is applied as follows (Fig. 340 a): the unfolded triangle is laid with one end over the shoulder of

behind the neck. The point is finally pinned neatly round the elbow.

Sling for the elbow is applied in much the same way, with this exception: that the point of the triangle is placed under the wrist, while the centre of the base supports the elbow (Fig. 341 a). The bandage is completed by turning the point up over the wrist and pinning it

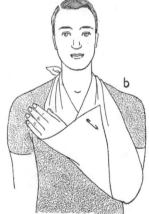

FIG. 340.—*a*, Sling for forearm ; *b*, sling for wrist.

Fig. 341.—Sling for elbow ; *a*, first stage ; *b*, finished.

the sound side, the centre of the base at the wrist of the injured limb, and the point of the bandage at the elbow of the injured limb. The other end is carried up in front of the injured limb, over the shoulder, and the two ends are tied

to the part of the bandage above (Fig. 341 b).

Sling for the shoulder is applied, as in the case of the sling for the elbow, with the centre of the base at the elbow, and the front end is carried over the opposite shoulder. The other end passes up behind the upper arm and across the back, the two ends being tied upon the sound shoulder. The object of this sling is to support, while avoiding pressure on the injured shoulder, as in fracture of the collar-bone. (*See* FRACTURES.)

SLOUGH means a dead part separated by natural processes from the living body. The term is applied to hard external parts which the lower animals cast off naturally in the course of growth, like the skin of snakes or the shell of crabs. In man, however, the process is generally associated with disease, and is then known as 'gangrene'. (*See* GANGRENE.) Sloughs may be of very small size, as in the case of the 'core' of a boil, or they may include a whole limb, but in general a slough involves a limited area of skin or of the underlying tissues. The process of separation of a slough is described under gangrene.

SMALLPOX, or VARIOLA (*varus*, a pimple), is an acute infectious disease characterized by fever and by the appearance on the surface of the body of an eruption which, after passing through various stages, dries up, leaving more or less distinct scars. Few diseases have been so destructive to human life as smallpox, and it has ever been regarded with horror, alike from its fatality, its loathsome accompaniments and disfiguring effects, and from the fact that no age or condition of life is exempt from liability to its occurrence. Although in most civilized countries its ravages have greatly decreased since the introduction of vaccination, yet epidemic outbreaks are far from uncommon, affecting especially those who are unprotected, or whose protection has become weakened by lapse of time.

Much obscurity surrounds the early history of smallpox. It appears to have been imported into Europe from Asia, where it had been known and recognized from remote antiquity. The earliest accounts of its existence reach back to the sixth century, when it was described by Procopius and Gregory of Tours as occurring in epidemic form in Arabia, Egypt, and the south of

Europe. The most reliable statements as to the early existence of the disease are found in Rhazes (*c*. A.D. 900), by whom its symptoms were clearly described, its pathology explained by a fermentation theory, and directions given for its treatment. During the period of the Crusades smallpox appears to have spread extensively through Europe, and hospitals for its treatment were erected in many countries. Smallpox was known in England as early as the thirteenth century, and had probably existed there before. It appears to have been introduced into America shortly after the discovery of that continent, and there, as in Europe and throughout the known world, destructive epidemics were of frequent occurrence during succeeding centuries.

Causes.—Smallpox is one of the most contagious of all diseases. It is due to infection with a virus. Its outbreak in epidemic form in a locality may frequently be traced to the introduction of a single case from a distance. By far the most common cause of conveyance of the disease is contact with the persons or the immediate surroundings of those already affected, but infection can also be carried by the clothes of third persons not themselves infected. The most infectious period extends from the appearance of the eruption till the drying up of the pustules. No age is exempt from susceptibility to smallpox. Dark-skinned races are said to suffer more readily and severely than whites. One attack of smallpox, as a rule, confers immunity from any recurrence. Overcrowding and all insanitary surroundings favour the spread of smallpox where it has broken out; but the most influential condition of all is the amount of protection afforded to a community by previous attacks and especially, in the present day, by vaccination. Such protection, although for a time most effectual, tends to become exhausted, unless renewed. Hence in a large population there is always likely to be an increasing number of individuals who have become susceptible to smallpox. This probably explains its occasional and even apparently periodic epidemic outbreaks in large centres, and the well-known fact that the most severe cases occur at the beginning of an epidemic—those least protected being necessarily more liable to be first and most seriously attacked.

Symptoms.—The onset of the symptoms is preceded by a period of incubation, during which the patient may or may not complain. This period is from seven to sixteen (usually twelve) days. The invasion is sudden and severe, in the form of a rigor followed by fever (the *primary fever*), in which the temperature rises to 103° or 104° F.(39·4° or 40° C.) or higher (Fig. 342). A quick pulse is present, together with thirst and constipation, while intense headache, vomiting, and pain in the back are among the most characteristic of the initial symptoms. Occasionally the disease is ushered in by convulsions. These symptoms continue with greater or less intensity throughout two days, and during their course there may occasionally be noticed on various parts of the body, especially on the lower part of the abdomen and inner sides of the thighs, a diffuse redness accompanied by slight spots of extravasation (*petechiæ*), the appearance somewhat resembling that of scarlet fever. These ' prodromal rashes ', as they are termed, appear to be more frequent in some epidemics than in others, and they do not seem to have any special significance. On the third day the characteristic eruption begins to make its appearance. It is almost always first seen on the face, particularly about the forehead and roots of the hair, in the form of a general redness ; but upon this surface there may be felt by the finger numerous elevated points more or less thickly set together. The eruption, which is accompanied by heat and itching, spreads over the face, trunk, and extremities in the course of a few hours—continuing, however, to come out more abundantly for one or two days. It is always most marked on the exposed parts ; but in such a case as that now described the individual ' pocks ' are separated from each other (discrete). On the second or third day after its appearance the eruption undergoes a change—the pocks becoming vesicles filled with a clear fluid. These vesicles attain to about the size of a pea, and in their centre there is a slight depression, giving the characteristic umbilicated appearance to the pock. The clear contents of these vesicles gradu-

820

ally become turbid, and by the eighth or ninth day of the disease they are changed into ' pustules ' containing yellow matter, while at the same time they increase still further in size and lose the central depression. Accompanying this change, there are great surrounding inflammation and swelling of the skin, which, where the eruption is thickly set, produce much disfigurement and render the features unrecognizable, while the affected parts emit an offensive odour, particularly if, as often happens, the pustules break. The eruption is present not only on the skin but on mucous membranes, that of the mouth and throat being affected at an early period ; and the swelling produced here is not only a source of great discomfort but even of danger from the obstruction thus occasioned in the upper portion of the air passages. The mucous membrane of the nostrils is similarly affected, while that of the eyes may also be involved, to the danger of permanent impairment of sight. The febrile symptoms, which ushered in the disease, undergo marked abatement on the appearance of the eruption on the third day, but on the eighth or ninth, when the vesicles become converted into pustules, there is a return of the fever (*secondary* or *suppurative fever*) (Fig. 342), often to a severe extent, and frequently accompanied by nervous symptoms, such as great restlessness, delirium, or coma. On the eleventh or twelfth day the pustules show signs of drying up (desiccation), and along with this the fever abates. Great itching of the skin attends this stage. The scabs produced by the dried pustules gradually fall off and reddish-brown spots remain, which, according to the depth of skin involved in the disease, leave a permanent, white, depressed scar—this ' pitting ', so characteristic of smallpox, being especially marked on the face. Convalescence in this form of the disease is, as a rule, uninterrupted.

In some outbreaks the type of the disease is much more severe than in others, and the mortality consequently greater. Smallpox is most fatal at the extremes of life, except in the case of vaccinated infants, in whom there is an immunity from the disease. Numerous and often dangerous complications are apt to occur at or after the supervention of the secondary fever. The most important are inflammatory affections of the respiratory organs, such as bronchitis, pleurisy, pneumonia, suppurative conditions of the throat, and swelling of the mucous membrane of the larynx and windpipe. Destructive ulceration affecting the eyes or ears is a well-known and formidable danger, whilst various affections of the skin, in the form of erysipelas, abscess, or carbuncles, are of occasional occurrence. Persons of enfeebled health, and those whose constitution is impaired by intemperance, readily succumb to attacks of smallpox

the pocks after they are formed. This is apt to be accompanied by bleeding from various mucous surfaces (particularly in the case of females), occasionally to a dangerous degree. Many of such cases also prove fatal. *Malignant smallpox* is a still more serious form, in which, as in the malignant forms of other infectious diseases (*see* MEASLES and SCARLATINA), the patient is from the outset overwhelmed with the poison and quickly succumbs — the rash scarcely appearing at all. Such cases are, however, rare. *Varioloid*, or *modified smallpox*, is the term applied to those cases which occur in people

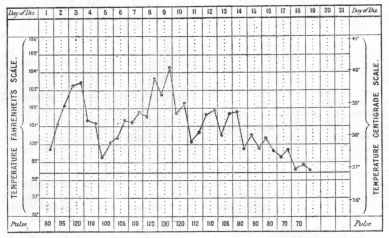

FIG. 342.—Temperature chart of a case of smallpox, showing the primary and secondary fevers.

even of comparatively mild character, as do also pregnant women, to whom this disease is peculiarly dangerous.

Varieties.—*Confluent smallpox* shows much severer symptoms from the onset than those just described, and the eruption, instead of showing itself in isolated pocks, appears in large patches run together, giving a blistered appearance to the skin. This confluent condition is almost entirely confined to the face, and produces shocking disfigurement and deep scars. The mortality in these cases is very high, and it is generally estimated that at least 50 per cent. of the cases of confluent smallpox prove fatal, whilst in those who survive, convalescence is apt to be slow and interrupted. *Hæmorrhagic smallpox* is a form in which bleeding takes place into

who are little susceptible to the disease, or in whom the protective influence of vaccination or of a previous attack of smallpox still exists to some extent.

Laboratory tests are now available to assist in diagnosis in difficult cases. The most reliable of these is the growing of the virus on the chorio-allantois of a fertile hen's egg. This is done by inoculating a sample of scrapings from the skin, or of fluid from a vesicle, into the egg.

Treatment.—In the prevention of smallpox, with regard to the safety both of the individual and of the community, no measure has been so effective as vaccination. (*See* VACCINATION.)

The treatment of cases of smallpox is conducted upon the same general principles as that for the other infectious diseases. (*See* CHOLERA, DIPHTHERIA, MEASLES, SCARLET FEVER.) The establishment of smallpox hospitals separated as far as possible from populous localities, and the prompt removal of cases of the disease where practicable, as well as the diligent prosecution of vaccination and re - vaccination, are among the first requirements. The patient should lie on a soft bed in a well-ventilated but somewhat darkened room, and be fed with the lighter forms of nutriment, such as milk, soups, etc. The skin should be sponged occasionally with tepid water, and the mouth and throat washed or sprayed with a solution of chlorate of potash, permanganate of potassium, or other safe disinfectant. In a severe case, with evidence of much prostration, stimulants are required. The patient should be always carefully watched, and special vigilance is called for when delirium exists.

Many applications have been proposed for preventing pitting, but probably the best are cold or tepid compresses of light weight kept constantly applied over the face and eyes. The fluid out of which these are wrung may be a weak lotion of boracic acid, with which the eyes should also be frequently irrigated. When the pustules have dried up, the itching thus produced may be much relieved by the application of carbolized vaseline. Complications are to be dealt with as they arise, and the severer forms of the disease treated with reference to the special symptoms presented. Ventilation should be free, and all clothing, etc., should be afterwards burnt.

SMEGMA (σμῆγμα, soap) is a thick, cheesy secretion formed by the sebaceous glands of the glans penis. A bacillus, closely resembling the tubercle bacillus morphologically, develops readily in this secretion.

SMELL (see NOSE, DISEASES OF ; for bad smell, see DEODORANTS, EUCALYPTUS, PERMANGANATE OF POTASSIUM, etc.).

SMELLING SALTS (see AMMONIA).

SMOKING (see TOBACCO).

SNAKE-BITE (see BITES, etc.).

822

SNAKE-ROOT is a popular term for several plants, including senega and serpentaria. Black snake-root is the name applied to *cimicifuga*, which is used in extract or tincture in treatment of chronic rheumatism.

SNARE is a wire loop used by the ear, nose, and throat surgeon for removing polypi from the nose.

SNEEZING means a sudden expulsion of air through the nose, designed to expel irritating materials from the upper air passages. In sneezing, a powerful expiratory effort is made, the vocal cords are kept shut till the pressure in the chest has risen high, and air is then suddenly allowed to escape upward, being directed into the back of the nose by the soft palate.

Sneezing may be caused by the presence of irritating particles in the nose, such as snuff, the pollen of grasses and flowers, etc. It is also an early symptom of colds, influenza, measles, and hay-fever, being then accompanied or followed by running at the nose.

SNORING is due to vibrations of the soft palate, and usually occurs in mouth-breathers. The principal cause is blockage of the nose, such as occurs during the course of the common cold or chronic nasal catarrh. Such blockage also occurs in some cases of deviation of the nasal septum or nasal polypi (*see* NOSE, DISEASES OF). In children, mouth-breathing, with resulting snoring, is often due to enlarged tonsils and adenoids. A further cause of snoring is loss of tone in the soft palate and surrounding tissues due to smoking, overwork, fatigue, obesity, and general poor health.

Treatment therefore consists of the removal of any of these causes of mouth-breathing that may be present. Should these not succeed in preventing snoring, then measures should be taken to prevent the victim from sleeping lying on his back, as this is a habit which strongly conduces to snoring. Simple measures include sleeping with several pillows so that the head is raised quite considerably when asleep. Alternatively, a small pillow may be put under the nape of the neck. If all these measures fail, there is much to be said for the old traditional method of sewing a hair-brush, or some other hard object such as a stone, into the back of the snorer's pyjamas. This means that if he does turn on to his back while asleep, he is quickly awakened and therefore able to turn on his side again. (*See also* STERTOR.)

SNUFFLES is the name applied to noisy breathing in children due to the constant presence of nasal discharge. (For treatment, *see* NOSE DISEASES.)

SOAP is a substance made by boiling a fat or oil with an alkali. The most commonly used oil is olive oil, and the most frequent alkali is caustic soda. In the process of manufacture the fatty acids of the oil unite with the alkali, glycerin separating out. In soft soap or green soap, caustic potash is used in place of soda ; marine soap is made with cocoanut oil ; curd soap has tallow for its fat ; while many toilet soaps have palm oil or almond oil. Barilla soap is made from soda got by burning plants ; in superfatted soaps care is taken that the fatty part is in excess, so that no crude alkali is left to irritate the skin ; whilst glycerin soaps have a specially emollient action. Medicated soaps of various kinds are prepared, the chief drugs added to soap being of an antiseptic nature, such as carbolic acid, coal-tar, formalin, ether, terebene.

Uses.—The chief use of soap is, mixed with water, as a cleansing agent. Internally, hard soap is often used to make up the bulk of pills containing very active ingredients. As a purgative enema, soap is used made up into a strong solution in warm water. Soap liniment, better known as ' opodeldoc ', is widely used as a popular remedy for stiffness or sprains.

SODA (*see* ALKALI, SODIUM).

SODIUM is a metal, the salts of which are white, crystalline, and very soluble. The fluids of the body contain naturally a considerable quantity of sodium chloride, or common salt, and therefore the salts of sodium, when used as drugs, have little effect, depending upon their metallic base. They act similarly to the corresponding salts of potassium (*see* POTASSIUM).

SODIUM CARBONATE, commonly known as SODA or WASHING SODA, has

a powerful softening action upon the tissues.

SODIUM BICARBONATE, or BAKING SODA, is used as an ' antacid ' in relieving indigestion associated with increased acidity of the gastric secretion. It is taken in doses of 10 or 20 grains (600 or 1,200 mg.), as a rule. (*See* ACIDITY.) The citrate and the acetate of sodium are used as diuretics and in the treatment of inflammatory conditions of the kidneys and bladder, although the corresponding potassium salts are more frequently employed.

SODIUM CALCIUMEDETATE is the ' approved ' name for the calcium complex of diamine tetra-acetic acid, which is proving of value in the treatment of lead poisoning and of chrome ulceration.

SODIUM CHLORIDE is the chemical name for common salt.

SOFTENING OF THE BRAIN (*see* APOPLEXY ; BRAIN, DISEASES OF).

SOFT SORE, or CHANCROID, is an infective venereal ulceration due specially to the *Hæmophilus ducreyi*, and probably to other organisms as well. It is a local condition, not spreading beyond the glands in the neighbourhood of the original ulcer, although there is always a possibility that syphilis may be contracted along with this disease and may show itself later. The condition begins within a few hours after inoculation as a pimple which enlarges rapidly and ulcerates. The glands in the groin speedily become affected, and as these may soften and ulcerate, the condition sometimes results in a tedious illness.

Treatment consists in the administration of full doses of one of the sulphonamides by mouth, and careful cleansing of the affected part with dilute potassium permanganate (1 in 8000 dilution). The affected glands are not drained, but if they become fluctuant the pus may be aspirated with a needle and syringe. In resistant cases, streptomycin or aureomycin may be tried.

SOLAPSONE is a sulphone derivative which is used in the treatment of leprosy. It can be given by mouth or by injection.

SOLARIUM is the term applied to a room enclosed by glass in which sun baths are taken while protection is afforded from the weather. This form of treatment is especially used against tuberculosis.

SOLDIER'S HEART, or DISORDERED ACTION OF THE HEART (D.A.H.), or EFFORT SYNDROME, is a term applied to a set of symptoms arising under conditions of great anxiety and unusual physical strain, and consisting of palpitation, shortness of breath, speedy exhaustion, depression, and irritability. The condition also occurs in civil life, but received its name on account of the frequency with which it was noticed during the 1914–18 War. (*See* HEART DISEASES.)

SOLOMON'S SEAL is a popular name for *Polygonatum officinale*. The fluid extract has astringent properties and is used as an application to bruises.

SOMATIC (σωματικός) means anything belonging to the framework of the body as distinguished from the internal organs.

SOMNAMBULISM (*somnus*, sleep; *ambulo*, I walk) means sleep-walking. (*See* SLEEP.)

SOPORIFICS (*sopor*, heavy sleep; *facio*, I make) are measures which induce sleep. (*See* HYPNOTICS.)

SORDES (*sordes*, filth) is the name applied to the thick offensive material which gathers on the lips, teeth, and tongue of persons who are very weak from fever or other cause. In healthy people the constant movements of the tongue and lips serve to keep them free of growing bacteria, remnants of food, and cells cast off from the mucous membrane of the mouth, which in the enfeebled state collect and form a brown or black putrefying deposit.

Treatment.—The lips, tongue, and teeth should be wiped occasionally with a rag dipped in borax and honey, or glycerin of borax, and the rag then burned. Syringing out the mouth with bicarbonate of soda solution, one teaspoonful to a tumblerful of warm water, is also helpful in very weak persons. If the person be strong enough, he may

rinse his mouth with weak solution of permanganate of potassium in water, diluted to a pale pink colour.

SORE is a popular term for ulcer (*see* ULCER).

SORE THROAT (*see* THROAT, DISEASES OF; *and* TONSILLITIS).

SOUND is a rod with a curve at one end, for passing into the bladder to determine whether a stone is present or not. (*See* BLADDER, DISEASES OF.)

SOUR MILK (*see* LACTIC ACID BACILLI).

SOUTHEY'S TUBES are long, fine tubes for drawing off water slowly from cases of dropsy. (*See* ASPIRATION.)

SOYA BEAN is the bean of *Glycine hispida* or *Soja max*, a leguminous plant related to peas and beans. The outstanding characteristic of the soya bean is its very high protein and fat content. There is an almost complete absence of starch. There is a large amount of mineral matter. Soya flour contains 40 per cent. of protein and 20 per cent. of fat. It yields 470 calories per 100 grammes as compared with 370 calories for white wheat flour. Soya flour contains 0·2 per cent. of calcium (about ten times as much as in white flour). It also contains a variable but large amount of iron—6·7 to 30 mg. per 100 grammes of soya flour compared with 1 mg. in white flour and 3 mg. in 100 grammes of wholemeal flour. It is a good source of vitamin B_1 and riboflavine, and of vitamin A in the form of carotene. As a concentrated food it proved a valuable addition to the national diet during war-time rationing.

SPANISH FLY is a popular term for cantharides, which is used as a blistering agent. (*See* CANTHARIDES.)

SPASM (σπάσμα, a convulsion) means an involuntary, and, in severe cases, painful contraction of a muscle or of a hollow organ with a muscular wall. Spasm may be due to affections in the muscle where the spasm takes place, or it may originate in some disturbance of that part of the nervous system which controls the spasmodically acting muscles. Spasms of a general nature are usually spoken of as ' convulsions ', spasms of a painful nature are known as ' cramp ' when they affect the muscles of the limbs, and as ' colic ' when they are situated in the stomach, bowels, or other organs of the abdomen. Spasm of the heart receives the name of ' breast-pang ' or ' angina pectoris ', and is both a serious and an agonizing condition. When the spasm is a prolonged firm contraction, it is spoken of as ' tonic ' spasm ; when it consists of a series of twitches or quick alternate contractions and relaxations, it is known as ' clonic ' spasm. Spasm is a symptom of many diseases.

SPASMODIC TORTICOLLIS, or WRY-NECK, is the term applied to a condition in which there is continuous or interrupted spasm of the muscles of one side or of both sides of the neck, the head being held or jerked either backwards or to one side. It is a nervous disorder.

SPASMOLYTICS are drugs which relieve spasm (see ANTISPASMODICS).

SPASMOPHILIA (σπασμός, spasm ; φιλέω, I love) is a term applied to a condition affecting certain persons, especially in childhood, in which the motor nerves are unusually sensitive to irritation. Such patients show an abnormal tendency to convulsions and spasms on very slight cause.

SPASMUS NUTANS is the term for describing the rhythmic nodding of the head sometimes seen in infants during the first year of life.

SPASTIC (σπαστικός, drawing) is a term applied to any condition showing a tendency to spasm, e.g. spastic gait. This is specially associated with some disease affecting the upper part of the nervous system connected with movement (upper neurone), so that its controlling influence is lost and the muscles are in a state of over-excitability.

SPATULA is the name of a flat, knife-like instrument used for spreading plasters and ointments, and also for depressing the tongue when the throat is being examined.

SPECIFIC (species, a particular kind ; facio, I make) is a term used in various ways. It is applied to remedies which appear to have a definitely curative effect in certain diseases, as, for example, to salicylate of soda, which is said to be specific in rheumatism, or to quinine, which is a specific for malaria. Again, it is applied to bacteria and other agents which form the chief cause of certain diseases, though there may be other minor contributing causes ; for example, the comma bacillus is the specific cause of cholera, the sarcoptes parasite is the specific cause of the itch. The term is also used to designate diseases that have an identity of their own, have a definite cause, and do not consist merely of a group of symptoms ; for example, scarlet fever, measles, typhoid fever are specific as compared with vague ailments such as enlargement of the glands in the neck, diarrhœa, or dyspepsia. The word specific is also sometimes used as a euphemism for venereal disease.

SPECTACLES are worn on account of some defect in the refractive (i.e. focusing) power of the eye, or owing to the axis of the eye being misdirected (i.e. squinting), or simply as a protection from bright light, wind, or dust.

Refractive errors consist of four types : (1) SHORT-SIGHT or MYOPIA, in which the refractive power of the eye is too strong or the globe of the eye too long from before backwards, so that rays of light from distant objects are brought to a focus in front of the retina, upon which blurred images are therefore formed. Spectacles containing concave lenses are used in order to correct this in viewing distant objects. Children with short-sight have difficulty in following their lessons, because they cannot see clearly maps, figures on blackboards, and other objects at a distance. They should therefore be early provided with appropriate glasses, since the error, if uncorrected, is liable to become more pronounced.

(2) LONG-SIGHT or HYPERMETROPIA, in which the globe of the eye is so short from before backwards, that rays of light from objects close at hand would come to a focus behind the retina and therefore produce blurred images, although the vision for distant objects

825

may be perfect. In this case, convex spectacles are used for near work in order to increase the converging power of the lens of the eyes. Long-sighted eyes in school children and students are apt to be inflamed and productive of headache in consequence of the constant overstrain required to focus near objects, such as a printed page, upon the retina. The condition is very apt to pass unnoticed, since, except in extreme degrees of this malformation, the child or student has good vision for distant things. Constantly inflamed eyes, headache, and especially occasional blurring of the print after the eyes have been used for some hours in reading, should attract attention to this condition.

(3) ASTIGMATISM, in which the curvature of the cornea is not symmetrical, so that the rays of light in one plane cannot be focused upon the retina along with those in the plane at right angles to it. Such an eye, accordingly, sees objects, whether they be near at hand or far off, in a distorted manner ; a circle, for example, being seen as an ellipse and blurred at two points opposite one another. For the correction of this error extreme care is necessary. Spectacles have to be fitted in which the glasses, instead of being lens-shaped, consist of a slice from the side of a cylinder. That is to say, the glasses are flat in one direction, and curved in the axis at right angles to it. The axis of the cylinder must be set with great care in the spectacle frame at right angles to the axis of astigmatism. Astigmatism may occur in long-sighted or in short-sighted eyes, or, the eye may be long-sighted in one meridian, short-sighted in the meridian at right angles to it (mixed astigmatism).

(4) PRESBYOPIA, or the condition which is a natural consequence of increasing age, in which the lens of the eye gradually hardens and so loses its power to become more convex and thus accommodate itself for the vision of near objects. This condition necessitates that reading, sewing, etc., shall be carried on, after the age of forty or forty-five, at an inconvenient distance, if the details of the work are to be sharply focused on the retina. The condition is treated by wearing convex glasses for near work. although the

eyes remain perfectly good for viewing objects at a distance. Thus it becomes possible for elderly people, aided by spectacles, whose strength is proportioned to their age, to read, sew, etc., at the convenient distance of 12 or 14 inches (30 or 35 cm.). One sometimes hears it said that a certain person has required no glasses for reading even in advanced old age, but this is simply equivalent to stating that the person has had short-sight all his days and has never had perfect vision for distant objects. In these persons the length of the eye is well adapted for focusing near objects, without artificial aid. Also in cases of commencing cataract in old people the vision for near objects improves a little at first. People of normal sight are usually benefited by spectacles for near work after passing the age of forty-five, and certainly after fifty, since the effort to accommodate for near vision after this age fatigues the eyes and is productive of headache.

Squinting is usually caused by the excessive efforts made by long-sighted children to accommodate their eyes for near vision. In squints due to this cause the squint is remedied by convex glasses. Many other cases of squint (latent squint) are remedied by wearing prismatic glasses. (*See* SQUINTING.)

Protection of the eyes is afforded usually by glass, tinted grey or black according to the degree of protection from light that is required. The disease in which protection is specially required is iritis.

The forms of spectacles, then, are concave and convex lenses, cylinders, prisms, and plane glasses. In many cases a cylinder has to be combined with a lens, and then the lens shape is usually ground upon one side of the glass, the cylinder upon the other. The nature of the glass can be told by holding it close to the eye and moving from side to side. If the lens be convex, the objects seen through it appear to move in the opposite direction to that in which the glass travels. If it be concave, they move with the glass. If the glass contain a cylinder, the rate at which objects travel varies as the glass is moved up and down or from side to side. Often a person has to wear one pair of glasses for near, and another pair for distant work. and it is usual to combine these by making the upper half of each glass the lens suitable for distant work, and adapting the lower half of each for near work. For the method of testing for spectacles see *under* VISION.

The frame in which lenses are set is important. It should be light, and, for persons who use glasses constantly, the spectacle form is best. For occasional use, some *pince-nez* form of frame is usually more convenient, but great care must be taken, especially if the lenses are strong, that the centre of each lens comes before the centre of the eye. For this reason the best form of eyeglasses is one in which the frame has a rigid bridge and is supported by springs that do not alter the position of the lenses.

SPECULUM (*speculum*) is an instrument designed to aid the examination of the various openings on the surface of the body. Many specula are provided with small electric lamps so placed as to light up the cavity brilliantly.

SPEECH (*see* VOICE AND SPEECH).

SPERMATIC is the name applied to the blood-vessels and other structures associated with the testicle.

SPERMATORRHŒA is the name applied to the passage of semen without erection of the penis or orgasm.

SPES PHTHISICA is the term applied to the curious mental condition sometimes observed in a patient with advanced pulmonary tuberculosis, wherein he becomes hopeful of recovery and mildly exalted, and has a false sense of well-being. It appears to be a compensatory reaction to an inner knowledge of impending dissolution.

SPHACELUS (σφάκελος) is another name for gangrene. (*See* GANGRENE.)

SPHENOID (σφήν, a wedge; εἶδος, form) is a bone lying in the centre of the base of the skull, and supporting the others like a wedge or keystone (FIG. 335).

SPHINCTER (σφιγκτήρ) means a circular muscle which surrounds the opening from an organ, and by maintaining constantly a state of moderate contraction prevents the escape of the contents of the organ. Sphincters close the outlet from the bladder and rectum, and in certain nervous diseases their action is interfered with, so that the power to relax or to keep moderately contracted is lost, and retention or incontinence of the evacuation results.

SPHYGMOGRAPH (σφυγμός, the pulse; γράφω, I write) is an instrument for recording the pulse. (*See* PULSE.)

SPHYGMOMANOMETER (σφυγμός, pulse; μανός, thin; μέτρον, measure) is the name of an instrument for measuring blood-pressure in the arteries. It usually consists of a pneumatic armlet, the interior of which communicates by a rubber tube with an air-pressure pump and a gauge. The armlet is bound about the upper arm and pumped up sufficiently to obliterate the pulse as felt at the wrist or as heard in the artery at the bend of the elbow. The pressure registered on the gauge at this point is regarded as the pressure of the blood at each heart-beat (systolic pressure). The pressure at which the sound heard in the artery suddenly changes its character marks the diastolic pressure.

SPICA BANDAGE (*spica*, a head of grain) is a method of applying the ordinary roller bandage in order to cover a joint. When it is finished the overlapping turns of bandage give it the appearance of a head of wheat. (*See* BANDAGES.)

SPINAL COLUMN, also known as the SPINE, CHINE, BACKBONE, and VERTEBRAL COLUMN, forms an important part of the skeleton, acting both as the rigid pillar which supports the upper parts of the body and as a protection to the spinal cord and nerves arising from it. The spinal column is built up of a number of bones placed one upon another, which, in consequence of having a slight degree of turning-movement, are known as the vertebræ. The possession of a spinal cord supported by a vertebral column distinguishes the higher animals from the lower types, and gains for them the general name of vertebrates. Of the vertebrates, man alone stands absolutely erect, and this erect carriage of the body gives to the skull and vertebral column certain distinctive characters.

The human backbone is about 28 inches (70 cm.) in length, and varies little in full-grown persons; differences in height depend mainly upon the length of the lower limbs. The number of vertebræ is 33 in children, although in adult life 5 of these fuse together to form the sacrum, and the lowest 4 unite in the

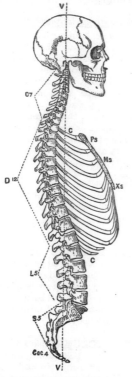

FIG. 343.—The spinal column. C7, Cervical; D12, dorsal; L5, lumbar vertebræ; S5, sacrum; Coc4, coccyx; C, C, the twelve ribs of the left side; Ps, Ms, Xs, three parts of the sternum; V, V, vertical axis of the spine showing its four curves. (Turner's Anatomy.)

coccyx, so that the number of separate bones is reduced to 26. Of these there are 7 in the neck, known therefore as *cervical vertebræ*; 12 with ribs attached, in the region of the thorax, and known as *thoracic* or *dorsal vertebræ*; 5 in the loins, called *lumbar vertebræ*; 5 fused to form the *sacrum*; and 4 joined in the *coccyx*. These numbers are ex-
828

pressed in a formula thus: $C7$, $D12$, $L5$, $S5$, $Coc4 = 33$. The formula in different animals varies considerably, but throughout the class of mammalia the number of cervical vertebræ is almost constantly seven, even in long-necked animals like the giraffe and short-necked animals like the whale. Although the vertebræ in each of these regions have distinguishing features, all the vertebræ are constructed on the same general plan. Each has a thick, rounded, bony part in front, known as the body, and these bodies form the main thickness of the column. Behind the body of each is a ring of bone, the neural ring, these rings placed one above another forming the spinal canal of bone which lodges the spinal cord. From each side of the ring a short process of bone known as the transverse process stands out, and from the back of the ring a larger process, the spine, projects. These processes give attachment to the strong ligaments and muscles which unite, support, and bend the column. The spines can be seen or felt beneath the skin of the back lying in the centre of a groove between the muscular masses of the two sides, and they give to the column its name of the spinal column. One of these spines, viz. that of the 7th cervical vertebra, is especially large and forms a distinct bony prominence, where the neck joins the back. Between the bodies of the vertebræ lies a series of thick discs of fibro-cartilage, and to these 23 discs the upper part of the spine owes much of its pliability, as well as a great deal of its resiliency and power of diminishing the effect of jars and blows communicated through the feet or head. There is also a small joint at each side upon the ring of the vertebra so that each vertebra comes in contact with the one above and the one beneath in three places.

The first and second cervical vertebræ are modified in a very special manner. The first vertebra is devoid of a body, but has a specially large and strong ring with two hollows upon which the skull rests, thus permitting of nodding movements. The second vertebra has a pivot upon its body which fits into the first vertebra and thus permits of free rotation of the head from side to side.

PLATE XVII

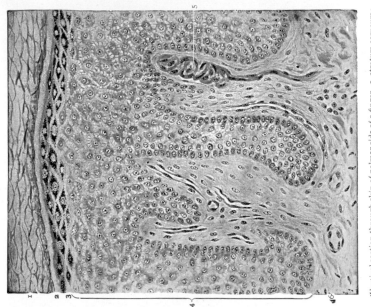

Vertical section through skin of palmar side of a finger. 1, stratum corneum; 2, stratum lucidum; 3, stratum granulosum; 4, rete mucosum; 5, tactile corpuscle; 6, cutis vera. (From Schafer's *Histology*. Longmans, Green & Co., Ltd.) *See* NERVES, SKIN and TOUCH.

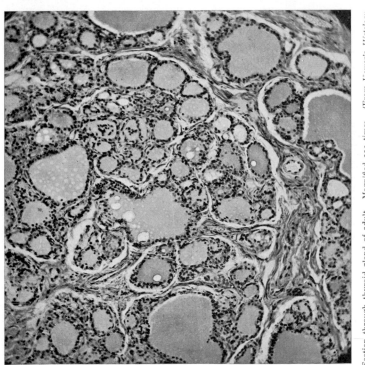

Section through thyroid gland of adult. Magnified 112 times. (From Fewer's *Histology*. Wm. Heinemann Ltd.) *See* THYROID GLAND.

PLATE XVIII

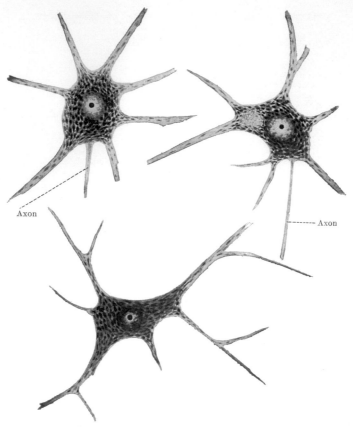

Axon

Axon

Three nerve cells from the anterior column of the spinal cord. (From Cunningham's *Anatomy.* Oxford University Press.) *See* NERVES and SPINAL CORD.

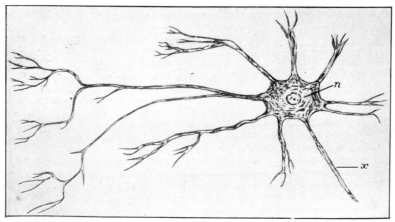

Nerve cell from anterior horn of grey matter of spinal cord, *x*, axon; *n*, nucleus. (From Hill's *Manual of Human Physiology.* Edward Arnold & Co.) *See* NERVES and SPINAL CORD.

A very important feature of the spinal column, and one which is especially marked in human beings, consists in the presence of four curves from behind forwards. Thus the cervical vertebræ are arranged with a curve whose hollow looks backwards, the dorsal vertebræ have a marked curve with the hollow forwards; in the lumbar region the

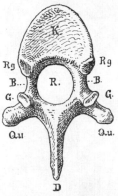

IG. 344.—Human dorsal vertebra seen from above. *K*, Body of vertebra; *R*, neural ring enclosing the spinal cord; *B*, *B*, notches by which the nerves emerge; *D*, spinous process; *Qu*, *Qu*, transverse processes; *G*, *G*, articular processes for the vertebra above; *Rg*, *Rg*, those for the head of the corresponding ribs. (Schmeil's *Zoology*.)

hollow is directed backwards, while the sacrum and coccyx form a marked hollow to the front. The effect of the dorsal and sacral curves is greatly to increase the size of the cavities of chest and pelvis, while the compensating curves of the neck and loins serve to keep the general axis of the spinal column in a vertical line. The curves have, further, an action very similar to that of the springs of a vehicle, in minimizing jolting and jarring of the internal organs. There is usually a very slight curve to one side in the upper dorsal region, resulting from the greater development and use of the right arm.

The neural rings placed one above another form a canal, which is wide in the neck, smaller and almost round in the dorsal region, and wide again in the lumbar vertebræ. This canal lodges the spinal cord, and the nerves that issue from the cord pass out from the canal by openings between the vertebræ which are produced by notches on the

upper and lower margins of each ring. The intervertebral foramina formed by these notches are so large in comparison with the nerves passing through them that there is no chance of pressure upon the latter, except in very serious injuries which dislocate and fracture the spine.

SPINAL CORD is the lower portion of the central nervous system which is situated within the spinal column. Above, it forms the direct continuation of the medulla oblongata, this part of the brain changing its name to spinal cord at the *foramen magnum*, the large opening in the base of the skull through which it passes into the spinal canal. Below, the spinal cord extends to about the upper border of the second lumbar vertebra, where it tapers off into a fine thread, known as the 'filum terminale', that is attached to the coccyx at the lower end of the spine. The spinal cord is thus considerably shorter than the spinal column, being only 15 to 18 inches (37 to 45 cm.) in length. In its course from the base of the skull to the lumbar region the cord gives off thirty-one nerves on each side, each of which arises by an anterior and a posterior root that join before the nerve emerges from the spinal canal. The openings for the nerves formed by notches on the ring of each vertebra have been mentioned under SPINAL COLUMN. To reach these openings the upper nerves pass almost directly outwards, whilst lower in the series their obliquity increases, until below the point where the cord terminates there is a sheaf of nerves, known as the cauda equina, running downwards to leave the spinal canal at their appropriate openings. In shape the cord is a cylinder, about the thickness of the little finger, and slightly flattened from before backwards. It has two slightly enlarged portions, one in the lower part of the neck, the other at the last dorsal vertebra, and from these thickenings arise the nerves that pass to the upper and lower limbs (*see* NERVES). The spinal cord, like the brain, is surrounded by three membranes, the dura mater, arachnoid mater, and pia mater, from without inwards. The arrangement of the dura and arachnoid is much looser in the case of the cord than their application to the brain. The dura especially forms a wide tube which is separated from the cord by fluid and from the vertebral canal by blood-vessels, fat, etc., this arrangement protecting the cord from the brain the grey matter is superficial. The arrangement of grey matter, as seen in a section across the cord, resembles the letter H (Fig. 347; Plate XV), each half of the cord possessing an anterior

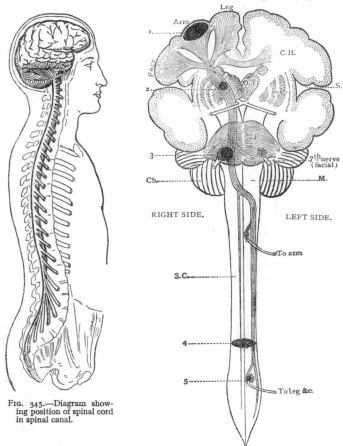

FIG. 345.—Diagram showing position of spinal cord in spinal canal.

FIG. 346.—Diagram showing the course of the motor tracts through the brain and spinal cord. The front half of the brain is supposed to have been removed, and the reader is looking at its interior. *CH*, Cerebral hemisphere; *Cb*, cerebellum; *OT*, optic thalamus; *LN*, lenticular nucleus; *M*, medulla; *P*, pons; *SC*, spinal cord. Note that the great majority of nerve-fibres cross over in the medulla from the right side to form the crossed pyramidal tract on the left side of the cord, while a smaller number continue straight down as the anterior pyramidal tract on the right side. (For the numbers, see under PARALYSIS.)

pressure in any ordinary movements of the spine.

IN SECTION, the spinal cord consists partly of grey, but mainly of white matter. It differs from the upper parts of the brain in that the white matter in the cord is arranged on the surface, surrounding a mass of grey matter, while in

and a posterior horn, and the masses of the two sides being joined by a wide posterior grey commisure. In the middle of this commisure lies the central canal of the cord, a small tube which is the continuation of the ventricles in the brain. The horns of grey matter reach almost to the surface of the cord, and from their ends arise the roots of the nerves that leave the cord, but elsewhere the grey is completely surrounded by white matter. The white matter is divided almost completely into two halves by a posterior septum and anterior fissure that project inwards from the back and front surfaces, the posterior septum reaching down to the grey commissure, but the anterior fissure being separated from it by a small anterior white commissure that joins the white matter of the two sides together. The white matter is further divided into three columns, on each side, by the horns of grey matter and

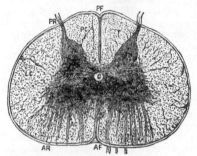

Fig. 347.—Transverse section of the spinal cord in the lumbar region. *AF, PF,* Anterior and posterior fissures ; *AR, PR,* anterior and posterior nerve roots ; *AC, LC, PC,* anterior, lateral, and posterior columns, *C,* central canal of the cord. The dark mass in the interior of the cord is the grey matter. Magnified about 3 times. (Turner's *Anatomy.*)

the nerve roots passing from them to the surface; these are known as the anterior, lateral, and posterior columns.

Minute structure.—The *grey matter* is found upon microscopic examination to consist largely of neuroglia, the connective tissue of the central nervous system, which is made up of small cells with long branching processes. This neuroglia forms a sort of felt-work, in the meshes of which lie numbers of multipolar nerve-cells (Plate XVII) and the nerve-fibres that spring from them and unite one cell to another or pass out into the nerves. The *white matter* consists almost entirely of bundles of nerve-fibres provided in general with a medullary sheath, the white colour being due to the collective appearance of these sheaths. (*See* NERVES.) There is also in the white matter a small quantity of supporting connective

tissue. Most of the nerve-fibres run vertically, so that a cross-section of the cord shows them as a collection of dots, each surrounded by a clear space. Blood-vessels are found in the cord both in grey and in white matter.

Functions.—The cord is, in part, a receiver and originator of nerve impulses, and in part merely a conductor of such impulses along fibres which pass through it to the brain. The presence of centres in the cord, capable of receiving sensory impressions and originating motor impulses, is proved by several facts. For example, it has been calculated that the number of nerve-fibres entering or leaving the cord by the spinal nerves is twice as great as the number of fibres contained in the upper end of the cord, where it is continued into the brain. Again, if the cord be severed in the dorsal region, as by a fracture of the spine, the centres which govern the evacuation of the bladder and bowel do not lose their power of controlling these organs immediately upon being severed from the brain. Many of these centres are known to exist in the cord, such as centres for regulating the size of the blood-vessels, for altering the size of the pupil of the eye, for sweating, for breathing, etc., and the position of several has been ascertained. Over most, if not all, of these centres, however, the brain exerts a controlling influence, and before any incoming sensation can produce an effect upon consciousness, it is in all probability necessary that it should obtain a clear passage up to the brain.

Many of these centres act in a rhythmical or *automatic* way. Other cells of the cord are capable of originating movements in response to impulses brought direct to them through sensory nerves, such activity being known as *reflex* action. (For a fuller description of the activities of the spinal cord, *see* NERVES.)

By observing the process of degeneration that takes place when nerve-fibres are cut off by disease or injury from the cells to which they belong, and by observing also the manner in which the fibres in different portions of the cord develop, it has been found possible to divide the three white columns of the cord into tracts, in each of which the fibres have a special function

(Fig. 348). Thus the posterior column consists of the *fasciculus gracilis* and the *fasciculus cuneatus* both conveying sensory impressions upwards. The lateral column contains the anterior and the posterior spino-cerebellar tracts passing to the cerebellum, the crossed pyramid tract of motor fibres carrying outgoing impulses downwards together with the rubro-spinal, the spino-thalamic, the spino-tectal, and

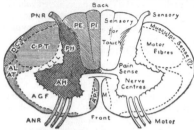

FIG. 348.—Diagram of a section of the cord in the region of the neck. On one side the chief nerve tracts are shown, on the other side the function of these is indicated. *PE*, *PI*, Postero-external and postero-internal tracts; *CPT*, crossed pyramidal tract; *DCT*, direct cerebellar tract; *LLL*, lateral limiting layer; *ALAT*, antero-lateral ascending tract; *AGF*, anterior ground fibres; *APT*, anterior pyramidal tract; *PH*, posterior horn, and *AH*, anterior horn of grey matter; *ANR*, anterior nerve root; *PNR*, posterior nerve root.

the postero-lateral tracts. And, finally, the anterior column contains the direct pyramidal tract of motor fibres and an anterior mixed zone. The pyramidal tracts have the best-known course (Fig. 346). Starting from cells near the fissure of Rolando on the brain (*see* BRAIN), the motor nerve-fibres run down through the internal capsule, pons, and medulla, in the lower part of which many of those coming from the right side of the brain cross to the left side of the spinal cord, and vice versa. Thence the fibres run down in the crossed pyramidal tract to end beside nerve-cells in the anterior horn of the cord. From these nerve-cells other fibres pass outwards to form the nerves that go direct to the muscles. Thus the motor nerve path from brain to muscle is divided into two sections or neurons, of which the upper exerts a controlling influence upon the lower, while the lower is concerned in maintaining the muscle in a state of health and good nutrition, and in directly calling it into action.

SPINE AND SPINAL CORD, DISEASES AND INJURIES OF.—These are considered together, because the chief danger of interference with the spinal column lies in the risk of injury to the spinal cord and nerves. Only some of the chief diseases will be dealt with.

LATERAL CURVATURE OF THE SPINE, or SCOLIOSIS, consists chiefly in bending of the spine over to one side, although, in consequence of the vertebræ being broader in front than behind, this is accompanied by a certain amount of twisting of the vertebræ round their vertical axis. The shape of the chest becomes, in consequence, markedly altered, the ribs on one side projecting behind at their angles, and causing the shoulder-blade to be very prominent, while on the other side the chest is flattened. (*See* CHEST DEFORMITIES.) The shoulder of the bulging side is usually considerably elevated. This condition may be started by slight injuries of the spine, by rickets in early life, or by diseases in the chest, such as pleurisy, which cause partial collapse of one side. But by far its most common occurrence is in young persons of feeble muscular power, especially in rapidly growing girls from about twelve to sixteen years of age, who adopt some bad habit of posture. Such a habit may consist in always crossing one leg over the other in sitting, leaning constantly on the same elbow at lessons, standing habitually with the weight of the body on one foot, or frequently carrying a heavy burden on one arm.

The consequences of this deformity are a bad carriage and awkward gait, while, if it be very marked, the lungs and other internal organs are liable to be attacked by various diseases, although there is no tendency for the spinal cord to suffer any damage.

Treatment consists in avoiding the bad posture mentioned above, and in making sure that the general health is maintained as high as possible by tonics, fresh air, and exercise. Above all, some special form of gymnastics, combined sometimes with massage, is advisable in order to strengthen the feeble muscles of the back. It is only in extremely marked cases that the strait-jackets and other mechanical supports, formerly so much in vogue, are needed to prevent increase in the deformity.

ANGULAR CURVATURE OF THE SPINE is a very much more serious condition. It not only produces more evident deformity, but many cases are accompanied by a certain degree of pressure upon the spinal cord. The condition was described by the famous surgeon, Percival Pott (1713–88), after whom it is also called *Pott's curvature*. This deformity is produced in the great majority of cases by caries of the vertebræ, the result of tuberculosis; the body of one or more vertebræ crumbles away, and the spinal column curves sharply forwards, so that the spinous processes stand out prominently at the site of the

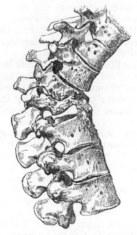

FIG. 349.—Caries of the spine, producing angular curvature. (Miller's *Surgery*, after Liston.)

disease (Fig. 349). A similar condition occasionally comes on after a fall in the case of a young child, or a severe blow upon the back of an older person. The symptoms are not at all well marked in the early stages. There is a general loss of health and strength, and the person becomes easily tired. The affected part of the spine is tender when pressure is made on the back, and the child holds himself stiffly. If the neck be diseased the head is not turned from side to side, and the child often supports the chin on his hand. If the back be the part concerned, the child holds himself very erect, and when he wishes to pick something off the floor, goes down upon

27

his knees rather than bend the back. When the lumbar region of the spine is diseased a frequent result is the formation of a psoas abscess which burrows towards the back or into the groin.

Treatment applicable to tuberculous disease affecting any other organ, *e.g.* good food, fresh air, and chemotherapy, is most important. In an early case, the patient must rest for many months, and in more advanced cases some form of mechanical support is in addition necessary. The region of the thorax, where the condition is commonest, is often supported by a jacket of poroplastic felt or of plaster of Paris; and when the disease attacks the neck, a padded collar or a jury-mast is used to support the head. Good results are often obtained by an operation in which diseased bone is scraped away and new bone transplanted, *e.g.* from a leg to the back of the spine. After the disease has been arrested and the bone has healed up, a considerable amount of permanent stiffness and deformity result.

Excellent results have been obtained from heliotherapy. The back is exposed for several hours daily to the sun's rays, while the patient lies supported on a pillow under the stomach and upon his elbows. Not only does this position relieve pressure upon the diseased part of the spine and gradually correct the deformity, but it allows the patient, during the long period necessary for treatment, to carry on light forms of work in perfect comfort.

CARIES OF THE SPINE is the condition of tuberculous disease leading to angular curvature (*see above*).

COMPRESSION OF THE CORD may arise from various causes. The seriousness of most diseases affecting the spine is, in fact, measured by their tendency to interfere with the spinal cord. This condition may be caused suddenly by a severe crush or blow upon the back, which produces a fracture of the spine with displacement of the fragments. Or it may come on slowly, and is then in the great majority of cases due to Pott's disease (*see above*). Compression of the cord in the neck is speedily fatal as a rule, owing to the involvement of important vital centres; but when it occurs in the region of the chest, the person may live a long time a more or less helpless invalid (Fig. 350).

Symptoms comprise interference with sensation below the level of compression, and, in chronic cases, pain round the body at this level ; more or less complete rigidity and paralysis of the lower limbs ; interference with the functions of the bladder and rectum, and a special tendency to bed sores in the paralysed parts.

Treatment, in cases due to accident, is not as a rule hopeful, since the spinal cord is generally lacerated, as well as compressed, by the damage to the spine. But cases which come on slowly,

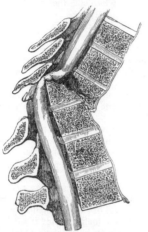

FIG. 350.—Fracture of the spinal column, causing compression of the cord. (Miller's *Surgery*.)

for example, as the result of Pott's disease, very frequently yield to treatment. This consists in the prolonged rest and support to the spine mentioned above ; whilst brilliant results are often obtained, even after several months of complete paralysis, by an operation designed to remove the bone or inflammatory product which is pressing upon the cord. Apart from the question of recovery, these cases require special care and watchfulness in nursing because of the great tendency that is present to the formation of bed sores, and because the patient loses to a great extent the power of voluntary control over the bladder and bowels, so that septic inflammation of the bladder and kidneys is very apt to

834

ensue and to terminate the patient's life.

SPONDYLITIS, or inflammation of the vertebræ of the spine, may occur at any age, but the most important form is *ankylosing spondylitis*. This is a disease predominantly of young males between the ages of 20 and 40. Unless treated in the early stages, it tends to run an inexorable course, leading in the end to complete fixation of the spine as a result of bony ankylosis between the vertebræ.

Treatment consists of deep X-ray therapy and, if given early in the disease, the results are excellent. Even in the later stages it may give considerable relief and slow the progress of the disease. Promising results are also being obtained from the use of the drug known as phenylbutazone.

MENINGITIS, or inflammation of the membranes surrounding the cord, is treated under MENINGITIS.

MYELITIS, or inflammation situated in the spinal cord itself, may be of an acute or chronic nature, and gives rise to symptoms much resembling those of compression though unaccompanied by pain. (*See* MYELITIS.) A special form of myelitis (poliomyelitis), affecting only the grey matter of the cord, is a frequent disease of young children, and causes the symptoms known as 'infantile paralysis '. (*See* POLIOMYELITIS.)

SCLEROSIS is a very chronic condition of the cord in which certain parts become increasingly hard in consequence of a disappearance of the white nerve-fibres and their replacement by an overgrowth of the connective tissue of the cord. This change is due to various causes, and the symptoms which it produces depend mainly upon the particular tracts of fibres that are affected. Sclerosis in the posterior part of the cord, for example, produces the disease known as locomotor ataxia (*see* LOCOMOTOR ATAXIA) ; whilst another disease, known as disseminated sclerosis, in which the degenerated patches are scattered through the nervous system, affects mainly the lateral portions of the cord. (*See* DISSEMINATED SCLEROSIS.)

PROGRESSIVE MUSCULAR ATROPHY is the chief member of a group of diseases in which the main characteristic is loss of power and muscular wasting, due to a gradual degeneration in the grey matter of the spinal cord and brain. (*See* PARALYSIS.)

SYRINGOMYELIA is a disease in which fissures and cavities exist in the cord together with an overgrowth of the supporting neuroglia. (*See* SYRINGO-MYELIA.)

SPINA BIFIDA is a defect in development affecting the spinal column, and in severe cases also the spinal cord, in the lumbar region. Children with this disease are born with a gap in the ring of some of the lumbar vertebræ so that the spinal canal in this region is protected only by the skin. The membranes surrounding the cord bulge out and produce a swelling in the small of the back, which may be the size of a hen's egg or even larger. Surgical treatment is in some cases very satisfactory in its results.

INJURIES TO THE SPINE AND CORD are of various grades of severity. *Sprains* of the back due to a twist and leading to tearing of muscles, ligaments, etc., and to deep-seated effusion of blood, may be productive of long-continued pain and even of a considerable amount of paralysis. In most cases this is probably due to some injury of the spinal nerves, but the symptoms pass off in general with rest and time. *Fracture of the spine* has been mentioned above under the heading of Compression. *Concussion of the cord* is a term which includes a number of possible injuries that may have been inflicted upon the cord by severe jarring or shaking of the body.

SPIRAMYCIN is an antibiotic isolated from *Streptomyces ambofaciens* which is useful in the treatment of certain cases of staphylococcal infection.

SPIRILLUM (diminutive of *spira*, a twist) is a form of micro-organism of wavy or spiral shape. (*See* BACTERIOLOGY.)

SPIRIT is a strong solution of alcohol in water. The term includes those beverages which contain sufficient alcohol to be inflammable, viz. brandy, whisky, rum, etc. (*See* ALCOHOL.) Proof spirit is one containing 57 per cent. of alcohol by volume or 49 per cent. by weight, and is so named because it

can stand the proof of just catching fire. Rectified spirit contains 90 per cent. of alcohol by volume or over 85 per cent. by weight. Proof spirit is generally used in the preparation of tinctures. Spirits of various drugs contain a solution of any given drug in rectified spirit. Among the most commonly used spirits are spirit of chloroform (also known as chloric ether), sweet spirit of nitre (spirit of nitrous ether), aromatic spirit of ammonia (sal volatile), spirit of ether, spirit of Cologne (eau-de-Cologne), spirit of camphor, and spirit of various volatile oils. Methylated spirit (also known as wood naphtha or wood spirit) is distilled from wood. When taken internally, the latter is a dangerous poison producing neuritis with great readiness, and especially neuritis of the optic nerves which may result in blindness. Mineralized or denatured methylated spirit is one to which crude pyridine and mineral naphtha have been added in small proportions, together with a minute quantity of methyl violet for colouring, in order to prevent its being drunk.

The term spirit is also used popularly in a loose application to various active substances, *e.g.* ' spirit of turpentine ' (oil of turpentine), ' spirit of hartshorn ' (ammonia in water), ' spirit of nitre ' (nitric acid), ' Mindererus spirit ' (liquor ammonii acetatis), and ' spirit of salt ' (hydrochloric acid).

Uses (for the internal uses of plain spirit, *see* ALCOHOL).—Externally, plain spirit or eau-de-Cologne is used to sprinkle on the skin or to apply on lint, as an evaporating lotion for its cooling and soothing effect (*see* LOTIONS). Spirit is also used to harden the skin for the prevention of bed sores and foot soreness. The spirits of the various oils form a convenient method of administering these oils as expectorants, or for colic, flatulence, etc. (*see* OILS).

SPIROCHÆTE (σπεῖρα, coil ; χαίτη, hair) is the name given to an order of bacteria which have a spiral form.

SPIROCHÆTOSIS ICTERO-HÆMORRHAGICA, or WEIL's DISEASE, or INFECTIOUS JAUNDICE, is the term applied to an acute infection with the *Spirochæta icterohæmorrhagiæ* which is transmitted to man by rats, these animals excreting the organism in their urine; hence the liability of sewer workers to the disease. The condition is characterized by fever, jaundice, enlarged liver, nephritis, and bleeding from mucous membranes.

SPIRONOLACTONE belongs to the group of substances known as spiro-lactones. These are steroids similar to aldosterone (*q.v.*) in structure but lacking its action. They can antagonize the action of aldosterone in the renal tubules. As there is evidence that there is an increased output of aldosterone in dropsical conditions, such as congestive heart failure, which accentuates the dropsy (or œdema), spironolactone is used, along with other diuretics, in resistant cases of œdema—to antagonize the fluid-retaining action of aldosterone.

SPLANCHNIC (σπλαγχνικός) means anything belonging to the internal organs of the body as distinguished from its framework.

SPLEEN is an organ deeply placed in the abdomen.
Position and size.—The spleen lies behind the stomach, high up on the left side of the abdomen, and corresponds to the position of the 9th, 10th, and 11th ribs, from which it is separated by the diaphragm. It is a soft, highly vascular, plum-coloured organ, and has a smooth surface, being almost completely covered by peritoneum. There are two wide peritoneal ligaments that support the spleen, the one attaching it to the stomach, the other to the kidney. Through the latter ligament. the large vessels that supply the spleen with blood make their way. The size of the spleen varies widely. It is usually about 5 to 6 inches (12·5 to 15 cm.) in length, and weighs about 6 ounces (170 grammes) or more, but these dimensions depend upon the amount of blood contained in it, for it contracts from time to time, and after meals is much smaller than at other times. In diseased conditions the organ may reach a weight of 18 to 20 pounds (8 to 9 kg.).
Structure.—(Plate XV.) The spleen is enveloped by peritoneal membrane like the stomach and intestines, and this smooth coat greatly facilitates its

movements. Beneath the peritoneum is a strong elastic tunic, composed partly of fibrous tissue containing many elastic fibres, and partly of unstriped muscle. This elastic coat allows of the free expansion and contraction of the

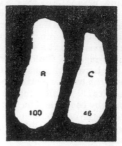

Fig. 351.—Sketch showing changes in volume of spleen of dog as a result of emotional excitement *R*, at rest; *C*, dog sees cat. Numbers represent relative size of spleen. (From Best and Taylor, *The Physiological Basis of Medical Practice.* Williams & Wilkins Co.)

organ according to the varying amount of blood present in it. From the inner surface of the membrane fibrous partitions known as 'trabeculæ' run down into the substance and form a network in which the dark spleen 'pulp' is contained. If the spleen be cut open and the pulp washed away, these trabeculæ stand out as shaggy projections on the cut surface. The 'pulp' consists of delicate connective tissue fibres passing between the various trabeculæ and of white and red blood corpuscles lying in this meshwork. Round the smaller arteries there are condensed areas of this pulp formed of developing white blood corpuscles, and known as Malpighian bodies.

VESSELS pass to the spleen, and are of so large a size compared with the size which would be necessary in order simply to carry nutritive material to the spleen as to render it clear that the organ has some important action connected with the maintenance of the blood. The arteries which enter the spleen at the 'hilum' become smaller and smaller till they end in capillaries, which open freely into the pulp. The blood thus escapes readily into the substance of the spleen, and, after passing through its meshwork, is collected by veins that unite into larger trunks till they form the splenic vein, which leaves the organ and joins the portal vein. There are also numerous lymphatics in the organ, which run in the trabeculæ or surround the veins.

Functions.—These are at best only vaguely known. The organ certainly plays some part in the formation of the white corpuscles of the blood, because a great number of these is to be found in blood drawn from the splenic vein, and because, if the spleen be stimulated to contract by an application of electricity to the surface overlying it, the number of white corpuscles in the blood is found much increased. In some animals the spleen also forms red blood corpuscles, and it appears to do this in the human fœtus, though not after birth. There are reasons for supposing that, in human beings, useless or worn-out red blood corpuscles are broken up by this organ. Nevertheless the spleen does not appear to be absolutely essential to life, since its removal is followed by increase in size of the lymphatic glands all over the body, and does not necessarily cause death.

SPLEEN, DISEASES OF.—In certain diseases associated with marked changes in the blood, such as leukæmia, waxy disease, and malaria, the organ becomes chronically enlarged. In some of the acute infectious diseases, the spleen becomes congested and acutely enlarged ; for example, in typhoid fever, anthrax, and plague. The condition, however, which most frequently attracts attention is rupture of the spleen. This accident may occur, like rupture of other internal organs, in consequence of extreme violence, but in malarious countries, where many people have the spleen greatly enlarged and softened as the result of malaria, rupture of this organ occurs now and then as the result of some very trivial blow upon the left side. The spleen, in consequence of its structure, bleeds excessively when torn, so that this accident is generally followed by collapse, signs of internal hæmorrhage, and death.

SPLENECTOMY means removal of the spleen. This operation may be necessary if the spleen has been severely injured or in the treatment of the severe form of purpura known as purpura hæmorrhagica (*q.v.*).

SPLENIC ANÆMIA (also known as BANTI'S DISEASE) is a chronic disease, of unknown cause, characterized by enlargement of the spleen and anæmia. In the later stages the liver becomes enlarged, and there may be severe hæmorrhage from the stomach. The condition usually begins before the age of 30 years. There is no specific treatment, but some cases respond to removal of the spleen. In the majority of cases, however, all that can be done is to maintain, so far as possible, the general health of the patient and to treat the anæmia with full doses of iron. Blood transfusion is necessary if hæmorrhage occurs.

SPLENOMEGALY means enlargement of the spleen beyond its normal size.

SPLINTS are supports for an injured or wounded part. They are most commonly employed in cases where a bone is fractured, and consist then of some rigid substance designed to take the place of the broken bone in maintaining the shape of the limb, as well as to keep the broken ends at rest and in contact, and thus to ensure their union. Splints are most commonly made of wood either shaped to the limb or consisting merely of strips of wood about the width of the injured limb, and carefully padded with wool or similar soft material. Splints are also made of metal, poroplastic felt, leather, and cotton stiffened with plaster of Paris, as well as other materials. Splints may be improvised for first-aid out of walking-sticks, rifles, broom-handles, branches, folded-up newspapers, and in fact anything of suitable length and rigidity. (*See* FRACTURES.)

SPONDYLITIS (σπόνδυλος, a vertebra) is another name for arthritis of the spine. (*See* SPINAL DISEASES.)

SPONDYLOSIS is the condition characterized by ankylosis (*q.v.*) of the vertebræ.

SPONGES are animals of lowly organization which develop on the bottom of shallow seas, and are gathered chiefly in the Levant and the West Indies. Small sponges which have been steeped in some antiseptic are still sometimes used by surgeons for wiping up blood at operations, but their place is generally taken by swabs of sterilized gauze. A domestic sponge should not be used to wash a wound, because the animal tissue it contains is likely to swarm with microbes. As a medicinal agent, burnt sponge was used for some time in treating goitre (see GOITRE).

SPORADIC (σποραδικός, scattered) is the term applied to cases of disease occurring here and there as opposed to epidemic outbreaks.

SPOTTED FEVER (see MENINGITIS, EPIDEMIC CEREBRO-SPINAL; also TYPHUS FEVER).

SPRAINS are injuries in the neighbourhood of joints, consisting usually in tearing of a ligament with effusion of blood. (See JOINTS, DISEASES OF.)

SPRAYS (see INHALATIONS).

SPRUE, or PSILOSIS, is a disease of uncertain origin, characterized by diarrhœa with the passage of large, fatty stools, anæmia, sore tongue, and loss of weight. The name was first given to the condition in 1879 by Sir Patrick Manson, and it was then considered to be a disease of tropical climates. Subsequent investigations have shown that a similar condition occurs in individuals who have never been in the tropics. To this latter condition the name ' nontropical sprue ' is usually given. The following description applies predominantly to the condition as it occurs in the tropics.

Causes.—Many theories have been advanced concerning the cause of sprue, but the general consensus of opinion to-day is that it is due to an inborn error of metabolism characterized primarily by inability to absorb fats from the intestine. This explains the bulky, frothy stools due to excess of fat. Subsequently there is interference with the absorption of carbohydrate, vitamins, and minerals. The poor absorption of vitamins is responsible for the anæmia and sore tongue, whilst the decreased absorption of calcium is responsible for the low level of calcium in the blood. One advantage of this theory is that it correlates three somewhat similar conditions : (1) tropical sprue ; (2) non-tropical sprue ; (3) 838

cœliac disease, which is a condition found in children. In all these the fundamental cause is the same. In children with cœliac disease the error of metabolism is so marked that the condition appears early in life. In adults the error is less marked and requires either some precipitating factor to provoke it, or else the normal ageing process. In the case of tropical sprue these precipitating factors are one or more of the following : an attack of dysentery ; the strain of living in a hot, damp climate ; dietetic indiscretions ; the highly spiced diet so commonly eaten by Europeans in the tropics.

Tropical sprue is found chiefly in India, Burma, Malaya, the East Indies, and China. It also occurs in the Southern States of U.S.A., the West Indies, and South America. It is more common in Europeans than in natives, and is more common in women than in men. As a rule it occurs after long residence in the tropics, and the onset is usually after the rains. There is quite often a preceding history of dysentery.

Symptoms.—The onset may be gradual or rapid, Initially there is weakness, soreness of the tongue, difficulty in swallowing, indigestion, and diarrhœa. The diarrhœa is usually worst in the morning, and the stools are pale, bulky, and frothy. The appetite is usually poor. There is a marked degree of anæmia, usually of the macrocytic type, i.e. there is a high colour index. The tongue is smooth and red. Gastric acidity is low. Other characteristic findings are that the rise in the blood sugar level following the taking of sugar is less than normal, and there is an increase in the amount of fat in the stools. In untreated cases the patient steadily loses weight and becomes emaciated. Death is usually due to exhaustion and some intercurrent infection. The prognosis depends largely upon the stage at which treatment is begun.

Treatment.—The essentials of treatment are rest in bed, a high-protein diet, and treatment of the anæmia and any other deficiency that may be present. It is usual to start the diet with skimmed milk and gradually add other items such as meat. Some authorities, on the other hand, recommend beginning with a diet consisting largely of beef. Whichever diet is used, the essential fact to be borne in mind is that the patient cannot tolerate fats, but that a high caloric intake is necessary to ensure that the patient is adequately nourished. This can best be done by a diet consisting predominantly of protein. For the anæmia folic acid and cyanocobalamin are required. Large doses of the vitamin B complex are also helpful, *e.g.* marmite. As the blood calcium level is also diminished, vitamins A and D should be given, and it is sometimes useful to supplement this by calcium lactate. As has already been pointed out, convalescence is often prolonged, resulting sometimes in marked depression on the part of the patient. Satisfactory results are seldom obtained unless the patient is sent home to a temperate climate for a long leave. An individual who has had sprue should never return to residence in the tropics unless it is absolutely essential.

SPUTUM (*sputum*) means material spat out of the mouth. It may consist of saliva from the mouth, of mucous secretions from the throat or back of the nose, but is generally expectorated by coughing from the lower air passages. (*See* EXPECTORATION.)

SQUILL is the sliced bulb of *Urginea maritima*, a plant from the shores of the Mediterranean. It contains several substances which exert an irritating, or, in small doses, a stimulating effect upon the kidneys and the mucous membrane of the stomach and bronchial tubes.

Uses. — The tincture, syrup, and vinegar of squills are now used mainly as constituents of expectorant (or cough) mixtures. Squill is also a constituent of Guy's pill which is used in the treatment of dropsy due to heart failure.

SQUINTING is a condition in which the two eyes do not look in the same direction at one time. The movements of the eyeballs depend upon the action of six muscles, four being straight and two oblique. (*See* EYE.) Of these muscles the outer and inner straight (*recti*) muscles turn the eye from side to side and enable the two eyes to act together. The external rectus muscle and the internal rectus muscle are therefore the most important of the six, and defects connected with them produce inward or outward squint. Other squints upwards or downwards are occasionally, though only rarely, met with, and will not be further referred to.

Causes. — A squint which appears in early childhood is very often due to some optical error in the eye, generally in the direction of LONG-SIGHTEDNESS. Such a defect causes squinting inwards of one or both eyes, especially when the child looks at something close at hand. The reason for this is that the person with the long-sighted (hypermetropic) eye makes an excessive effort in accommodating his vision for near objects. The muscle of accommodation is supplied by the same nerve (third cranial) as the internal rectus muscle, and the excessive effort also affects the muscles which pull the eye inwards. The two eyes, when thus directed across one another, cannot act together, and the person therefore uses only one at a time, directing it straight forward and turning the other still farther inwards. If the eyes are equally good, the person adopts a habit of looking straight forward first with one eye, then with the other, and is said to have an alternating squint. If, however, the refractive error in one eye be much greater than that in the other, the better eye is always used, and the squint in the other becomes a permanent squint. The power of vision may be so little developed in the brain centre corresponding to a permanently squinting eye that even at an early age it may be almost lost, although the person is unaware of the fact till careful examination reveals it.

SHORT-SIGHT is also productive of a squint which is usually outwards in persons who are not provided with proper spectacles. In reading, writing, and other near work such people bring their work much closer up to the eyes than is natural, and the internal recti muscles of the two eyes get a disproportionate amount of work in constantly making the eyes converge. These muscles increase in power therefore and produce the permanent degree of convergence which is occasionally seen in short-sighted students.

DEFECTIVE VISION in one eye is another, though much less frequent, cause of squinting. That is to say, there is, quite apart from mere refractive errors which can be corrected by spectacles, some defect in power of seeing. In such a case the defective eye is not controlled by its muscles, as no attempt is made to use the eyes together, and it has a great tendency to roll outwards at times.

PARALYSIS, caused by some affection of the brain or of the nerves supplying the eye muscles, is the usual cause of a squint which suddenly appears after the person has passed the years of childhood. The sixth nerve, which has a long course over the base of the skull and supplies the external rectus muscle, is especially liable to suffer in this way. This produces a strong inward squint of one eye, when the glance is directed towards the side to which the eye belongs, since the eye cannot be turned outwards.

Treatment.—In order to obtain the best results it is essential that treatment should be begun as soon as a squint is noticed in a child. Treatment may take one or more of four forms. When the squint is due to hypermetropia (*i.e.* long-sightedness) all that may be necessary may be the wearing of suitable *spectacles*. In cases in which the hypermetropia has persisted for some time before treatment it may be necessary to supplement the wearing of spectacles by *occlusion* of the good eye. This is done so as to ensure that the child uses the bad eye, which otherwise he would not do. At a more advanced stage *orthoptic* supervision will be necessary. This consists of a carefully graduated series of exercises for the muscles of the eye, whereby the child is trained to use his eye muscles correctly and thereby overcome the squinting defect which is his untrained (and wrong) method of overcoming the defect. Finally, *operation* may be required, either to strengthen a poorly acting eye muscle or to weaken an over-acting one.

STABS (*see* WOUNDS).

STAMMERING is a condition in which a person hesitates in the act of speaking, being unable for a time to pronounce certain syllables or repeating the same syllable over and over. For

example, in pronouncing such a word as ' Peter ' the person may at the beginning of the word be unable to sound the ' P ' for a time, remaining with the mouth open, or with the lips compressed, and often making vigorous movements with the hands or feet in the fruitless endeavour. Or he may repeat this sound, pronouncing ' Pe-pe-peter ', and being unable for a time to pass off the ' P ' to the rest of the word. The latter variety of stammering is generally called ' stuttering '.

Causes.—Stammering is not due to any defect in the brain or in the speech organs, and may be described as a functional disease, or a bad habit, or a sign of diffidence. It begins usually in childhood, and is a practice which one child readily learns from another, just as any peculiarity of speech in one person is liable to be unconsciously mimicked by those around. It is more common in twins. The actual cause of the stammering is a want of co-ordination between the various parts concerned in speech. The speech mechanism consists of three parts, and may be roughly compared to an organ. The chest corresponds to the bellows of the organ, the larynx, where the voice sounds are produced, to the keyboard and pipes of the organ by which the different notes are sounded, and the changes in the mouth effected by the tongue, palate, lips, etc., resemble the stops of the organ which modulate the notes. Just as these three parts of the organ must be worked in unison for the production of perfect music, so the three parts of the speech apparatus must work together. In stammering there is some error ; either the mouth does not shape itself at once to produce the necessary consonants when the stream of air is turned on and the larynx thrown into action, or the mouth is rigidly held in the proper attitude but no laryngeal note is sounded.

Treatment.—This consists of education in proper voice and speech production, and of psychological treatment. The importance of the psychological element is becoming more and more recognized. The stammerer, if a child, should in the first instance be removed from the others from whom he is learning to stammer. Later on, the cure depends upon the amount of care with which the person strives to regulate his vocal organs. (*See* VOICE AND SPEECH.) One of the most important points for the stammerer to recognize is the difference between those syllables and letters which are produced with full voice and those which have little voice. For example, in the words ' Peter ' and ' Beater ' the initial letter is hardly sounded in the first, the stress being thrown upon the *e*, while in ' Beater ' the *B* receives its full sound. The stammerer's difficulty in many cases arises from a reversal of this process, and disappears when he learns to recognize this difference. Sometimes, before commencing a course of treatment with a view to cure, the stammerer does well to remain absolutely silent for a week, with the view of losing his faulty method of speech.

STAPHYLOCOCCUS (σταφυλή, a bunch of grapes ; κόκκος, a kernel) is the name given to a bacterium which under the microscope appears in small masses like bunches of grapes. It is found in the pus discharged from acute abscesses, ulcers, boils, etc. (Plate VIII).

STARCH is a substance belonging to that group of carbohydrates known as the amyloses. It is converted into sugar when treated with heat in presence of a dilute acid. It is changed largely into dextrin when exposed to a considerable degree of dry heat, as in toasting bread ; and a similar change into dextrin and malt-sugar takes place under the action of various ferments such as the ptyalin of the saliva. Starch forms the chief constituent of the carbohydrate foods (*see* DIET *and* FARINACEOUS FOODS), and in the process of digestion the above-mentioned change takes place in order to prepare it for absorption.

Starch is used externally to form a poultice for softening the skin in skin diseases (*see* POULTICES). It is also used as a constituent of dusting powders for application to chafed or irritable areas of the skin (*see* CHAFING). Starch enema is administered in inflammatory conditions of the bowel, and is made by boiling two tablespoonfuls of starch in a pint of water and then adding hot water till the mixture is reduced to a syrupy consistency. This starch

27 *a*

enema is used as the basis for several kinds of soothing enema. For example, a teaspoonful of laudanum may be added to the starch. (*See* ENEMA.)

STARVATION (*see* FASTING). Partial starvation, as a method of treatment, is used in certain diseases associated with previous excess of food, particularly obesity (*see* CORPULENCE). When a person is completely deprived of food for a time, not only is there very great loss of weight but the chemical processes of the body are altered, and a poisoning effect is produced by the formation of acetone and other ketone bodies. In cases of slow starvation, the vitality of the tissues is reduced and they become more liable to the attack of tuberculosis and other diseases.

STASIS (στάσις, halt) is a term applied to stoppage of the flow of blood in the vessels or of the food materials down the intestinal canal. (For Blood Stasis, *see* CIRCULATION, DISORDERS OF.)

STATUS LYMPHATICUS is another name for lymphatism (*q.v.*).

STAVESACRE is the seeds of *Delphinum stophisagria*, which are crushed and made into an ointment for use as a parasiticide.

STEATORRHŒA is any condition characterized by the passing of stools containing an excess of fat. (*See* MALABSORPTION SYNDROME.)

STENOSIS (στενός, narrow) is a term applied to a condition of unnatural narrowing in any passage or orifice of the body. The word is specially used in connection with the four openings of the heart at which the valves are situated. (*See* HEART DISEASES.)

STEPPAGE GAIT is the name given to the peculiar walk characteristic of neuritis affecting the muscles of the leg and causing drop-foot. The feet are lifted high so that the toes may clear the ground.

STEREOGNOSIS (στερεός, solid ; γνῶσις, knowledge) means the faculty of recognizing the solidity of objects, and thus their nature, by handling them.

STERILIZATION means the process of rendering various objects which come in contact with wounds, various foods, etc., free from microbes. This may be effected in many ways, and different methods are used in different cases, for it is evident that processes applicable to clothing or to a room may be quite unsuited for the sterilization of food.

The manner of sterilizing bedding, furniture, etc., after contact with a case of infectious disease, is given under DISINFECTION, whilst the sterilization of instruments, dressings, and skin surfaces, necessary before surgical procedures, is mentioned in the same article and also under ANTISEPTICS, ASEPSIS, and WOUNDS. For general purposes, one of the cheapest and most effective agents is boiling water or steam.

Use of sterilization.—Milk is the chief article of food that calls for special sterilization. With regard to other foods, ordinary cooking has this for one of its chief objects. Milk, even from healthy cows, is contaminated by the hands of milkers and by organisms that fall into it from the surrounding air, so that an ounce of milk may be found to contain as many as 2,800,000 bacteria within a short time after milking. Further, milk may be drawn from tuberculous cows. For healthy adults these impurities may not be of such great importance as they undoubtedly are in the case of children liable to tuberculosis, those suffering from summer diarrhœa, and persons of weak digestive powers. The origin of epidemics, too, is frequently traced back to a dairy, especially in the case of typhoid fever and scarlet fever.

For all these reasons it is necessary to sterilize cow's milk, particularly before giving it to children. In the case of infants, the milk is often 'humanized' by the addition of water, sugar, and cream (see INFANT FEEDING) before it is sterilized ; and for dyspeptics it is a common practice to peptonize it (see PEPTONIZED FOODS) prior to sterilization.

Method of sterilization.—One of the most effective modes is simply to boil the milk for a prolonged period in a covered pan ; but this changes its taste considerably, and is therefore unsuitable for children and invalids.

842

Another method is to place the milk in a flask or bottle of which the neck is closed by a plug of cotton-wool, and set it in a pot of water, from the bottom of which it is separated by a triangle of wire or other means. The pot is placed upon the fire and the water boiled for three-quarters of an hour, by which time the milk is sufficiently sterilized without appreciably affecting its taste. Many forms of sterilizer, among which may be mentioned those of Aymard and Soxhlet, are on the market at a small cost, but all depend upon this principle of having an inner vessel or set of bottles suspended within an outer pot containing water, which is boiled for three-quarters of an hour to one hour. Care must be taken that the milk is not uncovered, after being sterilized, until just before it is to be used.

Pasteurization is a slightly different method of treatment, which seems to be sufficient to destroy the microbes that cause summer diarrhœa, as well as the infection of tuberculosis, scarlet fever, and typhoid fever, while preserving the natural state of the milk. (See PASTEURIZATION.)

Koch's method of sterilization is used in bacteriological investigation, where even the spores of bacteria must be destroyed. It is carried out by steaming the objects to be sterilized on three successive days. (See BACTERIOLOGY.)

STERNUM (στέρνον, the chest) is another name for the breast-bone.

STERNUTATORIES (sternuto, I sneeze) are substances that provoke sneezing.

STEROID is the group name for compounds that resemble cholesterol chemically. The group includes the sex hormones and bile acids.

STERTOR (sterto, I snore) is a term applied to noisy breathing resembling snoring. It is due usually to flapping of the soft palate between a stream of air entering by the nose and one entering by the mouth. In ordinary snoring (q.v.) this results from the habit of sleeping with the mouth open, and in certain serious disorders it arises from paralysis of the soft palate. Some of these conditions affecting the nervous system and thus leading to paralysis of the soft palate are—apoplexy, suffocation, concussion of the brain, drunkenness, poisoning by opium or by chloroform. (For the means of distinguishing between these conditions see OPIUM POISONING.) In some of these paralytic conditions the snoring is very loud, and the noise is due then, not to flapping of the soft palate, but to lolling back of the tongue against the back of the throat as the patient lies upon his back. In this case the breathing is at once relieved by pulling forward the lower jaw, by pulling the tongue out of the mouth, or by turning the patient upon one side, as is done, for example, in suffocation due to drowning or in chloroform poisoning.

Stertorous breathing is not to be confused with *sniffing* breathing produced by paralysis of the muscles that should hold the nostrils still and open ; nor with *puffing* breathing due to paralysis of the muscles in the cheeks and lips ; though all three conditions may be produced by the same causes. Nor must it be mistaken for *stridor*, or crowing breathing, due to spasmodic narrowing in the larynx (*see* LARYNGISMUS) ; nor for the prolonged. noisy, *wheezing* breathing of asthma produced by narrowing of the bronchial tubes.

STERULE is a term applied to a glass capsule containing sterile solution for hypodermic administration.

STETHOSCOPE (στῆθος, chest ; σκόπεω, I examine) is an instrument used for listening to the sounds produced by the action of the lungs, heart, and other internal organs. (*See* AUSCULTATION.)

STHENIC (σθένος, strength) is a term applied to certain diseases, especially fevers, to indicate that they are not associated with prostration.

STIBOPHEN is an organic antimony compound which is used in the treatment of schistosomiasis (*see* PARASITES).

STIFFNESS is a condition which may be due to a change in the joints, ligaments, tendons, or muscles, or to the influence of the nervous system over the muscles of the part affected. Stiffness is associated with various forms

of rheumatism. Stiffness of the neck muscles resulting in bending backward the head, and of the hamstring muscles, causing difficulty in straightening the lower limbs, are signs of meningitis. Stiffness or spasticity also occurs in certain diseases of the central nervous system.

STIGMA (στίγμα, mark) means any spot or impression upon the skin. The term ' stigmata of degeneration ' is applied to physical defects that are found in mentally defective persons. (*See* MENTAL DEFECTIVENESS.)

STILBŒSTROL is the name given to a synthetic œstrogen discovered by Sir Charles Dodds and his co-workers. Its physiological actions are closely similar to those of the natural ovarian hormone, and it has the great merit of being active when taken by mouth. An interesting property of stilbœstrol is seen in the relief it affords when given to patients suffering from cancer of the prostate, inducing in some cases, it appears, regression of the primary tumour and of secondary deposits in bone. (*See* HEXŒSTROL *and* ŒSTROGEN.)

STILET, or STILETTE, means the delicate probe or the wire used to clear a catheter or hollow needle.

STILLBIRTH (*see* BIRTH).

STILL'S DISEASE is a disease of childhood first described by Sir Frederic Still. It is characterized by inflammation of several joints (similar to the changes found in rheumatoid arthritis), enlarged spleen and lymph glands, and fever.

STIMULANTS (*stimulo*, I goad) are drugs and other agents employed to call forth special powers of the body or of individual organs in order to effect some special purpose or to offer resistance to some acute attack of disease. The use of stimulants presupposes a certain amount of reserve power on the part of the body or of the organ stimulated, which is lying dormant and requires an appropriate stimulus before it can be brought into action. In its broadest sense, the term ' stimulant ' includes all remedies which are not simply foods destined to supply the wear and tear of the body and to provide it with a store of energy-producing material. It also excludes remedies which have a sedative action upon the nervous system or other organs, and remedies which act directly upon the causes of disease without any reference to the body, such as antiseptics.

(For drugs which stimulate the intestines, see PURGATIVES; for those that stimulate the liver, see CHOLAGOGUES; for those that stimulate the kidneys, see DIURETICS; and for those that increase the activity of the skin secretion, see DIAPHORETICS.) Many substances, such as aromatics, spices, and bitters, stimulate the function of the stomach.

STINGS (see BITES, STINGS, etc.).

STIPP is a name formed of the initial letters of sodium tetriodophenolphthalein. (See IODOPHTHALEIN.)

STITCH is a popular name for a sharp pain in the side. It is generally due to cramp following unusually hard exertion (see CRAMP), but care must be taken that this trivial condition is not taken for pleurisy or for a fractured rib.

(For the stitches used to unite the edges of wounds, see WOUNDS.)

STOKES-ADAMS SYNDROME is a term applied to a condition in which slowness of the pulse is associated with attacks of unconsciousness, and which is due to a state of heart-block.

STOMACH.—The stomach is a dilated portion of the alimentary canal, which in man has a shape somewhat resembling that of a pear. The larger end, known as the fundus, lies in the hollow of the left side of the diaphragm, and at one side of this is the opening from the gullet. The greater part of the stomach, into which the gullet opens, is known as the cardiac part, whilst the lower and narrower portion is known as the pyloric part. The two openings into and out of the stomach are known as the cardia and the pylorus. The stomach is slightly flattened from before backwards, and the two edges are known as the lesser curvature, which runs from one opening to the other direct, and the greater curvature, which sweeps

round the fundus from the cardia to the pylorus (Fig. 353).

Size and position. — The stomach hangs freely suspended in the upper and left part of the abdomen (Fig. 352),

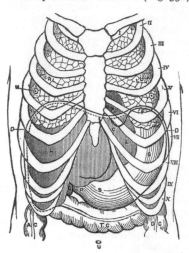

FIG. 352.—Diagram showing the position of the stomach with regard to the ribs and the other organs. *DD*, Diaphragm; *LL*, left, and *RL*, right lung; *P*, pericardium covering heart; *SS*, stomach with *F*, its fundus, *C*, its cardiac opening, and *P*, its pyloric opening; *L, L*, liver; *G*, gall-bladder; *AC, TC, DC*, part of the colon or large intestine; *U*, navel; *M*, nipple; *I–X*, upper ten ribs. (Turner's *Anatomy*, after Luschka.)

so that changes in position and shape take place readily according to the amount of food it contains. On the surface, the stomach corresponds to the ribs on the left side from about the fifth to the ninth, and extends below their protecting margin about half-way down to the navel, while the person is recumbent, and slightly below the navel when he stands up. The fundus lies immediately below the heart and base of the left lung, separated from them only by the diaphragm and their enveloping membranes. This explains the embarrassment of the heart's action and of breathing sometimes experienced by dyspeptics. The stomach is attached at the cardiac opening to the gullet, and at this point it is further secured to the diaphragm by a ligament. A broad band of peritoneum (small omentum) attaches the lesser curvature to the under surface of the liver, and a similar peritoneal fold unites its hinder surface to the spleen. The pyloric end, like the cardiac opening, is to a great extent fixed in position, but the greater curvature is quite freely movable.

The greatest length of the stomach from the fundus to the greater curvature near the pylorus is about one foot (30 cm.), and the greatest breadth does not exceed 4 to 5 inches (10 to 12·5 cm.).

mucous membrane is composed of a single layer of columnar cells, and these also line the pits referred to above. Each gland is composed of large cubical cells so arranged as to form a tube, open at the upper end where it meets the pit, and closed beneath. These cells secrete the gastric juice which exudes from all the minute tubes as digestion is proceeding. In the cardiac

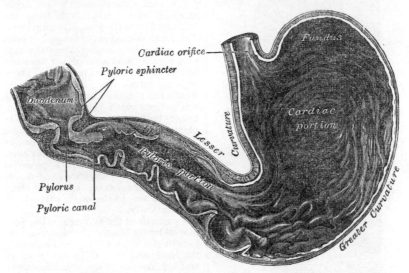

Fig. 353.—The interior of the stomach. (From Gray's *Anatomy*. Longmans, Green & Co. Ltd.)

The capacity varies greatly in different persons, but is usually about 1 to 1½ quarts (1 to 1½ litres).

Structure.—The stomach possesses four coats similar to those of the intestine, which are, from within outwards, a mucous membrane, sub-mucous layer, muscular coat, and peritoneal coat (Fig. 354).

MUCOUS MEMBRANE lines the interior of the stomach and is of smooth, soft texture, though raised up into ridges when the stomach is empty. The surface can be seen with the naked eye to be thickly covered by minute pits into each of which several tube-shaped glands are found, on microscopic section, to open. The mucous membrane in fact consists almost entirely of these glands placed side by side, and supported by a small quantity of connective tissue and by fibres of unstriped muscle. The surface of the

end of the stomach there are other larger cells in addition, mingled with those just described, and the large cells are supposed to secrete the acid of the gastric juice. Between the tubular glands lies some supporting connective tissue in which run numerous blood-capillaries and lymph-vessels.

SUBMUCOUS COAT is a loose connective tissue layer which joins the mucous coat to the muscular coat, and in which the large blood-vessels of the stomach run. The loose arrangement of its fibres allows the mucous membrane to glide freely over the muscular coat in the movements and variations in size of the stomach.

MUSCULAR COAT is of considerable thickness in the stomach, and is of great importance in varying the size of the organ according to the amount of food it contains, in making the peristaltic movements which mix the food with the digestive juice, and finally in expelling the softened food from the stomach into the small intestine. This coat consists of three layers, an outer one in which the fibres run lengthwise, a middle one

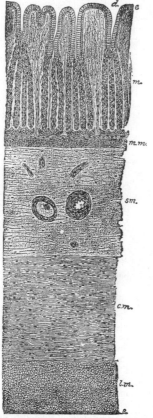

FIG. 354.—Diagram of section through wall of stomach. *M*, mucous membrane; *e*, epithelium; *d*, surface of gland duct; *m.m.*, muscularis mucosæ; *sm*, submucosa; *c.m.*, circular muscular layer; *l.m.*, longitudinal muscle layer; *s*, serous coat. (From Schafer's *Histology*. Longmans, Green & Co. Ltd.)

where they are circular, and an inner layer in which they run obliquely across the stomach.

PERITONEAL COAT is similar to the peritoneum covering the other organs of the abdomen. (*See* PERITONEUM.)

VESSELS.—The stomach is abundantly supplied with blood from the cœliac axis, a short, wide artery which comes directly from the aorta and like-

wise gives branches to the liver, pancreas, and spleen. There is a large arterial arch round either curvature, and from these two arches smaller branches run into the wall of the stomach and reach the submucous coat, from which minute branches are distributed to the other coats. The blood is collected by veins which ultimately return it to the portal vein.

NERVES.—The stomach is very richly supplied with nerves both from the brain and from the sympathetic system. The tenth cranial nerve (vagus) of each side has a long course down the side of the gullet, and after giving branches to the larynx, heart, lungs, and other organs, terminates in the stomach, which has therefore important nervous connections with these vital organs. Other branches come from the solar plexus of the sympathetic system. These nerves form a plexus in the submucous coat and another in the muscular coat, which undoubtedly exert a powerful influence over the secretions and movements of the organ, although these functions are, in the main, carried out automatically.

Functions of the stomach.—The part played by the stomach in digestion consists in storing, warming, and softening the food, and then in passing it on in small quantities to the intestine, where the more important digestive processes that prepare it for absorption take place. The action of the gastric juice upon the food has been described under DIGESTION. The action of the muscular coat of the stomach is also very important. In birds, which have no teeth, the gizzard is a powerful muscular organ that grinds down the grain and other food into a pulp, but in man the muscular action is much gentler. This, together with other facts regarding the stomach, was first carefully observed between 1825 and 1833 by the American physician W. Beaumont in the case of a man named Alexis St. Martin, whose stomach had been so exposed by a gunshot wound that a large opening existed through which its interior could be inspected. The movements, as seen by the aid of X-rays, consist of a series of waves, each of which takes about half a minute to pass along the stomach. These movements have also the effect of separating the more fluid parts from lumps still left in the later stages of digestion which are retained in the cardiac part of the stomach while the pylorus relaxes as each wave reaches it to allow some of the softened mass to pass through into the small intestine. This muscular movement takes place in health without causing any sensation, but in irritable conditions of the stomach, when digestion is not proceeding naturally, it may increase in force and give rise to irregular spasms which come and go, and which are attended by much pain. (*See* DYSPEPSIA.)

STOMACH, DISEASES OF.—Only the more common and serious varieties of gastric disease can be considered here. The majority of them exhibit, as their most marked and sometimes their only feature, the symptoms of dyspepsia (*see* DYSPEPSIA). Hence the diagnosis of the forms of stomach disease is frequently a matter of much difficulty.

ACUTE GASTRITIS or ACUTE CATARRH.—Causes.—Of these, the most important are : (1) Dietetic indiscretions, *e.g.* a large indigestible meal, or the excessive consumption of alcohol ; (2) food poisoning ; (3) infections, *e.g.* influenza, septicæmia ; (4) toxins, *e.g.* uræmia, gout ; (5) the swallowing of poisons, *e.g.* acids, alkalies.

Symptoms.—The chief change the stomach undergoes affects its mucous membrane, which is in a state of congestion, either throughout or in parts. The symptoms are those well known as characterizing an acute 'bilious attack', consisting in loss of appetite, sickness or nausea, and headache, frontal or occipital, often accompanied with giddiness. The tongue is furred, the breath fœtid, and there is pain or discomfort in the region of the stomach, with sour eructations, and frequently vomiting, first of food and then of bilious matter. An attack of this kind tends to subside in a few days, especially if the exciting cause be removed. Sometimes, however, the symptoms recur with such frequency as to lead to the more serious chronic form of the disease.

Treatment.—The patient must be kept in bed. If the irritant causing the gastritis has not been got rid of by vomiting, vomiting should be induced

by giving the patient half a pint of water, containing a teaspoonful of sodium bicarbonate, to drink. Hot applications, *e.g.* a rubber hot-water bottle, to the abdomen are the best way of relieving pain and easing vomiting. If there is constipation a saline aperient should be given. Nothing but sips of water should be given by mouth until the vomiting has ceased. Subsequently warm milk diluted with water should be given in small amounts at frequent intervals, *e.g.* hourly, and the diet gradually increased until the patient is again taking a normal diet.

CHRONIC GASTRITIS or CHRONIC CATARRH may arise after repeated attacks of the acute form or may come on independently. It is of several types. The result of the chronic irritation of the gastric mucous membrane may be an excessively acid gastric juice, which gives rise to an acid dyspepsia. (*See* DYSPEPSIA.) After a long period of irritation an atrophy of the secreting structures of the stomach may be produced, and there is then little or no secretion of gastric juice, a condition known as *gastritis anacida*. In addition to this failure to secrete a proper gastric juice, the interior of the stomach becomes constantly coated with tough mucus, which further prevents digestion from proceeding normally. The mucous membrane is permanently in a state of congestion, it becomes thickened and thrown into deep ridges and furrows, and frequent hæmorrhages take place from its dilated veins. At a later stage, great thickening of the other coats may take place (cirrhosis), leading to still further impairment of digestion, since the stomach becomes small, its movements impeded, and the outlet often blocked by thickening in the region of the pylorus.

Causes. — Chronic catarrh is frequently associated with previous disease in other organs, such as the lungs, heart, liver, or kidneys, and it is specially common in persons addicted either to over-eating or to alcoholic excess.

Symptoms.—The symptoms are those of dyspepsia in an aggravated form (*see* DYSPEPSIA), of which loss of appetite, discomfort and pain after food, with distension and frequent vomiting, are the chief.

Treatment.—This consists essentially

of ensuring that the affected individual is having a bland diet which is well cooked and that meals are taken regularly. Careful chewing of food must be insisted upon, and this is often facilitated by not drinking with meals. Alcohol and smoking should be avoided. Particular care must be taken not to eat coarse foods, fruit skins or pips, or pickles or sauces. Neither bitters nor alkaline mixtures should be taken until careful dieting has been given a full trial. Any underlying cause for the gastritis should be treated. Careful dental treatment is necessary if there is any evidence of dental sepsis or if there are not sufficient teeth to ensure adequate chewing of food.

ULCER OF THE STOMACH, GASTRIC ULCER, is of frequent occurrence, and may be a disease of much gravity. It occurs more frequently than is generally supposed, the result of autopsies showing that one person in every twenty or thereabout suffers from gastric ulcer at some period of life.

Causes.—These are not fully understood, yet the following points may be regarded as generally admitted : (1) gastric ulcer is two to three times more common in men than in women ; (2) it becomes more frequent as age increases.

It is held that when any degenerative change takes place in the mucous membrane of the stomach the part is less able to resist the action of the gastric juices upon it, and is apt to undergo disintegration all the more readily. Hence an ulcer is formed. This ulcer is usually of small size ($\frac{1}{4}$ to 1 inch in diameter), of round or oval form, and tends to advance, not superficially, but to penetrate through the coats of the stomach. Its most usual site is upon the posterior wall towards the upper or lesser curvature of the stomach and near to the pyloric orifice. This is the point at which the mucous membrane is subjected to most friction by the food as it leaves the stomach. The ulcer may undergo a healing process at any stage, in which case it may leave but little trace of its existence ; on the other hand, its scar may produce such an amount of contraction as to lead to narrowing of the pylorus, and later dilatation of the stomach.

848

Also, perforation may take place, which, if not quickly operated upon, may be rapidly fatal, unless previously the stomach has become, as it may, adherent to another organ, by which the dangerous effects of this occurrence may be averted. Usually there is only one ulcer, but sometimes there are more.

Symptoms.—The symptoms to which this disease gives rise are sometimes indefinite and obscure, and in some cases the diagnosis has been first made by the sudden occurrence of a perforation. First among the symptoms is *pain*, which is usually worse before food. This pain is situated either in front, at the lower end of the breast-bone, or behind, about the middle of the back. It is often severe, and is usually accompanied with much tenderness to touch, and also with a sense of oppression and inability to wear tight clothing. Accompanying the pain there is frequently *vomiting*, either very soon after the food is swallowed or at a later period. This tends in some measure to relieve the pain and discomfort, and in many instances the patient rather encourages this act. *Vomiting of blood* (hæmatemesis) occurs in about 25 per cent. of cases and is most important diagnostically. It may show itself either to a slight extent, and in the form of a brown or coffee-like mixture, or as a copious discharge of pure blood of dark colour and containing clots. The source of the blood is some vessel or vessels which the ulcerative process has ruptured. Vomiting of blood, however, does not always indicate the presence of a gastric ulcer. Blood is also found mixed with the discharges from the bowels, rendering them dark and 'tarry'-looking. The tongue presents a red, irritable appearance, and there is usually constipation of the bowels. X-ray examination gives little evidence of the presence of an acute ulcer, beyond showing that there is much irritation near the pyloric opening, with spasm to the rest of the stomach ; but in chronic cases the deep ulcer often fills up with the barium that has been administered for the examination, and its outline can then be readily seen.

The course of a case of gastric ulcer is very variable. In some instances it is acute, making rapid progress to a tavourable or unfavourable termination. In others, however, the disease is chronic, lasting for months or years, and in those cases where the ulcers are multiple or of extensive size, incomplete healing may take place and relapses of the symptoms occur from time to time. Ulcers are sometimes present and yet give rise to no marked symptoms, and one occasionally meets with cases where fatal perforation has suddenly taken place and where *post-mortem* examination reveals the existence of a long-standing ulcer which has furnished little or no evidence of its presence during life. Again, an unsuspected ulcer may run a favourable course, and the contraction of its scar may, at a later period of life, cause interference with the exit of food by the pylorus and consequent dilatation of the organ, and thus give the only evidence that an ulcer has at one time been present.

Although the majority of cases of gastric ulcer respond satisfactorily to a course of medical treatment, the relapse rate is high. More than half the cases treated medically relapse within three years, and about three-quarters within five years. Further, there is also the possibility of three serious complications developing : (i) hæmorrhage ; (ii) perforation ; (iii) obstruction of the pylorus as a result of contraction of the wall of the stomach produced by the ulcer.

Duodenal ulcer, in which a condition similar to gastric ulcer is found just beyond the pyloric opening, has symptoms like those of gastric ulcer, but is six to twelve times more common in males than females, and tends to occur at an earlier stage. (*See* DUODENAL ULCER.)

Treatment.—Most important is the careful adjustment of the diet. The essentials of an effective diet are small feeds every two hours, starting off with milk, or equal parts of milk and cream, and gradually working up to a diet which the individual can take while going about his daily work. In practice, this means breakfast, lunch and dinner (or supper) with a glass of milk in mid-morning, mid-afternoon, and at bedtime.

Of medicinal remedies, the most serviceable are large doses of alkalis, with which it may be helpful to con-

join belladonna and a small dose of barbiturate.

When hæmorrhage occurs, it is treated by complete rest in bed, morphine, and small two-hourly feeds of diluted milk for the first twenty-four hours. When much blood has been lost a transfusion may be necessary. In the event of perforation, treatment is by an immediate operation in which the peritoneal cavity is cleansed and the opening in the stomach wall stitched together. Such an operation must be performed at the earliest possible moment in order to afford good hope of recovery.

Surgical treatment, usually in the form of removal of that part of the stomach containing the ulcer, is indicated : (i) in the presence of perforation of the ulcer ; (ii) in the presence of severe pyloric obstruction ; (iii) in the absence of satisfactory response to medical treatment.

CANCER OF THE STOMACH is the most common form of cancer in men. It occurs for the most part in persons at or after middle life, and is more common in men. A hereditary tendency may sometimes be traced.

The most common varieties of cancer affecting the stomach are scirrhus, medullary, and colloid, and the parts affected are usually at the inlet or outlet ; but the disease may spread widely in the stomach wall. When it is situated in the neighbourhood of the pylorus, a stricture is frequently produced as the disease advances. The cancerous growth usually commences in the submucous tissue, but as it progresses it tends to ulcerate through the mucous membrane, and in this process bleeding and vomiting of blood may occur. The early symptoms of this disease are in many instances so indefinite as to render the diagnosis for a long time conjectural. They are mostly those of dyspepsia, with more or less pain, discomfort, and vomiting, particularly after meals. The vomited material is often of coffee-ground appearance, due to admixture with blood, but copious hæmatemesis is less frequent than in cases of gastric ulcer. The patient loses flesh and strength, and soon comes to acquire the cachectic aspect commonly associated with cancer. (*See* CANCER.) The diagnosis is rendered all the more certain when, as is frequently the case, a tumour can be detected on examination over the region of the stomach; but where no such evidence is obtained, the nature of the disease is left to be made out by the age of the patient, by absence of free hydrochloric acid from the gastric juice, by progressive loss of weight, and by X-ray examination. Cases of cancer of the stomach advance with more or less rapidity to a fatal termination. In most instances death takes place in from nine to eighteen months. The treatment can often be only palliative, but much relief may be afforded by a careful attention to diet, by the treatment applicable to dilatation of the stomach, by the use of morphine and other drugs which relieve pain. In early cases an operation can sometimes be performed by which the disease is completely removed, or, when this cannot be carried out, vomiting, pain, and other symptoms of obstruction are relieved by making a communication between the stomach and a loop in the small intestine (gastroenterostomy).

DILATATION OF THE STOMACH may occur without giving rise to any symptoms, the person in question being simply possessed of a gastric organ of more than usual capacity ; but in those cases in which portions of the food are retained for a long time in the stomach, giving rise to fermentation, to spasmodic and ineffectual efforts of the muscular wall to empty the organ, or to great irritation of the mucous membrane, the condition is both painful and has a serious effect upon the general health.

Causes.—The condition may arise in consequence of weakness of the muscular wall of the stomach as the result of any chronic wasting disease. The dilatation may also follow upon a downward displacement of the stomach which is an inborn peculiarity of certain persons aggravated by a bad habit of posture (*gastroptosis*). Such a defect gives rise to a minor degree of dilatation, the stomach being less active in its movements, and heavy meals being retained in it for many hours or even several days. More common as a cause, however, is narrowing of the outlet from the stomach in consequence of the scar of an old ulcer at the pylorus, or

850

owing to a cancer in this position. The condition is also met in newly born children as the result of a very narrow outlet from the stomach (*congenital pyloric stenosis*). In these conditions food collects in the lower part of the stomach, stretches the wall, and causes the dilatation to become persistent.

Symptoms.—The symptoms of dilatation have been to some extent mentioned under the heading of DYSPEPSIA. The condition gives rise to much discomfort, which is increased a few hours after meals, when digestion should be in full progress. Heartburn and the feeling of a heavy load under the ribs are often complained of. As the stomach in advanced cases is never completely emptied between meals, only a portion of the food escaping into the small intestine, fermentation goes on in the residue, growths of *sarcinæ* and *yeasts* being especially evident in the large volume of fermenting material that is vomited up every few days. Various substances, such as lactic acid, butyric acid, and even sometimes explosive gases, are formed as the result of this fermentation, and, owing to the great disturbance of digestion, severe constipation is a very common symptom. Naturally the patient derives little benefit from his food, and becomes weak and thin, the condition, for this reason, being sometimes mistaken for cancer.

Treatment. — Washing out the stomach daily, and thus removing the fermenting residue, either at night or in the morning, is found to give great relief, and often to effect a complete cure. (*See* DYSPEPSIA.) Further relief is gained by the patient lying on his right side so as to permit of the more ready escape of the digested food from the stomach, and in some cases by wearing a special belt over the lower part of the abdomen, which supports the dilated stomach. In those cases in which the dilatation is due to scarring as a result of an old ulcer in the region of the pylorus, the operation of gastro-enterostomy is performed. This consists in opening the abdomen, making an aperture at the lowest part of the stomach and one in a coil of the small intestine, uniting the two by sutures, and closing the abdominal wound.

Operation is also usually necessary in cases of congenital pyloric stenosis.

NEUROSES OF THE STOMACH include those conditions which do not appear to be associated with any disease in the organ.

Attacks of severe vomiting, called ' crises ', also form a symptom of the disease known as locomotor ataxia.

STOMACH TUBE is a soft rubber tube with rounded end, and usually about 30 inches (75 cm.) in length, which is used for drawing off the contents of the stomach with the view of chemically testing them, or in order to wash out the stomach when it contains some poisonous material, or when it is dilated and filled with fermenting food. For the purpose of washing out the stomach a long tube and funnel are attached to the stomach tube (Fig. 355). For the method of

FIG. 355.—Stomach tube of india-rubber connected by glass junction with india-rubber tube and funnel.

its use see under DYSPEPSIA. A narrower rubber tube, about the thickness of a quill and of 36 or more inches (90 cm.) in length, is used for the purpose of examining the stomach throughout the digestion of a meal. By means of such a tube (Fig. 356), which can be retained without discomfort by a patient for several hours, small samples of the gastric juice can be drawn off every quarter of an hour or thereabout and tested. Such a tube can also be allowed

to pass out of the stomach into the duodenum so that the contents of the upper part of the small intestine are similarly

FIG. 356.—Ryle's stomach (or duodenal) tube. (From Pye's *Surgical Handicraft.* John Wright & Sons Ltd.)

obtained for analysis. Such an examination is known as ' fractional gastric analysis '.

STOMATITIS (στόμα, the mouth) means inflammation of the mouth. (*See* MOUTH, DISEASES OF.)

-STOMY (στόμα, mouth) is a suffix signifying formation of an opening in an organ by operation, *e.g.* gastrostomy and colostomy.

STONE (*see* CONCRETIONS; BLADDER, DISEASES OF ; GALL-STONES).

STOOLS consist of the remainder of the food after it has passed through the alimentary canal and been subjected to the action of the digestive juices, and after the nutritious parts have been absorbed by the intestinal mucous membrane. The stools also contain various other matters, such as pigment, derived from the bile, and large quantities of bacteria. The stools are passed once daily by most persons, but infants, who are fed frequently, have several evacuations of the bowels in twenty-four hours. To some persons the habit of opening the bowels only once or twice a week seems to be quite natural, though such cases are not common.

The *amount* of the stool passed varies considerably, being roughly about 5 ounces (140 grammes), or about one-eighth of the daily food, but when diarrhœa is present, and there is much fluid in the stool, it is increased in amount, whilst in constipation it is diminished and hardened, and when astringents such as iron or tannin are taken, their effect is still further to harden the stools. Although in a healthy condition the stool of grown persons is cylindrical, and forms a cast of the interior of the rectum, in young children it is a soft pultaceous mass. The appearance of the stools is also much modified when any tumour is present in the lower bowel. In this case, they may be very small or may be squeezed out into a flattened tape - like form. A similar appearance is caused by that form of constipation which is due to a spastic condition of the bowel.

The *colour* of the stools is naturally of a dark brown, due to a pigment known as stercobilin, derived from the bile. This colour may be changed to green by the action of certain bacteria when decomposition is proceeding to a greater extent than usual in the bowels, and a deep green colour is also produced by some vegetables, such as spinach. White stools, having an appearance like that of clay or putty, are found in cases where the outlet of bile into the small intestine is stopped, and where jaundice is consequently present (acholic stools). When an excess of fat is taken in the food, as in the case of children fed on great quantities of cream, the digestive organs are unable to deal with it, and much of it is passed in the stools, giving the stools in these circumstances also a whitish colour. Black or slaty-grey stools are produced when certain drugs are taken, as, for example, iron and bismuth ; and a tarry blackness known as ' melæna ' is sometimes imparted to them when bleeding takes place from the stomach, the iron in the blood being acted upon by the sulphuretted hydrogen always present in the stools to produce the black sulphide of iron. Bright yellow stools are produced in diarrhœa, when the bile is passed almost unchanged, and a similar colour is caused by rhubarb, senna, and some other drugs. Mucus in the stools, whether in strings, or mixed with the food remnants, or in the form of membranes coating the hardened stools, is almost always a sign of irritation or inflammation in the mucous membrane low down in the bowel (colitis). Red blood in the stools signifies some diseased condition situated near the lower end of the bowel, such as an ulcer or piles. When the blood proceeds from a point higher up, such as an ulcer of the stomach, it is changed by the action of the digestive juices as already described.

852

Incontinence of the bowels, or inability to retain the stools, is found in several diseases of a prostrating nature in which the sphincter muscles, that naturally keep the bowel closed, relax. It is also a symptom of disease in, or injury to, the spinal cord.

Pain at stool is a characteristic symptom of a ' fissure ' at the anus or of inflamed piles, and in such cases is of a very sharp nature. Pain of a duller character associated with the movements of the bowels is often caused by inflammation in the other pelvic organs.

CONSTIPATION and DIARRHŒA have been considered under separate headings.

STOUTNESS (*see* CORPULENCE).

STRABISMUS (στραβισμός) is another name for squinting.

STRAMONIUM is the leaf of *Datura stramonium* (thorn-apple, devil's apple, Jimson weed). It contains an alkaloid named daturine, which is almost identical with atropine, and upon which its action depends. Certain preparations of stramonium are used similarly to those of atropine or of belladonna for various conditions (*see* ATROPINE).

STRANGULATION (*strangulo*, I choke) is the term applied to the stoppage of circulation which sometimes occurs in a hernia, owing to the pressure caused by the edges of the opening through which the affected organ protrudes. A strangulated hernia must be operated on immediately.

STRANGURY (στραγγουρία) is the name given to a condition in which there is constant desire to pass water, accompanied by a straining sensation, though only a few drops can be voided. It is a symptom of inflammation situated in the kidneys, bladder, or urinary passages.

STRAPPING means the application of strips of adhesive plaster, one overlapping the other, so as to cover a part and make pressure upon it. This method of treatment is used in cases of injury or disease when it is desired to keep a part at rest ; for example, strapping is applied to the chest in cases of pleurisy and fracture of the ribs. Also, it is frequently used to prevent the movement of joints which are sprained or otherwise injured.

STREPTOCOCCUS (στρεπτός, a necklace ; κόκκος, a kernel) is the name given to a variety of bacterium which under the microscopic has much the appearance of a string of beads. It is responsible for erysipelas and other virulent forms of inflammation. (*See* BACTERIOLOGY.)

STREPTOKINASE is a substance produced by certain streptococci, which has the property of removing blood clot and inflammatory material. It is now available on a commercial scale and is being used in the treatment of bruises and inflammatory conditions in order to facilitate the absorption of extravasated blood and inflammatory exudates.

STREPTOMYCIN is an anti-bacterial substance obtained from the soil mould, *Actinomyces griseus*. It was first isolated in 1944 by Dr. Waksman in the United States of America. Its outstanding therapeutic advantages are twofold. In the first place, it is the most active known anti-tuberculous substance which can safely be used in the treatment of tuberculosis in man. Carefully controlled clinical trials have shown that it is of value in all acute forms of tuberculous infection.

Its second great advantage is that it is active against a range of Gram-negative bacteria which are relatively (or wholly) insensitive to penicillin. These particular organisms are responsible for certain chronic infections, particularly of the genito-urinary tract, which have hitherto proved resistant to all other known forms of treatment. Tularæmia (*q.v.*), an important disease in the United States of America, also responds to streptomycin, as do certain infections of the intestine.

Streptomycin, unfortunately, has also two big disadvantages. The most important of these is the tendency of organisms to become resistant to streptomycin. This means that the administration of this antibiotic must be care-

fully supervised to ensure that correct dosage is being used. This disadvantage can be overcome to a certain extent by combining it with the administration of para-aminosalicylic acid or isoniazid. The other disadvantage is that streptomycin produces toxic effects more easily than penicillin, especially disturbance of the vestibular apparatus, resulting in giddiness or unsteadiness.

STREPTOTHRIX (στρεπτός, a necklace ; θρίξ, hair) is the name of a group of micro-organisms closely allied to the moulds. They consist of filaments which show true branching and interlace to form a mycelium. The most important member of this group is *Streptothrix actinomyces*, the causative organism of actinomycosis (*q.v.*).

STRETCHERS (*see* INJURED, REMOVAL OF).

STRIÆ ATROPHICÆ is the term applied to atrophied strips of skin where this has been excessively stretched, as, for example, in pregnancy, when the greyish atrophied strips are known as STRIÆ GRAVIDARUM.

STRICTURE (*strictura*) means a narrowing in any of the natural passages of the body, such as the gullet, the bowel, or the urethra. It may be due to the development of some growth in the wall of the passage affected, or to pressure upon it by such a growth in some neighbouring organ, but in the majority of cases a stricture is the result of previous ulceration on the inner surface of the passage, followed by contraction of the scar. (*See* INTESTINE, DISEASES OF ; THROAT, DISEASES OF ; URETHRA, DISEASES OF, etc.)

STROKE is a popular name for apoplexy (*q.v.*).

STROMA (στρῶμα, a covering) is the name applied to the tissue which forms the framework and covering of an organ.

STROPHANTHUS is the seed of an East African climbing plant, *Strophanthus kombé*, from which the natives made Kombé arrow-poison. From these seeds an active principle, strophanthin, can be separated, and upon this substance the activity of the drug depends. Its action upon the heart is almost identical with that of digitalis (*see* DIGITALIS). Strophanthin-K must be distinguished from ouabain (*q.v.*), which is strophanthin-G.

Uses.—It is specially in cases of heart disease in which the heart is beating feebly and the pulse weak and irregular —*i.e.* cases of atrial fibrillation—that strophanthus is used. The effects of this drug, like those of digitalis, are often remarkable in removing dropsy, breathlessness, dyspepsia, and various other symptoms due to some defect in the heart. (*See also* OUABAIN.)

STROPHULUS, or RED GUM, is a rash consisting of numerous small red pimples, which appears in young children usually about teething-time, and is associated with a damp skin. It is relieved by careful attention to the diet, and by frequent use of some astringent dusting powder.

STRUMA (*struma*) is an old term which was applied to swellings in the neck : either tuberculous glands or enlargement of the thyroid gland. In the former sense it is equivalent to scrofula (*see* SCROFULA). (For the second meaning, *see* GOITRE.) The term 'strumous' is equivalent to 'tuberculous'.

STRYCHNINE is an alkaloid derived from nux vomica, the seed of an East Indian tree, as well as from the seeds of several other closely allied trees and shrubs. It is a white crystalline body possessed of an intensely bitter taste, more bitter perhaps than that of any other substance, and it is not very soluble in water. Strychnine in small doses is still a widely used stimulating drug, although in larger amounts it is a dangerous poison.

Action.—This drug acts mainly on the nervous system. When taken in small doses over a considerable time, it sharpens the mental powers and increases sensibility so that sight and hearing are improved and the sense of touch becomes more acute. The heart beats both more quickly and more strongly under its use, the breathing

becomes deeper, and the movements of the bowels are rendered less sluggish. But it is chiefly upon the spinal cord that strychnine acts ; all the functions of the cord are more quickly and more vigorously carried out, reflex action is increased, the muscles are kept in a state of greater ' tone ', and there is a general sense of increased bodily well-being. When over-large doses are taken, however, this readiness of the spinal cord to produce muscular action becomes so great that convulsions result from slight sensory impressions, such as a loud noise or cold draught.

Uses.—Strychnine is used chiefly as a tonic combined with other remedies during convalescence from weakening diseases, in fatigue brought on by overwork, and in various nervous conditions. Most tonic syrups with a bitter taste contain strychnine.

Strychnine is also added to purgative medicines for its stimulating action on the bowels ; it is used as a general stimulant when failure of the heart's action is imminent ; and small doses form a useful bitter tonic taken after meals in cases of atonic dyspepsia.

STRYCHNINE POISONING is fortunately of rare occurrence. It shows itself, as stated above, in convulsions, which come on very speedily after the person has taken the poison. These convulsions are brought on by slight causes, and the sufferer becomes quite flaccid between them. The mental faculties remain unaffected, and the symptoms end in death or recovery within a few hours. These symptoms serve to distinguish strychnine poisoning from tetanus or lock-jaw, the only malady which it resembles (*see* TETANUS).

Treatment.—The patient should be kept quiet by himself in a darkened room, all noise and disturbance being reduced to a minimum. At the earliest moment a barbiturate is injected intravenously in a large enough dose to stop the convulsions and put the patient to sleep : sodium pentobarbital or sodium amytal can be used for this purpose. If the patient is seen early enough after taking the poisonous dose, potassium permanganate, tannic acid, or charcoal may be given by mouth. To wash out the stomach or to induce vomiting in a patient with convulsions is not free from risk. If the muscles of respiration are fixed in spasm, artificial respiration is needed.

STUPE (*stuppa*, tow) is the name applied to a hot fomentation with turpentine sprinkled on it. (*See* FOMENTATIONS.)

STUTTERING (*see* STAMMERING).

STYE, or STY (*see* EYE, DISEASES OF).

STYPTICS (στυπτικός, astringent) are applications which check bleeding, either by making the blood-vessels contract more firmly or by causing rapid clotting in the blood. Some possess both modes of action.

Varieties. — Many substances have this action on account of their chemical or physical properties. Among them may be mentioned ice ; hot water at 120° F. (49° C.) if brought directly in contact with the bleeding surface ; perchloride of iron ; acetate of lead and Goulard's water ; nitrate of silver ; sulphate of copper ; sulphate of zinc ; alum ; tannin ; hazeline ; ergot ; adrenaline ; and Russell-viper venom.

Uses.—The use of styptics is mentioned under HÆMORRHAGE.

SUB- (*sub*, under) is a prefix signifying under, near, or moderately.

SUBARACHNOID HÆMORRHAGE is a hæmorrhage into the subarachnoid space. It is usually the result of an aneurysm on the circle of Willis (*q.v.*).

SUBARACHNOID SPACE is the space between the arachnoid and the pia mater, two of the membranes covering the brain (*q.v.*).

SUBCLAVIAN is the name applied to a large artery and vein which pass to the upper arm between the collar bone and the first rib.

SUBCONSCIOUS is the term applied to a state of being partially conscious, or to the condition in which mental processes occur and outside objects and events are perceived with the mind nearly or quite unconscious of them. Such subconscious impressions or events may be forgotten at the time and may nevertheless exert a continued influence over the conscious mind, or may at a subsequent time come fully into consciousness. Much importance is attached at the present time to the influence of painful or unpleasant experiences which, though forgotten, continue to influence the mind, and these are held to be largely responsible for neurasthenic and similar states. This injurious influence is removed when the subconscious impressions come fully into consciousness and are then remembered and clearly seen in their relative importance.

SUBCUTANEOUS (*sub*, under ; *cutis*, the skin) means anything pertaining to the loose cellular tissue beneath the skin, *e.g.* a subcutaneous injection. (*See* HYPODERMIC INJECTION.)

SUBINVOLUTION is a term used to indicate that the womb has failed to undergo the usual 'involution', or decrease in size, which naturally takes place within one month after a child is born.

SUBJECTIVE is a term applied to symptoms, sensations, etc., perceived only by the affected individual. For example, numbness is a purely subjective sensation, whilst the jerk given by the leg on tapping the tendon of the knee is an objective sign.

SUBLIMATION (*sublimatio*) is a term applied to the processes of converting a solid substance into a vapour and recondensing it. The term is also used in a mental sense for the process of converting instinctive sexual desires to new aims and objects of a higher type devoid of sexual significance.

SUBLUXATION (*sub*, under ; *luxatio*, a dislocation) means a partial dislocation, and is a term sometimes applied to a sprain.

SUBMAXILLA is the Latin term for the lower jaw-bone.

SUBSTITUTION is a term used in pharmacy for the replacing of one substance by another, frequently in a fraudulent manner.

SUBSULTUS (*subsulto*, I leap) means the twitching of the muscles that sometimes occurs in weakening fevers.

SUCCINYLSULPHATHIAZOLE. — A sulphonamide drug which is absorbed only slowly from the intestine, and on that account used in the treatment of intestinal infections.

SUCCUSSION (*succussio*, a shaking) is a method of examination by shaking the body of a patient in order to elicit splashing sounds, with a view to determining the presence of gas and fluid in a cavity such as the interior of the stomach or the pleural cavity.

SUCKLING (*see* INFANT FEEDING; BREASTS, DISEASES OF).

SUDAMINA (*sudo*, I sweat) are small vesicles which appear underneath the surface layer of the skin during diseases associated with constant perspiration, such as rheumatic fever.

SUDORIFICS (*sudor*, sweat; *facio*, I make) are drugs and other agents which produce copious perspiration. (*See* DIAPHORETICS.)

SUFFOCATION (*see* ASPHYXIA *and* CHOKING).

SUGAR is a substance containing the elements carbon, hydrogen, and oxygen, and belonging therefore to the chemical group of carbohydrates. This group includes three subdivisions as follows :

(1) Monosaccharides, or glucoses ($C_6H_{12}O_6$)
    e.g. Glucose, or dextrose or grape-sugar.
    Lævulose or fructose.
    Galactose.
(2) Disaccharides, or sucroses ($C_{12}H_{22}O_{11}$)
    e.g. Cane-sugar.
    Lactose or milk-sugar.
    Maltose or malt-sugar.
(3) Polysaccharides, or amyloses ($C_6H_{10}O_5$)
    e.g. Starch.
    Glycogen or animal starch.
    Dextrin and other gums.

Grape-sugar is found in various kinds of fruit, and is the form of sugar produced by the tissues and excreted in large amount by the kidneys in diabetes.

856

Cane-sugar is very widely distributed through the vegetable kingdom, though it is specially plentiful in the juice of the sugar-cane, beetroot, and maple. When taken as a food, it is converted by the digestive juices into grape-sugar before it is absorbed, this process being known as ' inversion '. Cane-sugar is a valuable food, being utilized in the production of heat and energy, although it is also to a certain extent a tissue-builder so far as fat is concerned. It is to be avoided by persons who tend to corpulence, as well as by diabetics.

Milk-sugar is found in milk, and it is to the fermentation of this sugar and consequent production of lactic acid by certain bacteria that the souring of milk is due. The extent to which it is present in the milk of different animals is mentioned under INFANT FEEDING. Milk-sugar has little sweetening power compared with cane-sugar, but it is used sometimes as a laxative.

Malt-sugar is produced by the action of the ferment diastase upon the starch contained in barley, and also by the ferments of the saliva and pancreatic juice, although it appears to be still further changed by the latter ferments into glucose before it is absorbed.

Invert sugar is a natural mixture of dextrose and lævulose resulting from a chemical decomposition of cane-sugar or of starch.

Starch is mentioned under a separate heading, and its use as a food under DIET and CEREALS.

The energy-producing value of sugars generally is taken as being, on the average, 4 calories for each gramme of sugar.

SUGAR OF LEAD (*see* LEAD).

SUGGESTION TREATMENT (*see* PSYCHOTHERAPY).

SUICIDE (*see under* INSANITY).

SULCUS is the term applied to any groove or furrow, but especially to a fissure of the brain.

SULPHACETAMIDE, or *p*-amino-benzene-sulphonacetamide, is one of the sulphonamides. It is principally used in the treatment of infections of the urinary tract, as it is active against

E. coli. As the sodium salt it is used locally in the treatment of infections of the eye.

SULPHADIAZINE, or 2-(*p*-amino-benzene - sulphonamido) - pyrimidine, is one of the sulphonamides. It is a highly active drug and in moderate dosage produces a high and persistent blood concentration. It is relatively non-toxic and is particularly useful in the treatment of meningitis.

SULPHADIMETHOXINE is one of the new long-acting sulphonamides, only one dose of which is required daily.

SULPHADIMIDINE, or 2-(*p*-amino-benzene-sulphonamido)-4 : 6-dimethyl-pyrimidine, is comparable in activity to sulphadiazine, and has the advantage of being even more non-toxic and of producing higher blood concentrations.

SULPHAFURAZOLE, or dimethyl-sulphanilamido-isoxazole, is one of the more recent additions to the range of sulphonamide drugs. It has a wide range of anti-bacterial action, but, in view of its high solubility, it is particularly useful in infections of the urinary tract.

SULPHAGUANIDINE, or *p*-amino-benzene - sulphonyl - guanidine mono-hydrate, is a sulphonamide which is not readily absorbed from the intestine, and is therefore of value in the treatment of bacillary dysentery.

SULPHAMERAZINE is the term for the sulphonamide drug, 2-(*p*-amino-benzene-sulphonamido)-4-methylpyrimidine. It is absorbed rapidly from the gut and is excreted slowly by the kidneys. The concentration of the drug in the blood therefore remains high for a long time, and so its action against bacterial infection is correspondingly maintained. Its therapeutic use is similar to that of sulpha-diazine (*q.v.*).

SULPHAMETHOXAZOLE is one of the new long-acting sulphonamides. It is related to sulphafurazole, has a duration of action of 12 hours, and is said to be particularly effective against streptococci.

SULPHAMETHOXYPYRIDAZINE is one of the new long-acting sulphona-mides, only one dose of which is required daily.

SULPHAMEZATHINE is another term for SULPHADIMIDINE (*q.v.*).

SULPHANILAMIDE, or *p* - amino-benzene-sulphonamide, is a drug the discovery of which is one of the most important in medicine in the twentieth century. In 1935 the German chemist Domagk announced the discovery of the effect of prontosil on streptococci. It was later found that this action was due to conversion in the body of prontosil into sulphanilamide, which acts by inhibiting the growth of various bacteria, especially the ubiquitous and dangerous *Streptococcus hæmolyticus.* Although several other sulphonamides with various advantages have been subsequently introduced, sulphanil-amide is still used, particularly for the treatment of moderately severe infec-tions, with the hæmolytic streptococcus, infections of the urinary tract, and as a local application in the treatment of wounds and peritonitis. (*See also* SULPHONAMIDE.)

SULPHAPHENAZOLE is one of the new long-acting sulphonamides.

SULPHASALAZINE is a sulphon-amide which is proving of value in the treatment of ulcerative colitis.

SULPHASOMIZOLE is one of the new long-acting sulphonamides.

SULPHATES are salts of sulphuric acid, and their action and uses vary much according to the metal with which the acid is combined. The sulphates of the heavy metals, which are soluble in water, viz. the sulphates of iron (green vitriol), zinc (white vitriol), and copper (blue vitriol), have a powerful astringent action ; whilst sulphates of the alkalis, viz. the sulphates of sodium, potassium, and magnesium (Epsom salts), are used as saline purgatives.

SULPHATHIAZOLE, another drug related to sulphanilamide, and dis-covered later than sulphapyridine, is effective against a variety of germs.

It is the only sulphonamide active against staphylococci. Its liability to produce toxic effects is steadily reducing its use.

SULPHETRONE is a sulphone, a group of drugs allied to the sulphonamides. It was originally introduced as an anti-tuberculous drug, but is proving more promising in the treatment of leprosy.

SULPHINPYRAZONE is a derivative of phenylbutazone (q.v.) which is proving of value in the treatment of gout.

SULPHONAL is a slow-acting hypnotic with a prolonged action. It is therefore unsuitable for frequent use. The dose is 5 to 20 grains.

SULPHONAMIDE.—A drug having the sulphonamide grouping—SO_2NH_2. In 1935 Domagk, a German chemist, announced the discovery of the effect of prontosil on streptococci. Subsequent work showed that this action was due to the conversion in the body of prontosil to sulphanilamide. The action of the sulphonamides is bacteriostatic and not bactericidal, i.e. they do not directly kill the bacteria but so interfere with their growth that they are unable to multiply. This action of the sulphonamides is now believed to be due to the similarity of their chemical structure to that of p-aminobenzoic acid. This latter substance is essential for the growth of many bacteria. If the bacteria is surrounded by a sulphonamide in greater concentration than p-aminobenzoic acid, then the bacteria take up the sulphonamide. This interferes with their development and they therefore never mature nor are they able to reproduce themselves.

Of the many sulphonamides which have been produced, the following are the most important : sulphacetamide, sulphadiazine, sulphadimidine, sulphaguanidine, sulphamerazine, sulphathiazole, and phthalylsulphathiazole. Further information concerning each of these will be found in the appropriate sections. Although the sulphonamides are being replaced to an increasing
858

extent by penicillin, which is active against many of the same organisms, they are still a useful addition to our ability to control diseases due to bacterial infection.

SULPHONES are a group of drugs allied to the sulphonamides. They are used in the treatment of leprosy. The most important members of this group are dapsone, solapsone (or sulphetrone), diasone, and promin.

SULPHUR is a non-metallic element widely used in medicine. The crude sulphur is obtained in volcanic districts, and from it ' sublimed sulphur ' is prepared by heating. This sublimed sulphur is either run into moulds as ' rolled sulphur ', or allowed to deposit as ' flowers of sulphur ', which consists of a fine gritty powder and is the most commonly used form. The sublimed sulphur may be boiled with slaked lime and treated with hydrochloric acid, when the sulphur settles down in the form of a fine greyish-yellow powder— ' precipitated sulphur '.

Action.—The action of sulphur depends partly upon the grittiness of the ' flowers of sulphur ', and mainly upon the readiness with which sulphur enters into chemical combinations to form sulphides and sulphates. In consequence of this property, it is possessed of disinfectant and antiparasitic powers. When taken internally, the sulphides that are formed stimulate the action of the bowels, and, being excreted partly from the surface of the skin and mucous membranes of the air passages, they also stimulate these.

Uses.—Sulphur is burned in order to produce sulphurous acid gas, which is widely used as a disinfectant (see DISINFECTION). Externally, sulphur ointment is one of the remedies against the minute parasite that is responsible for the itch ; and milk of sulphur is used in lotions for acne on the face. Sulphur is also used in baths for its stimulating action on the skin in cases of skin disease, rheumatism, etc. For this purpose either plain sulphur or, more commonly, sulphuret of potash is added in the amount of a quarter or half a pound (113 or 226 grammes) to 30 gallons (135 litres) of hot water. Internally, sulphur is a time-honoured remedy for constipation, in doses of a teaspoonful or thereabout made into a paste with treacle. It may be used for the same purpose in the more palatable form of lozenges, several of these being taken at one time, and has a gentle laxative action. In old persons who suffer from rheumatism and who are liable to constipation and to bronchitis, sulphur has been long used in combination with various anti-rheumatic drugs in the confection known as ' Chelsea Pensioner ' (see CONFECTIONS).

SULPHURET OF POTASH, also known on account of its appearance as ' liver of sulphur ', is used in baths for the treatment of skin diseases. (*See* SULPHUR.)

SULPHURIC ACID, or OIL OF VITRIOL, is, in its undiluted state, one of the most powerful of the mineral acids. It is a heavy, colourless liquid of oily consistence and is largely used in various manufacturing operations, so that poisoning by sulphuric acid is not uncommon. It chars any organic substance with which it is brought in contact, and acts as a violent corrosive poison. The treatment of sulphuric acid poisoning is that for corrosive poisons generally, viz. to administer weak alkalis such as baking soda, whitening, magnesia, or soap in water, and to apply oil to the injured surfaces. **Uses.**—Dilute sulphuric acid, or aromatic sulphuric acid containing cinnamon and ginger, and commonly known as ' elixir of vitriol ', is used in cases of diarrhœa for its astringent properties, in doses of 5 or 20 drops well diluted in water. A lemonade is also made, containing small quantities of sulphuric acid, for use by lead-workers ; since it forms an insoluble sulphate with lead, and thus prevents absorption of any lead which may be accidentally swallowed at work.

SULPHURIC ETHER is a name sometimes applied to the ether used for anæsthetic purposes, because sulphuric acid is employed in its preparation. (*See* ANÆSTHETICS, ETHER.)

SULPHUROUS ACID is a gas derived from burning sulphur. It has an ex-tremely pungent odour and strong disinfectant power. Dissolved in water mixed with glycerin it is used for application to the skin in various parasitic skin diseases.

SUMMER DIARRHŒA (*see* DIARRHŒA *and* INFANT FEEDING).

SUNBURN includes the various effects produced upon the skin by the sun's rays. Similar effects are produced by exposure to the heat of furnaces, and also on the skin of those who are exposed for long periods close to electric arc lamps or X-ray apparatus. The effect produced on the skin by strong sunlight is due to the ultra-violet rays. The actual changes vary greatly in different individuals, fair-haired, delicate, thin-skinned people suffering to a much greater extent, as a rule, than the strong and swarthy.

Symptoms.—In its simplest form sunburn consists in the development of dark pigment in the deeper layer of the epithelium, which gives the skin a brown hue and acts as a natural protection from the heat rays. In a severer form there are marked flushing of the skin (erythema), tingling, itching, and finally peeling off of the cuticle in flakes. This process may be very severe, painful, and accompanied by the formation of blisters. After long periods of sunburn, the skin is apt to become permanently dry and wrinkled as well as browned.

Treatment.—Mere tanning of the skin under the sun's rays is a healthy sign which requires no treatment, but the severer forms are not only unsightly but often very painful. Prevention may be effected by the use of sunshades, veils, etc., those of a brown colour being most effective. The redness may be relieved by applying calamine lotion or by dabbing on an evaporating fluid such as eau-de-Cologne, elder-flower water, or rose water. The effects of heat may also be to some extent prevented by sponging the exposed parts with an astringent such as Goulard's water or hazeline, or by the ancient practice of oiling the skin, or of applying an ointment such as cold cream after a bath.

SUNLIGHT (*see* LIGHT TREATMENT).

SUNSTROKE, HEAT - STROKE, INSOLATION, COUP DE SOLEIL, and THERMIC FEVER are terms applied to the effects produced upon the central nervous system, and through it upon other organs of the body, by exposure to the sun or to overheated air. Although most frequently observed in tropical regions, this disease occurs also in temperate climates during hot weather. A moist condition of the atmosphere, which interferes with cooling of the overheated body, greatly increases the liability to suffer from this ailment.

Causes.—The fundamental cause of the condition is exposure of the body to amounts of radiant energy for which it cannot compensate. The radiant energy may take the form of heat rays or of sunlight. This inability to compensate to excessive exposure to heat or sunlight results in overheating of the body and loss of fluid. In any given case one or other of these factors, or both, may come into play. In the more acute cases the condition is characterized by failure of the sweating mechanism, and these are the cases which are rapidly fatal unless treatment is instituted immediately. When excessive sweating occurs in the early stages this loss of fluid is usually accompanied by a corresponding loss of salt, resulting in a disturbance of the electrolyte balance of the body fluids. Unless this loss of water and of sodium chloride is compensated for, one of three things may occur : (i) the individual may be seized with severe cramp in the muscles, *i.e.* heat cramps ; (ii) the blood volume is diminished and the circulation of the body is seriously disturbed, resulting in a condition analogous to surgical shock ; (iii) the sweating mechanism may break down, with resultant further rise in the temperature of body, leading to a fatal termination.

Predisposing factors are bad living or working conditions, lack of acclimatization to tropical conditions, unsuitable clothing, poor health, and dietetic and alcoholic indiscretions.

Symptoms.—The symptoms, which obviously depend upon the disorganization of the normal heat-regulating mechanism as well as of the functions of circulation and respiration, vary in their intensity and likewise to some

860

extent in their form. Five chief types of the disease are usually described.

(1) HEAT COLLAPSE.—This is the mildest form of the condition. It is characterized by fatigue, giddiness, and temporary loss of consciousness. The blood pressure is low and the pulse is slow. In the more severe cases there is a state of collapse, with cold, clammy skin and a subnormal temperature. Vomiting is not uncommon and there may be muscular cramps. The urine is much diminished in volume, is highly coloured and has a high specific gravity, *e.g.* over 1020. This type of case practically always recovers.

(2) HEAT EXHAUSTION.—The mild case of heat exhaustion is very similar to one of heat collapse. The more severe case tends to occur towards the end of the hot season in the tropics. The onset is characterized by increasing weakness, dizziness, and insomnia, and this is accompanied by defective sweating in the majority of cases. Cramps and vomiting seldom occur, but large volumes of urine are voided. The temperature is usually about 100–101° F. (37·8–38·3° C.), the pulse rate is within normal limits, and there are seldom signs of dehydration, the skin usually having quite a good colour.

(3) HEAT CRAMPS.—These have been recognized for many years and occur in individuals who perform hard physical work in high temperatures. Hence the many different names by which they have been known, *e.g.* miners' cramps, stokers' cramps, bakers' cramps. The characteristic feature is agonizing cramp, usually in the legs, arms, or back. Occasionally the abdominal muscles are involved, and in these cases the intensity of the pain may suggest some acute condition of the stomach or gut. The cramps are accompanied by sweating, pallor of the skin, and a feeling of intense anxiety. There may be headache and giddiness. The temperature is seldom raised very much.

(4) HEAT HYPERPYREXIA.—This is the most serious type of all. The initial manifestations are loss of energy and irritability. Then follow mental confusion and diminution or cessation of sweating. Gradually, or sometimes with startling suddenness, this passes into restlessness and then coma and the temperature rises rapidly to 107° F.

(41·7° C.) or even higher. Unless treatment is instituted immediately, there is soon a fatal termination.

(5) SUNSTROKE.—This term is usually restricted to the condition resulting from exposure to intense sunlight. In mild cases it may consist only of headache and a sense of lassitude, persisting for a few hours. In more severe cases there may be intense headache, aversion to light, vomiting, and delirium. The skin is dry, the pulse is rapid, and there is a moderate rise in temperature. Recovery may be slow in severe cases, and for a long period subsequently there may be loss of memory and inability to concentrate. It is seldom wise for such severe cases to continue to live in tropical countries.

Prevention.—Careful selection of personnel who have to perform hard physical work under tropical conditions or in high temperatures such as pertain in stokeholds, is essential. Even in the case of such selected individuals acclimatization is necessary and they should not be allowed to perform severe physical exertion at high temperatures until a period of several weeks' training has elapsed. In the tropics elderly people should move to a cool area, e.g. the hills in India during the hot season. Personal hygiene is important. Only light clothing should be worn, with a minimum of constrictions such as tight belts.

Diet should be light and nourishing and ample fluids should be taken. Salads and fruit should constitute an important part of the diet, and fluids should be bland, e.g. fruit drinks, tea, iced coffee. Alcoholic drinks should be taken in moderation, and only after sundown. In the case of individuals performing hard physical exertion at high temperatures, water containing salt (i.e. sodium chloride) should be drunk freely. Unless the water contains a certain amount of salt, there is an increased tendency to develop cramps. In industries where men work under such conditions, they are now provided with salt and water flavoured with lemon to disguise the salty flavour. Attention to ventilation and air-conditioning is also essential. In the tropics, when air-conditioning is not available, houses should be closed up in the early morning and opened up again at sundown. This reduces the amount of hot air entering the house during the day and allows of free circulation of the cool night air. Fans are also of value, and, in hot, dry conditions, sprinkling the compound with water during the afternoon sometimes helps to keep the house cool.

Treatment.—In the case of *heat cramps, heat collapse,* and *heat exhaustion,* treatment consists of removal of the affected individual to a cool place and the administration of normal saline. In severe cases the normal saline can be given intravenously, but it can usually be given by mouth. *Heat hyperpyrexia* is an emergency which requires immediate attention with a view to reducing the temperature. The individual should be placed in the shade, stripped, and drenched with water. To increase the cooling property of the water the surface of the body should be fanned. The patient is then wrapped in a sheet soaked in as cool water as possible, and the fanning is continued. This treatment must be stopped when the rectal temperature falls to 102° F. (38·9° C.) and the patient then be wrapped in a dry blanket. The reason for stopping at this temperature is that the temperature continues to fall after treatment is stopped, and therefore if treatment was continued until the temperature became normal, the further fall in temperature might have serious consequences. As soon as the patient is conscious he should be given normal saline to drink, and this usually provokes sweating—a favourable sign. Whenever possible, further treatment should be carried out in hospital, as there is always a risk of circulatory collapse occurring. Convalescence may be prolonged, and the advisability of the affected individual returning permanently to a cooler climate must always be given careful consideration.

The individual with *sunstroke* should be put to bed in a darkened, cool room. Wet compresses to the head are soothing, and in mild cases this is all that is required. If the patient is restless or suffering from insomnia, sedatives should be given. Ample fluids should be drunk and alcohol should be forbidden. In all except the mildest cases, only a fluid diet should be given during the first two days. In severe cases, convalescence may be prolonged and troublesome, and transfer to a temperate climate is essential.

SUPER- (*super*, above) is a prefix signifying above or implying excess.

SUPERFŒTATION is the term applied to the condition in which there is fertilization of a second ovum in a woman already pregnant.

SUPERINVOLUTION is a term applied to the process by which the womb decreases in size after childbirth, when, instead of stopping at the point when the womb reaches its usual size, more or less complete wasting away of this organ takes place.

SUPINATION (*supinatio*) means the turning of the forearm and hand so that the palm faces upwards.

SUPPOSITORY (*suppositorius*, something introduced beneath) is a small conical mass made of oil of theobroma, to which white beeswax is sometimes added, or glycerin-jelly, and containing drugs intended for introduction into the rectum. This method of using drugs may be chosen for various reasons. For example, the suppository, as in the case of soap or glycerin suppositories, is often used to produce an aperient action. Other suppositories, such as those of morphine, are used to quiet pain and check the action of the bowels. Others are used for the sake of their influence on neighbouring organs.

The following official suppositories are those commonly employed : suppository of bismuth subgallate, of glycerin, of hammamelis and zinc oxide, and of morphine.

Method of use.—The suppository is placed with its pointed end against the anus and with a firm but gentle screwing movement is pushed upwards. With the point of the forefinger, it must be pushed onwards for about 1 inch (25 mm.), past the sphincter muscle, otherwise it will not be retained. It must be quickly introduced, as the material of which it is composed rapidly softens when brought into contact with the body.

862

SUPPRESSION is the name applied to a failure on the part of the kidneys to secrete urine. This is sometimes a complication of fevers or of acute nervous affections, such as meningitis, but it is chiefly found in acute Bright's disease, and leads then to the dangerous condition known as uræmia (*see* URÆMIA). Sometimes in children during a feverish attack the urine is almost completely suppressed for some days with little ill result.

SUPPURATION (*suppuratio*) means the process of pus formation. When pus forms on a raw surface the process is called 'ulceration', whilst a deep-seated collection of pus is known as an 'abscess'. (For more detailed information, *see* ABSCESS, INFLAMMATION, PHAGOCYTOSIS, ULCER, WOUNDS.)

SUPRA- (*supra*, above) is a prefix signifying above or upon.

SUPRAPUBIC (*supra*, above ; *pubes*, the private parts) operation is one in which the abdomen is opened in its lower part, immediately above the pubic bones. (*See* LITHOTOMY.)

SUPRARENAL GLANDS (*supra*, above ; *renes*, the kidneys), also known as SUPRARENAL CAPSULES, or ADRENAL BODIES, are two organs situated one upon the upper end of each kidney. Each measures about 2 inches (5 cm.) in length from above downwards, rather less than that from side to side ; and each is about a quarter of an inch (6 mm.) thick. The two together weigh about a quarter of an ounce (7 grammes).

Structure.—Each suprarenal gland has an enveloping layer of fibrous tissue. Within this the gland shows two distinct parts, an outer, firm, deep-yellow, *cortical* layer, and a central, soft, dark-brown, *medullary* portion. The cortical part consists of columns of cells running from the surface inwards, whilst in the medullary portion the cells are arranged irregularly and separated from one another by large capillary blood-vessels. Both the blood-vessels and the nerves of the suprarenal glands are very large and numerous, considering the small size of the organ.

Functions.—It has long been known

that removal of the suprarenal glands in animals is speedily followed by great muscular prostration and death in a few days. In human beings, disease of the suprarenal glands is apt to bring on Addison's disease, in which the chief symptoms are increasing weakness and bronzing of the skin. The medulla of the glands produces a substance—adrenaline—the effects of which very closely resemble those brought about by activity of the sympathetic nervous system : dilated pupil, hair standing on end, quickening and strengthening of the heart-beat, immobilization of the gut, increased output of sugar from the liver into the blood-stream. From the cortex of the gland are produced a series of hormones which play a vital, though as yet incompletely elucidated, rôle in the metabolism of the body. Some (such as aldosterone) control the electrolyte balance of the body, others are concerned in carbohydrate metabolism, whilst others again are concerned with sex physiology. One of the most important is deoxycortone, lack of which produces Addison's disease (*q.v.*). Cortisone is another suprarenal cortical hormone which is now known to be of value in the treatment of rheumatoid arthritis and certain other rheumatic diseases.

SURAMIN is the *British Pharmacopœia* name for a drug which has been much used, and with success, in the treatment of trypanosomiasis.

SURROGATE (*surrogatus*, substituted) is a term applied in medicine to a substance used as a substitute for another.

SUSPENDED ANIMATION (*see* Death, Signs of ; *and* Sleep).

SUSPENSORY means anything serving to hold up a part, and is a term specially applied to bandages for the breast, testicle, and other dependent parts.

SUTURE (*sutura*, a seam) is the name given either to the close union between two neighbouring bones of the skull, or to the series of stitches by which a wound is closed. (*See* Wounds.)

SWAB is a term applied to a small piece of gauze, lint, or similar material used for wiping out the mouth of a helpless patient or for drying out a wound. The term is also applied to a tuft of sterilized cotton-wool wrapped round a wire and enclosed in a sterile glass tube used for obtaining matter or membrane from the throat, from wounds, etc., in order that this may be subjected to bacteriological examination.

SWEAT (*see* Perspiration).

SWEAT-GLANDS (*see* Skin).

SWEATING SICKNESS was the name given to a malady that appeared in Europe, and especially in England, during the fifteenth and sixteenth centuries. It was named after its most prominent symptom, appears to have been a disease of sudden onset which caused extreme prostration, and was very fatal. There were several epidemics during the centuries mentioned, and the disease seems to have been regarded with great dread, although it is difficult to identify it with any infectious malady at present known.

SWEETBREAD is a popular term applied to several glands used for food, including the thymus gland of young animals (neck sweetbread), the pancreas (stomach sweetbread), and the testis.

SWEET SPIRIT OF NITRE, also known as Spirit of nitrous ether, consists of a mixture of water, alcohol, aldehyde, and various nitrous bodies. It is prepared by a complicated process of distillation from nitric acid and rectified spirit. Like other drugs containing nitrites, sweet spirit of nitre has an action in checking spasm of all sorts and in dilating the blood-vessels. (*See* Nitroglycerin.) In certain circumstances it is a diaphoretic, causing copious perspiration and thus reducing feverishness. In other circumstances it acts as a diuretic, increasing the action of the kidneys. When kept in unstoppered bottles, however, it rapidly loses strength and, therefore, to be of any value, must be used fresh.

SYCOSIS (σῦκον, fig) is the name given to a skin disease in which **the** hair follicles, especially of the chin, are inflamed, forming pustules round the hairs, surrounded by a swollen and reddened area of skin. The disease is directly due to infection of the hair follicles with staphylococcus or ringworm. The infection is generally attributed to a barber's utensils, and the condition is sometimes known as ' barber itch ', ' foul shave ', or ' ringworm of the beard '. (For treatment, see RINGWORM.)

SYMPATHETIC is a term applied to certain diseases or symptoms which arise in one part of the body in consequence of disease in some distant part. Inflammation may arise in one eye, in consequence of injury to the other, by the spread of organisms along the lymphatic channels connecting the two, and is then known as sympathetic inflammation. Pain also may be of a sympathetic nature (see PAIN).

SYMPATHETIC SYSTEM is that part of the nervous system from which most of the nerves that connect and regulate the various internal organs appear to take their origin. It consists of scattered collections of grey matter known as ganglia, united by an irregular network of nerve-fibres, those portions where the ganglia are placed most closely and the network of fibres is specially dense being known as ' plexuses'. The chief part of the sympathetic system consists of two ' ganglionated cords ' that run through the neck, chest, and abdomen, lying close in front of the spine. (For further details, see NERVES.)

SYMPATHOMIMETIC DRUGS are those producing an effect comparable to those produced by stimulation of the sympathetic nervous system: e.g. adrenaline (q.v.).

SYMPTOM (σύμπτωμα) is a term applied to any evidence of disease. The term ' physical sign ' is generally applied to symptoms of which the patient does not complain but which are elicited upon examination. For the symptoms indicative of the various diseases see under the headings of each disease.

SYN- (σύν, with) is a prefix signifying union.

864

SYNAPSE (σύν, with ; ἅπτω, I touch) is the term applied to the anatomical relation of one nerve-cell with another which is effected at various points by contact of their branching processes. The state of shrinkage or relaxation at these points (synapses) is supposed in some cases to determine the readiness with which a nervous impulse is transmitted from one part of the nervous system to another. Many drugs also are supposed to act upon the nervous system through their effect in closing or widening these junctions.

SYNCOPE (συγκοπή) is another name for fainting. (See FAINTING.)

SYNDACTYLY is the condition which a child is born with, in which two or more fingers or toes are fused together to a varying extent. The condition is popularly known as webbed fingers or toes (q.v.).

SYNDROME (συνδρομή, concurrence) is a term applied to a group of symptoms occurring together regularly and thus constituting a disease to which some particular name is given : e.g. Stokes-Adams Syndrome, of slow pulse and giddiness, forming a sign of degeneration of the heart-muscle causing heart-block ; Korsakoff Syndrome, of loss of appreciation of time and place combined with talkativeness, forming signs of alcoholic delirium.

SYNECHIA (συνέχεια, continuity) is the term applied to adhesions between the iris and the cornea or lens.

SYNOSTOSIS (σύν, together ; ὀστέον, bone) is the term applied to a union by bony material of adjacent bones usually separate.

SYNOVIAL MEMBRANE forms the lining of the soft parts that enclose the cavity of a joint. (See JOINTS.)

SYNOVITIS means inflammation of the membrane lining a joint. It is usually painful and accompanied by effusion of fluid within the synovial sac of the joint. It is found in acute rheumatism, various injuries and inflammations of joints, and in chronic form in tuberculosis.

SYNTHETIC is a term applied to substances produced by chemical processes in the laboratory or by artificial building up.

SYPHILIS is a contagious disease of slow development, which, at its commencement, shows a characteristic sore at the site of infection, later brings on constitutional effects resembling those of other infectious diseases, and at a still later period produces certain changes resembling some of those caused by leprosy and tuberculosis. Because, in the majority of cases the disease is acquired as a result of sexual intercourse with an infected individual, it is classed as one of the *venereal* diseases. Syphilis affects only human beings, though it has been experimentally produced in anthropoid apes.

The disease seems to have first attracted public attention about or soon after the year 1494 in consequence of a severe and widespread outbreak among the French soldiers then occupied in the siege of Naples. For long it was known as the Neapolitan disease, French Pox, or Great Pox ; and, in consequence probably of the licentiousness and the want of cleanliness that then prevailed in persons and dwellings, it spread in epidemic form. Later, it came to be called syphilis, the name being derived from that of the chief character in a Latin poem published by Fracastorius in 1536. It has been suggested that the disease existed in ancient times among the natives of America, and that the infection was brought to Europe by the followers of Columbus, but there are also grounds for supposing that the disease occurred among the Eastern races in ancient times, although it was most likely confounded with leprosy and tuberculosis.

Causes.—The causative organism is the *Treponema pallidum* (or *Spirochæta pallida*), a long, thread-like, wavy organism with pointed tapering ends. It is found in large numbers in the sores in the primary stage of the disease and in the skin lesions in the secondary stage. This organism was discovered in 1905.

Syphilis may be ACQUIRED from persons already suffering from the disease, or it may be INHERITED from one or both parents. The acquired form is usually got by sexual intercourse, but it may also result from kissing or from contact with a sore upon another person through some wound or abrasion. The epithelium covering the general surface of the skin seems to be an efficient protection, but the infective material apparently has the power of penetrating mucous membranes. Not only may the disease be spread as a venereal affection, but cups, spoons, towels, sponges, sheets, which have been used by the diseased, have been known to convey the contagion to others, although fortunately such inanimate articles appear to retain their infectiveness only for a short time. The acquired form of the disease is infectious from contact with sores, both in its primary and secondary stages ; whilst infants suffering from the inherited form are also highly infectious. Accordingly any one acting as wet-nurse to, or even frequently handling such an infant, runs great risk of infection, although the mother may handle it with impunity (Colles's Law).

Symptoms.—The *acquired form* of the disease is commonly divided into three stages — PRIMARY, SECONDARY, and TERTIARY, although in many cases the tertiary stage is wanting, whilst in others there is no dividing line between the secondary and tertiary symptoms. To certain late affections, which may appear after the lapse of several years, such as locomotor ataxia and general paralysis, the terms parasyphilis and QUATERNARY syphilis are sometimes applied. The disease presents great variations of intensity, being occasionally of a ' malignant ' type, in which widespread ulceration speedily comes on and even causes death ; and in other cases showing little more than a slight skin eruption, although probably it exerts, even in such mild cases, a highly prejudicial effect upon the constitution. In doubtful cases of the disease the Wassermann reaction is regarded as an almost certain diagnostic feature.

The incubation period ranges from 10 to 90 days, though most frequently it occupies about four weeks. Then a small ulcer appears at the site of infection, which is accompanied by a typical ' cartilaginous ' hardness of the tissues immediately round and beneath it, and characterized by its resistance to all healing treatment. This, which is known as the PRIMARY SORE (or *chancre*), may be very much inflamed, or it may be so small and occasion so little trouble as to pass almost or quite unnoticed. A few days after this sore has appeared, the lymphatic glands in its neighbourhood, and later those all over the body, become swollen and hard. This condition lasts for several weeks as a rule, and then the sore slowly heals and the glands subside. After a variable period, which, however, may in most cases be placed at about two months from the date of infection, the SECONDARY SYMPTOMS appear and resemble the symptoms of an ordinary fever in so far as they include rise of temperature and feverishness, loss of appetite, vague pains through the body, and a faint red rash seen best upon the front of the chest. The rash may also show other characters. The Wassermann test now gives a positive reaction. Other symptoms very often present at this stage include falling out of the hair, bloodlessness, the appearance of sores in the mouth and throat (mucous patches), headache with, occasionally, mental deterioration, and painful swellings on the bones due to periostitis. There is also general enlargement of the lymphatic glands. The duration of this stage is largely dependent upon the efficiency with which it is treated.

In untreated or inadequately treated cases manifestations of the TERTIARY STAGE develop after the lapse of some months or years. These consist in the growth, here and there throughout the body, of masses of granulation tissue known as ' gummata '. These gummata may appear as hard nodules in the skin, or form tumour-like masses in the muscles, or cause great thickening of bones, or they may develop in the brain and spinal cord, where their presence causes very serious symptoms. Those which lie beneath the skin or a mucous membrane may break down and form deep ulcers with characteristic thickened, sharply cut edges. These often leave rounded brownish scars when they heal. Gummata yield readily, as a rule, to appropriate treatment, and generally disappear speedily when this is secured.

866

Still later effects are apt to follow, such as disease of the arteries, leading to aneurysm (*see* ARTERIES, DISEASES OF, *and* ANEURYSM), to apoplexy, and to early mental failure (*see* MENTAL ILLNESS) ; also certain nervous diseases, of which locomotor ataxia and general paralysis are the chief.

The *inherited form* of syphilis, or *congenital syphilis* as it is usually known, may affect the child before birth, leading then as a rule to miscarriage, or to dead-birth of the child, if it be born at full time. Or it may show its first symptoms a few weeks after birth, the appearances then corresponding to the secondary manifestations of the acquired form. The child, apparently at first quite healthy, begins to waste, so that the skin appears loose and wrinkled. Eruptions develop and the breathing is of a ' snuffling ' character, in consequence of inflammation in the mucous membrane of the mouth and nose. Deafness is also a common result of inflammation in the delicate structures of the inner ear. On the other hand, no symptoms may appear till later in life, when the nose becomes sunken and broad at the bridge, and the eyes are dull as the result of inflammation affecting the cornea (keratitis) or iris (iritis). These changes often appear about the age of 12 or 14, causing dimness of vision. When the permanent teeth appear, the central incisors are frequently notched at the edge (Hutchinson's teeth).

Treatment.—Any person who suffers from this disease forms a source of infection to those around, and it is his duty to take precautions that he may not spread it. He should bear in mind the fact that, whilst the natural secretions of the body are harmless, the discharge from any sore or abraded surface is highly contagious. He should, if suffering from any sore about the lips or mouth, be most careful not to drink from any public drinking utensil, and he should never allow any one else to use his sponge or towel or to wear any of his clothes. He must remember, too, the fact that the disease is transmissible to his offspring so long as he shows any manifestation of its presence ; and in this relation it is usual for physicians to advise a person suffering from syphilis not to marry till at least a year has elapsed since any sign of the disease has been present, and then only if an energetic course of treatment has been carried out.

For generations, salts of mercury were the traditional drugs for the treatment of syphilis, given by mouth or by inunction, and later by intramuscular injection. Following the discovery by Ehrlich, in 1910, of the anti-syphilitic action of organic arsenical preparations, these became the essential part of the treatment of the condition, supplemented by bismuth salts. The first organic arsenical preparation introduced by Ehrlich was long known as '606' because it was the 606th preparation of the kind prepared by him in his search for an effective anti-syphilitic drug. Its official name was arsphenamine (*q.v.*), and later it was replaced by a less toxic derivative known as neoarsphenamine.

For nearly forty years the organic arsenical preparations, in one form or another, constituted the first line of attack on syphilis. During the last twenty years, however, they have been replaced gradually by penicillin which, used in the correct dosage, is now accepted as the drug of choice in the treatment of syphilis in all its stages.

The successful introduction of penicillin, however, has not altered the three essential bases of successful treatment : (1) treatment must be instituted as soon as possible after infection is acquired ; (2) a full course of treatment is essential in every case, no matter how mild the disease may appear to be; (3) periodic blood examinations, including the Wassermann or Kahn reactions (*q.v.*), must be carried out on every patient for at least two years after he or she has been apparently cured.

SYRINGE (σῦριγξ) is the name of an instrument for injecting liquids into the body. Syringes vary considerably in shape and size according to the purpose for which they are used. (For the method of using a hypodermic syringe, see HYPODERMIC.) For larger syringes the important points in construction are that the syringe should have a bulbous or cone-shaped nozzle, so that its point cannot inflict injury on the passage through which it is used ; also that the syringe should be capable of disinfection.

SYRINGOMYELIA (σῦριγξ, a pipe ; μυελός, the marrow) is a rare disease affecting the spinal cord, in which are found irregular cavities surrounded by an excessive amount of the connective tissue of the central nervous system. These cavities encroach upon the nerve tracts in the cord, producing especially loss of the sense of pain or of that for heat and cold in parts of the limbs, although the sensation of touch is retained. Another symptom sometimes present is wasting of certain muscles in the limbs. Changes affecting outlying parts like the fingers are also found. On account of their insensitiveness to pain, the fingers, for example, are often burnt or wounded, and troublesome ulcers, or losses of parts of the fingers, result. The condition of the spinal cord is probably present at birth, though the symptoms do not usually appear till the period of youth is reached. The disease is slowly progressive, and the treatment consists simply in the maintenance of general good health.

SYRUP, formed of a mixture of sugar and water, is a fluid frequently used for the administration of drugs. It is employed partly on account of its pleasant taste, and largely also because it retards changes in drugs which deteriorate on exposure to the air. The dose of most syrups is about a teaspoonful.

SYSTOLE (συστολή) means the contraction of the heart, and alternates with the resting phase, known as diastole. The two occupy respectively about one-third and two-thirds of the cycle of cardiac action.

T

TABES (*tabes*) means, literally, a wasting disease, and is an old name applied to various diseases, such as consumption, locomotor ataxia, tuberculosis accompanied by enlargement of glands, etc. At present the name *tabes dorsalis* is used for locomotor ataxia (*see* LOCOMOTOR ATAXIA) and *tabes mesenterica* is used for tuberculosis affecting the glands in the abdomen, these two diseases being, however, totally different in their nature and cause.

TABLET is the name given to a solid disc-like preparation made by compression and containing drugs mixed usually with sugar and other indifferent material. Tablets are widely used because of their convenience and accurate dosage. The word 'tabloid' indicates a proprietary preparation.

TACHE CÉRÉBRALE (Fr.) is a sign frequently observed in meningitis. The sign consists in the production of a bright-red line of congestion when the finger-nail is drawn across the patient's skin—for example, across his abdomen.

TACHYCARDIA (ταχύς, rapid ; καρδία, the heart) is the name applied to a disturbance of the heart's action which produces great acceleration of the pulse. (*See* HEART DISEASES.)

TACHYPNŒA means unusual quickness of breathing.

TÆNIA (*tænia*, a ribbon) means a tape-worm. (*See* PARASITES.)

TÆNICIDE is a drug which destroys tape-worms.

TAKADIASTASE (*see* DIASTASE).

TALC is a soft mineral consisting of magnesium silicate, which in powder gives an oily sensation to the tongue. It is much used as an ingredient of dusting powders.

TALIPES (*talus*, the ankle ; *pes*, the foot) is the technical name for club-foot.

868

TAMARIND is the preserved pulp of the fruit of *Tamarindus indica*, a West Indian tree. It contains a large amount of vegetable acid, is eaten as a confection, and has a laxative action.

TANNIN, or TANNIC ACID, is an uncrystallizable white or yellowish-white powder, which is very soluble in water or glycerin. It is a complicated organic acid with the empirical formula of $C_{76}H_{52}O_{46}$. It is extracted from oak-galls in large amount, but it is also present in almost all vegetable infusions. Tannic acid, when brought in contact with any mucous membrane, acts as an astringent and diminishes its secretion. It coagulates albuminous substances and thus hardens animal food with which it is mixed, and also leads to rapid clotting of blood with which it is brought in contact.

Uses.—Tannin is used largely as a styptic to apply directly to bleeding wounds or surfaces with which it can be brought in contact, as the mouth, interior of the stomach, or of the rectum, and since its action in coagulating albumin is powerful, it speedily causes a clot to form. It is applied to relaxed mucous membranes, employed, for instance, in lozenges when the throat is relaxed, or applied in ointment for piles. Glycerin of tannin is also a convenient method of applying this substance as an astringent, by painting, to the throat. Tannin is used to check diarrhœa, administered either in the form of some vegetable astringent infusion, or in a chemical combination which is not destroyed in the stomach, such as tannalbin, tannigen, or tanocol.

As tannin neutralizes many poisonous alkaloids, it is often administered as an antidote to vegetable poisons.

Many vegetable astringents owe their usefulness to the tannin they contain, as, for example, catechu, kino, and rhatany.

TAPE-WORM (*see* PARASITES).

TAPPING is the popular name for the withdrawal of dropsical fluid from the cavities or the subcutaneous tissues of the body. (*See* ASPIRATION.)

TAR, or PIX LIQUIDA, is a thick, dark, oily substance obtained by the destructive distillation of several species of pine-tree. It is slightly soluble in water, more readily so in alcohol, oils, and strong alkaline solutions. Other tars of similar physical and medicinal properties are obtained from other woods, as well as from coal, shale, and peat ; for example, birch-tar, well known for the aroma it imparts to Russian leather. Tar is a substance of very complex chemical composition, varying not only according to the source from which it is derived, but still more with the temperature at which it has been distilled. Generally speaking, wood-tar contains resin, creosote, and turpentine in considerable quantities, also benzol, carbolic acid, acetic acid, wood-spirit or methyl alcohol, methyl acetate, acetone, and wood-naphtha. The aniline dyes, many antipyretic bodies, saccharin, and various other medicinal substances and disinfectants are obtained indirectly from coal-tar.

Action.—In consequence of the numerous medicinally active bodies it contains, tar exerts many marked effects upon the body. By reason of the creosote, carbolic acid, and methyl alcohol that it contains, it possesses an antiseptic and preservative power. Certain of its ingredients are of an irritating nature, and tar therefore stimulates the action of any skin surface with which it is brought in contact, as well as the respiratory and other mucous membranes by which it is excreted after being taken internally.

Uses. — Bishop Berkeley in 1744 published his *Siris*, a treatise upon the virtues of tar-water, in which he extolled this substance as an almost universal remedy.

Externally, tar is one of the most efficient preservatives of animal and vegetable tissues that we possess. For its germicidal action and stimulating properties it is largely used in chronic skin diseases, particularly psoriasis and dry eczema. To this end it is employed most commonly in the form of tar ointment. An alcoholic extract known as coal tar solution is also used to cleanse areas of skin affected by the disease.

Internally, it is sometimes used in chronic bronchitis as an expectorant. It both checks excessive expectoration and renders coughing easier. For this purpose it is most commonly used in the form of *tar-water*, made by shaking up one part of tar with ten of water, allowing to settle, and decanting the clear liquid. This tar-water may be taken in wine-glassful doses. Syrup of tar is tar-water sweetened with sugar.

TARAXACUM, or DANDELION, is a very old remedy for dyspepsia associated with torpidity of the liver. The fresh milky juice of the flower-stalks is also sometimes used as a remedy for warts.

TARSUS (ταρσός) is the name applied to the region of the instep with its seven bones, the chief of which are the astragalus supporting the leg-bones and the calcaneum or heel-bone, the others being the scaphoid, cuboid, and three cuneiform bones.

TARTAR is a concretion that forms on the teeth near the margin of the gum, consisting chiefly of phosphate of lime deposited from the saliva. Mixed with this are food particles, and in it flourish numberless bacteria. It is important that it should be prevented from forming by regular brushing of the teeth, or removal after it has formed, because it gives rise to wasting of the gums and loosening of the teeth, as well as to dyspepsia, bad breath, and ill-health.

TARTAR EMETIC, TARTARATED ANTIMONY, or TARTRATE OF POTASSIUM AND ANTIMONY, is a white crystalline substance, which in minute doses acts as a diaphoretic and expectorant, in larger doses (1 to 2 grains (60 to 120 mg.)) as an emetic, and in very large quantities or in small quantities administered over a long period as an irritant poison. It must not be confounded with cream of tartar, another name for bi-tartrate of potassium, a harmless substance.

For the use of tartar emetic *see* ANTIMONY.

When this substance has been taken in poisonous amount, it produces a strong metallic taste and soreness of the mouth and throat, followed speedily by vomiting, pain in the abdomen, and purging, and at a later stage by great depression and collapse. The treatment of acute poisoning consists of encouraging vomiting by copious draughts of warm water, milk, flour in water, or other mucilaginous substances which have the further benefit of soothing the irritated mucous membranes. Tannin acts as a direct antidote to this poison by forming a harmless tannate of antimony, and therefore a strong infusion of tea, coffee, oak-bark, or other substance containing much tannin should next be prepared and administered.

TARTARIC ACID is almost identical with citric acid in appearance, chemical properties, and medicinal uses. Tartaric acid is obtained from grapes, whilst citric acid is contained in many fruits like the lemon, lime, and orange. (*See* CITRIC ACID.)

TASTE (*see* TONGUE).

TAXIS (τάξις, an arranging) is the name given to the method of pushing back, into the abdominal cavity, a loop of bowel which has passed through the wall in consequence of a rupture.

TEA (*see* COFFEE AND TEA).

TEARS (*see* EYE).

TEETH are hard organs developed in connection with the mucous membrane of the mouth and implanted in the jaw-bones. In man they serve for biting and grinding the food, as well as aiding in speech, whilst in many animals they are adapted as weapons.

Structure.—Each tooth is composed of four substances : dentine, enamel, cement or *crusta petrosa*, and pulp (Figs. 357, 358, 359).

DENTINE, or IVORY, makes up the greater part of each tooth, both in the crown, where it is covered by a layer of enamel, and in the fang, where it is surrounded by cement ; whilst in the centre of the tooth it is hollowed out to lodge the pulp. The dentine is composed of an intimate mixture of animal matter and earthy matter, chiefly lime salts, in the proportion of 72 per cent. of earthy, and 28 per cent. of animal. When examined in thin slices, the dentine is found to consist of a dense yellowish-

white substance pierced by minute tubes that run in a wavy manner from the pulp cavity, giving off branches as they go, to end under the enamel and cement. At their widest part, these tubes are about $\frac{1}{4500}$ inch (5·5 microns) across, and each lodges a fine thread-like fibril that runs out through the

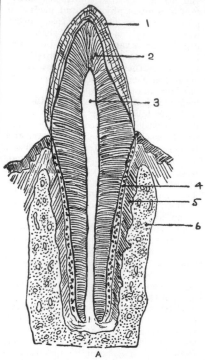

FIG. 357.—Diagram of vertical section through incisor tooth. 1, enamel ; 2, dentine ; 3, pulp cavity ; 4, cement ; 5, dental periosteum ; 6, bone of jaw. (From Hewer's *Histology*. Wm. Heinemann Ltd.)

tooth from the pulp. In some animals the dentine closely resembles bone in structure.

ENAMEL is a brilliant white layer forming a sort of cap to the tooth. It is thickest on the cutting or grinding surface and thins away towards the gum, disappearing at the neck of the tooth. It is the hardest tissue in the body and contains 96·5 per cent. of earthy matter, mainly phosphate of lime. It is composed of long rods or prisms placed side by side, with one end resting on the dentine, the other forming part of the surface of the tooth. When the tooth appears, there is a thin, horny layer, known as Nasmyth's membrane, or the skin of the tooth, covering

PULP is one of the most important parts of the tooth. In structure it is soft, consisting of connective tissue, the cells which form the dentine, the blood-

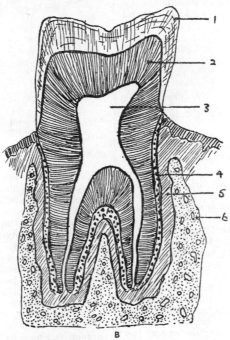

B

FIG. 358.—Diagram of vertical section through molar tooth. 1, enamel; 2, dentine; 3, pulp cavity; 4, cement; 5, dental periosteum; 6, bone of jaw. (From Hewer's *Histology*. Wm. Heinemann Ltd.)

the enamel, but this is speedily worn away when the teeth come into use. Indeed, in persons who live on very hard food the upper surface of the tooth may, in advanced years, be worn quite flat and the dentine exposed.

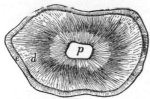

FIG. 359.—Transverse section across the crown of a tooth. *p*, Pulp cavity; *d*, dentine; *e*, enamel. Magnified by 6. (Turner's *Anatomy*.)

CEMENT, *crusta petrosa*, or tooth bone, is simply a thin layer of bone covering the dentine in the fang where enamel is absent.

vessels, and the nerve-fibres derived from the fifth cranial nerve, that enter by the tip of the fang and nourish the tooth. From its cells spring the fibrils that run into the tubes of the dentine, and upon this connection the sensitiveness of the tooth depends.

Arrangement and form.—Teeth are present in most mammals and nearly all have two sets—temporary or milk teeth in early life, and permanent or adult teeth developed later. In some animals, like the toothed whales, all the teeth are similar, but in most mammals and in man there are four different shapes of teeth, viz. incisors, canines or eye-teeth, premolars or bicuspids, and molars or grinders. Each tooth possesses a *crown* which projects into the cavity of the mouth and a root or *fang* which is embedded in a socket in the jaw-bone ; at the point where crown

871

and fang join, there is usually a constriction known as the *neck* (Fig. 360).

The shape of the teeth is adapted very much to the habits and character of their owner. Thus in rodents the incisor teeth are long, chisel-shaped, and

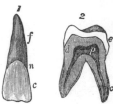

FIG. 360.—1, A human upper incisor tooth; *c*, crown; *n*, neck; *f*, fang. 2, A section through a molar tooth; *e*, cap of enamel; *c*, cement; *d*, dentine; *p*, pulp cavity. (Turner's *Anatomy*.)

keep on growing all the animal's life at the same rate as they are worn away by gnawing. In some animals, such as the dog and boar, the canine teeth are elongated so as to be dangerous offensive weapons. In carnivorous animals generally, the back teeth are not flat-topped grinders, but have a jagged cutting edge, so that the upper and lower teeth tear the prey like a pair of shears. In herbivorous animals the teeth are flat-topped for crushing herbs and fruit. The elephant has peculiarly modified incisors in the upper jaw (tusks), and molars which appear one at a time ; and in the narwhal, one of the canine teeth is developed into a long spear-like organ.

In man, the shape of the various teeth indicates that they are adapted for the mixed diet that custom has found most convenient. The adult set consists of two chisel-shaped incisors in each half jaw, one pointed canine tooth, two pre-molars, each with two cusps on the crown, and three flat-topped molars; thirty-two in all (Fig. 361). In the child the molars have no predecessors, so that the teeth are two incisors, one canine, and two pre-molars in each half-jaw, or twenty teeth in all.

Development.—The first stage in the formation of the teeth consists of a groove produced in the soft connective tissue underlying the mucous membrane of the gum by the down-growth of a ridge of cells derived from the epithelium on the surface of the mucous membrane. Here and there at the bottom of this

872

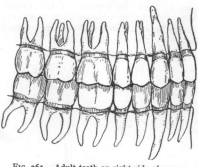

FIG. 361.—Adult teeth on right side of upper and lower jaw.

groove, papillæ of connective tissue appear, similar to those of the skin upon which hairs are developed. From each of these papillæ, ten in number in the lower jaw, and ten in the upper jaw, the pulp, dentine, and cement of a milk tooth are produced, while the caps of epithelial cells lying on the papillæ form their enamel. The neck of epithelial cells which joins the enamel of each tooth to the surface is next cut off and each tooth becomes surrounded by a sac. Finally, when the child reaches a certain age, each tooth begins to develop a fang, which, as it grows, pushes the tooth out of its sac and through the mucous membrane of the gum. The permanent teeth are developed in a similar manner, and their formation commences before the milk teeth are completely formed (Fig. 362).

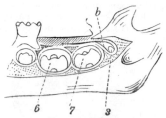

FIG. 362.—Lower jaw of a child about six years old. The hindmost milk tooth is shown with the permanent tooth ready to grow up into its place. 6, 7, 8, Permanent molars developing in their cavities. (Turner's *Anatomy*.)

When the time approaches for the milk tooth to be shed, its fang is gradually absorbed and the growing permanent tooth pushes out the crown. If this process of absorption does not take place properly, the new teeth are apt to come through crooked.

Time of appearance. — The teeth appear in a definite order and at definite periods, but there may be several months' delay without this being of any significance. The order for the milk teeth is as follows :

Middle incisors about 6th month
Lateral incisors ,, 9th ,,
First molars ,, 12th ,,
Canines (eye-teeth) ,, 18th ,,
Second molars ,, 24th ,,

As regards the permanent teeth, the first molars appear when the child is six years old, the incisors about seven and eight, the bicuspids about nine and ten, the canines about twelve, the second molars about thirteen, and the wisdom teeth frequently do not cut the gum till the age of twenty or twenty-five.

TEETH, DISEASES OF.—From the fact that the teeth are highly sensitive, that any interference with their use causes marked disturbance of digestion, and that good teeth form a highly æsthetic feature, disorders of these structures are of great importance. Only the most common disorders will be mentioned here ; some conditions affecting the gums are mentioned under MOUTH, DISEASES OF (*see also* GUMBOIL, *and* NOSE, DISEASES OF).

TEETHING, or the process of eruption of the teeth, may be accompanied by certain symptoms due to the irritation produced by the erupting tooth as it pushes through the resistant gum. The most common symptoms are irritability and loss of sleep. The infant may also refuse feeds, and this may lead to loss of weight. Occasionally with infants it is apt to be specially troublesome and to give rise to such general symptoms as diarrhœa, cough, skin eruptions, and even convulsions. The source of irritation is generally quite evident, as the child continually rubs the part of his gums beneath which the growing teeth are situated. These symptoms are often aggravated when parents have delayed the vaccination of the child so long that the child is troubled by the two sources of irritation at one time. Even adults possessed of a small lower jaw sometimes suffer great pain during the

28 *a*

cutting of the lower wisdom teeth, the reason being that there is not enough space left for the new tooth in the corner between the second molar and the vertical portion of the jaw.

Treatment.—In children, comfort is often obtained when the child is given some hard object, such as a bone or a rusk, against which it can press the gums. In the young adult it is occasionally necessary to extract the wisdom tooth or the tooth in front of it.

TOOTHACHE is a symptom of several affections of the teeth and neighbouring parts. The pain may vary from slight annoyance to great agony, and it often comes on at fairly regular intervals.

Causes.—Much the commonest cause of toothache is caries or decay affecting one or more teeth, particularly when the cavity in a tooth reaches near to, or exposes, the pulp. A gumboil, consisting of an inflammatory condition connected with the root of the tooth, which often proceeds to the formation of an abscess, is another cause of dull, throbbing pain (*see* GUMBOIL). The want of effective cleansing of the mouth, leading to the presence of acid secretion on the gums and between the teeth, which eats gradually into the enamel, is another cause of very annoying though less severe toothache. Certain general causes also, especially digestive disturbances, general debility, and pregnancy, render persons much more liable to suffer from toothache than when they are in ordinary health. Given some of these conditions, an attack of toothache is started by exposure to cold, a hot drink, or some sweet or acid article of food.

Treatment.—The careful avoidance of the above causes, and particularly the prevention of decay, will relieve persons who are liable to attacks of toothache (*see below*). During an attack of toothache affecting a whole row of teeth relief can often be obtained by rinsing the mouth with warm bicarbonate of soda solution. If a tooth with a large cavity be affected, the pain can generally be at once eased by filling the hole with a small piece of cotton-wool dipped in an essential oil, such as oil of cloves, or in a mixture of chloral and menthol, or of zinc oxide and oil of cloves. In any case, pain can be temporarily abolished by an injection, with a hypodermic syringe, of procaine into the space between the root of the tooth and the jaw. If the tooth be so far decayed as to be useless for chewing, it should be extracted. (*See also* NEURALGIA.)

CARIES OF THE TEETH is an extremely common condition among civilized peoples, and is most frequent in childhood and early adult life. A high percentage of all children attending school have at least one carious tooth, while many show advanced dental disease.

Causes.—The cause of caries is still unknown, although micro-organisms which flourish in the food particles and tartar on the teeth, and which produce acids that dissolve their lime salts, undoubtedly play a role in many cases.

In areas where the fluorine content of drinking water is 0·75 to 1 part per million, the incidence of caries in young children is much less than in areas where the fluorine content of the water is lower. In some persons, however, the teeth decay much more readily and more quickly than in others. This is in many cases due to bad quality of the teeth, in others due to overcrowding or a bad arrangement in the jaw which allows food particles to accumulate between the teeth and prevents opposing teeth from meeting one another properly in chewing. Decay rarely appears on free, smooth surfaces that are exposed to the rubbing of the lips and tongue and the scouring of the food ; nor among primitive peoples who subsist on coarse food that requires a great deal of chewing. It begins usually in some groove or pit in the enamel or between the teeth, and when the process has made a small opening through the enamel it may spread widely in the dentine, so that the first sign the person gets, apart from discoloration of the tooth, may be its sudden caving in during a meal. For this reason the teeth should be carefully inspected by a dentist once or twice every year.

Treatment.—In early life the provision of suitable and sufficient food is of great importance in forming strong teeth. The prevention of caries, though not always successful, may be greatly assisted by constant care of the teeth.

This consists mainly in cleansing the teeth with a soft brush after every meal and before retiring to bed at night. Any simple tooth-powder or tooth-paste should be used. Substances like charcoal, which impart a brilliant polish to the teeth, should not be often used, since they scratch the enamel and help to erode it. Persons taking medicines containing acids, like some of the iron preparations, should rinse the mouth out with water immediately after each dose.

The question of food is important, especially in children. The chewing of hard foods scours the teeth and stimulates the circulation in the jaw and gum. It is important, also, for the child, and for the pregnant mother, to have foods with calcium salts in them, such as milk, cheese, and green vegetables. For the calcium to be of use to the body, vitamin D is necessary, which is present in eggs, milk, butter, liver, and fish-liver oils. Equally important is the avoidance of too much confectionery. Children should never be allowed to eat sweets between meals or just before going to bed at night. They should be encouraged to eat as much fresh fruit as possible, especially apples.

Promising results have been reported from many countries, including Britain, U.S.A. and New Zealand, from the adding of very small amounts of fluorine (up to 1 part per million) to drinking water, in the prevention of caries. Indeed, these reports are so overwhelmingly convincing that there are good grounds for recommending that fluoridation should be adopted on a national scale. (*See* FLUORINE.)

IRREGULARITY OF THE TEETH, when the permanent set appears, may be due to defective development of the jaw, to a highly arched palate, or very often to slowness in casting off the temporary set. Slight irregularities disappear as the jaw grows, but if the deformity be great, much may be done to remedy it by judicious extraction of some teeth and by wearing an elastic apparatus in the mouth which maintains a steady pressure upon others.

LOOSENING OF THE TEETH may be due to accident, to wasting of the gums in consequence of the irritation set up by tartar on the teeth, or to the degenerative processes of advancing age. A tooth knocked out by injury may be washed and replaced in its socket, when it will usually again become firmly fixed, and the same is true of teeth which have been merely loosened. When the gums are receding and the teeth loosening in consequence of a deposit of tartar and inflamed gums, the tartar should be removed by a dentist and some antiseptic mouth-wash used.

INFLAMMATION OF THE GUMS or GINGIVITIS, may occur as an acute or as a chronic condition. The acute form, which is often part of a general-ized infection of the mouth, *i.e.* gingivo-stomatitis, occurs principally in children and young adults. The chronic form is more liable to occur at a later age, and is more common in women than in men. The gums are congested, often bleed either when food is chewed or when the teeth are brushed, and fre-quently show a certain amount of ulceration and purulent discharge at their edges. There is a considerable amount of tenderness leading to solid food being swallowed without proper chewing, and hence producing dyspep-sia. Tartar, at the same time, collects on the teeth and the inflammation in severe cases spreads to the palate and the interior of the cheek. Various bac-teria and spirochætes are found on the inflamed parts. At a later stage, the gums waste and their margins shrink away from the teeth, leaving the necks of these exposed. The person whose teeth show either of these changes generally suffers from indigestion and frequently from diarrhœa and may have a considerable degree of anæmia. There is, however, no discharge of pus from the sockets of the teeth, a condition which distinguishes this disease from pyorrhœa. The tartar should be care-fully scraped from the teeth and a mild antiseptic mouth-wash should be used daily. The gums should be regularly brushed with a soft tooth-brush and antiseptic aromatic tooth-paste, or, if too tender for this, should be wiped with tincture of myrrh on a pledget of cotton-wool. Daily massage of the gums with the fingers improves the circula-tion in the gums and their nutrition. Penicillin lozenges are frequently of value in the more acute stages.

PYORRHŒA ALVEOLARIS, or RIGG'S DISEASE, now usually known as PARODONTAL DISEASE, is a condition characterized in the final stages by the promotion of pockets of purulent material around the teeth and loosen-ing of the affected teeth. Although the precise cause is still a matter of debate, the general consensus of opinion is that the condition is the resultant of inadequate roughage in the diet and inadequate care of the teeth. These two factors lead to stagnation of food between the teeth and excessive forma-tion of tartar. This in turn leads to proliferation of bacteria. The prolonged contact of tartar, food débris, and organisms with the surface of the gum results in ulceration of the gum and chronic inflammatory changes.

The effect of the condition upon the general health is variable, but there is no doubt that the condition tends to become worse if the individual develops some other illness. It is also liable to worsen during pregnancy. Pain is not a feature of parodontal disease, but it often gives rise to an unpleasant taste in the mouth and an unpleasant odour of the breath (halitosis). A char-acteristic feature in the later stages is a tendency for the gums to bleed easily. It is often accompanied by dyspepsia.

Treatment.—At one time, almost wholesale extraction of teeth was per-formed in an attempt to eradicate the disease. It is now realized that much can be done to cure the condition by careful hygiene of the mouth, including regular removal of tartar and attention to prevent food stagnating between the teeth by use of wooden points. In more advanced cases the free edge of the gum which forms the outer wall of the pocket, is removed.

INFLAMMATION OF THE TOOTH FANG (periodontitis) is a condition which may be present in various degrees. There may be simple acute inflammation following a blow on the tooth ; less acute inflammation due to the presence of an imperfect stopping ; and in the severest form pyorrhœa.

Symptoms.—There are pain and in-flammation in a tooth or teeth without any obvious cause in the form of decay. Tenderness is present when the affected tooth is touched, and especially when the tooth is used for biting. The tooth usually appears to the individual to stand up a little higher than the other teeth and congestion is often visible in the neighbouring gum. Such a condition may come and go for a long time. If an X-ray photograph is taken of the teeth, a clear or rarefied area may be seen round the fang or as a small rounded area at its tip (*root abscess*). This condition may at times cure itself by the formation of an acute abscess, which distends the socket and bursts through the gum (*see* GUMBOIL), or it may remain for many years and ultimately develop into the condition of pyorrhœa.

Treatment.—In early stages, painting the gum with weak tincture of iodine or other counter-irritant is sufficient to abate inflammation, but the tooth may require to be extracted. In more advanced conditions a certain amount of extraction of the teeth is necessary. All decayed teeth which cannot be satisfactorily stopped, all roots which have lost their crown, and all teeth which are unopposed in the opposite jaw or which show a considerable amount of pyorrhœa should be extracted. The other teeth should be treated by the application of antiseptic lotions night and morning. Vaccines prepared from the tooth sockets are sometimes used, and the mouth should be kept clean by the use of an aromatic mouthwash. The general condition of the patient as regards dyspepsia and anæmia, often requires considerable attention also.

TELANGIECTASIS means an abnormal dilatation of arterioles and capillaries, forming sometimes a tumour or TELANGIOMA.

TEMPERAMENT (*temperamentum*) is a term that includes those vague general peculiarities of mind and body that render some persons more liable than others to be affected by particular diseases. (*See* CONSTITUTION, IDIOSYNCRASY, IMMUNITY, *and also* ALCOHOLISM, HYSTERIA, MENTAL ILLNESS, NEURASTHENIA.)

TEMPERATURE (*temperatura*) of the body is a subject of great importance and will be dealt with here. For the proper temperature of rooms, baths,

876

etc., see NURSING; BATHS; COLD, USES OF.

Animals are generally divided as regards their temperature into two classes, viz. *cold-blooded animals*, including reptiles, amphibians, fishes, and invertebrates generally, whose temperature varies to a great extent according to that of the surrounding medium ; and *warm-blooded animals*, including mammals and birds, whose temperature remains almost constant, no matter how the surrounding temperature falls or rises. In warm-blooded animals, this constancy of body temperature is effected by a perpetual balancing of the various forces which produce heat and give off heat. The chief heat producer in the body is the oxidizing action that takes place on muscular contraction, and the chief cooling agents are the skin and lungs, which act by the exposure of the blood circulating in them to the air, and by the evaporation of moisture from their surfaces. The temperature of different warm-blooded animals varies considerably, being high in birds, viz. about 105° to 107° F. (40·5° to 41·7° C.), whilst in man it is somewhere between 98° and 99° F. (36·7° and 37·2° C.). It varies in different persons, but is generally stated at about 98·4° F., or 37° C., in man. Even in a given healthy individual the temperature is constantly changing, and may vary by 1° or 2° F. in the day, being lowest in the early morning and highest in the evening. The chief reason for this change is to be found probably in the variations as regards activity at different periods of the day. The temperature also varies in different parts of the body, that of the skin being about half a degree lower than that taken within the hollow organs of the body ; and in stout people this difference between the surface and the interior is still more marked. In parts exposed to cold or provided with a feeble blood supply, such as paralysed limbs, the temperature may sink very low.

Temperature in disease.—The maintenance of a nearly equal temperature is the result of a constant process of balancing between heat-production and heat-loss, controlled probably by a special centre in the nervous system. In disease, one or other of these processes may be impaired or the controlling mechanism may be thrown completely out of gear. The general temperature may rise as high as 110° F. (43·3° C.), or sink to 90° (32·2° C.) for a time ; but the risk to life is great when it passes above 106° F. (41° C.) or below 95° F. (35° C.).

Fall of temperature may be due to many causes. Thus it generally accompanies great loss of blood, starvation, and the collapsed condition which sometimes results from severe attacks of fever, peritonitis, and other devitalizing acute diseases. Certain chronic diseases are generally accompanied by a subnormal temperature ; of these, myxœdema, diabetes, and Bright's disease are the most outstanding.

Rise of temperature is a characteristic of acute diseases, and of diseases due to micro-organisms, the poisonous products of which lead to increased waste of the tissues. Injuries to the nervous system, even unpleasant sensations in children and nervous people, may have a similar effect. In persons dying in a feverish condition, the temperature often rises very high immediately before death, owing probably to failure of the circulation and other conditions which diminish the body heat. Rapid rise of temperature in such a case is therefore a very ominous sign.

Many diseases have a characteristic course of temperature, so that in hospital a glance at the temperature chart is often sufficient to acquaint a physician with the disease from which the patient is suffering. Thus advanced consumption, pneumonia, enteric fever, measles, and malaria show, as a rule, quite recognizable temperature records. Characteristic temperature charts are given under the headings of these diseases.

High temperature in some diseases is a much less serious feature than in others. Thus in enteric fever or pneumonia 105° F. (40·5° C.) is an ordinary temperature, whilst in rheumatic fever and diphtheria the temperature generally ranges between 101° and 103° F. (38·3° and 39·5° C.), so that in these diseases a temperature of 104° F. (40° C.) gives cause for anxiety.

In most diseases the temperature gradually abates as the patient recovers, but others, for example pneumonia and typhus fever, end rapidly by a *crisis* in

which the temperature falls, perspiration breaks out, the pulse becomes slower, and the breathing quieter. The reason for the sudden change lies probably in the fact that in favourable cases, after the disease has lasted a certain time, the resisting power of the body becomes able fully to neutralize the poisons produced by the organisms of the disease. This crisis is often preceded by an increase of all the symptoms, including an epicritical rise of temperature.

Record of temperature. — Temperature is generally measured by a thermometer, those intended for clinical use

FIG. 363.—Clinical thermometer.

possessing a long, narrow bulb, an index registering from 95° to 110° F., and being so made that the column of mercury does not fall back into the bulb till it is shaken down.

There are two scales in common use, the Fahrenheit scale, generally employed in Great Britain and in the United States, and the Centigrade or Celsius scale, used on the Continent of Europe. The difference consists in this, that in the Centigrade scale the freezing-point of water is marked 0° and the boiling-point 100°, while in the Fahrenheit scale these are 32° and 212° respectively. Accordingly 100 divisions on the Centigrade scale are equivalent to 180 divisions on the Fahrenheit scale, and 1 degree C. equals 1·8 degrees F. To convert from degrees F. to degrees C. the following formula may be used :

$$n° \text{ Fahr.} = [(n-32) \times \tfrac{5}{9}] \text{ C.,}$$

and to convert from degrees C. to degrees F. the following :

$$n° \text{ C.} = [(n \times \tfrac{9}{5}) + 32] \text{ Fahr.}$$

For examples :

$$98·6° \text{ Fahr.} = [(98·6 - 32) \times \tfrac{5}{9}] = 66·6 \times \tfrac{5}{9}$$
$$= 37° \text{ C.}$$

$$38° \text{ C.} = [(38 \times \tfrac{9}{5}) + 32] = 68·4 + 32$$
$$= 100·4° \text{ Fahr.}$$

The Réaumur scale, in which the freezing-point is 0° and the boiling-point 80°, is also used in some countries, *e.g.* France, though not for scientific purposes.

As to the part of the body where temperature is taken, the mouth is preferable, the bulb of the thermometer

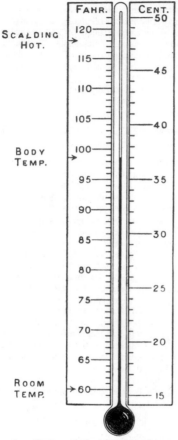

FIG. 364.—Thermometer scale ranging from room temperature to that of water used for douches, etc., and showing the corresponding points upon Fahrenheit and Centigrade scales.

being placed beneath the tongue. A more correct reading is thus obtained in a shorter time. The instrument must be carefully washed with cold water before use, so that it does not convey infection, and the patient must be directed to keep the mouth shut and breathe through the nose. It is essential to ensure that the patient has not just had a hot drink. The thermometer must be kept in the mouth for

at least three minutes. After use the thermometer must be thoroughly rinsed under running cold water and the mercury shaken down to below 96° F. When taken in the armpit the skin should be wiped dry, the bulb of the thermometer placed as high as possible, and the arm tightly folded across the chest. To obtain a correct reading, it is necessary to leave the thermometer in place for at least 5 minutes, because the skin surfaces do not at once represent the internal temperature of the body. Occasionally, and especially in infectious cases, the temperature is

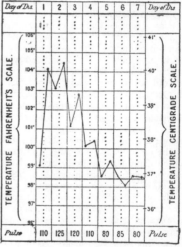

FIG. 365.—Temperature chart from a case of scarlatina, showing the method of registering the temperature.

taken by inserting the thermometer bulb about 2 inches (5 cm.) into the rectum, a method which gives the most correct result of all, and is the most satisfactory in infants.

To keep a record, a piece of paper ruled with vertical lines to represent the periods at which the temperature is taken, and with horizontal lines corresponding to degrees, is used. A large dot is marked in the proper place each time the temperature is taken and the successive dots are afterwards joined by straight lines.

Treatment of high temperature is mentioned under ANTIPYRETICS; COLD, USES OF; and FEVER.

TEMPLE (*tempus*) is the name given to the side of the head above the line between the eye and ear. The term temporal is applied to the muscles, nerves, artery, etc., of this region. The hair usually begins to turn grey first at the temples.

TENDERNESS is the term usually applied in medical nomenclature to pain experienced when a diseased part is handled, the term ' pain ' being reserved for unpleasant sensations felt apart from any manipulation.

TENDON (τένων), SINEW, or LEADER is the cord that attaches the end of a muscle to the bone or other structure upon which the muscle acts when it contracts. Tendons are composed of bundles of white fibrous tissue arranged in a very dense manner, and are of great strength. Some are rounded, some flattened bands, whilst others are very short, the muscle-fibres being attached almost directly to the bone. Most tendons are surrounded by sheaths lined with membrane similar to the synovial membrane lining joint-cavities. In this sheath the tendon glides smoothly over surrounding parts. The fibres of a tendon pass into the substance of the bone and blend with the fibres composing it. One of the largest tendons in the body is the tendo Achilles, which attaches the muscle of the calf to the calcaneum or heel-bone.

TENDOVAGINITIS means inflammation of a tendon and of the sheath enveloping it.

TENESMUS (τεινεσμός) is a term applied to a symptom of disease affecting the lower part of the large intestine, such as dysentery, piles, or tumour. It consists of a constant sense of weight about the lower bowel and desire to go to stool, coupled with straining at stool and the passage of little but mucus and perhaps some blood.

TENNIS ELBOW (*see* ELBOW).

TENO- (τένων, tendon) is a prefix denoting some relation to a tendon.

TENOSYNOVITIS, or TENOSITIS, means inflammation of a tendon.

TENOTOMY (τένων, a tendon ; τέμνω, I cut) means an operation in which one or more tendons are divided, usually with the object of remedying some deformity. The operation is, in general, a slight one.

TENTORIUM (*tentorium*, tent) is the name of a wide process of dura mater forming a partition between the cerebrum and cerebellum and supporting the former.

TENTS (*tendo*, I stretch) are instruments used for dilating narrow openings. The tent consists of some substance, like sea-tangle or sponge, which shrivels up when dried, and expands powerfully as it absorbs mixture. It is introduced dry into the opening it is to dilate, and expands in the course of some hours without producing pain.

TERATOGENESIS is the production of physical defects in the fœtus. A teratogenic drug is a drug which, when administered to a pregnant mother, induces some physical defect in her unborn child. The term has come into common usage since the thalidomide disaster.

Thalidomide was a most effective non-barbiturate hypnotic which had passed the most stringent tests before being released for general use. In spite of this it produced a large number of congenital defects, especially of the limbs, in children born to mothers who had taken the drug while pregnant. As soon as this was discovered the drug was withdrawn from use.

Subsequently the Government set up a Committee of Drug Safety to try and ensure that there was no recurrence of such a distressing episode with subsequent drugs.

Even the most stringent precautions, however, cannot ensure the complete elimination of this risk. Fortunately the risk is a remote one, but it is now realized that no drug should be given to a pregnant woman, particularly during the first few months of pregnancy unless it is absolutely essential for her health or that of her unborn child.

TERATOMA is the term applied to a tumour that consists of partially developed embryonic tissues. The most common sites of this tumour are the ovary and the testicle.

TEREBENE is a clear, colourless fluid, with an odour like fresh pine sawdust, prepared by the action of sulphuric acid upon turpentine. It is used as an expectorant in bronchitis.

TEREBINTHINA is the Latin name for turpentine.

TERRAMYCIN (*see* OXYTETRA-CYCLINE.)

TERTIAN FEVER (*tertianus*, belonging to the third day) is the name applied to that type of malaria in which the ague-fit reappears every other day. (*See* MALARIA.)

TESTICLE.—The testes or testicles are the two male sexual glands. Each is developed in the corresponding loin, but before birth they descend through openings in the lower part of the front of the abdomen into a fold or pouch of skin known as the scrotum. This fold is strengthened by a layer of muscle fibres and fibrous tissues, and within it each testicle possesses a separate covering known as the tunica vaginalis. This tunic is a double layer of serous membrane similar in structure to the peritoneum or pleura, and it is derived from the peritoneum while the testicle is still within the abdomen. Occasionally, as the result of defective development, a more or less open channel of communication is left between the peritoneum and tunica vaginalis, and down this channel a hernia is liable to form in childhood or later. Throughout life, the openings in the abdominal wall remain, but these inguinal canals should be just large enough to allow the passage of the two spermatic cords, each of which is composed of the vas deferens or duct of the testicle, together with the blood-vessels, nerves, and lymphatics proceeding to the gland. Within the tunica vaginalis lies a dense fibrous coat known as the tunica albuginea, which affords protection to the gland. On microscopic examination, each testicle is found to consist of a series of minute tubes from eight hundred to one thousand in number, supported by fibrous tissue in which the nerves and blood-vessels run, and lined by cells from which the spermatozoa are formed.

880

These tubes communicate with one another near the centre of the testicle, and are connected by a much convoluted tube, the epididymis, with the vas deferens, which enters the abdomen and passes on to the base of the bladder. This duct, after joining a reservoir known as the vesicula seminalis, opens, close to the duct from the other side of the body, into that part of the urethra which is surrounded by the prostate gland. Owing to the convolutions of these ducts leading from the testicles to the urethra, and their indirect route, the passage from testicle to urethra is over twenty feet in length. In addition to producing spermatozoa, the testicle also forms an internal secretion which is responsible for the development of male characteristics. This hormone has been isolated and is known as testosterone.

TESTICLE, DISEASES OF. — The pouch of skin in which the testicles lie is liable to various general skin diseases, but particularly to eczema, which is in many cases very irritable and very difficult of cure. Cancer of the skin in this region seems to be specially common among chimney-sweeps and cotton spinners, the result, it is supposed, of some irritating substance. Hernia, which in some cases passes into the scrotum, is treated under a special heading. Sometimes, owing to defective development, the testicles are retained within the abdomen.

HYDROCELE is a local dropsy affecting one tunica vaginalis, and distending that side of the scrotum with fluid. (*See* HYDROCELE.)

VARICOCELE is a condition in which the veins of the spermatic cord, especially on the left side, become unusually numerous and distended, the causes being much the same as those of varicose veins in other parts. The chief symptom is a dragging sensation in the testicle, which in some cases becomes at times very painful. This symptom is specially marked in warm weather and after exertion, the mass of veins at such a time becoming very distinct and resembling a ' bag of worms ', though they empty quickly when the person lies down. Cold sponging of the part, careful regulation of the bowels, and the support of a suspensory net bandage afford all the treatment that is necessary in most cases ; but an operation may sometimes be advisable.

INFLAMMATION of an acute type (orchitis) may arise in persons suffering from cystitis, stone in the bladder, and various forms of inflammation in the urinary organs, the most common cause of all being gonorrhœa. It may follow also upon some cases of mumps. The symptoms are intense pain and swelling with redness of the skin over the affected testicle ; and the usual treatment consists of rest in bed, the application of opium fomentations, suppositories of morphine, and administration of a saline purgative. In some cases the condition goes on to the formation of an abscess which bursts through the skin with immediate relief of pain. The condition is then treated as an abscess elsewhere.

TUBERCULOSIS occurs in the testicle occasionally, especially when some other organ, such as the bladder, is already the seat of the disease. It causes practically no pain, and is therefore often far advanced before it attracts attention. In cases where no other organ is affected, the testicle is usually removed in order to prevent the spread of the disease to other parts of the body.

INJURIES of the testicles are relatively rare. A severe blow may lead to shock and symptoms of severe collapse for a time, and may cause an effusion of blood into the tunica vaginalis. These symptoms are usually relieved by rest in bed.

TEST MEAL is a term originally applied to a meal given for the purpose of testing the digestive powers. At the present day the original gruel meal has been replaced by the injection of histamine (*q.v.*), which is a powerful stimulator of gastric juice. In this *histamine test meal*, as it is known, samples of the fasting gastric juice are withdrawn through a Ryle's tube before and after a subcutaneous injection of histamine. A modification of this test is the *augmented histamine test meal*, in which a larger dose of histamine is injected preceded by a dose of an antihistamine drug. This allows a larger dose of histamine to be given because the antihistamine counteracts its unpleasant effects, and the response to the larger dose provides a more accurate picture of the degree of acidity of the gastric juice.

Tubeless test meals, so-called because they do not involve the passage of a stomach tube, have been evolved. These depend upon the dissociation of a cation-exchange resin (*see* ION EXCHANGE RESINS) by the hydrochloric acid in the gastric juice. The cation is then absorbed and the amount excreted in the urine is measured. The results, however, are not particularly reliable, and these tests are therefore only used when it is difficult or impossible to pass a stomach tube.

TESTOSTERONE is the name given to the male sex hormone secreted by the testes. It has also been prepared synthetically and has a formula $C_{19}H_{28}O_2$. In true eunuchoid conditions it has the power of restoring male sexual characteristics.

TEST-TUBE is a tube of thin glass closed at one end, which is used for observing chemical reactions or for bacterial culture.

TETANUS ($\tau\acute{\epsilon}\tau\alpha\nu o\varsigma$), or LOCKJAW, is a disorder of the nervous system, consisting in a greatly increased excitability of the spinal cord and manifesting itself by painful and lengthened spasm of the voluntary muscles throughout the body. The disease was well known in former wars, and Hippocrates (400 B.C.) refers to its rapidly fatal character.

Causes.—The onset of the disease generally follows a wound, especially a deeply punctured, lacerated, or gunshot wound, usually appearing some 4 or 5 days after the wound has been inflicted, although it may be delayed for 3 or 4 weeks, by which time the wound is likely to be completely healed up. The presence in a wound of some foreign body, such as a splinter of wood or a portion of a bullet, seems to favour the onset of tetanus.

The direct cause of tetanus was discovered in 1889 by Kitasato, a Japanese observer, to be a bacillus—*Clostridium tetani*. This organism has a characteristic appearance, being long and bearing often at one end a large spore which gives to it a ' drumstick ' outline (Plate VIII). It inhabits earth and dust, living especially a little distance below the surface in places where the manure of horses and cattle is collected. Hence it is found especially in the neighbourhood of stables, and is liable to infect wounds soiled with earth. The bacillus develops a poison or toxin in the wound, and this, being absorbed, appears to find its way up the motor nerves to the spinal cord, which it renders excessively sensitive, so that its cells are excited by mild stimuli that under ordinary conditions would produce no reaction. After death, patients who have died of tetanus show very few lesions except congestion of the brain and spinal cord and degenerative changes in the cells of the latter.

In England and Wales, in 1966, there were 18 deaths assigned to tetanus. Another 9 deaths were complicated by tetanus assigned to injury.

Symptoms.—There is an incubation period of 2 to 14 days following the wound. Cases which develop very seriously have as a rule a short incubation period, and, if the incubation period is delayed for ten days or more, the chances are that the attack of tetanus will not be fatal. The first signs of the disease usually show themselves as stiffness in the muscles near the wound, followed later, no matter where the wound is situated, by stiffness about the muscles of the jaw, causing difficulty in opening the mouth, which soon increases to *lockjaw* or trismus. This is accompanied by spasm in neighbouring muscles, and the drawn features and exposed teeth give to the countenance the peculiar expression known as *risus sardonicus*. The rigidity extends to the muscles of the neck, back, chest, abdomen, and extremities, and the body frequently assumes a bent attitude, either backward (*opisthotonos*), forward (*emprosthotonos*), or laterally (*pleurosthotonos*). This general muscular rigidity, which at first is not constant but occasionally undergoes relaxation, is accompanied by frequently recurring convulsive seizures, which are readily excited by the slightest irritation, such as from a draught of cool air, a bright light, the closing of a door, etc. In such attacks there is great suffering and the expression of the face is indicative of agony. The function of respiration may be seriously involved and asphyxia threaten or actually take place. The

temperature of the body sometimes rises to a high degree, and copious perspiration is also a constant symptom. These acute symptoms may subside after a few days and the patient gradually recover. More frequently the symptoms increase in severity and death ensues either by asphyxia from prolonged spasm of the respiratory muscles, or exhaustion consequent on the violence of the symptoms, together with the absence of sleep. Throughout the whole course of the disease the mind is clear, and the patient waits with anxiety for the next convulsive attack. In milder cases the symptoms are less severe, the course more chronic, and recoveries more common. Tetanus sometimes occurs in new-born children, showing itself within a week of birth by obvious difficulty in the acts of sucking and swallowing ; by the supervention of lockjaw, together with prolonged contraction of the muscles of the limbs and body, accompanied by convulsive seizures. *Local cases* of tetanus occur in which the muscles of a limb in the neighbourhood of the wound show spasms, but these do not become general, or they pass off after appearing to a slight extent. Such cases often show stiffness for several months.

The symptoms of strychnine poisoning bear a strong resemblance to those of tetanus, but in the former case they are more acute, less prolonged than the spasms of tetanus, come on after something has been swallowed, and end either in death or in recovery within a few hours. Hydrophobia, too, resembles tetanus.

Prevention.—The outlook in tetanus has been entirely altered by the introduction of tetanus antitoxin and of tetanus toxoid. The latter provides effective protection against the disease, as was amply demonstrated during the 1939–45 War, when its use reduced the incidence of the disease among the troops to a very low level. Although the disease is not very common among civilians in this country, many authorities recommend that all children should be immunized against the disease. Certainly, all children living in areas such as East Anglia, where there is a relatively high incidence, should be protected in this way.

Whilst antitoxin is of primary value

from the point of view of treatment, it is of great prophylactic value if given immediately after an individual has received a wound which may be contaminated with the tetanus organism.

Treatment.—Tetanus tends especially to follow wounds infected by stable refuse, by street dust, or by the deeper soil thrown up by shells on the battlefield. In all such cases, 1500 international units of antitoxin must be injected as soon as possible, unless it is definitely known that the individual has been completely immunized by a previous course of toxoid.

If symptoms of tetanus appear, much larger doses are given into the muscles near the wound, the nerve trunks, and especially into the spinal canal.

Various drugs, which diminish the reflex excitability of the spinal cord and relax spasm, help in relieving the patient's sufferings and in carrying him over the period during which the toxin of the disease is being excreted. These include thiopentone, barbiturates, paraldehyde, and one of the muscle - relaxant drugs. Quietness around the patient, a darkened room, and the absence of all noise and excitement are of great importance in preventing convulsions, and the patient must receive fluid nourishment of a stimulating character.

TETANY (Fr. *tétanie*, from τέτανος) is a condition characterized by spasm of muscle usually caused by a fall in the ionic calcium of the blood. This fall in ionic calcium results in hyperexcitability of the muscles, which are thus liable to go into spasm on the slightest stimulus. This is well demonstrated in two of the classical signs of the disease : *Chvostek's sign*, in which the muscles of the face contract when the cheek is tapped over the facial nerve as it emerges on the cheek ; *Erb's sign*, in which muscles go into spasm in response to an electrical stimulus which normally causes only a contraction of the muscle. Tetany is most common in infants, in whom it may arise as a result of rickets, excessive vomiting, or certain forms of nephritis. It may also be due to lack of the active principle of the parathyroid glands. Overbreathing may

also cause it. Treatment consists of the administration of calcium salts, and in severe cases this is done by giving calcium gluconate intravenously or intramuscularly. Parathormone, the active principle of the parathyroid glands, is given in cases in which the tetany is due to deficiency of this principle.

TETRACYCLINES are a group of antibiotics which include chlortetracycline, oxytetracycline, tetracycline, demethylchlortetracycline, methacycline and lymecycline. Chlortetracycline, which is derived from *Streptomyces aureofaciens*, was the first to be discovered, followed by oxytetracycline which is derived from *Streptomyces rimosus*. Subsequently it was discovered that the active constituent of both these antibiotics was tetracycline, which can be prepared on a large scale by the catalytic hydrogenation of chlortetracycline. Methacycline and lymecycline are subsequently discovered derivatives.

From the point of view of antibacterial activity, all six preparations are virtually identical, being active against both Gram-negative and Grampositive bacteria, as well as certain rickettsiae (*q.v.*) and some of the larger viruses, including those causing Q fever, typhus, psittacosis, virus pneumonia and lymphogranuloma inguinale.

It is this wide range of activity, which has given them the name of broad-spectrum antibiotics, combined with the fact that they are given by mouth, that has made them such a useful contribution to the treatment of infective diseases.

TETRALOGY OF FALLOT is the most common form of cyanotic congenital heart disease. The tetralogy consists of : (*a*) stenosis of the pulmonary valve ; (*b*) a defect in the septum separating the two ventricles ; (*c*) the aorta over-rides both ventricles ; (*d*) marked hypertrophy of the right ventricle.

TETRAMINE, which is the ' approved ' name for triethylene melamine, is a preparation which is of value in the treatment of certain forms of malignant disease, including Hodgkin's disease and chronic leukæmia.

TETTER is a vague name for skin diseases of the eczema type.

THALAMENCEPHALON, also known as the INTERBRAIN or TWEENBRAIN, is the part of the brain lying below the cerebrum, around the third ventricle and containing the optic tracts, the grey matter of the optic thalami, the infundibulum, pineal body, and other parts.

THALASSÆMIA, also known as Cooley's anæmia, is a condition characterized by severe anæmia, due to the individual having an abnormal form of hæmoglobin in his blood.

THEINE is the alkaloidal principle which gives to tea its stimulating properties. (*See* CAFFEINE.)

THENAR EMINENCE (θέναρ) is the name given to the projecting mass at the base of the thumb.

THEOBROMINE is the alkaloidal principle upon which the stimulating action of cocoa and chocolate depends. (*See* CHOCOLATE *and* DIURETIN.)

THEOPHYLLINE is an alkaloid similar to theobromine and occurs in small amounts in tea. It is a diuretic, usually administered in the form of theophylline and sodium acetate or of theophylline with ethylenediamine (aminophylline).

THERAPEUTICS (θεραπευτική) is the general name applied to the science and art of healing.

THERAPY (θεραπεία), means the treatment of disease.

THERIAC (θηριακή, an antidote to bites) means an antidote or substance given to neutralize poison. The name was specially given to Venice treacle, a celebrated mixture of 64 drugs prescribed in olden times as an antidote for poisons and a preventative of disease.

THERMO- (θέρμη, heat) is a prefix implying some relation to heat.

THERMOMETER SCALES (*see* TEMPERATURE).

THERMOPHORE (θέρμη, heat; φέρω, I bear) is the name applied to a box or rubber bag filled with a mixture of glue, acetate of soda, chloride of soda, and sulphate of calcium. When it is placed in hot water for some time it has the property of retaining its heat for several hours and is used as a warm application.

THIACETAZONE is the ' approved ' name for 4-acetamidobenzaldehyde thiosemicarbazone. This substance was introduced into medicine by Domagk, the discoverer of the original sulphonamide, for the treatment of tuberculosis. It is also proving of value in the treatment of leprosy. It is administered by mouth.

THIAMBUTOSINE is a diphenyl-thio-urea that is proving of value in the treatment of patients with leprosy who are intolerant of, or hypersensitive to, dapsone.

THIAMINE is another name for vitamin B_1 (*see under* VITAMINS).

THIERSCH'S GRAFT is the term given to a method of skin grafting in which strips of skin are shaved from a normal area and placed on the abnormal area to be grafted.

THIGH is the portion of the lower limb above the knee. The thigh is supported by the femur or thigh-bone, the longest and strongest bone in the body. This fits by a rounded head at its upper end into the acetabulum, a hollow at the side of the pelvis, and at the lower end two large rounded condyles or knuckles rest upon the head of the tibia, and, along with the patella or knee-cap, form the knee-joint. A large four-headed muscle, the quadriceps, forms most of the fleshy mass on the front and sides of the thigh and serves to straighten the leg in walking and to maintain the erect posture of the body in standing. At the back of the thigh, lie the hamstring muscles ; and on the inner side the adductor muscles, attached above to the pelvis and below to the femur, pull the lower limb inwards. The large femoral vessels emerge from the abdomen in the middle of the groin, the vein lying to the inner side of the artery. These pass downwards with an inclination inwards deeply placed between the muscles, and at the knee they lie behind the joint. The large internal saphenous vein lies near the surface and can be seen towards the inner side of the thigh passing up to the groin, where it joins the femoral vein. The anterior crural nerve accompanies the large vessels and controls the muscles on the front and inner side of the thigh ; while the great sciatic nerve, about the thickness of a lead pencil, lies close to the back of the femur and supplies the muscles at the back of the thigh and muscles below the knee. Deep wounds on the inner side of the thigh are dangerous by reason of the risk of damage to the large vessels. Pain in the back of the thigh is often due to inflammation of the sciatic nerve (*see* NEURALGIA). The veins on the inner side of the thigh are specially liable to become dilated (*see* VARICOSE VEINS).

THIOPENTONE SODIUM is the *British Pharmacopœia* name for ethyl-(1-methylbutyl)-thiobarbituric acid, a commonly used intravenous anæsthetic.

THIOSULPHATE OF SODIUM, or sodium hyposulphite, is much used in photography as a solvent of silver, and in medicine is administered by intravenous or intramuscular injection in doses of 5 to 20 grains (300 to 1,200 mg.) as an antidote in cases of over-dosage with preparations of arsenic, mercury, bismuth, or gold.

THIOTEPA is one of the alkylating agents that is proving of value in the treatment of certain forms of malignant disease, including cancer of the breast and ovary.

THIOURACIL (*see* THIOUREA).

THIOUREA, the chemical formula of which is CH_4N_2S, has the property of interfering with the synthesis of thyroxine in the thyroid gland. It was therefore introduced, with success, for the treatment of Graves' disease, or thyrotoxicosis. Subsequently it was found that more satisfactory results were obtained from the use of a derivative, THIOURACIL, and this is now widely used for the treatment of thyrotoxicosis, either as the methyl or the propyl salt. The use of thiouracil is not without its risks, but these are negligible provided the drug is only used under medical supervision. Thiouracil is used in one of two ways : (*a*) to control thyrotoxicosis, and for this purpose it usually needs to be taken

for long periods ; (*b*) as a pre-operative measure in cases in which it has been decided that operation is necessary.

THIRST, like appetite, is an instinctive craving for something necessary to the continuance of bodily activity. The sensation of thirst is generally referred to the back of the throat, because, when there is a deficiency of water in the system, the throat and mouth especially become parched by evaporation of moisture from their surface. The mere swallowing of water, however, is not sufficient to abolish thirst, as appears in cases where a fistulous opening into the gullet exists, through which the water escapes. Thirst is increased by heat, and is a constant symptom of fever ; it is also present in diseases which remove a considerable amount of fluid from the system, such as diarrhœa, chronic Bright's disease, diabetes, and after great loss of blood by hæmorrhage. A desire for water is also a feature of many conditions associated with great exhaustion.

THORACIC DUCT is the large lymph-vessel which collects the contents of the lymphatics proceeding from the lower limbs, the abdomen, the left arm, and left side of the chest, neck, and head. It is about the size of a goose quill, is provided with very numerous valves, and opens into the veins at the left side of the neck. (*See* GLANDS *and* LYMPHATICS.)

THORACOCENTESIS (θώραξ, the chest ; κέντησις, a pricking) means the withdrawal of fluid from the pleural cavity. (*See* ASPIRATION.)

THORACOPLASTY is the term applied to the operation of removing a varying number of ribs so that the lung, lying adjacent to the spaces left, collapses. This form of 'collapse therapy' is used for pulmonary tuberculosis and bronchiectasis, when other methods of treatment fail.

THORAX (θώραξ) is another name for the chest.

THORN-APPLE is a popular name for stramonium. (*See* STRAMONIUM.)

THREAD-WORM (*see* PARASITES).

THREE-DAY FEVER, also known as PHLEBOTOMUS FEVER, SANDFLY FEVER, and PAPPATACI FEVER, is a short, sharp fever occurring in the eastern Mediterranean and other places, due to a virus conveyed by the bite of a small hairy midge (*Phlebotomus papatasii*). The incubation period is two to seven days.

Symptoms. — There are headache, feverishness, general sensations like those of influenza, flushed face and bloodshot eyes, but no signs of catarrh. As the name implies, the fever passes off in three days, but the patient may take some time to convalesce.

Treatment.—As there is no specific remedy, prophylaxis is important. This consists of the spraying of rooms with D.D.T. or Gammexane; the application of insect repellents such as dimethyl phthallate to the exposed parts of the body (*e.g.* ankles, wrists, and face), particularly at sunset; and the use of sand-fly nets at night. Once the infection is acquired, treatment consists of rest in bed, light diet, and aspirin and codeine.

THRILL is a tremor or vibration felt on applying the hand to the surface of the body. It is felt particularly over the region of the heart in conditions in which the valve openings are narrowed or an aneurysm is present.

THROAT is, in popular language, a vague term applied indifferently to the region in front of the neck, to the larynx or organ of voice, and to the cavity at the back of the mouth. The last-mentioned use of the word, to denote the pharynx or cavity into which the nose, mouth, gullet, and larynx all open, is the correct one. (*See* PHARYNX. Information will also be found *under* NECK, LARYNX, TONSILS, NOSE.)

THROAT, DISEASES OF.—Strictly speaking, the term 'throat diseases' should include only affections of the pharynx or throat proper, the general cavity into which the nose, mouth, larynx, gullet, and Eustachian tubes open; but for convenience the chief diseases that affect also the larynx and gullet are considered here.

(Information will also be found *under the headings*, CHOKING, CLERGYMAN'S

886

SORE THROAT, CROUP, DIPHTHERIA, LARYNGISMUS; MOUTH, DISEASES OF; NOSE, DISEASES OF; TONSILLITIS.)

LARYNGITIS, or inflammation of the mucous membrane of the larynx, may be either acute or chronic.

ACUTE LARYNGITIS.—Causes.— This complaint is usually produced by exposure to cold, either directly or through a catarrh extending from the nose above or from the bronchial tubes beneath to the mucous membrane of the larynx. It accompanies some of the infectious diseases in which the throat is liable to suffer, such as measles, scarlatina, diphtheria, smallpox, and erysipelas. Excessive use of the voice, as in loud and prolonged speaking or singing, sometimes produces laryngitis. Further, the inhalation of irritating particles and vapours, and the swallowing of very hot fluids are well recognized causes.

Symptoms. — The chief changes in the larynx are great redness and swelling, which affect the whole interior of the cavity, but are specially marked where the tissues are loose, such as the neighbourhood of the epiglottis and of the vocal cords. The effect is to produce narrowing of the channel for the entrance of air, and to this the chief dangers are due. The symptoms vary with the intensity of the attack, but, along with more or less feverishness and constitutional disturbance, there is usually a sense of heat, dryness, and pain in the throat, attended with some difficulty in the act of swallowing. Cough is a constant symptom, and is either loud, barking, or clanging, or else husky and toneless. It is at first dry, but afterwards is accompanied with expectoration. The voice, like the cough, is rough, husky, or may for a few days disappear almost entirely. The breathing shows evidence of laryngeal obstruction, both inspiration and expiration being prolonged and difficult, with a somewhat hissing sound, and with almost no interval between the two acts. In severe cases, the face and surface generally become livid, and suffocation threatens, particularly during the paroxysms of coughing. In favourable cases, which form the majority, the attack tends to abate in a few days, but on the other hand, death may occur suddenly in a suffocative paroxysm, particularly in the case of children. Many cases of acute laryngitis are so comparatively slight as to make themselves known only by hoarseness and the character of the cough ; nevertheless, in every instance the attack demands serious attention.

Treatment.—The treatment consists in keeping the patient in bed in an atmosphere of 65° to 70° F. (18·3° to 21° C.), made moist by steam (*see* BRONCHITIS). The use of warm gargles, and the frequent inhalation of the vapour of hot water, containing such soothing substances as benzoin or menthol, and the application of hot fomentations to the front of the neck, will be found of much value. Spraying the larynx with a warm mixture of glycerin and water (1 part of glycerin to 2 parts of water) is also of value, particularly in children. Internally, diaphoretics, such as small doses of Dover's powder, are also to be recommended. In most severe cases the use of penicillin or the sulphonamides must be considered. Their efficacy is dependent upon the laryngitis being due to a penicillin- or sulphonamide-sensitive organism. Such remedies usually suffice to relieve the attack, but in very severe cases more active interference may be necessary. When there is much swelling of the mucous membrane in the upper portion of the larynx, as shown by great obstruction of the breathing, scarification of the parts with the aid of the laryngoscope may afford relief, and even tracheotomy may have to be performed where death appears to be imminent from suffocation. Attacks of laryngitis may be largely prevented in those liable to them by a regimen calculated to invigorate the system, such as the cold bath, regular open-air exercise, etc.

CHRONIC LARYNGITIS.—

Causes.—This may occur as a result of repeated attacks of the acute form, or may arise independently owing to such causes as habitual exposure (especially where along with this there is over-indulgence in alcohol), the habitual over-use of the vocal organs, etc. Any interference with the entrance of air through the nose, leading to the bad habit of mouth-breathing, has a great influence in setting up chronic laryngitis. The changes taking place

in the parts are more permanent than in the acute form, consisting mainly in thickening of the mucous membrane, vocal cords, etc. Some cases are due to tuberculosis, syphilis, and other chronic inflammatory diseases, and these are apt to produce ulceration of the vocal cords and other parts of the larynx and ultimately destruction of its cartilages.

Symptoms. — The symptoms vary according to the extent and amount, as well as the duration of the inflammation. Thus there may simply be a certain huskiness or hoarseness on attempts at the use of the voice, this condition being well exemplified in the so-called clergyman's sore throat or *dysphonia clericorum* (*see* CLERGYMAN'S SORE THROAT) ; on the other hand, there may be not only complete loss of voice, but severe pain in the act of swallowing, and great difficulty in breathing, accompanied sometimes with expectoration of large quantities of matter in the cases in which ulceration is present. Under this variety of the disease may be included the ulceration due to syphilis and that occurring in the course of pulmonary tuberculosis, both of which are attended with the symptoms now mentioned. The diagnosis and the treatment of all such cases are greatly aided by the use of the laryngoscope, by which a view of the affected parts can be obtained, and the proper remedies more readily applied.

Treatment.—In the treatment of the chronic forms of laryngitis, rest to the parts is essential, any attempts at continuing the use of the voice only aggravating the condition ; while tonic remedies and regimen should be employed to strengthen the system generally. Applications to the affected parts in the forms of solutions of lactic acid, nitrate of silver, alum, tannin, etc., either by means of a brush or syringe introduced into the cavity or by the simpler method of spraying, are often beneficial. The insufflation of powders, such as iodoform, or starch mixed with a minute quantity of morphine, is also practised, as are likewise inhalations of vapours of iodine, carbolic acid, turpentine, eucalyptus, etc. The diet must be made as simple as possible, and all irritating condiments such as mustard, pickles, and spices should be avoided. Alcohol is also highly prejudicial, especially in the form of strong spirits, and should be avoided. The habit of smoking must be abandoned. The improper use of the voice has been dealt with under the simple but very troublesome form of laryngitis known as CLERGYMAN'S SORE THROAT, which is prone to affect those who use the voice a great deal.

TUBERCULOUS LARYNGITIS practically always occurs as a result of infection spreading from the lungs. Until recently one of the most serious complications of pulmonary tuberculosis, the outlook has been completely changed by the introduction of streptomycin, as this has proved to be one of the forms of tuberculosis which responds best to streptomycin.

TUMOURS and various *inflammatory growths* are frequently met with in the larynx and may give rise to symptoms of chronic laryngitis. Such growths may be of simple character, in the form of isolated fibrous formations attached by a peduncle to some portion of the laryngeal mucous membrane, or as warty excrescences occurring upon or in the neighbourhood of the vocal cords. They are detected by means of the laryngoscope, and can often be dealt with effectually by a very slight operation, though one requiring great skill. Cancer of the larynx may often be removed successfully if the disease is detected in its early stages. *Hoarseness may then be the only symptom.* Hence arises the great importance of a careful examination of the larynx by an expert in every case of hoarseness which has lasted for some weeks or more. In the more serious malignant tumours which either take origin in the larynx or spread into it from adjacent parts, interference by surgical measures can only afford temporary relief, although even in very bad cases the serious operation of entirely removing the larynx and tumour may prolong life over many months. In hopeless cases, tracheotomy is often performed so as to prevent the act of breathing from irritating the diseased part, by providing an entrance for air beneath the larynx. This usually gives considerable relief.

NERVOUS AFFECTIONS of the larynx occur independently of any local disease. One of the most important of these is *laryngismus stridulus*, otherwise

called *child-crowing* or *spasmodic croup.* This condition occurs chiefly during the early years of childhood, and manifests itself by a suffocative attack accompanied by peculiar 'crowing' breathing, as the result of spasmodic approximation of the vocal cords which causes great interference with the entrance of air. The causes and treatment of the condition are dealt with under LARYNGISMUS.

Symptoms not unlike those of laryngismus sometimes occur in adults as the result of irritation of the recurrent laryngeal nerve, by the pressure upon it of an aneurysm or tumour situated in the chest. Such pressure, if long continued, results in paralysis of the nerve, with loss of voice. (*See* RECURRENT LARYNGEAL NERVE.)

In the condition known as *nervous aphonia,* which occurs mostly in women of hysterical temperament or in circumstances of enfeebled health, the voice becomes reduced to a whisper, but there is seldom any affection of the breathing, or cough, and the laryngoscope reveals a perfectly healthy state of the parts. In such cases the remedies must be directed to the improvement of the general health and reassurance of the patient that there is no disease underlying the loss of voice. The use of electricity (faradism) applied to the neck is often attended with marked benefit. This condition may, like other hysterical conditions, be present for years, causing even complete loss of voice, and then may suddenly disappear as the result of a powerful mental impression.

PHARYNGITIS is an inflammatory condition affecting the wall of the pharynx or throat proper. It may be due to infection, which may either be confined to the pharynx (the common ' sore throat ') or may also involve the rest of the upper respiratory tract, *i.e.* the nose and larynx. It may be associated with derangements of the digestive organs, or be caused by the irritation of highly spiced food or of constant spirit-drinking, or even by excessive tobacco-smoking. On looking into the back of the throat, while the tongue is held down, one sees the mucous membrane unduly red and glazed, with enlarged lymph-follicles like sago-grains scattered over it. Small varicose veins are often seen here and there, and when these burst, the person may spit up blood, which he is apt to attribute wrongly to some disease in his lungs. It produces considerable irritation, cough, tickling in the throat, and discomfort, which may last long if not treated. Treatment consists in the use of gargles or sprays, whilst much relief may be obtained from the sucking of medicated pastilles or lozenges. In more acute cases a short course of penicillin or sulphonamides may be necessary. The diet should be bland, and the use of irritants such as smoking and highly spiced foods should be forbidden.

NARROWING OF THE GULLET. —The *œsophagus* or gullet may be the seat of catarrhal or inflammatory conditions causing discomfort in swallowing, but the more important ailments affecting this tract are those which arise from local injuries, such as the swallowing of scalding or corrosive substances. This may cause ulceration followed by the formation of a scar which narrows the passage and produces the symptoms of *stricture* of the œsophagus—namely, pain and difficulty in swallowing, with regurgitation of the food. The severity of the case will necessarily depend upon the amount of narrowing and consequent mechanical obstruction, but in some instances this has occurred to such an extent as practically to close the canal. Cases of œsophageal stricture of the kind now referred to may sometimes be dilated by the use of suitable instruments.

A still more serious and frequent cause of œsophageal stricture is that due to cancerous growth in the canal, which may occur at any part, but is most common at the lower end, in the vicinity of the entrance into the stomach. The chief symptoms of this condition are increasing difficulty in the passage downwards of the food, steady decline in strength, together with enlargement of the glands in the neck, whilst the diagnosis is rendered the more certain by the absence of any cause, such as local injury, for the formation of a stricture, and by the age (as a rule at or beyond middle life). In many cases treatment can only be palliative while life continues, which

in general is not long. Recent advances in surgery, however, have meant that promising results are occasionally obtained from operation. In certain cases treatment with radium produces relief, if not cure. Feeding by the bowel (enemata) may be resorted to as supplementary to efforts to administer liquid nutriment in the usual way. It is to be observed in all cases of organic stricture that the food does not necessarily return at once, but seems as if it had passed into the stomach. In reality, however, it has passed into the dilated or pouched portion of the canal, which is almost always present immediately above the seat of stricture, where it remains until, from its amount, it regurgitates back into the mouth, when it can be seen, by the absence of any evidence of digestion, that it has never been in the stomach. Life may be prolonged for a considerable time and freedom from pain obtained by fluid food ; and the operation of gastrostomy, by which an opening is made through the front of the abdomen, allows food to be directly introduced into the stomach.

Strictures of the œsophagus may also be produced by the pressure of tumours or aneurysms within the cavity of the chest but external to the canal.

An important cause of difficulty in swallowing is the condition known as *cardiospasm* or *achalasia of the cardia*. The latter is the more accurate description as the condition is due to failure of the cardiac sphincter (the sphincter at the lower end of the œsophagus) to relax when food is swallowed. The cause is not known. The condition occurs usually in young adults, who complain of food sticking behind the chest-bone. This results in vomiting and, of course, loss of weight. Treatment consists of passing special bougies down the œsophagus to dilate the sphincter. As this may need to be done before every meal for several months, the patient learns to pass the bougie himself. Such treatment, though prolonged, is usually successful.

Finally, difficulty in swallowing sometimes occurs in certain serious nervous diseases from paralysis affecting the nerves supplying the muscular coats of the pharynx, which thus loses its propulsive power (bulbar paralysis).

When such complications occur, they usually denote an advanced stage of the brain disease with which they are connected, and a speedily fatal termination.

INJURIES OF THE THROAT from without have been briefly referred to under CUT-THROAT.

FOREIGN BODIES sometimes lodge in the throat, being either of the nature of food which has been swallowed in too large or too hard pieces, or of the nature of indigestible substances like coins which children are apt to place in the mouth. Bodies which lodge in the respiratory part of the throat, *i.e.* at the entrance to, or in the cavity of, the larynx, set up immediate symptoms of choking (*see* CHOKING). Bodies which lodge in the gullet, on the contrary, do not usually set up any immediately serious symptoms, although their presence causes a considerable degree of discomfort. Such bodies are divided, for practical purposes, into two classes. One class includes smooth bodies like coins or fruit stones, which may be pushed down into the stomach or pulled up into the mouth by means of a bougie or a special instrument known as a 'coin-catcher', or, better still, by forceps passed down under the direct guidance of the œsophagoscope. The other, and more dangerous, class comprises bodies which are too large to be pushed down into the stomach and safely passed by the bowels, or too rough to be pulled back into the mouth, such as large pieces of bone, or large plates of artificial teeth. In cases where it is impossible to dislodge a foreign body up or down, it becomes necessary to perform an operation in order to remove the body from the gullet directly through the side of the neck.

THROMBOANGIITIS OBLITERANS,

also known as BUERGER'S DISEASE after the American surgeon who gave the first co-ordinated description of it in 1908, is an inflammatory disease involving the blood-vessels of the limbs, particularly the lower limbs. The cause is not known, but the use of tobacco is an important factor in its causation. It is almost entirely confined to males, and is more common in Jews than in Gentiles. Pain is the

outstanding symptom, accompanied by pallor of the affected part. Sooner or later ulceration and gangrene tend to develop in the feet or hands. There is no specific treatment, but, if seen in the early stages, considerable relief may be given to the patient.

THROMBOSIS (θρόμβωσις, a curdling) means the formation of a blood-clot within the vessels or heart during life. The process of clotting depends upon the same factors as in clotting of blood outside the body, involving the fibrinogen and lime salts circulating in the blood, as well as a body set free from the white corpuscles when clotting is about to occur. The indirect cause of thrombosis is usually some damage to the smooth lining of the blood - vessels brought about by inflammation, or the result of atheroma, a chronic disease of the vessel walls. The blood is also specially prone to clot in certain general conditions such as anæmia, the ill-health of wasting diseases like cancer, and in consequence of the feeble circulation of old age.

Thrombosis may occur in the heart and terminate some chronic wasting disease ; it frequently takes place in the vessels of the brain and thus causes apoplexy in persons whose arteries are much diseased ; it is sometimes a salutary thing, as in aneurysm, where the deposition of a clot within the sac forms the natural cure of this condition.

Thrombosis of a coronary artery of the heart is a very serious condition which affects, as a rule, middle-aged or elderly persons, appearing suddenly during rest and causing great pain in front of the chest or upper part of the abdomen, with pallor, feeble pulse, breathlessness, and sometimes vomiting. These symptoms may last for several hours or days, the pain being lessened by injections of morphine; but recovery takes place from about one-half of such attacks after a period of prolonged rest lasting three months or more.

THRUSH is a type of inflammation affecting the mouth of weakly children and causing a patchy white appearance on the lips, tongue, or palate. It is caused by the growth of a fungus on the surface of the mucous membrane. (*See* MOUTH, DISEASES OF.)

THYMOL is a white, crystalline substance derived from oil of thyme and other volatile oils. It has an antiseptic action, but its main use is to expel worms from the intestinal canal, especially the hook-worm and the whip-worm. Thymol is also used, either alone or in combination with menthol, as a local application for the relief of pruritus (*i.e.* itching of the skin).

THYMUS GLAND, so called by Galen in the second century A.D. because of its resemblance to a bunch of thyme flowers, has two lobes and lies in the lower part of the neck and the upper part of the chest. Each lobe is made up of a number of lobules divided into an outer portion, or cortex, and a central portion, or medulla. The cortex resembles lymphoid tissue and is made up of masses of small round cells (thymocytes), whilst the medulla contains small round masses known as Hassel's corpuscles. A striking feature of the gland is that it decreases in size after puberty. The function of the thymus gland is still unknown. Enlargement occurs in disturbances of certain other endocrine glands, and has been reported in cases of acromegaly and eunuchoidism, and following castration. One theory concerning its function is that it is concerned with general physical development and sexual maturation. Although this suggestion is supported by the fact that the gland begins to involute at puberty, there is no firm evidence in its favour. The observation that certain cases of myasthenia gravis (*q.v.*) are associated with enlargement of, or a tumour of, the thymus gland has led to the use of removal of the gland (*i.e. thymectomy*) as a means of treatment of this condition. Enlargement of the thymus is part of the condition known as status thymolymphaticus or status lymphaticus (*q.v.*).

THYROID CARTILAGE (θυρεοειδής, shield-shaped) is the largest cartilage in the larynx and forms the prominence of the Adam's apple in front of the neck. (*See* LARYNX.)

THYROID GLAND (θυρεοειδής, shield-shaped).—This is a highly vascular organ situated in front of the neck. It consists of a narrow isthmus cross-ing the windpipe close to its upper end, and joining together two lateral lobes which run upwards, one on each side of the larynx. The gland is therefore shaped somewhat like a horseshoe, each lateral lobe being about 2 inches (5 cm.) long and the isthmus about ½ inch (12 mm.) wide, and it is firmly bound to the larynx. The weight of the thyroid gland is about one ounce (28·5 grammes), but it is larger in females than in males, underoes in many w omen a periodic increase at each time of menstruation, and often reaches an enormous size in the condition known as goitre.

Minute structure. — The gland is enveloped in a layer of fibrous tissue and possesses a rich blood supply. It is composed of multitudes of closed vesicles, each formed by a layer of cubical cells and containing a thick yellow (colloid) (Plate XVI). Round the vesicles there is a dense network of capillary blood-vessels, whilst the finest lymphatic vessels communicate with the interior of these vesicles.

Function.—The chief function of the thyroid gland is to produce a hormone rich in iodine. The main active ingredient of this hormone is thyroxine, and its probable mode of manufacture is :

iodine + tyrosine = di-iodotyrosine
2 molecules of di-iodotyrosine = thyroxine.

This hormone, or secretion, which passes directly from the thyroid into the blood-stream, is deiodinated in the body cells to triiodothyronine which exerts the physiological action of the thyroid hormone. This hormone is one of the most important in the body and controls the rate of metabolism. Thus, if it is deficient in children they fail to grow, a condition known as CRETINISM (*q.v.*). If the deficiency develops in adult life, the individual becomes obese, lethargic, and develops a coarse skin, a condition known as MYXŒDEMA (*q.v.*). Over-action of the thyroid, or HYPERTHYROIDISM (*q.v.*), results in loss of weight, rapid heart action, and a highly strung nervous temperament. The condition known as EXOPHTHALMIC GOITRE, THYROTOXICOSIS, or GRAVES' DISEASE, is practically the same as hyperthyroidism, but, in certain cases at least, there is evidence to suggest that not only is the output of the secretion of the thyroid increased, in addition there is some abnormality in it.

The production of the thyroid hormone is controlled by a hormone of the pituitary gland—the thyrotrophic hormone.

THYROID GLAND, DISEASES OF (see CRETINISM, GOITRE, MYXŒDEMA).

THYROID GLAND, USES OF.—The thyroid gland of the sheep was introduced as a remedy for myxœdema, in consequence of the researches of several persons (see MYXŒDEMA). An extract, the official *British Pharmacopœia* name of which is thyroid, is administered in doses of 30 to 250 mg. It is usually made up into tablets. These tablets are also used in the treatment of cretinism, excessive stoutness when this is associated with other signs of hypothyroidism, and some cases of widespread psoriasis. Overdoses of the gland are apt to produce violent headache and feebleness of the heart's action.

THYROTOXICOSIS (see GOITRE.)

THYROXINE is a crystalline substance, containing iodine, isolated from the thyroid gland and possessing the properties of thyroid extract. It has also been synthesized. It may be used instead of the extract of the gland in cases of defective function of the thyroid, such as goitre, cretinism, and myxœdema.

TIBIA (*tibia*) is the name of the larger of the two bones in the leg. One surface of the tibia lies immediately beneath the skin in front and towards the inner side of the leg, forming the shin, and fractures of this bone are accordingly very liable to wound the skin and become compound. The thigh-bone rests upon the larger upper end of the tibia at the knee-joint, whilst below, the tibia and fibula together enter into the ankle-point, the two bosses or malleoli at the ankle belonging, the inner to the tibia, the outer to the fibula.

TIC is the term applied to the habit spasm which forms a personal peculiarity in neurotic subjects. (See CRAMP.)

TIC DOULOUREUX (Fr.) is another name for facial neuralgia due to some affection of the fifth cranial nerve, and

characterized by pain, situated somewhere about the temple, forehead, face, or jaw, and sometimes by spasm in the muscles of the affected region. (See NEURALGIA.)

TICK is the general name given to a group of arachnid insects, some of which act as transmitters of diseases.

TINCTURE (*tinctura*, a dye) is an alcoholic solution, generally of some vegetable substance. The official tinctures include tincture of the following drugs : belladonna, colchicum, hyoscyamus, ipecacuanha, nux vomica, opium, orange, stramonium. There are compound tinctures of cardamoms, gentian, rhubarb, and a camphorated tincture of opium. Most tinctures are given in doses of ½ to 1 teaspoonful, but those of the more powerful drugs, such as belladonna, colchicum, nux vomica, opium, and stramonium, are given in smaller doses, usually 5 to 30 minims (0·5 to 2 ml.).

TINEA (*tinea*, a moth) is the technical name for ringworm. (See RINGWORM.)

TINNITUS (*tinnitus*) means a noise heard in the ear without any objective cause. It is a frequent accompaniment of deafness. (See DEAFNESS *and* EAR, DISEASES OF.)

TIN-POISONING from canned food seldom occurs at the present day. When it does occur, the tin comes from the solder used in sealing the tin in the hole and cap variety, and in modern canning the food has practically no contact with the solder. Tin has been found occasionally in cheese wrapped in tin-foil, due to the action of free lactic acid.

The strong soluble salts of tin used by dyers, calico-printers, etc., act as irritant poisons. (See POISONS.)

TISANE (Fr.) is a name sometimes given to barley-water (see BARLEY-WATER). The term is also applied to a light variety of champagne wine.

TISSUES OF THE BODY are the simple elements from which, on microscopic examination, the various parts and organs are found to be built. All the body originates from the union of a pair of cells, but as growth proceeds the new cells produced from these form tissues of varying character and complexity (*see* CELL). It is customary to divide the tissues into five groups :

(1) Epithelial tissues, including the cells covering the skin, those lining the alimentary canal, those forming the secretions of internal organs, etc. (*See* EPITHELIUM.)
(2) Connective tissues, including fibrous tissue, fat, bone, cartilage. (*See* these headings.)
(3) Muscular tissues (*see* MUSCLE).
(4) Nervous tissues (*see* NERVES).
(5) Wandering corpuscles of the blood, lymph, etc. (*See* BLOOD.)

Many of the organs are formed of a single one of these tissues or of one with a very slight admixture of another, such as cartilage, or white fibrous tissue. Other parts of the body that are widely distributed are very simple in structure and consist of two or more simple tissues in varying proportion. Such are blood-vessels (*see* ARTERIES, VEINS), lymphatic vessels (*see* LYMPHATICS), lymphatic glands (*see* GLANDS), serous membranes (*see* SEROUS MEMBRANE), synovial membranes (*see* JOINTS), mucous membranes (*see* MUCOUS MEMBRANE), secreting glands (*see* GLANDS, SALIVARY GLANDS, THYROID GLAND, etc.), and skin (*see* SKIN).

The structure of the more complex organs of the body is dealt with under the heading of each organ.

TITRATION is the term applied to a form of chemical analysis by means of standard solutions of known strength.

TITUBATION (*titubatio*) means a staggering or reeling condition, especially due to disease of the spinal cord or cerebellum.

TOAST WATER is a fluid for administration to invalids, containing a small amount of protein and carbohydrate nourishment. To prepare it, take two or three slices of bread, toast them thoroughly without burning, put them into a large jug, and pour over them a quart of boiling water. This is strained when cold, sweetened with sugar, and flavoured with lemon.

TOBACCO is the leaf of several species of Nicotiana, especially of the American plant *Nicotiana tabacum*. It is not used in medicine, but demands some notice here on account of its popular use and the effects it produces.

The practice of smoking has probably been known for ages, but did not come into use in Europe till it was introduced from the West Indies by the followers of Columbus. The use of tobacco was popularized in England during the sixteenth century by Sir John Hawkins and Sir Walter Raleigh, and the plant was at the time successfully grown in England and Scotland. From the first, smoking was bitterly opposed by many who did not care for the practice. Popes issued edicts against it ; in Turkey and Russia it was made a punishable offence, and in England James I was constrained to issue his *Counterblasts to Tobacco*, in which he described smoking as ' a custom loathsome to the eye, hateful to the nose, harmful to the brain, dangerous to the lungs, . . . resembling the horrible Stygian smoke of the pit that is bottomless.'

Composition.—In addition to vegetable fibre, tobacco leaves contain a large quantity of ash, the nature of this depending largely upon the minerals present in the ground where the tobacco plant has been grown, but amounting to 12 or 20 per cent. of the whole. Of the organic constituents the brown fluid alkaloid known as nicotine is far the most important, as the special action of tobacco depends upon it. The nicotine content of tobacco ranges from 1·5 to 3 per cent. of the dried leaf in Havana tobacco to 6 to 8 per cent. in Virginian tobacco. Some Algerian tobaccos contain much larger amounts. The amount of nicotine entering the mouth of a smoker is 0·92 mg. per cigarette, 3·6 to 7·9 mg. per cigar, and 2·7 mg. per gramme of pipe tobacco. The amount of nicotine absorbed depends upon whether or not the smoker inhales. Most of the nicotine inhaled into the smaller air-passages of the lungs is absorbed, whereas without inhalation, much less per cigarette is absorbed. As a cigarette or cigar is smoked the stub becomes richer in nicotine. It has been estimated that if not more than two-thirds of a cigarette is smoked, some two-thirds of the nicotine is retained in the stub.

Other constituents of tobacco smoke include pyridine, ammonia, and carbon monoxide. The last is the most abundant of these, but American workers have stated that an individual walking along a street with heavy motor traffic would absorb more carbon monoxide than he would from heavy smoking.

Action and use.—The action of tobacco depends largely upon the constitution of the smoker, his habituation to the drug, and the circumstances under which he smokes.

A very small amount of nicotine, such as that derived from a single cigarette, has a stimulating effect upon the mental and bodily powers.

In larger amount, the action is a depressant and narcotic one, which in habitual smokers is modified to a sedative and quieting effect upon the nervous system, without much depression of the heart or other organs. The most suitable time for smoking is generally admitted to be after meals, and especially in the evening after the day's work is at an end, when the sedative action is most beneficial to the nervous system. Different people vary widely in their susceptibility to the influence of tobacco ; for in some, and particularly in young persons, very small quantities suffice to cause depression and irritability of the nervous system, the heart's action, and the digestive and other powers ; whilst others, especially those who lead an open-air life, are not in the least affected by large amounts. Generally speaking, excessive smoking is a harmful thing, particularly for young people.

Among the evil effects of smoking may be mentioned the temporary nausea, depression, giddiness, and vomiting which affect the unaccustomed smoker. These effects, however, pass off quickly, and the tendency to their occurrence disappears as the person becomes habituated to tobacco. Of more importance is the group of symptoms produced by continued and excessive smoking, especially of cigarettes. These include palpitation and irregularity of the heart, giddiness, and a tendency to sudden attacks of faintness, symptoms often grouped together under the popular name of ' tobacco heart '. Other common symptoms are liability to fatigue on slight exertion, dyspepsia, and dimness of vision associated with

impairment of power for seeing colours, especially green and red. These symptoms also pass off gradually when smoking is discontinued, or when the amount of tobacco consumed is reduced within suitable bounds ; but, while they last, they may cause great impairment of the health.

The greatest hazard of smoking, however, is the correlation that has been shown to exist between excessive cigarette smoking and cancer of the lung. On the available evidence there seems to be little doubt that anyone who smokes 20 or more cigarettes a day is definitely increasing the risk that he or she will develop cancer of the lung. Hence the justification for the current campaign to persuade youngsters never to start smoking, and adult cigarette smokers to cut down their daily consumption.

Almost equally serious is the undoubted correlation between heavy cigarette smoking on the one hand, and chronic bronchitis and duodenal ulcer on the other, and there is a growing volume of evidence of a correlation between cigarette smoking and coronary heart disease.

Another set of symptoms frequently arising in those who smoke, and often attributed to a mistaken cause, consists of irritable cough and soreness of the throat. These symptoms pass off when smoking is discontinued. (*See* THROAT DISEASES.)

Acute nicotine-poisoning seldom occurs. It may be due to the accidental swallowing of nicotine insecticides, or to the inhaling of tobacco dust in industrial processes. Occasionally it may occur in children as a result of swallowing tobacco. Nicotine is one of the most rapidly fatal poisons. The fatal dose for man is about 40 mg. The fatal dose of tobacco is about 2 grammes. The symptoms vary from those of smoking in the unaccustomed smoker to immediate prostration leading rapidly to collapse and death. Treatment consists of washing out the stomach, the administration of charcoal or permanganate, and artificial respiration.

TOES (*see* CORNS, FEET, NAILS).

TOLAZAMIDE is a sulponylurea compound, like tolbutamide (*q.v.*), which is proving of value in the treatment of certain forms of diabetes mellitus when given by mouth. One of its practical advantages is that it only needs to be taken once a day.

TOLAZOLINE is 2-benzylimidazoline hydrochloride. It antagonizes some of the effects of adrenaline, and is used in the treatment of peripheral vascular disorders due to arterial spasm or occlusion.

TOLBUTAMIDE is N-butyl-N'-toluene-p-sulphonylurea, a sulphonamide derivative which lowers the level of the blood sugar in diabetes mellitus. Its action is comparable to that of carbutamide (*q.v.*), but it is less toxic, and is the most generally used of the oral hypoglycæmic agents at the moment. As it is rapidly excreted from the body, it has to be taken twice daily. (*See also* DIABETES MELLITUS.)

TOLNAFTATE is a preparation which, in the form of a 1 per cent. solution, is proving useful as a local application of the treatment of certain forms of ringworm.

TOLU (*see* BALSAM).

TOLUOL, or METHYL BENZOL, is an oily substance with properties similar to those of benzol.

-TOMY (τομή, a cutting) is a suffix indicating an operation by cutting.

TONGUE.—The tongue is made up of several muscles, is richly supplied with blood-vessels and nerves, and is covered by highly specialized mucous membrane. It consists of a free part known as the tip, a body, and a hinder fixed part or root. The under surface lies upon the floor of the mouth, whilst the upper surface is curved from side to side, and still more from before backwards so as to adapt it to the roof of the mouth. At its root, the tongue is in contact with, and firmly united to, the upper edge of the larynx ; so that in some persons who can depress the tongue readily the tip of the epiglottis may be seen projecting upwards at its hinder part.

Structure. — The *substance* of the tongue consists almost entirely of muscles running in various directions. One runs along the upper surface and

another along the lower surface from root to tip. Other fibres run vertically from the upper to the lower surface, whilst the chief bulk of the tongue is made up of muscle-fibres running from side to side. These various fibres are chiefly concerned in making changes in the shape of the tongue and moving it within the mouth. In addition to these, the tongue has numerous outside attachments ; one muscle on each side unites it to the lower jaw-bone just behind the chin, and this muscle serves to protrude the tongue from the mouth ; other muscles, which retract the tongue, attach it to the hyoid bone, the larynx, the palate, and the styloid process on the base of the skull.

The *mucous membrane* on the under surface of the tongue is very thin, so that the large ranine vessels on each side can easily be seen through it. In the middle line a fold of mucous membrane, the frenum, passes from the under surface to the floor of the mouth, and, when this frenum is attached too far forwards towards the tip of the tongue, the movements of the organ are impeded, and the condition is known as tongue-tie. On the upper surface or dorsum of the tongue the mucous membrane is thicker, and in its front two-thirds is studded with little projections of three kinds. The majority of these projections or *papillæ* are of *conical* shape, and when the tongue becomes furred the appearance is due to an unhealthy collection of epithelium upon them. Some of them end in long filaments, and are then known as *filiform* papillæ. The roughness of the tongue in cats and other carnivorous animals is due to large backwardly directed conical papillæ, which assist in cleaning the flesh off bones. On the tip, and towards the edges of the tongue, small red rounded *fungiform* papillæ are seen, which act in all probability as end-organs for the sense of taste. On a line dividing the front two-thirds from the hinder one-third, and set in the shape of a V, is a row of seven to twelve large flat-topped *circumvallate* papillæ, each placed in a corresponding depression and just visible, in most mouths, when the tongue is pressed firmly down with some flat instrument. These also act as end-organs for the nerves of taste. Each circumvallate papilla is surrounded by a trench, and upon both sides of the trench open numerous *taste-buds* (Fig. 366). A taste-bud is shaped somewhat like a barrel, with an outer

the food between the teeth for mastication, and then mould it into a bolus preparatory to swallowing ; (b) as the organ of the sense of taste, and as an organ provided with a delicate sense of

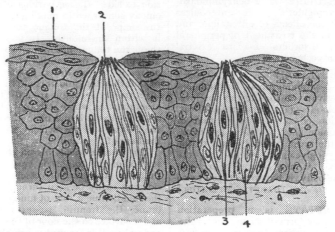

Fig. 366.—Section showing taste-buds, magnified 420 times : 1, stratified epithelium ; 2, gustatory pore ; 3, gustatory cell with hairlet ; 4, sustentacular cell. (From Hewer's *Histology*. Wm. Heinemann Ltd.)

covering of flattened stave-like cells, enclosing a bundle of spindle-shaped cells which end in hairlike processes at the mouth of the bud, and are connected at their deeply placed end with some filaments from the nerves of taste. These taste-buds are also found in the fungiform papillæ, though in smaller numbers, and they are scattered over the throat, fauces, and palate ; so that the popular expression ' a fine palate ', as applied to the sense of taste, is quite correct.

Nerves.—No fewer than five nerves supply branches to each side of the tongue. These are the *lingual* branch of the 5th nerve, which is the nerve of ordinary sensation, to the front two-thirds of the tongue ; the *chorda tympani* branch from the 7th nerve, which is supposed to be the nerve of taste, for a similar extent ; the *glosso-pharyngeal* or 9th nerve, which conveys sensations both of touch and taste from the hinder third ; the *superior laryngeal* branch of the 10th nerve, also sensory ; and the *hypoglossal* or 12th nerve, which supplies the muscles of the tongue.

Functions.—The chief uses of the tongue are of three kinds : (a) to push

touch ; and (c) to play a part in the production of speech (*see* VOICE AND SPEECH).

As to taste, the Greeks recognized nine varieties, but it is usual to classify any taste as—

1. Sweet,	3. Bitter,
2. Salt,	4. Acid,

since finer distinctions are largely dependent upon the sense of smell. The loss of keenness in taste brought about by a cold in the head, or even by holding the nose while swallowing, is well known. Sweet tastes seem to be best appreciated by the tip of the tongue, acids on its edges, and bitters at the back. It is possible too, by chewing the leaves of an Indian plant, *Gymnæma sylvesive*, to do away with the power of tasting bitter and sweet substances, while the sensation for acids and salts remains, so that in all probability there are different nerve-fibres and end-organs for the different varieties of taste. Many tastes depend upon the ordinary sensations of the tongue, such as the ' constringing ' taste of tannin and the ' metallic ' taste of a weak galvanic current passed through the tongue.

Like other sensations, taste can be very highly educated for a time, as in tea-tasters and wine-tasters, but this special adaptation is lost after some years.

TONGUE, DISEASES OF (*see* MOUTH, DISEASES OF).

TONGUE, FURRING OF (*see* MOUTH, DISEASES OF).

TONICS (τόνος, strength) are ' substances whose continued administration gives strength and vigour to the body, without producing sudden excitement or subsequent depression '. This is a 100-year old definition of a term which is gradually passing out of medical phraseology. In the old days, when knowledge of disease processes and of how to treat them was much less than it is to-day, there was a real place for remedies which would help to combat the weakness, lassitude, and loss of appetite which accompanied and followed most illnesses. At the present day it is so often possible to treat the underlying cause that tonics are seldom required. It is also recognized now that to treat symptoms of a disease, without discovering their cause, may do more harm than good. For instance, a middle-aged man's loss of appetite may be due to cancer of the stomach. To treat this by a ' bitter ' is obviously wrong, because the only hope of cure is an early operation. Similarly, the young woman's lassitude may be the first manifestation of pulmonary tuberculosis, the treatment of which is not a ' tonic ' but admission to a sanatorium. Or, to take one other example, an individual's lack of concentration may be due to diminished activity of the thyroid gland, *i.e.* myxœdema, a condition which can be immediately and effectively controlled by the administration of thyroid extract.

Thus, the use of tonics is very much less than it was. But there are still occasions when they may be of value ; for instance, in convalescence from a serious illness. Even in those cases in which they are still used, however, tonics are tending to be used with more discrimination and need not necessarily take the form of drugs. For the over-worked professional man or business executive who finds that he is unable to carry out his duties satis-

factorily, is losing his appetite, and is not sleeping well, the best tonic is a holiday. To give such a man a ' bitter ' to stimulate his appetite, a ' nerve tonic ' such as strychnine to ' buck him up ', and a sedative to allow him to sleep, is simply equivalent to whipping a tired horse to make renewed efforts. There may well be a response, but merely a temporary one achieved at the risk of doing permanent harm.

For individuals who are ' run down ', and in whom no disease or special cause can be found, the best tonics include a well-balanced diet, adequate sleep, ample fresh air and exercise. Cold baths or sprays are also of value in youngsters. During convalescence bitters such as strychnine, nux vomica, quinine, quassia, and gentian may be useful adjuncts to re-stimulating an active interest in food, although this can usually be achieved much more satisfactorily by presenting the patient with a well-cooked variety of food served in an attractive manner.

An unbalanced diet is often a cause for debility, particularly in children and adolescents. Here the best tonic is a well-balanced diet, ensuring an adequate supply of all the vitamins, first-class protein, and essential salts and metals such as iron and calcium. Vitamin deficiency is no longer a major problem in Great Britain, but this state of affairs can only be maintained if every individual up to the age of at least 18 years receives supplementary doses of vitamins A, D, and C during the winter months. Milk, eggs, and meat are the best sources of first-class protein.

Iron is often given as a tonic, but this is only of value when the individual is suffering from an iron-deficiency anæmia. Its use for this purpose is often indicated in adolescent girls in whom there is a heavy loss of blood during the menstrual period. Although there is not usually a marked degree of anæmia in these girls, there is often sufficient lack of iron in the diet to render beneficial the administration of additional iron. There is no justification for the use of liver extracts as a tonic. Apart from the treatment of the form of anæmia known as pernicious anæmia, their use is seldom indicated in Great Britain.

The best heart tonic is rest. Digitalis is sometimes described as a heart tonic but this is not justified. Whilst digitalis is the sheet-anchor in the treatment of heart failure, it is always used in conjunction with rest. To give digitalis to an individual with a failing heart, and not restrict his activities, is merely putting an unnecessary strain on the heart muscle.

No account of tonics would be complete without at least a brief reference to three iron-containing tonics which are still widely used : Parrish's food (compound syrup of iron phosphate), Easton's syrup (syrup of iron phosphate with quinine and strychnine), and syrup of iron iodide. The first of these is still a favourite for use in children, whilst Easton's syrup is a useful ' bitter ' for adults. None of them contain sufficient iron to relieve an iron-deficiency anæmia. If such be present, iron must be given in much larger doses.

TONSILLITIS means inflammation of the tonsils and may be either acute or chronic.

ACUTE TONSILLITIS. — It must never be forgotten that the infection is never entirely confined to the tonsils ; there is always some involvement of the surrounding throat. Just as in many cases of ' sore throat ' the tonsils are involved in the generalized inflammation of the throat.

Causes.—The most common cause is the hæmolytic streptococcus. Its highest incidence is between October and March. In children it is particularly important because it may be the precursor of rheumatic fever. When it occurs in hospitals or institutions it may be highly infectious, and, particularly in children's hospitals, care must be taken to prevent spread of the infection. In the early stages it may be difficult to differentiate from diphtheria, and should there be any doubt as to the diagnosis, a throat swab must be taken and sent immediately to the nearest laboratory so that the infecting organism can be determined. Occasionally the infection may spread to the surrounding tissues and cause abscess formation—a peritonsillar abscess or quinsy.

Symptoms.—The onset is usually

sudden, with pain in swallowing, a sensation of chilliness and fever. On examination, one or both tonsils are found to be enlarged, engorged, and covered with a varying amount of whitish or grey material. This material, or exudate as it is known, consists of purulent discharge from the tonsil. It may occur as scattered areas over the surface of the tonsil, the condition known as follicular tonsillitis and usually due to the hæmolytic streptococcus. In other areas there may be a more extensive exudate covering practically the whole of the tonsil ; this is the type of tonsillitis which is most difficult to differentiate from diphtheria. The inflammatory process is seldom restricted to the tonsil (or tonsils), and the whole of the throat is reddened and inflamed. The tongue, particularly the posterior part, is covered with a thick fur, and the breath has often an unpleasant odour. On pressure on the tonsils further purulent material may be pressed out of them. The glands underneath the angle of the jaw are enlarged and tender ; the enlargement may be marked. There is sometimes pain in the ear on the affected side ; this may indicate spread of the infection to the Eustachian tube. Particular attention must be paid to this in children, as it may lead to infection of the ear—with serious consequences.

Occasionally an abscess develops around the affected tonsil—a peritonsillar abscess or quinsy. This manifests itself by increased swelling in front of the tonsil, which is pushed backwards and also bulges farther into the throat. This is not a particularly serious complication provided it is treated properly. It may develop quite early in an attack of tonsillitis ; in other cases it comes on as the tonsillitis is apparently settling.

Treatment.—This consists of rest in bed so long as the temperature is raised. Except in mild cases, full doses of sulphonamides are given by mouth or penicillin is given intramuscularly or by mouth. The sucking of penicillin lozenges is of little use in the treatment of tonsillitis. In view of the pain on swallowing, the diet must be bland and fluid, e.g. milk, milk puddings, boiled or poached eggs. The patient should be encouraged to drink freely, and if he is taking plenty milk (2 pints daily (1 litre)) and fruit drinks there is no need to worry about the amount he is eating during the acute phase. The sucking of pastilles helps to overcome the unpleasant dryness of the mouth which is so often complained of. Local applications to the throat or tonsils are of little value in acute tonsillitis, but hot menthol inhalations through the mouth are sometimes comforting. When the glands in the neck are enlarged, kaolin poultices to the neck are useful. To relieve the general discomfort and to ensure a good night's rest the best remedies are Dover's powder, aspirin, or a combination of aspirin, phenacetin, and codeine.

Particular attention must be paid to tonsillitis in children because it may be the precursor of rheumatic fever or of acute nephritis (*i.e.* Bright's disease). The best way of reducing the risk of such complications is to keep the child strictly confined to bed until the temperature has been settled for two days. Such complications are most likely to occur when the infecting organism is the hæmolytic streptococcus. Some authorities recommend that full doses of penicillin should be given routinely to children with a hæmolytic streptococcal tonsillitis in order to diminish the risk of rheumatic fever developing. Because of the risk of nephritis developing, the urine must be examined regularly in all cases. When a hæmolytic streptococcal tonsillitis develops in an individual who has had rheumatic fever, the administration of penicillin is essential and the individual must be confined to bed for at least a week.

The treatment of quinsy is as for acute tonsillitis, except that the abscess is incised under a general anæsthetic when it is fully formed.

CHRONIC TONSILLITIS may occur either as a result of one attack of acute tonsillitis or, more commonly, as the result of recurrent attacks. In children there is usually also chronic inflammation of the adenoid tissue in the pharynx (*see* NOSE, DISEASES OF). Chronic tonsillitis is more likely to occur in debilitated children or in those who are living under unhygienic conditions, *e.g.* overcrowded houses, inadequate exercise and fresh air, and poor diet.

The condition manifests itself by chronic enlargement of the tonsils, which tend to have a dull-red colour instead of the normal bright-red colour. On pressure on the tonsil, purulent material can often be exuded from it. If the adenoids are also enlarged, the child breathes through the mouth instead of the nose. Such individuals are liable to be susceptible to repeated ' colds ', sore throats, or infections of the sinuses.

Removal of the tonsils is indicated : (*a*) when the tonsils and adenoids are permanently so enlarged as to interfere with breathing — in such cases the adenoids are removed as well as the tonsils ; (*b*) when the individual is subject to recurrent attacks of acute tonsillitis ; (*c*) when there is definite evidence of persistent active inflammation of the tonsils which will not respond to medical treatment. Such treatment consists of local applications to the tonsils, *e.g.* Mandl's paint or an astringent paint, a nourishing diet, full doses of cod-liver oil and vitamin C, and iron if there be any anæmia. Steps must also be taken to ensure that the child is living under as satisfactory conditions as possible, and a holiday in the country or at the sea often works wonders. In dealing with suspected cases of chronic tonsillitis in children it must never be forgotten that an enlarged tonsil is not necessarily an inflamed or abnormal one.

TONSILS (*tonsillæ*) are two almond-shaped glands situated one on each side of the narrow fauces where the mouth joins the throat. Each has a structure resembling that of a lymphatic gland, and consists of an elevation of the mucous membrane presenting twelve to fifteen openings, which lead into pits or lacunæ. The mucous covering is formed by the ordinary mucous membrane of the mouth, which also lines the pits ; and the main substance of the gland is composed of loose connective tissue containing lymph corpuscles in its meshes, and packed here and there into denser nodules or follicles. The tonsils play an important rôle in the protective mechanism of the body against infection.

TOOTHACHE (*see* TEETH, DISEASES OF).

TOPHUS (*tophus*, tufa) is the name given to the concretions which form in connection with joints or tendon sheaths as the result of attacks of gout. At first the tophus is a soft mass, but later becomes quite hard. It is composed of biurate of soda. (*See* CONCRETIONS, GOUT.)

TORMINA (*tormina*) a technical name for griping pains felt round the navel, as the result of spasmodic action of the muscular coat in the small intestine. (*See* COLIC.)

TORPOR (*torpor*) is a condition of bodily and mental inactivity, not amounting to sleep, but interfering greatly with the ordinary habits and pursuits. It is often found in persons suffering from fever, and is a common symptom in aged people whose arteries are diseased. It may annoy young persons after meals when they are the subjects of constipation or of dyspepsia, due to eating too much animal or indigestible food.

TORSION (*torsio*) means twisting. The term is applied to the process in which organs, tumours, etc., which are attached to the rest of the body by a narrow neck or pedicle, become twisted so as to narrow the blood-vessels or other structures in the pedicle. Torsion is also the term applied to the twisting of the small arteries severed at an operation, by which bleeding from them is stopped.

TORTICOLLIS (*tortus*, twisted ; *collum*, the neck) means wry-neck. (*See* CRAMP, WRY-NECK, SPASMODIC TORTICOLLIS.)

TORULA (*torulus*, a little lump) is another name for yeast. (*See* BACTERIOLOGY.)

TORULOSIS is a disease due to a yeast, *Torula histolytica*, which is usually characterized by meningitis or meningo-encephalitis.

TOUCH, according to the popular idea, is the fifth sense diffused all over the body, by which we become conscious of our surroundings otherwise than by the four special senses of hearing, seeing, tasting, and smelling. But when this diffused sensitiveness is ex-

900

amined it is found to consist of a group of senses, several of which have special end-organs situated in the skin, muscles, etc., and special nerve-paths to convey their impressions to the brain. It is convenient, however, to adopt the popular view so far, and to consider all these under one heading. The cutaneous sense, then, is made up of the following :

Touch sense proper, by which we perceive a touch or stroke and estimate the size and shape of bodies with which we come in contact, but which we do not see.

Pressure sense, by which we judge the heaviness of weights laid upon the skin, or appreciate the hardness of objects by pressing against them.

Heat sense, by which we perceive that a body is warmer than the skin.

Cold sense, by which we perceive that a body touching the skin is cold.

Pain sense, by which we appreciate pricks, pinches, and other painful impressions.

To these we may for convenience add :

Muscular sensitiveness, by which the painfulness of a squeeze is perceived. It is produced probably by direct pressure upon the nerve-fibres in the muscles.

Muscular sense, by which we test the weight of an object held in the hand, or gauge the amount of energy expended on an effort.

Sense of locality, by which we can, without looking, tell the position and attitude of any part of the body.

Common sensation, which is a vague term used to mean composite sensations produced by several of the foregoing, like tickling, or creeping, and the vague sense of well-being or the reverse that the mind receives from internal organs. (See the article on PAIN.)

The structure of the end-organs situated in the skin (Plate XVI), which receive impressions from the outer world, and of the nerve-fibres which conduct these impressions to the central nervous system, have been described under NERVES.

Touch affects the Meissner's or touch corpuscles (Fig. 367) placed beneath the cuticle, and, as these differ in closeness in different parts of the skin, the delicacy of the sense of touch varies greatly. Thus the points of a pair of compasses can be felt as two on the tip of the tongue when separated by only

$\frac{1}{24}$ of an inch, on the tips of the fingers they must be separated to twice that distance, whilst on the arm or leg they cannot be felt as two points unless

FIG. 367.—Tactile corpuscle of Meissner in a skin papilla. (From Hewer's *Histology*. Wm. Heinemann Ltd.)

separated by over an inch, and on the back they must be separated by over two inches. On the parts covered by hair, the nerves ending round the roots of the hairs also take up impressions of touch. Pressure is estimated probably through the same nerve-endings and nerves that have to do with touch, but it depends upon a difference in the sensations of parts pressed on and those of surrounding parts. Heat-sense, cold-sense, and pain-sense all depend upon different nerve-endings in the skin ; and thus, with care and delicate instruments like needles, bristles in holders, and metal pencils through which hot or cold water can be made to circulate, the skin may be mapped out into a mosaic of little areas where the different kinds of impressions are registered. Whilst the tongue and finger-tips are the parts most sensitive to touch, they are comparatively insensitive to heat, and can easily bear temperatures which the cheek or elbow could not tolerate. The muscular-sense, in all probability, depends on the sensory organs known as muscle-spindles, which are scattered through the substance of the muscles, and the sense of locality is dependent partly upon these and partly upon the nerves which end in tendons, ligaments, and joints.

Disorders of the sense of touch occur in various diseases.

HYPERÆSTHESIA (more correctly called hyperalgesia) is a condition in which a mere touch or gentle handling causes acute pain. It is found in various diseases of the spinal cord immediately above the level of the disease, combined often with loss of sensation below the diseased part. It is also present in neuralgia, the skin of the neuralgic area becoming excessively tender to touch, heat, or cold. Heightened sensibility to pain is seen sometimes in drunkards, who wince at a mere touch when not under the influence of alcohol. Heightened sensibility to temperature is a frequent symptom of neuritis. (*See* PAIN.)

ANÆSTHESIA, or diminution of the sense of touch, causing often a feeling of numbness, is present in many diseases affecting the nerves of sensation or their continuations up the posterior part of the spinal cord. The condition of *disassociated analgesia*, in which a touch is quite well felt, though there is complete insensibility to pain, is present in the disease of the spinal cord known as syringomyelia, and affords a proof that the nerve-fibres for pain and those for touch are quite separate. In locomotor ataxia there is sometimes loss of the sense of touch on feet or arms ; but in other cases of this disease there is no loss of the sense of touch, although there is a complete loss of the sense of locality in the lower limbs, thus proving that these two senses are quite distinct.

PARÆSTHESIÆ are peculiar forms of perverted sensation such as creeping, tingling, pricking, or hot flushes.

TOURNIQUET (Fr.) is an instrument used for the temporary stoppage of the circulation in a limb, to control bleeding (Fig. 368). There are various forms of tourniquet, the simplest being a *tourniquet improvised* from a band such as that made by a handkerchief folded cravat-wise, tied round the limb, and then twisted up by means of a rigid object passed beneath it. *Petit's tourniquet* has a linen strap passing over two pairs of brass rollers, which can be separated from one another by a screw, thus tightening the strap after it has been buckled round the limb. *Esmarch's tourniquet* consists of an elastic band which is wrapped with moderate tightness round the limb, and then prevented from unwrapping by tapes. It is the form generally used. (*See* HÆMORRHAGE.) A rubber tube knotted, or

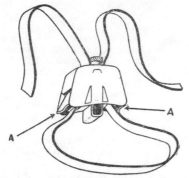

FIG. 368.—The L.P.L. tourniquet. The tourniquet is released by approximating the finger grips (A). (From Pye's *Surgical Handicraft.* John Wright & Sons Ltd.)

fixed with a clip, round the limb is also frequently used for arresting the blood-flow. In applying a tourniquet for bleeding, it must be rendered sufficiently tight to stop the circulation completely. Otherwise if the veins only are com-

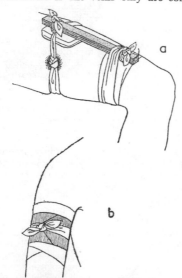

FIG. 369.—Two simple forms of tourniquet. *a*, An improvised tourniquet, the knot being over the femoral artery, and the lower band being intended simply to keep the handle of the tourniquet from unwinding; *b*, Esmarch's elastic band tourniquet.

pressed and the arteries still open, the bleeding is made worse. A tourniquet must not be left in position longer than is absolutely necessary; otherwise gangrene of the limb may result.

TOW is a form of jute which is very hygroscopic, absorbing up to 25 per cent. of moisture.

TOXÆMIA (τοξικόν, poison; αἷμα, blood) is a term applied to forms of blood-poisoning due to the absorption of bacterial products (toxins) formed at some local site of infection, such as abscesses. In other cases the toxæmia is due to defective action of some excretory organ, such as the kidney.

As regards treatment, the most important consideration is to remove the source of infection. Vaccines made from the bacteria responsible for the inflammation are also used in the treatment of this condition.

TOXICOLOGY (τοξικόν, poison; λόγος, discourse) is the science dealing with poisons. (*See* POISONS.)

TOXINS (τοξικόν, poison) are poisons produced by the action of bacteria upon the tissues of the body or other material in which the bacteria develop. (*See* BACTERIOLOGY, IMMUNITY, SERUM THERAPY.) Toxins are usually soluble, easily destroyed by heat, sometimes of the nature of crystalline substances, and sometimes albumins. When injected into animals in carefully graduated doses, they bring about the formation of substances called antitoxins which neutralize the action of the toxin. These antitoxins are generally produced in excessive amount, and the serum of the animal when withdrawn can be used for conferring antitoxic powers upon other animals or human beings to neutralize the disease in question. The best known of these antitoxins are those of diphtheria and tetanus. Substances like toxins are found in many plants and in snake venom. Some toxins are not set free by the bacteria, but remain in the substance of the latter and then are known as endotoxins and are not capable of producing antitoxins.

TOXOID is toxin (*q.v.*) which has been rendered non-toxic by certain chemicals, or by heat, or by being partly neutralized by antitoxin. The best-known example is diphtheria toxoid. (*See* IMMUNITY.)

TOXOPLASMOSIS is a relatively rare disease which is due to infection with protozoa of the genus *Toxoplasma*. It predominantly involves the central nervous system, and in most cases the infection occurs before birth, so that the infant is born with the disease.

TRACE ELEMENTS are chemical elements that are distributed throughout the tissues of the body in very small amounts and are essential for the nutrition of the body. Nine such elements are now recognized : cobalt, copper, fluorine, iodine, iron, manganese, molybdenum, selenium and zinc.

TRACHEA (τραχύς, rough) is another name for the windpipe. (*See* AIR PASSAGES.)

TRACHEITIS means inflammation of the trachea. It may occur along with bronchitis, or independently, due to similar causes.

TRACHEOTOMY (*trachea*, and τέμνω, I cut) is the operation in which the windpipe is opened from the front of the neck, so that air may obtain direct entrance into the lower air passages. It is usual to classify the operations as *high tracheotomy* when the trachea is opened above the isthmus of the thyroid gland, which crosses opposite the third and fourth cartilaginous rings of the trachea, and *low tracheotomy* when the opening is made below this level ; although in actual practice the thyroid gland is often cut across.

The higher the trachea is opened, the easier is the operation, because the trachea recedes from the surface as it passes downwards, and in the lower part of the neck is placed close to large blood-vessels. Nevertheless, the condition for relief of which the operation is performed frequently renders it necessary that the operation should be performed as low down as possible.

Reasons for operation. — Inflammatory conditions, which lead to narrowing of the opening into the larynx and threaten to prevent the entrance of air, form the chief class of conditions that demand tracheotomy, in order to provide an opening lower down. Chief among these is diphtheria. Wounds of the larynx, followed by inflammation, as in cut-throat, require it sometimes for the same reason. Or the blockage of the larynx may be due to some foreign body which has gone down into the air passages, or to some tumour growing in the larynx, or tuberculous disease of the vocal cords. In young children the operation of *intubation* is sometimes preferred, and, as the tube in this case is pushed in through the mouth, no cutting operation is required. Although intubation of the larynx has several points of advantage, tracheotomy is generally more successful when an operation becomes absolutely necessary.

Tracheotomy tubes. — When the trachea has been opened by a vertical slit on its front surface, after division of the skin and separation of the fatty tissue on the neck, it is necessary to introduce a tube in order to keep the opening from closing. The tubes are made either of hard rubber or more often of metal ; and there is always an *outer tube* which is fixed in position by tapes passing round the neck, and an *inner tube* which slides freely out of and into the other, so that it may be removed at any time for cleansing, and is readily coughed out should it happen to become blocked by mucus.

A dressing of boracic lint is generally applied between the edges of the outer tube and the wound ; while the entrance to the inner tube is protected by a few layers of gauze wrung out of hot water and sprinkled with terebene, so as to form a filter for the air entering the trachea.

The inner tube must be removed and washed several times daily, and if at any time it gets blocked by coughed-up mucus, it must be instantly removed and wiped. The outer tube is not removed till one or two days have elapsed after the operation, and then it is replaced by a fresh tube carefully introduced.

After-treatment.—When the operation has been performed for some permanent obstruction, the tube must be worn permanently ; and the double metal tube is in such cases replaced after a short time by a soft rubber single one. When the operation has

903

relieved some passing condition like diphtheria, the tube is left out now and then for a few hours, and finally, at the end of a week or so, is removed altogether, after which the wound quickly heals up.

TRACHOMA (*see* EYE DISEASES).

TRACTOTOMY (*see* CORDOTOMY.)

TRADE DISEASES.—The increasing complexity of industrial and manufacturing processes, and the large proportion of the population of the country who are employed in industry, render trade diseases, or, as they are sometimes called, occupational or industrial diseases, of increasing importance. Whenever a new process is introduced into industry every care is taken to ensure that it will involve no hazards to those employed in it. Even so, it is not always possible to foreseee all possible risks, and therefore the management and the industrial medical officer must always be on the look-out so as to be able to detect any such hazard at the earliest possible stage before irreparable harm is done to the health of men or women handling the process. In many cases freedom from the hazards to health inherent in industrial or manufacturing processes is, in part at least, dependent upon the active co-operation of workmen and involves such simple procedures as the wearing of respirators, careful washing of the hands before eating, the application of barrier creams to the hands and arms, and the like. The obtaining of such co-operation is one of the main aims of efficient industrial management at the present day. The magnitude of the problem involved can be gathered from the fact that it is estimated that there are about 2000 diseases which can be attributed to an individual's occupation. It says much, therefore, for the efficiency of the precautionary measures, and the care and skill with which they are employed, that there are so relatively few industrial diseases in any given year in such a highly industrialized country as Great Britain. This satisfactory state of affairs is the result of close and cordial co-operation between employers, industrial medical officers, and the Chief Inspector of Factories and his staff.

Although many industrial diseases entitle the victims to compensation, only a few are compulsorily notifiable. The following are the diseases which, if contracted in a factory, must be notified by the medical practitioner to the Chief Inspector of Factories : poisoning by lead, phosphorus, manganese, arsenic, mercury, carbon bisulphide, and aniline ; chronic benzene poisoning, toxic jaundice, anthrax, epitheliomatous ulceration, chrome ulceration, compressed air illness, and toxic anæmia.

Lead is used widely throughout industry, and the following are some of the occupations in which it constitutes a hazard to health unless adequate precautions are taken : smelting, plumbing and soldering, shipbreaking, printing, pottery industry, electric accumulator works, painting. In the case of pottery and printing the risk has been almost entirely eliminated by the use of modern methods. The lead salts used in industry which are most dangerous to health are the oxide, the carbonate, and the chromate. The lead usually enters the body by the inhalation of dust or fumes. One of the practical difficulties in detecting and preventing lead-poisoning is that it is often insidious in onset. (*See* LEAD-POISONING.)

Phosphorus has practically been eliminated as a cause of industrial poisoning in Great Britain. The first cases to be reported in this country since 1919 occurred during the 1939–45 war—one in 1941 and 1944. Yellow and white phosphorus are the dangerous forms. The red phosphorus used in the making of safety matches is relatively harmless. The match industry, in the days when white phosphorus was used for this purpose, was the classical source of phosphorus poisoning. The phosphorus gained admission through abrasions in the gums and caused destruction of the jaw, the condition known as ' phossy jaw '. Luminous paints are another potential source of danger, principally when used to paint luminous watch dials. (*See* PHOSPHORUS POISONING.)

Manganese is not a common cause of industrial disease, but it is important because the results are so serious. It affects the brain and causes a condition very like post-encephalitic Parkinsonism (*q,v.*) and leaves the victim a permanent invalid. The dioxide is the dangerous salt, and the risk occurs in the handling of manganese ore, or in the handling of manganese dioxide itself, from exposure to the dust.

Arsenic is encountered in industry in the smelting and refining of ores, the subliming of white arsenic, and the manufacture of sheep dip, Scheele's green, and Paris green. White arsenic is used as a preservative of furs, hides, and skins, whilst Paris green is used as an insecticide for fruit trees. The replacement of Scheele's green by aniline colours has abolished the historical rôle of the manufacture of green wallpapers and artificial flowers as a cause of arsenical poisoning. Poisoning from arsenic in industry usually results from inhalation of, or contact with, the dust of arsenic compounds, and results in eczema and neuritis. Occasionally it takes a more serious and acute form, when it results from the inhalation of arseniuretted hydrogen. (*See* ARSENIC, NEURITIS.)

Mercury constitutes an industrial hazard in three forms : (i) exposure to the dust or vapour of metallic mercury ; (ii) contact with mercury fulminate ; (iii) exposure to organic mercury compounds. The industries or processes in which exposure to mercury may occur include : mercury mining and the separation of the metal from the ore ; the manufacture of barometers, thermometers, and certain types of electric bulbs ; water gilding ; the felt-hat industry. Mercury fulminate is used in the making of explosives, and is particularly liable to attack the skin. Organic mercury compounds are mainly used in the manufacture of seed dressings and fungicides, and in the pharmaceutical industry. (*See* MERCURY POISONING.)

Carbon bisulphide, for long used in the ' cold curing ' of rubber and as a solvent for rubber, oil, and fats, has in more recent years been used in large amounts in the manufacture of certain forms of artificial silk. One of its dangers is that it vaporizes at ordinary temperatures, and the breathing of 1150 parts per million parts of air for

30 to 60 minutes is dangerous. Its main effect is upon the nervous system : neuritis, anxiety, depression, and impairment of memory.

Aniline is used in a wide variety of industrial processes : dyeing, painting, varnishing, rubber processing, and the manufacture of dyes, explosives, pharmaceutical products, and photographic chemicals. Absorption takes place mainly through the skin but may also occur through the lungs. The chief early manifestation of poisoning is a greyish-blue colour of the skin followed by shortness of breath. In chronic cases anæmia develops.

Benzene, a coal-tar derivative, is used on a large scale—the distillation of coal tar, the blending of motor fuels, and in the chemical industry. It is also used as a solvent in the rubber, aeroplane, linoleum, and celluloid industries and in the manufacture of paints, varnishes, glue, and artificial manure. The main manifestation of chronic benzene poisoning is anæmia due to a toxic effect of the benzene upon the bone marrow. Benzene is absorbed by inhalation.

Nitrobenzene is used in the manufacture of aniline dyes and explosives, and is a constituent of shoe and floor polish. It is also used as a perfume in cheap soaps. The main route of absorption is through the skin. It acts upon the nervous system, causing headache, giddiness, and numbness in the limbs, and upon the blood, causing anæmia and cyanosis.

Dinitrobenzene, which is used in the manufacture of dyes and explosives, is absorbed through the skin. Its principal toxic effect is upon the blood, resulting in cyanosis, which manifests itself by a blue discoloration of the skin. It also causes anæmia.

Trinitrotoluene, better known as T.N.T., is used in the making of explosives. It is mainly absorbed through the skin, and causes dermatitis, jaundice, and anæmia.

Chrome, used in chromium plating, attacks the skin, causing dermatitis. It also attacks the septum of the nose, leading to chrome ulceration and perforation of the septum. It is the cartilaginous part of the septum and not the bone which is attacked.

Toxic jaundice may be caused by

trinitrotoluene, tetrachlorethane, arseniuretted hydrogen, carbon tetrachloride, and certain benzene derivatives.

Epitheliomatous ulceration, a form of cancer, may arise among workers with tar, pitch, bitumen, or mineral oil. The best known form is mule-spinner's cancer.

Anthrax may occur among workers in wool, hides, and hair infected with the anthrax bacillus. The infection may be acquired through the skin, where it causes the so-called ' malignant pustule ', or through the lungs by breathing in the bacillus, when pulmonary anthrax results. Its incidence among people handling infected wool gave rise to the name ' woolsorters' disease '. (*See* ANTHRAX.)

Polymer fume fever, an influenza-like illness that occurs in people who work with polytetrafluoroethylene (Teflon.) (*See* POLYMER FUME FEVER.)

Pneumoconioses.—This is a group of diseases of the lungs due to the inhalation of dust. The most important dust in this connection is silica. The resulting disease is known as silicosis (*q.v.*). Other diseases in this category are asbestosis (*q.v.*), bagassosis (*q.v.*), berylliosis (*q.v.*), byssinosis (*q.v.*), and farmer's lung (*q.v.*).

Dermatitis is now one of the most important industrial diseases. It may be caused by a wide variety of agents, including alkalies, oil, petrol, paraffin, French polish, various chemicals, etc. Its importance lies in the fact that, with reasonable care, it can often be avoided, or, if it be detected early, it responds well to treatment. On the other hand, if allowed to persist for any length of time, it may become resistant to all but one form of treatment, *i.e.* change of occupation to one in which the individual will not come into contact with the offending substance. Preventive measures ensure adequate washing facilities and their full use by all workpeople exposed to risk ; maximum cleanliness at work, which reduces the risk of the individual coming into contact with the offending substance ; the wearing of protective clothing ; the use of barrier creams where this is possible.

Cramps and Paralyses.—Cramps may occur in individuals whose work involves repeated use of the same groups of muscles. Perhaps the best known examples of this are *telegraphist's cramp* and *writer's cramp*. Another example is *twister's cramp* which occurs in the cotton and woollen industries among those whose job is the twisting of cotton or woollen yarns. Although in a somewhat different category, reference may also be made here to the painful condition which develops in the arms of those handling *powerful pneumatic tools*. This condition is liable to be accompanied by insomnia and tremors. No effective treatment is known.

Miner's nystagmus is a distressing condition, characterized by persistent uncontrollable movements of the eye, which occurs in coal-miners. It is now generally accepted that the main cause is inadequate illumination, and the introduction of adequate lighting into mines should go far towards reducing its incidence.

Compressed air illness, formerly known as caisson disease, occurs in divers and in those who work in caissons. It is due to the affected individuals being ' decompressed ' too quickly. Divers and caisson workers work under high pressures, and if this pressure is reduced too quickly, bubbles of nitrogen are released in the body which cause pain in various areas— usually muscles or joints. These painful areas are known as ' bends '. Adherence to official decompression tables should prevent such accidents, but when they do occur, the treatment consists of recompression until the pain goes, followed by slow decompression.

TRAGACANTH is a gummy exudation obtained from *Astragalus gummifer*, which swells out and forms a mucilage when mixed with water. It is used as a demulcent, or in mixtures to suspend heavy particles, such as bismuth.

TRAINING (*see* DIET, EXERCISE).

TRANCE is the term applied to a profound sleep from which a person cannot for a time be aroused, but which is not due to organic disease. The power of voluntary movement is lost, though sensibility and even consciousness may remain. It is usually due to hysteria, and may be induced by hypnotism. (*See* CATALEPSY, ECSTASY, *and* SLEEP.)

TRANQUILLIZER.—A tranquillizer is a drug which induces a mental state free from agitation and anxiety, and renders the patient calm, serene, and peaceful. Strictly speaking, tobacco, alcohol, and the barbiturates might be included in this category, but the term ' tranquillizer ' is usually restricted to certain new groups of drugs whose main action is the control of anxiety and psychomotor agitation without producing hypnosis or clouding of consciousness. Among the more widely used drugs in this group are chlorpromazine, reserpine, meprobamate, and chlordiazepoxide.

TRANSFUSION OF BLOOD is an old method of restoring a person believed to be dying by passing blood from another person into his veins. The practice was much in vogue during the seventeenth century, and was performed either by bleeding a healthy person into a basin, and, by means of a syringe, injecting the blood into a cannula previously tied in one of the sick person's veins ; or by uniting a vein in the healthy person with one in the sick person by means of two cannulæ and a connecting tube, so that the blood passed directly from one to the other. In spite of all speed, the blood introduced by either of these methods was apt to clot ; and the practice was adopted of whipping the blood with fine twigs, or straining it through muslin so as to remove its fibrin, and thus introduce merely the serum and blood corpuscles.

Apart from the difficulty caused by the tendency to clot, the major drawback to transfusion is that the corpuscles are liable to break up in the new circulation into which they are introduced ; and the person into whom the new blood is transfused may suffer to a dangerous degree from symptoms such as nettle-rash, difficulty of breathing, purging, and signs of shock, whilst the immediate destruction of the red blood corpuscles leads to the passage of blood pigment in the urine and jaundice in some cases. A fatal result may quickly supervene.

To avoid this, it is necessary to find out that the blood of the donor is compatible with the blood already in the circulation of the recipient. Whenever possible, this should be done by persons specially trained in the technique. In an emergency in a remote area, however, where such facilities are not available, compatibility of blood can be investigated by a relatively simple technique. A little blood is drawn from the recipient, and a drop of its serum mixed with a minute drop of blood from the donor, which has been allowed to drop into citrate of soda solution. If, in the course of a few minutes, the serum of the recipient causes clotting or breaking up of the donor's corpuscles, the two bloods are incompatible, and another donor of new blood must be chosen and similarly tested. Standard serums can also be obtained for testing the ' group ' to which the blood of the donor and that of the recipient belong.

Various methods of transfusion have been used at different times : such as by uniting a vessel in the donor with a vessel in the recipient by means of a short tube, while the two lie side by side ; by withdrawing the blood into a syringe and then injecting it through a cannula into the recipient's vein ; or, most commonly, by withdrawing the blood from the donor into a large glass vessel, which has been coated with paraffin, and which contains a small amount of citrate of soda solution intended to prevent clotting.

In Great Britain, however, all these methods have been largely given up since the inception, in 1946, of the National Blood Transfusion Service, which is responsible for the collection of blood from voluntary donors and for its storage in blood-banks throughout the country. A standard transfusion bottle has been evolved, with special apparatus for the taking and the giving of blood. When such a set is used with the proper technique, the blood can be safely stored at a temperature of 2° to 6° C. for three weeks before use. In addition to whole blood, plasma or serum may be used for transfusion

907

purposes. When stored in the dried form, human plasma and serum have proved to be valuable substitutes for whole blood. In the dried state human plasma is stable for five years provided it is stored at a moderate temperature (4·4° to 21·1° C.) and is not exposed to direct sunlight. It is reconstituted by adding pyrogen-free distilled water.

EXCHANGE TRANSFUSION is the method of treatment in severe cases of hæmolytic disease of the newborn (*q.v.*). It consists of replacing the whole of the baby's blood with Rh-negative blood of the correct blood group for the baby.

TRANSILLUMINATION means the inspection of the interior of a cavity, *e.g.* of one of the sinuses connected with the nose, by means of a strong light passed through its walls, in a dark room. The condition of the cavity as regards the presence of pus or a tumour can thus be readily demonstrated.

TRANSPLANTATION of organs of the body has become a practical possibility within recent years. It is still in its infancy, however, and many problems have to be solved before it can be used on anything like a large scale. The major outstanding problem is how to prevent the recipient's body from rejecting and destroying the transplanted organ. Such rejection of a foreign body is part of the normal protective mechanism of the body and is essential for the maintenance of the integrity of the body.

Hitherto the major success has been achieved with transplantation of the kidney, and this has only been successful when the transplanted kidney has come from an identical twin. Partial success has been achieved when the kidney has come from a non-identical twin or some other near relative.

Drugs are now available that can temporarily depress the immune reactions of the recipient, which are responsible for the rejection of the transplanted organ. By means of these drugs it has proved possible to transplant kidneys, not only from near relatives, but also from cadavers. Although none of these transplantations has been permanently successful, they hold

out hope that in time a method will be evolved whereby successful transplantation of organs of the body can be successfully achieved.

TRANSVESTITISM, or TRANSVESTISM, is the term given to a psychosexual abnormality in which a person goes about dressed in the clothes of the opposite sex.

TRAPS (*see* WATER-CLOSETS).

TRAUMA, TRAUMATIC (τραῦμα, a wound), are terms used to indicate disorders due to wounds or injuries. Psychic trauma is the term applied to an emotional shock.

TRAVEL SICKNESS (*see* SEA-SICKNESS).

TREATMENT. — Special forms of treatment are considered under such headings as DIET, ELECTRICITY IN MEDICINE, LIGHT TREATMENT, SERUM THERAPY, PROTEIN THERAPY, etc. The treatment appropriate to each disease will be found under the headings of the various diseases.

TREMOR (*tremor*) means a very fine kind of jerking spasm. Tremors may be seen in projecting parts like the hands, head, and tongue, or they may involve muscles or even the individual fibres of a muscle here and there. They are of various grades of fineness. Very coarse tremors, which prevent a person from drinking a glass of water without spilling it, are found in disseminated sclerosis and in St. Vitus's dance (*see under* these headings) ; somewhat finer tremors, which produce trembling of the hands or tongue when they are stretched out, are caused by alcoholism (*see* ALCOHOLISM, CHRONIC), by poisoning with other substances like lead, by trembling palsy (*see* PARALYSIS), and by the weakness which follows some acute disease or characterizes old age ; very fine tremors, visible in the muscles of face or limbs, and known as ' fibrillary tremors ', are present in general paralysis of the insane, and in progressive muscular atrophy or wasting palsy. (*See* GENERAL PARALYSIS.)

TRENCH FEVER is an infectious disease caused by *Rickettsia quintana* which is transmitted by the body louse. Large epidemics occurred among troops on active service during the 1914–18 War, but the disease has scarcely been seen since then.

TREPHINING, or TREPANNING τρύπανον, a trephine), is an operation in which a portion of the cranium is removed. Originally the operation was performed with an instrument resembling a carpenter's brace and known as the trephine or trepan, which removes a small circle of bone ; but now this instrument is only used, as a rule, for making small openings, whilst, for wider operations, gouge forceps, circular saws driven by electric motor, or wire saws are employed in order to give greater ease and speed.

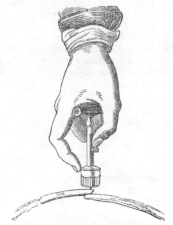

FIG. 370.—The form of trephine which has been in use since ancient times, showing its method of use. (Miller's *Surgery*.)

The operation is one requiring nicety of manipulation, but is neither difficult nor serious, and was one of the commonest major operations of antiquity. It is said, from the appearances presented by skulls found in old French burial mounds, to have been practised by prehistoric peoples ; at all events Hippocrates describes fully the operation and the conditions that call for it, whilst Galen mentions two varieties of the instrument in common use. Both among the Greeks and Romans, and in the Middle Ages, resort seems to have been made to trephining, on very slight provocation, for conditions traceable to the head.

At the present time, the conditions under which it may be thought advisable to trephine the skull are chiefly as follows. In cases of fracture, with splintering of the skull, the operation is performed to remove the fragments of bone and any foreign bodies, like a bullet, which may have entered, in order that the wound may be thoroughly cleansed. In compression of the brain with unconsciousness following an injury, the skull is trephined and any blood-clots removed, or torn vessels ligatured. When an abscess is present within the skull, the operation is called for in order to evacuate the pus. In epilepsy, or in continued headache, when the symptoms point to a definite part of the brain being involved, the skull is often trephined over this area, so that any clot, scar, thickening of the bone, or cyst, which is setting up the irritation, may be discovered and removed. For a cerebral tumour, trephining is often performed either with the view of removing the tumour, if that be possible, or at all events of relieving the great pressure within the skull caused by the growing mass.

TREPONEMA (τρέπω, I turn ; νῆμα, thread) is the name of a genus of spirochætal micro-organisms which consist of slender spirals and which progress by means of bending movements. *Treponema pallidum* (formerly called *Spirochæta pallida*) is the causative organism of syphilis.

TRIAMCINOLONE is one of the newer corticosteroids, which has a potency equivalent to that of prednisone, but is less likely to cause retention of sodium.

TRIAMTERINE is a recently introduced diuretic which is active when taken by mouth.

TRICHIASIS (τριχίασις) means a diseased condition of the eyelids, generally the result of old-standing inflammation, in which the eyelashes grow inwards towards the eye so as to cause great pain and irritation. (*See* EYE, DISEASES OF.)

TRICHINIASIS (*see* TRICHINOSIS).

TRICHINOSIS (τρίχινος, hair-like) is the name of a disease set up by eating diseased pork, in which the immature *Trichinella spiralis* is encysted. (*See* PARASITES.)

TRICHLOROETHYLENE, also known as TRILENE, is a volatile anæsthetic which has the advantages of being non-irritant and of inducing anæsthesia rapidly and pleasantly. It has been used mainly for inducing analgesia or light anæsthesia in obstetrics and dentistry. In an impure form it is used commercially in the dry-cleaning industry.

TRICHO- (θρίξ, hair) is a prefix denoting relation to hair.

TRICHOCEPHALUS (θρίξ, hair, κεφαλή, the head), or WHIP-WORM, is the name of a parasite that infests the lower part of the bowel. It is especially common in France. (*See* PARASITES.)

TRICHOMONAS VAGINALIS. — A protozoon normally present in the vagina of about 30–40 per cent. of women. It sometimes becomes pathogenic and causes inflammation of the genital passages, with vaginal discharge. A man may become infected and have a urethral discharge as a result ; it may also cause prostatitis.

TRICHOPHYTON (θρίξ, hair ; φυτόν, a plant) is the name of the vegetable parasite that causes ringworm. (*See* RINGWORM.)

TRICHORRHŒA is the term applied to the falling-out of hair. It is usually due to some general disease such as scarlet fever or typhoid fever. When there is no obvious cause, such as this, treatment consists of attention to the general hygiene of the scalp. Vigorous massage is to be avoided.

TRICHOTILLOMANIA is the term given to the condition in which a mentally disordered person has an obsessional impulse to pull out his own hair.

TRICRESOL is the name of a clear, colourless, strongly antiseptic mixture of the three forms of cresol. It may be mixed with water in any proportions. (For uses *see* CRESOL.)

TRICUSPID VALVE is the valve provided with three cusps or flaps, that guards the opening from the right atrium into the right ventricle of the heart. (*See* HEART.)

TRIGEMINAL NERVE, or TRIFACIAL NERVE, is the fifth cranial nerve. It consists of three divisions : (1) the ophthalmic nerve, which is purely sensory in function, being distributed mainly over the forehead and front part of the scalp ; (2) the superior maxillary nerve, which is also sensory and distributed to the skin of the cheek, the mucous membrane of the mouth and throat, and the upper teeth ; and (3) the inferior maxillary nerve, which is the nerve of sensation to the lower part of the face, the tongue, and the lower teeth, as well as being the motor nerve to the muscles concerned in chewing. This nerve is of special interest, owing to its liability to neuralgia.

TRIGGER FINGER, or SNAPPING FINGER, is the condition in which when the fingers are straightened on unclenching the fist one finger, usually the ring or middle finger, remains bent. The cause is obscure. In severe cases treatment consists of opening up the sheath surrounding the tendon of the affected finger.

TRIGONE (τρίγωνον, triangle) is the base of the bladder between the openings of the two ureters and of the urethra.

TRIIODOTHYRONINE is the substance which exerts the physiological action of thyroid hormone. It is formed in the body cells by the deiodination of thyroxine (tetraiodothyronine) which is the active principle secreted by the thyroid gland. It has also been synthesized, and is now available for the treatment of myxœdema (*q.v.*). It is three times as potent as thyroxine. (*See also* THYROID GLAND.)

TRILENE (*see* TRICHLOROETHYL-ENE).

TRIMUSTINE is a nitrogen mustard derivative (*q.v.*) used in the treatment of certain forms of malignant disease. It is administered intravenously.

TRINITRIN (*see* NITROGLYCERIN).

TRINITROPHENOL (*see* PICRIC ACID).

TRISMUS (τρίζω, I grind the teeth) is another name for lockjaw. (*See* TETANUS.)

TROCAR (Fr. *trois quart*) is an instrument provided with a sharp three-sided point fitted inside a tube or cannula, and used for puncturing cavities of the body in which fluid has collected.

TROCHANTER (τροχαντήρ, the round head of the thigh-bone) is the name given to the prominence at the upper end of the thigh-bone which can be felt on the outer side of the thigh. A small prominence on the inner side of this bone receives the name of the small trochanter.

TROCHES (τροχός, a disc) is another name for lozenges. (*See* LOZENGES.)

TROCHLEAR NERVE (*trochlea*, pulley) is the name of the fourth cranial nerve, which acts upon the superior oblique muscle of the eye.

TROMEXAN, to which the ' approved ' name of ethyl biscoumacetate has been given, is an anticoagulant (*q.v.*) which is active when given by mouth.

TROPHIC (τρέφω, I nourish) is a term applied to the influence that nerves exert with regard to the healthiness and nourishment of the parts to which they run. When the nerves become diseased or injured, this influence is lost and the muscles waste, while the skin loses its healthy appearance and is liable to break down into ulcers. (*See* NERVOUS DISEASES, BED SORES.)

TROPHOBLAST is the outer layer of the fertilized ovum which attaches the ovum to the wall of the uterus (or womb) and supplies nutrition to the embryo.

TROPICAL DISEASES.—This term includes some diseases that occur in temperate climates, but are more common or more severe in hot latitudes ; as well as some that are found only in the tropics. (*See* BERI-BERI; BLACK-WATER FEVER ; CHOLERA, ASIATIC ; CLIMATE ; CLOTHING ; DENGUE ; DYS-ENTERY; ELEPHANTIASIS; FRAMBŒSIA ; LEPROSY ; LIVER, DISEASES OF ; MAL-ARIA ; ORIENTAL SORE ; PARASITES ; PLAGUE ; PRICKLY HEAT ; SLEEPING SICKNESS ; SUNBURN ; SUNSTROKE ; YELLOW FEVER.)

TROXIDONE is the *British Pharma-copœia* name for tridione, the chemical formula of which is 3 : 5 : 5-trimethyl-oxazolidine-2 : 4-dione. It has proved to be one of the most effective drugs for the treatment of *petit mal.*

TRUSS is an instrument used to support a hernia, or to retain the protruding organ within the cavity from which it tends to pass.

Varieties of truss. — The nature of trusses varies according to the situation

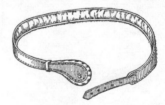

FIG. 371.—Simple truss for right inguinal hernia.

of the opening which the truss has to cover ; but every truss possesses a pad of some sort to cover the opening and a belt or spring to keep it in position.

VENTRAL TRUSSES intended for a hernia protruding through the wall of the abdomen, either at the navel or at some weak spot caused by a strain or by a wound, consist of a large flat pad kept in position by a belt passing round the waist. Sometimes a small pad made to fit the opening is adopted, but this is a mistake, as its pressure tends to enlarge the aperture.

INGUINAL TRUSSES are much more

commonly required than any other, and though many forms are made by different makers, all possess an oval obliquely placed pad with a spring pressing upon it. In the *ordinary truss*, there is a spring firmly fixed at one end to the pad, from which it passes right round the waist, to be bound at the other end by a short strap to the pad. Also there is a short strap passing down between the

Fig. 372.—Truss for double inguinal hernia.

legs and fastened to the truss before and behind so as to keep the pad from slipping upwards as the person moves. This is one of the cheapest and most generally used forms. The *Mocmain truss* differs from the ordinary truss in having a soft band to go round the waist and a short lever-spring to press upon the pad. The *Salmon and Ody truss* has a large pad pressing upon the small of the back, a

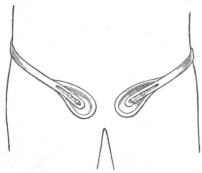

FIG. 373.—Double truss with celluloid pads in position.

wide spring which runs right round the side of the body opposite to that upon which the hernia exists, and crosses to the hernia, upon which it presses by a large pad with a ball-and-socket joint. *Double trusses* are often worn. They are fashioned like the ordinary truss, but have a pad for each side, and are advisable in the case of very stout people, in whom the retention of a

hernia upon one side is sometimes apt to produce a hernia at the other side. *Bath trusses* are made of vulcanite, india-rubber, lacquered metal, and other materials which will not spoil by wetting. Such trusses are also convenient for children, and many people who perspire copiously prefer them for general use. *Bag trusses*, consisting of a hollow pad kept in position by belts, etc., are sometimes necessary for the protection of a hernia which cannot be reduced.

FEMORAL TRUSSES are made in various forms similar to those of inguinal trusses. The pad, which comes down on the thigh, is small and triangular, so as not to press upon the femoral vessels. Such a truss is difficult to keep in position, and this is sometimes effected by having attached to the pad a thigh-piece which can be laced on the outer side of the thigh.

TRYPANOSOMA (τρύπανον, a gimlet; σῶμα, body) is the name of a genus of microscopic parasites of which several are responsible for causing sleeping sickness and some allied diseases. (*See* SLEEPING SICKNESS.)

TRYPANOSOMIASIS (*see* SLEEPING SICKNESS).

TRYPARSAMIDE is a complicated organic preparation of arsenic (sodium N - phenyl - glycineamide - *p* - arsonate) which was first used in the treatment of sleeping sickness. Because of its liability to cause blindness, it is now largely replaced by Mel B.

TRYPSIN is the name applied to the chief protein ferment of the pancreatic secretion. It changes proteins into peptones and forms the main constituent of pancreatic extracts used for digestion of food. (*See* PEPTONIZED FOOD.)

TSETSE FLY is the name of an African fly of the genus *Glossina*. One or more of these is responsible for carrying the trypanosome which causes sleeping sickness and thus spreads the disease among cattle and from cattle to men. (Fig. 339.)

TSUTSUGAMUSHI, or JAPANESE RIVER FEVER, is a disease of the typhus group. (*See* TYPHUS.)

TUBERCLE (*tuberculum*, a little lump) is a term used in two distinct senses. As a descriptive term in anatomy, a *tubercle* means a small elevation or roughness upon a bone, such as the tubercles of the ribs. In the pathological sense, a *tubercle* is a small mass, barely visible to the naked eye, formed in some organ as the starting-point of the disease which is now known as tuberculosis (Plate XI). The name of *tubercle bacillus* is given to the microorganism that causes this disease, although the official name is now *Mycobacterium tuberculosis*. The term tubercular should strictly be applied to anything connected with or resembling tubercles or nodules, and the term *tuberculous* to anything pertaining to the disease tuberculosis.

When tubercle bacilli have gained entrance to an organ, no matter whether inhaled on dust, or whether absorbed from food and circulated through the lymphatics or blood-vessels, the following results ensue. The individual bacilli multiply, and around each group forms a minute tubercle, or granule, which is of a size almost invisible to the naked eye, and greyish in colour. These tubercles fuse together, and, at the same time, soften to a cheesy substance, so as to form yellow bodies about the size of pin-heads. Each grey tubercle, under the microscope, shows the appearance of a group of cells of medium size (epithelioid cells), surrounded by many smaller cells (connective tissue cells and white blood corpuscles), attracted to the spot as a result of the inflammation set up. Scattered between these cells lie the tubercle bacilli. Near the centre of the older tubercles there are often seen one or more large cells with many nuclei (giant cells). The larger yellow tubercles form a more or less structureless mass in the centre, but show numbers of the small grey tubercles round their edge. Thus the process spreads, the healthy tissue being broken down and giving place to the soft, cheesy mass, which, in the case of the lungs, finally bursts into a bronchial tube, is coughed up, and leaves a ragged cavity in its place. Another change, however, takes place at the same time, for, in consequence of the irritation set up by the tubercle, strands of fibrous tissue are built up round its edge, and, when the process is a very chronic one, these come to form a dense capsule for the tuberculous area, cutting it off from further advance on healthy tissue, and forming Nature's cure.

TUBERCULIDE is the term given to any skin lesion which is the result of infection with the tubercle bacillus, or *Mycobacterium tuberculosis* as it is now known.

TUBERCULIN is the name originally given by Koch in 1890 to a preparation derived from the tubercle bacillus, or *Mycobacterium tuberculosis* as it is now known, and intended for the diagnosis or treatment of tuberculosis.

Varieties.—*Old Tuberculin* (O.T.) is made from a six-weeks-old culture of tubercle bacilli in glycerol broth, which is concentrated and then sterilized by heat filtration. It thus contains no bacilli but does contain substances produced by the bacilli during growth and substances resulting from the disintegration of the bacilli. *New Tuberculin* (T.R.) contains bacilli which have been ground up in 50 per cent. glycerol. Many other forms have been used at different times. The following are a few of those still in use : *Albumin-free Tuberculin* (T.A.F.), which differs from O.T. only in that the bacilli are grown in a special culture medium. *Bacillary Emulsion* (B.E.) is an emulsion of the entire substance of the bacilli. *Tuberculo-protein* (T.P.T.) has been specially treated so that it really contains only the bacillary substance responsible for the skin reaction. *Purified Protein Derivative* (P.P.D.) is probably the preparation least likely to give false, or unnecessarily severe, skin reactions.

Under the Therapeutic Substances Act, tuberculin is defined as ' preparations of fluid media in which *Bacillus tuberculosis* has been grown in artificial culture and which have been freed by filtration from the bacilli '. No Old Tuberculin preparation may be issued for use until it has been tested, and found satisfactory, in comparison with a standard preparation of Old Tuberculin which is kept in the National Institute for Medical Research, London.

Uses.—The basis of the tuberculin

reaction is that any person who has been infected with the *Mycobacterium tuberculosis* gives a reaction when a small amount of tuberculin is injected into the skin. This reaction consists of an inflammatory area, at least 5 mm. in diameter, which develops at the site of the test within two to four days of the test being made. If the area is less than 5 mm. in diameter the reaction is said to be negative. A negative reaction means that either the individual has never been infected with the tubercle bacillus, or that the infection has been too recent to have allowed of sensitivity developing. The only exceptions are that occasionally a negative reaction may be obtained in tuberculous subjects (*a*) in severe forms of the disease, (*b*) during pregnancy, (*c*) during an intercurrent infection.

To avoid serious reactions the test must be carried out in the first instance with a dilution of tuberculin of 1/10,000. If no reaction is obtained, the strength can be gradually increased: 1/1000; 1/100; 1/10. The amount used of any dilution is 0·1 millilitre.

There are various methods of carrying out the test, of which the following are the most commonly used. The *Mantoux Test* is the most satisfactory of all and has the advantage that the size of the reaction is a guide to the severity of the tuberculous infection. It is performed by injecting the tuberculin into the skin on the forearm. The *Heaf Multiple Puncture Test* is being used on an increasing scale because of its simplicity and reliability. It is carried out with the multiple puncture apparatus, or Heaf Gun, which enables six punctures to be made of equal depth : 2 mm. for adults, 1 mm. for children, depending upon which of the two detachable endpieces is used. The *Vollmer Patch Test* is particularly useful in children because of the ease with which it can be carried out. A piece of filter paper impregnated with tuberculin is fastened to the skin with adhesive plaster and left in position for forty-eight hours. *The von Pirquet Test* is carried out by placing a drop of undiluted Old Tuberculin on the skin and making a scratch in the skin through the drop, without drawing blood. The drop is then allowed to

dry. *Moro's reaction* is based upon rubbing a small piece of 50 per cent. tuberculin ointment into a small area of the skin of the chest.

TUBERCULOSIS (*tuberculum*, a little lump) is the general name for the whole group of diseases associated with the presence of the *Mycobacterium tuberculosis*, of which pulmonary tuberculosis is the most important. (*See* BACTERIOLOGY ; JOINTS, DISEASES OF.)

Tuberculosis not only affects the lungs, but may invade almost any organ, being seldom found, however, in the muscles or in tissues with few blood-vessels, like cartilage and sinews. The disease spreads usually by way of the lymphatic vessels. The severity of the disease varies considerably, according to the organ attacked—thus tuberculosis affecting the membranes of the brain and causing meningitis is a particularly dangerous disease, particularly in infants and young children. Chronic inflammation of bones and white swelling of joints are manifestations of the disease, having less influence upon the general health. The enlargement of glands, most common in the neck, to which the name of scrofula (Latin *scrofa*, a pig) was formerly given, because the swollen neck gives to the physiognomy a pig-like expression, is a well-known form of tuberculous disease. This form of the disease seems to have been much more widespread in former times, and was known also as ' king's-evil ', from the superstition that a touch of the royal hand conveyed a cure to the affected person. Many chronic abscesses are tuberculous in origin, arising from this affection in a bone, a gland, or the cellular tissue. The disfiguring skin disease known as lupus vulgaris is another of the manifestations of the disease. Other sites in which tuberculosis is apt to occur are the bowels and the genito-urinary tract, *i.e.* the kidneys, bladder, and epididymis.

Consumption, or phthisis (*consumo*, I destroy ; φθίσις, a wasting) is the name given, in popular language, to tuberculosis. It dates from the days when there was no effective treatment for tuberculosis, and the disease tended to be characterized by a rapid or gradual wasting away of the body. The term, phthisis, was usually restricted to that form of the disease in which the infection was restricted to the lungs : *i.e.* pulmonary tuberculosis.

The essential part of the disease, from which it receives its name of tuberculosis, is the formation in the substance of an organ of 'tubercles' (Plate XII), fine granules of a size barely visible to the naked eye, these tubercles multiplying and changing in such a way as to lead finally to the destruction of the organ in which they are found.

Nature of the disease.—Tuberculosis has been recognized as a disease from the earliest times. Hippocrates (460–380 B.C.) bestowed the name of phthisis upon the disease as it affects the lungs, and descriptions of the condition are found in the writings of classical authors. About A.D. 980 Haly Abbas of Baghdad, and again in 1779 Cullen, recognized the infectious nature of phthisis, but not till after the middle of the nineteenth century was it proved, by means of inoculating animals with tuberculous material from phthisical patients, that tuberculosis is really an infective disease, and that the 'tubercles' result from an inflammatory process, due to some poison introduced with the diseased products. The nature of the poison was much disputed till 1882, when Koch announced the discovery of the tubercle bacillus, or *Mycobacterium tuberculosis* as it is known (Plate VIII), and so answered this important question.

The manner in which these bacilli gain access to the body is important. There are three possible channels :

(*a*) BY INOCULATION. — A person may prick himself with a knife, etc., contaminated by the sputum of a tuberculous patient, or may rub some of this material into a cut. Generally this results merely in a local skin disease, and it occurs only in doctors, nurses, and others busied about consumptive hospitals.

(*b*) BY INHALATION. — The sputum and other discharges from tuberculous persons swarm with bacilli. It has been calculated that a person suffering from a cavity in the lung may spit up 4,000,000,000 bacilli in the course of twenty-four hours, and each of these, when dried and blown about on dust, is potent for evil. Neither drying, nor freezing, nor putrefaction, nor the lapse of months destroys these bacilli, but direct sunlight is speedily fatal to them, so that dust which has lain for a short time in the open on a bright day becomes rapidly harmless. In rooms inhabited by tuberculous patients, and in hospital wards, the dust from the floor frequently contains *Mycobacterium tuberculosis*.

Probably almost all cases in which this disease primarily affects the lungs are due to inhalation of dust laden with the bacilli or inhalation of droplets coughed into the air by a tuberculous patient, whilst those cases in which the glands of the neck are first attacked arise by absorption of the bacilli through the tonsils.

That this manner of infection is of great importance is shown by the fact that, of all persons dying of tuberculous diseases generally in England and Wales over nine-tenths die from this disease as it affects the lungs.

(*c*) BY INGESTION.—It has long been known that tuberculosis, like other infectious diseases, can be conveyed by means of milk and other articles of food, and, acting upon this belief, sanitary authorities have enforced regulations designed to protect the public from the effects of consuming diseased meat and milk. In the case of meat there is practically no danger, as the muscular tissues are exempt from the disease, and those parts which are diseased being, in the 'dressing' of the meat, carefully removed, any accidental contact with them is rendered harmless by the cooking of the meat.

The Royal Commission on Tuberculosis in its report issued in 1907, as well as various other observers, found that the bovine tubercle bacillus is present in a large proportion of diseased glands in children. It has also been found that in tuberculosis affecting the bones and joints of children from one-third to one-half are caused by the bovine bacillus, the rest by the human bacillus.

We may therefore conclude that the tissues of healthy human adults are more capable of resisting the bacillus of bovine source than are those of children, but that bovine tuberculosis may be, and often is, communicated through milk to children.

Much progress has been made of

recent years in eradicating tuberculosis from cattle in this country, and on October 1, 1960, the Ministry of Agriculture, Fisheries, and Food declared the whole of Great Britain an attested area, thus marking the successful completion of the official scheme to eradicate bovine tuberculosis as a disease of cattle on a nation-wide scale. Even though milk from such attested cattle, as they are known, is safe to drink from the point of tuberculosis, it is still a wise precaution to allow children to drink only pasteurized milk.

Mortality.—The figures in Table 27 show the steady decline in the number of deaths due to tuberculosis.

	Respiratory	Other forms	All forms
1851–1860	1,336	1,926	1,438
1861–1870	1,236	1,872	1,346
1871–1880	1,063	1,796	1,190
1881–1890	863	1,682	1,004
1891–1900	675	1,525	815
1901–1910	540	1,232	649
1911–1920	479	898	541
1921–1930	336	524	362
1931–1939	223	336	245
1940–1944	209	309	221
1945–1949	169	204	174
1950–1954	85	82	85
1955–1959	37	31	36
1966	16	14	16

TABLE 27.—Tuberculosis Standardized Mortality Ratios for England and Wales.

A very much larger number of the population suffer from early tuberculosis (it may be quite unsuspected) and recover. This is proved by the frequent presence on X-ray examination of old calcified tuberculous glands and by healed scars in the lungs found at autopsy.

Causes.—From what has been said it will be seen that the direct cause of the disease is the tubercle bacillus, or *Mycobacterium tuberculosis*, discovered by Koch. (*See* BACTERIOLOGY.) But, in view of the fact that many people suffer from the disease in a mild degree and afterwards recover, and that many limited cases of tuberculosis in bones, skin, glands, etc., are successfully treated, it appears that there are other factors which determine whether a given case is serious or not, and whether it is likely to proceed towards recovery, if properly treated, or to end inevitably in death.

HEREDITY.—There is probably a hereditary element in the predisposi-

916

tion to the disease. Over a long period those who are susceptible are gradually eliminated by the disease.

AGE is an important point. Young children, as above stated, are liable to tuberculosis affecting the bowels and the glands connected with them. At a slightly later age there is a greater tendency to that type of the disease formerly known as scrofula, the glands of the neck particularly being affected, and the greatest mortality from lung consumption takes place after the age of twenty is reached.

SEX.—As is shown in Table 28, in women a higher proportion of the cases of respiratory tuberculosis occur in early adult life than in the case of men.

Age-group	Notifications		Deaths	
	Males	Females	Males	Females
0–14	605	586	5	2
15–24	945	781	4	3
25–44	2,334	1,511	95	83
45 and over	4,339	1,208	1,455	447
All ages	8,250	4,105	1,599	531

TABLE 28.—Notifications of, and Deaths from, Respiratory Tuberculosis according to Sex and Age in England and Wales in 1966.

ATMOSPHERE.—The character of the atmosphere in which work is carried on has much to do with the onset of tuberculosis. Those who habitually live and work in ill-ventilated rooms are at a great disadvantage compared with those who lead an open-air life, or, at all events, keep their rooms well ventilated. It has been noticed that soldiers, sailors, and convicts have a much less liability to contract this disease than men of the same classes living in unhygienic homes. Further, the amount and nature of the dust in the air is highly important. Thus among agricultural labourers there are few deaths from tuberculosis; among wool-workers, carpet-makers, and masons there are about twice as many; among iron, steel, and copper workers three times; whilst cutlers, scissors-grinders, and file-makers head the list with four times as many consumptives as the agricultural labourers. It is a noteworthy fact, however, that coal-miners, whose lungs are literally black from inhaled coal dust, die in appreciably fewer numbers from tuberculosis than do even open-air workers, the coal dust or the nature of the work having, apparently, some protective effect.

OTHER DISEASES are of great importance in relation to tuberculosis. For example, a person who has long suffered from asthma or bronchitis may develop tuberculosis in the end, and diabetics not uncommonly contract this disease, but this has occurred less frequently since the introduction of insulin. It must be remembered, too, that several lung diseases closely resemble tuberculosis : for example, chronic catarrh following on a simple cold, bronchiectasis, and interstitial pneumonia. Further, it is not uncommon that a person suffers from tuberculosis and apparently recovers ; then, when some business reverse or family trouble comes, the disease reappears and he rapidly succumbs.

Varieties.—The forms of tuberculosis other than pulmonary tuberculosis, such as tuberculous disease of joints and bones, meningitis, lupus, etc., are

but the whole body becomes studded with the tubercles of the disease distributed by the blood, and the sufferer dies, from fever and exhaustion, in two or three weeks. This is the most rapid form, and, with the second variety, goes under the popular name of ' Galloping Consumption '.

2. ACUTE CASEOUS TUBERCULOSIS is a slightly slower form. The lungs only are affected, and, either in consequence of the bacilli inhaled into the lungs being specially virulent, or, more likely, owing to the person having acquired no immunity to the disease, or being in a particularly weak state, or of unhealthy constitution, tubercles form, undergo the caseous change, and break down to form cavities with great rapidity (Fig. 375), the patient dying in two or three months.

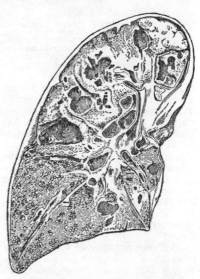

FIG. 375.—Lung showing acute caseous tuberculosis, with large masses of caseous material in the upper half, breaking down to form numerous large cavities. In the lower part are numerous scattered tubercles. (Miller.)

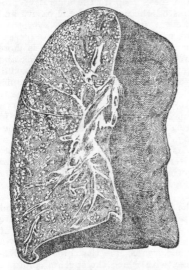

FIG. 374.—Lung showing acute miliary tuberculosis. The small masses of tubercles are seen scattered as white specks on the cut surface. (Miller.)

considered under these headings. The lung disease has, however, itself several varieties, differing much from one another.

1. ACUTE MILIARY TUBERCULOSIS.— In this form not only the lungs (Fig. 374),

3. FIBRO-CASEOUS TUBERCULOSIS is the usual form and may last for years. The change which occurs in the lungs is very much the same as in the last form, but, in addition, and in consequence of greater resisting power on the sufferer's part, there is an attempt at nature's cure, and much fibrous tissue is formed. The lung becomes denser, cavities

gradually form here and there (Fig. 376), and the downward progress is slow or may be arrested.

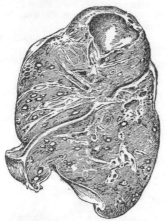

FIG. 376.—Lung showing chronic fibro-caseous tuberculosis, with marked tendency to healing. A large cavity and the healed scar of another are seen near the apex. Numerous scattered nodules of fibro-caseous material, all showing signs of healing, are scattered through the lung. (Miller.)

4. FIBROID TUBERCULOSIS is a form in which areas of the lung are converted into fibrous masses, which are in reality scars of previous disease that has undergone nature's cure, and there are no cavities.

Symptoms.—In the following brief account, the symptoms of an average case, in which fibrous formation and the caseous change leading to production of a cavity take place side by side, will be described. They fall conveniently into three stages of the disease :

(a) EARLY STAGE.—In this stage the tubercles are being deposited in the lung, almost always near the apex ; and this part of the lung becomes, in consequence, more solid. There is cough of an irritative nature, particularly in the morning, either without any expectoration or accompanied by a little clear mucus. Sometimes, the first sign of all is the spitting up of blood (hæmoptysis), which is never copious at this stage, and is due to congestion caused by the irritation of the tubercles. (See HÆMORRHAGE.) There is generally, from the first, loss of appetite, colour, and strength, followed soon by actual emaciation and loss of weight. Per-

spiration upon slight exertion is usual, and, very often, night sweats are a symptom. A very important sign is a regular rise of temperature, either in the forenoon, or more often in the early afternoon, with a fall below normal in the early morning, but this is not an invariable symptom of phthisis at this stage. The digestive functions are usually thrown out of gear, and there is apt to be sickness, diarrhœa, or constipation. A slight attack of pleurisy, causing pain in the chest, is very often a precursor of, or accompanies, these symptoms. This is the stage in which the disease is readily curable.

(b) STAGE OF ADVANCING DISEASE.—By this time, the tubercles have fused to form caseous masses, and these are breaking down and being spat up, leaving a ragged cavity, while the disease is slowly advancing to new areas of the lung. The surface of the cavity becomes infected sooner or later with other organisms inhaled on dust, and these keep up the ulcerative process on the surface of the cavity and prevent its healing. The symptoms are mainly an increase of those present in the first stage. The cough is more troublesome and the spit is thick and yellow, contains large numbers of bacilli, which can be stained and microscopically examined, and is occasionally streaked with blood. The sufferer is much weaker, and has greatly lost in weight. The temperature is of a swinging ' hectic ' type, rising to 100° or 101° F. (37·8° or 38·3° C.) in the late afternoon and falling, sometimes below normal, in the early part of the day (Fig. 377). Drenching night sweats are apt to break out during sleep in the early hours of the morning, and attacks of vomiting or diarrhœa are not infrequent. The disease may at this stage be found in both lungs or in other organs, like the throat or intestine, with which the sputum comes in contact. An important sign is that of falling in of the chest over the excavated area, so that a flat place or depression is found in its upper part.

(c) LATE STAGE.—In this stage, large cavities have usually formed in the lung, or there has been a production of fibrous tissue, the lung being shrunken and consisting of a mass of matted fibrous tissue and smaller cavities.

Accordingly, the whole side has usually fallen in considerably. The second lung is by this time extensively affected; the voice may be husky on account of disease in the throat, or there may be troublesome diarrhœa, due to affection of the bowels. Hæmorrhage is not uncommon in this stage, and death may be brought about by this means. The emaciation is now extreme, and bed-sores are apt to form. The swinging temperature and the excess-

(a) PREVENTIVE TREATMENT.—The problem of prevention is partly social and partly medical. Tuberculosis is commoner among the ill-fed and the badly housed. Abolition of over-crowding, provision of good homes, an adequate supply of ' protective ' foods and enough money to buy them have all gone a long way towards diminishing the incidence of tuberculosis. To a con-siderable extent, tuberculosis is a social disease. On the medical side, the

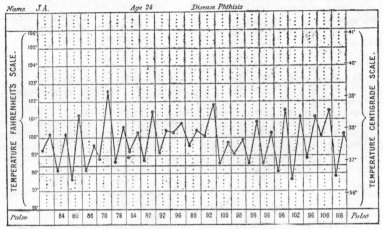

FIG. 377.—Typical temperature chart in a case of pulmonary, tuberculosis, showing the swinging temperature, as taken twice daily.

ive sweats continue, and the cough is often most troublesome. All through the disease, even to the very end, there is often a curious mental state known as the ' spes phthisica ', the sufferer being buoyed up by the daily recurring belief that he is better, and is beginning to recover.

The duration of the illness is largely dependent upon four factors : the acuteness of the infection, the age of the patient, the stage at which efficient treatment is started, and the natural resistance of the patient to the disease, Acute miliary tuberculosis, for instance. is rapidly fatal unless treatment is initiated at an early stage, and the disease runs a more rapid course in children, adolescents, and young adults than in the middle-aged.

Treatment.—This falls very natur-ally into two classes—(a) preventive, and (b) remedial.

problem is essentially to prevent un-infected susceptible people—especially children—from coming into contact with the infecting agent—the *Myco-bacterium tuberculosis*. The great risk to the child is coming into contact with an adult who has the causative organism in his or her sputum. So every attempt must be made (1) to detect all sufferers from tuberculosis, (2) to treat them and isolate them until they know how to safeguard other people by the proper use of sputum pots, etc., and (3) to examine and ' fol-low up ' all ' contact ' cases—especially children known to have been in close contact with adults suffering from tuberculosis.

Two of the most important preven-tive measures introduced of recent years have been B.C.G. vaccination (*q.v.*) and mass miniature radiography (*q.v.*). By means of the former an immunity to the disease can be given to those who have not acquired a natural immunity. By means of mass miniature radiography the disease can often be detected at an early stage when it is most likely to respond to treatment.

(b) REMEDIAL TREATMENT. — This consists of general treatment, collapse therapy, surgical treatment, and chemotherapy.

Early cases are much benefited by a change of air. Sea-voyages in many cases, mountain air in others, and a winter spent in a dry, bright climate in still a third group are most valuable (see CLIMATE). When these are impossible or inadvisable, the sufferer should spend his nights in a well-ventilated, large bedroom, and during the day should pass the whole time walking, sitting, or lying in the open air, protected from rain and wind by a veranda, or in one of the shelters used at sanatoria. While lying out in the open air, the sufferer must be particularly well wrapped up, especial care being taken to keep the hands and feet warm.

FIG. 378.—Open-air shelter protected on three sides from the weather.

Excessive exercises, like running or football, are bad for any case and tend to bring on hæmorrhage. The amount of exercise advisable depends greatly upon the nature of the individual case. At many sanatoria patients are graduated for exercise according to the length of time they have been in residence and the stage of their general symptoms, somewhat as follows :

1. Walking exercise, morning and afternoon, graduated from one to eight miles per diem.
2. *Grade 1.*—Very light gardening, such as weeding and tidying the garden.

Grade 2.—Ditto and hoeing and planting.

Grade 3.—Light gardening, such as planting and transplanting, mowing the lawns with assistance, and the light work of a kitchen garden.

Grade 4.—Sawing and chopping wood and digging with a small fork or spade.

Grade 5.—Digging and trenching the garden with full-size tools, and garden truck work.

All the above rest an hour before the midday meal.

Grade 6.—Same as Grade 5, without the said hour's rest.

The lower grades are employed more in the general garden, and the higher ones in the kitchen garden.

Other forms of labour are tree-felling and the care of pigs and poultry.

A limited amount of painting, glazing, and carpentering is also done.

All patients keep their own wards clean.

Diet is one of the essentials of treatment. What is required is a well-balanced diet containing 3000 to 4000 calories daily. In practice this means a diet containing 100 to 120 grammes of protein (milk, meat, fish and eggs), 400 grammes of carbohydrate and 200 grammes of fat. The diet should be varied and appetizing. It is essential to maintain a high intake of vitamin D. This can be partly achieved by including plenty fish in the diet but, in addition, it is advisable to give extra supplements of both vitamin D (2500 international units), and vitamin A (18,000 international units) daily.

Collapse Therapy.—Rest for the affected lung is of great importance. It is gained sufficiently in early cases by the gentleness of breathing maintained through general rest and careful avoidance of all violent movement. In advancing cases when one lung only is affected, this lung is often immobilized by introducing air into the pleural cavity (pneumothorax). This simple operation is carried out by a puncture between the ribs and introduction of a measured quantity of air. The lung collapses towards its root, and goes to a large extent out of action, thus allowing healing to take place in and around the cavities. The operation must be repeated at frequent intervals, as the air is quickly absorbed, until, after several months of treatment, the lung is allowed to expand again. In some cases, particularly if the disease is predominantly in the lower lobes of the lungs, the same effect may be obtained by introducing air into the peritoneal cavity (pneumoperitoneum). This pushes the diaphragm upwards and immobilizes it, thereby collapsing, or very much reducing the movement, of the lower lobes of the lungs.

Surgical Treatment.—In certain cases where adhesions have formed between the lung and the chest wall, it is found impossible to produce a complete pneumothorax. If a partial collapse can be obtained through the introduction of a certain amount of air, the collapse in some cases can be made complete by cutting or burning the adhesions through a thoracoscope. A state of partial and permanent rest for the affected lung may, however, be obtained by putting one-half of the diaphragm out of action through the operation of cutting the phrenic nerve in the neck (phrenicectomy).

In advanced cases with firm adhesions between lung and chest and with large cavities which cannot close, a good result sometimes follows an operation by which several ribs are removed and the cavities thus permitted to close. This operation (thoracoplasty), in the hands of a skilled surgeon, often gives excellent results in the right type of case. Surgical technique has now reached such a high standard that in certain cases in which the disease process has reached an advanced stage but is confined to one lung, it is possible to remove the affected lung.

Chemotherapy.—The outlook in tuberculosis has been revolutionized by the introduction of effective antituberculous drugs. Since the isolation, in 1944, of streptomycin, the first chemotherapeutic substance to be of any value in the treatment of tuberculosis, several other drugs have been introduced for this purpose, but the two important ones are para-aminosalicylic acid (P.A.S.) and isoniazid. This triad—streptomycin, P.A.S., and isoniazid—now constitute the basis of treatment of all forms of tuberculosis. Each of these is discussed under its name, but there are two general aspects of the chemotherapy that should be

mentioned here. The first is that the *Mycobacterium tuberculosis* has the unfortunate habit of becoming resistant to each of these drugs if it is given by itself. This can be prevented by giving two or more of them together. Thus, the routine treatment of tuberculosis now consists of the administration of (a) streptomycin combined with either P.A.S. or isoniazid ; or (b) P.A.S. and isoniazid. The second is that whilst their introduction has marked a big advance in the treatment of tuberculosis, they are merely ancillary to the other well-established lines of treatment which have been outlined in this section, *e.g.* rest, fresh air, and good food. It is when they are carefully integrated into a well-planned programme of treatment, under the supervision of a skilled physician, that they bring most benefit to the patient.

Eradication of Tuberculosis.—Since the turn of the century there has been a marked fall in the incidence of tuberculosis, as is well shown in Table 27, which gives the standardized mortality ratios for England and Wales from the decade, 1851–1860, to 1960. This shows that the ratio for pulmonary tuberculosis fell from 1336 in 1851–60 to 17 in 1964.

The figures for recent years are the most striking of all. Thus, in England and Wales the standardized mortality ratio for pulmonary tuberculosis fell from 85 in 1950–1954 to 17 in 1964.

Apart from the treatment of individual cases, the general measures adopted for its eradication are :

1. THE DISPENSARY SYSTEM, introduced by Sir Robert Philip in 1887, by which cases of tuberculosis are classified, treated, serious ones sent to sanatoria, and their dwellings and families investigated so as to deal with other early cases and educate those exposed to infection how best to avoid it.

2. PREVENTION OF BOVINE INFECTION, especially by obtaining a pure supply of milk, cream, and butter from healthy cows ; or if the milk be suspected, by sterilization of all milk to be consumed by children. (*See* MILK.)

3. B.C.G. VACCINE, for the protection of infants born to tuberculous mothers,

and of young adults particularly exposed to risk of infection, *e.g.* medical students and nurses.

4. MASS MINIATURE RADIOGRAPHY for the detection of cases at an early stage of the disease, when it is most amenable to treatment. This is also a valuable means of detecting the disease in individuals who, unbeknown to themselves and others, are suffering from the disease and spreading it to others with whom they live or work.

TUBEROSE SCLEROSIS, or EPILOIA, is a disease, usually hereditary, characterized by mental deficiency, epilepsy, and multiple cutaneous tumours of the cheeks and face. The condition is considered to be a developmental abnormality of the brain.

TUBULAR (*tubulus*, a small pipe) is a term used in two distinct senses. It is applied to disease affecting the small tubes of an organ, *e.g.* tubular bronchitis, tubular nephritis. It is also applied to the high-pitched breath-sounds heard on auscultation over a very dense area of consolidation in the lung.

TULARÆMIA is a disease of rodents such as rabbits and rats, caused by the *Pasteurella tularense*, and spread either by flies or by direct inoculation, for example, into the hands of a person engaged in skinning rabbits. In man the disease takes the form of a slow fever lasting several weeks, with much malaise and depression, followed by considerable emaciation. It was first described in the district of Tulare in California, and is found widely spread in North America and in Europe, but not in Great Britain. Streptomycin, the tetracyclines and chloramphenicol, have proved effective in treatment.

TUMOUR (*tumor*) means literally any swelling, but, by common consent, the term is held not to include passing swellings caused by acute inflammation, whilst the collections of diseased material arising in the course of chronic inflammation, like tuberculosis, syphilis, leprosy, and glanders, sometimes are and sometimes are not classed as tumours, according to their size and appearance.

Varieties.—Some are of an infective nature, as already stated ; some arise undoubtedly as the result of injury ; several contributing factors are mentioned under the heading of CANCER, but for the rest, the causes of tumours are really still undiscovered.

An old idea divides tumours into two great classes. On the one hand, some are *simple* or *benign*, growing slowly at one spot, pressing neighbouring parts aside but not invading them, not recurring after removal, and having little tendency to ulcerate ; whilst others are *malignant*, spreading quickly from point to point, invading and destroying surrounding tissues, tending to recur after apparently complete removal, and being very liable to ulcerate. This distinction is as old as the days of Hippocrates, who gave to gnawing tumours the name of carcinoma (καρκίνωμα). Although in the majority of cases it is easy to decide whether a given tumour is of simple or malignant character, there is no sharp dividing line between the two kinds. Thus an expert sometimes has difficulty in stating from the microscopic characters of an *adenoma* (glandular tumour) growing in the breast or in the bowel, whether its progress will show a simple or malignant course. Again, *rodent ulcer*, a small ulcerating tumour situated generally on the face, may remain restricted to a single spot for twenty or thirty years, although it has the microscopic characters of a malignant tumour and finally spreads like one. Another fact connecting the two groups is that some simple tumours, persisting as such through middle life, are liable to assume a malignant character when old age is reached.

Formerly tumours were named according to some peculiarity of shape, colour, etc. Thus a fungoid tumour was one resembling a mushroom, a polypus one which seemed to have one stalk with many feet, a mole was a dark hairy growth resembling the animal of that name, and sarcoma (σάρκωμα) was originally the name given by Galen to a tumour of fleshy appearance. The use of the microscope, however, has brought about a more precise grouping, and tumours are now classed according to the tissues of which they are built, somewhat as follows :

(1) Simple tumours of normal tissue.
(2) Hollow tumours or cysts, generally of simple nature.
(3) Malignant tumours: (a) of imperfect cellular structure, resembling the cells of skin, mucous membrane, or secreting glands ; (b) of imperfect connective tissue.

(1) SIMPLE TUMOURS OF NORMAL TISSUE.—ADENOMA is a tumour growing from a gland and composed of gland-like tissue. These tumours are specially common in the breasts of young women ; there may be several together, but usually they are easily removed.

ANGIOMA is a tumour formed by a mass of small blood-vessels or spaces in which blood circulates. These tumours may exist in internal organs, or on the skin, when they do not project much, and are known as nævi or 'mothers' marks '.

CHONDROMA is a tumour mainly formed of cartilage. These tumours develop especially on the fingers and toes.

FIBROMA is the name given to a tumour consisting mainly of fibrous tissue. Soft fibromas are often seen as wrinkled brownish tags upon the face or body.

LIPOMA means a tumour mainly composed of fat. Such tumours may be found in any part of the body, but they are especially common just beneath the skin. It is sometimes hard to distinguish such a tumour, which is very soft, from a chronic abscess ; but the fatty tumour generally has a firm edge and can be seen to be attached at several points to the skin, which is puckered by these attachments.

MYOMA is a tumour composed largely of muscle fibres, usually unstriped muscle. These tumours are far more commonly found in the wall of the womb than in any other position, being known as fibroid tumours.

NEUROMA is a tumour growing upon a nerve, and therefore in many cases producing pain.

OSTEOMA is a tumour composed of bone. These are usually of small size and cause little trouble, except in so far as their position occasions discomfort.

PAPILLOMA is a tumour projecting from the surface of the skin or of a mucous membrane. It is composed of a core of fibrous tissue, which represents an over-development of the papillæ naturally found in these situations, covered by masses of cells. Warts are examples of papillomas on the skin (see WARTS), whilst soft papillomas sometimes develop in the bladder or bowel and cause much bleeding.

(2) HOLLOW TUMOURS are described under a special heading. (See CYSTS.)

(3) MALIGNANT TUMOURS of imperfect cellular structure resembling the cells of skin, mucous membranes, or secreting glands, are known generally as CANCERS. This group and the following group are treated together under the heading of CANCER AND SARCOMA. Many names are applied to cancers of different parts and according to their appearance. The name CARCINOMA is generally reserved at the present day for malignant epithelial tumours. EPITHELIOMA is a cancer springing from the skin surface, and ADENOCARCINOMA means one originating in glandular tissue. SCIRRHUS is a hard cancer in which much fibrous tissue has been developed ; MEDULLARY or SOFT cancer is one in which the softer cellular element forms large masses ; and COLLOID cancer is one in which a characteristic glue-like transformation takes place. (See Plate VII.)

Malignant tumours of imperfect connective tissue are at the present day known as SARCOMAS ; and, according to the shape of the embryonic cells, or the nature of attempts at the formation of connective tissues, these are subdivided as ROUND-CELLED, SPINDLE-CELLED, MELANOTIC, MYELOID, etc. (Plate VII.)

Symptoms.—The symptoms of simple tumours are, as a rule, nothing beyond the presence of a swelling, and such accidental symptoms as those set up by its pressure upon neighbouring important organs, by the inconvenience of its size, its position, and the like. (For special symptoms of malignant tumours, see CANCER and SARCOMA.)

Treatment. — The treatment of a tumour is, in general, its removal by operation. With regard to simple tumours, the advantage gained by removal is frequently not worth the inconvenience caused by an operation, and such tumours may be left alone. In particular cases the unsightliness of the tumour, the inconvenience of its size, or the tendency that some simple tumours have to become malignant may call for removal. If a tumour be malignant, or if there be any doubt as to its character, an operation should be performed at the earliest possible opportunity. For some surface tumours, and also for inoperable tumours in internal organs, the application of radium and X-rays has, in recent years, played a great part (*see* RADIUM *and* X-RAYS).

TUNNEL-WORM is another name for the ankylostoma. (*See* PARASITES.)

TURBINATE, or TURBINAL (*turbo*, top), is the name applied to the three processes on the outer side of each nasal fossa, formed by bony projections covered by thick mucous membrane. These serve to warm and moisten the air as it passes over them into the upper air passages on its way to the lungs. The lowest of these, the inferior turbinate process, is apt to become inflamed and enlarged, leading in some cases to blockage of the nose. In such cases it requires to be reduced in size by various astringent applications or by the electro-cautery, or to be removed by operation.

TURNING (*see* VERSION).

TURNER'S SYNDROME is a congenital malformation characterized by webbing of the neck, deformity of the forearm, dwarfism and persistent infantilism.

TURN OF LIFE is a term applied to the menopause. (*See* CLIMACTERIC.)

TURPENTINE is the oleo-resin which exudes from trees of the pine family when the bark is injured. The oil distilled from this is known as oil of turpentine, rectified turpentine, or spirit of turpentine, the residue being the resin or rosin. The natural turpentine, containing resin, is not used in medicine,

924

since it is highly irritating; and when the word turpentine is used, the distilled product is always understood. The turpentine obtained from the ordinary yellow pine is the common form, that obtained from the silver fir is known as Canada balsam or balm of Gilead, and that got from the larch as Venice turpentine. Chian turpentine is got from the *Pistachia terebinthus*, an Eastern tree.

Action.—Turpentine has an action similar to that of other essential oils. It is highly irritating to any surface with which it is brought in contact, is antispasmodic, and, especially when it has been exposed to the air, is powerfully antiseptic.

Uses. — *Externally*, turpentine is used as a counter-irritant. It forms one of the most common ingredients of liniments and embrocations for application to sprains and bruises. It is used with hot fomentations when a specially strong action is desired, a fomentation sprinkled with turpentine being known as a 'stupe (*see* FOMENTATIONS). In chronic bronchitis, rubbing the chest with turpentine is a favourite household remedy.

Internally, turpentine is seldom administered now. In lumbago and other forms of chronic rheumatism, 5 drops of turpentine taken upon a lump of sugar thrice daily over a long period is an old household remedy. As an enema, an ounce of oil of turpentine may be mixed with half a pint of soapy water in order to relieve severe cases of flatulence.

TWILIGHT SLEEP is the name given to a method of anæsthesia at one time used in child-birth, but now practically discarded. The unconsciousness of pain was brought about by the hypodermic injection of morphine in full dose, with a small dose of scopolamine which was repeated about once an hour throughout the course of the labour or until the patient was unconscious.

TYMPANIC MEMBRANE is the ear-drum.

TYMPANITES (τυμπανίτης) means distension of the abdomen due to the presence of gas or air in the intestine or in the peritoneal cavity. The abdomen, when struck with the fingers, gives under these conditions a drum - like (tympanitic) note.

TYMPANUM (*tympanum*, a drum) is another name for the middle ear. (*See* EAR.)

TYPEWRITER'S CRAMP (*see* CRAMP, TRADE DISEASES).

TYPHLITIS (τυφλόν, the blind end of the large intestine) means inflammation of the cæcum or first part of the large intestine, into which the small intestine and the appendix vermiformis open. As the associated condition of appendicitis is of far greater importance than typhlitis, the latter name is little used.

TYPHOID FEVER (*see* ENTERIC FEVER).

TYPHOMALARIAL is a term applied to fevers which are of malarial origin but show typhoid symptoms.

TYPHUS FEVER (from τῦφος, smoke mist, in allusion to or the stupor of the disease) is an infective disease of world-wide distribution, the manifestations phus, and louse-borne typhus, is an acute infection of abrupt onset which, in the absence of treatment, persists for fourteen days. It is of world-wide distribution, but is particularly common in Eastern Europe, Russia, Northern Africa, and China. The causative organism is the *Rickettsia prowazeki*, so-called after Ricketts and Prowazeki, two brilliant investigators of typhus, both of whom died of the disease. It is transmitted by the louse. The rickettsiæ can survive in the dried fæces of lice for 60 days, and these infected fæces are probably the main source of infection of man.

Symptoms.—The incubation period is usually 10 to 14 days. The onset is preceded by headache, pain in the back and limbs, and rigors. On the third day the temperature rises suddenly, and the face and eyes become congested. At the same time the headache becomes more intense, and the patient is drowsy or delirious. Sometimes on this day, but more usually on the fifth or sixth day, the characteristic rash appears on the abdomen and inner aspect of the arms, to spread over the chest, back, and trunk, but seldom involving the face except in severe cases. It has been described as a

Typhus fevers (Rickettsiasis)

Epidemic (exanthematic) 'Louse' typhus

Non-epidemic typhus

Flea (murine) typhus (Brill's disease)

Tick typhus   Mite typhus (Tsutsugamushi)

Rocky Mountain spotted fever
Bullis fever
Fièvre Boutonneuse
South African 'tick-bite fever'

FIG. 378 a.—Classification of the typhus fevers.

of which vary in different localities. The causative organisms of all forms of typhus fever belong to the genus Rickettsia. These are organisms which are intermediate between bacteria and viruses in their properties and measure $0.5\,\mu$ or less in diameter. The following classification of the typhus fevers by Manson-Bahr provides a practical basis for discussion of the subject (Fig. 378 a).

Epidemic Typhus Fever, also known as exanthematic typhus, classical ty- 'mulberry rash' and consists essentially of reddish spots on a dusky background. During the second week a low muttering delirium develops, the patient becomes restless, and great prostration develops. In cases which are not going to recover, death usually occurs from heart failure about the fourteenth day. In those who recover, the temperature falls by crisis about this time (Fig. 379). In severe cases, and in neglected cases, gangrene is liable to occur. In diagnosis the Weil-Felix reaction is helpful. The death-rate is variable, varying from nearly 100 per cent. in epidemics among debilitated refugees to about 10 per cent.

Murine Typhus Fever, also known as flea typhus and Brill's disease (after N. E. Brill who first described it in New York in 1898), is world-wide in its distribution and is found wherever individuals are crowded together in insanitary, rat-infested areas. Hence

group consist of Rocky Mountain Spotted Fever, Fièvre Boutonneuse, and Tick-bite Fever.

Rocky Mountain Spotted Fever was reported originally in the mountainous western states of the U.S.A., but it is now found in many of the eastern states. The causal organism is *Rickettsia rickettsii*. The usual transmitters are the wood tick (*Dermacentor andersoni*) and the dog tick (*Dermacentor variabilis*) but there is evidence that other ticks

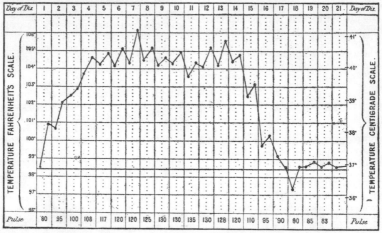

FIG. 379.—Chart showing the ordinary course of the temperature in a case of typhus fever. The fall by sudden crisis differs markedly from the gradual subsidence in typhoid fever.

the old names of jail-fever and ship typhus. The causative organism, *Rickettsia muricola* (or *mooseri*), which is closely related to *R. prowazeki*, is transmitted to man by the rat-flea, *Xenopsyalla cheopis*. The rat is the main reservoir of infection. Once man is infected, the human louse may act as a transmitter of the Rickettsia from man to man. This explains how the disease may become epidemic under insanitary, crowded conditions. As a rule, however, the disease is only acquired when man comes into close contact with infected rats.

Symptoms.—These are similar to those of louse-borne typhus, but the disease usually runs a milder course, and the mortality rate is very low (about 1·5 per cent.).

TICK TYPHUS, in which the infecting Rickettsia is transmitted by ticks, occurs in various parts of the world. The three best-known conditions in this

may occasionally transmit the disease. The highest incidence of the disease is in the spring and early summer, when the ticks are most active.

Symptoms.—The incubation period is three to twelve days. After a day or two of headache, backache, and loss of appetite the onset is rapid, with intensification of the headache, rigors, sickness, and congestion of the eyes. The temperature rises by steps to 103–106° F. (39·4 to 41·1° C.). The rash usually appears on the second to fourth day, first in the wrist and ankles, and then spreading over the whole body. It is usually more florid than the rash of louse typhus. The temperature settles slowly by lysis after two or three weeks. Convalescence is slow. The mortality rate varies, averaging about 20 per cent. ; it is low in children and high in adults and the elderly.

Fièvre Boutonneuse, also known as Marseilles fever, is a mild form of tick

typhus which occurs in the south of France and along the north coast of Africa. The causative organism is *Rickettsia conori*, which is probably identical with *Rickettsia rickettsii*. It is transmitted by a dog tick, *Rhipicephalus sanguineus*. One of the distinctive features of the disease is the development of a small area of gangrene at the site of the tick bite—the *tache noire*.

Tick-bite Fever occurs in South Africa, the Rhodesias, and East Africa. The Rickettsia is conveyed by a number of ticks which are conveyed to man by dogs and cattle. The initial infection takes place through a bite in the skin or through the conjunctiva. The manifestations of the disease are similar to those of Rocky Mountain spotted fever, but usually runs a much milder course, with a death rate of less than 1 per cent. The fever persists for about a fortnight.

MITE TYPHUS, or TSUTSUGAMUSHI, is also known as Japanese river fever, scrub typhus, and tropical typhus. The disease has been known in Japan for over a thousand years. Its distribution is now known to include Japan, the East Indies, and Queensland. The causative organism is *Rickettsia orientalis*, which is transmitted by various mites which become infected from wild rodents. The disease is most common among farmers, field workers, hunters, and surveyors. Whilst in Malaya it occurs all the year round, in Japan it is most common between June and October.

Symptoms.—The incubation period is 5 to 21 days. The onset is usually sudden, with headache, backache, rigors, and congestion of the eyes, as in other forms of typhus. A small ulcer usually develops at the site of the mite-bite, and the lymph glands draining this area are often enlarged. The temperature rises rapidly to 101–102° F. (38·3–38·9° C.), and then climbs to about 104° F. (40° C.). The rash appears about the fourth or fifth day—on the chest and abdomen, and then spreading to the limbs, and sometimes to the face. Nervous manifestations are usually marked : apathy during the day ; insomnia and delirium at night. The temperature usually subsides during the third week. The mortality rate ranges from 30 per cent. in Japan to 15 per cent. in Malaya. The disease is frequently fatal in old people.

Treatment.—The general principles of treatment are the same in all forms of typhus, and can be divided into prophylactic and curative.

Prophylaxis consists of either avoidance of, or destruction of, the vector. In the case of louse-typhus and flea-typhus, the outlook has been revolutionized by the introduction of efficient insecticides such as D.D.T. and gammexane. The value of the former has been well shown by its use during the post-1939–45-War period, which has resulted in almost complete freedom from the epidemics of typhus which ravaged Eastern Europe after the 1914–18 War. Efficient rat control is another measure which reduces the risk of typhus very considerably. In areas such as Malaya, where the mites are infected from a wide variety of rodents scattered over large areas, the wearing of protective clothing is the most practicable method of prophylaxis.

Curative treatment has also been revolutionized by the introduction of four new antibiotics : chloramphenicol, chlortetracycline, oxytetracycline, and tetracycline. These antibiotics have altered the prognosis in typhus fever very considerably, and the mortality figures which have been mentioned earlier in this section apply to the state of affairs before these antibiotics became available. The discovery of the anti-rickettsial action of these four antibiotics, which are taken by mouth, is as outstanding a discovery as that of the anti-bacterial action of penicillin. Their introduction, however, does not diminish the need for efficient nursing care in all cases.

U

ULCER (*ulcus*) means a breach on the surface of the skin or on the surface of the membrane lining any cavity within the body, which does not tend to heal quickly. The process by which an ulcer spreads and which involves the death of and gives a puckered appearance to the scar. If anything interferes with these natural processes, the ulcer is prevented from healing.

Varieties.—Ulcers are sometimes classified as *local* when they are found at

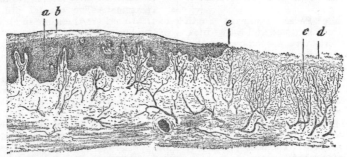

minute portions of tissue round its edge is known as ulceration. The process of ulceration and that of abscess formation are the same, since both are inflammatory processes, although ulceration takes place along a surface from which its discharge escapes at once, whilst an abscess spreads in every direction from a centre and its products are for a time retained. The microscopic changes that take place when an ulcer forms will therefore not be described in detail, as the features of an inflammatory process have been already described under ABSCESS, ACUTE.

An ulcer consists of a floor or surface, which, in consequence of the loss of tissue, is usually depressed below the surrounding healthy surface, and an ' edge ' where the healthy tissues end (Fig. 380). The floor of a healing ulcer is composed of granulations, which are small masses of cells engaged in forming connective tissue and richly supplied with capillary blood-vessels that give the ulcer a bright-red appearance; whilst the edge shows a blue line of growing epithelial cells, which are constantly spreading inwards. In the process of healing, the fibrous tissue formed by the granulations contracts and thus draws the edges of the ulcer together

one spot only, such as the varicose ulcer found on the lower part of the leg ; and *constitutional* when there are usually several ulcers on different parts of the body, produced chiefly by some constitutional defect. LOCAL ULCERS are further subdivided as follows, according to their symptoms or appearance.

SIMPLE or SLOWLY HEALING ULCER has been already described. The floor is moderately red and slightly sunk, the skin around is healthy up to the margin of the ulcer, and at the edge there is a blue line, which is of great importance as showing the progress of the healing. Such an ulcer has a very slight white discharge and is quite free from smell.

INFLAMED ULCER is one which, as the result usually of the presence of bacteria, or in consequence of continued irritation, is still spreading. The floor of such an ulcer is very red and bleeds easily, the skin around is red and swollen, there is a thick discharge of pus from the surface, and portions of the reddened skin at its edge or in its neighbourhood tend to die and thus form new ulcers.

WEAK ULCER is an appearance which the ulcers of weakly people, especially those suffering from dropsy, tend to

assume. The granulations are soft, project above the surface, forming what is popularly known as 'proud flesh ', bleed easily, and prevent the healing edge of the ulcer from growing inwards.

CALLOUS ULCER is the type of chronic ulcer most frequently met. The edge is thick and hard, the colour pale, few granulations are present, and the discharge in consequence is thin and small

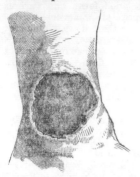

Fig. 381.—Callous or indolent ulcer, with smooth floor and thick hard margin. (Miller's *Surgery*.)

in amount, though often very offensive in smell (Fig. 381).

IRRITABLE ULCER is one which resembles in a mild degree the inflamed ulcer, and has the special character of being extremely painful to touch.

VARICOSE ULCER may belong to any of the above types. It generally comes on as the result of scratching the skin of a leg which has been rendered eczematous by the bad circulation. It will not heal so long as the patient walks about, and has a great tendency to develop into a callous ulcer.

INTERNAL ULCERS develop sometimes in the mouth (*see* MOUTH, DISEASES OF); in the stomach (*see* STOMACH, DISEASES OF) ; in the bowels (*see* INTESTINE, DISEASES OF) ; in the lining membrane of the heart (*see* HEART, DISEASES OF) ; and in other parts. Some of these are of a local character, though many are constitutional.

CONSTITUTIONAL ULCERS are generally the result of some widespread disease such as syphilis or tuberculosis. SYPHILITIC ULCERS have the characters of possessing a very abrupt edge, as if punched out, and of leaving behind after healing a brownish discoloured scar. TUBERCULOUS ULCERS may arise from

the bursting of a tuberculous abscess under the skin ; whilst the skin disease known as lupus vulgaris is a variety of tuberculous disease.

MALIGNANT ULCERS are developed when a cancer spreads so as to involve the skin. Such an ulcer has often a very offensive smell, requiring the use of deodorant substances.

TROPHIC ULCERS are apt to appear as the result of weakened nerve influence, *e.g.* the deep perforating ulcer on the sole of the foot in locomotor ataxia, or bed sores in people sick of some lingering disease. (*See* BED SORES.)

Causes.—An ulcer may be set up by any cause which damages the surface of the body and prevents immediate healing. Naturally, any constitutional condition which diminishes the vitality or the healing power of the body acts in this way, and among these causes may be mentioned old age, general illhealth, scurvy, diabetes, gout, syphilis, and tuberculosis, so that wounds produced in persons suffering from any of these conditions are apt to form ulcers. Defective circulation in the direction either of a poor blood supply or of the stagnation which takes place in varicose veins is another important cause. Constant movement of any part on which there is a wound is quite sufficient to delay its healing and produce an ulcer. Every one knows, for example, how difficult it is to heal a small crack at the corner of the mouth. Irritation of the ulcer by pressure, or by discharges pent up under dressings that are too seldom changed, or even by the application of strong lotions to the ulcer, may prevent its healing.

Dangers.—A person afflicted with a large ulcer is to a great extent incapacitated from active work, and the presence of any such septic condition has a prejudicial effect upon the general health. Further, the person always runs the risk of an attack of acute inflammation starting from the ulcer. A varicose ulcer has a danger of its own, consisting in the liability of the veins to become ulcerated and to burst, causing profuse bleeding. Even after a very chronic ulcer has healed, its scar contracts, and in doing so may cause disfigurement or may even interfere with the usefulness of a limb, if situated near a joint. Finally, ulcers which

have lasted many years may become the seat of cancer.

Treatment.—In treating an ulcer, three objects must be kept in view: (1) to remove the cause of ulceration; (2) to render the floor and edge of the ulcer healthy so that healing may commence; (3) to assist the healing process and ward off any source of irritation.

(1) REMOVAL OF THE CAUSE.—Any constitutional condition underlying the development of the ulcer must first of all be treated; otherwise the tissues surrounding the ulcer are unable to exert their power of healing. Thus syphilis or tuberculosis, if present, requires the special remedies suited to these diseases, whilst old age, scurvy, diabetes, and other conditions demand appropriate treatment. Bodily rest is also of great importance for the healing of an ulcer; and especially is this the case in ulcers of the leg, where constant movement combines with bad circulation to prevent healing. Accordingly, large varicose ulcers may refuse to heal till the person takes to bed, but when this is done, improvement is often rapid. This beneficial effect is still further aided, in the case of varicose ulcers, by raising the leg on a pillow or by elevating the foot of the bed on props so that the ulcer is brought above the level of the heart. When for any reason the person cannot lie in bed for several weeks, the evils of movement and the dependent position of the leg can be neutralized to some extent by wearing an elastic bandage over the dressing, which is applied every morning before the patient gets out of bed. Although this treatment will benefit any ulcer of the leg, it is not likely to cure a large one. (*See* VEINS, DISEASES OF.)

(2) RENDERING THE ULCER HEALTHY aims at converting any of the severer forms, *e.g.* the inflamed, weak, irritable, or callous ulcer, into the simple type, which is the first step necessary in the healing process. When the ulcer is *inflamed*, it must be treated with active antiseptics such as eusol, acriflavine, or perchloride of mercury lotion, and the dressing covered by oil-silk or gutta-percha tissue. Penicillin is most effective when the causative organism is penicillin-sensitive. As soon as the ulcer has been purified, however, these strong antiseptics must be discon-

tinued, since they retard the healing process. Sometimes the ulcer is purified quickly by the surgeon, who makes an application of undiluted carbolic acid to its surface, or scrapes away the diseased tissues thoroughly under an anæsthetic. Oxygen is sometimes used as a purifying agent, the gas being led under a closed vessel placed over the ulcer. In mild cases of inflammation, charcoal, iodoform, and various weak antiseptics are sometimes used. *Weak ulcers* are treated with blue-stone, red lotion, silver salts, or other substances which have an astringent effect upon the 'proud flesh' and stimulate the edge and floor of the ulcer. *Callous ulcer* is by far the most common variety that needs special treatment. The reparative material, which has been accumulated in the edges and floor, and which obstructs the circulation near the ulcer, and prevents healing, must be absorbed. This is effected sometimes in slight cases by massage of the skin near the ulcer, in other cases by blistering the thick edge all round the ulcer. Generally, continued pressure is the method chosen, and this is effected in one or other of two ways. The old method was by 'strapping' the ulcer; which consists in wrapping several overlapping strips of adhesive plaster round the limb so that the ends of the strips cross the ulcer and press its sides together. The more modern and more frequently used method is to wear during the day a special supporting bandage, which is applied to the leg from the ball of the foot up to the knee, passing over the dressing upon the ulcer with a very slight degree of pressure. There is now a range of such bandages, and medical advice should be sought as to the best one to use. To be successful, this treatment must be combined with complete rest and elevation of the ulcerated part. An *irritable ulcer* is treated by applying some form of caustic to the surface of the ulcer in order to destroy the sensitive nerve-endings in it. In slighter cases, when the mere contact of the dressings appears to irritate the ulcer, this may be avoided by leaving off all dressings and covering the ulcer simply with a little wire cage or a celluloid shield, and washing the ulcer daily with boric lotion.

(3) ASSISTANCE OF THE HEALING PROCESS.—When the ulcer has been purified and its floor and edges rendered healthy, a very simple dressing must be used. Care should be taken in dressing not to irritate the ulcer and make it bleed, and the very greatest care must be taken of the blue line at the ulcer's margin, as this is the healing part. The frequency of dressing the ulcer is a point of great importance ; for, if the dressing be too frequently renewed, the healing tissues are unnecessarily disturbed and damaged, whilst if the dressing be very seldom changed, pus is apt to collect, and by its decomposition to inflame the ulcer. The usual interval allowed to elapse between the successive dressings of a healing ulcer is two or three days, or less if there be much discharge. The ulcer must be washed with some mild fluid like weak boracic lotion, and strong lotions like carbolic are quite inadmissible for a healing ulcer. The best dressing is a piece of clean lint or gauze, but this should be kept from actual contact with the ulcer by a piece of oil-silk perforated here and there and just large enough to cover the red ' granulations ' of the ulcer's floor without touching the edge. At each dressing, the lint, etc., must be thoroughly soaked before removal, not pulled away roughly ; otherwise the healing tissues, especially the ' blue line ' at the edge, are damaged and torn. At each dressing, too, the piece of oil-silk is reduced in size. When an ulcer has become quite clean and is healing rapidly, one of the best forms of dressing consists of a weak boracic ointment spread on lint.

The healing of a large ulcer, after it has been rendered clean, may often be hastened by grafting its surface with skin from another part. (See SKIN-GRAFTING.)

For the treatment of internal ulcers, see under the headings of the organs in which they occur.

ULITIS (οὖλον, gum) means inflammation of the gums.

ULNA is the name of the inner of the two bones in the forearm. It is wide at its upper end, and its olecranon process forms the point of the elbow. In its lower part it is more fragile and is liable to be broken by a fall upon the forearm while something is grasped in the hand. Chipping off of the olecranon process is a frequent result of falls upon the elbow. (See FRACTURES.)

ULOGLOSSITIS means inflammation of the gums and of the tongue.

ULTRA- (ultra, beyond) is a prefix denoting excess.

ULTRASONICS relate to sound in the frequency above 15 kilocycles per second—that is, well above the upper frequency limit of the human ear. These frequencies are now being used to an increasing extent in medicine. In diagnosis they are proving useful in obstetrics in assessing the stage of pregnancy, and also in the diagnosis of brain tumours. They are also being used in the treatment of Ménière's disease (q.v.) and of bruises and strains.

ULTRA-VIOLET RAYS (see LIGHT).

UMBILICUS (umbilicus) is another name for the navel.

UNCINARIA (uncus, hook) is another name for hookworm. (See PARASITE.)

UNCINATE FIT is the term applied to a state in which the patient has a hallucination of smell or of taste ; it may be a manifestation of epilepsy, or the result of a tumour pressing on that part of the brain concerned with the appreciation of smell and taste.

UNCONSCIOUSNESS is a condition depending usually on some disorder of the brain, and may be of various degrees.

Varieties.—Sleep is a natural form of unconsciousness due to a resting condition of the brain (see SLEEP), and when the brain remains irregularly active various peculiar forms of unconsciousness or of disturbed consciousness are apt to ensue, such as delirium, somnambulism, hypnotism, catalepsy, ecstasy. (See under these headings.) In syncope or fainting, the brain ceases to act for a time in consequence of a bloodless state, brought on by feebleness of the heart's action. In the lesser forms of epilepsy (petit mal), the epileptic sometimes becomes unconscious of his surroundings, though able to perform such a simple act as to take

931

off his clothing, or to run some distance, or even to attack another person.

STUPOR is the name given to a partial state of unconsciousness from which the person can be roused for a moment by some powerful stimulus such as a shout.

COMA means a condition of complete oblivion very near to death.

Causes.—Fainting is due to deficient supply of blood to the brain. Among injuries to the brain, apoplexy, compression and concussion of the brain, and inflammation affecting the brain or its membranes are the chief causes. Epilepsy is also a cause of passing unconsciousness, either accompanied by a fit, or, in the slighter forms, without any such seizure. Narcotic poisons also produce stupor. The poisons that accumulate in the blood during various diseases, such as Bright's disease and diabetes, may produce coma, that due to the latter disease being curable by insulin.

Treatment.—The cause of unconsciousness must first of all be determined. Fainting brings with it its own cure, and little is necessary beyond leaving the unconscious person recumbent (see FAINTING). The means of distinguishing the effects of narcotic poisons from those of apoplexy are given under OPIUM, and this distinction is important, since in apoplexy the main requirement is absolute quiet, whilst in poisoning cases energetic treatment is necessary. Unconsciousness, due to compression of the brain resulting from severe injury to the head, may have to be treated by trephining the skull. The unconsciousness of uræmia due to Bright's disease is perhaps the form most liable to be mistaken or overlooked, but doubts as to this are set at rest by examination of the urine. In this case also prompt treatment is essential if life is to be saved. For the treatment of unconsciousness due to other causes, the special symptoms present will in general indicate the cause, and the treatment is given under other headings.

UNDECYLENIC ACID is a long chain fatty acid which is of value in the treatment of tinea pedis (see RINGWORM).

UNDINE is the name given to a small glass flask with drawn-out neck and an

opening which can be closed by the finger. It is used for irrigating the eye with fluid. (See EYE DISEASES.)

UNDULANT FEVER is another name for Malta fever, but especially for a variety of this disorder which occurs in temperate climates and caused by the *Brucella abortus*. This organism produces contagious abortion in cattle, and is apt to be conveyed to man by contact with them or by their milk, when it gives rise to the symptoms described under MALTA FEVER.

UNGUENTUM is the Latin name for ointment.

UNIT (*unus*, one) is the term applied to a quantity assumed as a standard for measurement. The *diphtheria antitoxin unit* is the specific neutralizing activity for diphtheria toxin contained in such an amount (in 1962 this was 0·0628 mg.) of the standard preparation as the Medical Research Council may from time to time indicate as the quantity exactly equivalent to the unit accepted for international use. The tetanus antitoxin unit is similarly determined. The *unit of insulin* is the specific activity contained in such an amount (in 1962 this was 0·04167 mg.) of the standard preparation as the Medical Research Council may from time to time indicate as the quantity exactly equivalent to the unit accepted for international use. The standard preparation consists of pure, dry, crystalline insulin.

URACHUS (οὐραχός) is the name of a corded structure which extends from the bladder up to the navel, and represents the remains of the canal which in the foetus joins bladder with allantois.

URÆMIA (οὖρον, urine; αἷμα, blood) is the condition which results from failure of renal function, as in Bright's disease (*q.v.*). Whilst it is generally accepted that it is due to retention in the body of substances that normally are excreted by the kidneys, there is no definite evidence as to which of these substances is responsible for the condition.

Symptoms.—Uræmia is sometimes classed as *acute, i.e.* those cases in which the symptoms develop in a few hours or days, and *chronic*, including cases in which the symptoms are less marked and last over weeks, months, or years. There is, however, no dividing line between the two, for in the chronic variety, which may be said to consist of the symptoms of chronic Bright's disease, an acute attack is at any time liable to come on.

Headache in the front or back of the head, accompanied often by insomnia at night and drowsiness during the day, is one of the commonest symptoms, although it is apt to be attributed to some other cause. Unconsciousness of a profound type, which may be accompanied by convulsions resembling those of epilepsy, is the most outstanding feature of an acute attack and is a very dangerous condition.

Another group of symptoms is associated with the lungs and may consist of great difficulty in breathing when the patient attempts to lie down, repeated attacks resembling asthma, or the peculiar type of breathing known as Cheyne-Stokes breathing. (*See* RESPIRATION.)

Still another symptom, which often precedes an acute attack, is severe vomiting without apparent cause. The appetite is always poor, and the onset of diarrhœa is a serious sign.

Treatment.—The treatment of the chronic type of uræmia includes all the measures which should be taken by a person suffering from chronic Bright's disease. Cheyne-Stokes respiration is relieved by the intravenous administration of theophylline ethylene-diamine.

URAMUSTINE is a nitrogen mustard derivative (*q.v.*) used in the treatment of certain forms of malignant disease. It is given by mouth in capsule form.

URANORRHAPHY (*οὐρανός*, palate ; *ῥαφή*, seam) is the name applied to an operation for closure of a cleft palate.

URATES (*see* URIC ACID).

UREA (*οὖρον*, urine), or CARBAMIDE, is a crystalline substance of the chemical formula $CO(NH_2)_2$, which is very soluble in water or alcohol. It is the chief waste product discharged from the body in the urine, being formed in the liver and carried to the kidneys

in the blood. The amount varies considerably with the quantity and nature of the food taken, rising greatly upon an animal (protein) dietary. It also rises during the continuance of a fever. The average amount excreted daily, during health, on a mixed diet is about 33 to 35 grammes, or slightly over one ounce.

Urea is administered for its diuretic action and also as a test of kidney efficiency, in doses of 15 to 30 grammes.

Urea is rapidly changed, by a yeast-like micro-organism, into carbonate of ammonia ; and to this chemical change the ammoniacal smell of badly kept latrines is due.

URETER (*οὐρητήρ*) is the tube, about the thickness of a goose-quill, which on each side leads from the corresponding kidney down to the bladder. Each ureter begins above at the pelvis of its kidney and after a course of 14 to 16 inches (35 to 40 cm.) through the loins and pelvis it opens by a narrow slit into the base of the bladder. The lower end pierces the wall of the bladder so obliquely (lying embedded in the wall for about ¾ inch) that, though urine runs freely into the bladder, it is prevented from returning up the ureter as the bladder becomes distended.

URETHANE is the official *British Pharmacopœia* name for ethyl carbamate. It is of value in the treatment of chronic leukæmia. Injection of quinine and urethane is used as a sclerosing agent.

URETHRA (*οὐρήθρα*) is the tube which leads from the bladder to the exterior, and by which the urine is voided. It is about 8 inches (20 cm.) long in the male and 1½ inches (3.5 cm.) long in the female.

URETHRA, DISEASES OF.—The chief conditions which cause pain in the urethra, or interfere with the passage of urine, are urethritis or inflammation of the mucous lining, and stricture or narrowing of the tube.

URETHRITIS is often difficult to tell from inflammation of the bladder (cystitis), which, however, it may accompany and of which it is frequently the cause.

Causes. — The most frequent cause of urethritis is gonorrhœa, and this disease produces the most severe type of inflammation. Another common cause is the condition known as non-specific, or abacterial urethritis—so-called because the cause is not known. Like gonorrhœa, it is a venereal disease. Gout is another cause, producing its effects either owing to the repeated passage of irritating gravel with the urine, or to a highly acid state of this excretion. The damage caused by the passage of a rough stone from the bladder or of a catheter unskilfully introduced may also occasion a severe urethritis ; and various drugs or articles of diet, such as alcohol or arsenic, may bring on an attack in those who are liable to suffer from it.

Symptoms.—The symptoms consist chiefly in the constant oozing out of a small quantity of pus from the orifice of the urethra, a sense of scalding pain whenever urine is passed, increased redness of the mucous membrane as seen at the orifice, and tenderness along the course of the urethra. Subsequently, inflammation in neighbouring organs, *e.g.* the bladder, testicle, or even kidney, may be set up.

Treatment. — This varies with the cause of the inflammation, but in all cases the drinking of milk, water, and other bland fluids in large quantities is of advantage in order to flush out the urethra. The sulphonamide drugs and penicillin are highly effective in the treatment of gonorrhœa. The disease causing the inflammation requires special treatment according to its nature.

STRICTURE is an abrupt narrowing of the tube at one or more places.

Varieties and causes. — SPASMODIC or CONGESTIVE STRICTURE is a temporary condition which is not of much importance. It follows upon exposure to cold, excessive exercise like bicycling, alcoholic indulgence, and frequently upon operations near the urethra, such as that for piles. It prevents the passage of urine for a few hours or days. It is treated simply by a warm sitz-bath or warm fomentations to the fork, and, if necessary, the urine is drawn off by means of a soft or flexible catheter passed along the urethra and through the stricture.

934

ORGANIC STRICTURE is a much more serious condition. It is a scar, due to previous injury or ulceration of the mucous membrane, which, by contracting after the manner of all scars, produces narrowing of the urethral tube. This scar is almost always due to one or other of two conditions : severe laceration of the urethra as the result of injury, or long-continued chronic inflammation.

A stricture almost always occurs at one of two points ; either just within the orifice of the urethra or in the fork where the urethra turns upwards as it enters the pelvis.

Symptoms.—An organic stricture is of very slow development, and gives rise at first to few symptoms beyond those of the urethritis, etc., which cause it. As the stricture narrows, the stream of urine becomes smaller than natural, and there is straining and pain each time it is voided. Occasional attacks of spasmodic stricture are brought on by injudicious acts on the part of the person who already has an organic stricture ; and this further narrowing of the tube causes complete stoppage of the urine for a time, accompanied by great pain, which results from distension of the bladder. After a stricture has lasted some years, unless it has been very carefully treated, and the person has led a well-ordered life, inflammation of the bladder almost certainly comes on, and the death of the patient may ultimately ensue from the spread of this inflammation upwards to the kidneys.

The existence, position, and calibre of a stricture are verified by the surgeon, who passes metal bougies of various sizes along the urethra.

Treatment.—The person who is the subject of a stricture must above all things live a moderate, well-regulated life, free from excesses of every kind. Highly spiced food, alcoholic beverages, and some forms of exercise, such as cycling and horseback riding, should be avoided. The diet should be simple and constipation must be prevented. By these means unnecessary irritation of the stricture is avoided, and thus spasmodic attacks with retention of the urine are warded off.

To check the gradual narrowing of the stricture some operative procedure is necessary, and, according to the situation and nature of the stricture, it is either *dilated* by means of bougies passed along the urethra, or it is divided by a special instrument passed along the urethra (*internal urethrotomy*), or by an incision made through the fork (*external urethrotomy*). After-treatment consisting in the passage of a bougie at regular intervals of some weeks or months, is necessary after any of these operations, in order to counteract the permanent tendency of the stricture to contract.

INJURIES TO THE URETHRA may follow a severe crush which has fractured the pelvis, or a fall astride of some object. The signs of this are the presence of blood in the urine, or inability to pass urine at all, after such an accident. The great risks are the occurrence of an abscess round the urethra, and the formation of a stricture at a later period.

URIC ACID (οὖρον, urine) is a crystalline substance, very slightly soluble in water, of chemical formula $C_5N_4H_4O_3$. It is white in the pure state, but when found as a urinary deposit it is reddish-brown, presenting a supposed resemblance to cayenne pepper. The bi-urate of sodium and urate of ammonium occur in considerable amount in the urine during a feverish state or after great exertion, and produce, as the urine cools, a dense pink or yellow sediment. The average daily quantity of uric acid passed by human beings is 0·5 to 1 gramme. In the urine of birds and reptiles uric acid is the chief nitrogenous constituent, taking the place of the urea excreted by human beings. Uric acid is formed in the liver and removed by the kidneys from the blood. The amount is increased in the following conditions :

(a) Excessive consumption of meat, combined with sedentary habits.
(b) Gout (*see* GOUT).
(c) Diseases in which the white corpuscles of the blood are increased, *e.g.* leukæmia.

Owing to their insolubility, uric acid and the various urates frequently produce deposits in the urinary passages, which are known as urinary sand, gravel, or stones according to their size.

URINARY ORGANS form the system by which the urine is extracted from the blood, stored up, and from time to time discharged from the body. They comprise the two kidneys placed in the loins, two ureters leading from them to the bladder which is situated in the front of the pelvis, and the urethra which leads from the floor of the bladder out beneath the pubic bones to the exterior. (*See* KIDNEYS, URETERS, BLADDER, URETHRA.)

URINE (*urina*) is the excretion produced by the kidneys, and consists chiefly of waste substances resulting from the activity of the body, dissolved in water. The function of the kidneys consists almost entirely in selecting these substances from the blood ; their actual formation takes place in the liver, muscles, etc. The urine and the perspiration are to a great extent interdependent ; thus, if the kidneys are acting vigorously, the skin becomes very dry, whilst if there has been much perspiration, as in fevers, the urine is small in amount and highly concentrated. The amount of water lost from the body daily by perspiration is, in health, about half the amount passed as urine, and, though the sweat contains little of the waste material present in the urine, the glands of the skin can be made to take up the function of the kidneys to a great extent when the latter organs are diseased. (*See* BRIGHT'S DISEASE.) Many poisons taken into the body are excreted by way of the urine, *e.g.* morphine and strychnine, and so also are the germs of many diseases, *e.g.* those of typhoid fever.

Composition.—About 96 per cent. of the urine is water, the remaining 4 per cent. being solids dissolved in it. Of the solids, far the most important is urea, of which there is, on an average, 25 grammes in 1000 millilitres. Common salt stands next in quantity, the average amount in 1 litre of urine being 9 grammes. Phosphates and sulphates are also important constituents combined with potassium, sodium, calcium, and magnesium, whilst there is less than 1 gramme each of creatinine, uric acid, and ammonia.

Pigments are also present in the urine, and to them its colour is due. These pigments, known as urobilin, urochrome, etc., are derived indirectly from the colouring matter of the blood, and are produced also by the liver.

Amount. — The amount of urine passed daily is about 50 ounces (1500 millilitres), subject to the variations mentioned above. A child of course passes much less than an adult ; the average daily amount is : 15 ounces (430 ml.) at two years ; 20 ounces (570 ml.) at four years ; 30 ounces (850 ml.) at seven years ; and 40 ounces (1140 ml.) at twelve years.

The amount of urine is *increased* in some diseases, of which diabetes and chronic Bright's disease of the cirrhotic type may be mentioned as the chief. In other conditions it is *diminished*, notably in acute Bright's disease, in fevers and feverish states generally, and in heart diseases.

COMPLETE STOPPAGE of the urine may occur for a time in the feverish conditions of children, or it may be due to acute Bright's disease, when the condition is a very serious one. When the stoppage is due to failure of the kidneys to secrete any urine, the condition is known as *suppression* or *anuria*. When the stoppage is due to such a cause as blockage of the ureters by stones or of the urethra by a stricture, although secretion by the kidneys still goes on, it is known as *retention*. Stoppage of the urine, to whatever cause it be due, may often be relieved by placing the patient in a hot bath and administering to him sweet spirits of nitre or other diaphoretic.

Colour.—The tint of normal urine is generally described as straw or amber coloured, but it may be considerably changed by various diseases or drugs.

PALLOR, giving the urine a watery appearance, is found in diabetes and in chronic Bright's disease, also in persons who drink large quantities of water.

ORANGE or RED COLOUR may appear when senna or rhubarb has been taken ; when blood is present the colour may be pink or bright red ; urates cause a turbid red or yellow appearance.

SMOKY TINT, depriving the urine of transparency, is caused by small quantities of blood.

GREEN or GREENISH-YELLOW urine is usually due to bile, or may be produced by taking santonin or quinine.

BLACK URINE may be due to absorption of carbolic acid from surgical dressings or from taking carbolic acid, lysol, or similar substances internally. It is often passed by those who are taking guaiacol or creosote. It may also be due to the presence of indican in cases of intestinal stasis, and is found in the form of sarcoma known as melanotic sarcoma when this involves the liver.

Odour.—Healthy urine has a faint aromatic odour, but when it begins to decompose, an unpleasant ammoniacal smell is given off. Thus the presence of cystitis or of dribbling of the urine is betrayed by the odour of the patient's personal or bed clothes. When turpentine and some other aromatic drugs have been taken, the urine acquires an odour of violets, and in diabetes it presents an aroma similar to that of new-mown hay.

Specific gravity of urine varies in health from 1015 to 1025 (distilled water being 1000). A urine of lower specific gravity suggests the presence of chronic Bright's disease, whilst a higher specific gravity may be due to diabetes, or to a feverish state.

Reaction.—When the urine is tested with litmus paper it is found to be acid in general, and this is of importance, because the acid has an antiseptic action. This acidity is due, not to free acids, but to acid salts such as acid phosphate of sodium. In consequence of the secretion of acid from the blood into the gastric juice that is poured into the stomach shortly after meals, the urine may at such times become alkaline. In herbivorous animals and in vegetarians, owing to the great quantities of alkaline salts eaten in the diet, the urine is permanently alkaline.

Deposits.—In healthy urine there is usually a fleecy deposit of mucus secreted by the mucous membrane of the urinary passages. A pink or yellow deposit, that settles as soon as the urine begins to cool, and that often leaves a stain upon the utensil in which the urine has stood, is due to urates (*see* URIC ACID). Uric acid is a rare deposit, and, when present, falls in very scanty yellow or brownish grains. A white deposit that collects upon the bottom of the utensil after the urine has stood undisturbed for some time may be due to phosphates, to pus, or to debris from diseased kidneys known as tube-casts.

Abnormal substances. — Many un-usual substances taken into or formed in the body are got rid of in the urine, sometimes just as they have entered the body, in other cases considerably changed, *e.g.* drugs, and the poisons of various diseases. Further, various bac-teria and parasites can be discovered in the urine in some diseases. Elaborate chemical or microscopical examination is necessary in order to reveal these, but there are six substances the detection of which is of great importance, and which are discovered with comparative ease. These substances are (1) albumin; (2) blood ; (3) sugar ; (4) pus and tube-casts ; (5) bile ; (6) acetone.

(1) ALBUMIN is present in various conditions mentioned under ALBUMIN-URIA, and may be recognized by the following tests :

(*a*) *Boiling*, after the addition of a few drops of acid, produces a copious white cloud of coagulated albumin.

(*b*) *Heller's test*.—Place some strong nitric acid in the bottom of a test-tube and carefully pour in urine above it. If the urine contains albumin a dense white line forms where the two fluids meet.

(*c*) *Salicyl-sulphonic acid*.—Drop 25 per cent. solution of salicyl-sulphonic acid into a test-tube containing urine. If albumin is present, each drop carries down a white cloud of coagulated albumin.

(2) BLOOD is present in acute Bright's disease, in congestion of the kidneys, or when a stone, ulcer, or tumour is present in any of the urinary organs. If a drop or two of tincture of guaiac resin is mixed with a little of the suspected urine to form a white fluid in a test-tube, and some ozonic ether or oxidized turpentine is poured in above this mixture, a deep-blue colour appears where the two fluids join, when blood is present. A similar result is given, how-ever, by the urine of patients who have been taking iodide of potassium, so that for absolute certainty a drop of the urine must be examined under the microscope to find if blood-cells are actually present.

(3) SUGAR is a sign of diabetes mel-litus (*see* DIABETES) when it is present

constantly in the urine. It may also be found following upon a diet that con-tains a great deal of sugar—a harmless condition known as ' alimentary glyco-suria '. In some cases the difficulty lies in the kidneys—' renal diabetes ', which is also of little importance.

(*a*) *Fehling's test.* — A special blue-coloured solution composed of copper sulphate, Rochelle salt, and caustic potash is placed in a test tube and heated almost to boiling point. While it is hot, an equal volume of the sus-pected urine, which has also been heated in a separate test tube, is added, and, if sugar is present, red and yellow cuprous salts are formed.

(*b*) *Benedict's test.* — Benedict's re-agent contains copper sulphate, sodium carbonate, potassium citrate, potas-sium thiocyanate, and potassium ferro-cyanide, dissolved in distilled water. When urine containing sugar is boiled along with this pale-blue solution, the colour disappears. This reagent is commonly used for estimating the amount of sugar present, the calcula-tion being based upon the fact that 25 ml. of the reagent are completely reduced by exactly 50 mg. of glucose, and rendered colourless.

(*c*) *Fermentation test.*—A little yeast is shaken up with some of the urine, placed in a special glass which is closed at the upper end, and allowed to stand in a warm place overnight. If the urine contains sugar it will ferment and bubbles of carbonic acid gas collect at the upper end of the glass.

(4) PUS AND TUBE-CASTS are the sign of inflammation or of ulceration some-where in the urinary passages. Pus alone is generally a sign that the bladder is affected ; tube-casts always point to involvement of the kidneys. If tincture of guaiac resin is added to urine con-taining much pus, a greenish tinge is produced, or if liquor potassæ is added the urine becomes ' ropy '. These, how-ever, are unreliable tests, and for the detection of pus or tube-casts in small amounts a drop of urine must be placed on a glass slide and examined with the microscope.

(5) BILE in the urine is a sign that the bile ducts are obstructed, and that bile is being absorbed into the blood. Sometimes the jaundice that accom-panies this condition is so slight as to

escape notice, so that the detection of bile in the urine is an important sign. Place some of the urine in a large conical glass, dilute it with water till quite transparent, and pour impure nitric acid down the side of the glass. If bile is present in the urine, a brilliant play of colours—yellow, red, violet, and green—takes place where the urine and acid meet. It is the green colour that is characteristic of bile.

(6) ACETONE may appear in the urine in cases of diabetes, general acidosis, and some other conditions.

Rothera's test.—Place in a test tube crystals of ammonium sulphate to a depth of about an inch. Then add a few grains of sodium nitroprusside. Add sufficient urine to produce a saturated solution of the ammonium sulphate. This requires vigorous shaking of the test tube, and, if the solution is saturated, there will be some undissolved crystals in the solution. A solution of strong ammonia is then added, and, if a purple colour develops, this denotes the presence of acetone bodies.

DIACETIC ACID, which is often also present with acetone, may be tested by adding to $1\frac{1}{2}$ inches (3·5 cm.) of urine in a test tube, solution of 10 per cent. ferric chloride, drop by drop. A precipitate of iron phosphate first forms, which is filtered off. If diacetic acid be present, a dark-red colour next develops, which disappears on boiling the urine. This is known as *Gerhardt's test.*

URINE, EXCESS OF.—The amount of urine passed in 24 hours is often markedly increased in diabetes, a fact which sometimes, without any other symptom, attracts the patient's attention. The bladder also requires to be emptied more than usual in the chronic forms of Bright's disease, but this is due rather to greater frequency than to increased quantity of urine. The increase in this case is noticed especially during the night. Any source of irritation or inflammation in the kidneys or bladder may also produce this symptom, such as the formation of gravel or of a stone, tuberculosis of the kidney, inflammation of the bladder (cystitis), or enlargement of the prostate gland. The bladder, however, varies greatly in size in different individuals, and the necessity to pass water frequently may simply be a life-long personal peculiarity due to smallness of its capacity.

An annoying form of increase in the urine at night leads to wetting of the bed by children. (*See* NOCTURNAL ENURESIS.)

Treatment. — Any increase in the amount of urine or the frequency with which it is passed calls for testing as to the presence of sugar, albumin, gravel, pus, etc. The treatment consists in that suited to any disease that may be discovered.

URINE, RETENTION OF.—The term ' retention ' is applied to cases in which urine is duly secreted by the kidneys, but for some reason is retained in the bladder ; while the more serious condition, in which the kidneys fail to produce urine, is known as ' suppression ' or anuria. (*See* URINE, AMOUNT.)

Causes.—The urine may be retained either because the bladder is too weak to expel it, or because of some obstruction to the passage by which it should be voided. Weakness is a rare condition and is generally the result of some damage to the nervous system, this being one of the troublesome symptoms that follow an injury to the spinal cord ; it is accompanied by dribbling away of the urine when the bladder becomes fully distended. A similar condition results from long-continued distension produced by some obstruction to the outflow.

Among the cases due to obstruction, some are acute and merely temporary, such as the difficulty of passing water that follows upon any operation near the bladder, *e.g.* one for piles, or that is apt to follow child-birth. In these cases the difficulty commonly is due to spasm, and does not persist more than a day or two. Among the more chronic cases of retention the commonest are those caused by enlargement of the prostate gland and consequent blockage of the outlet from the bladder ; this condition is common in old men. In these the retention usually comes on gradually, and it is a common experience to find that the bladder never empties completely as it ought to do, but forms a sort of reservoir from which an overflow is discharged every few hours. The condition that leads to the most complete form of retention is a stricture or narrowing of the urethra due to the scar of previous injury or ulceration (*see* URETHRA, DISEASES OF.) Similar blockage results also, in rare instances, from the pressure of some tumour upon the urethra, or the displacement of a neighbouring organ such as the womb in women.

Treatment.—Cases in which retention is due to weakness of the bladder, in a chronic invalid, are treated by the regular use of a soft rubber catheter, and this forms one of the most important duties in the nursing of such a case.

In any case of retention where the urine accumulates in and causes painful distension of the bladder, the condition may often be relieved by the sufferer placing himself in a warm bath. This produces so much relaxation that the bladder often succeeds in emptying itself, a result which is still further assisted by the use of soothing draughts or the giving of an enema.

If relief is not gained by these means, the medical attendant withdraws the urine by means of a catheter passed along the urethra. (*See* CATHETERS.) The instrument chosen varies according to the cause of the retention ; thus, in cases due to weakness of the bladder or to moderate spasm at the outlet, a soft rubber catheter only is necessary. In cases of severer spasm, and in cases where the prostate gland is enlarged, a flexible instrument or a hard rubber catheter with a bend upon the point (known as a *coudé* catheter) is generally chosen ; while, in cases of very narrow stricture, the surgeon may require to pass a rigid metal instrument. As a rule, great difficulty is experienced only in the last-named class of cases ; and in them it may occasionally be necessary to tap the bladder above the pubis by means of a hollow needle. After its contents have escaped, the patient gains immediate relief and can generally pass urine, when it next becomes necessary, by natural means.

URINOMETER (*οὖρον*, urine ; *μέτρον*, measure), or DENSIMETER, is an instrument designed for estimating the specific gravity of urine. It consists of a graduated stem supported upon a large glass bulb containing air which floats partly submerged, and which is kept upright by a smaller bulb containing mercury placed at its lower end. The urine is poured into a tall glass vessel, the urinometer placed in it, and, when it is floating motionless, the point on the scale which is at the surface of the urine registers the specific gravity.

UROGASTRONE is a depressant of gastric acidity which has been isolated from urine. Its precise function in the body and its constitution are not known. Attempts have been made to use it in the treatment of peptic ulcer, but so far without convincing success.

UROLOGY is that branch of medicine which treats of disorders and diseases of the kidney, ureters, bladder, prostate, and urethra.

URTICARIA (*urtica*, a stinging nettle) is another name for nettle-rash (*q.v.*).

UTERUS (*uterus*), or WOMB, is a hollow organ suspended in the cavity of the pelvis. In shape, it is triangular from side to side, and flattened from before backwards. The lower angle is prolonged into a rounded neck (*cervix*) which communicates through a narrow opening or mouth (*os uteri*) with the vagina, the passage leading to the exterior of the body. In size, the normal uterus is only about 3 inches long, 2 inches in its greatest width, and 1 inch in thickness from front to back, while the walls are so thick that the cavity consists of a mere slit. During pregnancy, however, it enlarges to an enormous extent, and the walls increase still further in thickness (*see* MUSCLE). The cavity is lined by a thick, soft, mucous membrane, and the wall is chiefly composed of muscle fibres arranged in three layers. The outer surface, like that of other abdominal organs, is covered by a layer of peritoneum. The uterus has a copious supply of blood derived from the uterine and ovarian arteries. It has also many lymphatic vessels, and its nerves establish wide connections with other organs (*see* PAIN). The position of the uterus is in the centre of the pelvis, where it is suspended by several ligaments between the bladder in front and the rectum behind. On each side of the uterus are the broad ligaments passing outwards to the side of the pelvis, the utero-sacral ligament passing back to the sacral bone, the utero-vesical ligament passing forwards to the bladder, and the round ligament uniting the uterus to the front of the abdomen.

UTERUS, DISEASES OF.—Most diseases of this organ are of a chronic type, occur in married women, and, although their symptoms in the great majority of cases are not of an extreme nature, they are apt to constitute a drain upon the general health. Among the most common symptoms are pain or irregularity in the menstrual functions, the presence of a white discharge (*leucorrhœa*), constant pain or sense of weakness in the back, and often the inability to bear children.

MALFORMATIONS sometimes occur and give rise to trouble in child-birth ; for example, the uterus may be double, may have a partition down the middle, etc. The cervix may be long and furnished with a very narrow mouth, which is sometimes a cause of pain in menstruation. Overgrowth may occur, usually as the result of chronic inflammation.

DISPLACEMENTS are of more importance. The uterus is slung in the centre of the pelvic cavity, and has great freedom of movement up and down and from before backwards. It lies naturally with its long axis directed upwards and forwards between the bladder and rectum, but its position at any time varies considerably according to the state of distension of one or other of these organs. A flabby state of the muscular wall of the uterus, or a contraction of some of the ligaments that suspend it, may produce a bend upon the organ itself, or may permanently tilt it forwards or backwards. Bending forwards is known as *anteflexion*, tilting forwards is called *anteversion*, and the corresponding conditions towards the back are known as *retroflexion* and *retroversion*. In the treatment of these conditions, two objects are kept in view, the one being to diminish the inflammation that is apt to accompany them, and the other consisting in the support of the uterus in its proper position by a suitably shaped instrument known as a pessary ;

or by an operation, when the displacement is very marked.

Downward displacement is known as *prolapse*, and in this condition the uterus slips bodily downwards in the space between the bladder and bowel, till, in bad cases, it may actually protrude from the vagina. The condition comes on in older women, usually those who are becoming stout, have a considerable amount of work to do, and have in child-birth suffered laceration of the parts that should support the uterus. When the condition is slight it is relieved by wearing a suitably shaped pessary, and in cases which are not relieved by this simple measure an operation (colporrhaphy), designed to repair the injury previously done, will often remedy the displacement.

INFLAMMATION is, perhaps, the commonest type of uterine disorder. It is of several forms, but the general term *endometritis* is applied to inflammation affecting the mucous membrane, *metritis* to the rarer condition in which the muscular substance is involved. This condition is frequently due to child-birth which has not passed off quite successfully ; and it is still more often due to miscarriage. Inflammation spreading upwards from the vagina, and displacements of the uterus are other, though less common, causes. The usual treatment consists in rest, the employment of hot, antiseptic douches and other applications to the vagina, and various remedies to improve the general health, such as tonics, baths, change of air. The sulphonamides or penicillin are given in severe cases. The interior of the uterus can often be brought quickly to a healthy condition by the operation of curetting, which consists in scraping away the unhealthy mucous membrane with a special instrument, the curette. After this operation the patient must observe the greatest caution till the next menstrual period shall have passed.

TUMOURS of the uterus are by no means uncommon. The two most important ones are fibroids and cancer.

Fibroid tumours, or fibromyomata, are the most common form of tumour in any part of the body. They consist of masses of muscle fibres, similar to those of the uterus, and white fibrous tissue. They vary in size from that of a small seed to a mass weighing several pounds. The cause is not known, but they are much more common in women who have never borne children than in those with children. Whilst they may occur any time between puberty and the change of life, they are usually first recognized between the ages of 35 and 45. The symptoms depend upon the size and site of the tumour, and many fibroids give rise to no symptoms at all. Speaking generally, the larger the tumour, and the more it involves the inner aspect of the uterus, the more likely is it to produce signs of its presence. The more important symptoms and signs are menstrual irregularity consisting of excessive loss of blood or excessive length of the period, sterility, frequency of micturition, and retention of urine. Pain is seldom a marked feature. Only those fibroids causing symptoms require treatment. If the symptoms are at all severe, operation is the treatment of choice. In some cases this involves removal of part, or the whole, of the uterus; in others it is possible to remove the tumour itself and leave the rest of the uterus intact. In cases with only mild symptoms, or in women approaching the menopause, when the tumour may decrease in size, medical treatment is sometimes used. This consists of rest in bed during menstruation, the administration of ergot to control the excessive bleeding, and full doses of iron to combat the anæmia usually present. In more severe cases, or in those in which such treatment fails, X-rays or radium are sometimes used with benefit.

Cancer of the uterus is one of the most common forms of cancer in women. It may occur in either the neck (or cervix) of the uterus or in the body of the uterus. Cancer of the cervix of the uterus is more common than cancer of the body of the uterus, and 95 per cent. of cases occur in women who have borne children. Cancer of the body of the uterus, on the other hand, is more common in unmarried women or women who have never borne children. Both forms occur most commonly between the ages of 40 and 55. Cancer of the body of the uterus is rare before the menopause. The first sign is usually a blood-stained discharge. Treatment consists of either radium or surgery. The results with radium have been particularly gratifying, and figures from the Marie Curie Hospital, London, show that 83 per cent. of patients in whom cancer of the neck of the uterus was recognized at an early stage and treated by irradiation were still alive five years later. The importance of early diagnosis is well demonstrated by the fact that at the same hospital the five-year survival rate was only 7·4 per cent. among those cases not recognized until a late stage of the disease. This is why it is so important that any woman over the age of 40 who has either excessive loss at the period, or irregular bleeding, should report at once to her doctor. In most cases there will be nothing serious to worry about, but if the bleeding should be due to cancer, then early diagnosis will permit of treatment being carried out at a stage when the expectation of cure is high.

UVEA is a term applied to the middle coat of the eye, including the iris, ciliary body and choroid.

UVEITIS is inflammation of the uvea. It is responsible for 2 to 3 per cent. of the blind population in England. It is rare in childhood and old age.

UVULA (*uvula*) is the small mass of muscle covered by mucous membrane that hangs down from the middle of the soft palate. It may be elongated in relaxed conditions of the throat, but should not be cut, since it recovers its proper size as the condition of the throat improves. Its elongation, when sufficient to make it reach the tongue, may set up a constant irritative cough and tendency to retch.

V

VACCINATION (*vacca*, a cow) means inoculation with the material of cow-pox, performed for the purpose of affording protection to the inoculated person against an attack of smallpox, or at all events with the view of diminishing the seriousness of, and averting a fatal result from, any such attack. The material now used is almost always glycerinated calf lymph, obtained by inoculating healthy calves with lymph derived from cow-pox, and afterwards adding glycerin to the material got from the vesicles. The glycerin has the effect of destroying any disease-producing organisms that may be present, and thus of rendering the lymph harmless.

Effectiveness of vaccination.—Among Eastern nations there existed a very ancient practice of inoculating healthy persons with the material from mild cases of smallpox, in the expectation of producing in them a mild attack which rendered them immune from accidental infection that might produce a serious attack at a later period. This practice was introduced into England from Turkey by Lady Mary Wortley Montagu about 1717, and the necessity for some such measure may be judged when it is stated that one in every twelve of the deaths in London during the eighteenth century was due to smallpox. This practice, however, involved a considerable element of danger, and after the introduction of vaccination it was abolished in Britain by Act of Parliament in 1840.

There had long been a tradition among the country people in the west of England that an attack of cow-pox— an eruption upon the udders of cows liable to be communicated to the hands of milkers—afforded protection against a subsequent attack of smallpox. In 1796 Edward Jenner, a surgeon of Berkeley, performed his first experiment in this matter by inoculating James Phipps, a boy of eight, with cow-pox material from the hand of Sarah Nelmes, a dairymaid. Six weeks later the boy was inoculated with smallpox material, but no disease followed. Subsequently, the experiment was successfully repeated both by Jenner and by other persons, and by 1801 Jenner states that over 100,000 persons had been vaccinated in England alone. With regard to the nature of cow-pox, opinions have varied as to whether it is simply a modified smallpox or is a different disease. At the present day the general opinion agrees with that held by Jenner, that cow-pox is simply smallpox much modified by passage through the cow. It might be supposed that this fact would be one easy of demonstration, and cows have by many observers, *e.g.* by Woodville in 1799, by Ceely, by Badcock, and by Thiele of Kazan in 1838, been experimentally inoculated with smallpox, but in most cases the disease, when thus artificially produced in cows, appears to retain a considerable degree of virulence, and to produce general though slight symptoms when again communicated to human beings, instead of the purely local symptoms of ordinary vaccination. So important did vaccination appear to the Governments of foreign countries, that its practice was in a few years made compulsory by several, although in England it was not enforced till 1853. Nevertheless from its first introduction to the present day, vaccination has had its opponents, who have attacked it upon the grounds both of uselessness and of danger. A *prima facie* case of the strongest kind, however, is established in its favour by the evidence of statistics.

Thus, as regards ENGLAND, whilst Farr, quoted by Edwards, gives the smallpox death-rate for London in the eighteenth century, just before the introduction of vaccination, as 4000 per million living in every year, and Lyon Playfair, quoted by the same authority, gives the general rate for England as 3000 per million at this time, we find, from the Registrar-General's returns, that, in the beginning of the twentieth century, the death-rate from smallpox for England and Wales is only about 75 in every million living. That is to say, during the century in which vaccination was practised, smallpox decreased to one-fortieth of its previous importance as a cause of death.

SWEDEN, which early adopted compulsory vaccination, gives important confirmation, according to statistics quoted from Edwards. In that country, where vaccination was introduced in 1801, and became compulsory after 1816, the deaths in each year from smallpox per million of inhabitants show a striking decrease :

Period.	Deaths from Smallpox.
1774–1800 . .	2049 per million yearly
1802–1811 . .	623 ,, ,,
1812–1821 . .	133 ,, ,,
1890–1899 . .	1 ,, ,,

TABLE 29.—Deaths from Smallpox in Sweden.

GERMANY, however gave perhaps the most notable example of the change in the mortality from small-pox which was associated with the introduction of compulsory vaccination for infants in 1835, and showed an even more notable decrease in smallpox mortality following upon the enforcement of revaccination for school children, which became law in 1874.

Period.	Deaths from Smallpox.
1803 . . .	4000 per million yearly
1854–1863 . .	224 ,, ,,
1889–1898 . .	2 ,, ,,

TABLE 30.—Deaths from Smallpox in Prussia.

If the whole German Empire be taken, the death-rate from smallpox was even less in the last-mentioned decade, being only 1·4 per million ; and this notwith-standing the fact that in the neighbour-ing countries of Russia and Austria, where vaccination was not so rigorous, the death-rates were respectively 463 and 99 per million.

A ROYAL COMMISSION on vaccination was appointed by the British Govern-ment in 1889, and after exhaustive and careful examination of all the objections to vaccination, this Commission issued its report in 1896. The conclusions as to the value of vaccination in relation to smallpox arrived at by the Commission were as follows : ' We think—

' 1. That it diminishes the liability to be attacked by the disease.

' 2. That it modifies the character of the disease, and renders it (a) less fatal, and (b) of a milder or less severe type.

' 3. That the protection it affords against attacks of the disease is greatest during the years immediately succeed-ing the operation of vaccination. It is impossible to fix with precision the length of this period of highest protec-tion. Although not in all cases the same, if a period is to be fixed, it might, we think, fairly be said to cover in general a period of nine or ten years.

' 4. That after the lapse of the period of highest protective potency the efficacy of vaccination to protect against attack rapidly diminishes, but that it is still considerable in the next quinquennium, and possibly never alto-gether ceases.

' 5. That its power to modify the character of the disease is also greatest in the period in which its power to pro-tect from attack is greatest, but that its power thus to modify the disease does not diminish as rapidly as its pro-tective influence against attacks, and its efficacy during the later periods of life to modify the disease is still very considerable.

' 6. That revaccination restores the protection which lapse of time has dim-inished, but the evidence shows that this protection again diminishes, and that to ensure the highest protection which vaccination can give the opera-tion should be at intervals repeated.

' 7. That the beneficial effects of vac-cination are most experienced by those in whose case it has been most thorough. We think it may fairly be concluded that where the vaccine matter is inserted in three or four places it is more effectual than when introduced into one or two places only ; and that if the vaccina-tion marks are of an area of half a square inch, they indicate a better state of protection than if their area be at all considerably below this.'

Dangers of vaccination.—There can be no doubt that the dangers attendant upon vaccination have been enormously exaggerated by those opposed to the practice. On its first introduction the opponents of vaccination declared that it would be the means of engrafting cow-like characters upon the human race, but the absurdity of this has been proved by over a century's experience. The production of skin diseases has also been alleged against vaccination. Some-times a general rash accompanies the formation of the vesicles, and occasion-ally an eczematous condition of the scalp is observed to follow vaccination, but these are trifling disorders which speedily subside. The transmission of syphilis from one child to another was an occasional, though extremely rare, misfortune in the days when the lymph obtained from the arm of one child was inoculated upon the next ; but now that calf lymph is used, this accident is impossible, since the calf is immune from this disease. Erysipelas and the production of ulcers at the site of inoculation form the only real dangers attending upon this little operation, and they may be entirely avoided by scrupulous cleansing of the child's arm before vaccination, and of the instruments used.

Method of vaccination. — In the United Kingdom vaccination against smallpox ceased to be compulsory with the advent of the National Health Service in July 1948. Previously it had been compulsory, although parents had been able to obtain exemption if they claimed to have conscientious objections to it.

If the child suffers from any skin disorder, or from diarrhœa, or if there is any severe epidemic in the neighbourhood by which the child is likely to be infected, vaccination should be delayed till the child is better. If, however, there be smallpox in the child's vicinity, nothing should interfere with its vaccination.

For long the usual time for smallpox vaccination was at the age of 2 to 4 months. Now, however, when it is usual for a child to receive inoculations against several diseases—*e.g.* diphtheria, poliomyelitis, whooping-cough—the recommended time for smallpox vaccination is either at the age of 5 or 6 months or towards the end of the first year of life.

The two main methods of vaccination are the multiple pressure method and the scratch method. The former is the technique used in the United States of America, and is preferred by many experts in Great Britain. The advantages claimed for it are that it produces less severe reactions and smaller scars, and a larger number of ' takes '. Many, however, still prefer the scratch method which is officially recognized as an alternative procedure in Great Britain.

The part is either covered by a simple dry dressing or is left exposed, care being taken not to wet it. No change is noticed till about the third day, when a slight elevation appears

944

at the vaccinated spots. By the fifth or sixth day this has developed into a distinct vesicle, with a central depression, and the vesicle has attained its full development and become of a pearl colour one week from the day on which the lymph was inserted. There is often a red ring of inflammation round each vesicle, and both this and the vesicle increase in extent for the next day or two, the arm at the same time becoming slightly swollen and the glands in the armpit enlarged. After this the inflammation subsides, the vesicle at the end of a fortnight dries up and forms a hard brown scab, which falls off about the end of the third week, leaving a permanent, depressed scar.

The performance of vaccination, then, is extremely simple and virtually free from danger. It appears also, from more than a hundred years' experience, that its practice has been accompanied by a great diminution in the frequency and severity of smallpox, which formed one of the most terrible scourges of humanity in the eighteenth century. It is therefore a matter for great regret that any parents should neglect the adoption of this simple and harmless procedure for their children. In 1966, only 38 per cent. of children in the first two years of life were vaccinated in England and Wales.

It is eminently advisable that persons of maturer years who are either proceeding to some country where smallpox is rife, or who are liable to be exposed to smallpox infection, should have themselves revaccinated as a precautionary measure. Indeed, in many countries recent revaccination is compulsory and no one is allowed into the country without a duly recognized certificate of vaccination. Anyone proceeding abroad, therefore, should first acquaint himself with the regulations on the subject pertaining to the particular country or countries to which he is going. Such information is obtainable from Medical Officers of Health.

VACCINE is the name applied generally to a substance of the nature of dead or attenuated living infectious material introduced into the body with the object of increasing its power to resist or to get rid of a disease.

In cases where healthy people are

inoculated with vaccine as a protection against a particular disease, this is done with the object of producing 'antibodies' which will confer immunity against a subsequent attack of the disease. In cases where a vaccine is used to cure acute inflammation already fully developed, it is supposed to stir up the general resisting power of the whole body to overcome what has previously been a limited condition. It is doubtful whether this principle really comes into action, and the value of the latter type of vaccine treatment has probably been greatly exaggerated.

Vaccines may be divided into two classes : stock vaccines, prepared from bacteria known to cause a particular disease and kept in readiness for use against that disease ; and autogenous vaccines, prepared from bacteria which are already in the patient's body and to which the disease is due. Vaccines intended to protect against the onset of disease are necessarily of the stock variety. Phylacogen is the name given to an extract of a vaccine from which the bacteria have been filtered out so that only their products remain.

Autogenous vaccines are prepared from the cultivation of bacteria found in the expectoration, the urine, the fæces, and in areas of inflammation such as boils. This type of vaccine was introduced by Wright about 1903. (*See* OPSONINS.)

Anthrax vaccine was introduced by Pasteur about 1882 for the protection of sheep and cattle against this disease. A safe and effective vaccine for use in human beings has now been evolved.

B.C.G. vaccine is used to provide protection against tuberculosis. (*See* B.C.G. VACCINE.)

Catarrhal vaccine is used as a preventive of colds and bronchitis, for persons who are liable to these and similar catarrhal attacks every winter. The vaccine treatment is administered in the autumn before the season of catarrhs begins. Various organisms are used to make the vaccine, but the commonest combination consists of *Hæmophilus influenzæ*, *Pneumococcus*, *Streptococcus*, and *Micrococcus catarrhalis*.

Cholera vaccine was introduced by Haffkine in India about 1894. A weak

vaccine is first injected and later one of exalted virulence. The method appears to be free from risk and reduces the susceptibility to cholera.

Hay fever vaccine. — A vaccine prepared from the pollen of various grasses is used in gradually increasing doses for prevention of hay fever in persons susceptible to this disease.

Rabies vaccine was introduced by Pasteur in 1885 for administration, during the long incubation period, to persons bitten by a mad dog, in order to prevent the disease from developing. The vaccine is usually made from spinal cords containing the virus, but vaccines are now available made directly from attenuated rabies virus. (*See* RABIES.)

Influenza vaccine.—A vaccine is now available for protection against influenza due to the influenza viruses A and B.

Plague vaccine was introduced by Haffkine, and appears to give useful protection, but the duration of protection is relatively short—from two to twenty months.

Poliomyelitis vaccine is now available which gives a high degree of protection against the disease. The Salk-type of vaccine, in which the virus is killed by formaldehyde, contains all three known types of poliomyelitis virus. Three intramuscular injections are required, with an interval of four to six weeks between the first and second, and seven to twelve months between the second and third. There is a growing volume of evidence that a fourth injection prolongs the duration of the protection provided by the vaccine.

The Salk vaccine has now been largely replaced by the live attenuated vaccine which is taken by mouth—a few drops on a lump of sugar.

Smallpox vaccine was the first introduced. (*See* VACCINATION.)

Staphylococcus vaccine was at one time widely used in the treatment of infections, such as boils and carbuncles, due to the *Staphylococcus aureus*, but it is seldom used nowadays.

Typhoid vaccine was introduced by Wright and Semple for the protection of troops in the South African War and in India. Two doses usually are given, one of 500,000,000 bacilli followed ten days later by 1,000,000,000, and with this are usually combined two other vaccines of paratyphoid A and paratyphoid B bacilli respectively, each in half the amount of the typhoid bacilli. This is known as T.A.B. vaccine. The skin of arm or back is painted with tincture of iodine or other antiseptic, and the hypodermic syringe with which the vaccine is inoculated is also carefully sterilized by boiling or by drawing into it alcohol or hot oil prior to use. After an inoculation no heavy work is done for two days, any appreciable reaction having usually passed off by that time.

Results of antityphoid inoculation.— If a drop of blood from the person who has been inoculated be examined about ten days after the first inoculation it is found to have developed a striking power. A drop of ordinary blood-serum mixed with a drop of emulsion of living typhoid bacilli and examined under the microscope has the power of stopping their activity and causing them to adhere together when diluted about 10 times with salt solution. A similar observation made upon the blood of the person who has been inoculated discovers that his blood possesses this power even if diluted about 100 times with fluid. After a second inoculation this agglutinating power of the blood for typhoid bacilli is increased to about 300 times that of normal blood. The effect is at its highest point about three weeks after the first inoculation, and thereafter it gradually diminishes, the protective influence passing off completely in three or four years.

The protective influence has been very marked among troops. Thus in an investigation carried out on 24 units involving about 20,000 men, of whom roughly one-half had been inoculated, the occurrence of typhoid fever was 5·6 times greater among uninoculated than among inoculated men, while the deaths among the former were 10·7 times more numerous. The following table gives the numbers of typhoid fever cases among all the British troops in India during the year 1903 before inoculation was introduced, and during the year 1913 when it had been in extensive use for eight years :

	Number of Cases.	Deaths.
1903	1384	296
1913	85	16

The difference is partly due to improved general sanitary conditions, but partly, in all probability, to the protective influence of inoculation. During both World Wars, protective inoculation with typhoid and paratyphoid vaccine was rigorously carried out, and no widespread epidemic of these diseases occurred.

Whooping-cough vaccine is prepared from the bacillus of Bordet and Gengou, or *Bordetella pertussis*, and is proving of value in prophylaxis against whooping-cough.

Yellow fever vaccine is prepared from chick embryos injected with the living, attenuated strain (17D) of pantropic virus. Only one injection is required, and immunity persists for many years. Reinoculation, however, is desirable every six years.

(*See also* IMMUNITY.)

VACCINIA is another term for cowpox, a disease in which vesicles form on the udders and teats, due to the same virus as is responsible for smallpox in man.

VAGINA is the name given to the front passage leading from the exterior to the womb.

VAGINISMUS is the term applied to spasmodic contraction of the orifice of the vagina on attempted coitus. It is usually psychological in origin, due, for instance, to a neurotic temperament or to frigidity, but it may also be due to some local inflammatory condition.

VAGINITIS is inflammation of the vagina. (*See* WHITES.)

VAGITUS UTERINUS is the term applied to the crying of a child just before birth and while it is still in the uterus.

VAGOTOMY is the operation of cutting the fibres of the vagus nerve to the stomach. It is sometimes performed as part of the surgical treatment of duodenal ulcer, the aim being to reduce the flow or acidity of the gastric juice.

VAGUS (*vagus*, wandering), or PNEUMOGASTRIC, nerve is the tenth cranial nerve. Unlike the other cranial nerves, which are concerned with the special senses, or distributed to the skin and muscles of the head and neck, this nerve, as its names imply, strays downwards into the chest and abdomen, supplying branches to the throat, lungs, heart, stomach, etc. It contains motor, secretory, sensory, and vaso-dilator fibres.

VALERIAN is the root of *Valeriana officinalis*, a European plant. Its action, which is a sedative one upon the nervous system, depends mainly upon a volatile oil that it contains, and also to some extent upon valerianic acid.

Uses.—Valerian was at one time widely used, chiefly in the form of the tincture of valerian, to quiet nervous-ness, insomnia, and hysterical attacks, being taken in doses of a teaspoonful. The oil of valerian, in doses of two or three drops on sugar, is an old remedy for the relief of dyspepsia associated with spasm of the stomach.

VALETUDINARIAN (*valetudinarius*) is a term applied to an invalid ; also to a person who is constantly thinking about his own state of health.

VALGUS (*valgus*) means literally knock-kneed, and is a bending inward at the knees (*genu valgum*), or at the ankle, as occurs in flat-foot (*pes valgus*).

VALVES are found in the heart, veins, and lymphatic vessels, for the purpose of maintaining the circulation of the blood and lymph always in one direction. (*See* HEART, VEINS.)

VALVULAR DISEASE (*see* HEART DISEASES).

VANCOMYCIN is an antibiotic de-rived from a streptomyces, which is active against a wide range of Gram-positive organisms, including the staphylococcus.

VAN DEN BERGH TEST is one per-formed on a specimen of serum of the blood in cases of jaundice, to decide whether this is due to ordinary bile (immediate reaction) or incompletely formed bile pigment (delayed reac-tion).

VAPOUR BATHS (*see* BATHS).

VARICELLA is another name for chickenpox (*q.v.*).

VARICOCELE (*varix*, a dilated vein ; κήλη, tumour) means a condition in which the veins of the testicle are dis-tended. (*See* TESTICLE, DISEASES OF.)

VARICOSE VEINS (*varix*, a dilated vein) are veins that have become stretched and dilated. (*See* VEINS, DISEASES OF.)

VARIOLA (*varus*, a blotch on the face) is another name for smallpox (*q.v.*).

VARIOLOID is the name applied to a mild type of smallpox.

VARIX means an enlarged and tor-tuous vein.

VARUS, meaning bow-legged, is the term applied to a bulging condition at the hip (*coxa vara*), at the knee (*genu varum*), or at the ankle (*talipes varus*).

VAS is the Latin term for a vessel, especially a blood-vessel.

VASELINE is the trade mark for petroleum jelly and other products.

VASOMOTOR NERVES are the small nerve fibres that lie upon the walls of blood-vessels and connect the muscle fibres of their middle coat with the nervous system. Through these nerves the blood-vessels are retained in a state of moderate contraction. There are also vasodilator nerves, through which are transmitted impulses that dilate the vessels, and, in the case of the skin-vessels, produce the condition of blush-ing. Various drugs produce dilatation or contraction of the blood-vessels and several of the substances produced by ductless glands in the body have these effects.

VASOPRESSIN is the fraction isolated from extract of the posterior pituitary lobe which stimulates intestinal activity, constricts blood-vessels, and inhibits the secretion of urine. It is also known as pitressin.

VEGETARIANISM means the principle of subsisting on a diet of vegetables. (*See* ' Quality of Food ' *under* Diet.)

VEGETATIONS is the term applied to roughenings that appear upon the valves of the heart, usually as the result of acute rheumatism, and that lead in time to narrowing of the openings from the cavities of the heart, or to incompetence of the valves that close these openings. (*See* Heart Diseases.)

VEGETATIVE SYSTEM is a term applied to that part of the nervous system which acts in an involuntary manner, to a large extent independently of the brain and spinal cord, and which regulates and connects movements and secretions of internal organs. The term includes the ' sympathetic ' and ' parasympathetic ' nervous systems.

VEINS are the vessels which carry blood to the heart after it has circulated through the tissues of the body. In general the veins lie alongside corresponding arteries that carry outwards to the tissues the blood which afterwards returns by the veins. The veins are, however, both more numerous and more capacious than the arteries, and, as a rule, there are two accompanying veins for each artery of moderate size. In addition to these deeply placed veins, there are superficial veins in the limbs, which can be readily seen in their distended state lying immediately beneath the skin.

Structure. — A vein is of similar structure to an artery, consisting of three coats, viz. outer fibrous, middle of muscular and elastic fibres, and inner composed of elastic membrane and flattened cells. Any vein has, however,

948

a much thinner wall than its corresponding artery, especially as regards the middle coat. Most veins are provided with valves similar in structure to the aortic and pulmonary valves of the heart, and consisting each of two segments or pouches, which lie flat

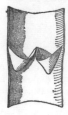

Fig. 382.—A vein slit open to show the two pockets of a valve on its inner surface. (Turner's *Anatomy*.)

against the wall of the vein as the blood passes in the proper direction, or which meet and close the passage whenever the blood tends to run backwards. The position of these valves can easily be seen upon the arm or leg by running the finger backwards along a large vein, when the distended vein shows a little swelling at each valve. The valves are most numerous in the veins of the lower limb, those in the arm stand next in point of numbers, whilst there are few valves in the veins of internal organs.

Chief veins.—Four *pulmonary veins* open into the left auricle of the heart, two coming from each lung. Into the right auricle there open some small veins that run upon the walls of the heart, and two great vessels, superior vena cava and inferior vena cava, that bring back blood from the body generally. The *superior vena cava* brings the blood from the head, neck, and upper limbs. It is formed by the union of two *innominate veins*, each of which results from the junction, at the root of the neck, of the internal jugular vein, from the neck, and the subclavian vein, from the upper limb. The *internal jugular vein* receives the blood from within the skull and collects branches from the face and neck as it runs downwards alongside the carotid artery under cover of the thick sterno-mastoid muscle. One of its most important branches is the *external jugular vein*, which runs beneath the skin from the angle of the jaw straight downwards to the middle of the collar-bone. This vessel can be readily seen when the veins of the neck are distended, and is very liable to be opened in wounds of this region. The *subclavian vein* is the last section of the system of veins that accompany the arteries in the arm, each vein being named after its corresponding artery. The superficial veins of the arm are of special interest, because the large *basilic vein* that runs up the inner side of the upper arm is the vein usually opened in blood-letting, and the vein used for punctures to get blood for various tests or in order to give intravenous injections. (*See* BLOOD-LETTING.)

The *inferior vena cava*, which lies to the right side and in front of the spinal column, commencing at the junction of the two common iliac veins about the level of the navel, collects the blood from the lower limbs and abdomen. In the lower limbs and in the pelvis, the deeply placed veins correspond in name and in position to the arteries, while the surface veins of the lower limb empty their contents into an *external saphenous vein* on the back of the leg, and an *internal saphenous vein* that runs from the instep up the inner side of the leg, knee, and thigh. These veins, and especially the internal saphenous vein, are of special interest because of their liability to become distended or ' varicose ' as the result of some impediment in the return of blood to the heart. Within the abdomen, the inferior vena cava receives branches corresponding to several branches of the aorta, its largest branches being the *hepatic veins*, which return not only the blood that has reached the liver in the hepatic arteries, but also blood which comes from the digestive organs in the *portal vein* to undergo a second capillary circulation in the liver. (*See* PORTAL VEIN.)

It appears from what has been said that the blood circulating in the uppermost parts of the body is returned to the heart by the superior vena cava, that from below the diaphragm by the inferior vena cava. There are, however, several connections between these two great vessels, the most important being three *arygos veins* that lie upon the sides of the spinal column, the veins on the front of the abdomen, and some veins that emerge from the abdomen at the navel and connect the portal system with those of the inferior and superior vena cava. By these means the circulation is maintained even when one of these large vessels has been blocked by some disease within the chest or the abdomen.

VEINS, DISEASES OF. — These vessels are subject to degenerative and inflammatory changes.

INFLAMMATION of a vein is a condition which is serious mainly on account of the clotting of blood that usually takes place within the inflamed part (thrombosis), and the risk that such a clot may break up and portions be swept away by the circulation to lodge in other vessels (embolism). *Phlebitis*, or *thrombophlebitis*, is the name commonly applied to general inflammation of a vein, while the term *peri-phlebitis* is used when the inflammation is limited to the loose connective tissue immediately surrounding the vessel. Occasionally the inflammation is of a very acute character, the vein becoming filled with a clot containing bacteria, which are carried to distant parts of the body and there produce abscesses. This condition, known as pyæmia, is an extremely grave one (*see* BLOOD-POISONING). As a rule, however, phlebitis is of a more chronic type, running a course of three or four

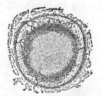

FIG. 383.—Inflamed vein filled with clot, which is beginning to ' organize '.

weeks and then improving under careful treatment.

Causes.—Thrombophlebitis may occur as a result of local injury to the affected part, *e.g.* a bruise or a fracture, or it may be due to involvement of the vein from a neighbouring inflammatory or suppurative process. It not infrequently occurs in varicose veins. Most of the cases, however, occur following child-birth or an operation, and in these cases the main factor responsible for the condition is stagnation of the blood-flow through the veins (*see also* WHITE LEG). It may also occur in certain infectious diseases, particularly typhoid fever, and in certain non-infectious diseases, including gout. In all these conditions the actual cause is

FIG. 384.—Organization proceeding and vein reopening at the edge.

probably one or more of three factors : (1) injury or inflammation of the lining endothelium of the vein ; (2) slowing of the blood-stream in the vein ; (3) some alteration in the blood which makes it more liable to clot.

Symptoms.—In a typical case, the skin near the inflamed vein becomes red ; the affected part becomes hot, and indeed the general temperature of the body may sometimes be raised ; there is swelling both around the vein and of the part beyond it, so that, if a vein in the leg be inflamed, the foot is

FIG. 385.—Organization of clot nearly complete and passage through vein restored.

swollen ; finally, considerable pain and tenderness to touch are experienced along the vein. When a clot forms in the vein, as it commonly does, the vessel can be felt as a hard line, and this blocked condition may persist for the rest of life, the vein being converted into a firm, fibrous cord ; or a

passage may be tunnelled through the clot after the inflammation has subsided in the course of three or four weeks (Figs. 383, 384, 385).

Treatment.—When the veins of the lower limbs are involved, the patient should rest in bed with the affected limb elevated and resting on pillows. Hot wet packs are applied to relieve the pain and to help to maintain an adequate circulation. If the pain is severe, sedatives may be required. Of recent years, anticoagulants such as dicoumarol (*q.v.*) and heparin (*q.v.*) have also been given to prevent the clot increasing in size and to reduce the risk of pulmonary embolism. Within three days of going to bed, the patient should be encouraged to move the affected limb and foot, as this speeds the process of recovery. It is now recognized that prolonged rest in bed tends to delay recovery.

VARICOSE VEINS are veins that have become stretched and dilated out of proportion to the amount of blood they have to carry. There are three positions in which the veins have a special tendency to become varicose. These are the veins about the lower end of the bowel, producing the condition known as hæmorrhoids or piles (*see* PILES) ; the veins of the testicle, producing varicocele (*see* TESTICLE, DISEASES OF) ; and the internal saphenous vein, with its branches on the inner side of the leg, knee, and thigh. Further, small veins are apt to become varicose here and there on a mucous membrane that is the seat of chronic catarrh and congestion ; these minute varicose veins are found especially on the mucous membranes of the throat and stomach, and may give rise, now and then, to hæmorrhage, particularly in the case of persons addicted to alcoholism. Only the varicose veins of the limbs are considered here, the others having been dealt with elsewhere.

Causes.—Undoubtedly some persons are more liable to the formation of varicose veins than others. The veins vary greatly in thickness in different persons and at different portions of the same vein, so that the formation of the vessel wall and the condition of surrounding parts have much to do with its dilatation. Thus the tendency to varicose veins is often hereditary. Employments that necessitate long-continued standing, with little vigorous muscular exertion, not only throw a great strain upon the veins of the leg, but fail to provide the pumping action that muscular contractions exert in emptying the veins. Thus barmaids, shopmen, and washerwomen frequently suffer from varicose veins. The evil effects of prolonged standing are increased by tight garters. Pregnancy is another common cause of varicose veins, though the condition tends to disappear after the child is born.

An important consideration is that, after a vein has begun to dilate, its walls become weaker and its valves useless. Thus the weight of the column of blood in the limb presses down with increasing force, the condition tends to grow worse and worse, and to spread into neighbouring veins.

Symptoms.—At first the only symptoms are a feeling of weight and aching in the limbs, accompanied sometimes by cramps. This is experienced either at night, after a long day's standing, or in the morning when the feet are first put to the ground. After the condition becomes marked, there is often swelling of the feet, especially above the ankles, that quickly disappears when the patient lies down. Varicose veins that have lasted many years are liable to become inflamed, and to produce eczema and ulceration of the skin. (*See* ULCERS.) Another risk attached to untreated varicose veins, particularly in older individuals, is that a blow on them may lead to severe hæmorrhage.

Treatment.—Varicose veins, as stated above, tend, when untreated, to become worse and worse. Treatment which is directed merely towards checking their increase and towards preventing ulceration is known as palliative treatment, whilst the entire removal of the distended veins is known as radical treatment.

PALLIATIVE TREATMENT.—In slight cases, it is often sufficient to avoid the use of garters, to remedy constipation, to avoid standing as much as possible, and, after the day's work is done, to sit with the feet elevated on a couch or chair. In more marked cases, some mechanical support for the superficial veins is necessary, in order to counteract the downward pressure of the blood in the long saphenous vein, whose valves have become useless. For this purpose one may use an elastic or crêpe bandage, or elastic stockings. Elastic bandages are probably the most satisfactory method of support. They can be cleaned with soap and water, and, if carefully handled, will last for a year. There are two main types of elastic bandages—the two-way stretch bandage and the one-way stretch bandage. The former is rather more difficult to apply, but is the bandage of choice in severe cases. For many cases the one-way stretch bandage is eminently satisfactory. Elastic bandages must be removed at night before retiring to bed and reapplied before getting out of bed in the morning. Crêpe bandages are used in a similar manner. Some persons find elastic stockings more comfortable than bandages. There must be no tight band at the top of the stocking, but slipping down may be prevented by suspenders; while, of the various kinds, the spiral silk elastic stocking is generally regarded as the best. For the treatment of varicose ulcers *see* ULCERS.

Successful results are sometimes obtained from the injection, here and there into the veins, of some irritating substance, such as quinine-urethane or sodium morrhuate. A clot forms at once in the vein, which later becomes solid. This treatment is practically painless and devoid of later discomfort.

RADICAL TREATMENT is adopted when the veins are excessively dilated, when they cause much annoyance, or when the person suffering from them wishes to enter one of the public services. The most successful method consists in turning up a flap of skin on the inner side of the thigh or knee, ligaturing the vein in two places and removing the intervening dilated portions *en masse*. The wound heals quickly, and, in most cases, the cure is complete.

WOUNDS IN VEINS are not in general serious; for, although a considerable amount of dark blood flows steadily from that end of the vein more distant from the heart, it can be stopped by gentle pressure, and soon ceases of itself. When a varicose vein ruptures, as it may do if an ulcer be present, the condition is more serious. Blood, in this case, flows copiously from the end next the heart in consequence of the defects in the vein's valves, as well as from the other end ; and the loss of blood may be great unless pressure be speedily applied. This also can be checked easily by pressure above and below the wound, and by raising the limb. Another danger, attaching to wounds of the veins in the neck, is that air may be drawn into them by the act of breathing, and great interference with the circulation may ensue.

VENA CAVA (*vena*, vein ; *cava*, hollow) is the name applied to either of the two large vessels that open into the right atrium of the heart. (*See* VEINS.)

VENEREAL DISEASES are certain contagious maladies which are, as a rule, communicated from one person to another by sexual intercourse. These diseases are three in number, viz. syphilis, soft sore, and gonorrhœa. (*See* articles under these headings.)

Much public interest has of late centred on the treatment of these diseases. The number of patients with early syphilis attending venereal disease clinics in England and Wales for the first time in 1964 was 1381. The comparable figure for gonorrhœa was 37,665. In 1964, in England and Wales the number of deaths directly attributable to syphilitic disease was 791. This figure, however, does not by any means represent the amount of serious invalidism caused to the persons who have suffered from one of these diseases and to their children. The direct results of the diseases are mentioned under the headings GONORRHŒA and SYPHILIS, whilst the results of inherited syphilis include deafness, various forms of skin and bone diseases, and a large number of all the cases of mental defectiveness. At one time a large proportion of cases of blindness in young persons were due to gonorrhœal ophthalmia contracted at birth, but efficient treatment has now made this one of the rarer causes of blindness.

Among the means which have been proposed for reducing the amount of these diseases are : general instruction of the public in regard to their disastrous effects ; provision of means for immediate self-disinfection ; early

treatment ; and compulsory treatment of all persons found to be affected, the last measure almost necessarily implying notification of these diseases in the same manner as one of the ordinary infectious diseases. Such compulsory notification has never been favoured in Great Britain, though it is in force in certain European countries. For purposes of efficient treatment, clinics, where treatment may be obtained gratuitously, have been established in almost all the large towns in Great Britain.

VENESECTION (*vena*, a vein ; *seco*, I cut) means the withdrawal of blood by opening a vein. (*See* BLOOD-LETTING.)

VENOGRAPHY is the study of the veins, particularly by means of X-rays after the veins have been injected with a radio-opaque substance.

VENOMOUS BITES (*see* BITES).

VENTER is the Latin term for the belly.

VENTILATION. — Ventilation consists in the continuous dilution or removal, by pure fresh air, of the vitiated products from respiration, combustion, putrefaction of animal and vegetable material, and from industrial processes and trades. It includes the ventilation of houses, factories, buildings of every description, as well as of streets, alleys, courts, and sewers. Different methods must be adopted for each variety of case. In streets and courts, reliance must be placed on the influence of winds, the height of the buildings, and the width of the street or space. In the confined areas of houses, means must be adopted for the ingress and exit of the air. Similar provision must be made in the case of sewers, the exit for which, however, must be placed where there is least chance of danger.

It is now recognized that lack of oxygen or excess of carbon dioxide plays little part in producing the discomfort of badly ventilated rooms. Nor is there any evidence that there is any organic poison in exhaled air. The main factor responsible is heat stagnation due to excess of moisture and lack of air movement. In other words, ventilation and warming must be considered together. A desirable atmosphere has been defined as ' cool rather than hot ; dry rather than damp ; and moving rather than still '. Various methods have been evolved for correlating these different factors, the most important of which include : the *kata-thermometer* which indicates the cooling power of the air. The *eupatheoscope*, an instrument which corresponds approximately to the human body in its sensitivity to air currents, and is read on a scale of equivalent temperature. The *globe thermometer*, which gives an index of the combined influence of air temperature and radiant heat. Another standard, used in the U.S.A., is the *effective temperature*, which is defined as ' that temperature of saturated motionless air which would produce the same sensation of coolness as that produced by the combination of temperature, humidity, and air motion under observation '. In Great Britain the optimum conditions for sedentary work are a dry kata-thermometer cooling power of 6 ; an equivalent temperature of 62° F. ; a globe thermometer reading of 65° F. ; an effective temperature of 61° F.

In the provision of ventilation, the amount of cubic space and the superficial area allotted to each individual are important, the amount of floor space per person being a better standard than the amount of cubic space. With a greater cubic space the air can more readily be supplied without the production of a draught. Thus, other things being equal, a wide, low room is better ventilated than a high, narrow one. Some idea of the standards at present being observed may be obtained from the fact that the size of house recommended by the Ministry of Health for five persons is 800 to 900 square feet. One of the official criteria of overcrowding is where more than one person is sleeping in a room with a floor area of ' 70 square feet or more, but less than 90 square feet '.

In ventilation, we are either dependent on processes of Nature or on artificial interference, and ventilation may there-fore be described as natural or artificial (mechanical).

Natural ventilation depends on the use of certain physical processes. The prevalence of winds by which volumes of air are driven ahead into spaces, or masses of air are aspirated as the wind passes horizontally over chimneys ; the law of the diffusion of gases ; and the fact that air, when heated, expands, and so becoming lighter bulk for bulk, rises, allowing colder air to rush in to take its place, all play their part in natural ventilation.

Room.	Air Supply per Hour.
Living-room (4 persons)	2400 cubic feet
Bedroom (2 persons)	1200 ,, ,,
Bedroom (1 person)	600 ,, ,,
Kitchen	1000 ,, ,,
Halls and passages	1 air-change
Bathroom and W.C.s	2 ,, ,, (or more)

TABLE 31.—Minimum Standards of Ventilation.

In the ordinary dwelling-house, no special provision is usually made for the inlet of fresh air. The windows, doors, and spaces between the skirting-boards and sashes act as inlets. The chimney provides the exit or exhaust. The chief objections, where there are no special inlets, are that one cannot control the source of the supply or ensure thorough mixture of the fresh and vitiated air.

Inlets, if the air can be warmed, should be placed preferably at the floor level. In cold climates like that of Britain, however, if the air is not specially warmed, the inlet should be placed above the occupants, with the stream directed upwards so that it may at once be well mixed with the general air of the room. A convenient special form of inlet is provided by double windows, the lower sash of the outer window being raised, and the upper sash of the inner window lowered. The air then enters between the windows.

Hinckes Bird's method of raising the lower sash about four inches by an accurately fitting wooden board, gives an inlet between the two sashes of a window (Fig. 386). Louvres, preferably on the lowest plane of the upper sash, and Cooper's revolving glass discs covering or exposing holes in the window when required, are largely used. Windows with the upper portion hinged to fall inwards and thus directing the current upwards, are commonly employed. Sheringham's valves, in which the air passes through a perforated

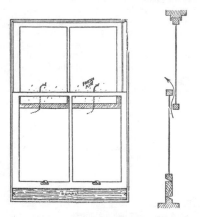

FIG. 386.—Hinckes Bird's ventilator from inside room.

FIG. 387.—Vertical section of a window, showing the board introduced beneath the lower sash.

plate and impinges on a hinged valve, serve the same end (Fig. 388). Tobin's tubes, frequently used, have the air entering through a perforated plate at the floor level, from which it is conducted by a tube of about 6 feet in height through the wall and up its

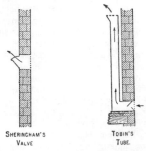

SHERINGHAM'S VALVE

TOBIN'S TUBE.

FIG. 388.—Vertical section of a house wall with a grating on the outer side and the valve on the inside.

FIG. 389.—Vertical section showing the wall, grating, and flanges to direct the air over a tray of water on the floor and Tobin's tube running upwards about 6 feet.

inner side (Fig. 389). Ellison's bricks are bricks pierced with conical holes which

954

have a small opening to the outside and a wide opening to the inside of the building. The air in this way is diffused as it enters. These bricks are much used for halls, stables, cowsheds, etc.

The air may be warmed if required by passing a coil of hot pipes through the inlet or by conducting it to a chamber behind the fire grate. In towns it may have to be filtered by passing through muslin, or moistened if the air be too dry.

Outlets should be placed at the highest parts of the room, or, if they can be heated, at any part. They should be protected by cowls to aid aspiration by wind, and to prevent their being closed or acting as channels for rain. They should be straight and smooth to lessen the retardation of the air by friction. The chimney with an open fire is the usual outlet in rooms, or the heat of the fire may be utilized by shafts round the smoke-flue opening from the upper parts of the room, or again a valve may open directly into the chimney, but so arranged as to prevent the reflux of smoke.

In the 'sunlight gas burners' in public buildings the products of combustion are led off in an inner tube. This heated inner tube is encased in an outer one, which conducts off the foul air of the room. In McKinnell's circular tubes we have both an inlet and an outlet (Fig. 390). The inner tube is the longer, projecting both upwards and downwards, the lower end being flanged. The air enters by the outer tube, and is directed along the upper parts of the room by the flanges of the inner tube. The inner tube acts as the outlet.

Artificial ventilation consists in the propulsion into a building of the required fresh air, or the extraction of foul air, by mechanical means. Heat may be utilized, as in the case of an ordinary chimney, or as in the heating of the upcast shaft still in use at some collieries. In large buildings, tubes may be conducted from several rooms into the chimney shaft near the fire. A steam jet has been used as the extracting force, especially in collieries, a jet of steam being able to set in motion a volume of air equivalent to 217 times its own bulk. Various forms of air-conditioning plants are now in use which purify, heat, and moisten the air, and automatically change the air in a room so many times an hour.

The advantages of artificial ventilation are : the greater certainty that the source of fresh air is pure ; the ease with

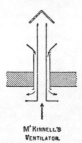

M'KINNELL'S
VENTILATOR.

FIG. 390.—A roof provided with this ventilator, showing inlet and outlet shafts.

which the supply can be regulated, filtered, warmed, or cooled; the more effective distribution of the air, and its independence of the weather conditions.

Air sterilization.—In order to reduce the risk of cross-infection, particularly in schools, dormitories, and offices, much attention has been devoted in recent years to the problem of killing pathogenic organisms in the air of a room. Ultra-violet light has been used, but its use for this purpose is restricted. It has been used mainly in operating theatres. The more promising method is by means of bactericidal mists or ærosols, using glycols.

VENTOUSE, or VACUUM EXTRACTOR, is being used to an increasing extent in obstetrics. It is based upon a suction-cup technique, whereby the baby is sucked out of the uterus instead of being drawn out by forceps.

VENTRAL (*venter*, the belly) means belonging to the belly.

VENTRICLE (*ventriculus*, the stomach) is the term applied to the two lower cavities of the heart (*see* HEART), and also to the cavities within the brain.

VENTRICULOGRAPHY is the term applied to the process of taking an X-ray photograph of the brain after the fluid in the lateral ventricles of the

brain has been replaced by air ; in this way any alteration in the outline of the ventricles (*e.g.* from pressure by a tumour) can be detected.

VENUPUNCTURE is the name applied to inserting a needle into a vein, usually for the purpose of injecting a drug.

VERATRINE is a mixture of alkaloids, derived from the seeds of *Asagrœa officinalis*, which has a paralysing effect upon nerves. The ointment of veratrine is used for the relief of pain in cases of rheumatism or of neuralgia.

VERATRUM, also known as green hellebore, Indian poke, and poke root, is the root of *Veratrum viride*, a plant of the United States. It acts as a sedative and depressant of the heart and nervous system by virtue of veratrine and other alkaloids that it contains. Alkaloids obtained from it are now being used in the treatment of high blood-pressure. (*See* ESSENTIAL HYPERTENSION.)

VERBIGERATION (*verbigero*, I chatter) means the insane repetition of meaningless words and sentences.

VERDIGRIS is a basic acetate of copper. It may be formed by the action of fruit juice on copper saucepans or dishes which are not kept clean, and is said to have given rise to poisoning. (*See* COPPER POISONING.)

VERMES (*see* PARASITES).

VERMICIDES, or VERMIFUGES (*vermis*, a worm ; *cædo*, I kill ; *fugo*, I drive away) are substances that kill, or expel, parasitic worms from the intestines. (*See* PARASITES.)

VERMIN (*vermis*, worm) is a term applied in medicine to parasites on the surface of the body. (*See* INSECTS.)

VERONAL (*see* BARBITONE).

VERRUCA is the Latin term for a wart.

VERRUCOSE (*verrucosus*) means covered with warts.

VERSION, or TURNING, is the name given to an operation in obstetrics which consists in turning the child in cases in which the lie of the child is abnormal.

VERTEBRA (*vertebra*) is one of the irregularly shaped bones that together form the vertebral column. (*See* SPINAL COLUMN.)

VERTIGO (*vertigo*, a whirling round) or giddiness is a condition in which the affected person loses the power of balancing himself, and has a false sensation as to his own movements or as to those of surrounding objects. The power of balancing depends upon sensations derived partly through the sense of touch, partly from the eyes, but mainly from the semicircular canals of the internal ears, and vertigo is in general due to some interference with this mechanism or with the centres in the cerebellum and cerebrum with which it is connected. Giddiness is very apt to be associated with headache, nausea, and vomiting.

Causes.—The simplest cause of vertigo is some mechanical disturbance of the body affecting the fluid in the internal ear ; such as that produced by moving in a swing with the eyes shut, the motion of a boat causing sea-sickness, or a sudden fall (*see* SEA-SICKNESS). The cause which produces the most severe and most sudden giddiness is Ménière's disease, a condition in which there is loss of function of the labyrinth of the inner ear. The most serious form is that in which sudden hæmorrhage takes place into the semicircular canals, producing an apoplectic-like fall, often of great violence. A condition of similar nature, though less violent and less permanent in its effects, is sometimes produced by the removal of wax from the ear, or even by syringing out the ear. (*See* EAR, DISEASES OF.) A third group of causes for vertigo is found in disorders of the stomach. Refractive errors in the eyes which have not received appropriate treatment by glasses, an overstrained nervous system, an attack of migraine,

a mild attack of epilepsy, and gross diseases of the brain, such as tumours, form another set of causes acting more directly upon the central nervous system. Finally, giddiness may be due to some disorder of the circulation, *e.g.* bloodlessness of the brain produced by fainting, or by disease of the heart.

Treatment, while the attack lasts, consists in maintaining a recumbent posture, in a darkened, quiet room. Sedatives are the drugs which have most influence in diminishing giddiness when it is distressing. After the attack is over, careful examination is necessary in order to determine the cause, for upon this depends the appropriateness of treatment.

VESICAL (*vesica*, a bladder or blister) is the term applied to structures connected with, or diseases of, the bladder. (*See* BLADDER.)

VESICANTS (*vesica*, a blister) are blistering agents. (*See* BLISTERS.)

VESICLE (*vesicula*, a little blister) means a small collection of fluid in the cuticle. The fluid in some cases consists of a drop of sweat collected at the mouth of a sweat-gland, but in general it is serum from the blood. The skin disease specially associated with the formation of vesicles is herpes ; in this disease the vesicles usually burst and then scab over. Some infectious diseases show an eruption composed of vesicles, *e.g.* smallpox and chickenpox. When a large number of white corpuscles from the blood find their way into a vesicle, it becomes a ' pustule '.

The term vesicle is also applied to minute sacs of normal structure, such as the air-vesicles in which the finest bronchial tubes end in the lungs.

VIABLE is a term applied to a newly born child to signify that it is capable of living separately from the mother. (*See* BIRTH.)

VIBRATOR is the name of an instrument used for vibratory massage in the mechanical treatment of disease. For its use *see* MASSAGE.

VIBRIO (*vibro*, I quiver) is the name applied to a bacterium of curved shape, such as the vibrio of cholera.

VIBURNUM, or BLACK HAW, is the bark of *Viburnum prunifolium* or of *Viburnum lentago*, of which the liquid extract is used in doses of 60 to 120 minims (4 to 8 ml.) for treating painful menstruation.

VICARIOUS is a term applied to the temporary discharge by one organ of the functions of another. The word is chiefly used in connection with vicarious menstruation, when the blood that should be got rid of from the uterus runs from the nose, bowels, stomach, etc.

VICHY WATER is an alkaline mineral water from springs at Vichy in France, and is used in various constitutional disorders.

VILLUS (*villus*, hair) is the name given to one of the minute processes which are thickly planted upon the inner surface of the small intestine, giving it, to the naked eye, a velvety appearance, and greatly assisting absorption. (*See* DIGESTION, INTESTINE.)

VINBLASTINE is an alkaloid (*q.v.*) derived from the periwinkle plant (*Vinca rosea* Linn.) which is of value in the treatment of certain forms of malignant disease, particularly choriocarcinoma and Hodgkin's disease.

VINCENT'S ANGINA is an ulcerative inflammation of the throat, often foul smelling, and caused by large, spindle-shaped bacilli and spirilla.

VINEGAR (*see* ACETIC ACID).

VINESTHENE is an inhalational anæsthetic. It is a mixture of 75 per cent. di-ethyl ether and di-vinyl ether.

VINUM is the Latin name for wine. The wines used as medicinal remedies include wines of colchicum, antimony, ipecacuanha, citrate of iron, quinine, and orange. They are seldom used now.

VIOMYCIN is an antibiotic obtained from *Streptomyces punicens* and *Streptomyces floridæ*, which is active against the *Mycobacterium tuberculosis*, but less active than streptomycin or isoniazid.

VIRGINIAN PRUNE BARK, or WILD CHERRY BARK, is the bark of *Prunus serotina*, which yields an oil containing hydrocyanic acid. It possesses tonic and sedative properties and in the form of tincture and syrup is used as a remedy for cough.

VIRILISM is the term applied to the condition in which masculine characteristics develop in the female, and is commonly the result of an overactive suprarenal gland, or of a tumour of its cortex.

VIRUS (*virus*, poison) is the term applied to a group of infective agents which are so small that they are able to pass through the pores of collodion filters. They are responsible for some of the most important diseases affecting man, *e.g.* influenza, poliomyelitis, smallpox, and yellow fever. Some idea of their size may be obtained from the fact that the virus of influenza measures 80 mμ, whereas the staphylococcus measures 1000 mμ. (1 mμ = 0·000001 millimetre.)

VISCERA (*viscus*, the bowels) is the general name given to the larger organs lying within the cavities of the chest and abdomen. The term viscus is also applied individually to these organs.

VISCEROPTOSIS, also known as splanchnoptosis, means a falling down of the viscera, especially those of the abdomen. It is often associated with faulty posture in standing. In elderly women it may be associated with prolapse of the womb (*see* PROLAPSE).

VISION.—The functions of the eye as an optical instrument which brings rays of light to the endings of the optic nerve, have been already considered (*see* EYE) ; in this article, vision will be dealt with as a sensation.

Rays of light pass, in the first place, through the cornea, then through the aqueous humour that fills the anterior chamber of the eye (Fig. 391). The

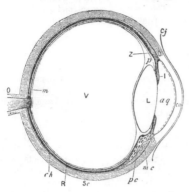

FIG. 391.—Horizontal section through the left eye. *co*, Cornea; *aq*, aqueous humour; *L*, lens; *V*, vitreous humour; *m*, macula or spot of clearest vision; *O*, optic nerve. (For other letters, *see* EYE.) (Turner's *Anatomy*.)

light then enters the hinder part of the eye through the pupil, a round hole in the iris which is automatically narrowed according to the strength of the entering light. Next it passes through the lens, which, by a similar automatic action, brings the rays to a correct locus upon the retina, where they finally arrive after passing through the vitreous humour, a jelly-like substance that fills out the eyeball. (*See* ACCOMMODATION.)

In the retina, the sensory endings appear to be the rods and cones, minute structures placed closely side by side (Fig. 171). The number of cones in a single eye has been estimated at 3,000,000, whilst the rods are considerably in excess of the cones. At the *fovea centralis* or point of clearest vision, situated near the centre of the back of the eye, there are no rods, but only cones.

Light perception. — The retina is extremely delicate in its power of perceiving a faint amount of light and very short flashes of light. Thus a flash from a rapidly revolving mirror lasting only one eight-millionth of a second is perceived. According to Weber's law, however, if the eye be subjected to a constant light, the light must be increased in strength by $\frac{1}{100}$ before any difference can be observed; for ex-

ample, if a room be lighted by 1000 candles and the light be increased, no difference in brightness will be noticed if fewer than ten more candles be brought in at one time. The intensity of a sensation of light bears no relation to the time during which the light falls upon the eye, but a very important fact is that any image formed in the eye takes an appreciable time to fade away, lasting about $\frac{1}{8}$ of a second. Thus, if an appearance be repeated more frequently than eight times in a second it produces an impression of permanence, and, for this reason, the spokes of a quickly revolving wheel produce an appearance as if the wheel were solid.

Acuteness of vision.—As in the case of the sense of touch, a sharp contrast between any object and its surroundings renders it more perceptible, whilst movement renders anything more easily seen, just as it makes a touch more easily felt. In order that an object may be distinguished, it must be of a certain size. Two points will not be seen as two unless they are at least so far apart that the lines joining them to the centre of the eye enclose between them an angle of about one-sixtieth of a degree. This distance enables the images of the two points to fall upon two cones, the centres of the cones, which are closely placed at the *fovea centralis*, being about $\frac{1}{7000}$ of an inch (3·5 microns) apart. In order that a complex object, such as a letter or figure, may be recognized, it must subtend an angle of about five times this size, that, is one-twelfth of a degree. Upon this principle Snellen's types for testing the acuteness of vision are constructed (Fig. 392). The largest letters are of such a size that at 60 metres distance they occupy an angle

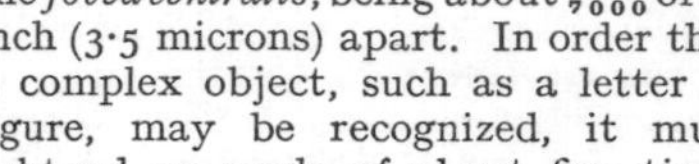

E V O

FIG. 392.—Three test types of Snellen's scale (D = 6). These letters should be clearly visible to normal eyes at a distance of 6 metres.

of one-twelfth degree, and should therefore be clearly seen ; whilst the smallest are of such a size that they occupy this angle at 6 metres distance, and should

there be correctly read. The vision of
a normal-sighted person, who can read
these last types at 6 metres distance,
is represented by the fraction $\frac{6}{6}$, whilst
that of a person who can read only the
largest type at the same distance is $\frac{6}{60}$,
and intermediate degrees of faulty
vision are $\frac{6}{12}$, $\frac{6}{18}$, $\frac{6}{24}$, etc. Still smaller
types are used for testing the acuteness
of near vision. It must be noted that
efficiency of vision is not proportional
to acuity of vision. Thus a man with
' vision $= \frac{6}{12}$' has half the visual acuity
of a man with vision $= \frac{6}{6}$', but he has
very little less efficiency. Indeed, for
ordinary manual work, vision of $\frac{6}{12}$
gives practically full efficiency. This
point is important in connection with
accidents to the eye.

Colour sense is one of the most difficult to understand of the visual powers.
It corresponds, broadly speaking, to the
perception of the pitch of notes by the
ear, depending upon the difference in
rapidity of vibration of various rays of
light. White light is supposed to be
compounded of a mixture in certain
proportions of the other colours, into
which it may be split by refraction
through the prism. This band of
colours, or spectrum, may be again
compounded into white light by passage
through a second prism ; or the same
effect may be got by rotating rapidly
before the eyes a disc with segments
variously coloured. White light may
also be formed by a disc of two colours,
which are therefore known as complementary colours. These are red with
bluish-green, orange with blue, or violet
with yellow. Again, any colour may be
produced by mixtures in varying proportions of red, green, and violet, these
three being therefore known as cardinal
or fundamental colours. Three theories
have been suggested as to the manner in
which various colours are produced.

(1) YOUNG-HELMHOLTZ THEORY is
the one that finds most acceptance. It
teaches that there are in the retina
separate elements, probably cones, capable of being stimulated by the rays in
different parts of the spectrum. Some
of these react to red but not to green or
violet, others to green but not to red
or violet, and a third set to violet
though not to red or green ; whilst an
appearance of white results when all
are fairly equally stimulated.

(2) HERING'S THEORY demands the
existence of chemical substances in the
retina, three in number, which are constantly being either formed or broken
down under the action of light. Each
substance is supposed to correspond
with a pair of colours, one with black or
white sensations, one with red or green,
and the third with yellow or blue.
Destruction of each substance by light
produces one colour of a pair, construction produces the other. Intermediate
colours of the spectrum, such as orange,
result from light affecting two of these
substances.

(3) TELEPHONE THEORY is one that
has been suggested, but has not found
much favour. By it the rays of all
wave-lengths are supposed to be
received on the retina, where they set
up differing nerve vibrations that are
conveyed to the brain, where for the
first time they are analysed into different
sensations of colour, just as a telephone
ear-piece reproduces the voice with all
its original pitch and modulations.

Field of vision.—When one looks
straight forwards with one eye at a time,

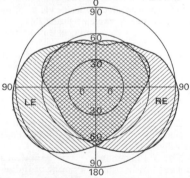

FIG. 393.—Diagram of the fields of vision. The
outer circle represents the half of space lying
in front of the observer. As he looks directly
forwards, the figure o is straight above his
head, 180 straight beneath his feet, and 90
straight out on either side. The two smaller
circles rise 30° and 60° above the horizon.
The two shaded areas represent the field
visible to either eye, LE to the left eye, and
RE to the right eye. The darker area, where
the two overlap, is the part seen by both eyes.

one sees with special clearness the
object towards which the eye is directed
and more vaguely objects for some
distance around. The extent that can
be seen without moving the eye is
known as the 'field of vision' (Fig. 393).

It is oval in shape and extends much farther outwards than in other directions. Towards the temple, indeed, the eye of a sharp-sighted person looking straight forwards can see white objects about ten degrees behind the person. The fields of vision of the two eyes overlap to a great extent, so that objects around the centre and to the inner side of each field are viewed by both eyes. Accordingly there are ' corresponding points ' in the two retinæ, an object to the right of the observer producing an image on the inner side of his right eye, but on the outer side of his left eye.

The optic nerves are arranged in correspondence with this, the nerve fibres from the left half of each retina passing to the left hemisphere of the brain, and those fibres from the two right halves going to the right hemisphere. Thus half of each optic nerve crosses from one eye to the other side of the brain at the optic chiasma.

It is interesting to note that the field of vision forms an inverted image on the retina, objects to the right falling upon the left side of each retina, those above upon its lower part, and vice versa. The mind, however, as the result of experience, analyses these images and so this inversion is not perceived.

The field of vision varies for different colours, that for white being largest, yellow next, then blue, red, while green is only seen for a short distance round the centre of the field when the coloured areas are of equal size.

The existence of a blind spot is mentioned and the proof of its presence detailed under EYE.

Visual judgements.—The sensations of sight imply a great amount of judgement, for whilst the other senses are influenced by direct physical impressions, in sight we have to examine an inverted image of microscopic size produced by ether waves upon each retina. We are, however, conscious neither of the minuteness of the visual image, nor of its inversion ; nor are we aware of the blind spot in each field of vision, unless we search for it in the manner described under EYE.

The manner in which we estimate size and distance was inquired into by Bishop Berkeley in his *Essay towards a*

New Theory of Vision, published in 1709, and his conclusions still in the main hold the field. He concluded that our idea of near distances was derived from three arbitrary signs : (a) the sense of muscular effort in converging the eyes when they are directed to something very close at hand, and of relaxation when they diverge to view some object farther off ; (b) the blurred appearance presented by nearer objects, when we are looking at an object situated farther off, or vice versa ; (c) the muscular effort of accommodating the eye for near or for distant vision (see ACCOMMODATION). In distant vision, too, he held that we are mainly dependent on the three signs : (a) evidence derived from experience mainly of the sense of touch ; a certain combination of colours and form, for example, being associated with the idea of a man felt at close quarters, the same colours and form of smaller size suggest a man some distance off ; (b) the sense of blurring of distant objects, already mentioned, when we look at objects close at hand ; (c) faintness in appearance of an object suggests distance, clearness suggests that the object is near at hand. When objects are seen under unusual conditions of faintness or clearness it becomes very difficult to estimate their size and distance. Thus the moon low down near the horizon and partly obscured by mists rising from the earth, or figures of men on a foggy day, loom much larger than natural, because we over-estimate their distance, owing to their faintness.

Berkeley, however, took little note of the value of binocular vision and of the partial overlapping of the two fields already mentioned. He based his theory largely upon the axiom that ' distance being a line directed endwise to the eye, it projects only one point in the fund of the eye—which point remains invariably the same, whether the distance be longer or shorter '. This, however, applies only to a one-eyed man, and, in binocular vision, each eye corrects this deficiency of the other, seeing as it were across the other eye's line of vision. Thus we can see in some degree behind or round the corners of nearer objects, and so we obtain to a great extent our idea of depth, or solidity.

VISION, DISORDERS OF. — Many disorders which indirectly affect the power of vision owing to inflammation or to a painful condition of the eye have been mentioned under EYE, DISEASES OF. Here we shall consider more permanent and direct disturbances of sight under the heads of : (a) Dimness of vision ; (b) Colour-blindness ; (c) Decreased visual field ; (d) Night-blindness.

Dimness of vision.—The most frequent cause of dim vision, or even of total blindness, is some obstruction to the entrance of light through the parts that ought to be transparent.

CORNEAL OPACITIES may produce a ground-glass-like condition of the naturally transparent cornea, so that light may be prevented from gaining access to the eye at all. Thus a dark shadow is caused upon the vision, or complete blindness is produced, according to the breadth and density of the opacity. Practically nothing can be done to remove dimness of vision due to this cause. The most common diseases leading to this condition are keratitis and corneal ulcers. (*See under* EYE, DISEASES OF.)

REFRACTIVE ERRORS produced by malformations of the cornea, the lens, or the globe of the eye, are by far the commonest causes of defective vision. They are also the most important, both because they cause great interference with the ordinary pursuits of life and may lead to a great degree of general ill-health, and still more because the recognition and appropriate treatment of these errors are easily effected by the expert. The symptoms due to refractive errors are sometimes grouped as the result of *eye-strain*, and include in the first place headache, inflammation of the eyes (*conjunctivitis* and *iritis*), and inability to use the eyes for long at one time. Children, especially, who have uncorrected errors of refraction have difficulty in keeping up with their fellows at school because of blurring of the page in reading (long-sight) or inability to see clearly maps, blackboards, and other objects at a distance (short-sight). The strain produced may even lead, in delicate children, to headaches or more serious nervous disorders, or to impairment of the general health. Further, children with such defects are apt to adopt a crouching position at lessons, and to evince a distaste for outdoor sports. This leads to curvature of the spine, defective chest development, and liability to lung diseases. The varieties and treatment of refractive errors are dealt with under SPECTACLES.

CATARACT is an opaque condition of the lens coming on slowly, as a rule, in elderly people. Its symptoms, etc., are treated under CATARACT.

VITREOUS HUMOUR OPACITIES are apt to be seen by any one who looks steadily at a bright surface, particularly when the general health is not perfect. These may be due to the remains of former inflammation in the choroid coat, but as a rule they are simply the shadows of unimportant cells and fibres floating in the vitreous humour, and need not cause any worry.

DISEASE IN THE FUNDUS of the eye, consisting of chronic inflammation in the retina or choroid coat, or in both, is often a reason of diminishing vision, characterized especially by inability to see in a dim light. (*See* EYE, DISEASES OF ; CHOROIDITIS.)

DISEASES OF THE BRAIN OR OF THE OPTIC NERVE may lead to temporary dimness of vision, and sometimes blindness.

Colour-blindness is a much more common disorder than is generally supposed, being present to an appreciable extent in about one person out of every fifty, and much more common in men than in women. It is usually congenital, and persists through life, although it may be acquired as the result of poisoning by various substances, notably by excessive tobacco smoking.

Red-green blindness is the most common form, and is present in all grades of completeness, from that of a person for whom red simply loses its brilliance at a distance, to that of a person for whom vivid green and brilliant scarlet appear as one and the same colour. In one variety of red-green blindness the red, orange, yellow, and green of the spectrum appear all of one colour, ' green ' ; while the blue and violet both appear as ' blue ', with a gap in the spectrum where the normal eye sees a bluish-green colour.

One test for colour-blindness consists

31

in giving the person a skein of green or red wool, and asking him to select from many other skeins the colours which appear to him to match the one he holds. The colour-blind person confuses red with brown, greenish-brown, and yellowish-brown ; and he confuses green with bluish-green, rose, and grey. This test, however, has been largely replaced by the Ishihara test (*q.v.*).

The importance in testing for colour-blindness any one who is to be a signal-man or engine-driver is evident.

Decreased visual field is another form of visual defect. Complete blindness in one eye which has lasted since birth is frequently discovered only by accident in middle life, because the healthy eye has always had an unrestricted field. Another and rarer condition, which is more noticeable to the patient, consists in loss of one-half of the visual field, so that the person can see objects only at one side and must turn his head in order to appreciate his surroundings. This is due to some defect in one-half of the brain or in the optic tract. In this defect a corresponding part of each retina is thrown out of action. Local causes of decrease in the visual field of each eye are found in atrophy of the optic nerve and certain forms of inflammation of the retina. Some general conditions also produce a temporary narrowing of the field, notably great bloodlessness, and over-dosage with quinine.

These defects can be mapped out accurately by the help of an instrument called the perimeter.

Night-blindness, or NYCTALOPIA, an abnormal inability to see things in the night, is thought to be due in many cases to vitamin A deficiency ; sometimes the condition is hereditary.

Yellow vision may appear from taking santonin or excessive doses of digitalis, or in jaundice.

VIS MEDICATRIX NATURÆ is a Latin term meaning the healing power of Nature, and is often used to indicate the tendency of wounds to heal and of the bodily powers to subdue disease, when left to the operation of time and rest.

VITAMIN (*vita*, life) is a term applied to a group of substances which exist in minute quantities in natural foods,

and which are necessary to normal nutrition, especially in connection with growth and development. Several of them have now been synthesized. When they are absent from the food, defective growth takes place in young animals and children, and in adults various diseases arise ; whilst short of the production of actual disease, persistent deprivation of one or other vitamin is apt to lead to a state of lowered general health. Certain deficiencies in diet have long been known to be the cause of scurvy, beri-beri, and rickets, but the so-called ' vitamine hypothesis ' was not introduced until the twentieth century.

Vitamin A is usually taken in more than ample quantity in the food, and is stored in the liver. It is developed originally by plants as a yellow colouring matter, carotene, for example in carrots, and it is also found in egg yolk, liver, milk, butter, and most green vegetables. When stored in the liver it is colourless and has a slight chemical difference from carotene. The two richest sources of this vitamin are halibut-liver oil, which contains 5,000,000 international units per gramme, and cod-liver oil, which contains 100,000 international units per gramme. The daily requirement of vitamin A is in the region of 4000 international units. Children and pregnant women require relatively more than adults. Deficiency of vitamin A is responsible for serious inflammation of the eyes known as xerophthalmia, which in India is one of the chief causes of blindness ; also for night blindness, various skin eruptions, defective development of the teeth, and particularly for want of vitality in the tissues, which leads to localized inflammations.

Vitamin B₁, also known as ANEURINE and THIAMINE, is found in the husks of cereal grains. Its deficiency may be produced by too careful milling of rice in the East, or by a diet of white bread to the exclusion of brown bread and other cereal sources of this vitamin, The resulting disease is a form of neuritis with muscular weakness, heart failure, etc., which in Japan and other parts of the East is known as beri-beri. Vitamin B_1 has now been isolated in crystalline form, and a minute dose of this rapidly cures the symptoms of beri-beri. The best sources of this vitamin are whole-meal flour, bacon, liver, egg-yolk, yeast, and the pulses. The daily requirement is dependent, among other things, upon the total food intake, and has been estimated to be in the region of 0·5 mg. of aneurine per 1000 calories, increased during pregnancy to 2 mg. daily as a minimum.

Vitamin B2 is now divided into different fractions, and the term is being restricted to the vitamin known as RIBOFLAVINE (q.v.), which has been isolated in crystal form. It seems to be essential for growth and the health of the skin. In human beings sore lips and inflamed mouth are thought to be due to deficiency of riboflavine. That part of the vitamin B₂ complex responsible for the prevention of pellagra has now been identified as NICOTINIC ACID (q.v.). Other substances separated from the ' vitamin B₂ complex' are PYRIDOXINE (q.v.), or vitamin B₆, and PANTOTHENIC ACID (q.v.).

Vitamin B₁₂ (see CYANOCOBALAMIN).

Vitamin C is especially found in fresh fruits such as the orange, and also in fresh green vegetables, and to a smaller extent in milk, meat, and other fresh foods. Canned vegetables such as tomatoes also retain it if their reaction is acid. It is quickly destroyed by high temperature, by excess baking soda and other alkalies, and gradually by oxidation in process of keeping. Its deficiency in a few months leads to symptoms of scurvy, including muscular weakness, hæmorrhages under the skin, swelling and inflammation of the gums with loss of teeth, and serious damage to joints by hæmorrhage ; it occurs in sailors and other persons long deprived of fresh foods, and also in babies fed persistently on artificial foods. This vitamin has not only been obtained in a pure state, but has been manufactured in a crystalline form as ascorbic acid. The daily requirement of vitamin C (in terms of ascorbic acid) is 30 mg. for adults and 60 mg. for children.

Vitamin D is of special importance for the growth of children, and its deficiency produces rickets with softening and irregular growth of bones, so that swollen joints, distorted limbs, deformities of the chest and similar malforma-tions arise. It was formerly common in the dark and narrow streets of large manufacturing towns and is still found when children are kept too much indoors. Osteomalacia, a similar disease affecting the bones of adult women, results from the same causes when lime salts are absorbed from the bones during pregnancy. Rickets is also common among young dogs and other animals. It has long been known that cod-liver oil was the chief remedy for rickets, and for a time it was supposed that its anti-rachitic action depended upon Vitamin A, but it is now known to be vitamin D. Vitamin D can be produced by the action of ultra-violet rays upon a waxy constituent of animal and vegetable tissues known as ergosterol, from which vitamin D can afterwards be separated. To this synthetic vitamin D the name of calciferol has been given, and it is 400,000 times more potent than cod-liver oil in preventing or curing rickets. This substance is also formed naturally in the fatty tissues of the body when the skin is exposed to the action of sunlight, or, when this is not available, to ultra-violet rays from an arc lamp. It can also be formed in food such as milk when this is similarly exposed to light. Only a few foods contain vitamin D naturally, including cod-liver oil and other fish liver oils (especially that from halibut liver), whilst egg yolk contains a smaller quantity ; other fats and milk contain very small quantities. The mode of action of vitamin D is to aid the absorption of phosphorus and calcium from the food, increase their amount in the blood, and thus in the bones. In the case of this vitamin bad effects may follow over-dosage, or hypervitaminosis, because if too much calcium and phosphorus are maintained in the blood the bones and teeth become overcalcified, the arteries may become unduly hardened and calculi may be formed in the kidneys and other organs. The daily requirement for infants and nursing mothers is 400 to 800 international units, whilst for adults it is probably about 400 units.

Vitamin E has been known since the year 1922, when it was found that its absence in the case of rats caused failure to produce young. It is derived especially from the oil contained in seeds and in green leaves, and also is present in smaller amounts in other fresh fats. It is readily stored, like vitamin A, in the body, and thus is unlikely to be found wanting in human beings except in cases of very severe under-nutrition. It is possible, however, that miscarriages may occasionally be due to its deficiency.

Vitamin H (*see* BIOTIN).

Vitamin K, or the anti-hæmorrhagic vitamin, is essential for the proper clotting of blood. It has been given successfully in cases of bleeding in infants, and to patients with jaundice, who have a special tendency to bleeding. Bleeding in these conditions is thought to be due to deficiency of vitamin K. Synthetic chemical products with an identical physiological action have now been made. In the natural form it is widespread in nature, the main sources being spinach, leafy vegetables, tomatoes, and liver. The daily requirement of man is not known.

Vitamin P, CITRIN, or HESPERIDIN, present in citrus fruits, appears to be responsible for the resistance of the capillaries to pressure. If there is a deficiency of vitamin P in the diet the capillaries rupture easily, resulting, for example, in purpura.

It should be said in conclusion, with regard to the supply of vitamins, that any person using a diet containing the ' protective foods ', such as milk, eggs, butter, cheese, fat, fish, wholemeal bread, fresh vegetables and fruit, should obtain an ample supply of vitamins. Infants should have a teaspoonful daily of cod-liver oil and two teaspoonfuls of orange juice or of tomato juice.

VITELLUS, or VITELLUM, is the Latin name for yolk of egg.

VITILIGO is the term given to a skin disease in which smooth light-coloured patches appear either on the skin or in the hair.

VITRELLA is a small, crushable, glass capsule enclosed in an absorptive and protective fabric, used for the dispensing of medicines such as amyl nitrite which are to be inhaled.

VITREOUS BODY (*vitreus*, glassy) is a semi-fluid transparent substance which fills most of the globe of the eye behind the lens.

VITRIOL, OIL OF, is an old name for sulphuric acid.

VOCAL RESONANCE is the term applied to the buzzing sound that is heard when the ear is applied to the chest as the patient speaks.

VOICE AND SPEECH are two terms applied to the system of sounds which are produced in the upper air passages and in the mouth, and which form one of the means of communication between human beings.

Voice means the set of fundamental notes and tones produced by the larynx, which are modified in various ways during their passage through the mouth so as to form speech or song. Speech differs from song in being less sustained and of smaller compass with regard to pitch, and in presenting sounds which have not a musical character.

Voice is produced in the larynx of most animals, although birds have a special organ known as the ' syrinx ' in which their song takes origin. The question was formerly much debated as to what musical instrument most closely resembles the larynx. Ferrein held that the violin formed the nearest artificial approach, and hence the name of vocal ' cords '. Other observers have, in a somewhat fanciful way, compared the air which the chest drives upwards to the bow, the larynx to the violin, and the tongue, lips, etc., which modify the laryngeal notes, to the string-hand of the violinist. It is generally admitted, however, that the larynx more nearly resembles a wind instrument with a pair of vibrating reeds. Many persons have made a careful study of voice production by the aid of the laryngoscope (*see* LARYNX), an instrument which enables the changes that take place in the larynx, when different notes are sounded, to be clearly seen.

Musical notes vary in three characters, viz. loudness, pitch, and quality or timbre. The *loudness* of the voice depends upon the volume of air which is available for agitating the vocal cords, and therefore upon the size of the chest and vigour with which its muscles can be made to act.

The *pitch* of the voice is determined by several things, the chief points being the size of the larynx ; the degree of tenseness at which the vocal cords are, for the time being, maintained by the laryngeal muscles ; the fact as to whether the cords vibrate as a whole or merely at their edges ; and the shape which is given to the cavity of the larynx by movements of the arytenoid and epiglottic cartilages. In any given voice, the range of pitch seldom exceeds two and a half octaves, although the particular part of the musical scale that can be produced varies according as the voice is bass, tenor, contralto, soprano, etc. Generally speaking, a large larynx with long vocal cords produces low notes, and hence men have a deeper voice than women. For the same reason the small larynx of childhood produces a shrill voice, whilst the rapid growth of the larynx at the time of puberty, and consequent uncertainty of muscular control over the vocal cords, produces the ' breaking ' of the voice that occurs in boys at this time. The manner in which the muscles of the larynx act upon the cords allows the pitch to change at will. Thus if the thick part of each cord be held rigid and only the sharp free edge be allowed to vibrate, a high note is the result, and a still higher note is reached in men when only the front part of this free edge is allowed to move, as in the ' falsetto ' voice. On the other hand, by allowing a greater thickness of the cord to vibrate, the person loads the vibrating edge, and thus produces a much deeper note.

The *timbre* of the voice is partly due to these differences in the larynx, but chiefly to peculiarities and to voluntary changes in shape of the mouth and other cavities associated with the air passages. These changes in shape of the mouth, etc., are chiefly concerned with the alterations of the fundamental notes which produce speech, and they are considered in detail below.

It should be remembered, however, that while the muscular arrangements of the larynx are chiefly concerned with the pitch of the voice, and the shape of the mouth with its modulation, the *loudness* is varied by the movements of the chest. The neglect of this fact is often responsible for the bad voice-production which leads to great straining of the throat, and is largely responsible for the throat affections of many of those who use the voice much. (*See* CLERGYMAN'S SORE THROAT.)

There are certain peculiar forms of voice production. The *falsetto voice* has been already mentioned. *Whispering* is a form of speech in which voice is completely absent, the larynx being wide open, and the sound produced entirely in the mouth. *Ventriloquism* is a form of speech in which the voice is produced by the indrawing of air, instead of in the usual way of expiration. Since it is always difficult to localize the source of sound, the ventriloquist can easily suggest to his audience a false place of origin for the unusual voice.

Speech consists of a series of rapid modifications of the voice, produced by changes in position of the palate, tongue, and lips. EACH VOWEL has an appropriate pitch as ordinarily spoken, although it is possible to pronounce any of the vowels in any note within the compass of the voice. The appropriate pitch of *u* (pronounced $\overline{oo}$) is lowest, and the vowels rise through *o*, *a* (pronounced *ah*), *e* (pronounced *eh*), to *i* (pronounced $\overline{ee}$). Apart from this slight difference in pitch, the distinguishing character of each vowel is gained by alterations in the shape of the mouth cavity through which the stream of air passes. Any one can at once prove this fact by opening his mouth widely and sounding musical notes of various pitch. All of these will have the character of *a*, nor can the vowel be changed till the mouth is shut somewhat and certain changes made in the position of the tongue and lips. These changes in the shape of the mouth have the effect of intensifying certain of the overtones in the fundamental laryngeal note, and thus the vowels are produced. The shape of the mouth in speaking the different vowels is somewhat as follows. In pronouncing *a* (ah) the mouth is something like a funnel open to the front, the lips and teeth being held wide apart. For sounding *e* (eh) the shape is slightly modified, the mouth being more closed. When *u* ($\overline{oo}$) is pronounced the cavity of the mouth is shaped like a wide flask with a very narrow neck at the lips, which are protruded as far as possible. For *o* the flask shape is modified slightly, the neck being made shorter and wider by bringing the lips nearer the teeth and opening them a little. In pronouncing *i* (ēē) the tongue is brought up to the teeth, so that the air passes through a long narrow cavity, and obtains free exit, the lips being drawn well back. Although the English language is usually said to include only five vowels, many others can be formed by slight variations in the shape of the mouth, as, for example, in the case of the modified *ō* and *ü*, and other vowels of Continental languages. Diphthongs, like *ai, oi, ae*, are produced simply by a rapid change from one mouth-shape to another while air is issuing through the larynx.

Consonants are sudden sounds produced by cutting off the stream of air either wholly or partially, or by suddenly beginning it. Of necessity, a consonant forms either the beginning or end of a vowel sound, and the particular consonant produced depends upon the point at which the stream of air is checked. According to Brücke, there are four ' stop-positions ' :

(1) Between the lips.
(2) Between tip of tongue and roof of mouth.
(3) Between root of tongue and palate.
(4) In the larynx.

The character of the consonant varies also according as the stoppage of air is complete or its commencement sudden (*explosive consonants*) ; as the stoppage is only partial or the commencement gradual (*aspirate consonants*) ; or as the margins of the opening are thrown into vibration (*vibrative consonants*). Again, in the case of some consonants, the mouth is closed at different stop positions, and the air stream is allowed to pass out by the nose (*resonant consonants*). On this principle, consonants are classified as follows :

	Explosives.	Aspirates.	Vibratives.	Resonants.
1st Stop Position	P, B	F, V, W		M
2nd Stop Position	T, D	S, Z, L Sch, Th	R	N
3rd Stop Position	K, G	Ch, J	Palatal R	-Ng
4th Stop Position		H	Saxon R	

TABLE 32.—Classification of Consonants.
966

Another distinction, which is of great importance in the treatment of stammering, consists in the amount of force which is necessary to open the stop and sound the consonant, and the amount of voice which therefore accompanies it at the beginning of a syllable.

	Explosives.	Aspirates.
Voiceless	P, T, K	F, S, Sch, Th (as in *throw*), Ch
Voiced	B, D, G	V, Z, L, Th (as in *then*), J, H

The vibratives and resonants are all voiced.
TABLE 33.—Classification of Explosives and Aspirates.

One can test this by comparing, for example, the words ' Peter ' and ' Beater '. In ' Peter ' the *P* has little sound, the voice becoming full only on the *E*, while in ' Beater ' the full volume of sound comes out at once on the *B* and dies away on the *E*. One cause of stammering is the attempt to pronounce, with full voice, the consonants at the commencement of words which should be voiceless, instead of touching off the consonant lightly and passing on at once to emphasize the vowel.

Defects of speech.—The apparatus for speech being so complicated, and the changes which must take place constantly in its different parts so varied, it follows that the act of speech has a very elaborate controlling mechanism in the nervous system. Further, the power of speech is gained in early life by children hearing the sounds made by others and mimicking them, so that the centres for speech in the brain are intimately connected with those concerned in the sense of hearing.

Mutism, or the entire absence of the power to speak, may be due to various causes, the most effectual being some mental deficiency which denies to the child sufficient intelligence to mimic the actions of those around him. In other cases the child seems to be quite intelligent, but, owing apparently to some defect in the nervous control of the voice and speech organs, or in these organs themselves, he is unable to make any sounds. A very common cause of mutism is complete deafness present at birth, or caused by some ear diseases in early childhood. The child in this case cannot learn to speak, simply because he cannot hear, but, if properly educated, he can be taught to speak fluently and to understand what is said by watching the lips and throat of others. (*See* DUMBNESS.)

STAMMERING is a bad habit of speech due to want of co-ordination between the different parts of the speech mechanism. (*See* STAMMERING.)

TWANGS of various kinds are assumed very easily, and, indeed, often unconsciously, from those around. The ease with which the exact pronunciation of a foreign tongue is picked up by a person living in the country in question is well known. Many differences between different languages are to be explained by slight differences in shape between the speech organs of different races. Other differences are to be explained by different habits of opening the lips and mouth in various tribes of the same stock, due perhaps to external conditions, such as climate. Such minor peculiarities in speech as ' burrs ' and ' lisps ' are due to peculiarities in the action of the tongue or palate, whilst the deformities of tongue-tie and cleft-palate are accompanied by still greater defects of speech. When the nose is blocked by any condition, such as cold in the head or polypus, the pronunciation of the resonants *m*, *n*, and *ng* is interfered with, these being heard as *b*, *d*, and *g* respectively, for a reason which can be seen on consulting the first table given above.

APHASIA is a condition in which various forms of inability to speak, or to understand speech, come on late in life as the result of brain disease. (*See* APHASIA.)

APHONIA, or loss of voice, causes speaking to be carried on in a whisper. It is usually either due to some disorder of the vocal cords, as in the laryngitis which may form part of a cold (*see* THROAT DISEASES), or is a symptom of hysteria. It is generally of short duration.

VOLAR (*vola*, palm or sole) means something pertaining to the palm or sole.

VOLKMANN'S CONTRACTURE is the term applied to the condition in which, as a result of too great a pressure from splint or bandage in the treatment of a broken arm, the flexor muscles of the forearm contract and thus obstruct free flow of blood in the veins ; the muscles then swell and ultimately become fibrosed.

VOLSELLA is a Latin term for a forceps with hooked blades.

VOLVULUS (*volvo*, I twist) means an obstruction of the bowels produced by the twisting of a loop of bowel round itself. (*See* INTESTINE, DISEASES OF.)

VOMICA (*vomica*, an abscess) means a cavity in the lung produced by ulceration, which is usually a sign of tuberculosis.

VOMITING (*vomo*, I vomit) means the expulsion of the stomach contents through the mouth. When the effort of vomiting is made, but nothing is brought up, the process is known as ' retching '. When vomiting occurs, the chief effort is made by the muscles of the abdominal wall and by the diaphragm contracting together and squeezing the stomach. The contraction of the stomach wall is no doubt also a factor, and an important step in the act consists in the opening at the right moment of the cardiac or upper orifice of the stomach. This concerted action of various muscles is brought about by a ' vomiting centre ' situated on the floor of the fourth ventricle in the brain.

Causes.—Vomiting is brought about by some irritation of this nervous centre, but in the great majority of cases this is effected through sensations derived from the stomach itself. Thus, of the drugs which cause vomiting some act only after being absorbed into the blood and carried to the brain, although most are irritants to the mucous membrane of the stomach (*see* EMETICS) ; dyspepsia also acts thus, and lies at the root of most sick-headaches ; and various diseases of the stomach, such as chronic catarrh, cancer, ulcer, and dilatation, act in a similar way. Irritation, not only of the nerves of the stomach, but also of those proceeding from other abdominal organs, produces vomiting ; thus in obstruction of the bowels, peritonitis, gall-stone colic, renal colic, and even during pregnancy, vomiting is a prominent symptom.

Strong impressions of an unpleasant nature made upon the nerves of sense are very apt to produce vomiting. Thus an offensive smell, a disagreeable sight, any interference with the balancing sense as in sea-sickness, irritation or even tickling of the throat, and the pain of an injury or operation are all likely to be attended by vomiting.

Direct disturbance of the brain itself is naturally a cause, and often a very obscure cause, of vomiting ; for example, a blow on the head, a cerebral tumour, a cerebral abscess, meningitis. Many cases of hysteria also show attacks of vomiting as one of their prominent symptoms.

Finally, the vomiting centre may be brought into action by various poisons introduced into the blood, like tartar emetic and apomorphine ; or by the poisons of various acute and chronic diseases, *e.g.* Bright's disease, smallpox, scarlet fever, typhus, and cholera. Vomiting, indeed, forms an important early symptom of these diseases.

Characters of the vomit. — FOOD, more or less softened and made sour and bitter by digestion, constitutes the vomit in the simpler cases, such as those due to emetics, sea-sickness, etc. It should be remembered that when milk is vomited up curdled, this indicates simply that the first step in its digestion has taken place, and it is a mistake to conclude, as is often done, that the curdling indicates some intolerance of the stomach for milk.

WATERY FLUID, brought up irrespective of meals, forms the vomitus in conditions where the vomiting is due to disturbances of the brain, *e.g.* brain tumours, and in certain other conditions such as the vomiting in the early months of pregnancy. When the vomiting continues long, it tends to bring up mucus and bile also.

MUCUS, when vomited in considerable amount in strings, and especially when sour in taste and brought up in the morning, is a sign of catarrh of the stomach, particularly that form associated with constant indulgence in alcohol.

BILE may be brought up by any long-continued attack of vomiting, after the

contents of the stomach have been expelled and retching still continues, for example, in sea-sickness, or in migraine. Usually the bile is golden-yellow in colour; but sometimes it is grass-green.

FROTHY MATERIAL, with a yeasty smell, which divides into three distinct layers, viz. froth on the surface, and a sediment of undigested food, with a layer of clearer fluid between, is highly characteristic of the vomit from a dilated stomach in which fermentative dyspepsia is taking place.

BLOOD may be red in colour, and brought up mixed with the food or in clots ; but, much more frequently, it is vomited as a brown granular material, very much resembling 'coffee-grounds'. As a general rule, the vomiting of blood indicates some ulceration in the interior of the stomach, but the amount of blood is no guide to the size of the ulcer, because serious bleeding sometimes occurs from hardly perceptible 'erosions' of the mucous membrane. Large quantities of blood are also occasionally brought up in chronic catarrh of the stomach (especially the alcoholic variety) which is accompanied by congestion.

Treatment must have two objects in view : (1) to relieve the source of the irritation, and (2) to soothe the nervous centre.

In the first place, the cause of the vomiting must be sought for, and in general this will be found to be some disorder of the stomach. If an indigestible meal has been taken some time previously, and its remnants be still loading the stomach, an emetic or a copious draught of warm water has the effect of getting rid of the indigestible material and allowing the irritation to subside. Various substances which have a soothing action upon the stomach may also be taken when the sickness continues, such as cream of magnesia, or a powder composed of rhubarb (2 parts), soda (2 parts), and bismuth (4 parts), in teaspoonful doses, or a tablespoonful of chloroform water.

The application of some counter-irritant, such as a mustard leaf, over the pit of the stomach, has often a marked sedative effect. (*See* BLISTERS.) In irritable stomach conditions, posture is an important matter ; the sufferer should lie with the head on a low pillow, and on his left side, so that the stomach is supported by the ribs.

The vomiting due to such serious conditions as peritonitis subsides under the treatment appropriate to these conditions.

The special measures applicable to sea-sickness are given under SEA-SICK-NESS.

Vomiting due to inflammation or some other source of irritation in the throat is greatly relieved by soothing gargles, or by sucking lozenges containing ammonium chloride or chlorate of potash.

Fresh air is of great importance, and the drawing of deep breaths has a distinct effect in checking the tendency to vomit. Mental quiet and a darkened room also assist in soothing the nervous system.

VULVA is the general term applied to the external female genitals.

VULVO-VAGINITIS is inflammation of the vulva and the vagina. It is more common in young girls than in adult women. It may be a manifestation of infection elsewhere in the body, or may indicate the presence of some infection in the vagina. (*See* WHITES.)

WAFER PAPERS are thin circular discs made of flour and water, which become pliable when wetted, and form a convenient wrapper for swallowing nauseous drugs without tasting them. (For the method of use, see POWDERS.)

WALK (*see* GAIT).

WALLS (*see under* SANITATION).

WARBURG'S TINCTURE is a complex liquid containing no fewer than fourteen ingredients, of which the chief is quinine. It used to enjoy a great reputation in the treatment of malaria.

WARFARIN is an anticoagulant which is active whether given by mouth, intramuscularly, intravenously or rectally. It is usually given by mouth, when its maximum effect occurs within about 36 hours. Its action passes off within 48 hours of cessation of treatment.

WARMING (*see* LIGHTING).

WARTS, or VERRUCAE, are small, solid growths, arising from the surface of the skin. They are due to a virus infection of the skin.

Varieties and causes. — COMMON WARTS develop on the skin of children and young persons in positions where the growth of the skin is exuberant and the surface is exposed to much irritation, for example, on the knuckles, on the backs of the hands, and on the face. Occasionally such warts come out in a crop. In structure, these warts consist of a bundle of fibres produced by overgrowth of the papillæ in the true skin, each bundle enveloped by a cap of the horny cells that cover the surface of the cuticle, and the whole mass being surrounded by a ring of thickened cuticle. These fibres can easily be seen when the surface of the wart becomes worn away, and especially if the top of the wart be accidentally cut or knocked off, so that it bleeds. The dirty-brown colour of

warts is due to dirt becoming lodged between these fibres. PLANTAR WARTS occur on the soles of the feet. They are found most commonly in older children and adolescents. Epidemics are not uncommon in schools, the infection being spread by the children walking with bare feet. They are usually painful. SENILE WARTS are usually hard, wrinkled, and slightly raised areas of skin found in old people. SOFT WARTS, consisting of little tags of skin, are found especially upon the neck, chest, ears, or eyelids of persons whose skin has been subjected for long to some irritation, such as that of working among paraffin. HORNS are formed sometimes upon the face or hands, as the result of the drying up of the sebaceous material exuding from the skin that covers a wart, and, as the secretion goes on, these horns occasionally reach a length of some inches. TUBERCULOUS WARTS are developed sometimes as the result of a wound in the skin of the hands, especially of those who have come in contact with persons or animals suffering from some form of tuberculosis, *e.g.* pathologists and butchers.

Treatment. — As a rule, warts are removed painlessly by the application of some substance which dissolves the horny surface and cauterizes the parts beneath. The local application of carbon dioxide snow is a most effective form of treatment, provided there are not too many warts. Caustic potash, nitric acid, or lunar caustic is also used, but care must be taken that the drop of nitric acid or caustic potash applied to a wart does not run over the neighbouring skin. Several applications, as a rule, are necessary to each wart. The same result may be attained, especially as regards warts on the feet, by the use of the salicylic acid application mentioned under CORNS. Warts that hang by a pedicle are best removed by snipping off with scissors, the bleeding being easily checked by some astringent. Tuberculous warts should be completely excised.

WASHING (*see* BATHS, DISINFECTION).

WASHING OUT BLADDER (*see* BLADDER, DISEASES OF, *and* DOUCHES).

WASHING OUT STOMACH is performed for various reasons, particularly in order to remove a narcotic poison that has been recently swallowed, before it shall have had time to act. Washing out is also employed to cleanse the stomach in cases in which the food tends to collect in the organ and to ferment. (For the method, *see* Fermentative Dyspepsia under DYSPEPSIA.)

WASP STINGS. (*See* BITES.)

WASSERMANN REACTION is a test introduced for the diagnosis of syphilis by examination of the blood. With the exception of leprosy, yaws, and some of the acute infectious diseases, the only condition in which the blood appears to give this reaction is syphilis ; and, as the diseases mentioned are not likely to cause confusion, the test forms a valuable method for the diagnosis of the latter condition in at least 90 per cent. of cases.

The reaction depends upon the principle known as fixation of complement, and is only capable of being satisfactorily performed in a laboratory. In every blood there exists a substance known as complement. If a poison capable of destroying blood corpuscles be introduced into the blood, some of this complement must be absorbed or fixed by the poison before the corpuscles can be broken up. In the Wassermann reaction some of the suspectedly syphilitic blood serum is mixed in a tube with an animal extract and with a definite quantity of complement, and then a test is done to find whether the complement has been fixed to the extract or not. If it has been fixed, then the suspected serum must have contained a substance capable of joining it to the extract, and the person from whom the serum was taken has syphilis. If the complement is unfixed and still free to act, then the person's blood may be pronounced healthy.

Method of use.—Blood is drawn from the suspected person by puncturing a vein in the arm or elsewhere with the needle of a large hypodermic syringe, filling the syringe, and squeezing the blood into a sterile test tube which is sent to the laboratory. The reaction is done in two stages :

STAGE 1. — To give the syphilitic material, if present, a chance to ' fix complement '. In a small test tube there are mixed : (*a*) a small quantity of the serum separated from the clot of the suspected blood, which has already been heated for half an hour at 55° C., in order to destroy the natural complement which it contains, and diluted with normal salt solution ; (*b*) a little alcoholic extract of some animal tissue, *e.g.* liver ; (*c*) the same quantity of a healthy serum, *e.g.* that of a guinea-pig, which supplies the necessary complement. This tube is placed in an incubator for $1\frac{1}{2}$ hours to allow fixation of complement to occur, if it can take place.

STAGE 2.—To find whether fixation of complement has taken place or not. To the tube are now added (*d*) 1 ml. of fluid containing 1 part of sheep (or ox) blood corpuscles, carefully washed free from serum, in 20 parts of normal salt solution ; and (*e*) a sufficient amount of a special serum derived from an animal, *e.g.* a rabbit, which has previously had sheep (or ox) corpuscles injected into its blood and has in consequence developed an anti-body capable of breaking up these foreign corpuscles. The tube is returned to the incubator for another hour.

If then the blood corpuscles have settled uninjured to the bottom of the tube, the complement must all have been fixed in the first stage, so that the anti-body could not act in the second stage ; and syphilis is therefore present. The reaction is said to be positive.

If the corpuscles are broken up, as shown by a diffuse red colour through the tube, then the complement was left free to act in the second stage and no syphilitic substance was present to fix it in the first stage. The reaction is said to be negative.

WASTING (*see* ATROPHY).

WASTING PALSY is a popular name for the disease more commonly known as progressive muscular atrophy. (*See* PARALYSIS.)

WATER-BEDS

WATER-BEDS are flat, closed sacks of heavy india-rubber material, with a funnel-shaped orifice at one corner through which water can be poured, and which can be closed by a screw-stopper. They are made in various sizes, some being sufficiently large to cover a whole bedstead, though more frequently, for convenience in handling, they are of smaller size, and occasionally are made as small cushions, as rings with a hollow in the centre, or in horseshoe shape. Those of the largest size possess a special outlet at one corner through which air escapes as water enters at the opposite corner.

Water-beds have been replaced to a great extent by air-beds (*q.v.*).

WATERBRASH, or PYROSIS,

WATERBRASH, or PYROSIS, is a condition in which, during the course of digestion, the mouth fills with tasteless or sour fluid, which is generally saliva, but sometimes seems to be brought up from the stomach. At the same time, a burning pain is often felt at the pit of the stomach or in the chest. The condition is a symptom of excessive acidity of the stomach contents, due sometimes to an irritating diet, and often characteristic of a duodenal ulcer.

WATER CANKER

WATER CANKER is another name for cancrum oris. (*See* CANCRUM ORIS.)

WATER-CLOSETS, DRAINS, and SEWERS

WATER-CLOSETS, DRAINS, and SEWERS.—This principle of removing excreta and soiled water is known as the 'water-carriage system'. In this method, special channels and receptacles are provided for the waste waters of houses, and into these drains and sewers the human excreta are swept and removed by the flow of the water. The other great method of disposal in which the excreta are removed along with the animal and vegetable refuse of households is known as the 'dry method of disposal', or the 'conservancy system', and is treated in a special article. (*See* REFUSE AND SEWAGE DISPOSAL.)

Forms of water-closet basin.—Various water-closets are utilized, depending upon the special circumstances of the place, especially with reference to the adequacy of the water supply.

SLOP CLOSETS, in which the household waste waters form the flush, were in use in some places but are now rarely seen. The waste waters may be directly conducted to the basin of the closet, or may be collected in an automatic tipper, an iron or earthenware

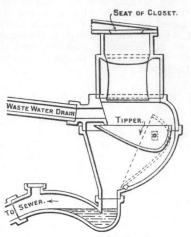

FIG. 394.—Diagram of Day's waste-water closet, in which a tipper receives the excreta and the water for flushing. (Modified from Parkes's *Hygiene*.)

vessel balanced on pivots, which, when full, tips over and sends the contents, usually two or three gallons, as a sudden

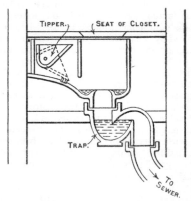

FIG. 395.—Diagram of a waste-water closet with a tipper at the side of the closet basin. (Modified from Notter and Firth's *Hygiene*.)

flush into the basin of the closet. The 'tipper' may be the basin of the closet itself, receiving the excreta, and, when full, projecting its contents down the drain (Fig. 394). In another arrangement, a large siphon trap is placed on the drain, beyond the ' tipper ', and the closet, a vertical shaft, is placed over this trap (Fig. 395). This form of closet has the advantage of being economical, no special water being needed, and also of preventing the liability to freezing of pipes. But the closets are difficult to keep clean, since the sides of the closet get fouled, and the waste waters do not cleanse them ; while the sewage, being more concentrated, is more liable to putrefaction than if a closet with a special fresh-water flush were employed.

TROUGH CLOSETS, used frequently in connection with schools and factories, consist of a long trough of iron or earthenware, partly filled with water

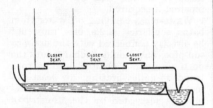

FIG. 396.—Diagram of a trough water-closet.

passing beneath the seats of a number of closets. These troughs are automatically flushed with water from time to time from a tilting receiver, the waste waters of houses being utilized occasionally for this purpose (Fig. 396).

In houses at the present time, the chief varieties of water-closets in use are the pan or container closet, the valve or plug closet, the long-hopper closet, the wash-out and the wash-down closets.

A good water-closet must have a basin composed of some non-absorbent material shaped so as to receive the water used in flushing, and so formed as to prevent the excreta adhering to the sides, and to allow them to fall directly into the water.

PAN CLOSETS, still found in old houses but now prohibited in new buildings by the by-laws of the Ministry of Health of England, consist of a basin surrounded by a container (Fig. 397).

At the bottom of the basin is a movable pan, which contains a small quantity of water and receives the excreta.

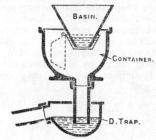

FIG. 397.—Diagram of a pan closet with D-trap. Both this form of closet and this form of trap are objectionable, owing to the readiness with which they become fouled.

The pan swings back when the handle is raised and the excreta pass with the flush of water through the container, frequently fouling the sides with the splashing. This form of water-closet is usually also provided with a D-trap, a highly objectionable form of trap. (See TRAPS, below.)

LONG-HOPPER CLOSETS consist of a deep basin ending in a siphon trap (Fig. 398). Their length and general construction make them liable to

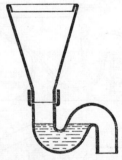

FIG. 398.—Diagram of a long-hopper closet. Also an unsuitable form.

fouling, and a better form of closet should be employed when it can be obtained.

VALVE CLOSETS have a movable valve, which supports a quantity of water into which the excreta are received before being projected into the water of the trap beneath, by the swinging aside of the valve as the handle is raised.

973

WASH-OUT CLOSETS, made of a single piece of earthenware, hold water in a basin formed by a ridge, and into this basin the excreta are received, to be later on swept over into the trap by the flush. The flush in this closet, if the ridge is too high, may not be sufficient to wash the excreta away. The ridge, again, may be too small to dam up sufficient water to cover the excreta, and fouling of the sides may result (Fig. 399).

FIG. 399.—Diagram of a wash-out closet.

WASH - DOWN CLOSETS, or SHORT HOPPERS, in which a flushing rim is provided giving an adequate flush all round the basin, form an excellent type of closet (Fig. 400).

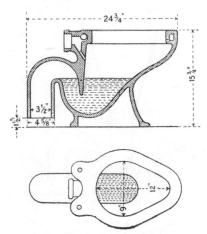

FIG. 400.—Diagram of a wash-down or short-hopper closet. This is the best form, being very simple and not liable to become fouled.

The *flush* of water given to a closet should be about three gallons, but not less than two gallons, delivered by a pipe at least $1\frac{1}{4}$ inches in diameter, and

every closet should be provided with its own special flushing cistern, usually formed of iron, with siphonic action, and having an overflow pipe discharging directly into the outer air and not into any pipe connected with the closet.

Water-closets should be placed at some outer part of the building (not in some convenient recess in the centre of the house), against an external wall, so that the soil-pipe may be led straight to the exterior. The room should be provided with a window opening right up to the ceiling, and should be well ventilated, if possible by two windows placed opposite each other, or, when this is impossible, by at least one window and a perforated iron plate. Formerly it was customary to box in the water-closet with wood, but at the present time the whole closet is usually left uncovered, so that all parts are more easily seen and can be cleaned or repaired if required.

Waste-pipes carrying off water from baths, sculleries, sinks, etc., must not be directly connected with the drain or soil-pipe, but should discharge into the open air upon a channel leading to a trapped gulley-grating at least 18 inches distant from the end of the waste-pipe, as suggested by the Ministry of Health in their model by-laws. Frequently, however, the waste-pipe discharges directly over a grating above a trapped gulley or even under the grating, as shown in Fig. 401.

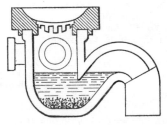

FIG. 401.—Diagram of a yard gulley with waste-pipe entering from behind and a grating for rain-water, cleansing, etc. This is a common form of gulley but not so satisfactory as the arrangement shown in Fig. 408. (Modified from Whitelegge's *Hygiene*.)

Soil-pipes, for carrying off sewage, are usually formed of drawn lead, circular in shape, about 4 inches in diameter, and seamless. They should be fixed outside the house, and for the purpose of ventilation should be carried in their full diameter above the eaves, away from windows, and protected by cowls or wires drawn across. If formed of lead they should be placed away from the sun as much as possible, because the heating may lead to twisting from the expansion of the metal. The soil-pipes are also frequently formed of heavy cast-iron with caulked lead joints.

Traps are contrivances which prevent the sewer air from gaining entrance into the house from the drains, water being used for this purpose. The simplest form of trap is, therefore, simply a bend in the pipe which retains water. The water, however, may not be altogether efficient, for it may absorb some of the sewer gases and give them off from its surface. If, further, it is allowed to become stagnant, bubbles of gas may be discharged into the house. If, however, the water in the trap be renewed from time to time, and if the drain be well ventilated, there is little danger of the air accumulating in such quantities as to force the seal, and thus the ' Water seal ', as it is called, will be efficient.

Traps, to be efficient, must be self-cleansing as far as possible, smooth in the interior, free from angles, and have a sufficient depth of water, at least $1\frac{1}{2}$ inches. A good type of trap is shown in the accompanying sketch (Fig. 402).

FROM HOUSE.   →To Sewer.

WATER SEAL.

FIG. 402.—Diagram showing a suitable form of trap for disconnecting the house drain from the sewer. The opening on the house side is for ventilation, that on the sewer side for cleansing.

It is provided on the house side of the water seal with a ventilating shaft, which is taken up to the surface of the ground away from the windows of the house, and covered with an iron grating. Beyond the seal is another shaft, which is used for inspecting the drain and for cleansing. This should be built up to the surface of the ground and covered

with a slab, so that access may readily be obtained.

Buchan's trap is efficient and answers the chief requirements of a good trap. It has the ventilating pipe on the house side, the shaft for cleansing on the side next the sewer, a good fall for the sewage, and a sufficient depth of the water seal.

As a sample of a bad but sometimes-used form of trap, the one represented in Fig. 403 may be taken. There is no provision made for ventilation on the house side of the trap, and no access is given beyond the seal for cleansing. The central shaft may, if covered with

FROM HOUSE.   →To Sewer.

FILTH

FIG. 403.—Diagram of an unsuitable though common form of trap. The central opening does not give efficient ventilation and does not admit of complete cleansing. The trap also is unprovided with a base on which to stand evenly.

a grating, act as a ventilator, or, if covered with a heavy slab, simply gives an opening for cleansing. This shaft at the bend, however, just tends to collect filth, which is also apt to be deposited on the side of the trap, as the ' dip ' is not sufficient to wash out the trap.

One of the old types of traps still found is the 'dipstone' trap. It consists of a box with a partition, the sewage entering at one side of the box and leav-

FIG. 404.—Diagram of a dipstone trap. An old and objectionable form of trap.

ing at the same height on the other. The water in the trap reaches a short distance up the partition, and thus forms the water seal. Filth and waste matters tend to collect at the bottom, and as the force of water is not usually sufficient to wash out the trap, it simply becomes a miniature cesspool and requires cleaning repeatedly (Fig. 404).

The D-trap so frequently found in

FIG. 405.—Diagram of a siphon trap attached to baths, wash-basins, and sinks.

connection with pan-closets is highly objectionable (Fig. 397). Its angles tend to prevent cleanliness and accumulate filth. Ministry of Health model by-laws, if adopted by sanitary authorities, prevent its employment in new buildings.

In the traps placed on the waste-pipes from baths and sinks generally, the simple siphon S-bend on the pipe is sufficient, and, on the bends, access screw plugs are usually placed, through which a suitable and easy entrance is obtained for cleansing (Fig. 405).

Sometimes, to prevent the admission of too much grease and sand to the drain, *a grease-intercepting chamber* is placed in connection with the pipe from the scullery sink (Fig. 406). It

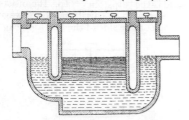

FIG. 406.—Diagram of a grease trap, sometimes attached to scullery sinks in large houses.

consists of a stoneware chamber, into which the waste water flows, and the grease rising to the surface and solidifying as it cools can be easily removed from time to time, while the sand sinks to the floor of the chamber, the water leaving by the mouth near the bottom. The grease trap can be opened periodically and cleansed, but, except in very

large households, this trap is hardly necessary, and should not be used where its use can be dispensed with, as it is simply of the nature of a cesspool.

Gulley traps for waters from courtyards, rain-pipes, and waste waters from baths and sinks usually consist of the type shown in the sketch (Fig. 407).

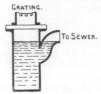

FIG. 407.—Diagram of a gulley trap for rainwater, etc. Solid refuse is deposited at the bottom and must be periodically removed.

They are easily cleaned and should be so treated periodically. All waste-pipes from baths and sinks, and all pipes for carrying off waste waters from a new building, should, according to the by-laws of the Ministry of Health, discharge over a channel leading to a trapped gulley at least 18 inches distant, in the external air (Fig. 408).

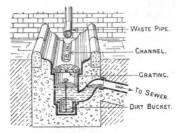

FIG. 408.—Waste-water pipe discharging over a channel leading to a trapped gulley, in accordance with the requirements of the Ministry of Health. The front of the figure shows a vertical section through the gulley. (Altered from Knight's *Annotated Model Bye-laws*.)

A trap may be rendered inefficient in several ways by the breaking of the water seal. If the trap is but little employed, the water may evaporate, while if the drain is not ventilated the pressure inside the drain may force sewer air through the water seal. Further, if the momentum of the water discharged is too great, the water may rush straight through the trap and leave it empty. When more than one

pipe discharges into the same common pipe, or when the fall beyond is
sudden and great in a pipe which is too
small and running full, the water may
be drawn out of the trap by siphonic
action. To prevent these defects it is
advisable to have a ventilating opening
at the crown of the trap, and also to
see that the pipe is not too small.

Drains are the pipes outside one
house or building, which carry away as
quickly as possible to the sewer or
cesspool the ordinary sewage of the
building. They must, to prevent pollution of the surrounding soil, be made
water-tight, and, except for ventilating
purposes at special points, air-tight as
well. Drain-pipes are usually, therefore, formed of glazed stoneware or
cast-iron, in sizes varying from 4 or 5
inches for ordinary houses up to 6 or 9
inches for large institutions. They
should be laid, if possible, in a straight
line, on a foundation made firm by a
layer of concrete. Each pipe should fit
firmly into the next, special sockets
being provided on the pipes for this
purpose, and the socket being always so
placed as to point away from the sewer
(Fig. 409, *a* and *b*). The joint should be

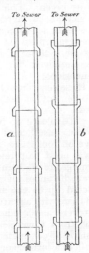

FIG. 409.—Diagram of the laying of drain-pipes.
a, Shows correct manner ; *b*, incorrect manner,
which leads to leakage.

made firm by cement. Drains should
be provided with cleaning branches
consisting of V-shaped junction pipes,

by which ready access is given. Where
two drains meet, specially curved pipes
must be employed according to the
junction required, as no junctions of

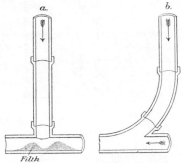

FIG. 410.—Diagram of the junction of a side drain
with a main drain, showing the special junction
pieces required. *a*, Shows an incorrect mode
of junction, liable to produce choking of the
pipe ; *b*, correct mode.

drains at right angles are permissible,
since they interfere too much with the
flow of the sewage (Fig. 410, *a* and *b*).
No drains should, if possible, be taken
under a house, but if this must be done,
the pipe should be placed in a bed of
concrete at least 6 inches thick. Sufficient fall must be given to the drain to
allow of the flow of the sewage. The
gradient needed will vary with the
size of the pipe, but as a rule a fall of
1 in 40 must be given for a 4-inch drain,
and for a 6-inch drain 1 in 60 will be
required. Where sufficient gradient
cannot be obtained, flush tanks should
be provided, working automatically,
but with their water supply under
control, so that they may discharge
only at such regular intervals as may
be desired (Fig. 411). Before using a
new house-drain, the presence of leaks
should be tested for. This can be
readily done by various methods. Testing by plugging the lower end, filling
the drain with water until it reaches a
certain level in an inspection chamber,
and watching if the water falls, is an
effective but drastic method of detecting defects. Pumping smoke into the
drain and soil-pipes after all natural
outlets have been first stopped, and
then watching for leakages betrayed
by the issue of smoke, is another method
now commonly employed. The custom

of pouring some highly volatile oil down the soil-pipe and then washing it down

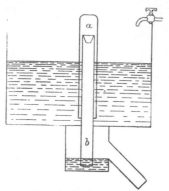

FIG. 411.—Diagram of Field's annular siphon flush tank, very frequently used for automatically flushing drains, public urinals, etc. *a*, Outer tube open at the bottom, enclosing *b*, the inner tube, which has a funnel-shaped opening above and free discharge below. (Modified from Parkes's *Hygiene*.)

with several gallons of water, the oil being smelt where any defect is present, is still occasionally used, though it is not so satisfactory as the test by smoke.

Sewers are underground channels used to carry off by gravitation the rainfall, waste waters from houses, the excreta of man and animals where the water-carriage system is in vogue, and the waste waters of trades and manufacturing processes. Originally sewers were used only to carry off the rainfall, and as constructed at first of brickwork acted as drains for the subsoil waters, and had thus a beneficial effect. In some places where the rainfall is excessive, separate sewers are provided, one set for the rain and waters used in washing the streets, the other set for the ordinary sewage. This method allows the formation of smaller sewers, with the advantage of easier flushing, whilst the sewage to be dealt with is more uniform in character and so can be more easily treated. Where the separate system is not employed, sewers should therefore be made large enough for the general needs of the district, consideration being given to the possibility of rain-storms, and allowance in size being made accordingly. The fall of the sewer must be sufficient to give in large pipes, over

978

24 inches in diameter, a velocity of at least 2 feet per second, and a greater velocity for pipes that are smaller. The sewers should be laid as far as possible in straight lines, and, as in drains, should never join each other at right angles. The shape of large brick

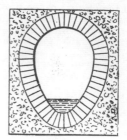

FIG. 412.—Cross-section of a large sewer, showing the egg shape.

sewers in section should be that of an egg with the smaller end downwards (Fig. 412), thus giving a greater depth of the sewage and producing a better cleansing effect ; although for the largest outfall sewer the circular form may be used because of the greater strength thus given. The surface of the sewer should be smooth, glazed earthenware pipes set in cement being used for sewers up to 18 inches in diameter, while well burnt, impervious bricks are employed for sewers of greater dimensions. All bricks and pipes used in sewers should be firmly jointed with cement, as leakages must be prevented.

Sewage, particularly if it becomes stagnant from insufficient gradient, tends to give off foul gases, and therefore the sewer must be properly ventilated. Openings are made in the sewer, preferably at distances of about 100 feet, conducted up to the street level and covered there with a grating. Sometimes, to prevent any chance of nuisance arising from these sewer ventilators, the shaft is conducted into the chimney-stalk of a furnace or led up the sides of the neighbouring buildings.

Flushing of sewers may be required where the fall is insufficient or the sewage is tending to quick decomposition in very dry seasons. The flushing may be carried out by means of a hose from the nearest hydrant. The sewage itself may be dammed up for a short time and then allowed to rush on, thus flushing the sewer, but it is better to employ some other method, as by the automatic flush siphon mentioned in the flushing of drains (Fig. 411).

Manholes, or disconnecting chambers, should be introduced whenever

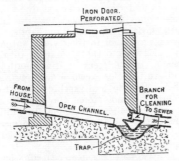

FIG. 413.—Diagram of a manhole for disconnection at a junction between drains, and for ventilation and cleansing purposes. (Modified from Notter and Firth's *Hygiene.*)

two sewers or drains join, or whenever there is a change in direction. They should be built of brickwork set in cement, and the drains or sewers passing through along the floor should consist of half-open pipes, the surface of the cement being raised a little above the pipes to prevent sewage flowing over on to the floor. The manholes should be provided at the street level with a perforated plate, while a trap below will catch any dust or debris and prevent it entering the sewer (Fig. 413).

Defects.—Soil - pipes often exhibit defects in that they are frequently carried through the interior of houses, are imperfectly jointed, are made with seams, are unventilated, or are connected with the overflow pipe of cisterns for holding drinking water—a most objectionable process, as the foul air may gain access to the cistern and be absorbed by the water. The soil-pipe may be ventilated by too small a pipe, or the rain-pipe may be joined to the soil-pipe and made to act as the ventilator — a most unsatisfactory method, as during a period of rainstorm, when the rain-pipe is running full, there will be no exit at all for foul air.

Waste-pipes and rain-pipes are some-

times found joining each other and reaching the drain-pipe untrapped, and thus the drain air may readily enter the house.

Drains formed of porous material, such as bricks badly jointed, are sometimes found running under the dwelling, whilst a cesspool is occasionally got under the cellar. Drains are sometimes laid with straight pipes to form the bends, thus producing a leaky joint ; often they have insufficient fall, or they may be found with junctions at right angles (Fig. 410, *a*), or with branches fixed so that the sewage entering from the small branch flows in the opposite direction to that in the main drain. The soil-pipes, waste-pipes, and house drains may be found to enter the main sewers without any traps intervening, or may be provided with inefficient forms of traps. Defective forms of water-closets are still sometimes seen in old houses, such as the pan-closet with its filthy receptacle and D-trap, whilst some water-closets may even be discovered receiving their supply direct from the water main—a system which may lead to pollution of the water through foul air being admitted to the water-pipes during an intermission in the supply.

WATER-HAMMER PULSE is a name given to the peculiarly sudden pulse that is associated with incompetence of the aortic valve of the heart, and suggests the philosophical toy after which it is named. (*See* PULSE.)

WATERING-PLACES suited for the treatment of various diseases are mentioned under these headings, and the general principles underlying the choice of a watering-place are described under CLIMATE IN RELATION TO DISEASE.

WATER ON THE BRAIN is a popular name for hydrocephalus and for meningitis. (*See* HYDROCEPHALUS, MENINGITIS.)

WATER SUPPLY.—Sources.—RAINFALL forms the primary source of all water supplies. If collected under careful conditions, the vessels in which it is received being free from contamination and filth, it constitutes the purest and softest of waters, containing only such impurities as it has washed down or dissolved in its course through the atmosphere. In its passage through the air it becomes highly aerated and, except in the neighbourhood of towns and densely populated districts, where manufactories abound and the pollution of the atmosphere with impurities may be considerable, it is practically pure. The rainfall is usually collected from the roofs of houses and buildings by the gutters and rain-pipes, which should be regularly cleaned. These conduct the water to specially prepared cisterns or receptacles, preferably formed of slates, bricks set in cement, or good cement concrete. Sometimes special collecting surfaces are provided, portions of land being set aside, the surface of which is rendered impermeable with a layer of slates, and the water being conducted into a tank by a pipe to which the surface of the impermeable layer has been sloped. The first rain that falls should be rejected, as it will contain most of the impurities washed from the atmosphere and the collecting surface.

Rain-water, on account of its softness, is invaluable for washing. This quality of softness, however, renders it especially liable to dissolve lead, and consequently it should be stored in cisterns formed of slate or similar material. Its great disadvantage, as a sole source of supply, arises from the variability in the rainfall, and therefore it is advisable to have some other means of supply.

SPRINGS.—The portion of the rainfall which percolates through the soil absorbs from the ground-air carbonic acid, which aids it in dissolving many of the mineral constituents with which it comes in contact, thus rendering it in many instances unsuitable for drinking purposes. On the other hand, however, spring water is frequently rendered clear and bright by the purification it undergoes in moving through the strata of the earth before it reaches its point of issue, this natural filtration, if the water has penetrated far enough, being sufficient to remove completely the organic matter with which the water came in contact in the upper regions of the soil.

Springs are due to the water percolating through the soil and being prevented from going deeper by some impermeable stratum, above which the water accumulates as if in a reservoir. The point of issue of the spring is determined by the position where this impermeable layer crops out upon the surface of the soil. Where the collection of underground water is due to an impervious layer of clay just under a thin surface of gravel or sand, the springs are poor in their yield, subject to variations with the nature of the season, intermittent in their supply, and are therefore termed *land springs*. These intermittent springs are frequently found along the course of rivers in valleys bounded by hills, where the level of the underground water varies considerably with the seasons.

Main springs are deep-seated, where the water has percolated through thick masses of porous geological formations, such as chalk, overlying impermeable layers. Where the demand is not great, they usually yield throughout the whole year a sufficient supply of water which is clear, sparkling, well aerated, and cool, due to the natural purification it has undergone. It may be impregnated with various mineral salts, which render it hard and so interfere with its value for washing and cooking, although it may still be extremely palatable for drinking.

As the water from springs may be contaminated at the point of issue, the spring should be walled in and provided with a discharging pipe that passes some distance below the surface, thus conducting the water to the surface.

WELLS consist of two main forms, ' shallow ' and ' deep ', a special form of the latter being known as ' Artesian '. The shallow wells (Fig. 414, *a*) reach the same kind of water as was described in the case of ' land ' springs, and are liable to pollution by soakings through the soil from leaking cesspools and drains, from surface washings and manure, from animal and vegetable debris spread on the fields, the depth of such a well not being usually sufficient to allow of natural purification. ' Deep ' wells (Fig. 414, *c*), in which the water is usually brought to the surface by pumping, tap the same kind of water as ' main ' springs, yielding usually an excellent, palatable supply, and, in order to protect them from pollution by surface and subsoil waters, they should be lined with bricks embedded in cement down to the depth of the impermeable layer, and built up and closed in above the ground to prevent them further from being contaminated at the surface.

Artesian wells pass through an upper impermeable layer to reach a store of water in a water-bearing stratum lying upon a second impermeable formation. This water-bearing permeable stratum has its ' outcrop ' at a higher level than

and pure, but if it is obtained from a river after it has received the washings and drainage of manured fields, the soakage from cesspools, and the sewage of hamlets and towns, it may be highly contaminated and unfit for drinking purposes. Every river in its course tends naturally to purify its water. The bulk of water dilutes any sewage entering the river, the grosser impurities are broken up against the stones of the river's bed or destroyed by fish, and the oxygen which the moving water absorbs in large quantity from the air decomposes the organic matter into harmless substances. This natural purification is considerable where there is abundance

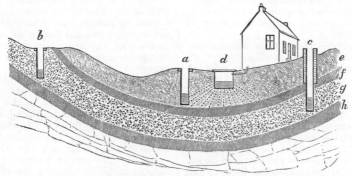

FIG. 414.—Diagram of a section across the bottom of a little valley, showing a water supply by wells. *a*, Surface well polluted by *d*, a neighbouring cesspool ; *b*, surface well at a safe distance ; *c*, deep well (safe) lined with masonry down to the first impervious stratum, and protected above ground ; *e* and *g*, permeable strata ; *f* and *h*, impervious strata.

where the well has been sunk, and consequently the water in its endeavour to find its own level rises up the well and issues at the top.

Tube wells are made by driving tubes, one section of which is screwed on to the next, down into the soil, the first one being provided with a steel point and perforated at the bottom for about 2 feet. These can be used to provide a small temporary supply of water, the water entering the tube through the perforations and being pumped up if the pressure is not sufficient to raise the water to the surface.

RIVER WATER.—The quality of the water derived from rivers differs greatly according to the nature of the source from which it is obtained. Where the supply is drawn from a river high up near its origin among granite-bound hills, the water may be perfectly potable

of pure fresh water in the stream to mix with the sewage; but where there is extensive contamination from sewage, rivers and streams form a supply in which the process of natural purification will not have been sufficient to render the water free from danger.

UPLAND SURFACE WATER.—The supply of water from such a source is usually good alike for domestic purposes and trade requirements. The water taken from streams near their source or from upland lakes closely resembles rain-water in composition, because it contains little dissolved solid matter, whilst the organic matter present is mainly of vegetable, not of animal origin. These waters are usually highly palatable and pure, with the additional advantage of softness, which renders them suitable for trade purposes. Peaty matter is frequently found in such upland waters, giving the water a slight yellow discoloration and imparting a peaty taste, but this does not interfere with its potability, and the peaty matter may be removed, if desired, by filtration through filters of sand.

These upland waters form such good sources of supply, being removed largely from danger of contamination by human excretions, that many of the principal towns in Great Britain now obtain their supplies in this manner. Glasgow, Manchester, and Liverpool, to mention three examples, have all tapped such sources of supply many miles from their boundaries, and the water thus obtained for the inhabitants has contributed in no small degree to the health and general prosperity of the cities.

Quality.—Apart from actual contamination, or the tendency to convey diseases (*see below*), water may be either ' soft ' or ' hard '. The hardness is usually described as either temporary or permanent. Temporary hardness is due to the presence of the bicarbonates of calcium and magnesium held in solution by carbonic acid gas, which may be driven off by boiling the water. This carbonic acid gas may also be got rid of by adding slaked lime to the water, which causes the production of still more carbonate of lime. This, however, settles, with the carbonate originally present, in a sediment ; and thus the temporary hardness is removed (*see* FILTRATION *below*). Permanent hardness is due to the presence of the sulphates of calcium and magnesium, as well as iron and alumina, which cannot be got rid of by boiling.

In describing the quality of a given water, it is usual to express it in degrees of hardness which correspond to the number of grains of carbonate of lime or chalk in each gallon. Rain-water is the softest of all waters, containing seldom more than $\frac{1}{2}$ grain of carbonate of lime to the gallon, *i.e.* its hardness is about $\frac{1}{2}$ degree. Water is said to be hard when it contains more than 10 grains per gallon. The degree of hardness in a given water is estimated very simply by placing a measured quantity in a flask. A standard soap solution is then run in and the water shaken all the while, till finally a lather forms on the

982

surface which remains permanent for five minutes. The number of cubic centimetres of soap solution which have been used give the number of degrees of hardness.

Soft water is invaluable for washing and cooking, since hard water forms a precipitate with the fats of the soap, and thus prevents it from lathering till all the hardness has been neutralized. Hard water, therefore, entails a great waste of soap, and it is said that each degree of hardness means the waste of a pound of soap in every 1000 gallons of water used. In cooking, too, hard water deposits a layer on kettles and pots, and even on the food, thus preventing the boiling water from penetrating it. Among the minor diseases caused by unduly hard drinking-water are constipation and dyspepsia, whilst goitre and the formation of urinary calculi have also been attributed to this cause.

Storage.—In obtaining a supply of water for a town from gathering-grounds, it is customary to store the water in a reservoir so placed as to allow the water to pass into the distributing pipes by gravitation, and be so conveyed through the district supplied. The usual arrangement consists in carefully selecting the site for the impounding reservoir so that no leakage will occur, a dam being constructed across the valley to which the waters naturally flow, at such a place as will store up sufficient water for four to six months' supply, and where the construction of this barrier will entail as little expense as possible. The foundation of the dam consists in earthwork and masonry, a wall of puddled clay being carried down through the centre into a deep trench, so as to render the wall water-tight. Provision is also made to regulate the admission of water into the reservoir, since compensation water must be allowed to flow on in the streams for the working of mills on their banks and other purposes, while an arrangement may be made to allow turbid storm water to pass on without entering the reservoir. Sluices and valves must be placed on the outlet culvert to regulate the discharge of the water to the town, and special service reservoirs for each district of the town may be formed at suitable places, so that the supply to each portion of the town may be known and regulated.

Filtration.—The water supplied to a district should be selected from a source as little liable to pollution as can be obtained, but if there is the slightest chance that it is contaminated in any form, filtration and purification should be carried out before distribution, whilst the consumer may, if he so desires, add to this public filtration, purification by domestic filters at his house. The main objects of filtration consist in the removal of deleterious ingredients such as mineral matters, *e.g.* the salts of magnesia and lime leading to hardness, suspended materials, dissolved organic matters, and micro-organisms.

PUBLIC FILTRATION on a large scale is usually carried out in sand filter-beds, which consist of layers of fine sand about 3 feet in thickness, resting on layers of fine gravel, gradually increasing in size from above downwards till the last layer of coarse gravel and pebbles is reached, in which are found the mouths of the outlet pipes (Fig. 415), The water is conducted on to the surface of the filter-beds to a suitable depth (usually not more than 2 feet), and allowed slowly to percolate downwards. The upper layers of fine sand become, after some time, coated with sediment, and must consequently be cleaned, which is done by scraping off the sand at the surface and having it thoroughly washed, whilst, to add to the efficiency of the filter-beds, they are allowed to

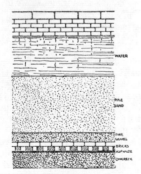

FIG. 415.—Filter-bed in section.

remain empty from time to time to permit of aeration.

By this system of filtration, water is rendered pure and potable, the suspended matters being removed by the superficial layers of sand, mineral particles being detained in the same manner, whilst the organic matter present is, in the deeper portions of the filter, aerated and rendered innocuous to a certain extent. Such filters remove micro-organisms from the water in a large degree. This is accomplished by a gelatinous film which forms on the surface of the sand and consists of the suspended materials and masses of bacteria. If proper precautions as to aeration, rate of filtration, and cleansing of the sand are carried out, such sand filters remove bacteria from the water in satisfactory proportions.

Sterilization.—Filtration is usually followed by sterilization. This is usually carried out by chlorination or by the addition of *excess lime*. *Chlorination* is dependent upon the powerful bactericidal properties of chlorine which is added to the water either in the form of bleaching powder or of chlorine gas. The latter is used when large quantities of water have to be dealt with. For efficient sterilization filtered water requires about 0·25 part of chlorine per million parts of water.

Domestic purification may be carried out, where required, in various ways. *Distillation* provides an excellent, pure water, which is, however, insipid because deficient as to aeration, and which acts easily on certain metals, such as copper. The water may be aerated by passing it in a finely divided spray through the air. *Boiling* renders the water softer and destroys micro-organisms, but leaves the water insipid, and therefore the water should be aerated again before use.

Domestic filters, so commonly employed, are frequently worse than useless, giving an idea of false security and rendering the water after so - called filtration more impure than it was before. Therefore, when a domestic filter is employed, it must be regularly and systematically cleansed, for in certain forms the organic matter, if not removed, accumulates and constitutes an excellent nidus for the growth of bacteria, which still further pollute the water that is being filtered.

Animal charcoal filters, the charcoal of which is obtained from bones calcined in closed boxes, oxidize to some extent the organic matters, but at the same time add phosphate of lime to the water and thus aid the growth of micro-organisms. This form of domestic filter therefore requires a great deal of attention and cleaning, and does not provide an efficient filtration.

Spongy iron has also been used in domestic filters, whilst other forms, such as the *filtre rapide* of Maignen, are provided with a mixture of powdered charcoal and lime over a straining-cloth of asbestos. The ordinary forms of ' *sponge* ' *filters* simply remove suspended impurities, harbour organisms, and require constant cleansing. They do not protect against the passage of organisms into the filtered water, but may add considerably to the pollution.

Of the filters which remove micro-organisms from the water, the *Pasteur-Chamberland filter* forms a good example. Briefly, it consists of a cylinder or series of cylinders formed of specially prepared unglazed porcelain, porous to a certain extent, through which the water is forced under pressure such as is usually obtained from a water service main pipe. Such a filter removes the bacteria from the water, thus sterilizing it and rendering it safe for domestic requirements. This filter can be cleansed by boiling and brushing under hot water. Another good filter is the *Berkefeld filter*, in which the filtering cylinder is made of compressed diatomaceous earth known as *Kieselguhr*. It supplies filtered water in a similar method under pressure, and may also be sterilized by boiling. It may be washed by simply turning a second tap. (*See* Fig. 416.)

Distribution.—In some countries and districts where the conditions render it unavoidable, the water supply is still distributed by means of carriers, but where the water is drawn from any distance, the method of distribution by pipes or aqueducts should be adopted. Where reservoirs are provided, the water is received into an outlet-pipe bent upwards at its commencement so as to receive none of the water near the bottom of the reservoir, where the sediment is lying. This outlet or aqueduct may be in the form of an open

channel, in which the water gets aerated to some extent, or may be, as is most usually the case, composed of large iron pipes, the dimensions of which will vary with the supply required. These pipes are buried some

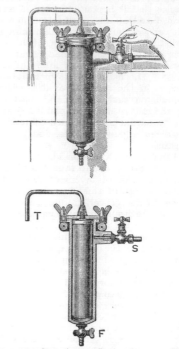

FIG. 416.—One of the effective forms of filter (Berkefeld Filter) removing bacteria as well as other solid impurities from the water. The upper figure shows the filter fixed to a wall. The lower figure shows it in section. *S,* Supply pipe from the main ; *T,* tap through which the filtered water is delivered ; *F,* flushing tap, by turning which the filter can be washed out and a free supply of unfiltered water obtained.

feet under the soil, and in order to prevent the water acting on the pipes they are treated by some special process, such as by producing the magnetic oxide of iron on the surface or coating them with hot pitch or a vitreous glaze.

DISTRIBUTING PIPES, which run along the street, are similar in structure to those above mentioned, and should be similarly protected against the action of the water. Provision for fire extinguishing is made on their course by hydrants. The *direct communication pipes* for the house come off from the street mains, the junction being effected by a brass screwed ferrule. These house pipes are usually formed of lead on account of the numerous turnings necessary in the piping inside the house, and are controlled by the provision of stop-cocks on their course where required.

Water is distributed to houses on two distinct systems—the constant and the intermittent systems. The difference between the two consists in the fact that where the supply is intermittent, or only for a certain period in the day, provision must be made at every house for storage, in the form of large cisterns holding at least sufficient supply for a day. In the constant system, small cisterns only need be made for the water-closets and kitchen boilers.

The advantages of a *constant system* include a free supply of good water, clear and unpolluted by storing in cisterns, fresh from the main, with an abundant supply in case of danger from fire ; but the system is weak in the fact that there is a tendency to too great consumption and waste on the part of the user, the supply being so easily obtained ; whilst during periods of scarcity, such as long drought or prolonged frost, the neglect of active central control may make the careful consumer suffer for the fault of the wasteful.

The *intermittent system*, which is gradually being abolished, though it regulates wastage, has the strong defect that cisterns are provided in which the water is apt to become stagnant and foul, the cistern being uncovered and receiving all forms of impurities from the air and the dust, and to become perhaps impregnated by sewer gas and liquid filth when the main pipes are empty. Especially is this the case when, in the houses of the poorer classes, the same cistern is made to do duty for flushing the water-closet and providing the drinking supply. It is also believed that the intermittent supply, in which the pipes are alternately full and empty, tends greatly to the solution of lead ; while the cistern may be formed of galvanized iron, from which the zinc becomes dissolved, so that the iron rusts and discolours the water. Lead cisterns at first allow some solution, but

become later coated with carbonates which protect the lead from dissolving. In old, poor houses, cisterns may still be found constructed of wood, which forms an inefficient cistern, as the wood rots and aids in pollution.

If an intermittent system is in use, certain precautions must, therefore, be adopted. The cistern should be formed of slate, stoneware, or galvanized iron, large enough to hold an abundant supply, covered, well ventilated, easily accessible, not directly connected with the water-closet cistern, nor should it have its overflow pipe discharging directly into the sewerage system, but into the open air, where it can be easily seen. The cistern also must be periodically inspected and cleansed.

Diseases spread by water.—Impure water may cause disease simply in general forms such as diarrhœa, sickness, and dyspepsia due to the suspended materials present, whilst excessive presence of mineral matters and hardness may lead to digestive disturbance and constipation. Peaty matters, if in excess, may give rise to similar disturbance, whilst the presence of polluting sewage may create severe abdominal disturbance in the form of colic, vomiting, and purging. A more serious mode in which water may give rise to disease is in its being able to convey the special germs of disease, such as enteric fever. Enteric fever epidemics have not infrequently originated by the water supply becoming infected from the undestroyed discharges of a patient, huge epidemics thus originating from a single case. Outbreaks of Asiatic cholera have frequently been proved to be due to the water supply of a district becoming infected by the specific organism in the excreta from a cholera patient, and many of the towns in Great Britain owe their improved gravitation water supplies to the attention devoted to the water question in consequence of the cholera epidemics which formerly invaded this country Various parasites may find their way into drinking-water and be received into the stomach of man in the form of eggs or embryos, such as the *Ascaris lumbricoides* or roundworm, the *Filaria dracunculus* or Guinea-worm, and the *Bilharzia hæmatobium*. (*See* PARASITES.)

Poisoning by various metals may arise from trade-washings that pass into a stream, or by the solution of the metallic constituents of the water-pipes. Lead-poisoning may arise from the latter cause, especially where the water contains a free acid, as in the case of peaty waters ; but, if the water contains carbonate of lime, an insoluble protective coating is formed on the interior of the pipes. Many moorland waters have been found to act on lead, but this may be effectually prevented by treating the water with filters composed of sand and limestone. It is also possible to avoid the use of lead pipes where the water is known to act on the lead. It is generally considered that 0·1 part per million of lead is safe, that 0·5 part is the maximum permissible, and that 0·7 part is likely to lead to chronic lead-poisoning.

WATER TREATMENT (see BATHS ; COLD, USES OF ; DOUCHES ; TYPHOID FEVER ; WET PACK).

WAX is used in medicine as an ingredient of ointments, plasters, and suppositories. It is used either as yellow wax derived directly from honeycomb, or as white wax, which is the same substance bleached.

For wax in the ear, see EAR, DISEASES OF.

WAXY DISEASE, also known as LARDACEOUS DISEASE, or AMYLOID DEGENERATION, is a condition in which the fibrous tissues undergo degeneration into a substance of an albuminous nature, which resembles wax in certain of its chemical reactions. It is usually caused by one or other of three chronic diseases, viz. tuberculosis affecting the bones, lungs, or other organs ; syphilis ; and long-continued suppuration ; and it forms one of the dangers that are apt to attend one of these diseases when it has lasted for a long time. The organs affected by waxy disease undergo a change which makes them larger, harder, heavier, more translucent, and so changed in consistence that they may be cut into the sharpest angles and edges and into extremely thin slices.

986

WEAKNESS (see ATROPHY, CACHEXIA, PARALYSIS, TONICS, and under the heads of various weakening diseases, e.g. TUBERCULOSIS, DYSPEPSIA, NEURASTHENIA).

WEALS, or WHEALS, are raised white areas on the skin with reddened margins, which may result from sharp blows, or may be a symptom of nettle-rash.

WEANING (see INFANT FEEDING).

WEBBED FINGERS or TOES constitute a deformity sometimes present at birth, and liable to run in families. The web may be quite a thin structure, or the fingers may be closely united by solid tissue. In any case, separation is a matter of considerable difficulty, because, if the web be simply divided, it heals up as before. A special operation is necessary, consisting in turning back a flap of the web upon each of the united fingers, or some other device to produce healing in the new position.

WEIGHT and HEIGHT.—The weight of a child at birth is about 7 to 8 pounds (3·2 to 3·6 kg.) and the height 20 inches (50 cm.). During the first six months the infant puts on weight at the rate of about 5 oz. (140 G.) per week if no illness occurs, and during the second six months of life about 1 pound (0·5 kg.) per month. At the age of one year he weighs from 18 to 24 pounds (8·2 to 10·9 kg.). In the first year he increases in height about 10 inches (25 cm.), and measures almost 30 inches (75 cm.) at one year old.

In both boys and girls the growth in height amounts to 3 inches (7·5 cm.) per year from the second to the fifth years. Boys continue to grow at the rate of 2 inches (5 cm.) per year from the sixth to the fifteenth years, whilst girls continue to grow at this rate from the sixth to the eleventh years. In general, it may be said that the height is doubled at the end of five years, and trebled in the thirteenth or fourteenth year. After adolescence growth is more vigorous in boys, but girls attain their full height earlier than boys. Increase in height is greatest in the late spring and early summer, and least in the winter.

As a rule increase in height and increase in weight run parallel. At 2½ years the birth-weight has usually been increased fourfold, whilst at 5 years it has been increased fivefold. The general tendency of weight increase can be summarized as follows : (1) rapid increase in infancy and early childhood ; (2) slow but constant increase from 3 to 12 years ; (3) marked acceleration during puberty; (4) very slow increase to age of 25 or 30 years.

The following tables give a guide to the expected height and weight of children, but their interpretation in any one particular case must be made with care and discretion. Height, particularly, is a variable factor, and, if a child is under the average height for his age, this need not necessarily be of serious import. Family variations must be taken into consideration, as well as weight and the child's general health. Failure to gain weight is of more significance. Whilst this may be due to some underlying disease, the commonest cause is a diet containing inadequate calories.

In the case of adults (pp. 990-91), views have changed of recent years concerning 'ideal' weight. Life insurance statistics have shown that maximal life expectancy is obtained if the average weight at ages 25 to 30 years is maintained throughout the rest of life. These insurance statistics also suggest that it is of advantage to be slightly over average weight before the age of 30 years, to be of average weight from ages 30 to 40, and to be under-weight after the age of 40. In the past it has been usual, in assessing the significance of an adult's weight, to allow a 10 per cent. range on either side of normal for variations in body build. A closer correlation has been found between thoracic and abdominal measurements and weight. As average weights are still often referred to, the tables of these in men and women have been retained in this edition, but two further tables have been added showing ideal weights in men and women.

AGE	HEIGHT				WEIGHT			
	BOYS		GIRLS		BOYS		GIRLS	
	Inches	Centi-metres	Inches	Centi-metres	Pounds	Kilo-grams	Pounds	Kilo-grams
Birth	20·0	50·9	19·5	49·5	7·5	3·4	7·3	3·3
2 weeks	20·3	51·7	20·1	51·0	7·5	3·4	7·3	3·3
3 months	23·7	60·2	23·2	58·8	12·9	5·8	12·0	5·5
6 months	26·2	66·7	25·6	65·0	17·4	7·9	16·4	7·4
9 months	28·0	71·2	27·4	69·6	20·4	9·2	19·2	8·7
1 year	29·6	75·1	29·1	73·9	22·8	10·3	21·7	9·8
2 years	34·0	86·4	33·7	85·5	27·0	12·2	25·7	11·6
3 years	37·8	95·9	36·9	93·8	31·5	14·3	30·4	13·8
4 years	40·6	103·0	40·0	101·6	35·6	16·2	34·5	15·7
5 years	43·1	109·5	42·9	108·9	40·2	18·3	39·4	17·9

TABLE 34.—Mean Height and Weight of infants and young children (Thomson).

WEIGHT AND HEIGHT

Age	Average Height, Inches	Average Weight, Pounds	Age	Average Height, Inches	Average Weight, Pounds
Under 1 month	21⅛	9⅛	8 months, under 9	27¾	19
1 month, under 2	22½	10⅞	9 ,, ,, 10	28¼	19⅝
2 months, ,, 3	23⅝	12⅝	10 ,, ,, 11	28⅝	20¼
3 ,, ,, 4	24½	14⅛	11 ,, ,, 12	29	20¾
4 ,, ,, 5	25⅝	15⅜	1 year	29½	21⅜
5 ,, ,, 6	26⅛	16¼	2 years	33⅝	26⅝
6 ,, ,, 7	26¾	17½	3 ,,	36⅝	30¾
7 ,, ,, 8	27¼	18¼	4 ,,	38	34

	Weight in Pounds								
Height in Inches	5 years	6 years	7 years	8 years	9 years	10 years	11 years	12 years	13 years	14 years
---	---	---	---	---	---	---	---	---	---	---
38	34	34								
39	35	35								
40	36	36								
41	38	38	38							
42	39	39	39	39						
43	41	41	41	41						
44	44	44	44	44						
45	46	46	46	46	46					
46	47	48	48	48	48					
47	49	50	50	50	50	50				
48		52	53	53	53	53				
49		55	55	55	55	55	55			
50		57	58	58	58	58	58	58		
51			61	61	61	61	61	61		
52			63	64	64	64	64	64	64	
53			66	67	67	67	67	68	68	
54				70	70	70	70	71	71	72
55				72	72	73	73	74	74	74
56				75	76	77	77	77	78	78
57					79	80	81	81	82	83
58					83	84	84	85	85	86
59						87	88	89	89	90
60						91	92	92	93	94
61							95	96	97	99
62							100	101	102	103
63							105	106	107	108
64								109	111	113
65								114	117	118
66									119	122
67									124	128
68										134
69										137
70										143
71										148

The above table prepared by Bird T. Baldwin and Thomas D. Wood, accepted by the American Medical Association, from Bridges' *Dietetics for the Clinician*. Courtesy of Lea & Febiger and Henry Kimpton.

TABLE 34A.—HEIGHT, WEIGHT, AND AGE—BOYS

Age	Average Height, Inches	Average Weight, Pounds	Age	Average Height, Inches	Average Weight, Pounds
Under 1 month	$20\frac{7}{8}$	$8\frac{5}{8}$	8 months, under 9	$27\frac{1}{4}$	$17\frac{3}{4}$
1 month, under 2	$21\frac{7}{8}$	$10\frac{1}{8}$	9 ,, ,, 10	$27\frac{5}{8}$	$18\frac{1}{2}$
2 months, ,, 3	$23\frac{1}{8}$	$11\frac{3}{4}$	10 ,, ,, 11	$28\frac{1}{8}$	19
3 ,, ,, 4	24	13	11 ,, ,, 12	$28\frac{1}{2}$	$19\frac{1}{2}$
4 ,, ,, 5	$24\frac{7}{8}$	$14\frac{1}{4}$	1 year	$28\frac{7}{8}$	20
5 ,, ,, 6	$25\frac{1}{2}$	$15\frac{3}{8}$	2 years	$33\frac{1}{8}$	$25\frac{1}{8}$
6 ,, ,, 7	$26\frac{1}{8}$	$16\frac{1}{4}$	3 ,,	$36\frac{1}{4}$	$29\frac{1}{2}$
7 ,, ,, 8	$26\frac{3}{4}$	$17\frac{1}{8}$	4 ,,	38	33

Height in Inches	Weight in Pounds									
	5 years	6 years	7 years	8 years	9 years	10 years	11 years	12 years	13 years	14 years
38	33	33								
39	34	34								
40	36	36	36							
41	37	37	37							
42	39	39	39							
43	41	41	41	41						
44	42	42	42	42						
45	45	45	45	45	45					
46	47	47	47	48	48					
47	49	50	50	50	50	50				
48		52	52	52	52	53	53			
49		54	54	55	55	56	56			
50		56	56	57	58	59	61	62		
51			59	60	61	61	63	65		
52			63	64	64	64	65	67		
53			66	67	67	68	68	69	71	
54				69	70	70	71	71	73	
55				72	74	74	74	75	77	78
56					76	78	78	79	81	83
57					80	82	82	82	84	88
58						84	86	86	88	93
59						87	90	90	92	96
60						91	95	95	97	101
61							99	100	101	105
62							104	105	106	109
63								110	110	112
64								114	115	117
65								118	120	121
66									124	124
67									128	130
68									131	133
69										135
70										136
71										138

The above table prepared by Bird T. Baldwin and Thomas D. Wood, accepted by the American Medical Association, from Bridges' *Dietetics for the Clinician*. Courtesy of Lea & Febiger and Henry Kimpton.

TABLE 35.—HEIGHT, WEIGHT, AND AGE—GIRLS

WEIGHT AND HEIGHT

Height		Small Frame	Medium Frame	Large Frame
Feet	Inches			
5	2	116–125	124–133	131–142
5	3	119–128	127–136	133–144
5	4	122–132	130–140	137–149
5	5	126–136	134–144	141–153
5	6	129–139	137–147	145–157
5	7	133–143	141–151	149–162
5	8	136–147	145–156	153–166
5	9	140–151	149–160	157–170
5	10	144–155	153–164	161–175
5	11	148–159	157–168	165–180
6	0	152–164	161–173	169–185
6	1	157–169	166–178	174–190
6	2	163–175	171–184	179–196
6	3	168–180	176–189	184–202

(Weight in pounds with clothes. Height in feet and inches, with shoes on.)

TABLE 36.—IDEAL WEIGHTS FOR **MEN**

Height		Small Frame	Medium Frame	Large Frame
Feet	Inches			
4	11	104–111	110–118	17–127
5	0	105–113	112–120	119–129
5	1	107–115	114–122	121–131
5	2	110–118	117–125	124–135
5	3	113–121	120–128	127–138
5	4	116–125	124–132	131–142
5	5	119–128	127–135	133–145
5	6	123–132	130–140	138–150
5	7	126–136	134–144	142–154
5	8	129–139	137–147	145–158
5	9	133–143	141–151	149–162
5	10	136–147	145–155	152–166
5	11	139–150	148–158	155–169

From Metropolitan Life Insurance Company (as noted by Rynearson and Gastineau).

(Weight in pounds with clothes. Height in feet and inches, with shoes on.)

TABLE 37.—IDEAL WEIGHTS FOR **WOMEN**

Age.	Feet and Inches of Height with Shoes.																	
	5–0	5–1	5–2	5–3	5–4	5–5	5–6	5–7	5–8	5–9	5–10	5–11	6–0	6–1	6–2	6–3	6–4	6–5
16	109	111	114	117	120	124	128	132	136	140	144	149	154	159	164	169	174	179
18	113	115	118	121	124	128	132	136	140	144	148	153	158	163	168	173	178	183
20	117	119	122	125	128	132	136	140	144	148	152	156	161	166	171	176	181	186
22	119	121	124	127	131	135	139	142	146	150	154	158	163	168	173	178	183	188
24	121	123	126	129	133	137	141	144	148	152	156	160	165	171	177	182	187	192
26	123	125	127	130	134	138	142	146	150	154	158	163	168	174	180	186	191	196
28	125	127	129	132	135	139	143	147	151	155	159	164	170	176	182	188	193	198
30	126	128	130	133	136	140	144	148	152	156	161	166	172	178	184	190	196	201
32	127	129	131	134	137	141	145	149	154	158	163	168	174	180	186	192	198	203
34	128	130	132	135	138	142	146	150	155	160	165	170	176	182	188	194	200	206
36	129	131	133	136	139	143	147	151	156	161	166	171	177	183	190	196	202	208
38	130	132	134	137	140	144	148	152	157	162	167	173	179	185	192	198	204	210
40	131	133	135	138	141	145	149	153	158	163	168	174	180	186	193	200	206	212
42	132	134	136	139	142	146	150	154	159	164	169	175	181	187	194	201	208	214
44	133	135	137	140	143	147	151	155	160	165	170	176	182	188	195	202	209	215
46	134	136	138	141	144	148	152	156	161	166	171	177	183	189	196	203	210	216
48	134	136	138	141	144	148	152	156	161	166	171	177	183	190	197	204	211	217
50	134	136	138	141	144	148	152	156	161	166	171	177	183	190	197	204	211	217
52	135	137	139	142	145	149	153	157	162	167	172	178	184	191	198	205	212	218
54	135	137	139	142	145	149	153	158	163	168	173	178	184	191	198	205	212	219

TABLE 38.—AVERAGE WEIGHT OF **MEN** IN POUNDS WITH CLOTHES

Age.	Feet and Inches of Height with Shoes.																
	4–8	4–9	4–10	4–11	5–0	5–1	5–2	5–3	5–4	5–5	5–6	5–7	5–8	5–9	5–10	5–11	6–0
16	102	104	106	108	109	111	114	117	120	124	128	132	136	139	143	148	153
18	104	106	108	110	112	114	117	120	123	126	130	134	138	141	145	150	155
20	106	108	110	112	114	116	119	122	125	128	132	136	140	143	147	151	156
22	107	109	111	113	115	117	120	123	126	129	133	137	141	145	149	153	157
24	109	111	113	115	117	119	121	124	127	130	134	138	142	146	150	154	158
26	110	112	114	116	118	120	122	125	128	131	135	139	143	147	151	155	159
28	111	113	115	117	119	121	123	126	130	133	137	141	145	149	153	156	160
30	112	114	116	118	120	122	124	127	131	134	138	142	146	150	154	157	161
32	113	115	117	119	121	123	125	128	132	136	140	144	148	152	155	158	162
34	115	117	119	121	123	125	127	130	134	138	142	146	150	154	157	160	163
36	116	118	120	122	124	126	128	131	135	139	143	147	151	155	158	161	164
38	117	119	121	123	125	127	130	133	137	141	145	149	153	157	160	163	166
40	119	121	123	125	127	129	132	135	138	142	146	150	154	158	161	164	167
42	120	122	124	126	128	130	133	136	139	143	147	151	155	159	162	166	169
44	122	124	126	128	130	132	135	138	141	145	149	153	157	161	164	168	171
46	123	125	127	129	131	133	136	139	142	146	150	154	158	162	165	169	172
48	124	126	128	130	132	134	137	140	143	147	152	156	160	164	167	171	174
50	125	127	129	131	133	135	138	141	144	148	152	156	161	165	169	173	176
52	125	127	129	131	133	135	138	141	144	148	152	157	162	166	170	174	177
54	125	127	129	131	133	135	138	141	144	148	153	158	163	167	171	174	177

TABLE 39.—AVERAGE WEIGHT OF **WOMEN** IN POUNDS WITH CLOTHES

WEIGHTS AND MEASURES—

APOTHECARIES' WEIGHT

						Metric Equivalent in Grammes.
Troy grains	20		=	1 scruple (Э)	=	1·29
,, ,,	60	= 3 scruples	=	1 dram (Ʒ)	=	3·88
,, ,,	480	= 8 drams	=	1 ounce (Ƹ)	=	31·1
,, ,,	5760	= 12 ounces	=	1 pound (lb.)	=	373

AVOIRDUPOIS WEIGHT

						Metric Equivalent in Grammes.
Troy grains	437·5	= 16 drams	=	1 ounce (oz.)	=	28·35
,, ,,	7000	= 16 ounces	=	1 pound (lb.)	=	453·60

APOTHECARIES' FLUID (WINE) MEASURE
(Used in America)

						Metric Equivalent in Millilitres.
Minims (♏)	60		=	1 fluid dram (fl. Ʒ)	=	3·55
,,	480	= 8 fluid drams	=	1 fluid ounce (fl. Ƹ)	=	30·00*
,,	7,680	= 16 fluid ounces	=	1 pint (O)	=	454·6
,,	61,440	= 8 pints	=	1 gallon (C)	=	3636·7

* More accurately, 28·412 millilitres. 1 pint = 27·7 cubic inches.

IMPERIAL FLUID MEASURE
(Used in Great Britain)

						Metric Equivalent in Millilitres.
Minims (♏)	60		=	1 fluid dram (fl. Ʒ)	=	3·55
,,	480	= 8 fluid drams	=	1 fluid ounce (fl. Ƹ)	=	30·00*
,,	9,600	= 20 fluid ounces	=	1 Imperial pint	=	568·25
,,	19,200	= 2 Imperial pints	=	1 Imperial quart	=	1136·5
,,	76,800	= 4 Imperial quarts	=	1 Imperial gallon	=	4546·0

N.B.—1 Imperial pint = 1 pint 4 fluid ounces Apothecaries' Measure.
* More accurately 28·412 millilitres.

METRIC WEIGHT AND MEASURE UNITS

The metre or unit of length = 39·370432 inches (approx. 40 inches)
The litre or unit of capacity = 35·196 fluid ounces (approx. 35 fluid ounces)
The gramme or unit of weight = 15·4323 troy grains (approx. 15½ grains)
The millilitre = 16·896 minims Imperial (approx. 17 minims)

METRIC MEASURES OF LENGTH

1 Kilometre (Km.)	= 1000·0 metres	= 0·6214 mile
1 Hectometre (Hm.)	= 100·0 metres	= 109·30 yards
1 Dekametre (Dm.)	= 10·0 metres	= 32·81 feet
1 Metre (M.)	= 1·0 metre	= 39·37 inches
1 Decimetre (dm.)	= 0·1 metre	= 3·93 inches
1 Centimetre (cm.)	= 0·01 metre	= 0·394 inch
1 Millimetre (mm.)	= 0·001 metre	= 0·039 inch

METRIC MEASURES OF WEIGHT

*1 Kilogram (Kg.)	= 1000·0 G.	= 2·205 pounds (avoirdupois)
1 Hectogram	= 100·0 G.	= 3·527 ounces (avoirdupois)
1 Dekagram	= 10·0 G.	= 154·323 grains
1 Gramme (G.)	= 1·0 G.	= 15·432 grains
1 Decigram	= 0·1 G.	= 1·543 grains
1 Centigram (cg.)	= 0·01 G.	= 0·154 grain
1 Milligram (mg.)	= 0·001 G.	= 0·015 grain

* Commonly called 1 kilo

WEIGHTS AND MEASURES

METRIC MEASURES OF CAPACITY

1 Kilolitre (Kl.)	= 1000·0 litres	= 220·15 Imperial gallons
1 Hectolitre (Hl.)	= 100·0 litres	= 22·01 Imperial gallons
1 Dekalitre (Dl.)	= 10·0 litres	= 2·2 Imperial gallons
1 Litre (L.)	= 1·0 litre	= 35·196 Imperial fluid ounces
1 Decilitre (dl.)	= 0·1 litre	= 3·5 Imperial fluid ounces
1 Centilitre (cl.)	= 0·01 litre	= 0·35 Imperial fluid ounce
1 Millilitre (ml.)	= 0·001 litre	= 16·89 Imperial minims
1 Decimil (dml.)	= 0·0001 litre	= 1·68 Imperial minims
1 Centimil (cml.)	= 0·00001 litre	= 0·16 Imperial minim

N.B.—1 Millilitre is approximately equivalent to one cubic centimetre (c.c.).

FACTORS FOR CONVERTING FROM ONE SCALE TO THE OTHER

To convert grammes into grains	× 15·432
„ „ „ ounces, avoirdupois	× 0·03527
„ kilograms into pounds	× 2·2046
„ grains into grammes	× 0·0648
„ avoirdupois ounces into grammes	× 28·35
„ troy ounces into grammes	× 31·104
„ cubic centimetres into fluid ounces, Imperial . .	× 0·0352
„ litres into fluid ounces, Imperial	× 35·2
„ fluid ounces into millilitres	× 28·42
„ pints into litres	× 0·568
„ metres into inches	× 39·37
„ inches into metres	× 0·0254

IMPERIAL MEASURES OF MASS WITH APPROXIMATE METRIC EQUIVALENTS

Imperial.	Metric.	Imperial.	Metric.
gr. $\frac{1}{100}$	= 0·0006 G.	gr. 10	= 0·6 G.
„ $\frac{1}{64}$	= 0·001 „	„ 15	= 1·0 „
„ $\frac{1}{2}$	= 0·03 „	„ 20	= 1·3 „
„ 1	= 0·06 „	„ 25	= 1·6 „
„ 2	= 0·12 „	„ 30	= 2·0 „
„ 3	= 0·2 „	„ 40	= 2·5 „
„ 4	= 0·25 „	„ 60	= 4 „
„ 5	= 0·3 „	„ 90	= 6 „
„ 6	= 0·36 „	„ 120	= 8 „
„ 7	= 0·45 „	oz. $\frac{1}{4}$ (avoir.)	= 7·5 „
„ 8	= 0·5 „	„ $\frac{1}{2}$ „	= 15 „
„ 9	= 0·58 „	„ 1 „	= 30* „

* More accurately 28·3 G.

IMPERIAL MEASURES OF CAPACITY WITH APPROXIMATE METRIC EQUIVALENTS

Imperial.	Metric.	Imperial.	Metric.
min. $\frac{1}{2}$	= 0·03 ml.	min. 25	= 1·5 ml.
„ 1	= 0·06 „	„ 30	= 1·8 „
„ 2	= 0·12 „	„ 50	= 3·0 „
„ 3	= 0·18 „	„ 60	= 3·6 „
„ 4	= 0·2 „	„ 90	= 6 „
„ 5	= 0·3 „	drams 2	= 8 „
„ 8	= 0·5 „	„ 4	= 16 „
„ 10	= 0·6 „	„ 6	= 24 „
„ 15	= 0·9 „	ounce 1	= 30 „
„ 20	= 1·2 „		

WEIGHTS AND MEASURES

Metric Measures of Mass with Approximate Imperial Equivalents

Metric.		Imperial.	Metric.	Imperial.
1 mg.	(0·001 G.)	= $\frac{1}{66}$ grain	2 G.	= 30$\frac{7}{8}$ grains
2 ,,	(0·002 ,,)	= $\frac{1}{32}$,,	3 ,,	= 46$\frac{1}{4}$,,
3 ,,	(0·003 ,,)	= $\frac{1}{20}$,,	4 ,,	= 61$\frac{3}{4}$,,
4 ,,	(0·004 ,,)	= $\frac{1}{16}$,,	5 ,,	= 77$\frac{1}{8}$,,
5 ,,	(0·005 ,,)	= $\frac{1}{13}$,,	7·5 G.	= 115$\frac{3}{4}$,,
8 ,,	(0·008 ,,)	= $\frac{1}{8}$,,	10 G.	= 154$\frac{1}{2}$,,
1 cg.	(0·01 ,,)	= $\frac{1}{6}$,,	15 ,,	= 231$\frac{1}{2}$,,
2 ,,	(0·02 ,,)	= $\frac{1}{3}$,,	20 ,,	= 308$\frac{3}{5}$,,
3 ,,	(0·03 ,,)	= $\frac{1}{2}$,,	30 ,,	= 1 oz. 25$\frac{1}{2}$ grains
5 ,,	(0·05 ,,)	= $\frac{3}{4}$,,	40 ,,	= 1 ,, 179$\frac{4}{5}$,,
10 ,,	(0·1 ,,)	= 1$\frac{1}{2}$,,	50 ,,	= 1 ,, 334 ,,
1 dgm.	(0·1 ,,)	= 1$\frac{1}{2}$,,	75 ,,	= 2 ,, 282$\frac{1}{2}$,,
2 ,,	(0·2 ,,)	= 3 grains	100 ,,	= 3 ,, 230$\frac{3}{4}$,,
3 ,,	(0·3 ,,)	= 4$\frac{1}{2}$,,	150 ,,	= 5 ,, 127$\frac{1}{2}$,,
4 ,,	(0·4 ,,)	= 6$\frac{1}{4}$,,	250 ,,	= 8 ,, 358 ,,
5 ,,	(0·5 ,,)	= 7$\frac{3}{4}$,,	600 ,,	= 1 lb. 1 oz. 278 gr.
10 ,,	(1·0 ,,)	= 15$\frac{1}{2}$,,	750 ,,	= 1 ,, 10 ,, 200 ,,
1 G.		= 15$\frac{1}{2}$ (15·432) gr.	1 kg.	= 2 ,, 3 ,, 120 ,,

Metric Measures of Capacity with Approximate Imperial Equivalents

Metric.	Imperial.	Metric.	Imperial.
1 ml.	= 17 (16·9) min.	25 ml.	= 7 fl. dr. 2 min.
2 ,,	= 33$\frac{4}{5}$ min.	30 ,,	= ,, 27 ,,
3 ,,	= 50$\frac{3}{4}$,,	40 ,,	= 1 fl. oz. 3 fl. dr. 16 min.
4 ,,	= 1 fl. dr. 7 min.	50 ,,	= 1 ,, 6 ,, 5 ,,
5 ,,	= 1 ,, 24 ,,	75 ,,	= 2 ,, 5 ,, 7 ,,
6 ,,	= 1 ,, 41 ,,	100 ,,	= 3 ,, 4 ,, 10 ,,
7 ,,	= 1 ,, 58 ,,	125 ,,	= 4 ,, 3 ,, 12 ,,
8 ,,	= 2 ,, 15 ,,	150 ,,	= 5 ,, 2 ,, 15 ,,
9 ,,	= 2 ,, 32 ,,	200 ,,	= 7 ,, 0 ,, 20 ,,
10 ,,	= 2 ,, 49 ,,	300 ,,	= 10 ,, 4 ,, 30 ,,
15 ,,	= 4 ,, 13 ,,	500 ,,	= 17 ,, 4 ,, 50 ,,
20 ,,	= 5 ,, 38 ,,	1 litre	= 35 ,, 1 ,, 34 ,,

Approximate Value of Domestic Measures

Tumbler	= 10 fluid ounces	Table-spoon (small)	= $\frac{1}{2}$ fluid ounce
Breakfast-cup	= 8 ,, ,,	Dessert-spoon	= 120 minims
Tea-cup	= 5 ,, ,,	Tea-spoon	= 60 minims
Wine-glass (large)	= 2$\frac{1}{4}$,, ,,	Drop (of water)	= 1 minim

Note.—When medicine is measured this should be done by means of a standardized measure, because domestic utensils vary greatly in size.

WEIL'S DISEASE is a form of jaundice due to infection with a spirochæte, also known as infectious jaundice and as SPIROCHÆTOSIS ICTERO-HÆMORRHAGICA (*q.v.*).

WEIR MITCHELL TREATMENT is a form of treatment which consists in absolute rest of body and mind, administration of highly nutritious and easily digestible food in large quantities, and massage to take the place of muscular exercise. (*See* NEURASTHENIA.)

WELLS (*see* WATER SUPPLY).

WENS are small cystic tumours in the skin, consisting of a collection of sebaceous material, due to blockage of the outlet from a sebaceous gland. They occur most commonly about the face and scalp, where they form smooth, rounded, elastic tumours, often of a considerable size, but give rise to no trouble save that occasioned by their position, by their unsightliness, and by the fact that they are liable to become inflamed from the pressure of the hat, etc.

Treatment consists in opening the cyst, squeezing out its fatty contents, and carefully removing the lining membrane. If any part of the membrane lining the interior be left behind, the wound heals in such a way that the wen is apt to refill. On the scalp this membrane is tough and can generally be pulled out entire, but on the face greater care is necessary, and the thin skin over the wen, to which the lining membrane is adherent, is also removed. The little operation is usually performed under a local anæsthetic, and is accompanied by very little pain.

WET BRAIN is a term applied to an œdematous state of the brain caused by chronic alcoholism and associated with mental failure and delusions.

WET CUP is a form of cupping in which the cupping glass is applied after scarification of the skin. (*See* CUPPING.)

WET PACK is a method of treatment much in vogue in some countries and with some physicians, for the purpose of applying a moderate degree of cold or of heat, for some time, to a patient's skin.

Uses.—The conditions in which cold is beneficial are detailed under COLD, USES OF, and the wet pack is a specially convenient method of applying cold when it is desired to exert a gentle cooling influence over a prolonged period, one hour or more, and at the same time to maintain the patient in a condition of absolute quiet and rest. It is used, for example, in such conditions as neurasthenia, and exhaustion due to heat. When a more rapid degree of cooling is desired, the patient is changed from one wet pack to another every quarter of an hour or thereabout, two beds being placed near one another for this purpose. Very rapid cooling may be achieved by wrapping the patient in a wet pack and rubbing down the sheet in which he is enveloped with pieces of ice.

Hot wet packs are also applied, *e.g.* in Bright's disease.

Method of application. — (1) COLD PACK.—A mackintosh sheet covered by a large blanket is spread upon the bed, and, when the patient is ready, a sheet is dipped in cold water, wrung out fairly dry, and laid over the blanket. The patient, stripped, is laid upon the sheet. which is quickly turned over him from both sides, and pushed between his legs and between each arm and the chest, so that skin does not touch skin anywhere. This must be done quickly, and the sheet being neatly tucked in round the neck and folded beneath the feet, every part of the body is covered saving the head and face. The head may also be wrapped in a wet towel. Finally the sides of the blanket are turned over the patient, and wrapped round him so as to lie smoothly everywhere. The patient, enveloped in this pack, lies absolutely helpless and should on no account be left by the attendant till the pack is removed, when he is put back into bed.

(2) HOT PACK.—A mackintosh sheet is spread on the bed as for a cold pack. Upon this is laid a dry blanket. A

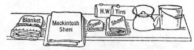

FIG. 417.—Requisites for hot pack.

FIG. 418.—Hot pack, first stage. Pail containing sheet for wringer and blanket for pack.

FIG. 419.—Hot pack, second stage. Wringing out the blanket inside the sheet.

second blanket (which retains heat better than a sheet) is placed in a pail and boiling water is poured over it (Fig. 418). The blanket is then taken out of the pail, wrung, shaken, and rolled up (Fig. 419). It is next applied to the patient in the same way as the sheet in the case of the cold pack (Fig. 420). The dry blanket is then also wrapped round the patient outside the wet blanket ; a second mackintosh sheet is spread over him (Fig. 421) ; hot-water bottles, if desired, are placed alongside him ; and

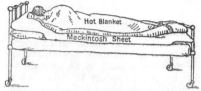

FIG. 420.—Hot pack, third stage. Applying the hot wet blanket.

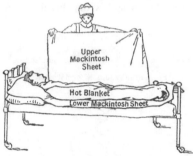

FIG. 421. — Hot pack, fourth stage. Blanket tucked round patient, and upper mackintosh being laid over.

several more blankets are laid on top of the mackintosh sheet. The patient may lie enveloped in the hot pack for twenty minutes ; he is then quickly dried with warm towels, a warm flannel night-dress reapplied, and he is put back in bed. The patient must on no account be left alone while he is in the hot pack.

(3) WHISKY PACK.—(*See* ALCOHOL.)

(4) MUSTARD PACK.—A pack containing mustard is sometimes used as a last resort in cases of collapse or of failure of breathing in young children. The pack is made by mixing mustard with warm water to the consistency of cream and saturating a smooth hand-towel with a breakfast-cupful of the mixture. The child is laid on a mackintosh, and the towel is wrapped round its chest, abdomen, and limbs, the face being meantime protected by the hand of the nurse or by a dry towel. A second mackintosh is laid over the pack and a strip of cotton-wool is tucked round the neck to keep the fumes from the face and eyes. The child, after 10 or 15 minutes, is

transferred to a warm bath, the skin is thoroughly rinsed to remove the mustard, and an ordinary hot wet pack is applied for 20 or 30 minutes. In the latter, a marked reaction should take place.

WHEEZING is a popular name applied to the various sounds produced in the chest when the bronchial tubes are inflamed. It is applied particularly to the long-drawn breathing of asthma, and to the whistling or purring noises that accompany breathing in cases of bronchitis. (*See* ASTHMA, BRONCHITIS.)

WHELK is a term applied to a weal, and also to a red protuberance on the face or nose seen in the case of a hard drinker. (*See* ACNE ROSACEA.)

WHEY (*see* JUNKET).

WHIPWORM is a popular name for *Trichuris trichiura*. (*See* PARASITES.)

WHISKY (*see* ALCOHOL).

WHITE LEG is a fairly common and well-known condition in which a limb, usually one of the lower limbs, becomes enlarged, white, and painful.

Causes.—Most commonly the condition occurs after child-birth ; sometimes it occurs during convalescence from an acute febrile disease, especially typhoid fever or pneumonia. It is usually due to inflammation in, and blocking of, the veins of the limb, or may be caused by the spread of infection into the lymphatics of the limb from those within the pelvis, or to some morbid change in the blood causing it to clot.

Symptoms.—The disease comes on during convalescence from one of the conditions mentioned above, beginning with slight feverishness and pain down the leg which is to be affected. The limb gradually swells, and in a few days may be greatly enlarged, hard, glossy, and of a strikingly white colour. The veins can generally be felt as solid lines down the inner side of the thigh, and the affected parts may be very tender to the touch. These symptoms persist for a week or so, but generally begin to subside within a fortnight from the onset, and about three-fourths of all cases recover completely in a few weeks. In other cases, some degree of muscular weakness, swelling, or aching of the limb remains permanently, but the condition, though a serious one demanding most careful treatment, is very seldom fatal.

Treatment consists chiefly of rest in bed with the affected limb supported on a pillow. Pain is relieved by laudanum fomentations or simply by wrapping the limb in cotton-wool. Anticoagulants such as heparin and dicoumarol are sometimes given to prevent the process spreading.

This is one of the conditions, however, in which it is now recognized that preventive measures can be most effective. These consist principally of not allowing patients to stay in bed longer than necessary, or of giving massage to the legs in cases which are confined to bed for long periods.

WHITE PRECIPITATE is the popular name for ammonio-chloride of mercury, a substance much used in the form of an ointment for application to various skin diseases. (*See* MERCURY.)

WHITES, or LEUCORRHŒA, is a symptom of many diseases peculiar to women, and may be of an acute nature, when the discharge is thick and white, consisting mainly of pus; or is more often chronic and catarrhal, when the discharge is usually thinner, sometimes of a clear mucous nature; in other cases acrid and offensive. In slighter cases, the discharge precedes or follows the menstrual flow; in severer cases it continues throughout the whole intervening periods. Persons affected in this manner are generally unhealthy in appearance, the face is pale and sallow, weariness is felt easily upon exertion, and a dull gnawing pain is often experienced in the lower part of the back.

Causes.—Leucorrhœa may arise as a result of infection anywhere in the genital tract in women, *i.e.* in the uterus, cervix, or vagina. The commonest cause is some chronic inflammation of the womb following on childbirth, and associated with some displacement of this organ or some laceration of its neck. Another important cause is gonorrhœa. In other cases it is due to infection of the vagina with the *Trichomonas vaginalis* (*q.v.*). The condition may occur as a symptom of general debility accompanied by congestion of internal organs. An occasional cause of very offensive discharge is found in the irritation set up by the presence of a foreign body, such as a pessary that has been introduced for the support of a displaced womb, and then forgotten. In young children the condition is not common, but may arise from the irritation set up by threadworms, as the result of general debility combined with want of cleanliness, or following upon some acute infective disease.

Treatment.—Constitutional remedies are of importance in almost all cases, and include good diet, the administration of iron for anæmia, and bracing treatment, such as the daily cold bath. Frequently, change of air is recommended. As regards local measures, the careful regulation of the bowels is of great importance, and the cleansing and soothing action of the warm douche is the chief method of treatment (*see* DOUCHE). In simpler cases it is often sufficient to use plain water for the douche, or water tinted to a pink colour with permanganate of potassium. The douche should be large in amount, at least a quart, and should be regularly used, either once or twice daily. In more intractable cases, various astringents such as alum, sulphate of zinc, and vegetable infusions containing tannin, are added to the water of the douche.

If, however, the condition be due to some definite disease, these measures are no more than palliative, so long as it remains untreated, and some special form of treatment becomes necessary. (*See* UTERUS, DISEASES OF.)

WHITE SWELLING is a popular name applied to tuberculous disease of joints. (*See* JOINTS, DISEASES OF.)

WHITLOW is a popular term applied to all acute inflammations of the deep-seated tissues in the fingers, whether the structure affected be the root of the nail, the pulp of the finger-tip, the sheaths of the tendons that run along the back and front of the fingers, or the bone. Acute inflammation of the bones in the finger is very rare, and in general a whitlow begins in the last part of one finger, being, when situated towards the back, a small abscess at the root of the nail, and, when commencing in front, an abscess in the fat and fibrous tissue that compose the pulp of the finger. Suppuration may also begin in the sheath of the tendon, generally in front of the finger.

WHOOPING-COUGH, also known as HOOPING-COUGH, PERTUSSIS, and CHIN-COUGH, is an infectious disease of the mucous membrane lining the air passages, which manifests itself by frequently recurring attacks of convulsive coughing, followed by peculiar, loud indrawing of the breath, and often by vomiting. It occurs for the most part in children, and seldom more than once in a lifetime.

Causes.—The direct cause of whooping-cough is a bacillus discovered by Bordet and Gengou in 1906 and found in the sputum. It is often referred to as the ' bacillus of Bordet and Gengou ', but generally goes under the name of *Bordetella pertussis*. Although specially a disease of childhood, whooping-cough is by no means limited to that period, but may occur at any time of life, even to old age, should there have been no previous attack. It is most prevalent between the ages of one and four, and is uncommon after ten. Whooping-cough can be a dangerous disease in infants, but is a much less serious malady in older children. It has been occasionally observed in newly born infants, and is more common in female than in male children. Whooping-cough is infectious during any stage of its progress, but chiefly at its commencement. It is not only communicated by the breath, but may be conveyed by the medium of clothing. It prevails mostly in spring and autumn, doubtless owing to these seasons increasing the predisposition to affections of the respiratory passages. Epidemics of whooping - cough have often been noticed to succeed or to accompany those of measles, although no causal connection between these diseases appears to be traceable. The incubation period is usually 10 to 14 days.

In 1966, there were 19,427 cases of

whooping-cough in England and Wales, with 23 deaths. Twenty-two of these deaths occurred under the age of 1 year.

Symptoms.—Three stages of the disease are recognized, viz. (1) the catarrhal stage, (2) the spasmodic stage, (3) the stage of decline.

The *first stage* is characterized by the usual symptoms of a catarrh, with sneezing, watering of the eyes, irritation of the throat, feverishness, and cough, but in general there is nothing in the symptoms to indicate that they are to develop into whooping-cough. The catarrhal stage usually lasts from ten to fourteen days.

The *second stage* is marked by the abatement of the catarrhal symptoms, but at the same time by increase in the cough, which now occurs in irregular paroxysms both by day and by night. Each paroxysm consists in a series of violent and rapid expiratory coughs, succeeded by a loud sonorous or crowing inspiration—the ' whoop '. During the coughing efforts the air is driven with great force out of the lungs, and, as none can enter the chest, the symptoms of impending asphyxia appear. The patient grows deep-red or livid in the face, the eyes appear as if they would burst from their sockets, and suffocation seems imminent till relief is brought by the ' whoop '. Occasionally blood runs from the nose or mouth, or is extravasated into the conjunctiva of the eyes. A single fit rarely lasts beyond from half to three-quarters of a minute, but after the ' whoop ' another recurs, and of these a number may come and go for several minutes. The paroxysm ends by the coughing or vomiting up of a viscid tenacious secretion, and usually after this the patient seems comparatively well, or, it may be, somewhat wearied and fretful. The frequency of the paroxysms varies according to the severity of the case, being in some instances only to the extent of one or two in the whole day, whilst in others there may be several in the course of a single hour. Slight causes serve to bring on the fits of coughing, such as the acts of swallowing, talking, laughing, crying, or they may occur without any apparent exciting cause. In general, children come to recognize an impending attack by a feeling of tickling in the throat, and they cling with dread to their mother or nurse, or take hold of some object near them for support during the paroxysm; but, although exhausted by the severe fit of coughing, they soon resume their play, apparently little the worse. The attacks are on the whole most severe at night. This stage of the disease usually continues during four to seven weeks, but it may be shorter or longer. It is during this time that complications are apt to arise which may become a source of danger greater even than the malady itself. The chief of these are inflammatory affections of the bronchial tubes and lungs, and convulsions, any of which may prove fatal. A milder but very frequent complication is the formation of a small ulcer under the tongue from rubbing against the teeth in coughing. Hernia and prolapse of the rectum sometimes are produced by the strain of violent coughing.

When, however, the disease progresses favourably, as it usually does, it passes into the *third* or *terminal stage*, in which the cough becomes less frequent and generally loses in great measure its ' whooping ' character. The patient's general condition undergoes improvement, and the symptoms disappear in from one to three weeks. It is to be observed, however, that for a long period afterwards in any simple catarrh from which the patient suffers the cough often assumes a spasmodic character, which may suggest the erroneous notion that a relapse of the whooping-cough has occurred.

In severe cases it sometimes happens that the disease leaves behind it such structural changes in the lungs (emphysema, etc.) as entail permanent shortness of breathing, or a liability to attacks of asthma. Occasionally the violence of the cough may rupture a blood-vessel in the brain, with hemiplegia as a result.

Treatment.—As regards the treatment of whooping-cough in mild cases, little is necessary beyond keeping the patient warm and carefully attending to the general health. The remedies applicable in the case of catarrh or the milder forms of bronchitis are of service here, whilst gentle counter-irritation to the chest by stimulating liniments may be employed all through the attack. In mild weather the patient may be in the open air. In the more severe forms, efforts have to be employed to modify the severity of the paroxysms. Numerous remedies are recommended, the chief of which are phenobarbitone, camphorated tincture of opium, and atropine methonitrate. During convalescence, when the cough still continues to be troublesome, a change of air will often effect its removal.

The tetracyclines and chloramphenicol are of value, but it is not recommended that they should be used routinely. The main indications for their use are in young children and when there are complications.

A vaccine has now been prepared which is effective as a prophylactic. Children should be vaccinated as early in life as possible, and should be given a reinforcing dose at 12 to 18 months. A hyper-immune serum is also available which appears to be of value in the prevention of the disease, and in the modification of the disease when given early enough.

WIDAL REACTION (*see* AGGLUTINATION).

WILSON'S DISEASE, or HEPATOLENTICULAR DEGENERATION, is a familial disease in which there is an increased accumulation of copper in the liver, brain, and other tissues including the kidneys. Its main manifestation is the development of tremor and rigidity, with difficulty in speech. In some cases there is improvement following the administration of dimercaprol or penicillamine ; these two substances cause an increased excretion of copper.

WINDPIPE is the popular name for the trachea, which extends from the larynx above to the point in the upper part of the chest where it divides into the two large bronchial tubes, one to each lung. It thus extends through the lower part of the neck and upper part of the chest, and is about four inches in length. It consists of a fibrous tube kept permanently open by about twenty strong horizontally placed hoops of cartilage, each of which forms about two-thirds of a circle, but is defective behind where the two ends are united by muscle-fibres. This fibro-cartilaginous tube is lined by a smooth mucous membrane, richly supplied with mucous glands and covered by a single layer of ciliated epithelium. (*See also* AIR PASSAGES.)

WIND SUCKING (*see* AEROPHAGY).

WINE (*see* VINUM *and* ALCOHOL).

WINTER COUGH is a name sometimes given to chronic bronchitis which affects old people specially. The cough passes off during the summer and returns with the damp weather each winter. (*See* BRONCHITIS.)

WINTERGREEN (*see* GAULTHERIA).

WISDOM TOOTH is a popular name for the last molar tooth on either side of each jaw. These teeth are the last to appear and should develop in early adult life, but frequently they do not cut the gum till the age of twenty or twenty-five, or indeed they may sometimes remain permanently impacted in the jaw-bone.

WITCH-HAZEL is a preparation of the bark, twigs, and dried leaves from *Hamamelis virginiana*, a plant of the United States possessed of strong astringent properties. It is used to check hæmorrhages and excessive mucous discharges, and also for piles. The most commonly used preparation is the liquid extract, which is sometimes given internally and more often used in the strength of 60 minims (4 ml.) to 3 ounces (85 ml.) of cold water, either as a lotion for bruises or as an enema for bleeding piles. Extract of hamamelis is employed as an application for varicose veins and ulcers; and ointments known as hazeline snow, hazeline cream, etc., are much used as applications for irritable states of the skin.

WOLF'S-BANE is another name for aconite (*q.v.*).

WOMB (*see* UTERUS).

WOOD ALCOHOL is another name for methyl alcohol. (*See* SPIRIT.)

WOOD WOOL is the name of a fabric prepared from wood fibre, and much used for padding splints and other

surgical purposes where the more expensive and softer cotton-wool is not necessary.

WOOLSORTERS' DISEASE is another name for anthrax. (*See* ANTHRAX.)

WORD BLINDNESS is the term applied to a condition in which, as the result of disease in the brain, a person becomes unable to associate their proper meanings with words, although he may be quite able to spell the letters. WORD DEAFNESS is an associated condition in which, though hearing remains perfect, the patient has lost the power of referring the names he hears to the articles they denote. (*See* APHASIA.)

WORMS (*see* PARASITES).

WORMSEED is a popular name for santonin. (*See* SANTONIN.)

WORMWOOD (*see* ABSINTHISM).

WOUNDS.—A wound is any breach suddenly produced in the tissues of the body by direct violence. An extensive injury of the deeper parts without corresponding injury of the surface is known as a bruise or contusion.

Varieties.—Classified according to the immediate effect produced, four varieties are usually described, viz. *incised, punctured, lacerated,* and *contused.*

INCISED WOUNDS are usually inflicted with some sharp instrument, and are clean cuts, in which the tissues are simply divided without any damage to parts around. The bleeding from such a wound is apt to be very free, but it can be readily controlled.

PUNCTURED WOUNDS, or stabs, are inflicted with a pointed instrument. These wounds are the most dangerous, partly because their depth involves the danger of wounding vital organs, partly because bleeding from a stab is hard to control, and largely on account of the difficulty of purification. The wound produced by the modern nickel-nosed bullet is a puncture, much less severe than the ugly lacerated wound caused by an expanding bullet, or by a ricochet, and, if no clothing has been carried in by the bullet, the wound is clean and usually heals at once.

LACERATED WOUNDS are those in which great tearing takes place, such as injuries caused by machinery. The blood-vessels being torn and twisted, little bleeding is apt to result, and a limb may be torn completely away without great loss of blood. Such wounds are, however, specially liable to the danger of suppuration.

CONTUSED WOUNDS are those accompanied by much bruising of surrounding parts, as in the case of a blow from a cudgel or poker. In these wounds also there is little bleeding, but healing is slow on account of damage to the edges of the wound.

Any of these varieties may become infected by pus-forming germs and develop into a POISONED WOUND.

First-aid treatment.—The first duty of a bystander who renders help to a wounded person is to check any bleeding. This may be done by pressure upon the edges of the wound with a clean handkerchief, or, if the bleeding is serious, by putting the finger in the wound and pressing it upon the spot from which the blood is coming. If necessary, the person may then at his leisure apply other methods described under HÆMORRHAGE and TOURNIQUET.

If a medical man is to see a wound within a few hours, it should not be interfered with further than is necessary to stop the bleeding and to cover the wound with a clean dry handkerchief or piece of lint. In cases in which expert assistance is not soon obtainable, one of the following procedures may be adopted. The bleeding being checked, the next step is to cleanse the wound and surrounding skin.

(a) *By painting freely with acriflavine or dettol* the wound and the surrounding skin, and covering with a piece of clean dry lint ; this answers well in the case of small wounds and abrasions. A small piece of sterilized lint attached to a strip of sticking plaster may be purchased ready for use and forms a convenient and quickly applied dressing.

(b) *By washing with clean water (i.e.* boiled). For this purpose, one requires two *clean* bowls scalded out quickly with boiling water, and filled with *clean* warm water ; also several *clean* cloths, which may be handkerchiefs, squares of lint (preferably boracic lint), or newly washed rags.

32 *a*

(1) First, it is essential that the person who is to dress the wound should wash his own hands, and especially the nails, thoroughly with soap and water.

(2) Press a clean cloth upon the wound to prevent the entrance into it of dirty water, and carefully wash the skin around the wound with water. from one of the bowls, using soap if necessary.

(3) Wring out a fresh cloth from the clean water in the second bowl, and with it gently dab the wound. Remove, replace by another clean cloth similarly wrung out, and fix it on the wound with a folded handkerchief. (*See* BANDAGES.)

(4) The injured part is finally fixed so that movement is prevented or minimized. A wounded hand or arm is fixed with a sling (*see* SLINGS), a wounded leg with a splint.

(5) If the injury has caused severe shock, stimulants may be necessary. (*See* SHOCK.)

Healing of wounds. — The reaction of the tissues to an injury is similar to that produced by any other irritation, viz. an inflammation which finally heals the part. If the wound has been accompanied by loss of substance which has to be made good, or by death of a piece of tissue which has to be cast off as a slough, or by infection with bacteria which has to be overcome, the process of repair is tedious and in some cases permanent damage is produced. The new tissue formed in the wound is mainly fibrous tissue, like that composing the supporting framework of the body.

HEALING BY FIRST INTENTION.—In a clean, incised wound of moderate severity, the immediate effect is bleeding from the ends of the vessels which have been cut. This, however, is soon arrested by the contraction and retraction of the coats of the divided vessels, and by the formation of blood-clots in their open ends. A small quantity of blood remains in the wound and clots. The blood-vessels round the injured part dilate, the blood flow becomes slowed, and there passes out from the blood a fluid known as lymph, which coagulates upon the surface of the wound, forming a sticky layer of fibrin which, if the injured surfaces are in contact, causes them to adhere to one another. This forms the temporary scaffolding within which the tissues of repair will be built, and possesses the other valuable property of being strongly germicidal to any organisms which may come in contact with it. White corpuscles also migrate through the walls of the dilated blood-vessels and pass into this exudate in the wound. This fact is of the greatest importance, since the white corpuscles eat up and destroy any foreign or dead substance which has to be removed in the process of repair. (See PHAGOCYTOSIS.) They remove the minute portions of tissue which have been killed by the injury, and the small quantity of blood which has accumulated in the wound. Following the entrance of the white blood corpuscles, within twenty-four hours after the infliction of the wound, there comes a host of cells produced by the rapid multiplication of the cells in the tissues around the wound. Some of these also have the power of phagocytosis, and others, called fibroblasts, become transformed into delicate fibrous tissue. Next, minute buds shoot in from the walls of the smallest blood-vessels and form minute blood channels, which pass from side to side of the wound, or form loops if a gap has been left. The tissue so formed is known as granulation tissue, because, when its surface is closely examined, it has a red, granular appearance due to these loops of vessels covered by masses of the cells mentioned above. The same form of tissue is readily seen on a healing ulcer. Epithelial cells from the surface of the skin now grow over and cover the wound, the whole process being completed usually in less than a week. The delicately formed tissue of the healed wound is gradually replaced by firm fibrous tissue containing fewer blood-vessels, and in less than a year the angry, red scar of the recently healed wound is replaced by a white scar. With minor modifications, this process of repair takes place in all healing wounds (Fig. 182, p. 363).

HEALING BY SECOND INTENTION takes place where the granulation tissue is exposed to view. It occurs in wounds which have broken down owing to suppuration, or where there is an ulcer, and the edges are gradually drawn together by the contraction of the

newly formed fibrous tissue. This results in a wider, weaker, and more noticeable scar.

HEALING BY SCAB FORMATION occurs where the lymph dries up, and union is continued under the dry cake so formed.

HEALING OF POISONED WOUNDS. — Where a wound becomes poisoned, the multiplication of the germs in it dissolves the fibrin and destroys many of the cells engaged in repair. The reaction of the tissues becomes intense, and the inflammation is so evident that the wound is popularly said to be inflamed. As a result of the destruction, many of the cells are discharged as pus. Granulation tissue is gradually formed around the site of infection, the bacteria are cast off in the pus, and healing by second intention takes place. A certain amount of the poison produced by the bacteria, however, escapes into the circulation and causes the symptoms of general ill-health which are present with a poisoned wound.

Dangers of wounds.—BLOOD-POISONING usually means that the germs themselves have entered the circulation, which is a grave occurrence and may be fatal. (See BLOOD-POISONING.)

ERYSIPELAS, TETANUS, and GAS GANGRENE are conditions in which germs enter the lymphatics and produce widespread effects. (See ERYSIPELAS, TETANUS, and GANGRENE.)

HÆMORRHAGE. — *Primary hæmorrhage* means bleeding which occurs at the time of the injury. A large vein or artery may have been divided and may require to be tied. (See HÆMORRHAGE.) A wound of a large vessel like the femoral or the popliteal artery may cause death in a few minute if untreated. *Reactionary hæmorrhage* takes place sometimes from wounds which do not bleed much when they are first inflicted. The explanation is that the shock caused by the injury enfeebles the action of the heart, and, when the wounded person recovers from the shock in a few hours, the increased force of the heart's beating causes bleeding to recommence in the wound. *Secondary hæmorrhage* occurs only in the case of poisoned wounds. The spread of the infection breaks down the blood-clot which has formed in the open end of a blood-vessel and allows the escape of blood. It is usually preceded by a slight oozing of blood, which serves to forewarn the medical attendant. This form of bleeding seldom occurs earlier than a week from the date of the injury.

PARALYSIS.—In a wound of a limb, one of the nerves may be divided. When this has happened, a definite area of skin is found to have lost the sense of touch and pain, and the muscles supplied by the divided nerve have completely lost their power. The tendons, which attach the muscles to the bones, may also be divided, as, for example, by a wound behind or in front of the wrist, causing loss of power in the injured part. If either or both of these complications be present, it is of the greatest importance that the divided ends should be stitched together as early as possible, or a permanent loss of power may result.

SCALP WOUNDS usually heal well, but in deep scalp wounds there is a danger that suppuration may result and may pass within the skull. Again, a severe blow producing a scalp wound may cause fracture of the skull and concussion or compression of the brain. (See BRAIN DISEASES.)

CHEST WOUNDS.—Stabs of the chest are serious chiefly because of the fatal bleeding likely to follow any wound of the heart or large vessels ; and a less serious danger attends wounds of the pleural cavity causing collapse of the lung or empyema.

ABDOMINAL WOUNDS.—A penetrating wound of the abdomen, particularly when the bowel has been cut, is frequently fatal from the acute general peritonitis which it causes.

General treatment of wounds.—The treatment of wounds was revolutionized between 1918 and 1939 by two measures. The first was the closed-plaster technique of treating open wounds, especially when associated with a fracture of bone. In this, the wound was excised and drained and then enclosed in plaster of Paris, the idea being to give the injured tissues complete rest. The second measure was the local application to wounds of one of the sulphonamide drugs or of penicillin. Propamidine and proflavine are other antiseptics applied locally

to the wound with successful results. The first-aid treatment, already described, has for its chief objects the arrest of bleeding and the covering of the wound by a clean dressing, so as to prevent the entrance of germs and to get rid of those which have gained entrance from the skin, or upon the object that inflicted the wound.

To prevent infection of a wound at an operation or in applying a permanent dressing, everything which comes in contact with it must be sterilized or rendered germ-free. To destroy the germs, the best and most easily obtained material is boiling water or steam. If subjected to the action of boiling water for one hour, all known germs are killed, whilst five minutes' boiling is found sufficient for practical purposes. Chemical agents, such as carbolic acid or perchloride of mercury, when used in solutions of given strength, are antiseptics or germicides, and are employed where heat is not applicable. The antiseptic method of treatment for a wound, as originally laid down by Lord Lister, was carried out by using, in addition to the preliminary sterilization of everything which could possibly contaminate the wound, antiseptic lotions with which to douche it. The disadvantage of this form of treatment is that an antiseptic powerful enough to kill any germs in the wound, will also kill the tissue cells. The aseptic method of treatment, on the other hand, is carried out when everything that can possibly convey infection to the wound is rendered free from germs, but none of the fluids or dressings which come in contact with the wound contain antiseptics. In hospitals it is usual to employ the aseptic method, and all gauze, lint, wool, and bandages are treated in a steam sterilizer before use, and kept covered till required.

CHANGING THE DRESSING.—If the wounded surfaces are in contact, the dressing should not be changed unless pain is felt in the wound, discharge from the wound soaks through the dressing, a rise of temperature occurs, or the part feels uncomfortable, until the eighth to tenth day, when the dressing is removed.

DRESSINGS AND LOTIONS.—The most satisfactory dressing is sterilized gauze but should this not be available, then either boracic lint or cyanide gauze may be used. Cyanide gauze is gauze impregnated with the double cyanide of mercury and zinc.

Although the local application of penicillin or of one of the sulphonamides to wounds is being used to an increasing extent, there is still scope for the use of antiseptic solutions. Of all these, the *flavines* are probably the most useful—acriflavine and proflavine are the most widely used. *Eusol* (*q.v.*) is also of value, particularly in wounds known to be infected ; its major practical disadvantage is that it only retains its antiseptic properties for two or three weeks, and must therefore be made up fresh at regular intervals. *Iodine*, in 2 to 5 per cent. alcoholic solutions is a useful antiseptic if used with discrimination. *Biniodide of mercury* (1 in 500 solution in 75 per cent. methylated spirit) is a potent antiseptic. *Perchloride of mercury* (1 in 2000 parts of water) is less potent but correspondingly safer. *Carbolic acid* (*q.v.*), 1 part in 20 parts of water, is less widely used than at one time, but is still a useful application to small, infected wounds. It must not be used for large wounds, nor must it be used with dressings impermeable to the air, because of the risk of excessive absorption leading to carbolic acid poisoning. *Saponaceous solution of cresol*, *B.P.* (perhaps better known as lysol), 1 part in 100 to 200 parts of water, is also used. Three widely used antiseptics at the moment are *cetrimide*, *chlorhexidine*, and *dettol*.

STITCHES.—If the wound be of the incised variety, with wide separation of the edges, it may require to be stitched. Horse-hair, silkworm gut, silver wire, silk, or catgut may be employed for this purpose. One of the first three is used in cases where there is a risk that the wound may become poisoned. Catgut, which is prepared from the intestine of the sheep, possesses the advantage over all the others that it is absorbed by the tissues, and thus does not require to be removed. Where stitches of any of the others have been used, they are generally removed about the tenth day. Sometimes a continuous suture is used for a long wound, but more commonly each stitch is put in and tied singly.

DRAINAGE TUBES.—Sterilized india-

rubber tubing is inserted down to the bottom of the wound in all cases where suppuration is likely to occur in a deep wound, when there is much bruising of the tissues, or when blood is liable to accumulate in the wound. If the wound remains clean, the drainage tube will be removed on the third day. If suppuration occurs, it will be replaced and kept in until the discharge ceases or the deep wound closes up so far as to become a healing ulcer. For small wounds, a strip of gauze or a few strands of worsted or a folded strip of thin rubber tissue is often used as a drain instead of a tube.

Treatment of discharging wounds.— If a wound should suppurate, it must receive treatment which will enable the pus to escape freely while the wound slowly closes. This is provided by inserting a drainage tube into the wound. To prevent the pus drying up and retaining the discharge, and to draw the pus out of the wound, a moist dressing is applied. A piece of lint soaked in sterilized water, or boracic lotion (1 in 60), or perchloride of mercury lotion (1 in 3000), is applied to the wound. The lint is covered with a larger piece of waterproof material, such as gutta-percha tissue, oil-silk, or tin-foil ; over this a still larger piece of cotton-wool is applied, and the whole is fixed by a bandage. This dressing is changed daily until the discharge ceases. If the pus is abundant and not escaping freely, the wound is, in addition, washed out with sterilized water or with lotion at each dressing. When improvement is very slow, a hot boracic fomentation, changed every four hours, is to be recommended. Should blood-poisoning develop, special treatment is required, directed against the infection which is present throughout the blood. This includes the administration of penicillin or one of the sulphonamides.

WRIST is the joint situated between the arm above and the hand below. The region of the wrist contains the eight small carpal bones, which intervene between the arm bones and the five metacarpal bones in the hand, and which have the effect of diminishing jars communicated to the hand in virtue of a certain amount of sliding movement over one another, of which they are capable. These small bones are closely bound to one another by short, strong ligaments, and the wrist-joint is the union of the composite mass thus formed with the radius and ulna in the forearm. Three of the nearer row of carpal bones—the scaphoid, lunar, and cuneiform bones—form the lower surface of the joint, whilst the radius and a triangular cartilage that covers the end of the ulna form the upper surface. These two surfaces are united by strong outer and inner lateral ligaments, and by weaker ligaments before and behind, whilst the powerful tendons passing to the hand and fingers give it a great measure of strength.

The joint is capable of movement in all directions, and, on account of its shape and its numerous ligaments, is very little liable to dislocation, although stretching or tearing of some of these ligaments is a common accident, constituting a sprain. (*See* Joints, Diseases and Injuries of.) Inflamma-

tion of the tendon-sheaths before and behind the wrist, causing the presence of fluid, also results occasionally from an injury, and produces a sense of weakness in the wrist. A fairly common condition is that known as a ganglion, in which an elastic swelling full of fluid develops on the back or front of the wrist in connection with the sheaths of the tendons. (*See* Ganglion.)

WRIST-DROP (*see* Drop-wrist).

WRITER'S CRAMP (*see* Cramp).

WRY-NECK is a condition in which the head is twisted to one side. It may be caused by the contraction of a scar, such as that resulting from a burn or by paralysis of some of the muscles, but in the great majority of cases it is a spasmodic condition due to excessive tendency of certain muscles to contract. (*See* Cramp *and* Spasmodic Torticollis.)

X

X-RAYS, or RÖNTGEN RAYS.—The discovery of these was recorded in January 1896 by Professor Röntgen, at that time professor of physics at Würzburg. This epoch-making discovery had been preceded by a series of experiments carried out by Crookes and Lenard. Crookes, employing vacuum tubes with residual air at $\frac{1}{1000000}$ of an atmosphere, produced cathodal rays from the negative pole on the passage of a high-potential electric current. Lenard passed these rays into the air through an aluminium window in the tube, and found that they could produce fluorescence of certain bodies, would pass through certain substances opaque to ordinary light, and would act on a photographic plate. Röntgen, using a still higher vacuum, succeeded in producing X-rays from the walls of the tube, these rays being unaffected by a magnet, and possessing greater power of penetration.

From these simple beginnings the science of Radiography and Radiotherapy has been slowly developed, until at the present day countless sets of apparatus are in daily use in X-ray departments of hospitals throughout the world. The uses of X-rays are, however, manifold. Hardly any scientific laboratory of the present day is complete without an X-ray installation. In industry the X-rays are used in work of investigation; with high-tension apparatus giving up to 300,000 volts, steel is examined for faults, and hidden faults can be discovered in the wood used for aeroplane construction.

Apparatus.—Electricity of high potential is the first essential, and it can be produced by: (1) an induction coil; (2) a static machine; (3) a set of about 20,000 galvanic cells (*see* ELECTRICITY IN MEDICINE); (4) the continuous current mains of an electrical supply; or (5) the alternating mains of an electrical supply. Low-tension current from any of these sources is converted into a current of high potential, which is essential for the energizing of an X-ray tube. This current may be obtained from:

(1) INDUCTION COILS (Fig. 422) giving 1- to 2-inch sparks between the terminals of the secondary wire in the coil

were used in the early experiments in X-ray work, but one possessing a spark of 6 to 20 inches is generally employed to excite the X-ray tube. The current may be derived from a main-electric

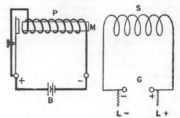

FIG. 422.—Diagram of induction coil. *P*, Primary coil, with *M*, magnet, and *B*, battery or other source of electrical energy; *S*, secondary coil, with *G*, spark-gap, and *L*, *L*, leads to X-ray tube.

circuit led through a switch-board with shunt resistances, and as a rule this is the source of supply used. For portable apparatus, accumulators are generally employed; even galvanic cells might be used. Where convenient, a switch-board with voltmeter and ammeter and arrangements to vary the current from, say, 10 to 100 volts and 3 to 15 amperes, is the most satisfactory arrangement. Accumulators or galvanic cells should have a strength of 12 to 24 volts. The interruptor is one of the most troublesome parts. The old-fashioned Neef's hammer will not work with high voltages, and is generally replaced with advantage by a motor mercury, electrolytic, or other interruptor.

(2) A STATIC MACHINE (Wimshurst or Holtz) is also used as a means of exciting the X-ray tube. In some hands these machines do good work, but they are suited only for dry climates and are large and cumbersome.

(3) GALVANIC CELLS in large numbers (20,000 or thereabout) might be used, but are far too expensive ever to be of any practical value.

Of these methods, the induction coil seems to meet all purposes best. If the interruptor is thoroughly understood and carefully kept in repair, little difficulty is met with. Recently an advance has been made by eliminating even this, the current being led from an alternating dynamo through a closed-circuit transformer. A high-voltage *equally alternating* current is thus produced—differing from the current of an induction coil, which, although alternating, has the current made at breaking the circuit so much more powerful than

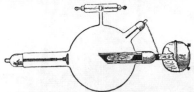

FIG. 423.—Diagram of vacuum tube for production of X-rays. In this type there is a water-jacket to cool the anode, and, above, an accessory tube for regulating the vacuum.

that produced on making the circuit that the latter can practically be ignored. To make the current unidirectional it is passed through valve vacuum tubes, such as the Soupape type, which only allows passage of one phase, or a mechanical rectifier may be used.

A more recent method is to use hot cathode valve tubes similar to those used in ' wireless '. These cut out one phase of the alternating current and so produce a unidirectional current (Coolidge type of tube).

THE VACUUM or X-RAY TUBE.—The X-rays were originally produced from the walls of the tube, but Jackson improved upon this by using the anode or +pole as the reflecting target for the X-rays. Alterations in the vacuum within the tube produce variations

In this type of tube, when the current is passing correctly, fluorescence of the half of the bulb opposite the reflector is observed—this being generally apple-green in colour, as the tube is made of soda-glass, but varying if other ingredients are used. If this half be not distinctly marked, and fluorescence at other parts be more evident, probably the negative and positive poles are not connected to the corresponding poles on the coil, and the current should be reversed or the tube turned round. With the tube now in position and fixed on a stand, the ray effects can be tested either by the fluorescent screen or the photographic plate.

COOLIDGE TUBE. — The standard Coolidge tube consists of a bulb 7 in. in diameter with the usual hot cathode consisting of a spiral wire, heated by a current of 3 to 5 amperes at about 12 volts, supplied through a screw cap fitting at the end of the cathode neck, and an anticathode in the form of a block of tungsten (Figs. 423, 424). This tube is capable of withstanding heavy discharges through it.

FLUORESCENT SCREEN.—Fluorescence is produced in various substances by the action of X-rays, but the two most used are barium platinocyanide and calcium tungstate, one of which, sprinkled on cardboard, forms the fluorescent screen in common use. In a darkened room, if a hand be placed close against the screen, between it and the tube which is

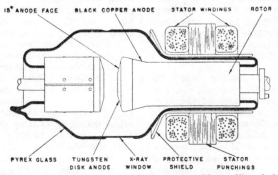

FIG. 424.—Diagram of rotating anode X-ray tube. ˙ (Newton Victor Ltd.)

in the ray production ; for, with a low vacuum, the rays have less penetrating power than those produced by a tube in which the vacuum is very high (Fig. 423).

emitting the rays, the screen will appear brightly illuminated, except in the region where, owing to the obstruction of the rays, there is a faint shadow of the flesh, a denser shadow of the bones, and, if there be a ring on the finger, a still darker shadow from the ring. It has been stated that the ray-production varies with the condition of the

considerably with the voltage in the primary circuit ; for instance, a *hard tube* (*i.e.* one with a high vacuum) may only allow ·25 milliampere, and a soft

Fig. 425.—Coolidge rotating anode X-ray tube. (Newton Victor Ltd.)

vacuum, and the effect can now be carefully studied.

(1) The spark-gap varies directly with the vacuum. A movable rod runs between the terminals of the secondary coil, and gives an alternative path for the current. If the tube be very resistant, owing to a high vacuum (small residue of air), the electric discharge will prefer to spark over a space of 6 or more inches ; on the other hand, if there be a low vacuum (large residue of air), it may not even spark over a space of ½ inch

(2) The screen - shadow, when the vacuum is low, is very black, owing to the lessened penetration of the rays, and there is little differentiation of the bones to be made out. If the vacuum is raised, this differentiation becomes more evident, until, if carried too far, the penetration may be so great that very little shadow is observable, and details of the bones are lost owing to too great penetration.

(3) A milliamperemeter, in circuit with the tube and the secondary wire, indicates the number of milliamperes passing through. This quantity varies

tube (*i.e.* one with a low vacuum) as much as 3 or 4 milliamperes, to pass with 20 volts, but if the voltage be raised to 80, the hard tube may allow 1 milliampere and the soft tube 5 or 6 milliamperes.

Applying the three tests to a medium tube, with pressure of 20 volts in the primary coil, it would be found probably that there was an alternating spark-gap of 2 inches, that the bones of the hand threw clear, black shadows on the screen, and that about 1·5 milliamperes were passing through.

After X-ray tubes of the gas type have been worked for some time, they tend to get harder, although, with high voltages, they may become temporarily softer owing to heating of the anode. The explanation of this hardening is that the residual air accumulates on the anode, and many devices are used to prevent this. Heating the tube does well as a temporary measure, but rest for a month or so is more satisfactory. Many ingenious arrangements are also in use, which, up to a certain point, are successful, and of these the chief are side tubes containing a chemical salt, which, when heated, gives off gas; or mica, which, when heated by the current, gives off absorbed air.

To counteract the heating of the anode, it is often made of thick metal, or has a water-cooled tube behind it.

Radiography. — X-rays act on a sensitized photographic plate in the same manner as ordinary light, but, as they penetrate paper, the exposure can be made in daylight by enclosing the plate in a black paper envelope, through which the daylight cannot pass. It must be remembered that the X-ray photograph differs from a photograph taken by ordinary light in that it is really a shadow-picture or skiagram. A skiagram differs from an ordinary photograph in that no lens is used; the X-rays pass in parallel lines from the focus spot on the anticathode. X-rays cannot be focused upon the object as in ordinary photography for the above reason. Briefly, in order to obtain a skiagram, the method is as follows. The plate—a rapid one—is placed first in a yellow envelope, this again in a black one, the whole being placed close beneath the part to be photographed. The tube is situated directly opposite, with the limb or other object to be photographed a little distance off, but between the tube and the plate. The tube must be arranged so that the rays fall as perpendicularly as possible on to the part, careful centring by a plumb-line and weight being used where suitable. The distance of the tube from the object and the duration of exposure are matters of experience; but the farther apart they are, the less chance there is of distortion. At two metres or more the amount of distortion is practically negligible; so that when working at that distance between the anticathode of the tube and the surface of the film or plate, the actual size of an organ within the body can be measured. This is taken advantage of in cardiac examinations, when measurements of the size of the heart can be obtained.

In order to show the position, shape, etc., of the stomach and intestine, some opaque but harmless material, such as carbonate of bismuth or sulphate of barium, is administered by the mouth. This throws a dense shadow, corresponding to the interior of the organ examined, upon the screen or photo-graphic plate. For examination of the lungs, gall-bladder, etc., other opaque substances, such as harmless compounds of iodine, are injected so as to pass into their interior.

For examination of other organs, such as the brain and abdominal organs, oxygen is sometimes injected into the cavities in the brain or the peritoneal cavity, so as to render the outlines sharper when an X-ray photograph is taken.

THE EXPOSURE IN RADIOGRAPHY.— The nearer we can get to an instantaneous exposure, the clearer is the outline, especially when we are dealing with the abdomen or thorax. In the early days, very long exposures were required because of the very low currents available and the imperfect development of the X-ray tube. At the present time it is possible to get exposures in as short a time as $\frac{1}{100}$ of a second through the thickness of the body of an average patient.

Amongst other uses for X-rays in diagnosis attention must be called to the localization of foreign bodies in various parts of the body. For this purpose localizers of various patterns and arrangements for taking stereoscopic photographs have been devised. These are of great importance in surgery for the purpose of fixing the position of foreign bodies, like steel chips in the eye or bullets in the body, and also give valuable aid in determining the nature and position of fractures and other injuries of the bones.

Accelerating screens made of cardboard covered with fluorescent material are sometimes used. This screen is placed in contact with the photographic plate. Being caused to glow where the light falls upon it, the screen still affects the plate after the exposure is over. When the apparatus is not powerful enough to give very short exposures, the accelerating screens are used. In this way an instantaneous photograph can be made in $\frac{1}{10}$ second or less from a distance of several feet. Thus the beating heart or the contractions of the stomach in digestion can be taken in a series of flashes and demonstrated on a cinematograph film.

Radiotherapy, or Treatment by X-rays.—The two chief sources of the ionizing radiations used in radiotherapy are the gamma rays of radium (*q.v.*) and the penetrating X-rays generated by apparatus working at various voltages. For superficial lesions energies of around 40 kilovolts are used, but for deep-seated conditions, such as cancer of the internal organs, much higher voltages are required. X-ray machines are now in use which work at two million volts. Even higher voltages are now available through the development of the linear accelerator, which makes use of the frequency magnetron which is the basis of radar. The linear accelerator receives its name from the fact that it accelerates a beam of electrons down a straight tube, 3 metres in length, and in this process a voltage of eight million is attained. The use of these very high voltages has led to the development of a highly specialized technique which has been devised for the treatment of cancer and like diseases.

Like the photographic effect, the therapeutic effects were discovered almost accidentally—it being observed that prolonged exposures to the rays caused inflammation, and even ulceration of the skin, and further, that they caused loss of hair, and that they improved various diseased conditions. Repeated exposures, for example, of the hands of physicians using this method of treatment, have been observed to produce permanent baldness, pigmentation of the skin, excessive growth of its horny layer, and even epithelioma. X-rays are particularly hurtful to the testes and ovaries of young persons ; and when these are exposed to the rays repeatedly, the genital glands must be covered by sheet-lead or some such protection, lest sterility result. Too severe a reaction to the irritating effect of the rays upon the patient's skin at a single sitting must also be avoided. It is important to protect the surrounding areas, and this is done by the use of masks of sheet-lead, with a hole cut out over the affected area, and by enclosing the tube in a metal-lined box, with an opening opposite the affected spot. By these means, as well as by wearing lead-lined gloves, and by frequently anointing the skin with some simple ointment, persons constantly applying the rays are effectually protected.

The greatest value of radiotherapy is in the treatment of malignant disease. In many cases it can be used for the treatment of malignant growths which are not accessible to surgery, whilst in others it is used in conjunction with surgery.

Leukæmia and other conditions, in which the spleen is enlarged, are often greatly benefited by exposure of the spleen or long bones to X-rays or radium.

In simple conditions, particularly superficial ones, X-rays have been used very successfully, but are being used less and less, in view of the increasing necessity to reduce to the absolute minimum the amount of irradiation to which the citizen of to-day is exposed.

XANTHOMA, also known as XANTHELASMA and VITILIGOIDEA, is a relatively rare skin disease in which yellow plates form in the surface of the skin, especially on the eyelids.

XERODERMA (ξηρός, dry ; δέρμα, skin) is the name applied to a rough, dry condition of the skin accompanied by the copious formation of scales.

XEROPHTHALMIA. — A dry, thickened state of the conjunctiva associated with chronic conjunctivitis, the result of deficiency of vitamin A in the diet.

XEROSIS (ξηρός, dry) means abnormal dryness, especially of the eye.

XEROSTOMIA is the condition of dryness of the mouth due to lack of saliva.

XIPHISTERNUM, or XIPHOID CARTILAGE, is the lowest part of the breastbone.

XYLOCAINE (*see* LIGNOCAINE).

Y

YAWS, known also as FRAMBŒSIA and PIAN, is a disease of the tropics, especially of Africa and the West Indies, affecting both white and black races. It consists in the appearance of small tumours covered with yellow crusts, scattered over the surface of the body.

Cause.—The disease is directly contagious from person to person, and the infection is probably also carried by flies, and certainly by clothing and by the unclean huts of the natives. The direct cause is a spirochæte known as *Treponema pertenue*, and the occurrence of the disease in a person of unhealthy constitution, or one who is suffering from another disease, such as syphilis or tuberculosis, renders the attack very much more serious.

Symptoms.—The disease does not appear for a fortnight or more after infection, and during this time fever, malaise, pains, and itching of the skin may come on. It begins as a scaly eruption about the body and legs, in which small lumps form, and grow till they reach a size even of several inches in diameter. The surface of these is covered by a yellow crust of dried-up secretion, and in unhealthy people the tumours may break down and produce deep ulcers. After a duration of weeks or months the tumours gradually shrink and disappear.

Treatment.—The outlook in yaws has been transformed by the introduction of penicillin, the effects of which are dramatic in this disease.

YEAST is a ferment consisting of *Saccharomyces cerevisiæ* obtained in the brewing of beer, making of bread, etc. It may be used in its natural form as a remedy, of which a tablespoonful or thereabout is stirred up in milk or water. It can also be obtained in a dry powder, of which a teaspoonful is similarly taken. Its main value as a medicine lies in the fact that it contains a large amount of vitamin B. Yeast is an old-fashioned remedy for boils, and there is evidence suggesting that it is of value in increasing the resistance to infection.

YELLOW FEVER, also known as YELLOW JACK and VOMITO AMARILLI, is an acute disease of certain tropical localities, characterized by fever and jaundice.

Distribution.—It is endemic in the West Indies, some parts of the Spanish Main, such as at Vera Cruz and Rio de Janeiro, and in West and East Africa. From these parts it occasionally spreads in epidemics to neighbouring regions. In 1793 a very serious epidemic spread over the Northern United States, and, in Philadelphia alone, over 10 per cent. of the total population were swept off in the course of four months. Numerous other epidemics invaded the States in the end of the eighteenth and during the course of the nineteenth centuries, the last severe one taking place in 1878. In Europe the disease has from time to time invaded some of the Portuguese and Spanish ports, but it has never gained any permanent hold. When cases of yellow fever arrive at British or other northern European ports, no spread of the disease takes place. It is also unknown in the Far East.

Causes.—The disease is due to a virus which is transmitted to man by the *Aëdes egypti* mosquito (Fig. 426).

FIG. 426.—*Aëdes egypti* (female). The transmitter of yellow fever and dengue. (From Manson's *Tropical Diseases*. Cassell & Co. Ltd.)

Monkeys are an important reservoir of infection in areas where the disease is endemic. The virus is found in the blood of infected individuals during the first three or four days of the disease. The blood of one patient is directly infectious, and the deaths of three of the great investigators of the disease, Stokes, Noguchi, and Young, all of whom died of yellow fever, were probably due to direct contact with infected blood.

Apart from the direct cause, many factors are of known importance in assisting to spread the disease or to render it more severe. Thus all epidemics take place during the hot season, and it is much more dangerous for a susceptible person to visit some centre of yellow fever during the hot months than during the cooler ones. Further, a threatened epidemic is sometimes cut short by a spell of cool weather or by heavy rains. The disease is usually limited to the sea coast and to the sides of swampy rivers, and seldom rises above an altitude of 1000 feet. No race or age is exempt, although negroes are believed to be less severely attacked than white men. A slight attack of yellow fever, however, and even prolonged residence in an infected district, is believed to confer a considerable degree of immunity from further attack.

Symptoms. — Different cases vary greatly in severity, but the disease is apt to be especially serious during the prevalence of an epidemic, or when it affects persons newly arrived from healthier parts. The incubation period is usually 3 to 5 days, but may be up to 10 days.

Three stages are usually described in a severe case. The *first stage* begins suddenly with headache, chill, pains in the back and limbs, and rise of temperature. The eyes are bloodshot. Vomiting also occurs, the tongue is furred, and the bowels are constipated. A very important point is that the urine decreases in amount, and, if tested, is found to contain albumin, the result of inflammation of the kidneys. The degree in which these signs are present forms a valuable indication of the severity of the case and of the need for special treatment.

These symptoms last for about three days and then sometimes abate to some extent for a day and the patient appears better. This constitutes the *second stage*.

The *third stage* begins usually about the fourth day. The patient now becomes very weak and the ' black

vomit ' comes on. This consists in bringing up constantly from the stomach a clear fluid containing black flakes formed of blood that has been acted upon by the gastric juice. Although this black vomit is regarded as an alarming sign, it is by no means an index that the patient is sure to die. Jaundice also appears with the third stage, and is the symptom to which the disease owes its name. Usually it amounts only to a pale yellow discoloration of the skin, but it may become mahogany brown in hue, and small hæmorrhages under the skin and mucous membranes are also common. In fatal cases examined after death, the principal changes found are fatty degeneration of the liver, acute inflammation of the kidneys, and an inflamed and congested state of the stomach, which contains some of the black fluid mentioned above.

Treatment. — PREVENTIVE TREATMENT is important, and consists of vaccination of everyone travelling to and from those parts of the world where the disease occurs. Such vaccination is compulsory, not only for the inhabitants of endemic zones and for travellers going to these areas, but, in addition, many countries outside endemic areas require that travellers who have come from, or have passed through, yellow fever areas shall have been vaccinated. The sick must be kept for the first three days of illness in rooms protected by mosquito-netting, so that they may not infect mosquitoes which would pass on the disease to healthy persons. The same general measures as in the case of malaria should be taken against mosquitoes.

CURATIVE TREATMENT must be directed towards checking symptoms as they arise. Vomiting is allayed by sucking ice or sipping iced water, and by the administration of dilute hydrocyanic acid in doses of two drops in water. Food should be, to a great extent, withheld in the early stage, but the patient must have plenty of water in small draughts, containing glucose, and flavoured with lime, orange, or grapefruit juice. Later on, the only food should be milk, thin soups, and similar liquid nourishment. When the patient is greatly prostrated, alcohol may be given, and, of this, champagne is the most approved form. The high temperature, which sometimes shows itself, is relieved by sponging or by the wet pack. One of the most important symptoms to treat is stoppage of the urine, and for this hot-air baths are employed, as in acute Bright's disease.

YOGHURT is the name applied to sour milk curdled with one of the lactic-acid producing bacilli, such as *Lactobacillus acidophilus* or *Lactobacillus bulgaricus*. It contains all the protein, fat, calcium, and vitamins of the original milk, and is therefore a nutritious food, but there is no evidence that it has any unique beneficial properties of its own. In countries where standards of hygiene are low it has the advantage of having been sterilized by boiling and is therefore unlikely to be contaminated with dangerous micro-organisms.

YOHIMBINE is an alkaloid obtained from the bark of *Corynanthe johimbe*. It is reputed to be an aphrodisiac.

YOMESAN (*see* NICLOSAMIDE.)

Z

ZANDER APPARATUS is a collection of machines devised by J. G. W. Zander, a Swedish physician, for permitting within the limits of a gymnasium various active forms of exercise usually attainable only out of doors. It includes devices for exercising the muscles employed in rowing, those used in bicycling, horseback riding, etc., as well as apparatus for moving individual joints and so increasing their suppleness after injury or disease.

ZINC is a metal of which several salts are used in medicine for external application. Its salts fall into two classes : soluble and insoluble. The important soluble salts are the acetate of zinc, sulphate of zinc, and chloride of zinc, of which the first two, in a concentrated form, are powerfully irritating, whilst the third corrodes any tissues with which it comes in contact. All, and especially the chloride, are powerful antiseptics. The insoluble salts that are of importance are the oxide and carbonate, which have simply an astringent action.

Uses.—The acetate or the sulphate of zinc is much used in the strength of about 2 grains to each ounce of water, to form a lotion for inflammation of the eyes or an astringent douche. The chloride of zinc forms the basis of Sir W. Burnett's disinfectant solution. It was formerly used either dissolved in its own weight of water to form a liquor, or made up with flour into a paste, as a caustic for destroying foul ulcers or cancers whose removal by excision was, for some reason, impossible.

Oxide of zinc, stearate of zinc, and carbonate of zinc are made up in dusting powders, in ointments, or suspended in water as lotions for the astringent action they exert upon abraded surfaces of the skin.

Internally, oxide of zinc is administered in pills designed to exert an astringent action on the bowels. Sulphate of zinc, administered in doses of 20 grains in water, forms a valuable emetic.

ZONA and ZOSTER (ζώνη, ζωστήρ, a girdle) are two names for the eruption popularly known as shingles. (*See* HERPES.)

ZONULOLYSIS is the process whereby the ciliary zonule, which is the suspensory ligament of the lens of the eye, is lysed, or digested, by chymotrypsin, which is an enzyme obtained from mammalian pancreas. Zonulolysis is now being used as an aid in cataract surgery.

ZOONOSES are animal diseases which can be transmitted to man. There are over 80 infections of domestic and wild vertebrates which can be transmitted in this way, including bovine tuberculosis, brucellosis, and rabies.

ZYGOMA (ζύγωμα) is the name given to a bridge of bone formed by the union of a process from the temporal bone with one from the malar bone. It lies in the region of the temple, gives attachment to the powerful masseter muscle which moves the lower jaw, and forms a protection to the side of the head.

ZYMOTIC DISEASES (ζύμη, ferment) is an old term for the acute infectious maladies. As originally employed by Dr. Farr of the British Registrar-General's department, the term included the diseases which were ' epidemic, endemic, and contagious ', and owed their origin to the presence of some morbific principle in the system acting in a manner analogous to, although not identical with, the process of fermentation. A very large number of diseases were accordingly included under this designation. The term, however, came to be restricted to the chief fevers and contagious diseases (*e.g.* typhus and typhoid fevers, smallpox, scarlet fever, measles, erysipelas, cholera, whooping-cough, diphtheria, etc.), but is seldom used nowadays, on account of the theory which it suggests.

PRINTED BY R. & R. CLARK, LTD., EDINBURGH